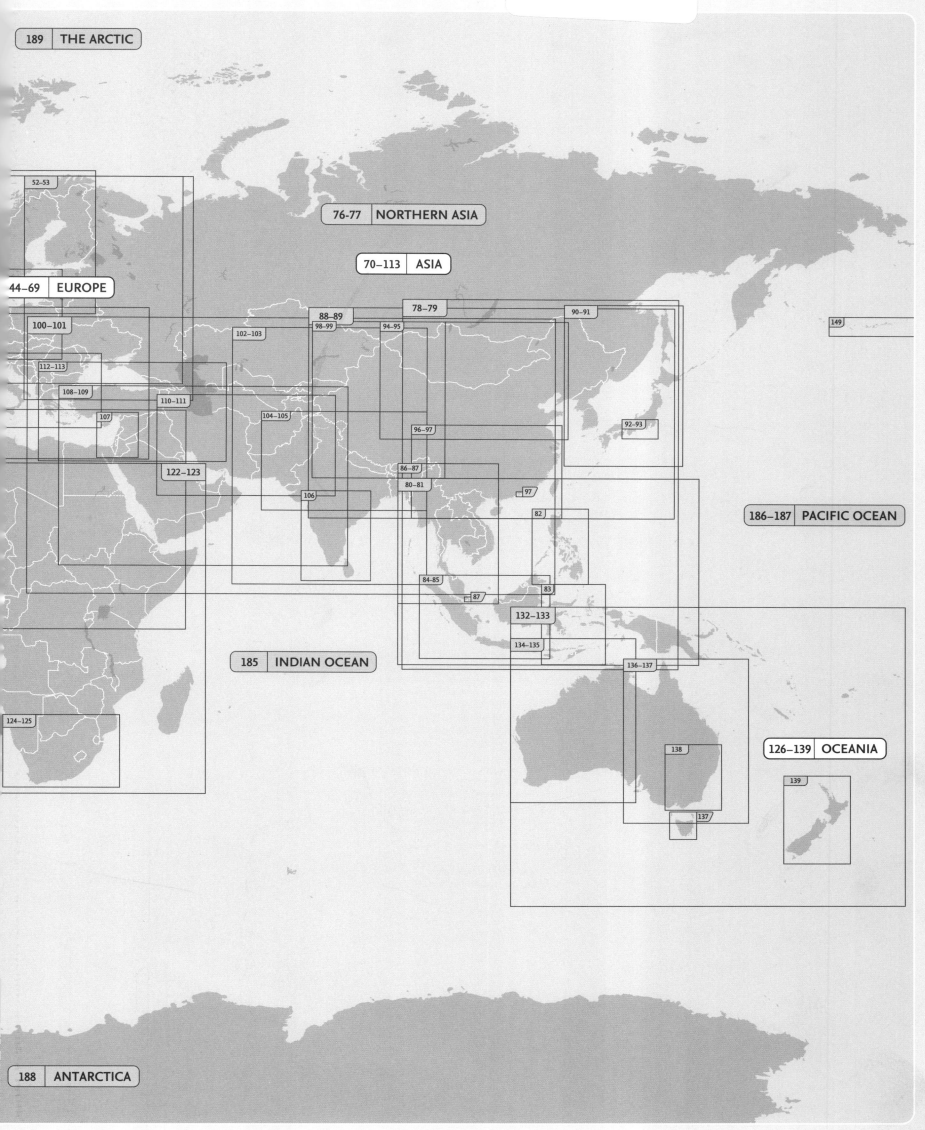

189 | THE ARCTIC

52–53

76-77 | NORTHERN ASIA

70–113 | ASIA

44–69 | EUROPE

78–79

90–91

149

100–101

88–89
98–99

94–95

102–103

112–113

108–109

110–111

104–105

96–97

92–93

107

86–87

80–81

122–123

106

97

82

186–187 | PACIFIC OCEAN

84–85

83

87

132–133

134–135

185 | INDIAN OCEAN

136–137

124–125

138

126–139 | OCEANIA

139

137

188 | ANTARCTICA

Find your map

Collins World Atlas – Complete Edition

Collins
An imprint of HarperCollins Publishers
Westerhill Road,
Bishopbriggs, Glasgow G64 2QT

First published 2008
Second Edition 2012

Printed in Hong Kong.

ISBN 978-0-00-745610-9
Imp 001

All mapping in this title is generated
from Collins Bartholomew™ digital databases.
Collins Bartholomew™, the UK's leading independent geographical
information supplier, can provide a digital, custom, and premium
mapping service to a variety of markets.
For further information:
Tel: +44 (0) 208 307 4515
e-mail: collinsbartholomew@harpercollins.co.uk
or visit our website: www.collinsbartholomew.com

If you would like to comment on any aspect of this atlas,
please write to
Collins Maps, HarperCollins Publishers,
Westerhill Road, Bishopbriggs, Glasgow G64 2QT
e-mail: collinsmaps@harpercollins.co.uk

Follow us on twitter: @collinsmaps

www.CollinsMaps.com
Discover the world through maps

Collins World Atlas

COMPLETE EDITION

Collins

Contents

Contents

Map Symbols

Southern Europe

Japan

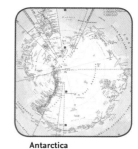

Antarctica

Settlements

Population	National capital	Administrative capital	Other city or town
over 10 million	BEIJING ✪	Karachi ◉	New York ◉
5 million to 10 million	JAKARTA ✪	Tianjin ◉	Nova Iguaçu ◉
1 million to 5 million	KĀBUL ✪	Sydney ◉	Kaohsiung ◉
500 000 to 1 million	BANGUI ✪	Trujillo ◉	Jeddah ◉
100 000 to 500 000	WELLINGTON ✪	Mansa ◉	Apucarana ◉
50 000 to 100 000	PORT OF SPAIN ✪	Potenza ◉	Arecibo ◉
10 000 to 50 000	MALABO ✪	Chinhoyi ◦	Ceres ◦
under 10 000	VALLETTA ✪	Ati ◦	Venta ◦

⬭ Built-up area

Boundaries

——— International boundary

–·–·– Disputed international boundary or alignment unconfirmed

– – – – Disputed territory boundary

——— Administrative boundary

········· Ceasefire line

////// UN Buffer zone

Miscellaneous

---------- National park

············ Reserve or Regional park

✱ Site of specific interest

⊂⊃⊂⊃ Wall

Land and sea features

Desert

▾ Oasis

Lava field

Marsh

1234
△ Volcano
height in metres

Ice cap or Glacier

Escarpment

Coral reef

↲ *1234* Pass
height in metres

Lakes and rivers

Lake

Impermanent lake

Salt lake or lagoon

Impermanent salt lake

Dry salt lake or salt pan

123 Lake height
surface height above
sea level, in metres

——— River

——— Impermanent river or watercourse

‖ Waterfall

| Dam

| Barrage

Relief

Contour intervals and layer colours

Height

metres		feet
5000		16404
3000		9843
2000		6562
1000		3281
500		1640
200		656
below sea level		0
0		0
200		656
2000		6562
4000		13124
6000		19686

Depth

1234
▲ Summit
height in metres

-123 Spot height
height in metres

123 Ocean deep
depth in metres

Transport

→ ····· Motorway (tunnel; under construction)

→ – – – Main road (tunnel; under construction)

→ – – – Secondary road (tunnel; under construction)

········· Track

—•—•— Main railway (tunnel; under construction)

——•—— Secondary railway (tunnel; under construction)

——•—— Other railway (tunnel; under construction)

——— Canal

✈ Main airport

✈ Regional airport

Satellite imagery - The thematic pages in the atlas contain a wide variety of photographs and images. These are a mixture of terrestrial and aerial photographs and satellite imagery. All are used to illustrate specific themes and to give an indication of the variety of imagery available today. The main types of imagery used in the atlas are described in the table below. The sensor for each satellite image is detailed on the acknowledgements page.

Main satellites/sensors

Satellite/sensor name	Launch dates	Owner	Aims and applications	Internet links	Additional internet links
Landsat 1, 2, 3, 4, 5, 7	July 1972–April 1999	National Aeronautics and Space Administration (NASA), USA	The first satellite to be designed specifically for observing the Earth's surface. Originally set up to produce images of use for agriculture and geology. Today is of use for numerous environmental and scientific applications.	landsat.gsfc.nasa.gov	earth.jsc.nasa.gov
					earthnet.esrin.esa.it
					earthobservatory.nasa.gov
SPOT 1, 2, 3, 4, 5 (Satellite Pour l'Observation de la Terre)	February 1986–March 1998	Centre National d'Etudes Spatiales (CNES) and Spot Image, France	Particularly useful for monitoring land use, water resources research, coastal studies and cartography.	www.spotimage.fr	gs.mdacorporation.com
					modis.gsfc.nasa.gov
Space Shuttle	Regular launches from 1981	NASA, USA	Each shuttle mission has separate aims. Astronauts take photographs with high specification hand held cameras.	nasascience.nasa.gov www.jpl.nasa.gov/srtm	seawifs.gsfc.nasa.gov
ASTER	1999	Japan Ministry of Economy, Trade and Industry, partnered with NASA	Produced GDEM.	asterweb.jpl.nasa.gov	topex-www.jpl.nasa.gov
					visibleearth.nasa.gov
IKONOS	September 1999	GeoEye	First commercial high-resolution satellite. Useful for a variety of applications mainly Cartography, Defence, Urban Planning, Agriculture, Forestry and Insurance.	www.geoeye.com	www.usgs.gov
GeoEye-1	September 2008	GeoEye	Another commercial high-resolution satellite which is of use for numerous environmental, scientific, economic and national defence applications.	www.geoeye.com	
Suomi NPP (Suomi National Polar-orbiting Partnership)	October 2011	NASA	The first of a new generation of satellites, with five different imaging systems, covering a wide variety of applications.	npp.gsfc.nasa.gov	

Time Zones

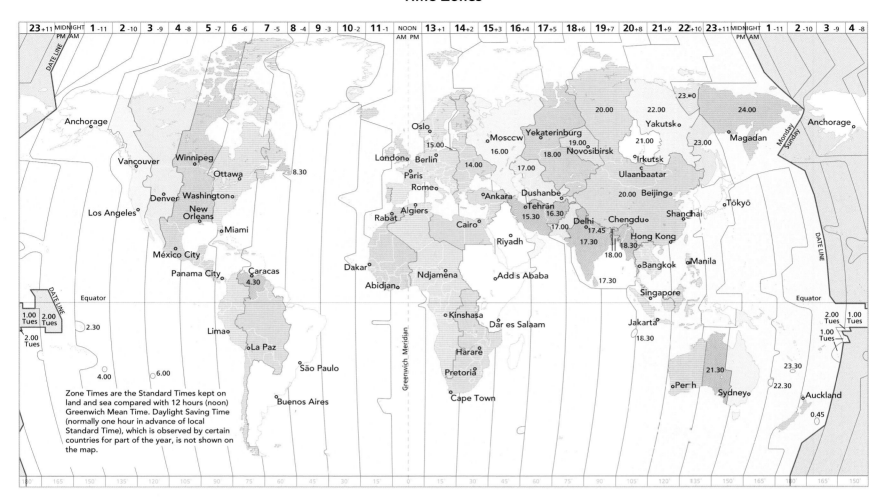

Zone Times are the Standard Times kept on land and sea compared with 12 hours (noon) Greenwich Mean Time. Daylight Saving Time (normally one hour in advance of local Standard Time), which is observed by certain countries for part of the year, is not shown on the map.

International Organizations

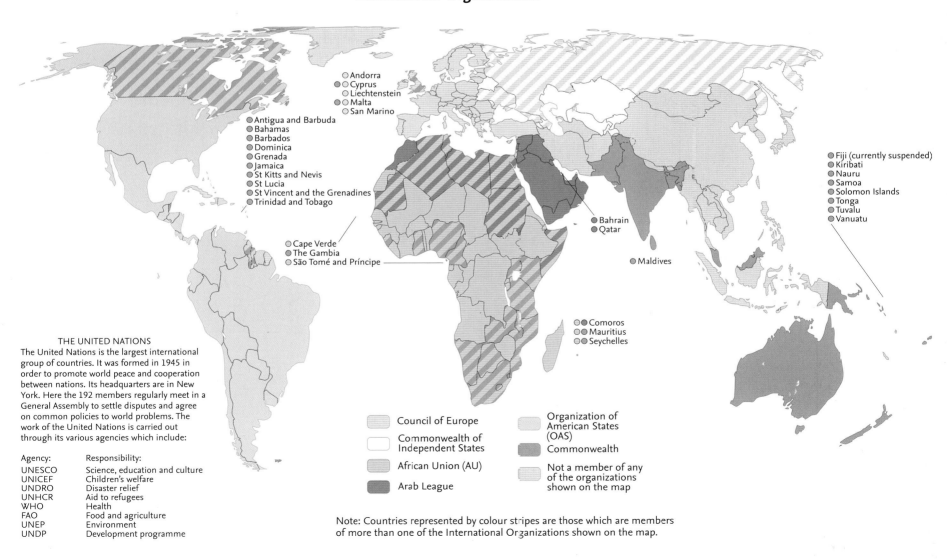

THE UNITED NATIONS
The United Nations is the largest international group of countries. It was formed in 1945 in order to promote world peace and cooperation between nations. Its headquarters are in New York. Here the 192 members regularly meet in a General Assembly to settle disputes and agree on common policies to world problems. The work of the United Nations is carried out through its various agencies which include:

Agency:	Responsibility:
UNESCO	Science, education and culture
UNICEF	Children's welfare
UNDRO	Disaster relief
UNHCR	Aid to refugees
WHO	Health
FAO	Food and agriculture
UNEP	Environment
UNDP	Development programme

Andorra
Cyprus
Liechtenstein
Malta
San Marino

Antigua and Barbuda
Bahamas
Barbados
Dominica
Grenada
Jamaica
St Kitts and Nevis
St Lucia
St Vincent and the Grenadines
Trinidad and Tobago

Cape Verde
The Gambia
São Tomé and Príncipe

Bahrain
Qatar

Maldives

Comoros
Mauritius
Seychelles

Fiji (currently suspended)
Kiribati
Nauru
Samoa
Solomon Islands
Tonga
Tuvalu
Vanuatu

Council of Europe

Commonwealth of Independent States

African Union (AU)

Arab League

Organization of American States (OAS)

Commonwealth

Not a member of any of the organizations shown on the map

Note: Countries represented by colour stripes are those which are members of more than one of the International Organizations shown on the map.

The Earth's physical features, both on land and on the sea bed, closely reflect its geological structure. The current shapes of the continents and oceans have evolved over millions of years. Movements of the tectonic plates which make up the Earth's crust have created some of the best-known and most spectacular features. The processes which have shaped the Earth continue today with earthquakes, volcanoes, erosion, climatic variations and man's activities all affecting the Earth's landscapes.

The total topographic range of the Earth's surface is nearly 20 000 metres, from the highest point Mount Everest, to the lowest point in the Mariana Trench. Major mountain ranges include the Himalaya, the Andes and the Rocky Mountains, each of which gives rise to some of the world's greatest rivers. In contrast, the deserts of the Sahara, Australia, the Arabian Peninsula and the Gobi cover vast areas and each provides unique landscapes.

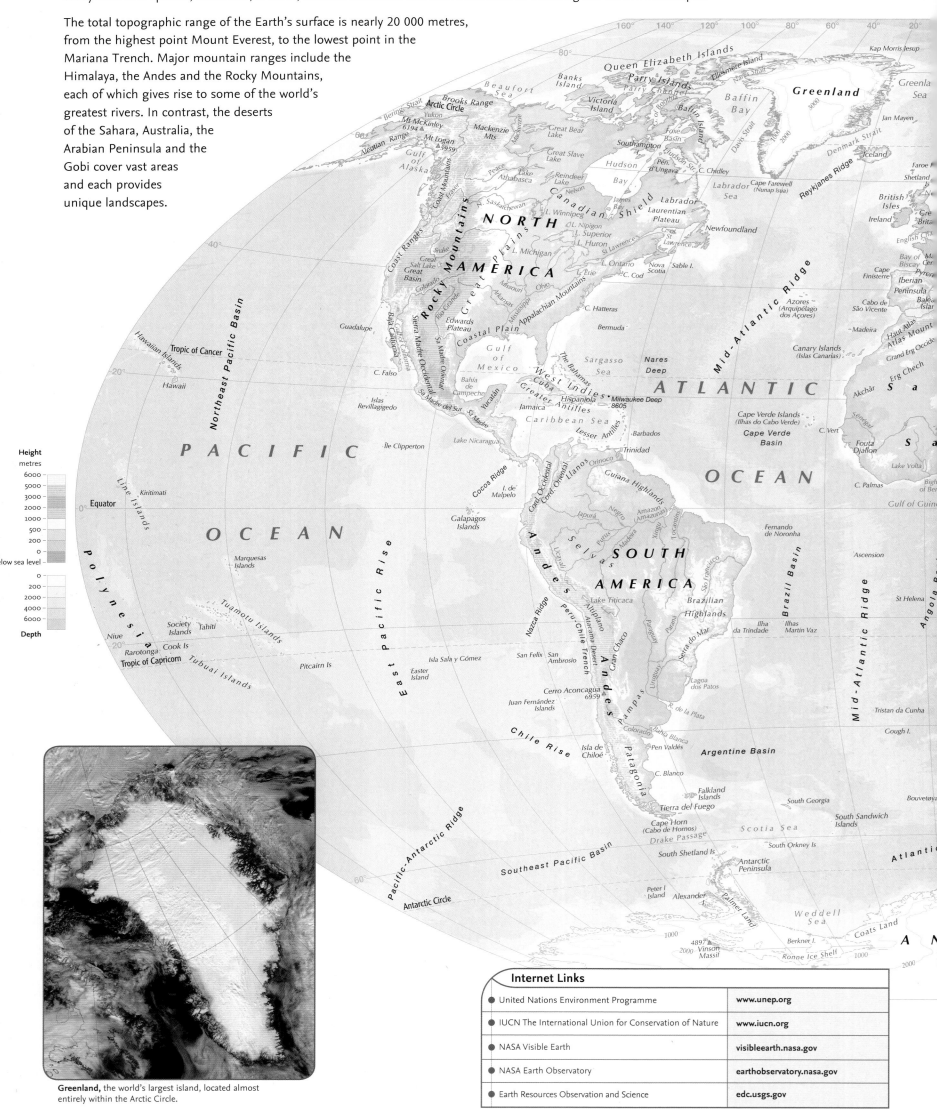

Height
metres
6000
5000
3000
2000
1000
500
200
0
below sea level

0
200
2000
4000
6000
Depth

Greenland, the world's largest island, located almost entirely within the Arctic Circle.

Internet Links	
● United Nations Environment Programme	**www.unep.org**
● IUCN The International Union for Conservation of Nature	**www.iucn.org**
● NASA Visible Earth	**visibleearth.nasa.gov**
● NASA Earth Observatory	**earthobservatory.nasa.gov**
● Earth Resources Observation and Science	**edc.usgs.gov**

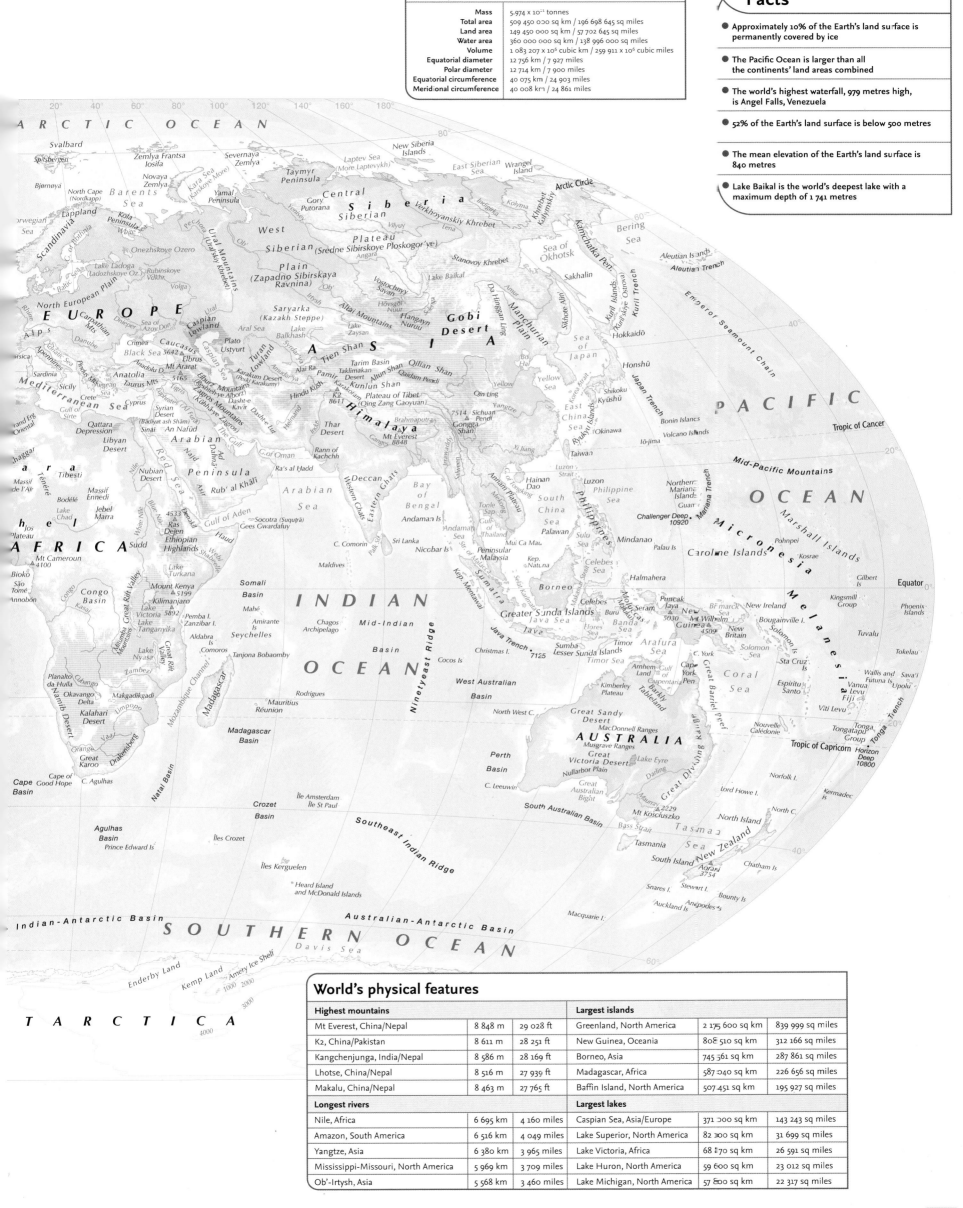

Earth's dimensions	
Mass	5 974 450 x 10²¹ tonnes
Total area	509 450 000 sq km / 196 698 645 sq miles
Land area	149 450 000 sq km / 57 702 645 sq miles
Water area	360 000 000 sq km / 138 996 000 sq miles
Volume	1 083 207 x 10⁶ cubic km / 259 911 x 10⁶ cubic miles
Equatorial diameter	12 756 km / 7 927 miles
Polar diameter	12 714 km / 7 900 miles
Equatorial circumference	40 075 km / 24 903 miles
Meridional circumference	40 008 km / 24 861 miles

Facts

- Approximately 10% of the Earth's land surface is permanently covered by ice
- The Pacific Ocean is larger than all the continents' land areas combined
- The world's highest waterfall, 979 metres high, is Angel Falls, Venezuela
- 52% of the Earth's land surface is below 500 metres
- The mean elevation of the Earth's land surface is 840 metres
- Lake Baikal is the world's deepest lake with a maximum depth of 1 741 metres

World's physical features

Highest mountains			Largest islands		
Mt Everest, China/Nepal	8 848 m	29 028 ft	Greenland, North America	2 175 600 sq km	839 999 sq miles
K2, China/Pakistan	8 611 m	28 251 ft	New Guinea, Oceania	808 510 sq km	312 166 sq miles
Kangchenjunga, India/Nepal	8 586 m	28 169 ft	Borneo, Asia	745 561 sq km	287 861 sq miles
Lhotse, China/Nepal	8 516 m	27 939 ft	Madagascar, Africa	587 040 sq km	226 656 sq miles
Makalu, China/Nepal	8 463 m	27 765 ft	Baffin Island, North America	507 451 sq km	195 927 sq miles
Longest rivers			**Largest lakes**		
Nile, Africa	6 695 km	4 160 miles	Caspian Sea, Asia/Europe	371 000 sq km	143 243 sq miles
Amazon, South America	6 516 km	4 049 miles	Lake Superior, North America	82 100 sq km	31 699 sq miles
Yangtze, Asia	6 380 km	3 965 miles	Lake Victoria, Africa	68 870 sq km	26 591 sq miles
Mississippi-Missouri, North America	5 969 km	3 709 miles	Lake Huron, North America	59 600 sq km	23 012 sq miles
Ob'-Irtysh, Asia	5 568 km	3 460 miles	Lake Michigan, North America	57 800 sq km	22 317 sq miles

World
Countries

The current pattern of the world's countries and territories is a result of a long history of exploration, colonialism, conflict and politics. The fact that there are currently 196 independent countries in the world – the most recent, South Sudan, only being created in July 2011 – illustrates the significant political changes which have occurred since 1950 when there were only eighty-two. There has been a steady progression away from colonial influences over the last fifty years, although many dependent overseas territories remain.

The shapes of countries and the pattern of international boundaries reflect both physical and political processes. Some borders follow natural features – rivers, mountain ranges, etc – others are defined according to political agreement or as a result of war. Some are still subject to dispute between two or more countries, and many remain undefined on the ground.

Facts

- The longest single continuous land border stretches for 6 416 kilometres between Canada and the USA
- Both China and the Russian Federation have land borders with 14 different countries
- Vatican City, the smallest independent country, was created in 1929 as an enclave within Rome, the capital of Italy
- All countries of the world are members of the United Nations except Kosovo, Taiwan and Vatican City

Internet Links

United Nations	www.un.org
Foreign and Commonwealth Office	www.fco.gov.uk
International Boundaries Research Unit	www.dur.ac.uk/ibru
Permanent Committee on Geographical Names	www.pcgn.org.uk
U.S. Board on Geographic Names	geonames.usgs.gov

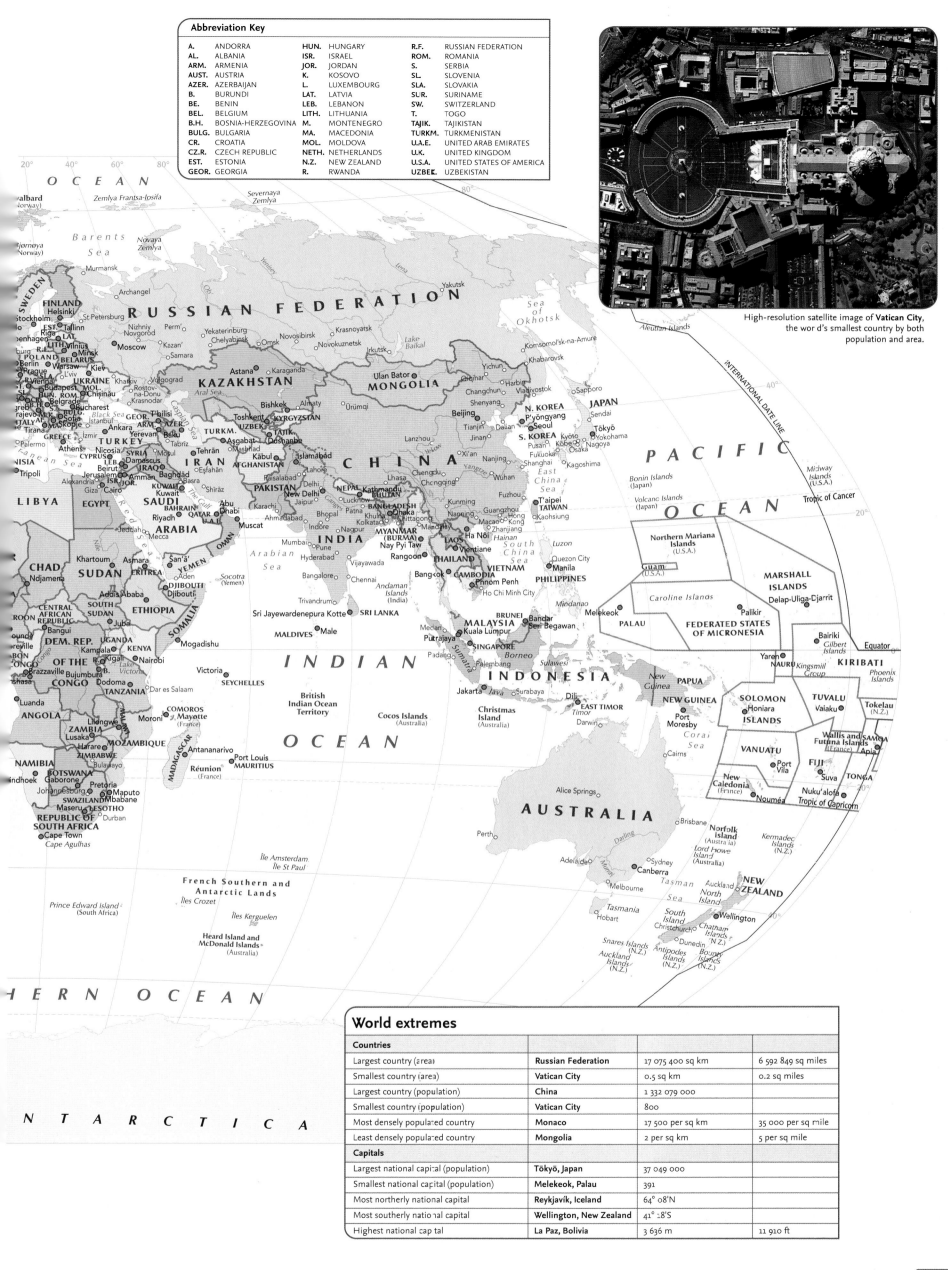

Abbreviation Key

A.	ANDORRA	HUN.	HUNGARY	R.F.	RUSSIAN FEDERATION
AL.	ALBANIA	ISR.	ISRAEL	ROM.	ROMANIA
ARM.	ARMENIA	JOR.	JORDAN	S.	SERBIA
AUST.	AUSTRIA	K.	KOSOVO	SL.	SLOVENIA
AZER.	AZERBAIJAN	L.	LUXEMBOURG	SLA.	SLOVAKIA
B.	BURUNDI	LAT.	LATVIA	SUR.	SURINAME
BE.	BENIN	LEB.	LEBANON	SW.	SWITZERLAND
BEL.	BELGIUM	LITH.	LITHUANIA	T.	TOGO
B.H.	BOSNIA-HERZEGOVINA	M.	MONTENEGRO	TAJIK.	TAJIKISTAN
BULG.	BULGARIA	MA.	MACEDONIA	TURKM.	TURKMENISTAN
CR.	CROATIA	MOL.	MOLDOVA	U.A.E.	UNITED ARAB EMIRATES
CZ.R.	CZECH REPUBLIC	NETH.	NETHERLANDS	U.K.	UNITED KINGDOM
EST.	ESTONIA	N.Z.	NEW ZEALAND	U.S.A.	UNITED STATES OF AMERICA
GEOR.	GEORGIA	R.	RWANDA	UZBEK.	UZBEKISTAN

High-resolution satellite image of **Vatican City**, the world's smallest country by both population and area.

World extremes

Countries			
Largest country (area)	**Russian Federation**	17 075 400 sq km	6 592 849 sq miles
Smallest country (area)	**Vatican City**	0.5 sq km	0.2 sq miles
Largest country (population)	**China**	1 332 079 000	
Smallest country (population)	**Vatican City**	800	
Most densely populated country	**Monaco**	17 500 per sq km	35 000 per sq mile
Least densely populated country	**Mongolia**	2 per sq km	5 per sq mile
Capitals			
Largest national capital (population)	**Tōkyō, Japan**	37 049 000	
Smallest national capital (population)	**Melekeok, Palau**	391	
Most northerly national capital	**Reykjavík, Iceland**	64° 08'N	
Most southerly national capital	**Wellington, New Zealand**	41° 18'S	
Highest national capital	**La Paz, Bolivia**	3 636 m	11 910 ft

World
Earthquakes and Volcanoes

Earthquakes and volcanoes hold a constant fascination because of their power, their beauty, and the fact that they cannot be controlled or accurately predicted. Our understanding of these phenomena relies mainly on the theory of plate tectonics. This defines the Earth's surface as a series of 'plates' which are constantly moving relative to each other, at rates of a few centimetres per year. As plates move against each other enormous pressure builds up and when the rocks can no longer bear this pressure they fracture, and energy is released as an earthquake. The pressures involved can also melt the rock to form magma which then rises to the Earth's surface to form a volcano. The distribution of earthquakes and volcanoes therefore relates closely to plate boundaries. In particular, most active volcanoes and much of the Earth's seismic activity are centred on the 'Ring of Fire' around the Pacific Ocean.

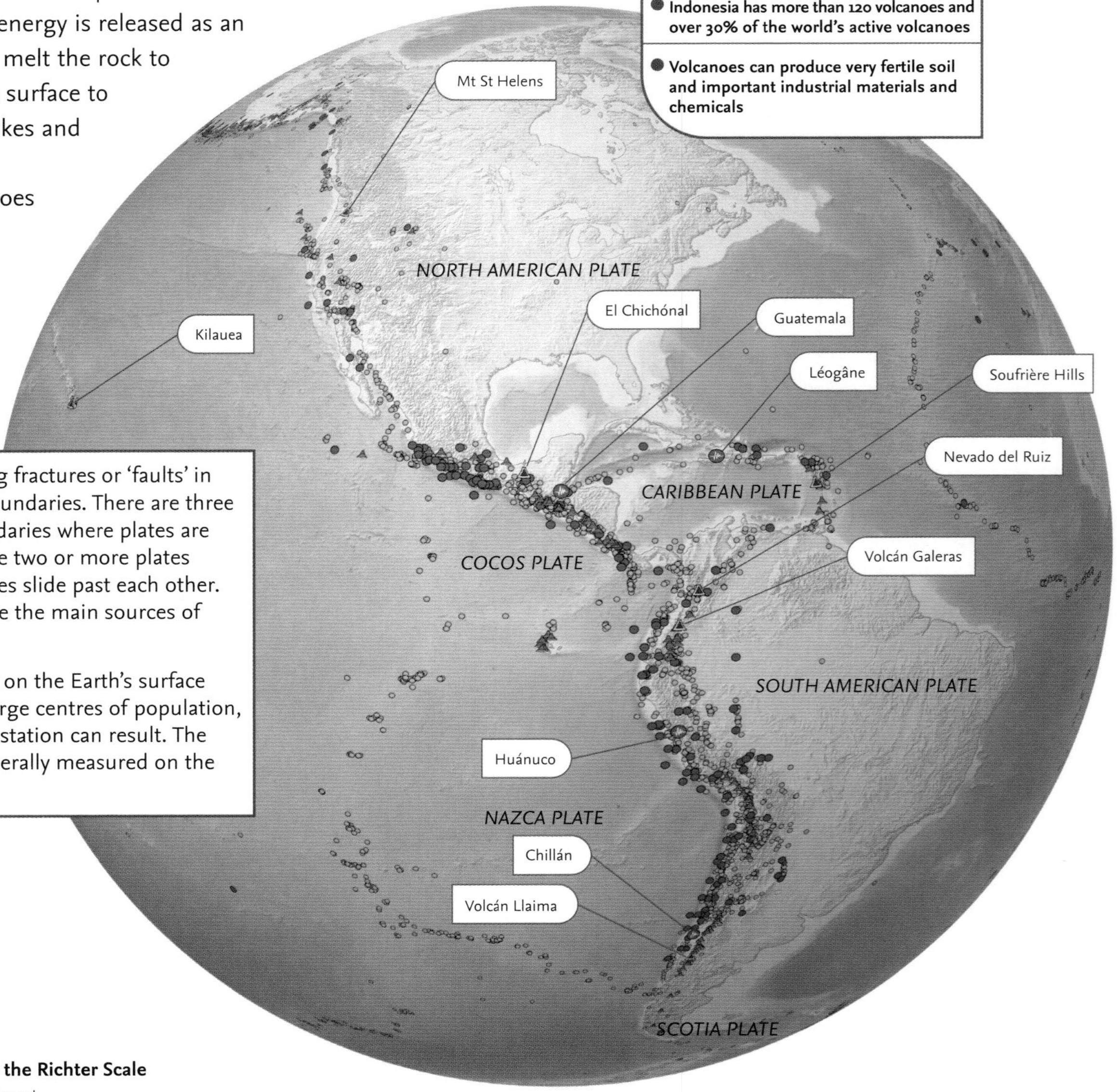

Earthquakes

Earthquakes are caused by movement along fractures or 'faults' in the Earth's crust, particularly along plate boundaries. There are three types of plate boundary: constructive boundaries where plates are moving apart; destructive boundaries where two or more plates collide; conservative boundaries where plates slide past each other. Destructive and conservative boundaries are the main sources of earthquake activity.

The epicentre of an earthquake is the point on the Earth's surface directly above its source. If this is near to large centres of population, and the earthquake is powerful, major devastation can result. The size, or magnitude, of an earthquake is generally measured on the Richter Scale.

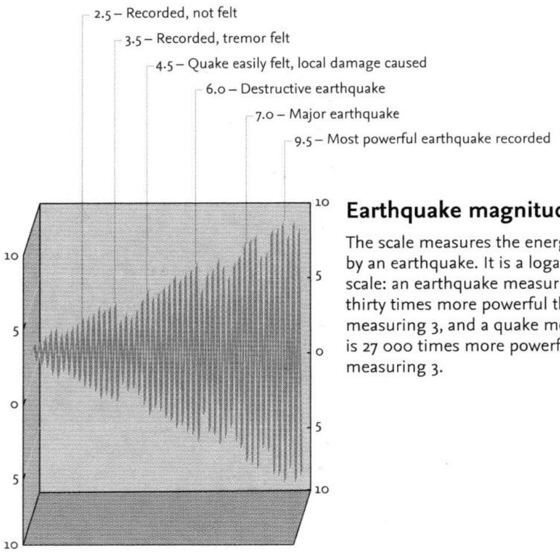

Labels on globe (North/South America)
Mt St Helens, Kilauea, NORTH AMERICAN PLATE, El Chichónal, Guatemala, Léogâne, Soufrière Hills, Nevado del Ruíz, CARIBBEAN PLATE, COCOS PLATE, Volcán Galeras, SOUTH AMERICAN PLATE, Huánuco, NAZCA PLATE, Chillán, Volcán Llaima, SCOTIA PLATE

Richter Scale key
- 2.5 – Recorded, not felt
- 3.5 – Recorded, tremor felt
- 4.5 – Quake easily felt, local damage caused
- 6.0 – Destructive earthquake
- 7.0 – Major earthquake
- 9.5 – Most powerful earthquake recorded

Earthquake magnitude – the Richter Scale

The scale measures the energy released by an earthquake. It is a logarithmic scale: an earthquake measuring 4 is thirty times more powerful than one measuring 3, and a quake measuring 6 is 27 000 times more powerful than one measuring 3.

Chlef

SOUTH AMERICAN PLATE

Plate boundaries

Labels
EURASIAN PLATE, NORTH AMERICAN PLATE, ARABIAN PLATE, PHILIPPINE PLATE, PACIFIC PLATE, CARIBBEAN PLATE, COCOS PLATE, SOUTH AMERICAN PLATE, AFRICAN PLATE, SOUTH AMERICAN PLATE, INDO-AUSTRALIAN PLATE, NAZCA PLATE, SCOTIA PLATE, ANTARCTIC PLATE, SCOTIA PLATE

- Constructive boundary
- Destructive boundary
- Conservative boundary

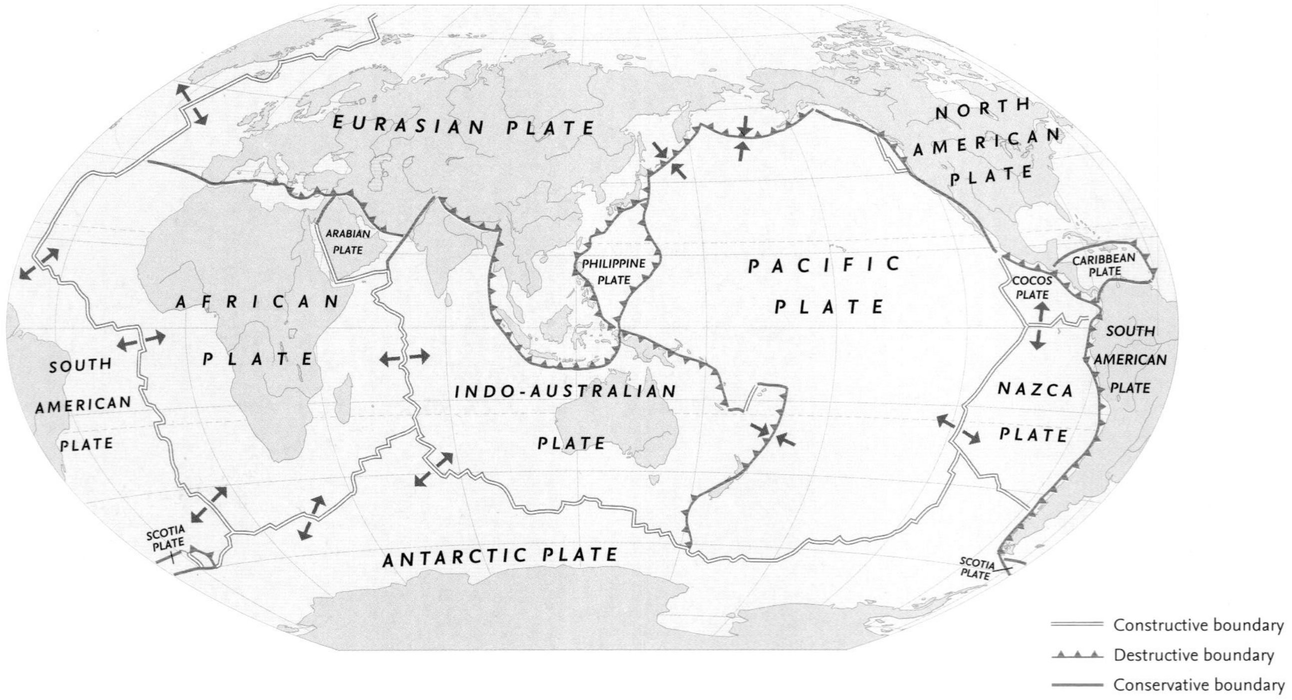

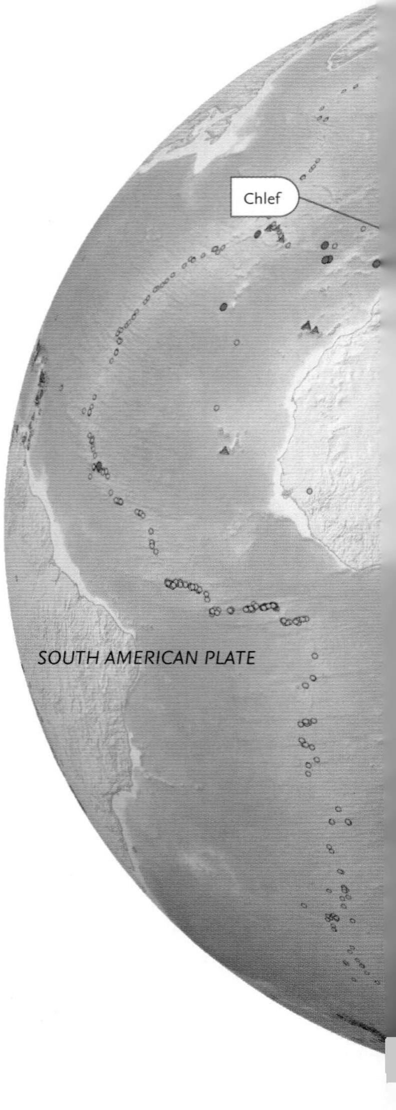

- ◑ Deadliest earthquake
- ● Earthquake of magnitude 7.5 or greater
- ○ Earthquake of magnitude 5.5 – 7.4
- ▲ Major volcano
- ▲ Other volcano

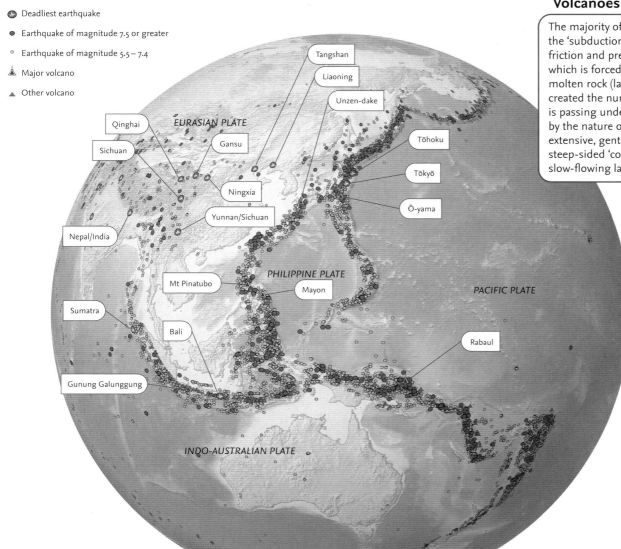

Volcanoes

The majority of volcanoes occur along destructive plate boundaries in the 'subduction zone' where one plate passes under another. The friction and pressure causes the rock to melt and to form magma which is forced upwards to the Earth's surface where it erupts as molten rock (lava) or as particles of ash or cinder. This process created the numerous volcanoes in the Andes, where the Nazca Plate is passing under the South American Plate. Volcanoes can be defined by the nature of the material they emit. 'Shield' volcanoes have extensive, gentle slopes formed from free-flowing lava, while steep-sided 'continental' volcanoes are created from thicker, slow-flowing lava and ash.

Major volcanic eruptions 1980–2011

Volcano	Country	Date
Mt St Helens	USA	1980
El Chichónal	Mexico	1982
Gunung Galunggung	Indonesia	1982
Kilauea	Hawaii, USA	1983
Ō-yama	Japan	1983
Nevado del Ruiz	Colombia	1985
Mt Pinatubo	Philippines	1991
Unzen-dake	Japan	1991
Mayon	Philippines	1993
Volcán Galeras	Colombia	1993
Volcán Llaima	Chile	1994
Rabaul	Papua New Guinea	1994
Soufrière Hills	Montserrat	1997
Hekla	Iceland	2000
Mt Etna	Italy	2001
Nyiragongo	Dem. Rep. of the Congo	2002
Eyjafjallajökull	Iceland	2010

Deadliest earthquakes since 1900

Year	Location	Deaths
1905	Kangra, India	19 000
1907	west of Dushanbe, Tajikistan	12 000
1908	Messina, Italy	110 000
1915	Abruzzo, Italy	35 000
1917	Bali, Indonesia	15 000
1920	Ningxia Province, China	200 000
1923	Tōkyō, Japan	142 807
1927	Qinghai Province, China	200 000
1932	Gansu Province, China	70 000
1933	Sichuan Province, China	10 000
1934	Nepal/India	10 700
1935	Quetta, Pakistan	30 000
1939	Chillán, Chile	28 000
1939	Erzincan, Turkey	32 700
1948	Aşgabat, Turkmenistan	19 800
1962	northwest Iran	12 225
1970	Huánuco Province, Peru	66 794
1974	Yunnan and Sichuan Provinces, China	20 000
1975	Liaoning Province, China	10 000
1976	central Guatemala	22 778
1976	Tangshan, Hebei Province, China	255 000
1978	Khorāsān Province, Iran	20 000
1980	Chlef, Algeria	11 000
1988	Spitak, Armenia	25 000
1990	Manjil, Iran	50 000
1999	İzmit (Kocaeli), Turkey	17 000
2001	Gujarat, India	20 000
2003	Bam, Iran	26 271
2004	off Sumatra, Indian Ocean	> 225 000
2005	northwest Pakistan	74 648
2008	Sichuan Province, China	> 60 000
2009	Abruzzo region, Italy	308
2009	Sumatra, Indonesia	> 1 100
2010	Léogâne, Haiti	222 570
2011	Tōhoku, Japan	14 500

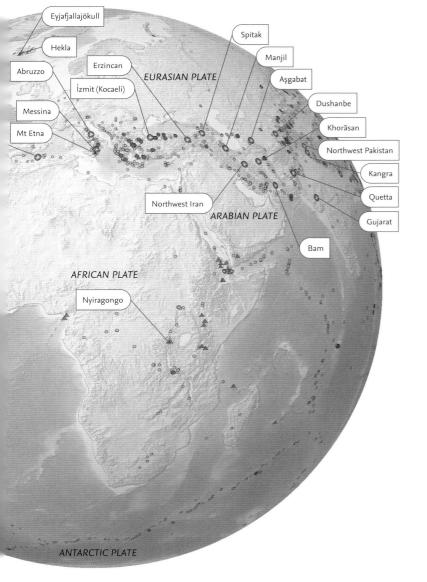

Internet Links

● USGS National Earthquake Hazards Program	earthquake.usgs.gov/regional/neic
● USGS Volcano Hazards Program	volcanoes.usgs.gov
● British Geological Survey	www.bgs.ac.uk
● NASA Natural Hazards	earthobservatory.nasa.gov/NaturalHazards
● Volcano World	volcano.oregonstate.edu

World
Climate and Weather

The climate of a region is defined by its long-term prevailing weather conditions. Classification of Climate Types is based on the relationship between temperature and humidity and how these factors are affected by latitude, altitude, ocean currents and winds. Weather is the specific short term condition which occurs locally and consists of events such as thunderstorms, hurricanes, blizzards and heat waves. Temperature and rainfall data recorded at weather stations can be plotted graphically and the graphs shown here, typical of each climate region, illustrate the various combinations of temperature and rainfall which exist worldwide for each month of the year. Data used for climate graphs are based on average monthly figures recorded over a minimum period of thirty years.

World Statistics: see pages **190–196**

Major climate regions, ocean currents and sea surface temperatures

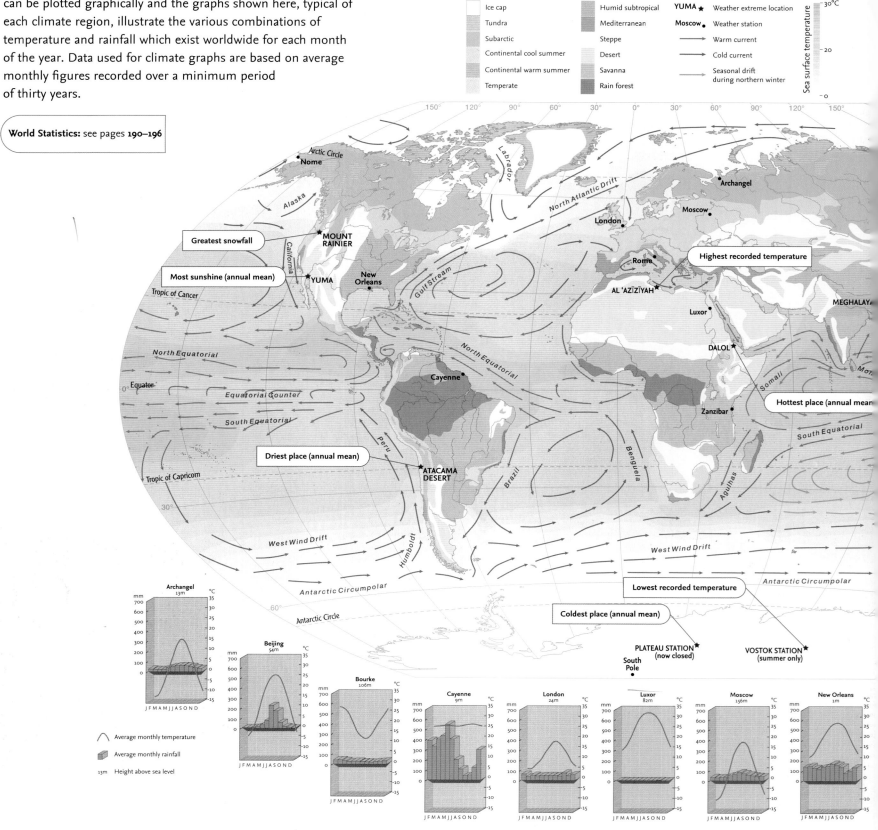

Ice cap	Humid subtropical	YUMA ★ Weather extreme location
Tundra	Mediterranean	Moscow ● Weather station
Subarctic	Steppe	→ Warm current
Continental cool summer	Desert	→ Cold current
Continental warm summer	Savanna	→ Seasonal drift during northern winter
Temperate	Rain forest	

Average monthly temperature

Average monthly rainfall

13m Height above sea level

Climate change

The temperatures in 2010 were the warmest on record, along with 2005 and 1998. Globally, the ten hottest years have all been since 1998 and the global average temperature in 2010 was 0.53°C above the 1961–90 mean. Most of this warming is caused by human activities which result in a build-up of greenhouse gases, mainly carbon dioxide, allowing heat to be trapped within the atmosphere. Carbon dioxide emissions have increased since the beginning of the industrial revolution due to burning of fossil fuels, increased urbanization, population growth, deforestation and industrial pollution.

Annual climate indicators such as number of frost-free days, length of growing season, heat wave frequency, number of wet days, length of dry spells and frequency of weather extremes are used to monitor climate change. The map opposite shows how future changes in temperature will not be spread evenly around the world. Some regions will warm faster than the global average, while others will warm more slowly. The Arctic is warming twice as fast as other areas mainly due to ice melting and there being less to reflect sunlight to keep the surface cool.

Facts

- Arctic Sea ice thickness has declined 40% in the last 40 years
- El Niño and La Niña episodes occur at irregular intervals of 2–7 years
- Sea levels are rising by one centimetre per decade
- Precipitation in the northern hemisphere is increasing
- Droughts have increased in frequency and intensity in parts of Asia and Africa

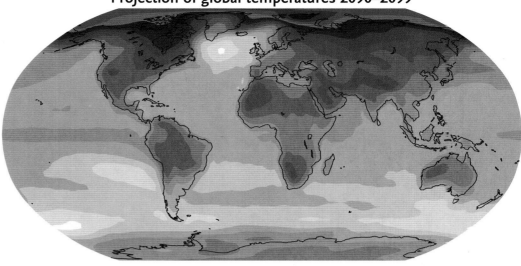

0.5 1 1.5 2 2.5 3 3.5 4 4.5 5 5.5 6 6.5 7 7.5

Change in average surface temperature (°C)

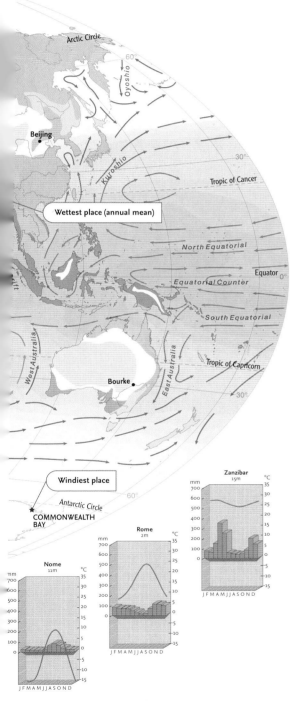

Arctic Circle

60°

Oyoshio

Beijing

Kuroshio

30°

Tropic of Cancer

Wettest place (annual mean)

North Equatorial

Equatorial Counter

Equator 0°

South Equatorial

West Australia

East Australia

Bourke

Tropic of Capricorn

30°

Windiest place

60°

Antarctic Circle

COMMONWEALTH BAY

Nome
11m

Rome
2m

Zanzibar
15m

Tracks of tropical storms

Tennessee-Alabama-Ohio 2002
East Coast 2004
Louisiana 2005, 2008
Florida-New Jersey 1996
Texas 1997, 2008
S. Carolina-Virginia 1996, 2003
N.W. Mexico 1995
South Korea 1995, 1999
Bahamas-E. USA 1999, 2004, 2005
W. Mexico 1995, 1997, 2002, 2004, 2009, 2011
Florida Alabama 2004, 2005
Zhejiang 1994, 1997
Kyūshū 1934, 2005
Caribbean 1994, 1998, 2004, 2005, 2008, 2010, 2011
1994, 1997, 2007, 2009, 2011
Bangladesh 1996
Puerto Rico, Virgin Is 1996
Orissa 1999
Taiwan 1994, 1996, 1997, 2005, 2006, 2009
S. Mexico 1997, 2005
N.E. Caribbean
Oman 2007
Myanmar 2008, 2010
Philippines 1994, 1995, 1998, 2004, 2006, 2009, 2011
Central America 1998, 2005
Colombia 1995, 1998, 2004, 2007, 2009, 2010
West India 1996, 1998
Andhra Pradesh 1996
S. Vietnam, Cambodia 1997
Costa Rica 1996
Tamil Nadu 1996
Sabah 1996
Papua New Guinea 2007
Mozambique 1994, 2000
Madagascar 1997, 2000, 2008
N. Coast 2005
Queensland 2006, 2011
N.W. Coast 2005, 2007, 2009
2005

→ Cyclone track
→ Hurricane track
→ Typhoon track
● Major tropical storm
Source area of tropical storms
Tornado high risk areas

Tropical storms

Tropical storms are among the most powerful and destructive weather systems on Earth. Of the eighty to one hundred which develop annually over the tropical oceans, many make landfall and cause considerable damage to property and loss of life as a result of high winds and heavy rain. Although the number of tropical storms is projected to decrease, their intensity, and therefore their destructive power, is likely to increase.

Hurricane Ophelia near Puerto Rico, September 2011.

Weather extremes	
Highest recorded temperature	57.8°C/136°F Al'Azīzīyah, Libya (September 1922)
Hottest place - annual mean	34.4°C/93.9°F Dalol, Ethiopia
Driest place - annual mean	0.1mm/0.004 inches Atacama Desert, Chile
Most sunshine - annual mean	90% Yuma, Arizona, USA (over 4000 hours)
Lowest recorded temperature	-89.2°C/-128.6°F Vostok Station, Antarctica (July 1983)
Coldest place - annual mean	-56.6°C/-69.9°F Plateau Station, Antarctica
Wettest place annual mean	11 873 mm/467.4 inches Meghalaya, India
Greatest snowfall	31 102 mm/1 224.5 inches Mount Rainier, Washington, USA (February 1971 – February 1972)
Windiest place	322 km per hour/200 miles per hour (in gales) Commonwealth Bay, Antarctica

Internet Links	
● Met Office	www.metoffice.gov.uk
● BBC Weather Centre	www.bbc.co.uk/weather
● National Oceanic and Atmospheric Administration	www.noaa.gov
● National Climatic Data Center	www.ncdc.noaa.gov
● United Nations World Meteorological Organization	www.wmo.ch

World
Land Cover

The oxygen- and water-rich environment of the Earth has helped create a wide range of habitats. Forest and woodland ecosystems form the predominant natural land cover over most of the Earth's surface. Tropical rainforests are part of an intricate land-atmosphere relationship that is disturbed by land cover changes. Forests in the tropics are believed to hold most of the world's bird, animal, and plant species. Grassland, shrubland and deserts collectively cover most of the unwooded land surface, with tundra on frozen subsoil at high northern latitudes. These areas tend to have lower species diversity than most forests, with the notable exception of Mediterranean shrublands, which support some of the most diverse floras on the earth. Humans have extensively altered most grassland and shrubland areas, usually through conversion to agriculture, burning and introduction of domestic livestock. They have had less immediate impact on tundra and true desert regions, although these remain vulnerable to global climate change.

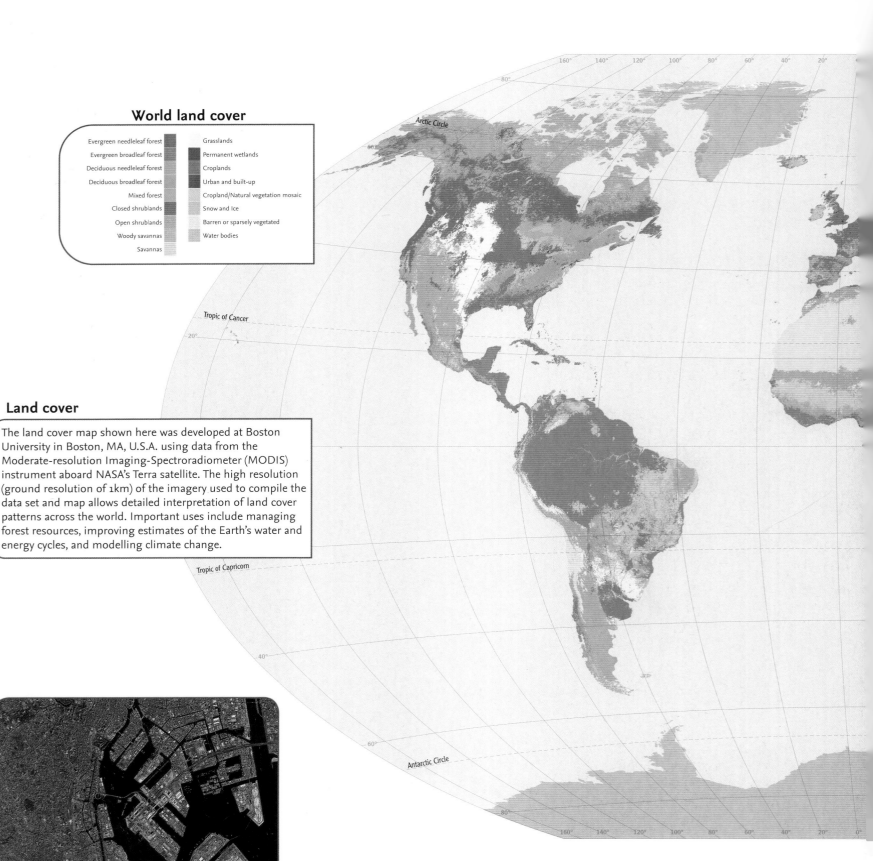

World land cover

Evergreen needleleaf forest	Grasslands
Evergreen broadleaf forest	Permanent wetlands
Deciduous needleleaf forest	Croplands
Deciduous broadleaf forest	Urban and built-up
Mixed forest	Cropland/Natural vegetation mosaic
Closed shrublands	Snow and Ice
Open shrublands	Barren or sparsely vegetated
Woody savannas	Water bodies
Savannas	

Land cover

The land cover map shown here was developed at Boston University in Boston, MA, U.S.A. using data from the Moderate-resolution Imaging-Spectroradiometer (MODIS) instrument aboard NASA's Terra satellite. The high resolution (ground resolution of 1km) of the imagery used to compile the data set and map allows detailed interpretation of land cover patterns across the world. Important uses include managing forest resources, improving estimates of the Earth's water and energy cycles, and modelling climate change.

Urban, Tōkyō, capital of Japan and the largest city in the world.

Land cover composition and change

The continents all have different characteristics. There are extensive croplands in North America and eastern Europe, while south of the Sahara are belts of grass/shrubland which are at risk from desertification. Tropical forests are not pristine areas either as they show signs of human activity in deforestation of land for crops or grazing.

Cropland, near Consuegra, Spain.

Barren/Shrubland, Mojave Desert, California, United States of America.

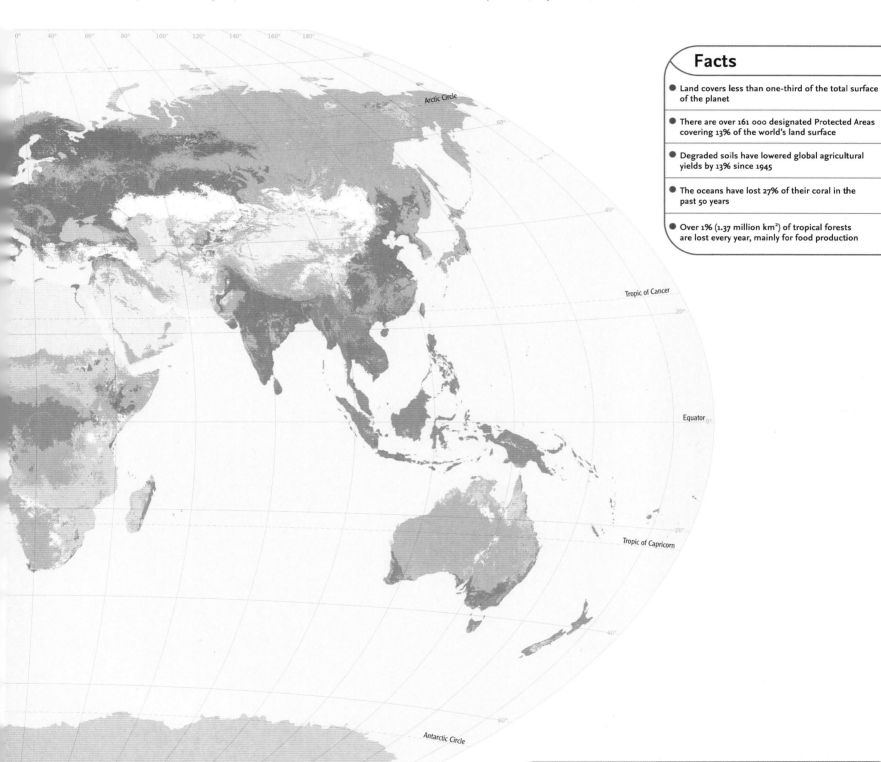

Internet Links

World Resources Institute	www.wri.org
World Conservation Monitoring Centre	www.unep-wcmc.org
United Nations Environment Programme (UNEP)	www.unep.org
IUCN, International Union for Conservation of Nature	www.iucn.org
MODIS Land Cover Group at Boston University	www-modis.bu.edu/landcover/index.html

Snow and ice, Larsen Ice Shelf, Antarctica.

World
Population

After increasing very slowly for most of human history, world population more than doubled in the last half century. Whereas world population did not pass the one billion mark until 1804 and took another 123 years to reach two billion in 1927, it then added the third billion in 33 years, the fourth in 14 years and the fifth in 13 years. Just twelve years later on October 12, 1999 the United Nations announced that the global population had reached the six billion mark, with seven billion being reached only eleven years later, on October 31, 2011. It is expected that another two billion people will have been added to the world's population by 2043.

World Statistics: see pages 190–196

World population distribution
Population density (2005), continental populations (2011)
and continental population change (2010–2015)

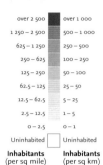

over 2 500	over 1 000
1 250 – 2 500	500 – 1 000
625 – 1 250	250 – 500
250 – 625	100 – 250
125 – 250	50 – 100
62.5 – 125	25 – 50
12.5 – 62.5	5 – 25
2.5 – 12.5	1 – 5
0 – 2.5	0 – 1
Uninhabited	Uninhabited

Inhabitants (per sq mile) / Inhabitants (per sq km)

World population change

Population growth since 1950 has been spread very unevenly between the continents. While overall numbers have been growing rapidly since 1950, a massive 89 per cent increase has taken place in the less developed regions, especially southern and eastern Asia. In contrast, Europe's population level has been almost stationary and is expected to decrease in the future. India and China alone are responsible for over one-third of current growth. Most of the highest rates of growth are to be found in Sub-Saharan Africa and, until population growth is brought under tighter control, the developing world in particular will continue to face enormous problems of supporting a rising population.

North America
Total population 360 956 000
Population change 0.9%

Europe
Total population 771 195 000
Population change 0.1%

Latin America and the Caribbean
Total population 605 602 000
Population change 1.1%

World
Total population 7 084 322 000
Population change 1.1%

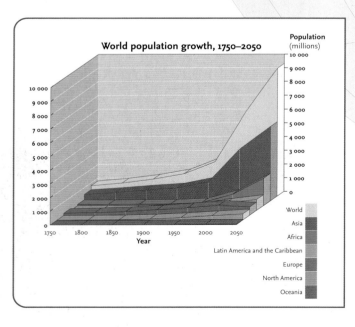

World population growth, 1750–2050

Population (millions)

Year

World
Asia
Africa
Latin America and the Caribbean
Europe
North America
Oceania

Top 10 countries by population, 2011

Rank	Country	Population
1	China	1 347 565 324
2	India	1 241 491 960
3	United States of America	313 085 380
4	Indonesia	242 325 638
5	Brazil	196 655 014
6	Pakistan	176 745 364
7	Nigeria	162 470 737
8	Bangladesh	150 493 658
9	Russian Federation	142 835 555
10	Japan	126 497 241

The island nation of **Singapore**, the world's second most densely populated country.

Facts

- ● The world's population is growing at an annual rate of 83 million people per year

- ● Today's population is only 6.5% of the total number of people who ever lived on the Earth

- ● It is expected that in 2050 there will be more people aged over 60 than children aged less than 14

- ● More than 90% of the 82 million inhabitants of Egypt are located around the River Nile

- ● India's population reached 1 billion in August 1999

Asia
Total population 4 257 672 000
Population change 1.0%

Africa
Total population 1 050 654 000
Population change 2.3%

Oceania
Total population 38 242 000
Population change 1.5%

Top 10 countries by population density, 2010
(persons per square kilometre)

Rank	Country*	Population density
1	Bangladesh	1 045
2	South Korea	486
3	India	378
4	Belgium	352
5	Japan	335
6	Philippines	316
7	Vietnam	268
8	United Kingdom	257
9	Germany	230
10	Pakistan	222

*Only countries with a population of over 10 million are considered

Kuna Indians inhabit this congested island off the north coast of Panama.

World
Urbanization and Cities

The world is becoming increasingly urban but the level of urbanization varies greatly between and within continents. At the beginning of the twentieth century only fourteen per cent of the world's population was urban and by 1950 this had increased to thirty per cent. In the more developed regions and in Latin America and the Caribbean over seventy per cent of the population is urban while in Africa and Asia the figure is forty per cent. In recent decades urban growth has increased rapidly to over fifty per cent and there will be nearly 500 cities with over 1 000 000 inhabitants. It is in the developing regions that the most rapid increases are taking place and it is expected that by 2030 over half of urban dwellers worldwide will live in Asia. Migration from the countryside to the city in the search for better job opportunities is the main factor in urban growth.

World Statistics: see pages 190–196

World Statistics: see pages 190–196

Facts

- From 2008, cities occupying less than 2% of the Earth's land surface will house over 50% of the human population
- Urban growth rates in Africa are the highest in the world
- Antarctica is uninhabited and most settlements in the Arctic regions have less than 5 000 inhabitants
- By 2015 India will have 52 cities with over one million inhabitants
- London was the first city to reach a population of over 5 million

Level of urbanization and the world's largest cities

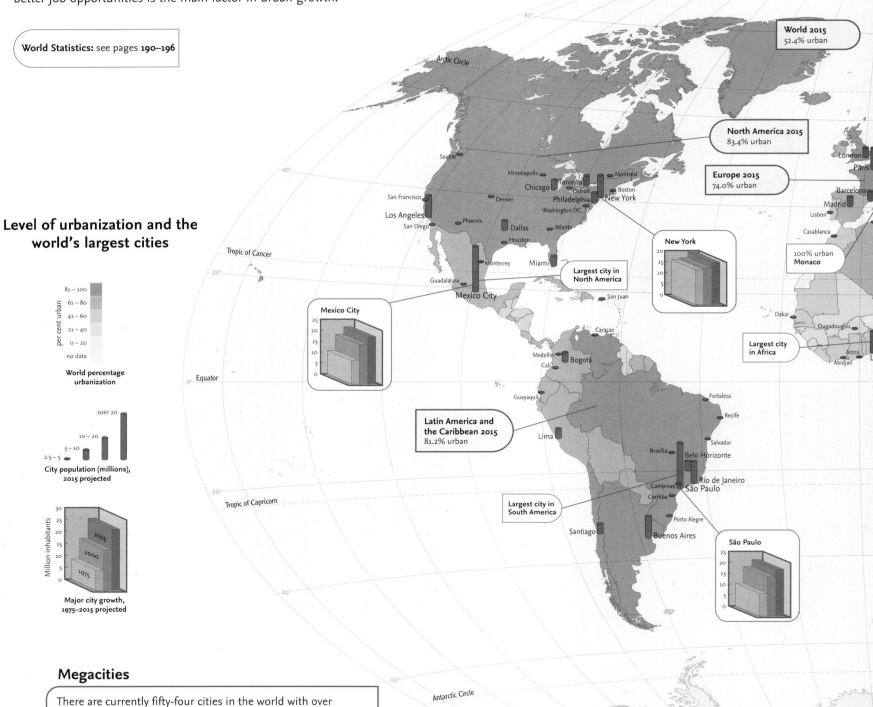

per cent urban
- 81 – 100
- 61 – 80
- 41 – 60
- 21 – 40
- 0 – 20
- no data

World percentage urbanization

City population (millions), 2015 projected
- over 20
- 10 – 20
- 5 – 10
- 2.5 – 5

Major city growth, 1975–2015 projected
Million inhabitants
2015
2000
1975

World 2015
52.4% urban

North America 2015
83.4% urban

Europe 2015
74.0% urban

New York
Largest city in North America

100% urban
Monaco

Largest city in Africa

Mexico City

Latin America and the Caribbean 2015
81.2% urban

Largest city in South America

São Paulo

Megacities

There are currently fifty-four cities in the world with over 5 000 000 inhabitants. Twenty-one of these, often referred to as megacities, have over 10 000 000 inhabitants and one has over 30 000 000. Tōkyō, with 37 049 000 inhabitants, has remained the world's largest city since 1970 and is likely to remain so for the next decade. Other cities expected to grow to over 20 000 000 by 2015 are Mumbai, São Paulo, Delhi and Mexico City. Ten of the world's megacities are in Asia, all of them having over 10 000 000 inhabitants.

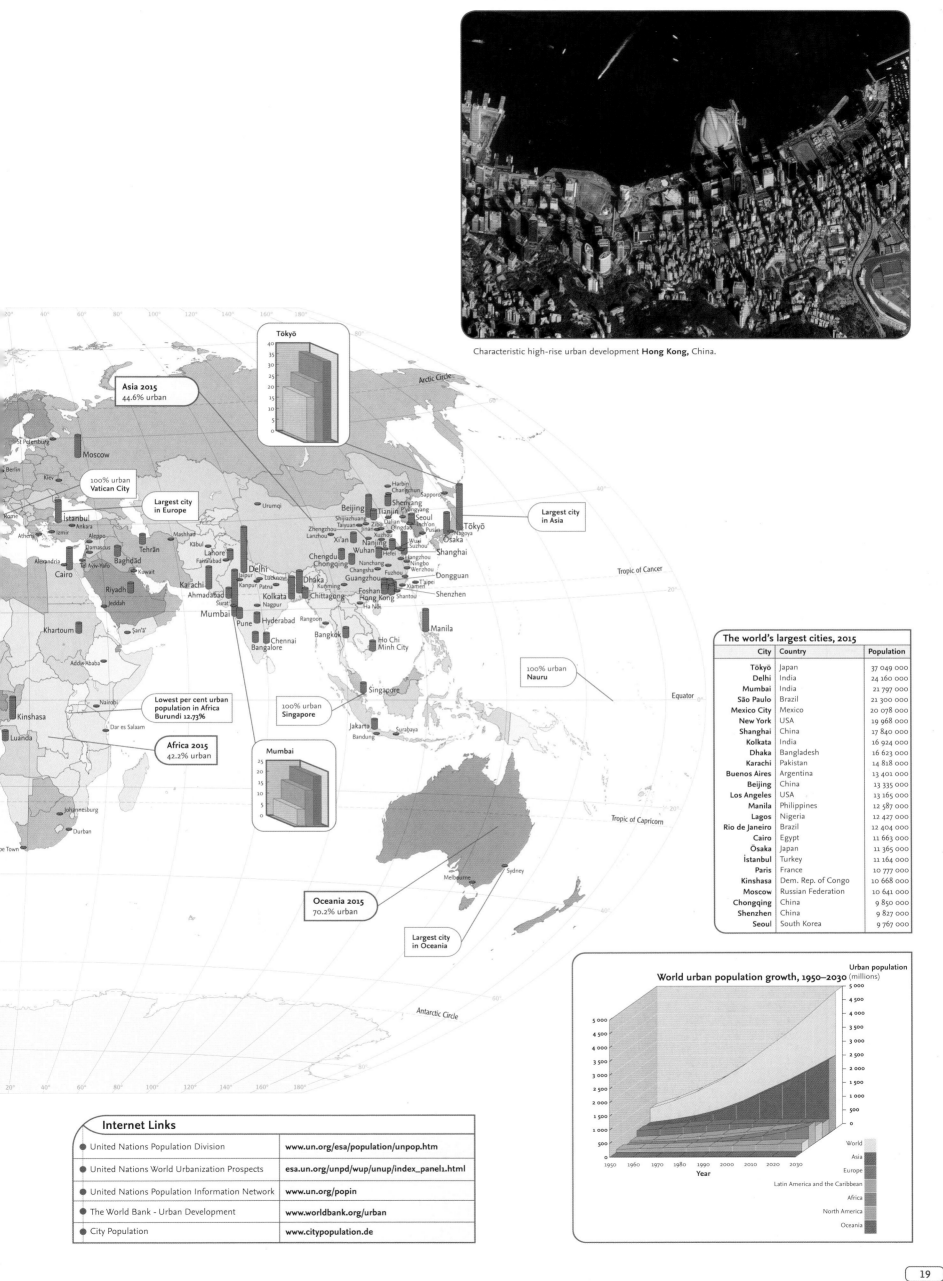

Characteristic high-rise urban development **Hong Kong**, China.

Tōkyō

Asia 2015
44.6% urban

100% urban
Vatican City

Largest city
in Europe

Largest city
in Asia

100% urban
Nauru

Lowest per cent urban
population in Africa
Burundi 12.73%

100% urban
Singapore

Africa 2015
42.2% urban

Mumbai

Oceania 2015
70.2% urban

Largest city
in Oceania

St Petersburg
Moscow
Berlin
Kiev
Rome
İstanbul
Ankara
İzmir
Athens
Aleppo
Damascus
Tel Aviv-Yafo
Baghdād
Kuwait
Alexandria
Cairo
Riyadh
Jeddah
Şan'ā'
Khartoum
Addis Ababa
Nairobi
Dar es Salaam
Kinshasa
Luanda
Johannesburg
Durban
Cape Town
Mashhad
Tehrān
Kābul
Lahore
Faisalabad
Karachi
Ahmadabad
Surat
Mumbai
Pune
Hyderabad
Bangalore
Chennai
Kolkata
Nagpur
Delhi
Jaipur
Kanpur
Lucknow
Patna
Dhaka
Chittagong
Rangoon
Bangkok
Ho Chi
Minh City
Singapore
Jakarta
Bandung
Surabaya
Manila
Urumqi
Harbin
Changchun
Sapporo
Beijing
Tianjin
Shenyang
Pyongyang
Seoul
Inch'on
Pusan
Tōkyō
Nagoya
Ōsaka
Shanghai
Shijiazhuang
Taiyuan
Zibo
Dalian
Zhengzhou
Jinan
Qingdao
Lanzhou
Xuzhou
Xi'an
Nanjing
Wuhan
Hefei
Chengdu
Nanchang
Chongqing
Changsha
Hangzhou
Ningbo
Wenzhou
Fuzhou
Guangzhou
Kunming
Foshan
Dongguan
Hong Kong
Shantou
Shenzhen
T'aipei
Xiamen
Ha Nôi

Arctic Circle
Tropic of Cancer
Equator
Tropic of Capricorn
Antarctic Circle

Melbourne
Sydney

The world's largest cities, 2015

City	Country	Population
Tōkyō	Japan	37 049 000
Delhi	India	24 160 000
Mumbai	India	21 797 000
São Paulo	Brazil	21 300 000
Mexico City	Mexico	20 078 000
New York	USA	19 968 000
Shanghai	China	17 840 000
Kolkata	India	16 924 000
Dhaka	Bangladesh	16 623 000
Karachi	Pakistan	14 818 000
Buenos Aires	Argentina	13 401 000
Beijing	China	13 335 000
Los Angeles	USA	13 165 000
Manila	Philippines	12 587 000
Lagos	Nigeria	12 427 000
Rio de Janeiro	Brazil	12 404 000
Cairo	Egypt	11 663 000
Ōsaka	Japan	11 365 000
İstanbul	Turkey	11 164 000
Paris	France	10 777 000
Kinshasa	Dem. Rep. of Congo	10 668 000
Moscow	Russian Federation	10 641 000
Chongqing	China	9 850 000
Shenzhen	China	9 827 000
Seoul	South Korea	9 767 000

World urban population growth, 1950–2030 (millions)

Urban population

Year
1950 1960 1970 1980 1990 2000 2010 2020 2030

World
Asia
Europe
Latin America and the Caribbean
Africa
North America
Oceania

Internet Links

● United Nations Population Division	www.un.org/esa/population/unpop.htm
● United Nations World Urbanization Prospects	esa.un.org/unpd/wup/unup/index_panel1.html
● United Nations Population Information Network	www.un.org/popin
● The World Bank - Urban Development	www.worldbank.org/urban
● City Population	www.citypopulation.de

World
Communications

Increased availability and ownership of telecommunications equipment since the beginning of the 1970s has aided the globalization of the world economy. Over half of the world's fixed telephone lines have been installed since the mid-1980s and the majority of the world's internet hosts have come on line since 1997. There are now over one billion fixed telephone lines in the world. The number of mobile cellular subscribers has grown dramatically from sixteen million in 1991 to almost six billion today.

The internet is the fastest growing communications network of all time. It is relatively cheap and now links over 556 million host computers globally. Its growth has resulted in the emergence of hundreds of Internet Service Providers (ISPs) and internet traffic is now doubling every six months. In 1993 the number of internet users was estimated to be just under ten million, there are now over two billion.

Internet users

Internet users per
100 inhabitants 2010

- 80 – 100
- 60 – 79.9
- 40 – 59.9
- 20 – 39.9
- 0 – 19.9
- no data

Total internet users
Top ten countries

China
485 000 000

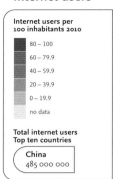

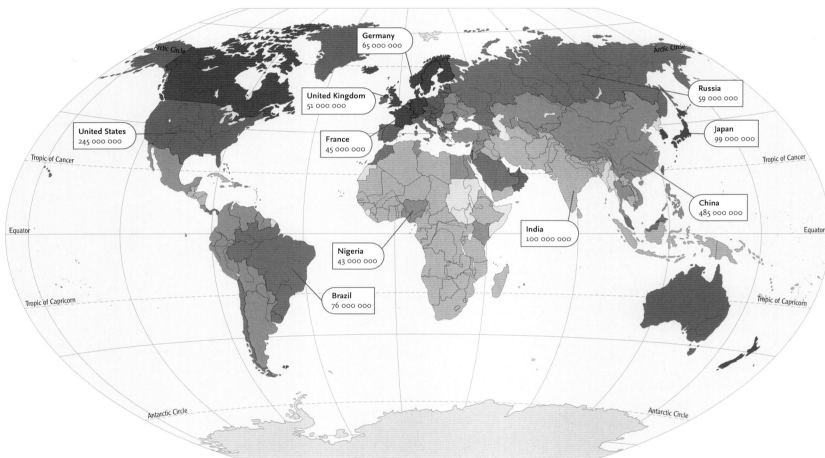

Germany
65 000 000

United Kingdom
51 000 000

United States
245 000 000

France
45 000 000

Russia
59 000 000

Japan
99 000 000

China
485 000 000

India
100 000 000

Nigeria
43 000 000

Brazil
76 000 000

The Internet

The Internet is a global network of millions of computers around the world, all capable of being connected to each other. Internet Service Providers (ISPs) provide access via 'host' computers, of which there are now over 556 million. It has become a vital means of communication and data transfer for businesses, governments and financial and academic institutions, with a steadily increasing proportion of business transactions being carried out on-line. Personal use of the Internet – particularly for access to the World Wide Web information network, and for e-mail communication – has increased enormously and there are now estimated to be over two billion users worldwide.

Top Broadband Economies 2011
Countries with the highest broadband penetration rate – subscribers per 100 inhabitants

	Top Economies	Rate
1	Netherlands	38.1
2	Switzerland	37.9
3	Denmark	37.7
4	South Korea	35.7
5	Norway	35.3
6	Iceland	34.1
7	France	33.9
8	Luxembourg	33.2
9	Sweden	31.8
10	Germany	31.7
11	United Kingdom	31.6
12	Belgium	31.5
13	Hong Kong, China	29.9
14	Canada	29.8
15	Finland	28.6
16	USA	27.6
17	Malta	27.5
18	Japan	26.9
19	Estonia	25.1
20	Singapore	24.9

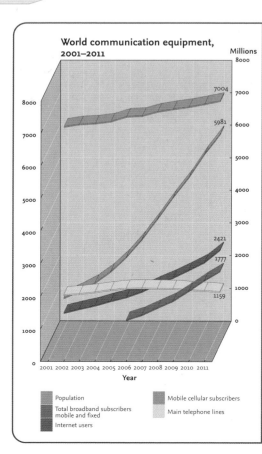

World communication equipment, 2001–2011

Millions

7004
5981
2421
1777
1159

2001 2002 2003 2004 2005 2006 2007 2008 2009 2010 2011
Year

- Population
- Total broadband subscribers mobile and fixed
- Internet users
- Mobile cellular subscribers
- Main telephone lines

Mobile phone subscribers

In 2011, there were almost six billion mobile cellular subscribers and it was estimated that out of every one hundred people, eighty-seven of them owned a mobile. One area showing a recent change with the development of new mobile cellular technology, is mobile broadband where subscribers are now double the number of fixed broadband subscribers in all regions. The total number of Short Message Service (SMS) or text messages sent globally tripled between 2007 and 2010 to over 6 trillion messages, around 200 000 every second. Many phone packages now include "unlimited" free text messages encouraging many shorter messages to be sent.

The rise of 3G

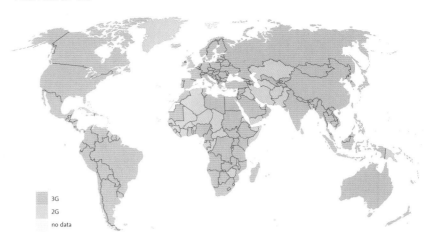

3G
2G
no data

Mobile phone subscribers

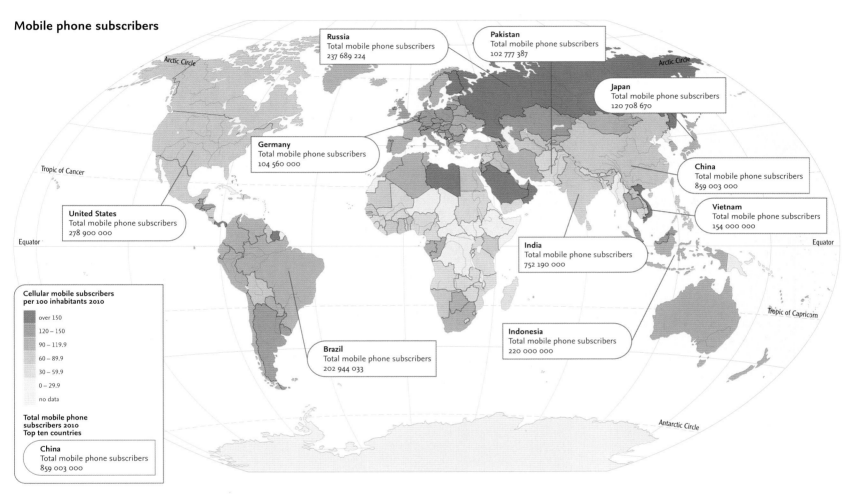

Russia
Total mobile phone subscribers
237 689 224

Pakistan
Total mobile phone subscribers
102 777 387

Japan
Total mobile phone subscribers
120 708 670

Germany
Total mobile phone subscribers
104 560 000

China
Total mobile phone subscribers
859 003 000

Vietnam
Total mobile phone subscribers
154 000 000

United States
Total mobile phone subscribers
278 900 000

India
Total mobile phone subscribers
752 190 000

Indonesia
Total mobile phone subscribers
220 000 000

Brazil
Total mobile phone subscribers
202 944 033

Cellular mobile subscribers per 100 inhabitants 2010

over 150
120 – 150
90 – 119.9
60 – 89.9
30 – 59.9
0 – 29.9
no data

Total mobile phone subscribers 2010
Top ten countries

China
Total mobile phone subscribers
859 003 000

Fixed telephone lines

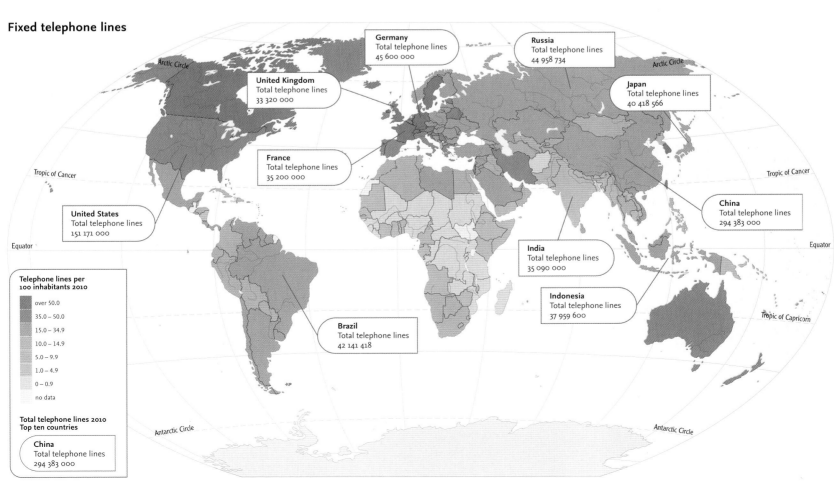

Germany
Total telephone lines
45 600 000

Russia
Total telephone lines
44 958 734

United Kingdom
Total telephone lines
33 320 000

Japan
Total telephone lines
40 418 566

France
Total telephone lines
35 200 000

China
Total telephone lines
294 383 000

United States
Total telephone lines
151 171 000

India
Total telephone lines
35 090 000

Indonesia
Total telephone lines
37 959 600

Brazil
Total telephone lines
42 141 418

Telephone lines per 100 inhabitants 2010

over 50.0
35.0 – 50.0
15.0 – 34.9
10.0 – 14.9
5.0 – 9.9
1.0 – 4.9
0 – 0.9
no data

Total telephone lines 2010
Top ten countries

China
Total telephone lines
294 383 000

Countries are often judged on their level of economic development, but national and personal wealth are not the only measures of a country's status. Numerous other indicators can give a better picture of the overall level of development and standard of living achieved by a country. The availability and standard of health services, levels of educational provision and attainment, levels of nutrition, water supply, life expectancy and mortality rates are just some of the factors which can be measured to assess and compare countries.

While nations strive to improve their economies, and hopefully also to improve the standard of living of their citizens, the measurement of such indicators often exposes great discrepancies between the countries of the 'developed' world and those of the 'less developed' world. They also show great variations within continents and regions and at the same time can hide great inequalities within countries.

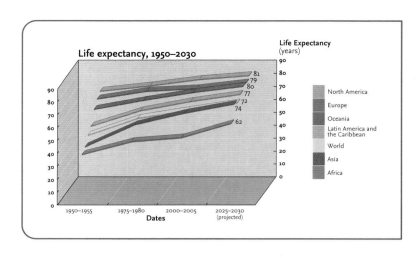

Life expectancy, 1950–2030

World Statistics: see pages 190–196

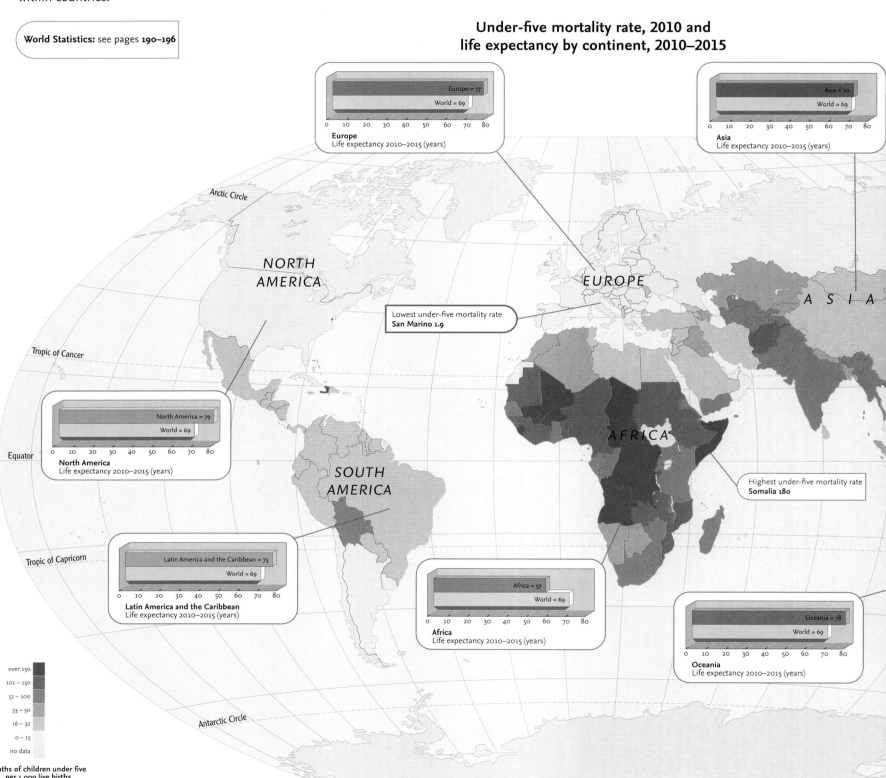

Under-five mortality rate, 2010 and life expectancy by continent, 2010–2015

Europe = 77
World = 69
Europe
Life expectancy 2010–2015 (years)

Asia = 70
World = 69
Asia
Life expectancy 2010–2015 (years)

Lowest under-five mortality rate
San Marino 1.9

North America = 79
World = 69
North America
Life expectancy 2010–2015 (years)

Highest under-five mortality rate
Somalia 180

Latin America and the Caribbean = 75
World = 69
Latin America and the Caribbean
Life expectancy 2010–2015 (years)

Africa = 57
World = 69
Africa
Life expectancy 2010–2015 (years)

Oceania = 78
World = 69
Oceania
Life expectancy 2010–2015 (years)

over 150
101 – 150
51 – 100
33 – 50
16 – 32
0 – 15
no data

Deaths of children under five per 1 000 live births

Health and education

Perhaps the most important indicators used for measuring the level of national development are those relating to health and education. Both of these key areas are vital to the future development of a country, and if there are concerns in standards attained in either (or worse, in both) of these, then they may indicate fundamental problems within the country concerned. The ability to read and write (literacy) is seen as vital in educating people and encouraging development, while easy access to appropriate health services and specialists is an important requirement in maintaining satisfactory levels of basic health.

Literacy rate

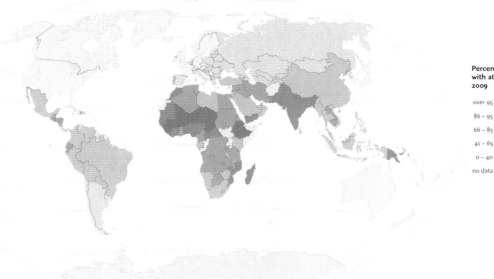

Percentage of population aged 15 and over with at least a basic ability to read and write
2009

over 95	
86 – 95	
66 – 85	
41 – 65	
0 – 40	
no data	

Arctic Circle

Tropic of Cancer

Equator

Tropic of Capricorn

OCEANIA

Antarctic Circle

Doctors per 100 000 people

over 350	
250 – 350	
150 – 249	
50 – 149	
0 – 49	
no data	

Number of trained doctors
per 100 000 people
2009

UN Millennium Development Goals
From the Millennium Declaration, 2000

Goal 1	Eradicate extreme poverty and hunger
Goal 2	Achieve universal primary education
Goal 3	Promote gender equality and empower women
Goal 4	Reduce child mortality
Goal 5	Improve maternal health
Goal 6	Combat HIV/AIDS, malaria and other diseases
Goal 7	Ensure environmental sustainability
Goal 8	Develop a global partnership for development

Internet Links

United Nations Development Programme	www.undp.org
World Health Organization	www.who.int
United Nations Statistics Division	unstats.un.org
United Nations Millennium Development Goals Indicators	www.un.org/millenniumgoals

World
Economy and Wealth

The globalization of the economy is making the world appear a smaller place. However, this shrinkage is an uneven process. Countries are being included in and excluded from the global economy to differing degrees. The wealthy countries of the developed world, with their market-led economies, access to productive new technologies and international markets, dominate the world economic system. Great inequalities exist between and within countries. There may also be discrepancies between social groups within countries due to gender and ethnic divisions. Differences between countries are evident by looking at overall wealth on a national and individual level.

Many of the world's largest financial institutions can be found in the **City of London**.

World Statistics: see pages 190–196

Poverty and inequality

In 2005, 25 per cent of the population of low- and middle-income economies lived in extreme poverty. With continued growth of average incomes, that number is expected to fall to less than 900 million by 2015. Even then there will be more than 2 billion people living on less than $2.00 a day or $730 a year. The greatest number of the extreme poor live in the large, lower-middle income economies of Asia – India and China – which together account for almost half of the people living in extreme poverty. But these are fast growing economies, where poverty rates have been falling rapidly. The highest rates of poverty are found in Sub-Saharan Africa, where economic growth was slowest in the 1990s and the regional poverty rate has only recently fallen below 50 per cent and is expected to reach 36 per cent by 2015. Since the mid-1990s, income inequality, as measured by the Gini index, has increased in slightly more than half of developing countries with available data.

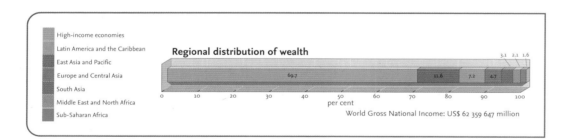

High-income economies
Latin America and the Caribbean
East Asia and Pacific
Europe and Central Asia
South Asia
Middle East and North Africa
Sub-Saharan Africa

Regional distribution of wealth

3.1 2.1 1.6

69.7   11.6   7.2   4.7

0   10   20   30   40   50   60   70   80   90   100
per cent

World Gross National Income: US$ 62 359 647 million

Income inequality

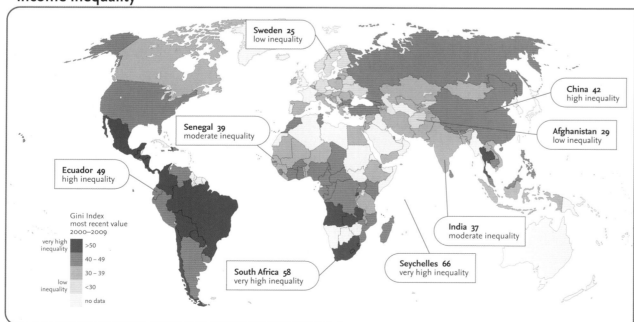

Sweden 25
low inequality

China 42
high inequality

Senegal 39
moderate inequality

Afghanistan 29
low inequality

Ecuador 49
high inequality

India 37
moderate inequality

South Africa 58
very high inequality

Seychelles 66
very high inequality

Gini Index
most recent value
2000–2009

very high inequality >50
40 – 49
30 – 39
low inequality <30
no data

40 000 – 184 000
20 000 – 40 000
10 000 – 20 000
2 000 – 10 000
1 000 – 2 000
0 – 1 000
no data

US$

Arctic Circle
U.S.A.
U N
O
Tropic of Cancer
MEXIC
20°
Equator
KIRIBATI
20°
Tropic of Capricorn
40°
60°
Antarctic Circle

Rural village, **Malawi** – most of the world's poorest countries are in Africa.

Gross National Income per capita

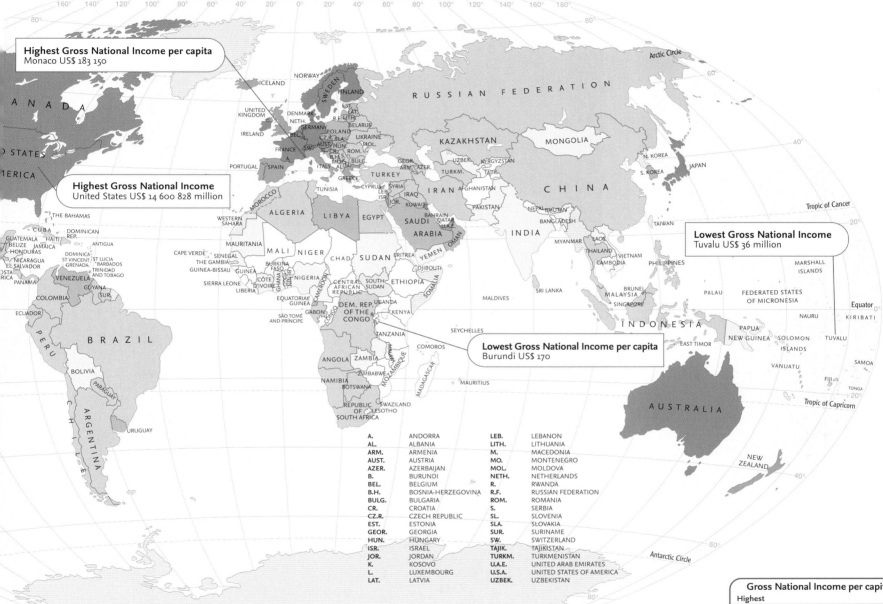

Highest Gross National Income per capita
Monaco US$ 183 150

Highest Gross National Income
United States US$ 14 600 828 million

Lowest Gross National Income
Tuvalu US$ 36 million

Lowest Gross National Income per capita
Burundi US$ 170

A.	ANDORRA	LEB.	LEBANON
AL.	ALBANIA	LITH.	LITHUANIA
ARM.	ARMENIA	M.	MACEDONIA
AUST.	AUSTRIA	MO.	MONTENEGRO
AZER.	AZERBAIJAN	MOL.	MOLDOVA
B.	BURUNDI	NETH.	NETHERLANDS
BEL.	BELGIUM	R.	RWANDA
B.H.	BOSNIA-HERZEGOVINA	R.F.	RUSSIAN FEDERATION
BULG.	BULGARIA	ROM.	ROMANIA
CR.	CROATIA	S.	SERBIA
CZ.R.	CZECH REPUBLIC	SL.	SLOVENIA
EST.	ESTONIA	SLA.	SLOVAKIA
GEOR.	GEORGIA	SUR.	SURINAME
HUN.	HUNGARY	SW.	SWITZERLAND
ISR.	ISRAEL	TAJIK.	TAJIKISTAN
JOR.	JORDAN	TURKM.	TURKMENISTAN
K.	KOSOVO	U.A.E.	UNITED ARAB EMIRATES
L.	LUXEMBOURG	U.S.A.	UNITED STATES OF AMERICA
LAT.	LATVIA	UZBEK.	UZBEKISTAN

Measuring wealth

One of the indicators used to determine a country's wealth is its Gross National Income (GNI). This gives a broad measure of an economy's performance. This is the value of the final output of goods and services produced by a country plus net income from non-resident sources. The total GNI is divided by the country's population to give an average figure of the GNI per capita. From this it is evident that the developed countries dominate the world economy with the United States having the highest GNI. China is a rapidly growing world economic player with the second highest GNI figure and a relatively high GNI per capita (US$4 260) in proportion to its huge population.

Gross National Income per capita

Highest

Rank	Country	US$
1	Monaco	183 150
2	Liechtenstein	137 070
3	Norway	85 340
4	Luxembourg	79 630
5	Switzerland	70 030
6	Denmark	59 210
7	San Marino	50 400
8	Sweden	50 000
9	Netherlands	49 750
10	Kuwait	47 790

Lowest

Rank	Country	US$
179	Guinea	400
180	Ethiopia	390
181	Niger	370
182	Eritrea	340
182	Sierra Leone	340
184	Malawi	330
185	Afghanistan	290
186	Liberia	200
187	Congo	180
188	Burundi	170

Geo-political issues shape the countries of the world and the current political situation in many parts of the world reflects a long history of armed conflict. Since the Second World War conflicts have been fairly localized, but there are numerous 'flash points' where factors such as territorial claims, ideology, religion, ethnicity and access to resources can cause friction between two or more countries. Such factors also lie behind the recent growth in global terrorism.

Military expenditure can take up a disproportionate amount of a country's wealth – East Timor, with a Gross National Income (GNI) per capita of US$ 2 220 spends eleven per cent of its total GDP on military activity. There is an encouraging trend towards wider international cooperation, mainly through the United Nations (UN) and the North Atlantic Treaty Organization (NATO), to prevent escalation of conflicts and on peacekeeping missions.

Military spending, 2009 and conflicts since 1946

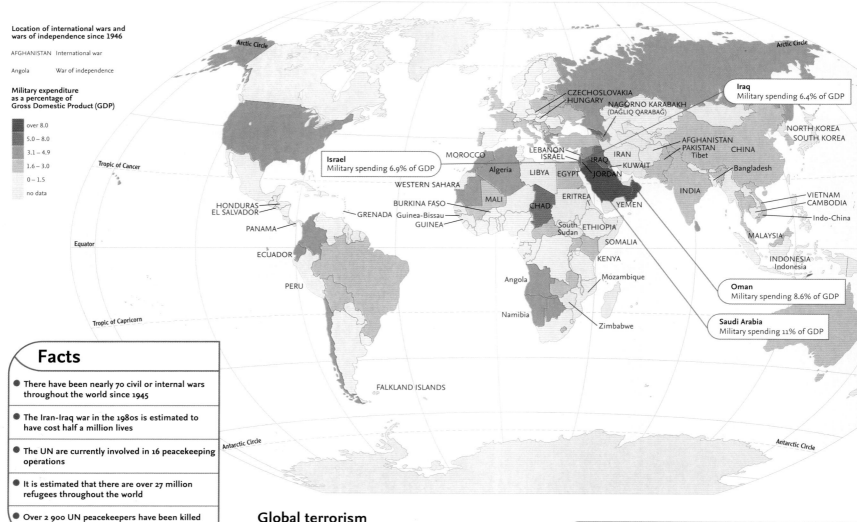

Location of international wars and wars of independence since 1946

AFGHANISTAN   International war

Angola   War of independence

Military expenditure as a percentage of Gross Domestic Product (GDP)

- over 8.0
- 5.0 – 8.0
- 3.1 – 4.9
- 1.6 – 3.0
- 0 – 1.5
- no data

Israel
Military spending 6.9% of GDP

Iraq
Military spending 6.4% of GDP

Oman
Military spending 8.6% of GDP

Saudi Arabia
Military spending 11% of GDP

Facts

- There have been nearly 70 civil or internal wars throughout the world since 1945
- The Iran-Iraq war in the 1980s is estimated to have cost half a million lives
- The UN are currently involved in 16 peacekeeping operations
- It is estimated that there are over 27 million refugees throughout the world
- Over 2 900 UN peacekeepers have been killed since 1948

Global terrorism

Terrorism is defined by the United Nations as "All criminal acts directed against a State and intended or calculated to create a state of terror in the minds of particular persons or a group of persons or the general public". The world has become increasingly concerned about terrorism and the possibility that terrorists could acquire and use nuclear, chemical and biological weapons. One common form of terrorist attack is suicide bombing. Pioneered by Tamil secessionists in Sri Lanka, it has been widely used by Palestinian groups fighting against Israeli occupation of the West Bank and Gaza. In recent years it has also been used by the Al Qaida network in its attacks on the western world. Suicide bombings have also been used in Iraq and Afghanistan.

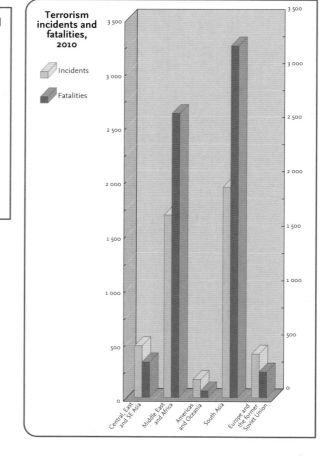

Terrorism incidents and fatalities, 2010

- Incidents
- Fatalities

United Nations peacekeeping

United Nations peacekeeping was developed by the Organization as a way to help countries torn by conflict create the conditions for lasting peace. The first UN peacekeeping mission was established in 1948, when the Security Council authorized the deployment of UN military observers to the Middle East to monitor the Armistice Agreement between Israel and its Arab neighbours. Since then, there have been a total of 66 UN peacekeeping operations around the world.

UN peacekeeping goals were primarily limited to maintaining ceasefires and stabilizing situations on the ground, so that efforts could be made at the political level to resolve the conflict by peaceful means. Today's peacekeepers undertake a wide variety of complex tasks, from helping to build sustainable institutions of governance, to human rights monitoring, to security sector reform, to the disarmament, demobilization and reintegration of former combatants.

United Nations peacekeeping operations 1948–2011
Current peacekeeping operations are named on the map

Many refugees from Myanmar (Burma) live in villages in **Thailand**.

Major terrorist incidents				
Date	Location	Summary	Killed	Injured
December 1988	Lockerbie, Scotland	Airline bombing	270	5
March 1995	Tōkyō, Japan	Sarin gas attack on subway	12	5 510
April 1995	Oklahoma City, USA	Bomb in the Federal building	168	over 800
August 1998	Nairobi, Kenya and Dar es Salaam, Tanzania	US Embassy bombings	225	over 4 000
August 1998	Omagh, Northern Ireland	Town centre bombing	29	220
September 2001	New York and Washington D.C., USA	Airline hijacking and crashing	3 018	over 6 200
October 2002	Bali, Indonesia	Car bomb outside nightclub	202	over 200
October 2002	Moscow, Russian Federation	Theatre siege	170	over 600
March 2004	Baghdād and Karbalā', Iraq	Suicide bombing of pilgrims	181	over 400
March 2004	Madrid, Spain	Train bombings	191	1 800
September 2004	Beslan, Russian Federation	School siege	385	over 700
July 2005	London, UK	Underground and bus bombings	56	700
July 2005	Sharm ash Shaykh, Egypt	Bombs at tourist sites	88	200
July 2006	Mumbai, India	Train bombings	209	700
August 2007	Qahtaniya, Iraq	Suicide bombing in town centres	796	over 1 500
November 2008	Mumbai, India	Coordinated shootings at eight sites	183	over 300
October 2009	Baghdad, Iraq	Two vehicles detonated	155	over 520
January 2010	Lakki Marwat, Pakistan	Suicide car bomb	105	over 100
October 2011	Mogadishu, Somalia	Suicide truck bomb	139	over 90

Number of terrorist incidents 2004-2010

- over 2000
- 500 – 2000
- 100 – 499
- 10 – 99
- 0 – 9
- no data

☆ Major terrorist incident location

With the process of globalization has come an increased awareness of, and direct interest in, issues which have global implications. Social issues can now affect large parts of the world and can impact on large sections of society. Perhaps the current issues of greatest concern are those of national security, including the problem of international terrorism, health, crime and natural resources. The three issues highlighted here reflect this and are of immediate concern.

The international drugs trade, and the crimes commonly associated with it, can impact on society and individuals in devastating ways; scarcity of water resources and lack of access to safe drinking water can have major economic implications and cause severe health problems; and the AIDS epidemic is having disastrous consequences in large parts of the world, particularly in sub-Saharan Africa.

The **opium poppy** is the plant from which opium is extracted.

The drugs trade

The international trade in illegal drugs is estimated to be worth over US$400 billion. While it may be a lucrative business for the criminals involved, the effects of the drugs on individual users and on society in general can be devastating. Patterns of drug production and abuse vary, but there are clear centres for the production of the most harmful drugs – the opiates (opium, morphine and heroin) and cocaine. The 'Golden Triangle' of Laos, Myanmar and Thailand, and western South America respectively are the main producing areas for these drugs. Significant efforts are expended to counter the drugs trade, and there have been signs recently of downward trends in the production of heroin and cocaine.

The international drugs trade

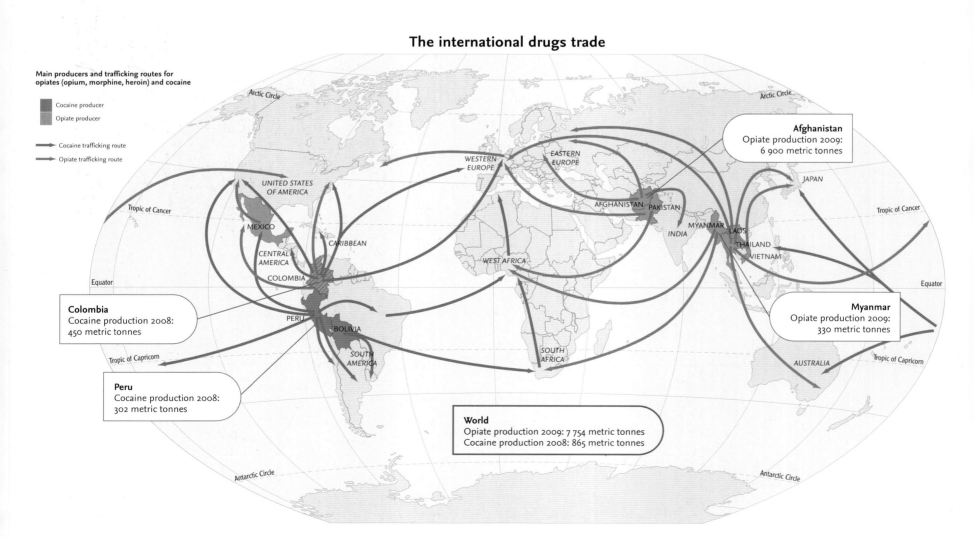

Main producers and trafficking routes for opiates (opium, morphine, heroin) and cocaine

- Cocaine producer
- Opiate producer

→ Cocaine trafficking route
→ Opiate trafficking route

Afghanistan
Opiate production 2009:
6 900 metric tonnes

Myanmar
Opiate production 2009:
330 metric tonnes

Colombia
Cocaine production 2008:
450 metric tonnes

Peru
Cocaine production 2008:
302 metric tonnes

World
Opiate production 2009: 7 754 metric tonnes
Cocaine production 2008: 865 metric tonnes

AIDS epidemic

With over 33 million people living with HIV/AIDS (Human Immunodeficiency Virus/Acquired Immune Deficiency Syndrome) and more than 20 million deaths from the disease, the AIDS epidemic poses one of the biggest threats to public health. The UNAIDS project estimated that 2.6 million people were newly infected in 2009 and that 1.8 million AIDS sufferers died. This is nearly one fifth fewer new infections than the peak of 3.2 million in 1997. As well as the death count itself, in 2009 there were almost 15 million living African children, between the ages of 10 and 17, that had been orphaned as a result of the disease. Treatment to prevent HIV transmission to babies has resulted in 24 per cent drop in infections.

Facts

- The majority of people infected with HIV, if not treated, develop signs of AIDS within 8 to 10 years

- Agriculture uses 70 per cent of all the water taken from aquifers, streams and lakes

- Nearly 4 million people die each year from water-related diseases such as cholera and dysentery

- Estimates suggest that 200 million people consume illegal drugs around the world

Population living with HIV/AIDS, 2009

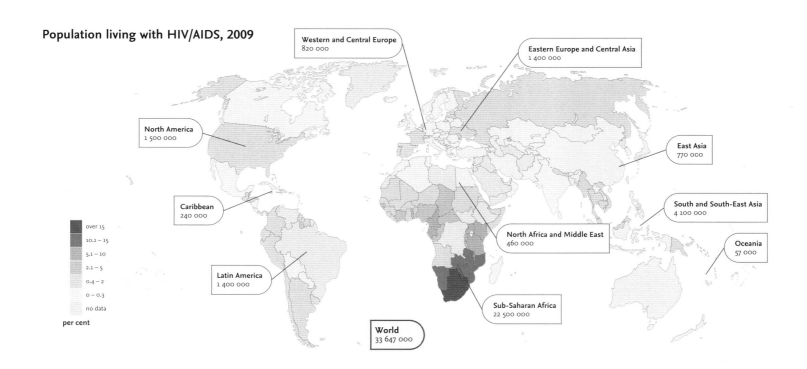

Western and Central Europe
820 000

Eastern Europe and Central Asia
1 400 000

North America
1 500 000

East Asia
770 000

Caribbean
240 000

South and South-East Asia
4 100 000

North Africa and Middle East
460 000

Oceania
57 000

Latin America
1 400 000

Sub-Saharan Africa
22 500 000

World
33 647 000

over 15
10.1 – 15
5.1 – 10
2.1 – 5
0.4 – 2
0 – 0.3
no data

per cent

Water resources

Water is one of the fundamental requirements of life, and yet in some countries it is becoming more scarce due to increasing population and climate change. Safe drinking water, basic hygiene, health education and sanitation facilities are often virtually nonexistent for impoverished people in developing countries throughout the world. WHO/UNICEF estimate that the combination of these conditions results in over 4 000 deaths every day, most of these being children. Currently over 884 million people drink untreated water and expose themselves to serious health risks, while political struggles over diminishing water resources are increasingly likely to be the cause of international conflict.

Domestic use of **untreated water** in Varanasi, India

Access to safe water, 2008
Percentage of population using improved drinking water

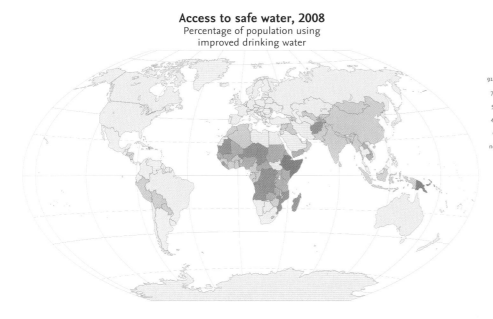

91 – 100
71 – 90
51 – 70
41 – 50
0 – 40
no data

per cent

Internet Links

UNESCO	www.unesco.org
UNAIDS	www.unaids.org
WaterAid	www.wateraid.org.uk
World Health Organization	www.who.int
UNODC United Nations Office on Drugs and Crime	www.unodc.org

The Earth has a rich and diverse environment which is under threat from both natural and man-induced forces. Forests and woodland form the predominant natural land cover with tropical rain forests – currently disappearing at alarming rates – believed to be home to the majority of animal and plant species. Grassland and scrub tend to have a lower natural species diversity but have suffered the most impact from man's intervention through conversion to agriculture, burning and the introduction of livestock. Wherever man interferes with existing biological and environmental processes degradation of that environment occurs to varying degrees. This interference also affects inland water and oceans where pollution, over-exploitation of marine resources and the need for fresh water has had major consequences on land and sea environments.

Facts

- The Sundarbans stretching across the Ganges delta is the largest area of mangrove forest in the world, covering 10 000 square kilometres (3 861 square miles) and forming an important ecological area, home to 260 species of birds, the Bengal tiger and other threatened species

- Over 90 000 square kilometres of precious tropical forest and wetland habitats are lost each year

- The surface level of the Dead Sea has fallen by more than 28 metres over the last 50 years

- Climate change and mismanagement of land areas can lead to soils becoming degraded and semi-arid grasslands becoming deserts – a process known as desertification

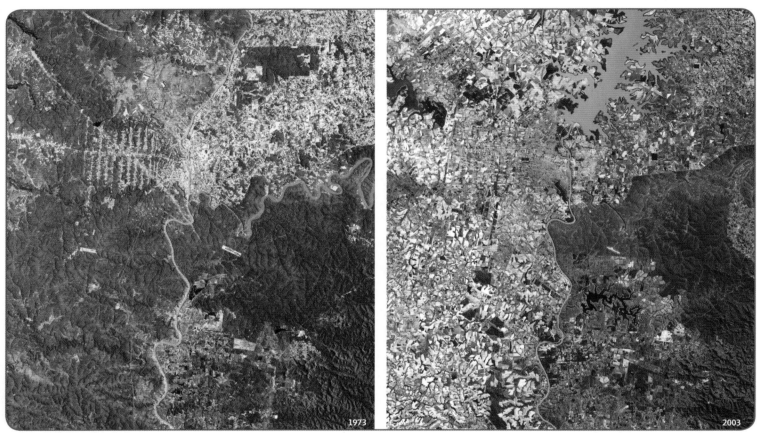

1973   2003

Deforestation and the creation of the **Itaipu Dam** on the Paraná river in Brazil have had a dramatic effect on the landscape and ecosystems of this part of South America. Some forest on the right of the images lies within Iguaçu National Park and has been protected from destruction.

Environmental change

Whenever natural resources are exploited by man, the environment is changed. Approximately half the area of post-glacial forest has been cleared or degraded, and the amount of old-growth forest continues to decline. Desertification caused by climate change and the impact of man can turn semi-arid grasslands into arid desert. Regions bordering tropical deserts, such as the Sahel region south of the Sahara and regions around the Thar Desert in India, are most vulnerable to this process. Coral reefs are equally fragile environments, and many are under threat from coastal development, pollution and over-exploitation of marine resources.

Water resources in certain parts of the world are becoming increasingly scarce and competition for water is likely to become a common cause of conflict. The Aral Sea in central Asia was once the world's fourth largest lake but it now ranks only sixteenth after shrinking by more than 51 000 square kilometres since the 1960s. This shrinkage has been due to climatic change and to the diversion, for farming purposes, of the major rivers which feed the lake. The change has had a devastating effect on the local fishing industry and the exposure of chemicals on the lake bed has caused health problems for the local population.

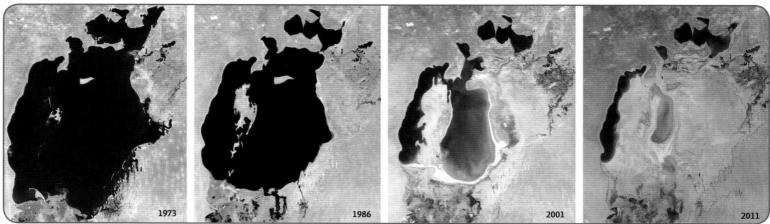

Aral Sea, Kazakhstan/Uzbekistan 1973–2011 Climate change and the diversion of rivers have caused its dramatic shrinkage.

Environmental Impacts

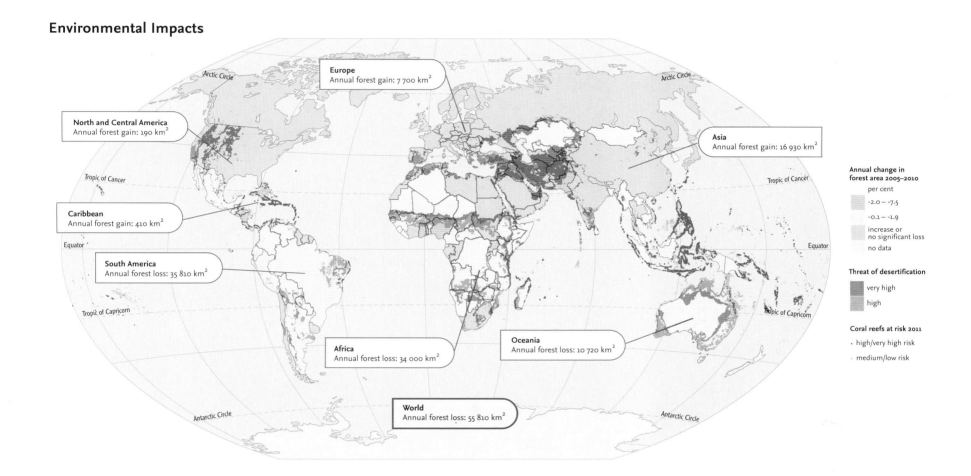

North and Central America
Annual forest gain: 190 km²

Europe
Annual forest gain: 7 700 km²

Asia
Annual forest gain: 16 930 km²

Caribbean
Annual forest gain: 410 km²

South America
Annual forest loss: 35 810 km²

Africa
Annual forest loss: 34 000 km²

Oceania
Annual forest loss: 10 720 km²

World
Annual forest loss: 55 810 km²

Annual change in forest area 2005–2010
per cent
-2.0 – -7.5
-0.1 – -1.9
increase or no significant loss
no data

Threat of desertification
very high
high

Coral reefs at risk 2011
high/very high risk
medium/low risk

Internet links

United Nations Environment Programme (UNEP)	**www.unep.org**
IUCN International Union for Conservation of Nature	**www.iucn.org**
UNESCO World Heritage	**whc.unesco.org**

Environmental protection

Top 10 protected areas by size

Rank	Protected area	Country	Size (sq km)	Designation
1	Northeast Greenland	Greenland	972 000	National Park
2	Rub' al-Khālī	Saudi Arabia	640 000	Wildlife Management Area
3	Chagos Marine Protected Area	BIOT	545 000	Marine Protected Area
4	Kavango-Zambezi	Angola, Botswana, Namibia, Zambia, Zimbabwe	444 000	Transfrontier Conservation Area
5	Phoenix Islands	Kiribati	408 250	Marine Protected Area
6	Papahānaumokuākea Marine National Monument	United States	360 000	Coral Reef Ecosystem Reserve
7	Great Barrier Reef	Australia	345 500	Marine Park
8	Qiangtang	China	298 000	Nature Reserve
9	Macquarie Island	Australia	162 060	Marine Park
10	Sanjiangyuan	China	152 300	Nature Reserve

Great Barrier Reef, Australia, the world's seventh largest protected area.

Many parts of the world are undergoing significant changes which can have widespread and long-lasting effects. The principal causes of change are environmental factors – particularly climatic – and the influence of man. However, it is often difficult to separate these causes because man's activities can influence and exaggerate environmental change. Changes, whatever their cause, can have significant effects on the local population, on the wider region and even on a global scale. Major social, economic and environmental impacts can result from often irreversible changes – deforestation can affect a region's biodiversity, land reclamation can destroy fragile marine ecosystems, major dams and drainage schemes can affect whole drainage basins, and local communities can be changed beyond recognition through such projects.

Facts

● Earth-observing satellites can now detect land detail, and therefore changes in land use, of less than 1 metre extent

● Hong Kong International Airport, opened in 1998 and covering an area of over 12 square kilometres, was built almost entirely on reclaimed land

● The UN have estimated that 1800 million people will be living in places with absolute water scarcity by 2025

● Approximately 35% of cropland in Asia is irrigated

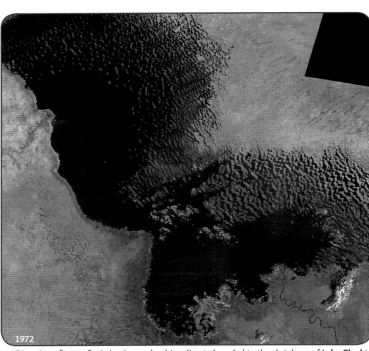
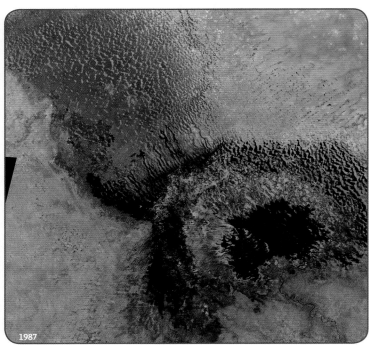

Diversion of water for irrigation and a drier climate have led to the shrinkage of **Lake Chad** in Africa.

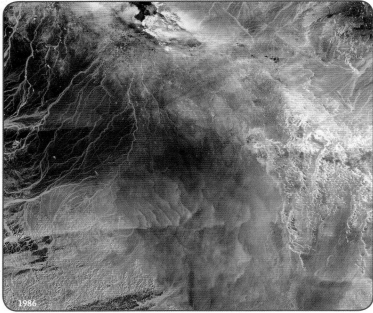

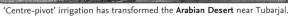

'Centre-pivot' irrigation has transformed the **Arabian Desert** near Tubarjal.

Effects of change

Both natural forces and human activity have irreversibly changed the environment in many parts of the world. Satellite images of the same area taken at different times are a powerful tool for identifying and monitoring such change. Climate change and an increasing demand for water can combine to bring about dramatic changes to lakes and rivers, while major engineering projects, reclamation of land from the sea and the expansion of towns and cities, create completely new environments. Use of water for the generation of hydro-electric power or for irrigation of otherwise infertile land leads to dramatic changes in the landscape and can also be a cause of conflict between countries. All such changes can have major social and economic impacts on the local population. However time also heals scars as regeneration of landcover gradually returns a damaged landscape to a healthier state.

Yellowstone National Park suffered a major fire in 1988 and the scars show as bright red areas in the Landsat images as they use both visible and infrared light. With infrequent fires the landscape gradually recovers, but there is concern that with climate becoming warmer and drier more frequent fires could lead to the dense conifer forest cover being lost.

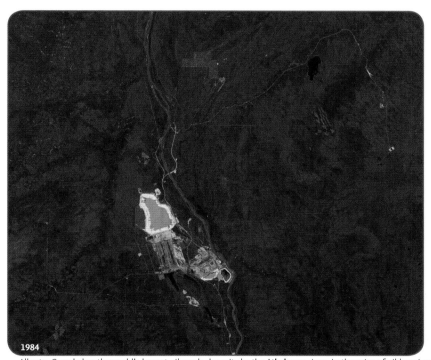

Alberta, Canada has the world's largest oil sands deposits by the **Athabasca** river. As the price of oil has risen over the past decade, mining here has become more profitable and the expansion of operations can be seen clearly. The process is toxic and releases more greenhouse gases than other oil extraction methods. However, strict Canadian environmental laws demand land restoration, and this process has been started with a restored pond.

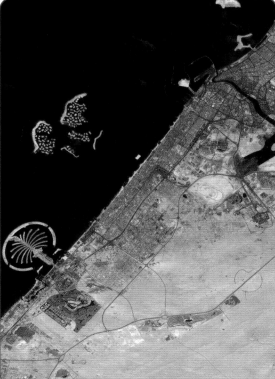

Dubai has changed dramatically since the turn of the century, both offshore and on land. Offshore the development of the Palm Jumeirah in the bottom of the picture, "The World" and Palm Deira are clearly visible, while on the land the expansion of the urban area is extensive. Also noticeable in these infrared images are the many red areas that indicate irrigated land.

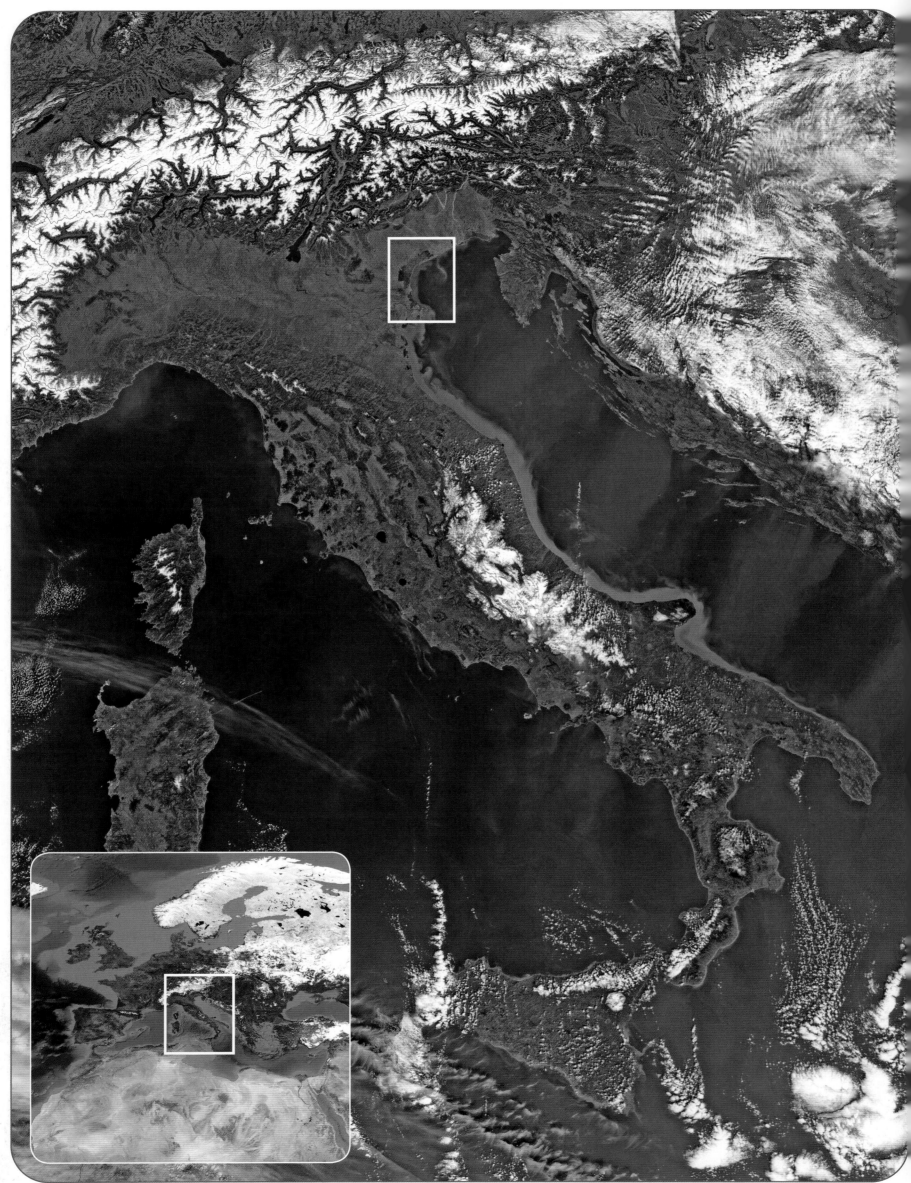

This sequence of satellite images at progressively higher resolutions illustrates the value of such imagery in observing and monitoring features on the Earth. From world, continental and regional views to detailed images picking out individual features on the ground less than 1 m (3.3 feet) in size, images like this can be used for many scientific, environmental and planning purposes.

Satellite sensors commonly collect many types of data which allow very detailed analysis of vegetation and climatic conditions. The fact that Earth-observing satellites regularly revisit the same location adds to this the valuable ability to monitor change over time.

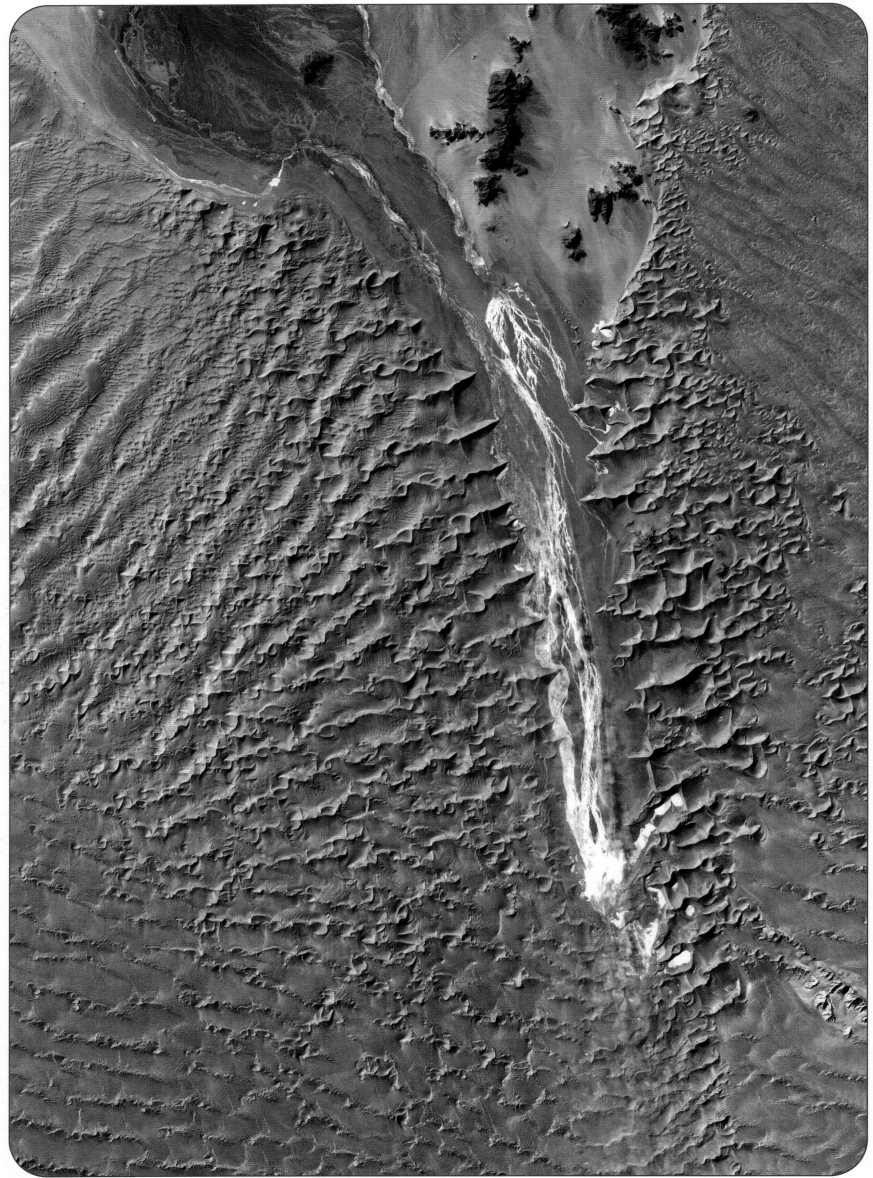

This image shows the intermittent Tsauchab River, one of the few sources of water in the Namib Desert in southwest Africa. Sporadic rains can turn the river into a raging torrent within twenty-four hours. Like other ephemeral rivers flowing into the desert it ends in a vlei, or mud flat – the clearing in the sand dunes at the top of this image.

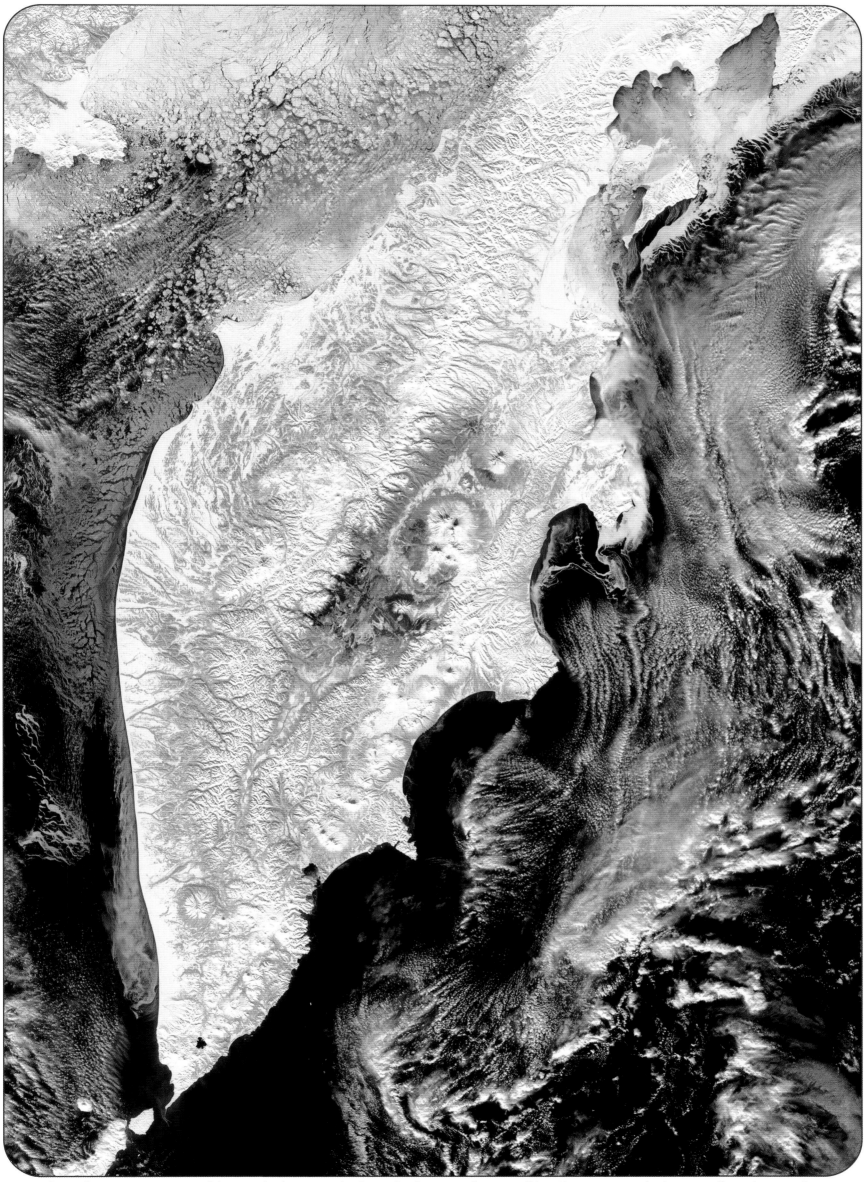

This early springtime image of the Kamchatka Peninsula shows the distinctive feature still largely snow covered. The snow allows this complex mountainous landscape to be clearly seen. The eastern edge of the peninsula is marked by numerous active volcanoes – this region forms part of the Pacific 'Ring of Fire', a zone of volcanic and seismic activity circling the Pacific Ocean.

Central **London** has many notable buildings. Buckingham Palace can be seen at the bottom of this image, with The Mall running along by St James' Park. St Stephen's Tower, home of Big Ben can just be seen casting its shadow over traffic approaching Westminster Bridge, while on the opposite bank of the Thames is the London Eye, a great spot for views of the cityscape.

The numerous space-rocket launch pads and the Space Shuttle landing strip, 4.8 km (3 miles) in length, can be easily identified in this ASTER satellite image of the John F. Kennedy Space Center located on Cape Canaveral on the east coast of Florida, USA.

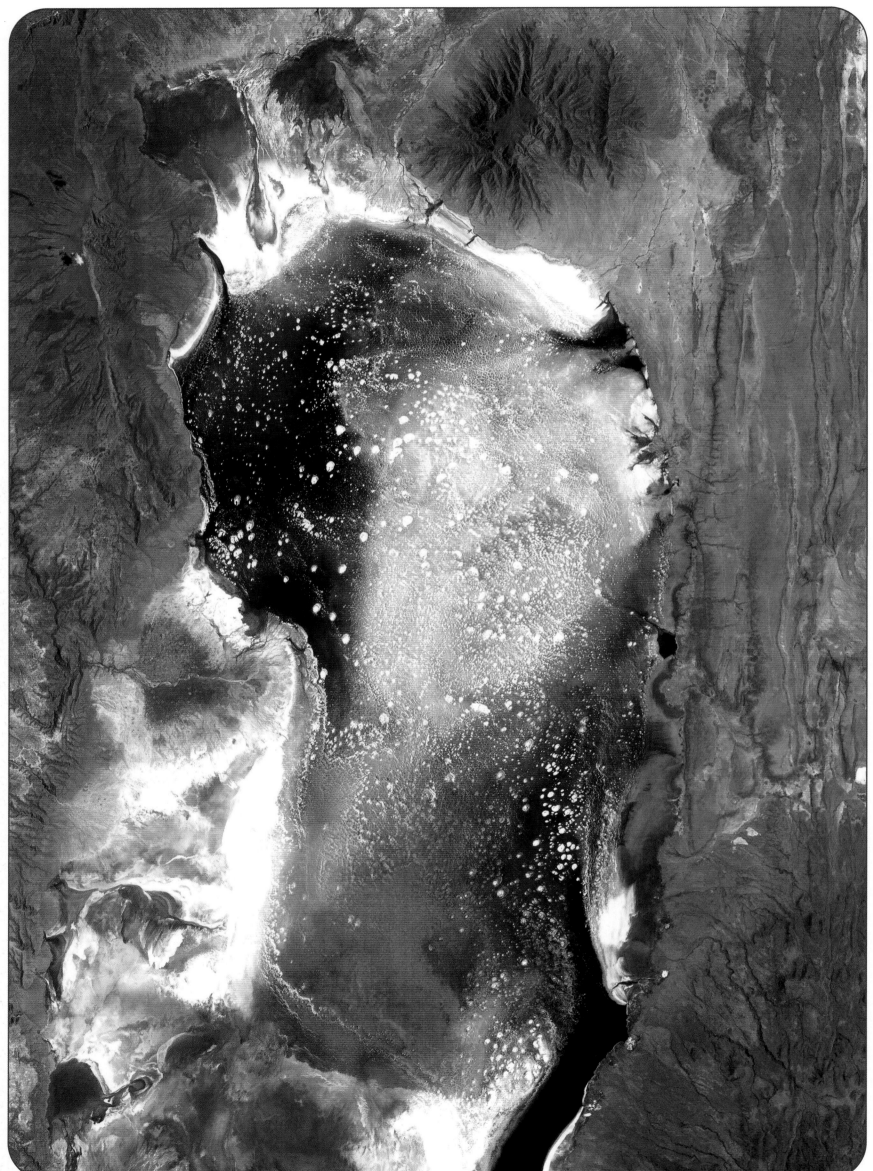

Lake Natron is a unique soda lake landscape in Tanzania. Despite being the most caustic lake in the world due to deposits of volcanic ash, it hosts algae called Spirulina whose bright red pigments colour the lake, and also Lesser Flamingos who eat the algae and use the hostile environment as a relatively safe place to raise their young. However due to the hot springs, temperatures in the lake can reach as high as 50°C and the pH can reach over 10, a very alkaline state, so even the flamingos need to take care.

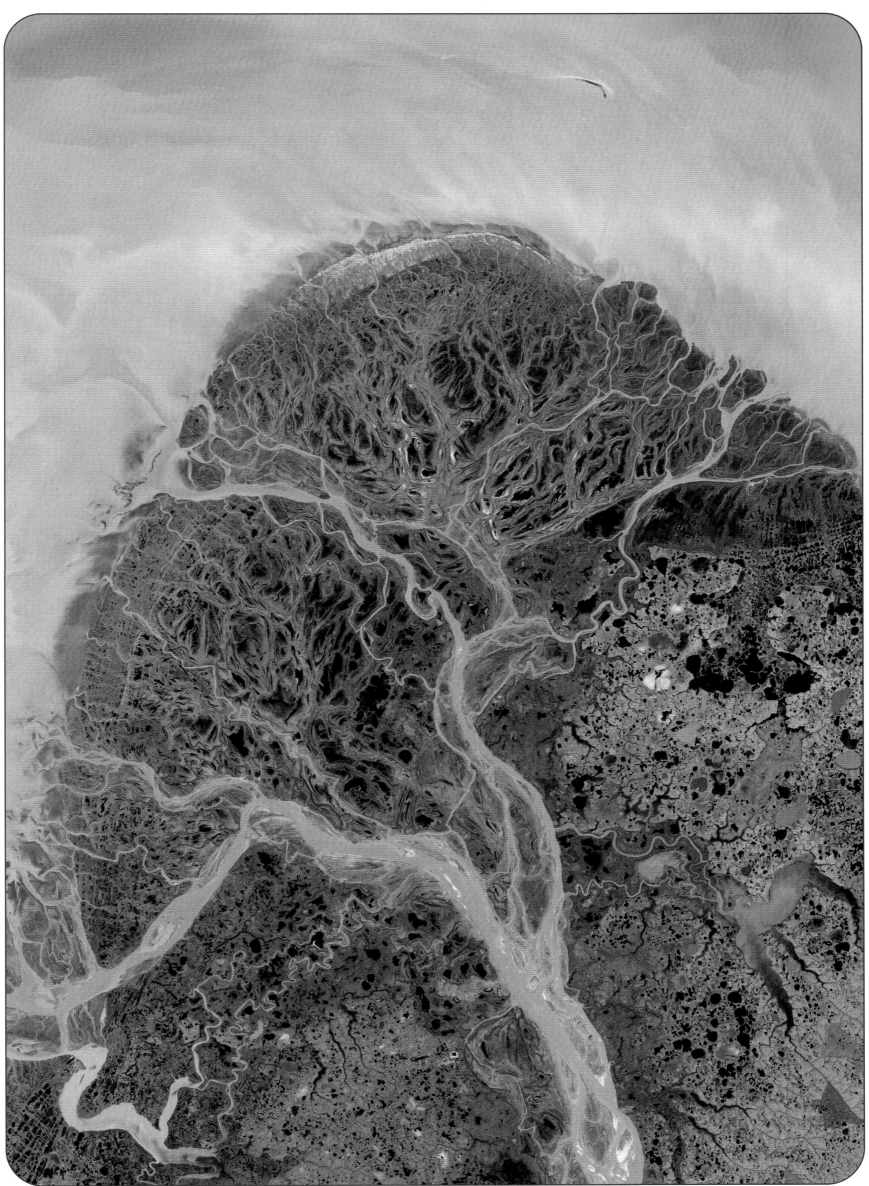

The **Yukon** river flows north through Canada, before entering Alsaka in the USA and heading for the coast. The delta is an important place as it is home to many of the Yup'ik people making it one of the more populated parts of Alaska. The delta is also a National Wildlife Refuge, important for migrating birds and waterfowl. The river channels change course constantly and the heavy sediment load can be clearly seen in the lighter colours of the sea.

ENVIRONMENT

The Earth has a rich environment with a wide range of habitats. Forest and woodland form the predominant natural land cover and tropical rain forests are believed to be home to the majority of the world's bird, animal and plant species. These forests are part of a delicate land-atmosphere relationship disturbed by changes in land use. Grassland, shrubland and deserts cover most of the unwooded areas of the earth with low-growing tundra in the far northern latitudes. Grassland and shrubland regions in particular have been altered greatly by man through agriculture, livestock grazing and settlements.

ORGANIZATION	WEB ADDRESS	THEME
NASA Earth Observatory	earthobservatory.nasa.gov	Observing the earth
USGS Earthquakes Hazards Center	earthquake.usgs.gov	Monitoring earthquakes
Rainforest Action Network	ran.org	Rainforest information and resources
Scripps Institution of Oceanography	sio.ucsd.edu	Exploration of the oceans
Visible Earth	visibleearth.nasa.gov	Satellite images of the earth
USGS Volcanoes Hazard Program	volcanoes.usgs.gov	Volcanic activity
UNESCO World Heritage Centre	whc.unesco.org	World Heritage Sites
British Geological Survey	www.bgs.ac.uk	Geology
The World Conservation Union	www.iucn.org	World and ocean conservation
IUCN Red List	www.iucnredlist.org	Threatened species
United Nations Environment Programme	www.unep.org	Environmental protection by the UN
World Conservation Monitoring Centre	www.unep-wcmc.org	Conservation and the environment
World Resources Institute	www.wri.org	Monitoring the environment and resources

OCEANS

Between them, the world's oceans cover approximately 70 per cent of the earth's surface. They contain 96 per cent of the earth's water and a vast range of flora and fauna. They are a major influence on the world's climate, particularly through ocean currents – the circulation of water within and between the oceans. Our understanding of the oceans has increased enormously over the last twenty years through the development of new technologies, including that of satellite images, which can generate vast amounts of data relating to the sea floor, ocean currents and sea surface temperatures.

ORGANIZATION	WEB ADDRESS	THEME
International Maritime Organisation	www.imo.org	Shipping and the environment
General Bathymetric Chart of the Oceans	www.gebco.net	Mapping the oceans
National Oceanography Centre, Southampton	www.noc.soton.ac.uk	Researching the oceans
Scott Polar Research Institute	www.spri.cam.ac.uk	Polar research

CLIMATE

The Earth's climate system is highly complex. It is recognized and accepted that man's activities are affecting this system, and monitoring climate change, including human influences upon it, is now a major issue. Future climate change depends critically on how quickly and to what extent the concentration of greenhouse gases in the atmosphere increase. Change will not be uniform across the globe and the information from sophisticated mathematical climate models is invaluable in helping governments and industry to assess the impacts climate change will have.

ORGANIZATION	WEB ADDRESS	THEME
BBC Weather Centre	www.bbc.co.uk/weather	UK weather forecasts
University of East Anglia Climatic Research Unit	www.cru.uea.ac.uk	Climatic research in the UK
Met Office	www.metoffice.gov.uk	Weather information and climatic research
National Climatic Data Center	www.ncdc.noaa.gov/oa/ncdc.html	Global climate data
NOAA/National Weather Service National Hurricane Center	www.nhc.noaa.gov	Tracking hurricanes
National Oceanic and Atmospheric Administration	www.noaa.gov	Monitoring climate and the oceans
United Nations World Meteorological Organization	www.wmo.int	The world's climate
El Niño	www.elnino.noaa.gov	El Niño research and observations

POPULATION

The world's population reached seven billion in 2011. Rates of population growth vary between continents, but overall, the rate of growth has been increasing and it is predicted that by 2043 another two billion people will inhabit the planet. The process of urbanization, in particular migration from countryside to city, has led to the rapid growth of many cities. In 2008, for the first time in history, more people were living in urban areas than in rural areas. There are now over 500 cities with over one million inhabitants and twenty-one with over ten million.

ORGANIZATION	WEB ADDRESS	THEME
UK Office for National Statistics	www.ons.gov.uk/ons/guide-method/census/2011/the-2011-census/index.html	The UK 2011 census
City Populations	www.citypopulation.de	Statistics and maps about population
US Census Bureau	www.census.gov	US and world population
United Nations World Urbanization Prospects	esa.un.org/unpd/wup/index.htm	Urban population estimates and projections
United Nations Population Information Network	www.un.org/popin	World population statistics
UN Population Division	www.un.org/esa/population/unpop.htm	Monitoring world population

COUNTRIES

The present picture of the political world is the result of a long history of exploration, colonialism, conflict and negotiation. In 1950 there were eighty-two independent countries. Since then there has been a significant trend away from colonial influences and although many dependent territories still exist, there are now 196 independent countries. The newest country is South Sudan which gained independence from Sudan in July 2011. The shapes of countries reflect a combination of natural features, such as mountain ranges, and political agreements. There are still areas of the world where boundaries are disputed or only temporarily settled as ceasefire lines.

ORGANIZATION	WEB ADDRESS	THEME
European Union	europa.eu/index_en.htm	Gateway to the European Union
Permanent Committee on Geographical Names	www.pcgn.org.uk	Place names research in the UK
The World Factbook	https://www.cia.gov/library/publications/the-world-factbook/index.html	Country profiles
US Board on Geographic Names	geonames.usgs.gov	Place names research in the USA
United Nations	www.un.org/en	The United Nations
International Boundaries Research Unit	www.dur.ac.uk/ibru	International boundaries resources and research
Organisation for Economic Co-operation and Development	www.oecd.org	Economic statistics
World Bank	data.worldbank.org	World development indicators

TRAVEL

Travelling as a tourist or on business to some countries, or travelling within certain areas can be dangerous because of wars and political unrest. The UK Foreign Office provides the latest travel advice and security warnings. Some areas of the world, particularly tropical regions in the developing world, also carry many risks of disease. Advice should be sought on precautions to take and medications required.

ORGANIZATION	WEB ADDRESS	THEME
UK Foreign Office	www.fco.gov.uk	Travel, trade and country information
US Department of State	www.state.gov	Travel advice
World Health Organization	www.who.int	Health advice and world health issues
Centers for Disease Control and Prevention	wwwnc.cdc.gov/travel	Advice for travellers
Airports Council International	www.airports.org	The voice of the world's airports
Travel Daily News	www.traveldailynews.com	Travel and tourism newsletter

ORGANIZATIONS

Throughout the world there are many international, national and local organizations representing the interests of individual countries, groups of countries, regions and specialist groups. These can provide enormous amounts of information on economic, social, cultural, environmental and general geographical issues facing the world. The following is a selection of such sites.

ORGANIZATION	WEB ADDRESS	THEME
United Nations	www.un.org/en	The United Nations
United Nations Educational, Scientific and Cultural Organization	www.unesco.org	International collaboration
United Nations Children's Fund	www.unicef.org	Health, education, equality and protection for children
United Nations High Commissioner for Refugees	www.unhcr.org	The UN refugee agency
Food and Agriculture Organization	www.fao.org	Agriculture and defeating hunger
United Nations Development Programme	www.undp.org	The UN global development network
North Atlantic Treaty Organization	www.nato.int	North Atlantic freedom and security
European Environment Agency	www.eea.europa.eu	Europe's environment
European Centre for Nature Conservation	www.ecnc.org	Nature conservation in Europe
Europa - The European Union On-line	europa.eu/index_en.htm	European Union facts and statistics
World Health Organisation	www.who.int	Health issues and advice
Association of Southeast Asian Nations	www.aseansec.org	Economic, social and cultural development
International Water Management Institute	www.iwmi.cgiar.org	Water and land resources management
The Joint United Nations Convention on AIDS	www.unaids.org	The AIDS crisis
African Union	www.au.int/en	African international relations
World Lakes	www.worldlakes.org/lakes.asp	Lakes around the world
The Secretariat of the Pacific Commmunity	www.spc.int	The Pacific community
The Maori world	www.maori.org.nz	Maori culture
US National Park Service	www.nps.gov	National Parks of the USA
Parks Canada	www.pc.gc.ca/eng/index.aspc	Natural heritage of Canada
The Panama Canal	www.pancanal.com/eng/index.html	Explore the Panama Canal
The Caribbean Community Secretariat	www.caricom.org	Caribbean Community
Organization of American States	www.oas.org	Inter-American cooperation
The Latin American Network Information Center	lanic.utexas.edu	Latin America
World Wildlife Fund	www.worldwildlife.org	Global environmental conservation
The Amazon Conservation Team	www.amazonteam.org	Conservation in tropical America

Europe

The generally densely vegetated continent of Europe
contains some dramatic geographical features.
Its northern and western limits are marked by the
complex coastlines of Iceland, Scandinavia and
northwestern Russian Federation, while the British
Isles sit on the flat, wide continental shelf. Europe's
mountain ranges divide the continent – in the
southwest, the Pyrenees separate France from the
drier Iberian Peninsula, the wide arc of the Alps
separates Italy from the rest of western Europe, the
Carpathian Mountains, appearing as a dark curve
between the Alps and the Black Sea, mark the edge
of the vast European plains, and the Caucasus,
stretching between the Black Sea and the Caspian
Sea, create a prominent barrier between Europe and
Asia. Two of Europe's greatest rivers are also clearly
visible on this image – the Volga, Europe's longest
river, flowing south from the Ural Mountains into
the Caspian Sea and the Dnieper flowing
across the plains into the northern Black Sea.

Europe
Landscapes

Europe, the westward extension of the Asian continent and the second smallest of the world's continents, has a remarkable variety of physical features and landscapes. The continent is bounded by mountain ranges of varying character – the highlands of Scandinavia and northwest Britain, the Pyrenees, the Alps, the Carpathian Mountains, the Caucasus and the Ural Mountains. Two of these, the Caucasus and Ural Mountains, define the eastern limits of Europe, with the Black Sea and the Bosporus defining its southeastern boundary with Asia.

Across the centre of the continent stretches the North European Plain, broken by some of Europe's greatest rivers, including the Volga and the Dnieper and containing some of its largest lakes. To the south, the Mediterranean Sea divides Europe from Africa. The Mediterranean region itself has a very distinct climate and landscape.

Facts

- The Danube flows through 7 countries and has 7 different name forms

- Lakes cover almost 10% of the total land area of Finland

- The Strait of Gibraltar, separating the Atlantic Ocean from the Mediterranean Sea and Europe from Africa, is only 13 kilometres wide at its narrowest point

- The highest mountain in the Alps is Mont Blanc, 4 810 metres, on the France/Italy border

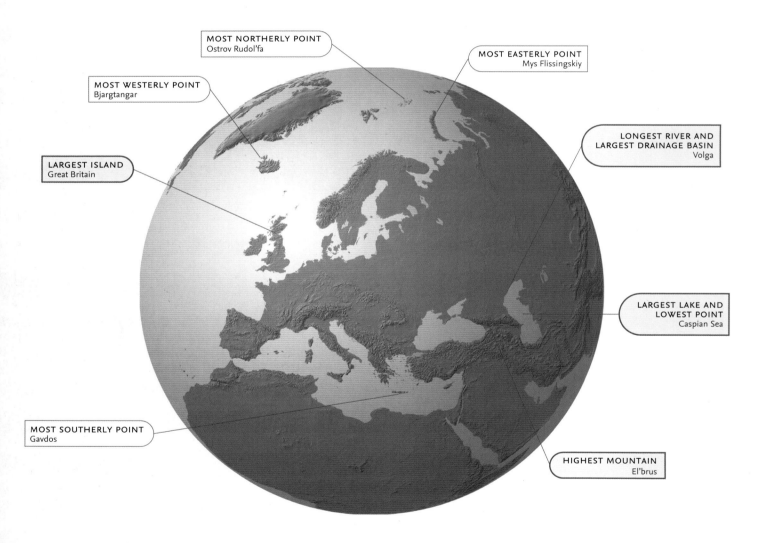

MOST NORTHERLY POINT
Ostrov Rudol'fa

MOST EASTERLY POINT
Mys Flissingskiy

MOST WESTERLY POINT
Bjargtangar

LONGEST RIVER AND
LARGEST DRAINAGE BASIN
Volga

LARGEST ISLAND
Great Britain

LARGEST LAKE AND
LOWEST POINT
Caspian Sea

MOST SOUTHERLY POINT
Gavdos

HIGHEST MOUNTAIN
El'brus

Europe's greatest physical features

Highest mountain	El'brus, Russian Federation	5 642 metres	18 510 feet
Longest river	Volga, Russian Federation	3 688 km	2 292 miles
Largest lake	Caspian Sea	371 000 sq km	143 243 sq miles
Largest island	Great Britain, United Kingdom	218 476 sq km	84 354 sq miles
Largest drainage basin	Volga, Russian Federation	1 380 000 sq km	532 818 sq miles

Europe's extent

TOTAL LAND AREA	9 908 599 sq km / 3 825 710 sq miles
Most northerly point	Ostrov Rudol'fa, Russian Federation
Most southerly point	Gavdos, Crete, Greece
Most westerly point	Bjargtangar, Iceland
Most easterly point	Mys Flissingskiy, Russian Federation

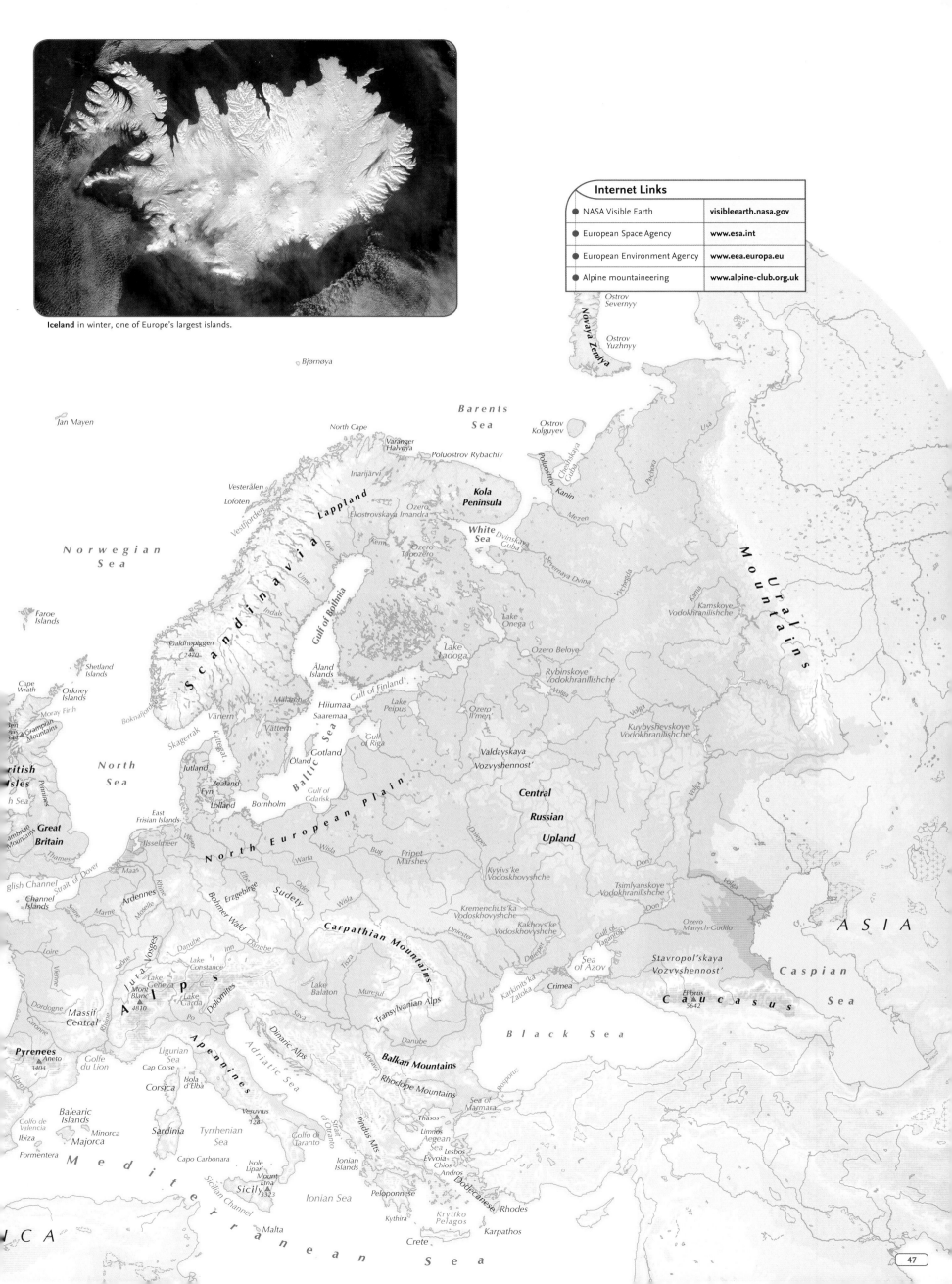

Iceland in winter, one of Europe's largest islands.

Internet Links	
● NASA Visible Earth	**visibleearth.nasa.gov**
● European Space Agency	**www.esa.int**
● European Environment Agency	**www.eea.europa.eu**
● Alpine mountaineering	**www.alpine-club.org.uk**

Europe
Countries

The predominantly temperate climate of Europe has led to it becoming the most densely populated of the continents. It is highly industrialized, and has exploited its great wealth of natural resources and agricultural land to become one of the most powerful economic regions in the world.

The current pattern of countries within Europe is a result of numerous and complicated changes throughout its history. Ethnic, religious and linguistic differences have often been the cause of conflict, particularly in the Balkan region which has a very complex ethnic pattern. Current boundaries reflect, to some extent, these divisions which continue to be a source of tension. The historic distinction between 'Eastern' and 'Western' Europe is no longer made, following the collapse of Communism and the break up of the Soviet Union in 1991.

Facts

- The European Union was founded by six countries: Belgium, France, Germany, Italy, Luxembourg, and the Netherlands. It now has 27 members

- The newest members of the European Union, Bulgaria and Romania joined in 2007

- Europe has the 2 smallest independent countries in the world – Vatican City and Monaco

- Vatican City is an independent country entirely within the city of Rome, and is the centre of the Roman Catholic Church

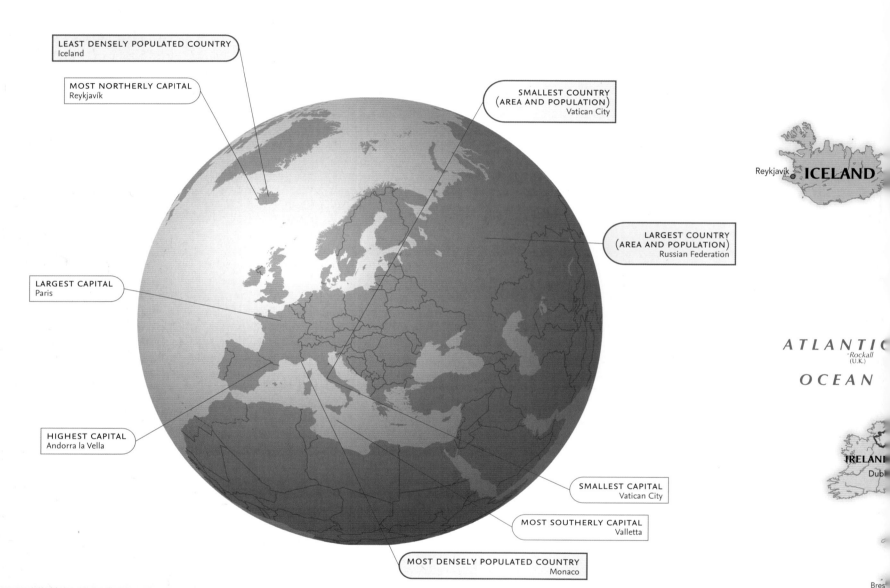

LEAST DENSELY POPULATED COUNTRY
Iceland

MOST NORTHERLY CAPITAL
Reykjavík

SMALLEST COUNTRY
(AREA AND POPULATION)
Vatican City

LARGEST COUNTRY
(AREA AND POPULATION)
Russian Federation

LARGEST CAPITAL
Paris

HIGHEST CAPITAL
Andorra la Vella

SMALLEST CAPITAL
Vatican City

MOST SOUTHERLY CAPITAL
Valletta

MOST DENSELY POPULATED COUNTRY
Monaco

Reykjavik · ICELAND

ATLANTIC
·Rockall
(U.K.)

OCEAN

IRELAND
Dub

Bres

Azores
(Portugal)

Bay o
Biscay

Cape Finisterre · A Coruña
Bilbao
Oporto · Douro
Salamanca
Madrid
PORTUGAL SPAIN
Lisbon · Tagu
Cabo de
São Vicente
Seville · Córdoba
Cádiz · Málaga
Cartage
Str. of
Gibraltar · Gibraltar

A F

Bosporus, Turkey, a narrow strait of water which separates Europe from Asia.

Europe's capitals

Largest capital (population)	Paris, France	10 777 000	
Smallest capital (population)	Vatican City	800	
Most northerly capital	Reykjavík, Iceland	64° 39'N	
Most southerly capital	Valletta, Malta	35° 54'N	
Highest capital	Andorra la Vella, Andorra	1 029 metres	3 376 feet

Europe's countries

Largest country (area)	Russian Federation	17 075 400 sq km	6 592 849 sq miles
Smallest country (area)	Vatican City	0.5 sq km	0.2 sq miles
Largest country (population)	Russian Federation	142 836 000	
Smallest country (population)	Vatican City	800	
Most densely populated country	Monaco	17 500 per sq km	35 000 per sq mile
Least densely populated country	Iceland	3 per sq km	8 per sq mile

Internet Links

● European Union	europa.eu/
● UK Foreign and Commonwealth Office	www.fco.gov.uk
● CIA World Factbook	www.cia.gov/library/publications/the-world-factbook/index.html

Europe
Northern Europe

112 →

Europe
Western Russian Federation

57 ↓

Europe

Scandinavia and the Baltic States

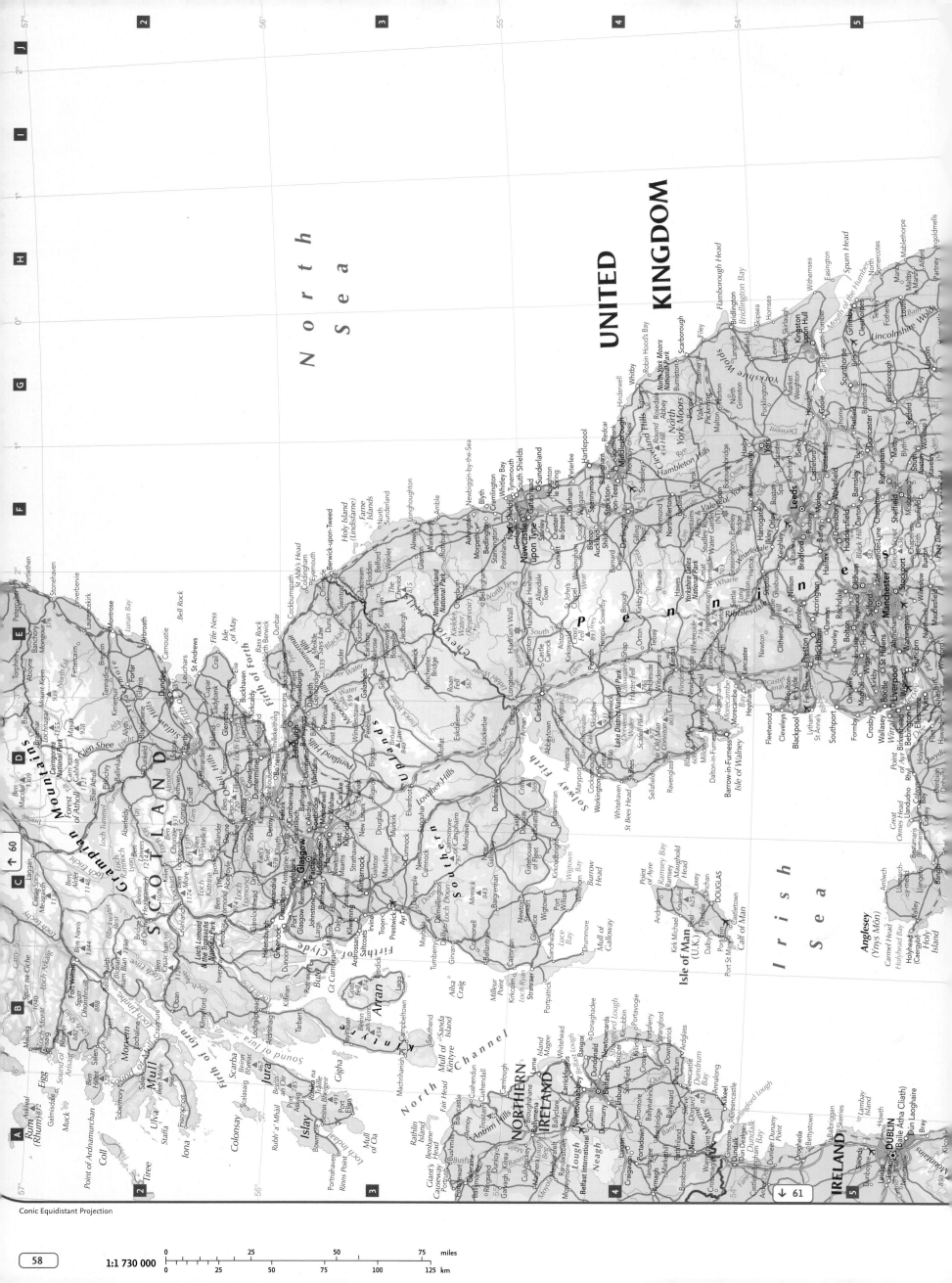

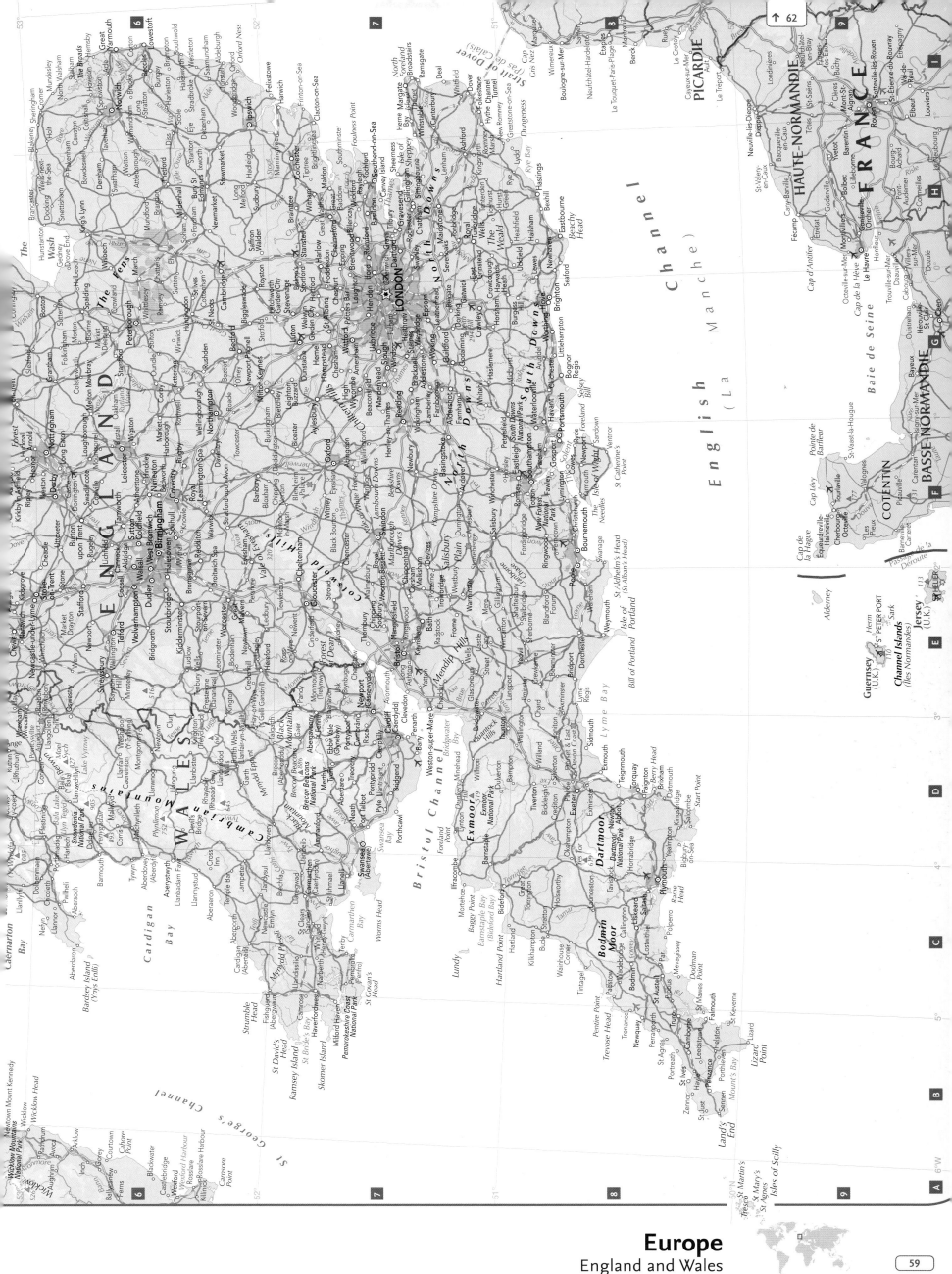

Europe
England and Wales

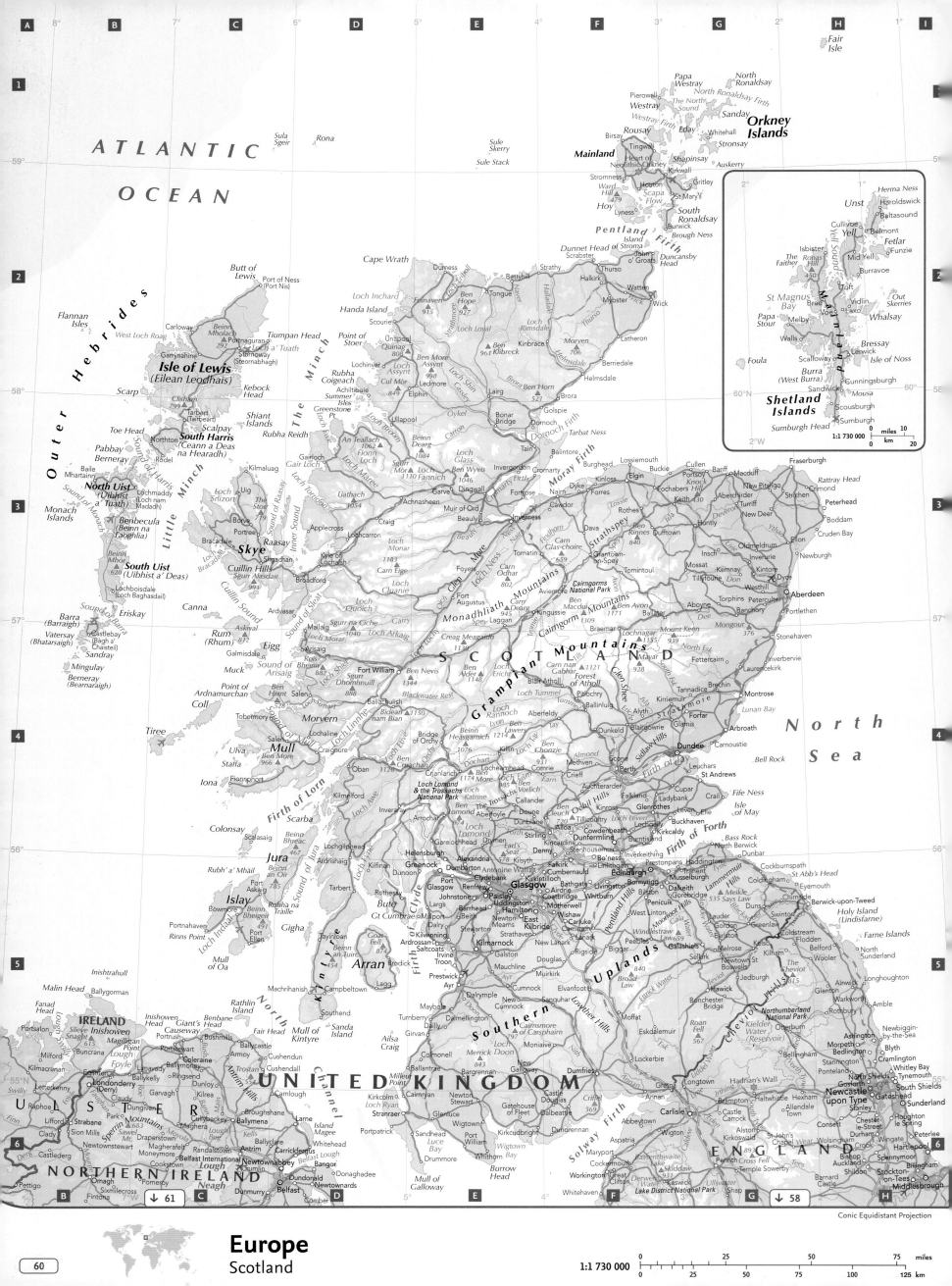

Europe
Scotland

1:1 730 000

Conic Equidistant Projection

Europe
Ireland

1:1 730 000

Conic Equidistant Projection

61

Europe
Southern Europe and the Mediterranean

↑ 56

Conic Equidistant Projection

Europe
France

1:4 300 000

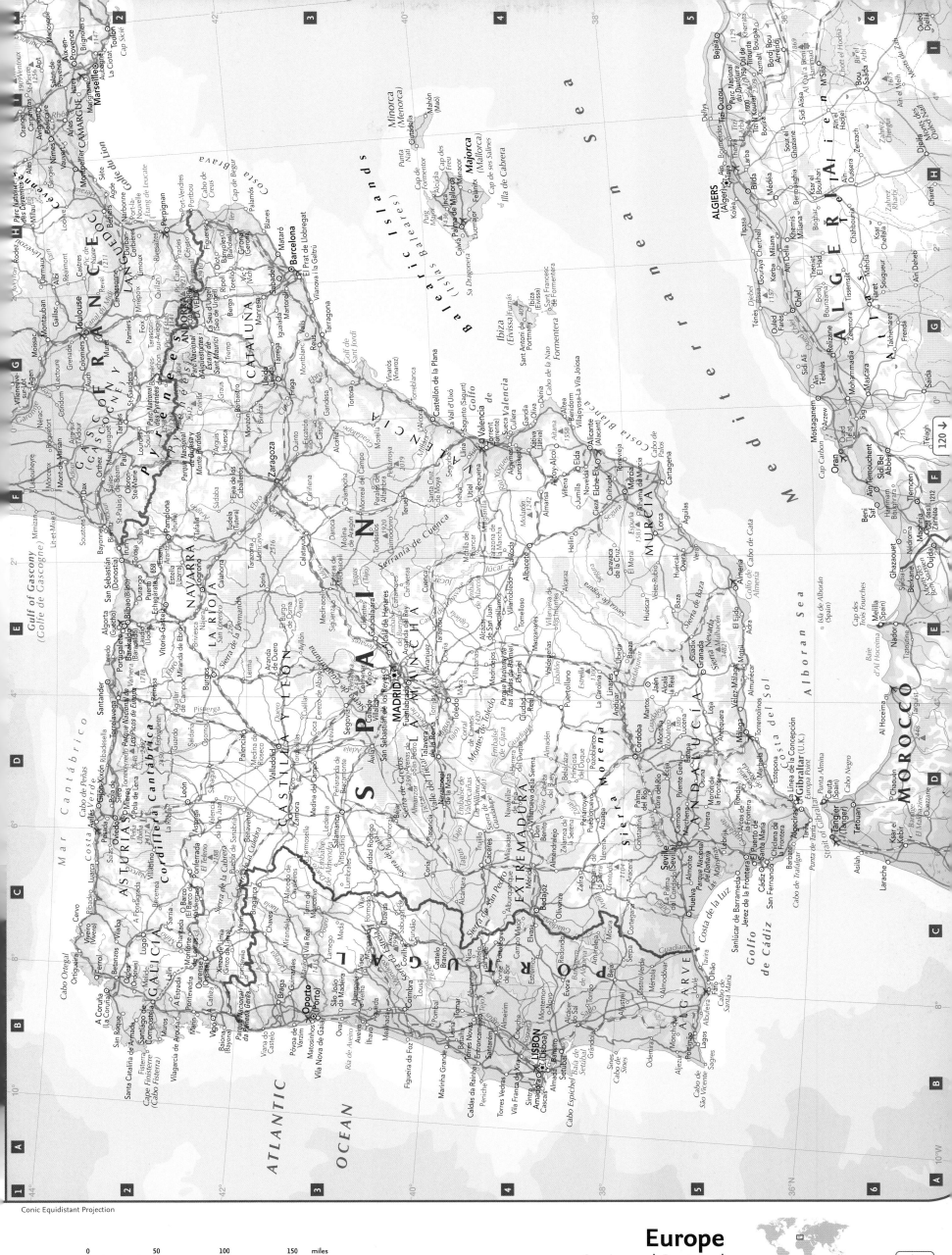

1:4 300 000

| 0 | 50 | 100 | 150 | miles |

| 0 | 50 | 100 | 150 | 200 | 250 km |

Europe
Spain and Portugal

Conic Equidistant Projection

1:4 300 000

| 0 | 50 | 100 | 150 | miles |

| 0 | 50 | 100 | 150 | 200 | 250 | km |

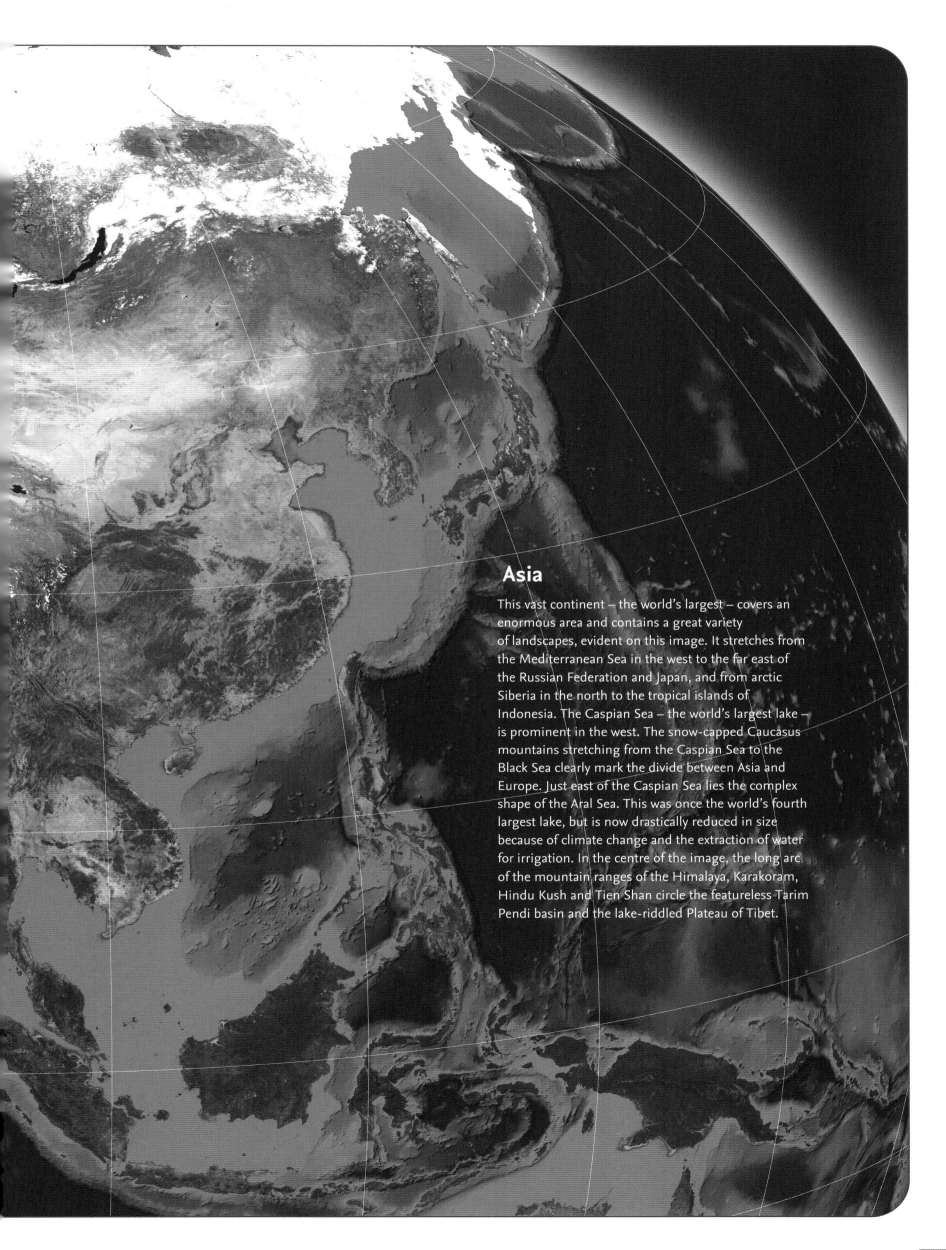

Asia

This vast continent – the world's largest – covers an enormous area and contains a great variety of landscapes, evident on this image. It stretches from the Mediterranean Sea in the west to the far east of the Russian Federation and Japan, and from arctic Siberia in the north to the tropical islands of Indonesia. The Caspian Sea – the world's largest lake – is prominent in the west. The snow-capped Caucasus mountains stretching from the Caspian Sea to the Black Sea clearly mark the divide between Asia and Europe. Just east of the Caspian Sea lies the complex shape of the Aral Sea. This was once the world's fourth largest lake, but is now drastically reduced in size because of climate change and the extraction of water for irrigation. In the centre of the image, the long arc of the mountain ranges of the Himalaya, Karakoram, Hindu Kush and Tien Shan circle the featureless Tarim Pendi basin and the lake-riddled Plateau of Tibet.

Asia
Landscapes

Asia is the world's largest continent and occupies almost one-third of the world's total land area. Stretching across approximately 165° of longitude from the Mediterranean Sea to the easternmost point of the Russian Federation on the Bering Strait, it contains the world's highest and lowest points and some of the world's greatest physical features. Its mountain ranges include the Himalaya, Hindu Kush, Karakoram and the Ural Mountains and its major rivers – including the Yangtze, Tigris-Euphrates, Indus, Ganges and Mekong – are equally well-known and evocative.

Asia's deserts include the Gobi, the Taklimakan, and those on the Arabian Peninsula, and significant areas of volcanic and tectonic activity are present on the Kamchatka Peninsula, in Japan, and on Indonesia's numerous islands. The continent's landscapes are greatly influenced by climatic variations, with great contrasts between the islands of the Arctic Ocean and the vast Siberian plains in the north, and the tropical islands of Indonesia.

The **Yangtze,** China, Asia's longest river, flowing into the East China Sea near Shanghai.

Asia's physical features

Highest mountain	Mt Everest, China/Nepal	8 848 metres	29 028 feet
Longest river	Yangtze, China	6 380 km	3 965 miles
Largest lake	Caspian Sea	371 000 sq km	143 243 sq miles
Largest island	Borneo	745 561 sq km	287 861 sq miles
Largest drainage basin	Ob'-Irtysh, Kazakhstan/Russian Federation	2 990 000 sq km	1 154 439 sq miles
Lowest point	Dead Sea	-423 metres	-1 388 feet

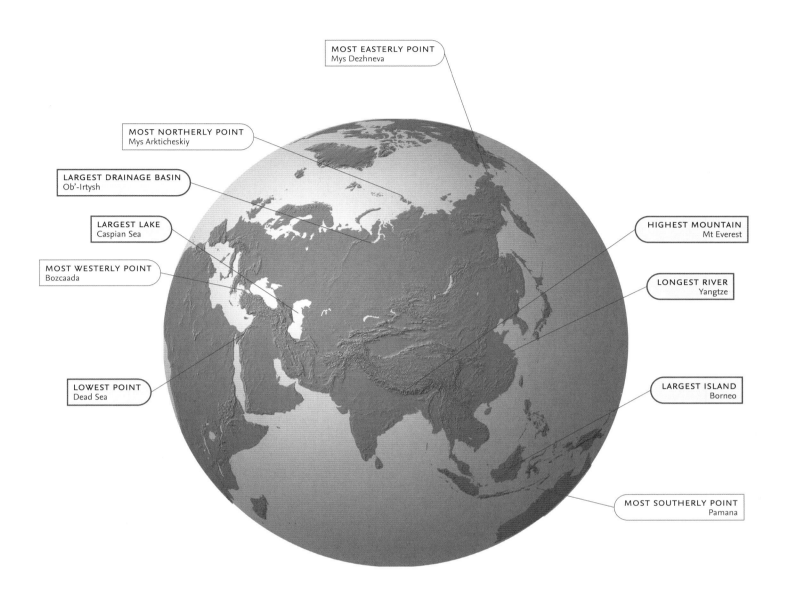

MOST EASTERLY POINT
Mys Dezhneva

MOST NORTHERLY POINT
Mys Arkticheskiy

LARGEST DRAINAGE BASIN
Ob'-Irtysh

LARGEST LAKE
Caspian Sea

MOST WESTERLY POINT
Bozcaada

LOWEST POINT
Dead Sea

HIGHEST MOUNTAIN
Mt Everest

LONGEST RIVER
Yangtze

LARGEST ISLAND
Borneo

MOST SOUTHERLY POINT
Pamana

Hahajima-rettō
Bonin Islands
Volcano Islands

Palau Islands

CIFIC CEAN

Jazirah Doberai
Puncak Jaya
▲ *5030*
New Guinea

Kepulauan Aru
Kepulauan Tanimbar
Arafura Sea

Asia's extent

TOTAL LAND AREA	45 036 492 sq km / 17 388 686 sq miles
Most northerly point	Mys Arkticheskiy, Russian Federation
Most southerly point	Pamana, Indonesia
Most westerly point	Bozcaada, Turkey
Most easterly point	Mys Dezhneva, Russian Federation

Facts

- 90 of the world's 100 highest mountains are in Asia

- The Indonesian archipelago is made up of over 13 500 islands

- The height of the land in Nepal ranges from 60 metres to 8 848 metres

- The deepest lake in the world is Lake Baikal, Russian Federation, with a maximum depth of 1 741 metres

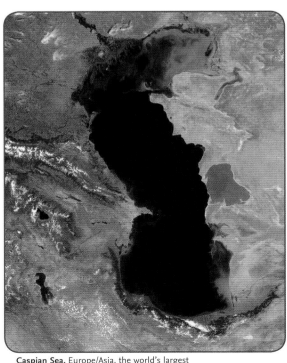

Caspian Sea, Europe/Asia, the world's largest expanse of inland water.

Asia
Countries

With approximately sixty per cent of the world's population, Asia is home to numerous cultures, people groups and lifestyles. Several of the world's earliest civilizations were established in Asia, including those of Sumeria, Babylonia and Assyria. Cultural and historical differences have led to a complex political pattern, and the continent has been, and continues to be, subject to numerous territorial and political conflicts – including the current disputes in the Middle East and in Jammu and Kashmir.

Separate regions within Asia can be defined by the cultural, economic and political systems they support. The major regions are: the arid, oil-rich, mainly Islamic southwest; southern Asia with its distinct cultures, isolated from the rest of Asia by major mountain ranges; the Indian- and Chinese-influenced monsoon region of southeast Asia; the mainly Chinese-influenced industrialized areas of eastern Asia; and Soviet Asia, made up of most of the former Soviet Union.

Timor island in southeast Asia, on which East Timor, Asia's newest independent state, is located.

Internet Links

● UK Foreign and Commonwealth Office	www.fco.gov.uk
● CIA World Factbook	www.cia.gov/library/publicaions/the-world-factbook/index.html
● Asian Development Bank	www.adb.org
● Association of Southeast Asian Nations (ASEAN)	www.aseansec.org
● Asia-Pacific Economic Cooperation	www.apec.org

Asia's countries

Largest country (area)	Russian Federation	17 075 400 sq km	6 592 849 sq miles
Smallest country (area)	Maldives	298 sq km	115 sq miles
Largest country (population)	China	1 332 079 000	
Smallest country (population)	Palau	21 000	
Most densely populated country	Singapore	8 118 per sq km	21 004 per sq mile
Least densely populated country	Mongolia	2 per sq km	5 per sq mile

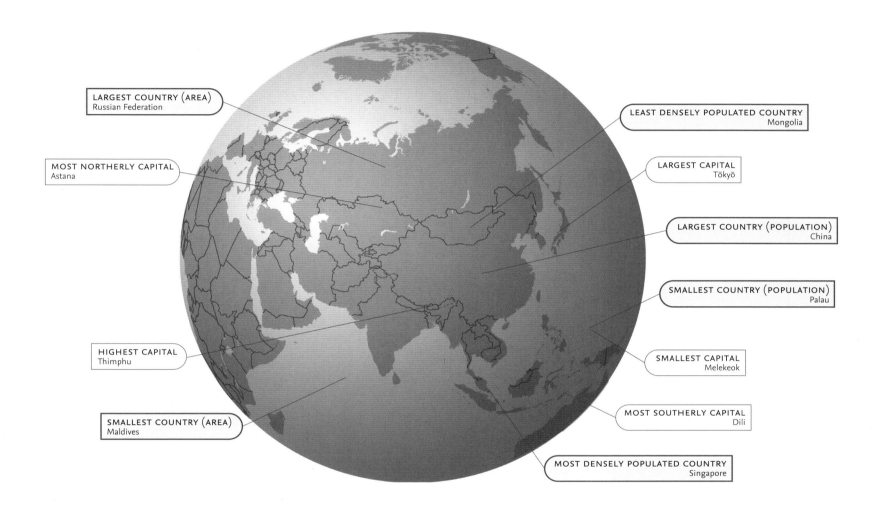

LARGEST COUNTRY (AREA)
Russian Federation

MOST NORTHERLY CAPITAL
Astana

HIGHEST CAPITAL
Thimphu

SMALLEST COUNTRY (AREA)
Maldives

LEAST DENSELY POPULATED COUNTRY
Mongolia

LARGEST CAPITAL
Tōkyō

LARGEST COUNTRY (POPULATION)
China

SMALLEST COUNTRY (POPULATION)
Palau

SMALLEST CAPITAL
Melekeok

MOST SOUTHERLY CAPITAL
Dili

MOST DENSELY POPULATED COUNTRY
Singapore

Bonin Islands (Japan)

Volcano Islands (Japan)

Melekeok
PALAU

Jayapura

New Guinea

Asia's capitals

Largest capital (population)	Tōkyō, Japan	37 049 000
Smallest capital (population)	Melekeok, Palau	391
Most northerly capital	Astana, Kazakhstan	51° 10'N
Most southerly capital	Dili, East Timor	8° 35'S
Highest capital	Thimphu, Bhutan	2 423 metres 7 949 feet

Facts

● Over 60% of the world's population live in Asia

● Asia has 10 of the world's 20 largest cities

● The Korean peninsula was divided into North Korea and South Korea in 1948 approximately along the 38th parallel

Beijing, capital of China, the most populous country in the world.

Conic Equidistant Projection

1:17 300 000

| 0 | 200 | 400 | 600 miles |

| 0 | 200 | 400 | 600 | 800 | 1000 km |

O C E A N

Severnaya
Zemlya
Ostrov
Oktyabr'skoy
Revolyutsii
Ostrov
Bol'shevik

Peninsula
v Taymyr
Gory
Byrranga
Ozero
Taymyr
Lowland
Nizmennost')

T

S

R

Q

P

O

N

M

L

New Siberia Islands
(Novosibirskiye Ostrova)

Laptev
Sea
(More Laptevykh)

East Siberian Sea
(Vostochno-Sibirskoye More)

Wrangel Island
(Ostrov
Vrangelya)

Chukchi
Sea

Seward Peninsula

Arctic Circle

Point
Hope

Nome

U.S.A.

Bering Strait

Aleutian Islands

Pribilof
Islands

St Matthew
Island (U.S.A.)

St Lawrence
Island (U.S.A.)

B e r i n g   S e a

Attu
Island
(U.S.A.)

Kiska
Island (U.S.A.)

Khrebet Kolymskiy

Koryakskoye Nagor'ye

Kamchatka Peninsula
(Poluostrov Kamchatka)

Petropavlovsk-
Kamchatskiy

Sredinnyy Khrebet

Khrebet Cherskogo

Sea
of
Okhotsk
(Okhotskoye More)

Kuril Islands
(Kuril'skiye Ostrova)

ADMINISTERED BY
RUSSIAN FEDERATION,
CLAIMED BY JAPAN

Central Siberian
Plateau

(Sredne-Sibirskoye
Ploskogor')

S I B E R I A

R U S S I A N   F E D E R A T I O N

Yakutsk

Stanovoy Khrebet

Sikhote-Alin'

Sakhalin

Yuzhno-Sakhalinsk

PACIFIC
OCEAN

Severo-
Baykal'skoye

Nagor'ye

Stanovoye
Nagor'ye

Vitimskoye
Ploskogor'ye

Khabarovsk

HOKKAIDO

Sapporo

Irkutsk

Ulan-Ude

Lake Baikal

Chita

M A N C H U R I A

Qiqihar

Daqing
(Anda)

Harbin

Jiamusi

Hegang

Vladivostok

Sea
of
Japan
(East Sea)

JAPAN

Sendai

TŌKYŌ
Yokohama

ULAN BATOR
(Ulaanbaatar)

M O N G O L I A

Hövsgöl
Nuur

Darhan

Changchun

Jilin
(Kirin)

NORTH
KOREA

PYONGYANG

Nagoya
Kyōto
Ōsaka
Kōbe

Gobi   Desert

INNER MONGOLIA

Chifeng
(Ulanhad)

Shenyang

Fushun

Anshan
Benxi

SEOUL
(Sŏul)

SOUTH KOREA

Taegu

Pusan

Hiroshima

Fukuoka

Hohhot

Baotou

BEIJING
(Peking)

Datong

Tianjin

Tangshan

Dalian
(Lüda)

Yantai

Bo Hai

Yellow
Sea
(Huang Hai)

Kwangju

Kyūshū

C H I N A

↓ 78

L   M   N   O

Asia

Eastern and Southeast Asia

Asia
Southeast Asia

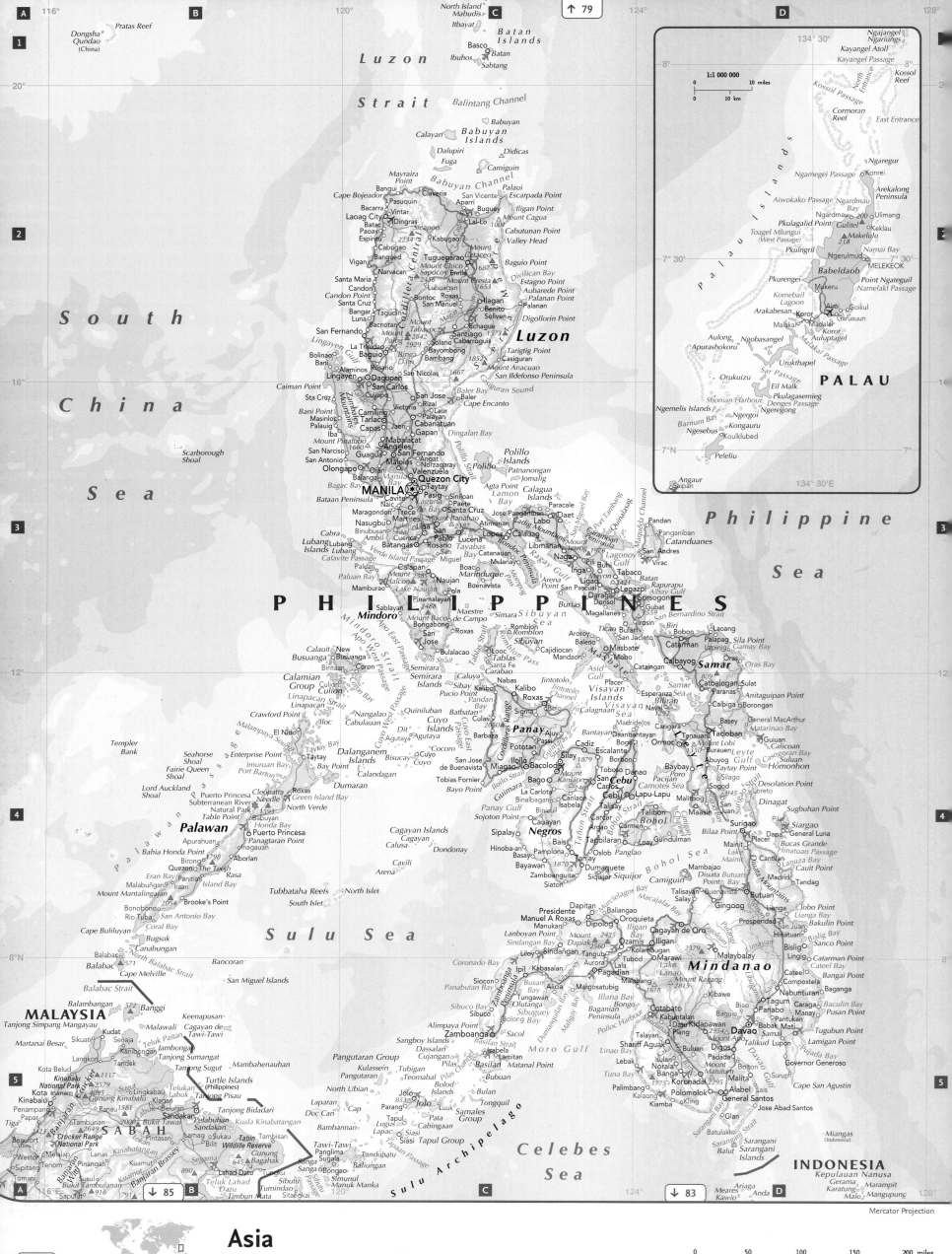

Asia
Philippines

Mercator Projection

1:5 500 000

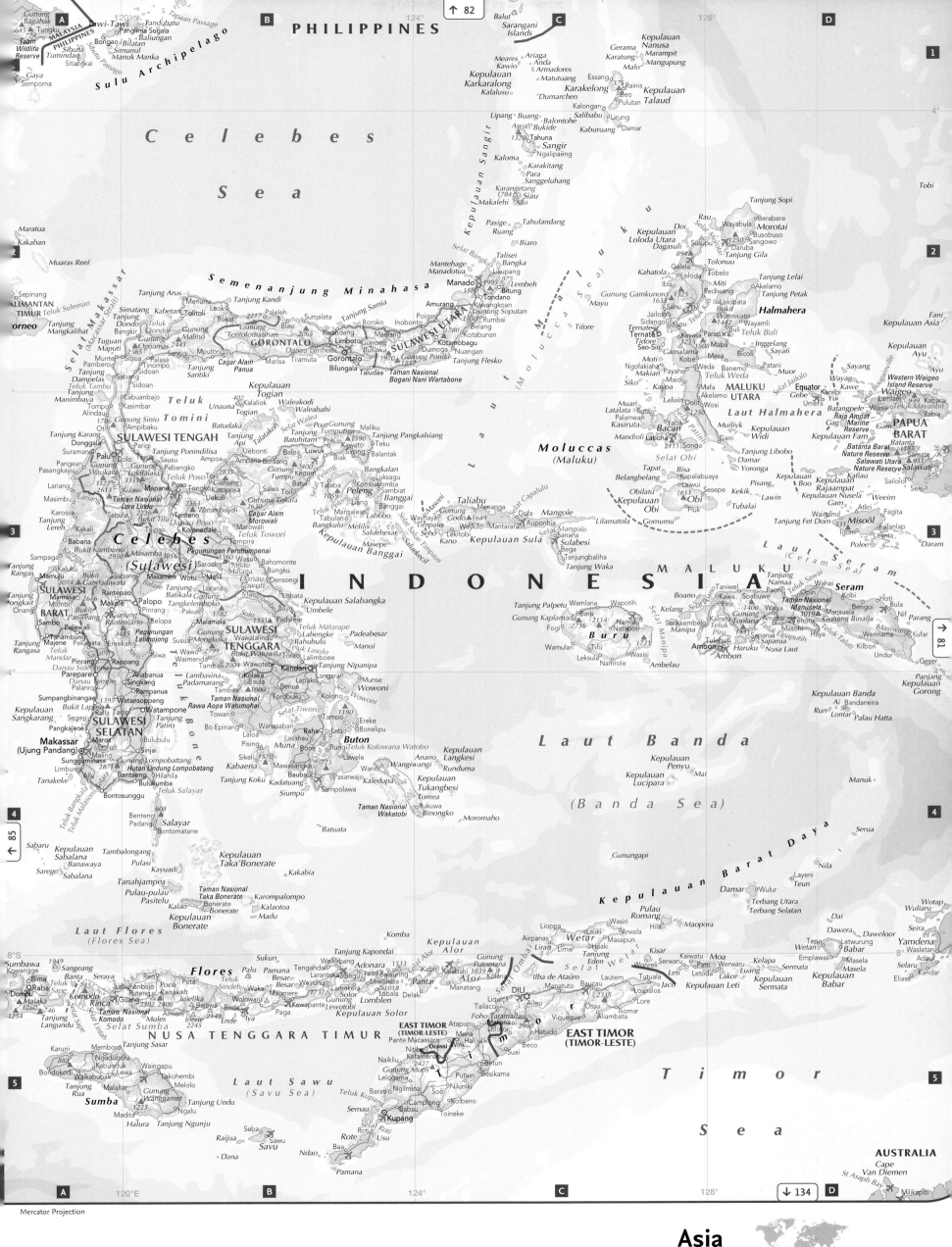

PHILIPPINES

Celebes Sea

Sulu Archipelago

Celebes Sea

Semenanjung Minahasa

SULAWESI UTARA

GORONTALO

Halmahera

MALUKU UTARA

Laut Halmahera

PAPUA BARAT

SULAWESI TENGAH

Teluk Tomini

Celebes (Sulawesi)

SULAWESI BARAT

SULAWESI TENGGARA

I N D O N E S I A

Moluccas (Maluku)

M A L U K U

Seram

Buru

SULAWESI SELATAN

Makassar (Ujung Pandang)

Buton

Laut Banda

(Banda Sea)

Laut Flores (Flores Sea)

NUSA TENGGARA TIMUR

Flores

DILI

EAST TIMOR (TIMOR-LESTE)

EAST TIMOR (TIMOR-LESTE)

Kepulauan Barat Daya

Laut Sawu (Savu Sea)

Sumba

Kupang

Timor Sea

AUSTRALIA

Cape Van Diemen

St Asaph Bay

Mercator Projection

1:5 500 000

0 50 100 150 200 miles
0 50 100 150 200 250 300 km

Asia
Central Indonesia

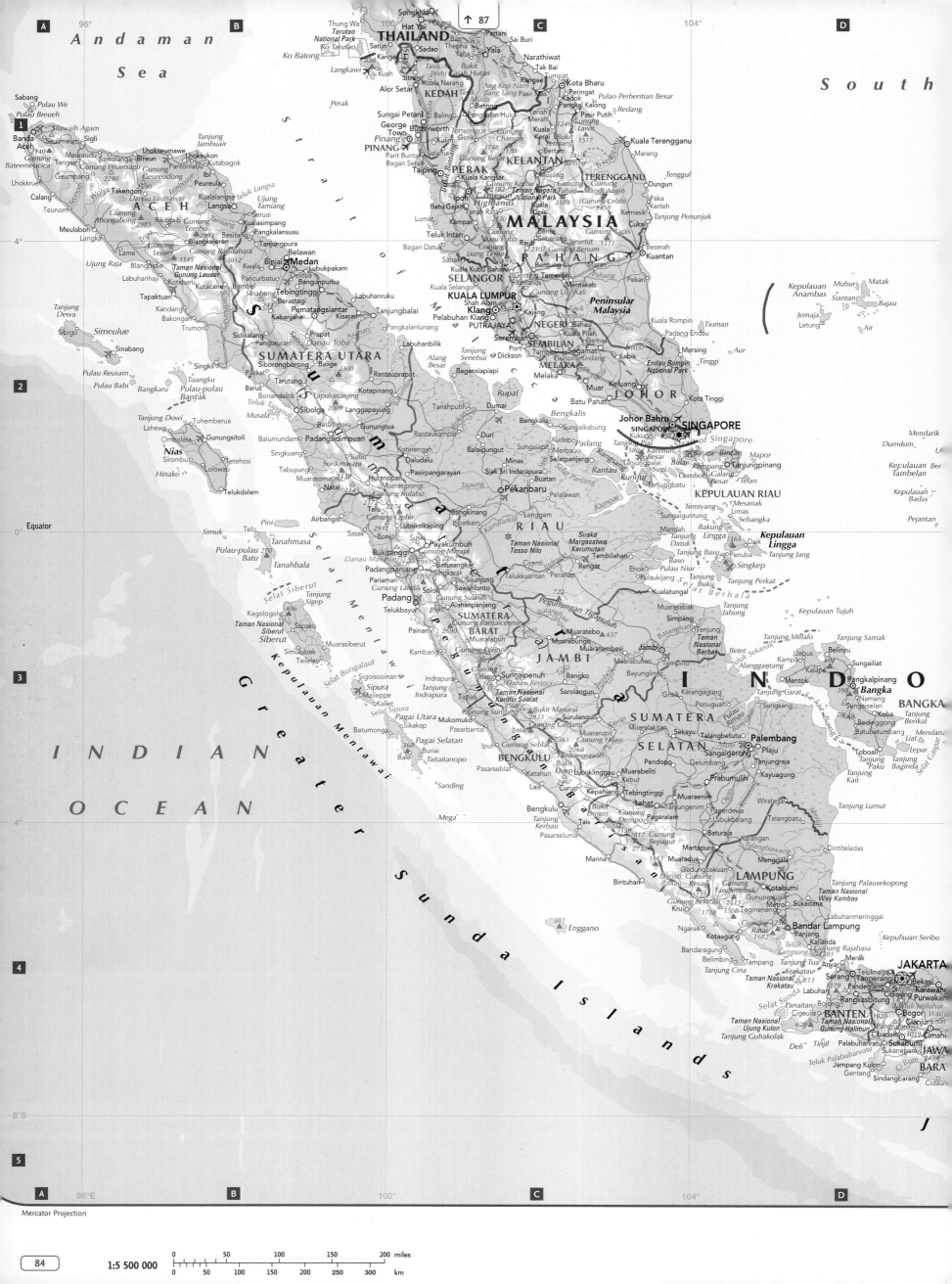

China Sea

Charlotte Bank
108°

112°

116°

PHILIPPINES

Sulu Sea

Cagayan de Tawi-Tawi

G

SABAH

BRUNEI

BANDAR SERI
BEGAWAN

LABUAN
Labuan

Celebes Sea

**KALIMANTAN
UTARA**

M   A   L   A   Y   S   I   A

SARAWAK

Kuching

**KALIMANTAN
BARAT**

Pontianak

B   o   r   n   e   o

K   A   L   I   M   A   N   T   A   N

**KALIMANTAN
TIMUR**

Samarinda

Balikpapan

**SULAWESI
TENGAH**

Palu

**SULAWESI
BARAT**

**Celebes
(Sulawesi)**

I   N   D   O   N   E   S   I   A

Singkawang

Selat Karimata

ELITUNG

Belitung

Manggar

**KALIMANTAN
TENGAH**

Palangkaraya

**KALIMANTAN
SELATAN**

Banjarmasin
Martapura

Equator

*Selat Makassar
(Macassar Strait)*

**SULAWESI
SELATAN**

**Makassar
(Ujung Pandang)**

L   a   u   t   J   a   w   a
(J   a   v   a   S   e   a)

Kepulauan Sangkarang

*Kepulauan
Laut Kecil*

4

Madura

Bandung

JAWA TENGAH

Semarang

Surabaya

**JAWA
TIMUR**

Surakarta

YOGYAKARTA

Malang

Selat Madura

*Laut Bali
(Bali Sea)*

BALI

Denpasar

Bali

Lombok

NUSA TENGGARA BARAT

*Laut
Flores
(Flores Sea)*

Sumbawa

*Taman Nasional
Komodo*

a   v   a
(J   a   w   a)

108°

112°

116°

G

5

Asia
West Indonesia and Malaysia

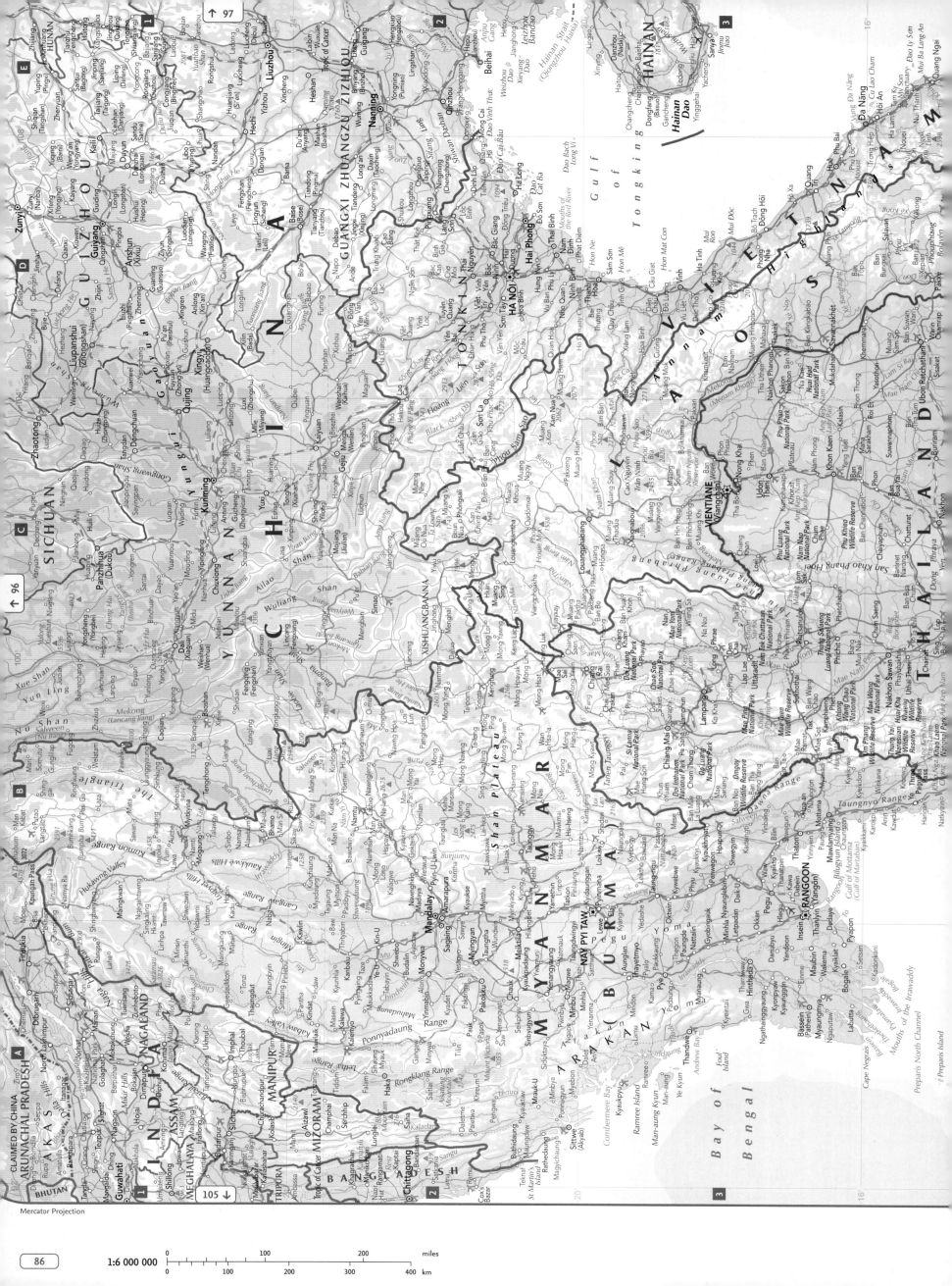

Asia

Myanmar, Thailand, Peninsular Malaysia and Indo-China

Albers Conic Equal Area Projection

1:13 000 000

| 0 | 200 | 400 | miles |

| 0 | 200 | 400 | 600 | 800 | km |

Asia
Eastern Asia

Asia

Japan, North Korea and South Korea

→ 89

P A C I F I C   O C E A N

Sea of Japan (East Sea)

Yellow Sea (Huang Hai)

East China Sea (Dong Hai)

NORTH KOREA

SOUTH KOREA

PYŎNGYANG

SEOUL (Sŏul)

J A P A N

TOKYO

Kyūshū

Shikoku

Ryukyu Islands (Nansei-shotō) (Japan)

Tokara-rettō

Bonin Islands (Ogasawara-shotō) (Japan)

Asia
Japan – Central Honshū

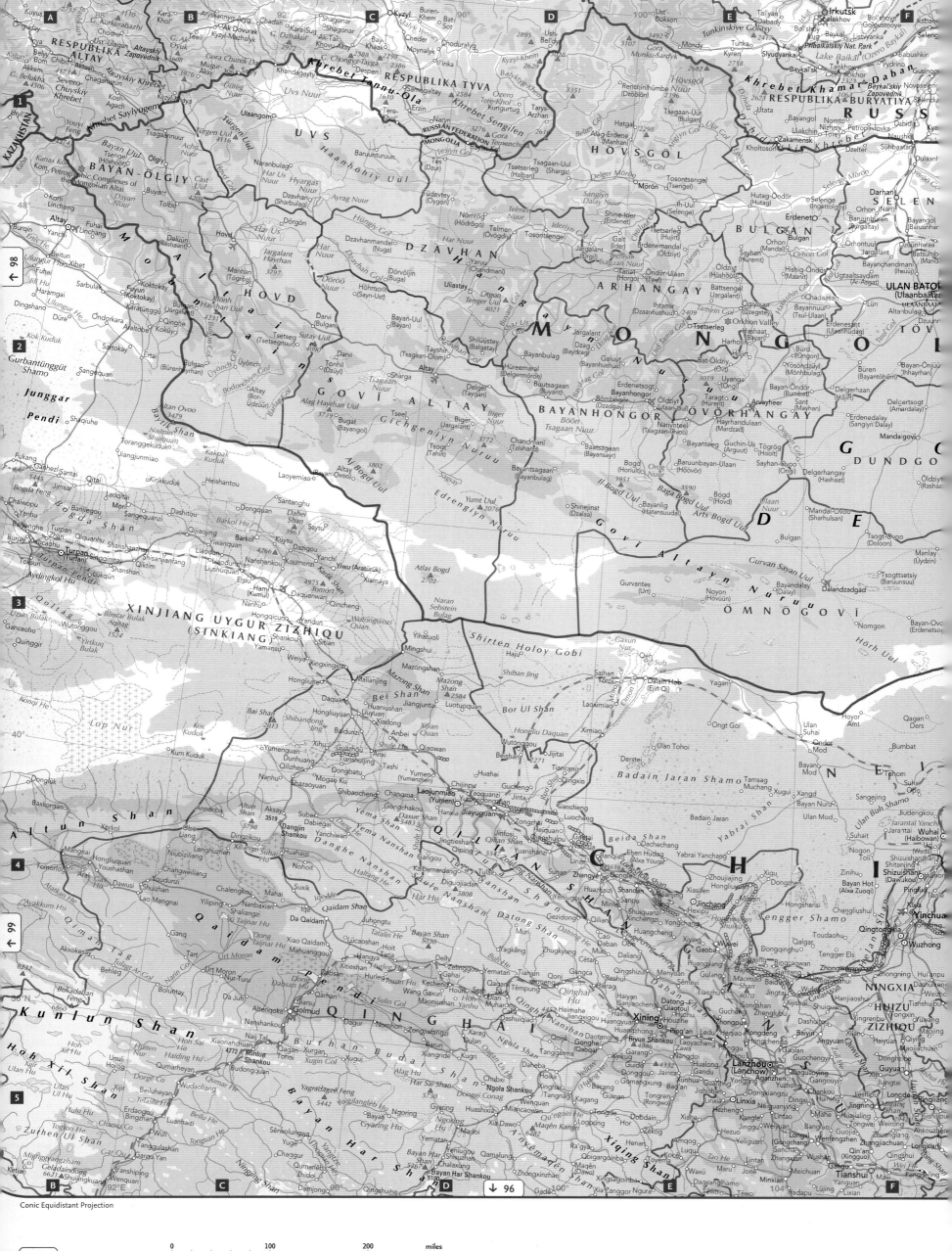

Asia

Northern China and Mongolia

Conic Equidistant Projection

1:6 000 000

Conic Equidistant Projection

1:6 000 000

0   100   200   miles

0   100   200   300   400   km

Asia

West China

Albers Conic Equal Area Projection

1:17 300 000

| 0 | 200 | 400 | 600 miles |

| 0 | 200 | 400 | 600 | 800 | 1000 km |

RUSSIAN FEDERATION

MONGOLIA

Gobi Desert

INNER MONGOLIA

KYRGYZSTAN

TAJIKISTAN

XINJIANG

Tarim Basin
(Tarim Pendi)

Taklimakan Desert
(Taklimakan Shamo)

Tien Shan

Kunlun Shan

Altun Shan

Hoh Xil Shan

Qaidam Pendi

Qilian Shan

CHINA

Plateau of Tibet
(Qingzang Gaoyuan)

TIBET

Tanggula Shan

PAKISTAN

JAMMU AND KASHMIR

NEPAL

BHUTAN

BANGLADESH

DHAKA
(Dacca)

INDIA

Deccan

Western Ghats

Eastern Ghats

MYANMAR
BURMA

NAY PYI TAW

Bay
of
Bengal

Andaman
Islands
(India)

Andaman
Sea

LAOS

THAILAND

BANGKOK
Krung Thep

CAMBODIA

PHNOM PENH

VIETNAM

Ho Chi Minh City
(Saigon)

Gulf of
Thailand

South
China
Sea

Hainan
Dao

SRI
LANKA

MALDIVES

Nicobar Islands
(India)

Ten Degree Channel

Nine Degree
Channel

Eight Degree Channel

Peninsular
Malaysia

MALAYSIA

KUALA
LUMPUR
PUTRAJAYA

SINGAPORE

INDONESIA

Asia

Central and Southern Asia

Albers Equal Area Conic Projection

1:11 000 000

0 100 200 300 400 500 miles
0 100 200 300 400 500 600 700 800 km

Asia
Northern India, Nepal, Bhutan and Bangladesh

Asia
Southern India and Sri Lanka

↓ 103

Conic Equidistant Projection

1:6 000 000

Administrative divisions in India
numbered on the map:

1. DADRA AND NAGAR HAVELI (B1)
2. DAMAN AND DIU (A1, B1)
3. PUDUCHERRY (C4)

TURKEY
MERCIN
ADANA
KARAMAN

CYPRUS
ADMINISTERED AS NORTHERN CYPRUS
GREEN LINE
NICOSIA (Lefkosa)

SYRIA

Mediterranean Sea

LEBANON

BEIRUT (Beyrouth)

DAMASCUS (Dimashq)

IRAQ

CEASE-FIRE LINES 1974

ADMINISTERED BY ISRAEL CLAIMED BY SYRIA

Haifa (Hefa)

WEST BANK

Tel Aviv-Yafo

JERUSALEM (Yerushalayim) (El Quds)

GAZA

AMMAN

Syrian Desert (Badiyat ash Sham)

PALESTINE

ISRAEL

JORDAN

MOAB

EDOM

BUR SA'ID

EGYPT

Negev

SHAMAL SINA'

JANUB SINA'

Sinai (Shibh Jazirat Sina')

SAUDI ARABIA

HUWAYTAT

Conic Equidistant Projection

Asia
Middle East

1:2 600 000

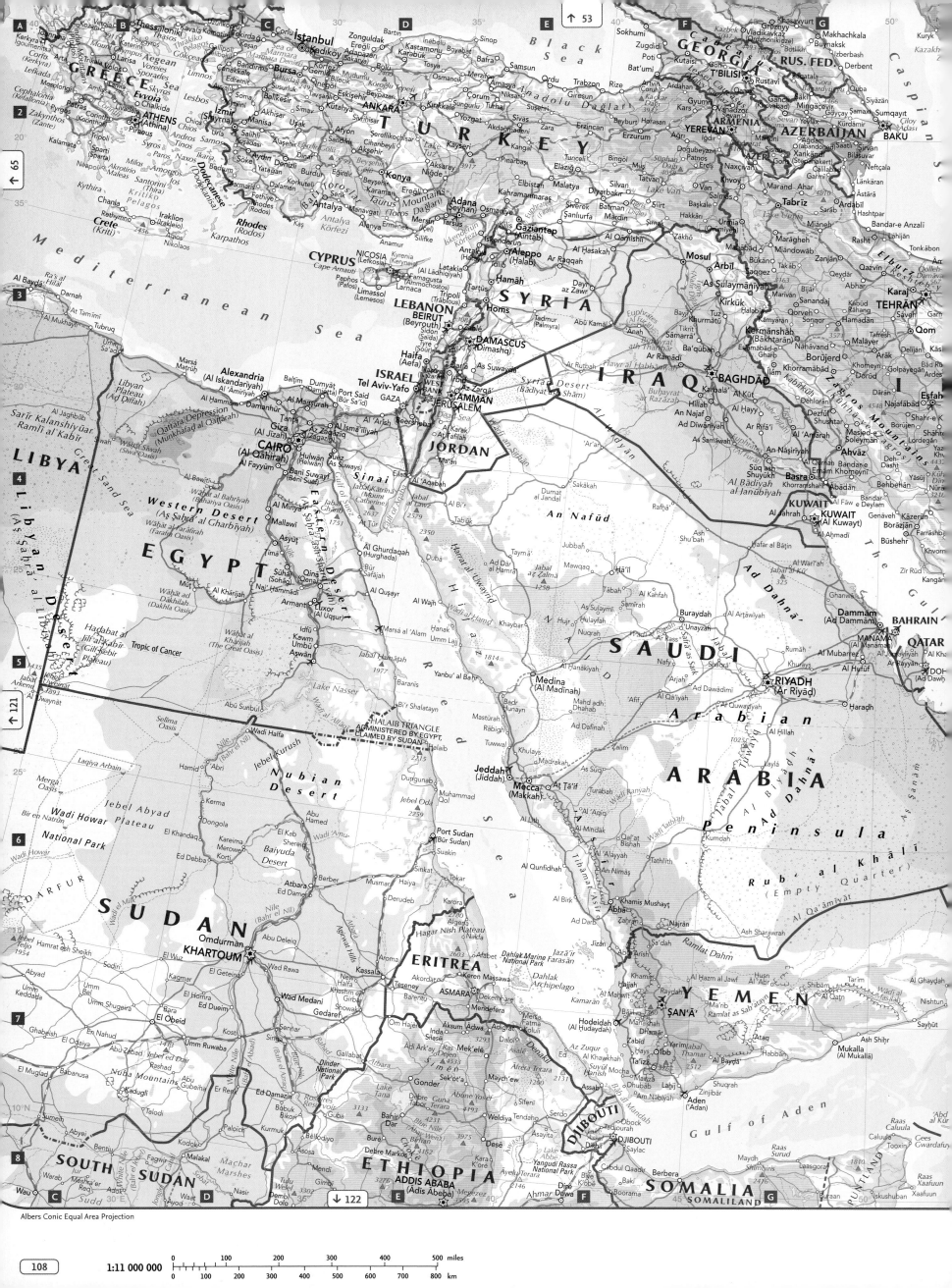

Administrative divisions in Russian Federation
numbered on the map:

1. RESPUBLIKA KALMYKIYA - KHALM'G-TANGCH (G1)
2. RESPUBLIKA DAGESTAN (G2)
3. CHECHENSKAYA RESPUBLIKA (G2)
4. RESPUBLIKA INGUSHETIYA (G2)
5. RESPUBLIKA SEVERNAYA OSETIYA - ALANIYA (G2)
6. KABARDINO-BALKARSKAYA RESPUBLIKA (F2)
7. KARACHAYEVO-CHERKESSKAYA RESPUBLIKA (F2)
8. RESPUBLIKA ADYGEYA (F1)

← 69

← 121

↓ 121

Conic Equidistant Projection

1:6 000 000

0   100   200   miles
0   100   200   300   400   km

Asia
Eastern Mediterranean, the Caucasus and Iraq

Africa

This image of Africa clearly shows the change in vegetation through the equatorial regions from the vast, dry Sahara desert covering much of the north of the continent, through the rich forests of the Congo basin – the second largest drainage basin in the world – to the high plateau of southern Africa. Lake Victoria dominates central east Africa and the Nile and its delta create a distinctive feature in the desert in the northeast. The path of the Great Rift Valley can be traced by the pattern of linear lakes in east Africa, to Ethiopia, and along the Red Sea. The dark fan-shaped feature in central southern Africa is the Okavango Delta in Botswana – one of the world's most ecologically sensitive areas. To the east of the continent lies Madagascar, and in the Indian Ocean northeast of this is the Mascarene Ridge sea feature stretching from the Seychelles in the north to Mauritius and Réunion in the south.

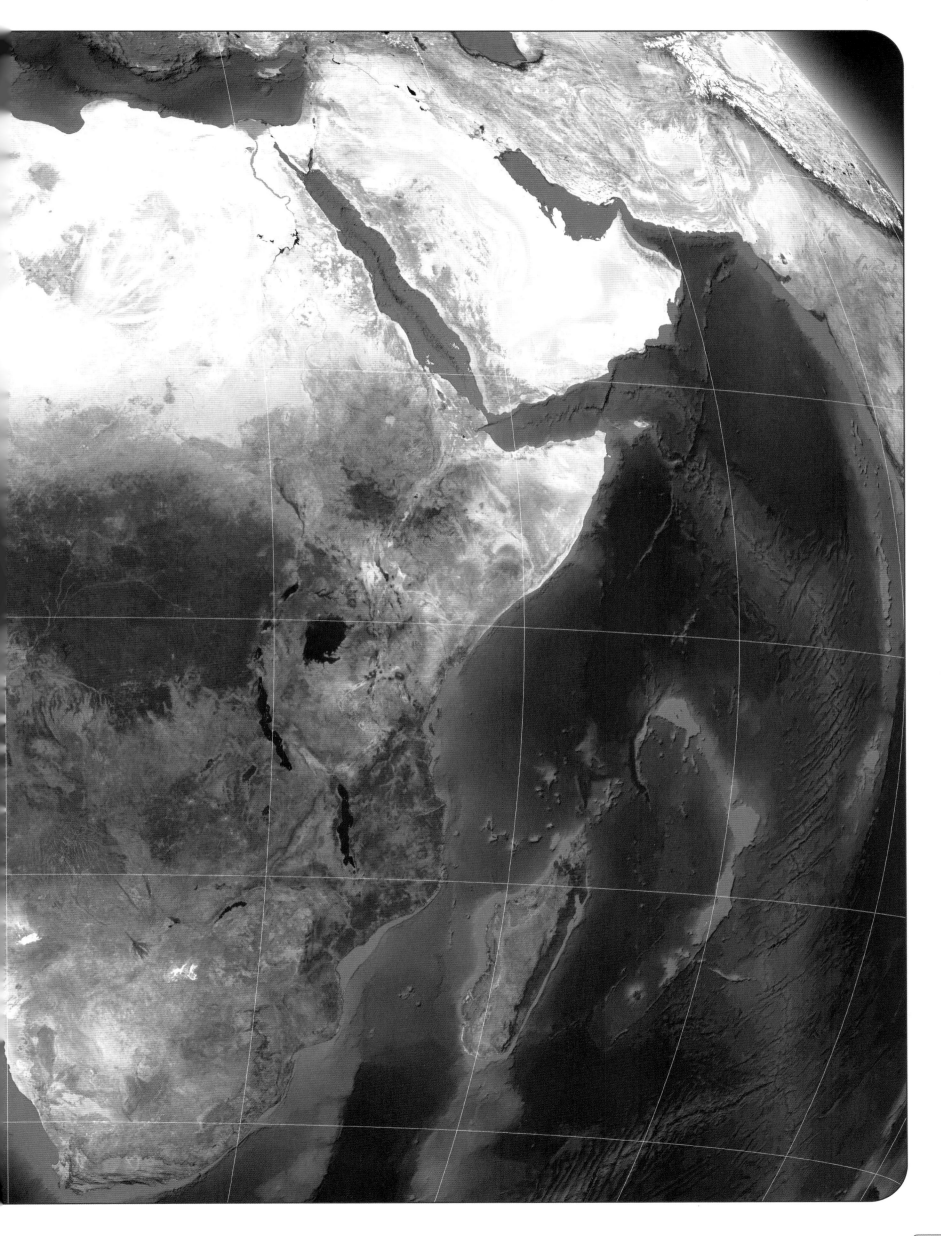

Africa
Landscapes

Some of the world's greatest physical features are in Africa, the world's second largest continent. Variations in climate and elevation give rise to the continent's great variety of landscapes. The Sahara, the world's largest desert, extends across the whole continent from west to east, and covers an area of over nine million square kilometres. Other significant African deserts are the Kalahari and the Namib. In contrast, some of the world's greatest rivers flow in Africa, including the Nile, the world's longest, and the Congo.

The Great Rift Valley is perhaps Africa's most notable geological feature. It stretches for nearly 3 000 kilometres from Jordan, through the Red Sea and south to Mozambique, and contains many of Africa's largest lakes. Significant mountain ranges on the continent are the Atlas Mountains and the Ethiopian Highlands in the north, the Ruwenzori in east central Africa, and the Drakensberg in the far southeast.

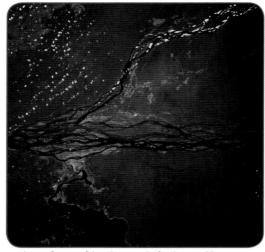

The confluence of the Ubangi and Africa's second longest river, the **Congo**.

Africa's extent

TOTAL LAND AREA	30 343 578 sq km / 11 715 655 sq miles
Most northerly point	La Galite, Tunisia
Most southerly point	Cape Agulhas, South Africa
Most westerly point	Santo Antão, Cape Verde
Most easterly point	Raas Xaafuun, Somalia

Internet Links	
● NASA Visible Earth	visibleearth.nasa.gov
● NASA Astronaut Photography	eol.jsc.nasa.gov
● Peace Parks Foundation	www.peaceparks.org

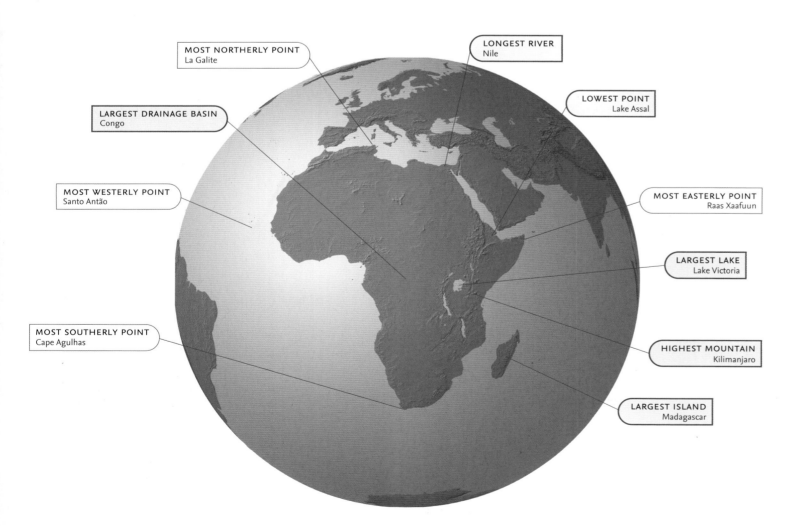

MOST NORTHERLY POINT
La Galite

LONGEST RIVER
Nile

LARGEST DRAINAGE BASIN
Congo

LOWEST POINT
Lake Assal

MOST WESTERLY POINT
Santo Antão

MOST EASTERLY POINT
Raas Xaafuun

MOST SOUTHERLY POINT
Cape Agulhas

LARGEST LAKE
Lake Victoria

HIGHEST MOUNTAIN
Kilimanjaro

LARGEST ISLAND
Madagascar

Madeira

Canary Islands
Tenerife
Gran Canaria

Akchâr

Aoul

Cape Verde *Santo Antão*
Ilhas do Cabo Verde
Boa Vista
Fogo *Santiago*
Cap Vert
Sénégal
Gambia
Fouta Djallon

Ascension

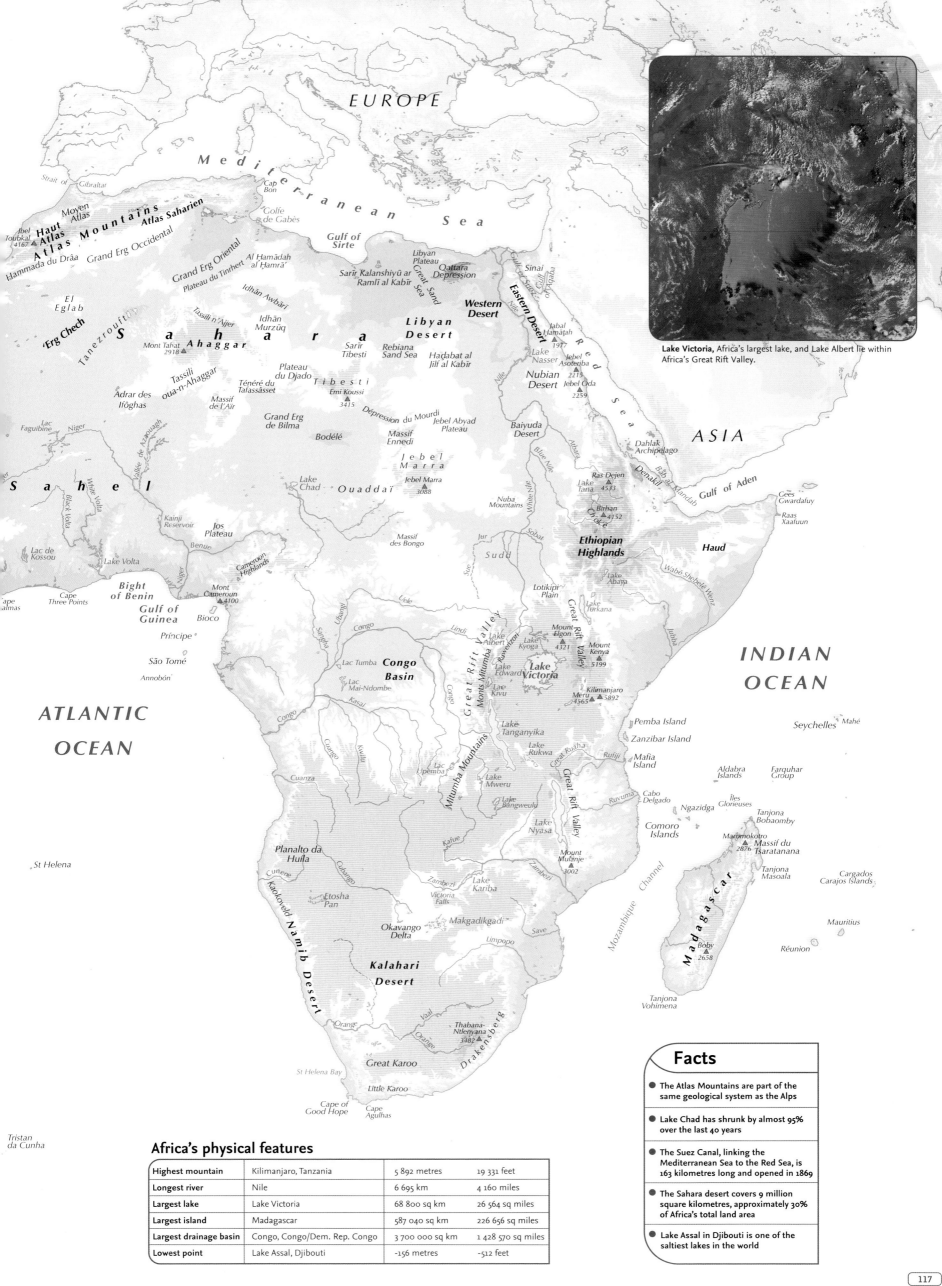

EUROPE

Strait of Gibraltar

Mediterranean Sea

Cap Bon
Golfe de Gabès
Gulf of Sirte

Moyen Atlas
Ibel Haut Toubkal △ Atlas 4167
Atlas Mountains Atlas Saharien
Hammada du Drâa Grand Erg Occidental
El Eglab
'Erg Chech
Tanezrouft
Adrar des Ifôghas
Tassili oua-n-Ahaggar
Massif de l'Aïr

S a h a r a
Grand Erg Oriental
Plateau du Tinrhert
Idhān Awbārī
Al Ḩamādah al Ḩamrā'
Sarīr Kalanshiyū ar Ramlī al Kabīr
Idhān Murzūq
Sarīr Tibesti
Rebiana Sand Sea
Plateau du Djado
Ténéré du Tafassâsset
Grand Erg de Bilma
Bodélé
Dépression du Mourdi
Mont Tahat △ 2918 **Ahaggar**
Tassili n'Ajjer
T i b e s t i
Emi Koussi △ 3415
Massif Ennedi
Jebel Abyad Plateau

Libyan Plateau
Great Sand Sea
Qattara Depression
Western Desert
Libyan Desert
Sinai
Eastern Desert
Ḩadabat al Jilf al Kabīr
Jabal Ḩamāṭah △ 1977

Gulf of Suez
Lake Nasser
Jebel Asoteriba △ 2215
Jebel Oda △ 2259
Nubian Desert
Baiyuda Desert
Nuba Mountains

Red Sea
Dahlak Archipelago
Denakil

A S I A

Gulf of Aden
Gees Gwardafuy
Raas Xaafuun
Bab al Mandab

Lac Faguibine
Niger
Lac de Kossou
Black Volta
White Volta
S a h e l
Vallée de l'Azaouagh
Kainji Reservoir
Benue
Jos Plateau
Lake Volta
Jebel Marra △ 3088
Lake Chad
Ouaddaï
Massif des Bongo
Jur
Sue
Sobat
Sudd
Blue Nile
Atbara
Lake Tana
Birhan △ 4152
Ras Dejen △ 4533
Choke
Jebel Marra

Ethiopian Highlands
Lake Abaya
Wabē Shebelē Wenz
Haud

Bight of Benin
Cape Three Points
Cape Palmas
Mont Cameroun △ 4100
Gulf of Guinea
Cameroon Highlands
Bioco
Príncipe
São Tomé
Annobón

Lotikipi Plain
Lake Turkana
Juba

ATLANTIC OCEAN

St Helena

Ubangi
Uele
Congo Basin
Congo
Sangha
Lac Tumba
Lac Mai-Ndombe
Kasai
Lindi
Congo
Lomami
Kwilu
Cuango
Cuanza
Lac Upemba
Kasai

Lake Albert
Ruwenzori
Lake Edward
Lake Kivu
Mount Elgon △ 4321
Lake Kyoga
Lake Victoria
Mount Kenya △ 5199
Meru △ 4565
Kilimanjaro △ 5892
Great Rift Valley
Monts Mitumba
Mitumba Mountains
Lake Tanganyika
Lake Rukwa
Great Ruaha
Rufiji
Ruvuma

Pemba Island
Zanzibar Island
Mafia Island

INDIAN OCEAN

Seychelles
Mahé

Lake Mweru
Lac Bangweulu
Kafue
Zambezi
Lake Nyasa
Mount Mulanje △ 3002
Cabo Delgado
Comoro Islands
Ngazidga
Îles Glorieuses
Aldabra Islands
Farquhar Group

Planalto da Huíla
Cunene
Cubango
Zambezi
Lake Kariba
Victoria Falls
Makgadikgadi
Limpopo
Save
Mozambique Channel

Maromokotro △ 2876
Massif du Tsaratanana
Tanjona Bobaomby
Tanjona Masoala
Cargados Carajos Islands
Mauritius
Réunion

Kaokoveld
Namib Desert
Etosha Pan
Okavango Delta
Kalahari Desert

M a d a g a s c a r
Boby △ 2658
Tanjona Vohimena

Orange
Vaal
Orange
Thabana-Ntlenyana △ 3482
Drakensberg
Great Karoo
Little Karoo
St Helena Bay
Cape of Good Hope
Cape Agulhas

Tristan da Cunha

Lake Victoria, Africa's largest lake, and Lake Albert lie within Africa's Great Rift Valley.

Africa's physical features

Highest mountain	Kilimanjaro, Tanzania	5 892 metres	19 331 feet
Longest river	Nile	6 695 km	4 160 miles
Largest lake	Lake Victoria	68 800 sq km	26 564 sq miles
Largest island	Madagascar	587 040 sq km	226 656 sq miles
Largest drainage basin	Congo, Congo/Dem. Rep. Congo	3 700 000 sq km	1 428 570 sq miles
Lowest point	Lake Assal, Djibouti	-156 metres	-512 feet

Facts

- The Atlas Mountains are part of the same geological system as the Alps

- Lake Chad has shrunk by almost 95% over the last 40 years

- The Suez Canal, linking the Mediterranean Sea to the Red Sea, is 163 kilometres long and opened in 1869

- The Sahara desert covers 9 million square kilometres, approximately 30% of Africa's total land area

- Lake Assal in Djibouti is one of the saltiest lakes in the world

Africa
Countries

Africa is a complex continent, with over fifty independent countries and a long history of political change. It supports a great variety of ethnic groups, with the Sahara creating the major divide between Arab and Berber groups in the north and a diverse range of groups, including the Yoruba and Masai, in the south.

The current pattern of countries in Africa is a product of a long and complex history, including the colonial period, which saw European control of the vast majority of the continent from the fifteenth century until widespread moves to independence began in the 1950s. Despite its great wealth of natural resources, Africa is by far the world's poorest continent. Many of its countries are heavily dependent upon foreign aid and many are also subject to serious political instability.

Facts

- Africa has over 1 000 linguistic and cultural groups
- Only Liberia and Ethiopia have remained free from colonial rule throughout their history
- Over 30% of the world's minerals, and over 46% of the world's diamonds, come from Africa
- 9 of the 10 poorest countries in the world are in Africa

LARGEST COUNTRY (AREA)
Algeria

MOST NORTHERLY CAPITAL
Tunis

LARGEST CAPITAL
Cairo

LARGEST COUNTRY (POPULATION)
Nigeria

HIGHEST CAPITAL
Addis Ababa

SMALLEST CAPITAL
Victoria

SMALLEST COUNTRY
(AREA AND POPULATION)
Seychelles

LEAST DENSELY POPULATED COUNTRY
Namibia

MOST DENSELY POPULATED COUNTRY
Mauritius

MOST SOUTHERLY CAPITAL
Cape Town

Madeira
(Portugal)

Canary Island
(Spain)

Laâyoune

WESTERN
SAHARA

Nouâdhibou

MAURITAN

Nouakchott

Sénégal

St-Louis

CAPE
VERDE

Dakar

Kaye

SENEGAL

Praia

Kaolack

Banjul

THE GAMBIA

Bissau

GUINEA-
BISSAU

GUINEA

Conakry

Kar

Freetown

SIERRA
LEONE

Monrovia

LIBER

Ascension
(U.K.)

Internet Links

UK Foreign and Commonwealth Office	www.fco.gov.uk
CIA World Factbook	www.cia.gov/library/publications/the-world-factbook/index.html
Southern African Development Community	www.sadc.int
GeoEye	www.GeoEye.com

EUROPE

Strait of
Gibraltar
Tangier
Casablanca
Rabat
Fès
Beni Mellal
Marrakech
Béchar

Atlas Mountains

MOROCCO

Oran
Algiers
Ech Chélif
Sidi Bel Abbès
Skikda
Bejaïa
Annaba
Constantine
Tunis
Laghouat

TUNISIA
Tripoli
Sfax
Gabès
Mişrātah
Al Bayḑā'
Benghazi

ALGERIA

LIBYA

Sahara

Mediterranean Sea

Gulf of Sirte

Libyan Desert

EGYPT
Alexandria
Tanţā
Cairo
Giza
Suez
Port Said
Al Minyā
Asyūţ
Luxor
Qinā
Aswān
Lake Nasser
Nile

Red Sea

ASIA

MALI
Gao
Mopti
Ségou
Bamako
Niger

Niamey
Ouagadougou
Dioulasso
obo
BURKINA FASO
Tamale

NIGER
Agadez
Zinder
Sokoto
Kano
Zaria
Maiduguri
Maroua
Kumo
Lake Chad
Ndjamena

CHAD
Abéché
El Obed

SUDAN
Omdurman
Khartoum
Wad Medani
Gedaref
Blue Nile

ERITREA
Asmara
Mek'elē

DJIBOUTI
Djibouti
Berbera
SOMALILAND
Hargeysa

CÔTE D'IVOIRE
(IVORY COAST)
Bouaké
Yamoussoukro
Kumasi
GHANA
TOGO
BENIN
Parakou
Abidjan
Cape Coast
Accra
Lomé
Porto-Novo

NIGERIA
Abuja
Ibadan
Ogbomosho
Lagos
Onitsha
Warri
Uyo
Port Harcourt
Malabo
Douala
Lake Volta

Ngaoundéré
Bossángoa
Moundou
Sarh
Bangui
Congo

CENTRAL AFRICAN REPUBLIC

SOUTH SUDAN
Wau
Juba

Bahir Dar
Addis Ababa
ETHIOPIA

Dirē Dawa
Gulf of Aden

EQUATORIAL GUINEA
São Tomé
SÃO TOMÉ AND PRÍNCIPE
Libreville
Port-Gentil

GABON
CONGO
Franceville
Brazzaville
Pointe-Noire
CABINDA (Angola)
Matadi
Kinshasa

DEMOCRATIC REPUBLIC OF THE CONGO
Mbandaka
Kisangani
Bandundu
Kikwit
Kananga
Mbuji-Mayi
Kamina

UGANDA
Kampala
RWANDA
Kigali
BURUNDI
Bujumbura
Kigoma
Kalemie
Bukavu
Kisumu
Nakuru
Mount Kenya 5199
Lake Victoria
Mwanza

KENYA
Nairobi
Mombasa
Kismaayo
Mogadishu

SOMALIA
Wabē Shabēlē

INDIAN OCEAN

Victoria
SEYCHELLES

TANZANIA
Tabora
Dodoma
Iringa
Mbeya
Arusha
Kilimanjaro 5892
Tanga
Zanzibar
Zanzibar Island
Dar es Salaam
Lake Tanganyika

Aldabra Islands

ATLANTIC OCEAN

Luanda
Cuanza

ANGOLA
Lobito
Benguela
Huambo
Namibe
Lubango

Likasi
Lubumbashi
Solwezi
Kasama
Mansa
Ndola
Chingola
Kabwe
Lusaka
Mongu

ZAMBIA

MALAWI
Lake Nyasa
Chipata
Lilongwe
Blantyre
Tete
Nampula
Nacala
Pemba

COMOROS
Moroni
Antsiranana

Mayotte (France)
Mahajanga

St Helena
(U.K.)
St Helena, Ascension
and Tristan da Cunha
(U.K.)

Cubango

NAMIBIA
Windhoek
Namib Desert
Etosha Pan
Okavango Delta

Orange

BOTSWANA
Gaborone

ZIMBABWE
Harare
Chitungwiza
Mutare
Gweru
Bulawayo
Francistown
Livingstone

MOZAMBIQUE
Quelimane
Beira
Inhambane
Xai-Xai
Maputo

MADAGASCAR
Toamasina
Antananarivo
Fianarantsoa
Toliara

Port Louis
MAURITIUS
Réunion
(France)

Johannesburg
Carletonville
Pretoria (Tshwane)
Soweto
Mbabane
SWAZILAND
LESOTHO
Maseru

Kimberley
Bloemfontein

REPUBLIC OF SOUTH AFRICA

Cape Town
Khayelitsha
Cape of Good Hope
Cape Agulhas
Port Elizabeth
East London
Durban

Tristan da Cunha
(U.K.)

Gulf of Guinea

Cape Town, legislative capital of the Republic of South Africa and the most southerly African capital city.

Africa's capitals

Largest capital (population)	Cairo, Egypt	11 663 000
Smallest capital (population)	Victoria, Seychelles	25 500
Most northerly capital	Tunis, Tunisia	36° 46'N
Most southerly capital	Cape Town, Republic of South Africa	33° 57'S
Highest capital	Addis Ababa, Ethiopia	2 408 metres 7 900 feet

Africa's countries

Largest country (area)	Algeria	2 381 741 sq km	919 595 sq miles
Smallest country (area)	Seychelles	455 sq km	176 sq miles
Largest country (population)	Nigeria	162 471 000	
Smallest country (population)	Seychelles	87 000	
Most densely populated country	Mauritius	640 per sq km	1 659 per sq mile
Least densely populated country	Namibia	3 per sq km	7 per sq mile

A   B   C   D

ATLANTIC
OCEAN

Arquipélago
da Madeira   Ilha de Porto Santo
FUNCHAL   Madeira
(Portugal)

Canary Islands
(Spain)   Lanzarote
La Palma   Santa Cruz
2426   de la Palma   Santa Cruz   Arrecife
La Gomera   3718   de Tenerife   Fuerteventura
El Hierro   Pico del Teide   Las Palmas de
Tenerife   Gran Canaria
Gran   LAÂYOUNE
Canaria

MOROCCO

SPAIN

ALGIERS
(Alger)

TUNIS

TUNISIA

ALGERIA

WESTERN
SAHARA

ADMINISTERED BY MOROCCO

Tropic of Cancer

MAURITANIA   EL MREYYÉ

MALI

NIGER

NOUAKCHOTT

DAKAR

SENEGAL

THE GAMBIA
BANJUL

GUINEA BISSAU
BISSAU

Arquipélago
dos Bijagós

GUINEA

CONAKRY

FREETOWN

SIERRA LEONE

MONROVIA

LIBERIA

BURKINA FASO

BAMAKO

OUAGADOUGOU

NIAMEY

NIGERIA

KANO

KADUNA

ABUJA

CÔTE D'IVOIRE
(IVORY COAST)

GHANA

YAMOUSSOUKRO

ABIDJAN

ACCRA

BENIN

TOGO

LOMÉ

PORTO
NOVO

Lagos

Cotonou

Gulf
of Guinea

Bight
of Benin

Slave Coast

CAMEROON
YAOUNDÉ

Douala

MALABO

EQUATORIAL
GUINEA

SÃO TOMÉ
AND
PRÍNCIPE

SÃO TOMÉ

LIBREVILLE

GABON

CAPE VERDE

Ilhas do
Cabo Verde

PRAIA

1:14 000 000

ATLANTIC

OCEAN

Lambert Azimuthal Equal Area Projection

Africa
Northern Africa

ATLANTIC

OCEAN

NAMIBIA

BOTSWANA

GHANZI

KWENENG

SOUTHERN

REPUBLIC OF

SOUTH AFR

WESTERN CAPE

NORTHERN OF CAPE

KHOMAS

ERONGO

OTJOZONDJUPA

OMAHEKE

HARDAP

KARAS

GRIQUALAND WEST

Kalahari Desert

Kgalagadi

Namib Desert

Great Namaqualand

Namaqualand

Great Karoo

Little Karoo

CAPE TOWN

Lambert Azimuthal Equal Area Projection

1:4 300 000

0   50   100   150   miles

0   50   100   150   200   250 km

Africa
Republic of South Africa

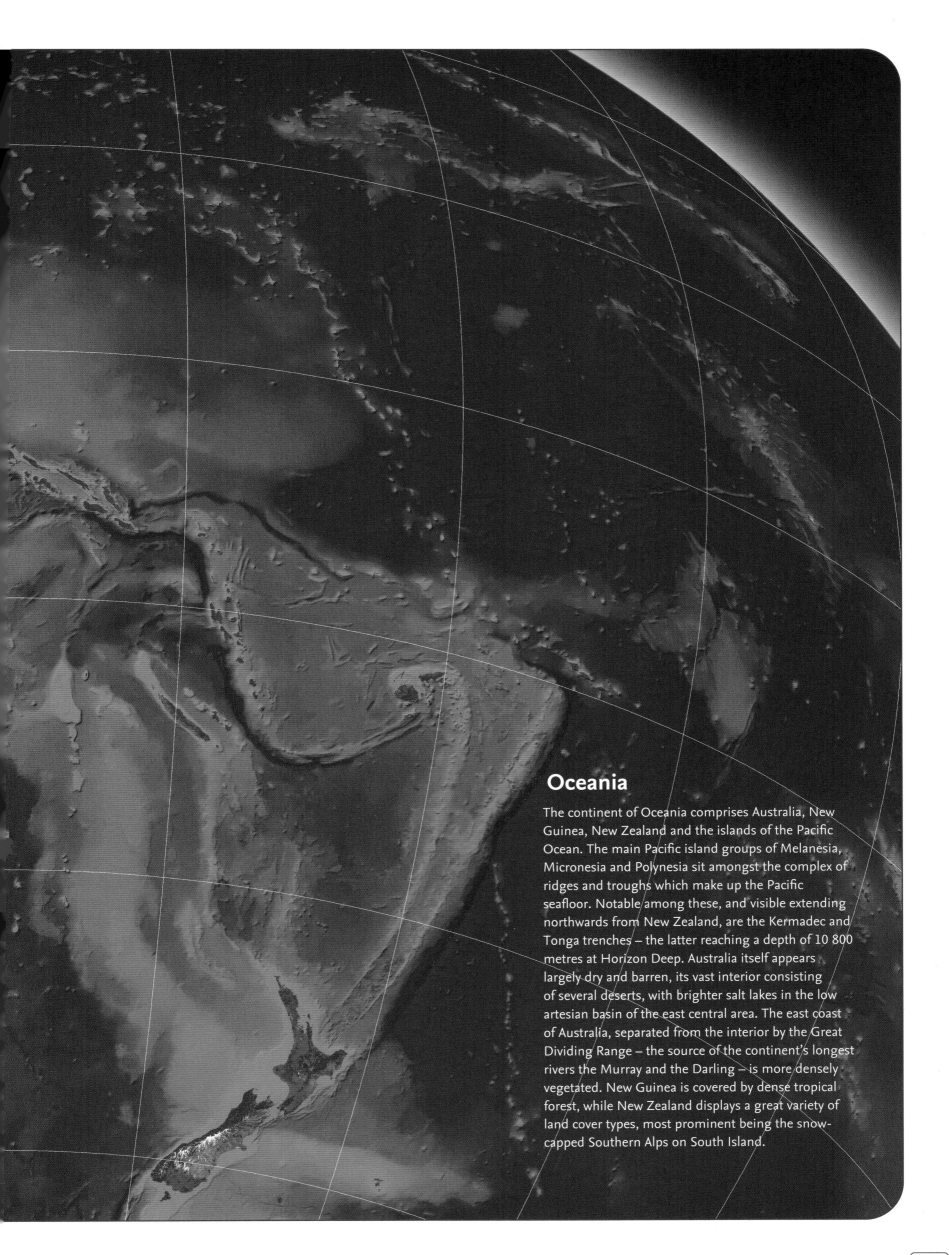

Oceania

The continent of Oceania comprises Australia, New Guinea, New Zealand and the islands of the Pacific Ocean. The main Pacific island groups of Melanesia, Micronesia and Polynesia sit amongst the complex of ridges and troughs which make up the Pacific seafloor. Notable among these, and visible extending northwards from New Zealand, are the Kermadec and Tonga trenches – the latter reaching a depth of 10 800 metres at Horizon Deep. Australia itself appears largely dry and barren, its vast interior consisting of several deserts, with brighter salt lakes in the low artesian basin of the east central area. The east coast of Australia, separated from the interior by the Great Dividing Range – the source of the continent's longest rivers the Murray and the Darling – is more densely vegetated. New Guinea is covered by dense tropical forest, while New Zealand displays a great variety of land cover types, most prominent being the snow-capped Southern Alps on South Island.

Oceania comprises Australia, New Zealand, New Guinea and the islands of the Pacific Ocean. It is the smallest of the world's continents by land area. Its dominating feature is Australia, which is mainly flat and very dry. Australia's western half consists of a low plateau, broken in places by higher mountain ranges, which has very few permanent rivers or lakes. The narrow, fertile coastal plain of the east coast is separated from the interior by the Great Dividing Range, which includes the highest mountain in Australia.

The numerous Pacific islands of Oceania are generally either volcanic in origin or consist of coral. They can be divided into three main regions - Micronesia, north of the equator between Palau and the Gilbert islands; Melanesia, stretching from mountainous New Guinea to Fiji; and Polynesia, covering a vast area of the eastern and central Pacific Ocean.

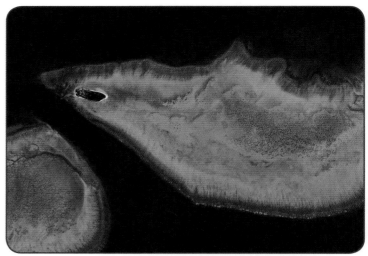

Heron Island, surrounded by coral reefs, lies at the southern end of Australia's Great Barrier Reef.

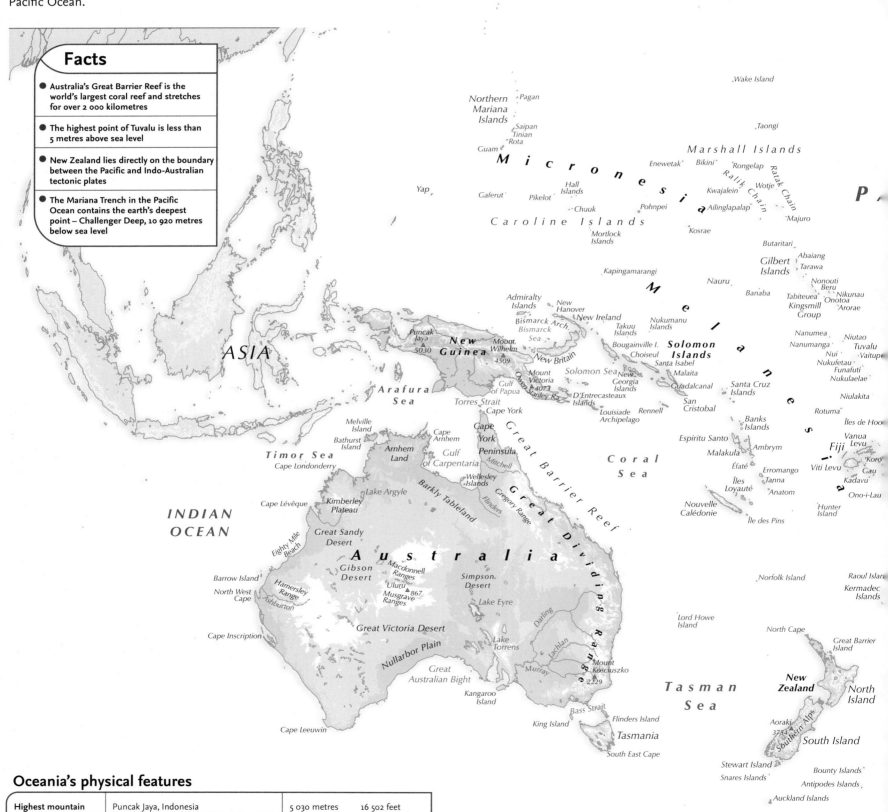

Facts

- Australia's Great Barrier Reef is the world's largest coral reef and stretches for over 2 000 kilometres

- The highest point of Tuvalu is less than 5 metres above sea level

- New Zealand lies directly on the boundary between the Pacific and Indo-Australian tectonic plates

- The Mariana Trench in the Pacific Ocean contains the earth's deepest point – Challenger Deep, 10 920 metres below sea level

Oceania's physical features

Highest mountain	Puncak Jaya, Indonesia	5 030 metres	16 502 feet
Longest river	Murray-Darling, Australia	3 672 km	2 282 miles
Largest lake	Lake Eyre, Australia	0–8 900 sq km	0–3 436 sq miles
Largest island	New Guinea, Indonesia/Papua New Guinea	808 510 sq km	312 166 sq miles
Largest drainage basin	Murray-Darling, Australia	1 058 000 sq km	408 494 sq miles
Lowest point	Lake Eyre, Australia	-16 metres	-53 feet

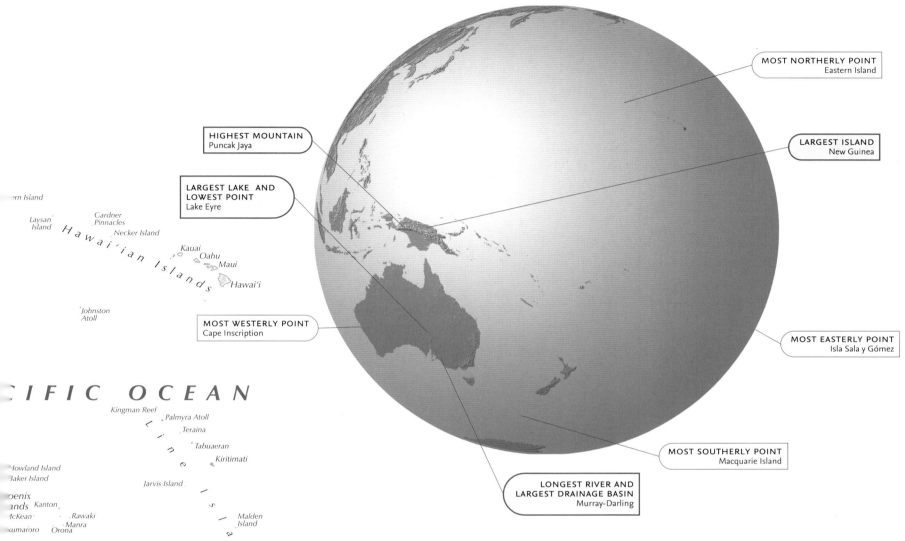

MOST NORTHERLY POINT
Eastern Island

HIGHEST MOUNTAIN
Puncak Jaya

LARGEST ISLAND
New Guinea

LARGEST LAKE AND LOWEST POINT
Lake Eyre

MOST WESTERLY POINT
Cape Inscription

MOST EASTERLY POINT
Isla Sala y Gómez

MOST SOUTHERLY POINT
Macquarie Island

LONGEST RIVER AND LARGEST DRAINAGE BASIN
Murray-Darling

ern Island

Laysan Island

Cardner Pinnacles

Necker Island

Hawaiʻian Islands

Kauai
Oahu
Maui
Hawaiʻi

Johnston Atoll

CIFIC OCEAN

Kingman Reef
Palmyra Atoll
Teraina
Tabuaeran
Kiritimati

Line Islands

Howland Island
Baker Island
Jarvis Island

oenix
ands *Kanton*
cKean *Rawaki*
Manra
kumaroro *Orona*

Malden Island

Starbuck Island

Atafu *Tokelau*
Nukunonu *Fakaofo*
Swains Island

Rakahanga *Penrhyn*
Pukapuka *Manihiki*
Nassau
Vostok Island
Caroline Island
Flint Island

Nuku Hiva
Marquesas Islands
Hiva Oa

P
o
l
y
n
e
s
i
a

llis **Samoan Islands**
Savaiʻi *Manuʻa Islands*
Upolu *Rose Island*
Tutuila
Tafahi
Niuatoputopu
Vavaʻu Group
fua **Tonga** *Niue*
Tongatapu Group

Suwarrow

Îles du Roi Georges
Îles du Désappointement

Îles Palliser
Manuae *Motu One*
Huahine *Raroia* *Pukapuka*
Palmerston *Raiatea* *Fakarava*
Aitutaki *Tahiti* *Anaa* *Hao*
Cook Islands *Atiu* *Mehetia*
Rarotonga *Mauke* *Hervey Islands*
Maria *Héréhérétué*
Mangaia *Society Islands*
Îles du Duc de Gloucester *Groupe Actéon*
Ruruta *Rimatara* *Tubuai* *Mururoa*
Raivavae
Îles Gambier
Tubuai Islands
Rapa *Oeno*
Marotiri *Pitcairn Island* *Henderson Island*
Ducie Island

Tuamotu Islands

Oceania's extent

TOTAL LAND AREA (includes New Guinea and Pacific Island nations)	8 844 516 sq km / 3 414 868 sq miles
Most northerly point	Eastern Island, North Pacific Ocean
Most southerly point	Macquarie Island, South Pacific Ocean
Most westerly point	Cape Inscription, Australia
Most easterly point	Isla Sala y Gómez, South Pacific Ocean

hatham Islands
itt Island

HERN OCEAN

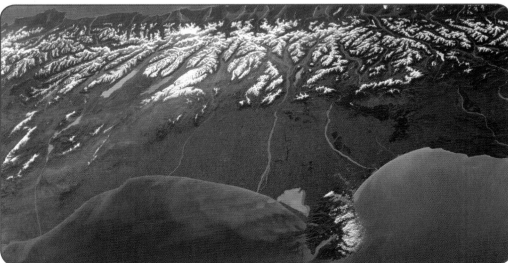

Banks Peninsula, Canterbury Plains and the **Southern Alps**, South Island, New Zealand.

Oceania
Countries

Stretching across almost the whole width of the Pacific Ocean, Oceania has a great variety of cultures and an enormously diverse range of countries and territories. Australia, by far the largest and most industrialized country in the continent, contrasts with the numerous tiny Pacific island nations which have smaller, and more fragile economies based largely on agriculture, fishing and the exploitation of natural resources.

The division of the Pacific island groups into the main regions of Micronesia, Melanesia and Polynesia – often referred to as the South Sea islands – broadly reflects the ethnological differences across the continent. There is a long history of colonial influence in the region, which still contains dependent territories belonging to Australia, France, New Zealand, the UK and the USA.

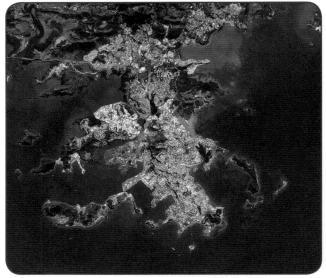

Nouméa, capital of the French dependency of New Caledonia in the southern Pacific Ocean.

Facts

- Over 91% of Australia's population live in urban areas

- The Maori name for New Zealand is Aotearoa, meaning 'land of the long white cloud'

- Auckland, New Zealand, has the largest Polynesian population of any city in Oceania

- Over 800 different languages are spoken in Papua New Guinea

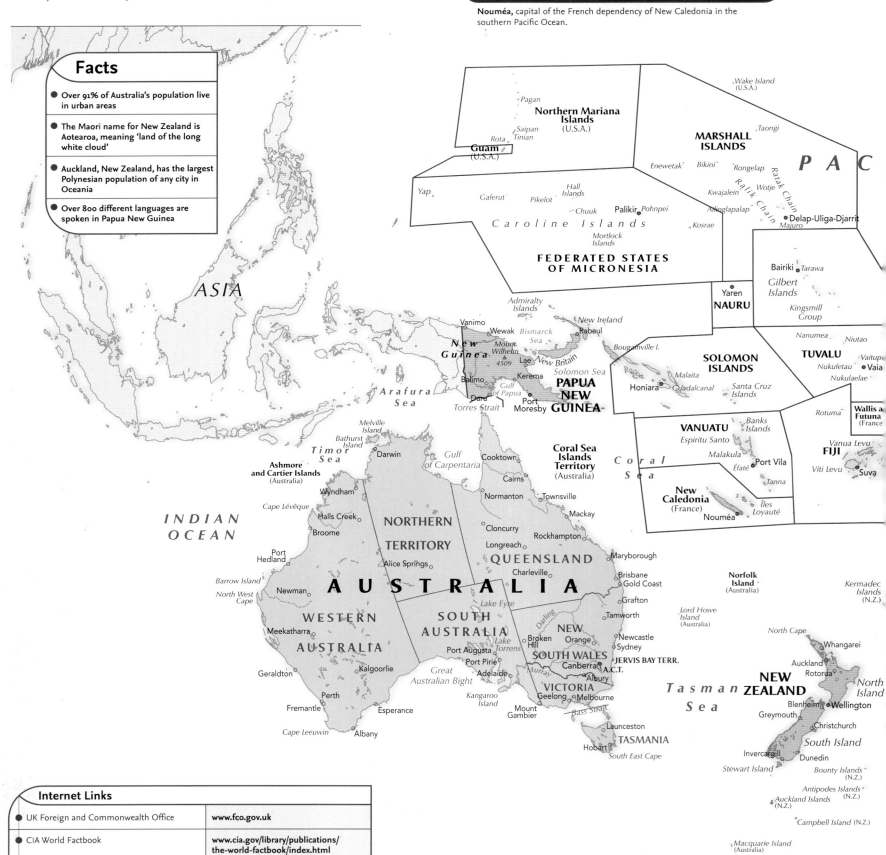

Internet Links

UK Foreign and Commonwealth Office	www.fco.gov.uk
CIA World Factbook	www.cia.gov/library/publications/the-world-factbook/index.html
Geoscience Australia	www.ga.gov.au

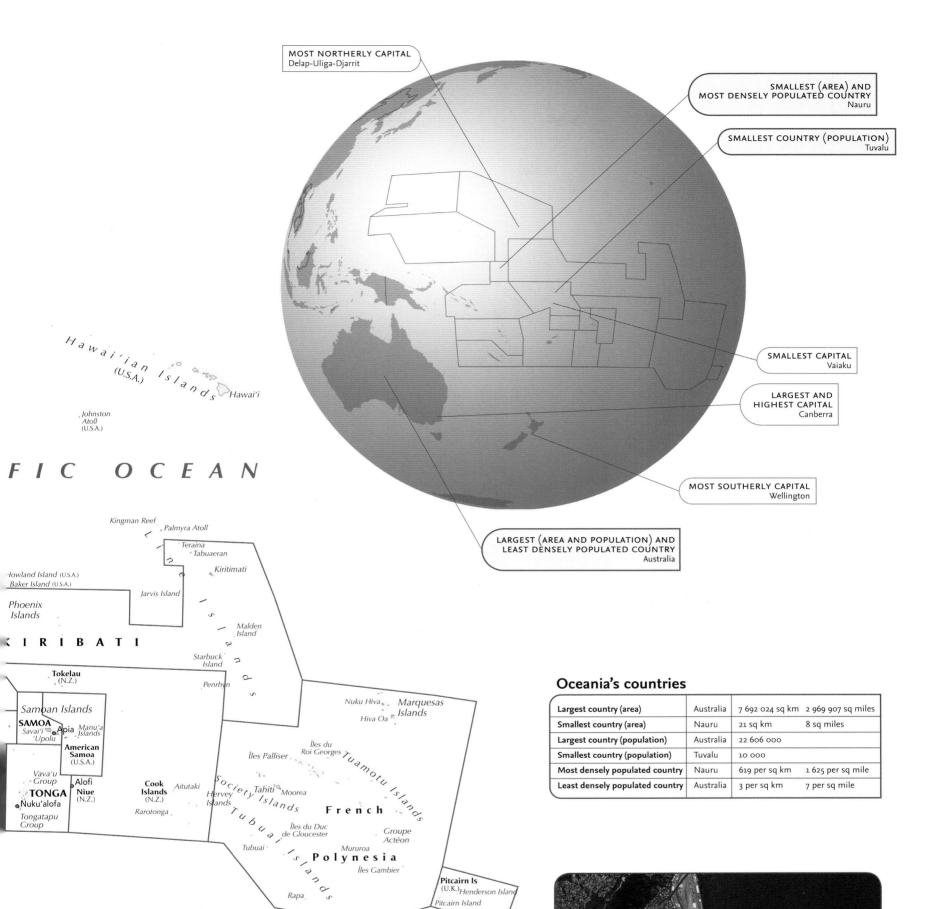

MOST NORTHERLY CAPITAL
Delap-Uliga-Djarrit

SMALLEST (AREA) AND
MOST DENSELY POPULATED COUNTRY
Nauru

SMALLEST COUNTRY (POPULATION)
Tuvalu

SMALLEST CAPITAL
Vaiaku

LARGEST AND
HIGHEST CAPITAL
Canberra

MOST SOUTHERLY CAPITAL
Wellington

LARGEST (AREA AND POPULATION) AND
LEAST DENSELY POPULATED COUNTRY
Australia

Hawai'ian Islands (U.S.A.)
Hawai'i

Johnston Atoll (U.S.A.)

FIC OCEAN

Kingman Reef
Palmyra Atoll
Teraina
Tabuaeran
Kiritimati

Howland Island (U.S.A.)
Baker Island (U.S.A.)
Jarvis Island

Phoenix Islands

KIRIBATI

Line Islands

Malden Island

Starbuck Island

Tokelau (N.Z.)

Penrhyn

Samoan Islands

SAMOA
Savai'i
'Upolu
Apia
Manu'a Islands

American Samoa (U.S.A.)

Vava'u Group
TONGA
Nuku'alofa
Alofi
Niue (N.Z.)

Tongatapu Group

Cook Islands (N.Z.)
Aitutaki
Rarotonga

Society Islands
Îles Palliser
Hervey Islands
Tahiti
Moorea

Nuku Hiva
Hiva Oa
Marquesas Islands

Îles du Roi Georges
Tuamotu Islands

French
Îles du Duc de Gloucester
Groupe Actéon
Tubuai
Tubuai Islands
Mururoa
Polynesia
Îles Gambier
Rapa

Pitcairn Is (U.K.)
Henderson Island
Pitcairn Island

Chatham Islands (N.Z.)

OCEAN

Oceania's countries

Largest country (area)	Australia	7 692 024 sq km	2 969 907 sq miles
Smallest country (area)	Nauru	21 sq km	8 sq miles
Largest country (population)	Australia	22 606 000	
Smallest country (population)	Tuvalu	10 000	
Most densely populated country	Nauru	619 per sq km	1 625 per sq mile
Least densely populated country	Australia	3 per sq km	7 per sq mile

Oceania's capitals

Largest capital (population)	Canberra, Australia	358 000	
Smallest capital (population)	Vaiaku, Tuvalu	516	
Most northerly capital	Delap-Uliga-Djarrit, Marshall Islands	7° 7'N	
Most southerly capital	Wellington, New Zealand	41° 18'S	
Highest capital	Canberra, Australia	581 metres	1 906 feet

Wellington, capital of New Zealand.

G · 160° · 170° · H · 180° · I · 170° · J

Howland Island (U.S.A.)
Baker Island (U.S.A.)

1

Aranuka
Nonouti
Nonouti
Nikunau
YAREN
Nauru
Banaba
(Ocean Island)
Beru
Tabiteuea
Onotoa
Kingsmill Group
Tamana
Arorae

NAURU

K I R I B A T I

Phoenix
Islands
Kanton
McKean
Rawaki
Nikumaroro
Orona
Manra

2

Takuu
Islands
Nukumanu
Islands
Ontong
Java Atoll
Choiseul
Roncador
Reef
Santa
Isabel
Buala
Malu'u
Stewart
Islands
Nanumea
Nanumanga
Niutao

Nui
Vaitupu

New
Georgia
Florida
Islands
Malaita
Maramasike
HONIARA
Avuavu
Ulawa Island
Guadalcanal
Santa
Ana
San Cristobal
(Makira)
Nupani
Swallow
Islands
Duff
Islands
Santa Cruz Islands
(Solomon Islands)
Nukufetau

TUVALU
Funafuti VAIAKU

Nukulaelae

Tokelau
(New Zealand)
Atafu
Nukunonu
Fakaofo

**SOLOMON
ISLANDS**

Rennell
Indispensable
Reefs
Ndeni
Utupua
Vanikoro
Islands
Tikopia
Mitre
Island
Cherry
Island
Niulakita

Swains Island

Pukapuka
(Danger Islands)
Nassau

10°

al Sea
Torres Islands
Uréparapara
Banks
Islands
Vanua Lava
Santa Maria Island
Rotuma
(Fiji)

Wallis and
Futuna Islands
(France)
Îles
Wallis
MATĀ'UTU
SAMOA
Savai'i
APIA
'Upolu
Manu'a
Islands (U.S.A.)
**American
Samoa**
Tutuila FAGATOGO
Rose
Island

Suwarrow

Espiritu Santo
Mount
Tabwémasana
1879
Aoba
Maéwo
Pentecost Island
Îles de Hoorn
Niuafo'ou
210
Tafahi
Niuatoputapu

3

VANUATU
Norsupo
Ambrym
Malakula
Émaé
1270 Epi
Shepherd
Islands
PORT VILA
Efaté

Great Sea Reef Vanua Levu
Yasawa
Group
Labasa
(Lembasa)
Taveuni
Northern
Lau Group
Niuafo'ou
Tafahi
Cook Islands
(New Zealand)

Récifs
d'Entrecasteaux
Grand Passage
Erromango
Tanna 361
Anatom
(Aneityum)

Viti Levu
Lautoka
Tomanivi
(Mt Victoria)
Koro
Koro
Sea
SUVA Nasinu
Gau
FIJI
Kadavu Passage
Kadavu
Moala
Lakeba
Southern
Lau Group
Kabara
Vava'u
Group
ALOFI **Niue**
(New Zealand)
Palmerston

Îles Chesterfield
(France)
Grand Récif
de Cook
Îles Belep
Récif des
Français
Koumac
Nouvelle Calédonie
Ouvéa
Îles loyauté
(France)
Lifou
Tadin
Maré
Bourail
New Caledonia
(France)
NOUMÉA
Yaté
Île des Pins
Hunter
Island
100
Ceva-i-Ra
(Conway Reef)
Futuna
Matuku
Vatoa
Tofua 500
Doi Ono-i-Lau
Ha'apai
Group
TONGA
NUKU'ALOFA
Tongatapu
Group

Grand Récif
du Sud
Ata
20°

Minerva Reefs

160°
Tropic of Capricorn

P A C I F I C   O C E A N

4

Norfolk Island
(Australia)
KINGSTON

Lord Howe Island
(Australia)

Raoul Island
Kermadec Islands
(New Zealand)
Macauley Island
Curtis Island
Havre Rock
L'Espérance Rock

30°

Three Kings
Islands
Cape
Maria van Diemen
North
Cape
Awanui
Whangarei
North Island
Great Barrier Island

**NEW
ZEALAND**
Takapuna
Auckland
Manukau
Hamilton
Te Kuiti
Tokoroa
Tauranga
Whakatane
East Cape
Gisborne
New
Plymouth
Mount Taranaki
(Mount Egmont)
Taupo
Mount
2518 Ruapehu
Wairoa
Mahia Peninsula
Napier
Hastings

man Sea

5

Cape Farewell
Hawera
Wanganui
Tasman
Bay
Nelson
Picton
Blenheim
Levin
Palmerston North
Masterton
Lower Hutt
WELLINGTON
Cook Strait

Westport
**South
Island**
Hokitika
Greymouth
Aoraki
(Mount Cook)
3754
Southern Alps
Mount
Aspiring
3030
Queenstown
Ashburton
Timaru
Christchurch
Banks Peninsula

Chatham Islands
(New Zealand)
Chatham Island
Waitangi
Pitt Island

40°

Cape Providence
Mount
Christina
2502
Gore
Oamaru
Dunedin

Cape Providence
Stewart Island
Invercargill
Foveaux Strait
South West Cape

6

'Snares
Islands
Auckland Islands
(New Zealand)
Antipodes Islands
(New Zealand)
Bounty Islands
(New Zealand)

160°
G
170°
H
180°
I
170°
J
160°
K
150°W
L

Oceania
Western Australia

Oceania
Eastern Australia

Oceania
Southeast Australia

Lambert Azimuthal Equal Area Projection

1:4 300 000

Conic Equidistant Projection

1:4 500 000

Oceania
New Zealand

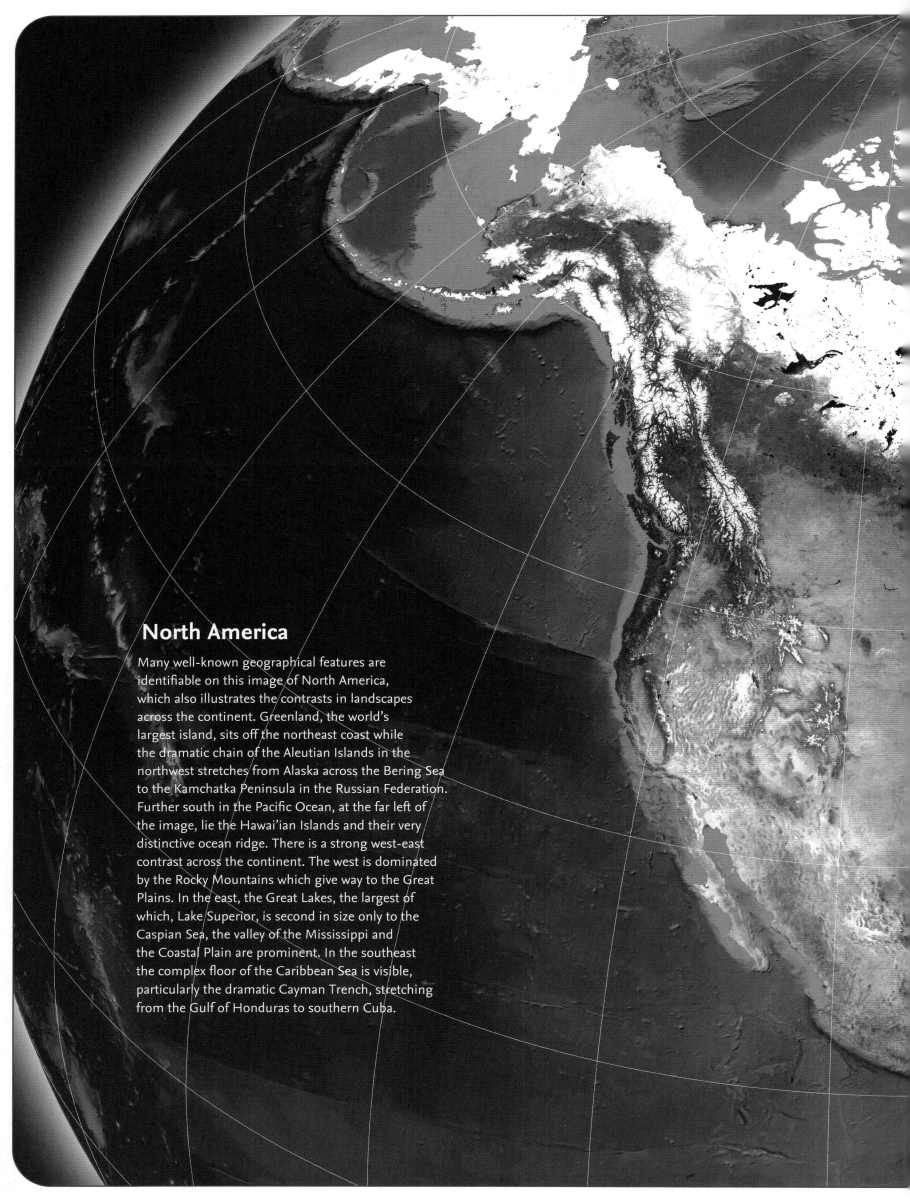

North America

Many well-known geographical features are identifiable on this image of North America, which also illustrates the contrasts in landscapes across the continent. Greenland, the world's largest island, sits off the northeast coast while the dramatic chain of the Aleutian Islands in the northwest stretches from Alaska across the Bering Sea to the Kamchatka Peninsula in the Russian Federation. Further south in the Pacific Ocean, at the far left of the image, lie the Hawai'ian Islands and their very distinctive ocean ridge. There is a strong west-east contrast across the continent. The west is dominated by the Rocky Mountains which give way to the Great Plains. In the east, the Great Lakes, the largest of which, Lake Superior, is second in size only to the Caspian Sea, the valley of the Mississippi and the Coastal Plain are prominent. In the southeast the complex floor of the Caribbean Sea is visible, particularly the dramatic Cayman Trench, stretching from the Gulf of Honduras to southern Cuba.

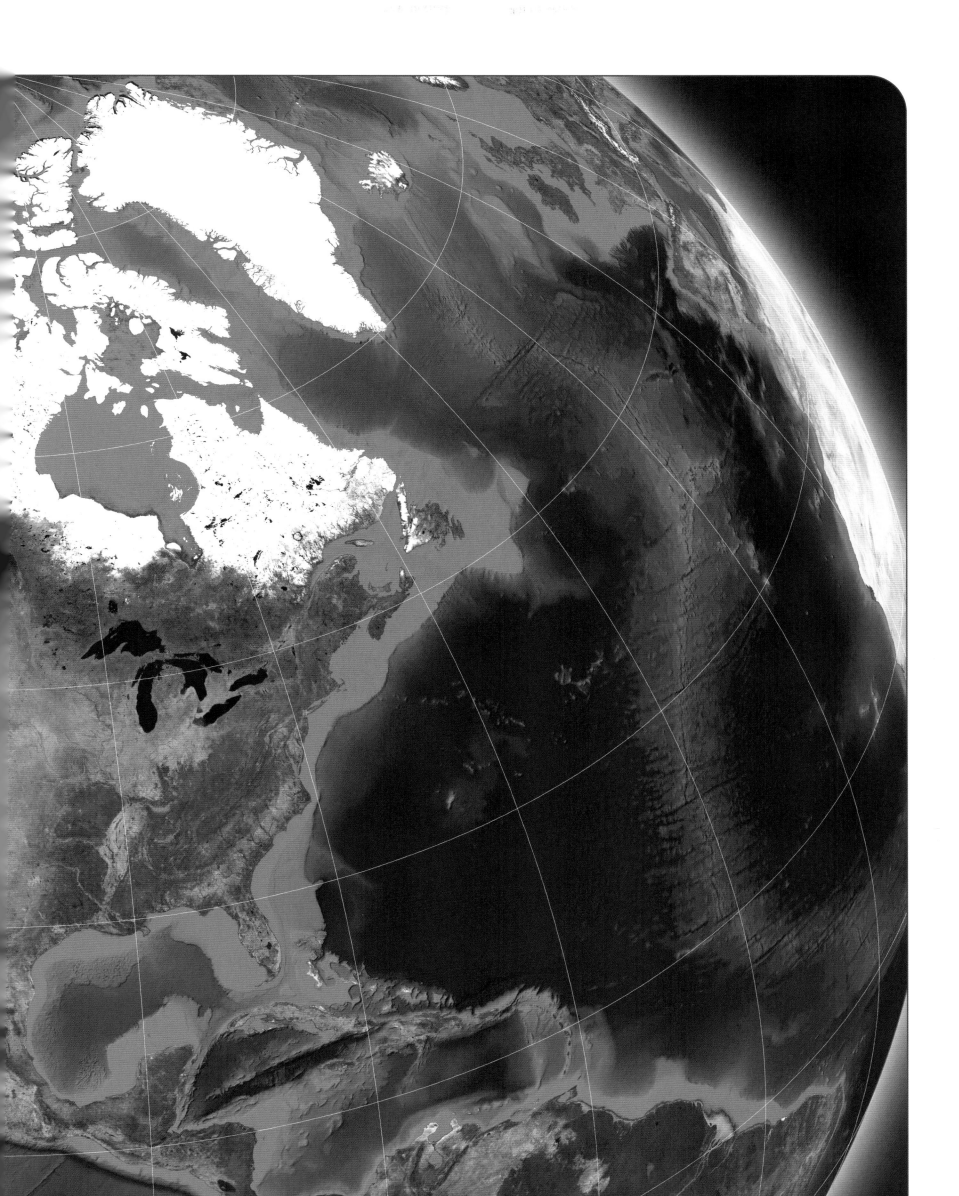

North America, the world's third largest continent, supports a wide range of landscapes from the Arctic north to sub-tropical Central America. The main physiographic regions of the continent are the mountains of the west coast, stretching from Alaska in the north to Mexico and Central America in the south; the vast, relatively flat Canadian Shield; the Great Plains which make up the majority of the interior; the Appalachian Mountains in the east; and the Atlantic coastal plain.

These regions contain some significant physical features, including the Rocky Mountains, the Great Lakes – three of which are amongst the five largest lakes in the world – and the Mississippi-Missouri river system which is the world's fourth longest river. The Caribbean Sea contains a complex pattern of islands, many volcanic in origin, and the continent is joined to South America by the narrow Isthmus of Panama.

Internet Links

● NASA Visible Earth	visibleearth.nasa.gov
● U.S. Geological Survey	www.usgs.gov
● Natural Resources Canada	www.nrcan.gc.ca/home
● SPOT Image satellite imagery	www.spotimage.com

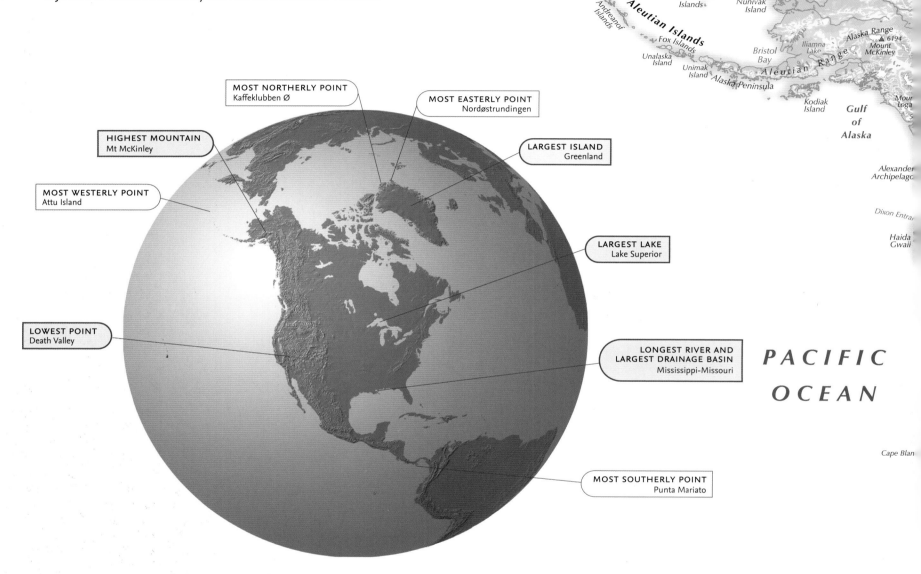

MOST NORTHERLY POINT
Kaffeklubben Ø

MOST EASTERLY POINT
Nordøstrundingen

HIGHEST MOUNTAIN
Mt McKinley

LARGEST ISLAND
Greenland

MOST WESTERLY POINT
Attu Island

LARGEST LAKE
Lake Superior

LOWEST POINT
Death Valley

LONGEST RIVER AND
LARGEST DRAINAGE BASIN
Mississippi-Missouri

MOST SOUTHERLY POINT
Punta Mariato

PACIFIC OCEAN

Chukchi Sea

Bering Strait

Seward Peninsula

Norton Sound

Pribilof Islands

Nunivak Island

Yukon

Aleutian Islands

Andreanof Islands

Fox Islands

Unalaska Island

Bristol Bay

Iliamna Lake

Alaska Range

▲ 6 194 Mount McKinley

Unimak Island

Alaska Peninsula

Aleutian Range

Kodiak Island

Gulf of Alaska

Mour Loga

Alexander Archipelago

Dixon Entran

Haida Gwaii

Cape Blan

North America's physical features

Highest mountain	Mt McKinley, USA	6 194 metres	20 321 feet
Longest river	Mississippi-Missouri, USA	5 969 km	3 709 miles
Largest lake	Lake Superior, Canada/USA	82 100 sq km	31 699 sq miles
Largest island	Greenland	2 175 600 sq km	839 999 sq miles
Largest drainage basin	Mississippi-Missouri, USA	3 250 000 sq km	1 254 825 sq miles
Lowest point	Death Valley, USA	-86 metres	-282 feet

North America's longest river system, the **Mississippi-Missouri**, flows into the Gulf of Mexico through the Mississippi Delta.

North America's extent

TOTAL LAND AREA (including Hawai'ian Islands)	24 680 331 sq km / 9 529 076 sq miles
Most northerly point	Kaffeklubben Ø, Greenland
Most southerly point	Punta Mariato, Panama
Most westerly point	Attu Island, USA
Most easterly point	Nordøstrundingen, Greenland

The **Panama Canal**, Panama, linking the Pacific Ocean to the Atlantic Ocean.

ARCTIC OCEAN

Point Barrow

Beaufort Sea

Kaffeklubben Ø

Greenland Sea

Shannon Ø

Kong Oscars Fjord

Kong Frederik VIII Land

Kangertittivaq

Denmark Strait

Ellesmere Island

Axel Heiberg Island

Ellef Ringnes Island

Borden Island

Prince Patrick Island

Queen Elizabeth Islands

Parry Islands

Melville Island

Devon Island

Parry Channel

Banks Island

Victoria Island

Prince of Wales Island

Somerset Island

Brodeur Peninsula

Boothia Peninsula

Gulf of Boothia

King William Island

Queen Maud Gulf

Melville Peninsula

Greenland

Kong Christian X Land

Kong Christian IX Land

Kong Frederik VI Kyst

3000

2000

1000

Qimusseriarsuaq

Bylot Island

Baffin Bay

Qeqertarsuaq

Davis Strait

Cape Farewell

Baffin Island

Prince Charles Island

Cumberland Peninsula

Cumberland Sound

Nettilling Lake

Amadjuak Lake

Foxe Basin

Foxe Pen.

Frobisher Bay

Home Bay

Rocky Mountains

Coast Mountains

Mackenzie Mountains

Selwyn Mountains

Cassiar Mountains

Porcupine

Yukon

Liard

Mackenzie

Great Bear Lake

Dubawnt Lake

Caribou Mountains

Peace

Athabasca

Great Slave Lake

Lake Athabasca

Wollaston Lake

Reindeer Lake

Southern Indian Lake

Churchill

Nelson

Southampton Island

Coats Island

Mansel Island

Hudson Bay

Belcher Islands

Péninsule d'Ungava

Ungava Bay

C. Chidley

Hudson Strait

Labrador Sea

Labrador

Lac Caniapiscau

Smallwood Reservoir

Lac Bienville

Laurentian Plateau

Newfoundland

Cape Race

Île d'Anticosti

Gulf of St Lawrence

Cabot Strait

Cape Breton Island

ATLANTIC OCEAN

Mount Robson 3954

Fraser

North Saskatchewan

South Saskatchewan

Saskatchewan

Lake Winnipeg

Lake Winnipegosis

Canadian Shield

James Bay

Albany

Réservoir La Grande 2

Severn

Lake of the Woods

Lake Nipigon

Great Lakes

Lake Superior

St Lawrence

Ottawa

Nova Scotia

Sable Island

Cape Sable

Bay of Fundy

Massachusetts Bay

Cape Cod

Vancouver Island

Mount Rainier 4392

Cascade Range

Coast Ranges

Bitterroot Range

F. D. Roosevelt Lake

Columbia

Fort Peck Reservoir

Yellowstone

Missouri

Snake

Lake Sakakawea

Great Plains

Lake Oahe

Missouri

Platte

Illinois

Mississippi

Lake Michigan

Lake Huron

Lake Erie

Lake Ontario

Hudson

Long Island

Appalachian Mountains

Allegheny Mts

Chesapeake Bay

Cape Hatteras

Great Salt Lake

Great Basin

Sierra Nevada

Death Valley

San Joaquin

Sangre de Cristo Range

Colorado

Mount Elbert 4398

Grand Canyon

Colorado Plateau

Arkansas

Lake of the Ozarks

Ozark Plateau

Ohio

Tennessee

Alabama

Canadian

Red

Mount Mitchell 2037

Cape Fear

Guadalupe

Baja California

Gila

Pecos

Conchos

Rio Grande

Llano Estacado

Edwards Plateau

Brazos

Coastal Plain

Cape Canaveral

Gulf of California

Sierra Madre Occidental

Yaqui

Cabo Falso

Cabo Corrientes

Rio Grande

Sierra Madre Oriental

Mississippi Delta

Gulf of Mexico

Padre Island

Grand Bahama

Great Abaco

The Bahamas

Andros

Straits of Florida

West Indies

Acklins Island

Turks and Caicos Islands

Great Inagua

Puerto Rico

Virgin Islands

Anguilla

Guadaloupe

Dominica

St Lucia

Martinique

Barbados

Islas Revillagigedo

Volcán Popocatépetl 5452

Bahía de Campeche

Yucatán

Yucatán Channel

Cayman Islands

Cuba

Jamaica

Hispaniola

Greater Antilles

Lesser Antilles

Caribbean Sea

Tobago

Trinidad

Aruba

Curaçao

Île Clipperton

Sierra Madre del Sur

Sierra Madre

Islas de la Bahía

Gulf of Tehuantepec

Bahía de Campeche

Golfo de Fonseca

Lake Nicaragua

Peninsula de Nicoya

Cordillera Central

Panama Canal

Ishmus of Panama

Golfo del Darién

Gulf of Panamá

SOUTH AMERICA

Facts

- Devon Island, Canada, is the world's largest uninhabited island
- Canada has the longest coastline of any country in the world
- Lake Superior is the world's largest freshwater lake
- Over 320 000 square kilometres of the USA is protected for conservation purposes

North America
Countries

North America has been dominated economically and politically by the USA since the nineteenth century. Before that, the continent was subject to colonial influences, particularly of Spain in the south and of Britain and France in the east. The nineteenth century saw the steady development of the western half of the continent. The wealth of natural resources and the generally temperate climate were an excellent basis for settlement, agriculture and industrial development which has led to the USA being the richest nation in the world today.

Although there are twenty-three independent countries and fourteen dependent territories in North America, Canada, Mexico and the USA have approximately eighty-five per cent of the continent's population and eighty-eight per cent of its land area. Large parts of the north remain sparsely populated, while the most densely populated areas are in the northeast USA, and the Caribbean.

Internet Links	
● UK Foreign and Commonwealth Office	www.fco.gov.uk
● CIA World Factbook	www.cia.gov/library/publications/the-world-factbook/index.html
● U.S. Board on Geographic Names	geonames.usgs.gov
● NASA Astronaut Photography	eol.jsc.nasa.gov

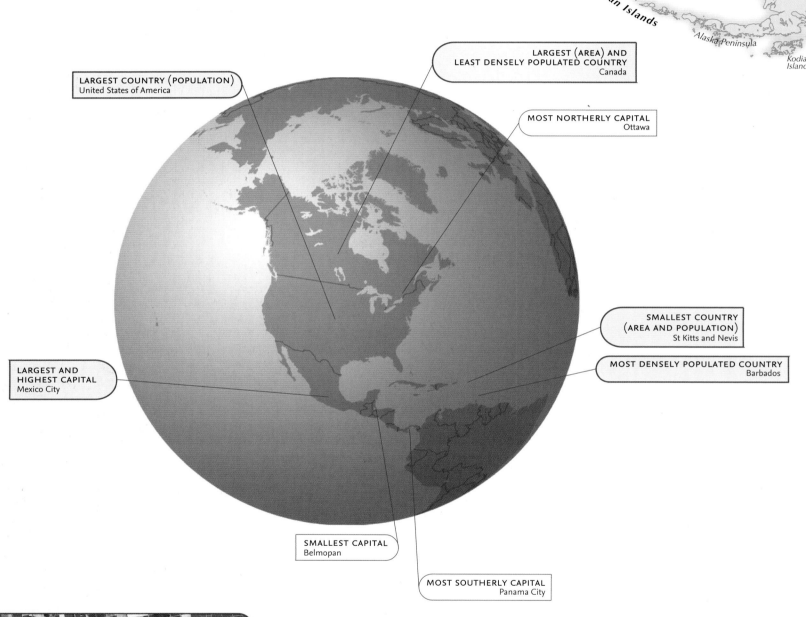

LARGEST COUNTRY (POPULATION)
United States of America

LARGEST (AREA) AND LEAST DENSELY POPULATED COUNTRY
Canada

MOST NORTHERLY CAPITAL
Ottawa

SMALLEST COUNTRY (AREA AND POPULATION)
St Kitts and Nevis

MOST DENSELY POPULATED COUNTRY
Barbados

LARGEST AND HIGHEST CAPITAL
Mexico City

SMALLEST CAPITAL
Belmopan

MOST SOUTHERLY CAPITAL
Panama City

False-colour satellite image of the **Mexico-USA** boundary at Mexicali.

North America's countries

Largest country (area)	Canada	9 984 670 sq km	3 855 103 sq miles
Smallest country (area)	St Kitts and Nevis	261 sq km	101 sq miles
Largest country (population)	United States of America	313 085 000	
Smallest country (population)	St Kitts and Nevis	53 000	
Most densely populated country	Barbados	637 per sq km	1 650 per sq mile
Least densely populated country	Canada	3 per sq km	8 per sq mile

North America's capitals

Largest capital (population)	Mexico City, Mexico	20 078 000
Smallest capital (population)	Belmopan, Belize	13 600
Most northerly capital	Ottawa, Canada	45° 25'N
Most southerly capital	Panama City, Panama	8° 56'N
Highest capital	Mexico City, Mexico	2 300 metres 7 546 feet

The Bahamas, a chain of islands in the North Atlantic Ocean, lying southeast of Florida, USA.

Facts

- The Panama Canal, opened in 1914, cut the journey between the Atlantic and the Pacific by over 14 000 km

- Mexico City is the highest city in North America and houses approximately 18% of Mexico's population

- The state of Alaska was bought by the USA from Russia in 1867

- The territory of Nunavut is Canada's newest administrative division, created in 1999 from the eastern part of Northwest Territories

145

Lambert Conformal Conic Projection

↓ 154

1:14 000 000

| 0 | 200 | 400 | miles |

| 0 | 200 | 400 | 600 | 800 | km |

North America
Canada

Lambert Conformal Conic Projection

1:6 000 000

0	100	200		miles
0	100	200	300	400 km

North America

Alaska

Conic Equidistant Projection

1:6 000 000

← 151

↓ 162

Conic Equidistant Projection

1:6 000 000

| 0 | 100 | 200 | miles |

| 0 | 100 | 200 | 300 | 400 | km |

50°

Queen Charlotte Strait
Cape Scott
Kyuquot
Cape McNeill
Tofino
Vancouver
Island
Alberni
Cape Flattery
Juan de Fuca

Chilanko
Williams
Lake
Alexis
Creek
Quesnel
Lake
100 Mile
House
Dawsons
Landing
Pemberton
Mount
Waddington
4042
Chilko
Lake
Mount
Robson
3954

Valemount
Brûlé
Lake
Jasper
Mount
Columbia
3747
Drayton Valley

Edmonton

Fort
Saskatchewan
Vermilion
Bonnyville
Green Lake
Delaronde
Lake
Candle
Lake

Weyakwin
North
Saskatchewan

Flin Flon
Cranberry
Portage
The
Westray
Wabowden
Nor
La P

**BRITISH
COLUMBIA**

ALBERTA

SASKATCHEWAN

C A

MAN

Mount
Waddington
4042

Campbell River
Powell River
Courtenay
Nanaimo
Victoria
Vancouver
Bellingham

Lillooet
Thompson
Sound
Golden
Hinde
2201
Cott
Peak
2050

Cache
Creek
Kamloops
Chase
Barrière

Mica
Creek
Mount
Farnham
3457

Kicking
Horse Pass
1627
Banff

Red Deer
Lacombe
Ponoka
Camrose
Wetaskiwin

Maidstone
North
Battleford

Lloydminster
Rosthern

Tisdale
Melfort
Humboldt

Prince Albert
Red Deer Lake

Tobin
Lake
Smeaton

Candle
Cedar
Lake

Easterville
Grand
Rapids

Vancouver
Victoria
Nanaimo
Chilliwack
Hope
Okanagan
Lake
Kelowna
Penticton
Vernon
Salmon
Arm
Revelstoke

Selkirk
Mountains

Mount
Sir Sandford
3522

Kimberley
Cranbrook

Calgary
Airdrie
Cochrane
High River

Drumheller
Hanna

Bassano
Brooks

Saskatoon
Outlook

Rosetown
Biggar

Watrous
Lanigan
Wadena
Foam
Lake

Quill
Lakes

Kelvington
Preeceville

Canora
Kamsack

Swan
River

Duck
Bay

Reinde
Baldy
Mountain
831
Dauphin
Lake

WASHINGTON

Seattle
Everett
Bellevue
Tacoma
Olympia

Mount
Baker
3285

Glacier Peak
3213

Skagit Lake

Franklin D
Roosevelt
Lake

Newport
Bonners
Ferry

Eureka
Libby
Kalispell

Shelby
Conrad
Cut Bank

Havre
Malta
Milk
Fort
Benton

Glasgow
Plentywood
Crosby

Stanley
Williston
Minot
New Town
Harvey
Carrington

Rugby
Devils
Lake

Portal
Westhope

OREGON

Portland
Oregon
City
Salem
Albany
Corvallis
Eugene
Cottage
Grove

Astoria
McMinnville
Newport

Vancouver
Mount
St Helens
2550

Mount
Hood
3427
The Dalles
Pendleton

Ellensburg
Yakima
Sunnyside
Richland
Walla
Walla

Moses
Lake

Spokane
Pullman
Moscow
Lewiston
Orofino

Coeur
d'Alene
St Maries

Missoula
Deer Lodge
Anaconda
Butte
Helena
Townsend

Great
Falls

Bearpaw Mts
2116
Fort
Peck
Reservoir

Lewistown
Jordan

Sidney
Watford
City
Glendive

Dickinson
White Butte
1076
Mandan
Bismarck
Linton

MONTANA

NORTH DAKOTA

Coos Bay
Cape Blanco
Brookings
Crescent City

Grants
Pass
Roseburg
Medford
Ashland
Klamath
Falls

Bend
Madras
John Day

La Grande
Baker

Blue
Mountains

Eagle
Cap
2925

Salmon
River
Mountains

McCall
McGuire Mtn
2156
Salmon
Grangeville

Challis

Bozeman
Livingston

Dillon
Targhee
Pass

Billings
Hardin
Colstrip

Forsyth
Miles
City
Baker

Broadus

Bowman
Lemmon
Mobridge
Aberdeen
Ellendale

SOUTH DAKOTA

Eureka
Redding
Red Bluff

Yreka
Mount
Shasta
4317
Weaverville
Alturas
Lakeview

High
Desert

Harney Basin
Burns

Steens
Mountain
McDermitt

Owyhee

St Anthony
Rexburg

Idaho Falls
American Falls
Reservoir
Pocatello

Grand Teton
4190
Jackson
4203

Cody
Greybull
Worland

Thermopolis

Cloud
Peak
4016

Sheridan
Buffalo
Gillette

Belle
Fourche
Sturgis
Newcastle
Rapid
City

Spearfish
Redfield
Gettysburg

Pierre
Miller
Huron
Mitchell

IDAHO

WYOMING

Boise
Nampa
Caldwell
Fayette
Payette

Mountain
Home

Twin
Falls
Burley

Jerome

Snake River Plain

Preston
Soda
Springs

Pinedale

Riverton

Casper
Douglas

Lusk

Chadron
Pine Ridge

Valentine
Ainsworth
O'N

Hot Springs
Martin
Winner

NEBRASKA

Fort
Bragg
Ukiah
Point
Arena

Willits
Paradise
Chico
Oroville

Susanville
Eagle
Lake

Winnemucca

Battle
Mountain

Elko

Logan
Brigham City
Ogden

Kemmerer
Green
River
Evanston

Rawlins
Saratoga
Laramie

Rock
Springs

Medicine Bow Mts
3667
Kims Peak
4123

Cheyenne
Sidney

Fall River
Pass
3713

Kimball

Scottsbluff
Bridgeport
Alliance

Thedford

Lake McConaughy

Chadron

McCook
Holdrege
Minden

NEVADA

Santa Rosa
Napa
Vallejo
Sacramento
San Francisco
Berkeley
Oakland
Concord
San Jose
Santa Cruz

Lodi
Stockton
Modesto

Pyramid
Lake
Sparks
Reno

Virginia City
Carson City
South
Lake Tahoe
2160
Fallon

Austin

Eureka

Ely

Wendover
Great
Salt
Lake

Great
Salt Lake
Desert

Tooele
American Fork
Provo

Salt Lake City
Heber City
Uinta
Mountains

Vernal

Craig
Steamboat
Springs
Meeker

Berthoud
Pass

Boulder
Longmont
Greeley
Sterling

North Platte
Ogallala
Lexington
Kearney

Holyoke

Julesburg

Akron

UTAH

Salinas
Monterey Bay

Merced
Madera
Fresno
Visalia

Los Banos

Mount
Jefferson
3642

Tonopah
Goldfield

Warm Springs

Delta
Nephi
Price

Wheeler
Peak
3983

Mount
Peale
3877

Grand
Junction
Delta
Montrose
Gunnison

Glenwood Springs
Aspen
4398

Leadville
Castle Rock

Denver
Aurora

Colorado
Springs

Limon
Burlington
Colby
WaKeeney
Hays

Smoky
Hills

Concord

COLORADO

King City
Paso Robles
San Luis Obispo
Santa Maria

Coalinga

Bishop
White
Mountain Peak
4342

Mount Jefferson

Independence

Beatty

Charleston Peak
3632

Lone
Pine

Death Valley

Indian
Springs
Overton

Las
Vegas
Henderson
Boulder City

St George
Kanab

Lake
Powell

Cedar
City

Richfield
Beaver

Pioche
Caliente

Delano
Peak
3710

Monticello
Silverton

Cortez
Durango

Monarch
Pass

Salida

Pueblo
Canon
City
Florence
Fowler

Sangre de Cristo Mts
4011

Walsenburg

La Junta
Lamar
Syracuse

Scott
City
Great Bend

Garden
City
Dodge
City

Ulysses

Liberal

KANS

McPher
Hutchinson
Pratt

CALIFORNIA

Point Conception
Santa Barbara
Santa Cruz Island
Santa Rosa
Island
San Nicolas
Island
Channel Islands
San Clemente
Island

Bakersfield
Wasco
Porterville

Mojave Desert

Lancaster
Barstow

Baker

Los Angeles
Pasadena
Santa Ana
Long
Beach
San Bernardino
Riverside
Oceanside
Escondido
San Diego
Tijuana
Mexicali

Needles
Chino Valley
Prescott
Wickenburg
Quartzsite
Blythe

Kingman

Williams
Flagstaff
Humphreys
Peak
3851

Winslow
Holbrook

Grand
Canyon
Tuba
City

Kayenta

**Colorado
Plateau**

Gallup
Grants

Chinle
Ganado

Los Alamos
Santa Fe

Albuquerque
Rio Rancho

Las Vegas

Tucumcari

Vaughn

Clovis
Portales

Dumas
Stratford
Dalhart

Amarillo
Canyon

Clinton
Elk
Shamrock
Memphis

Hereford
Tulia
Plainview

El Reno
OKL

Hobart
Chickasha
Altus
Lawton
Wichita Falls

ARIZONA

Yuma

Gila Bend
Casa
Grande

Phoenix
Glendale
Mesa
Chandler
Florence

Globe
Clifton
Safford
Willcox
Benson

Tucson

Nogales

Sierra
Vista

Show
Low
Springerville
Baldy Peak
3476

Socorro

Truth or
Consequences

Silver City
Lordsburg
Deming
Las Cruces

Alamogordo

Roswell

Carlsbad

**NEW
MEXICO**

Vaughn
Fort Sumner

Carrizozo

Whitewater
Baldy
3320

Artesia
Hobbs

Lovington
Brownfield
Levelland
Lubbock

Seminole
Andrews
Big Spring

Paducah
Vernon
Seymour

Abilene
Weatherf

Sweetwater
Snyder

Stephenville
Gatesville

**Llano
Estacado**

TEXAS

**PACIFIC
OCEAN**

Ensenada

Guadalupe
(Mexico)

Picacho
del Diablo
3096

San
Vicente

Isla
Cedros

Bahía
Sebastián
Vizcaíno

Punta Eugenia

Punta San
Hipólito

Vicente Guerrero

San Felipe

El Sahuaro

Puerto
Libertad

Cananea
Naco
Douglas
Agua
Prieta

Nogales

El Paso
Ciudad Juárez

Fort
Stockton

Alpine

Guadalupe
Peak
2667

Kermit
Odessa
Midland

San Angelo
Big Lake

Ballinger
Coleman

Brownwood
Brady
Junction

**Edwards
Plateau**

Georgetown
Austin
San Marcos
New
Braunfels

Cabo
San Quintín

Rosario

Bahía
Tortugas

Guerrero
Negro
1908

Sierra Vizcaíno

Volcán Las
Tres Vírgenes
1996

Santa
Rosalía

Mulegé

Benjamín Hill
Arizpe

Carbó

Opodepe

Magdalena

Santa
Ana

Fronteras

Janos

Ascensión
Nuevo Casas
Grandes
Villa
Ahumada

El Porvenir Van
Horn

Mount
Livermore
2554

Presidio
Ojinaga

Marfa

Sanderson

Del Rio
Acuña
Eagle Pass

Uvalde
Hondo

Sabinal
Pearsall

San Antonio

**Baja
California**

Isla Ángel
de la Guarda

Isla Tiburón

Hermosillo

Mazatán

Tepache

Moctezuma

Madera

Las
Varas

San José
de Bavicora

Gómez
Farías

Ciudad
Camargo

Chihuahua

Ciudad
Delicias

Ciudad
Camargo

Bolsón
de Mapimí

Monclova

Piedras
Negras

Nava

Crystal
City

Carrizo
Springs

Beeville

Alice

Gulf of California

Bahía
Magdalena

Isla
Santa
Margarita

Isla
San José

La Paz
3118

Volcán Las
Tres Vírgenes

Ciudad
Obregón
Navojoa

Presa
Macuzari

Huatabampo

El Fuerte

Los
Mochis

Guasave

Guamúchil

Indé

Hidalgo
del Parral

Llano de los
Caballos Mesteños

Santa Bárbara
Ceballos

Saucillo

Allende

El Oro

Cuatro Ciénegas
Buenaventura

Múzquiz
Sabinas

Nueva
Rosita

Nadadores

Castaños

Sabinas
Hidalgo
Lampazos

Laredo
Nuevo
Laredo

Kingsville
Zapata

Raymond
Rio Gra

Punta San
Hipólito

Cabo
San Lázaro

Villa
Insurgentes

Ciudad
Constitución

Tropic of Cancer

San José
de Comondú

Loreto

La Paz

San José
del Cabo

Isla
San José

Isla
Espíritu Santo
Isla Cerralvo

San Pedro

Todos Santos

El Dorado
Costa Rica

Culiacán

Navolato

Tamazula

Villa
Unión

Escuinapa

Ciudad
Guadalupe
Victoria

Juan
Aldama

Durango

Nombre de
Dios

Mezquital

Nazas

Gómez
Palacio
Torreón

Matamoros

Parras

Viesca

Garza García
Monterrey

Saltillo

Ramos
Arizpe

Santa
Catarina

Montemorelos

Linares

Galeana

Monteros

General
Terán

China

Cerralvo

Reynosa
McAllen
Edinburg
Hidalgo

San
Fernando

Burgos

El Salvador

Villagrán

El Fernó

MEXICO

1:10 000 000

0   100   200   300   400   miles
0   100   200   300   400   500   600   700   km

Lambert Conformal Conic Projection

1:6 000 000

| 0 | 100 | 200 | miles |

| 0 | 100 | 200 | 300 | 400 | km |

North America
Western United States

PACIFIC

OCEAN

CALIFORNIA

NEVADA

UNIT

OF

BAJA CA
M

Lambert Conformal Conic Projection

1:3 000 000

0   50   100   miles
0   50   100   150   200 km

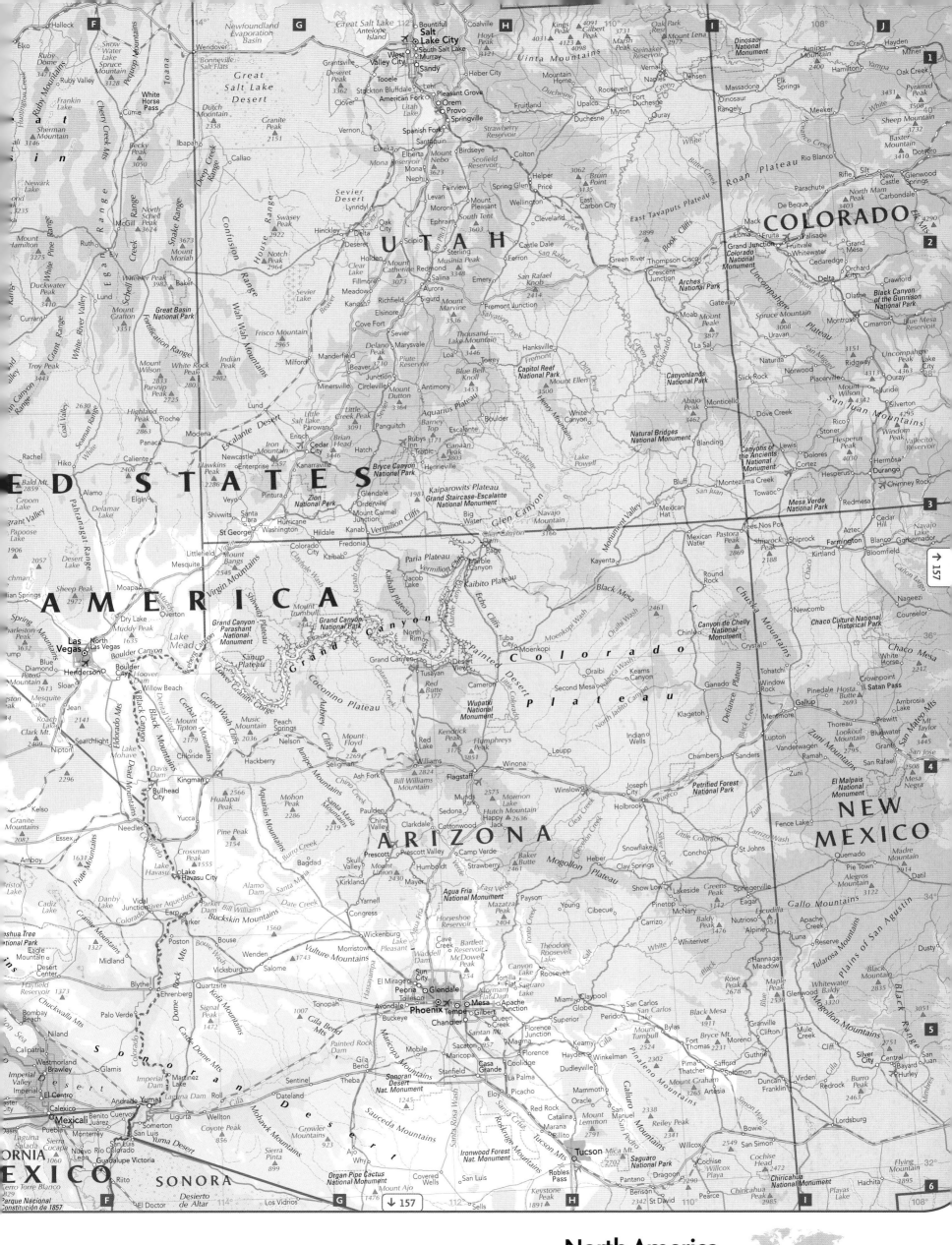

Lambert Conformal Conic Projection

1:6 000 000

miles
km

North America
Central United States

CANADA

QUÉBEC

ONTARIO

NEW BRUNSWICK

MAINE

VERMONT

NEW HAMPSHIRE

NEW YORK

Adirondack Mts

Lake Ontario

Lake Erie

Lake Huron

Georgian Bay

Lake Superior

MICHIGAN

WISCONSIN

MINNESOTA

Lake Michigan

ILLINOIS

IOWA

INDIANA

OHIO

PENNSYLVANIA

WEST VIRGINIA

VIRGINIA

MARYLAND

NEW JERSEY

KENTUCKY

TENNESSEE

MISSOURI

UNITED STATES

Gulf of Maine

Cape Cod

Chesapeake Bay

Montréal

Ottawa

Toronto

Buffalo

Detroit

Cleveland

Pittsburgh

Chicago

Milwaukee

Indianapolis

Columbus

Cincinnati

Louisville

Boston

New York

Philadelphia

Baltimore

WASHINGTON D.C.

Richmond

Virginia Beach

↑ 153

↑ 152

↑ 160

Lambert Conformal Conic Projection

1:3 000 000

0   50   100   miles

0   50   100   150   200 km

North America
Northeast United States

A **B** **C** **D**

San Diego
Chula Vista
Tijuana

El Centro
Mexicali

Florence
Truth or
Consequences

1

ARIZONA

NEW MEXICO

Tucson

El Paso
Ciudad Juárez

UNITED

2

BAJA
CALIFORNIA

SONORA

Hermosillo

CHIHUAHUA

Chihuahua

3

BAJA
CALIFORNIA
SUR

Guaymas

Ciudad Obregón

Los Mochis

Culiacán

DURANGO

Torreón

4

Tropic of Cancer

Mazatlán

MÉX

Tropic of Cancer

BELIZE
GUATEMALA

HONDURAS
TEGUCIGALPA

EL SALVADOR

Caribbean
Sea

NAYARIT

Tepic

Guadalajara

JALISCO

5

NICARAGUA
MANAGUA

Lake Nicaragua

PACIFIC
OCEAN

COLIMA

6

COSTA RICA
SAN JOSE

PANAMA
PANAMA CITY

PACIFIC

7

8

COLOMBIA

H **I** **J** **K**

Lambert Conformal Conic Projection

1:6 300 000
miles
km

166

North America
Mexico and Central America

1:6 300 000
miles
km

Lambert Conformal Conic Projection

1:12 000 000

| 0 | 200 | 400 | miles |
| 0 | 200 | 400 | 600 | 800 km |

H WEST I Richmond J K L M 1

ATLANTIC

OCEAN

HAMILTON Bermuda
(U.K.)

THE
BAHAMAS

West

Indies

Turks and
Caicos Islands
(U.K.)

GRAND TURK
(Cockburn Town)

Virgin
Islands
(U.K.)

Leeward Islands

HAVANA
(La Habana)

CUBA

Hispaniola

SAN
JUAN

Anguilla

ANTIGUA
AND BARBUDA

HAITI
PORT-AU-
PRINCE

SANTO
DOMINGO

Puerto Rico
(U.S.A.)

Virgin
Islands
(U.S.A.)

ST KITTS
AND NEVIS

Montserrat
(U.K.)

Guadeloupe
(France)

DOMINICA

Cayman
Islands
(U.K.)

JAMAICA

KINGSTON

DOMINICAN
REPUBLIC

Lesser

FORT-DE-FRANCE
Martinique
(France)

CASTRIES ST LUCIA

BARBADOS
BRIDGETOWN

ST VINCENT
AND
THE GRENADINES

GRENADA

Antilles

Caribbean Sea

Lesser Antilles

Aruba Curaçao
(Neth.) (Neth.)
ORANJESTAD WILLEMSTAD
Bonaire
(Neth.)

TRINIDAD
AND
TOBAGO
PORT-
OF-SPAIN

EGUCIGALPA

NICARAGUA
MANAGUA

CARACAS

Maracaibo

Valencia

Maracay

COSTA RICA
SAN
JOSÉ

PANAMA
PANAMA
CITY

CARTAGENA

Barranquilla

Bucaramanga

VENEZUELA

GUYANA

Medellín

BOGOTÁ

COLOMBIA

BRAZIL

North America
Central America and the Caribbean

South America

The Andes mountains stretch along the whole length of the west coast of South America, widening into the high plains of the Altiplano in Bolivia and Peru in the centre of the continent. Lake Titicaca, the world's highest large navigable lake, lies on the Altiplano, straddling the Bolivia-Peru border. Running parallel to the Andes, just off the west coast, is the Peru-Chile Trench which marks the active boundary between the Nazca and South American tectonic plates. Movement between these plates gives rise to numerous volcanoes in the Andes. The Amazon river runs across almost the whole width of the continent in the north, meeting the Atlantic Ocean in its wide delta on the northeast coast. The vast Amazon basin is one of the most ecologically diverse areas of the Earth. In the south, the wide continental shelf stretches eastward from the tip of the continent to the Falkland Islands and South Georgia on the bottom edge of the image.

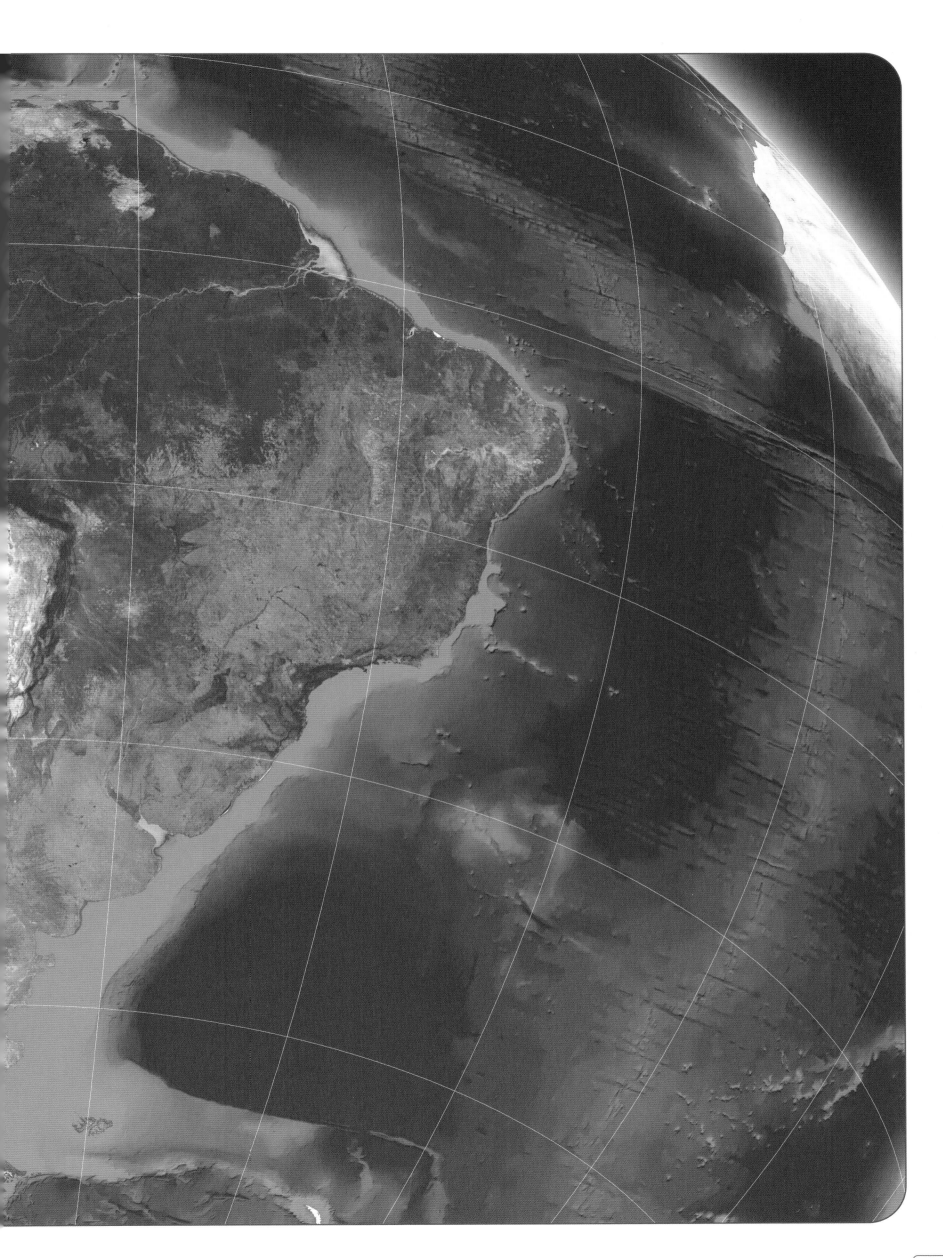

South America
Landscapes

South America is a continent of great contrasts, with landscapes varying from the tropical rainforests of the Amazon Basin, to the Atacama Desert, the driest place on earth, and the sub-Antarctic regions of southern Chile and Argentina. The dominant physical features are the Andes, stretching along the entire west coast of the continent and containing numerous mountains over 6 000 metres high, and the Amazon, which is the second longest river in the world and has the world's largest drainage basin.

The Altiplano is a high plateau lying between two of the Andes ranges. It contains Lake Titicaca, the world's highest navigable lake. By contrast, large lowland areas dominate the centre of the continent, lying between the Andes and the Guiana and Brazilian Highlands. These vast grasslands stretch from the Llanos of the north through the Selvas and the Gran Chaco to the Pampas of Argentina.

Confluence of the **Amazon** and **Negro** rivers at Manaus, northern Brazil.

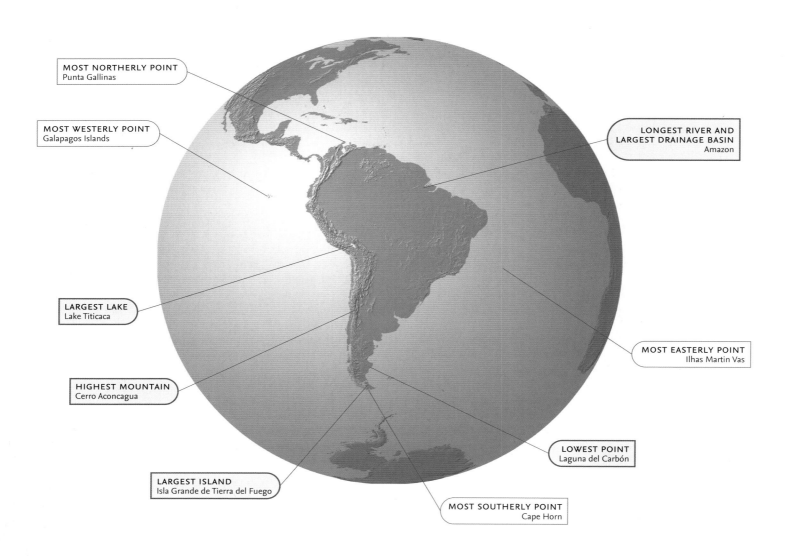

MOST NORTHERLY POINT
Punta Gallinas

MOST WESTERLY POINT
Galapagos Islands

LONGEST RIVER AND
LARGEST DRAINAGE BASIN
Amazon

LARGEST LAKE
Lake Titicaca

MOST EASTERLY POINT
Ilhas Martin Vas

HIGHEST MOUNTAIN
Cerro Aconcagua

LOWEST POINT
Laguna del Carbón

LARGEST ISLAND
Isla Grande de Tierra del Fuego

MOST SOUTHERLY POINT
Cape Horn

South America's physical features

Highest mountain	Cerro Aconcagua, Argentina	6 959 metres	22 831 feet
Longest river	Amazon	6 516 km	4 049 miles
Largest lake	Lake Titicaca, Bolivia/Peru	8 340 sq km	3 220 sq miles
Largest island	Isla Grande de Tierra del Fuego, Argentina/Chile	47 000 sq km	18 147 sq miles
Largest drainage basin	Amazon	7 050 000 sq km	2 722 005 sq miles
Lowest point	Laguna del Carbón, Argentina	-105 metres	-345 feet

Internet Links

● NASA Visible Earth	**visibleearth.nasa.gov**
● NASA Astronaut Photography	**eol.jsc.nasa.gov**
● World Rainforest Information Portal	**www.ran.org**
● Peakware World Mountain Encyclopedia	**www.peakware.com**

NORTH AMERICA

Caribbean Sea

PACIFIC
OCEAN

ATLANTIC
OCEAN

Facts

- Water flow along the Amazon is over 1 500 times that of the River Thames

- Cerro Aconcagua, 6 959 metres, is the highest point in the western hemisphere

- The Amazon rainforest supports approximately half of all the world's living species

- The Pantanal in Brazil is the largest area of wetland in the world

- The world's driest desert is the Atacama, where only 1mm of rain may fall as infrequently as once every 5–20 years

Isla Grande de Tierra del Fuego,
South America's largest island, situated at the southernmost tip of the continent.

South America's extent

TOTAL LAND AREA	17 815 420 sq km / 6 878 534 sq miles
Most northerly point	Punta Gallinas, Colombia
Most southerly point	Cape Horn, Chile
Most westerly point	Galapagos Islands, Ecuador
Most easterly point	Ilhas Martin Vas, Atlantic Ocean

South America
Countries

French Guiana, a French Department, is the only remaining territory under overseas control on a continent which has seen a long colonial history. Much of South America was colonized by Spain in the sixteenth century, with Britain, Portugal and the Netherlands each claiming territory in the northeast of the continent. This colonization led to the conquering of ancient civilizations, including the Incas in Peru. Most countries became independent from Spain and Portugal in the early nineteenth century.

The population of the continent reflects its history, being composed primarily of indigenous Indian peoples and mestizos – reflecting the long Hispanic influence. There has been a steady process of urbanization within the continent, with major movements of the population from rural to urban areas. The majority of the population now lives in the major cities and within 300 kilometres of the coast.

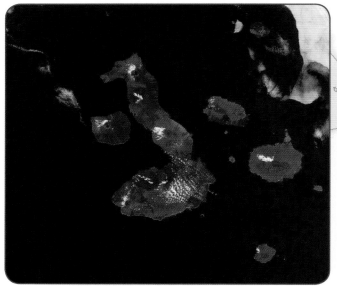

Galapagos Islands, an island territory of Ecuador which lies on the equator in the eastern Pacific Ocean over 900 kilometres west of the coast of Ecuador.

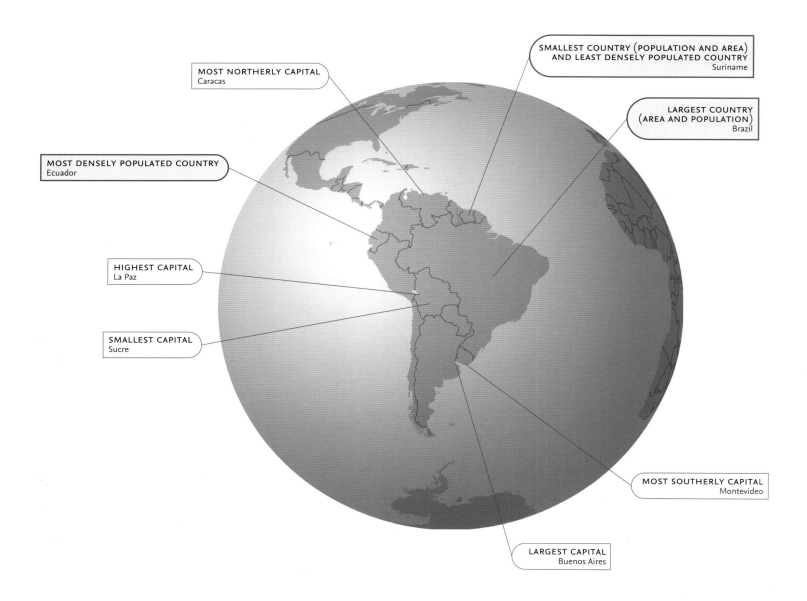

MOST NORTHERLY CAPITAL
Caracas

SMALLEST COUNTRY (POPULATION AND AREA)
AND LEAST DENSELY POPULATED COUNTRY
Suriname

LARGEST COUNTRY
(AREA AND POPULATION)
Brazil

MOST DENSELY POPULATED COUNTRY
Ecuador

HIGHEST CAPITAL
La Paz

SMALLEST CAPITAL
Sucre

MOST SOUTHERLY CAPITAL
Montevideo

LARGEST CAPITAL
Buenos Aires

South America's countries

Largest country (area)	Brazil	8 514 879 sq km	3 287 613 sq miles
Smallest country (area)	Suriname	163 820 sq km	63 251 sq miles
Largest country (population)	Brazil	196 655 000	
Smallest country (population)	Suriname	529 000	
Most densely populated country	Ecuador	53 per sq km	139 per sq mile
Least densely populated country	Suriname	3 per sq km	8 per sq mile

Internet Links

● UK Foreign and Commonwealth Office	www.fco.gov.uk
● CIA World Factbook	www.cia.gov/library/publications/the-world-factbook/index.html
● Caribbean Community (Caricom)	www.caricom.org
● Latin American Network Information Center	lanic.utexas.edu

North America

Caribbean Sea

Punta Gallinas

Barranquilla
Cartagena
Maracaibo
Cabimas
Maracay
Caracas
Cumaná
Valencia
Barquisimeto
Montería
San Cristóbal
Ciudad Bolívar

VENEZUELA
GUYANA
Georgetown
Paramaribo
Cayenne
SURINAME
French Guiana

Medellín
Tunja
Ibagué
Bogotá
Cali
Neiva
Puerto Ayacucho
Boa Vista

COLOMBIA
Guaviare
Meta
Orinoco

Isla de Malpelo (Colombia)

Esmeraldas
Pasto
Caquetá
Quito
Manta
ECUADOR
Guayaquil
Cuenca
Iquitos
Amazon
Japurá
Putumayo

Galapagos Islands (Ecuador)

Sullana
Marañón
Tarapoto
Chiclayo
Trujillo
Pucallpa
Cruzeiro do Sul
Río Branco
Porto Velho

PERU
Ucayali
Yavari
Juruá
Purus
Madeira

Tonantins
Carauari

Manaus
Santarém
Belém
São Luís
Parnaíba
Fortaleza
Teresina
Natal
João Pessoa
Floresta
Recife
Maceió
Aracaju
Salvador
Ilhéus

B R A Z I L

Negro
Branco
Represa de Balbina
Amazon
Mouths of the Amazon
Tapajós
Tocantins
Xingu
Teles Pires
Iriri
Araguaia
Paraíba
São Francisco
Represa Tucuruí

Marabá

Callao
Lima
Huancayo
Ica
Cusco
Juliaca
Arequipa
Arica
Iquique

Puerto Maldonado
Riberalta
Beni
Mamoré
Lago de San Luis
Trinidad
Lake Titicaca
La Paz

BOLIVIA
Cochabamba
Sucre
Potosí
Tarija
Santa Cruz

Cuiabá
Pantanal
Campo Grande
Goiânia
Brasília
Patos de Minas
Uberaba
Teófilo Otoni
Belo Horizonte
Vitória
Araçatuba
Ribeirão Preto
Campinas
Maringá
Nova Iguaçu
Rio de Janeiro
São Paulo

Paraná
Paranaíba
Grande
Velhas
Paranapanema

PARAGUAY
Pedro Juan Caballero
Asunción
Pilcomayo
Teuco
Paraguay

San Salvador de Jujuy
San Miguel de Tucumán
Formosa
Resistencia
Corrientes
Encarnación
Posadas
Santa Maria
Foz do Iguaçu
Iguaçu
Curitiba
Joinville
Florianópolis
Porto Alegre

Antofagasta
Copiapó
Catamarca
La Rioja
San Juan
Córdoba
Santa Fe
Paraná
Concordia
Paysandú
Rosario
Uruguay
Salado
Río Grande
Lagoa dos Patos

Cerro Aconcagua 6959
Valparaíso
Santiago
Mendoza
San Rafael
Talca
San Luis
Buenos Aires
La Plata
Montevideo
URUGUAY
Río de la Plata

Concepción
Chillán
Santa Rosa
Neuquén
Bahía Blanca
Mar del Plata

ARGENTINA
C H I L E
Colorado
Negro

Valdivia
Viedma

Puerto Montt
Isla de Chiloé
Trelew

Archipiélago de los Chonos
Comodoro Rivadavia
Golfo de San Jorge

Islas Desventuradas (Chile)

Archipiélago Juan Fernández (Chile)

Punta Medanosa

Falkland Islands (U.K.)

Patagonia
Bahía Grande
Puerto Natales
Río Gallegos
Stanley
Punta Arenas
Isla Grande de Tierra del Fuego
Ushuaia
Cape Horn

P A C I F I C   O C E A N

A T L A N T I C   O C E A N

South America's capitals

Largest capital (population)	Buenos Aires, Argentina	13 401 000
Smallest capital (population)	Sucre, Bolivia	284 000
Most northerly capital	Caracas, Venezuela	10° 28'N
Most southerly capital	Montevideo, Uruguay	34° 52'S
Highest capital	La Paz, Bolivia	3 630 metres 11 909 feet

Facts

- South America is often referred to as 'Latin America', reflecting the historic influences of Spain and Portugal

- The largest city in each South American country is the capital, except in Brazil and Ecuador

- South America has only two landlocked countries – Bolivia and Paraguay

- Chile is over 4 000 kilometres long but has an average width of only 177 kilometres

Falkland Islands, an overseas UK territory in the South Atlantic Ocean.

South Georgia
(U.K.)

PACIFIC

OCEAN

Galapagos Islands
(Islas Galápagos)
(Ecuador)

Parque Nacional
Galápagos

Equator

Isla
Fernandina

Isla
Isabela

Isla
Santa María

Isla
San Salvador

Isla
Santa Cruz

Puerto
Ayora

Isla
San Cristóbal

Puerto
Baquerizo Moreno

1:12 000 000

miles   100

km   150

NICARAGUA
MANAGUA

COSTA RICA

SAN JOSÉ

PANAMA

PANAMA CITY

COLOMBIA

BOGOTÁ

MEDELLÍN

Cali

ECUADOR

QUITO

Guayaquil

PERU

LIMA

Callao

Trujillo

Arequipa

BOLIVIA

LA PAZ

SUCRE

Santa Cruz

VENEZUELA

Maracaibo

CARACAS

Valencia

GRENADA
ST GEORGE'S

TRINIDAD AND TOBAGO
PORT OF SPAIN

ARGENTINA

CHILE

Lambert Azimuthal Equal Area Projection

1:12 000 000

miles
0   200   400

km
0   200   400   600   800

South America
Southern South America

1:12 000 000

Lambert Azimuthal Equal Area Projection

0   200   400   miles
0   200   400   600   800 km

MATO GROSSO

TOCANTINS

BAHIA

GOIÁS

BRAZIL

DISTRITO FEDERAL

BRASÍLIA

MINAS GERAIS

Belo Horizonte

ESPÍRITO SANTO

Vitória

SÃO PAULO

São Paulo

Campinas

Santos

RIO DE JANEIRO

Rio de Janeiro

PARANÁ

Curitiba

SANTA CATARINA

Florianópolis

RIO GRANDE DO SUL

Porto Alegre

Salvador (Bahia)

Goiânia

Tropic of Capricorn

ATLANTIC OCEAN

52°W
48°
44°
40°

16°

20°

24°

28°

Lambert Azimuthal Equal Area Projection

South America
Southeast Brazil

1:6 000 000

0   100   200   miles
0   100   200   300   400 km

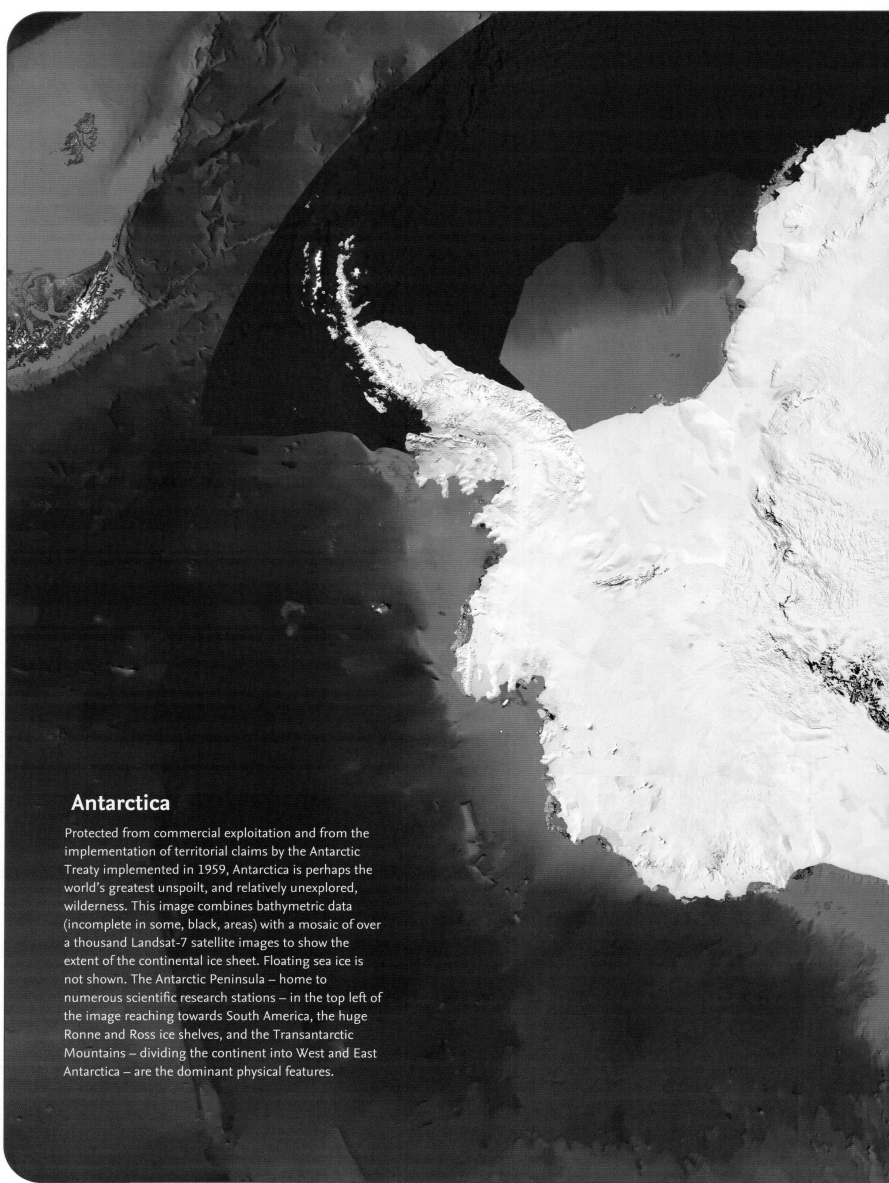

Antarctica

Protected from commercial exploitation and from the implementation of territorial claims by the Antarctic Treaty implemented in 1959, Antarctica is perhaps the world's greatest unspoilt, and relatively unexplored, wilderness. This image combines bathymetric data (incomplete in some, black, areas) with a mosaic of over a thousand Landsat-7 satellite images to show the extent of the continental ice sheet. Floating sea ice is not shown. The Antarctic Peninsula – home to numerous scientific research stations – in the top left of the image reaching towards South America, the huge Ronne and Ross ice shelves, and the Transantarctic Mountains – dividing the continent into West and East Antarctica – are the dominant physical features.

Between them, the world's oceans and polar regions cover approximately seventy per cent of the earth's surface. The oceans contain ninety-six per cent of the Earth's water and a vast range of flora and fauna. They are a major influence on the world's climate, particularly through ocean currents. The Arctic and Antarctica are the coldest and most inhospitable places on the Earth. They both have vast amounts of ice which, if global warming continues, could have a major influence on sea level across the globe.

Our understanding of the oceans and polar regions has increased enormously over the last twenty years through the development of new technologies, particularly that of satellite remote sensing, which can generate vast amounts of data relating to, for example, topography (both on land and the seafloor), land cover and sea surface temperature.

The oceans

The world's major oceans are the Pacific, the Atlantic and the Indian Oceans. The Arctic Ocean is generally considered as part of the Atlantic, and the Southern Ocean, which stretches around the whole of Antarctica is usually treated as an extension of each of the three major oceans.

One of the most important factors affecting the earth's climate is the circulation of water within and between the oceans. Differences in temperature and surface winds create ocean currents which move enormous quantities of water around the globe. These currents re-distribute heat which the oceans have absorbed from the sun, and so have a major effect on the world's climate system. El Niño is one climatic phenomenon directly influenced by these ocean processes.

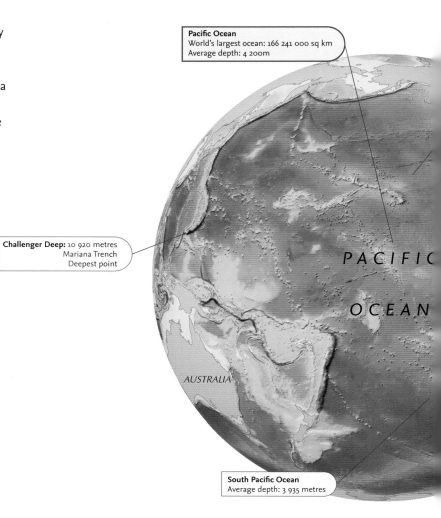

Pacific Ocean
World's largest ocean: 166 241 000 sq km
Average depth: 4 200m

Challenger Deep: 10 920 metres
Mariana Trench
Deepest point

PACIFIC

OCEAN

AUSTRALIA

South Pacific Ocean
Average depth: 3 935 metres

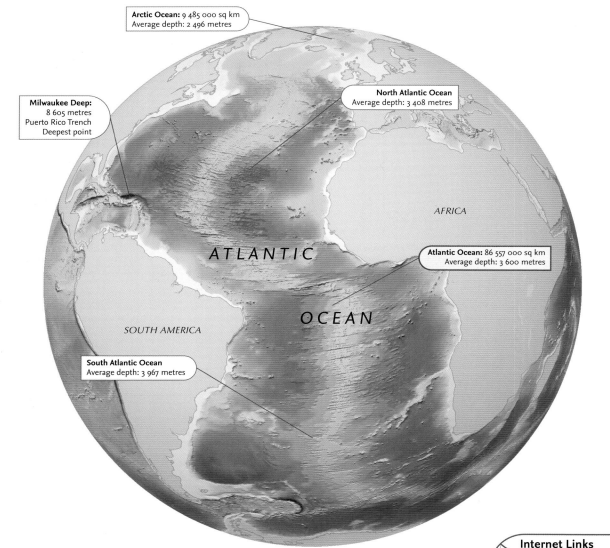

Arctic Ocean: 9 485 000 sq km
Average depth: 2 496 metres

Milwaukee Deep:
8 605 metres
Puerto Rico Trench
Deepest point

North Atlantic Ocean
Average depth: 3 408 metres

AFRICA

ATLANTIC

Atlantic Ocean: 86 557 000 sq km
Average depth: 3 600 metres

OCEAN

SOUTH AMERICA

South Atlantic Ocean
Average depth: 3 967 metres

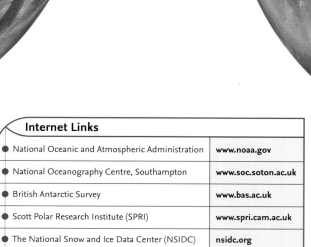

Indian Ocean: 73 427 000 sq km
Average depth: 4 000 metres

AFRICA

Internet Links

● National Oceanic and Atmospheric Administration	www.noaa.gov
● National Oceanography Centre, Southampton	www.soc.soton.ac.uk
● British Antarctic Survey	www.bas.ac.uk
● Scott Polar Research Institute (SPRI)	www.spri.cam.ac.uk
● The National Snow and Ice Data Center (NSIDC)	nsidc.org

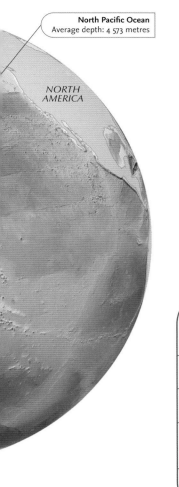

North Pacific Ocean
Average depth: 4 573 metres

NORTH AMERICA

Facts

- If all of Antarctica's ice melted, world sea level would rise by more than 60 metres
- The Arctic Ocean produces up to 50 000 icebergs per year
- The Mid-Atlantic Ridge in the Atlantic Ocean is the earth's longest mountain range
- The world's greatest tidal range – 21 metres – is in the Bay of Fundy, Nova Scotia, Canada
- The Circumpolar current in the Southern Ocean carries 125 million cubic metres of water per second

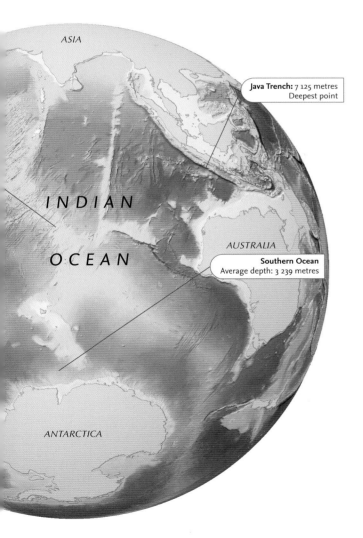

ASIA

Java Trench: 7 125 metres
Deepest point

INDIAN

OCEAN

AUSTRALIA

Southern Ocean
Average depth: 3 239 metres

ANTARCTICA

Polar regions

Although a harsh climate is common to the two polar regions, there are major differences between the Arctic and Antarctica. The North Pole is surrounded by the Arctic Ocean, much of which is permanently covered by sea ice, while the South Pole lies on the huge land mass of Antarctica. This is covered by a permanent ice cap which reaches a maximum thickness of over four kilometres. Antarctica has no permanent population, but Europe, Asia and North America all stretch into the Arctic region which is populated by numerous ethnic groups. Antarctica is subject to the Antarctic Treaty of 1959 which does not recognize individual land claims and protects the continent in the interests of international scientific cooperation.

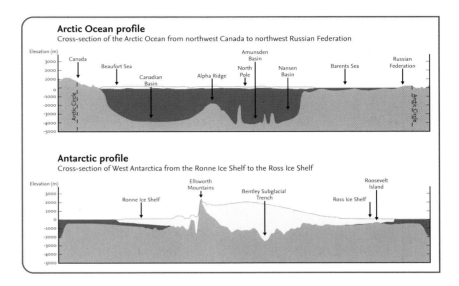

Arctic Ocean profile
Cross-section of the Arctic Ocean from northwest Canada to northwest Russian Federation

Antarctic profile
Cross-section of West Antarctica from the Ronne Ice Shelf to the Ross Ice Shelf

Antarctica's physical features

Highest mountain: Vinson Massif	4 897 m	16 066 ft
Total land area (excluding ice shelves)	12 093 000 sq km	4 669 107 sq miles
Ice shelves	1 559 000 sq km	601 930 sq miles
Exposed rock	49 000 sq km	18 919 sq miles
Lowest bedrock elevation (Bentley Subglacial Trench)	2 496 m below sea level	8 189 ft below sea level
Maximum ice thickness (Astrolabe Subglacial Basin)	4 776 m	15 669 ft
Mean ice thickness (including ice shelves)	1 859 m	6 099 ft
Volume of ice sheet (including ice shelves)	25 400 000 cubic km	6 094 628 cubic miles

The **Antarctic Peninsula** and the **Larsen Ice Shelf** in western Antarctica.

Atlantic Ocean
Indian Ocean

185

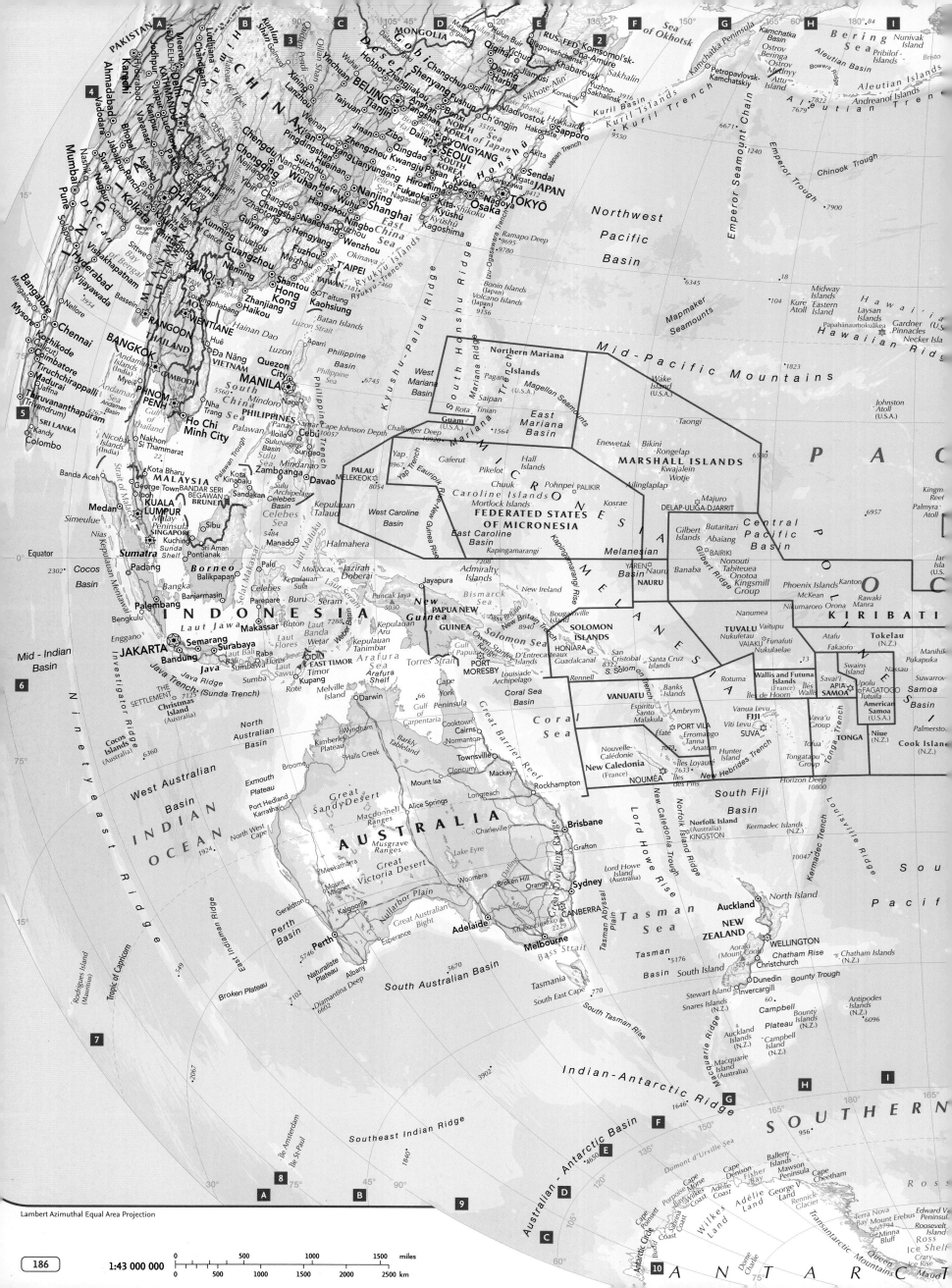

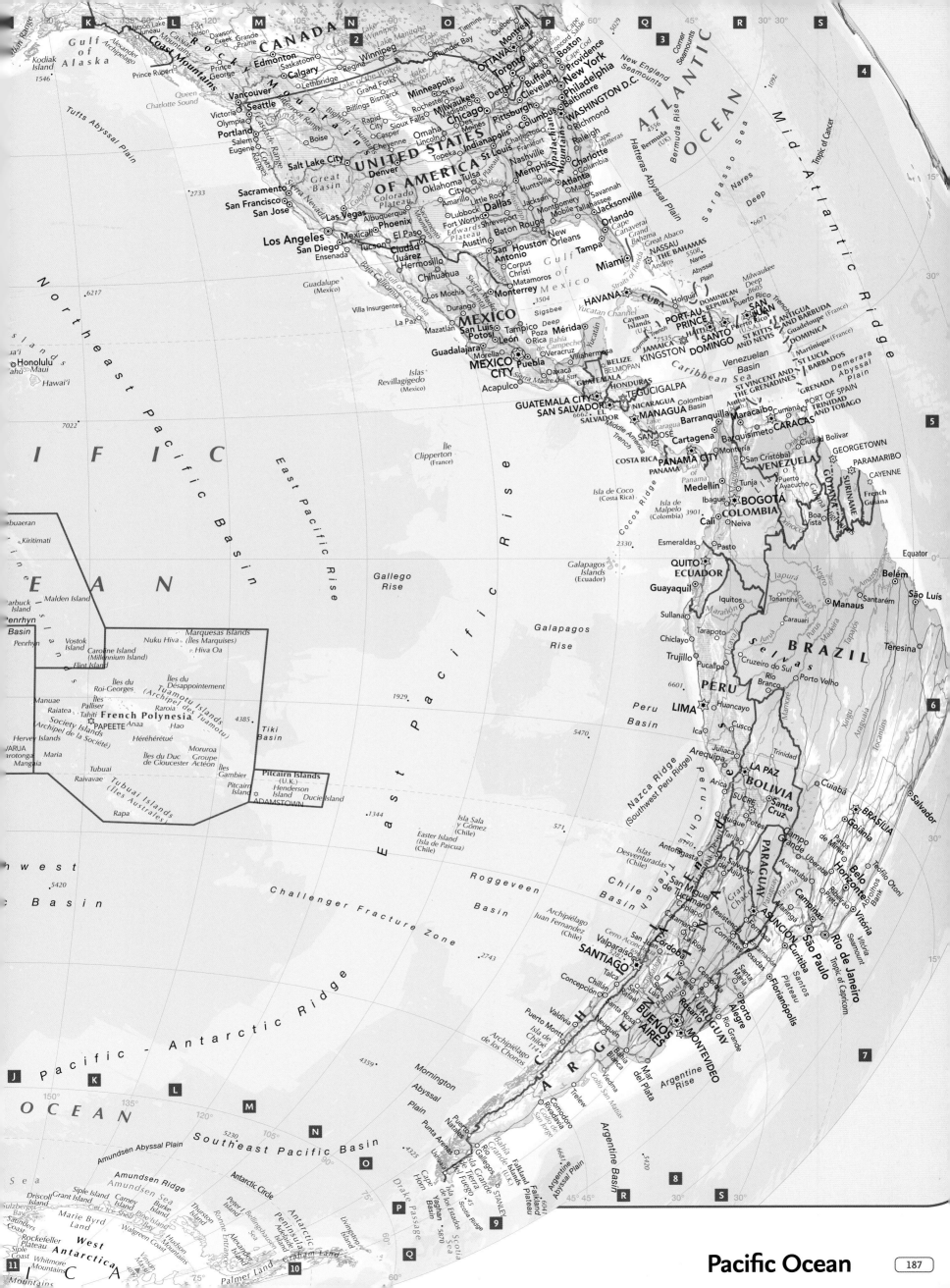

Pacific Ocean

187

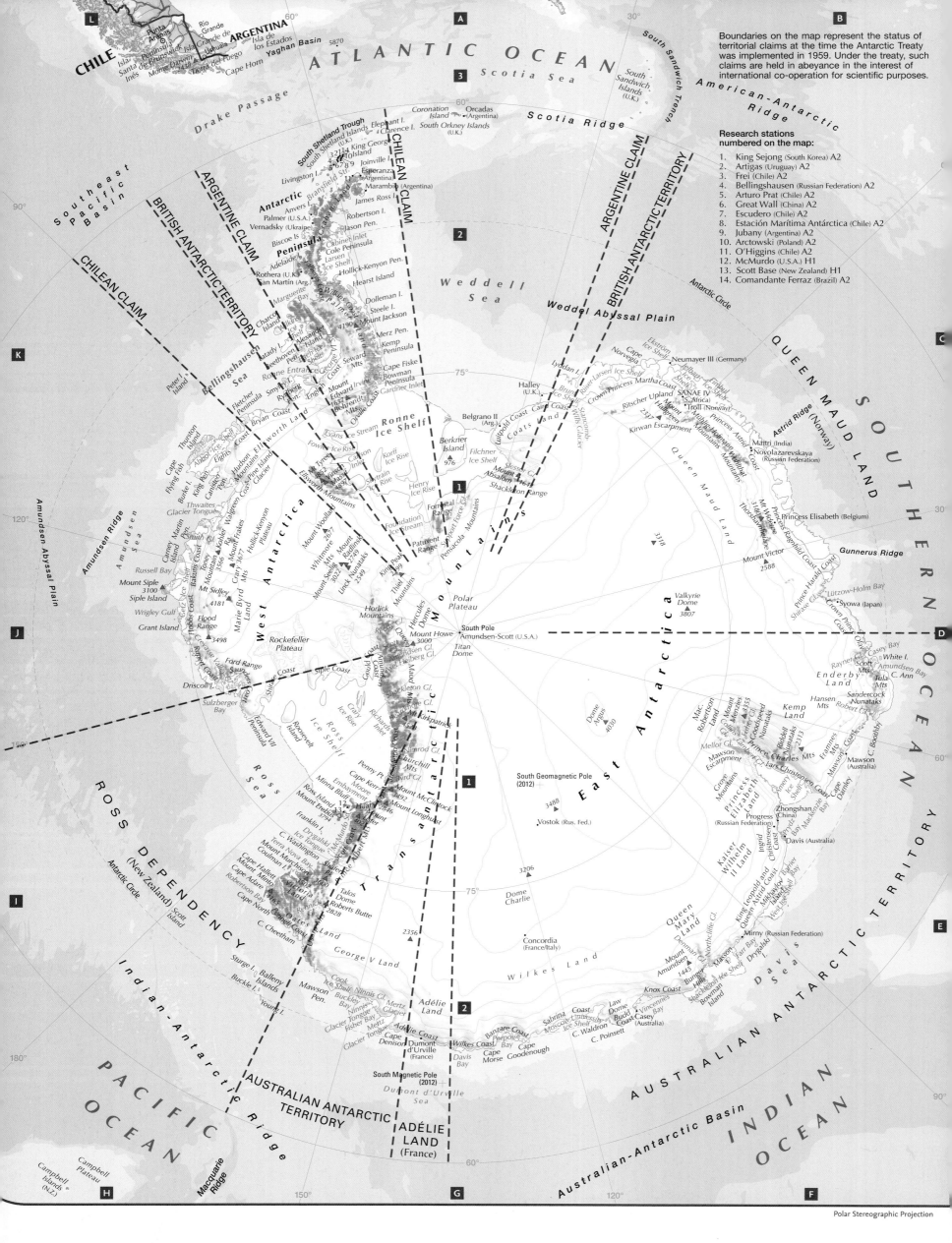

CHILE · ARGENTINA

ATLANTIC OCEAN

Scotia Sea

South Sandwich Islands (U.K.)

Drake Passage

Scotia Ridge

American-Antarctic Ridge

Boundaries on the map represent the status of territorial claims at the time the Antarctic Treaty was implemented in 1959. Under the treaty, such claims are held in abeyance in the interest of international co-operation for scientific purposes.

Research stations numbered on the map:

1. King Sejong (South Korea) A2
2. Artigas (Uruguay) A2
3. Frei (Chile) A2
4. Bellingshausen (Russian Federation) A2
5. Arturo Prat (Chile) A2
6. Great Wall (China) A2
7. Escudero (Chile) A2
8. Estación Marítima Antárctica (Chile) A2
9. Jubany (Argentina) A2
10. Arctowski (Poland) A2
11. O'Higgins (Chile) A2
12. McMurdo (U.S.A.) H1
13. Scott Base (New Zealand) H1
14. Comandante Ferraz (Brazil) A2

SOUTHERN OCEAN

CHILEAN CLAIM

ARGENTINE CLAIM

BRITISH ANTARCTIC TERRITORY

Bellingshausen Sea

Weddell Sea

Weddel Abyssal Plain

QUEEN MAUD LAND

Antarctic Circle

Ronne Ice Shelf

West Antarctica

Transantarctic Mountains

South Pole
Amundsen-Scott (U.S.A.)

Polar Plateau

East Antarctica

South Geomagnetic Pole (2012)

Vostok (Rus. Fed.)

Dome Charlie

Concordia (France/Italy)

Ross Dependency (New Zealand)

Ross Sea

Ross Ice Shelf

Wilkes Land

AUSTRALIAN ANTARCTIC TERRITORY

Indian-Antarctic Ridge

PACIFIC OCEAN

South Magnetic Pole (2012)

Dumont d'Urville Sea

AUSTRALIAN ANTARCTIC TERRITORY

ADÉLIE LAND (France)

Australian-Antarctic Basin

Australian-Antarctic Ridge

INDIAN OCEAN

Campbell Plateau

Campbell Islands (N.Z.)

Macquarie Ridge

Antarctica

1:22 500 000

Polar Stereographic Projection

0 200 400 600 800 1000 miles
0 200 400 600 800 1000 1200 1400 1600 km

The Arctic

1:22 500 000

Polar Stereographic Projection

See page 196 for explanatory table and sources

| | Population | | | | | | | Economy | | | | | |
	Total population	Population change (%)	% urban	Total fertility	Population by age (%)		2050 projected population	Total Gross National Income (GNI) (US$M)	GNI per capita (US$)	Debt service ratio (% GNI)	Total debt service (US$)	Aid receipts (% GNI)	Military spending (% GDP)
					0–14	60 or over							
WORLD	6 974 036 000	1.2	49.2	2.6	28.2	10.4	9 306 128 000	62 359 648	9 116	...	...	0.2	2.7
AFGHANISTAN	32 358 000	3.5	22.6	6.0	50.1	4.3	76 250 000	14 259	290	...	10 600 000	...	...
ALBANIA	3 216 000	0.4	51.9	1.5	22.9	15.0	2 990 000	12 677	3 960	2.2	264 494 000	3.0	2.1
ALGERIA	35 980 000	1.5	66.5	2.1	27.1	7.5	46 522 000	157 939	4 450	0.7	1 026 992 000	0.2	3.8
ANDORRA	86 000	1.5	88.0	5.1	...	...	137 000	3 447	41 750				
ANGOLA	19 618 000	2.7	58.5	...	46.8	4.2	42 334 000	75 150	3 940	5.1	3 507 521 000	0.3	4.2
ANTIGUA AND BARBUDA	90 000	1.0	30.3	...	...	...	112 000	939	10 590	...	...	0.6	
ARGENTINA	40 765 000	1.0	92.4	2.2	24.7	17.0	50 560 000	343 636	8 500	4.1	12 126 778 000	0.0	0.8
ARMENIA	3 100 000	0.2	64.2	1.7	20.2	17.3	2 931 000	9 556	3 090	4.9	430 568 000	6.1	4.1
AUSTRALIA	22 606 000	1.1	89.1	1.9	19.7	23.6	31 385 000	956 912	43 590	...	...	...	1.9
AUSTRIA	8 413 000	0.4	67.6	1.3	14.7	28.0	8 427 000	391 511	46 690	...	...	...	0.9
AZERBAIJAN	9 306 000	1.1	51.9	2.1	21.5	10.2	11 578 000	45 983	5 080	1.0	397 457 000	0.6	3.5
THE BAHAMAS	347 000	1.2	84.1	1.9	22.3	11.4	445 000	6 972	20 610	...	...	...	...
BAHRAIN	1 324 000	2.1	88.6	2.4	31.3	5.7	1 801 000	19 714	18 730	...	...	...	3.6
BANGLADESH	150 494 000	1.4	28.1	2.2	28.3	6.6	194 353 000	104 478	700	1.0	956 569 000	1.3	1.1
BARBADOS	274 000	0.3	44.5	1.6	18.5	20.6	264 000	3 453	12 660	...	...	0.3	...
BELARUS	9 559 000	-0.5	74.7	1.5	15.0	21.6	8 001 000	58 169	6 130	2.5	1 247 665 000	0.2	1.8
BELGIUM	10 754 000	0.5	97.4	1.8	16.9	28.4	11 587 000	493 526	45 360	...	...	...	1.1
BELIZE	318 000	2.1	52.2	2.7	34.9	6.5	529 000	1 288	3 740	8.1	99 602 000	2.3	...
BENIN	9 100 000	3.2	42.0	5.1	42.0	4.8	21 734 000	6 945	780	0.6	36 915 000	10.3	...
BHUTAN	738 000	1.7	34.7	2.3	30.2	7.9	962 000	1 361	1 880	6.1	75 497 000	10.2	...
BOLIVIA	10 088 000	1.8	66.5	3.2	35.7	7.6	16 769 000	17 982	1 810	3.5	589 709 000	4.4	1.6
BOSNIA-HERZEGOVINA	3 752 000	-0.1	48.6	1.1	15.0	21.8	2 952 000	18 015	4 790	3.7	645 768 000	2.4	1.5
BOTSWANA	2 031 000	1.5	61.1	2.6	33.0	6.7	2 503 000	13 633	6 790	0.4	46 665 000	2.4	3.2
BRAZIL	196 655 000	1.0	86.5	1.8	25.4	11.7	222 843 000	1 830 392	9 390	2.8	44 317 041 000	0.0	1.6
BRUNEI	406 000	1.9	75.7	2.0	25.7	6.3	602 000	12 460	31 800	...	...	...	3.1
BULGARIA	7 446 000	-0.6	71.5	1.5	13.7	28.2	5 459 000	47 159	6 250	11.1	5 210 101 000	...	2.3
BURKINA FASO	16 968 000	3.4	25.7	5.8	45.8	3.9	46 721 000	9 031	550	0.5	41 701 000	13.5	1.3
BURUNDI	8 575 000	2.9	11.0	4.1	37.3	4.8	13 703 000	1 402	170	1.5	19 345 000	42.3	...
CAMBODIA	14 305 000	1.6	20.1	2.4	30.0	6.2	18 965 000	10 686	760	0.5	49 453 000	7.3	...
CAMEROON	20 030 000	2.3	58.4	4.3	39.9	5.7	38 472 000	23 169	1 180	1.8	394 624 000	2.9	1.5
CANADA	34 350 000	1.0	80.6	1.7	16.5	23.9	43 642 000	1 475 864	41 950	...	...	...	1.4
CAPE VERDE	501 000	1.4	61.1	2.3	30.7	7.9	632 000	1 620	3 270	2.1	32 871 000	12.7	...
CENTRAL AFRICAN REPUBLIC	4 487 000	1.9	38.9	4.4	39.4	6.3	8 392 000	2 067	470	1.6	31 869 000	12.3	1.8
CHAD	11 525 000	2.8	27.6	5.7	44.3	4.7	27 252 000	6 929	620	1.3	78 176 000	9.2	6.4
CHILE	17 270 000	1.0	89.0	1.8	22.1	15.2	20 059 000	170 284	9 950	10.2	15 283 023 000	0.1	3.1
CHINA	1 332 079 000	0.6	47.0	1.6	19.3	13.5	1 295 604 000	5 700 018	4 260	0.8	41 830 332 000	0.0	2.0
COLOMBIA	46 927 000	1.5	75.1	2.3	28.7	9.7	61 764 000	255 290	5 510	3.9	8 839 690 000	0.5	4.1
COMOROS	754 000	2.3	28.2	4.7	45.3	4.8	1 700 000	550	750	2.2	11 834 000	9.5	...
CONGO	4 140 000	1.9	62.1	4.4	43.7	6.5	8 801 000	8 698	180	2.4	163 343 000	4.1	...
CONGO, DEM. REPUBLIC OF THE	67 758 000	2.8	35.2	5.5	45.0	4.4	148 523 000	11 951	2 150	6.7	699 927 000	22.6	1.1
COSTA RICA	4 727 000	1.4	64.4	..	25.0	11.0	6 001 000	30 518	6 550	4.3	1 229 366 000	0.4	...
CÔTE D'IVOIRE (IVORY COAST)	20 153 000	2.3	50.6	4.2	37.5	5.8	40 674 000	22 976	1 160	5.0	1 106 880 000	10.7	1.8
CROATIA	4 396 000	-0.2	57.7	1.5	15.0	27.1	3 859 000	60 965	13 780	...	...	0.3	1.8
CUBA	11 254 000	0.0	75.2	1.5	17.4	19.9	9 898 000	62 203	5 520	...	...	...	2.2
CYPRUS	1 117 000	1.0	70.3	1.5	22.3	23.7	1 347 000	23 654	30 480	...	...	...	1.5
CZECH REPUBLIC	10 534 000	0.4	73.5	1.5	14.1	25.6	10 638 000	188 269	17 890	...	...	...	1.4
DENMARK	5 573 000	0.2	86.9	1.9	18.2	27.7	5 920 000	328 252	59 210	...	...	...	...
DJIBOUTI	906 000	1.8	76.2	3.6	36.2	5.8	1 620 000	1 105	1 270	2.6	29 308 000	14.5	...
DOMINICA	68 000	0.0	67.2	...	...	...	65 000	367	5 410	5.0	17 840 000	10.1	...
DOMINICAN REPUBLIC	10 056 000	1.4	69.2	2.5	30.1	10.0	12 942 000	49 662	5 000	3.0	1 326 417 000	0.3	0.6
EAST TIMOR (TIMOR-LESTE)	1 154 000	3.3	28.1	5.9	44.4	4.8	3 006 000	2 493	2 220	...	...	9.0	11.0
ECUADOR	14 666 000	1.1	66.9	2.4	31.9	10.7	19 549 000	62 106	4 290	11.4	6 368 500 000	0.4	3.7
EGYPT	82 537 000	1.8	43.4	2.6	30.3	8.4	123 452 000	197 922	2 440	1.6	2 941 613 000	0.5	2.1
EL SALVADOR	6 227 000	0.4	64.3	2.2	32.0	11.1	7 607 000	20 820	3 360	6.0	1 223 450 000	1.4	0.6
EQUATORIAL GUINEA	720 000	2.6	39.7	5.0	39.7	4.9	1 493 000	10 182	14 540	...	...	0.4	...
ERITREA	5 415 000	3.1	21.6	4.2	41.8	4.4	11 568 000	1 792	340	1.2	21 553 000	7.9	...
ESTONIA	1 341 000	-0.1	69.5	1.7	15.4	27.1	1 233 000	19 247	14 370	...	...	...	2.3
ETHIOPIA	84 734 000	2.6	16.7	3.8	40.5	5.5	145 187 000	32 409	390	0.3	103 202 000	12.0	1.3
FIJI	868 000	0.6	51.9	2.6	29.3	8.4	1 017 000	3 085	3 580	0.9	25 572 000	2.5	...
FINLAND	5 385 000	0.4	85.1	1.9	16.6	29.6	5 611 000	252 958	47 160	...	...	...	1.5
FRANCE	63 126 000	0.5	85.3	2.0	18.4	28.4	72 442 000	2 749 821	42 390	...	...	...	2.4
GABON	1 534 000	1.8	86.0	3.2	35.6	7.3	2 784 000	11 655	7 740	4.7	468 107 000	0.8	...
THE GAMBIA	1 776 000	2.8	58.1	4.7	43.4	3.6	4 036 000	770	450	3.7	25 641 000	18.5	...
GEORGIA	4 329 000	-1.1	52.7	1.5	17.1	23.0	3 186 000	11 976	2 690	2.5	262 986 000	8.5	5.6

Social Indicators					Environment				Communications				
Child mortality rate	Life expectancy	Literacy rate (%)	Access to safe water (%)	Doctors per 100 000 people	Forest area (%)	Annual change in forest area (%)	Protected land area (%)	CO_2 emissions (metric tonnes per capita)	Main telephone lines per 100 people	Cellular phone subscribers per 100 people	Internet users per 10 000 people	International dialling code	Time zone
57.9	**69.3**	**87.6**	**87**	**152**	**31.1**	**-0.1**	**12**	**4.6**	**17.2**	**78.0**	**29.7**	**...**	**...**
149.2	49.3	...	48	21	2.1	0.0	0	0.0	0.5	41.4	4.0	93	+4.5
18.4	77.1	95.9	97	115	28.3	-0.2	10	1.3	10.4	141.9	45.0	355	+1
36.0	73.5	72.6	83	121	0.6	-0.6	6	4.1	8.2	92.4	12.5	213	+1
3.8	...	...	100	372	34.0	0.0	6	6.6	45.0	77.2	81.0	376	+1
160.5	51.7	70.0	50	8	46.9	-0.2	12	1.4	1.6	46.7	10.0	244	+1
8.1	...	99.0	...	...	22.7	0.0	7	5.1	47.1	184.7	80.0	1 268	-4
13.8	76.1	97.7	97	321	10.7	-0.8	5	4.7	24.7	141.8	36.0	54	-3
19.6	74.4	99.5	96	370	9.2	-1.5	8	1.6	19.1	125.0	37.0	374	+4
4.9	82.1	...	100	299	19.4	-0.6	11	17.7	38.9	101.0	76.0	61	+8 to +10.5
4.2	81.1	...	100	475	47.1	0.1	23	8.3	38.7	145.8	72.7	43	+1
45.9	70.9	99.5	80	379	11.3	0.0	7	3.7	16.3	99.1	36.0	994	+4
16.1	75.9	...	...	...	51.4	0.0	14	6.5	37.7	124.9	43.0	1 242	-5
10.2	75.3	91.4	...	144	1.3	3.3	1	24.2	18.1	124.2	55.0	973	+3
47.8	69.4	55.9	80	30	11.1	-0.2	2	0.3	0.6	46.2	3.7	880	+6
19.6	77.1	...	100	181	18.6	0.0	0	5.0	50.3	128.1	70.2	1 246	-4
6.0	70.8	99.7	100	511	42.5	0.5	7	6.9	43.1	107.7	31.7	375	+2
4.4	80.0	...	100	299	22.4	0.2	1	9.7	43.3	113.5	79.3	32	+1
16.5	76.3	...	99	83	61.1	-0.7	28	1.4	9.7	62.3	14.0	501	-6
115.4	56.8	41.7	75	6	41.2	-1.1	24	0.5	1.5	79.9	3.1	229	+1
56.1	67.7	52.8	92	2	84.6	0.3	28	0.8	3.6	54.3	13.6	975	+6
54.2	67.1	90.7	86	...	52.8	-0.5	18	1.4	8.5	72.3	20.0	591	-4
8.4	75.9	97.8	99	142	42.7	0.0	1	7.7	26.6	80.1	52.0	387	+1
47.7	52.7	84.1	95	34	20.0	-1.0	31	2.6	6.9	117.8	6.0	267	+2
19.4	74.0	90.0	97	172	61.4	-0.4	28	1.9	21.6	104.1	40.7	55	-2 to -4
7.3	78.2	95.3	...	142	72.1	-0.5	43	20.1	20.0	109.1	50.0	673	+8
12.7	73.7	98.3	100	364	36.2	1.5	9	6.8	29.4	141.2	46.2	359	+2
176.2	56.1	28.7	76	6	20.6	-1.0	14	0.1	0.9	34.7	1.4	226	GMT
141.9	51.1	66.6	72	3	6.7	-1.0	5	0.0	0.4	13.7	2.1	257	+2
51.0	63.7	77.6	61	23	57.2	-1.2	24	0.3	2.5	57.7	1.3	855	+7
136.2	52.5	70.7	74	19	42.1	-1.1	9	0.3	2.5	41.6	4.0	237	+1
5.9	81.2	...	100	191	34.1	0.0	8	16.9	50.0	70.7	81.6	1	-3.5 to -8
35.6	74.2	84.8	84	57	21.1	0.4	2	0.6	14.5	75.0	30.0	238	-1
158.8	49.5	55.2	67	8	36.3	-0.1	15	0.1	0.3	23.2	2.3	236	+1
173.4	50.1	33.6	50	4	9.2	-0.7	9	0.0	0.5	23.3	1.7	235	+1
8.8	79.3	98.6	96	128	21.8	0.2	16	4.3	20.2	116.0	45.0	56	-4
18.4	73.8	94.0	89	142	22.2	1.4	17	5.0	22.0	64.0	34.3	86	+8
19.1	74.0	93.2	92	143	54.5	-0.2	20	1.4	14.7	93.8	36.5	57	-5
85.6	61.7	74.2	95	15	1.6	-9.7	0	0.2	2.9	22.5	5.1	269	+3
93.4	58.0	...	71	10	65.6	-0.1	10	0.4	0.2	94.0	5.0	242	+1
169.9	48.9	67.0	46	11	68.0	-0.2	9	0.0	0.1	17.2	0.7	243	+1 to +2
10.1	79.5	96.1	97	...	51.0	0.9	21	1.8	31.8	65.1	36.5	506	-6
123.0	56.4	55.3	80	14	32.7	0.0	23	0.3	1.1	75.5	2.6	225	GMT
5.5	76.9	98.8	99	268	34.3	0.2	7	5.6	42.4	144.5	60.3	385	+1
5.9	79.3	99.8	94	640	27.0	1.3	6	2.4	10.3	8.9	15.1	53	-5
3.8	79.9	97.9	100	230	18.7	0.0	11	7.7	37.6	93.7	53.0	357	+2
4.0	77.9	...	100	363	34.4	0.1	15	12.1	21.0	136.6	68.8	420	+1
3.9	79.0	...	100	342	12.8	0.4	5	9.1	47.3	124.4	88.7	45	+1
91.1	58.5	...	92	23	0.3	0.0	0	0.6	2.1	18.6	6.5	253	+3
12.4	...	...	...	...	60.0	-0.6	22	1.8	22.9	144.9	47.5	1 767	-4
26.5	73.8	88.2	86	...	40.8	0.0	22	2.2	10.2	89.6	39.5	1 809	-4
54.8	63.2	50.6	69	10	49.9	-1.4	6	0.2	0.2	53.4	0.2	670	+9
20.1	75.9	84.2	94	...	39.7	-1.9	25	2.2	14.4	102.2	24.0	593	-5
21.8	73.5	66.4	99	283	0.1	0.9	6	2.4	11.9	87.1	26.7	20	+2
16.2	72.5	84.1	87	160	13.9	-1.5	1	1.1	16.2	124.3	15.0	503	-6
120.8	51.5	93.3	...	30	58.0	-0.7	19	7.4	1.9	57.0	6.0	240	+1
60.8	62.2	66.6	61	5	15.2	-0.3	5	0.1	1.0	3.5	5.4	291	+3
5.4	75.1	99.8	98	341	52.3	-0.3	20	15.2	36.0	123.2	74.1	372	+2
105.9	60.0	29.8	38	2	12.3	-1.1	18	0.1	1.1	7.9	0.8	251	+3
17.4	69.4	...	...	45	55.5	0.3	1	1.7	15.9	116.2	14.8	679	+12
3.0	80.2	...	100	274	72.9	0.0	9	12.1	23.3	156.4	86.9	358	+2
4.1	81.7	...	100	350	29.1	0.3	15	5.8	56.1	99.7	80.1	33	+1
73.5	63.3	87.7	87	29	85.4	0.0	15	1.4	2.0	106.9	7.2	241	+1
98.1	59.0	46.5	92	4	48.0	0.4	2	0.2	2.8	85.5	9.2	220	GMT
22.4	74.1	99.7	98	454	39.5	-0.1	4	1.4	13.7	73.4	27.0	995	+4

See page 196 for explanatory table and sources

| | Population | | | | | | | Economy | | | | | |
	Total population	Population change (%)	% urban	Total fertility	Population by age (%) 0 – 14	Population by age (%) 60 or over	2050 projected population	Total Gross National Income (GNI) (US$M)	GNI per capita (US$)	Debt service ratio (% GNI)	Total debt service (US$)	Aid receipts (% GNI)	Military spending (% GDP)
GERMANY	82 163 000	-0.1	73.8	1.5	13.5	31.2	74 781 000	3 537 180	43 290	...	...	...	1.4
GHANA	24 966 000	2.1	51.5	4.0	38.7	6.4	49 107 000	30 080	1 230	0.9	232 805 000	6.1	0.4
GREECE	11 390 000	0.2	61.4	1.5	14.8	29.6	11 647 000	308 596	27 260	...	...	...	4.0
GRENADA	105 000	0.4	39.3	2.2	27.7	11.5	95 000	580	26 020	3.5	20 416 000	8.3	...
GUATEMALA	14 757 000	2.5	49.5	3.8	41.5	7.2	31 595 000	39 345	2 730	4.6	1 686 423 000	1.0	0.4
GUINEA	10 222 000	2.3	35.4	5.0	41.5	5.3	23 006 000	3 972	400	3.5	129 087 000	5.8	...
GUINEA-BISSAU	1 547 000	2.2	30.0	4.9	38.0	5.2	3 185 000	890	590	1.2	9 981 000	17.8	...
GUYANA	756 000	-0.1	28.6	2.2	33.3	7.1	766 000	2 491	3 300	0.8	19 474 000	7.5	...
HAITI	10 124 000	1.6	52.1	3.2	35.3	6.9	14 178 000	6 464	650	0.7	44 723 000	17.3	...
HONDURAS	7 755 000	2.0	51.6	3.0	36.7	7.1	12 939 000	14 302	1 880	3.0	413 664 000	3.3	0.8
HUNGARY	9 966 000	-0.2	68.1	1.4	14.7	26.5	9 243 000	129 923	12 980	...	...	...	1.3
ICELAND	324 000	2.2	93.4	2.1	20.3	19.7	431 000	10 787	33 990	...	...	...	0.1
INDIA	1 241 492 000	1.4	30.0	2.5	30.8	8.3	1 692 008 000	1 566 636	1 340	1.1	16 150 121 000	0.2	2.7
INDONESIA	242 326 000	1.2	44.3	2.1	27.9	9.2	293 456 000	599 148	2 500	4.8	24 851 671 000	0.2	0.9
IRAN	74 799 000	1.2	70.8	1.6	22.6	8.3	85 344 000	330 399	4 520	0.8	2 578 336 000	0.0	...
IRAQ	32 665 000	2.2	66.2	4.5	43.4	5.2	83 357 000	74 885	2 340	...	...	4.6	6.4
IRELAND	4 526 000	1.8	61.9	2.1	20.6	18.8	6 038 000	182 474	40 720	...	...	...	0.6
ISRAEL	7 562 000	1.7	91.9	2.9	27.7	18.0	12 029 000	207 195	27 170	...	...	...	6.9
ITALY	60 789 000	0.5	68.4	1.5	14.2	32.6	59 158 000	2 125 845	35 150	...	...	...	1.7
JAMAICA	2 751 000	0.5	52.0	2.3	29.2	12.6	2 569 000	12 892	4 770	12.1	1 450 059 000	1.2	...
JAPAN	126 497 000	-0.1	66.8	1.4	13.3	36.6	108 549 000	5 369 116	42 130	...	...	...	1.0
JORDAN	6 330 000	3.0	78.5	2.9	35.9	6.0	9 882 000	26 520	4 390	2.3	584 689 000	3.0	5.5
KAZAKHSTAN	16 207 000	0.7	58.5	2.5	24.9	11.3	21 210 000	121 383	7 440	39.7	40 686 217 000	0.3	1.2
KENYA	41 610 000	2.6	22.2	4.6	42.1	4.5	96 887 000	31 810	790	1.3	382 036 000	6.1	1.9
KIRIBATI	101 000	1.5	43.9	...	...	...	156 000	200	2 010	...	...	15.6	...
KOSOVO	2 180 686	...	...	...	...	...	...	5 981	3 300	4.1	230 281 000	14.2	...
KUWAIT	2 818 000	2.4	98.4	2.3	24.0	3.9	5 164 000	116 969	47 790	...	...	...	4.1
KYRGYZSTAN	5 393 000	1.2	34.5	2.6	28.9	7.0	7 768 000	4 701	880	8.0	361 389 000	7.0	...
LAOS	6 288 000	1.8	33.2	2.5	33.2	6.2	8 384 000	6 474	1 040	4.1	242 022 000	7.1	...
LATVIA	2 243 000	-0.5	67.7	1.5	13.9	27.1	1 902 000	26 056	11 620	...	...	...	2.6
LEBANON	4 259 000	0.8	87.2	1.8	24.6	11.4	4 678 000	38 374	9 080	12.4	4 242 798 000	1.9	4.1
LESOTHO	2 194 000	0.9	26.9	3.1	39.0	7.2	2 788 000	2 248	1 040	1.7	37 656 000	5.4	2.6
LIBERIA	4 129 000	4.1	47.8	5.0	42.3	4.5	9 660 000	782	200	8.7	63 956 000	69.9	0.8
LIBYA	6 423 000	2.0	77.9	2.4	29.5	6.9	8 773 000	77 140	12 320	...	...	0.1	...
LIECHTENSTEIN	36 000	0.8	14.3	...	...	...	45 000	4 903	137 070	...	...	...	...
LITHUANIA	3 307 000	-1.0	67.0	1.5	15.2	25.2	2 813 000	37 838	11 390	17.4	6 528 064 000	...	1.7
LUXEMBOURG	516 000	1.2	85.2	1.7	18.2	23.3	708 000	40 281	79 630	...	...	...	...
MACEDONIA (F.Y.R.O.M.)	2 064 000	0.1	59.3	1.4	17.8	18.9	1 881 000	9 319	4 520	6.0	551 454 000	2.1	2.1
MADAGASCAR	21 315 000	2.7	30.2	4.5	44.3	5.3	53 561 000	8 820	430	0.5	45 446 000	5.3	...
MALAWI	15 381 000	2.8	19.8	6.0	43.5	5.0	49 719 000	4 886	330	0.8	35 789 000	16.6	...
MALAYSIA	28 859 000	1.7	72.2	2.6	30.9	8.4	43 455 000	220 417	7 760	5.9	11 069 598 000	0.1	2.0
MALDIVES	320 000	1.4	40.1	1.7	26.8	7.6	405 000	1 340	4 240	5.5	69 196 000	2.6	...
MALI	15 840 000	2.4	35.9	6.1	54.4	4.3	42 130 000	9 146	600	0.9	80 515 000	11.5	2.0
MALTA	418 000	0.4	94.7	1.3	15.2	24.9	415 000	7 957	18 430	...	...	...	0.6
MARSHALL ISLANDS	55 000	1.6	71.8	1.8	19.4	23.9	...	187	3 450	...	...	32.1	...
MAURITANIA	3 542 000	2.4	89.0	4.4	40.4	4.7	7 085 000	3 571	1 030	2.5	77 665 000	9.3	3.8
MAURITIUS	1 307 000	0.7	41.4	1.6	21.9	12.4	1 367 000	9 925	7 750	1.4	125 216 000	1.7	...
MEXICO	114 793 000	1.0	77.8	4.2	29.8	10.6	143 925 000	1 012 316	8 930	4.6	39 953 214 000	0.0	0.5
MICRONESIA, FED. STATES OF	112 000	0.3	22.7	2.2	36.6	6.6	139 000	300	2 700	...	...	40.9	...
MOLDOVA	3 545 000	-1.0	47.0	3.3	16.7	18.1	2 661 000	6 456	1 810	6.7	386 689 000	4.3	0.5
MONACO	35 000	0.0	100.0	1.5	...	...	36 000	6 479	183 150	...	...	...	...
MONGOLIA	2 800 000	1.2	62.0	2.4	28.2	6.7	4 093 000	5 106	1 850	2.6	111 873 000	8.5	...
MONTENEGRO	632 000	0.0	61.5	1.6	19.4	20.2	604 000	4 183	6 620	1.7	70 697 000	1.8	1.4
MOROCCO	32 273 000	1.2	58.2	2.2	27.6	8.9	39 200 000	94 053	2 900	3.8	3 410 754 000	1.0	3.3
MOZAMBIQUE	23 930 000	2.3	38.4	4.7	44.1	5.5	50 192 000	10 344	440	0.5	43 317 000	20.8	0.9
MYANMAR	48 337 000	0.9	33.6	1.9	24.4	8.2	55 296 000	...	...	...	28 931 000	...	...
NAMIBIA	2 324 000	1.9	38.0	3.1	37.6	6.4	3 599 000	10 286	4 500	...	...	3.6	3.3
NAURU	10 000	0.6	100.0	...	...	...	11 000	...	...	...	...	...	...
NEPAL	30 486 000	1.9	18.6	2.6	36.3	6.8	46 495 000	14 529	480	1.4	176 553 000	6.6	1.5
NETHERLANDS	16 665 000	0.4	82.9	1.8	17.7	25.6	17 151 000	826 491	49 750	...	...	...	1.5
NEW ZEALAND	4 415 000	0.9	86.2	2.1	20.8	22.1	5 678 000	124 176	29 050	...	...	...	1.1
NICARAGUA	5 870 000	1.3	57.3	2.5	34.3	7.2	7 846 000	6 282	1 090	8.3	491 894 000	13.0	0.7
NIGER	16 069 000	3.9	17.1	6.9	47.8	3.9	55 435 000	5 689	370	0.9	44 660 000	9.0	...
NIGERIA	162 471 000	2.3	49.8	5.4	42.9	5.7	389 615 000	186 406	1 180	0.3	509 515 000	1.0	0.9
NORTH KOREA	24 451 000	0.4	60.2	2.0	23.2	15.1	26 382 000	...	...	...	...	...	...
NORWAY	4 925 000	0.9	79.4	1.9	18.8	25.9	6 063 000	416 905	85 340	...	...	...	1.5

Social Indicators					Environment				Communications				
Child mortality rate	Life expectancy	Literacy rate (%)	Access to safe water (%)	Doctors per 100 000 people	Forest area (%)	Annual change in forest area (%)	Protected land area (%)	CO$_2$ emissions (metric tonnes per capita)	Main telephone lines per 100 people	Cellular phone subscribers per 100 people	Internet users per 10 000 people	International dialling code	Time zone
4.1	80.6	...	100	353	31.8	0.0	40	9.6	55.4	127.0	81.9	49	+1
74.4	64.7	66.6	82	9	21.7	-2.2	14	0.4	1.1	71.5	8.6	233	GMT
4.1	80.1	97.2	100	604	30.3	0.8	5	8.8	45.8	108.2	44.4	30	+2
11.1	76.2	96.0	...	...	50.0	0.0	14	2.3	27.2	116.7	33.5	1 473	-4
31.8	71.5	74.5	94	...	34.1	-1.5	31	1.0	10.4	125.6	10.5	502	-6
129.9	54.8	39.5	71	10	26.6	-0.5	7	0.1	0.2	40.1	1.0	224	GMT
149.5	48.8	52.2	61	5	71.9	-0.5	16	0.2	0.3	39.2	2.5	245	GMT
30.4	70.3	...	94	...	77.2	0.0	5	2.0	19.9	73.6	29.9	592	-4
164.8	62.5	48.7	63	...	3.7	-0.8	0	0.2	0.5	40.0	8.4	509	-5
24.0	73.6	83.6	86	...	46.4	-2.2	18	1.2	8.8	125.1	11.1	504	-6
6.4	74.7	99.4	100	310	22.6	0.5	5	5.6	29.8	120.3	65.3	36	+1
2.4	82.0	...	100	393	0.3	3.3	10	7.5	63.7	108.7	95.0	354	GMT
62.7	66.0	62.8	88	60	23.0	0.2	5	1.4	2.9	61.4	7.5	91	+5.5
35.3	70.1	92.2	80	29	52.1	-0.7	14	1.7	15.8	91.7	9.1	62	+7 to +9
25.8	73.3	85.0	...	89	6.8	0.0	7	6.9	36.3	91.2	13.0	98	+3.5
38.6	70.2	78.1	79	69	1.9	0.0	0	3.4	5.1	75.8	5.6	964	+3
3.9	80.8	...	100	319	10.7	1.2	1	10.2	46.5	105.2	69.9	353	GMT
4.5	82.0	...	100	363	7.1	-0.1	19	9.3	44.2	133.1	67.2	972	+2
3.7	82.0	98.9	100	424	31.1	0.9	10	7.7	35.7	135.4	53.7	39	+1
23.8	73.5	86.4	94	85	31.1	-0.1	19	5.2	9.6	113.2	26.1	1 876	-5
3.2	83.7	...	100	206	68.5	0.0	16	9.8	31.9	95.4	80.0	81	+9
21.7	73.6	92.2	96	245	1.1	0.0	9	3.8	7.8	107.0	38.0	962	+2
33.2	67.6	99.7	95	380	1.2	-0.2	3	14.7	25.0	123.3	34.0	7	+5 to +6
84.7	58.0	87.0	59	14	6.1	-0.3	12	0.3	1.1	61.6	21.0	254	+3
48.6	...	...	...	30	14.8	0.0	22	0.3	4.1	10.1	9.0	686	+12 to +14
...	...	...	...	...	...	...	...	...	...	...	...	381	+1
11.1	74.8	93.9	99	179	0.3	2.4	2	35.2	20.7	160.8	38.3	965	+3
37.7	68.3	99.2	90	230	5.0	1.9	7	1.2	9.4	91.9	20.0	996	+6
53.8	67.9	72.7	57	27	68.2	-0.5	16	0.3	1.7	64.6	7.0	856	+7
9.6	73.8	99.8	99	299	53.9	0.3	18	3.4	23.6	102.4	68.4	371	+2
22.1	72.9	89.6	100	354	13.4	0.1	0	3.2	21.0	68.0	31.0	961	+2
85.0	49.1	89.7	85	5	1.4	0.5	0	...	1.8	32.2	3.9	266	+2
102.6	57.5	59.1	68	1	44.9	-0.7	18	0.2	0.2	39.3	0.1	231	GMT
16.9	75.1	88.9	...	190	0.1	0.0	0	9.5	19.3	171.5	14.0	218	+2
2.1	...	...	...	...	43.8	0.0	42	...	54.4	98.5	80.0	423	+1
6.5	72.8	99.7	...	366	34.5	0.4	4	4.5	22.1	147.2	62.1	370	+2
3.1	80.2	...	100	286	33.6	0.0	20	22.6	53.7	143.3	90.6	352	+1
11.7	75.1	97.1	100	255	39.6	0.5	5	5.5	20.1	104.5	51.9	389	+1
62.1	66.9	64.5	41	16	21.6	-0.5	3	0.1	0.8	39.8	1.7	261	+3
92.1	55.1	73.7	80	2	34.4	-1.0	15	0.1	1.1	20.4	2.3	265	+2
6.3	74.6	92.5	100	94	62.3	-0.4	18	7.2	16.1	121.3	55.3	60	+8
15.0	77.3	98.4	91	160	3.3	0.0	...	3.0	15.2	156.5	28.3	960	+5
178.1	52.1	26.2	56	5	10.2	-0.6	2	0.0	0.7	47.7	2.7	223	GMT
6.0	80.0	92.4	100	307	...	0.0	17	6.7	59.4	109.3	63.0	356	+1
26.3	80.6	...	94	56	72.2	0.0	3	1.9	8.1	7.0	3.6	692	+12
111.2	59.2	57.5	49	13	0.2	-2.0	1	0.6	2.1	79.3	3.0	222	GMT
15.1	73.6	87.9	99	106	17.2	0.1	4	3.1	29.8	91.7	24.9	230	+4
16.7	77.2	93.4	94	289	33.3	-0.2	11	4.3	17.5	80.6	31.0	52	-6 to -8
42.1	69.3	...	...	56	91.4	0.0	4	0.6	7.6	24.8	20.0	691	+10 to +11
19.0	69.8	98.5	90	267	11.7	1.2	1	1.3	32.5	88.6	40.0	373	+2
4.3	...	...	100	...	0.0	...	24	...	96.4	74.3	80.0	377	+1
31.6	68.9	97.5	76	276	7.0	-0.7	13	4.0	7.0	91.1	10.2	976	+8
8.0	74.9	...	98	199	40.4	0.0	13	...	26.8	185.3	52.0	382	+1
35.5	72.5	56.1	81	62	11.5	0.2	2	1.5	11.7	100.1	49.0	212	GMT
135.0	51.0	55.1	47	3	49.6	-0.5	16	0.1	0.4	30.9	4.2	258	+2
66.2	66.0	92.0	71	46	48.6	-1.0	6	0.3	1.3	1.2	0.2	95	+6.5
40.1	62.7	88.5	92	37	8.9	-1.0	14	1.4	6.7	67.2	6.5	264	+1
...	69.1	...	...	...	...	...	...	...	0.0	60.5	6.0	674	+12
49.5	80.9	59.1	88	21	25.4	0.0	17	0.1	2.8	30.7	6.8	977	+5.75
4.3	77.0	...	100	392	10.8	0.0	12	10.6	43.2	116.2	90.7	31	+1
6.0	80.8	...	100	238	31.4	-0.1	26	7.7	42.8	114.9	83.0	64	+12 to +12.75
26.9	74.4	78.0	85	37	25.9	-2.1	37	0.8	4.5	65.1	10.0	505	-6
143.3	55.3	28.7	48	2	1.0	-1.0	7	0.1	0.5	24.5	0.8	227	+1
142.9	52.5	60.8	58	40	9.9	-4.0	13	0.6	0.7	55.1	28.4	234	+1
33.2	69.1	100.0	100	329	47.1	-2.1	4	2.9	4.9	1.8	0.0	850	+9
3.4	81.3	...	100	408	32.9	0.8	14	9.1	34.9	113.1	93.4	47	+1

See page 196 for explanatory table and sources

	Population							Economy					
	Total population	Population change (%)	% urban	Total fertility	Population by age (%) 0 – 14	Population by age (%) 60 or over	2050 projected population	Total Gross National Income (GNI) (US$M)	GNI per capita (US$)	Debt service ratio (% GNI)	Total debt service (US$)	Aid receipts (% GNI)	Military spending (% GDP)
OMAN	2 846 000	2.1	73.0	2.1	26.0	4.5	3 740 000	49 512	18 260	...	...	0.5	8.6
PAKISTAN	176 745 000	2.2	35.9	3.2	...	...	274 875 000	182 537	1 050	2.1	3 431 784 000	1.7	3.0
PALAU	21 000	...	83.4	...	33.2	6.6	28 000	133	6 470	...	...	27.9	...
PANAMA	3 571 000	1.6	74.8	2.4	29.0	10.9	5 128 000	24 531	6 980	4.3	981 556 000	0.3	...
PAPUA NEW GUINEA	7 014 000	2.4	12.5	3.8	38.9	4.9	13 549 000	8 935	1 300	6.9	542 507 000	5.3	0.5
PARAGUAY	6 568 000	1.8	61.5	2.9	33.5	8.6	10 323 000	19 008	2 940	3.2	443 910 000	1.1	0.9
PERU	29 400 000	1.2	76.9	2.4	29.5	9.8	38 832 000	138 978	4 780	3.1	3 782 964 000	0.4	1.2
PHILIPPINES	94 852 000	1.8	48.9	3.1	35.3	6.1	154 939 000	192 238	2 060	5.9	9 880 555 000	0.2	0.8
POLAND	38 299 000	-0.1	61.0	1.4	14.9	22.8	34 906 000	474 045	12 410	...	...	...	2.0
PORTUGAL	10 690 000	0.4	60.7	1.3	15.0	28.1	9 379 000	232 590	21 850	...	...	...	2.0
QATAR	1 870 000	10.7	95.8	2.2	15.7	2.3	2 612 000	...	...	...	...	...	...
ROMANIA	21 436 000	-0.4	57.5	1.4	15.4	23.7	18 535 000	168 208	7 840	10.0	16 333 827 000	...	1.4
RUSSIAN FEDERATION	142 836 000	-0.4	73.2	1.5	15.3	21.1	126 188 000	1 404 179	9 910	5.7	67 360 225 000	...	4.4
RWANDA	10 943 000	2.7	18.9	5.3	44.1	4.8	26 003 000	5 537	520	0.5	25 889 000	17.9	1.4
ST KITTS AND NEVIS	53 000	1.2	32.4	...	...	...	68 000	499	9 520	8.4	41 233 000	1.1	...
ST LUCIA	176 000	1.0	28.0	1.9	25.9	11.1	205 000	865	4 970	5.1	44 245 000	4.7	...
ST VINCENT AND THE GRENADINES	109 000	0.1	49.3	2.0	26.6	11.0	113 000	530	4 850	5.6	31 252 000	5.5	...
SAMOA	184 000	0.0	20.2	3.8	38.7	8.4	219 000	524	2 860	1.8	8 461 000	16.1	...
SAN MARINO	32 000	0.6	94.1	...	...	...	34 000	15 724	50 400	...	...	...	...
SÃO TOMÉ AND PRÍNCIPE	169 000	1.6	62.2	3.5	40.4	5.9	299 000	199	1 200	1.8	3 477 000	16.0	...
SAUDI ARABIA	28 083 000	2.1	82.1	2.6	31.7	5.3	44 938 000	434 119	16 190	...	...	...	11.1
SENEGAL	12 768 000	2.6	42.4	4.6	42.2	3.9	28 607 000	13 533	1 090	1.6	200 462 000	8.0	...
SERBIA	7 306 677	0.0	56.1	1.6	17.6	22.8	8 797 000	42 394	5 810	11.4	4 650 348 000	1.5	2.3
SEYCHELLES	87 000	...	55.3	...	...	...	91 000	845	9 760	9.0	62 834 000	3.3	0.8
SIERRA LEONE	5 997 000	2.7	38.4	4.7	43.2	3.7	11 088 000	2 009	340	0.4	7 271 000	24.3	...
SINGAPORE	5 188 000	2.5	100.0	1.4	18.3	16.6	6 106 000	210 326	41 430	...	...	...	4.2
SLOVAKIA	5 472 000	0.1	55.0	1.4	15.3	20.2	5 241 000	88 051	16 210	...	...	...	1.5
SLOVENIA	2 035 000	0.2	49.5	1.5	13.9	26.6	1 994 000	49 276	24 000	...	...	...	1.7
SOLOMON ISLANDS	552 000	2.5	18.6	4.0	39.9	5.4	1 163 000	552	1 030	2.1	9 953 000	43.5	...
SOMALIA	9 557 000	2.3	37.4	6.3	44.8	4.6	28 217 000	...	...	...	...	...	...
SOUTH AFRICA, REPUBLIC OF	50 460 000	1.0	61.7	2.4	29.9	7.9	56 757 000	304 591	6 090	2.8	7 651 085 000	0.4	1.4
SOUTH KOREA	48 391 000	0.4	83.0	1.4	16.3	17.6	47 050 000	972 299	19 890	...	...	...	2.9
SOUTH SUDAN*	8 260 490	...	...	...	...	...	...	...	...	...	...	...	...
SPAIN	46 455 000	1.0	77.4	1.5	15.2	27.7	51 354 000	1 462 894	31 750	...	...	...	1.3
SRI LANKA	21 045 000	0.9	14.3	2.2	25.4	14.1	23 193 000	46 738	2 240	3.4	1 417 751 000	1.7	3.5
SUDAN	36 371 510	2.2	40.1	4.2	40.4	6.1	90 962 000	55 277	1 270	1.0	482 524 000	4.6	...
SURINAME	529 000	1.0	69.4	2.3	28.6	10.4	614 000	3 076	5 920	...	...	4.8	...
SWAZILAND	1 203 000	1.3	21.4	3.2	37.9	5.6	1 679 000	3 119	2 630	1.6	44 229 000	2.1	...
SWEDEN	9 441 000	0.5	84.7	1.9	16.7	30.5	10 916 000	469 002	50 000	...	...	...	1.3
SWITZERLAND	7 702 000	0.4	73.6	1.5	15.4	27.8	7 870 000	548 012	70 030	...	...	...	0.8
SYRIA	20 766 000	3.3	55.7	2.8	33.5	5.9	33 051 000	57 003	2 790	1.2	642 558 000	0.5	4.0
TAIWAN	23 164 000	...	...	...	...	...	...	...	...	...	...	...	...
TAJIKISTAN	6 977 000	1.6	26.3	3.2	36.0	5.4	10 745 000	5 512	800	9.6	470 582 000	8.3	...
TANZANIA	46 218 000	2.9	26.4	5.5	44.5	5.2	138 312 000	23 366	530	0.8	164 202 000	13.7	1.0
THAILAND	69 519 000	0.7	34.0	1.5	20.8	14.8	71 037 000	286 676	4 150	5.0	12 623 339 000	0.0	1.8
TOGO	6 155 000	2.5	43.4	3.9	35.3	5.0	11 130 000	2 957	490	2.0	55 471 000	17.7	...
TONGA	105 000	0.5	23.4	3.8	37.5	9.3	138 000	353	3 390	1.2	3 832 000	11.9	...
TRINIDAD AND TOBAGO	1 346 000	0.4	13.9	1.6	20.6	11.9	1 288 000	20 664	15 400	...	...	0.0	...
TUNISIA	10 594 000	1.0	67.3	1.9	23.7	11.2	12 649 000	42 826	4 060	5.1	2 104 138 000	1.1	1.2
TURKEY	73 640 000	1.2	69.6	2.0	25.3	9.5	91 617 000	719 404	9 890	10.2	61 578 858 000	0.2	2.8
TURKMENISTAN	5 105 000	1.3	49.5	2.3	28.5	6.7	6 639 000	19 159	3 800	1.0	168 286 000	0.2	...
TUVALU	10 000	0.2	50.4	...	...	...	13 000	36	3 700	...	...	43.7	...
UGANDA	34 509 000	3.3	13.3	5.9	47.9	4.2	94 259 000	16 553	500	0.5	71 119 000	11.5	2.2
UKRAINE	45 190 000	-0.7	68.8	1.5	14.2	24.1	36 074 000	137 917	3 010	18.6	21 288 472 000	0.6	2.9
UNITED ARAB EMIRATES	7 891 000	2.8	84.1	1.7	27.2	1.8	12 152 000	290 912	28 340	...	...	...	...
UNITED KINGDOM	62 417 000	0.5	79.6	1.9	17.4	27.3	72 817 000	2 399 292	38 560	...	...	...	2.7
UNITED STATES OF AMERICA	313 085 000	1.0	82.3	2.1	19.6	21.7	403 101 000	14 600 828	47 240	...	...	...	4.7
URUGUAY	3 380 000	0.3	92.5	2.0	22.5	21.9	3 663 000	35 557	10 590	6.2	1 905 584 000	0.2	1.6
UZBEKISTAN	27 760 000	1.1	36.2	2.3	29.0	7.0	35 438 000	36 086	1 280	1.9	618 124 000	0.6	...
VANUATU	246 000	2.5	25.6	3.8	...	...	513 000	662	2 760	1.0	5 623 000	17.4	...
VATICAN CITY	800	0.1	100.0	...	37.3	5.7	< 1 000	...	...	...	...	...	...
VENEZUELA	29 437 000	1.7	93.4	2.4	29.4	9.6	41 821 000	334 113	11 590	1.2	3 963 814 000	0.0	1.3
VIETNAM	88 792 000	1.2	30.4	1.8	23.3	9.5	103 962 000	96 899	1 110	1.2	1 139 404 000	4.1	2.2
YEMEN	24 800 000	2.9	31.8	4.9	43.9	4.4	61 577 000	25 008	1 070	1.1	261 525 000	2.0	...
ZAMBIA	13 475 000	2.4	35.7	6.3	45.8	5.0	45 037 000	13 816	1 070	1.5	171 340 000	11.1	1.7
ZIMBABWE	12 754 000	0.3	38.3	3.1	38.6	6.6	20 614 000	5 841	460	1.9	101 008 000	13.7	...

* See Sudan for figures prior to formation of independent state

Social Indicators					Environment				Communications				
Child mortality rate	Life expectancy	Literacy rate (%)	Access to safe water (%)	Doctors per 100 000 people	Forest area (%)	Annual change in forest area (%)	Protected land area (%)	CO_2 emissions (metric tonnes per capita)	Main telephone lines per 100 people	Cellular phone subscribers per 100 people	Internet users per 10 000 people	International dialling code	Time zone
9.3	73.4	86.6	88	190	0.0	0.0	11	14.6	10.2	165.5	62.6	968	+4
86.5	65.8	55.5	90	81	2.2	-2.4	10	1.0	2.0	59.2	16.8	92	+5
19.0	...	...	...	130	87.0	0.0	2	10.6	34.1	70.9	27.0	680	+9
20.2	76.4	93.6	93	...	43.7	-0.4	19	2.2	15.7	184.7	42.8	507	-5
60.8	63.3	60.1	40	5	63.4	-0.5	3	0.5	1.8	27.8	1.3	675	+10
24.6	72.8	94.6	86	...	44.3	-1.0	5	0.7	6.3	91.6	23.6	595	-4
19.2	74.3	89.6	82	92	53.1	-0.2	14	1.5	10.9	100.1	34.3	51	-5
29.4	69.2	95.4	91	115	25.7	0.7	11	0.8	7.3	85.7	25.0	63	+8
6.0	76.4	99.5	100	214	30.7	0.3	22	8.3	24.7	120.2	62.3	48	+1
3.7	79.8	94.9	99	376	37.8	0.1	6	5.5	42.0	142.3	51.1	351	GMT
8.2	78.5	94.7	100	276	0.0	...	1	53.5	17.0	132.4	69.0	974	+3
13.6	77.8	97.7	...	192	28.6	0.6	7	4.4	20.9	114.7	39.9	40	+2
11.6	74.3	99.6	96	431	49.4	0.0	9	10.8	31.5	166.3	43.0	7	+3 to +12
91.1	69.2	70.7	65	2	17.6	2.5	10	0.1	0.4	33.4	7.7	250	+2
8.0	55.8	...	99	...	42.3	0.0	4	4.9	39.3	161.4	32.9	1 869	-4
15.9	74.9	...	98	...	77.0	0.0	14	2.3	23.6	102.9	36.0	1 758	-4
21.2	72.6	...	...	...	69.2	0.3	11	1.8	19.9	120.5	69.6	1 784	-4
20.2	72.8	98.8	...	27	60.4	0.0	...	0.9	19.3	91.4	7.0	685	+13
1.9	...	...	...	...	0.0	...	...	...	68.8	76.1	54.2	378	+1
79.9	65.0	88.8	89	49	28.1	0.0	11	0.8	4.6	62.0	18.8	239	GMT
17.5	74.2	86.1	...	94	0.5	0.0	31	15.8	15.2	187.9	41.0	966	+3
75.2	59.8	49.7	69	6	44.0	-0.5	24	0.5	2.8	67.1	16.0	221	GMT
7.1	74.7	...	99	204	30.7	1.9	6	...	40.5	129.2	40.9	381	+1
13.5	...	91.8	...	151	89.1	0.0	42	7.3	25.5	135.9	41.0	248	+4
174.0	48.2	40.9	49	2	38.1	-0.7	5	0.2	0.2	34.1	0.3	232	GMT
2.6	81.3	94.7	100	183	2.9	0.0	5	11.8	39.0	143.7	70.0	65	+8
8.2	75.8	...	100	300	40.2	0.0	23	6.8	20.1	108.5	79.4	421	+1
2.9	79.5	99.7	99	247	62.2	0.2	12	7.5	45.0	104.5	70.0	386	+1
26.7	68.4	...	...	19	79.1	-0.3	0	0.4	1.6	5.6	5.0	677	+11
180.0	51.7	...	30	4	10.8	-1.1	1	0.1	1.1	6.9	1.2	252	+3
56.6	53.8	88.7	91	77	4.7	0.0	7	9.0	8.4	100.5	12.3	27	+2
4.9	80.7	...	98	197	64.2	-0.1	2	10.4	59.2	105.4	83.7	82	+9
...	...	...	...	...	...	...	...	...	...	...	...	211	+3
4.8	81.8	97.7	100	371	36.4	1.0	9	8.0	43.2	111.8	66.5	34	+1
16.5	75.2	90.6	90	49	29.7	-0.8	21	0.6	17.2	83.2	12.0	94	+5.5
103.3	62.0	70.2	57	28	29.4	-0.1	5	0.3	0.9	40.5	10.2	249	+3
30.5	70.9	94.6	93	...	94.6	0.0	11	4.8	16.2	169.6	31.6	597	-3
77.7	49.2	86.9	69	16	32.7	0.8	3	0.9	3.7	61.8	8.0	268	+2
3.0	81.7	...	100	358	68.7	0.0	11	5.4	53.5	113.5	90.0	46	+1
4.6	82.5	...	100	407	31.0	0.4	23	5.0	58.6	123.6	83.9	41	+1
16.0	76.1	84.2	89	150	2.7	1.3	1	3.6	19.9	57.3	20.7	963	+2
...	...	...	...	...	...	...	...	...	70.8	119.9	71.5	886	+8
62.6	67.9	99.7	70	201	2.9	0.0	4	1.1	5.4	86.4	11.6	992	+5
75.8	59.3	72.9	54	1	37.7	-1.2	28	0.1	0.4	46.8	11.0	255	+3
13.0	74.4	93.5	98	30	37.1	0.1	20	4.1	10.1	100.8	21.2	66	+7
103.4	57.8	56.9	60	5	5.3	-5.8	11	0.2	3.6	40.7	5.4	228	GMT
15.6	72.5	99.0	100	...	12.5	0.0	15	1.7	29.8	52.2	12.0	676	+13
27.1	70.4	98.7	94	118	44.1	-0.3	31	27.9	21.9	141.2	48.5	1 868	-4
16.1	74.8	77.6	94	119	6.5	1.7	1	2.3	12.3	106.0	36.8	216	+1
17.6	74.3	90.8	99	164	14.7	1.1	2	4.1	22.3	84.9	39.8	90	+2
55.5	65.2	99.6	...	244	8.8	0.0	3	9.4	10.3	63.4	2.2	993	+5
32.5	...	...	97	64	33.3	0.0	0	...	16.5	25.4	25.0	688	+12
98.9	54.7	...	67	12	15.2	-2.7	10	0.1	1.0	38.4	12.5	256	+3
13.2	69.0	99.7	98	313	16.8	0.3	4	6.8	28.5	118.7	23.0	380	+2
7.1	76.8	90.0	100	193	3.8	0.3	6	25.1	19.7	145.5	78.0	971	+4
5.4	80.4	...	100	274	11.9	0.3	24	8.8	53.7	130.2	85.0	44	GMT
7.5	78.8	...	99	267	33.2	0.1	15	19.3	48.7	89.9	79.0	1	-5 to -10
10.8	77.3	98.3	100	374	10.0	2.8	0	1.9	28.6	131.7	43.4	598	-3
51.5	68.8	99.3	87	262	7.7	-0.1	2	4.3	6.8	76.3	20.0	998	+5
13.9	71.4	82.0	83	12	36.1	0.0	4	0.5	2.1	119.1	8.0	678	+11
...	...	...	...	...	0.0	0.0	...	...	...	...	...	39	+1
18.3	74.7	95.2	...	...	52.5	-0.6	54	6.0	24.4	96.2	35.6	58	-4.5
23.3	75.5	92.8	94	122	44.5	1.1	6	1.3	18.7	175.3	27.6	84	+7
77.0	66.1	62.4	62	30	1.0	0.0	1	1.0	4.4	46.1	10.9	967	+3
111.0	49.7	70.9	60	6	66.5	-0.3	36	0.2	0.7	37.8	6.7	260	+2
79.8	53.5	91.9	82	16	40.4	-2.0	28	0.8	3.0	59.7	11.5	263	+2

Definitions

Indicator	Definition
Population	
Total population	Interpolated mid-year population, 2011.
Population change	Percentage average annual rate of change, 2010–2015.
% urban	Urban population as a percentage of the total population, 2010.
Total fertility	Average number of children a woman will have during her child-bearing years, 2010–2015.
Population by age	Percentage of population in age groups 0–14 and 60 or over, 2010.
2050 projected population	Projected total population for the year 2050.
Economy	
Total Gross National Income (GNI)	The sum of value added to the economy by all resident producers plus taxes, less subsidies, plus net receipts of primary income from abroad. Data are in U.S. dollars (millions), 2010 or latest available. Formerly known as Gross National Product (GNP).
GNI per capita	Gross National Income per person in U.S. dollars using the World Bank Atlas method, 2010 or latest available.
Debt service ratio	Debt service as a percentage of GNI, 2009.
Total debt service	Sum of principal repayments and interest paid on long-term debt, interest paid on short-term debt and repayments to the International Monetary Fund (IMF), 2009.
Aid receipts	Aid received as a percentage of GNI from the Development Assistance Committee (DAC) countries of the Organization for Economic Co-operation and Development (OECD), 2009.
Military spending	Military-related spending, including recruiting, training, construction and the purchase of military supplies and equipment, as a percentage of Gross National Income, 2009.
Social Indicators	
Child mortality rate	Number of deaths of children aged under 5 per 1 000 live births, 2010.
Life expectancy	Average life expectancy, at birth in years, male and female, 2010–2015.
Literacy rate	Percentage of population aged 15 or over with at least a basic ability to read and write, 2009.
Access to safe water	Percentage of population using improved drinking water, 2008.
Doctors	Number of trained doctors per 100 000 people, 2009.
Environment	
Forest area	Percentage of total land area covered by forest, 2010.
Change in forest area	Average annual percentage change in forest area, 2005–2010.
Protected land area	Percentage of total land area designated as protected land, 2009.
CO_2 emissions	Emissions of carbon dioxide from the burning of fossil fuels and the manufacture of cement, divided by the population, expressed in metric tons per capita, 2007.
Communications	
Telephone lines	Main (fixed) telephone lines per 100 inhabitants, 2010.
Cellular phone subscribers	Cellular mobile subscribers per 100 inhabitants, 2010.
Internet users	Internet users per 10 000 inhabitants, 2010.
International dialling code	The country code prefix to be used when dialling from another country.
Time zone	Time difference in hours between local standard time and Greenwich Mean Time.

Main Statistical Sources	Internet Links
United Nations Department of Economic and Social Affairs (UDESA) World Population Prospects: The 2010 Revision. World Urbanization Prospects: The 2009 Revision.	www.un.org/esa/population/unpop
UNESCO Education Data Centre	stats.uis.unesco.org
UN Human Development Report 2011	hdr.undp.org
World Bank World Development Indicators online	www.worldbank.org/data
OECD: Development Co-operation Report 2011	www.oecd.org
UNICEF: The State of the World's Children 2011	www.unicef.org
Food and Agriculture Organization (FAO) of the UN: Global Forest Resources Assessment 2010	www.fao.org
World Resources Institute Biodiversity and Protected Areas Database	www.wri.org
International Telecommunications Union (ITU)	www.itu.int

World States and Territories

States and Territories

All 196 independent countries and all populated dependent and disputed territories are included in this list of the states and territories of the world; the list is arranged in alphabetical order by the conventional name form. For independent states, the full name is given below the conventional name, if this is different; for territories, the status is given. The capital city name is given in conventional English form with selected alternative, usually local, form in brackets.

Area and population statistics are the latest available and include estimates. The information on languages and religions is based on the latest information on 'de facto' speakers of the language or 'de facto' adherents of the religion. This varies greatly from country to country because some countries include questions in censuses while others do not, in which case best estimates are used. The order of the languages and religions reflects their relative importance within the country; generally, languages or religions are included when more than one per cent of the population are estimated to be speakers or adherents.

ABBREVIATIONS

CURRENCIES

CFA	Communauté Financière Africaine
CFP	Comptoirs Français du Pacifique

Membership of selected international organizations is shown by the abbreviations below; dependent territories do not normally have separate memberships of these organizations.

ORGANIZATIONS

APEC	Asia-Pacific Economic Cooperation
ASEAN	Association of Southeast Asian Nations
CARICOM	Caribbean Community
CIS	Commonwealth of Independent States
Comm.	The Commonwealth
EU	European Union
NATO	North Atlantic Treaty Organization
OECD	Organisation for Economic Co-operation and Development
OPEC	Organization of the Petroleum Exporting Countries
SADC	Southern African Development Community
UN	United Nations

Abkhazia
Disputed territory

Area Sq Km	8 700	Languages	Abkhaz, Russian, Georgian
Area Sq Miles	3 359	Religions	Abkhaz Orthodox Christianity, Sunni Muslim
Population	180 000		
Capital	Sokhumi (Aq"a)	Currency	Russian rouble, Abkhaz apsar

An autonomous republic within Georgia, Abkhazia has an active separatist movement seeking independence from Georgia. Although it is de jure part of Georgia, it effectively currently functions as an independent state with backing from the Russian Federation. This dispute has led to intermittent, but serious, armed conflict over the last twenty years. Abkhazia voted to separate from Georgia in 1992, a move rejected by Georgia and prompting a Georgian invasion. Abkhazian and Russian forces ousted Georgia and a cease-fire was established in 1994.

AFGHANISTAN
Islamic State of Afghanistan

Area Sq Km	652 225	Languages	Dari, Pushtu, Uzbek, Turkmen
Area Sq Miles	251 825	Religions	Sunni Muslim, Shi'a Muslim
Population	32 358 000	Currency	Afghani
Capital	Kābul	Organizations	UN

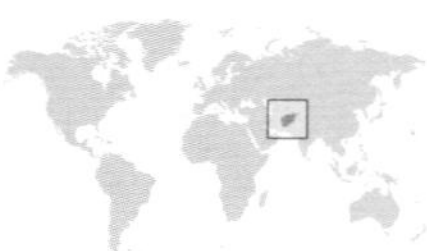

A landlocked country in central Asia with central highlands bordered by plains in the north and southwest, and by the Hindu Kush mountains in the northeast. The climate is dry continental. Over the last twenty-five years war has disrupted the economy, which is highly dependent on farming and livestock rearing. Most trade is with the former USSR, Pakistan and Iran.

ALBANIA
Republic of Albania

Area Sq Km	28 748	Languages	Albanian, Greek
Area Sq Miles	11 100	Religions	Sunni Muslim, Albanian Orthodox, Roman Catholic
Population	3 216 000	Currency	Lek
Capital	Tirana (Tiranë)	Organizations	NATO, UN

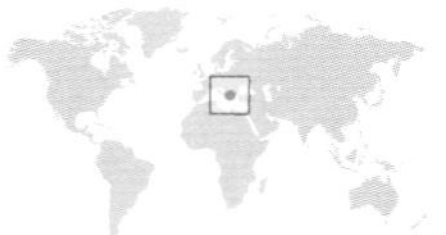

Albania lies in the western Balkan Mountains in southeastern Europe, bordering the Adriatic Sea. It is mountainous, with coastal plains where half the population lives. The economy is based on agriculture and mining. Albania is one of the poorest countries in Europe and relies heavily on foreign aid.

ALGERIA
People's Democratic Republic of Algeria

Area Sq Km	2 381 741	Languages	Arabic, French, Berber
Area Sq Miles	919 595	Religions	Sunni Muslim
Population	35 980 000	Currency	Algerian dinar
Capital	Algiers (Alger)	Organizations	OPEC, UN

Algeria, the largest country in Africa, lies on the Mediterranean coast of northwest Africa and extends southwards to the Atlas Mountains and the dry sandstone plateau and desert of the Sahara. The climate ranges from Mediterranean on the coast to semi-arid and arid inland. The most populated areas are the coastal plains and the fertile northern slopes of the Atlas Mountains. Oil, natural gas and related products account for over ninety-five per cent of export earnings. Agriculture employs about a quarter of the workforce, producing mainly food crops. Algeria's main trading partners are Italy, France and the USA.

American Samoa
United States Unincorporated Territory

Area Sq Km	197	Languages	Samoan, English
Area Sq Miles	76	Religions	Protestant, Roman Catholic
Population	70 000	Currency	United States dollar
Capital	Fagatogo		

Lying in the south Pacific Ocean, American Samoa consists of five main islands and two coral atolls. The largest island is Tutuila. Tuna and tuna products are the main exports, and the main trading partner is the USA.

ANDORRA
Principality of Andorra

Area Sq Km	465	Languages	Spanish, Catalan, French
Area Sq Miles	180	Religions	Roman Catholic
Population	86 000	Currency	Euro
Capital	Andorra la Vella	Organizations	UN

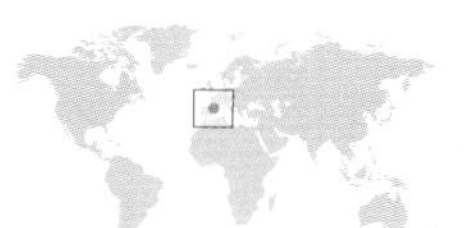

A landlocked state in southwest Europe, Andorra lies in the Pyrenees mountain range between France and Spain. It consists of deep valleys and gorges, surrounded by mountains. Tourism, encouraged by the development of ski resorts, is the mainstay of the economy. Banking is also an important economic activity.

ANGOLA
Republic of Angola

Area Sq Km	1 246 700	Languages	Portuguese, Bantu, local languages
Area Sq Miles	481 354	Religions	Roman Catholic, Protestant, traditional beliefs
Population	19 618 000	Currency	Kwanza
Capital	Luanda	Organizations	OPEC, SADC, UN

Angola lies on the Atlantic coast of south central Africa. Its small northern province, Cabinda, is separated from the rest of the country by part of the Democratic Republic of the Congo. Much of Angola is high plateau. In the west is a narrow coastal plain and in the southwest is desert. The climate is equatorial in the north but desert in the south. Over eighty per cent of the population relies on subsistence agriculture. Angola is rich in minerals (particularly diamonds), and oil accounts for approximately ninety per cent of export earnings. The USA, South Korea and Portugal are its main trading partners.

Anguilla
United Kingdom Overseas Territory

Area Sq Km	155	Languages	English
Area Sq Miles	60	Religions	Protestant, Roman Catholic
Population	16 000	Currency	East Caribbean dollar
Capital	The Valley		

Anguilla lies at the northern end of the Leeward Islands in the eastern Caribbean. Tourism and fishing form the basis of the economy.

ANTIGUA AND BARBUDA

Area Sq Km	442	Languages	English, Creole
Area Sq Miles	171	Religions	Protestant, Roman Catholic
Population	90 000	Currency	East Caribbean dollar
Capital	St John's	Organizations	CARICOM, Comm., UN

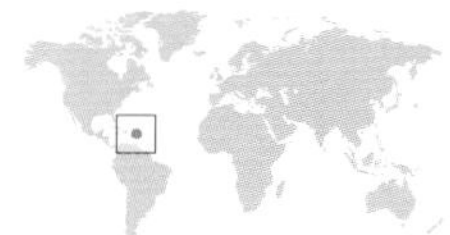

The state comprises the islands of Antigua, Barbuda and the tiny rocky outcrop of Redonda, in the Leeward Islands in the eastern Caribbean. Antigua, the largest and most populous island, is mainly hilly scrubland, with many beaches. The climate is tropical, and the economy relies heavily on tourism. Most trade is with other eastern Caribbean states and the USA.

ARGENTINA
Argentine Republic

Area Sq Km	2 766 889	Languages	Spanish, Italian, Amerindian languages
Area Sq Miles	1 068 302	Religions	Roman Catholic, Protestant
Population	40 765 000	Currency	Argentinian peso
Capital	Buenos Aires	Organizations	UN

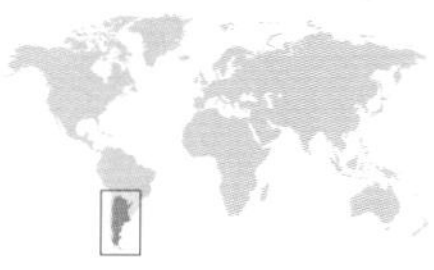

Argentina, the second largest state in South America, extends from Bolivia to Cape Horn and from the Andes mountains to the Atlantic Ocean. It has four geographical regions: subtropical forests and swampland in the northeast; temperate fertile plains or Pampas in the centre; the wooded foothills and valleys of the Andes in the west; and the cold, semi-arid plateaus of Patagonia in the south. The highest mountain in South America, Cerro Aconcagua, is in Argentina. Nearly ninety per cent of the population lives in towns and cities. The country is rich in natural resources including petroleum, natural gas, ores and precious metals. Agricultural products dominate exports, which also include motor vehicles and crude oil. Most trade is with Brazil and the USA.

ARMENIA
Republic of Armenia

Area Sq Km	29 800	Languages	Armenian, Azeri
Area Sq Miles	11 506	Religions	Armenian Orthodox
Population	3 100 000	Currency	Dram
Capital	Yerevan (Erevan)	Organizations	CIS, UN

A landlocked state in southwest Asia, Armenia lies in the south of the Lesser Caucasus mountains. It is a mountainous country with a continental climate. One-third of the population lives in the capital, Yerevan. Exports include diamonds, scrap metal and machinery. Many Armenians depend on remittances from abroad.

Aruba
Self-governing Netherlands Territory

Area Sq Km	193	Languages	Papiamento, Dutch, English
Area Sq Miles	75	Religions	Roman Catholic, Protestant
Population	108 000	Currency	Aruban florin
Capital	Oranjestad		

The most southwesterly of the islands in the Lesser Antilles in the Caribbean, Aruba lies just off the coast of Venezuela. Tourism, offshore finance and oil refining are the most important sectors of the economy. The USA is the main trading partner.

AUSTRALIA
Commonwealth of Australia

Area Sq Km	7 692 024	Languages	English, Italian, Greek
Area Sq Miles	2 969 907	Religions	Protestant, Roman Catholic, Orthodox
Population	22 606 000	Currency	Australian dollar
Capital	Canberra	Organizations	APEC, Comm., OECD, UN

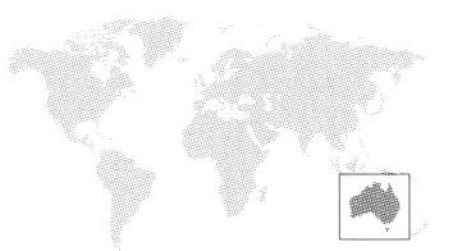

Australia, the world's sixth largest country, occupies the smallest, flattest and driest continent. The western half of the continent is mostly arid plateaus, ridges and vast deserts. The central eastern area comprises the lowlands of river systems draining into Lake Eyre, while to the east is the Great Dividing Range, a belt of ridges and plateaus running from Queensland to Tasmania. Climatically, more than two-thirds of the country is arid or semi-arid. The north is tropical monsoon, the east subtropical, and the southwest and southeast temperate. The majority of Australia's highly urbanized population lives along the east, southeast and southwest coasts. Australia has vast mineral deposits and various sources of energy. It is among the world's leading producers of iron ore, bauxite, nickel, copper and uranium. It is a major producer of coal, and oil and natural gas are also being exploited. Although accounting for only five per cent of the workforce, agriculture continues to be an important sector of the economy, with food and agricultural raw materials making up most of Australia's export earnings. Fuel, ores and metals, and manufactured goods, account for the remainder of exports. Japan and the USA are Australia's main trading partners.

Australian Capital Territory (Federal Territory)
Area Sq Km (Sq Miles) 2 358 (910) Population 359 700 Capital Canberra

Jervis Bay Territory (Territory)
Area Sq Km (Sq Miles) 73 (28) Population 611

New South Wales (State)
Area Sq Km (Sq Miles) 800 642 (309 130) Population 7 253 400 Capital Sydney

Northern Territory (Territory)
Area Sq Km (Sq Miles) 1 349 129 (520 902) Population 230 200 Capital Darwin

Queensland (State)
Area Sq Km (Sq Miles) 1 730 648 (668 207) Population 4 532 300 Capital Brisbane

South Australia (State)
Area Sq Km (Sq Miles) 983 482 (379 725) Population 1 647 800 Capital Adelaide

Tasmania (State)
Area Sq Km (Sq Miles) 68 401 (26 410) Population 508 500 Capital Hobart

Victoria (State)
Area Sq Km (Sq Miles) 227 416 (87 806) Population 5 567 100 Capital Melbourne

Western Australia (State)
Area Sq Km (Sq Miles) 2 529 875 (976 790) Population 2 306 200 Capital Perth

AUSTRIA
Republic of Austria

Area Sq Km	83 855	Languages	German, Croatian, Turkish
Area Sq Miles	32 377	Religions	Roman Catholic, Protestant
Population	8 413 000	Currency	Euro
Capital	Vienna (Wien)	Organizations	EU, OECD, UN

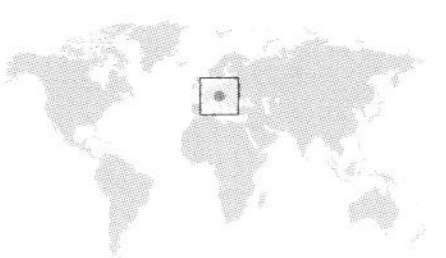

Two-thirds of Austria, a landlocked state in central Europe, lies within the Alps, with lower mountains to the north. The only lowlands are in the east. The Danube river valley in the northeast contains almost all the agricultural land and most of the population. Although the climate varies with altitude, in general summers are warm and winters cold with heavy snowfalls. Manufacturing industry and tourism are the most important sectors of the economy. Exports are dominated by manufactured goods. Germany is Austria's main trading partner.

AZERBAIJAN
Republic of Azerbaijan

Area Sq Km	86 600	Languages	Azeri, Armenian, Russian, Lezgian
Area Sq Miles	33 436	Religions	Shi'a Muslim, Sunni Muslim, Russian and Armenian Orthodox
Population	9 306 000	Currency	Azerbaijani manat
Capital	Baku	Organizations	CIS, UN

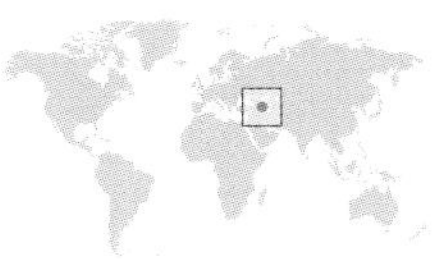

Azerbaijan lies to the southeast of the Caucasus mountains, on the Caspian Sea. Its region of Naxçıvan is separated from the rest of the country by part of Armenia. It has mountains in the northeast and west, valleys in the centre, and a low coastal plain. The climate is continental. It is rich in energy and mineral resources. Oil production, onshore and offshore, is the main industry and the basis of heavy industries. Agriculture is important, with cotton and tobacco the main cash crops.

THE BAHAMAS
Commonwealth of The Bahamas

Area Sq Km	13 939	Languages	English, Creole
Area Sq Miles	5 382	Religions	Protestant, Roman Catholic
Population	347 000	Currency	Bahamian dollar
Capital	Nassau	Organizations	CARICOM, Comm., UN

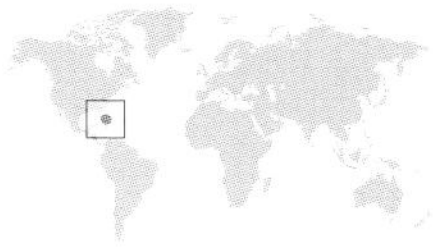

The Bahamas, an archipelago made up of approximately seven hundred islands and over two thousand cays, lies to the northeast of Cuba and east of the Florida coast of the USA. Twenty-two islands are inhabited, and two-thirds of the population lives on the main island of New Providence. The climate is warm for much of the year, with heavy rainfall in the summer. Tourism is the islands' main industry. Offshore banking, insurance and ship registration are also major foreign exchange earners.

BAHRAIN
Kingdom of Bahrain

Area Sq Km	691	Languages	Arabic, English
Area Sq Miles	267	Religions	Shi'a Muslim, Sunni Muslim, Christian
Population	1 324 000	Currency	Bahraini dinar
Capital	Manama (Al Manāmah)	Organizations	UN

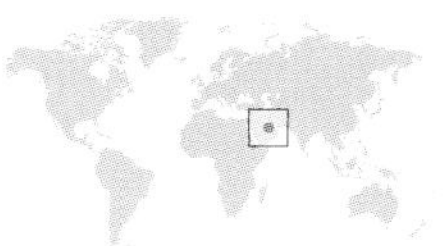

Bahrain consists of more than thirty islands lying in a bay in The Gulf, off the coasts of Saudi Arabia and Qatar. Bahrain Island, the largest island, is connected to other islands and to the mainland of Arabia by causeways. Oil production and processing are the main sectors of the economy.

BANGLADESH
People's Republic of Bangladesh

Area Sq Km	143 998	Languages	Bengali, English
Area Sq Miles	55 598	Religions	Sunni Muslim, Hindu
Population	150 494 000	Currency	Taka
Capital	Dhaka (Dacca)	Organizations	Comm., UN

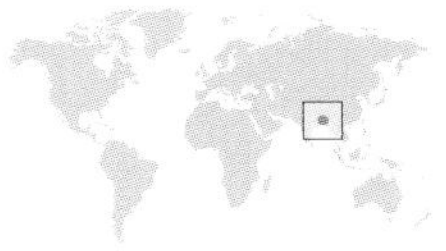

The south Asian state of Bangladesh is in the northeast of the Indian subcontinent, on the Bay of Bengal. It consists almost entirely of the low-lying alluvial plains and deltas of the Ganges and Brahmaputra rivers. The southwest is swampy, with mangrove forests in the delta area. The north, northeast and southeast have low forested hills. Bangladesh is one of the world's most densely populated and least developed countries. The economy is based on agriculture, though the garment industry is the main export sector. Storms during the summer monsoon season often cause devastating flooding and crop destruction. The country relies on large-scale foreign aid and remittances from workers abroad.

BARBADOS

Area Sq Km	430	Languages	English, Creole
Area Sq Miles	166	Religions	Protestant, Roman Catholic
Population	274 000	Currency	Barbados dollar
Capital	Bridgetown	Organizations	CARICOM, Comm., UN

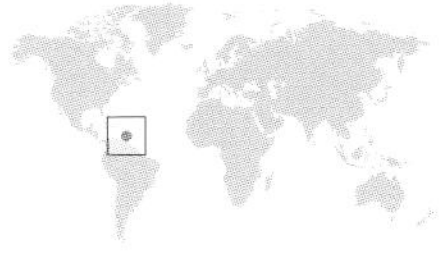

The most easterly of the Caribbean islands, Barbados is small and densely populated. It has a tropical climate and is subject to hurricanes. The economy is based on tourism, financial services, light industries and sugar production.

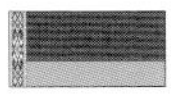

BELARUS
Republic of Belarus

Area Sq Km	207 600	Languages	Belorussian, Russian
Area Sq Miles	80 155	Religions	Belorussian Orthodox, Roman Catholic
Population	9 559 000	Currency	Belarus rouble
Capital	Minsk	Organizations	CIS, UN

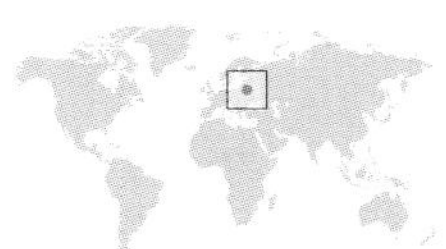

Belarus, a landlocked state in eastern Europe, consists of low hills and plains, with many lakes, rivers and, in the south, extensive marshes. Forests cover approximately one-third of the country. It has a continental climate. Agriculture contributes one-third of national income, with beef cattle and grains as the major products. Manufacturing industries produce a range of items, from construction equipment to textiles. The Russian Federation and Ukraine are the main trading partners.

BELGIUM
Kingdom of Belgium

Area Sq Km	30 520	Languages	Dutch (Flemish), French (Walloon), German
Area Sq Miles	11 784	Religions	Roman Catholic, Protestant
Population	10 754 000	Currency	Euro
Capital	Brussels (Bruxelles)	Organizations	EU, NATO, OECD, UN

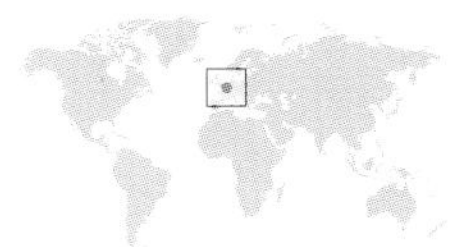

Belgium lies on the North Sea coast of western Europe. Beyond low sand dunes and a narrow belt of reclaimed land, fertile plains extend to the Sambre-Meuse river valley. The land rises to the forested Ardennes plateau in the southeast. Belgium has mild winters and cool summers. It is densely populated and has a highly urbanized population. With few mineral resources, Belgium imports raw materials for processing and manufacture. The agricultural sector is small, but provides for most food needs. A large services sector reflects Belgium's position as the home base for over eight hundred international institutions. The headquarters of the European Union are in the capital, Brussels.

BELIZE

Area Sq Km	22 965	Languages	English, Spanish, Mayan, Creole
Area Sq Miles	8 867	Religions	Roman Catholic, Protestant
Population	318 000	Currency	Belize dollar
Capital	Belmopan	Organizations	CARICOM, Comm., UN

Belize lies on the Caribbean coast of central America and includes numerous cays and a large barrier reef offshore. The coastal areas are flat and swampy. To the southwest are the Maya Mountains. Tropical jungle covers much of the country and the climate is humid tropical, but tempered by sea breezes. A third of the population lives in the capital. The economy is based primarily on agriculture, forestry and fishing, and exports include raw sugar, orange concentrate and bananas.

BENIN
Republic of Benin

Area Sq Km	112 620	Languages	French, Fon, Yoruba, Adja, local languages
Area Sq Miles	43 483	Religions	Traditional beliefs, Roman Catholic, Sunni Muslim
Population	9 100 000	Currency	CFA franc
Capital	Porto-Novo	Organizations	UN

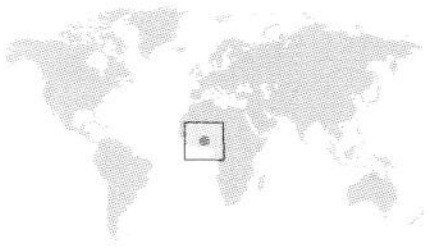

Benin is in west Africa, on the Gulf of Guinea. The climate is tropical in the north, equatorial in the south. The economy is based mainly on agriculture and transit trade. Agricultural products account for two-thirds of export earnings. Oil, produced offshore, is also a major export.

Bermuda
United Kingdom Overseas Territory

Area Sq Km	54	Languages	English
Area Sq Miles	21	Religions	Protestant, Roman Catholic
Population	65 000	Currency	Bermuda dollar
Capital	Hamilton		

In the Atlantic Ocean to the east of the USA, Bermuda comprises a group of small islands with a warm and humid climate. The economy is based on international business and tourism.

BHUTAN
Kingdom of Bhutan

Area Sq Km	46 620	Languages	Dzongkha, Nepali, Assamese
Area Sq Miles	18 000	Religions	Buddhist, Hindu
Population	738 000	Currency	Ngultrum, Indian rupee
Capital	Thimphu	Organizations	UN

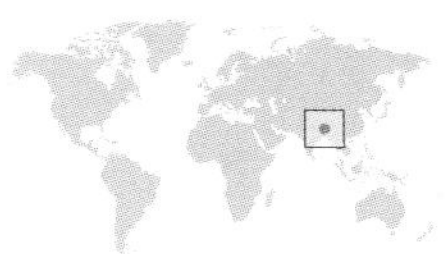

Bhutan lies in the eastern Himalaya mountains, between China and India. It is mountainous in the north, with fertile valleys. The climate ranges between permanently cold in the far north and subtropical in the south. Most of the population is involved in livestock rearing and subsistence farming. Bhutan is a producer of cardamom. Tourism is an increasingly important foreign currency earner and hydro-electric power is also sold to India from the Tala site in the south-west.

States and Territories

BOLIVIA
Plurinational State of Bolivia

Area Sq Km	1 098 581	Languages	Spanish, Quechua, Aymara
Area Sq Miles	424 164	Religions	Roman Catholic, Protestant, Baha'i
Population	10 088 000	Currency	Boliviano
Capital	La Paz/Sucre	Organizations	UN

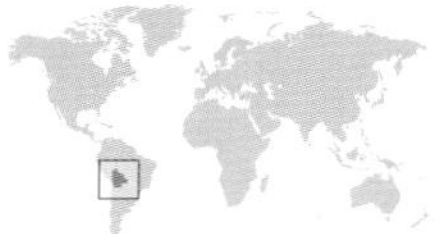

Bolivia is a landlocked state in central South America. Most Bolivians live on the high plateau within the Andes mountains. The lowlands range between dense rainforest in the northeast and semi-arid grasslands in the southeast. Bolivia is rich in minerals (zinc, tin and gold), and sales generate approximately half of export income. Natural gas, timber and soya beans are also exported. The USA is the main trading partner.

BOSNIA-HERZEGOVINA
Republic of Bosnia and Herzegovina

Area Sq Km	51 130	Languages	Bosnian, Serbian, Croatian
Area Sq Miles	19 741	Religions	Sunni Muslim, Serbian Orthodox, Roman Catholic, Protestant
Population	3 752 000	Currency	Marka
Capital	Sarajevo	Organizations	UN

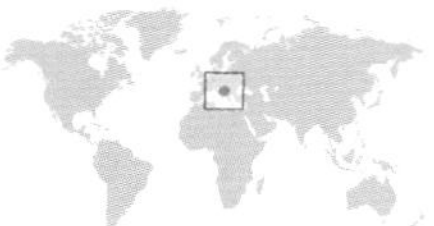

Bosnia-Herzegovina lies in the western Balkan Mountains of southern Europe, on the Adriatic Sea. It is mountainous, with ridges running northwest-southeast. The main lowlands are around the Sava valley in the north. Summers are warm, but winters can be very cold. The economy relies heavily on overseas aid.

BOTSWANA
Republic of Botswana

Area Sq Km	581 370	Languages	English, Setswana, Shona, local languages
Area Sq Miles	224 468	Religions	Traditional beliefs, Protestant, Roman Catholic
Population	2 031 000	Currency	Pula
Capital	Gaborone	Organizations	Comm., SADC, UN

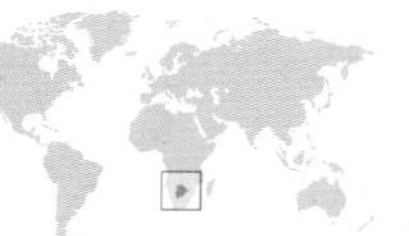

Botswana is a landlocked state in southern Africa. Over half of the country lies within the Kalahari Desert, with swamps to the north and salt-pans to the northeast. Most of the population lives near the eastern border. The climate is subtropical, but drought-prone. The economy was founded on cattle rearing, and although beef remains an important export, the economy is now based on mining. Diamonds account for seventy per cent of export earnings. Copper-nickel matte is also exported. Most trade is with other members of the Southern African Customs Union.

BRAZIL
Federative Republic of Brazil

Area Sq Km	8 514 879	Languages	Portuguese
Area Sq Miles	3 287 613	Religions	Roman Catholic, Protestant
Population	196 655 000	Currency	Real
Capital	Brasília	Organizations	UN

Brazil, in eastern South America, covers almost half of the continent, and is the world's fifth largest country. The northwest contains the vast basin of the Amazon, while the centre-west is largely a vast plateau of savanna and rock escarpments. The northeast is mostly semi-arid plateaus, while to the east and south are rugged mountains, fertile valleys and narrow, fertile coastal plains. The Amazon basin is hot, humid and wet; the rest of the country is cooler and drier, with seasonal variations. The northeast is drought-prone. Most Brazilians live in urban areas along the coast and on the central plateau. Brazil has well-developed agricultural, mining and service sectors, and the economy is larger than that of all other South American countries combined. Brazil is the world's biggest producer of coffee, and other agricultural crops include grains and sugar cane. Mineral production includes iron, aluminium and gold. Manufactured goods include food products, transport equipment, machinery and industrial chemicals. The main trading partners are the USA and Argentina. Economic reforms in Brazil have turned it into one of the fastest growing economies.

BRUNEI
State of Brunei Darussalam

Area Sq Km	5 765	Languages	Malay, English, Chinese
Area Sq Miles	2 226	Religions	Sunni Muslim, Buddhist, Christian
Population	406 000	Currency	Brunei dollar
Capital	Bandar Seri Begawan	Organizations	APEC, ASEAN, Comm., UN

The southeast Asian oil-rich state of Brunei lies on the northwest coast of the island of Borneo, on the South China Sea. Its two enclaves are surrounded by the Malaysian state of Sarawak. Tropical rainforest covers over two-thirds of the country. The economy is dominated by the oil and gas industries.

BULGARIA
Republic of Bulgaria

Area Sq Km	110 994	Languages	Bulgarian, Turkish, Romany, Macedonian
Area Sq Miles	42 855	Religions	Bulgarian Orthodox, Sunni Muslim
Population	7 446 000	Currency	Lev
Capital	Sofia (Sofiya)	Organizations	EU, NATO, UN

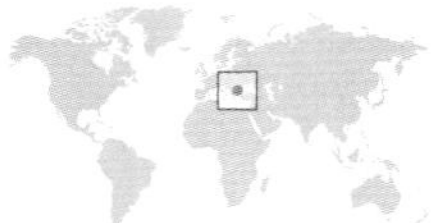

Bulgaria, in southern Europe, borders the western shore of the Black Sea. The Balkan Mountains separate the Danube plains in the north from the Rhodope Mountains and the lowlands in the south. The economy has a strong agricultural base. Manufacturing industries include machinery, consumer goods, chemicals and metals. Most trade is with the Russian Federation, Italy and Germany.

BURKINA FASO
Democratic Republic of Burkina Faso

Area Sq Km	274 200	Languages	French, Moore (Mossi), Fulani, local languages
Area Sq Miles	105 869	Religions	Sunni Muslim, traditional beliefs, Roman Catholic
Population	16 968 000	Currency	CFA franc
Capital	Ouagadougou	Organizations	UN

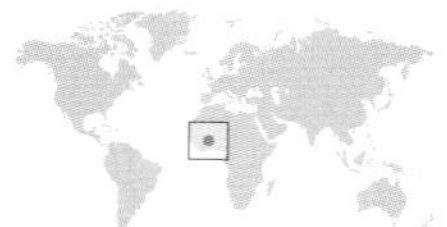

Burkina Faso, a landlocked country in west Africa, lies within the Sahara desert to the north and semi-arid savanna to the south. Rainfall is erratic, and droughts are common. Livestock rearing and farming are the main activities, and cotton, livestock, groundnuts and some minerals are exported. Burkina Faso relies heavily on foreign aid, and is one of the poorest and least developed countries in the world.

BURUNDI
Republic of Burundi

Area Sq Km	27 835	Languages	Kirundi (Hutu, Tutsi), French
Area Sq Miles	10 747	Religions	Roman Catholic, traditional beliefs, Protestant
Population	8 575 000	Currency	Burundian franc
Capital	Bujumbura	Organizations	UN

The densely populated east African state of Burundi consists of high plateaus rising from the shores of Lake Tanganyika in the southwest. It has a tropical climate and depends on subsistence farming. Coffee is its main export, and its main trading partners are Germany and Belgium. The country has been badly affected by internal conflict since the early 1990s.

CAMBODIA
Kingdom of Cambodia

Area Sq Km	181 000	Languages	Khmer, Vietnamese
Area Sq Miles	69 884	Religions	Buddhist, Roman Catholic, Sunni Muslim
Population	14 305 000	Currency	Riel
Capital	Phnom Penh	Organizations	ASEAN, UN

Cambodia lies in southeast Asia on the Gulf of Thailand, and occupies the Mekong river basin, with the Tônlé Sap (Great Lake) at its centre. The climate is tropical monsoon. Forests cover half the country. Most of the population lives on the plains and is engaged in farming (chiefly rice growing), fishing and forestry. The economy is recovering following the devastation of civil war in the 1970s, with rapid progress since 2000. Mineral resources are starting to be identified for development.

CAMEROON
Republic of Cameroon

Area Sq Km	475 442	Languages	French, English, Fang, Bamileke, local languages
Area Sq Miles	183 569	Religions	Roman Catholic, traditional beliefs, Sunni Muslim, Protestant
Population	20 030 000	Currency	CFA franc
Capital	Yaoundé	Organizations	Comm., UN

Cameroon is in west Africa, on the Gulf of Guinea. The coastal plains and southern and central plateaus are covered with tropical forest. Despite oil resources and favourable agricultural conditions Cameroon still faces problems of underdevelopment. Oil, timber and cocoa are the main exports. France is the main trading partner.

CANADA

Area Sq Km	9 984 670	Languages	English, French
Area Sq Miles	3 855 103	Religions	Roman Catholic, Protestant, Eastern Orthodox, Jewish
Population	34 350 000	Currency	Canadian dollar
Capital	Ottawa	Organizations	APEC, Comm., NATO, OECD, UN

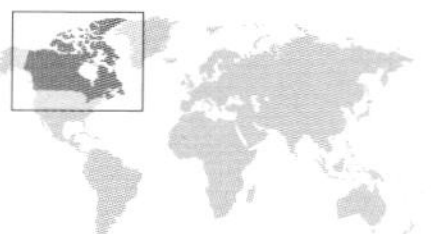

The world's second largest country, Canada covers the northern two-fifths of North America and has coastlines on the Atlantic, Arctic and Pacific Oceans. In the west are the Coast Mountains, the Rocky Mountains and interior plateaus. In the centre lie the fertile Prairies. Further east, covering about half the total land area, is the Canadian Shield, a relatively flat area of infertile lowlands around Hudson Bay, extending to Labrador on the east coast. The Shield is bordered to the south by the fertile Great Lakes-St Lawrence lowlands. In the far north climatic conditions are polar, while the rest has a continental climate. Most Canadians live in the urban areas of the Great Lakes-St Lawrence basin. Canada is rich in mineral and energy resources. Only five per cent of land is arable. Canada is among the world's leading producers of wheat, of wood from its vast coniferous forests, and of fish and seafood from its Atlantic and Pacific fishing grounds. It is a major producer of nickel, uranium, copper, iron ore, zinc and other minerals, as well as oil and natural gas. Its abundant raw materials are the basis for many manufacturing industries. Main exports are machinery, motor vehicles, oil, timber, newsprint and paper, wood pulp and wheat. Since the 1989 free trade agreement with the USA and the 1994 North America Free Trade Agreement, trade with the USA has grown and now accounts for around seventy-five per cent of imports and around eighty-five per cent of exports.

Alberta (Province)
Area Sq Km (Sq Miles) 661 848 (255 541) Population 3 742 753 Capital Edmonton

British Columbia (Province)
Area Sq Km (Sq Miles) 944 735 (364 764) Population 4 554 085 Capital Victoria

Manitoba (Province)
Area Sq Km (Sq Miles) 647 797 (250 116) Population 1 243 653 Capital Winnipeg

New Brunswick (Province)
Area Sq Km (Sq Miles) 72 908 (28 150) Population 753 232 Capital Fredericton

Newfoundland and Labrador (Province)
Area Sq Km (Sq Miles) 405 212 (156 453) Population 509 148 Capital St John's

Northwest Territories (Territory)
Area Sq Km (Sq Miles) 1 346 106 (519 734) Population 43 554 Capital Yellowknife

Nova Scotia (Province)
Area Sq Km (Sq Miles) 55 284 (21 345) Population 943 414 Capital Halifax

Nunavut (Territory)
Area Sq Km (Sq Miles) 2 093 190 (808 185) Population 33 303 Capital Iqaluit

Ontario (Province)
Area Sq Km (Sq Miles) 1 076 395 (415 598) Population 13 282 444 Capital Toronto

Prince Edward Island (Province)
Area Sq Km (Sq Miles) 5 660 (2 185) Population 143 481 Capital Charlottetown

Québec (Province)
Area Sq Km (Sq Miles) 1 542 056 (595 391) Population 7 942 983 Capital Québec

Saskatchewan (Province)
Area Sq Km (Sq Miles) 651 036 (251 366) Population 1 052 050 Capital Regina

Yukon (Territory)
Area Sq Km (Sq Miles) 482 443 (186 272) Population 34 306 Capital Whitehorse

CAPE VERDE
Republic of Cape Verde

Area Sq Km	4 033	Languages	Portuguese, Creole
Area Sq Miles	1 557	Religions	Roman Catholic, Protestant
Population	501 000	Currency	Cape Verde escudo
Capital	Praia	Organizations	UN

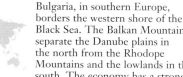

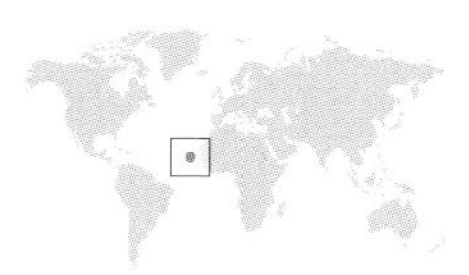

Cape Verde is a group of semi-arid volcanic islands lying off the coast of west Africa. The economy is based on fishing, subsistence farming and service industries. Windfarms on four islands supply around a quarter of all electricity.

Cayman Islands
United Kingdom Overseas Territory

Area Sq Km	259	Languages	English
Area Sq Miles	100	Religions	Protestant, Roman Catholic
Population	57 000	Currency	Cayman Islands dollar
Capital	George Town		

A group of islands in the Caribbean, northwest of Jamaica. There are three main islands: Grand Cayman, Little Cayman and Cayman Brac. The Cayman Islands are one of the world's major offshore financial centres. Tourism is also important to the economy.

CENTRAL AFRICAN REPUBLIC

Area Sq Km	622 436	Languages	French, Sango, Banda, Baya, local languages
Area Sq Miles	240 324	Religions	Protestant, Roman Catholic, traditional beliefs, Sunni Muslim
Population	4 487 000	Currency	CFA franc
Capital	Bangui	Organizations	UN

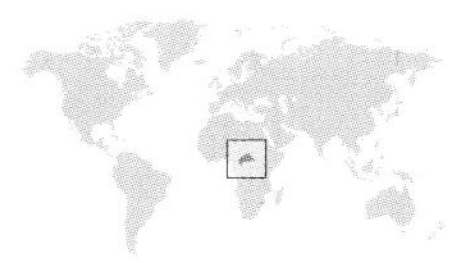

A landlocked country in central Africa, the Central African Republic is mainly savanna plateau, drained by the Ubangi and Chari river systems, with mountains to the east and west. The climate is tropical, with high rainfall. Most of the population lives in the south and west, and a majority of the workforce is involved in subsistence farming. Some cotton, coffee, tobacco and timber are exported, but diamonds account for around half of export earnings.

CHAD
Republic of Chad

Area Sq Km	1 284 000	Languages	Arabic, French, Sara, local languages
Area Sq Miles	495 755	Religions	Sunni Muslim, Roman Catholic, Protestant, traditional beliefs
Population	11 525 000	Currency	CFA franc
Capital	Ndjamena	Organizations	UN

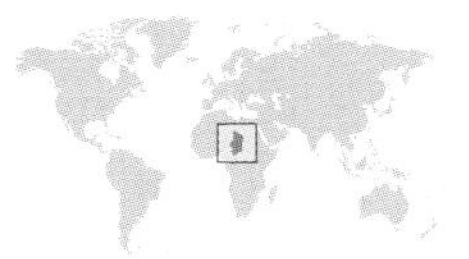

Chad is a landlocked state of north-central Africa. It consists of plateaus, the Tibesti mountains in the north and the Lake Chad basin in the west. Climatic conditions range between desert in the north and tropical forest in the southwest. With few natural resources, Chad relies on subsistence farming, exports of raw cotton, and foreign aid. The main trading partners are France, Portugal and Cameroon.

CHILE
Republic of Chile

Area Sq Km	756 945	Languages	Spanish, Amerindian languages
Area Sq Miles	292 258	Religions	Roman Catholic, Protestant
Population	17 270 000	Currency	Chilean peso
Capital	Santiago	Organizations	APEC, OECD, UN

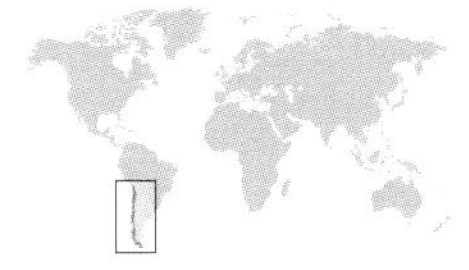

Chile lies along the Pacific coast of the southern half of South America. Between the Andes in the east and the lower coastal ranges is a central valley, with a mild climate, where most Chileans live. To the north is the arid Atacama Desert and to the south is cold, wet forested grassland. Chile has considerable mineral resources and is the world's leading exporter of copper. Nitrates, molybdenum, gold and iron ore are also mined. Agriculture (particularly viticulture), forestry and fishing are also important to the economy.

CHINA
People's Republic of China

Area Sq Km	9 584 492	Languages	Mandarin (Putonghua), Wu, Cantonese, Hsiang, regional languages
Area Sq Miles	3 700 593	Religions	Confucian, Taoist, Buddhist, Christian, Sunni Muslim
Population	1 332 079 000	Currency	Yuan, Hong Kong dollar, Macao pataca
Capital	Beijing (Peking)	Organizations	APEC, UN

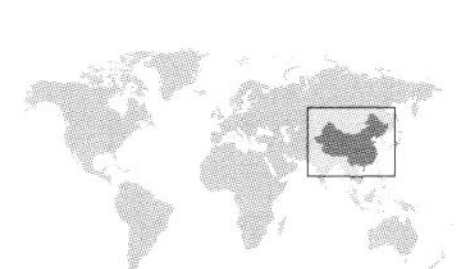

China, the world's most populous and fourth largest country, occupies a large part of east Asia, borders fourteen states and has coastlines on the Yellow, East China and South China Seas. It has a huge variety of landscapes. The southwest contains the high Plateau of Tibet, flanked by the Himalaya and Kunlun Shan mountains. The north is mountainous with arid basins and extends from the Tien Shan and Altai Mountains and the vast Taklimakan Desert in the west to the plateau and Gobi Desert in the centre-east. Eastern China is predominantly lowland and is divided broadly into the basins of the Yellow River (Huang He) in the north, the Yangtze (Chang Jiang) in the centre and the Pearl River (Xi Jiang) in the southeast. Climatic conditions and vegetation are as diverse as the topography: much of the country experiences temperate conditions, while the southwest has an extreme mountain climate and the southeast enjoys a moist, warm subtropical climate. Around fifty per cent of China's huge population lives in rural areas, and agriculture employs around thirty per cent of the working population. The main crops are rice, wheat, soya beans, peanuts, cotton, tobacco and hemp. China is rich in coal, oil and natural gas and has the world's largest potential in hydroelectric power. It is a major world producer of iron ore, molybdenum, copper, asbestos and gold. Economic reforms from the early 1980's led to an explosion in manufacturing development concentrated on the 'coastal economic open region'. The main exports are machinery, textiles, footwear, toys and sports goods. Japan and the USA are China's main trading partners.

Anhui (Province)
Area Sq Km (Sq Miles) 139 000 (53 668) Population 61 350 000 Capital Hefei

Beijing (Municipality)
Area Sq Km (Sq Miles) 16 800 (6 487) Population 16 950 000 Capital Beijing (Peking)

Chongqing (Municipality)
Area Sq Km (Sq Miles) 23 000 (8 880) Population 28 390 000 Capital Chongqing

Fujian (Province)
Area Sq Km (Sq Miles) 121 400 (46 873) Population 36 040 000 Capital Fuzhou

Gansu (Province)
Area Sq Km (Sq Miles) 453 700 (175 175) Population 26 280 000 Capital Lanzhou

Guangdong (Province)
Area Sq Km (Sq Miles) 178 000 (68 726) Population 95 440 000 Capital Guangzhou (Canton)

Guangxi Zhuangzu Zizhiqu (Autonomous Region)
Area Sq Km (Sq Miles) 236 000 (91 120) Population 48 160 000 Capital Nanning

Guizhou (Province)
Area Sq Km (Sq Miles) 176 000 (67 954) Population 37 930 000 Capital Guiyang

Hainan (Province)
Area Sq Km (Sq Miles) 34 000 (13 127) Population 8 540 000 Capital Haikou

Hebei (Province)
Area Sq Km (Sq Miles) 187 700 (72 471) Population 69 890 000 Capital Shijiazhuang

Heilongjiang (Province)
Area Sq Km (Sq Miles) 454 600 (175 522) Population 38 250 000 Capital Harbin

Henan (Province)
Area Sq Km (Sq Miles) 167 000 (64 479) Population 94 290 000 Capital Zhengzhou

Hong Kong (Special Administrative Region)
Area Sq Km (Sq Miles) 1 075 (415) Population 6 978 000 Capital Hong Kong

Hubei (Province)
Area Sq Km (Sq Miles) 185 900 (71 776) Population 57 110 000 Capital Wuhan

Hunan (Province)
Area Sq Km (Sq Miles) 210 000 (81 081) Population 63 800 000 Capital Changsha

Jiangsu (Province)
Area Sq Km (Sq Miles) 102 600 (39 614) Population 76 770 000 Capital Nanjing

Jiangxi (Province)
Area Sq Km (Sq Miles) 166 900 (64 440) Population 44 000 000 Capital Nanchang

Jilin (Province)
Area Sq Km (Sq Miles) 187 000 (72 201) Population 27 340 000 Capital Changchun

Liaoning (Province)
Area Sq Km (Sq Miles) 147 400 (56 911) Population 43 150 000 Capital Shenyang

Macao (Special Administrative Region)
Area Sq Km (Sq Miles) 17 (7) Population 552 000 Capital Macao

Nei Mongol Zizhiqu Inner Mongolia (Autonomous Region)
Area Sq Km (Sq Miles) 1 183 000 (456 759) Population 24 140 000 Capital Hohhot

Ningxia Huizu Zizhiqu (Autonomous Region)
Area Sq Km (Sq Miles) 66 400 (25 637) Population 6 180 000 Capital Yinchuan

Qinghai (Province)
Area Sq Km (Sq Miles) 721 000 (278 380) Population 5 540 000 Capital Xining

Shaanxi (Province)
Area Sq Km (Sq Miles) 205 600 (79 383) Population 37 620 000 Capital Xi'an

Shandong (Province)
Area Sq Km (Sq Miles) 153 300 (59 189) Population 94 170 000 Capital Jinan

Shanghai (Municipality)
Area Sq Km (Sq Miles) 6 300 (2 432) Population 18 880 000 Capital Shanghai

Shanxi (Province)
Area Sq Km (Sq Miles) 156 300 (60 348) Population 34 110 000 Capital Taiyuan

Sichuan (Province)
Area Sq Km (Sq Miles) 569 000 (219 692) Population 81 380 000 Capital Chengdu

Tianjin (Municipality)
Area Sq Km (Sq Miles) 11 300 (4 363) Population 11 760 000 Capital Tianjin

Xinjiang Uygur Zizhiqu Sinkiang (Autonomous Region)
Area Sq Km (Sq Miles) 1 600 000 (617 763) Population 21 310 000 Capital Ürümqi

Xizang Zizhiqu Tibet (Autonomous Region)
Area Sq Km (Sq Miles) 1 228 400 (474 288) Population 2 870 000 Capital Lhasa

Yunnan (Province)
Area Sq Km (Sq Miles) 394 000 (152 124) Population 45 430 000 Capital Kunming

Zhejiang (Province)
Area Sq Km (Sq Miles) 101 800 (39 305) Population 51 200 000 Capital Hangzhou

Taiwan: The People's Republic of China claims Taiwan as its 23rd Province

Christmas Island
Australian External Territory

Area Sq Km	135	Languages	English
Area Sq Miles	52	Religions	Buddhist, Sunni Muslim, Protestant, Roman Catholic
Population	1 403	Currency	Australian dollar
Capital	The Settlement (Flying Fish Cove)		

The island is situated in the east of the Indian Ocean, to the south of Indonesia. The economy was formerly based on phosphate extraction, although the mine is now closed. Tourism is developing and is a major employer.

Cocos Islands (Keeling Islands)
Australian External Territory

Area Sq Km	14	Languages	English
Area Sq Miles	5	Religions	Sunni Muslim, Christian
Population	621	Currency	Australian dollar
Capital	West Island		

The Cocos Islands consist of numerous islands on two coral atolls in the eastern Indian Ocean between Sri Lanka and Australia. Most of the population lives on West Island or Home Island. Coconuts are the only cash crop, and the main export.

COLOMBIA
Republic of Colombia

Area Sq Km	1 141 748	Languages	Spanish, Amerindian languages
Area Sq Miles	440 831	Religions	Roman Catholic, Protestant
Population	46 927 000	Currency	Colombian peso
Capital	Bogotá	Organizations	UN

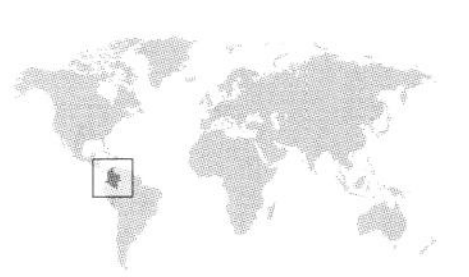

A state in northwest South America, Colombia has coastlines on the Pacific Ocean and the Caribbean Sea. Behind coastal plains lie three ranges of the Andes mountains, separated by high valleys and plateaus where most Colombians live. To the southeast are grasslands and the forests of the Amazon. The climate is tropical, although temperatures vary with altitude. Only five per cent of land is cultivable. Coffee (Colombia is the world's second largest producer), sugar, bananas, cotton and flowers are exported. Coal, nickel, gold, silver, platinum and emeralds (Colombia is the world's largest producer) are mined. Oil and its products are the main exports. Industries include the processing of minerals and crops. The main trade partner is the USA. Internal violence – both politically motivated and relating to Colombia's leading role in the international trade in illegal drugs – continues to hinder development.

COMOROS
United Republic of the Comoros

Area Sq Km	1 862	Languages	Shikomor (Comorian), French, Arabic
Area Sq Miles	719	Religions	Sunni Muslim, Roman Catholic
Population	754 000	Currency	Comoros franc
Capital	Moroni	Organizations	UN

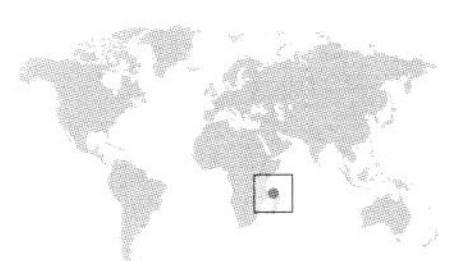

This state, in the Indian Ocean off the east African coast, comprises three volcanic islands of Ngazidja (Grande Comore), Nzwani (Anjouan) and Mwali (Mohéli), and some coral atolls. These tropical islands are mountainous, with poor soil and few natural resources. Subsistence farming predominates. Vanilla, cloves and ylang-ylang (an essential oil) are exported, and the economy relies heavily on workers' remittances from abroad.

States and Territories

CONGO
Republic of the Congo

Area Sq Km	342 000	Languages	French, Kongo, Monokutuba, local languages
Area Sq Miles	132 047	Religions	Roman Catholic, Protestant, traditional beliefs, Sunni Muslim
Population	4 140 000	Currency	CFA franc
Capital	Brazzaville	Organizations	UN

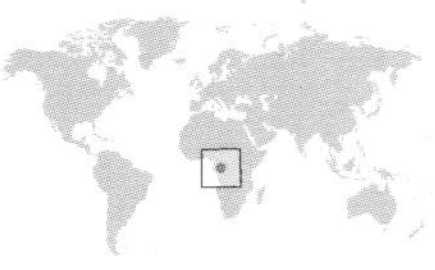

Congo, in central Africa, is mostly a forest or savanna-covered plateau drained by the Ubangi-Congo river systems. Sand dunes and lagoons line the short Atlantic coast. The climate is hot and tropical. Most Congolese live in the southern third of the country. Half of the workforce are farmers, growing food and cash crops including sugar, coffee, cocoa and oil palms. Oil and timber are the mainstays of the economy, and oil generates over fifty per cent of the country's export revenues.

CONGO, DEMOCRATIC REPUBLIC OF THE

Area Sq Km	2 345 410	Languages	French, Lingala, Swahili, Kongo, local languages
Area Sq Miles	905 568	Religions	Christian, Sunni Muslim
Population	67 758 000	Currency	Congolese franc
Capital	Kinshasa	Organizations	SADC, UN

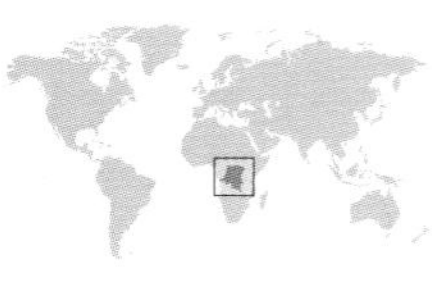

This central African state, formerly Zaire, consists of the basin of the Congo river flanked by plateaus, with high mountain ranges to the east and a short Atlantic coastline to the west. The climate is tropical, with rainforest close to the Equator and savanna to the north and south. Fertile land allows a range of food and cash crops to be grown, chiefly coffee. The country has vast mineral resources, with copper, cobalt and diamonds being the most important.

Cook Islands
Self-governing New Zealand Overseas Territory

Area Sq Km	293	Languages	English, Maori
Area Sq Miles	113	Religions	Protestant, Roman Catholic
Population	20 000	Currency	New Zealand dollar
Capital	Avarua		

These consist of groups of coral atolls and volcanic islands in the southwest Pacific Ocean. The main island is Rarotonga. Distance from foreign markets and restricted natural resources hinder development.

COSTA RICA
Republic of Costa Rica

Area Sq Km	51 100	Languages	Spanish
Area Sq Miles	19 730	Religions	Roman Catholic, Protestant
Population	4 727 000	Currency	Costa Rican colón
Capital	San José	Organizations	UN

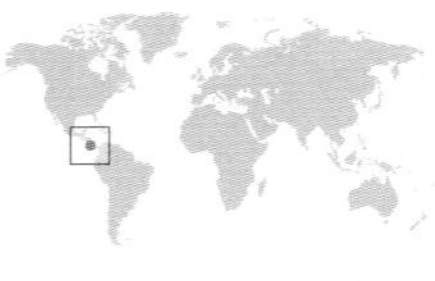

Costa Rica, in central America, has coastlines on the Caribbean Sea and Pacific Ocean. From tropical coastal plains, the land rises to mountains and a temperate central plateau, where most of the population lives. The economy depends on agriculture and tourism, with ecotourism becoming increasingly important. Main exports are textiles, coffee and bananas, and almost half of all trade is with the USA.

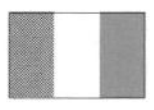

CÔTE D'IVOIRE (Ivory Coast)
Republic of Côte d'Ivoire

Area Sq Km	322 463	Languages	French, Creole, Akan, local languages
Area Sq Miles	124 504	Religions	Sunni Muslim, Roman Catholic, traditional beliefs, Protestant
Population	20 153 000	Currency	CFA franc
Capital	Yamoussoukro	Organizations	UN

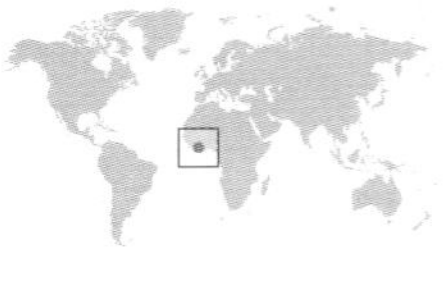

Côte d'Ivoire (Ivory Coast) is in west Africa, on the Gulf of Guinea. In the north are plateaus and savanna; in the south are low undulating plains and rainforest, with sand-bars and lagoons on the coast. Temperatures are warm, and rainfall is heavier in the south. Most of the workforce is engaged in farming. Côte d'Ivoire is a major producer of cocoa and coffee, and agricultural products (also including cotton and timber) are the main exports. Oil and gas have begun to be exploited.

CROATIA
Republic of Croatia

Area Sq Km	56 538	Languages	Croatian, Serbian
Area Sq Miles	21 829	Religions	Roman Catholic, Serbian Orthodox, Sunni Muslim
Population	4 396 000	Currency	Kuna
Capital	Zagreb	Organizations	NATO, UN

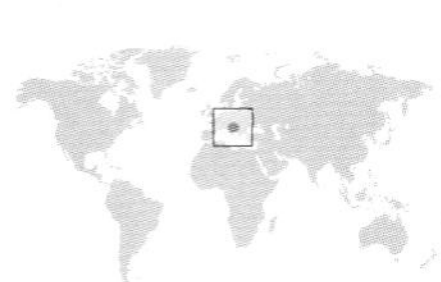

The southern European state of Croatia has a long coastline on the Adriatic Sea, with many offshore islands. Coastal areas have a Mediterranean climate; inland is cooler and wetter. Croatia was once strong agriculturally and industrially, but conflict in the early 1990s, and associated loss of markets and a fall in tourist revenue, caused economic difficulties from which recovery has been slow.

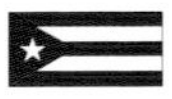

CUBA
Republic of Cuba

Area Sq Km	110 860	Languages	Spanish
Area Sq Miles	42 803	Religions	Roman Catholic, Protestant
Population	11 254 000	Currency	Cuban peso
Capital	Havana (La Habana)	Organizations	UN

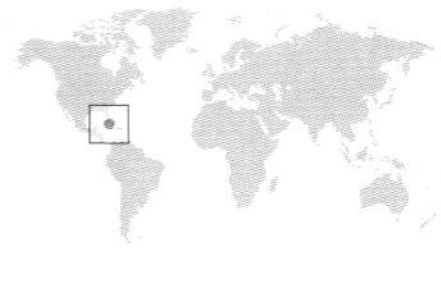

The country comprises the island of Cuba (the largest island in the Caribbean), and many islets and cays. A fifth of Cubans live in and around Havana. Cuba is slowly recovering from the withdrawal of aid and subsidies from the former USSR. Sugar remains the basis of the economy, although tourism is developing and is, together with remittances from workers abroad, an important source of revenue.

Curaçao
Self-governing Netherlands territory

Area Sq Km	444	Languages	Dutch, Papiamento
Area Sq Miles	171	Religions	Roman Catholic, Protestant
Population	142 180	Currency	Caribbean guilder
Capital	Willemstad		

Situated in the Caribbean Sea off the north coast of Venezuela, Curaçao was previously part of the Netherlands Antilles until they were dissolved in October 2010. It consists of the main island and the smaller uninhabited Klein Curaçao and is the largest and most populous of the Lesser Antilles. Oil refining and tourism form the basis of the economy.

CYPRUS
Republic of Cyprus

Area Sq Km	9 251	Languages	Greek, Turkish, English
Area Sq Miles	3 572	Religions	Greek Orthodox, Sunni Muslim
Population	1 117 000	Currency	Euro
Capital	Nicosia (Lefkosia)	Organizations	Comm., EU, UN

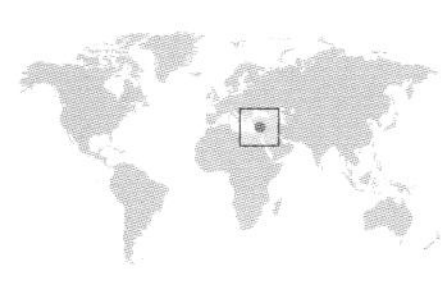

The eastern Mediterranean island of Cyprus has effectively been divided into two since 1974. The economy of the Greek-speaking south is based mainly on specialist agriculture and tourism, with shipping and offshore banking. The ethnically Turkish north depends on agriculture, tourism and aid from Turkey. The island has hot dry summers and mild winters. Cyprus joined the European Union in May 2004.

CZECH REPUBLIC

Area Sq Km	78 864	Languages	Czech, Moravian, Slovakian
Area Sq Miles	30 450	Religions	Roman Catholic, Protestant
Population	10 534 000	Currency	Koruna
Capital	Prague (Praha)	Organizations	EU, NATO, OECD, UN

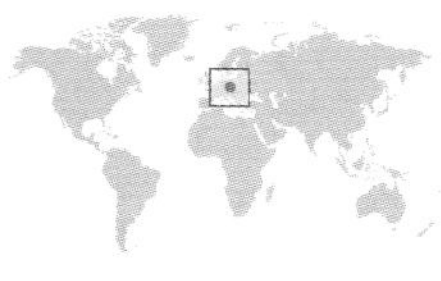

The landlocked Czech Republic in central Europe consists of rolling countryside, wooded hills and fertile valleys. The climate is continental. The country has substantial reserves of coal and lignite, timber and some minerals, chiefly iron ore. It is highly industrialized, and major manufactured goods include industrial machinery, consumer goods, cars, iron and steel, chemicals and glass. Germany is the main trading partner. The Czech Republic joined the European Union in May 2004.

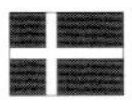

DENMARK
Kingdom of Denmark

Area Sq Km	43 075	Languages	Danish
Area Sq Miles	16 631	Religions	Protestant
Population	5 573 000	Currency	Danish krone
Capital	Copenhagen (København)	Organizations	EU, NATO, OECD, UN

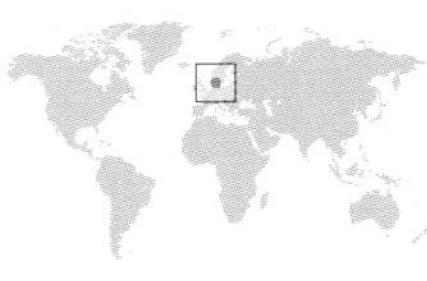

Denmark occupies the Jutland peninsula (Jylland) and nearly five hundred islands between the North and Baltic Seas in northern Europe. The country is low-lying. The climate is cool and temperate. A fifth of the population lives in and around the capital, Copenhagen (København), on the island of Zealand (Sjælland). Two-thirds of the area is fertile farmland, though agriculture only employs around six per cent of the workforce. Denmark is self-sufficient in oil and natural gas from the North Sea. Manufacturing, largely based on imported materials, accounts for over half of all exports, which include machinery, food, furniture, and pharmaceuticals. The main trading partners are Germany and Sweden.

DJIBOUTI
Republic of Djibouti

Area Sq Km	23 200	Languages	Somali, Afar, French, Arabic
Area Sq Miles	8 958	Religions	Sunni Muslim, Christian
Population	906 000	Currency	Djibouti franc
Capital	Djibouti	Organizations	UN

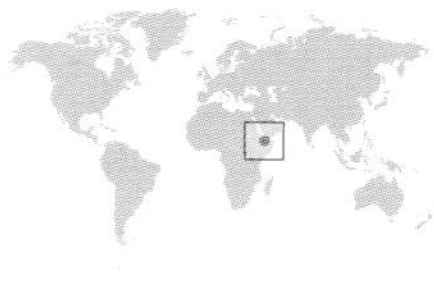

Djibouti lies in northeast Africa, on the Gulf of Aden at the entrance to the Red Sea. Most of the country is semi-arid desert with high temperatures and low rainfall. More than two-thirds of the population lives in the capital. There is some camel, sheep and goat herding, but with few natural resources the economy is based on services and trade. Djibouti serves as a free trade zone for northern Africa, and the capital's port is a major transhipment and refuelling destination. It is linked by rail to Addis Ababa in Ethiopia.

DOMINICA
Commonwealth of Dominica

Area Sq Km	750	Languages	English, Creole
Area Sq Miles	290	Religions	Roman Catholic, Protestant
Population	68 000	Currency	East Caribbean dollar
Capital	Roseau	Organizations	CARICOM, Comm., UN

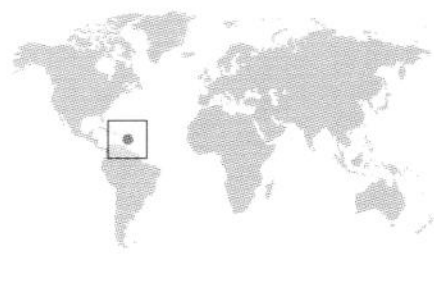

Dominica is the most northerly of the Windward Islands, in the eastern Caribbean. It is very mountainous and forested, with a coastline of steep cliffs. The climate is tropical and rainfall is abundant. Approximately a quarter of Dominicans live in the capital. The economy is based on agriculture, with bananas (the major export), coconuts and citrus fruits the most important crops. Tourism is a developing industry.

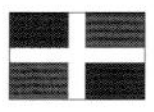

DOMINICAN REPUBLIC

Area Sq Km	48 442	Languages	Spanish, Creole
Area Sq Miles	18 704	Religions	Roman Catholic, Protestant
Population	10 056 000	Currency	Dominican peso
Capital	Santo Domingo	Organizations	UN

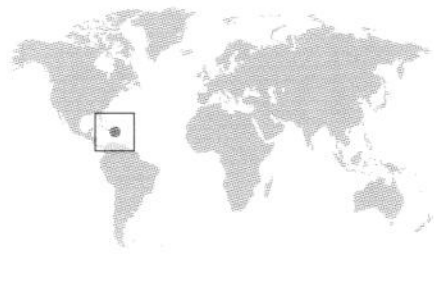

The state occupies the eastern two-thirds of the Caribbean island of Hispaniola (the western third is Haiti). It has a series of mountain ranges, fertile valleys and a large coastal plain in the east. The climate is hot tropical, with heavy rainfall. Sugar, coffee and cocoa are the main cash crops. Nickel (the main export), and gold are mined, and there is some light industry. The USA is the main trading partner. Tourism is the main foreign exchange earner.

EAST TIMOR (Timor-Leste)
Democratic Republic of Timor-Leste

Area Sq Km	14 874	Languages	Portuguese, Tetun, English
Area Sq Miles	5 743	Religions	Roman Catholic
Population	1 154 000	Currency	United States dollar
Capital	Dili	Organizations	UN

The island of Timor is part of the Indonesian archipelago, to the north of western Australia. East Timor (Timor-Leste) occupies the eastern section of the island, and a small coastal enclave (Ocussi) to the west. A referendum in 1999 ended Indonesia's occupation, after which the country was under UN transitional administration until full independence was achieved in 2002. The economy is in a poor state and East Timor is heavily dependent on foreign aid.

ECUADOR
Republic of Ecuador

Area Sq Km	272 045	Languages	Spanish, Quechua, and other Amerindian languages
Area Sq Miles	105 037	Religions	Roman Catholic
Population	14 666 000	Currency	United States dollar
Capital	Quito	Organizations	OPEC, UN

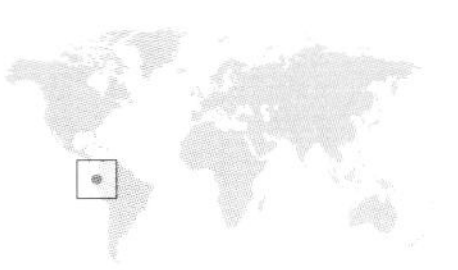

Ecuador is in northwest South America, on the Pacific coast. It consists of a broad coastal plain, high mountain ranges in the Andes, and part of the forested upper Amazon basin to the east. The climate is tropical, moderated by altitude. Most people live on the coast or in the mountain valleys. Ecuador is one of South America's main oil producers, and mineral reserves include gold. Most of the workforce depends on agriculture. Petroleum, bananas, shrimps, coffee and cocoa are exported. The USA is the main trading partner.

EGYPT
Arab Republic of Egypt

Area Sq Km	1 101 450	Languages	Arabic
Area Sq Miles	386 660	Religions	Sunni Muslim, Coptic Christian
Population	82 537 000	Currency	Egyptian pound
Capital	Cairo (Al Qāhirah)	Organizations	UN

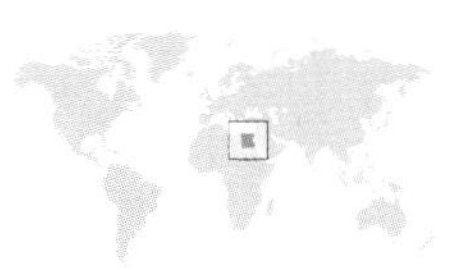

Egypt, on the eastern Mediterranean coast of north Africa, is low-lying, with areas below sea level in the Qattara depression. It is a land of desert and semi-desert except for the Nile valley, where ninety-nine per cent of Egyptians live. The Sinai peninsula in the northeast forms a land bridge between Africa and Asia. The summers are hot, the winters mild and rainfall is negligible. Less than four per cent of the land (chiefly around the Nile) is cultivated. Farming employs about one-third of the workforce; cotton is the main cash crop. Hydroelectric power is important. Main exports are oil and oil products, cotton, textiles and clothing.

EL SALVADOR
Republic of El Salvador

Area Sq Km	21 041	Languages	Spanish
Area Sq Miles	8 124	Religions	Roman Catholic, Protestant
Population	6 227 000	Currency	El Salvador colón, United States dollar
Capital	San Salvador	Organizations	UN

Located on the Pacific coast of central America, El Salvador consists of a coastal plain and volcanic mountain ranges which enclose a densely populated plateau area. The coast is hot, with heavy summer rainfall; the highlands are cooler. Coffee (the chief export), sugar and cotton are the main cash crops. The main trading partners are the USA and Guatemala.

EQUATORIAL GUINEA
Republic of Equatorial Guinea

Area Sq Km	28 051	Languages	Spanish, French, Fang
Area Sq Miles	10 831	Religions	Roman Catholic, traditional beliefs
Population	720 000	Currency	CFA franc
Capital	Malabo	Organizations	UN

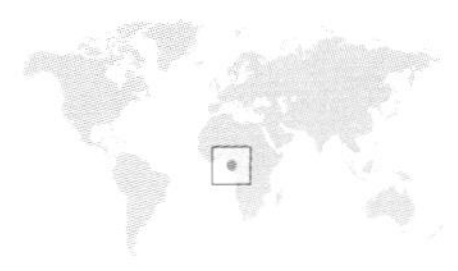

The state consists of Rio Muni, an enclave on the Atlantic coast of central Africa, and the islands of Bioco, Annobón and the Corisco group. Most of the population lives on the coastal plain and upland plateau of Rio Muni. The capital city, Malabo, is on the fertile volcanic island of Bioco. The climate is hot, humid and wet. Oil production started in 1992, and oil is now the main export, along with timber. The economy depends heavily on foreign aid.

ERITREA
State of Eritrea

Area Sq Km	117 400	Languages	Tigrinya, Tigre
Area Sq Miles	45 328	Religions	Sunni Muslim, Coptic Christian
Population	5 415 000	Currency	Nakfa
Capital	Asmara	Organizations	UN

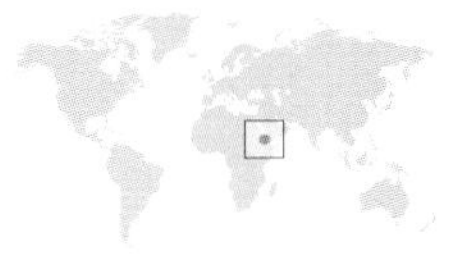

Eritrea, on the Red Sea coast of northeast Africa, consists of a high plateau in the north with a coastal plain which widens to the south. The coast is hot; inland is cooler. Rainfall is unreliable. The agriculture-based economy has suffered from over thirty years of war and occasional poor rains. Eritrea is one of the least developed countries in the world.

ESTONIA
Republic of Estonia

Area Sq Km	45 200	Languages	Estonian, Russian
Area Sq Miles	17 452	Religions	Protestant, Estonian and Russian Orthodox
Population	1 341 000	Currency	Euro
Capital	Tallinn	Organizations	EU, NATO, OECD, UN

Estonia is in northern Europe, on the Gulf of Finland and the Baltic Sea. The land, over one-third of which is forested, is generally low-lying with many lakes. Approximately one-third of Estonians live in the capital, Tallinn. Exported goods include machinery, wood products, textiles and food products. The main trading partners are the Russian Federation, Finland and Sweden. Estonia joined the European Union in May 2004.

ETHIOPIA
Federal Democratic Republic of Ethiopia

Area Sq Km	1 133 880	Languages	Oromo, Amharic, Tigrinya, local languages
Area Sq Miles	437 794	Religions	Ethiopian Orthodox, Sunni Muslim, traditional beliefs
Population	84 734 000	Currency	Birr
Capital	Addis Ababa (Ādīs Ābeba)	Organizations	UN

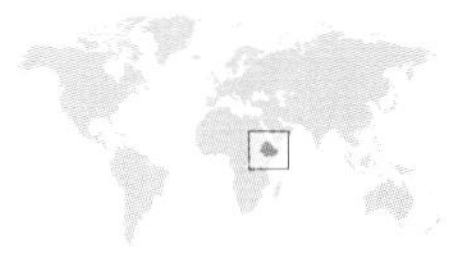

A landlocked country in northeast Africa, Ethiopia comprises a mountainous region in the west which is traversed by the Great Rift Valley. The east is mostly arid plateau land. The highlands are warm with summer rainfall. Most people live in the central–northern area. In recent years civil war, conflict with Eritrea and poor infrastructure have hampered economic development. Subsistence farming is the main activity, although droughts have led to frequent famines. Coffee is the main export and there is some light industry. Ethiopia is one of the least developed countries in the world.

Falkland Islands
United Kingdom Overseas Territory

Area Sq Km	12 170	Languages	English
Area Sq Miles	4 699	Religions	Protestant, Roman Catholic
Population	2 955	Currency	Falkland Islands pound
Capital	Stanley		

Lying in the southwest Atlantic Ocean, northeast of Cape Horn, two main islands, West Falkland and East Falkland and many smaller islands, form the territory of the Falkland Islands. The economy is based on sheep farming and the sale of fishing licences.

Faroe Islands
Self-governing Danish Territory

Area Sq Km	1 399	Languages	Faroese, Danish
Area Sq Miles	540	Religions	Protestant
Population	49 000	Currency	Danish krone
Capital	Thorshavn (Tórshavn)		

A self-governing territory, the Faroe Islands lie in the north Atlantic Ocean between the UK and Iceland. The islands benefit from the North Atlantic Drift ocean current, which has a moderating effect on the climate. The economy is based on deep-sea fishing.

FIJI
Republic of Fiji

Area Sq Km	18 330	Languages	English, Fijian, Hindi
Area Sq Miles	7 077	Religions	Christian, Hindu, Sunni Muslim
Population	868 000	Currency	Fiji dollar
Capital	Suva	Organizations	Comm., UN

The southwest Pacific republic of Fiji comprises two mountainous and volcanic islands, Vanua Levu and Viti Levu, and over three hundred smaller islands. The climate is tropical and the economy is based on agriculture (chiefly sugar, the main export), fishing, forestry, gold mining and tourism.

FINLAND
Republic of Finland

Area Sq Km	338 145	Languages	Finnish, Swedish
Area Sq Miles	130 559	Religions	Protestant, Greek Orthodox
Population	5 385 000	Currency	Euro
Capital	Helsinki (Helsingfors)	Organizations	EU, OECD, UN

Finland is in northern Europe, and nearly one-third of the country lies north of the Arctic Circle. Forests cover over seventy per cent of the land area, and ten per cent is covered by lakes. Summers are short and warm, and winters are long and severe, particularly in the north. Most of the population lives in the southern third of the country, along the coast or near the lakes. Timber is a major resource and there are important minerals, chiefly chromium. Main industries include metal working, electronics, paper and paper products, and chemicals. The main trading partners are Germany, Sweden and the UK.

FRANCE
French Republic

Area Sq Km	543 965	Languages	French, Arabic
Area Sq Miles	210 026	Religions	Roman Catholic, Protestant, Sunni Muslim
Population	63 126 000	Currency	Euro
Capital	Paris	Organizations	EU, NATO, OECD, UN

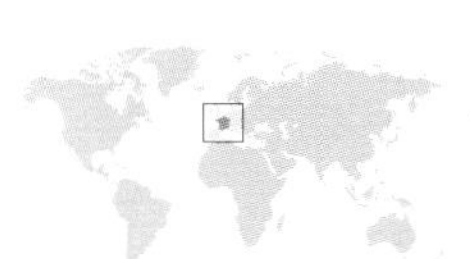

France lies in western Europe, on the Atlantic and the Mediterranean. There are mountain ranges in the southwest (the Pyrenees) and the east (the Alps, Jura and Vosges), and the Massif Central is an extensive hill region. The climate is temperate, the Mediterranean coast having hotter summers and milder winters. Over seventy per cent of the population lives in towns. There are coal reserves, and some oil and gas, but nuclear and hydroelectric power and imported fuels are vital. Industries include food processing, iron, steel and aluminium, chemicals, cars, electronics, oil refining, and tourism. Transport equipment, plastics and chemicals are exported. Trade is mainly with other EU countries.

French Guiana
French Overseas Department

Area Sq Km	90 000	Languages	French, Creole
Area Sq Miles	34 749	Religions	Roman Catholic
Population	237 000	Currency	Euro
Capital	Cayenne		

French Guiana, on the north coast of South America, is densely forested. The climate is tropical, with high rainfall. Most people live in the coastal strip, and agriculture is mostly subsistence farming. Forestry and fishing are important, but mineral resources are largely unexploited and industry is limited. French Guiana depends on French aid. The main trading partners are France and the USA.

French Polynesia
French Overseas Country

Area Sq Km	3 265	Languages	French, Tahitian, Polynesian languages
Area Sq Miles	1 261	Religions	Protestant, Roman Catholic
Population	274 000	Currency	CFP franc
Capital	Papeete		

Extending over a vast area of the southeast Pacific Ocean, French Polynesia comprises more than one hundred and thirty islands and coral atolls. The main island groups are the Marquesas Islands, the Tuamotu Archipelago and the Society Islands. The capital, Papeete, is on Tahiti in the Society Islands. The climate is subtropical, and the economy is based on tourism. The main export is cultured pearls.

GABON
Gabonese Republic

Area Sq Km	267 667	Languages	French, Fang, local languages
Area Sq Miles	103 347	Religions	Roman Catholic, Protestant, traditional beliefs
Population	1 534 000	Currency	CFA franc
Capital	Libreville	Organizations	UN

Gabon, on the Atlantic coast of central Africa, consists of low plateaus and a coastal plain lined by lagoons and mangrove swamps. The climate is tropical and rainforests cover over three-quarters of the land area. Over seventy per cent of the population lives in towns. The economy is heavily dependent on oil, which accounts for around seventy-five per cent of exports; manganese, uranium and timber are the other main exports. Agriculture is mainly at subsistence level.

THE GAMBIA
Republic of The Gambia

Area Sq Km	11 295	Languages	English, Malinke, Fulani, Wolof
Area Sq Miles	4 361	Religions	Sunni Muslim, Protestant
Population	1 776 000	Currency	Dalasi
Capital	Banjul	Organizations	Comm., UN

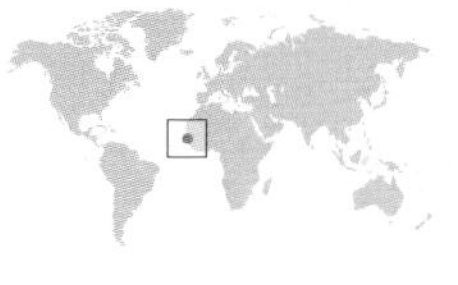

The Gambia, on the coast of west Africa, occupies a strip of land along the lower Gambia river. Sandy beaches are backed by mangrove swamps, beyond which is savanna. The climate is tropical, with most rainfall in the summer. Over seventy per cent of Gambians are farmers, growing chiefly groundnuts (the main export), cotton, oil palms and food crops. Livestock rearing and fishing are important, while manufacturing is limited. Re-exports, mainly from Senegal, and tourism are major sources of income.

Gaza
Disputed territory

Area Sq Km	363	Languages	Arabic
Area Sq Miles	140	Religions	Sunni Muslim, Shi'a Muslim
Population	1 535 120	Currency	Israeli shekel
Capital	Gaza		

Gaza is a narrow strip of land on the southeast corner of the Mediterranean Sea, between Egypt and Israel. This Palestinian territory has limited autonomy from Israel, but hostilities between Israel and the indigenous Arab population continue to restrict its economic development.

GEORGIA
Republic of Georgia

Area Sq Km	69 700	Languages	Georgian, Russian, Armenian, Azeri, Ossetian, Abkhaz
Area Sq Miles	26 911	Religions	Georgian Orthodox, Russian Orthodox, Sunni Muslim
Population	4 329 000	Currency	Lari
Capital	T'bilisi	Organizations	CIS, UN

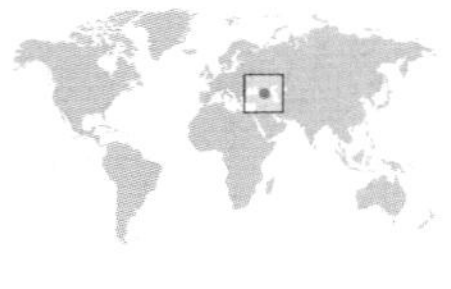

Georgia is in the northwest Caucasus area of southwest Asia, on the eastern coast of the Black Sea. Mountain ranges in the north and south flank the Kura and Rioni valleys. The climate is generally mild, and along the coast it is subtropical. Agriculture is important, with tea, grapes, and citrus fruits the main crops. Mineral resources include manganese ore and oil, and the main industries are steel, oil refining and machine building. The main trading partners are the Russian Federation and Turkey.

GERMANY
Federal Republic of Germany

Area Sq Km	357 022	Languages	German, Turkish
Area Sq Miles	137 847	Religions	Protestant, Roman Catholic
Population	82 163 000	Currency	Euro
Capital	Berlin	Organizations	EU, NATO, OECD, UN

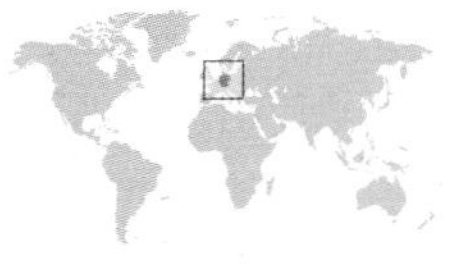

The central European state of Germany borders nine countries and has coastlines on the North and Baltic Seas. Behind the indented coastline, and covering about one-third of the country, is the north German plain, a region of fertile farmland and sandy heaths drained by the country's major rivers. The central highlands are a belt of forested hills and plateaus which stretch from the Eifel region in the west to the Erzgebirge mountains along the border with the Czech Republic. Farther south the land rises to the Swabian Alps (Schwäbische Alb), with the high rugged and forested Black Forest (Schwarzwald) in the southwest. In the far south the Bavarian Alps form the border with Austria. The climate is temperate, with continental conditions in eastern areas. The population is highly urbanized, with over eighty-five per cent living in cities and towns. With the exception of coal, lignite, potash and baryte, Germany lacks minerals and other industrial raw materials. It has a small agricultural base, although a few products (chiefly wines and beers) enjoy an international reputation. Germany is the world's fourth ranking economy after the USA, China and Japan. Its industries are amongst the world's most technologically advanced. Exports include machinery, vehicles and chemicals. The majority of trade is with other countries in the European Union, the USA and Japan.

Baden-Württemberg (State)
Area Sq Km (Sq Miles) 35 752 (13 804) Population 10 758 000 Capital Stuttgart

Bayern (State)
Area Sq Km (Sq Miles) 70 550 (27 240) Population 12 538 000 Capital Munich (München)

Berlin (State)
Area Sq Km (Sq Miles) 892 (344) Population 3 456 000 Capital Berlin

Brandenburg (State)
Area Sq Km (Sq Miles) 29 476 (11 381) Population 2 505 100 Capital Potsdam

Bremen
Area Sq Km (Sq Miles) 404 (156) Population 661 000 Capital Bremen

Hamburg (State)
Area Sq Km (Sq Miles) 755 (292) Population 2 834 221 Capital Hamburg

Hessen (State)
Area Sq Km (Sq Miles) 21 114 (8 152) Population 6 071 000 Capital Wiesbaden

Mecklenburg-Vorpommern (State)
Area Sq Km (Sq Miles) 23 173 (8 947) Population 1 645 000 Capital Schwerin

Niedersachsen (State)
Area Sq Km (Sq Miles) 47 616 (18 385) Population 7 922 000 Capital Hannover

Nordrhein-Westfalen (State)
Area Sq Km (Sq Miles) 34 082 (13 159) Population 17 851 000 Capital Düsseldorf

Rheinland-Pfalz (State)
Area Sq Km (Sq Miles) 19 847 (7 663) Population 4 006 000 Capital Mainz

Saarland (State)
Area Sq Km (Sq Miles) 2 568 (992) Population 1 019 000 Capital Saarbrücken

Sachsen (State)
Area Sq Km (Sq Miles) 18 413 (7 109) Population 4 152 000 Capital Dresden

Sachsen-Anhalt (State)
Area Sq Km (Sq Miles) 20 447 (7 895) Population 2 339 000 Capital Magdeburg

Schleswig-Holstein (State)
Area Sq Km (Sq Miles) 15 761 (6 085) Population 2 834 221 Capital Kiel

Thüringen (State)
Area Sq Km (Sq Miles) 16 172 (6 244) Population 2 237 000 Capital Erfurt

GHANA
Republic of Ghana

Area Sq Km	238 537	Languages	English, Hausa, Akan, local languages
Area Sq Miles	92 100	Religions	Christian, Sunni Muslim, traditional beliefs
Population	24 966 000	Currency	Cedi
Capital	Accra	Organizations	Comm., UN

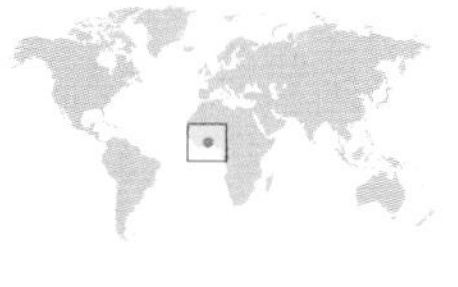

A west African state on the Gulf of Guinea, Ghana is a land of plains and low plateaus covered with savanna and rainforest. In the east is the Volta basin and Lake Volta. The climate is tropical, with the highest rainfall in the south, where most of the population lives. Agriculture employs around sixty per cent of the workforce. Main exports are gold, timber, cocoa, bauxite and manganese ore.

Gibraltar
United Kingdom Overseas Territory

Area Sq Km	7	Languages	English, Spanish
Area Sq Miles	3	Religions	Roman Catholic, Protestant, Sunni Muslim
Population	29 000	Currency	Gibraltar pound
Capital	Gibraltar		

Gibraltar lies on the south coast of Spain at the western entrance to the Mediterranean Sea. The economy depends on tourism, offshore banking and shipping services.

GREECE
Hellenic Republic

Area Sq Km	131 957	Languages	Greek
Area Sq Miles	50 949	Religions	Greek Orthodox, Sunni Muslim
Population	11 390 000	Currency	Euro
Capital	Athens (Athina)	Organizations	EU, NATO, OECD, UN

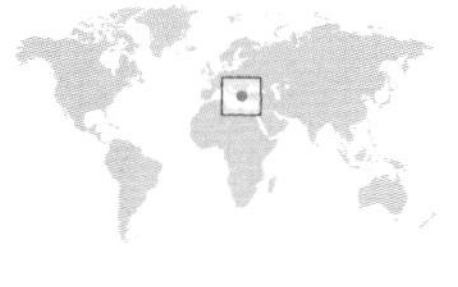

Greece comprises a mountainous peninsula in the Balkan region of southeastern Europe and many islands in the Ionian, Aegean and Mediterranean Seas. The islands make up over one-fifth of its area. Mountains and hills cover much of the country. The main lowland areas are the plains of Thessaly in the centre and around Thessaloniki in the northeast. Summers are hot and dry while winters are mild and wet, but colder in the north with heavy snowfalls in the mountains. One-third of Greeks live in the Athens area. Employment in agriculture accounts for approximately twenty per cent of the workforce, and exports include citrus fruits, raisins, wine, olives and olive oil. Aluminium and nickel are mined and a wide range of manufactures are produced, including food products and tobacco, textiles, clothing, and chemicals. Tourism is an important industry and there is a large services sector. Most trade is with other European Union countries.

Greenland
Self-governing Danish Territory

Area Sq Km	2 175 600	Languages	Greenlandic, Danish
Area Sq Miles	840 004	Religions	Protestant
Population	57 000	Currency	Danish krone
Capital	Nuuk (Godthåb)		

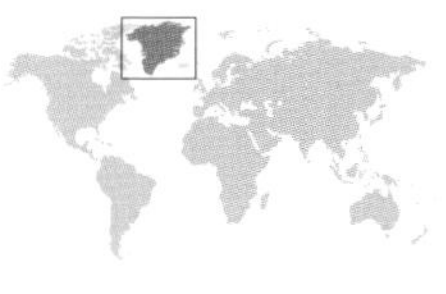

Situated to the northeast of North America between the Atlantic and Arctic Oceans, Greenland is the largest island in the world. It has a polar climate and over eighty per cent of the land area is covered by permanent ice cap. The economy is based on fishing and fish processing.

GRENADA

Area Sq Km	378	Languages	English, Creole
Area Sq Miles	146	Religions	Roman Catholic, Protestant
Population	105 000	Currency	East Caribbean dollar
Capital	St George's	Organizations	CARICOM, Comm., UN

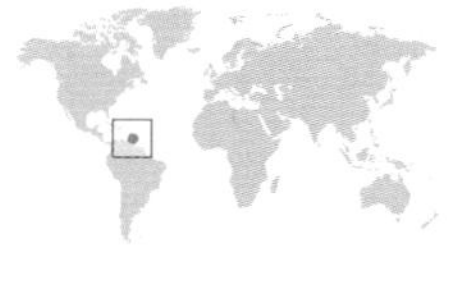

The Caribbean state comprises Grenada, the most southerly of the Windward Islands, and the southern islands of the Grenadines. Grenada has wooded hills, with beaches in the southwest. The climate is warm and wet. Agriculture is the main activity, with bananas, nutmeg and cocoa the main exports. Tourism is the main foreign exchange earner.

Guadeloupe
French Overseas Department

Area Sq Km	1 780	Languages	French, Creole
Area Sq Miles	687	Religions	Roman Catholic
Population	463 000	Currency	Euro
Capital	Basse-Terre		

Guadeloupe, in the Leeward Islands in the Caribbean, consists of two main islands (Basse-Terre and Grande-Terre, connected by a bridge), Marie-Galante, and a few outer islands. The climate is tropical, but moderated by trade winds. Bananas, sugar and rum are the main exports and tourism is a major source of income.

Guam
United States Unincorporated Territory

Area Sq Km	541	Languages	Chamorro, English, Tagalog
Area Sq Miles	209	Religions	Roman Catholic
Population	182 000	Currency	United States dollar
Capital	Hagåtña		

Lying at the south end of the Northern Mariana Islands in the western Pacific Ocean, Guam has a humid tropical climate. The island has a large US military base and the economy relies on that and on tourism.

GUATEMALA
Republic of Guatemala

Area Sq Km	108 890	Languages	Spanish, Mayan languages
Area Sq Miles	42 043	Religions	Roman Catholic, Protestant
Population	14 757 000	Currency	Quetzal, United States dollar
Capital	Guatemala City	Organizations	UN

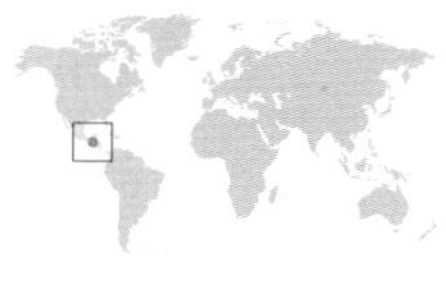

The most populous country in Central America after Mexico, Guatemala has long Pacific and short Caribbean coasts separated by a mountain chain which includes several active volcanoes. The climate is hot tropical in the lowlands and cooler in the highlands, where most of the population lives. Farming is the main activity and coffee, sugar and bananas are the main exports. There is some manufacturing of clothing and textiles. The main trading partner is the USA.

Guernsey
United Kingdom Crown Dependency

Area Sq Km	78	Languages	English, French
Area Sq Miles	30	Religions	Protestant, Roman Catholic
Population	65 264	Currency	Pound sterling
Capital	St Peter Port		

Guernsey is one of the Channel Islands, lying off northern France. The dependency also includes the nearby islands of Alderney, Sark and Herm. Financial services are an important part of the island's economy.

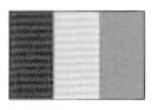

GUINEA
Republic of Guinea

Area Sq Km	245 857	Languages	French, Fulani, Malinke, local languages
Area Sq Miles	94 926	Religions	Sunni Muslim, traditional beliefs, Christian
Population	10 222 000		
Capital	Conakry	Currency	Guinea franc
		Organizations	UN

Guinea is in west Africa, on the Atlantic Ocean. There are mangrove swamps along the coast, while inland are lowlands and the Fouta Djallon mountains and plateaus. To the east are savanna plains drained by the upper Niger river system. The southeast is hilly. The climate is tropical, with high coastal rainfall. Agriculture is the main activity, employing nearly eighty per cent of the workforce, with coffee, bananas and pineapples the chief cash crops. There are huge reserves of bauxite, which accounts for more than seventy per cent of exports. Other exports include aluminium oxide, gold, coffee and diamonds.

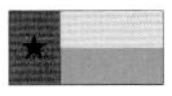

GUINEA-BISSAU
Republic of Guinea-Bissau

Area Sq Km	36 125	Languages	Portuguese, Crioulo, local languages
Area Sq Miles	13 948	Religions	Traditional beliefs, Sunni Muslim, Christian
Population	1 547 000		
Capital	Bissau	Currency	CFA franc
		Organizations	UN

Guinea-Bissau is on the Atlantic coast of west Africa. The mainland coast is swampy and contains many estuaries. Inland are forested plains, and to the east are savanna plateaus. The climate is tropical. The economy is based mainly on subsistence farming. There is little industry, and timber and mineral resources are largely unexploited. Cashews account for seventy per cent of exports. Guinea-Bissau is one of the least developed countries in the world.

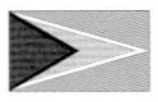

GUYANA
Co-operative Republic of Guyana

Area Sq Km	214 969	Languages	English, Creole, Amerindian languages
Area Sq Miles	83 000	Religions	Protestant, Hindu, Roman Catholic, Sunni Muslim
Population	756 000		
Capital	Georgetown	Currency	Guyana dollar
		Organizations	CARICOM, Comm., UN

Guyana, on the northeast coast of South America, consists of highlands in the west and savanna uplands in the southwest. Most of the country is densely forested. A lowland coastal belt supports crops and most of the population. The generally hot, humid and wet conditions are modified along the coast by sea breezes. The economy is based on agriculture, bauxite, and forestry. Sugar, bauxite, gold, rice and timber are the main exports.

HAITI
Republic of Haiti

Area Sq Km	27 750	Languages	French, Creole
Area Sq Miles	10 714	Religions	Roman Catholic, Protestant, Voodoo
Population	10 124 000	Currency	Gourde
Capital	Port-au-Prince	Organizations	CARICOM, UN

Haiti, occupying the western third of the Caribbean island of Hispaniola, is a mountainous state with small coastal plains and a central valley. The Dominican Republic occupies the rest of the island. The climate is tropical, and is hottest in coastal areas. Haiti has few natural resources, is densely populated and relies on exports of local crafts and coffee, and remittances from workers abroad. The country has not yet recovered from the 2010 earthquake.

HONDURAS
Republic of Honduras

Area Sq Km	112 088	Languages	Spanish, Amerindian languages
Area Sq Miles	43 277	Religions	Roman Catholic, Protestant
Population	7 755 000	Currency	Lempira
Capital	Tegucigalpa	Organizations	UN

Honduras, in central America, is a mountainous and forested country with lowland areas along its long Caribbean and short Pacific coasts. Coastal areas are hot and humid with heavy summer rainfall; inland is cooler and drier. Most of the population lives in the central valleys. Coffee and bananas are the main exports, along with shellfish and zinc. Industry involves mainly agricultural processing.

HUNGARY

Area Sq Km	93 030	Languages	Hungarian
Area Sq Miles	35 919	Religions	Roman Catholic, Protestant
Population	9 966 000	Currency	Forint
Capital	Budapest	Organizations	EU, NATO, OECD, UN

The Danube river flows north-south through central Hungary, a landlocked country in eastern Europe. In the east lies a great plain, flanked by highlands in the north. In the west low mountains and Lake Balaton separate a smaller plain and southern uplands. The climate is continental. Sixty per cent of the population lives in urban areas, and one-fifth lives in the capital, Budapest. Some minerals and energy resources are exploited, chiefly bauxite, coal and natural gas. Hungary has an industrial economy based on metals, machinery, transport equipment, chemicals and food products. The main trading partners are Germany and Austria. Hungary joined the European Union in May 2004.

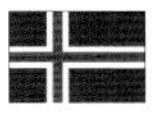

ICELAND
Republic of Iceland

Area Sq Km	102 820	Languages	Icelandic
Area Sq Miles	39 699	Religions	Protestant
Population	324 000	Currency	Icelandic króna
Capital	Reykjavik	Organizations	NATO, OECD, UN

Iceland lies in the north Atlantic Ocean near the Arctic Circle, to the northwest of Scandinavia. The landscape is volcanic, with numerous hot springs, geysers, and approximately two hundred volcanoes. One-tenth of the country is covered by ice caps. Only coastal lowlands are cultivated and settled, and over half the population lives in the Reykjavik area. The climate is mild, moderated by the North Atlantic Drift ocean current and by southwesterly winds. The mainstays of the economy are fishing and fish processing, which account for seventy per cent of exports. Agriculture involves mainly sheep and dairy farming. Hydroelectric and geothermal energy resources are considerable. The main industries produce aluminium, ferro-silicon and fertilizers. Tourism, including ecotourism, is growing in importance.

INDIA
Republic of India

Area Sq Km	3 064 898	Languages	Hindi, English, many regional languages
Area Sq Miles	1 183 364		
Population	1 241 492 000	Religions	Hindu, Sunni Muslim, Shi'a Muslim, Sikh, Christian
Capital	New Delhi	Currency	Indian rupee
		Organizations	Comm., UN

The south Asian country of India occupies a peninsula that juts out into the Indian Ocean between the Arabian Sea and Bay of Bengal. The heart of the peninsula is the Deccan plateau, bordered on either side by ranges of hills, the western Ghats and the lower eastern Ghats, which fall away to narrow coastal plains. To the north is a broad plain, drained by the Indus, Ganges and Brahmaputra rivers and their tributaries. The plain is intensively farmed and is the most populous region. In the west is the Thar Desert. The mountains of the Himalaya form India's northern border, together with parts of the Karakoram and Hindu Kush ranges in the northwest. The climate shows marked seasonal variation: a hot season from March to June; a monsoon season from June to October; and a cold season from November to February. Rainfall ranges between very high in the northeast Assam region to negligible in the Thar Desert. Temperatures range from very cold in the Himalaya to tropical heat over much of the south. Over seventy per cent of the huge population – the second largest in the world – is rural, although Delhi, Mumbai (Bombay) and Kolkata (Calcutta) all rank among the ten largest cities in the world. Agriculture, forestry and fishing account for a quarter of national output and two-thirds of employment. Much of the farming is on a subsistence basis and involves mainly rice and wheat. India is a major world producer of tea, sugar, jute, cotton and tobacco. Livestock is reared mainly for dairy products and hides. There are major reserves of coal, reserves of oil and natural gas, and many minerals, including iron, manganese, bauxite, diamonds and gold. The manufacturing sector is large and diverse – mainly chemicals and chemical products, textiles, iron and steel, food products, electrical goods and transport equipment; software and pharmaceuticals are also important. All the main manufactured products are exported, together with diamonds and jewellery. The USA, Germany, Japan and the UK are the main trading partners.

INDONESIA
Republic of Indonesia

Area Sq Km	1 919 445	Languages	Indonesian, local languages
Area Sq Miles	741 102	Religions	Sunni Muslim, Protestant, Roman Catholic, Hindu, Buddhist
Population	242 326 000		
Capital	Jakarta	Currency	Rupiah
		Organizations	APEC, ASEAN, OPEC, UN

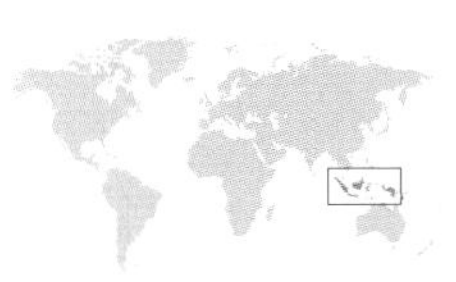

Indonesia consists of over thirteen thousand islands in Southeast Asia, between the Pacific and Indian Oceans. Sumatra, Java, Sulawesi (Celebes), Kalimantan (two-thirds of Borneo) and Papua (formerly Irian Jaya, western New Guinea) make up ninety per cent of the area. Most of Indonesia is covered with rainforest or mangrove swamps, and there are over three hundred volcanoes. Two-thirds of the population lives in the lowland areas of Java and Madura. The climate is tropical monsoon. Chief products are rice, palm oil, tea, coffee, rubber, tobacco, textiles, clothing, cement, tin, fertilizers and vehicles. Oil, gas, timber products and clothing are exported. Main trading partners are Japan, the USA and Singapore.

IRAN
Islamic Republic of Iran

Area Sq Km	1 648 000	Languages	Farsi, Azeri, Kurdish, regional languages
Area Sq Miles	636 296		
Population	74 799 000	Religions	Shi'a Muslim, Sunni Muslim
Capital	Tehrän	Currency	Iranian rial
		Organizations	OPEC, UN

Iran is in southwest Asia, and has coasts on The Gulf, the Caspian Sea and the Gulf of Oman. In the east is a high plateau, with large salt pans and a vast sand desert. In the west the Zagros Mountains form a series of ridges, and to the north lie the Elburz Mountains. Most farming and settlement is on the narrow plain along the Caspian Sea and in the foothills of the north and west. The climate is one of extremes, with hot summers and very cold winters. Most of the light rainfall is in the winter months. Agriculture involves approximately one-third of the workforce. Wheat is the main crop, but fruit (especially dates) and pistachio nuts are grown for export. Petroleum (the main export) and natural gas are Iran's leading natural resources. Manufactured goods include carpets, clothing, food products and construction materials.

IRAQ
Republic of Iraq

Area Sq Km	438 317	Languages	Arabic, Kurdish, Turkmen
Area Sq Miles	169 235	Religions	Shi'a Muslim, Sunni Muslim, Christian
Population	32 665 000		
Capital	Baghdäd	Currency	Iraqi dinar
		Organizations	OPEC, UN

Iraq, in southwest Asia, has at its heart the lowland valley of the Tigris and Euphrates rivers. In the southeast, where the two rivers join, are the Mesopotamian marshes and the Shatt al 'Arab waterway leading to The Gulf. The north is hilly, while the west is mostly desert. Summers are hot and dry, and winters are mild with light, unreliable rainfall. The Tigris-Euphrates valley contains most of the country's arable land. One in five of the population lives in the capital, Baghdad. The economy has suffered following the 1991 Gulf War and the invasion of US-led coalition forces in 2005. The latter resulted in the overthrow of the dictator Saddam Hussein, but there is continuing internal instability. Oil is normally the main export.

IRELAND
Republic of Ireland

Area Sq Km	70 282	Languages	English, Irish
Area Sq Miles	27 136	Religions	Roman Catholic, Protestant
Population	4 526 000	Currency	Euro
Capital	Dublin (Baile Átha Cliath)	Organizations	EU, OECD, UN

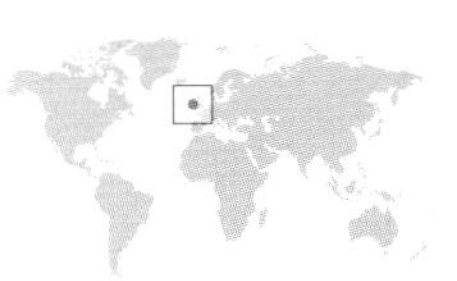

The Irish Republic occupies eighty per cent of the island of Ireland, in northwest Europe. It is a lowland country of wide valleys, lakes and peat bogs, with isolated mountain ranges around the coast. The climate is mild, modified by the North Atlantic Drift ocean current, and rainfall is plentiful, although highest in the west. Over sixty per cent of the population lives in urban areas. Resources include natural gas, peat, lead and zinc. Agriculture now employs less than ten per cent of the workforce. The main industries are electronics, pharmaceuticals, engineering, food processing, brewing and textiles. Service industries and tourism are also important. The UK is the main trading partner.

States and Territories

Isle of Man
United Kingdom Crown Dependency

Area Sq Km	572	Languages	English
Area Sq Miles	221	Religions	Protestant, Roman Catholic
Population	83 000	Currency	Pound sterling
Capital	Douglas		

The Isle of Man lies in the Irish Sea between England and Northern Ireland. The island is self-governing, although the UK is responsible for its defence and foreign affairs. It is not part of the European Union, but has a special relationship with the EU which allows for free trade. Eighty per cent of the economy is based on the service sector, particularly financial services.

ISRAEL
State of Israel

Area Sq Km	20 770	Languages	Hebrew, Arabic
Area Sq Miles	8 019	Religions	Jewish, Sunni Muslim, Christian, Druze
Population	7 562 000	Currency	Shekel
Capital	Jerusalem (Yerushalayim) (El Quds) De facto capital. Disputed.	Organizations	OECD, UN

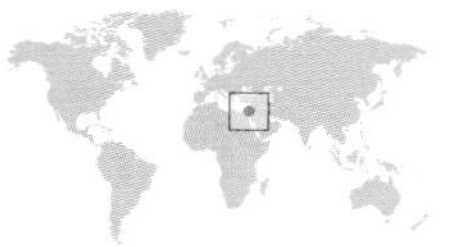

Israel lies on the Mediterranean coast of southwest Asia. Beyond the coastal Plain of Sharon are the hills and valleys of Samaria, with the Galilee highlands to the north. In the east is a rift valley, which extends from Lake Tiberias (Sea of Galilee) to the Gulf of Aqaba and contains the Jordan river and the Dead Sea. In the south is the Negev, a triangular semi-desert plateau. Most of the population lives on the coastal plain or in northern and central areas. Much of Israel has warm summers and mild, wet winters. The south is hot and dry. Agricultural production was boosted by the occupation of the West Bank in 1967. Manufacturing makes the largest contribution to the economy, and tourism is also important. Israel's main exports are machinery and transport equipment, software, diamonds, clothing, fruit and vegetables. The country relies heavily on foreign aid. Security issues relating to territorial disputes over the West Bank and Gaza have still to be resolved.

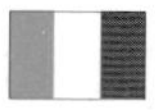

ITALY
Italian Republic

Area Sq Km	301 245	Languages	Italian
Area Sq Miles	116 311	Religions	Roman Catholic
Population	60 789 000	Currency	Euro
Capital	Rome (Roma)	Organizations	EU, NATO, OECD, UN

Italy occupies a peninsula in southern Europe jutting out into the Mediterranean. It includes Sicily and Sardinia and many smaller islands. The Alps are in the north, and the Apennines run along the peninsula. Population, agriculture and industry are concentrated in the northern lowlands. The climate is Mediterranean, but with colder, wetter winters in the north. Only one-fifth of the land is cultivated. Some oil, gas and coal are produced. Cereals, vines, fruit and vegetables are grown: Italy is the world's largest wine producer. Manufactures include industrial and domestic equipment, cars, textiles, chemicals and metal products. Tourism, finance and service industries are important. Most trade is with other EU countries.

JAMAICA

Area Sq Km	10 991	Languages	English, Creole
Area Sq Miles	4 244	Religions	Protestant, Roman Catholic
Population	2 751 000	Currency	Jamaican dollar
Capital	Kingston	Organizations	CARICOM, Comm., UN

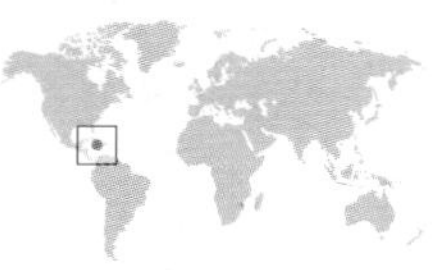

Jamaica, the third largest Caribbean island, has beaches and densely populated coastal plains traversed by hills and plateaus rising to the forested Blue Mountains in the east. The climate is tropical, but cooler and wetter on high ground. The economy is based on tourism, agriculture, mining and light manufacturing. Bauxite, aluminium oxide, sugar and bananas are the main exports. The USA is the main trading partner. Foreign aid is also significant.

JAPAN

Area Sq Km	377 727	Languages	Japanese
Area Sq Miles	145 841	Religions	Shintoist, Buddhist, Christian
Population	126 497 000	Currency	Yen
Capital	Tōkyō	Organizations	APEC, OECD, UN

Japan lies in the Pacific Ocean off the coast of eastern Asia and consists of four main islands – Hokkaidō, Honshū, Shikoku and Kyūshū – and more than three thousand smaller islands in the surrounding Sea of Japan, East China Sea and Pacific Ocean. The central island of Honshū accounts for sixty per cent of the total land area and contains eighty per cent of the population. Behind the long and deeply indented coastline, nearly three-quarters of the country is mountainous and heavily forested. Japan has over sixty active volcanoes, and is subject to frequent earthquakes and typhoons. The climate is generally temperate maritime, with warm summers and mild winters, except in western Hokkaidō and northwest Honshū, where the winters are very cold with heavy snow. Only fourteen per cent of the land area is suitable for cultivation, and its few raw materials (coal, oil, natural gas, lead, zinc and copper) are insufficient for its industry. Most materials must be imported, including about ninety per cent of energy requirements. Yet Japan has the world's third largest industrial economy, with a range of modern heavy and light industries centred mainly around the major ports of Yokohama, Ōsaka and Tōkyō. It is the world's largest manufacturer of cars, motorcycles and merchant ships, and a major producer of steel, textiles, chemicals and cement. It is also a leading producer of many consumer durables, such as washing machines, and electronic equipment, chiefly office equipment and computers. Japan has a strong service sector, banking and finance being particularly important, and Tōkyō has one of the world's major stock exchanges. Owing to intensive agricultural production, Japan is seventy per cent self-sufficient in food. The main food crops are rice, barley, fruit, wheat and soya beans. Livestock rearing (chiefly cattle, pigs and chickens) and fishing are also important, and Japan has one of the largest fishing fleets in the world. A major trading nation, Japan has trade links with many countries in southeast Asia and in Europe, although its main trading partner is the USA.

Jersey
United Kingdom Crown Dependency

Area Sq Km	116	Languages	English, French
Area Sq Miles	45	Religions	Protestant, Roman Catholic
Population	92 500	Currency	Pound sterling
Capital	St Helier		

One of the Channel Islands lying off the west coast of the Cherbourg peninsula in northern France. Financial services are the most important part of the economy.

JORDAN
Hashemite Kingdom of Jordan

Area Sq Km	89 206	Languages	Arabic
Area Sq Miles	34 443	Religions	Sunni Muslim, Christian
Population	6 330 000	Currency	Jordanian dinar
Capital	'Ammān	Organizations	UN

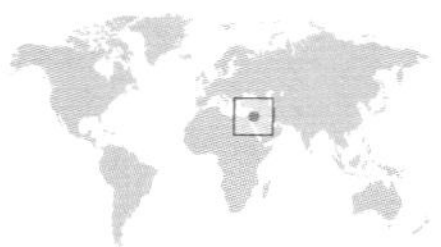

Jordan, in southwest Asia, is landlocked apart from a short coastline on the Gulf of Aqaba. Much of the country is rocky desert plateau. To the west of the mountains, the land falls below sea level to the Dead Sea and the Jordan river. The climate is hot and dry. Most people live in the northwest. Phosphates, potash, pharmaceuticals, fruit and vegetables are the main exports. The tourist industry is important, and the economy relies on workers' remittances from abroad and foreign aid.

KAZAKHSTAN
Republic of Kazakhstan

Area Sq Km	2 717 300	Languages	Kazakh, Russian, Ukrainian, German, Uzbek, Tatar
Area Sq Miles	1 049 155	Religions	Sunni Muslim, Russian Orthodox, Protestant
Population	16 207 000	Currency	Tenge
Capital	Astana (Akmola)	Organizations	CIS, UN

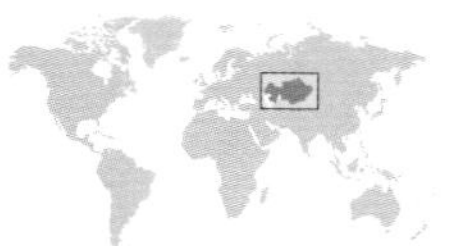

Stretching across central Asia, Kazakhstan covers a vast area of steppe land and semi-desert. The land is flat in the west, with large lowlands around the Caspian Sea, rising to mountains in the southeast. The climate is continental. Agriculture and livestock rearing are important, and cotton and tobacco are the main cash crops. Kazakhstan is very rich in minerals, including coal, chromium, gold, molybdenum, lead and zinc, and has substantial reserves of oil and gas. Mining, metallurgy, machine building and food processing are major industries. Oil, gas and minerals are the main exports, and the Russian Federation is the dominant trading partner.

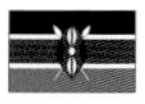

KENYA
Republic of Kenya

Area Sq Km	582 646	Languages	Swahili, English, local languages
Area Sq Miles	224 961	Religions	Christian, traditional beliefs
Population	41 610 000	Currency	Kenyan shilling
Capital	Nairobi	Organizations	Comm., UN

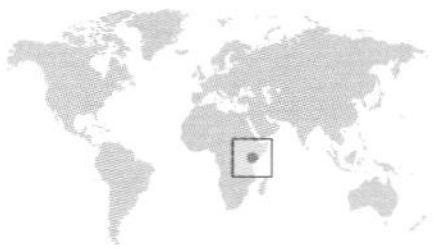

Kenya is in east Africa, on the Indian Ocean. Inland beyond the coastal plains the land rises to plateaus interrupted by volcanic mountains. The Great Rift Valley runs north-south to the west of the capital, Nairobi. Most of the population lives in the central area. Conditions are tropical on the coast, semi-desert in the north and savanna in the south. Hydroelectric power from the Upper Tana river provides most of the country's electricity. Agricultural products, mainly tea, coffee, fruit and vegetables, are the main exports. Light industry is important, and tourism, oil refining and re-exports for landlocked neighbours are major foreign exchange earners.

KIRIBATI
Republic of Kiribati

Area Sq Km	717	Languages	Gilbertese, English
Area Sq Miles	277	Religions	Roman Catholic, Protestant
Population	101 000	Currency	Australian dollar
Capital	Bairiki	Organizations	Comm., UN

Kiribati, in the Pacific Ocean, straddles the Equator and comprises coral islands in the Gilbert, Phoenix and Line Island groups and the volcanic island of Banaba. Most people live on the Gilbert Islands, and the capital, Bairiki, is on Tarawa island in this group. The climate is hot, and wetter in the north. Copra and fish are exported. Kiribati relies on remittances from workers abroad and foreign aid.

KOSOVO
Republic of Kosovo

Area Sq Km	10 908	Languages	Albanian, Serbian
Area Sq Miles	4 212	Religions	Sunni Muslim, Serbian Orthodox
Population	2 180 686	Currency	Euro
Capital	Prishtinë (Priština)		

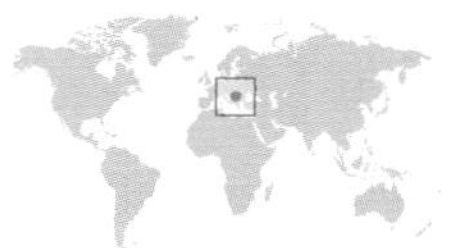

Kosovo, traditionally an autonomous southern province of Serbia, was the focus of ethnic conflict between Serbs and the majority ethnic Albanians in the 1990s until international intervention in 1999, after which it was administered by the UN. Kosovo declared its independence from Serbia in February 2008. The landscape is largely hilly or mountainous, especially along the southern and western borders.

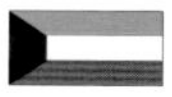

KUWAIT
State of Kuwait

Area Sq Km	17 818	Languages	Arabic
Area Sq Miles	6 880	Religions	Sunni Muslim, Shi'a Muslim, Christian, Hindu
Population	2 818 000	Currency	Kuwaiti dinar
Capital	Kuwait (Al Kuwayt)	Organizations	OPEC, UN

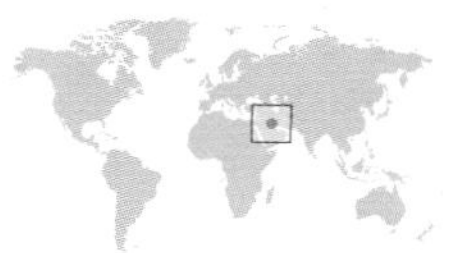

Kuwait lies on the northwest shores of The Gulf in southwest Asia. It is mainly low-lying desert, with irrigated areas along the bay, Kuwait Jun, where most people live. Summers are hot and dry, and winters are cool with some rainfall. The oil industry, which accounts for eighty per cent of exports, has largely recovered from the damage caused by the Gulf War in 1991. Income is also derived from extensive overseas investments. Japan and the USA are the main trading partners.

KYRGYZSTAN
Kyrgyz Republic

Area Sq Km	198 500	Languages	Kyrgyz, Russian, Uzbek
Area Sq Miles	76 641	Religions	Sunni Muslim, Russian Orthodox
Population	5 393 000	Currency	Kyrgyz som
Capital	Bishkek (Frunze)	Organizations	CIS, UN

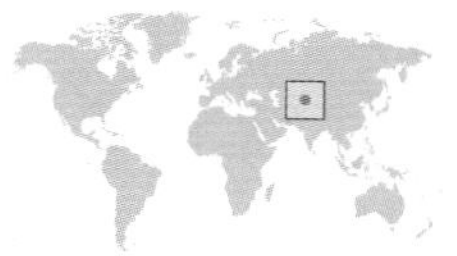

A landlocked central Asian state, Kyrgyzstan is rugged and mountainous, lying to the west of the Tien Shan mountain range. Most of the population lives in the valleys of the north and west. Summers are hot and winters cold. Agriculture (chiefly livestock farming) is the main activity. Some oil and gas, coal, gold, antimony and mercury are produced. Manufactured goods include machinery, metals and metal products, which are the main exports. Most trade is with Germany, the Russian Federation, Kazakhstan and Uzbekistan.

LAOS

Lao People's Democratic Republic

Area Sq Km	236 800	Languages	Lao, local languages
Area Sq Miles	91 429	Religions	Buddhist, traditional beliefs
Population	6 288 000	Currency	Kip
Capital	Vientiane (Viangchan)	Organizations	ASEAN, UN

A landlocked country in southeast Asia, Laos is a land of mostly forested mountains and plateaus. The climate is tropical monsoon. Most of the population lives in the Mekong valley and the low plateau in the south, where food crops, chiefly rice, are grown. Hydroelectricity from a plant on the Mekong river, timber, coffee and tin are exported. Laos relies heavily on foreign aid.

LATVIA

Republic of Latvia

Area Sq Km	64 589	Languages	Latvian, Russian
Area Sq Miles	24 938	Religions	Protestant, Roman Catholic, Russian Orthodox
Population	2 243 000	Currency	Lats
Capital	Rīga	Organizations	EU, NATO, UN

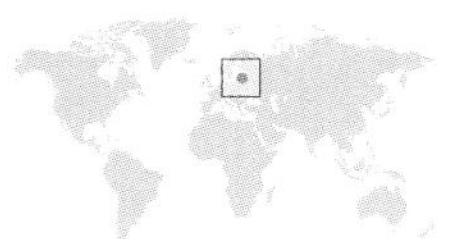

Latvia is in northern Europe, on the Baltic Sea and the Gulf of Riga. The land is flat near the coast but hilly with woods and lakes inland. The country has a modified continental climate. One-third of the people live in the capital, Rīga. Crop and livestock farming are important. There are few natural resources. Industries and main exports include food products, transport equipment, wood and wood products and textiles. The main trading partners are the Russian Federation and Germany. Latvia joined the European Union in May 2004.

LEBANON

Republic of Lebanon

Area Sq Km	10 452	Languages	Arabic, Armenian, French
Area Sq Miles	4 036	Religions	Shi'a Muslim, Sunni Muslim, Christian
Population	4 259 000	Currency	Lebanese pound
Capital	Beirut (Beyrouth)	Organizations	UN

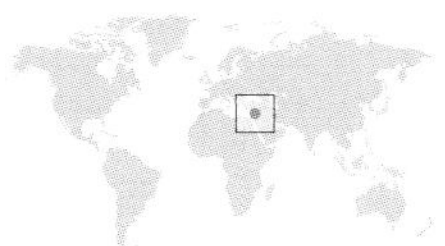

Lebanon lies on the Mediterranean coast of southwest Asia. Beyond the coastal strip, where most of the population lives, are two parallel mountain ranges, separated by the Bekaa Valley (El Beq'a). The economy and infrastructure have been recovering since the 1975–1991 civil war crippled the traditional sectors of financial services and tourism. Italy, France and the UAE are the main trading partners.

LESOTHO

Kingdom of Lesotho

Area Sq Km	30 355	Languages	Sesotho, English, Zulu
Area Sq Miles	11 720	Religions	Christian, traditional beliefs
Population	2 194 000	Currency	Loti, South African rand
Capital	Maseru	Organizations	Comm., SADC, UN

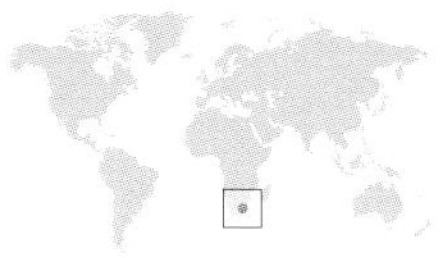

Lesotho is a landlocked state surrounded by the Republic of South Africa. It is a mountainous country lying within the Drakensberg mountain range. Farming and herding are the main activities. The economy depends heavily on South Africa for transport links and employment. A major hydroelectric plant completed in 1998 allows the sale of water to South Africa. Exports include manufactured goods (mainly clothing and road vehicles), food, live animals, wool and mohair.

LIBERIA

Republic of Liberia

Area Sq Km	111 369	Languages	English, Creole, local languages
Area Sq Miles	43 000	Religions	Traditional beliefs, Christian, Sunni Muslim
Population	4 129 000	Currency	Liberian dollar
Capital	Monrovia	Organizations	UN

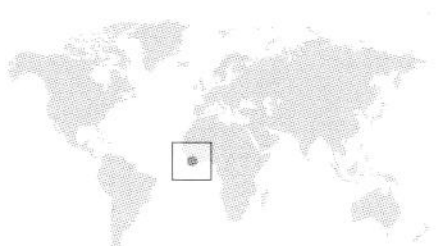

Liberia is on the Atlantic coast of west Africa. Beyond the coastal belt of sandy beaches and mangrove swamps the land rises to a forested plateau and highlands along the Guinea border. A quarter of the population lives along the coast. The climate is hot with heavy rainfall. Liberia is rich in mineral resources and forests. The economy is based on the production and export of basic products. Exports include diamonds, iron ore, rubber and timber. Liberia has a huge international debt and relies heavily on foreign aid.

LIBYA

Area Sq Km	1 759 540	Languages	Arabic, Berber
Area Sq Miles	679 362	Religions	Sunni Muslim
Population	6 423 000	Currency	Libyan dinar
Capital	Tripoli (Ṭarābulus)	Organizations	OPEC, UN

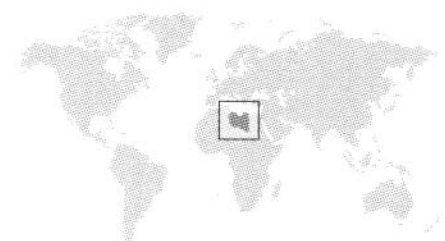

Libya lies on the Mediterranean coast of north Africa. The desert plains and hills of the Sahara dominate the landscape and the climate is hot and dry. Most of the population lives in cities near the coast, where the climate is cooler with moderate rainfall. Farming and herding, chiefly in the northwest, are important but the main industry is oil. Libya is a major producer, and oil accounts for virtually all of its export earnings. Italy and Germany are the main trading partners. As a result of the civil war in 2011 oil exports were disrupted and there was severe damage to the infrastructure of the country.

LIECHTENSTEIN

Principality of Liechtenstein

Area Sq Km	160	Languages	German
Area Sq Miles	62	Religions	Roman Catholic, Protestant
Population	36 000	Currency	Swiss franc
Capital	Vaduz	Organizations	UN

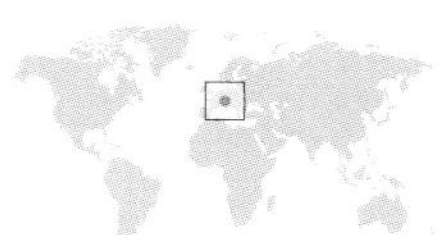

A landlocked state between Switzerland and Austria, Liechtenstein has an industrialized, free-enterprise economy. Low business taxes have attracted companies to establish offices which provide approximately one-third of state revenues. Banking is also important. Major products include precision instruments, ceramics and textiles.

LITHUANIA

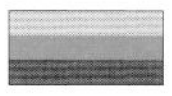

Republic of Lithuania

Area Sq Km	65 200	Languages	Lithuanian, Russian, Polish
Area Sq Miles	25 174	Religions	Roman Catholic, Protestant, Russian Orthodox
Population	3 307 000	Currency	Litas
Capital	Vilnius	Organizations	EU, NATO, UN

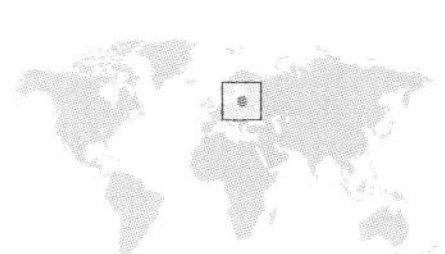

Lithuania is in northern Europe on the eastern shores of the Baltic Sea. It is mainly lowland with many lakes, rivers and marshes. Agriculture, fishing and forestry are important, but manufacturing dominates the economy. The main exports are machinery, mineral products and chemicals. The Russian Federation and Germany are the main trading partners. Lithuania joined the European Union in May 2004.

LUXEMBOURG

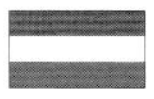

Grand Duchy of Luxembourg

Area Sq Km	2 586	Languages	Letzeburgish, German, French
Area Sq Miles	998	Religions	Roman Catholic
Population	516 000	Currency	Euro
Capital	Luxembourg	Organizations	EU, NATO, OECD, UN

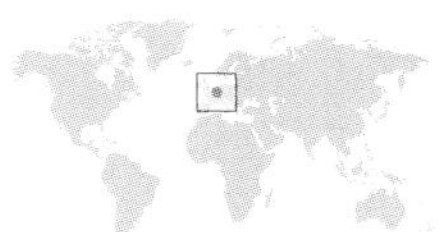

Luxembourg, a small landlocked country in western Europe, borders Belgium, France and Germany. The hills and forests of the Ardennes dominate the north, with rolling pasture to the south, where the main towns, farms and industries are found. The iron and steel industry is still important, but light industries (including textiles, chemicals and food products) are growing. Luxembourg is a major banking centre. Main trading partners are Belgium, Germany and France.

MACEDONIA (F.Y.R.O.M.)

Republic of Macedonia

Area Sq Km	25 713	Languages	Macedonian, Albanian, Turkish
Area Sq Miles	9 928	Religions	Macedonian Orthodox, Sunni Muslim
Population	2 064 000	Currency	Macedonian denar
Capital	Skopje	Organizations	NATO, UN

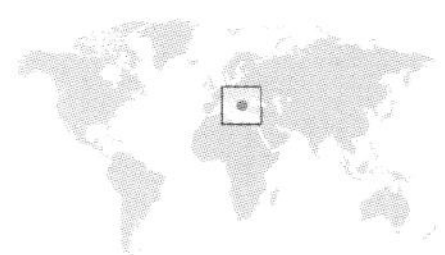

The Former Yugoslav Republic of Macedonia is a landlocked state in southern Europe. Lying within the southern Balkan Mountains, it is traversed northwest-southeast by the Vardar valley. The climate is continental. The economy is based on industry, mining and agriculture, but conflicts in the region have reduced trade and caused economic difficulties. Foreign aid and loans are now assisting in modernization and development of the country.

MADAGASCAR

Republic of Madagascar

Area Sq Km	587 041	Languages	Malagasy, French
Area Sq Miles	226 658	Religions	Traditional beliefs, Christian, Sunni Muslim
Population	21 315 000	Currency	Malagasy franc
Capital	Antananarivo	Organizations	SADC, UN

Madagascar lies off the east coast of southern Africa. The world's fourth largest island, it is mainly a high plateau, with a coastal strip to the east and scrubby plain to the west. The climate is tropical, with heavy rainfall in the north and east. Most of the population lives on the plateau. Although the amount of arable land is limited, the economy is based on agriculture. The main industries are agricultural processing, textile manufacturing and oil refining. Foreign aid is important. Exports include coffee, vanilla, cotton cloth, sugar and shrimps. France is the main trading partner.

MALAWI

Republic of Malawi

Area Sq Km	118 484	Languages	Chichewa, English, local languages
Area Sq Miles	45 747	Religions	Christian, traditional beliefs, Sunni Muslim
Population	15 381 000	Currency	Malawian kwacha
Capital	Lilongwe	Organizations	Comm., SADC, UN

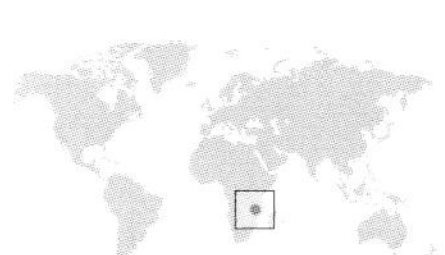

Landlocked Malawi in central Africa is a narrow hilly country at the southern end of the Great Rift Valley. One-fifth is covered by Lake Nyasa. Most of the population lives in rural areas in the southern regions. The climate is mainly subtropical, with varying rainfall. The economy is predominantly agricultural, with tobacco, tea and sugar the main exports. Malawi is one of the world's least developed countries and relies heavily on foreign aid. South Africa is the main trading partner.

MALAYSIA

Federation of Malaysia

Area Sq Km	332 965	Languages	Malay, English, Chinese, Tamil, local languages
Area Sq Miles	128 559	Religions	Sunni Muslim, Buddhist, Hindu, Christian, traditional beliefs
Population	28 859 000	Currency	Ringgit
Capital	Kuala Lumpur/ Putrajaya	Organizations	APEC, ASEAN, Comm., UN

Malaysia, in southeast Asia, comprises two regions, separated by the South China Sea. The western region occupies the southern Malay Peninsula, which has a chain of mountains dividing the eastern coastal strip from wider plains to the west. East Malaysia, consisting of the states of Sabah and Sarawak in the north of the island of Borneo, is mainly rainforest-covered hills and mountains with mangrove swamps along the coast. Both regions have a tropical climate with heavy rainfall. About eighty per cent of the population lives in Peninsular Malaysia. The country is rich in natural resources and has reserves of minerals and fuels. It is an important producer of tin, oil, natural gas and tropical hardwoods. Agriculture remains a substantial part of the economy, but industry is the most important sector. The main exports are transport and electronic equipment, oil, chemicals, palm oil, wood and rubber. The main trading partners are Japan, the USA and Singapore.

MALDIVES

Republic of the Maldives

Area Sq Km	298	Languages	Divehi (Maldivian)
Area Sq Miles	115	Religions	Sunni Muslim
Population	320 000	Currency	Rufiyaa
Capital	Male	Organizations	Comm., UN

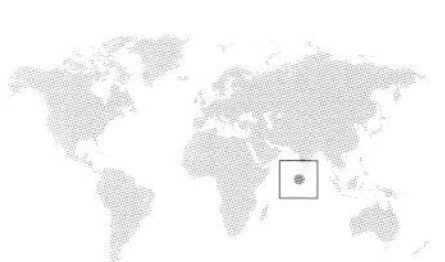

The Maldive archipelago comprises over a thousand coral atolls (around two hundred of which are inhabited), in the Indian Ocean, southwest of India. Over eighty per cent of the land area is less than one metre above sea level. The main atolls are North and South Male and Addu. The climate is hot, humid and monsoonal. There is little cultivation and almost all food is imported. Tourism has expanded rapidly and is the most important sector of the economy.

States and Territories

MALI
Republic of Mali

Area Sq Km	1 240 140	Languages	French, Bambara, local languages
Area Sq Miles	478 821	Religions	Sunni Muslim, traditional beliefs, Christian
Population	15 840 000	Currency	CFA franc
Capital	Bamako	Organizations	UN

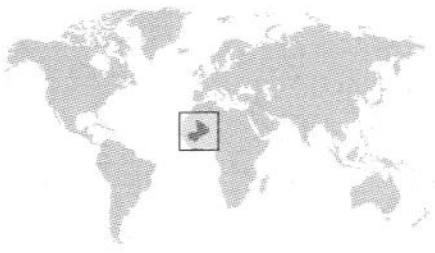

A landlocked state in west Africa, Mali is low-lying, with a few rugged hills in the northeast. Northern regions lie within the Sahara desert. To the south, around the Niger river, are marshes and savanna grassland. Rainfall is unreliable. Most of the population lives along the Niger and Falémé rivers. Exports include cotton, livestock and gold. Mali is one of the least developed countries in the world and relies heavily on foreign aid.

MALTA
Republic of Malta

Area Sq Km	316	Languages	Maltese, English
Area Sq Miles	122	Religions	Roman Catholic
Population	418 000	Currency	Euro
Capital	Valletta	Organizations	Comm., EU, UN

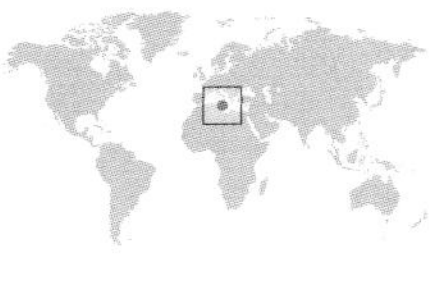

The islands of Malta and Gozo lie in the Mediterranean Sea, off the coast of southern Italy. The islands have hot, dry summers and mild winters. The economy depends on foreign trade, tourism and the manufacture of electronics and textiles. Main trading partners are the USA, France and Italy. Malta joined the European Union in May 2004.

MARSHALL ISLANDS
Republic of the Marshall Islands

Area Sq Km	181	Languages	English, Marshallese
Area Sq Miles	70	Religions	Protestant, Roman Catholic
Population	55 000	Currency	United States dollar
Capital	Delap-Uliga-Djarrit	Organizations	UN

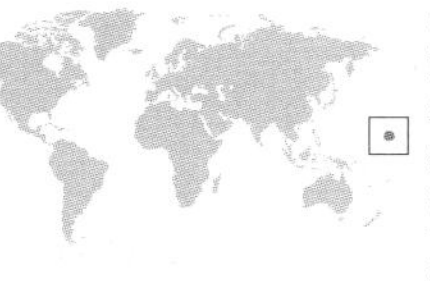

The Marshall Islands consist of over a thousand atolls, islands and islets, within two chains in the north Pacific Ocean. The main atolls are Majuro (home to half the population), Kwajalein, Jaluit, Enewetak and Bikini. The climate is tropical, with heavy autumn rainfall. About half the workforce is employed in farming or fishing. Tourism is a small source of foreign exchange and the islands depend heavily on aid from the USA.

Martinique
French Overseas Department

Area Sq Km	1 079	Languages	French, Creole
Area Sq Miles	417	Religions	Roman Catholic, traditional beliefs
Population	407 000	Currency	Euro
Capital	Fort-de-France		

Martinique, one of the Caribbean Windward Islands, has volcanic peaks in the north, a populous central plain, and hills and beaches in the south. Tourism is a major source of foreign exchange, and substantial aid is received from France. The main trading partners are France and Guadeloupe.

MAURITANIA
Islamic Arab and African Republic of Mauritania

Area Sq Km	1 030 700	Languages	Arabic, French, local languages
Area Sq Miles	397 955	Religions	Sunni Muslim
Population	3 542 000	Currency	Ouguiya
Capital	Nouakchott	Organizations	UN

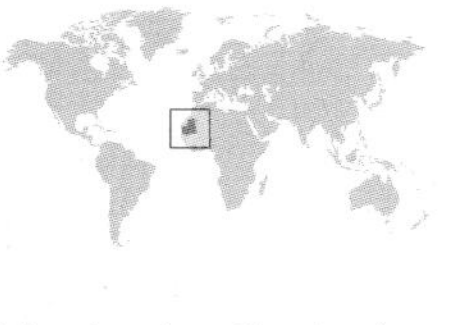

Mauritania is on the Atlantic coast of northwest Africa and lies almost entirely within the Sahara desert. Oases and a fertile strip along the Senegal river to the south are the only areas suitable for cultivation. The climate is generally hot and dry. About a quarter of Mauritanians live in the capital, Nouakchott. Most of the workforce depends on livestock rearing and subsistence farming. There are large deposits of iron ore which account for more than half of total exports. Mauritania's coastal waters are among the richest fishing grounds in the world. The main trading partners are France, Japan and Italy.

MAURITIUS
Republic of Mauritius

Area Sq Km	2 040	Languages	English, Creole, Hindi, Bhojpurī, French
Area Sq Miles	788	Religions	Hindu, Roman Catholic, Sunni Muslim
Population	1 307 000	Currency	Mauritius rupee
Capital	Port Louis	Organizations	Comm., SADC, UN

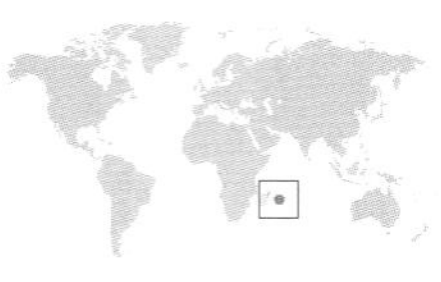

The state comprises Mauritius, Rodrigues and some twenty small islands in the Indian Ocean, east of Madagascar. The main island of Mauritius is volcanic in origin and has a coral coast, rising to a central plateau. Most of the population lives on the north and west sides of the island. The climate is warm and humid. The economy is based on sugar production, light manufacturing (chiefly clothing) and tourism.

Mayotte
French Overseas Department

Area Sq Km	373	Languages	French, Mahorian
Area Sq Miles	144	Religions	Sunni Muslim, Christian
Population	211 000	Currency	Euro
Capital	Dzaoudzi		

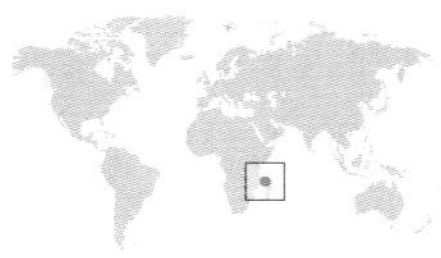

Lying in the Indian Ocean off the east coast of central Africa, Mayotte is geographically part of the Comoro archipelago. The economy is based on agriculture, but Mayotte depends heavily on aid from France.

MEXICO
United Mexican States

Area Sq Km	1 972 545	Languages	Spanish, Amerindian languages
Area Sq Miles	761 604	Religions	Roman Catholic, Protestant
Population	114 793 000	Currency	Mexican peso
Capital	Mexico City	Organizations	APEC, OECD, UN

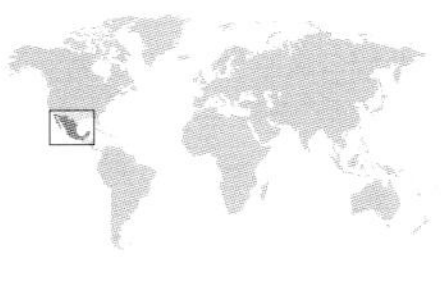

The largest country in Central America, Mexico extends south from the USA to Guatemala and Belize, and from the Pacific Ocean to the Gulf of Mexico. The greater part of the country is high plateau flanked by the western and eastern ranges of the Sierra Madre mountains. The principal lowland is the Yucatán peninsula in the southeast. The climate varies with latitude and altitude: hot and humid in the lowlands, warm on the plateau and cool with cold winters in the mountains. The north is arid, while the far south has heavy rainfall. Mexico City is the fifth largest conurbation in the world and the country's centre of trade and industry. Agriculture involves a fifth of the workforce; crops include grains, coffee, cotton and vegetables. Mexico is rich in minerals, including copper, zinc, lead, tin, sulphur, and silver. It is one of the world's largest producers of oil, from vast reserves in the Gulf of Mexico. The oil and petrochemical industries still dominate the economy, but a variety of manufactured goods are produced, including iron and steel, motor vehicles, textiles, chemicals and food and tobacco products. Tourism is growing in importance. Over three-quarters of all trade is with the USA.

MICRONESIA, FEDERATED STATES OF

Area Sq Km	701	Languages	English, Chuukese, Pohnpeian, local languages
Area Sq Miles	271	Religions	Roman Catholic, Protestant
Population	112 000	Currency	United States dollar
Capital	Palikir	Organizations	UN

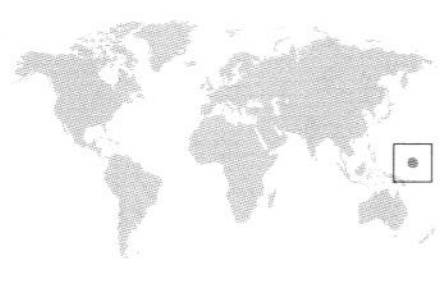

Micronesia comprises over six hundred atolls and islands of the Caroline Islands in the north Pacific Ocean. A third of the population lives on Pohnpei. The climate is tropical, with heavy rainfall. Fishing and subsistence farming are the main activities. Fish, garments and bananas are the main exports. Income is also derived from tourism and the licensing of foreign fishing fleets. The islands depend heavily on aid from the USA.

MOLDOVA
Republic of Moldova

Area Sq Km	33 700	Languages	Romanian, Ukrainian, Gagauz, Russian
Area Sq Miles	13 012	Religions	Romanian Orthodox, Russian Orthodox
Population	3 545 000	Currency	Moldovan leu
Capital	Chişinău (Kishinev)	Organizations	CIS, UN

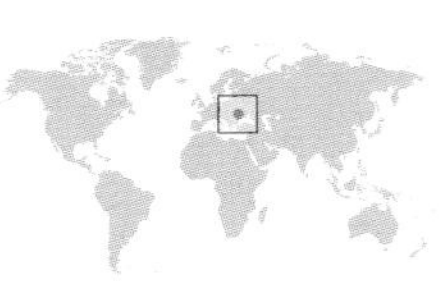

Moldova lies between Romania and Ukraine in eastern Europe. It consists of hilly steppe land, drained by the Prut and Dniester rivers. Moldova has no mineral resources, and the economy is mainly agricultural, with sugar beet, tobacco, wine and fruit the chief products. Food processing, machinery and textiles are the main industries. The Russian Federation is the main trading partner.

MONACO
Principality of Monaco

Area Sq Km	2	Languages	French, Monégasque, Italian
Area Sq Miles	1	Religions	Roman Catholic
Population	35 000	Currency	Euro
Capital	Monaco-Ville	Organizations	UN

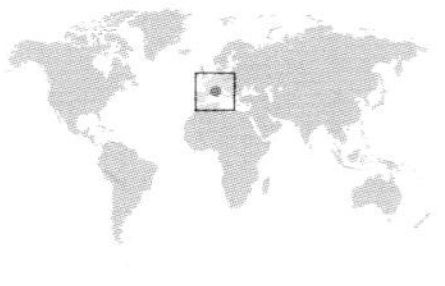

The principality occupies a rocky peninsula and a strip of land on France's Mediterranean coast. Monaco's economy depends on service industries (chiefly tourism, banking and finance) and light industry.

MONGOLIA

Area Sq Km	1 565 000	Languages	Khalka (Mongolian), Kazakh, local languages
Area Sq Miles	604 250	Religions	Buddhist, Sunni Muslim
Population	2 800 000	Currency	Tugrik (tögrög)
Capital	Ulan Bator (Ulaanbaatar)	Organizations	UN

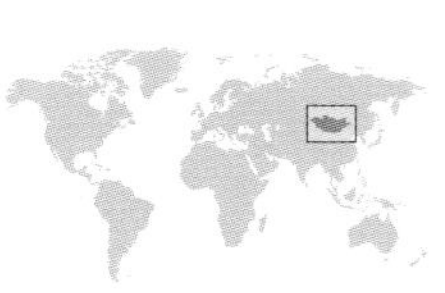

Mongolia is a landlocked country in eastern Asia between the Russian Federation and China. Much of it is high steppe land, with mountains and lakes in the west and north. In the south is the Gobi desert. Mongolia has long, cold winters and short, mild summers. A quarter of the population lives in the capital, Ulaanbaatar. Livestock breeding and agricultural processing are important. There are substantial mineral resources. Copper and textiles are the main exports. China and the Russian Federation are the main trading partners.

MONTENEGRO

Area Sq Km	13 812	Languages	Serbian (Montenegrin), Albanian
Area Sq Miles	5 333	Religions	Montenegrin Orthodox, Sunni Muslim
Population	632 000	Currency	Euro
Capital	Podgorica	Organizations	UN

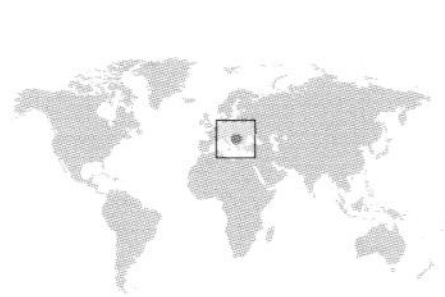

Montenegro, previously a constituent republic of the former Yugoslavia, became an independent nation in June 2006 when it opted to split from the state union of Serbia and Montenegro. Montenegro separates the much larger Serbia from the Adriatic coast. The landscape is rugged and mountainous, and the climate Mediterranean.

Montserrat
United Kingdom Overseas Territory

Area Sq Km	100	Languages	English
Area Sq Miles	39	Religions	Protestant, Roman Catholic
Population	4 655	Currency	East Caribbean dollar
Capital	Brades	Organizations	CARICOM

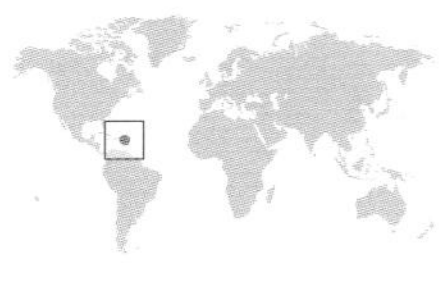

An island in the Leeward Islands group in the Lesser Antilles, in the Caribbean. From 1995 to 1997 the volcanoes in the Soufrière Hills erupted for the first time since 1630. Over sixty per cent of the island was covered in volcanic ash and Plymouth, the capital was, virtually destroyed. Many people emigrated, and the remaining population moved to the north of the island. Brades has replaced Plymouth as the temporary capital. Reconstruction is being funded by aid from the UK.

MOROCCO
Kingdom of Morocco

Area Sq Km	446 550	Languages	Arabic, Berber, French
Area Sq Miles	172 414	Religions	Sunni Muslim
Population	32 273 000	Currency	Moroccan dirham
Capital	Rabat	Organizations	UN

Lying in the northwest of Africa, Morocco has both Atlantic and Mediterranean coasts. The Atlas Mountains separate the arid south and disputed region of western Sahara from the fertile west and north, which have a milder climate. Most Moroccans live on the Atlantic coastal plain. The economy is based on agriculture, phosphate mining and tourism; the most important industries are food processing, textiles and chemicals.

MOZAMBIQUE
Republic of Mozambique

Area Sq Km	799 380	Languages	Portuguese, Makua, Tsonga, local languages
Area Sq Miles	308 642	Religions	Traditional beliefs, Roman Catholic, Sunni Muslim
Population	23 930 000	Currency	Metical
Capital	Maputo	Organizations	Comm., SADC, UN

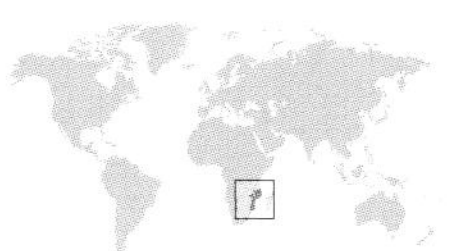

Mozambique lies on the east coast of southern Africa. The land is mainly a savanna plateau drained by the Zambezi and Limpopo rivers, with highlands to the north. Most of the population lives on the coast or in the river valleys. In general the climate is tropical with winter rainfall, but droughts occur. The economy is based on subsistence agriculture. Exports include shrimps, cashews, cotton and sugar, but Mozambique relies heavily on aid, and remains one of the least developed countries in the world.

MYANMAR (Burma)
Republic of the Union of Myanmar

Area Sq Km	676 577	Languages	Burmese, Shan, Karen, local languages
Area Sq Miles	261 228	Religions	Buddhist, Christian, Sunni Muslim
Population	48 337 000	Currency	Kyat
Capital	Nay Pyi Taw/ Rangoon (Yangôn)	Organizations	ASEAN, UN

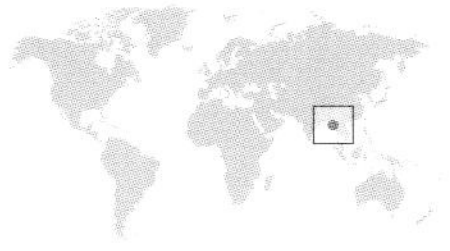

Myanmar (Burma) is in southeast Asia, bordering the Bay of Bengal and the Andaman Sea. Most of the population lives in the valley and delta of the Irrawaddy river, which is flanked by mountains and high plateaus. The climate is hot and monsoonal, and rainforest covers much of the land. Most of the workforce is employed in agriculture. Myanmar is rich in minerals, including zinc, lead, copper and silver. Political and social unrest and lack of foreign investment have affected economic development.

Nagorno-Karabakh (Dağlıq Qarabağ)
Disputed territory

Area Sq Km	6 000	Languages	Armenian
Area Sq Miles	2 317	Religions	Armenian Orthodox
Population	140 000	Currency	Armenian dram
Capital	Xankändi (Stepanakert)		

Established as an Autonomous Region within Azerbaijan in 1923, Nagorno-Karabakh is a disputed enclave of Azerbaijan. It is legally part of Azerbaijan, but is populated largely by ethnic Armenians who have established what amounts to a separatist de facto republic operating with support from Armenia. In 1991, the local Armenian population declared independence and Azerbaijan abolished the area's autonomous status. As a result of conflict, Nagorno-Karabakh/Armenia occupies approximately twenty per cent of Azerbaijan. A Russian-brokered cease-fire has been in place since 1994, with the cease-fire line enclosing the territory of Nagorno-Karabakh and the additional parts of Azerbaijan, up to the Armenian border, seized by Karabakh Armenians during the fighting. The area between the cease-fire line and the boundary of Nagorno-Karabakh is effectively a 'no-go' area.

NAMIBIA
Republic of Namibia

Area Sq Km	824 292	Languages	English, Afrikaans, German, Ovambo, local languages
Area Sq Miles	318 261	Religions	Protestant, Roman Catholic
Population	2 324 000	Currency	Namibian dollar
Capital	Windhoek	Organizations	Comm., SADC, UN

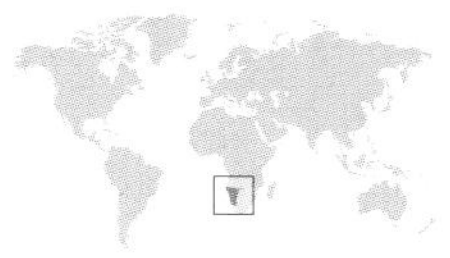

Namibia lies on the southern Atlantic coast of Africa. Mountain ranges separate the coastal Namib Desert from the interior plateau, bordered to the south and east by the Kalahari Desert. The country is hot and dry, but some summer rain in the north supports crops and livestock. Employment is in agriculture and fishing, although the economy is based on mineral extraction – diamonds, uranium, lead, zinc and silver. The economy is closely linked to the Republic of South Africa.

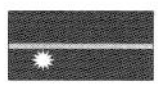

NAURU
Republic of Nauru

Area Sq Km	21	Languages	Nauruan, English
Area Sq Miles	8	Religions	Protestant, Roman Catholic
Population	10 000	Currency	Australian dollar
Capital	Yaren	Organizations	Comm., UN

Nauru is a coral island near the Equator in the Pacific Ocean. It has a fertile coastal strip and a barren central plateau. The climate is tropical. The economy is based on phosphate mining, but reserves are exhausted and replacement of this income is a serious long-term problem.

NEPAL
Federal Democratic Republic of Nepal

Area Sq Km	147 181	Languages	Nepali, Maithili, Bhojpuri, English, local languages
Area Sq Miles	56 827	Religions	Hindu, Buddhist, Sunni Muslim
Population	30 486 000	Currency	Nepalese rupee
Capital	Kathmandu	Organizations	UN

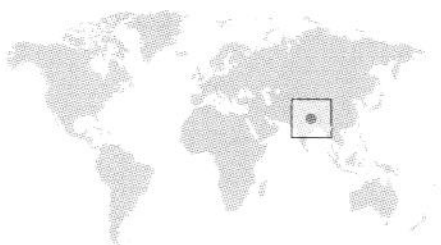

Nepal lies in the eastern Himalaya mountains between India and China. High mountains (including Everest) dominate the north. Most people live in the temperate central valleys and subtropical southern plains. The economy is based largely on agriculture and forestry. There is some manufacturing, chiefly of textiles and carpets, and tourism is important. Nepal relies heavily on foreign aid.

NETHERLANDS
Kingdom of the Netherlands

Area Sq Km	41 526	Languages	Dutch, Frisian
Area Sq Miles	16 033	Religions	Roman Catholic, Protestant, Sunni Muslim
Population	16 665 000	Currency	Euro
Capital	Amsterdam/ The Hague	Organizations	EU, NATO, OECD, UN

The Netherlands lies on the North Sea coast of western Europe. Apart from low hills in the far southeast, the land is flat and low-lying, much of it below sea level. The coastal region includes the delta of five rivers and polders (reclaimed land), protected by sand dunes, dykes and canals. The climate is temperate, with cool summers and mild winters. Rainfall is spread evenly throughout the year. The Netherlands is a densely populated and highly urbanized country, with the majority of the population living in the cities of Amsterdam, Rotterdam and The Hague. Horticulture and dairy farming are important activities, although they employ less than four per cent of the workforce. The Netherlands is an important agricultural exporter, and is a leading producer and exporter of natural gas from reserves in the North Sea. The economy is based mainly on international trade and manufacturing industry. The main industries produce food products, chemicals, machinery, electrical and electronic goods and transport equipment. Germany is the main trading partner, followed by other European Union countries.

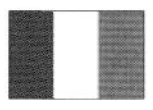

New Caledonia
French Overseas Collectivity

Area Sq Km	19 058	Languages	French, local languages
Area Sq Miles	7 358	Religions	Roman Catholic, Protestant, Sunni Muslim
Population	255 000	Currency	CFP franc
Capital	Nouméa		

An island group lying in the southwest Pacific, with a sub-tropical climate. New Caledonia has over one-fifth of the world's nickel reserves, and the main economic activity is metal mining. Tourism is also important. New Caledonia relies on aid from France.

NEW ZEALAND

Area Sq Km	270 534	Languages	English, Maori
Area Sq Miles	104 454	Religions	Protestant, Roman Catholic
Population	4 415 000	Currency	New Zealand dollar
Capital	Wellington	Organizations	APEC, Comm., OECD, UN

New Zealand comprises two main islands separated by the narrow Cook Strait, and a number of smaller islands. North Island, where three-quarters of the population lives, has mountain ranges, broad fertile valleys and a central plateau with hot springs and active volcanoes. South Island is also mountainous, with the Southern Alps running its entire length. The only major lowland area is the Canterbury Plains in the centre-east. The climate is generally temperate, although South Island has colder winters. Farming is the mainstay of the economy. New Zealand is one of the world's leading producers of meat (beef, lamb and mutton), wool and dairy products; fruit and fish are also important. Hydroelectric and geothermal power provide much of the country's energy needs. Other industries produce timber, wood pulp, iron, aluminium, machinery and chemicals. Tourism is the fastest growing sector of the economy. The main trading partners are Australia, the USA and Japan.

NICARAGUA
Republic of Nicaragua

Area Sq Km	130 000	Languages	Spanish, Amerindian languages
Area Sq Miles	50 193	Religions	Roman Catholic, Protestant
Population	5 870 000	Currency	Córdoba
Capital	Managua	Organizations	UN

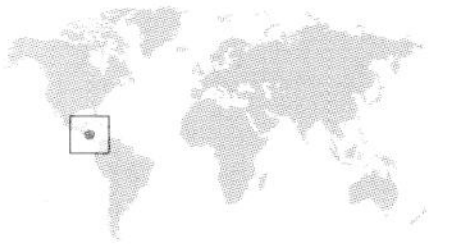

Nicaragua lies at the heart of Central America, with both Pacific and Caribbean coasts. Mountain ranges separate the east, which is largely rainforest, from the more developed western regions, which include Lake Nicaragua and some active volcanoes. The highest land is in the north. The climate is tropical. Nicaragua is one of the western hemisphere's poorest countries, and the economy is largely agricultural, but growth in tourism is having a positive effect on other areas. Exports include coffee, seafood, cotton and bananas. The USA is the main trading partner. Nicaragua has a huge national debt, and relies heavily on foreign aid.

NIGER
Republic of Niger

Area Sq Km	1 267 000	Languages	French, Hausa, Fulani, local languages
Area Sq Miles	489 191	Religions	Sunni Muslim, traditional beliefs
Population	16 069 000	Currency	CFA franc
Capital	Niamey	Organizations	UN

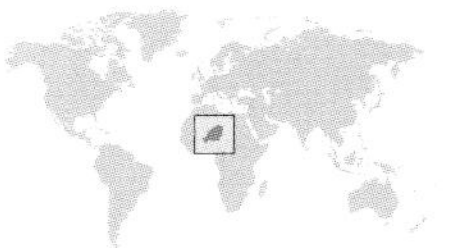

A landlocked state of west Africa, Niger lies mostly within the Sahara desert, but with savanna in the south and in the Niger valley area. The mountains of the Massif de l'Aïr dominate central regions. Much of the country is hot and dry. The south has some summer rainfall, although droughts occur. The economy depends on subsistence farming and herding, and uranium exports, but Niger is one of the world's least developed countries and relies heavily on foreign aid. France is the main trading partner.

NIGERIA
Federal Republic of Nigeria

Area Sq Km	923 768	Languages	English, Hausa, Yoruba, Ibo, Fulani, local languages
Area Sq Miles	356 669	Religions	Sunni Muslim, Christian, traditional beliefs
Population	162 471 000	Currency	Naira
Capital	Abuja	Organizations	Comm., OPEC, UN

Nigeria is in west Africa, on the Gulf of Guinea, and is the most populous country in Africa. The Niger delta dominates coastal areas, fringed with sandy beaches, mangrove swamps and lagoons. Inland is a belt of rainforest which gives way to woodland or savanna on high plateaus. The far north is the semi-desert edge of the Sahara. The climate is tropical, with heavy summer rainfall in the south but low rainfall in the north. Most of the population lives in the coastal lowlands or in the west. About half the workforce is involved in agriculture, mainly growing subsistence crops. Agricultural production, however, has failed to keep up with demand, and Nigeria is now a net importer of food. Cocoa and rubber are the only significant export crops. The economy is heavily dependent on vast oil resources in the Niger delta and in shallow offshore waters, and oil accounts for over ninety per cent of export earnings. Nigeria also has natural gas reserves and some mineral deposits, but these are largely undeveloped. Industry involves mainly oil refining, chemicals (chiefly fertilizers), agricultural processing, textiles, steel manufacture and vehicle assembly. Political instability in the past has left Nigeria with heavy debts, poverty and unemployment.

Niue
Self-governing New Zealand Overseas Territory

Area Sq Km	258	Languages	English, Nivean
Area Sq Miles	100	Religions	Christian
Population	1 496	Currency	New Zealand dollar
Capital	Alofi		

Niue, one of the largest coral islands in the world, lies in the south Pacific Ocean about 500 kilometres (300 miles) east of Tonga. The economy depends on aid and remittances from New Zealand. The population is declining because of migration to New Zealand.

Norfolk Island
Australian External Territory

Area Sq Km	35	Languages	English
Area Sq Miles	14	Religions	Protestant, Roman Catholic
Population	2 523	Currency	Australian dollar
Capital	Kingston		

In the south Pacific Ocean, Norfolk Island lies between Vanuatu and New Zealand. Tourism has increased steadily and is the mainstay of the economy and provides revenues for agricultural development.

Northern Mariana Islands
United States Commonwealth

Area Sq Km	477	Languages	English, Chamorro, local languages
Area Sq Miles	184	Religions	Roman Catholic
Population	61 000	Currency	United States dollar
Capital	Capitol Hill		

A chain of islands in the northwest Pacific Ocean, extending over 550 kilometres (350 miles) north to south. The main island is Saipan. Tourism is a major industry, employing approximately half the workforce.

NORTH KOREA
Democratic People's Republic of Korea

Area Sq Km	120 538	Languages	Korean
Area Sq Miles	46 540	Religions	Traditional beliefs, Chondoist, Buddhist
Population	24 451 000	Currency	North Korean won
Capital	P'yŏngyang	Organizations	UN

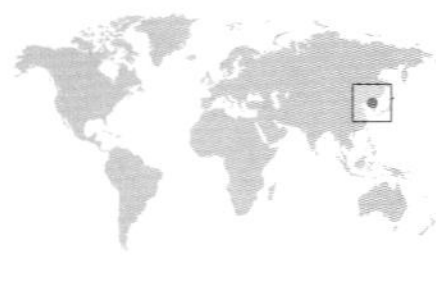

Occupying the northern half of the Korean peninsula in eastern Asia, North Korea is a rugged and mountainous country. The principal lowlands and the main agricultural areas are the plains in the southwest. More than half the population lives in urban areas, mainly on the coastal plains. North Korea has a continental climate, with cold, dry winters and hot, wet summers. Approximately one-third of the workforce is involved in agriculture, mainly growing food crops on cooperative farms. Various minerals, notably iron ore, are mined and are the basis of the country's heavy industries. Exports include minerals (lead, magnesite and zinc) and metal products (chiefly iron and steel). The economy declined after 1991, when ties to the former USSR and eastern bloc collapsed, and there have been serious food shortages.

NORWAY
Kingdom of Norway

Area Sq Km	323 878	Languages	Norwegian
Area Sq Miles	125 050	Religions	Protestant, Roman Catholic
Population	4 925 000	Currency	Norwegian krone
Capital	Oslo	Organizations	NATO, OECD, UN

Norway stretches along the north and west coasts of Scandinavia, from the Arctic Ocean to the North Sea. Its extensive coastline is indented with fjords and fringed with many islands. Inland, the terrain is mountainous, with coniferous forests and lakes in the south. The only major lowland areas are along the southern North Sea and Skagerrak coasts, where most of the population lives. The climate is modified by the effect of the North Atlantic Drift ocean current. Norway has vast petroleum and natural gas resources in the North Sea. It is one of western Europe's leading producers of oil and gas, and exports of oil account for approximately half of total export earnings. Related industries include engineering (oil and gas platforms) and petrochemicals. More traditional industries process local raw materials, particularly fish, timber and minerals. Agriculture is limited, but fishing and fish farming are important. Norway is the world's leading exporter of farmed salmon. Merchant shipping and tourism are major sources of foreign exchange.

OMAN
Sultanate of Oman

Area Sq Km	309 500	Languages	Arabic, Baluchi, Indian languages
Area Sq Miles	119 499	Religions	Ibadhi Muslim, Sunni Muslim
Population	2 846 000	Currency	Omani riyal
Capital	Muscat (Masqaṭ)	Organizations	UN

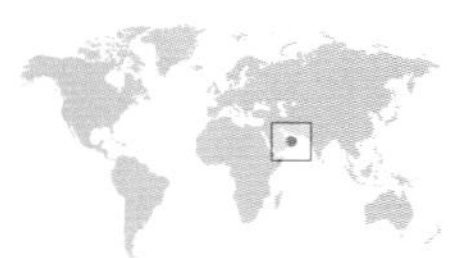

In southwest Asia, Oman occupies the east and southeast coasts of the Arabian Peninsula and an enclave north of the United Arab Emirates. Most of the land is desert, with mountains in the north and south. The climate is hot and mainly dry. Most of the population lives on the coastal strip on the Gulf of Oman. The majority depend on farming and fishing, but the oil and gas industries dominate the economy with around eighty per cent of export revenues coming from oil.

PAKISTAN
Islamic Republic of Pakistan

Area Sq Km	803 940	Languages	Urdu, Punjabi, Sindhi, Pushtu, English
Area Sq Miles	310 403	Religions	Sunni Muslim, Shi'a Muslim, Christian, Hindu
Population	176 745 000	Currency	Pakistani rupee
Capital	Islamabad	Organizations	Comm., UN

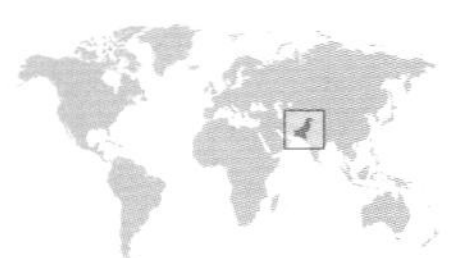

Pakistan is in the northwest part of the Indian subcontinent in south Asia, on the Arabian Sea. The east and south are dominated by the great basin of the Indus river system. This is the main agricultural area and contains most of the predominantly rural population. To the north the land rises to the mountains of the Karakoram, Hindu Kush and Himalaya mountains. The west is semi-desert plateaus and mountain ranges. The climate ranges between dry desert, and arctic tundra on the mountain tops. Temperatures are generally warm and rainfall is monsoonal. Agriculture is the main sector of the economy, employing approximately half of the workforce, and is based on extensive irrigation schemes. Pakistan is one of the world's leading producers of cotton and a major exporter of rice. Pakistan produces natural gas and has a variety of mineral deposits including coal and gold, but they are little developed. The main industries are textiles and clothing manufacture and food processing, with fabrics and ready-made clothing the leading exports. Pakistan also produces leather goods, fertilizers, chemicals, paper and precision instruments. The country depends heavily on foreign aid and remittances from workers abroad.

PALAU
Republic of Palau

Area Sq Km	497	Languages	Palauan, English
Area Sq Miles	192	Religions	Roman Catholic, Protestant, traditional beliefs
Population	21 000	Currency	United States dollar
Capital	Melekeok (Ngerulmud)	Organizations	UN

Palau comprises over three hundred islands in the western Caroline Islands, in the west Pacific Ocean. The climate is tropical. The economy is based on farming, fishing and tourism, but Palau is heavily dependent on aid from the USA.

PANAMA
Republic of Panama

Area Sq Km	77 082	Languages	Spanish, English, Amerindian languages
Area Sq Miles	29 762	Religions	Roman Catholic, Protestant, Sunni Muslim
Population	3 571 000	Currency	Balboa
Capital	Panama City	Organizations	UN

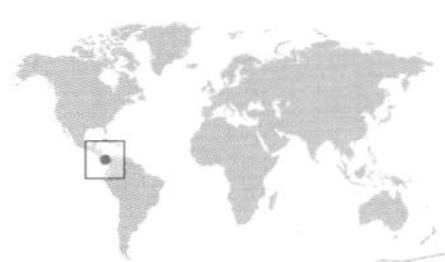

Panama is the most southerly state in central America and has Pacific and Caribbean coasts. It is hilly, with mountains in the west and jungle near the Colombian border. The climate is tropical. Most of the population lives on the drier Pacific side. The economy is based mainly on services related to the Panama Canal: shipping, banking and tourism. Exports include bananas, shrimps, coffee, clothing and fish products. The USA is the main trading partner.

PAPUA NEW GUINEA
Independent State of Papua New Guinea

Area Sq Km	462 840	Languages	English, Tok Pisin (Creole), local languages
Area Sq Miles	178 704	Religions	Protestant, Roman Catholic, traditional beliefs
Population	7 014 000	Currency	Kina
Capital	Port Moresby	Organizations	APEC, Comm., UN

Papua New Guinea occupies the eastern half of the island of New Guinea and includes many island groups. It has a forested and mountainous interior, bordered by swampy plains, and a tropical monsoon climate. Most of the workforce are farmers. Timber, copra, coffee and cocoa are important, but exports are dominated by minerals, chiefly gold and copper. The country depends on foreign aid. Australia, Japan and Singapore are the main trading partners.

PARAGUAY
Republic of Paraguay

Area Sq Km	406 752	Languages	Spanish, Guaraní
Area Sq Miles	157 048	Religions	Roman Catholic, Protestant
Population	6 568 000	Currency	Guaraní
Capital	Asunción	Organizations	UN

Paraguay is a landlocked country in central South America, bordering Bolivia, Brazil and Argentina. The Paraguay river separates a sparsely populated western zone of marsh and flat alluvial plains from a more developed, hilly and forested region to the east and south. The climate is subtropical. Virtually all electricity is produced by hydroelectric plants, and surplus power is exported to Brazil and Argentina. The hydroelectric dam at Itaipú is one of the largest in the world. The mainstay of the economy is agriculture and related industries. Exports include cotton, soya bean and edible oil products, timber and meat. Brazil and Argentina are the main trading partners.

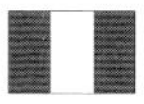

PERU
Republic of Peru

Area Sq Km	1 285 216	Languages	Spanish, Quechua, Aymara
Area Sq Miles	496 225	Religions	Roman Catholic, Protestant
Population	29 400 000	Currency	Nuevo sol
Capital	Lima	Organizations	APEC, UN

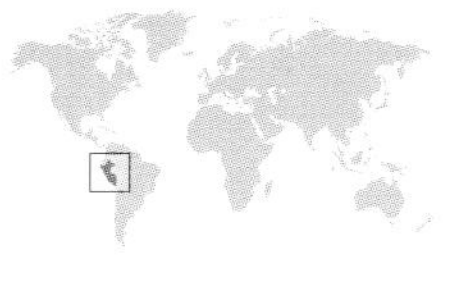

Peru lies on the Pacific coast of South America. Most Peruvians live on the coastal strip and on the plateaus of the high Andes mountains. East of the Andes is the Amazon rainforest. The coast is temperate with low rainfall while the east is hot, humid and wet. Agriculture involves one-third of the workforce and fishing is also important. Agriculture and fishing have both been disrupted by the El Niño climatic effect in recent years. Sugar, cotton, coffee and, illegally, coca are the main cash crops. Copper and copper products, fishmeal, zinc products, coffee, petroleum and its products, and textiles are the main exports. The USA and the European Union are the main trading partners.

PHILIPPINES
Republic of the Philippines

Area Sq Km	300 000	Languages	English, Filipino, Tagalog, Cebuano, local languages
Area Sq Miles	115 831	Religions	Roman Catholic, Protestant, Sunni Muslim, Aglipayan
Population	94 852 000	Currency	Philippine peso
Capital	Manila	Organizations	APEC, ASEAN, UN

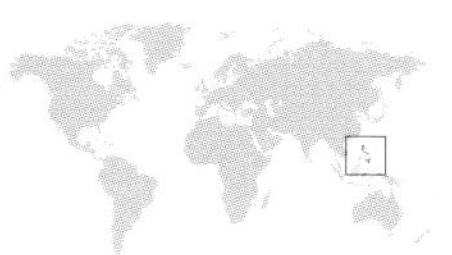

The Philippines, in southeast Asia, consists of over seven thousand islands and atolls lying between the South China Sea and the Pacific Ocean. The islands of Luzon and Mindanao account for two-thirds of the land area. They and nine other fairly large islands are mountainous and forested. There are active volcanoes, and earthquakes and tropical storms are common. Most of the population lives in the plains on the larger islands or on the coastal strips. The climate is hot and humid with heavy monsoonal rainfall. Rice, coconuts, sugar cane, pineapples and bananas are the main agricultural crops, and fishing is also important. Main exports are electronic equipment, machinery and transport equipment, garments and coconut products. Foreign aid and remittances from workers abroad are important to the economy, which faces problems of high population growth rate and high unemployment. The USA and Japan are the main trading partners.

Pitcairn Islands
United Kingdom Overseas Territory

Area Sq Km	45	Languages	English
Area Sq Miles	17	Religions	Protestant
Population	48	Currency	New Zealand dollar
Capital	Adamstown		

An island group in the southeast Pacific Ocean consisting of Pitcairn Island and three uninhabited islands. It was originally settled by mutineers from HMS *Bounty* in 1790.

POLAND
Polish Republic

Area Sq Km	312 683	Languages	Polish, German
Area Sq Miles	120 728	Religions	Roman Catholic, Polish Orthodox
Population	38 299 000	Currency	Złoty
Capital	Warsaw (Warszawa)	Organizations	EU, NATO, OECD, UN

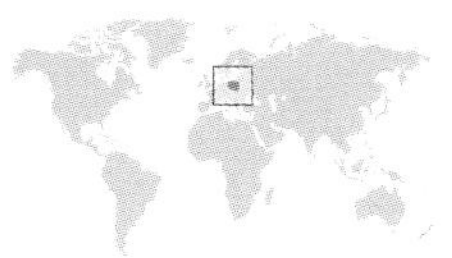

Poland lies on the Baltic coast of eastern Europe. The Oder (Odra) and Vistula (Wisła) river deltas dominate the coast. Inland, much of the country is low-lying, with woods and lakes. In the south the land rises to the Sudeten Mountains and the western part of the Carpathian Mountains, which form the borders with the Czech Republic and Slovakia respectively. The climate is continental. Around a quarter of the workforce is involved in agriculture, and exports include livestock products and sugar. The economy is heavily industrialized, with mining and manufacturing accounting for forty per cent of national income. Poland is one of the world's major producers of coal, and also produces copper, zinc, lead, sulphur and natural gas. The main industries are machinery and transport equipment, shipbuilding, and metal and chemical production. Exports include machinery and transport equipment, manufactured goods, food and live animals. Germany is the main trading partner. Poland joined the European Union in May 2004.

PORTUGAL
Portuguese Republic

Area Sq Km	88 940	Languages	Portuguese
Area Sq Miles	34 340	Religions	Roman Catholic, Protestant
Population	10 690 000	Currency	Euro
Capital	Lisbon (Lisboa)	Organizations	EU, NATO, OECD, UN

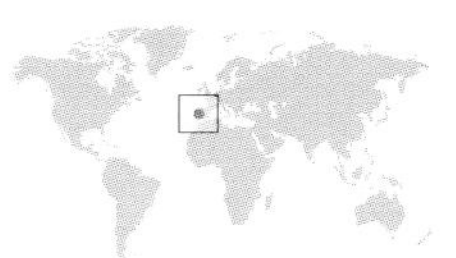

Portugal lies in the western part of the Iberian peninsula in southwest Europe, has an Atlantic coastline and is bordered by Spain to the north and east. The island groups of the Azores and Madeira are parts of Portugal. On the mainland, the land north of the river Tagus (Tejo) is mostly highland, with extensive forests of pine and cork. South of the river is undulating lowland. The climate in the north is cool and moist; the south is warmer, with dry, mild winters. Most Portuguese live near the coast, and more than one-third of the total population lives around the capital, Lisbon (Lisboa). Agriculture, fishing and forestry involve approximately ten per cent of the workforce. Mining and manufacturing are the main sectors of the economy. Portugal produces kaolin, copper, tin, zinc, tungsten and salt. Exports include textiles, clothing and footwear, electrical machinery and transport equipment, cork and wood products, and chemicals. Service industries, chiefly tourism and banking, are important to the economy, as are remittances from workers abroad. Most trade is with other European Union countries.

Puerto Rico
United States Commonwealth

Area Sq Km	9 104	Languages	Spanish, English
Area Sq Miles	3 515	Religions	Roman Catholic, Protestant
Population	3 746 000	Currency	United States dollar
Capital	San Juan		

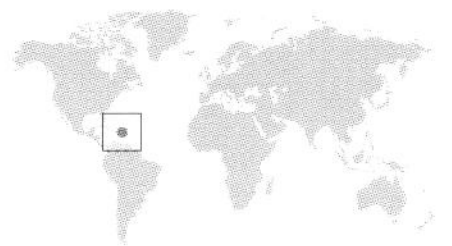

The Caribbean island of Puerto Rico has a forested, hilly interior, coastal plains and a tropical climate. Half of the population lives in the San Juan area. The economy is based on manufacturing (chiefly chemicals, electronics and food), tourism and agriculture. The USA is the main trading partner.

QATAR
State of Qatar

Area Sq Km	11 437	Languages	Arabic
Area Sq Miles	4 416	Religions	Sunni Muslim
Population	1 870 000	Currency	Qatari riyal
Capital	Doha (Ad Dawḩah)	Organizations	OPEC, UN

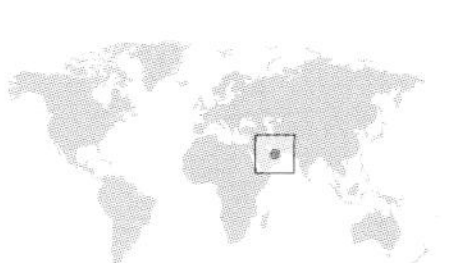

Qatar occupies a peninsula in southwest Asia that extends northwards from east-central Saudi Arabia into The Gulf. The land is flat and barren with sand dunes and salt pans. The climate is hot and mainly dry. Most people live in the area of the capital, Doha. The economy is heavily dependent on oil and natural gas production and the oil-refining industry. Income also comes from overseas investment. Japan is the largest trading partner.

Réunion
French Overseas Department

Area Sq Km	2 551	Languages	French, Creole
Area Sq Miles	985	Religions	Roman Catholic
Population	856 000	Currency	Euro
Capital	St-Denis		

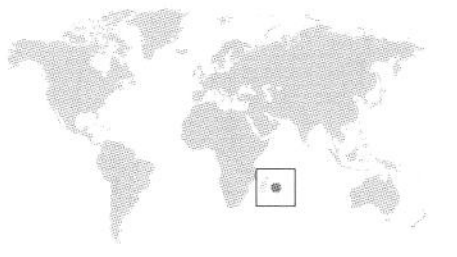

The Indian Ocean island of Réunion is mountainous, with coastal lowlands and a warm climate. The economy depends on tourism, French aid, and exports of sugar. In 2005 France transferred the administration of various small uninhabited islands in the seas around Madagascar from Réunion to the French Southern and Antarctic Lands.

ROMANIA

Area Sq Km	237 500	Languages	Romanian, Hungarian
Area Sq Miles	91 699	Religions	Romanian Orthodox, Protestant, Roman Catholic
Population	21 436 000	Currency	Romanian leu
Capital	Bucharest (București)	Organizations	EU, NATO, UN

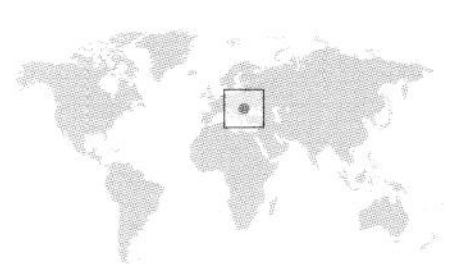

Romania lies in eastern Europe, on the northwest coast of the Black Sea. Mountains separate the Transylvanian Basin in the centre of the country from the populous plains of the east and south and from the Danube delta. The climate is continental. Romania has mineral resources (zinc, lead, silver and gold) and oil and natural gas reserves. Economic development has been slow and sporadic, but measures to accelerate change were introduced in 1999. Agriculture employs over one-third of the workforce. The main exports are textiles, mineral products, chemicals, machinery and footwear. The main trading partners are Germany and Italy.

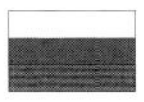

RUSSIAN FEDERATION

Area Sq Km	17 075 400	Languages	Russian, Tatar, Ukrainian, local languages
Area Sq Miles	6 592 849	Religions	Russian Orthodox, Sunni Muslim, Protestant
Population	142 836 000	Currency	Russian rouble
Capital	Moscow (Moskva)	Organizations	APEC, CIS, UN

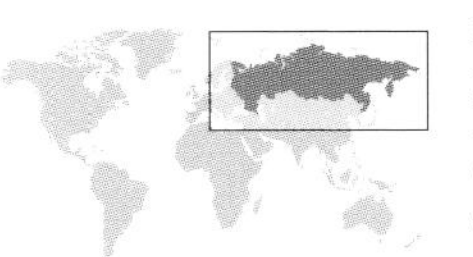

The Russian Federation occupies much of eastern Europe and all of northern Asia, and is the world's largest country. It borders fourteen countries to the west and south and has long coastlines on the Arctic and Pacific Oceans to the north and east. European Russia lies west of the Ural Mountains. To the south the land rises to uplands and the Caucasus mountains on the border with Georgia and Azerbaijan. East of the Urals lies the flat West Siberian Plain and the Central Siberian Plateau. In the south-east is Lake Baikal, the world's deepest lake, and the Sayan ranges on the border with Kazakhstan and Mongolia. Eastern Siberia is rugged and mountainous, with many active volcanoes in the Kamchatka Peninsula. The country's major rivers are the Volga in the west and the Ob', Irtysh, Yenisey, Lena and Amur in Siberia. The climate and vegetation range between arctic tundra in the north and semi-arid steppe towards the Black and Caspian Sea coasts in the south. In general, the climate is continental with extreme temperatures. The majority of the population (the ninth largest in the world), and industry and agriculture are concentrated in European Russia. The economy is dependent on exploitation of raw materials and on heavy industry. Russia has a wealth of mineral resources, although they are often difficult to exploit because of climate and remote locations. It is one of the world's leading producers of petroleum, natural gas and coal as well as iron ore, nickel, copper, bauxite, and many precious and rare metals. Forests cover over forty per cent of the land area and supply an important timber, paper and pulp industry. Approximately eight per cent of the land is suitable for cultivation, but farming is generally inefficient and food, especially grains, must be imported. Fishing is important and Russia has a large fleet operating around the world. The transition to a market economy has been slow and difficult, with considerable underemployment. As well as mining and extractive industries there is a wide range of manufacturing industry, from steel mills to aircraft and space vehicles, shipbuilding, synthetic fabrics, plastics, cotton fabrics, consumer durables, chemicals and fertilizers. Exports include fuels, metals, machinery, chemicals and forest products. The most important trading partners include Germany, the USA and Belarus.

RWANDA
Republic of Rwanda

Area Sq Km	26 338	Languages	Kinyarwanda, French, English
Area Sq Miles	10 169	Religions	Roman Catholic, traditional beliefs, Protestant
Population	10 943 000	Currency	Rwandan franc
Capital	Kigali	Organizations	Comm., UN

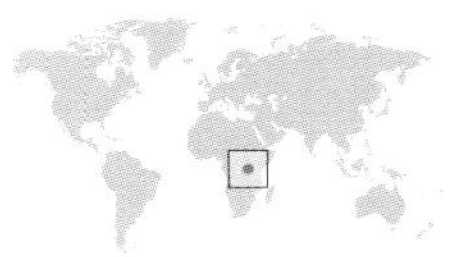

Rwanda, the most densely populated country in continental Africa, is situated in the mountains and plateaus to the east of the western branch of the Great Rift Valley in east Africa. The climate is warm with a summer dry season. Rwanda depends on subsistence farming, coffee and tea exports, light industry and foreign aid. The country is slowly recovering from serious internal conflict which caused devastation in the early 1990s.

St-Barthélemy
French Overseas Collectivity

Area Sq Km	21	**Languages**	French
Area Sq Miles	8	**Religions**	Roman Catholic
Population	8 823	**Currency**	Euro
Capital	Gustavia		

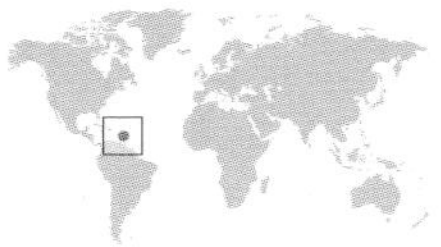

An island in the Leeward Islands in the Lesser Antilles, in the Caribbean south of St-Martin. It was separated from Guadeloupe politically in 2007. Tourism is the main economic activity.

St Helena, Ascension and Tristan da Cunha
United Kingdom Overseas Territory

Area Sq Km	410	**Languages**	English
Area Sq Miles	158	**Religions**	Protestant, Roman Catholic
Population	5 404	**Currency**	St Helena pound, Pound sterling
Capital	Jamestown		

St Helena along with Ascension and Tristan da Cunha are isolated island groups lying in the south Atlantic Ocean. St Helena is a rugged island of volcanic origin. The main activity is fishing, but the economy relies on financial aid from the UK. Main trading partners are the UK and South Africa.

ST KITTS AND NEVIS
Federation of Saint Kitts and Nevis

Area Sq Km	261	**Languages**	English, Creole
Area Sq Miles	101	**Religions**	Protestant, Roman Catholic
Population	53 000	**Currency**	East Caribbean dollar
Capital	Basseterre	**Organizations**	CARICOM, Comm., UN

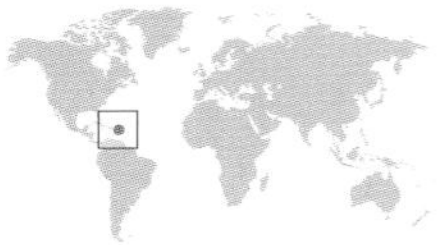

St Kitts and Nevis are in the Leeward Islands, in the Caribbean. Both volcanic islands are mountainous and forested, with sandy beaches and a warm, wet climate. About three-quarters of the population lives on St Kitts. Agriculture is the main activity, with sugar the main product. Tourism and manufacturing (chiefly garments and electronic components) and offshore banking are important activities.

ST LUCIA

Area Sq Km	616	**Languages**	English, Creole
Area Sq Miles	238	**Religions**	Roman Catholic, Protestant
Population	176 000	**Currency**	East Caribbean dollar
Capital	Castries	**Organizations**	CARICOM, Comm., UN

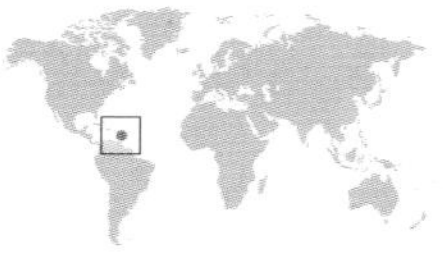

St Lucia, one of the Windward Islands in the Caribbean Sea, is a volcanic island with forested mountains, hot springs, sandy beaches and a wet tropical climate. Agriculture is the main activity, with bananas accounting for approximately forty per cent of export earnings. Tourism, agricultural processing and light manufacturing are increasingly important.

St-Martin
French Overseas Collectivity

Area Sq Km	54	**Languages**	French
Area Sq Miles	21	**Religions**	Roman Catholic
Population	37 163	**Currency**	Euro
Capital	Marigot		

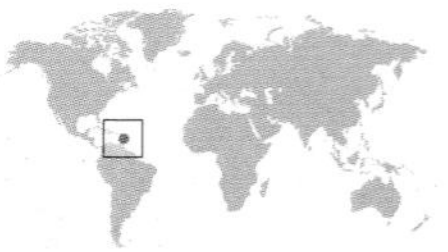

The northern part of St-Martin, one of the Leeward Islands, in the Caribbean. The other part of the island is part of the Netherlands Antilles (Sint Maarten). It was separated from Guadeloupe politically in 2007. Tourism is the main source of income.

St Pierre and Miquelon
French Territorial Collectivity

Area Sq Km	242	**Languages**	French
Area Sq Miles	93	**Religions**	Roman Catholic
Population	6 290	**Currency**	Euro
Capital	St-Pierre		

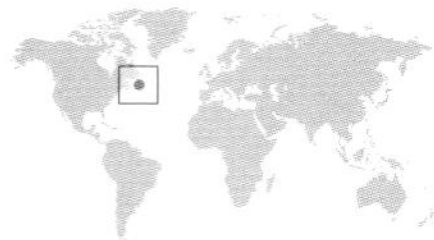

A group of islands off the south coast of Newfoundland in eastern Canada. The islands are largely unsuitable for agriculture, and fishing and fish processing are the most important activities. The islands rely heavily on financial assistance from France.

ST VINCENT AND THE GRENADINES

Area Sq Km	389	**Languages**	English, Creole
Area Sq Miles	150	**Religions**	Protestant, Roman Catholic
Population	109 000	**Currency**	East Caribbean dollar
Capital	Kingstown	**Organizations**	CARICOM, Comm., UN

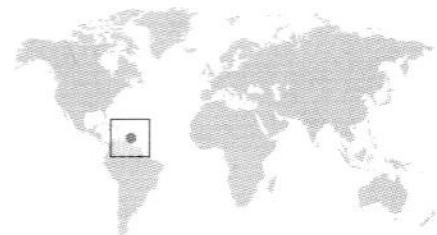

St Vincent, whose territory includes islets and cays in the Grenadines, is in the Windward Islands, in the Caribbean. St Vincent itself is forested and mountainous, with an active volcano, Soufrière. The climate is tropical and wet. The economy is based mainly on agriculture and tourism. Bananas account for approximately one-third of export earnings and arrowroot is also important. Most trade is with the USA and other CARICOM countries.

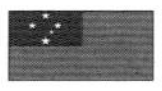

SAMOA
Independent State of Samoa

Area Sq Km	2 831	**Languages**	Samoan, English
Area Sq Miles	1 093	**Religions**	Protestant, Roman Catholic
Population	184 000	**Currency**	Tala
Capital	Apia	**Organizations**	Comm., UN

Samoa consists of two larger mountainous and forested islands, Savai'i and Upolu, and seven smaller islands, in the south Pacific Ocean. Over half the population lives on Upolu. The climate is tropical. The economy is based on agriculture, with some fishing and light manufacturing. Traditional exports are coconut products, fish and beer. Tourism is increasing, but the islands depend on workers' remittances and foreign aid.

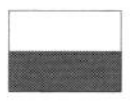

SAN MARINO
Republic of San Marino

Area Sq Km	61	**Languages**	Italian
Area Sq Miles	24	**Religions**	Roman Catholic
Population	32 000	**Currency**	Euro
Capital	San Marino	**Organizations**	UN

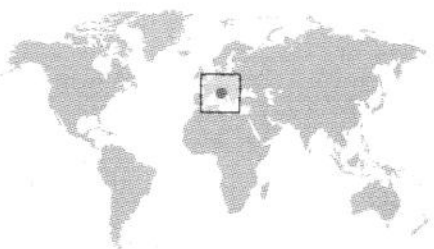

Landlocked San Marino lies in northeast Italy. A third of the people live in the capital. There is some agriculture and light industry, but most income comes from tourism. Italy is the main trading partner.

SÃO TOMÉ AND PRÍNCIPE
Democratic Republic of São Tomé and Príncipe

Area Sq Km	964	**Languages**	Portuguese, Creole
Area Sq Miles	372	**Religions**	Roman Catholic, Protestant
Population	169 000	**Currency**	Dobra
Capital	São Tomé	**Organizations**	UN

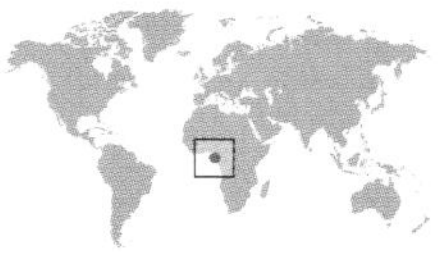

The two main islands and adjacent islets lie off the coast of west Africa in the Gulf of Guinea. São Tomé is the larger island, with over ninety per cent of the population. Both São Tomé and Príncipe are mountainous and tree-covered, and have a hot and humid climate. The economy is heavily dependent on cocoa, which accounts for around ninety per cent of export earnings.

SAUDI ARABIA
Kingdom of Saudi Arabia

Area Sq Km	2 200 000	**Languages**	Arabic
Area Sq Miles	849 425	**Religions**	Sunni Muslim, Shi'a Muslim
Population	28 083 000	**Currency**	Saudi Arabian riyal
Capital	Riyadh (Ar Riyāḍ)	**Organizations**	OPEC, UN

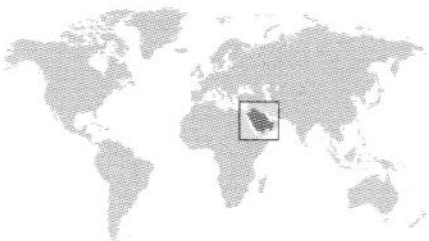

Saudi Arabia occupies most of the Arabian Peninsula in southwest Asia. The terrain is desert or semi-desert plateaus, which rise to mountains running parallel to the Red Sea in the west and slope down to plains in the southeast and along The Gulf in the east. Over eighty per cent of the population lives in urban areas. There are around four million foreign workers in Saudi Arabia, employed mainly in the oil and service industries. Summers are hot, winters are warm and rainfall is low. Saudi Arabia has the world's largest reserves of oil and significant natural gas reserves, both onshore and in The Gulf. Crude oil and refined products account for over ninety per cent of export earnings. Other industries and irrigated agriculture are being encouraged, but most food and raw materials are imported. Saudi Arabia has important banking and commercial interests. Japan and the USA are the main trading partners.

SENEGAL
Republic of Senegal

Area Sq Km	196 720	**Languages**	French, Wolof, Fulani, local languages
Area Sq Miles	75 954	**Religions**	Sunni Muslim, Roman Catholic, traditional beliefs
Population	12 768 000	**Currency**	CFA franc
Capital	Dakar	**Organizations**	UN

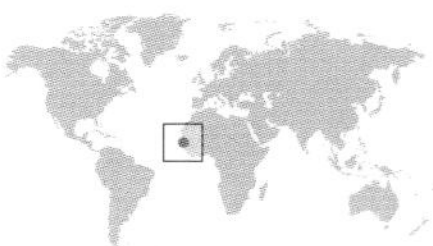

Senegal lies on the Atlantic coast of west Africa. The north is arid semi-desert, while the south is mainly fertile savanna bushland. The climate is tropical with summer rains, although droughts occur. One-fifth of the population lives in and around Dakar, the capital and main port. Fish, groundnuts and phosphates are the main exports. France is the main trading partner.

SERBIA
Republic of Serbia

Area Sq Km	77 453	**Languages**	Serbian, Hungarian
Area Sq Miles	29 904	**Religions**	Serbian Orthodox, Roman Catholic, Sunni Muslim
Population	7 306 677	**Currency**	Serbian dinar
Capital	Belgrade (Beograd)	**Organizations**	UN

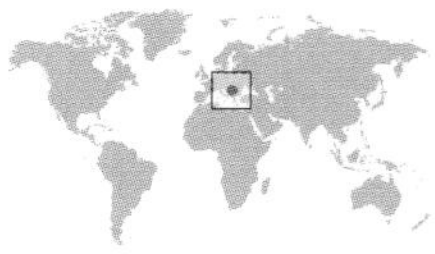

Following ethnic conflict and the break-up of Yugoslavia through the 1990s, the state union of Serbia and Montenegro retained the name Yugoslavia until 2003. The two then became separate independent countries in 2006. The southern Serbian province of Kosovo declared its independence from Serbia in February 2008. The landscape is rugged, mountainous and forested in the south, while the north is low-lying and drained by the Danube river system.

SEYCHELLES
Republic of Seychelles

Area Sq Km	455	**Languages**	English, French, Creole
Area Sq Miles	176	**Religions**	Roman Catholic, Protestant
Population	87 000	**Currency**	Seychelles rupee
Capital	Victoria	**Organizations**	Comm., SADC, UN

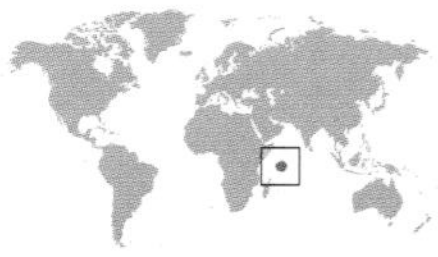

The Seychelles comprises an archipelago of over one hundred granitic and coral islands in the western Indian Ocean. Over ninety per cent of the population lives on the main island, Mahé. The climate is hot and humid with heavy rainfall. The economy is based mainly on tourism, fishing and light manufacturing.

SIERRA LEONE

Republic of Sierra Leone

Area Sq Km	71 740	Languages	English, Creole, Mende, Temne, local languages
Area Sq Miles	27 699	Religions	Sunni Muslim, traditional beliefs
Population	5 997 000	Currency	Leone
Capital	Freetown	Organizations	Comm., UN

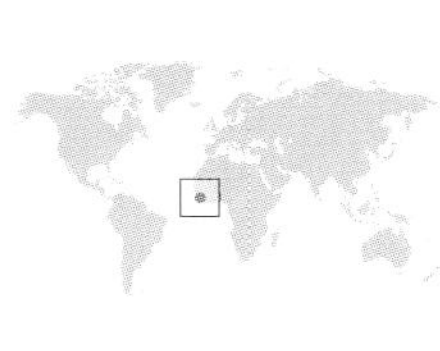

Sierra Leone lies on the Atlantic coast of west Africa. Its coastline is heavily indented and is lined with mangrove swamps. Inland is a forested area rising to savanna plateaus, with mountains to the northeast. The climate is tropical and rainfall is heavy. Most of the workforce is involved in subsistence farming. Cocoa and coffee are the main cash crops. Diamonds and rutile (titanium ore) are the main exports. Sierra Leone is one of the world's poorest countries, and the economy relies on substantial foreign aid.

SINGAPORE

Republic of Singapore

Area Sq Km	639	Languages	Chinese, English, Malay, Tamil
Area Sq Miles	247	Religions	Buddhist, Taoist, Sunni Muslim, Christian, Hindu
Population	5 188 000	Currency	Singapore dollar
Capital	Singapore	Organizations	APEC, ASEAN, Comm., UN

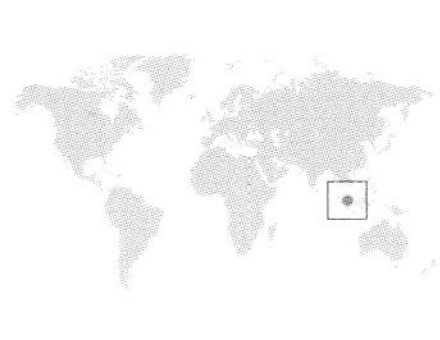

The state comprises the island of Singapore and over fifty others, at the tip of the Malay Peninsula in southeast Asia. Singapore is generally low-lying and includes areas of reclaimed land. The climate is hot and humid, with heavy rainfall all year. Most food has to be imported. Singapore lacks natural resources; industries and services have fuelled the nation's economic growth during recent decades. Main industries include electronics, oil refining, chemicals, pharmaceuticals, ship repair, food processing and textiles. Singapore is also a major financial centre. Its port is one of the world's largest and busiest. Tourism is also important. Japan, the USA and Malaysia are the main trading partners.

Sint Maarten

Self-governing Netherlands territory

Area Sq Km	34	Languages	Dutch, English
Area Sq Miles	13	Religions	Roman Catholic, Protestant
Population	37 429	Currency	Caribbean guilder
Capital	Philipsburg		

The southern part of one of the Leeward Islands, in the Caribbean; the other part of the island is a dependency of France. Sint Maarten was previously part of the Netherlands Antilles until they were dissolved in October 2010. Tourism and fishing are the most important industries.

SLOVAKIA

Slovak Republic

Area Sq Km	49 035	Languages	Slovakian, Hungarian, Czech
Area Sq Miles	18 933	Religions	Roman Catholic, Protestant, Orthodox
Population	5 472 000	Currency	Euro
Capital	Bratislava	Organizations	EU, NATO, OECD, UN

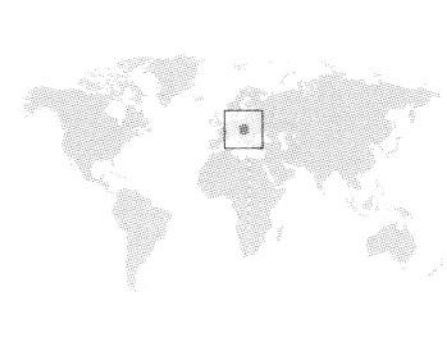

A landlocked country in central Europe, Slovakia is mountainous in the north, but low-lying in the southwest. The climate is continental. There is a range of manufacturing industries, and the main exports are machinery and transport equipment, but in recent years there have been economic difficulties and growth has been slow. Slovakia joined the European Union in May 2004. Most trade is with other EU countries, especially the Czech Republic.

SLOVENIA

Republic of Slovenia

Area Sq Km	20 251	Languages	Slovenian, Croatian, Serbian
Area Sq Miles	7 819	Religions	Roman Catholic, Protestant
Population	2 035 000	Currency	Euro
Capital	Ljubljana	Organizations	EU, NATO, OECD, UN

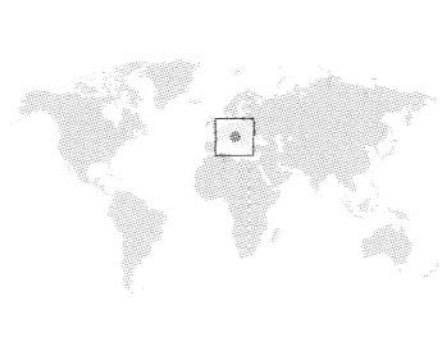

Slovenia lies in the northwest Balkan Mountains of southern Europe and has a short coastline on the Adriatic Sea. It is mountainous and hilly, with lowlands on the coast and in the Sava and Drava river valleys. The climate is generally continental inland and Mediterranean nearer the coast. The main agricultural products are potatoes, grain and sugar beet; the main industries include metal processing, electronics and consumer goods. Trade has been re-orientated towards western markets and the main trading partners are Germany and Italy. Slovenia joined the European Union in May 2004.

SOLOMON ISLANDS

Area Sq Km	28 370	Languages	English, Creole, local languages
Area Sq Miles	10 954	Religions	Protestant, Roman Catholic
Population	552 000	Currency	Solomon Islands dollar
Capital	Honiara	Organizations	Comm., UN

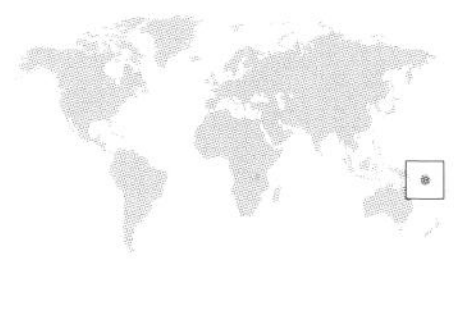

The state consists of the Solomon, Santa Cruz and Shortland Islands in the southwest Pacific Ocean. The six main islands are volcanic, mountainous and forested, although Guadalcanal, the most populous, has a large lowland area. The climate is generally hot and humid. Subsistence farming, forestry and fishing predominate. Exports include timber products, fish, copra and palm oil. The islands depend on foreign aid.

SOMALIA

Somali Republic

Area Sq Km	637 657	Languages	Somali, Arabic
Area Sq Miles	246 201	Religions	Sunni Muslim
Population	9 557 000	Currency	Somali shilling
Capital	Mogadishu (Muqdisho)	Organizations	UN

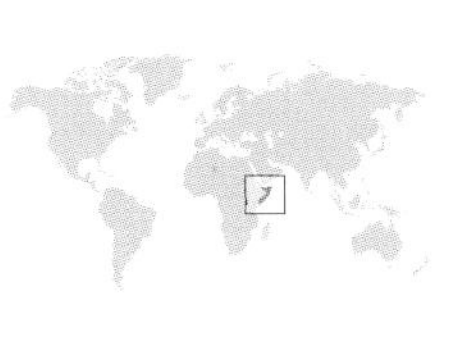

Somalia is in northeast Africa, on the Gulf of Aden and Indian Ocean. It consists of a dry scrubby plateau, rising to highlands in the north. The climate is hot and dry, but coastal areas and the Jubba and Webi Shabeelle river valleys support crops and most of the population. Subsistence farming and livestock rearing are the main activities. Exports include livestock and bananas. Frequent drought and civil war have prevented economic development. Somalia is one of the poorest, most unstable and least developed countries in the world.

Somaliland

Disputed territory

Area Sq Km	140 000	Languages	Somali, Arabic, English
Area Sq Miles	54 054	Religions	Sunni Muslim
Population	3 500 000	Currency	Somaliland shilling
Capital	Hargeysa		

After the collapse of the central Somali government in 1991 and at the start of the civil war, Somaliland, in the northwest of the country, covering the area of the former British Protectorate of Somaliland, declared its independence from Somalia as the Republic of Somaliland.

A referendum in 2001 saw a majority vote for secession, and Somaliland currently operates as a de facto independent country, with fairly close relations with Ethiopia. The Transitional Federal Government of Somalia does not recognize its independence and conflicts still arise between Somaliland and the neighbouring region of Puntland over ownership of the administrative regions of Sanaag and Sool.

SOUTH AFRICA, REPUBLIC OF

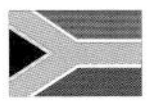

Area Sq Km	1 219 090	Languages	Afrikaans, English, nine other official languages
Area Sq Miles	470 693	Religions	Protestant, Roman Catholic, Sunni Muslim, Hindu
Population	50 460 000	Currency	Rand
Capital	Pretoria (Tshwane)/ Cape Town	Organizations	Comm., SADC, UN

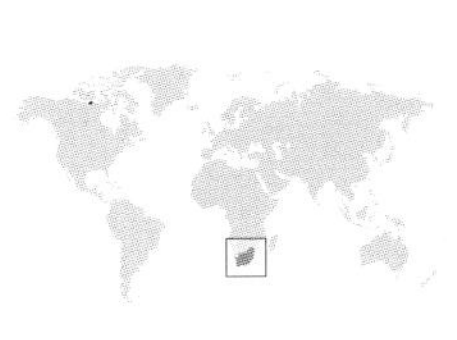

The Republic of South Africa occupies most of the southern part of Africa. It surrounds Lesotho and has a long coastline on the Atlantic and Indian Oceans. Much of the land is a vast plateau, covered with grassland or bush and drained by the Orange and Limpopo river systems. A fertile coastal plain rises to mountain ridges in the south and east, including Table Mountain near Cape Town and the Drakensberg range in the east. Gauteng is the most populous province, with Johannesburg and Pretoria its main cities. South Africa has warm summers and mild winters. Most of the country has the majority of its rainfall in summer, but the coast around Cape Town has winter rains. South Africa has the largest economy in Africa, although wealth is unevenly distributed and unemployment is very high. Agriculture employs approximately one-third of the workforce, and produce includes fruit, wine, wool and maize. The country is the world's leading producer of gold and chromium and an important producer of diamonds. Many other minerals are also mined. The main industries are mineral and food processing, chemicals, electrical equipment, textiles and motor vehicles. Financial services are also important.

SOUTH KOREA

Republic of Korea

Area Sq Km	99 274	Languages	Korean
Area Sq Miles	38 330	Religions	Buddhist, Protestant, Roman Catholic
Population	48 391 000	Currency	South Korean won
Capital	Seoul (Sŏul)	Organizations	APEC, OECD, UN

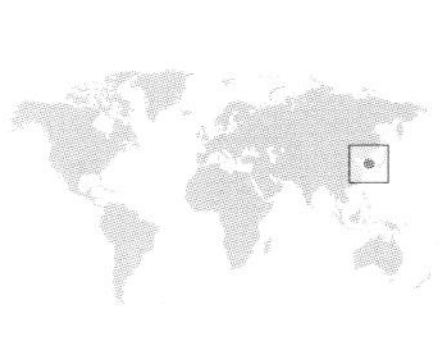

The state consists of the southern half of the Korean Peninsula in eastern Asia and many islands lying off the western and southern coasts in the Yellow Sea. The terrain is mountainous, although less rugged than that of North Korea. Population density is high and the country is highly urbanized; most of the population lives on the western coastal plains and in the river basins of the Han-gang in the northwest and the Naktong-gang in the southeast. The climate is continental, with hot, wet summers and dry, cold winters. Arable land is limited by the mountainous terrain, but because of intensive farming South Korea is nearly self-sufficient in food. Sericulture (silk) is important, as is fishing, which contributes to exports. South Korea has few mineral resources, except for coal and tungsten. It has achieved high economic growth based mainly on export manufacturing. The main manufactured goods are cars, electronic and electrical goods, ships, steel, chemicals and toys, as well as textiles, clothing, footwear and food products. The USA and Japan are the main trading partners.

South Ossetia

Disputed territory

Area Sq Km	4 000	Languages	Ossetian, Russian, Georgian
Area Sq Miles	1 544	Religions	Eastern Orthodox
Population	70 000	Currency	Russian rouble
Capital	Tskhinvali		

The formerly autonomous region of South Ossetia seeks independence from Georgia and looks to the Russian Federation, which recognizes its independence, as its principal ally. South Ossetia's autonomous status was removed in 1990. Violent conflicts followed between Georgia and the separatists, supported by Russia, who wished to unite with Russian North Ossetia. A cease-fire was agreed in 1992. Elections in 1996 were not recognized by Georgia, nor were elections and an independence referendum, voting in favour of independence, in 2006. Russian interference and interest in the area has continued to cause tensions with the Georgian government, the most recent conflict was in 2008 when Georgian troops attacked separatists. Russia responded and a week of fighting was ended by a cease-fire and resulted in Russia recognising South Ossetia's independence.

SOUTH SUDAN

Republic of South Sudan

Area Sq Km	644 329	Languages	English, Arabic, Dinka, Nuer, local languages
Area Sq Miles	248 775	Religions	Traditional beliefs, Christian
Population	8 260 490	Currency	South Sudan pound
Capital	Juba	Organizations	UN

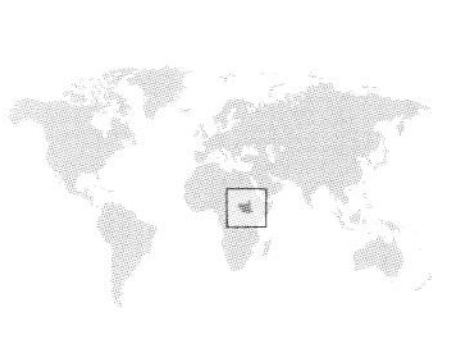

South Sudan in northeast Africa has grasslands, tropical forests and swamps in the north with higher lands in the south. The equatorial climate has moderate temperatures, high humidity and heavy rainfall. Independence from Sudan was gained in July 2011 as a result of a referendum held as part of the agreement which ended decades of civil war between north and south. The government plan to move the capital from Juba to Ramciel in the centre of the country. The economy is mostly agricultural, but the vast natural resources, including huge oil-reserves, are now being increasingly exploited. South Sudan is one of the world's least developed countries.

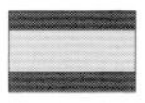

SPAIN
Kingdom of Spain

Area Sq Km	504 782	Languages	Spanish, Castilian, Catalan, Galician, Basque
Area Sq Miles	194 897	Religions	Roman Catholic
Population	46 455 000	Currency	Euro
Capital	Madrid	Organizations	EU, NATO, OECD, UN

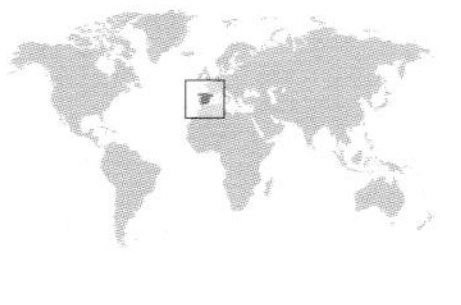

Spain occupies most of the Iberian peninsula in southwest Europe. It includes the Canary Islands, and two enclaves in north Africa. Much of the mainland is a high plateau, and the Pyrenees form the border with France. Summers are hot and winters cool, especially in the north. Most of the population is urban, and agriculture involves only a tenth of the workforce. Fruit, vegetables and wine are exported. Mineral resources include lead, copper, mercury and fluorspar. Some oil is produced, but Spain has to import energy. Manufacturing industries include machinery, transport equipment, vehicles and food products. Fishing, tourism and financial services are also important. Most trade is with other EU countries.

SRI LANKA
Democratic Socialist Republic of Sri Lanka

Area Sq Km	65 610	Languages	Sinhalese, Tamil, English
Area Sq Miles	25 332	Religions	Buddhist, Hindu, Sunni Muslim, Roman Catholic
Population	21 045 000	Currency	Sri Lankan rupee
Capital	Sri Jayewardenepura Kotte	Organizations	Comm., UN

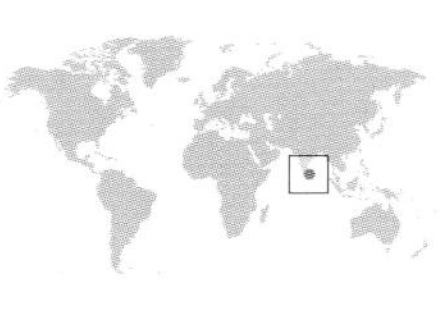

Sri Lanka lies in the Indian Ocean off the southeast coast of India in south Asia. It has rolling coastal plains, with mountains in the centre-south. The climate is hot and monsoonal. Most people live on the west coast. Manufactures (chiefly textiles and clothing), tea, rubber, copra and gems are exported. The economy relies on foreign aid and workers' remittances. The USA and the UK are the main trading partners.

SUDAN
Republic of the Sudan

Area Sq Km	1 861 484	Languages	Arabic, Dinka, Nubian, Beja, Nuer, local languages
Area Sq Miles	718 725	Religions	Sunni Muslim, traditional beliefs, Christian
Population	36 371 510	Currency	Sudanese pound (Sudani)
Capital	Khartoum	Organizations	UN

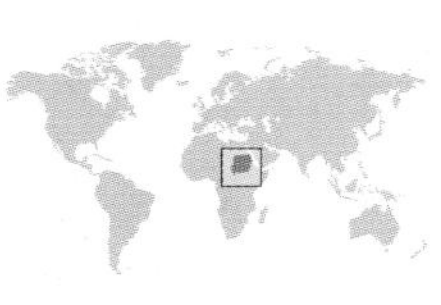

The Sudan is in the northeast of the continent of Africa, on the Red Sea. It lies within the upper Nile basin, much of which is arid plain but with swamps to the south. Mountains lie to the northeast, west and south. The climate is hot and arid with light summer rainfall, and droughts occur. Most people live along the Nile and are farmers and herders. Cotton, gum arabic, livestock and other agricultural products are exported. The government is working with foreign investors to develop oil resources, but the independence of South Sudan in July 2011 after civil war, and ethnic cleansing in Darfur continue to restrict the economy. Main trading partners are Saudi Arabia, China and Libya.

SURINAME
Republic of Suriname

Area Sq Km	163 820	Languages	Dutch, Surinamese, English, Hindi
Area Sq Miles	63 251	Religions	Hindu, Roman Catholic, Protestant, Sunni Muslim
Population	529 000	Currency	Suriname guilder
Capital	Paramaribo	Organizations	CARICOM, UN

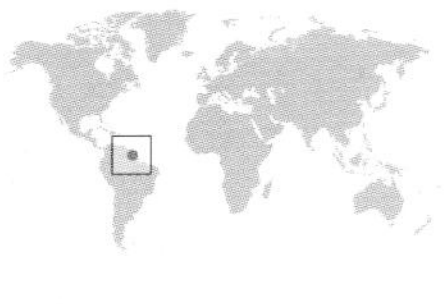

Suriname, on the Atlantic coast of northern South America, consists of a swampy coastal plain (where most of the population lives), central plateaus, and highlands in the south. The climate is tropical, and rainforest covers much of the land. Bauxite mining is the main industry, and alumina and aluminium are the chief exports, with shrimps, rice, bananas and timber also exported. The main trading partners are the Netherlands, Norway and the USA.

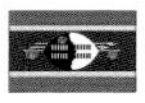

SWAZILAND
Kingdom of Swaziland

Area Sq Km	17 364	Languages	Swazi, English
Area Sq Miles	6 704	Religions	Christian, traditional beliefs
Population	1 203 000	Currency	Emalangeni, South African rand
Capital	Mbabane	Organizations	Comm., SADC, UN

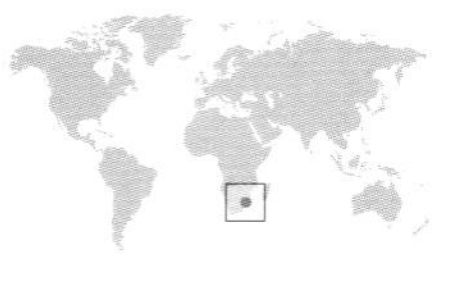

Landlocked Swaziland in southern Africa lies between Mozambique and the Republic of South Africa. Savanna plateaus descend from mountains in the west towards hill country in the east. The climate is subtropical, but temperate in the mountains. Subsistence farming predominates. Asbestos and diamonds are mined. Exports include sugar, fruit and wood pulp. Tourism and workers' remittances are important to the economy. Most trade is with South Africa.

SWEDEN
Kingdom of Sweden

Area Sq Km	449 964	Languages	Swedish
Area Sq Miles	173 732	Religions	Protestant, Roman Catholic
Population	9 441 000	Currency	Swedish krona
Capital	Stockholm	Organizations	EU, OECD, UN

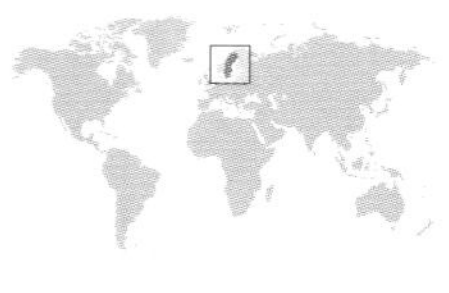

Sweden occupies the eastern part of the Scandinavian peninsula in northern Europe and borders the Baltic Sea, the Gulf of Bothnia, and the Kattegat and Skagerrak, connecting with the North Sea. Forested mountains cover the northern half, part of which lies within the Arctic Circle. The southern part of the country is a lowland lake region where most of the population lives. Sweden has warm summers and cold winters, which are more severe in the north. Natural resources include coniferous forests, mineral deposits and water resources. Some dairy products, meat, cereals and vegetables are produced in the south. The forests supply timber for export and for the important pulp, paper and furniture industries. Sweden is an important producer of iron ore and copper. Zinc, lead, silver and gold are also mined. Machinery and transport equipment, chemicals, pulp and wood, and telecommunications equipment are the main exports. The majority of trade is with other European Union countries.

SWITZERLAND
Swiss Confederation

Area Sq Km	41 293	Languages	German, French, Italian, Romansch
Area Sq Miles	15 943	Religions	Roman Catholic, Protestant
Population	7 702 000	Currency	Swiss franc
Capital	Bern	Organizations	OECD, UN

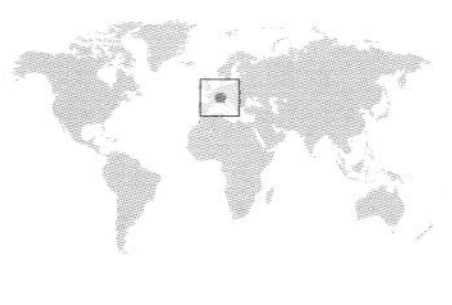

Switzerland is a mountainous, landlocked country in west-central Europe. The southern half lies within the Alps, and the Jura mountains are in the northwest. The rest is a high plateau, where most of the population lives. Climate varies depending on altitude, but in general summers are mild and winters are cold. Switzerland has a very high living standard, yet it has few mineral resources, and most food and raw materials are imported. Manufacturing (especially precision instruments and heavy machinery, chemicals and pharmaceuticals) and financial services are the mainstay of the economy. Tourism, and international organizations based in Switzerland, are also major foreign currency earners. Germany is the main trading partner.

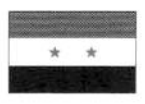

SYRIA
Syrian Arab Republic

Area Sq Km	185 180	Languages	Arabic, Kurdish, Armenian
Area Sq Miles	71 498	Religions	Sunni Muslim, Shi'a Muslim, Christian
Population	20 766 000	Currency	Syrian pound
Capital	Damascus (Dimashq)	Organizations	UN

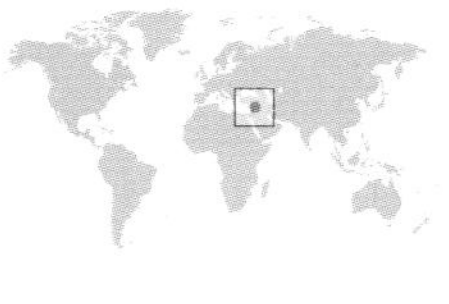

Syria is in southwest Asia, has a short coastline on the Mediterranean Sea, and stretches inland to a plateau traversed northwest-southeast by the Euphrates river. Mountains flank the southwest borders with Lebanon and Israel. The climate is Mediterranean in coastal regions, hotter and drier inland. Most Syrians live on the coast or in the river valleys. Cotton, cereals and fruit are important products, but the main exports are petroleum and related products, and textiles.

TAIWAN
Republic of China

Area Sq Km	36 179	Languages	Mandarin (Putonghua), Min, Hakka, local languages
Area Sq Miles	13 969	Religions	Buddhist, Taoist, Confucian, Christian
Population	23 164 000	Currency	Taiwan dollar
Capital	T'aipei	Organizations	APEC

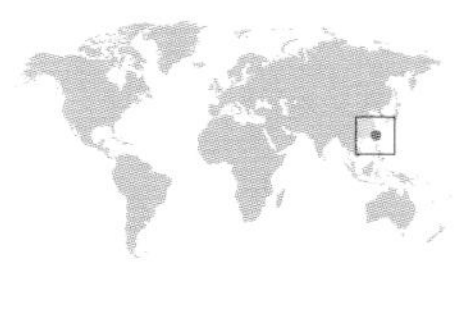

The east Asian state consists of the island of Taiwan, separated from mainland China by the Taiwan Strait, and several much smaller islands. Much of Taiwan is mountainous and forested. Densely populated coastal plains in the west contain most of the population and economic activity. The climate is tropical and monsoonal. The country is virtually self-sufficient in food, and exports some products. Coal, oil and gas are produced and a few minerals are mined. Taiwan depends heavily on imported raw materials. The main manufactures and exports are electrical goods (including televisions, computers and calculators), textiles, fertilizers, clothing, footwear and toys. The main trading partners are the USA, Japan and Germany. The People's Republic of China claims Taiwan as its 23rd Province.

TAJIKISTAN
Republic of Tajikistan

Area Sq Km	143 100	Languages	Tajik, Uzbek, Russian
Area Sq Miles	55 251	Religions	Sunni Muslim
Population	6 977 000	Currency	Somoni
Capital	Dushanbe	Organizations	CIS, UN

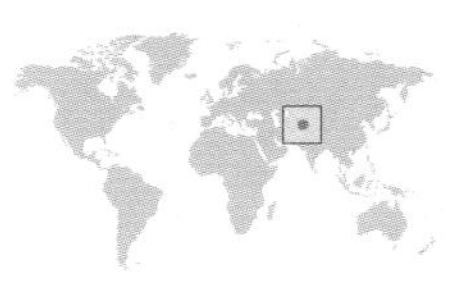

Landlocked Tajikistan in central Asia is a mountainous country, dominated by the mountains of the Alai Range and the Pamir. In the less mountainous western areas summers are warm, although winters are cold. Agriculture is the main sector of the economy, chiefly cotton growing and cattle breeding. Mineral deposits include lead, zinc, and uranium. Processed metals, textiles and clothing are the main manufactured goods; the main exports are aluminium and cotton. Uzbekistan, Kazakhstan and the Russian Federation are the main trading partners.

TANZANIA
United Republic of Tanzania

Area Sq Km	945 087	Languages	Swahili, English, Nyamwezi, local languages
Area Sq Miles	364 900	Religions	Shi'a Muslim, Sunni Muslim, traditional beliefs, Christian
Population	46 218 000	Currency	Tanzanian shilling
Capital	Dodoma	Organizations	Comm., SADC, UN

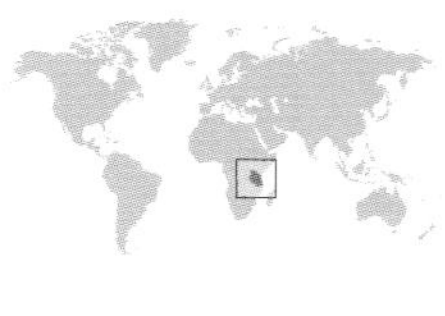

Tanzania lies on the coast of east Africa and includes the island of Zanzibar in the Indian Ocean. Most of the mainland is a savanna plateau lying east of the Great Rift Valley. In the north, near the border with Kenya, is Kilimanjaro, the highest mountain in Africa. The climate is tropical. The economy is predominantly based on agriculture, which employs an estimated ninety per cent of the workforce. Agricultural processing and gold and diamond mining are the main industries, although tourism is growing. Coffee, cotton, cashew nuts and tobacco are the main exports, with cloves from Zanzibar. Most export trade is with India and the UK. Tanzania depends heavily on foreign aid.

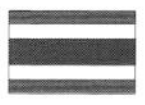

THAILAND
Kingdom of Thailand

Area Sq Km	513 115	Languages	Thai, Lao, Chinese, Malay, Mon-Khmer languages
Area Sq Miles	198 115	Religions	Buddhist, Sunni Muslim
Population	69 519 000	Currency	Baht
Capital	Bangkok (Krung Thep)	Organizations	APEC, ASEAN, UN

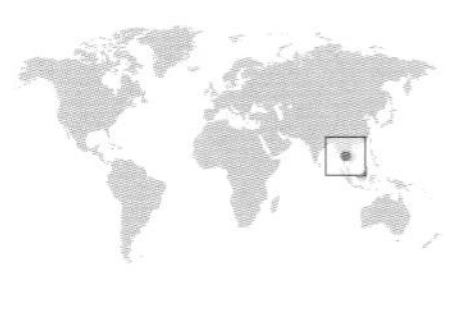

Thailand lies between the Gulf of Thailand and the Andaman Sea and includes the northern Malay Peninsula and many islands lining the coast. To the east of the extensive Chao Phraya basin is a plateau drained by the Mekong, while much of the rest is forested upland. The climate is hot, humid and monsoonal. Half the workforce is involved in agriculture, and fishing is also important, but tourism is the major earner. Minerals include gas, oil, lignite, tin, tungsten and baryte, and gemstones, and manufacturing includes electronics, clothing and food processing. Thailand is a leading exporter of rice, rubber, maize and tapioca. Japan and the USA are the main trading partners.

TOGO
Republic of Togo

Area Sq Km	56 785	Languages	French, Ewe, Kabre, local languages
Area Sq Miles	21 925	Religions	Traditional beliefs, Christian, Sunni Muslim
Population	6 155 000	Currency	CFA franc
Capital	Lomé	Organizations	UN

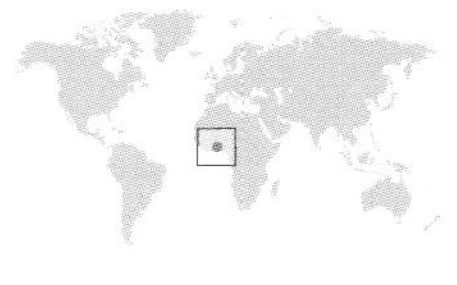

Togo is a long narrow country in west Africa with a short coastline on the Gulf of Guinea. The interior consists of plateaus rising to mountainous areas. The climate is tropical, and is drier inland. Agriculture is the mainstay of the economy. Phosphate mining and food processing are the main industries. Cotton, phosphates, coffee and cocoa are the main exports. Lomé, the capital, is an entrepôt trade centre.

Tokelau
New Zealand Overseas Territory

Area Sq Km	10	Languages	English, Tokelauan
Area Sq Miles	4	Religions	Christian
Population	1 466	Currency	New Zealand dollar

Tokelau consists of three atolls, Atafu, Nukunonu and Fakaofa, lying in the Pacific Ocean north of Samoa. Subsistence agriculture is the main activity, and the islands rely on aid from New Zealand and remittances from workers overseas.

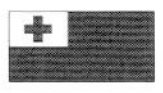

TONGA
Kingdom of Tonga

Area Sq Km	748	Languages	Tongan, English
Area Sq Miles	289	Religions	Protestant, Roman Catholic
Population	105 000	Currency	Pa'anga
Capital	Nuku'alofa	Organizations	Comm., UN

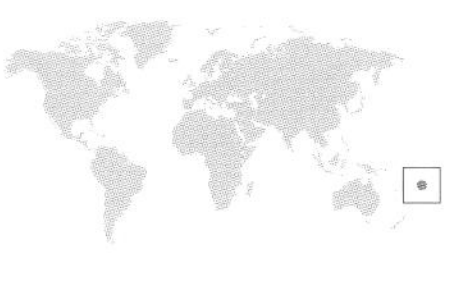

Tonga comprises some one hundred and seventy islands in the south Pacific Ocean, northeast of New Zealand. The three main groups are Tongatapu (where sixty per cent of Tongans live), Ha'apai and Vava'u. The climate is warm and wet, and the economy relies heavily on agriculture. Tourism and light industry are also important to the economy. Exports include squash, fish, vanilla beans and root crops. Most trade is with New Zealand, Japan and Australia.

Transnistria
Disputed territory

Area Sq Km	4 200	Languages	Russian, Ukrainian, Moldovan
Area Sq Miles	1 622	Religions	Eastern Orthodox, Roman Catholic
Population	520 000	Currency	Transnistrian rouble, Moldovan leu
Capital	Tiraspol		

Transnistria, the area of Moldova mainly between the Dniester river and the Ukrainian border, is a predominantly ethnic Russian, and Russian-speaking region. Campaigns for Transnistrian autonomy and independence led to civil war between Moldovan forces and separatists who had proclaimed the self-styled 'Dniester Republic', aligned to Russia, in 1990. A peace agreement with Russia in 1992 ended this war, granted Transnistria special status and established a security zone along its border with Moldova, controlled by Russian, Moldovan and Transnistrian troops. An agreement between Moldova and Transnistria in 1996 stated that Transnistria would remain a part of Moldova, but the campaign for independence continues and the status of the region remains to be resolved. It currently functions as a (predominantly Russian) de facto autonomous republic, separate from Moldova – the Pridnestrovian Moldavian Republic.

TRINIDAD AND TOBAGO
Republic of Trinidad and Tobago

Area Sq Km	5 130	Languages	English, Creole, Hindi
Area Sq Miles	1 981	Religions	Roman Catholic, Hindu, Protestant, Sunni Muslim
Population	1 346 000	Currency	Trinidad and Tobago dollar
Capital	Port of Spain	Organizations	CARICOM, Comm., UN

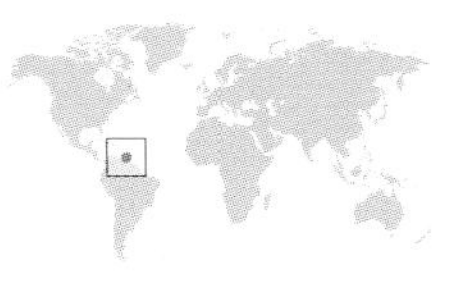

Trinidad, the most southerly Caribbean island, lies off the Venezuelan coast. It is hilly in the north, with a central plain. Tobago, to the northeast, is smaller, more mountainous and less developed. The climate is tropical. The main crops are cocoa, sugar cane, coffee, fruit and vegetables. Oil and petrochemical industries dominate the economy. Tourism is also important. The USA is the main trading partner.

TUNISIA
Republic Tunisian

Area Sq Km	164 150	Languages	Arabic, French
Area Sq Miles	63 379	Religions	Sunni Muslim
Population	10 594 000	Currency	Tunisian dinar
Capital	Tunis	Organizations	UN

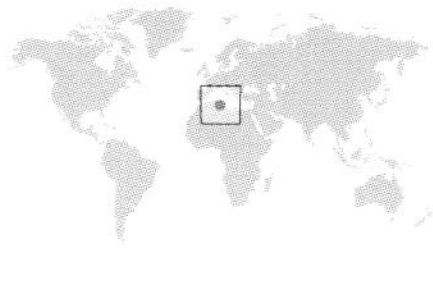

Tunisia is on the Mediterranean coast of north Africa. The north is mountainous with valleys and coastal plains, has a Mediterranean climate and is the most populous area. The south is hot and arid. Oil and phosphates are the main resources, and the main crops are olives and citrus fruit. Tourism is an important industry. Exports include petroleum products, textiles, fruit and phosphorus. Most trade is with European Union countries.

TURKEY
Republic of Turkey

Area Sq Km	779 452	Languages	Turkish, Kurdish
Area Sq Miles	300 948	Religions	Sunni Muslim, Shi'a Muslim
Population	73 640 000	Currency	Lira
Capital	Ankara	Organizations	NATO, OECD, UN

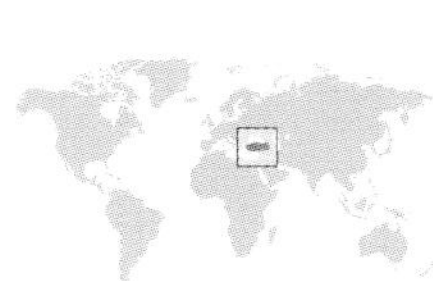

Turkey occupies a large peninsula in southwest Asia. It includes eastern Thrace, in southeastern Europe. The Asian mainland consists of the semi-arid Anatolian plateau, flanked to the north, south and east by mountains. The coast has a Mediterranean climate, but inland conditions are more extreme, with hot, dry summers and cold, snowy winters. Cotton, grains, tobacco, fruit, nuts and livestock are produced, and minerals include chromium, iron ore, lead, tin, borate, baryte, and some coal. Manufacturing includes clothing, textiles, food products, steel and vehicles. Tourism is a major industry. Germany and the USA are the main trading partners. Remittances from workers abroad are important to the economy.

TURKMENISTAN
Republic of Turkmenistan

Area Sq Km	488 100	Languages	Turkmen, Uzbek, Russian
Area Sq Miles	188 456	Religions	Sunni Muslim, Russian Orthodox
Population	5 105 000	Currency	Turkmen manat
Capital	Aşgabat (Ashkhabad)	Organizations	UN

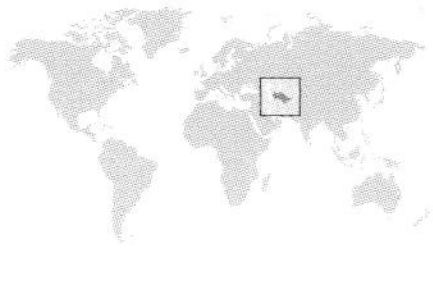

Turkmenistan, in central Asia, comprises the plains of the Karakum Desert, the foothills of the Kopet Dag mountains in the south, the Amudar'ya valley in the north and the Caspian Sea plains in the west. The climate is dry, with extreme temperatures. The economy is based mainly on irrigated agriculture (chiefly cotton growing), and natural gas and oil. Main exports are natural gas, oil and cotton fibre. Ukraine, Iran, Turkey and the Russian Federation are the main trading partners.

Turks and Caicos Islands
United Kingdom Overseas Territory

Area Sq Km	430	Languages	English
Area Sq Miles	166	Religions	Protestant
Population	39 000	Currency	United States dollar
Capital	Grand Turk (Cockburn Town)		

The state consists of over forty low-lying islands and cays in the northern Caribbean. Only eight islands are inhabited, and two-fifths of the people live on Grand Turk and Salt Cay. The climate is tropical, and the economy is based on tourism, fishing and offshore banking.

TUVALU

Area Sq Km	25	Languages	Tuvaluan, English
Area Sq Miles	10	Religions	Protestant
Population	10 000	Currency	Australian dollar
Capital	Vaiaku	Organizations	Comm., UN

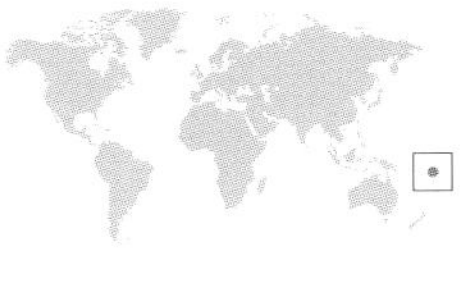

Tuvalu comprises nine low-lying coral atolls in the south Pacific Ocean. One-third of the population lives on Funafuti, and most people depend on subsistence farming and fishing. The islands export copra, stamps and clothing, but rely heavily on foreign aid. Most trade is with Fiji, Australia and New Zealand.

UGANDA
Republic of Uganda

Area Sq Km	241 038	Languages	English, Swahili, Luganda, local languages
Area Sq Miles	93 065	Religions	Roman Catholic, Protestant, Sunni Muslim, traditional beliefs
Population	34 509 000	Currency	Ugandan shilling
Capital	Kampala	Organizations	Comm., UN

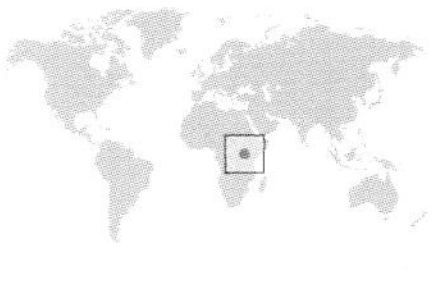

A landlocked country in east Africa, Uganda consists of a savanna plateau with mountains and lakes. The climate is warm and wet. Most people live in the southern half of the country. Agriculture employs around eighty per cent of the workforce and dominates the economy. Coffee, tea, fish and fish products are the main exports. Uganda relies heavily on aid.

UKRAINE

Area Sq Km	603 700	Languages	Ukrainian, Russian
Area Sq Miles	233 090	Religions	Ukrainian Orthodox, Ukrainian Catholic, Roman Catholic
Population	45 190 000	Currency	Hryvnia
Capital	Kiev (Kyiv)	Organizations	CIS, UN

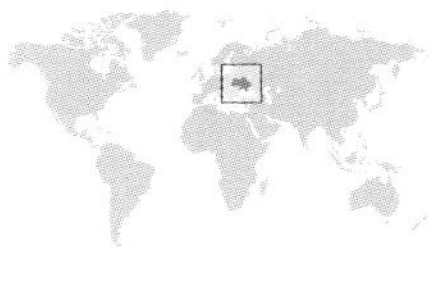

The country lies on the Black Sea coast of eastern Europe. Much of the land is steppe, generally flat and treeless, but with rich black soil, and it is drained by the river Dnieper. Along the border with Belarus are forested, marshy plains. The only uplands are the Carpathian Mountains in the west and smaller ranges on the Crimean peninsula. Summers are warm and winters are cold, with milder conditions in the Crimea. About a quarter of the population lives in the mainly industrial areas around Donets'k, Kiev and Dnipropetrovs'k. The Ukraine is rich in natural resources: fertile soil, substantial mineral and natural gas deposits, and forests. Agriculture and livestock rearing are important, but mining and manufacturing are the dominant sectors of the economy. Coal, iron and manganese mining, steel and metal production, machinery, chemicals and food processing are the main industries. The Russian Federation is the main trading partner.

UNITED ARAB EMIRATES
Federation of Emirates

Area Sq Km	77 700	Languages	Arabic, English
Area Sq Miles	30 000	Religions	Sunni Muslim, Shi'a Muslim
Population	7 891 000	Currency	United Arab Emirates dirham
Capital	Abu Dhabi (Abū Ẓaby)	Organizations	OPEC, UN

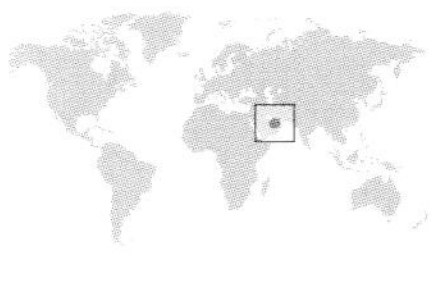

The UAE lies on the Gulf coast of the Arabian Peninsula. Six emirates are on The Gulf, while the seventh, Fujairah, is on the Gulf of Oman. Most of the land is flat desert with sand dunes and salt pans. The only hilly area is in the northeast. Over eighty per cent of the population lives in three of the emirates - Abu Dhabi, Dubai and Sharjah. Summers are hot and winters are mild, with occasional rainfall in coastal areas. Fruit and vegetables are grown in oases and irrigated areas, but the Emirates' wealth is based on hydrocarbons found in Abu Dhabi, Dubai, Sharjah and Ras al Khaimah. The UAE is one of the major oil producers in the Middle East. Dubai is an important entrepôt trade centre The main trading partner is Japan.

Abu Dhabi (Emirate)
Area Sq Km (Sq Miles) 67 340 (26 000) | Population 1 628 000 | Capital Abu Dhabi (Abū Ẓaby)

Ajman (Emirate)
Area Sq Km (Sq Miles) 259 (100) | Population 250 000 | Capital Ajman

Dubai (Emirate)
Area Sq Km (Sq Miles) 3 885 (1 500) | Population 1 722 000 | Capital Dubai

Fujairah (Emirate)
Area Sq Km (Sq Miles) 1 165 (450) | Population 152 000 | Capital Fujairah

Ra's al Khaymah (Emirate)
Area Sq Km (Sq Miles) 1 684 (650) | Population 241 000 | Capital Ra's al Khaymah

Sharjah (Emirate)
Area Sq Km (Sq Miles) 2 590 (1 000) | Population 1 017 000 | Capital Sharjah

Umm al Qaywayn (Emirate)
Area Sq Km (Sq Miles) 777 (300) | Population 56 000 | Capital Umm al Qaywayn

UNITED KINGDOM

United Kingdom of Great Britain and Northern Ireland

Area Sq Km	243 609	**Languages**	English, Welsh, Gaelic
Area Sq Miles	94 058	**Religions**	Protestant, Roman Catholic, Muslim
Population	62 417 000	**Currency**	Pound sterling
Capital	London	**Organizations**	Comm., EU, NATO, OECD, UN

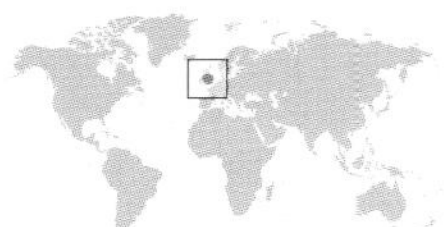

The United Kingdom, in northwest Europe, occupies the island of Great Britain, part of Ireland, and many small adjacent islands. Great Britain comprises England, Scotland and Wales. England covers over half the land area and supports over four-fifths of the population, at its densest in the southeast. The English landscape is flat or rolling with some uplands, notably the Cheviot Hills on the Scottish border, the Pennines in the centre-north, and the hills of the Lake District in the northwest. Scotland consists of southern uplands, central lowlands, the Highlands (which include the UK's highest peak) and many islands. Wales is a land of hills, mountains and river valleys. Northern Ireland contains uplands, plains and the UK's largest lake, Lough Neagh. The climate of the UK is mild, wet and variable. There are few mineral deposits, but important energy resources. Agricultural activities involve sheep and cattle rearing, dairy farming, and crop and fruit growing in the east and southeast. Productivity is high, but approximately one-third of food is imported. The UK produces petroleum and natural gas from reserves in the North Sea and is self-sufficient in energy in net terms. Major manufactures are food and drinks, motor vehicles and parts, aerospace equipment, machinery, electronic and electrical equipment, and chemicals and chemical products. However, the economy is dominated by service industries, including banking, insurance, finance and business services. London, the capital, is one of the world's major financial centres. Tourism is also a major industry, with approximately twenty-eight million visitors a year. International trade is also important, equivalent to around forty per cent of national income. Over half of the UK's trade is with other European Union countries.

England (Constituent country)
Area Sq Km (Sq Miles) 130 433 (50 360) **Population** 51 809 700 **Capital** London

Northern Ireland (Province)
Area Sq Km (Sq Miles) 13 576 (5 242) **Population** 1 788 900 **Capital** Belfast

Scotland (Constituent country)
Area Sq Km (Sq Miles) 78 822 (30 433) **Population** 5 194 000 **Capital** Edinburgh

Wales (Principality)
Area Sq Km (Sq Miles) 20 778 (8 022) **Population** 2 999 300 **Capital** Cardiff

UNITED STATES OF AMERICA

Area Sq Km	9 826 635	**Languages**	English, Spanish
Area Sq Miles	3 794 085	**Religions**	Protestant, Roman Catholic, Sunni Muslim, Jewish
Population	313 085 000	**Currency**	United States dollar
Capital	Washington D.C.	**Organizations**	APEC, NATO, OECD, UN

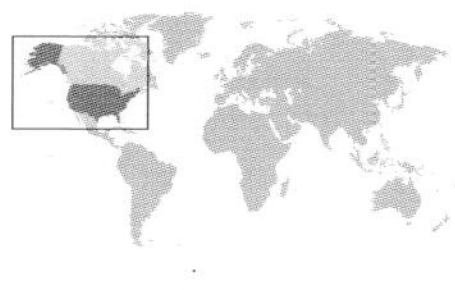

The USA comprises forty-eight contiguous states in North America, bounded by Canada and Mexico, plus the states of Alaska, to the northwest of Canada, and Hawaii, in the north Pacific Ocean. The populous eastern states cover the Atlantic coastal plain (which includes the Florida peninsula and the Gulf of Mexico coast) and the Appalachian Mountains. The central states occupy a vast interior plain drained by the Mississippi-Missouri river system. To the west lie the Rocky Mountains, separated from the Pacific coastal ranges by intermontane plateaus. The Pacific coastal zone is also mountainous, and prone to earthquakes. Hawaii is a group of some twenty volcanic islands. Climatic conditions range between arctic in Alaska to desert in the intermontane plateaus. Most of the USA has a temperate climate, although the interior has continental conditions. There are abundant natural resources, including major reserves of minerals and energy resources. The USA has the largest and most technologically advanced economy in the world, based on manufacturing and services. Although agriculture accounts for approximately two per cent of national income, productivity is high and the USA is a net exporter of food, chiefly grains and fruit. Cotton is the major industrial crop. The USA produces iron ore, copper, lead, zinc, and many other minerals. It is a major producer of coal, petroleum and natural gas, although being the world's biggest energy user it imports significant quantities of petroleum and its products. Manufacturing is diverse. The main industries are petroleum, steel, motor vehicles, aerospace, telecommunications, electronics, food processing, chemicals and consumer goods. Tourism is a major foreign currency earner, with approximately sixty million visitors a year. Other important service industries are banking and finance, Wall Street in New York being one of the world's major stock exchanges. Canada and Mexico are the main trading partners.

Alabama (State)
Area Sq Km (Sq Miles) 135 765 (52 419) **Population** 4 708 708 **Capital** Montgomery

Alaska (State)
Area Sq Km (Sq Miles) 1 717 854 (663 267) **Population** 698 473 **Capital** Juneau

Arizona (State)
Area Sq Km (Sq Miles) 295 253 (113 998) **Population** 6 595 778 **Capital** Phoenix

Arkansas (State)
Area Sq Km (Sq Miles) 137 733 (53 179) **Population** 2 889 450 **Capital** Little Rock

California (State)
Area Sq Km (Sq Miles) 423 971 (163 696) **Population** 36 961 664 **Capital** Sacramento

Colorado (State)
Area Sq Km (Sq Miles) 269 602 (104 094) **Population** 5 024 748 **Capital** Denver

Connecticut (State)
Area Sq Km (Sq Miles) 14 356 (5 543) **Population** 3 518 288 **Capital** Hartford

Delaware (State)
Area Sq Km (Sq Miles) 6 446 (2 489) **Population** 885 122 **Capital** Dover

District of Columbia (District)
Area Sq Km (Sq Miles) 176 (68) **Population** 599 657 **Capital** Washington

Florida (State)
Area Sq Km (Sq Miles) 170 305 (65 755) **Population** 18 537 969 **Capital** Tallahassee

Georgia (State)
Area Sq Km (Sq Miles) 153 910 (59 425) **Population** 9 829 211 **Capital** Atlanta

Hawaii (State)
Area Sq Km (Sq Miles) 28 311 (10 931) **Population** 1 295 178 **Capital** Honolulu

Idaho (State)
Area Sq Km (Sq Miles) 216 445 (83 570) **Population** 1 545 801 **Capital** Boise

Illinois (State)
Area Sq Km (Sq Miles) 149 997 (57 914) **Population** 12 910 409 **Capital** Springfield

Indiana (State)
Area Sq Km (Sq Miles) 94 322 (36 418) **Population** 6 423 113 **Capital** Indianapolis

Iowa (State)
Area Sq Km (Sq Miles) 145 744 (56 272) **Population** 3 007 856 **Capital** Des Moines

Kansas (State)
Area Sq Km (Sq Miles) 213 096 (82 277) **Population** 2 818 747 **Capital** Topeka

Kentucky (State)
Area Sq Km (Sq Miles) 104 659 (40 409) **Population** 4 314 113 **Capital** Frankfort

Louisiana (State)
Area Sq Km (Sq Miles) 134 265 (51 840) **Population** 4 492 076 **Capital** Baton Rouge

Maine (State)
Area Sq Km (Sq Miles) 91 647 (35 385) **Population** 1 318 301 **Capital** Augusta

Maryland (State)
Area Sq Km (Sq Miles) 32 134 (12 407) **Population** 5 699 478 **Capital** Annapolis

Massachusetts (State)
Area Sq Km (Sq Miles) 27 337 (10 555) **Population** 6 593 587 **Capital** Boston

Michigan (State)
Area Sq Km (Sq Miles) 250 493 (96 716) **Population** 9 969 727 **Capital** Lansing

Minnesota (State)
Area Sq Km (Sq Miles) 225 171 (86 939) **Population** 5 266 214 **Capital** St Paul

Mississippi (State)
Area Sq Km (Sq Miles) 125 433 (48 430) **Population** 2 951 996 **Capital** Jackson

Missouri (State)
Area Sq Km (Sq Miles) 180 533 (69 704) **Population** 5 987 580 **Capital** Jefferson City

Montana (State)
Area Sq Km (Sq Miles) 380 837 (147 042) **Population** 974 989 **Capital** Helena

Nebraska (State)
Area Sq Km (Sq Miles) 200 346 (77 354) **Population** 1 796 619 **Capital** Lincoln

Nevada (State)
Area Sq Km (Sq Miles) 286 352 (110 561) **Population** 2 643 085 **Capital** Carson City

New Hampshire (State)
Area Sq Km (Sq Miles) 24 216 (9 350) **Population** 1 324 575 **Capital** Concord

New Jersey (State)
Area Sq Km (Sq Miles) 22 587 (8 721) **Population** 8 707 739 **Capital** Trenton

New Mexico (State)
Area Sq Km (Sq Miles) 314 914 (121 589) **Population** 2 009 671 **Capital** Santa Fe

New York (State)
Area Sq Km (Sq Miles) 141 299 (54 556) **Population** 19 541 453 **Capital** Albany

North Carolina (State)
Area Sq Km (Sq Miles) 139 391 (53 819) **Population** 9 380 884 **Capital** Raleigh

North Dakota (State)
Area Sq Km (Sq Miles) 183 112 (70 700) **Population** 646 844 **Capital** Bismarck

Ohio (State)
Area Sq Km (Sq Miles) 116 096 (44 825) **Population** 11 542 645 **Capital** Columbus

Oklahoma (State)
Area Sq Km (Sq Miles) 181 035 (69 898) **Population** 3 687 050 **Capital** Oklahoma City

Oregon (State)
Area Sq Km (Sq Miles) 254 806 (98 381) **Population** 3 825 657 **Capital** Salem

Pennsylvania (State)
Area Sq Km (Sq Miles) 119 282 (46 055) **Population** 12 604 767 **Capital** Harrisburg

Rhode Island (State)
Area Sq Km (Sq Miles) 4 002 (1 545) **Population** 1 053 209 **Capital** Providence

South Carolina (State)
Area Sq Km (Sq Miles) 82 931 (32 020) **Population** 4 561 242 **Capital** Columbia

South Dakota (State)
Area Sq Km (Sq Miles) 199 730 (77 116) **Population** 812 383 **Capital** Pierre

Tennessee (State)
Area Sq Km (Sq Miles) 109 150 (42 143) **Population** 6 296 254 **Capital** Nashville

Texas (State)
Area Sq Km (Sq Miles) 695 622 (268 581) **Population** 24 782 302 **Capital** Austin

Utah (State)
Area Sq Km (Sq Miles) 219 887 (84 899) **Population** 2 784 572 **Capital** Salt Lake City

Vermont (State)
Area Sq Km (Sq Miles) 24 900 (9 614) **Population** 621 760 **Capital** Montpelier

Virginia (State)
Area Sq Km (Sq Miles) 110 784 (42 774) **Population** 7 882 590 **Capital** Richmond

Washington (State)
Area Sq Km (Sq Miles) 184 666 (71 300) **Population** 6 664 195 **Capital** Olympia

West Virginia (State)
Area Sq Km (Sq Miles) 62 755 (24 230) **Population** 1 819 777 **Capital** Charleston

Wisconsin (State)
Area Sq Km (Sq Miles) 169 639 (65 498) **Population** 5 654 774 **Capital** Madison

Wyoming (State)
Area Sq Km (Sq Miles) 253 337 (97 814) **Population** 544 270 **Capital** Cheyenne

URUGUAY

Oriental Republic of Uruguay

Area Sq Km	176 215	**Languages**	Spanish
Area Sq Miles	68 037	**Religions**	Roman Catholic, Protestant, Jewish
Population	3 380 000	**Currency**	Uruguayan peso
Capital	Montevideo	**Organizations**	UN

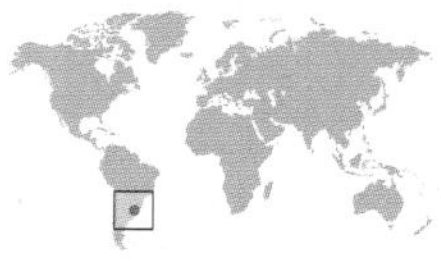

Uruguay, on the Atlantic coast of central South America, is a low-lying land of prairies. The coast and the River Plate estuary in the south are fringed with lagoons and sand dunes. Almost half the population lives in the capital, Montevideo. Uruguay has warm summers and mild winters. The economy is based on cattle and sheep ranching, and the main industries produce food products, textiles, and petroleum products. Meat, wool, hides, textiles and agricultural products are the main exports. Brazil and Argentina are the main trading partners.

UZBEKISTAN

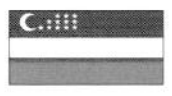

Republic of Uzbekistan

Area Sq Km	447 400	Languages	Uzbek, Russian, Tajik, Kazakh
Area Sq Miles	172 742	Religions	Sunni Muslim, Russian Orthodox
Population	27 760 000	Currency	Uzbek som
Capital	Toshkent (Tashkent)	Organizations	CIS, UN

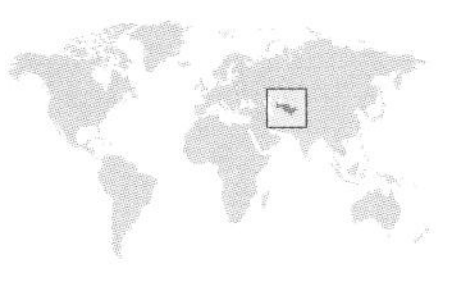

A landlocked country of central Asia, Uzbekistan consists mainly of the flat Kyzylkum Desert. High mountains and valleys are found towards the southeast borders with Kyrgyzstan and Tajikistan. Most settlement is in the Fergana basin. The climate is hot and dry. The economy is based mainly on irrigated agriculture, chiefly cotton production. Uzbekistan is rich in minerals, including gold, copper, lead, zinc and uranium, and it has one of the largest gold mines in the world. Industry specializes in fertilizers and machinery for cotton harvesting and textile manufacture. The Russian Federation is the main trading partner.

VANUATU

Republic of Vanuatu

Area Sq Km	12 190	Languages	English, Bislama (Creole), French
Area Sq Miles	4 707	Religions	Protestant, Roman Catholic, traditional beliefs
Population	246 000	Currency	Vatu
Capital	Port Vila	Organizations	Comm., UN

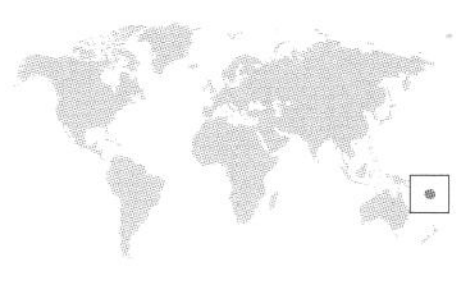

Vanuatu occupies an archipelago of approximately eighty islands in the southwest Pacific. Many of the islands are mountainous, of volcanic origin and densely forested. The climate is tropical, with heavy rainfall. Half of the population lives on the main islands of Éfaté and Espíritu Santo, and the majority of people are employed in agriculture. Copra, beef, timber, vegetables, and cocoa are the main exports. Tourism is becoming important to the economy. Australia, Japan and Germany are the main trading partners.

VATICAN CITY

Vatican City State or Holy See

Area Sq Km	0.5	Languages	Italian
Area Sq Miles	0.2	Religions	Roman Catholic
Population	800	Currency	Euro
Capital	Vatican City		

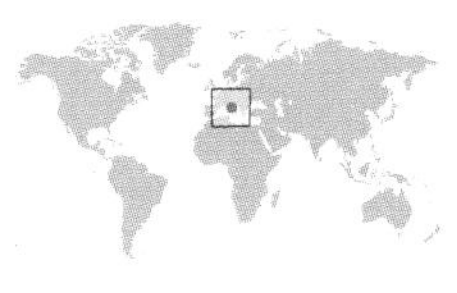

The world's smallest sovereign state, the Vatican City occupies a hill to the west of the river Tiber within the Italian capital, Rome. It is the headquarters of the Roman Catholic church, and income comes from investments, voluntary contributions and tourism.

VENEZUELA

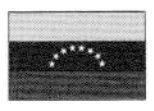

Bolivarian Republic of Venezuela

Area Sq Km	912 050	Languages	Spanish, Amerindian languages
Area Sq Miles	352 144	Religions	Roman Catholic, Protestant
Population	29 437 000	Currency	Bolívar fuerte
Capital	Caracas	Organizations	OPEC, UN

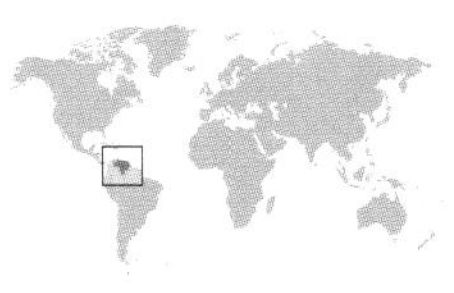

Venezuela is in northern South America, on the Caribbean. Its coast is much indented, with the oil-rich area of Lake Maracaibo at the western end, and the swampy Orinoco Delta to the east. Mountain ranges run parallel to the coast, and turn southwestwards to form a northern extension of the Andes. Central Venezuela is an area of lowland grasslands drained by the Orinoco river system. To the south are the Guiana Highlands, which contain the Angel Falls, the world's highest waterfall. Almost ninety per cent of the population lives in towns, mostly in the coastal mountain areas. The climate is tropical, with most rainfall in summer. Farming is important, particularly cattle ranching and dairy farming; coffee, maize, rice and sugar cane are the main crops. Venezuela is a major oil producer, and oil accounts for about seventy-five per cent of export earnings. Aluminium, iron ore, copper and gold are also mined, and manufactures include petrochemicals, aluminium, steel, textiles and food products. The USA and Puerto Rico are the main trading partners.

VIETNAM

Socialist Republic of Vietnam

Area Sq Km	329 565	Languages	Vietnamese, Thai, Khmer, Chinese, local languages
Area Sq Miles	127 246	Religions	Buddhist, Taoist, Roman Catholic, Cao Dai, Hoa Hao
Population	88 792 000	Currency	Dong
Capital	Ha Nôi	Organizations	APEC, ASEAN, UN

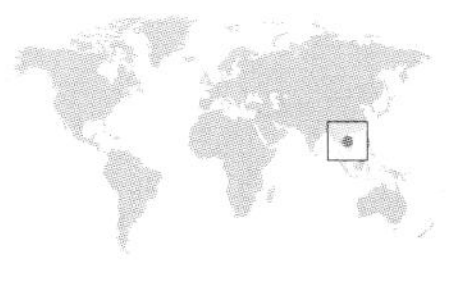

Vietnam lies in southeast Asia on the west coast of the South China Sea. The Red River delta lowlands in the north are separated from the huge Mekong delta in the south by long, narrow coastal plains backed by the mountainous and forested terrain of the Annam Highlands. Most of the population lives in the river deltas. The climate is tropical, with summer monsoon rains. Over three-quarters of the workforce is involved in agriculture, forestry and fishing. Coffee, tea and rubber are important cash crops, but Vietnam is the world's second largest rice exporter. Oil, coal and copper are produced, and other main industries are food processing, clothing and footwear, cement and fertilizers. Exports include oil, coffee, rice, clothing, fish and fish products. Japan and Singapore are the main trading partners.

Virgin Islands (U.K.)

United Kingdom Overseas Territory

Area Sq Km	153	Languages	English
Area Sq Miles	59	Religions	Protestant, Roman Catholic
Population	23 000	Currency	United States dollar
Capital	Road Town		

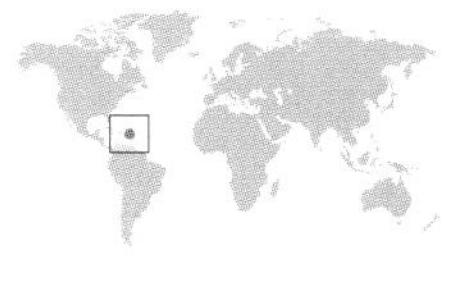

The Caribbean territory comprises four main islands and over thirty islets at the eastern end of the Virgin Islands group. Apart from the flat coral atoll of Anegada, the islands are volcanic in origin and hilly. The climate is subtropical, and tourism is the main industry.

Virgin Islands (U.S.A.)

United States Unincorporated Territory

Area Sq Km	352	Languages	English, Spanish
Area Sq Miles	136	Religions	Protestant, Roman Catholic
Population	109 000	Currency	United States dollar
Capital	Charlotte Amalie		

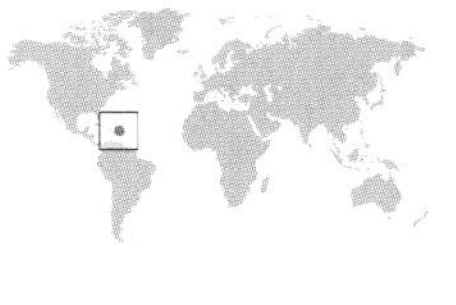

The territory consists of three main islands and over fifty islets in the Caribbean's western Virgin Islands. The islands are hilly, of volcanic origin, and the climate is subtropical. The economy is based on tourism, with some manufacturing, including a major oil refinery on St Croix.

Wallis and Futuna Islands

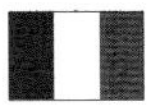

French Overseas Collectivity

Area Sq Km	274	Languages	French, Wallisian, Futunian
Area Sq Miles	106	Religions	Roman Catholic
Population	13 000	Currency	CFP franc
Capital	Matā'utu		

The south Pacific territory comprises the volcanic islands of the Wallis archipelago and the Hoorn Islands. The climate is tropical. The islands depend on subsistence farming, the sale of licences to foreign fishing fleets, workers' remittances from abroad and French aid.

West Bank

Disputed territory

Area Sq Km	5 860	Languages	Arabic, Hebrew
Area Sq Miles	2 263	Religions	Sunni Muslim, Jewish, Shi'a Muslim, Christian
Population	2 513 283	Currency	Jordanian dinar, Israeli shekel

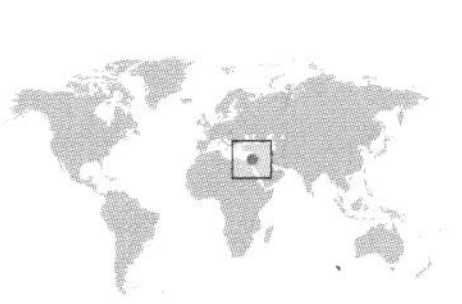

The territory consists of the west bank of the river Jordan and parts of Judea and Samaria. The land was annexed by Israel in 1967, but some areas have been granted autonomy under agreements between Israel and the Palestinian Authority. Conflict between the Israelis and the Palestinians continues to restrict economic development.

Western Sahara

Disputed territory

Area Sq Km	266 000	Languages	Arabic
Area Sq Miles	102 703	Religions	Sunni Muslim
Population	548 000	Currency	Moroccan dirham
Capital	Laâyoune		

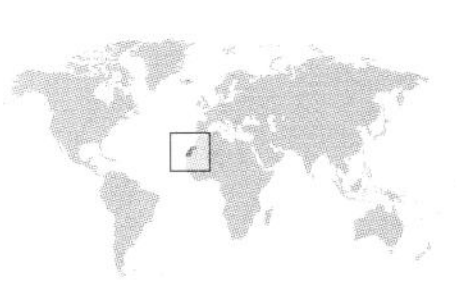

Situated on the northwest coast of Africa, the territory of the Western Sahara is now effectively controlled by Morocco. The land is low, flat desert with higher land in the northeast. There is little cultivation and only about twenty per cent of the land is pasture. Livestock herding, fishing and phosphate mining are the main activities. All trade is controlled by Morocco.

YEMEN

Republic of Yemen

Area Sq Km	527 968	Languages	Arabic
Area Sq Miles	203 850	Religions	Sunni Muslim, Shi'a Muslim
Population	24 800 000	Currency	Yemeni riyal
Capital	Şan'ā'	Organizations	UN

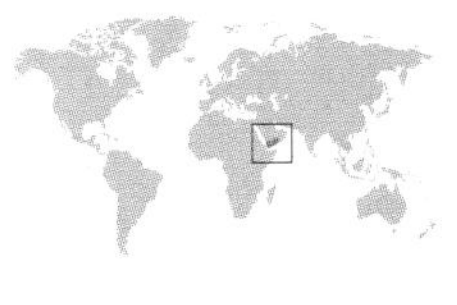

Yemen occupies the southwestern part of the Arabian Peninsula, on the Red Sea and the Gulf of Aden. Beyond the Red Sea coastal plain the land rises to a mountain range and then descends to desert plateaus. Much of the country is hot and arid, but there is more rainfall in the west, where most of the population lives. Farming and fishing are the main activities, with cotton the main cash crop. The main exports are crude oil, fish, coffee and dried fruit. Despite some oil resources Yemen is one of the poorest countries in the Arab world. Main trading partners are Thailand, China, South Korea and Saudi Arabia.

ZAMBIA

Republic of Zambia

Area Sq Km	752 614	Languages	English, Bemba, Nyanja, Tonga, local languages
Area Sq Miles	290 586	Religions	Christian, traditional beliefs
Population	13 475 000	Currency	Zambian kwacha
Capital	Lusaka	Organizations	Comm., SADC, UN

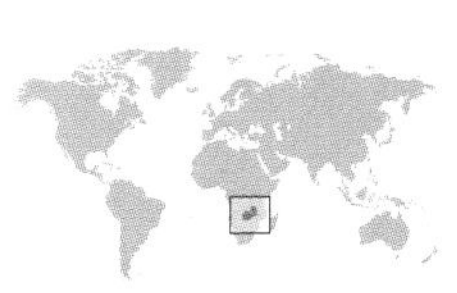

A landlocked state in south central Africa, Zambia consists principally of high savanna plateaus and is bordered by the Zambezi river in the south. Most people live in the Copperbelt area in the centre-north. The climate is tropical, with a rainy season from November to May. Agriculture employs approximately eighty per cent of the workforce, but is mainly at subsistence level. Copper mining is the mainstay of the economy, although reserves are declining. Copper and cobalt are the main exports. Most trade is with South Africa.

ZIMBABWE

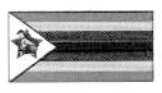

Republic of Zimbabwe

Area Sq Km	390 759	Languages	English, Shona, Ndebele
Area Sq Miles	150 873	Religions	Christian, traditional beliefs
Population	12 754 000	Currency	Zimbabwean dollar (suspended)
Capital	Harare	Organizations	SADC, UN

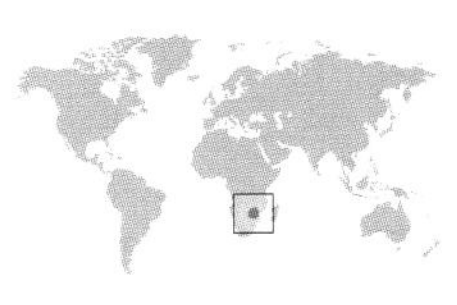

Zimbabwe, a landlocked state in south-central Africa, consists of high plateaus flanked by the Zambezi river valley and Lake Kariba in the north and the Limpopo river in the south. Most of the population lives in the centre of the country. There are significant mineral resources, including gold, nickel, copper, asbestos, platinum and chromium. Agriculture is a major sector of the economy, with crops including tobacco, maize, sugar cane and cotton. Beef cattle are also important. Exports include tobacco, gold, ferroalloys, nickel and cotton. South Africa is the main trading partner. The economy has suffered recently through significant political unrest and instability.

abrasion

A

abrasion The wearing away of the landscape by rivers, **glaciers**, the sea or wind, caused by the load of debris that they carry. *See also* **corrasion**.

abrasion platform *See* **wave-cut platform**.

acid rain Rain that contains a high concentration of pollutants, notably sulphur and nitrogen oxides. These pollutants are produced from factories, power stations burning **fossil fuels,** and car exhausts. Once in the **atmosphere**, the sulphur and nitrogen oxides combine with moisture to give sulphuric and nitric acids which fall as corrosive rain.

administrative region An area in which organizations carry out administrative functions; for example, the regions of local health authorities and water companies, and commercial sales regions.

adult literacy rate A percentage measure which shows the proportion of an adult population able to read. It is one of the measures used to assess the level of development of a country.

aerial photograph A photograph taken from above the ground. There are two types of aerial photograph – a vertical photograph (or 'bird's-eye view') and an oblique photograph where the camera is held at an angle. Aerial photographs are often taken from aircraft and provide useful information for map-making and surveys. *Compare* **satellite image**.

afforestation The conversion of open land to forest; especially, in Britain, the planting of coniferous trees in upland areas for commercial gain. *Compare* **deforestation**.

agglomerate A mass of coarse rock fragments or blocks of lava produced during a volcanic eruption.

agribusiness Modern **intensive farming** which uses machinery and artificial fertilizers to increase **yield** and output. Thus agriculture resembles an industrial process in which the general running and managing of the farm could parallel that of large-scale industry.

agriculture Human management of the **environment** to produce food. The numerous forms of agriculture fall into three groups: **commercial agriculture, subsistence agriculture** and **peasant agriculture**. *See also* **agribusiness**.

aid The provision of finance, personnel and equipment for furthering economic development and improving standards of living in the **Third World**. Most aid is organized by international institutions (e.g. the United Nations), by charities (e.g. Oxfam) (*see* **non-governmental organizations** (NGOs); or by national governments. Aid to a country from the international institutions is called *multilateral aid*. Aid from one country to another is called *bilateral aid*.

air mass A large body of air with generally the same temperature and moisture conditions throughout.

Warm or cold and moist air masses usually develop over large bodies of water (**oceans**). Hot or cold and dry air masses develop over large land areas (**continents**).

alluvial fan A cone of **sediment** deposited at an abrupt change of slope; for example, where a post-glacial stream meets the flat floor of a **U-shaped valley**. Alluvial fans are also common in arid regions where streams flowing off **escarpments** may periodically carry large loads of sediment during **flash floods**.

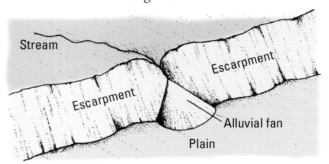

alluvial fan

alluvium Material deposited by a river in its middle and lower course. Alluvium comprises **silt**, sand and coarser debris eroded from the river's upper course and transported downstream. Alluvium is deposited in a graded sequence: coarsest first (heaviest) and finest last (lightest). Regular floods in the lower course create extensive layers of alluvium which can build up to a considerable depth on the **flood plain**.

alp A gentle slope above the steep sides of a glaciated valley, often used for summer grazing. *See also* **transhumance**.

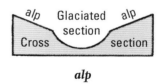

alp

anemometer An instrument for measuring the velocity of the wind. An anemometer should be fixed on a post at least 5 m above ground level. The wind blows the cups around and the speed is read off the dial in km/hr (or knots).

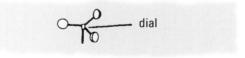

anemometer

antarctic circle Imaginary line that encircles the South Pole at **latitude** 66° 32'S

anthracite A hard form of **coal** with a high carbon content and few impurities.

anticline An arch in folded **strata**; the opposite of **syncline**. *See* **fold**.

barograph

anticyclone An area of high atmospheric pressure with light winds, clear skies and settled **weather**. In summer, anticyclones are associated with warm and sunny conditions; in winter, they bring frost and fog as well as sunshine.

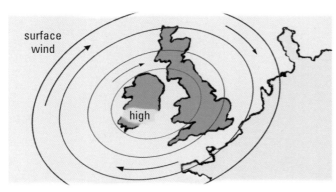

anticyclone

aquifer *See* **artesian basin**.

arable farming The production of cereal and root crops – as opposed to the keeping of livestock.

archipelago A group or chain of islands.

arctic circle Imaginary line that encircles the North Pole at **latitude** 66° 32'N

arête A knife-edged ridge separating two **corries** in a glaciated upland. The arête is formed by the progressive enlargement of corries by **weathering** and **erosion**. *See also* **pyramidal peak**.

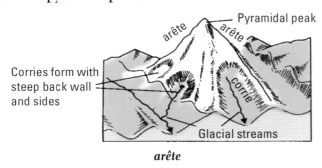

arête

artesian basin This consists of a shallow **syncline** with a layer of **permeable rock**, e.g. chalk, sandwiched between two impermeable layers, e.g. clay. Where the permeable rock is exposed at the surface, rainwater will enter the rock and the rock will become saturated. This is known as an *aquifer*. Boreholes can be sunk into the structure to tap the water in the aquifer.

asymmetrical fold Folded **strata** where the two limbs are at different angles to the horizontal.

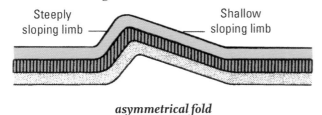

asymmetrical fold

atmosphere The air which surrounds the Earth, and consists of three layers: the *troposphere* (6 to 10 km from the Earth's surface), the *stratosphere* (50km from the Earth's surface), and the *mesosphere* and *ionosphere*, an ionised region of rarefied gases (1000km from the Earth's surface). The atmosphere comprises oxygen (21%), nitrogen (78%), carbon dioxide, argon, helium and other gases in minute quantities.

attrition The process by which a river's load is eroded through particles, such as pebbles and boulders, striking each other.

B

backwash The return movement of seawater off the beach after a wave has broken. *See also* **longshore drift** and **swash**.

bar graph A graph on which the values of a certain variable are shown by the length of shaded columns, which are numbered in sequence. *Compare* **histogram**.

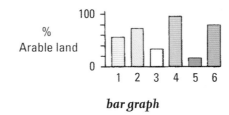

bar graph

barchan A type of crescent-shaped sand dune formed in desert regions where the wind direction is very constant. Wind blowing round the edges of the dune causes the crescent shape, while the dune may advance in a downwind direction as particles are blown over the crest.

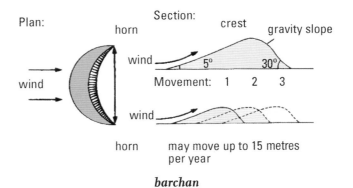

barchan

barograph An aneroid **barometer** connected to an arm and inked pen which records pressure changes continuously on a rotating drum. The drum usually takes a week to make one rotation.

barometer

barometer An instrument for measuring atmospheric pressure. There are two types, the *mercury barometer* and the *aneroid barometer*. The mercury barometer consists of a glass tube containing mercury which fluctuates in height as pressure varies. The aneroid barometer is a small metal box from which some of the air has been removed. The box expands and contracts as the air pressure changes. A series of levers joined to a pointer shows pressure on a dial.

barrage A type of dam built across a wide stretch of water, e.g. an estuary, for the purposes of water management. Such a dam may be intended to provide water supply, to harness wave energy or to control flooding, etc. There is a large barrage across Cardiff Bay in South Wales.

basalt A dark, fine-grained extrusive **igneous rock** formed when **magma** emerges onto the Earth's surface and cools rapidly. A succession of basalt **lava flows** may lead to the formation of a **lava plateau**.

base flow The water flowing in a stream which is fed only by **groundwater**. During dry periods it is only the base flow which passes through the stream channel.

batholith A large body of igneous material intruded into the Earth's **crust**. As the batholith slowly cools, large-grained **rocks** such as **granite** are formed. Batholiths may eventually be exposed at the Earth's surface by the removal of overlying rocks through **weathering** and **erosion**.

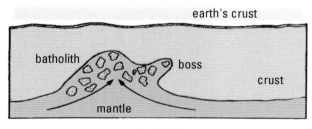

batholith

bay An indentation in the coastline with a **headland** on either side. Its formation is due to the more rapid **erosion** of softer rocks.

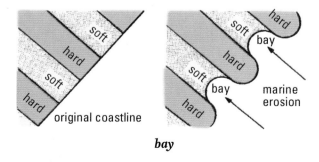

bay

beach A strip of land sloping gently towards the sea, usually recognized as the area lying between high and low tide marks.

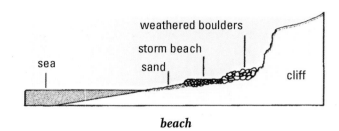

beach

bearing A compass reading between 0 and 360 degrees, indicating direction of one location from another.

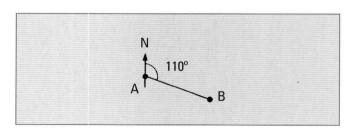

bearing *The bearing from A to B is 110°.*

Beaufort wind scale An international scale of wind velocities, ranging from 0 (calm) to 12 (hurricane).

bedrock The solid rock which usually lies beneath the soil.

bergschrund A large **crevasse** located at the rear of a **corrie** icefield in a glaciated region, formed by the weight of the ice in the corrie dragging away from the rear wall as the **glacier** moves downslope.

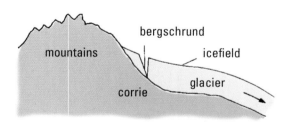

bergschrund

biodiversity The existence of a wide variety of plant and animal species in their natural environment.

biogas The production of methane and carbon dioxide, which can be obtained from plant or crop waste. Biogas is an example of a renewable source of energy (*see* **renewable resources, nonrenewable resources**).

biomass The total number of living organisms, both plant and animal, in a given area.

biome A complex community of plants and animals in a specific physical and climatic region. *See* **climate**.

biosphere The part of the Earth which contains living organisms. The biosphere contains a variety of **habitats**, from the highest mountains to the deepest oceans.

birth rate The number of live births per 1000 people in a population per year.

bituminous coal Sometimes called house coal – a medium-quality **coal** with some impurities; the typical domestic coal. It is also the major fuel source for **thermal power stations.**

block mountain *or* **horst** A section of the Earth's **crust** uplifted by faulting. Mt Ruwenzori in the East African Rift System is an example of a block mountain.

blowhole A crevice, **joint** or **fault** in coastal rocks, enlarged by marine **erosion**. A blowhole often leads from the rear of a cave (formed by wave action at the foot of a **cliff**) up to the cliff top. As waves break in the cave they erode the roof at the point of weakness and eventually a hole is formed. Air and sometimes spray are forced up the blowhole to erupt at the surface.

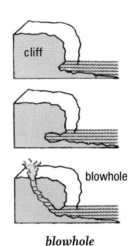

blowhole

bluff *See* **river cliff.**

boreal forest *See* **taiga.**

boulder clay *or* **till** The unsorted mass of debris dragged along by a **glacier** as *ground moraine* and dumped as the glacier melts. Boulder clay may be several metres thick and may comprise any combination of finely ground 'rock flour', sand, pebbles or boulders.

breakwater *or* **groyne** A wall built at right angles to a beach in order to prevent sand loss due to **longshore drift.**

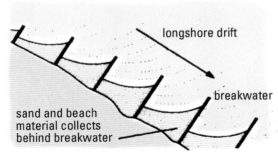

breakwater or groyne

breccia Rock fragments cemented together by a matrix of finer material; the fragments are angular and unsorted. An example of this is volcanic breccia, which

is made up of coarse angular fragments of **lava** and **crust** rocks welded by finer material such as ash and **tuff.**

bush fallowing *or* **shifting cultivation** A system of **agriculture** in which there are no permanent fields. For example in the **tropical rainforest**, remote societies cultivate forest clearings for one year and then move on. The system functions successfully when forest **regeneration** occurs over a sufficiently long period to allow the soil to regain its fertility.

bushfire An uncontrolled fire in forests and grasslands.

business park An out-of-town site accommodating offices, high-technology companies and light industry. *Compare* **science park.**

butte An outlier of a **mesa** in arid regions.

C

caldera A large crater formed by the collapse of the summit cone of a **volcano** during an eruption. The caldera may contain subsidiary cones built up by subsequent eruptions, or a crater lake if the volcano is extinct or dormant.

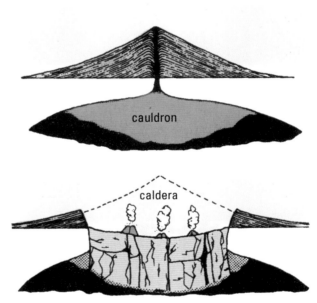

caldera

canal An artificial waterway, usually connecting existing **rivers**, **lakes** or **oceans**, constructed for navigation and transportation.

canyon A deep and steep-sided river valley occurring where rapid vertical **corrasion** takes place in arid regions. In such an **environment** the rate of **weathering** of the valley sides is slow. If the **rocks** of the region are relatively soft then the canyon profile becomes even more pronounced. The Grand Canyon of the Colorado River in the USA is the classic example. See diagram overleaf.

capital city

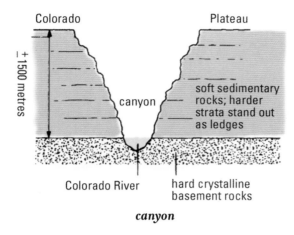

canyon

capital city Seat of government of a country or political unit.

catchment **1.** In **physical geography**, an alternative term to **river basin**.

2. In **human geography**, an area around a town or city – hence 'labour catchment' means the area from which an urban workforce is drawn.

cavern In **limestone** country, a large underground cave formed by the dissolving of limestone by subterranean streams. *See also* **stalactite, stalagmite**.

cay A small low **island** or bank composed of sand and coral fragments. Commonly found in the Caribbean Sea.

CBD (Central Business District) This is the central zone of a town or city, and is characterized by high accessibility, high land values and limited space. The visible result of these factors is a concentration of high-rise buildings at the city centre. The CBD is dominated by retail and business functions, both of which require maximum accessibility.

CFCs (Chlorofluorocarbons) Chemicals used in the manufacture of some aerosols, the cooling systems of refrigerators and fast-food cartons. These chemicals are harmful to the **ozone** layer.

chalk A soft, whitish **sedimentary rock** formed by the accumulation of small fragments of skeletal matter from marine organisms; the rock may be almost pure calcium carbonate. Due to the **permeable** and soluble nature of the rock, there is little surface **drainage** in chalk landscapes.

channel *See* **strait**.

chernozem A deep, rich soil of the plains of southern Russia. The upper **horizons** are rich in lime and other plant nutrients; in the dry **climate** the predominant movement of **soil** moisture is upwards (*contrast* with **leaching**), and lime and other chemical nutrients therefore accumulate in the upper part of the **soil profile**.

chloropleth map *See* **shading map**.

cirrus High, wispy or strand-like, thin **cloud** associated with the advance of a **depression**.

clay A soil composed of very small particles of

sediment, less than 0.002 mm in diameter. Due to the dense packing of these minute particles, clay is almost totally impermeable, i.e. it does not allow water to drain through. Clay soils very rapidly waterlog in wet weather.

cliff A steep rockface between land and sea, the profile of which is determined largely by the nature of the coastal rocks. For example, resistant rocks such as **granite** (e.g. at Land's End, England) will produce steep and rugged cliffs.

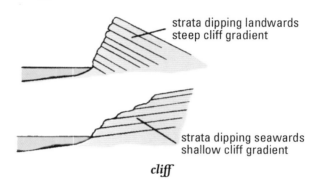

cliff

climate The average atmospheric conditions prevailing in a region, as distinct from its **weather**. A statement of climate is concerned with long-term trends. Thus the climate of, for example, the Amazon Basin is described as hot and wet all the year round; that of the Mediterranean Region as having hot dry summers and mild wet winters. *See* **extreme climate, maritime climate**.

clint A block of **limestone**, especially when part of a **limestone pavement**, where the surface is composed of clints and **grykes**.

cloud A mass of small water drops or ice crystals formed by the **condensation** of water vapour in the

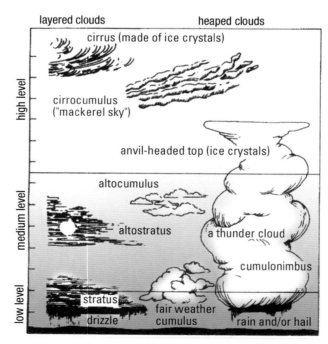

cloud

atmosphere, usually at a considerable height above the Earth's surface. There are three main types of cloud: **cumulus, stratus** and **cirrus**, each of which has many variations.

coal A **sedimentary rock** composed of decayed and compressed vegetative matter. Coal is usually classified according to a scale of hardness and purity ranging from **anthracite** (the hardest), through **bituminous coal** and **lignite** to **peat**.

cold front *See* **depression**.

commercial agriculture A system of **agriculture** in which food and materials are produced specifically for sale in the market, in contrast to **subsistence agriculture**. Commercial agriculture tends to be capital intensive. *See also* **agribusiness**.

Common Agricultural Policy (CAP) The policy of the European Union to support and subsidize certain crops and methods of animal husbandry.

common land Land which is not in the ownership of an individual or institution, but which is historically available to any member of the local community.

communications The contacts and linkages in an **environment**. For example, roads and railways are communications, as are telephone systems, newspapers, and radio and television.

commuter zone An area on or near to the outskirts of an urban area. Commuters are among the most affluent and mobile members of the urban community and can afford the greatest physical separation of home and work.

concordant coastline A coastline that is parallel to mountain ranges immediately inland. A rise in sea level or a sinking of the land cause the valleys to be flooded by the sea and the mountains to become a line of islands. *Compare* **discordant coastline**.

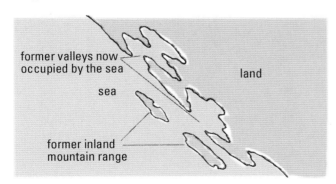

concordant coastline

condensation The process by which cooling vapour turns into a liquid. **Clouds**, for example, are formed by the condensation of water vapour in the **atmosphere**.

coniferous forest A forest of **evergreen** trees such as pine, spruce and fir. Natural coniferous forests occur considerably further north than forests of broad-leaved **deciduous** species, as coniferous trees are able to withstand harsher climatic conditions. The **taiga** areas

of the northern hemisphere consist of coniferous forests.

conservation The preservation and management of the natural **environment**. In its strictest form, conservation may mean total protection of endangered species and habitats, as in nature reserves. In some cases, conservation of the man-made environment, e.g. ancient buildings, is undertaken.

continent One of the earth's large land masses. The world's continents are generally defined as Asia, Africa, North America, South America, Europe, Oceania and Antarctica.

continental climate The climate at the centre of large landmasses, typified by a large annual range in temperature, with precipitation most likely in the summer.

continental drift The theory that the Earth's continents move gradually over a layer of semi-molten rock underneath the Earth's **crust**. It is thought that the present-day continents once formed the supercontinent, **Pangaea,** which existed approximately 200 million years ago. *See also* **Gondwanaland, Laurasia** *and* **plate tectonics**.

continental shelf The seabed bordering the continents, which is covered by shallow water – usually of less than 200 metres. Along some coastlines the continental shelf is so narrow it is almost absent.

contour A line drawn on a map to join all places at the same height above sea level.

conurbation A continuous built-up urban area formed by the merging of several formerly separate towns or cities. Twentieth-century **urban sprawl** has led to the merging of towns.

coombe *See* **dry valley**.

cooperative A system whereby individuals pool their **resources** in order to optimize individual gains.

core **1.** In **physical geography**, the core is the innermost zone of the Earth. It is probably solid at the centre, and composed of iron and nickel.
2. In **human geography**, a central place or central region, usually the centre of economic and political activity in a region or nation.

corrasion The abrasive action of an agent of **erosion** (rivers, ice, the sea) caused by its load. For example the pebbles and boulders carried along by a river wear away the channel bed and the river bank. *Compare* with **hydraulic action**.

corrie, cirque *or* **cwm** A bowl-shaped hollow on a mountainside in a glaciated region; the area where a valley **glacier** originates. In glacial times the corrie contained an icefield, which in cross section appears as in diagram *a* overleaf. The shape of the corrie is determined by the rotational erosive force of ice as the glacier moves downslope (diagram *b*).

corrosion

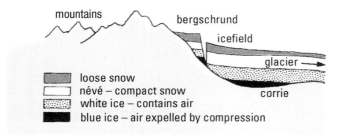

loose snow
névé – compact snow
white ice – contains air
blue ice – air expelled by compression

(a) A corrie in glacial times.

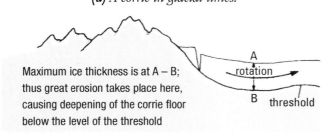

Maximum ice thickness is at A – B; thus great erosion takes place here, causing deepening of the corrie floor below the level of the threshold

A rotation B threshold

(b) Erosion of a corrie.

corrosion **Erosion** by solution action, such as the dissolving of **limestone** by running water.

crag Rocky outcrop on a valley side formed, for example, when a **truncated spur** exists in a glaciated valley.

crag and tail A feature of lowland **glaciation**, where a resistant rock outcrop withstands **erosion** by a **glacier** and remains as a feature after the **Ice Age**. Rocks of volcanic or metamorphic origin are likely to produce such a feature. As the ice advances over the crag, material will be eroded from the face and sides and will be deposited as a mass of boulder clay and debris on the leeward side, thus producing a 'tail'.

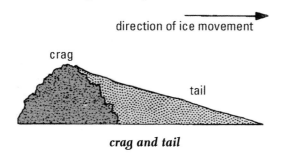

direction of ice movement

crag

tail

crag and tail

crevasse A crack or fissure in a **glacier** resulting from the stressing and fracturing of ice at a change in **gradient** or valley shape.

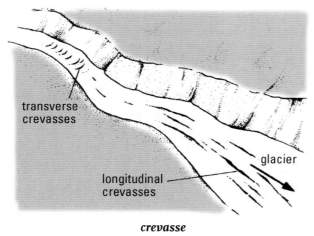

transverse crevasses

longitudinal crevasses

glacier

crevasse

cross section A drawing of a vertical section of a line of ground, deduced from a map. It depicts the **topography** of a system of **contours**.

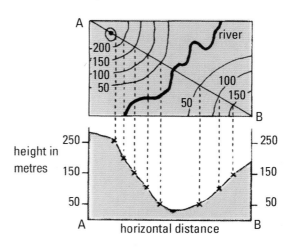

A river
200
150
100
50
100
150
50
B

height in metres
250
150
50

A horizontal distance B

cross section Map and corresponding cross section.

crust The outermost layer of the Earth, representing only 0.1% of the Earth's total volume. It comprises continental crust and oceanic crust, which differ from each other in age as well as in physical and chemical characteristics. The crust, together with the uppermost layer of the **mantle**, is also known as the *lithosphere*.

culvert An artificial drainage channel for transporting water quickly from place to place.

cumulonimbus A heavy, dark **cloud** of great vertical height. It is the typical thunderstorm cloud, producing heavy showers of rain, snow or hail. Such clouds form where intense solar radiation causes vigorous convection.

cumulus A large **cloud** (smaller than a **cumulonimbus**) with a 'cauliflower' head and almost horizontal base. It is indicative of fair or, at worst, showery **weather** in generally sunny conditions.

cut-off *See* **oxbow lake**.

cyclone *See* **hurricane**.

D

dairying A **pastoral farming** system in which dairy cows produce milk that is used by itself or used to produce dairy products such as cheese, butter, cream and yoghurt.

dam A barrier built across a stream, river or **estuary** to create a body of water.

death rate The number of deaths per 1000 people in a population per year.

deciduous woodland Trees which are generally of broad-leaved rather than **coniferous** habit, and which shed their leaves during the cold season.

deflation The removal of loose sand by wind **erosion** in desert regions. It often exposes a bare rock surface beneath.

developing countries

deforestation The practice of clearing trees. Much deforestation is a result of development pressures, e.g. trees are cut down to provide land for agriculture and industry. *Compare* **afforestation**.

delta A fan-shaped mass consisting of the deposited load of a river where it enters the sea. A delta only forms where the river deposits material at a faster rate than can be removed by coastal currents. While deltas may take almost any shape and size, three types are generally recognized, as shown in the following diagrams.

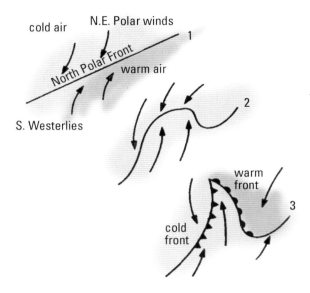

depression The development of a depression.

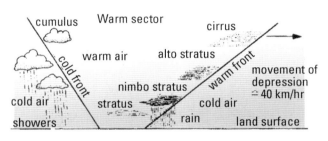

depression Characteristics.

Arcuate delta, e.g. Nile. Note bifurcation of river into distributaries in delta

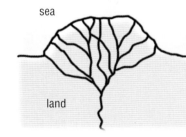

Bird's foot delta, e.g. Mississippi

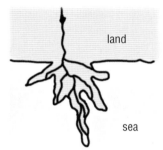

Estuarine delta, e.g. Amazon

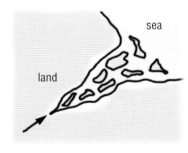

delta

denudation The wearing away of the Earth's surface by the processes of **weathering** and **erosion**.

depopulation A long-term decrease in the population of any given area, frequently caused by economic migration to other areas.

deposition The laying down of **sediments** resulting from **denudation**.

depression An area of low atmospheric pressure occurring where warm and cold air masses come into contact. The passage of a depression is marked by thickening cloud, rain, a period of dull and drizzly weather and then clearing skies with showers. A depression develops as in the diagrams on the right.

desert An area where all forms of **precipitation** are so low that very little, if anything, can grow.

Deserts can be broadly divided into three types, depending upon average temperatures:

(a) *hot deserts:* occur in tropical latitudes in regions of high pressure where air is sinking and therefore making rainfall unlikely. *See* **cloud**.

(b) *temperate deserts:* occur in mid-latitudes in areas of high pressure. They are far inland, so moisture-bearing winds rarely deposit rainfall in these areas.

(c) *cold deserts:* occur in the northern latitudes, again in areas of high pressure. Very low temperatures throughout the year mean the air is unable to hold much moisture.

desertification The encroachment of **desert** conditions into areas which were once productive. Desertification can be due partly to climatic change, i.e. a move towards a drier climate in some parts of the world (possibly due to **global warming**), though human activity has also played a part through bad farming practices. The problem is particularly acute along the southern margins of the Sahara desert in the Sahel region between Mali and Mauritania in the west, and Ethiopia and Somalia in the east.

developing countries A collective term for those nations in Africa, Asia and Latin America which are

dew point

undergoing the complex processes of modernization, **industrialization** and **urbanization**. *See also* **Third World**.

dew point The temperature at which the **atmosphere**, being cooled, becomes saturated with water vapour. This vapour is then deposited as drops of dew.

dip slope The gentler of the two slopes on either side of an escarpment crest; the dip slope inclines in the direction of the dipping **strata**; the steep slope in front of the crest is the **scarp slope**.

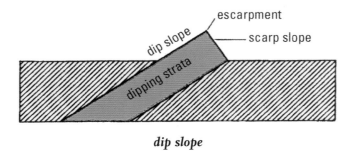

dip slope

discharge The volume of run-off in the channels of a **river basin**.

discordant coastline A coastline that is at right angles to the mountains and valleys immediately inland. A rise in sea level or a sinking of the land will cause the valleys to be flooded. A flooded river valley is known as a **ria**, whilst a flooded glaciated valley is known as a **fjord**. *Compare* **concordant coastline**.

discordant coastline

distributary An outlet stream which drains from a larger river or stream. Often found in a **delta** area. *Compare* **tributary**.

doldrums An equatorial belt of low atmospheric pressure where the **trade winds** converge. Winds are light and variable but the strong upward movement of air caused by this convergence produces frequent thunderstorms and heavy rains.

dormitory settlement A village located beyond the edge of a city but inhabited by residents who work in that city (*see* **commuter zone**).

drainage The removal of water from the land surface by processes such as streamflow and infiltration.

drainage basin *See* **river basin**.

drift Material transported and deposited by glacial action on the Earth's surface. *See also* **boulder clay**.

drought A prolonged period where rainfall falls below the requirement for a region.

dry valley *or* **coombe** A feature of **limestone** and **chalk** country, where valleys have been eroded in dry landscapes.

dune A mound or ridge of drifted sand, occurring on the sea coast and in deserts.

dyke **1.** An artificial **drainage** channel.
2. An artificial bank built to protect low-lying land from flooding.
3. A vertical or semi-vertical igneous intrusion occurring where a stream of **magma** has extended through a line of weakness in the surrounding **rock**. *See* **igneous rock**.

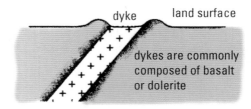

Metamorphosed zone: surrounding rocks close to intrusion are 'baked'

dyke Cross section of eroded dyke, showing how metamorphic margins, harder than dyke or surrounding rocks, resist erosion.

E

earthquake A movement or tremor of the Earth's crust. Earthquakes are associated with plate boundaries (*see* **plate tectonics**) and especially with subduction zones, where one plate plunges beneath another. Here the crust is subjected to tremendous stress. The rocks are forced to bend, and eventually the stress is so great that the rocks 'snap' along a **fault** line.

eastings The first element of a **grid reference**. *See* **northing**.

ecology The study of living things, their interrelationships and their relationships with the **environment**.

ecosystem A natural system comprising living organisms and their **environment**. The concept can be applied at the global scale or in the context of a smaller defined environment. The principle of the ecosystem is constant: all elements are intricately linked by flows of energy and nutrients.

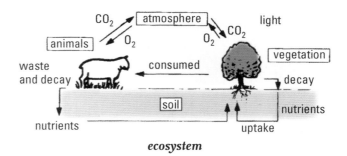

ecosystem

fault

El Niño The occasional development of warm ocean surface waters along the coast of Ecuador and Peru. Where this warming occurs the tropical Pacific trade winds weaken and the usual up-welling of cold, deep ocean water is reduced. El Niño normally occurs late in the calendar year and lasts for a few weeks to a few months and can have a dramatic impact on weather patterns throughout the world.

emigration The movement of population out of a given area or country.

employment structure The distribution of the workforce between the **primary, secondary, tertiary** and **quaternary sectors** of the economy. Primary employment is in **agriculture**, mining, forestry and fishing; secondary in manufacturing; tertiary in the retail, service and administration category; quaternary in information and expertise.

environment Physical surroundings: **soil**, vegetation, wildlife and the **atmosphere**.

equator The great circle of the Earth with a **latitude** of 0°, lying equidistant from the poles.

erosion The wearing away of the Earth's surface by running water (rivers and streams), moving ice (**glaciers**), the sea and the wind. These are called the *agents* of erosion.

erratic A boulder of a certain rock type resting on a surface of different geology. For example, blocks of **granite** resting on a surface of carboniferous **limestone**.

escarpment A ridge of high ground as, for example, the **chalk** escarpments of southern England (the Downs and the Chilterns).

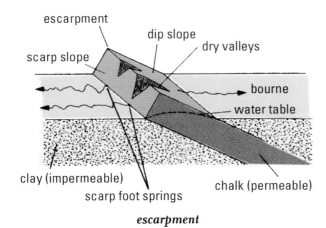

escarpment

esker A low, winding ridge of pebbles and finer **sediment** on a glaciated lowland.

estuary The broad mouth of a river where it enters the sea. An estuary forms where opposite conditions to those favourable for **delta** formation exist: deep water offshore, strong marine currents and a smaller **sediment** load.

ethnic group A group of people with a common identity such as culture, religion or skin colour.

evaporation The process whereby a substance changes from a liquid to a vapour. Heat from the sun evaporates water from seas, lakes, rivers, etc., and this process produces water vapour in the **atmosphere**.

evergreen A vegetation type in which leaves are continuously present. *Compare* **deciduous woodland**.

exfoliation A form of **weathering** whereby the outer layers of a **rock** or boulder shear off due to the alternate expansion and contraction produced by diurnal heating and cooling. Such a process is especially active in **desert** regions.

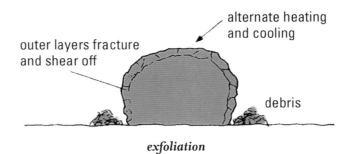

exfoliation

exports Goods and services sold to a foreign country (*compare* **imports**).

extensive farming A system of **agriculture** in which relatively small amounts of capital or labour investment are applied to relatively large areas of land. For example, sheep ranching is an extensive form of farming, and yields per unit area are low.

external processes Landscape-forming processes such as **weather** and **erosion**, in contrast to internal processes.

extreme climate A climate that is characterized by large ranges of temperature and sometimes of rainfall. *Compare* **temperate climate, maritime climate**.

F

fault A fracture in the Earth's crust on either side of which the **rocks** have been relatively displaced. Faulting occurs in response to stress in the Earth's crust; the release of this stress in fault movement is experienced as an **earthquake**. *See also* **rift valley**.

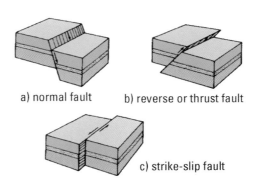

fault The main types.

fell

fell Upland rough grazing in a **hill farming** system, for example in the English Lake District.

fjord A deep, generally straight inlet of the sea along a glaciated coast. A fjord is a glaciated valley which has been submerged either by a post-glacial rise in sea level or a subsidence of the land.

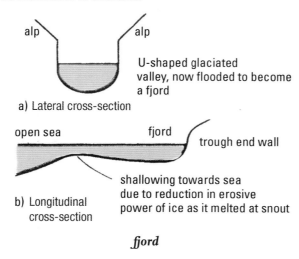

a) Lateral cross-section

alp alp

U-shaped glaciated valley, now flooded to become a fjord

b) Longitudinal cross-section

open sea fjord trough end wall

shallowing towards sea due to reduction in erosive power of ice as it melted at snout

fjord

flash flood A sudden increase in river **discharge** and overland flow due to a violent rainstorm in the upper **river basin.**

flood plain The broad, flat valley floor of the lower course of a river, levelled by annual flooding and by the lateral and downstream movement of **meanders.**

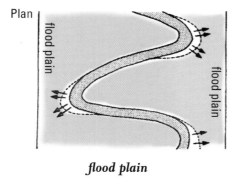

Plan

flood plain

flood plain

flood plain

flow line A diagram showing volumes of movement, e.g. of people, goods or information between places. The width of the flow line is proportional to the amount of movement, for example in portraying commuter flows into an urban centre from surrounding towns and villages.

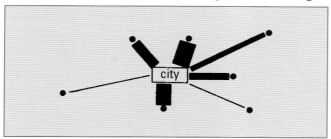

city

Flow line *Commuter flows into a city.*

fodder crop A crop grown for animal feed.

fold A bending or buckling of once horizontal rock **strata.** Many folds are the result of rocks being crumpled at plate boundaries (*see* **plate tectonics**), though **earthquakes** can also cause rocks to fold, as can igneous **intrusions.**

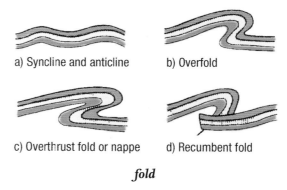

a) Syncline and anticline   b) Overfold

c) Overthrust fold or nappe   d) Recumbent fold

fold

fold mountains Mountains which have been formed by large-scale and complex folding. Studies of typical fold mountains (the Himalayas, Andes, Alps and Rockies) indicate that folding has taken place deep inside the Earth's **crust** and upper **mantle** as well as in the upper layers of the crust.

fossil fuel Any naturally occurring carbon or hydrocarbon fuel, notably coal, oil, peat and natural gas. These fuels have been formed by decomposed prehistoric organisms.

free trade The movement of goods and services between countries without any restrictions (such as quotas, tariffs or taxation) being imposed.

freeze-thaw A type of physical **weathering** whereby **rocks** are denuded by the freezing of water in cracks and crevices on the rock face. Water expands on freezing, and this process causes stress and fracture along any line of weakness in the rock. **Nivation** debris accumulates at the bottom of a rock face as **scree.**

front A boundary between two air masses. *See also* **depression.**

G

GDP *See* **Gross Domestic Product.**

geosyncline A basin (a large **syncline**) in which thick marine sediments have accumulated.

geothermal energy A method of producing power from heat contained in the lower layers of the Earth's **crust.** New Zealand and Iceland both use superheated water or steam from geysers and volcanic **springs** to heat buildings and for hothouse cultivation and also to drive steam turbines to generate electricity. Geothermal energy is an example of a renewable resource of energy (*see* **renewable resources, nonrenewable resources**).

glaciation A period of cold **climate** during which time **ice sheets** and **glaciers** are the dominant forces of **denudation.**

HDI (human development index)

glacier A body of ice occupying a valley and originating in a **corrie** or icefield. A glacier moves at a rate of several metres per day, the precise speed depending upon climatic and **topographic** conditions in the area in question.

global warming *or* greenhouse effect The warming of the Earth's atmosphere caused by an excess of carbon dioxide, which acts like a blanket, preventing the natural escape of heat. This situation has been developing over the last 150 years because of (a) the burning of **fossil fuels**, which releases vast amounts of carbon dioxide into the **atmosphere**, and (b) **deforestation**, which results in fewer trees being available to take up carbon dioxide (*see* **photosynthesis**).

globalization The process that enables financial markets and companies to operate internationally (as a result of deregulation and improved communications). **Transnational corporations** now locate their manufacturing in places that best serve their global market at the lowest cost.

GNI (gross national income) *formerly* GNP (gross national product) The total value of the goods and services produced annually by a nation, plus net property income from abroad.

Gondwanaland The southern-hemisphere super-continent, consisting of the present South America, Africa, India, Australasia and Antarctica, which split from **Pangaea** *c*.200 million years ago. Gondwanaland is part of the theory of **continental drift**. *See also* **plate tectonics**.

GPS (global positioning system) A system of earth-orbiting satellites, transmitting signals continuously towards earth, which enable the position of a receiving device on the earth's surface to be accurately estimated from the difference in arrival of the signals.

gradient **1.** The measure of steepness of a line or slope. In mapwork, the average gradient between two points can be calculated as:

$$\frac{\textit{difference in altitude}}{\textit{distance apart}}$$

2. The measure of change in a property such as density. In **human geography** gradients are found in, for example, **population density**, land values and **settlement** ranking.

granite An **igneous rock** having large crystals due to slow cooling at depth in the Earth's **crust**.

green belt An area of land, usually around the outskirts of a town or city on which building and other developments are restricted by legislation.

greenfield site A development site for industry, retailing or housing that has previously been used only for agriculture or recreation. Such sites are frequently in the **green belt**.

greenhouse effect *See* **global warming**.

Greenwich Meridian *See* **prime meridian**.

grid reference A method for specifying position on a map. *See* **eastings** and **northings**.

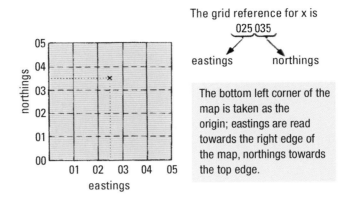

The grid reference for x is
025 035
eastings   northings

The bottom left corner of the map is taken as the origin; eastings are read towards the right edge of the map, northings towards the top edge.

Gross Domestic Product (GDP) The total value of all goods and services produced domestically by a nation during a year. It is equivalent to **Gross National Income (GNI)** minus investment incomes from foreign nations.

groundwater Water held in the bedrock of a region, having percolated through the **soil** from the surface. Such water is an important **resource** in areas where **surface run-off** is limited or absent.

groyne *See* **breakwater**.

gryke An enlarged joint between blocks of **limestone** (**clints**), especially in a **limestone pavement**.

gulf A large coastal indentation, similar to a **bay** but larger in extent. Commonly formed as a result of rising sea levels.

H

habitat A preferred location for particular species of plants and animals to live and reproduce.

hanging valley A tributary valley entering a main valley at a much higher level because of deepening of the main valley, especially by glacial erosion.

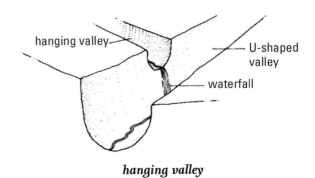

hanging valley

HDI (human development index) A measurement of a country's achievements in three areas: longevity, knowledge and standard of living. Longevity is measured by life expectancy at birth; knowledge is measured by a combination of the adult literacy rate and the combined gross primary, secondary and tertiary school enrolment ratio; standard of living is measured by **GDP** per capita.

headland

headland A promontory of resistant **rock** along the coastline. *See* **bay**.

hemisphere Any half of a globe or sphere. The earth has traditionally been divided into hemispheres by the **equator** (northern and southern hemispheres) and by the **prime meridian** and **International Date Line** (eastern and western hemispheres).

hill farming A system of **agriculture** where sheep (and to a lesser extent cattle) are grazed on upland rough pasture.

histogram A graph for showing values of classed data as the areas of bars.

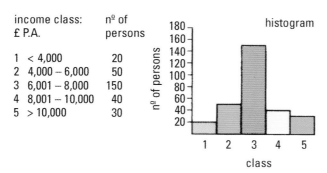

income class: £ P.A.	nº of persons
1 < 4,000	20
2 4,000 – 6,000	50
3 6,001 – 8,000	150
4 8,001 – 10,000	40
5 > 10,000	30

histogram

horizon The distinct layers found in the **soil profile**. Usually three horizons are identified – A, B and C, as in the diagram below.

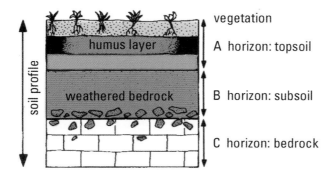

horizon A typical soil profile.

horst *See* **block mountain**.

horticulture The growing of plants and flowers for commercial sale. It is now an international trade, for example, orchids are grown in Southeast Asia for sale in Europe.

human geography The study of people and their activities in terms of patterns and processes of population, **settlement**, economic activity and **communications**. *Compare* **physical geography**.

hunter/gatherer economy A pre-agricultural phase of development in which people survive by hunting and gathering the animal and plant **resources** of the natural **environment**. No cultivation or herding is involved.

hurricane, cyclone *or* **typhoon** A wind of force 12 on the **Beaufort wind scale**, i.e. one having a velocity of more than 118 km per hour. Hurricanes can cause great damage by wind as well as from the storm waves and floods that accompany them.

hydraulic action The erosive force of water alone, as distinct from **corrasion**. A river or the sea will erode partially by the sheer force of moving water and this is termed 'hydraulic action'.

hydroelectric power The generation of electricity by turbines driven by flowing water. Hydroelectricity is most efficiently generated in rugged **topography** where a head of water can most easily be created, or on a large river where a dam can create similar conditions. Whatever the location, the principle remains the same – that water descending via conduits from an upper storage area passes through turbines and thus creates electricity.

hydrological cycle The cycling of water through sea, land and **atmosphere**.

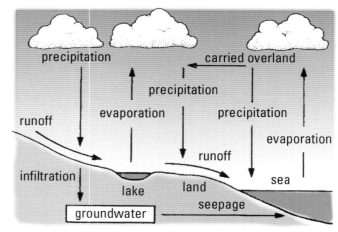

hydrological cycle

hydrosphere All the water on Earth, including that present in the **atmosphere** as well as in oceans, seas, **ice sheets**, etc.

hygrometer An instrument for measuring the relative humidity of the **atmosphere**. It comprises two thermometers, one of which is kept moist by a wick inserted in a water reservoir. Evaporation from the wick reduces the temperature of the 'wet bulb' thermometer, and the difference between the dry and the wet bulb temperatures is used to calculate relative humidity from standard tables.

I

Ice Age A period of **glaciation** in which a cooling of **climate** leads to the development of **ice sheets, ice caps** and valley **glaciers**.

ice cap A covering of permanent ice over a relatively small land mass, e.g. Iceland.

joint

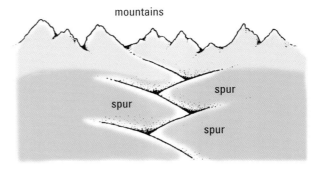

ice sheet A covering of permanent ice over a substantial continental area such as Antarctica.

iceberg A large mass of ice which has broken off an **ice sheet** or **glacier** and left floating in the sea.

igneous rock A **rock** which originated as **magma** (molten rock) at depth in or below the Earth's **crust**. Igneous rocks are generally classified according to crystal size, colour and mineral composition. *See also* **plutonic rock**.

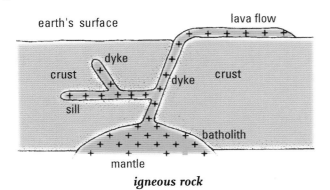

igneous rock

immigration The movement of people into a country or region from other countries or regions.

impermeable rock A rock that is non-porous and therefore incapable of taking in water or of allowing it to pass through between the grains. *Compare* **impervious rock**. *See also* **permeable rock**.

impervious rock A non-porous rock with no cracks or fissures through which water might pass.

imports Goods or services bought into one country from another (*compare* **exports**).

industrialization The development of industry on an extensive scale.

infiltration The gradual movement of water into the ground.

infrastructure The basic structure of an organization or system. The infrastructure of a city includes, for example, its roads and railways, schools, factories, power and water supplies and drainage systems.

inner city The ring of buildings around the **Central Business District (CBD)** of a town or city.

intensive farming A system of **agriculture** where relatively large amounts of capital and/or labour are invested on relatively small areas of land.

interglacial A warm period between two periods of **glaciation** and cold **climate**. The present interglacial began about 10,000 years ago.

interlocking spurs Obstacles of hard **rock** round which a river twists and turns in a V-shaped valley. **Erosion** is pronounced on the concave banks, and this ultimately causes the development of spurs which alternate on either side of the river and interlock as shown in the diagram top right.

interlocking spurs A V-shaped valley with interlocking spurs.

International Date Line An imaginary line which approximately follows 180° **longitude**. The area of the world just east of the line is one day ahead of the area just west of the line.

international trade The exchange of goods and services between countries.

intrusion A body of **igneous rock** injected into the Earth's **crust** from the **mantle** below. *See* **dyke, sill, batholith**.

ionosphere *See* **atmosphere**.

irrigation A system of artificial watering of the land in order to grow crops. Irrigation is particularly important in areas of low or unreliable rainfall.

island A mass of land, smaller than a continent, which is completely surrounded by water.

isobar A line joining points of equal atmospheric pressure, as on the meteorological map below.

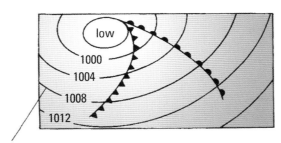

isobar, indicating atmospheric pressure in millibars

isobar

isohyet A line on a meteorological map joining places of equal rainfall.

isotherm A line on a meteorological map joining places of equal temperature.

J

joint A vertical or semi-vertical fissure in a **sedimentary rock**, contrasted with roughly horizontal bedding planes. In **igneous rocks** jointing may occur as a result of contraction on cooling from the molten state. Joints should be distinguished from **faults** in that they are on a much smaller scale and there is no relative displacement of the rocks on either side of the joint.

kame

Joints, being lines of weakness are exploited by **weathering**.

K

kame A short ridge of sand and gravel deposited from the water of a melted glacier.

karst topography An area of **limestone** scenery where **drainage** is predominantly subterranean.

kettle hole A small depression or hollow in a glacial outwash plain, formed when a block of ice embedded in the outwash deposits eventually melts, causing the **sediment** above to subside.

L

laccolith An igneous **intrusion**, domed and often of considerable dimensions, caused where a body of viscous **magma** has been intruded into the **strata** of the Earth's **crust**. These strata are buckled upwards over the laccolith.

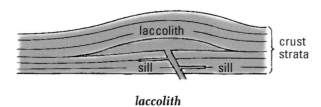

laccolith

lagoon **1.** An area of sheltered coastal water behind a bay bar or **tombolo**.
2. The calm water behind a coral reef.

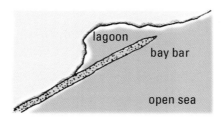

lagoon

lahar A landslide of volcanic debris mixed with water down the sides of a volcano, caused either by heavy rain or the heat of the volcano melting snow and ice.

lake A body of water completely surrounded by land.

land tenure A system of land ownership or allocation.

land use The function of an area of land. For example, the land use in rural areas could be farming or forestry, whereas urban land use could be housing or industry.

landform Any natural feature of the Earth's surface, such as mountains or valleys.

laterite A hard (literally 'brick-like') soil in tropical regions caused by the baking of the upper **horizons** by exposure to the sun.

latitude Distance north or south of the equator, as measured by degrees of the angle at the Earth's centre:

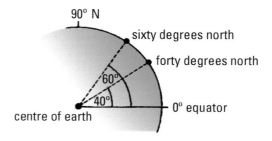

latitude

Laurasia The northern hemisphere supercontinent, consisting of the present North America, Europe and Asia (excluding India), which split from **Pangaea** *c.* 200 million years ago. Laurasia is part of the theory of **continental drift**. *See also* **plate tectonics**.

lava **Magma** extruded onto the Earth's surface via some form of volcanic eruption. Lava varies in viscosity (*see* **viscous lava**), colour and chemical composition. Acidic lavas tend to be viscous and flow slowly; basic lavas tend to be nonviscous and flow quickly. Commonly, **lava flows** comprise basaltic material, as for example in the process of sea-floor spreading (*see* **plate tectonics**).

lava flow A stream of **lava** issuing from some form of volcanic eruption. *See also* **viscous lava**.

lava plateau A relatively flat upland composed of layer upon layer of approximately horizontally bedded lavas. An example of this is the Deccan Plateau of India.

leaching The process by which soluble substances such as mineral salts are washed out of the upper soil layer into the lower layer by rain water.

levée The bank of a river, raised above the general level of the **flood plain** by **sediment** deposition during flooding. When the river bursts its banks, relatively coarse sediment is deposited first, and recurrent flooding builds up the river's banks accordingly.

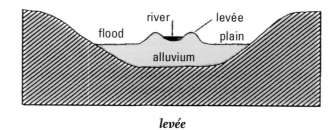

levée

lignite A soft form of **coal**, harder than **peat** but softer than **bituminous coal**.

limestone Calcium-rich **sedimentary rock** formed by the accumulation of the skeletal matter of marine organisms.

map

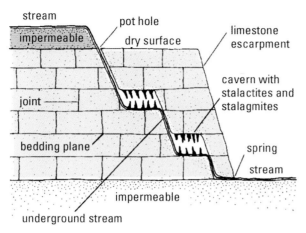

limestone

limestone pavement An exposed **limestone** surface on which the joints have been enlarged by the action of rainwater dissolving the limestone to form weak carbonic acid. These enlarged joints, or **grykes**, separate roughly rectangular blocks of limestone called **clints**.

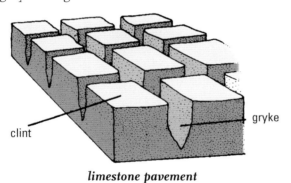

limestone pavement

location The position of population, settlement and economic activity in an area or areas. Location is a basic theme in **human geography**.

loess A very fine **silt** deposit, often of considerable thickness, transported by the wind prior to **deposition**. When irrigated, loess can be very fertile and, consequently, high **yields** can be obtained from crops grown on loess deposits.

longitude A measure of distance on the Earth's surface east or west of the Greenwich Meridian, an imaginary line running from pole to pole through Greenwich in London. Longitude, like **latitude**, is measured in degrees of angle taken from the centre of the Earth.

The precise location of a place can be given by a **grid**

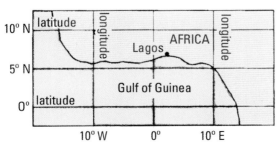

longitude A grid showing the location of Lagos, Nigeria.

reference comprising longitude and latitude. *See also* **map projection, prime meridian**.

longshore drift The net movement of material along a beach due to the oblique approach of waves to the shore. Beach deposits move in a zig-zag fashion, as shown in the diagram. Longshore drift is especially active on long, straight coastlines.

As waves approach, sand is carried up the beach by the **swash**, and retreats back down the beach with the **backwash**. Thus a single representative grain of sand will migrate in the pattern A, B, C, D, E, F in the diagram.

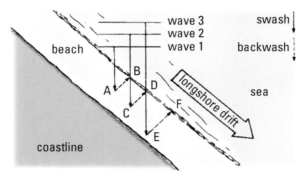

longshore drift

M

magma Molten rock originating in the Earth's **mantle**; it is the source of all **igneous rocks**.

malnutrition The condition of being poorly nourished, as contrasted with **undernutrition**, which is lack of a sufficient quantity of food. The diet of a malnourished person may be high in starchy foods but is invariably low in protein and essential minerals and vitamins.

mantle The largest of the concentric zones of the Earth's structure, overlying the **core** and surrounded in turn by the **crust**.

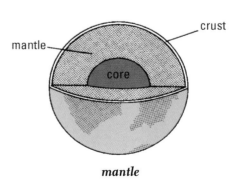

mantle

manufacturing industry The making of articles using physical labour or machinery, especially on a large scale. *See* **secondary sector**.

map Diagrammatic representation of an area – for example part of the earth's surface.

map projection

map projection A method by which the curved surface of the Earth is shown on a flat surface map. As it is not possible to show all the Earth's features accurately on a flat surface, some projections aim to show direction accurately at the expense of area, some the shape of the land and oceans, while others show correct area at the expense of accurate shape.

One of the projections most commonly used is the *Mercator projection*, devised in 1569, in which all lines of **latitude** are the same length as the equator. This results in increased distortion of area, moving from the equator towards the poles. This projection is suitable for navigation charts.

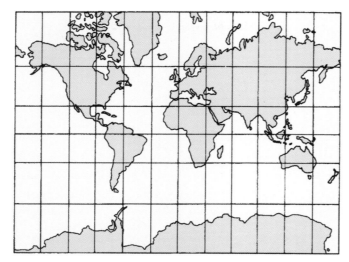

map projection *Mercator projection.*

The *Mollweide projection* shows the land masses the correct size in relation to each other but there is distortion of shape. As the Mollweide projection has no area distortion it is useful for showing distributions such as population distribution.

The only true representation of the Earth's surface is a globe.

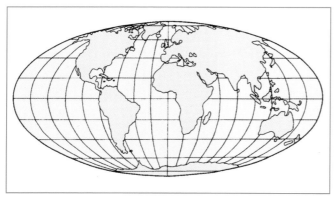

map projection *Mollweide projection.*

marble A whitish, crystalline **metamorphic rock** produced when **limestone** is subjected to great heat or pressure (or both) during Earth movements.

maritime climate A **temperate climate** that is affected by the closeness of the sea, giving a small annual range of temperatures – a coolish summer and a mild winter – and rainfall throughout the year. Britain has a maritime climate. *Compare* **extreme climate**.

market gardening An intensive type of **agriculture** traditionally located on the margins of urban areas to supply fresh produce on a daily basis to the city population. Typical market-garden produce includes salad crops, such as tomatoes, lettuce, cucumber, etc., cut flowers, fruit and some green vegetables.

maximum and minimum thermometer An instrument for recording the highest and lowest temperatures over a 24-hour period.

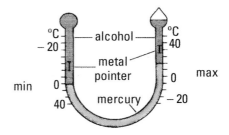

maximum and minimum thermometer

meander A large bend, especially in the middle or lower stages of a river's course. *See* **flood plain**. A meander is the result of lateral **corrasion**, which becomes dominant over vertical corrasion as the **gradient** of the river's course decreases. The characteristic features of a meander are summarized in the diagrams below. *See also* **oxbow lake**.

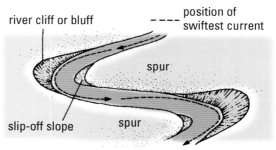

meander *A river meander.*

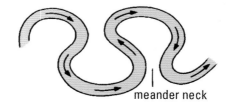

meander *Fully formed meanders.*

mesa A flat-topped, isolated hill in arid regions. A mesa has a protective cap of hard **rock** underlain by softer, more readily eroded **sedimentary rock**. A **butte** is a relatively small outlier of a mesa.

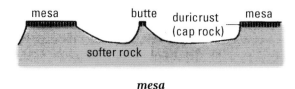

mesa

mesosphere *See* **atmosphere**.

metamorphic rock A **rock** which has been changed by intensive heat or pressure. Metamorphism implies an increase in hardness and resistance to **erosion**. Shale, for example, may be metamorphosed by pressure into **slate**; **sandstone** by heat into **quartzite**, **limestone** into **marble**. Metamorphism of pre-existing rocks is associated with the processes of **folding, faulting** and **vulcanicity**.

migration A permanent or semipermanent change of residence.

monoculture The growing of a single crop.

monsoon The term strictly means 'seasonal wind' and is used generally to describe a situation where there is a reversal of wind direction from one season to another. This is especially the case in South and Southeast Asia, where two monsoon winds occur, both related to the extreme pressure gradients created by the large land mass of the Asian continent.

moraine A collective term for debris deposited on or by **glaciers** and ice bodies in general. Several types of moraine are recognized: *lateral* moraine forms along the edges of a valley glacier where debris eroded from the valley sides, or weathered from the slopes above the glacier, collects; *medial* moraine forms where two lateral moraines meet at a glacier junction; *englacial* moraine is material which is trapped within the body of the glacier; and *ground* moraine is material eroded from the floor of the valley and used by the glacier as an abrasive tool. A *terminal* moraine is material bulldozed by the glacier during its advance and deposited at its maximum down-valley extent. *Recessional* moraines may be deposited at standstills during a period of general glacial retreat.

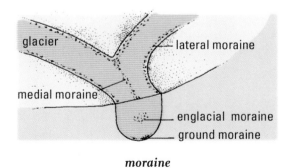

moraine

mortlake *See* **oxbow lake**.

mountain A natural upward projection of the Earth's surface, higher and steeper than a hill, and often having a rocky summit.

northings

N

national park An area of scenic countryside protected by law from uncontrolled development. A national park has two main functions:

(a) to conserve the natural beauty of the landscape;

(b) to enable the public to visit and enjoy the countryside for leisure and recreation.

natural hazard A natural event which, in extreme cases, can lead to loss of life and destruction of property. Some natural hazards result from geological events, such as **earthquakes** and the eruption of **volcanoes**, whilst others are due to weather events such as **hurricanes**, floods and droughts.

natural increase The increase in population due to the difference between **birth rate** and **death rate**.

neap tides *See* **tides**.

névé Compact snow. In a **corrie** icefield, for example, four layers are recognized: blue and white ice at the bottom of the ice mass; névé overlying the ice and powder snow on the surface.

new town A new urban location created (a) to provide overspill accommodation for a large city or **conurbation**; (b) to provide a new focus for industrial development.

newly industrialized country (NIC) A **developing country** which is becoming industrialized, for example Malaysia and Thailand. Some NICs have successfully used large-scale development to move into the industrialized world. Usually the capital for such developments comes from outside the country.

nivation The process of **weathering** by snow and ice, particularly through **freeze-thaw** action. Particularly active in cold **climates** and high altitudes – for example on exposed slopes above a **glacier**.

nomadic pastoralism A system of **agriculture** in dry grassland regions. People and stock (cattle, sheep, goats) are continually moving in search of pasture and water. The pastoralists subsist on meat, milk and other animal products.

non-governmental organizations (NGOs) Independent organizations, such as charities (Oxfam, Water Aid) which provide aid and expertise to economically developing countries.

nonrenewable resources Resources of which there is a fixed supply, which will eventually be exhausted. Examples of these are metal ores and **fossil fuels**. *Compare* **renewable resources**.

North and South A way of dividing the industrialized nations, found predominantly in the North from those less developed nations in the South. The gap which exists between the rich 'North' and the poor 'South' is called the *development gap*.

northings The second element of a **grid reference**. *See* **eastings**.

nuclear power station

nuclear power station An electricity-generating plant using nuclear fuel as an alternative to the conventional **fossil fuels** of **coal**, oil and gas.

nuée ardente A very hot and fast-moving cloud of gas, ash and rock that flows close to the ground after a violent ejection from a volcano. It is very destructive.

nunatak A mountain peak projecting above the general level of the ice near the edge of an **ice sheet**.

nutrient cycle The cycling of nutrients through the **environment**.

O

ocean A large area of sea. The world's oceans are the Pacific, Atlantic, Indian and Arctic. The Southern Ocean is made up of the areas of the Pacific, Atlantic and Indian Oceans south of latitude 60°S.

ocean current A movement of the surface water of an ocean.

opencast mining A type of mining where the mineral is extracted by direct excavation rather than by shaft or drift methods.

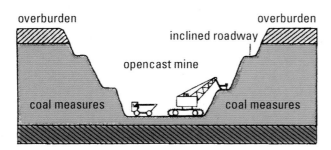

opencast mining

organic farming A system of farming that avoids the use of any artificial fertilizers or chemical pesticides, using only organic fertilizers and pesticides derived directly from animal or vegetable matter. Yields from organic farming are lower, but the products are sold at a premium price.

overfold *See* **fold**.

oxbow lake, mortlake *or* **cut-off** A crescent-shaped lake originating in a **meander** that was abandoned when

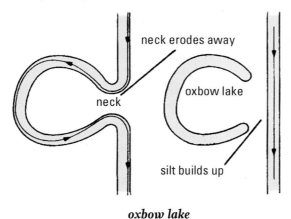

oxbow lake

erosion breached the neck between bends, allowing the stream to flow straight on, bypassing the meander. The ends of the meander rapidly silt up and it becomes separated from the river.

ozone A form of oxygen found in a layer in the **stratosphere**, where it protects the Earth's surface from ultraviolet rays.

P

Pangaea The supercontinent or universal land mass in which all continents were joined together approximately 200 million years ago. *See* **continental drift**.

passage *See* **strait**.

pastoral farming A system of farming in which the raising of livestock is the dominant element. *See also* **nomadic pastoralism**.

peasant agriculture The growing of crops or raising of animals, partly for subsistence needs and partly for market sale. Peasant agriculture is thus an intermediate stage between subsistence and commercial farming.

peat Partially decayed and compressed vegetative matter accumulating in areas of high rainfall and/or poor **drainage**.

peneplain A region that has been eroded until it is almost level. The more resistant rocks will stand above the general level of the land.

per capita income The **GNI** (gross national income) of a country divided by the size of its population. It gives the average income per head of the population if the national income were shared out equally. Per capita income comparisons are used as one indicator of levels of economic development.

periglacial features A periglacial landscape is one which has not been glaciated *per se*, but which has been affected by the severe **climate** prevailing around the ice margin.

permafrost The permanently frozen subsoil that is a feature of areas of **tundra**.

permeable rock Rock through which water can pass via a network of pores between the grains. *Compare* **pervious rock**. *See also* **impermeable rock**.

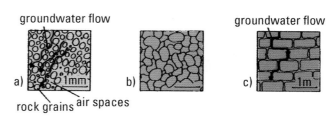

permeable rock (a) Permeable rock, (b) impermeable rock, (c) pervious rock.

population change

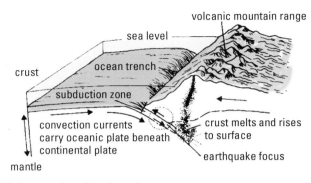

b) *Destructive plate boundary*
plate tectonics

pervious rock Rock which, even if non-porous, can allow water to pass through via interconnected joints, bedding planes and fissures. An example is **limestone**. *Compare* **permeable rock**. *See also* **impervious rock**.

photosynthesis The process by which green plants make carbohydrates from carbon dioxide and water, and give off oxygen. Photosynthesis balances **respiration**.

physical feature *See* **topography**.

physical geography The study of our **environment**, comprising such elements as geomorphology, hydrology, pedology, meteorology, climatology and biogeography.

pie chart A circular graph for displaying values as proportions:

The journey to work: mode of transport.
(Sample of urban population)

Mode	No.	%	Sector° (% x 3.6)
Foot	25	3.2	11.5
Cycle	10	1.3	4.7
Bus	86	11.1	40.0
Train	123	15.9	57.2
Car	530	68.5	246.6
Total	774	100	360
		per cent	degrees

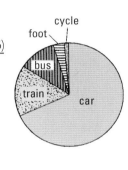

pie chart

plain A level or almost level area of land.

plantation agriculture A system of **agriculture** located in a tropical or semi-tropical **environment**, producing commodities for export to Europe, North America and other industrialized regions. Coffee, tea, bananas, rubber and sisal are examples of plantation crops.

plateau An upland area with a fairly flat surface and steep slopes. Rivers often dissect plateau surfaces.

plate tectonics The theory that the Earth's **crust** is divided into seven large, rigid plates, and several smaller ones, which are moving relative to each other over the upper layers of the Earth's **mantle**. *See* **continental drift**. **Earthquakes** and volcanic activity occur at the boundaries between the plates.

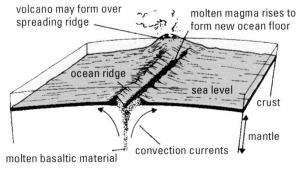

a) *Constructive plate boundary*
plate tectonics

plucking A process of glacial **erosion** whereby, during the passage of a valley **glacier** or other ice body, ice forming in cracks and fissures drags out material from a **rock** face. This is particularly the case with the backwall of a **corrie**.

plug The solidified material which seals the vent of a **volcano** after an eruption.

plutonic rock **Igneous rock** formed at depth in the Earth's **crust**; its crystals are large due to the slow rate of cooling. **Granite**, such as is found in **batholiths** and other deep-seated intrusions, is a common example.

podzol The characteristic **soil** of the **taiga** coniferous forests of Canada and northern Russia. Podzols are leached, greyish soils: iron and lime especially are leached out of the upper horizons, to be deposited as *hardpan* in the B **horizon**.

pollution Environmental damage caused by improper management of **resources**, or by careless human activity.

population change The increase of a population, the components of which are summarized in the following diagram.

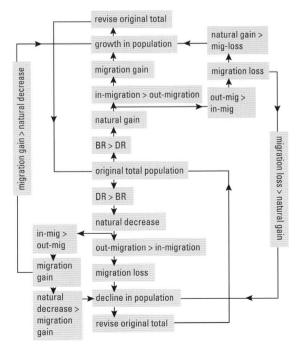

BR= birth rate   DR= death rate
population change

population density

population density The number of people per unit area. Population densities are usually expressed per square kilometre.

population distribution The pattern of population location at a given **scale**.

population explosion On a global **scale**, the dramatic increase in population during the 20th century. The graph below shows world **population growth**.

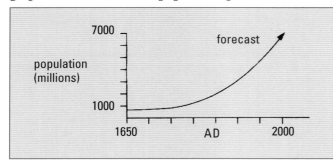

population explosion

population growth An increase in the population of a given region. This may be the result of natural increase (more births than deaths) or of in-migration, or both.

population pyramid A type of **bar graph** used to show population structure, i.e. the age and sex composition of the population for a given region or nation.

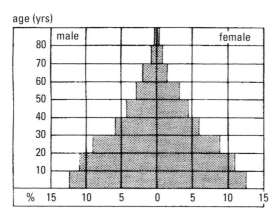

a) population pyramid Pyramid for India, showing high birth rates and death rates.

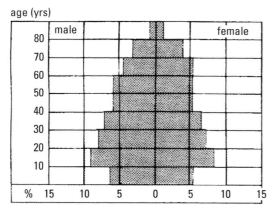

b) population pyramid Pyramid for England and Wales, showing low birth and death rates.

pothole **1.** A deep hole in limestone, caused by the enlargement of a **joint** through the dissolving effect of rainwater.
2. A hollow scoured in a river bed by the swirling of pebbles and small boulders in eddies.

precipitation Water deposited on the Earth's surface in the form of e.g. rain, snow, sleet, hail and dew.

prevailing wind The dominant wind direction of a region. Prevailing winds are named by the direction from which they blow.

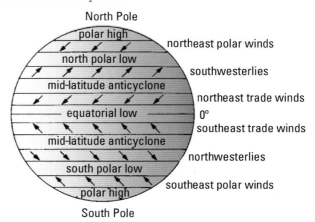

primary sector That sector of the national economy which deals with the production of primary materials: **agriculture**, mining, forestry and fishing. Primary products such as these have had no processing or manufacturing involvement. The total economy comprises the primary sector, the **secondary sector**, the **tertiary sector** and the **quaternary sector**.

primary source *See* **secondary source**.

prime meridian *or* **Greenwich Meridian** The line of 0° longitude passing through Greenwich in London.

pumped storage Water pumped back up to the storage lake of a **hydroelectric power** station, using surplus 'off-peak' electricity.

pyramidal peak A pointed mountain summit resulting from the headward extension of **corries** and **arêtes.** Under glacial conditions a given summit may develop corries on all sides, especially those facing north and east. As these erode into the summit, a formerly rounded profile may be changed into a pointed, steep-sided peak.

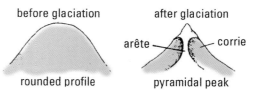

pyramidal peak

pyroclasts Rocky debris emitted during a volcanic eruption, usually following a previous emission of gases and prior to the outpouring of **lava** – although many eruptions do not reach the final lava stage.

ribbon lake

Q

quality of life The level of wellbeing of a community and of the area in which the community lives.

quartz One of the commonest minerals found in the Earth's **crust**, and a form of silica (silicon+oxide). Most **sandstones** are composed predominantly of quartz.

quartzite A very hard and resistant **rock** formed by the metamorphism of **sandstone**.

quaternary sector That sector of the economy providing information and expertise. This includes the microchip and microelectronics industries. Highly developed economies are seeing an increasing number of their workforce employed in this sector. *Compare* **primary sector, secondary sector, tertiary sector**.

R

rain gauge An instrument used to measure rainfall. Rain passes through a funnel into the jar below and is then transferred to a measuring cylinder. The reading is in millimetres and indicates the depth of rain which has fallen over an area.

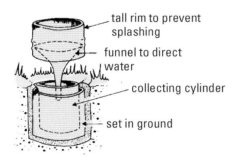

- tall rim to prevent splashing
- funnel to direct water
- collecting cylinder
- set in ground

rain gauge

raised beach *See* **wave-cut platform**.

range A long series or chain of mountains.

rapids An area of broken, turbulent water in a river channel, caused by a stratum of resistant **rock** that dips downstream. The softer rock immediately upstream and downstream erodes more quickly, leaving the resistant rock sticking up, obstructing the flow of the water. *Compare* **waterfall**.

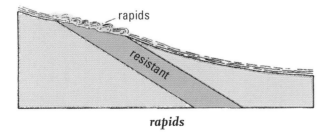

rapids

resistant

rapids

raw materials The **resources** supplied to industries for subsequent manufacturing processes.

reef A ridge of rock, sand or coral whose top lies close to the sea's surface.

regeneration Renewed growth of, for example, forest after felling. Forest regeneration is crucial to the long-term stability of many **resource** systems, from **bush fallowing** to commercial forestry.

region An area of land which has marked boundaries or unifying internal characteristics. Geographers may identify regions according to physical, climatic, political, economic or other factors.

rejuvenation Renewed vertical **corrasion** by rivers in their middle and lower courses, caused by a fall in sea level, or a rise in the level of land relative to the sea.

relative humidity The relationship between the actual amount of water vapour in the air and the amount of vapour the air could hold at a particular temperature. This is usually expressed as a percentage. Relative humidity gives a measure of dampness in the **atmosphere**, and this can be determined by a **hygrometer**.

relief The differences in height between any parts of the Earth's surface. Hence a relief map will aim to show differences in the height of land by, for example, **contour** lines or by a colour key.

remote sensing The gathering of information by the use of electronic or other sensing devices in satellites.

renewable resources Resources that can be used repeatedly, given appropriate management and conservation. *Compare* **non-renewable resources**.

representative fraction The fraction of real size to which objects are reduced on a map; for example, on a 1:50 000 map, any object is shown at 1/50 000 of its real size.

reserves Resources which are available for future use.

reservoir A natural or artificial lake used for collecting or storing water, especially for water supply or **irrigation**.

resource Any aspect of the human and physical **environments** which people find useful in satisfying their needs.

respiration The release of energy from food in the cells of all living organisms (plants as well as animals). The process normally requires oxygen and releases carbon dioxide. It is balanced by **photosynthesis.**

revolution The passage of the Earth around the sun; one revolution is completed in 365.25 days. Due to the tilt of the Earth's axis ($23\frac{1}{2}°$ from the vertical), revolution results in the sequence of seasons experienced on the Earth's surface. *See* diagram overleaf.

ria A submerged river valley, caused by a rise in sea level or a subsidence of the land relative to the sea. *See* diagram overleaf.

ribbon lake A long, relatively narrow lake, usually occupying the floor of a U-shaped glaciated valley. A ribbon lake may be caused by the *overdeepening* of a section of the valley floor by glacial **abrasion**.

Richter scale

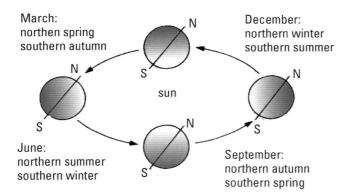

March:
northen spring
southern autumn

December:
northern winter
southern summer

sun

June:
northern summer
southern winter

September:
northern autumn
southern spring

revolution The seasons of the year.

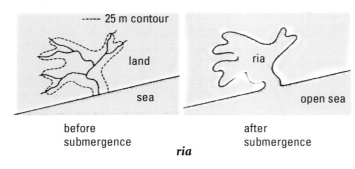

----- 25 m contour

land

sea

before
submergence

ria

after
submergence

open sea

ria

Richter scale A scale of **earthquake** measurement that describes the magnitude of an earthquake according to the amount of energy released, as recorded by **seismographs**.

rift valley A section of the Earth's **crust** which has been downfaulted. The **faults** bordering the rift valley are approximately parallel. There are two main theories related to the origin of rift valleys. The first states that tensional forces within the Earth's crust have caused a block of land to sink between parallel faults. The second theory states that compression within the Earth's crust has caused faulting in which two side blocks have risen up towards each other over a central block.

The most complex rift valley system in the world is that ranging from Syria in the Middle East to the river Zambezi in East Africa.

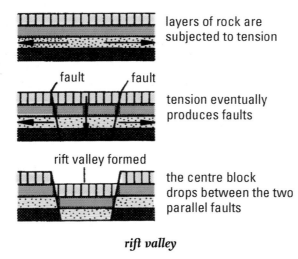

layers of rock are
subjected to tension

fault   fault

tension eventually
produces faults

rift valley formed

the centre block
drops between the two
parallel faults

rift valley

river A large natural stream of fresh water flowing along a definite course, usually into the sea.

river basin The area drained by a river and its tributaries, sometimes referred to as a **catchment** area.

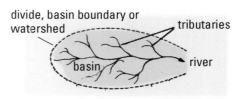

divide, basin boundary or
watershed

tributaries

basin

river

river basin

river cliff *or* **bluff** The outer bank of a **meander**. The cliff is kept steep by undercutting since river **erosion** is concentrated on the outer bank. *See* **meander** and **river's course**.

river's course The route taken by a river from its source to the sea. There are three major sections: the upper course, the middle course and the lower course.

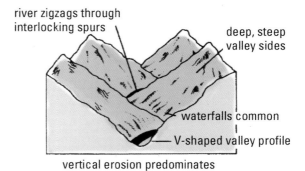

river zigzags through
interlocking spurs

deep, steep
valley sides

waterfalls common

V-shaped valley profile

vertical erosion predominates

river's course Upper course.

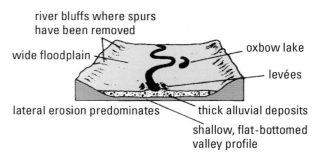

river bluffs where spurs
have been removed

wide floodplain

oxbow lake

levées

lateral erosion predominates

thick alluvial deposits

shallow, flat-bottomed
valley profile

river's course Lower course.

river terrace A platform of land beside a river. This is produced when a river is **rejuvenated** in its middle or lower courses. The river cuts down into its **flood plain**, which then stands above the new general level of the river as paired terraces.

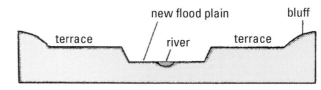

new flood plain

bluff

terrace

river

terrace

river terrace Paired river terraces above a flood plain.

roche moutonnée An outcrop of resistant **rock** sculpted by the passage of a **glacier**.

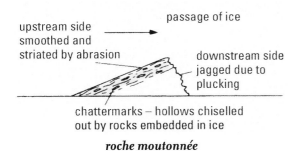

roche moutonnée

rock The solid material of the Earth's **crust**. *See* **igneous rock, sedimentary rock, metamorphic rock.**

rotation The movement of the Earth about its own axis. One rotation is completed in 24 hours. Due to the tilt of the Earth's axis, the length of day and night varies at different points on the Earth's surface. Days become longer with increasing latitude north; shorter with increasing latitude south. The situation is reversed during the northern midwinter (= the southern midsummer).

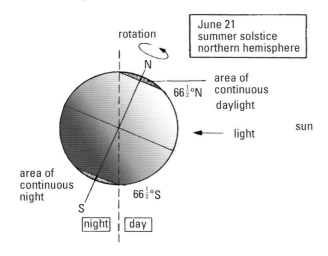

rotation The tilt of the Earth at the northern summer and southern winter solstice.

rural depopulation The loss of population from the countryside as people move away from rural areas towards cities and **conurbations.**

rural–urban migration The movement of people from rural to urban areas. *See* **migration** and **rural depopulation.**

S

saltpan A shallow basin, usually in a desert region, containing salt which has been deposited from an evaporated salt lake.

sandstone A common **sedimentary rock** deposited by either wind or water.

Sandstones vary in texture from fine- to coarse-grained, but are invariably composed of grains of **quartz**, cemented by such substances as calcium carbonate or silica.

satellite image An image giving information about an area of the Earth or another planet, obtained from a satellite. Instruments on an Earth-orbiting satellite, such as Landsat, continually scan the Earth and sense the brightness of reflected light. When the information is sent back to Earth, computers turn it into *false colour images* in which built-up areas appear in one colour (perhaps blue), vegetation in another (often red), bare ground in a third, and water in a fourth colour, making it easy to see their distribution and to monitor any changes. *Compare* **aerial photograph.**

savanna The grassland regions of Africa which lie between the **tropical rainforest** and the hot **deserts**. In South America, the *Llanos* and *Campos* regions are representative of the savanna type.

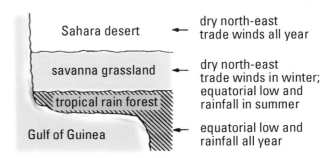

savanna The position of the savanna in West Africa.

scale The size ratio represented by a map; for example, on a map of scale 1:25 000, the real landscape is portrayed at 1/25 000 of its actual size.

scarp slope The steeper of the two slopes which comprise an **escarpment** of inclined **strata**. *Compare* **dip slope.**

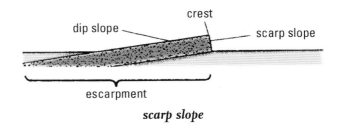

scarp slope

science park A site accommodating several companies involved in scientific work or research. Science parks are linked to universities and tend to be located on **greenfield** and/or landscaped sites. *Compare* **business park.**

scree *or* **talus** The accumulated **weathering** debris below a **crag** or other exposed rock face. Larger boulders will accumulate at the base of the scree, carried there by greater momentum. *See* diagram overleaf.

sea level

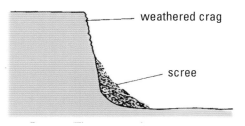

scree or talus

sea level The average height of the surface of the oceans and seas.

secondary sector The sector of the economy which comprises manufacturing and processing industries, in contrast with the **primary sector** which produces **raw materials**, the **tertiary sector** which provides **services**, and the **quaternary sector** which provides information.

secondary source A supply of information or data that has been researched or collected by an individual or group of people and made available for others to use; census data is an example of this. A *primary source* of data or information is one collected at first hand by the researcher who needs it; for example, a traffic count in an area, undertaken by a student for his or her own project.

sediment The material resulting from the **weathering** and **erosion** of the landscape, which has been deposited by water, ice or wind. It may be reconsolidated to form **sedimentary rock**.

sedimentary rock A rock which has been formed by the consolidation of **sediment** derived from pre-existing rocks. **Sandstone** is a common example of a rock formed in this way. **Chalk** and **limestone** are other types of sedimentary rock, derived from organic and chemical precipitations.

seif dune A linear sand dune, the ridge of sand lying parallel to the prevailing wind direction. The eddying movement of the wind keeps the sides of the dune steep.

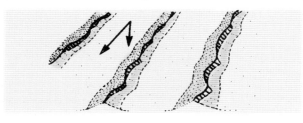

seif dunes

seismograph An instrument which measures and records the seismic waves which travel through the Earth during an **earthquake**.

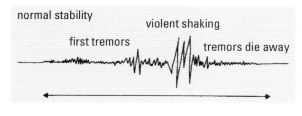

seismograph A typical seismograph trace.

seismology The study of **earthquakes**.

serac A pinnacle of ice formed by the tumbling and shearing of a **glacier** at an ice fall, i.e. the broken ice associated with a change in **gradient** of the valley floor.

service industry The people and organizations that provide a service to the public.

settlement Any location chosen by people as a permanent or semi-permanent dwelling place.

shading map *or* **choropleth map** A map in which shading of varying intensity is used. For example, the pattern of **population densities** in a region.

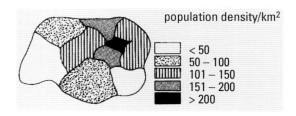

shading map

shanty town An area of unplanned, random, urban development often around the edge of a city. The shanty town is a major element of the structure of many **Third World** cities such as São Paulo, Mexico City, Nairobi, Kolkata and Lagos. The shanty town is characterized by high-density/low-quality dwellings, often constructed from the simplest materials such as scrap wood, corrugated iron and plastic sheeting – and by the lack of standard services such as sewerage and water supply, power supplies and refuse collection.

shifting cultivation *See* **bush fallowing**.

shoreface terrace A bank of **sediment** accumulating at the change of slope which marks the limit of a marine **wave-cut platform**.

Material removed from the retreating cliff base is transported by the undertow off the wave-cut platform to be deposited in deeper water offshore.

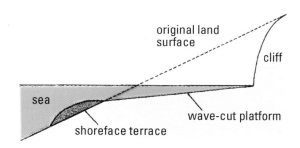

shoreface terrace

silage Any **fodder crop** harvested whilst still green. The crop is kept succulent by partial fermentation in a *silo*. It is used as animal feed during the winter.

sill **1.** An igneous intrusion of roughly horizontal disposition. *See* **igneous rock**.
2. (Also called **threshold**) the lip of a **corrie**.

stack

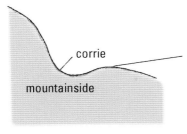

sill

silt Fine **sediment**, the component particles of which have a mean diameter of between 0.002 mm and 0.02 mm.

sinkhole *See* **pothole**.

slash and burn *See* **tropical rainforest**.

slate Metamorphosed shale or **clay**. Slate is a dense, fine-grained **rock** distinguished by the characteristic of *perfect cleavage*, i.e. it can be split along a perfectly smooth plane.

slip The amount of vertical displacement of **strata** at a **fault**.

smog A mixture of smoke and fog associated with urban and industrial areas, that creates an unhealthy **atmosphere**.

snow line The altitude above which permanent snow exists, and below which any snow that falls will not persist during the summer months.

socioeconomic group A group defined by particular social and economic characteristics, such as educational qualifications, type of job, and earnings.

soil The loose material which forms the uppermost layer of the Earth's surface, composed of the *inorganic fraction*, i.e. material derived from the **weathering** of bedrock, and the *organic fraction* – that is material derived from the decay of vegetable matter.

soil erosion The accelerated breakdown and removal of soil due to poor management. Soil erosion is particularly a problem in harsh **environments**.

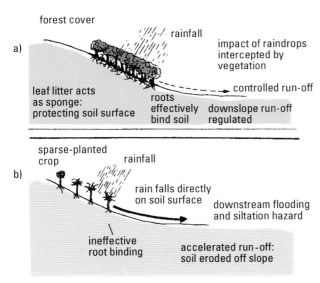

soil erosion *a) Stable environment, b) unstable environment.*

soil profile The sequence of layers or **horizons** usually seen in an exposed soil section.

solar power Heat radiation from the sun converted into electricity or used directly to provide heating. Solar power is an example of a renewable source of energy (*see* **renewable resources**).

solifluction A process whereby thawed surface soil creeps downslope over a permanently frozen **subsoil** (**permafrost**).

spatial distribution The pattern of locations of, for example, population or **settlement** in a region.

spit A low, narrow bank of sand and shingle built out into an **estuary** by the process of **longshore drift**.

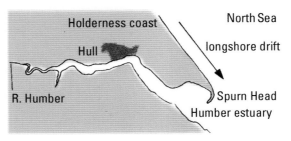

spit *Spurn Head, a coastal spit.*

spring The emergence of an underground stream at the surface, often occurring where **impermeable rock** underlies **permeable rock** or **pervious rock** or **strata**.

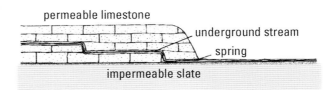

spring *Rainwater enters through the fissures of the limestone and the stream springs out where the limestone meets slate.*

spring tides *See* **tides**.

squatter settlement An area of peripheral urban settlement in which the residents occupy land to which they have no legal title. *See* **shanty town**.

stack A coastal feature resulting from the collapse of a natural arch. The stack remains after less resistant **strata** have been worn away by **weathering** and marine **erosion**.

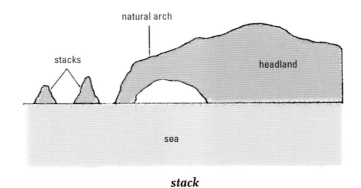

stack

stalactite

stalactite A column of calcium carbonate hanging from the roof of a **limestone** cavern. As water passes through the limestone it dissolves a certain proportion, which is then precipitated by **evaporation** of water droplets dripping from the cavern roof. The drops splashing on the floor of a cavern further evaporate to precipitate more calcium carbonate as a **stalagmite**.

stalagmite A column of calcium carbonate growing upwards from a cavern floor. *Compare* **stalactite**. Stalactites and stalagmites may meet, forming a column or pillar.

staple diet The basic foodstuff which comprises the daily meals of a given people.

Stevenson's screen A shelter used in weather stations, in which thermometers and other instruments may be hung.

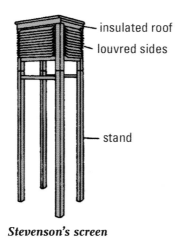

- insulated roof
- louvred sides
- stand

Stevenson's screen

strait, channel *or* **passage** A narrow body of water, between two land masses, which links two larger bodies of water.

strata Layers of **rock** superimposed one upon the other.

stratosphere The layer of the **atmosphere** which lies immediately above the troposphere and below the mesosphere and ionosphere. Within the stratosphere, temperature increases with altitutude.

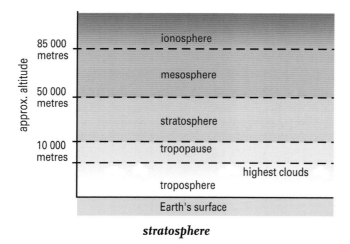

stratosphere

stratus Layer-cloud of uniform grey appearance, often associated with the warm sector of a **depression**. Stratus is a type of low **cloud** which may hang as mist over mountain tops.

striations The grooves and scratches left on bare **rock** surfaces by the passage of a **glacier**.

strip cropping A method of **soil** conservation whereby different crops are planted in a series of strips, often following **contours** around a hillside. The purpose of such a sequence of cultivation is to arrest the downslope movement of soil. *See* **soil erosion**.

subduction zone *See* **plate tectonics**.

subsistence agriculture A system of **agriculture** in which farmers produce exclusively for their own consumption, in contrast to **commercial agriculture** where farmers produce purely for sale at the market.

subsoil *See* **soil profile**.

suburbs The outer, and largest, parts of a town or city.

surface run-off That proportion of rainfall received at the Earth's surface which runs off either as channel flow or overland flow. It is distinguished from the rest of the rainfall, which either percolates into the soil or evaporates back into the **atmosphere**.

sustainable development The ability of a country to maintain a level of economic development, thus enabling the majority of the population to have a reasonable standard of living.

swallow hole *See* **pothole**.

swash The rush of water up the beach as a wave breaks. *See also* **backwash** and **longshore drift**.

syncline A trough in folded **strata**; the opposite of **anticline**. *See* **fold**.

T

taiga The extensive **coniferous forests** of Siberia and Canada, lying immediately south of the arctic **tundra**.

talus *See* **scree**.

tarn The postglacial lake which often occupies a **corrie**.

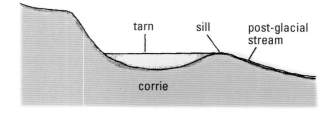

tarn   sill   post-glacial stream

corrie

temperate climate A climate typical of mid-latitudes. Such a climate is intermediate between the extremes of hot (tropical) and cold (polar) climates. Compare **extreme climate**. *See also* **maritime climate**.

terminal moraine *See* **moraine**.

terracing A means of **soil** conservation and land utilization whereby steep hillsides are engineered into a

tropical rainforest

series of flat ledges which can be used for **agriculture**, held in places by stone banks to prevent **soil erosion**.

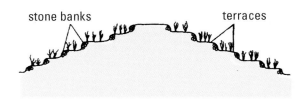

terracing

tertiary sector That sector of the economy which provides **services** such as transport, finance and retailing, as opposed to the **primary sector** which provides **raw materials**, the **secondary sector** which processes and manufactures products, and the **quaternary sector** which provides information and expertise.

thermal power station An electricity-generating plant which burns **coal**, oil or natural gas to produce steam to drive turbines.

Third World A collective term for the poor nations of Africa, Asia and Latin America, as opposed to the 'first world' of capitalist, developed nations and the 'second world' of formerly communist, developed nations. The terminology is far from satisfactory as there are great social and political variations within the 'Third World'. Indeed, there are some countries where such extreme poverty prevails that these could be regarded as a fourth group. Alternative terminology includes '**developing countries**', 'economically developing countries' and 'less economically developed countries' (LEDC). **Newly industrialized countries** are those showing greatest economic development.

threshold *See* **sill** (sense 2).

tidal range The mean difference in water level between high and low tides at a given location. *See* **tides**.

tides The alternate rise and fall of the surface of the sea, approximately twice a day, caused by the gravitational

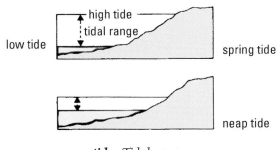

tides Tidal ranges.

pull of the moon and, to a lesser extent, of the sun.

till *See* **boulder clay**.

tombolo A **spit** which extends to join an island to the mainland.

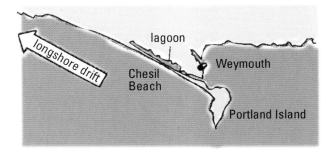

tombolo Chesil Beach, England.

topography The composition of the visible landscape, comprising both physical features and those made by people.

topsoil The uppermost layer of **soil**, more rich in organic matter than the underlying **subsoil**. *See* **horizon**, **soil profile**.

tornado A violent storm with winds circling around a small area of extremely low pressure. Characterized by a dark funnel-shaped cloud. Winds associated with tornadoes can reach speeds of over 300 mph (480 km/h).

trade winds Winds which blow from the subtropical belts of high pressure towards the equatorial belt of low pressure. In the northern hemisphere, the winds blow from the northeast and in the southern hemisphere from the southeast.

transhumance The practice whereby herds of farm animals are moved between regions of different climates. Pastoral farmers (*see* **pastoral farming**) take their herds from valley pastures in the winter to mountain pastures in the summer. *See also* **alp**.

transnational corporation (TNC) A company that has branches in many countries of the world, and often controls the production of the primary product and the sale of the finished article.

tributary A stream or river which feeds into a larger one. *Compare* **distributary**.

tropical rainforest The dense forest cover of the equatorial regions, reaching its greatest extent in the Amazon Basin of South America, the Congo Basin of

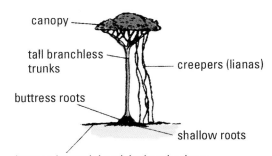

Intense bacterial activity breaks down fallen leaves, etc., to return nutrients to soil surface for immediate uptake by roots. Soils themselves are infertile: the nutrient cycle is concentrated in the vegetation and top few inches of soil.

a forest giant in the tropical rainforest

troposphere

Africa, and in parts of South East Asia and Indonesia. There has been much concern in recent years about the rate at which the world's rainforests are being cut down and burnt. The burning of large tracts of rainforest is thought to be contributing to **global warming**. Many governments and **conservation** bodies are now examining ways of protecting the remaining rainforests, which are unique **ecosystems** containing millions of plant and animal species.

tropics The region of the Earth lying between the *tropics of Cancer* ($23\frac{1}{2}°$N) and *Capricorn* ($23\frac{1}{2}°$S). *See* **latitude**.

troposphere *See* **atmosphere**.

trough An area of low pressure, not sufficiently well-defined to be regarded as a **depression**.

truncated spur A spur of land that previously projected into a valley and has been completely or partially cut off by a moving **glacier**.

tsunami A very large, and often destructive, sea wave produced by a submarine **earthquake**. Tsunamis tend to occur along the coasts of Japan and parts of the Pacific Ocean, and can be the cause of large numbers of deaths.

tuff Volcanic ash or dust which has been consolidated into **rock**.

tundra The barren, often bare-rock plains of the far north of North America and Eurasia where subarctic conditions prevail and where, as a result, vegetation is restricted to low-growing, hardy shrubs and mosses and lichens.

typhoon *See* **hurricane**.

U

undernutrition A lack of a sufficient quantity of food, as distinct from **malnutrition** which is a consequence of an unbalanced diet.

urban decay The process of deterioration in the **infrastructure** of parts of the city. It is the result of long-term shifts in patterns of economic activity, residential **location** and **infrastructure**.

urban sprawl The growth in extent of an urban area in response to improvements in transport and rising incomes, both of which allow a greater physical separation of home and work.

urbanization The process by which a national population becomes predominantly urban through a **migration** of people from the countryside to cities, and a shift from agricultural to industrial employment.

U-shaped valley A glaciated valley, characteristically straight in plan and U-shaped in **cross section**. *See* diagram. *Compare* **V-shaped valley**.

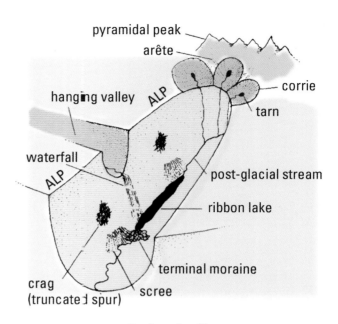

U-shaped valley

V

valley A long depression in the Earth's surface, usually containing a river, formed by **erosion** or by movements in the Earth's **crust**.

vegetation The plant life of a particular region.

viscous lava **Lava** that resists the tendency to flow. It is sticky, flows slowly and congeals rapidly. *Non-viscous* lava is very fluid, flows quickly and congeals slowly.

volcanic rock A category of **igneous rock** which comprises those rocks formed from **magma** which has reached the Earth's surface. **Basalt** is an example of a volcanic rock.

volcano A fissure in the Earth's **crust** through which **magma** reaches the Earth's surface. There are four main types of volcano:

(a) *Acid lava cone* – a very steep-sided cone composed entirely of acidic, **viscous lava** which flows slowly and congeals very quickly.

(b) *Composite volcano* – a single cone comprising alternate layers of ash (or other **pyroclasts**) and lava.

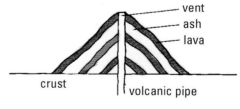

volcano *Composite volcano.*

(c) *Fissure volcano* – a volcano that erupts along a linear fracture in the crust, rather than from a single cone.

(d) *Shield volcano* – a volcano composed of very basic, non-viscous lava which flows quickly and congeals slowly, producing a very gently sloping cone.

wind vane

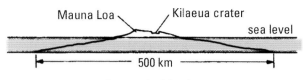

volcano Shield volcano.

V-shaped valley A narrow, steep-sided valley made by the rapid erosion of rock by streams and rivers. It is V-shaped in cross-section. *Compare* **U-shaped valley**.

vulcanicity A collective term for those processes which involve the intrusion of **magma** into the **crust**, or the extrusion of such molten material onto the Earth's surface.

W

wadi A dry watercourse in an arid region; occasional rainstorms in the desert may cause a temporary stream to appear in a wadi.

warm front *See* **depression**.

waterfall An irregularity in the long profile of a **river's course**, usually located in the upper course. *Compare* **rapids**.

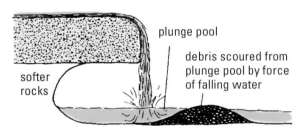

waterfall

watershed The boundary, often a ridge of high ground, between two **river basins**.

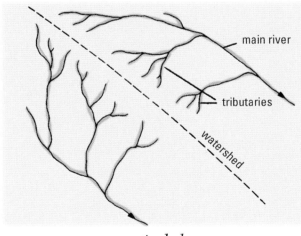

watershed

water table The level below which the ground is permanently saturated. The water table is thus the upper level of the **groundwater**. In areas where **permeable rock** predominates, the water table may be at some considerable depth.

wave-cut platform *or* **abrasion platform** A gently sloping surface eroded by the sea along a coastline.

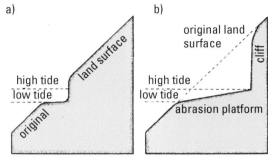

wave-cut platform a) Early in formation,
b) later in formation.

weather The day-to-day conditions of e.g. rainfall, temperature and pressure, as experienced at a particular location.

weather chart A map or chart of an area giving details of **weather** experienced at a particular time of day. Weather charts are sometimes called *synoptic charts*, as they give a synopsis of the weather at a particular time.

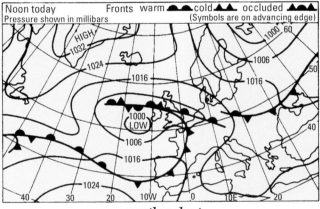

weather chart

weather station A place where all elements of the weather are measured and recorded. Each station will have a **Stevenson's screen** and a variety of instruments such as a **maximum and minimum thermometer**, a **hygrometer**, a **rain gauge**, a **wind vane** and an **anemometer**.

weathering The breakdown of rocks *in situ*; contrasted with **erosion** in that no large-scale transport of the denuded material is involved.

wet and dry bulb thermometer *See* **hygrometer**.

wind vane An instrument used to indicate wind direction. It consists of a rotating arm which always points in the direction from which the wind blows.

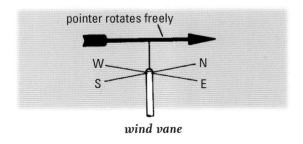

wind vane

yardang

Y

yardang Long, roughly parallel ridges of **rock** in arid and semi-arid regions. The ridges are undercut by wind **erosion** and the corridors between them are swept clear of sand by the wind. The ridges are oriented in the direction of the prevailing wind.

yield The productivity of land as measured by the weight or volume of produce per unit area.

Z

Zeugen *Pedestal rocks* in arid regions; wind **erosion** is concentrated near the ground, where **corrasion** by wind-borne sand is most active. This leads to undercutting and the pedestal profile emerges.

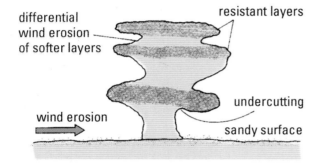

Zeugen

Introduction to the index

The index includes all names shown on the reference maps in the atlas. Each entry includes the country or geographical area in which the feature is located, a page number and an alphanumeric reference. Additional entry details and aspects of the index are explained below.

Name forms

The names policy in this atlas is generally to use local name forms which are officially recognized by the governments of the countries concerned. Rules established by the Permanent Committee on Geographical Names for British Official Use (PCGN) are applied to the conversion of non-roman alphabet names, for example in the Russian Federation, into the roman alphabet used in English.

However, English conventional name forms are used for the most well-known places for which such a form is in common use. In these cases, the local form is included in brackets on the map and appears as a cross-reference in the index. Other alternative names, such as well-known historical names or those in other languages, may also be included in brackets on the map and as cross-references in the index. All country names and those for international physical features appear in their English forms. Names appear in full in the index, although they may appear in abbreviated form on the maps.

Referencing

Names are referenced by page number and by grid reference. The grid reference relates to the alphanumeric values which appear on the edges of each map. These reflect the graticule on the map – the letter relates to longitude divisions, the number to latitude divisions. Names are generally referenced to the largest scale map page on which they appear. For large geographical features, including countries, the reference is to the largest scale map on which the feature appears in its entirety, or on which the majority of it appears.

Rivers are referenced to their lowest downstream point – either their mouth or their confluence with another river. The river name will generally be positioned as close to this point as possible.

Alternative names

Alternative names appear as cross-references and refer the user to the index entry for the form of the name used on the map.

For rivers with multiple names – for example those which flow through several countries – all alternative name forms are included within the main index entries, with details of the countries in which each form applies.

Administrative qualifiers

Administrative divisions are included in entries to differentiate duplicate names – entries of exactly the same name and feature type within the one country – where these division names are shown on the maps. In such cases, duplicate names are alphabetized in the order of the administrative division names.

Additional qualifiers are included for names within selected geographical areas, to indicate more clearly their location.

Descriptors

Entries, other than those for towns and cities, include a descriptor indicating the type of geographical feature. Descriptors are not included where the type of feature is implicit in the name itself, unless there is a town or city of exactly the same name.

Insets

Where relevant, the index clearly indicates [inset] if a feature appears on an inset map.

Alphabetical order

The Icelandic characters Þ and þ are transliterated and alphabetized as 'Th' and 'th'. The German character ß is alphabetized as 'ss'. Names beginning with Mac or Mc are alphabetized exactly as they appear. The terms Saint, Sainte, etc, are abbreviated to St, Ste, etc, but alphabetized as if in the full form.

Numerical entries

Entries beginning with numerals appear at the beginning of the index, in numerical order. Elsewhere, numerals are alphabetized before 'a'.

Permuted terms

Names beginning with generic geographical terms are permuted - the descriptive term is placed after, and the index alphabetized by, the main part of the name. For example, Mount Everest is indexed as Everest, Mount; Lake Superior as Superior, Lake. This policy is applied to all languages. Permuting has not been applied to names of towns, cities or administrative divisions beginning with such geographical terms. These remain in their full form, for example, Lake Isabella, USA.

Gazetteer entries

Selected entries have been extended to include gazetteer-style information. Important geographical facts which relate specifically to the entry are included within the entry.

Abbreviations

admin. dist.	administrative district	IL	Illinois	Phil.	Philippines
admin. div.	administrative division	imp. l.	impermanent lake	plat.	plateau
admin. reg.	administrative region	IN	Indiana	P.N.G.	Papua New Guinea
Afgh.	Afghanistan	Indon.	Indonesia	Port.	Portugal
AK	Alaska	Kazakh.	Kazakhstan	pref.	prefecture
AL	Alabama	KS	Kansas	prov.	province
Alg.	Algeria	KY	Kentucky	pt	point
AR	Arkansas	Kyrg.	Kyrgyzstan	Qld	Queensland
Arg.	Argentina	l.	lake	Que.	Québec
aut. comm.	autonomous community	LA	Louisiana	r.	river
aut. reg.	autonomous region	lag.	lagoon	reg.	region
aut. rep.	autonomous republic	Lith.	Lithuania	res.	reserve
AZ	Arizona	Lux.	Luxembourg	resr	reservoir
Azer.	Azerbaijan	MA	Massachusetts	RI	Rhode Island
b.	bay	Madag.	Madagascar	Rus. Fed.	Russian Federation
Bangl.	Bangladesh	Man.	Manitoba	S.	South, Southern
B.C.	British Columbia	MD	Maryland	S.A.	South Australia
Bol.	Bolivia	ME	Maine	salt l.	salt lake
Bos.-Herz.	Bosnia-Herzegovina	Mex.	Mexico	Sask.	Saskatchewan
Bulg.	Bulgaria	MI	Michigan	SC	South Carolina
c.	cape	MN	Minnesota	SD	South Dakota
CA	California	MO	Missouri	sea chan.	sea channel
Cent. Afr. Rep.	Central African Republic	Moz.	Mozambique	Sing.	Singapore
CO	Colorado	MS	Mississippi	Switz.	Switzerland
Col.	Colombia	MT	Montana	Tajik.	Tajikistan
CT	Connecticut	Mont.	Montenegro	Tanz.	Tanzania
Czech Rep.	Czech Republic	mt.	mountain	Tas.	Tasmania
DC	District of Columbia	mts	mountains	terr.	territory
DE	Delaware	N.	North, Northern	Thai.	Thailand
Dem. Rep. Congo	Democratic Republic of the Congo	nat. park	national park	TN	Tennessee
depr.	depression	N.B.	New Brunswick	Trin. and Tob.	Trinidad and Tobago
des.	desert	NC	North Carolina	Turkm.	Turkmenistan
Dom. Rep.	Dominican Republic	ND	North Dakota	TX	Texas
E.	East, Eastern	NE	Nebraska	U.A.E.	United Arab Emirates
Equat. Guinea	Equatorial Guinea	Neth.	Netherlands	U.K.	United Kingdom
esc.	escarpment	NH	New Hampshire	Ukr.	Ukraine
est.	estuary	NJ	New Jersey	U.S.A.	United States of America
Eth.	Ethiopia	NM	New Mexico	UT	Utah
Fin.	Finland	N.S.	Nova Scotia	Uzbek.	Uzbekistan
FL	Florida	N.S.W.	New South Wales	VA	Virginia
for.	forest	N.T.	Northern Territory	Venez.	Venezuela
Fr. Guiana	French Guiana	NV	Nevada	Vic.	Victoria
F.Y.R.O.M.	Former Yugoslav Republic of Macedonia	N.W.T.	Northwest Territories	vol.	volcano
g.	gulf	NY	New York	vol. crater	volcanic crater
GA	Georgia	N.Z.	New Zealand	VT	Vermont
Guat.	Guatemala	OH	Ohio	W.	West, Western
HI	Hawaii	OK	Oklahoma	WA	Washington
H.K.	Hong Kong	OR	Oregon	W.A.	Western Australia
Hond.	Honduras	PA	Pennsylvania	WI	Wisconsin
i.	island	Para.	Paraguay	WV	West Virginia
IA	Iowa	P.E.I.	Prince Edward Island	WY	Wyoming
ID	Idaho	pen.	peninsula	Y.T.	Yukon

1

1st Three Mile Opening sea chan. Australia 136 D2
2nd Three Mile Opening sea chan. Australia 136 C2
3-y Severnyy Rus. Fed. 51 S3
5 de Outubro Angola see Xá-Muteba
9 de Julio Arg. 178 D5
25 de Mayo Buenos Aires Arg. 178 D5
25 de Mayo La Pampa Arg. 178 C5
70 Mile House Canada 150 F5
150 Mile House Canada 150 F4

A

Aabenraa Denmark 55 F9
Aachen Germany 62 G4
Aalborg Denmark 55 F8
Aalborg Bugt b. Denmark 55 G8
Aalen Germany 63 K6
Aalesund Norway see Ålesund
Aaley Lebanon see Aley
Aalst Belgium 62 E4
Aanaar Fin. see Inari
Aarhus Denmark see Århus
Aarlen Belgium see Arlon
Aars Denmark 55 F8
Aarschot Belgium 62 E4
Aasiaat Greenland 147 M3
Aath Belgium see Ath
Aba China 96 D1
Aba Dem. Rep. Congo 122 D3
Aba Nigeria 120 D4
Abacaxis r. Brazil 177 G4
Ābādān Iran 110 C4
Abadan Turkm. 110 E2
Ābādeh Iran 110 D4
Ābādeh Ṭashk Iran 110 D4
Abadla Alg. 64 D5
Abaeté Brazil 179 B2
Abaetetuba Brazil 177 I4
Abagaytuy Rus. Fed. 95 I1
Abagnar Qi China see Xilinhot
Abag Qi China see Xin Hot
Abaiang atoll Kiribati 186 H5
Abajo Peak UT U.S.A. 159 I3
Abakaliki Nigeria 120 D4
Abakan Rus. Fed. 88 G2
Abakanskiy Khrebet mts Rus. Fed. 88 F2
Abalak Niger 120 D3
Abana Turkey 112 D2
Abancay Peru 176 D6
Abariringa atoll Kiribati see Kanton
Abarkūh Iran 110 D4
Abarkūh, Kavīr-e des. Iran 110 D4
Abarshahr Iran see Neyshābūr
Abashiri Japan 90 G3
Abashiri-wan b. Japan 90 G3
Abasolo Mex. 161 D7
Abau P.N.G. 136 E1
Abaya, Lake Eth. 122 D3
Ābaya Hāyk' l. Eth. see Abaya, Lake
Ābay Wenz r. Eth./Sudan see Blue Nile
Abaza Rus. Fed. 88 G2
Abba Cent. Afr. Rep. 122 B3
'Abbāsābād Eşfahān Iran 110 D3
'Abbāsābād Semnān Iran 110 E2
Abbasanta Sardinia Italy 68 C4
Abbatis Villa France see Abbeville
Abbe, Lake Djibouti/Eth. 108 F7
Abbeville France 62 B4
Abbeville AL U.S.A. 163 C6
Abbeville GA U.S.A. 163 D6
Abbeville LA U.S.A. 161 E6
Abbeville SC U.S.A. 163 D5
Abbey Canada 151 I5
Abbeyfeale Ireland 61 C5
Abbeytown U.K. 58 D4
Abborrträsk Sweden 54 K4
Abbot, Mount Australia 136 D4
Abbot Ice Shelf Antarctica 188 K2
Abbotsford Canada 150 F5
Abbott NM U.S.A. 157 G5
Abbott VA U.S.A. 164 E5
Abbottabad Pak. 111 I3
'Abd al 'Azīz, Jabal hill Syria 113 F3
'Abd al Kūrī i. Yemen 108 H7
'Abd Allah, Khawr sea chan. Iraq/Kuwait 110 C4
Abd al Ma'asīr well Saudi Arabia 107 D4
Ābdānān Iran 110 B3
'Abdollāhābād Iran 110 D3
Abdulino Rus. Fed. 51 Q5
Abéché Chad 121 F3
Abe-gawa r. Japan 93 E4
Abellinum Italy see Avellino
Abel Tasman National Park N.Z. 139 D5
Abengourou Côte d'Ivoire 120 C4
Åbenrå Denmark see Aabenraa
Abensberg Germany 63 L6
Abeokuta Nigeria 120 D4
Aberaeron U.K. 59 C6
Aberchirder U.K. 60 G3
Abercorn Zambia see Mbala
Abercrombie r. Australia 138 D4
Aberdare U.K. 59 D7
Aberdaron U.K. 59 C6
Aberdaugleddau U.K. see Milford Haven
Aberdeen Australia 138 E4
Aberdeen H.K. China 97 [inset]
Aberdeen S. Africa 124 G7
Aberdeen U.K. 60 G3
Aberdeen SD U.S.A. 160 D2
Aberdeen Lake Canada 151 L1
Aberdovey U.K. 59 C6
Aberdyfi U.K. see Aberdovey
Aberfeldy U.K. 60 F4
Aberford U.K. 58 F5
Aberfoyle U.K. 60 E4
Abergavenny U.K. 59 D7
Abergwaun U.K. see Fishguard
Aberhonddu U.K. see Brecon
Abermaw U.K. see Barmouth
Abernathy TX U.S.A. 161 C5
Aberporth U.K. 59 C6
Abersoch U.K. 59 C6
Abertawe U.K. see Swansea
Aberteifi U.K. see Cardigan
Aberystwyth U.K. 59 C6
Abeshr Chad see Abéché
Abez' Rus. Fed. 51 S2
Āb Gāh Iran 111 E5
Abhā Saudi Arabia 108 F6
Abhar Iran 110 C2
Abiad, Bahr el r. Africa 108 D6 see White Nile

▶Abidjan Côte d'Ivoire 120 C4
Former capital of Côte d'Ivoire (Ivory Coast).

Abijatta-Shalla National Park Eth. 122 D3
Ab-i-Kavīr salt flat Iran 110 E3
Abiko Japan 93 G3
Abilene KS U.S.A. 160 D4
Abilene TX U.S.A. 161 D5
Abingdon U.K. 59 F7
Abingdon VA U.S.A. 164 D5
Abington Reef Australia 136 E3
Abinsk Rus. Fed. 112 E1
Abitau Lake Canada 151 J2
Abitibi, Lake Canada 152 E4

▶Abkhazia aut. rep. Georgia 113 F2
Disputed Territory.

Ab Khūr Iran 110 E3
Abminga Australia 135 F6
Abnūb Egypt 112 C6
Åbo Fin. see Turku
Abohar India 104 C3
Aboisso Côte d'Ivoire 120 C4
Aboite IN U.S.A. 164 C3
Abomey Benin 120 D4
Abongabong, Gunung mt. Indon. 84 B1
Abong Mbang Cameroon 120 E4
Aborlan Palawan Phil. 82 B4
Abō-tōge pass Japan 92 D2
Abou Déia Chad 121 E3
Abovyan Armenia 113 G2
Aboyne U.K. 60 G3
Abqaiq Saudi Arabia 110 C5
Abraham's Bay Bahamas 163 F8
Abramovskiy, Mys pt Rus. Fed. 52 I2
Abrantes Port. 67 B4
Abra Pampa Arg. 178 C2
Abreojos, Punta pt Mex. 166 B3
'Abri Sudan 108 D5
Abrolhos Bank sea feature S. Atlantic Ocean 184 F7
Abruzzo, Parco Nazionale d' nat. park Italy 68 E4
Absalom, Mount Antarctica 188 B1
Absaroka Range mts WY U.S.A. 156 F3
Abtar, Jabal al hills Syria 107 C2
Abtsgmünd Germany 63 J6
Abū aḍ Ḍuhūr Syria 107 C2
Abū al Abyaḍ i. U.A.E. 110 D5
Abū al Ḥusayn, Qā' imp. l. Jordan 107 D3
Abū 'Alī i. Saudi Arabia 110 C5
Abū 'Āmūd, Wādī watercourse Jordan 107 C4
Abū 'Arīsh Saudi Arabia 108 F6
Abu 'Aweigīla well Egypt see Abū 'Uwayqilah
Abu Deleiq Sudan 108 D6

▶Abu Dhabi U.A.E. 110 D5
Capital of the United Arab Emirates.

Abū Du'ān Syria 107 D1
Abu Gubeiha Sudan 108 D7
Abū Ḥafnah, Wādī watercourse Jordan 107 D3
Abu Haggag Egypt see Ra's al Ḥikmah
Abū Ḥallūfah, Jabal hill Jordan 107 C4
Abu Hamed Sudan 108 D6

▶Abuja Nigeria 120 D4
Capital of Nigeria.

Abū Jifān well Saudi Arabia 110 B5
Abū Jurdhān Jordan 107 B4
Abū Kamāl Syria 113 F4
Abukuma-gawa r. Japan 93 G1
Abukuma-kōchi plat. Japan 93 G2
Abu Matariq Sudan 121 F3
Abumombazi Dem. Rep. Congo 122 C3
Abu Musa i. The Gulf 110 D5
Abū Mūsá, Jazīreh-ye i. The Gulf see Abu Musa
Abunā r. Bol. 176 E5
Abunã Brazil 176 E5
Ābune Yosēf mt. Eth. 108 E7
Abū Nujaym Libya 121 E1
Abū Qa'ṭūr Syria 107 C2
Abū Rawthah, Jabal mt. Egypt 107 B5
Aburazaka-tōge pass Japan 92 C3
Aburo mt. Dem. Rep. Congo 122 D3
Abu Road India 101 G4
Abū Rujmayn, Jabal mts Syria 107 D2
Abu Rûtha, Gebel mt. Egypt see Abū Rawthah, Jabal
Abū Sawādah well Saudi Arabia 110 C5
Abu Simbil Egypt see Abū Sunbul
Abū Sunbul Egypt 108 D5
Abū Ṭarfā', Wādī watercourse Egypt 107 A5
Abut Head hd N.Z. 139 C6
Abū 'Uwayqilah well Egypt 107 B4
Abuyog Leyte Phil. 82 D4
Abu Zabad Sudan 108 C7
Abū Ẓaby U.A.E. see Abu Dhabi
Abūzam Iran 110 C4
Abū Zanīmah Egypt 112 D5
Abu Zenîma Egypt see Abū Zanīmah
Abyad Sudan 108 C7
Abyaḍ, Jabal al mts Syria 107 C2
Abyār al Hakīm well Libya 112 A5
Abydos Australia 134 B5
Abyei Sudan 108 C8
Abyssinia country Africa see Ethiopia
Academician Vernadskiy research station Antarctica see Vernadsky
Academy Bay Rus. Fed. see Akademii, Zaliv
Acadia prov. Canada see Nova Scotia
Acadia National Park ME U.S.A. 162 G2
Açailândia Brazil 177 I5
Acajutla El Salvador 167 H6
Acamarachi mt. Chile see Pili, Cerro
Acambaro Mex. 167 E4
Acampamento de Caça do Mucusso Angola 123 C5
Acancéh Mex. 167 H4
Acandí Col. 176 C2
A Cañiza Spain 67 B2
Acaponeta Mex. 168 C4
Acapulco Mex. 168 E5
Acapulco de Juárez Mex. see Acapulco
Acará Brazil 177 I4
Acarai Mountains hills Brazil/Guyana 177 G3
Acaraú Brazil 177 J4
Acaray, Represa de resr Para. 178 E3
Acarigua Venez. 176 E2
Acatlán Mex. 168 E5
Acatzingo Mex. 167 F5
Acayucán Mex. 167 G5
Accho Israel see 'Akko
Accomac VA U.S.A. 165 H5
Accomack VA U.S.A. see Accomac

▶Accra Ghana 120 C4
Capital of Ghana.

Accrington U.K. 58 E5
Aceh admin. dist. Indon. 84 B1
Ach r. Germany 63 L6
Achacachi Bol. 176 E7
Achaguas Venez. 176 E2
Achalpur India 104 D5
Achampet India 106 C2
Achan Rus. Fed. 90 E2
Achayvayam Rus. Fed. 77 S3
Achchen Rus. Fed. 148 D2
Acheh admin. dist. Indon. see Aceh
Acheng China 90 B3
Achhota India 106 D1
Achi Japan 92 D3
Achicourt France 62 C4
Achill Ireland 61 C4
Achillbeg Island Ireland 61 C4
Achill Island Ireland 61 B4
Achiltibuie U.K. 60 D2
Achim Germany 63 J1
Achin admin. dist. Indon. see Aceh
Achinsk Rus. Fed. 76 K4
Achit Rus. Fed. 51 R4
Achit Nuur l. Mongolia 94 B1
Achkhoy-Martan Rus. Fed. 113 G2
Achna Cyprus 107 A2
Achnasheen U.K. 60 D3
Acıgöl l. Turkey 69 M6
Acıpayam Turkey 69 M6
Acireale Sicily Italy 68 F6
Ackerman MS U.S.A. 161 F5
Ackley IA U.S.A. 160 E3
Acklins Island Bahamas 163 F8
Acle U.K. 59 I6

▶Aconcagua, Cerro mt. Arg. 178 B4
Highest mountain in South America.

Acopiara Brazil 177 K5
A Coruña Spain 67 B2
Acoyapa Nicaragua 166 [inset] I7
Acqui Terme Italy 68 C2
Acra NY U.S.A. 165 H2
Acragas Sicily Italy see Agrigento
Acraman, Lake salt flat Australia 137 A7
Acre r. Brazil 176 E6
Acre Israel see 'Akko
Acre, Bay of Israel see Haifa, Bay of
Acri Italy 68 G5
Ács Hungary 57 Q7
Actaeon Group is Fr. Polynesia see Actéon, Groupe
Actéon, Groupe is Fr. Polynesia 187 K7
Acton Canada 164 E2
Acton CA U.S.A. 158 D4
Actopán Mex. 167 F4
Acungui Brazil 179 A4
Acunum Acusio France see Montélimar
Ada MN U.S.A. 160 D2
Ada OH U.S.A. 164 D3
Ada OK U.S.A. 161 D5
Ada WI U.S.A. 164 B2
Adabazar Turkey see Adapazarı
Adaja r. Spain 67 D3
Adak AK U.S.A. 148 [inset] C6
Adak Island AK U.S.A. 148 [inset] C6
Adalia Turkey see Antalya
Adam Oman 109 I5
Adam, Mount hill Falkland Is 178 E8
Adamantina Brazil 179 A3
Adams IN U.S.A. 164 C4
Adams KY U.S.A. 164 D4
Adams MA U.S.A. 165 I2
Adams NY U.S.A. 165 G2
Adams, Mount WA U.S.A. 156 C3
Adams Center NY U.S.A. 165 G2
Adams Lake Canada 150 G5
Adams Mountain AK U.S.A. 149 O5
Adam's Peak Sri Lanka 106 D5
Adams Peak CA U.S.A. 158 C2

▶Adamstown Pitcairn Is 187 L7
Capital of the Pitcairn Islands.

'Adan Yemen see Aden
Adana Turkey 107 B1
Adana prov. Turkey 107 B1
Adana Yemen see Aden
Adang, Teluk b. Indon. 85 G3
Adapazarı Turkey 69 N4
Adare Ireland 61 D5
Adare, Cape Antarctica 188 H2
Adavale Australia 137 D5
Ad Dabbah Sudan see Ed Debba
Ad Ḍabbīyah well Saudi Arabia 110 C5
Ad Dafinah Saudi Arabia 108 F5
Ad Dahnā' des. Saudi Arabia 108 G5
Ad Dakhla W. Sahara 120 B2
Ad Damir Sudan see Ed Damer
Ad Dammām Saudi Arabia see Dammam
Addanki India 106 C3
Ad Dār al Ḥamrā' Saudi Arabia 108 E4
Ad Darb Saudi Arabia 108 F6
Ad Dawādimī Saudi Arabia 108 F5
Ad Dawḥah Qatar see Doha
Ad Dawr Iraq 113 F4
Ad Daww plain Syria 107 C2
Ad Dayr Iraq 113 G5
Ad Dibdibah plain Saudi Arabia 110 B5
Ad Ḍiffah plat. Egypt see Libyan Plateau
Ad Dir'īyah Saudi Arabia 121 H2

▶Addis Ababa Eth. 122 D3
Capital of Ethiopia.

Addison NY U.S.A. 165 G2
Ad Dīwānīyah Iraq 113 G5
Addlestone U.K. 59 G7
Addo Elephant National Park S. Africa 125 G7
Addoo Atoll Maldives see Addu Atoll
Addu Atoll Maldives 103 D12
Ad Duwayd well Saudi Arabia 113 F5
Ad Duwaym Sudan see Ed Dueim
Ad Duwayris well Saudi Arabia 110 C6
Adegaon India 104 D5
Adel GA U.S.A. 163 D6
Adel IA U.S.A. 160 E3

▶Adelaide Australia 137 B7
Capital of South Australia.

Adelaide r. Australia 134 E3
Adelaide Bahamas 163 E7
Adelaide Island Antarctica 188 L2
Adelaide River Australia 134 E3
Adele Island Australia 134 C3
Adélie Coast Antarctica 188 G2
Adélie Land reg. Antarctica 188 G2
Adelong Australia 138 D5
Aden Yemen 108 F7
Aden, Gulf of Somalia/Yemen 108 G7
Adena OH U.S.A. 164 E3
Adenau Germany 62 G4
Adendorf Germany 63 K1
Aderbissinat Niger 120 D3
Aderno Sicily Italy see Adrano
Adesar India 104 B5
Adhan, Jabal mt. U.A.E. 110 E5
Adh Dhāyūf well Saudi Arabia 113 G6
'Adhfā' well Saudi Arabia 113 F5
'Ādhirīyāt, Jibāl al mts Jordan 107 C4
Adi i. Indon. 81 I7
Ādī Ārk'ay Eth. 108 E7
Adige r. Italy 68 E2
Ādīgrat Eth. 122 D2
Adilabad India 106 C2
Adilcevaz Turkey 113 F3
Adin CA U.S.A. 156 C4
Adīrī Libya 121 E2
Adirondack Mountains NY U.S.A. 165 H1
Ādīs Ābeba Eth. see Addis Ababa
Adi Ugri Eritrea see Mendefera
Adıyaman Turkey 112 E3
Adjud Romania 69 L1
Adlavik Islands Canada 153 K3
Admiralty Island Canada 147 H3
Admiralty Island AK U.S.A. 149 N4
Admiralty Island National Monument-Kootznoowoo Wilderness nat. park AK U.S.A. 150 C3
Admiralty Islands P.N.G. 81 L7
Ado-Ekiti Nigeria 120 D4
Adogawa Japan 92 C3
Ado-gawa r. Japan 92 C3
Adok South Sudan 108 D8
Adolfo L. Mateos Mex. 157 E8
Adolphus KY U.S.A. 164 B5
Adonara i. Indon. 83 B5
Adoni India 106 C3
Adorf Germany 63 M4
Adorf (Diemelsee) Germany 63 I3
Ado-Tymovo Rus. Fed. 90 F2
Adour r. France 66 D5
Adra Spain 67 E5
Adramyttium Turkey see Edremit
Adramyttium, Gulf of Turkey see Edremit Körfezi
Adrano Sicily Italy 68 F6
Adrar Alg. 120 C2
Adrar hills Mali see Ifôghas, Adrar des
Adré Chad 121 F3
Adrian MI U.S.A. 164 C3
Adrian TX U.S.A. 161 C5
Adrianople Turkey see Edirne
Adrianopolis Turkey see Edirne
Adriatic Sea Europe 68 E2
Adua Eth. see Ādwa
Adunara i. Indon. see Adonara
Adusa Dem. Rep. Congo 122 C3
Aduwa Eth. see Ādwa
Adverse Well Australia 134 C5
Ādwa Eth. 122 D2
Adycha r. Rus. Fed. 77 O3
Adyk Rus. Fed. 53 J7
Adzopé Côte d'Ivoire 120 C4
Aegean Sea Greece/Turkey 69 K5
Aegina i. Greece see Aigina
Aegyptus country Africa see Egypt
Aela Jordan see Al 'Aqabah
Aelana Jordan see Al 'Aqabah
Aelia Capitolina Israel/West Bank see Jerusalem
Aelōninae atoll Marshall Is see Ailinglaplap
Aenus Turkey see Enez
Aerzen Germany 63 J2
Aesernia Italy see Isernia
A Estrada Spain 67 B2
Afabet Eritrea 108 E6
Afanas'yevo Rus. Fed. 52 L4
Affreville Alg. see Khemis Miliana
Afghānestān country Asia see Afghanistan
Afghanistan country Asia 111 G3
Afgooye Somalia 122 E3
'Afīf Saudi Arabia 108 F5
Afiun Karahissar Turkey see Afyon
Åfjord Norway 54 G5
Aflou Alg. 64 E5
Afmadow Somalia 122 E3
Afogados da Ingazoira Brazil 177 K5
Afognak AK U.S.A. 148 I4
Afognak Island AK U.S.A. 148 I4
A Fonsagrada Spain 67 C2
Afonso Cláudio Brazil 179 C3
Āfrēra Terara vol. Eth. 108 F7
Africa Nova country Africa see Tunisia
'Afrīn Syria 107 C1
'Afrīn, Nahr r. Syria/Turkey 107 C1
Afşin Turkey 112 E3
Afsluitdijk barrage Neth. 62 F2
Afton WY U.S.A. 156 F4
Afuá Brazil 177 H4
'Afula Israel 107 B3
Afyon Turkey 69 N5
Afyonkarahisar Turkey see Afyon
Aga Germany 63 M4
Aga Rus. Fed. 95 H1
Aga r. Rus. Fed. 95 H1
Agadès Niger see Agadez
Agadez Niger 120 D3
Agadir Morocco 120 C1
Agadyr' Kazakh. 102 D2
Agalega Islands Mauritius 185 L6
Agalta, Sierra de mts Hond. 166 [inset] I6
Agana Guam see Hagåtña
Aganzhen China 94 E5
Agara Georgia 113 F2
Agartala India 105 G5
Agashi India 106 B2
Agate Canada 152 E4
Agathe France see Agde
Agathonisi i. Greece 69 L6
Agats Indon. 81 J8
Agatsuma Japan 93 E2
Agatsuma-gawa r. Japan 93 F2
Agatti i. India 106 B4
Agattu Island AK U.S.A. 148 [inset] A5
Agattu Strait AK U.S.A. 148 [inset] A5
Agboville Côte d'Ivoire 120 C4
Ağcabädi Azer. 113 G2
Ağdam (abandoned) Azer. 113 G3
Ağdaş Azer. 113 G2
Agdash Azer. see Ağdaş
Agde France 66 F5
Agdzhabedi Azer. see Ağcabädi
Agedabia Libya see Ajdābiyā
Agematsu Japan 92 D3
Agen France 66 E4
Ageo Japan 93 F3
Aggeneys S. Africa 124 D5
Aggteleki nat. park Hungary 57 R6
Aghil Dawan China 104 D1
Agiabampo Mex. 166 C3
Agiguan i. N. Mariana Is see Aguijan
Ağın Turkey 112 E3
Aginskoye Krasnoyarskiy Kray Rus. Fed. 88 G1
Aginskoye Zabaykal'skiy Kray Rus. Fed. 95 H1
Aginum France see Agen
Agios Dimitrios Greece 69 J6
Agios Efstratios i. Greece 69 K5
Agios Georgios i. Greece 69 J6
Agios Nikolaos Greece 69 K7
Agios Theodoros Cyprus 107 B2
Agiou Orous, Kolpos b. Greece 69 J4
Agirwat Hills Sudan 108 E6
Agisanang S. Africa 125 G4
Agnes, Mount hill Australia 135 E6
Agnew Australia 135 C6
Agnibilékrou Côte d'Ivoire 120 C4
Agnita Romania 69 K2
Agniye-Afanas'yevsk Rus. Fed. 90 E2
Ago Japan 92 C4
Agose Japan 93 F3
Ago-wan b. Japan 92 C4
Agra India 104 D4
Agrakhanskiy Poluostrov pen. Rus. Fed. 113 G2
Agram Croatia see Zagreb
Ağrı Turkey 113 F3
Agria Gramvousa i. Greece 69 J7
Agrigan i. N. Mariana Is see Agrihan
Agrigento Sicily Italy 68 E6
Agrigentum Sicily Italy see Agrigento
Agrihan i. N. Mariana Is 81 L3
Agrinio Greece 69 I5
Agropoli Italy 68 F4
Agryz Rus. Fed. 51 Q4
Ağsu Azer. 113 H2
Agta Point Phil. 82 C3
Agua, Volcán de vol. Guat. 168 F6
Agua Brava, Laguna lag. Mex. 166 D4
Água Clara Brazil 178 F2
Aguada Mex. 167 H5
Agua de Correra Mex. 167 E5
Aguadilla Puerto Rico 169 K5
Aguadulce Panama 166 [inset] J7
Agua Escondida Arg. 178 C5
Agua Fria r. AZ U.S.A. 159 G5
Agua Fria National Monument nat. park AZ U.S.A. 159 G4
Aguamilpa, Presa l. Mex. 166 D4
Aguanaval r. Mex. 161 C7
Aguanga CA U.S.A. 158 E5
Aguanish r. Canada 153 J4
Aguanqueterique Hond. 166 [inset] I6
Agua Nueva Mex. 166 D3
Aguapeí r. Brazil 179 A3
Agua Prieta Mex. 166 C2
Aguaro-Guariquito, Parque Nacional nat. park Venez. 176 E2
Aguaruto Mex. 166 D3
Aguascalientes Mex. 168 D4
Aguascalientes state Mex. 166 E4
Agudos Brazil 179 A3
Águeda Port. 67 B3
Aguemour reg. Alg. 120 D2
Agui Japan 92 C4
Aguié Niger 120 D3
Aguijan i. N. Mariana Is 81 L4
Aguilar CO U.S.A. 157 G5
Aguilar de Campoo Spain 67 D2
Águilas Spain 67 F5
Aguililla Mex. 166 E5

▶Agulhas, Cape S. Africa 124 E8
Most southerly point of Africa.

Agulhas Basin sea feature Southern Ocean 185 J9
Agulhas Negras mt. Brazil 179 B3
Agulhas Plateau sea feature Southern Ocean 185 J8
Agulhas Ridge sea feature S. Atlantic Ocean 184 I8
Agusan r. Mindanao Phil. 82 D4
Agutaya Phil. 82 C4
Agutaya i. Phil. 82 C4
Ağva Turkey 69 M4
Agvali Rus. Fed. 113 G2
Ahaggar plat. Alg. 120 D2
Ahaggar, Tassili oua-n- plat. Alg. 120 D2
Āhangarān Iran 111 F3
Ahar Iran 110 B2
Ahaura N.Z. 139 C6
Ahaus Germany 62 H2
Ahipara Bay N.Z. 139 D2
Ahiri India 106 D2
Ahklun Mountains AK U.S.A. 148 G4
Ahlen Germany 63 H3
Ahmadabad India 104 C5
Aḥmadābād Iran 111 E3
Aḥmad al Bāqir, Jabal mt. Jordan 107 B5
Ahmadī Iran 110 E5
Ahmadnagar India 106 B2
Ahmadpur East Pak. 111 H4
Ahmar mts Eth. 122 E3
Ahmar Mountains Eth. see Ahmar
Ahmedabad India see Ahmadabad
Ahmednagar India see Ahmadnagar
Ahome Mex. 166 C3
Ahorn Germany 63 K4
Ahr r. Germany 62 H4
Ahram Iran 110 C4
Ahrensburg Germany 63 K1
Āhtäri Fin. 54 N5
Ahtme Estonia 55 O7
Ahu China 97 H1
Āhū Iran 110 C4
Ahuacatlán Mex. 166 D4
Ahuachapán El Salvador 167 H6
Ahualulco Jalisco Mex. 166 E4
Ahualulco San Luis Potosí Mex. 167 E4
Ahun France 66 F3
Ahuzhen China see Ahu
Ahvāz Iran 110 C4
Ahwa India 106 B1
Ahwāz Iran see Ahvāz
Ai i. Maluku Indon. 83 D4
Ai-Ais Namibia 124 C4
Ai-Ais Hot Springs Game Park nature res. Namibia 124 C4
Aibag Gol r. China 95 G3
Aichi pref. Japan 92 D4
Aichi-kōgen Kokutei-kōen park Japan 92 D3
Aichilik r. AK U.S.A. 149 L1
Aichwara India 104 D4
Aid OH U.S.A. 164 D4
Aigialousa Cyprus 107 B2
Aigina i. Greece 69 J6
Aigio Greece 69 J5
Aigle de Chambeyron mt. France 66 H4
Aigüestortes i Estany de Sant Maurici, Parc Nacional d' nat. park Spain 67 G2
Ai He r. China 90 B4
Aihua China see Yunxian
Aihui China see Heihe
Aijal India see Aizawl
Aikawa Kanagawa Japan 93 F3
Aikawa Niigata Japan 91 E5
Aiken SC U.S.A. 163 D5
Ailao Shan mts China 96 D3
Aileron Australia 134 F5
Aileu East Timor 83 C5
Ailigandí Panama 166 [inset] K7
Ailinglabelab atoll Marshall Is see Ailinglaplap
Ailinglaplap atoll Marshall Is 186 H5
Ailly-sur-Noye France 62 C5
Ailsa Craig Canada 164 E2
Ailsa Craig i. U.K. 60 D5
Ailt an Chorráin Ireland 61 D3
Aimere Flores Indon. 83 B5
Aimorés, Serra dos hills Brazil 179 C2
Aïn Beïda Alg. 68 B7
'Aïn Ben Tili Mauritania 120 C2
'Aïn Dâlla spring Egypt see 'Ayn Dāllah
Aïn Defla Alg. 67 H5
Aïn Deheb Alg. 67 G6
Aïn el Hadjel Alg. 67 H6
'Aïn el Maqfi spring Egypt see 'Ayn al Maqfī
Aïn el Melh Alg. 67 I6
Aïn Mdila well Alg. 68 B7
Aïn-M'Lila Alg. 64 F4
Aïn Oussera Alg. 67 H6
Aïn Salah Alg. see In Salah
Aïn Sefra Alg. 64 D5
Ainsworth NE U.S.A. 160 D3
Aintab Turkey see Gaziantep
Aïn Taya Alg. 67 H5
Aïn Tédélès Alg. 67 G6
Aïn Temouchent Alg. 67 F6
'Ain Tibaghbagh spring Egypt see 'Ayn Tabaghbugh
'Ain Timeira spring Egypt see 'Ayn Tumayrah
'Ain Zeitûn Egypt see 'Ayn Zaytūn
Aiquile Bol. 176 E7
Air i. Indon. 84 D2
Airai Palau 82 [inset]
Airaines France 62 B5
Airbangis Sumatera Indon. 84 B2
Airdrie Canada 150 H5
Airdrie U.K. 60 F5
Aire r. France 62 E5
Aire, Canal d' France 62 C4
Aire-sur-l'Adour France 66 D5
Air Force Island Canada 147 K3
Airgin Sum China 95 G3
Airhitam r. Indon. 85 E3
Airhitam, Teluk b. Indon. 85 E3
Air Muda, Tasik l. Malaysia 84 C1
Airpanas Maluku Indon. 83 C4
Air Pedu, Tasik l. Malaysia 84 C1
Aisatung Mountain Myanmar 86 A2
Aisch r. Germany 63 L5
Ai Shan hill China 95 J4
Aishihik Canada 149 M3
Aishihik Lake Canada 149 M3
Aisne r. France 62 C5
Aïssa, Djebel mt. Alg. 64 D5
Aitamännikkö Fin. 54 N3
Aitana mt. Spain 67 F4
Aït Benhaddou tourist site Morocco 64 C5
Aiterach r. Germany 63 M6
Aitkin MN U.S.A. 160 E2
Aitō Japan 92 C3
Aiud Romania 69 J1
Aiwokako Passage Palau 82 [inset]
Aix France see Aix-en-Provence
Aix-en-Provence France 66 G5
Aix-la-Chapelle Germany see Aachen
Aix-les-Bains France 66 G4
Aiyina i. Greece see Aigina
Aiyion Greece see Aigio
Aizawl India 105 H5
Aizkraukle Latvia 55 N8
Aizpute Latvia 55 L8
Aizu-Wakamatsu Japan 91 E5
Ajaccio Corsica France 66 I6
Ajalpán Mex. 167 F5
Ajanta India 106 B1
Ajanta Range hills India see Sahyadriparvat Range
Ajaureforsen Sweden 54 I4
Ajax Canada 164 F2
Ajayameru India see Ajmer
Ajban U.A.E. 110 D5
Aj Bogd Uul mt. Mongolia 102 I3
Aj Bogd Uul mts Mongolia 94 C2
Ajdābiyā Libya 121 F1
a-Jiddét des. Oman see Ḥarāsīs, Jiddat al
Ajiro Japan 93 F3
'Ajlūn Jordan 107 B3
'Ajman U.A.E. 110 D5
Ajmer India 104 C4
Ajmer-Merwara India see Ajmer
Ajnala India 104 C3

Allende Nuevo León Mex. 167 E3
Allendorf (Lumda) Germany 63 I4
Allenford Canada 164 E1
Allenstein Poland see Olsztyn
Allensville KY U.S.A. 164 B5
Allentown PA U.S.A. 165 H3
Alleppey India see Alappuzha
Aller r. Germany 63 J2
Alliance NE U.S.A. 160 C3
Alliance OH U.S.A. 164 E3
Al Lībīyah country Africa see Libya
Allier r. France 66 F3
Al Liḥābah well Saudi Arabia 110 B5
Allinge-Sandvig Denmark 55 I9
Al Lisāfah well Saudi Arabia 110 B5
Al Lisān pen. Jordan 107 B4
Alliston Canada 164 F1
Al Līth Saudi Arabia 108 F5
Al Liwā' oasis U.A.E. 110 D6
Alloa U.K. 60 F4
Allons TN U.S.A. 164 C5
Allora Australia 138 F2
Allu Sulawesi Indon. 83 A4
Allur India 106 D3
Alluru Kottapatnam India 106 D3
Al Lussuf well Iraq 113 F5
Alma Canada 153 H4
Alma MI U.S.A. 164 C2
Alma NE U.S.A. 160 D3
Alma WI U.S.A. 160 F2
Al Ma'ānīyah Iraq 113 F5
Alma-Ata Kazakh. see Almaty
Almada Port. 67 B4
Al Madāfi' plat. Saudi Arabia 112 E5
Al Ma'danīyāt well Iraq 113 G5
Almaden Australia 136 D3
Almadén Spain 67 D4
Al Madīnah Saudi Arabia see Medina
Al Mafraq Jordan 107 C3
Al Maghrib country Africa see Morocco
Al Maghrib reg. U.A.E. 110 D6
Al Mahākik reg. Saudi Arabia 110 C6
Al Mahdum Syria 107 C1
Al Maḥiā depr. Saudi Arabia 112 E6
Al Maḥwīt Yemen 108 F6
Al Malsūnīyah reg. Saudi Arabia 110 C5
Almalyk Uzbek. see Olmaliq
Al Manadir reg. Oman 110 D6
Al Manāmah Bahrain see Manama
Al Manjūr well Saudi Arabia 110 B6
Almanor, Lake CA U.S.A. 158 C1
Almansa Spain 67 F4
Al Manṣūrah Egypt 112 C5
Almanzor mt. Spain 67 D3
Al Mariyyah U.A.E. 110 D6
Al Marj Libya 121 F1
Almas, Rio das r. Brazil 179 A1
Al Maṭarīyah Egypt 112 D5
Almatinskaya Oblast' admin. div. Kazakh. 98 B3

▶Almaty Kazakh. 102 E3
Former capital of Kazakhstan.

Al Mawṣil Iraq see Mosul
Al Mayādīn Syria 113 F4
Al Mazār Egypt 107 A4
Almaznyy Rus. Fed. 77 M3
Almeirim Brazil 177 H4
Almeirim Port. 67 B4
Almelo Neth. 62 G2
Almenara Brazil 179 C2
Almendra, Embalse de resr Spain 67 C3
Almendralejo Spain 67 C4
Almere Neth. 62 F2
Almería Spain 67 E5
Almería, Golfo de b. Spain 67 E5
Al'met'evsk Rus. Fed. see Al'met'yevsk
Al'met'yevsk Rus. Fed. 51 Q5
Älmhult Sweden 55 I8
Almina, Punta pt Spain 67 D6
Al Mindak Saudi Arabia 108 F5
Al Minyā Egypt 112 C5
Almirós Greece see Almyros
Al Mish'āb Saudi Arabia 110 C4
Almodôvar Port. 67 B5
Almoloya Mex. 167 E5
Almond r. U.K. 60 F4
Almont MI U.S.A. 164 D2
Almonte Spain 67 C5
Almora India 104 D3
Al Mu'ayzīlah hill Saudi Arabia 107 D5
Al Mubarrez Saudi Arabia 108 G4
Al Muḍaibī Oman 109 I5
Al Muḍairib Oman 110 E6
Al Muḥarraq Bahrain 110 C5
Al Mukallā Yemen see Mukalla
Al Mukhā Yemen see Mocha
Al Mukhaylī Libya 108 B3
Al Munbaṭiḥ des. Saudi Arabia 110 C6
Almuñécar Spain 67 E5
Al Muqdādīyah Iraq 113 G4
Al Mūrītānīyah country Africa see Mauritania
Al Murūt well Saudi Arabia 113 E5
Almus Turkey 112 E2
Al Musannāh ridge Saudi Arabia 110 B4
Al Musayyib Iraq 110 B3
Al Muwaqqar Jordan 107 C4
Almyros Greece 69 J5
Almyrou, Ormos b. Greece 69 K7
Alnwick U.K. 58 F3

▶Alofi Niue 133 J3
Capital of Niue.

Aloja Latvia 55 N8
Alon Myanmar 86 A2
Along India 105 H3
Alongshan China 90 A2
Alonnisos i. Greece 69 J5
Alor i. Indon. 83 C5
Alor, Kepulauan is Indon. 83 C5
Alor, Selat sea chan. Indon. 83 B5
Alor Setar Malaysia 84 C1
Alor Star Malaysia see Alor Setar
Alost Belgium see Aalst
Aloysius, Mount Australia 135 E6
Alozero (abandoned) Rus. Fed. 54 Q4
Alpen Germany 62 G3
Alpena MI U.S.A. 164 D1
Alpercatas, Serra das hills Brazil 177 J5
Alpha Australia 136 D4
Alpha Ridge sea feature Arctic Ocean 189 A1
Alpine AZ U.S.A. 159 I5
Alpine NY U.S.A. 165 G2
Alpine TX U.S.A. 161 C6
Alpine WY U.S.A. 156 F4
Alpine National Park Australia 138 C6
Alps mts Europe 66 H4
Al Qa'āmīyāt reg. Saudi Arabia 108 G6
Al Qaddāḥīyah Libya 121 E1
Al Qadmūs Syria 107 C2
Al Qaffāy i. U.A.E. 110 D5
Al Qāhirah Egypt see Cairo
Al Qā'īyah Saudi Arabia 108 F5
Al Qā'īyah well Saudi Arabia 110 B5
Al Qal'a Beni Hammad tourist site Alg. 67 I6
Al Qalībah Saudi Arabia 112 E5
Al Qāmishlī Syria 113 F3
Al Qar'ah Libya 112 B5
Al Qar'ah well Saudi Arabia 110 B5
Al Qar'ah lava field Syria 107 C3
Al Qardāḥah Syria 107 C2
Al Qarqar Saudi Arabia 107 C4
Al Qaryatayn Syria 107 C2
Al Qaṣab Ar Riyāḍ Saudi Arabia 110 B5
Al Qaṣab Ash Sharqīyah Saudi Arabia 110 C6
Al Qaṭīf Saudi Arabia 110 C5
Al Qaṭn Yemen 108 G6
Al Qaṭrānah Jordan 107 C4
Al Qaṭrūn Libya 121 E2
Al Qāyṣūmah well Saudi Arabia 113 F5
Alqueva, Barragem de resr Port. 67 C4
Al Qumur country Africa see Comoros
Al Qunayṭirah (abandoned) Syria 107 B3
Al Qunfidhah Saudi Arabia 108 F6
Al Qurayyāt Saudi Arabia 107 C4
Al Qurnah Iraq 113 G5
Al Quṣaymah Egypt 107 B4
Al Quṣayr Egypt 108 D4
Al Quṣayr Syria 107 C2
Al Qūṣīyah Egypt 112 C6
Al Qūṣūrīyah Saudi Arabia 110 B6
Al Quṭayfah Syria 107 C3
Al Quwayī' Saudi Arabia 110 B6
Al Quwayīyah Saudi Arabia 108 G5
Al Quwayrah Jordan 107 B5
Al Rabbād reg. U.A.E. 110 D6
Alroy Downs Australia 136 B3
Alsace admin. reg. France 63 H6
Alsace reg. France 66 H2
Alsager U.K. 59 E5
Al Samīt well Iraq 113 F5
Alsask Canada 151 I5
Alsatia reg. France see Alsace
Alsek r. AK U.S.A. 149 M4
Alsfeld Germany 63 J4
Alsleben (Saale) Germany 63 L3
Alston U.K. 58 E4
Alstonville Australia 138 F2
Alsunga Latvia 55 L8
Alta Norway 54 M2
Alta, Mount N.Z. 139 B7
Altaelva r. Norway 54 M2
Altafjorden sea chan. Norway 54 M1
Alta Floresta Brazil 177 G5
Alta Gracia Nicaragua 166 [inset] I7
Altai Mountains Asia 88 F3
Altamaha r. GA U.S.A. 163 D6
Altamira Brazil 177 H4
Altamira Costa Rica 166 [inset] I7
Altamira Mex. 167 F4
Altamirano Mex. 167 G5
Altamura Italy 68 G4
Altan Zabaykal'skiy Kray Rus. Fed. 95 G1
Altan Zabaykal'skiy Kray Rus. Fed. 95 G1
Altanbulag Mongolia 94 F2
Altan Emel China 95 I1
Altan Ovoo mt. China/Mongolia 94 B2
Altan Shiret China 95 G4
Altan Xiret China see Altan Shiret
Altar Mex. 166 C2
Altar r. Mex. 157 F7
Altar, Desierto de des. Mex. 166 B1
Altata Mex. 166 D3
Altavista VA U.S.A. 164 F5
Altay China 98 E3
Altay Govĭ-Altay Mongolia 94 C2
Altay Govĭ-Altay Mongolia 94 D2
Altay Hovd Mongolia 94 C2
Altay, Respublika aut. rep. Rus. Fed. 94 A1
Altayskiy Khrebet mts Asia see Altai Mountains
Altayskiy Zapovednik nature res. Rus. Fed. 94 B1
Altayskoye Rus. Fed. 102 G1
Altdorf Switz. 66 I3
Altea Spain 67 F4
Alteidet Norway 54 M1
Altenahr Germany 62 G4
Altenberge Germany 63 H2
Altenburg Germany 63 M4
Altenkirchen (Westerwald) Germany 63 H4
Altenqoke China 94 C4
Altin Köprü Iraq 113 G4
Altınoluk Turkey 69 L5
Altınözü Turkey 107 C1
Altıntaş Turkey 69 N5
Altiplano plain Bol. 176 E7
Altmark reg. Germany 63 L2
Altmühl r. Germany 63 L6
Alto, Monte hill Italy 68 D4
Alto Chicapa Angola 123 B5
Alto Cuchumatanes mts Guat. 167 H6
Alto de Pencoso hills Arg. 178 C4
Alto Garças Brazil 177 H7
Alto Madidi, Parque Nacional nat. park Bol. 176 E6
Alton CA U.S.A. 158 A1
Alton IL U.S.A. 160 F4
Alton MO U.S.A. 161 F4
Alton NH U.S.A. 165 J2
Altona Canada 150 F3
Altoona PA U.S.A. 165 F3
Alto Paraíso de Goiás Brazil 179 B1
Alto Parnaíba Brazil 177 I5
Alto Taquarí Brazil 177 H7
Altotonga Mex. 167 F5
Altötting Germany 57 N6
Altrincham U.K. 58 E5
Alt Schwerin Germany 63 M1
Altūn Kūbrī Iraq see Altin Köprü
Altun Shan mt. China 98 F5
Altun Shan mts China 99 D5
Alturas CA U.S.A. 156 C4
Altus OK U.S.A. 161 D5
Al 'Ubaylah Saudi Arabia 122 F1
Alucra Turkey 112 E2
Alūksne Latvia 55 O8
Alūm Iran 110 C3
Alum Bridge WV U.S.A. 164 E4
Al 'Uqaylah Libya 121 E1
Al 'Uqaylah Saudi Arabia see An Nabk
Al Uqṣur Egypt see Luxor
Alur India 106 C3
Al 'Urayq des. Saudi Arabia 112 E5
Al 'Urdun country Asia see Jordan
Alur Setar Malaysia see Alor Setar
'Ālūt Iran 110 B3
Aluva India see Alwaye
Al 'Uwayjā' well Saudi Arabia 110 C6
Al 'Uwaynāt Libya 108 B5
Al 'Uwayqīlah Saudi Arabia 113 F5
Al 'Uzayr Iraq 113 G5
Alva OK U.S.A. 161 D4
Alvand, Kūh-e mt. Iran 110 C3
Alvarado Mex. 167 G5
Alvarado TX U.S.A. 167 F1
Alvarães Brazil 176 F4
Alvaton KY U.S.A. 164 B5
Alvdal Norway 54 G5
Älvdalen Sweden 55 I6
Älvesta Sweden 55 I8
Ålvik Norway 55 E6
Alvik Sweden 54 J5
Alvin TX U.S.A. 161 E6
Alvorada do Norte Brazil 179 B1
Älvsbyn Sweden 54 L4
Al Wafrah Kuwait 110 B4
Al Wajh Saudi Arabia 108 E4
Al Wakrah Qatar 110 C5
Al Waqbā well Saudi Arabia 110 B4
Alwar India 104 D4
Al Warī'ah Saudi Arabia 108 G4
Al Wāṭiyah well Egypt 112 B5
Alwaye India 106 C4
Al Widyān plat. Iraq/Saudi Arabia 113 F4
Al Wusayṭ well Saudi Arabia 110 B4
Alxa Youqi China see Ehen Hudag
Alxa Zuoqi China see Bayan Hot
Al Yamāmah Saudi Arabia 110 B5
Al Yaman country Asia see Yemen
Alyangula Australia 136 B2
Al Yāsāt i. U.A.E. 110 C5
Alyth U.K. 60 F4
Alytus Lith. 55 N9
Alzette r. Lux. 62 G5
Alzey Germany 63 I5
Amacayacu, Parque Nacional nat. park Col. 176 D4
Amadeus, Lake salt flat Australia 135 E6
Amadjuak Lake Canada 147 K3
Amadora Port. 67 B4
Amaga-dake mt. Japan 93 E3
Amagasaki Japan 92 B4
Amagi-san vol. Japan 93 E4
Amagi-tōge pass Japan 93 E4
Amagiyugashima Japan 93 E4
Amagoi-dake mt. Japan 92 C3
Amahai Seram Indon. 83 D3
Amakazari-yama mt. Japan 93 D2
Amakusa-nada b. Japan 91 C6
Åmål Sweden 55 H7
Amalia S. Africa 125 G4
Amaliada Greece 69 I6
Amalner India 104 C5
Amamapare Indon. 81 J7
Amambaí Brazil 178 E2
Amambaí, Serra de hills Brazil/Para. 178 E2
Amami-Ō-shima i. Japan 91 C7
Amami-shotō is Japan 91 C8
Amamula Dem. Rep. Congo 122 C4
Amanab P.N.G. 81 K7
Amangel'dy Kazakh. 102 C1
Amankeldi Kazakh. see Amangel'dy
Amantea Italy 68 G5
Amanzimtoti S. Africa 125 J6
Amapá Brazil 177 H3
Amapala Hond. 166 [inset] I6
Amarante Brazil 177 J5
Amarapura Myanmar 86 B2
Amardalay Mongolia see Delgertsogt
Amareleja Port. 67 C4
Amargosa Brazil 179 D1
Amargosa watercourse CA U.S.A. 158 E3
Amargosa Desert NV U.S.A. 158 E3
Amargosa Range mts CA U.S.A. 158 E3
Amargosa Valley NV U.S.A. 158 E3
Amarillo TX U.S.A. 161 C5
Amarillo, Cerro mt. Arg. 178 C4
Amarkantak India 105 E5
Amarpur India 104 E5
Amasia Turkey see Amasya
Amasine W. Sahara 120 B2
Amasra Turkey 112 D2
Amasya Turkey 112 D2
Amata Australia 135 E6
Amatenango Mex. 167 G5
Amatique, Bahía de b. Guat. 166 [inset] H6
Amatitán Mex. 166 E4
Amatlán de Cañas Mex. 166 D4
Amatsu-Kominato Japan 93 G3
Amatulla India 105 H4
Amau P.N.G. 136 E1
Amay Belgium 62 F4
Amazar Rus. Fed. 90 A1
Amazar r. Rus. Fed. 90 A1

▶Amazon r. S. America 176 F4
Longest river and largest drainage basin in South America and 2nd longest river in the world.
Also known as Amazonas or Solimões

Amazon, Mouths of the Brazil 177 I3
Amazonas r. S. America 176 F4 see Amazon
Amazon Cone sea feature S. Atlantic Ocean 184 E5
Amazônia, Parque Nacional nat. park Brazil 177 G4
Ambajogai India 106 C2
Ambala India 104 D3
Ambalangoda Sri Lanka 106 D5
Ambalavao Madag. 123 E6
Ambam Cameroon 122 B3
Ambar Iran 110 E4
Ambarchik Rus. Fed. 77 R3
Ambarnyy Rus. Fed. 54 R4
Ambasa India see Ambassa
Ambasamudram India 106 C4
Ambassa India 105 G5
Ambathala Australia 137 D5
Ambato Ecuador 176 C4
Ambato Boeny Madag. 123 E5
Ambato Finandrahana Madag. 123 E6
Ambatolampy Madag. 123 E5
Ambatomainty Madag. 123 E5
Ambatondrazaka Madag. 123 E5
Ambejogai India see Ambajogai
Ambelau i. Maluku Indon. 83 C3
Ambeno enclave East Timor see Ocussi
Amberg Germany 63 L5
Ambergris Caye i. Belize 167 I5
Ambérieu-en-Bugey France 66 G4
Amberley Canada 164 E1
Ambgaon India 106 D1
Ambianum France see Amiens
Ambikapur India 105 E5
Ambil i. Phil. 82 C3
Ambilobe Madag. 123 E5
Ambition, Mount Canada 149 O4
Amble U.K. 58 F3
Ambler AK U.S.A. 148 H2
Ambler r. AK U.S.A. 148 H2
Ambleside U.K. 58 E4
Amblève r. Belgium 62 F4
Ambo India 105 F5
Amboasary Madag. 123 E6
Ambodifotatra Madag. 123 E5
Ambohimahasoa Madag. 123 E6
Ambohitra mt. Madag. 123 E5
Amboina Maluku Indon. see Ambon
Ambon Maluku Indon. 83 C3
Ambon i. Maluku Indon. 83 C3
Amboró, Parque Nacional nat. park Bol. 176 F7
Ambositra Madag. 123 E6
Ambovombe Madag. 123 E6
Amboy CA U.S.A. 159 F4
Ambre, Cap d' c. Madag. see Bobaomby, Tanjona
Ambrim i. Vanuatu see Ambrym
Ambriz Angola 123 B4
Ambrizete Angola see N'zeto
Ambrosia Lake NM U.S.A. 159 J4
Ambrym i. Vanuatu 133 G3
Ambunten Jawa Indon. 85 F4
Ambunti P.N.G. 81 K7
Ambur India 106 C3
Amchitka Island AK U.S.A. 148 [inset] B6
Amchitka Pass sea channel AK U.S.A. 148 [inset] C6
Am-Dam Chad 121 F3
Amded, Oued watercourse Alg. 120 D2
Amdo China 99 E6
Ameca Mex. 166 D4
Amecameca Mex. 167 F5
Ameland i. Neth. 62 F1
Amelia Court House VA U.S.A. 165 G5
Amellu India 99 C8
Amenia NY U.S.A. 165 I3
Amer, Erg d' des. Alg. 122 A1
Amereli India see Amreli
American, North Fork r. CA U.S.A. 158 C2
Americana Brazil 179 B3
American-Antarctic Ridge sea feature S. Atlantic Ocean 184 G9
American Falls ID U.S.A. 156 E4
American Falls Reservoir ID U.S.A. 156 E4
American Fork UT U.S.A. 159 H1

▶American Samoa terr. S. Pacific Ocean 133 J3
United States Unincorporated Territory.

Americus GA U.S.A. 163 C5
Amersfoort Neth. 62 F2
Amersfoort S. Africa 125 I4
Amersham U.K. 59 G7
Amery Canada 151 M3
Amery Ice Shelf Antarctica 188 E2
Ames IA U.S.A. 160 E3
Amesbury U.K. 59 F7
Amesbury MA U.S.A. 165 J2
Amet India 104 C4
Amethi India 105 E4
Amfissa Greece 69 J5
Amga Rus. Fed. 77 O3
Amgalang China 95 I1
Amgu Rus. Fed. 90 E3
Amguema Rus. Fed. 148 C2
Amguema r. Rus. Fed. 148 C1
Amguid Alg. 120 D2
Amgun' r. Rus. Fed. 90 E1
Amherst Canada 153 I5
Amherst Myanmar see Kyaikkami
Amherst MA U.S.A. 165 I2
Amherst OH U.S.A. 164 D3
Amherst VA U.S.A. 164 F5
Amherstburg Canada 164 D2
Amherst Island Canada 165 G1
Ami Japan 93 G2
Amiata, Monte mt. Italy 68 D3
Amida Turkey see Diyarbakır
Amidon ND U.S.A. 160 C2
Amiens France 62 C5
'Amīj, Wādī watercourse Iraq 113 F4
Amik Ovası marsh Turkey 107 C1
Amīnābād Iran 110 D4
Amindivi atoll India see Amini
Amindivi Islands India 106 B4
Amini atoll India 106 B4
Amino Eth. 122 E3
Amino Japan 92 B3
Aminuis Namibia 124 D2
Amīrābād Iran 110 B3
Amirante Islands Seychelles 185 L6
Amirante Trench sea feature Indian Ocean 185 L6
Amisk Lake Canada 151 K4
Amistad, Represa de resr Mex./U.S.A. see Amistad Reservoir
Amistad Reservoir Mex./U.S.A. 167 E2
Amisus Turkey see Samsun
Amite LA U.S.A. 161 F6
Amity Point Australia 138 F1
Amla India 104 D5
Amlash Iran 110 C2
Amlekhganj Nepal 105 F4
Åmli Norway 55 F7
Amlia Island AK U.S.A. 148 [inset] D5
Amlwch U.K. 58 C5

▶'Ammān Jordan 107 B4
Capital of Jordan.

Ammanazar Turkm. 110 D2
Ammanford U.K. 59 D7
Ämmänsaari Fin. 54 P4
'Ammār, Tall hill Syria 107 C3
Ammarnäs Sweden 54 J4
Ammaroo Australia 136 A4
Ammassalik Greenland 189 J2
Ammerland reg. Germany 63 H1
Ammern Germany 63 K3
Ammochostos Cyprus see Famagusta
Ammochostos Bay Cyprus 107 B2
Am Nābiyah Yemen 108 F7
Amne Machin Range mts China see A'nyêmaqên Shan
Amnok-kang r. China/N. Korea see Yalu Jiang
Amo Jiang r. China 96 D4
Āmol Iran 110 D2
Amorbach Germany 63 J5
Amorgos i. Greece 69 K6
Amory MS U.S.A. 161 F5
Amos Canada 152 F4
Amourj Mauritania 120 C3
Amoy China see Xiamen
Ampah Kalimantan Indon. 85 F3
Ampana Sulawesi Indon. 83 B3
Ampani India 106 D2
Ampanihy Madag. 123 E6
Ampara Sri Lanka 106 D5
Amparo Brazil 179 B3
Ampasimanolotra Madag. 123 E5
Ampenan Lombok Indon. 85 G5
Amphitheatre Australia 138 A6
Amphitrite Group is Paracel Is 80 E3
Ampibaku Sulawesi Indon. 83 B3
Ampoa Sulawesi Indon. 83 B3
Amqog China 94 E5
Amraoti India see Amravati
Amravati India 106 C1
Amrawad India 104 D5
Amreli India 104 B5
Amri Pak. 111 H5
Amring India 105 H4
'Amrīt Syria 107 B2
Amritsar India 104 C3
Amroha India 104 D3
Amsden OH U.S.A. 164 D3
Åmsele Sweden 54 K4
Amstelveen Neth. 62 E2

▶Amsterdam Neth. 62 E2
Official capital of the Netherlands.

Amsterdam S. Africa 125 J4
Amsterdam NY U.S.A. 165 H2
Amsterdam, Île i. Indian Ocean 185 N8
Amstetten Austria 57 O6
Am Timan Chad 121 F3
Amu Co l. China 99 E6
Amudar'ya r. Asia 111 F2
Amudaryo r. Asia see Amudar'ya
Amukta Island AK U.S.A. 148 E5
Amukta Pass sea channel AK U.S.A. 148 D5
Amund Ringnes Island Canada 147 I2
Amundsen, Mount Antarctica 188 F2
Amundsen Abyssal Plain sea feature Southern Ocean 188 J2
Amundsen Basin sea feature Arctic Ocean 189 H1
Amundsen Bay Antarctica 188 D2
Amundsen Coast Antarctica 188 J1
Amundsen Glacier Antarctica 188 I1
Amundsen Gulf Canada 146 F2
Amundsen Ridges sea feature Southern Ocean 188 J2
Amundsen-Scott research station Antarctica 188 C1
Amundsen Sea Antarctica 188 K2
Amuntai Kalimantan Indon. 85 F3
Amur r. China/Rus. Fed. 90 D2
also known as Heilong Jiang (China)
Amur r. Rus. Fed. 90 F1
'Amur, Wadi watercourse Sudan 108 D6
Amurang Sulawesi Indon. 83 C2
Amuro-Baltiysk Rus. Fed. 90 B1
Amur Oblast admin. div. Rus. Fed. see Amurskaya Oblast'
Amursk Rus. Fed. 90 E2
Amurskaya Oblast' admin. div. Rus. Fed. 90 C1
Amurskiy Liman strait Rus. Fed. 90 F1
Amurzet Rus. Fed. 90 C3
Amvrosiyivka Ukr. 53 H7
Amyderya r. Asia see Amudar'ya
Am-Zoer Chad 121 F3
An Myanmar 86 A3
Anaa atoll Fr. Polynesia 187 K7
Anabanua Sulawesi Indon. 83 B3
Anabar r. Rus. Fed. 77 M2
Anacapa Islands CA U.S.A. 158 D4
Anaconda MT U.S.A. 156 E3
Anacortes WA U.S.A. 156 C2
Anacuao, Mount Phil. 82 C2
Anadarko OK U.S.A. 161 D5
Anadolu reg. Turkey 112 D3
Anadolu Dağları mts Turkey 112 E2
Anadyr' Rus. Fed. 148 B2
Anadyrskaya Nizmennost' lowland Rus. Fed. 148 B2
Anadyrskiy Liman b. Rus. Fed. 148 B2
Anadyrskiy Zaliv b. Rus. Fed. 148 C3
Anafi i. Greece 69 K6
Anagé Brazil 179 C1
'Ānah Iraq 113 F4
Anaheim CA U.S.A. 158 E5
Anahim Lake Canada 150 E4
Anáhuac Mex. 167 E3
Anahuac TX U.S.A. 161 E6
Anaimalai Hills India 106 C4
Anaiteum i. Vanuatu see Anatom
Anajás Brazil 177 I4
Anakie Australia 136 D4
Anaktuvuk r. AK U.S.A. 149 J1
Anaktuvuk Pass AK U.S.A. 149 J1
Analalava Madag. 123 E5
Anamã Brazil 176 F4
Anambas, Kepulauan is Indon. 84 D2
Anamosa IA U.S.A. 160 F3
Anamur Turkey 107 A1
Anan Nagano Japan 93 D3
Anan Tokushima Japan 91 D6
Anand India 104 C5
Anandapur India 105 F5
Anan'evo Kyrg. 98 B4
Anano i. Indon. 83 C4
Anantapur India 106 C3
Ananthapur India see Anantapur
Anantnag India 104 C2
Anant Peth India 104 D4
Anantpur India see Anantapur
Ananyev Ukr. see Anan'yiv
Anan'yiv Ukr. 53 F7
Anapa Rus. Fed. 112 E1
Anápolis Brazil 179 A2
Anār Fin. see Inari
Anār Iran 110 D4
Anār Darah Afgh. 111 F3
Anatahan i. N. Mariana Is 81 L3
Anatajan i. N. Mariana Is see Anatahan
Anatom i. Vanuatu 133 G4
Añatuya Arg. 178 D3
Anaypazari Turkey see Gülnar
An Baile Breac Ireland 61 B6
Anbei China 94 D3
An Bun Beag Ireland 61 D2
Anbūr-e Kālārī Iran 110 D5
Anbyon N. Korea 91 B5
Ancenis France 66 D3
Anchorage AK U.S.A. 149 J3
Anchorage Island atoll Cook Is see Suwarrow
Anchor Bay MI U.S.A. 164 D2
Anchor Point AK U.S.A. 149 J4
Anchuthengu India 106 C4
Anci China see Langfang
An Clochán Liath Ireland 61 D3
An Cóbh Ireland see Cobh
Ancona Italy 68 E3
Ancud, Golfo de g. Chile 178 B6
Ancyra Turkey see Ankara
Anda Heilong. China see Daqing
Anda Heilong. China 90 B3
Anda i. Indon. 83 C1
Andacollo Chile 178 B4
Andado Australia 136 A5
Andahuaylas Peru 176 D6
An Daingean Ireland 61 B5
Andal India 105 F5
Åndalsnes Norway 54 E5
Andalucía aut. comm. Spain 67 D5
Andalusia aut. comm. Spain see Andalucía
Andalusia AL U.S.A. 163 C6
Andaman Basin sea feature Indian Ocean 185 O5
Andaman Islands India 87 A4
Andaman Sea Indian Ocean 87 A5
Andaman Strait India 87 A4
Andamooka Australia 137 B6
Andapa Madag. 123 E5
Andarāb, Darah-ye reg. Afgh. 111 H3
Ande China 96 E4
Andegavum France see Angers
Andelle r. France 62 B5
Andenes Norway 54 J2
Andenne Belgium 62 F4
Andéramboukane Mali 120 D3
Anderlecht Belgium 62 E4
Andermatt Switz. 66 I3
Andernos-les-Bains France 66 D4
Anderson r. Canada 149 O1
Anderson AK U.S.A. 149 J2
Anderson IN U.S.A. 164 C3
Anderson SC U.S.A. 163 D5
Anderson TX U.S.A. 161 E6
Anderson Bay Australia 137 [inset]
Anderson Lake Canada 150 F5
Andes mts S. America 178 C4
Andfjorden sea chan. Norway 54 J2
Andhiparos i. Greece see Antiparos
Andhra Lake India 106 B2
Andhra Pradesh state India 106 C2
Andijon Uzbek. 102 D3
Andikithira i. Greece see Antikythira
Andilamena Madag. 123 E5
Andilanatoby Madag. 123 E5
Andīmeshk Iran 110 C3
Andímilos i. Greece see Antimilos
Andípsara i. Greece see Antipsara
Andir He r. China 99 C5
Andırın Turkey 112 E3
Andirlangar China 99 C5
Andizhan Uzbek. see Andijon
Andkhōy Afgh. 111 G2
Andoany Madag. 123 E5
Andoas Peru 176 C4
Andogskaya Gryada hills Rus. Fed. 52 H4
Andol India 106 C2
Andong Liaoning China see Dandong
Andong Shandong China 95 I5
Andong S. Korea 91 C5
Andoom Australia 136 C2
Andorra country Europe 67 G2

▶Andorra la Vella Andorra 67 G2
Capital of Andorra.

Andorra la Vieja Andorra see Andorra la Vella
Andover U.K. 59 F7
Andover NY U.S.A. 165 G2
Andover OH U.S.A. 164 E3
Andøya i. Norway 54 I2
Andrade CA U.S.A. 159 F5
Andradina Brazil 179 A3
Andranomavo Madag. 123 E5
Andranopasy Madag. 123 E6
Andreafsky r. AK U.S.A. 148 G3
Andreafsky, East Fork r. AK U.S.A. 148 G3
Andreanof Islands AK U.S.A. 186 I2
Andreapol' Rus. Fed. 52 G4
Andreas Isle of Man 58 C4
Andrelândia Brazil 179 B3
Andrew Canada 151 H4
Andrew Bay Myanmar 86 A3
Andrews SC U.S.A. 163 E5
Andrews TX U.S.A. 161 C5
Andria Italy 68 G4
Androka Madag. 123 E6
Andropov Rus. Fed. see Rybinsk
Andros i. Bahamas 163 E7
Andros i. Greece 69 K6
Androscoggin r. ME/NH U.S.A. 165 K2
Andros Town Bahamas 163 E7
Andrott i. India 106 B4
Andselv Norway 54 K2
Andújar Spain 67 D4
Andulo Angola 123 B5
Anec, Lake salt flat Australia 135 E5
Āneen-Kio terr. N. Pacific Ocean see Wake Island
Anéfis Mali 120 D3
Anegada, Bahía b. Arg. 178 D6

Anegada Passage Virgin Is (U.K.) 169 L5
Aného Togo 120 D4
Aneityum *i.* Vanuatu *see* **Anatom**
'Aneiza, Jabal *hill* Iraq *see* **'Unayzah, Jabal**
Anemourion *tourist site* Turkey 107 A1
Anepmete P.N.G. 81 L8
Anet France 62 B6
Anetchom, Île *i.* Vanuatu *see* **Anatom**
Aneto *mt.* Spain 67 G2
Ānewetak *atoll* Marshall Is *see* **Enewetak**
Aney Niger 120 E3
Aneytioum, Île *i.* Vanuatu *see* **Anatom**
Anfu China 97 G3
Angalarri *r.* Australia 134 E3
Angamos, Punta *pt* Chile 178 B2
Ang'angxi China 95 J2

▶**Angara** *r.* Rus. Fed. 88 G1
Part of the Yenisey-Angara-Selenga, 3rd longest river in Asia.

Angarsk Rus. Fed. 88 I2
Angas Downs Australia 135 F6
Angat *Luzon* Phil. 82 C3
Angatuba Brazil 179 A3
Angaur *i.* Palau 81 I5
Ånge Sweden 54 I5
Angel, Salto *waterfall* Venez. *see* **Angel Falls**
Ángel de la Guarda, Isla *i.* Mex. 166 B2
Angeles *Luzon* Phil. 82 C3

▶**Angel Falls** *waterfall* Venez. 176 F2
Highest waterfall in the world.

Ängelholm Sweden 55 H8
Angellala Creek *r.* Australia 138 C1
Angels Camp *CA* U.S.A. 158 C2
Ångermanälven *r.* Sweden 54 J5
Angers France 66 D3
Anggana *Kalimantan* Indon. 85 G3
Angikuni Lake Canada 151 L2
Angiola *CA* U.S.A. 158 D4
Angkor *tourist site* Cambodia 87 C4
Anglesea Australia 138 B7
Anglesey *i.* U.K. 58 C5
Angleton *TX* U.S.A. 161 E6
Anglo-Egyptian Sudan *country* Africa *see* **Sudan**
Angmagssalik Greenland *see* **Ammassalik**
Ang Mo Kio Sing. 87 [inset]
Ango Dem. Rep. Congo 122 C3
Angoche Moz. 123 D5
Angohrān Iran 110 E5
Angol Chile 178 B5
Angola *country* Africa 123 B5
Angola *IN* U.S.A. 164 C3
Angola *NY* U.S.A. 164 F2
Angola Basin *sea feature* S. Atlantic Ocean 184 H7
Angora Turkey *see* **Ankara**
Angostura Mex. 157 F8
Angoulême France 66 E4
Angra dos Reis Brazil 179 B3
Angren Uzbek. 102 D3
Ang Thong Thai. 87 C4
Anguang China 95 J2

▶**Anguilla** *terr.* West Indies 169 L5
United Kingdom Overseas Territory.

Anguilla Cays *is* Bahamas 163 E8
Anguille, Cape Canada 153 K5
Angul India 106 E1
Anguli Nur *l.* China 95 H3
Anguo China 95 H4
Angus Canada 164 F1
Angutia Char *i.* Bangl. 105 G5
Angutikada Peak *AK* U.S.A. 148 H2
Anholt *i.* Denmark 55 G8
Anhua China 97 F2
Anhui *prov.* China 97 H1
Anhumas Brazil 177 H7
Anhwei *prov.* China *see* **Anhui**
Aniak *AK* U.S.A. 148 H3
Aniak *r.* *AK* U.S.A. 148 H3
Aniakchak National Monument and Preserve *nat. park* *AK* U.S.A. 146 C4
Animaki-san *hill* Japan 93 G2
Anin Myanmar 86 B4
Anini India 99 F7
Anitaguipan Point *Samar* Phil. 82 D4
Anitápolis Brazil 179 A4
Anıtlı Turkey 107 A1
Aniva Rus. Fed. 90 F3
Aniva, Mys *c.* Rus. Fed. 90 F3
Aniva, Zaliv *b.* Rus. Fed. 90 F3
Anizy-le-Château France 62 D5
Anjadip *i.* India 106 B3
Anjalankoski Fin. 55 O6
Anjengo India *see* **Anchuthengu**
Anji China 97 H2
Anjihai China 98 D3
Anjir Avand Iran 110 D3
Anjō Japan 92 D4
Anjoman *reg.* Afgh. 111 H3
Anjoman Iran 110 E3
Anjou *reg.* France 66 D3
Anjouan *i.* Comoros *see* **Nzwani**
Anjozorobe Madag. 123 E5
Anjuthengu India *see* **Anchuthengu**
Ankang China 97 F1

▶**Ankara** Turkey 112 D3
Capital of Turkey.

Ankaratra *mt.* Madag. 123 E5
Ankazoabo Madag. 123 E6
Ankeny *IA* U.S.A. 160 E3
An Khê Vietnam 87 E4
Ankleshwar India 104 C5
Anklesvar India *see* **Ankleshwar**
Ankola India 106 B3
Ankouzhen China 94 F5
Anling China *see* **Yanling**
An Lôc Vietnam 87 D5
Anlong China 96 E3
Anlu China 97 G2
Anmoore *WV* U.S.A. 164 E4
An Muileann gCearr Ireland *see* **Mullingar**
Anmyŏn-do *i.* S. Korea 91 B5
Ann, Cape Antarctica 188 D2
Ann, Cape *MA* U.S.A. 165 J2
Anna Rus. Fed. 53 I6
Anna, Lake *VA* U.S.A. 165 G4
Annaba Alg. 68 B6
Annaberg-Buchholtz Germany 63 N4
An Nabk Saudi Arabia 107 C4
An Nabk Syria 107 C2
An Nafūd *des.* Saudi Arabia 113 F5
Annaka Japan 93 E2
Annalee *r.* Ireland 61 E3
Annalong U.K. 61 G3
Annam *reg.* Vietnam 80 D3
Annam Highlands *mts* Laos/Vietnam 86 D3
Annan U.K. 60 F6
Annan *r.* U.K. 60 F6
'Annān, Wādī al *watercourse* Syria 107 D2
Annanba China 94 C4
Annandale *VA* U.S.A. 165 G4
Anna Plains Australia 134 C4

▶**Annapolis** *MD* U.S.A. 165 G4
Capital of Maryland.

Annapurna Conservation Area *nature res.* Nepal 105 F3

▶**Annapurna I** *mt.* Nepal 105 E3
10th highest mountain in Asia and the world.

Ann Arbor *MI* U.S.A. 164 D2
Anna Regina Guyana 177 G2
An Nás Ireland *see* **Naas**
An Naşrānī, Jabal *mts* Syria 107 C3
Annean, Lake *salt flat* Australia 135 B6
Anne Arundel Town *MD* U.S.A. *see* **Annapolis**
Annecy France 66 H4
Anne Marie Lake Canada 153 J3
Annen Neth. 62 G1
Annette Island *AK* U.S.A. 149 O5
An Nimārah Syria 107 C3
An Nimāş Saudi Arabia 108 F6
Anning China 96 D3
Anniston *AL* U.S.A. 163 C5
Annobón *i.* Equat. Guinea 120 D5
Annonay France 66 G4
An Nu'mānīyah Iraq 113 G4
An Nuşayrīyah, Jabal *mts* Syria 107 C2
Anō Japan 92 C4
Anonima *atoll* Micronesia *see* **Namonuito**
Anoón de Sardinas, Bahía de *b.* Col. 176 C3
Anorontany, Tanjona *hd* Madag. 123 E5
Ano Viannos Greece *see* **Viannos**
Anpu Gang *b.* China 97 F4
Anqing China 97 H2
Anqiu China 95 I4
Anren China 97 G3
Ans Belgium 62 F4
Ansai China 95 G4
Ansbach Germany 63 K5
Anser Group *is* Australia 138 C7
Anshan China 95 J3
Anshun *Guizhou* China 96 E3
Anshun *Sichuan* China 96 D2
An Sirhān, Wādī *watercourse* Saudi Arabia 112 E5
Ansley *NE* U.S.A. 160 D3
Anson *TX* U.S.A. 161 D5
Anson Bay Australia 134 E3
Ansongo Mali 120 D3
Ansonville Canada 152 E4
Ansted *WV* U.S.A. 164 E4
Ansu China *see* **Xushui**
Ansudu Indon. 81 J7
Antabamba Peru 176 D6
Antakya Turkey 107 C1
Antalaha Madag. 123 F5
Antalya Turkey 69 N6
Antalya *prov.* Turkey 107 A1
Antalya Körfezi *g.* Turkey 69 N6

▶**Antananarivo** Madag. 123 E5
Capital of Madagascar.

An tAonach Ireland *see* **Nenagh**

▶**Antarctica** 188
Most southerly and coldest continent, and the continent with the highest average elevation.

Antarctic Peninsula Antarctica 188 L2
Antas *r.* Brazil 179 A5
An Teallach *mt.* U.K. 60 D3
Antelope Island *UT* U.S.A. 159 G1
Antelope Range *mts* *NV* U.S.A. 158 E2
Antequera Spain 67 D5
Anthony *NM* U.S.A. 166 D1
Anthony Lagoon Australia 136 A3
Anti Atlas *mts* Morocco 64 C6
Antibes France 66 H5
Anticosti, Île d' *i.* Canada 153 J4
Anticosti Island Canada *see* **Anticosti, Île d'**
Antifer, Cap d' *c.* France 59 H9
Antigo *WI* U.S.A. 160 F2
Antigonish Canada 153 J5
Antigua *i.* Antigua and Barbuda 169 L5
Antigua Guat. *see* **Antigua Guatemala**
Antigua *country* West Indies *see* **Antigua and Barbuda**
Antigua and Barbuda *country* West Indies 169 L5
Antigua Guatemala Guat. 167 H6
Antiguo-Morelos Mex. 167 F4
Antikythira *i.* Greece 69 J7
Antikythiro, Steno *sea chan.* Greece 69 J7
Anti Lebanon *mts* Lebanon/Syria *see* **Sharqī, Jabal ash**
Antimilos *i.* Greece 69 K6
Antimony *UT* U.S.A. 159 H2
An tInbhear Mór Ireland *see* **Arklow**
Antioch Turkey *see* **Antakya**
Antioch *CA* U.S.A. 158 C2
Antiocheia ad Cragum *tourist site* Turkey 107 A1
Antiochia Turkey *see* **Antakya**
Antiparos *i.* Greece 69 K6
Antipodes Islands N.Z. 133 H6
Antipsara *i.* Greece 69 K5
Antium Italy *see* **Anzio**
Antlers *OK* U.S.A. 161 E5
Antofagasta Chile 178 B2
Antofagasta de la Sierra Arg. 178 C3
Antofalla, Volcán *vol.* Arg. 178 C3
Antoing Belgium 62 D4
Antonine Wall *tourist site* U.K. 60 E5
António Enes Moz. *see* **Angoche**
Antri India 104 D4
Antrim U.K. 61 F3
Antrim Hills U.K. 61 F2
Antrim Plateau Australia 134 E4
Antropovo Rus. Fed. 52 I4
Antsalova Madag. 123 E5
Antseranana Madag. *see* **Antsirañana**
Antsirabe Madag. 123 E5
Antsirañana Madag. 123 E5
Antsla Estonia 55 O8
Antsohihy Madag. 123 E5
Anttis Sweden 54 M3
Anttola Fin. 55 O6
An Tuc Vietnam *see* **An Khê**
Antwerp Belgium 62 E3
Antwerp *NY* U.S.A. 165 H1
Antwerpen Belgium *see* **Antwerp**
An Uaimh Ireland *see* **Navan**
Anuc, Lac *l.* Canada 152 G2
Anuchino Rus. Fed. 90 D4
Anugul India *see* **Angul**
Anupgarh India 104 C3
Anuradhapura Sri Lanka 106 D4
Anveh Iran 110 D5
Anvers Island Antarctica 188 L2
Anvik *AK* U.S.A. 148 G3
Anvik *r.* *AK* U.S.A. 148 G3
Anvil Range *mts* Canada 149 N3
Anxi *Fujian* China 97 H3
Anxi *Gansu* China 94 C3
Anxiang China 97 G2
Anxin China 95 H4
Anxious Bay Australia 135 F8
Anyang *Guangxi* China *see* **Du'an**
Anyang *Henan* China 95 H4
Anyang S. Korea 91 B5
Anyar *Jawa* Indon. 84 D4
A'nyêmaqên Shan *mts* China 94 D5
Anyuan *Jiangxi* China 97 G3
Anyuan *Jiangxi* China 97 G3
Anyue China 96 E2
Anyuy *r.* Rus. Fed. 90 E2
Anyuysk Rus. Fed. 77 R3
Anzac *Alta* Canada 151 I3
Anzac *B.C.* Canada 150 F4
Anze China 95 H4
Anzhero-Sudzhensk Rus. Fed. 76 J4
Anzi Dem. Rep. Congo 122 C4
Anzio Italy 68 E4
Aoba Japan 93 F3
Aoba *i.* Vanuatu 133 G3
Aoba-yama *hill* Japan 92 B3
Aogaki Japan 92 B3
Aoga-shima *i.* Japan 91 E6
Aohan Qi China *see* **Xinhui**
Ao Kham, Laem *pt* Thai. 87 B5
Aoki Japan 93 E2
Aomen China *see* **Macao**
Aomen Tebie Xingzhengqu *aut. reg.* China *see* **Macao**
Aomori Japan 90 F4
A'ong Co *l.* China 99 C6
Ao Phang Nga National Park Thai. 87 B5

▶**Aoraki** *mt.* N.Z. 139 C6
Highest mountain in New Zealand.

Aoraki/Mount Cook National Park N.Z. 139 C6
Aôral, Phnum *mt.* Cambodia 87 D4
Aorangi *mt.* N.Z. *see* **Aoraki**
Aosta Italy 68 B2
Aotearoa *country* Oceania *see* **New Zealand**
Aouk, Bahr *r.* Cent. Afr. Rep./Chad 121 E4
Aoukâr *reg.* Mali/Mauritania 120 C2
Aoulef Alg. 120 D2
Aoyama Japan 92 C4
Aozou Chad 121 E2
Apa *r.* Brazil 178 E2
Apache Creek *NM* U.S.A. 159 I5
Apache Junction *AZ* U.S.A. 159 H5
Apaiang *atoll* Kiribati *see* **Abaiang**
Apalachee Bay *FL* U.S.A. 163 C6
Apalachicola *FL* U.S.A. 163 C6
Apalachicola *r.* *FL* U.S.A. 163 C6
Apalachin *NY* U.S.A. 165 G2
Apamea Turkey *see* **Dinar**
Apan Mex. 167 F5
Apaporis *r.* Col. 176 E4
Apar, Teluk *b.* Indon. 85 G3
Aparecida do Tabuado Brazil 179 A3
Aparima N.Z. *see* **Riverton**
Aparri *Luzon* Phil. 82 C2
Apatity Rus. Fed. 54 R3
Apatzingán Mex. 168 D5
Apavawook Cape *AK* U.S.A. 148 E3
Ape Latvia 55 O8
Apeldoorn Neth. 62 F2
Apelern Germany 63 J2
Apennines *mts* Italy 68 C2
Apensen Germany 63 J1
Apex Mountain Canada 149 M3
Aphrewn *r.* *AK* U.S.A. 148 F3
Api *mt.* Nepal 104 E3
Api *i.* Vanuatu *see* **Epi**
Api, Tanjung *pt* Indon. 83 B3
Apia *atoll* Kiribati *see* **Abaiang**

▶**Apia** Samoa 133 I3
Capital of Samoa.

Apiacas, Serra dos *hills* Brazil 177 G6
Apiaí Brazil 179 A4
Apipilulco Mex. 167 F5
Apishapa *r.* *CO* U.S.A. 160 C4
Apiti N.Z. 139 E4
Apizaco Mex. 167 F5
Apizolaya Mex. 166 E3
Apkhazeti *aut. rep.* Georgia *see* **Abkhazia**
Aplao Peru 176 D7
Apo, Mount *vol.* *Mindanao* Phil. 82 D5
Apo East Passage Phil. 82 C3
Apoera Suriname 177 G2
Apolda Germany 63 L3
Apollo Bay Australia 138 A7
Apollonia Bulg. *see* **Sozopol**
Apolo Bol. 176 E6
Aporé Brazil 179 A2
Aporé *r.* Brazil 179 A2
Apostle Islands *WI* U.S.A. 160 F2
Apostolens Tommelfinger *mt.* Greenland 147 N3
Apostolos Andreas, Cape Cyprus 107 B2
Apoteri Guyana 177 G3
Apo West Passage Phil. 82 C3
Apozai Pak. 111 H4
Appalachian Mountains U.S.A. 164 D5
Appalla *i.* Fiji *see* **Kabara**
Appennino *mts* Italy *see* **Apennines**
Appennino Abruzzese *mts* Italy 68 E3
Appennino Tosco-Emiliano *mts* Italy 68 D3
Appennino Umbro-Marchigiano *mts* Italy 68 E3
Appingedam Neth. 62 G1
Applecross U.K. 60 D3
Appleton *MN* U.S.A. 160 D2
Appleton *WI* U.S.A. 164 A1
Apple Valley *CA* U.S.A. 158 E4
Appomattox *VA* U.S.A. 165 F5
Aprilia Italy 68 E4
Aprunyi India 96 B2
Apsheronsk Rus. Fed. 113 E1
Apsheronskaya Rus. Fed. *see* **Apsheronsk**
Apsley Canada 165 F1
Apt France 66 G5
Apucarana Brazil 179 A3
Apucarana, Serra da *hills* Brazil 179 A3
Apuka Rus. Fed. 77 R3
Apulum Romania *see* **Alba Iulia**
Apurahuan *Palawan* Phil. 82 B4
Apurashokoru *i.* Palau 82 [inset]
Aq"a Georgia *see* **Sokhumi**
'Aqaba Jordan *see* **Al 'Aqabah**
Aqaba, Gulf of Asia 112 D5
'Aqaba, Wâdi el *watercourse* Egypt *see* **'Aqabah, Wādī al**
'Aqabah, Birkat al *well* Iraq 110 A4
'Aqabah, Wādī al *watercourse* Egypt 107 A4
Aqadyr Kazakh. *see* **Agadyr'**
Aqal China 98 B4
Aqdoghmish *r.* Iran 110 B2
Aqitag *mt.* China 94 B3
Aqköl *Akmolinskaya Oblast'* Kazakh. *see* **Akkol'**
Aqköl *Atyrauskaya Oblast'* Kazakh. *see* **Akkol'**
Aqmola Kazakh. *see* **Astana**
Aqqan *Xinjiang* China 99 C5
Aqqan *Xinjiang* China 99 D5
Aqqikkol Hu *salt l.* China 99 E5
Aqra', Jabal al *mt.* Syria/Turkey 107 B2
'Aqran *hill* Saudi Arabia 107 D4
Aqsay Kazakh. *see* **Aksay**
Aqsayqin Hit *terr.* Asia *see* **Aksai Chin**
Aqshī Kazakh. *see* **Akshiy**
Aqshuqyr Kazakh. *see* **Akshukur**
Aqsū Kazakh. *see* **Aksu**
Aqsūat Kazakh. *see* **Aksuat**
Aqsū-Ayuly Kazakh. *see* **Aksu-Ayuly**
Aqtaū Kazakh. *see* **Aktau**
Aqtöbe Kazakh. *see* **Aktobe**
Aqtoghay Kazakh. *see* **Aktogay**
Aquae Grani Germany *see* **Aachen**
Aquae Gratianae France *see* **Aix-les-Bains**
Aquae Sextiae France *see* **Aix-en-Provence**
Aquae Statiellae Italy *see* **Acqui Terme**
Aquarius Mountains *AZ* U.S.A. 159 G4
Aquarius Plateau *UT* U.S.A. 159 H3
Aquaviva delle Fonti Italy 68 G4
Aquidauana Brazil 178 E2
Aquila Mex. 166 E5
Aquiles Mex. 166 D2
Aquincum Hungary *see* **Budapest**
Aquiry *r.* Brazil *see* **Acre**
Aquisgranum Germany *see* **Aachen**
Aquitaine *reg.* France 66 D5
Aquitania *reg.* France *see* **Aquitaine**
Aqzhayqyn Köli *salt l.* Kazakh. *see* **Akzhaykyn, Ozero**
Ara India 105 F4
Āra Ārba Eth. 122 E3
'Arab Afgh. 111 G4
Arab, Bahr el *watercourse* Sudan 121 F4
'Arab, Khalîg el *b.* Egypt *see* **'Arab, Khalīj al**
'Arab, Khalīj al *b.* Egypt 112 C5
'Arabah, Wādī al *watercourse* Israel/Jordan 107 B5
Arabian Basin *sea feature* Indian Ocean 185 M5
Arabian Gulf Asia *see* **The Gulf**
Arabian Peninsula Asia 108 G5
Arabian Sea Indian Ocean 109 K6
Araç Turkey 112 D2
Araça *r.* Brazil 176 F4
Aracaju Brazil 177 K6
Aracati Brazil 177 K4
Aracatu Brazil 179 C1
Araçatuba Brazil 179 A3
Aracena Spain 67 C5
Aracruz Brazil 179 C2
Araçuaí Brazil 179 C2
Araçuaí *r.* Brazil 179 C2
'Arad Israel 107 B4
Arad Romania 69 I1
'Arādah U.A.E. 110 D6
Arafune-yama *mt.* Japan 93 E2
Arafura Sea Australia/Indon. 132 D2
Arafura Shelf *sea feature* Australia/Indon. 186 E6
Aragarças Brazil 177 H7
Ara-gawa *r.* Japan 93 E1
Ara-gawa *r.* Japan 93 F3
Aragón *r.* Spain 67 F2
Araguaçu Brazil 179 A1
Araguaia *r.* Brazil 179 A1
Araguaia, Parque Nacional do *nat. park* Brazil 177 H6
Araguaiana Brazil 179 A1
Araguaína Brazil 177 I5
Araguari Brazil 179 A2
Araguari *r.* Brazil 177 H3
Araguatins Brazil 177 I5
Arai Brazil 179 B1
Arai *Niigata* Japan 93 E2
Arai *Shizuoka* Japan 92 D4
'Arâif el Naga, Gebel *hill* Egypt *see* **'Urayf an Nāqah, Jabal**
Araioses Brazil 177 J4
Arak Alg. 120 D2
Arāk Iran 110 C3
Arak Syria 107 D2
Arakai-yama *mt.* Japan 93 F1
Arakamchechen, Ostrov *i.* Rus. Fed. 148 D2
Arakan *reg.* Myanmar 86 A2
Arakan Yoma *mts* Myanmar 86 A2
Araki-gawa *r.* Japan 92 D2
Arakkonam India 106 C3
Araks *r.* Azer. *see* **Araz**
Araku India 106 D2
Aral China 99 E5
Aral Kazakh. *see* **Aral'sk**
Aral Tajik. *see* **Vose**

▶**Aral Sea** *salt l.* Kazakh./Uzbek. 102 B2
4th largest lake in Asia.

Aral'sk Kazakh. 102 B2
Aral'skoye More *salt l.* Kazakh./Uzbek. *see* **Aral Sea**
Aralsor, Ozero *l.* Kazakh. 53 K6
Aral Tengizi *salt l.* Kazakh./Uzbek. *see* **Aral Sea**
Araltobe China 94 B2
Aramac Australia 136 D4
Aramac Creek *watercourse* Australia 136 D4
Aramah *plat.* Saudi Arabia 110 B5
Aramberri Mex. 161 D7
Aramia *r.* P.N.G. 81 K8
Aran *r.* India 106 C2
Aranda de Duero Spain 67 E3
Arandai Indon. 81 I7
Aranđelovac Serbia 69 I2
Arandis Namibia 124 B2
Arang India 105 E5
Arani India 106 C3
Aran Islands Ireland 61 C4
Aranjuez Spain 67 E3
Aranos Namibia 124 D3
Aransas Pass *TX* U.S.A. 161 D7
Arantangi India 106 C4
Aranuka *atoll* Kiribati 133 H1
Aranyaprathet Thai. 87 C4
Arao Japan 91 C6
Araouane Mali 120 C3
Arapaho *OK* U.S.A. 161 D5
Arapgir Turkey 112 E3
Arapiraca Brazil 177 K5
Arapis, Akra *pt* Greece *see* **Arapis, Akrotirio**
Arapis, Akrotirio *pt* Greece 69 K4
Arapkir Turkey *see* **Arapgir**
Arapongas Brazil 179 A3
Araquari Brazil 179 A4
'Ar'ar Saudi Arabia 113 F5
Araracuara Col. 176 D4
Araraj India 99 D8
Araranguá Brazil 179 A5
Araraquara Brazil 179 A3
Araras Brazil 177 H5
Ararat Armenia 113 G3
Ararat Australia 138 A6
Ararat, Mount Turkey 113 G3
Araria India 105 F4
Araripina Brazil 177 J5
Aras *r.* Azer. *see* **Araz**
Aras Turkey 113 F3
Ar-Asgat Mongolia *see* **Ugtaaltsaydam**
Arashima-dake *mt.* Japan 92 C3
Arataca Brazil 179 D1
Aratürük China *see* **Yiwu**
Arauca Col. 176 D2
Arauca *r.* Venez. 176 E2
Aravalli Range *mts* India 104 C4
Aravete Estonia 55 N7
Arawa P.N.G. 132 F2
Araxá Brazil 179 B2
Araxes *r.* Azer. *see* **Araz**
Arayıt Dağı *mt.* Turkey 69 N5
Araz *r.* Azer. 113 H2
also spelt Araks (Armenia), Aras (Turkey), formerly known as Araxes
Arbailu Iraq *see* **Arbīl**
Arbat Iraq 113 G4
Arbela Iraq *see* **Arbīl**
Arberth U.K. *see* **Narberth**
Arbīl Iraq 113 G3
Arboga Sweden 55 I7
Arborfield Canada 151 K4
Arborg Canada 151 L5
Arbroath U.K. 60 G4
Arbuckle *CA* U.S.A. 158 B2
Arbū-ye Shamālī, Dasht-e *des.* Afgh. 111 F4
Arcachon France 66 D4
Arcade *NY* U.S.A. 165 F2
Arcadia *FL* U.S.A. 163 D7
Arcadia *LA* U.S.A. 161 E5
Arcadia *MI* U.S.A. 164 B1
Arcanum *OH* U.S.A. 164 C4
Arcas, Cayos *is* Mex. 167 H4
Arcata *CA* U.S.A. 156 B4
Arc Dome *mt.* *NV* U.S.A. 158 E2
Arcelia Mex. 168 D5
Archangel Rus. Fed. 52 I2
Archer *r.* Australia 79 G9
Archer Bend National Park Australia 136 C2
Archer City *TX* U.S.A. 161 D5
Arches National Park *UT* U.S.A. 159 I2
Archipiélago Los Roques, Parque Nacional *nat. park* Venez. 176 E1
Ärçivan Azer. 113 H3
Arckaringa *watercourse* Australia 137 A6
Arco *ID* U.S.A. 156 E4
Arcos Brazil 179 B3
Arcos de la Frontera Spain 67 D5
Arctic Bay Canada 147 J2
Arctic Institute Islands Rus. Fed. *see* **Arkticheskogo Instituta, Ostrova**
Arctic Lagoon *AK* U.S.A. 148 F2
Arctic Mid-Ocean Ridge *sea feature* Arctic Ocean 189 H1
Arctic National Wildlife Refuge *nature res.* *AK* U.S.A. 149 K1
Arctic Ocean 189 B1
Arctic Red *r.* Canada 149 N2
Arctic Red River Canada *see* **Tsiigehtchic**
Arctic Village *AK* U.S.A. 149 K1
Arctowski *research station* Antarctica 188 A2
Arda *r.* Bulg. 69 L4
also known as Ardas (Greece)
Ardabīl Iran 110 C2
Ardahan Turkey 113 F2
Ardakān Iran 110 D3
Årdalstangen Norway 55 E6
Ardara Ireland 61 D3
Ardas *r.* Bulg. *see* **Arda**
Arḑ aş Şawwān *plain* Jordan 107 C4
Ardatov *Nizhegorodskaya Oblast'* Rus. Fed. 53 I5
Ardatov *Respublika Mordoviya* Rus. Fed. 53 J5
Ardee Ireland 61 F4
Ardennes *plat.* Belgium 62 E5
Ardennes, Canal des France 62 E5
Arden Town *CA* U.S.A. 158 C2
Arderin *hill* Ireland 61 E4
Ardestān Iran 110 D3
Ardglass U.K. 61 G3
Ardila *r.* Port. 67 C4
Ardlethan Australia 138 C5
Ardmore *OK* U.S.A. 161 D5
Ardnamurchan, Point of U.K. 60 C4
Ardon Rus. Fed. 113 G2
Ardrishaig U.K. 60 D4
Ardrossan U.K. 60 E5
Ardvasar U.K. 60 D3
Areia Branca Brazil 177 K4
Arekalong Peninsula Palau 82 [inset]
Arel Belgium *see* **Arlon**
Arelas France *see* **Arles**
Arelate France *see* **Arles**
Aremberg *hill* Germany 62 G4
Arena *rf* Phil. 82 C4
Arena, Point *CA* U.S.A. 158 B2
Arena, Punta *pt* Mex. 166 C4
Arena de la Ventana, Punta *pt* Mex. 166 C3
Arenal, Volcán *vol.* Costa Rica 166 [inset] I7
Arena Point *Luzon* Phil. 82 C3
Arenas de San Pedro Spain 67 D3
Arendal Norway 55 F7
Arendsee (Altmark) Germany 63 L2
Areopoli Greece 69 J6
Areponapuchi Mex. 166 D3
Arequipa Peru 176 D7
Arere Brazil 177 H4
Arévalo Spain 67 D3
Arezzo Italy 68 D3
'Arfajah *well* Saudi Arabia 107 D4
Argadargada Australia 136 B4
Argalant Mongolia 95 G2
Argan China 98 E4
Arganda del Rey Spain 67 E3
Argao *Cebu* Phil. 82 C4
Argatay Mongolia *see* **Bayanjargalan**
Argel Alg. *see* **Algiers**
Argentan France 66 D2
Argentario, Monte *hill* Italy 68 D3
Argentera, Cima dell' *mt.* Italy 68 B2
Argenthal Germany 63 H5

▶**Argentina** *country* S. America 178 C5
2nd largest and 3rd most populous country in South America and 8th largest in the world.

Argentine Abyssal Plain *sea feature* S. Atlantic Ocean 184 E9
Argentine Basin *sea feature* S. Atlantic Ocean 184 F8
Argentine Republic *country* S. America *see* **Argentina**
Argentine Rise *sea feature* S. Atlantic Ocean 184 E8
Argentino, Lago *l.* Arg. 178 B8
Argenton-sur-Creuse France 66 E3
Argentoratum France *see* **Strasbourg**
Argeş *r.* Romania 69 L2
Arg-e Zārī Afgh. 111 G3
Arghandāb Rōd *r.* Afgh. 111 G4
Argi *r.* Rus. Fed. 90 C1
Argolikos Kolpos *b.* Greece 69 J6
Argos Greece 69 J6
Argos *IN* U.S.A. 164 B3
Argostoli Greece 69 I5
Arguis Spain 67 F2
Argun' *r.* China/Rus. Fed. 89 M2
Argun Rus. Fed. 113 G2
Argungu Nigeria 120 D3
Argunskiy Khrebet *mts* Rus. Fed. 95 I1
Argus Range *mts* *CA* U.S.A. 158 E4
Arguut Mongolia *see* **Guchin-Us**
Argyle Canada 153 I6
Argyle, Lake Australia 134 E4
Argyrokastron Albania *see* **Gjirokastër**
Arhangay *prov.* Mongolia 94 E2
Ar Horqin Qi China *see* **Tianshan**
Århus Denmark 55 G8
Arhymot Lake *AK* U.S.A. 148 G3
Ariaga *i.* Indon. 83 C1
Ariah Park Australia 138 C5
Ariamsvlei Namibia 124 D5
Ariana Tunisia *see* **L'Ariana**
Ariano Irpino Italy 68 F4
Ari Atoll Maldives 103 D11
Aribinda Burkina Faso 120 C3
Arica Chile 176 D7
Arid, Cape Australia 135 C8
Arida Japan 92 B4
Arida-gawa *r.* Japan 92 B4
Arigiyn Gol *r.* Mongolia 94 E1
Arigza China 96 C1
Arīḩā Syria 107 C2
Arīḩā West Bank *see* **Jericho**
Arikaree *r.* *CO* U.S.A. 160 C3
Arima Trin. and Tob. 169 L6
Arimine-ko *resr* Japan 92 D2
Ariminum Italy *see* **Rimini**
Arinos Brazil 179 B1
Ario de Rosáles Mex. 167 E5
Aripuanã Brazil 177 G6
Aripuanã *r.* Brazil 176 F5
Ariquemes Brazil 176 F5
Aris Namibia 124 C2
Arisaig U.K. 60 D4
Arisaig, Sound of *sea chan.* U.K. 60 D4
'Arīsh, Wādī al *watercourse* Egypt 107 A4
Aristazabal Island Canada 150 D4
Arixang China *see* **Wenquan**
Ariyalur India 106 C4
Arizaro, Salar de *salt flat* Arg. 178 C2
Arizona Arg. 178 C5
Arizona *state* U.S.A. 157 F6
Arizpe Mex. 166 C2
'Arjah Saudi Arabia 108 F5
Arjasa *Jawa* Indon. 85 F4
Arjeplog Sweden 54 J3
Arjuni *Chhattisgarh* India 106 D1
Arjuni *Mahar.* India 104 E5
Arkadak Rus. Fed. 53 I6
Arkadelphia *AR* U.S.A. 161 E5
Arkaig, Loch *l.* U.K. 60 D4
Arkalyk Kazakh. 102 C1
Arkansas *r.* *AR* U.S.A. 161 F5
Arkansas *state* U.S.A. 161 E5
Arkansas City *AR* U.S.A. 161 F5
Arkansas City *KS* U.S.A. 161 D4
Arkatag Shan *mts* China 99 E5
Arkell, Mount Canada 149 N3
Arkenu, Jabal *mt.* Libya 108 B5
Arkhangel'sk Rus. Fed. *see* **Archangel**
Arkhara Rus. Fed. 90 C2
Arkhipovka Rus. Fed. 90 D4
Árki *i.* Greece *see* **Arkoi**
Arklow Ireland 61 F5
Arkoi *i.* Greece 69 L6
Arkona Canada 164 E2

Arkona, Kap c. Germany 57 N3
Arkonam India see Arakkonam
Arkport NY U.S.A. 165 G2

▶Arkticheskiy, Mys c. Rus. Fed. 189 E1
Most northerly point of Asia.

Arkticheskogo Instituta, Ostrova is Rus. Fed. 76 J2
Arkul' Rus. Fed. 52 K4
Arlandag mt. Turkm. 110 D2
Arles France 66 G5
Arlington S. Africa 125 H5
Arlington NY U.S.A. 165 I3
Arlington OH U.S.A. 164 D3
Arlington SD U.S.A. 160 D2
Arlington VA U.S.A. 165 G4
Arlington Heights IL U.S.A. 164 A2
Arlit Niger 120 D3
Arlon Belgium 62 F5
Arm r. Canada 151 J5
Armadale Australia 135 A8
Armadores i. Indon. 83 C1
Armagh U.K. 61 F3
Armant Egypt 108 D4
Armavir Armenia 113 G2
Armavir Rus. Fed. 113 F1
Armenia country Asia 113 G2
Armenia Col. 176 C3
Armenopolis Romania see Gherla
Armeria Mex. 168 D5
Armidale Australia 138 E3
Armington MT U.S.A. 156 F3
Armit Lake Canada 151 N1
Armori India 106 D1
Armour SD U.S.A. 160 D3
Armoy U.K. 61 F2
Armstrong r. Australia 134 E4
Armstrong Canada 152 C4
Armstrong, Mount Canada 149 N3
Armstrong Island Cook Is see Rarotonga
Armu r. Rus. Fed. 90 E3
Armur India 106 C2
Armutçuk Dağı mts Turkey 69 L5
Armyanskaya S.S.R. country Asia see Armenia
Arnaoutis, Cape Cyprus see Arnauti, Cape
Arnaud r. Canada 153 H2
Arnauti, Cape Cyprus 107 A2
Årnes Norway 55 G6
Arnett OK U.S.A. 161 D4
Arnhem Neth. 62 F3
Arnhem, Cape Australia 136 B2
Arnhem Land reg. Australia 134 F3
Arno r. Italy 68 D3
Arno Bay Australia 137 B7
Arnold U.K. 59 F5
Arnold's Cove Canada 153 L5
Arnon r. Jordan see Mawjib, Wādī al
Arnprior Canada 165 G1
Arnsberg Germany 63 I3
Arnstadt Germany 63 K4
Arnstein Germany 63 J5
Arnstorf Germany 63 M6
Aroab Namibia 124 D4
Aroland Canada 152 D4
Arolsen Germany 63 J3
Aroma Sudan 108 E6
Arona Italy 68 C2
Aropuk Lake AK U.S.A. 148 G3
Arorae i. Kiribati 133 H2
Arore i. Kiribati see Arorae
Aroroy Masbate Phil. 82 C3
Aros r. Mex. 166 C2
Arossi i. Solomon Is see San Cristobal
Arpa Kyrg. 98 A4
Arqalyq Kazakh. see Arkalyk
Arquipélago da Madeira aut. reg. Port. 120 B1
Arrabury Australia 137 C5
Arrah India see Ara
Arraias Brazil 179 B1
Arraias, Serra de hills Brazil 179 B1
Ar Ramlah Jordan 107 B5
Ar Ramthā Jordan 107 C3
Arran i. U.K. 60 D5
Arranmore Island Ireland 61 D3
Ar Raqqah Syria 107 D2
Arras France 62 C4
Ar Rass Saudi Arabia 108 F4
Ar Rastān Syria 107 C2
Ar Rayyān Qatar 110 C5
Arrecife Canary Is 120 B2
Arretium Italy see Arezzo
Arriagá Mex. 168 F5
Arriaga Mex. 167 E4
Ar Rifā'ī Iraq 113 G5
Ar Rihāb salt flat Iraq 113 G5
Ar Rimāl reg. Saudi Arabia 122 F1
Arrington VA U.S.A. 165 F5
Ar Riyāḍ Saudi Arabia see Riyadh
Arrochar U.K. 60 E4
Arrojado r. Brazil 179 B1
Arrow, Lough l. Ireland 61 D3
Arrowsmith, Mount N.Z. 139 C6
Arroyo Grande CA U.S.A. 158 C4
Arroyo Seco Mex. 167 F4
Ar Rubay'iyah Saudi Arabia 110 B5
Ar Rummān Jordan 107 B3
Ar Ruq'ī well Saudi Arabia 110 B4
Ar Ruṣāfah Syria 107 D2
Ar Ruṣayfah Jordan 107 C3
Ar Rustāq Oman 110 E6
Ar Ruṭbah Iraq 113 F4
Ar Ruwaydah Saudi Arabia 110 B5
Ar Ruwaydah Saudi Arabia 110 B6
Ar Ruwayḍah Syria 107 C2
Års Denmark see Aars
Ars Iran 110 B2
Arseno Lake Canada 150 H1
Arsen'yev Rus. Fed. 90 D3
Arshaly Kazakh. 98 C2
Arsk Rus. Fed. 52 K4
Arta Greece 69 I5
Arteaga Coahuila Mex. 167 E3
Arteaga Michoacán Mex. 166 E5
Artem Rus. Fed. 90 D4
Artemisa Cuba 163 D8
Artemivs'k Ukr. 53 H6
Artemovsk Ukr. see Artemivs'k
Artenay France 66 E2
Artesia AZ U.S.A. 159 I5
Artesia NM U.S.A. 157 G6
Arthur Canada 164 E2
Arthur NE U.S.A. 160 C3
Arthur TN U.S.A. 164 D5
Arthur, Lake PA U.S.A. 164 E3
Arthur's Pass National Park N.Z. 139 C6
Arthur's Town Bahamas 163 F7
Arti Rus. Fed. 51 R4
Artigas research station Antarctica 188 A2
Artigas Uruguay 178 E4
Art'ik Armenia 113 F2
Artillery Lake Canada 151 I2
Artisia Botswana 125 H3
Artois reg. France 62 B4
Artois, Collines d' hills France 62 B4
Artos Dağı mt. Turkey 113 F3
Artova Turkey 112 E2
Artsakh terr. Azer. see Nagorno-Karabakh
Arts Bogd Uul mts Mongolia 94 E2
Artsiz Ukr. see Artsyz
Artsyz Ukr. 69 M2
Artur de Paiva Angola see Kuvango
Arturo Prat research station Antarctica 188 A2
Artux China 98 B5
Artvin Turkey 113 F2
Artyk Turkm. 110 E2
Aru, Kepulauan is Indon. 134 F1
Arua Uganda 122 D3
Aruanã Brazil 179 A1

▶Aruba terr. West Indies 169 K6
Self-governing Netherlands territory.

Arumã Brazil 176 F4
Arunachal Pradesh state India 105 H4
Arundel U.K. 59 G8
Arun Gol r. China 95 K2
Arun Qi China see Naji
Aruppukkottai India 106 C4
Arus, Tanjung pt Indon. 83 B2
Arusha Tanz. 122 D4
Arut r. Indon. 85 E3
Aruwimi r. Dem. Rep. Congo 122 C3
Arvada CO U.S.A. 156 G5
Arvagh Ireland 61 E4
Arvayheer Mongolia 94 E2
Arviat Canada 151 M2
Arvidsjaur Sweden 54 K4
Arvika Sweden 55 H7
Arvonia VA U.S.A. 165 F5
Arwā' Saudi Arabia 110 B6
Arwād i. Syria 107 B2
Arwala Maluku Indon. 83 C4
Arxan Nei Mongol China 95 I2
Arxan Xinjiang China 98 D4
Aryanah Tunisia see L'Ariana
Arys Kazakh. 102 C3
Arzamas Rus. Fed. 53 I5
Arzanah i. U.A.E. 110 D5
Arzberg Germany 63 M4
Arzew Alg. 67 F6
Arzgir Rus. Fed. 113 G1
Arzila Morocco see Asilah
Aš Czech Rep. 63 M4
Asaba Japan 93 D4
Asaba Nigeria 120 D4
Asad, Buḥayrat al resr Syria 107 D1
Asadābād Afgh. 111 H3
Asadābād Iran 110 C3
Asago Japan 92 A3
Asahan r. Indon. 84 B2
Asahi Aichi Japan 92 D3
Asahi Chiba Japan 93 G3
Asahi Fukui Japan 92 C3
Asahi Gifu Japan 92 D2
Asahi Ibaraki Japan 93 G2
Asahi Kanagawa Japan 93 F3
Asahi Mie Japan 92 C3
Asahi Nagano Japan 93 D2
Asahi Toyama Japan 92 D2
Asahi-dake vol. Japan 90 F4
Asahikawa Japan 90 F4
Asaka Japan 93 F3
Asakawa Japan 93 G1
Asake-gawa r. Japan 92 C3
'Asal Egypt 107 A5
Āsalē l. Eth. 122 E2
Asālem Iran 110 C2
'Asalūyeh Iran 110 D5
Asamaga-take hill Japan 92 C4
Asama-yama vol. Japan 93 E2
Asan-man b. S. Korea 91 B5
Asansol India 105 F5
Asao Japan 93 F3
Asar China 95 I2
Asashina Japan 93 E2
Āsayita Eth. 122 E2
Asbach Germany 63 H4
Asbestos Mountains S. Africa 124 F5
Asbury Park NJ U.S.A. 165 H3
Ascalon Israel see Ashqelon
Ascea Italy 68 F4
Ascensión Bol. 176 F7
Ascensión Chihuahua Mex. 166 D2
Ascensión Nuevo León Mex. 167 F3
Ascension atoll Micronesia see Pohnpei

▶Ascension i. S. Atlantic Ocean 184 H6
Part of St Helena, Ascension and Tristan da Cunha

Aschaffenburg Germany 63 J5
Ascheberg Germany 63 H3
Aschersleben Germany 63 L3
Ascoli Piceno Italy 68 E3
Asculum Italy see Ascoli Piceno
Asculum Picenum Italy see Ascoli Piceno
Ascutney VT U.S.A. 165 I2
Āseb Eritrea see Assab
Åseda Sweden 55 I8
Āsele Sweden 54 J4
Asenovgrad Bulg. 69 K3
Aşfar, Jabal al mt. Jordan 107 C3
Aşfar, Tall al hill Syria 107 C3

▶Aşgabat Turkm. 110 E2
Capital of Turkmenistan.

Asha Rus. Fed. 51 R5
Ashahi-dake mt. Japan 92 D2
Ashburn GA U.S.A. 163 D6
Ashburton watercourse Australia 134 A5
Ashburton N.Z. 139 C6
Ashburton Range hills Australia 134 F4
Ashdod Israel 107 B4
Ashdown AR U.S.A. 161 E5
Asheboro NC U.S.A. 162 E5
Asher OK U.S.A. 161 D5
Ashern Canada 151 L5
Asheville NC U.S.A. 162 D5
Asheweig r. Canada 152 D3
Ashford Australia 138 E2
Ashford U.K. 59 H7
Ash Fork AZ U.S.A. 159 G4
Ashgabat Turkm. see Aşgabat
Ashibetsu Japan 90 F4
Ashigawa Japan 93 E3
Ashikaga Japan 93 F2
Ashington U.K. 58 F3
Ashino-ko l. Japan 93 F3
Ashio Japan 93 F2
Ashio-sanchi mts Japan 93 F2
Ashiwada Japan 93 E3
Ashiya Japan 92 B4
Ashizuri-misaki pt Japan 91 D6
Ashkelon Israel see Ashqelon
Ashkhabad Turkm. see Aşgabat
Ashkum IL U.S.A. 164 B3
Ashkun reg. Afgh. 111 H3
Ashland AL U.S.A. 163 C5
Ashland ME U.S.A. 162 G2
Ashland NH U.S.A. 165 J2
Ashland OH U.S.A. 164 D3
Ashland OR U.S.A. 156 C4
Ashland VA U.S.A. 165 G5
Ashland WI U.S.A. 160 F2
Ashland City TN U.S.A. 164 B5
Ashley Australia 138 D2
Ashley MI U.S.A. 164 C2
Ashley ND U.S.A. 160 D2

▶Ashmore and Cartier Islands terr. Australia 134 C3
Australian External Territory.

Ashmore Reef Australia 134 C3
Ashmore Reefs Australia 136 D1
Ashmyany Belarus 55 N9
Ashqelon Israel 107 B4
Ash Shabakah Iraq 113 F5
Ash Shaddādah Syria 113 F3
Ash Shallūfah Egypt 107 A4
Ash Sham Syria see Damascus
Ash Shanāfīyah Iraq 113 G5
Ash Shaqīq well Saudi Arabia 113 F5
Ash Sharāh mts Jordan 107 B4
Ash Sharawrah Saudi Arabia 108 G6
Ash Shāriqah U.A.E. see Sharjah
Ash Sharqāṭ Iraq 113 F4
Ash Shaṭrah Iraq 113 G5
Ash Shaṭṭ Egypt 107 A5
Ash Shawbak Jordan 107 B4
Ash Shaybānī well Saudi Arabia 113 F5
Ash Shaykh Ibrāhīm Syria 107 D2
Ash Shiblīyāt hill Saudi Arabia 107 C5
Ash Shiḥr Yemen 108 G7
Ash Shu'aybah Saudi Arabia 113 F6
Ash Shu'bah Saudi Arabia 108 F4
Ash Shurayf Saudi Arabia see Khaybar
Ashta India 104 D5
Ashtabula OH U.S.A. 164 E3
Ashtarak Armenia 113 G2
Ashti Mahar. India 104 D5
Ashti Mahar. India 106 B2
Ashti Mahar. India 106 C2
Ashtīān Iran 110 C3
Ashton S. Africa 124 E7
Ashton ID U.S.A. 156 F3
Ashton-under-Lyne U.K. 58 E5
Ashuanipi r. Canada 153 I3
Ashuanipi Lake Canada 153 I3
Ashur Iraq see Ash Sharqāṭ
Ashville AL U.S.A. 163 C5
Ashwaubenon WI U.S.A. 164 A1
Asi r. Asia 112 E3 see 'Āṣī, Nahr al
'Āṣī r. Lebanon/Syria see Orontes
'Āṣī, Nahr al r. Asia 112 E3
also known as Asi or Orontes
Āsīā Bak Iran 110 C3
Asid Gulf Masbate Phil. 82 C3
Asientos Mex. 166 E4
Asifabad India 106 C2
Asika India 106 E2
Asilah Morocco 67 C6
Asinara, Golfo dell' b. Sardinia Italy 68 C4
Asino Rus. Fed. 76 J4
Asipovichy Belarus 53 F5
Asīr Iran 110 D5
'Asīr reg. Saudi Arabia 108 F5
Asisium Italy see Assisi
Askale Pak. 104 C2
Aşkale Turkey 113 F3
Asker Norway 55 G7
Askersund Sweden 55 I7
Askim Norway 55 G7
Askī Mawṣil Iraq 113 F3
Askino Rus. Fed. 51 R4
Askival hill U.K. 60 C4
Asl Egypt see 'Asal
Aslanköy r. Turkey 107 B1
Asmār reg. Afgh. 111 H3

▶Asmara Eritrea 108 E6
Capital of Eritrea.

Āsmera Eritrea see Asmara
Åsnen l. Sweden 55 I8
Asō Japan 93 G3
Aso-Kuju Kokuritsu-kōen Japan 91 C6
Asonli India 96 B3
Asop India 104 C4
Asori Indon. 81 J7
Āsosa Eth. 122 D2
Asotin WA U.S.A. 156 D3
Aspang-Markt Austria 57 P7
Aspara Kazakh. 98 A4
Aspatria U.K. 58 D4
Aspen CO U.S.A. 156 G5
Asperg Germany 63 J6
Aspermont TX U.S.A. 161 C5
Aspiring, Mount N.Z. 139 B7
Aspro, Cape Cyprus 107 A2
Aspromonte, Parco Nazionale dell' nat. park Italy 68 F5
Aspron, Cape Cyprus see Aspro, Cape
Aspur India 111 I6
Asquith Canada 151 J4
As Sa'an Syria 107 C2
Assab Eritrea 108 F7
As Sabsab well Saudi Arabia 110 C5
Assad, Lake resr Syria see Asad, Buḥayrat al
Aş Şadr U.A.E. 110 D5
Aş Şafā lava field Syria 107 C3
Aş Şafāqis Tunisia see Sfax
Aş Şaff Egypt 112 C5
As Safīrah Syria 107 C1
Aş Şaḥrā' al Gharbīyah des. Egypt see Western Desert
Aş Şaḥrā' ash Sharqīyah des. Egypt see Eastern Desert
Assake-Audan, Vpadina depr. Kazakh./Uzbek. 113 J2
'Assal, Lac l. Djibouti see Assal, Lake

▶Assal, Lake Djibouti 108 F7
Lowest point in Africa.

Aş Şāliḥīyah Syria 113 F4
As Sallūm Egypt 112 B5
As Salmān Iraq 113 G5
As Salṭ Jordan 107 B3
Assam state India 105 G4
Assamakka Niger 120 D3
As Samāwah Iraq 113 G5
As Samrā' Jordan 107 C3
Aş Şanām reg. Saudi Arabia 108 H5
As Sarīr reg. Libya 121 F2
Assateague Island MD U.S.A. 165 H4
As Sawādah reg. Saudi Arabia 110 B6
Assayeta Eth. see Āsayita
As Sayḥ Saudi Arabia 110 B6
Assen Neth. 62 G1
Assenede Belgium 62 D3
Assesse Belgium 62 F4
As Sidrah Libya 121 E1
As Sīfah Oman 110 E6
Assigny, Lac l. Canada 153 I3
As Sikak Saudi Arabia 110 C5
Assiniboia Canada 151 J5
Assiniboine r. Canada 151 L5
Assiniboine, Mount Canada 146 G4
Assis Brazil 179 A3
Assisi Italy 68 E3
Aßlar Germany 63 I4
Aş Şubayḥīyah Kuwait 110 B4
Aş Şufayrī well Saudi Arabia 110 B4
As Sukhnah Syria 107 D2
As Sulaymī Saudi Arabia 108 F4
Aş Şulb reg. Saudi Arabia 110 C5
Aş Şummān plat. Saudi Arabia 110 B5
Aş Şummān plat. Saudi Arabia 110 C6
As Sūq Saudi Arabia 108 F5
As Sūrīyah country Asia see Syria
Aş Şuwar Syria 113 F4
As Suwaydā' Syria 107 C3
As Suways Egypt see Suez
As Suways governorate Egypt 107 A4
Assynt, Loch l. U.K. 60 D2
Astacus Turkey see İzmit
Astakida i. Greece 69 L7
Astakos Greece 69 I5
Astalu Island Pak. see Astola Island

▶Astana Kazakh. 102 D1
Capital of Kazakhstan.

Astaneh Iran 110 C2
Astara Azer. 113 H3
Āstārā Iran 108 G2
Asterabad Iran see Gorgān
Asti Italy 68 C2
Astillero Peru 176 E6
Astin Tag mts China see Altun Shan
Astipálaia i. Greece see Astypalaia
Astola Island Pak. 111 F5
Astor Pak. 99 A6
Astor r. Pak. 111 I3
Astorga Spain 67 C2
Astoria OR U.S.A. 156 C3
Åstorp Sweden 55 H8
Astrabad Iran see Gorgān
Astrakhan' Rus. Fed. 53 K7
Astrakhan' Bazar Azer. see Cälilabad
Astravyets Belarus 55 N9
Astrida Rwanda see Butare
Asturias aut. comm. Spain 67 C2
Asturias, Principado de aut. comm. Spain see Asturias
Asturica Augusta Spain see Astorga
Astypalaia i. Greece 69 L6
Asubulak Kazakh. 98 C2
Asuka Japan 92 B4
Asuke Japan 92 D3
Asuncion i. N. Mariana Is 81 L3

▶Asunción Para. 178 E3
Capital of Paraguay.

Asuwa-gawa r. Japan 92 C2
Aswad Oman 110 E5
Aswân Egypt see Aswān
Aswān Egypt 108 D5
Asyût Egypt see Asyūṭ
Asyūṭ Egypt 112 C6
Ata i. Tonga 133 I4
Atacama, Desierto de des. Chile see Atacama Desert
Atacama, Salar de salt flat Chile 178 C2

▶Atacama Desert Chile 178 C3
Driest place in the world.

Atafu atoll Tokelau 133 I2
Atafu i. Tokelau 186 I6
Atago-san hill Japan 92 B3
Atago-yama hill Japan 93 F3
'Aṭā'iṭah, Jabal al mt. Jordan 107 B4
Atakent Turkey 107 B1
Atakpamé Togo 120 D4
Atalándi Greece see Atalanti
Atalanti Greece 69 J5
Atalaya Panama 166 [inset] J7
Atalaya Peru 176 D6
Ataléia Brazil 179 C2
Atambua Indon. 134 D2
Atami Japan 93 F3
Atamyrat Turkm. 111 G2
Ataniya Turkey see Adana
Atanur India 106 C2
Atapupu Timor Indon. 83 C5
'Ataq Yemen 108 G7
Atâr Mauritania 120 B2
Atari Pak. 111 I4
Atascadero CA U.S.A. 158 C4
Ātashān Iran 110 D3
Atasu Kazakh. 102 D2
Atatkan He r. China 99 E5
Ataúro, Ilha de i. East Timor 83 C5
Atáviros mt. Greece see Attavyros
Atayurt Turkey 107 A1
Atbara Sudan 108 D6
Atbara r. Sudan 108 D6
Atbasar Kazakh. 102 C1
At-Bashy Kyrg. 98 A4
Atchafalaya Bay LA U.S.A. 167 H2
Atchison KS U.S.A. 160 E4
Atchueelinguk r. AK U.S.A. 148 G3
Atebubu Ghana 120 C4
Atema-yama mt. Japan 93 E1
Ateransk Kazakh. see Atyrau
Atessa Italy 68 F3
Ath Belgium 62 D4
Athabasca r. Canada 151 I3
Athabasca, Lake Canada 151 I3
Athalia OH U.S.A. 164 D4
'Athāmīn, Birkat al well Iraq 110 A4
Atharan Hazari Pak. 111 I4
Athboy Ireland 61 F4
Athenae Greece see Athens
Athenry Ireland 61 D4
Athens Canada 165 H1

▶Athens Greece 69 J6
Capital of Greece.

Athens AL U.S.A. 163 C5
Athens GA U.S.A. 163 D5
Athens MI U.S.A. 164 C2
Athens OH U.S.A. 164 D4
Athens PA U.S.A. 165 G3
Athens TN U.S.A. 162 C5
Athens TX U.S.A. 161 E5
Atherstone U.K. 59 F6
Atherton Australia 136 D3
Athies France 62 C5
Athina Greece see Athens
Athínai Greece see Athens
Athleague Ireland 61 D4
Athlone Ireland 61 E4
Athnā', Wādī al watercourse Jordan 107 D3
Athni India 106 B2
Athol N.Z. 139 B7
Athol MA U.S.A. 165 I2
Atholl, Forest of reg. U.K. 60 E4
Athos mt. Greece 69 K4
Ath Thamad Egypt 107 B5
Ath Thāyat mt. Saudi Arabia 107 C5
Ath Thumāmī well Saudi Arabia 110 B5
Athy Ireland 61 F5
Ati Chad 121 E3
Aṭīābād Iran 110 E3
Atico Peru 176 D7
Atigun Pass AK U.S.A. 149 J1
Atikameg Canada 150 H4
Atikameg r. Canada 152 E3
Atik Lake Canada 151 M4
Atikokan Canada 147 I5
Atikonak Lake Canada 153 I3
Atimonan Luzon Phil. 82 C3
Atiquizaya El Salvador 167 H6
Ātish Khānah, Kōh-e hill Afgh. 111 F3
Atitlán Guat. 167 H6
Atitlán, Parque Nacional nat. park Guat. 167 H6
Atjeh admin. dist. Indon. see Aceh
Atka Rus. Fed. 77 Q3
Atka AK U.S.A. 148 [inset] D5
Atka Island AK U.S.A. 148 [inset] D5
Atkarsk Rus. Fed. 53 J6
Atkinson Point pt Canada 149 O1
Atkri Papua Indon. 83 D3

▶Atlanta GA U.S.A. 163 C5
Capital of Georgia.

Atlanta IN U.S.A. 164 B3
Atlanta MI U.S.A. 164 D1
Atlantic IA U.S.A. 160 E3
Atlantic NC U.S.A. 163 E5
Atlantic City NJ U.S.A. 165 H4
Atlantic-Indian-Antarctic Basin sea feature S. Atlantic Ocean 184 H10
Atlantic-Indian Ridge sea feature Southern Ocean 184 H9

▶Atlantic Ocean 184
2nd largest ocean in the world.

Atlantic Peak WY U.S.A. 156 F4
Atlantis S. Africa 124 D7
Atlas Bogd mt. Mongolia 94 D3
Atlas Méditerranéen mts Alg. see Atlas Tellien
Atlas Mountains Africa 64 C5
Atlas Saharien mts Alg. 64 E5
Atlas Tellien mts Alg. 67 H6
Atlin Lake Canada 149 N4
Atlixco Mex. 167 F5
Atmakur India 106 C3
Atmautluak AK U.S.A. 148 G3
Atmore AL U.S.A. 163 C6
Atocha Bol. 176 E8
Atoka OK U.S.A. 161 D5
Atotonilco el Alto Mex. 166 E4
Atouat mt. Laos 86 D3
Atouila, Erg des. Mali 120 C2
Atoyac de Álvarez Mex. 167 E5
Atqan China see Aqqan
Atqasuk AK U.S.A. 148 H1
Atrak r. Iran/Turkm. see Atrek
Atrato r. Col. 176 C2
Atrek r. Iran/Turkm. 110 D2
also known as Atrak, alt. Etrek
Atropatene country Asia see Azerbaijan
Atsonupuri vol. Rus. Fed. 90 G3
Atsugi Japan 93 F3
Atsumi Japan 92 D4
Atsumi-hantō pen. Japan 92 D4
Aṭ Ṭafīlah Jordan 107 B4
Aṭ Ṭā'if Saudi Arabia 108 F5
Attalea Turkey see Antalya
Attalia Turkey see Antalya
At Tamīmī Libya 112 A4
Attapu Laos 86 D4
Attavyros mt. Greece 69 L6
Attawapiskat Canada 152 E3
Attawapiskat r. Canada 152 E3
Attawapiskat Lake Canada 152 D3
Aṭ Ṭawīl mts Saudi Arabia 113 E5
At Taysīyah plat. Saudi Arabia 113 F5
Attendorn Germany 63 H3
Attersee l. Austria 57 N7
Attica IN U.S.A. 164 B3
Attica NY U.S.A. 165 F2
Attica OH U.S.A. 164 D3
Attigny France 62 E5
Attikamagen Lake Canada 153 I3
Attila Line Cyprus 107 A2
Attleborough U.K. 59 I6
Attopeu Laos see Attapu
Attu Greenland 147 M3
Attu AK U.S.A. 148 [inset] A5
Aṭ Ṭubayq reg. Saudi Arabia 107 C5

▶Attu Island AK U.S.A. 148 [inset] A5
Most westerly point of North America.

At Tūnisīyah country Africa see Tunisia
Aṭ Ṭūr Egypt 112 D5
Attur India 106 C4
Aṭ Ṭuwayyah well Saudi Arabia 113 F6
Atuk Mountain hill AK U.S.A. 148 E3
Åtvidaberg Sweden 55 I7
Atwari Bangl. 99 E8
Atwater CA U.S.A. 158 C3
Atwood KS U.S.A. 160 C4
Atwood Lake OH U.S.A. 164 E3
Atyashevo Rus. Fed. 53 J5
Atyrau Kazakh. 100 E2
Atyraū admin. div. Kazakh. see Atyrauskaya Oblast'
Atyrau Oblast admin. div. Kazakh. see Atyrauskaya Oblast'
Atyrauskaya Oblast' admin. div. Kazakh. 51 Q6
Aua Island P.N.G. 81 K7
Aub Germany 63 K5
Aubagne France 66 G5
Aubange Belgium 62 F5
Aubarede Point Luzon Phil. 82 C2
Aubenas France 66 G4
Aubergenville France 62 B6
Auboué France 62 F5
Aubrey Cliffs mts AZ U.S.A. 159 G4
Aubry Lake Canada 149 P2
Auburn r. Australia 137 E5
Auburn Canada 164 E2
Auburn AL U.S.A. 163 C5
Auburn CA U.S.A. 158 C2
Auburn IN U.S.A. 164 C3
Auburn KY U.S.A. 164 B5
Auburn ME U.S.A. 165 J1
Auburn NE U.S.A. 160 E3
Auburn NY U.S.A. 165 G2
Auburn Range hills Australia 136 E5
Aubusson France 66 F4
Auch France 66 E5
Auche Myanmar 86 B1
Auchterarder U.K. 60 F4

▶Auckland N.Z. 139 E3
5th most populous city in Oceania.

Auckland Islands N.Z. 133 G7
Auden Canada 152 D4
Audenarde Belgium see Oudenaarde
Audo mts Eth. 122 E3
Audo Range mts Eth. see Audo
Audruicq France 62 C4
Audubon IA U.S.A. 160 E3
Aue Germany 63 M4
Auerbach Germany 63 M4
Auerbach in der Oberpfalz Germany 63 L5
Auersberg mt. Germany 63 M4
Auezov Kazakh. 98 C2
Augathella Australia 137 D5
Augher U.K. 61 E3
Aughnacloy U.K. 61 F3
Aughrim Ireland 61 F5
Augrabies S. Africa 124 E5
Augrabies Falls S. Africa 124 E5
Augrabies Falls National Park S. Africa 124 E5
Au Gres MI U.S.A. 164 D1
Augsburg Germany 57 M6
Augusta Australia 135 A8
Augusta Sicily Italy 68 F6
Augusta AR U.S.A. 161 F5
Augusta GA U.S.A. 163 D5
Augusta KY U.S.A. 164 C4

▶Augusta ME U.S.A. 165 K1
Capital of Maine.

Augusta MT U.S.A. 156 E3
Augusta Auscorum France see Auch
Augusta Taurinorum Italy see Turin
Augusta Treverorum Germany see Trier
Augusta Vindelicorum Germany see Augsburg
Augustine Island AK U.S.A. 148 I4
Augusto de Lima Brazil 179 B2
Augustus, Mount Australia 135 B6
Auke Bay AK U.S.A. 149 N4
Aukštaitijos nacionalinis parkas nat. park Lith. 55 O9
Aulavik National Park Canada 146 G2
Auld, Lake salt flat Australia 134 C5
Auliye Ata Kazakh. see Taraz
Aulnoye-Aymeries France 62 D4
Aulon Albania see Vlorë
Aulong i. Palau 82 [inset]
Ault France 62 B4
Auluptagel i. Palau 82 [inset]
Aumale Alg. see Sour el Ghozlane
Aumale France 62 B5
Aundh India 106 B2
Aundhi India 106 D1
Aunglan Myanmar 86 A3
Auob watercourse Namibia/S. Africa 124 E4
Aupaluk Canada 153 H2
Auponhia Maluku Indon. 83 C3
Aur i. Malaysia 84 D2
Aura Fin. 55 M6
Auraiya India 104 D4
Aurangabad Bihar India 105 F4
Aurangabad Mahar. India 106 B2
Aure r. France 59 F9
Aurich Germany 63 H1
Aurigny i. Channel Is see Alderney
Aurilândia Brazil 179 A2
Aurillac France 66 F4
Aurkuning Kalimantan Indon. 85 E3
Aurora Mindanao Phil. 82 C5
Aurora CO U.S.A. 156 G5
Aurora IL U.S.A. 164 A3
Aurora MO U.S.A. 161 E4
Aurora NE U.S.A. 160 D3

Aurora *UT* U.S.A. **159** H2
Aurora Island Vanuatu *see* **Maéwo**
Aurukun Australia **136** C2
Aus Namibia **124** C4
Au Sable *MI* U.S.A. **164** D1
Au Sable Point *MI* U.S.A. **164** D1
Auskerry *i.* U.K. **60** G1
Austin *IN* U.S.A. **164** C4
Austin *MN* U.S.A. **160** E3
Austin *NV* U.S.A. **158** E2

▶**Austin** *TX* U.S.A. **161** D6
Capital of Texas.

Austin, Lake *salt flat* Australia **135** B6
Austintown *OH* U.S.A. **164** E3
Austral Downs Australia **136** B4
Australes, Îles *is* Fr. Polynesia *see* **Tubuai Islands**

▶**Australia** *country* Oceania **132** C4
Largest and most populous country in Oceania and 6th largest in the world.

Australian-Antarctic Basin *sea feature* S. Atlantic Ocean **186** C9
Australian Antarctic Territory *reg.* Antarctica **188** G2
Australian Capital Territory *admin. div.* Australia **138** D5
Australian Convict Sites *tourist site* Australia **137** D9
Austria *country* Europe **57** N7
Austvågøy *i.* Norway **54** I2
Autazes Brazil **177** G4
Autesiodorum France *see* **Auxerre**
Authie *r.* France **62** B4
Autlán Mex. **166** D5
Autti Fin. **54** O3
Auvergne *reg.* France **66** F4
Auvergne, Monts d' *mts* France **66** F4
Auxerre France **66** F3
Auxi-le-Château France **62** C4
Auxonne France **66** G3
Auyuittuq National Park Canada **147** L3
Auzangate, Nevado *mt.* Peru **176** D6
Ava *MO* U.S.A. **161** E4
Ava *NY* U.S.A. **165** H2
Avalik *r.* *AK* U.S.A. **148** H1
Avallon France **66** F3
Avalon *CA* U.S.A. **158** D5
Avalon Peninsula Canada **153** L5
Ávalos Mex. **167** E3
Avān Iran **113** G3
Avarau *atoll* Cook Is *see* **Palmerston**
Avaré Brazil **179** A3
Avaricum France *see* **Bourges**

▶**Avarua** Cook Is **187** J7
Capital of the Cook Islands, on Rarotonga.

Avawam *KY* U.S.A. **164** D5
Āvāz Iran **111** F3
Aveiro Port. **67** B3
Aveiro, Ria de *est.* Port. **67** B3
Āvej Iran **110** C3
Avellino Italy **68** F4
Avenal *CA* U.S.A. **158** C3
Avenhorn Neth. **62** E2
Avenio France *see* **Avignon**
Aversa Italy **68** F4
Avesnes-sur-Helpe France **62** D4
Avesta Sweden **55** J6
Aveyron *r.* France **66** E4
Avezzano Italy **68** E3
Aviemore U.K. **60** F3
Avignon France **66** G5
Ávila Spain **67** D3
Avilés Spain **67** D2
Avion France **62** C4
Avis *PA* U.S.A. **165** G3
Avlama Dağı *mt.* Turkey **107** A1
Avlona Albania *see* **Vlorë**
Avnyugskiy Rus. Fed. **52** J3
Avoca Australia **138** A6
Avoca *r.* Australia **138** A5
Avoca Ireland **61** F5
Avoca *IA* U.S.A. **160** E3
Avoca *NY* U.S.A. **165** G2
Avola *Sicily* Italy **68** F6
Avon *r.* *England* U.K. **59** E6
Avon *r.* *England* U.K. **59** E7
Avon *r.* *England* U.K. **59** F8
Avon *r.* *Scotland* U.K. **60** F3
Avon *NY* U.S.A. **165** G2
Avondale *AZ* U.S.A. **159** G5
Avonmore *r.* Ireland **61** F5
Avonmore *PA* U.S.A. **164** F3
Avonmouth U.K. **59** E7
Avranches France **66** D2
Avre *r.* France **62** C5
Avsuyu Turkey **107** C1
Avuavu Solomon Is **133** G2
Avveel Fin. *see* **Ivalo**
Avvil Fin. *see* **Ivalo**
A'waj *r.* Syria **107** B3
Awaji Japan **92** B4
Awaji-shima *i.* Japan **92** A4
Awakino N.Z. **139** E4
'Awālī Bahrain **110** C5
Awang *Lombok* Indon. **85** G5
Awano Japan **93** F2
Awanui N.Z. **139** D2
Awara Japan **92** C2
Awarawar, Tanjung *pt* Indon. **85** F4
Āwarē Eth. **122** E3
'Awāriḍ, Wādī al *watercourse* Syria **107** D2
Awarua Point N.Z. **139** B7
Āwash Eth. **122** E3
Āwash *r.* Eth. **122** E2
Awa-shima *i.* Japan **91** E5
Āwash National Park Eth. **122** D3
Awasib Mountains Namibia **124** B3
Awat China **98** C4
Awatere *r.* N.Z. **139** E5
Awbārī Libya **120** E2
Awbeg *r.* Ireland **61** D5
'Awdah *well* Saudi Arabia **110** C6
'Awdah, Hawr al *imp. l.* Iraq **113** G5
Aw Dheegle Somalia **121** H4
Awe, Loch *l.* U.K. **60** D4
Aweil South Sudan **121** F4
Awka Nigeria **120** D4
Awkal Afgh. **111** F3
Awo *r.* Indon. **83** B3
Awserd W. Sahara **120** B2
Awu *vol.* Indon. **83** C2
Awuna *r.* *AK* U.S.A. **148** I1
Axe *r.* *England* U.K. **59** D8
Axe *r.* *England* U.K. **59** E7
Axedale Australia **138** B6
Axel Heiberg Glacier Antarctica **188** I1
Axel Heiberg Island Canada **147** I2
Axim Ghana **120** C4
Axminster U.K. **59** E8
Axum Eth. *see* **Āksum**
Ay France **62** E5
Ay Kazakh. **98** C3
Ayabe Japan **92** B3
Ayachi, Jbel *mt.* Morocco **64** D5
Ayacucho Arg. **178** E5
Ayacucho Peru **176** D6
Ayadaw Myanmar **86** A2
Ayagoz Kazakh. **102** F2
Ayagoz *watercourse* Kazakh. **98** B3
Ayaguz Kazakh. *see* **Ayagoz**
Ayakkum Hu *salt l.* China **99** E5
Ayaköz Kazakh. *see* **Ayagoz**
Ayakulik *AK* U.S.A. **148** I4
Ayama Japan **92** C4
Ayan Rus. Fed. **77** O4
Ayancık Turkey **112** D2
Ayang N. Korea **91** B5
Ayaş Turkey **112** D2
Ayase Japan **93** F3
Āybak Afgh. **111** H2
Aybas Kazakh. **53** K7
Aydar *r.* Ukr. **53** H6
Aydarko'l ko'li *l.* Uzbek. **102** C3
Aydere Turkm. **110** E2
Aydın Turkey **69** L6
Aydıncık Turkey **107** A1
Aydın Dağları *mts* Turkey **69** L5
Aydingkol Hu *marsh* China **98** E4
Aýdyň Turkm. **110** D2
Āyelu Terara *vol.* Eth. **108** F7
Ayer *MA* U.S.A. **165** J2
Ayers Rock *hill* Australia *see* **Uluṟu**
Ayeyarwady *r.* Myanmar *see* **Irrawaddy**
Aygulakskiy Khrebet *mts* Rus. Fed. **98** D2
Aygyrzhal Kazakh. **98** C2
Ayila Ri'gyü *mts* China **99** B6
Áyios Dhimítrios Greece *see* **Agios Dimitrios**
Áyios Evstrátios *i.* Greece *see* **Agios Efstratios**
Áyios Nikólaos Greece *see* **Agios Nikolaos**
Áyios Yeóryios *i.* Greece *see* **Agios Georgios**
Aykol China **98** C4
Aylesbury N.Z. **139** D6
Aylesbury U.K. **59** G7
Aylett *VA* U.S.A. **165** G5
Ayllón Spain **67** E3
Aylmer *Ont.* Canada **164** E2
Aylmer *Que.* Canada **165** H1
Aylmer Lake Canada **151** I1
Aymangala India **106** C3
Aynabulak Kazakh. **98** B3
'Ayn al 'Abd *well* Saudi Arabia **110** C4
'Ayn al Baiḍā' Saudi Arabia **107** C4
'Ayn al Bayḍā' *well* Syria **107** C2
'Ayn al Ghazalah *well* Libya **112** A4
'Ayn al Maqfī *spring* Egypt **112** C6
'Ayn Dāllah *spring* Egypt **112** B6
Ayní Tajik. **111** H2
'Ayn 'Īsá Syria **107** D1
'Ayn Tabaghbugh *spring* Egypt **112** B5
'Ayn Tumayrah *spring* Egypt **112** B5
'Ayn Zaytūn Egypt **112** B5
Ayod South Sudan **108** D8
Ayon, Ostrov *i.* Rus. Fed. **77** R3
'Ayoûn el 'Atroûs Mauritania **120** C3
Ayr Australia **136** D3
Ayr Canada **164** E2
Ayr U.K. **60** E5
Ayr *r.* U.K. **60** E5
Ayr, Point of U.K. **58** D5
Ayrag Nuur *salt l.* Mongolia **94** C1
Ayrancı Turkey **112** D3
Ayre, Point of Isle of Man **58** C4
Aytos Bulg. **69** L3
Ayu *i.* *Papua* Indon. **83** D2
Ayu, Kepulauan *atoll* *Papua* Indon. **83** D2
A Yun Pa Vietnam **87** E4
Ayuthia Thai. *see* **Ayutthaya**
Ayutla *Guerrero* Mex. **167** F5
Ayutla *Jalisco* Mex. **166** D4
Ayutthaya Thai. **87** C4
Ayvacık Turkey **69** L5
Ayvalı Turkey **112** E3
Ayvalık Turkey **69** L5
Azai Japan **92** C3
Azak Rus. Fed. *see* **Azov**
Azalia *IN* U.S.A. **164** C4
Azamgarh India **105** E4
Azania *area* Somalia **122** E3
Azaouād *reg.* Mali **120** C3
Azaouagh, Vallée de *watercourse* Mali/Niger **120** D3
Azaran Iran *see* **Hashtrud**
Azärbaycan *country* Asia *see* **Azerbaijan**
Azărbayjan *country* Asia *see* **Azerbaijan**
Azare Nigeria **120** E3
A'zāz Syria **107** C1
Azbine *mts* Niger *see* **L'Aïr, Massif de**
Azdavay Turkey **112** D2
Azerbaijan *country* Asia **113** G2
Azerbaydzhanskaya S.S.R. *country* Asia *see* **Azerbaijan**
Azhikode India **106** B4
Aziscohos Lake *ME* U.S.A. **165** J1
'Azīzābād Iran **110** E4
Aziziye Turkey *see* **Pınarbaşı**
Azogues Ecuador **176** C4

▶**Azores** *terr.* N. Atlantic Ocean **184** G3
Autonomous Region of Portugal.

Azores-Biscay Rise *sea feature* N. Atlantic Ocean **184** G3
Azotus Israel *see* **Ashdod**
Azov Rus. Fed. **53** H7
Azov, Sea of Rus. Fed./Ukr. **53** H7
Azovs'ke More *sea* Rus. Fed./Ukr. *see* **Azov, Sea of**
Azovskoye More *sea* Rus. Fed./Ukr. *see* **Azov, Sea of**
Azraq, Bahr el *r.* Eth./Sudan **108** D6 *see* **Blue Nile**
Azraq ash Shīshān Jordan **107** C4
Azrou Morocco **64** C5
Aztec *NM* U.S.A. **159** I3
Azuaga Spain **67** D4
Azuchi Japan **92** C3
Azuero, Península de *pen.* Panama **166** [inset] J8
Azul *r.* Mex. **167** H5
Azul, Cordillera *mts* Peru **176** C5
Azul Meambar, Parque Nacional *nat. park* Hond. **166** [inset] I6
Azuma *Gunma* Japan **93** F2
Azuma *Gunma* Japan **93** F2
Azuma *Ibaraki* Japan **93** G3
Azuma-san *vol.* Japan **91** F5
Azumaya-san *mt.* Japan **93** E2
Azumi Japan **93** D2
Azusa-ko *resr* Japan **92** D2
'Azza Gaza *see* **Gaza**
Azzaba Alg. **68** B6
Aẓ Ẓahrān Saudi Arabia *see* **Dhahran**
Az Zaqāzīq Egypt **112** C5
Az Zarbah Syria **107** C1
Az Zarqā' Jordan **107** C3
Az Zawr, Ra's *pt* Saudi Arabia **113** H6
Aẓ Ẓa'yin *town* Qatar *see* **Al Dayyen**
Azzeffāl *hills* Mauritania/W. Sahara **120** B2
Az Zubayr Iraq **113** G5
Az Zuqur *i.* Yemen **108** F7

B

Ba, Sông *r.* Vietnam **87** E4
Baa Indon. **83** B5
Baabda Lebanon **107** B3
Baai *r.* Indon. **85** G2
Ba'albek Lebanon **107** C2
Ba'al Ḥazor *mt.* West Bank **107** B4
Baan Baa Australia **138** D3
Baardheere Somalia **122** E3
Baatsagaan Mongolia **94** D2
Bab India **104** D4
Bābā, Kōh-e *mts* Afgh. **111** H3
Baba Burnu *pt* Turkey **69** L5
Babadağ *mt.* Azer. **113** H2
Babadag Romania **69** M2
Babadurmaz Turkm. **110** E2
Babaeski Turkey **69** L4
Babahoyo Ecuador **176** C4
Babai India **104** D5
Babai *r.* Nepal **105** E3
Babak Phil. **82** D5
Bābā Kalān Iran **110** C4
Bāb al Mandab *strait* Africa/Asia **108** F7
Babana *Sulawesi Barat* Indon. **83** A3
Babanusa Sudan **108** C7
Babao *Qinghai* China *see* **Qilian**
Babao *Yunnan* China **96** E4
Babar *i.* *Maluku* Indon. **83** D4
Babar, Kepulauan *is* *Maluku* Indon. **83** D4
Babati Tanz. **123** D4
Babau *Timor* Indon. **83** B5
Babayevo Rus. Fed. **52** G4
Babayurt Rus. Fed. **113** G2
Babbage *r.* Canada **149** M1
Bābbdā Lebanon *see* **Baabda**
Babeldaob *i.* Palau **82** [inset]
Bab el Mandeb, Straits of Africa/Asia *see* **Bāb al Mandab**
Babelthuap *i.* Palau *see* **Babeldaob**
Babi, Pulau *i.* Indon. **84** B2
Babian Jiang *r.* China **96** D4
Babine *r.* Canada **150** E4
Babine Lake Canada **150** E4
Babine Range *mts* Canada **150** E4
Bābol Iran **110** D2
Bābol Sar Iran **110** D2
Babongo Cameroon **121** E4
Baboon Point S. Africa **124** D7
Baboua Cent. Afr. Rep. **122** B3
Babruysk Belarus **53** F5
Babstovo Rus. Fed. **90** D2
Babu China *see* **Hezhou**
Babuhri India **104** B4
Babusar Pass Pak. **111** I3
Babuyan *Palawan* Phil. **82** B4
Babuyan *i.* Phil. **82** C2
Babuyan Channel Phil. **82** C2
Babuyan Islands Phil. **82** C2
Bacaadweyn Somalia **122** E3
Bacabáchi Mex. **166** C3
Bacabal Brazil **177** J4
Bacalar Mex. **167** H5
Bacalar Chico, Boca *sea chan.* Mex. **167** I5
Bacan *i.* *Maluku* Indon. **83** C3
Bacang China **94** E5
Bacanora Mex. **166** C2
Bacarra *Luzon* Phil. **82** C2
Bacău Romania **69** L1
Baccaro Point Canada **153** I6
Bắc Giang Vietnam **86** D2
Bacha China **90** D2
Bach Ice Shelf Antarctica **188** L2
Bach Long Vi, Đao *i.* Vietnam **86** D2
Bachu China **98** B5
Bachuan China *see* **Tongliang**
Back *r.* Australia **136** C3
Back *r.* Canada **151** M1
Bačka Palanka Serbia **69** H2
Backbone Mountain *MD* U.S.A. **164** F4
Backbone Ranges *mts* Canada **149** O3
Backe Sweden **54** J5
Backstairs Passage Australia **137** B7
Bắc Liêu Vietnam **87** D5
Bắc Ninh Vietnam **86** D2
Bacnotan *Luzon* Phil. **82** C2
Baco, Mount *Mindoro* Phil. **82** C3
Bacoachi Mex. **166** C2
Bacoachi *watercourse* Mex. **157** F7
Bacobampo Mex. **166** C3
Bacolod *Negros* Phil. **82** C4
Bacqueville, Lac *l.* Canada **152** G2
Bacqueville-en-Caux France **59** H9
Bacubirito Mex. **166** D3
Baculin Bay *Mindanao* Phil. **82** D5
Bada China *see* **Xilin**
Bada *mt.* Eth. **122** D3
Bada *i.* Myanmar **87** B5
Badabaýhan Turkm. **111** F2
Bad Abbach Germany **63** M6
Badain Jaran China **94** E4
Badain Jaran Shamo *des.* China **94** E3
Badajoz Spain **67** C4
Badami India **106** B3
Badampaharh India **105** F5
Badanah Saudi Arabia **113** F5
Badaojiang China *see* **Baishan**
Badarpur India **105** H4
Badas Brunei **85** F1
Badas, Kepulauan *is* Indon. **84** D2
Badaun India *see* **Budaun**
Bad Axe *MI* U.S.A. **164** D2
Bad Bederkesa Germany **63** I1
Bad Bergzabern Germany **63** H5
Bad Berleburg Germany **63** I3
Bad Bevensen Germany **63** K1
Bad Blankenburg Germany **63** L4
Bad Camberg Germany **63** I4
Badderen Norway **54** M2
Bad Driburg Germany **63** J3
Bad Düben Germany **63** M3
Bad Dürkheim Germany **63** I5
Bad Dürrenberg Germany **63** M3
Bademli Turkey *see* **Aladağ**
Bademli Geçidi *pass* Turkey **112** C3
Bad Ems Germany **63** H4
Baden Austria **57** P6
Baden Switz. **66** I3
Baden-Baden Germany **63** I6
Baden-Württemberg *land* Germany **63** I6
Bad Essen Germany **63** I2
Bad Grund (Harz) Germany **63** K3
Bad Harzburg Germany **63** K3
Bad Hersfeld Germany **63** J4
Bad Hofgastein Austria **57** N7
Bad Homburg vor der Höhe Germany **63** I4
Badia Polesine Italy **68** D2
Badin Pak. **111** H5
Bad Ischl Austria **57** N7
Bādiyat ash Shām *des.* Asia *see* **Syrian Desert**
Bad Kissingen Germany **63** K4
Bad Königsdorff Poland *see* **Jastrzębie-Zdrój**
Bad Kösen Germany **63** L3
Bad Kreuznach Germany **63** H5
Bad Laasphe Germany **63** I4
Badlands *reg.* *ND* U.S.A. **160** C2
Badlands *reg.* *SD* U.S.A. **160** C3
Badlands National Park *SD* U.S.A. **160** C3
Bad Langensalza Germany **63** K3
Bad Lauterberg im Harz Germany **63** K3
Bad Liebenwerda Germany **63** N3
Bad Lippspringe Germany **63** I3
Bad Marienberg (Westerwald) Germany **63** H4
Bad Mergentheim Germany **63** J5
Bad Nauheim Germany **63** I4
Badnawar India **104** C5
Badnera India **106** C1
Bad Neuenahr-Ahrweiler Germany **62** H4
Bad Neustadt an der Saale Germany **63** K4
Badnor India **104** C4
Badong China **97** F2
Ba Đông Vietnam **87** D5
Badou China **95** I4
Badou Togo **120** D4
Bad Pyrmont Germany **63** J3
Badrah Iraq **113** G4
Bad Reichenhall Germany **57** N7
Badr Ḥunayn Saudi Arabia **108** E5
Bād Rūd Iran **110** D3
Bad Sachsa Germany **63** K3
Bad Salzdetfurth Germany **63** K2
Bad Salzuflen Germany **63** I2
Bad Salzungen Germany **63** K4
Bad Schwalbach Germany **63** I4
Bad Schwartau Germany **57** M4
Bad Segeberg Germany **57** M4
Bad Sobernheim Germany **63** H5
Badu Island Australia **136** C1
Badulla Sri Lanka **106** D5
Bad Vilbel Germany **63** I4
Bad Wilsnack Germany **63** L2
Bad Windsheim Germany **63** K5
Badzhal Rus. Fed. **90** D2
Badzhal'skiy Khrebet *mts* Rus. Fed. **90** D2
Bad Zwischenahn Germany **63** I1
Bae Colwyn U.K. *see* **Colwyn Bay**
Baeswelier Germany **62** G4
Baeza Spain **67** E5
Bafatá Guinea-Bissau **120** B3
Baffa Pak. **111** I3
Baffin Bay *sea* Canada/Greenland **147** L2

▶**Baffin Island** Canada **147** L3
2nd largest island in North America and 5th in the world.

Bafia Cameroon **120** E4
Bafilo Togo **120** D4
Bafing *r.* Africa **120** B3
Bafoulabé Mali **120** B3
Bafoussam Cameroon **120** E4
Bāfq Iran **110** D4
Bafra Turkey **112** D2
Bafra Burnu *pt* Turkey **112** D2
Bāft Iran **110** E4
Bafwaboli Dem. Rep. Congo **122** C3
Bafwasende Dem. Rep. Congo **122** C3
Baga Bogd Uul *mts* Mongolia **94** E2
Bagac Bay *Luzon* Phil. **82** C3
Bagaha India **105** F4
Bagahak, Gunung *hill* Malaysia **85** G1
Bagalkot India **106** B2
Bagalkote India *see* **Bagalkot**
Bagamoyo Tanz. **123** D4
Bagan China **96** C1
Bagan Datoh Malaysia *see* **Bagan Datuk**
Bagan Datuk Malaysia **84** C2
Baganga *Mindanao* Phil. **82** D5
Baganian Peninsula *Mindanao* Phil. **82** C5
Bagan Serai Malaysia **84** C1
Bagansiapiapi *Sumatera* Indon. **84** C2
Baganuur Mongolia **95** G2
Bagar China **99** F7
Bagata Dem. Rep. Congo **122** B4
Bagdad *AZ* U.S.A. **159** G4
Bagdarin Rus. Fed. **89** K2
Bagé Brazil **178** F4
Bagenalstown Ireland **61** F5
Bagerhat Bangl. **105** G5
Bageshwar India **104** D3
Baggs *WY* U.S.A. **156** G4
Baggy Point U.K. **59** C7
Bagh India **104** C5
Bàgh a' Chaisteil U.K. *see* **Castlebay**
Baghak Pak. **111** G4
Bagh Baghū Iran **111** F2

▶**Baghdād** Iraq **113** G4
Capital of Iraq.

Bāgh-e Malek Iran **110** C4
Bagherhat Bangl. *see* **Bagerhat**
Bāghīn Iran **110** E4
Baghlān Afgh. **111** H2
Baghrān Afgh. **111** G3
Baginda, Tanjung *pt* Indon. **84** D3
Bağırsak *r.* Turkey **107** C1
Bağırsak Deresi *r.* Syria/Turkey *see* **Sājūr, Nahr**
Bagley *MN* U.S.A. **160** E2
Bagley Icefield *AK* U.S.A. **149** J4
Baglung Nepal **105** E3
Bagnères-de-Luchon France **66** E5
Bagnuiti *r.* Nepal **99** D8
Bago Myanmar *see* **Pegu**
Bago *Negros* Phil. **82** C4
Bagong China *see* **Sansui**
Bagor India **111** I5
Bagrationovsk Rus. Fed. **55** L9
Bagrax China *see* **Bohu**
Bagrax Hu *l.* China *see* **Bosten Hu**
Baguio *Luzon* Phil. **82** C2
Baguio *Mindanao* Phil. **82** D5
Baguio Point *Luzon* Phil. **82** C2
Bagur, Cabo *c.* Spain *see* **Begur, Cap de**
Bagzane, Monts *mts* Niger **120** D3
Bahādorābād-e Bālā Iran **110** E4
Bahadurganj Nepal **99** C8
Bahalda India **105** F5
Bahāmabād Iran *see* **Rafsanjān**
Bahamas, The *country* West Indies **163** E7
Bahara Pak. **111** G5
Baharampur India **105** G4
Bahardipur Pak. **111** H5
Bahariya Oasis *oasis* Egypt *see* **Baḥrīyah, Wāḥāt al**
Bahau *r.* Indon. **85** G2
Bahau Malaysia **84** C2
Bahaur *Kalimantan* Indon. **85** F3
Bahawalnagar Pak. **111** I4
Bahawalpur Pak. **111** H4
Bahçe *Adana* Turkey **107** B1
Bahçe *Osmaniye* Turkey **112** E3
Baher Dar Eth. *see* **Bahir Dar**
Baheri India **104** D3
Bahia Brazil *see* **Salvador**
Bahia *state* Brazil **179** C1
Bahía, Islas de la *is* Hond. **166** [inset] I5
Bahía Asunción Mex. **157** E8
Bahía Blanca Arg. **178** D5
Bahia Honda Point *Palawan* Phil. **82** B4
Bahía Kino Mex. **166** C2
Bahía Laura Arg. **178** C7
Bahía Negra Para. **178** E2
Bahía Tortugas Mex. **166** B3
Bahir Dar Eth. **122** D2
Bahl India **104** C3
Bahlā Oman **110** E6
Bahomonte *Sulawesi* Indon. **83** B3
Bahraich India **105** E4
Bahrain *country* Asia **110** C5
Bahrain, Gulf of Asia **110** C5
Bahrām Beyg Iran **110** C2
Bahrāmjerd Iran **110** E4
Baḥrīyah, Wāḥāt al *oasis* Egypt **112** C6
Bahuaja-Sonene, Parque Nacional *nat. park* Peru **176** E6
Bahubulu *i.* Indon. **83** B3
Baia Mare Romania **69** J1
Baiazeh Iran **110** D3
Baicang China **105** G3
Baicheng *Henan* China *see* **Xiping**
Baicheng *Jilin* China **95** J2
Baicheng *Xinjiang* China **98** C4
Baidoa Somalia *see* **Baydhabo**
Baidoi Co *l.* China **99** D6
Baidu China **97** H3
Baidunzi *Gansu* China **94** F4
Baidunzi *Gansu* China **98** F4
Baie-aux-Feuilles Canada *see* **Tasiujaq**
Baie-Comeau Canada **153** H4
Baie-du-Poste Canada *see* **Mistissini**
Baie-St-Paul Canada **153** H5
Baie-Trinité Canada **153** I4
Baie Verte Canada **153** K4
Baigou He *r.* China **95** I4
Baiguan China *see* **Shangyu**
Baiguo *Hubei* China **97** G2
Baiguo *Hunan* China **97** G3
Baihanchang China **96** C3
Baihar India **104** E5
Baihe *Jilin* China **90** C4
Baihe *Shaanxi* China **97** F1
Bai He *r.* China **95** I3
Baiji Iraq *see* **Bayjī**
Baijiantan China **98** D3

▶**Baikal, Lake** Rus. Fed. **94** F1
Deepest and 2nd largest lake in Asia and 8th largest in the world.

Baikalu Shan *mt.* China **90** A1
Baikouquan China **98** D3
Baikunthpur India **105** E5
Bailang China **95** J2
Baile Átha Cliath Ireland *see* **Dublin**
Baile Átha Luain Ireland *see* **Athlone**
Baile Mhartainn U.K. **60** B3
Baile na Finne Ireland **61** D3
Băileşti Romania **69** J2
Bailey Range *hills* Australia **135** C7
Bailianhe Shuiku *resr* China **97** G2
Bailieborough Ireland **61** F4
Bailingmiao China **95** G3
Bailleul France **62** C4
Baillie *r.* Canada **151** J1
Baillie Islands Canada **149** O1
Bailong China *see* **Hadapu**
Bailong Jiang *r.* China **96** E1
Baima *Qinghai* China **96** D1
Baima *Xizang* China *see* **Baxoi**
Baima Jian *mt.* China **97** H2
Baimuru P.N.G. **81** K8
Bain *r.* U.K. **58** G5
Bainang China *see* **Norkyung**
Bainbridge *GA* U.S.A. **163** C6
Bainbridge *IN* U.S.A. **164** B4
Bainbridge *NY* U.S.A. **165** H2
Bainduru India **106** B3
Baingoin China **99** E7
Baini China *see* **Yuqing**
Baiona Spain **67** B2
Baiqên China **96** D1
Baiquan China **90** B3
Bā'ir Jordan **107** C4
Bā'ir, Wādī *watercourse* Jordan/Saudi Arabia **107** C4
Bairab Co *l.* China **99** C6
Bairat India **104** D4
Baird *TX* U.S.A. **161** D5
Baird, Mount Canada **149** N2
Baird Inlet *AK* U.S.A. **148** F3
Baird Mountains *AK* U.S.A. **148** H2

▶**Bairiki** Kiribati **186** H5
Capital of Kiribati, on Tarawa atoll.

Bairin Qiao China **95** I3
Bairin Youqi China *see* **Daban**
Bairin Zuoqi China *see* **Lindong**
Bairnsdale Australia **138** C6
Bais *Negros* Phil. **82** C4
Baise China **96** E4
Baisha *Chongqing* China **96** E2
Baisha *Hainan* China **97** F5
Baisha *Sichuan* China **97** F2
Baishan *Guangxi* China *see* **Mashan**
Baishan *Jilin* China *see* **Baishanzhen**
Baishan *Jilin* China **90** B4
Bai Shan *mt.* China **98** F4
Baishanzhen China **90** B4
Baishi Shuiku *resr* China **95** J3
Baishui *Shaanxi* China **95** G5
Baishui *Sichuan* China **96** E1
Baishui Jiang *r.* China **96** E1
Baisogala Lith. **55** M9
Baitadi Nepal **104** E3
Baitang China **96** C1
Bai Thương Vietnam **86** D3
Baitou Shan *mt.* China/N. Korea **90** C4
Baixi China *see* **Yibin**
Baixiang China **95** H4
Baixingt China **95** J3
Baiyanghe China **98** E4
Baiyashi China *see* **Dong'an**
Baiyin China **94** F4
Baiyü China **96** C2
Baiyuda Desert Sudan **108** D6
Baiyu Shan *mts* China **95** F4
Baja Hungary **68** H1
Baja, Punta *pt* Mex. **166** B2
Baja California *pen.* Mex. **166** B2
Baja California *state* Mex. **166** B2
Baja California Sur *state* Mex. **166** B3
Bajan Mex. **167** E3
Bajau *i.* Indon. **84** D2
Bajaur *reg.* Pak. **111** H3
Bajawa *Flores* Indon. **83** B5
Baj Baj India **105** G5
Bājgīrān Iran **110** E2
Bajiang China **97** F3
Bājil Yemen **108** F7
Bajo Boquete Panama **166** [inset] J7
Bajo Caracoles Arg. **178** B7
Bajoga Nigeria **120** E3
Bajoi China **96** D2
Bajrakot India **105** F5
Baka, Bukit *mt.* Indon. **85** F3
Bakala Cent. Afr. Rep. **121** F4
Bakanas Kazakh. **102** E3
Bakanas *watercourse* Kazakh. **98** B3
Bakar Pak. **111** H5
Bakaucengal *Kalimantan* Indon. **85** G3
Bakayan, Gunung *mt.* Indon. **85** G2
Bakel Senegal **120** B3
Baker *CA* U.S.A. **158** E4
Baker *ID* U.S.A. **156** E3
Baker *LA* U.S.A. **161** F6
Baker *MT* U.S.A. **156** G3
Baker *NV* U.S.A. **159** F2
Baker *OR* U.S.A. **156** D3
Baker *WV* U.S.A. **165** F4
Baker, Mount *vol.* *WA* U.S.A. **156** C2
Baker Butte *mt.* *AZ* U.S.A. **159** H4

▶**Baker Island** *terr.* N. Pacific Ocean **133** I1
United States Unincorporated Territory.

Baker Island *AK* U.S.A. **149** N5
Baker Lake *salt flat* Australia **135** D6
Baker Lake Canada **151** M1
Baker Lake *l.* Canada **151** M1
Baker's Dozen Islands Canada **152** F2
Bakersfield *CA* U.S.A. **158** D4
Bakersville *NC* U.S.A. **162** D4
Bâ Kêv Cambodia **87** D4
Bakhardok Turkm. *see* **Bokurdak**
Bākharz, Kūhhā-ye *mts* Iran **111** F3
Bakhasar India **104** B4
Bakhirevo Rus. Fed. **90** C2
Bakhmach Ukr. **53** G6
Bakhma Dam Iraq *see* **Békma, Sadd**
Bakhmut Ukr. *see* **Artemivs'k**
Bākhtarān Iran *see* **Kermānshāh**
Bakhtegan, Daryācheh-ye *l.* Iran **110** D4
Bakhtiari Country *reg.* Iran **110** C3
Bakı Azer. *see* **Baku**
Baki Somalia **122** E2
Bakırköy Turkey **69** M4
Bakkejord Norway **54** K2
Bakloh India **104** C2
Bako Eth. **122** D3
Bako National Park Malaysia **85** E2
Bakongan *Sumatera* Indon. **84** B2
Bakouma Cent. Afr. Rep. **122** C3
Baksan Rus. Fed. **113** F2
Bakty Kazakh. **98** C3

▶**Baku** Azer. **113** H2
Capital of Azerbaijan.

Baku Dem. Rep. Congo **122** D3
Bakulin Point *Mindanao* Phil. **82** D4
Bakung *i.* Indon. **84** D2
Bakutis Coast Antarctica **188** J2
Baky Azer. *see* **Baku**
Balâ Turkey **112** D3
Bala U.K. **59** D6
Bala, Cerros de *mts* Bol. **176** E6
Balabac Phil. **82** B4
Balabac *i.* Phil. **82** B5
Balabac Strait Malaysia/Phil. **80** F5
Balabalangan, Kepulauan *atolls* Indon. **85** G3
Baladeh *Māzandarān* Iran **110** C2
Baladeh *Māzandarān* Iran **110** C2

Baladek Rus. Fed. 90 D1
Balaghat India 104 E5
Balaghat Range hills India 106 B2
Bālā Ḥowz Iran 110 E4
Balaiberkuak Kalimantan Indon. 85 E3
Balaikarangan Kalimantan Indon. 85 E2
Balaipungut Sumatera Indon. 84 C2
Balairiam Kalimantan Indon. 85 E3
Balaka Malawi 123 D5
Balakān Azer. 113 G2
Balakhna Rus. Fed. 52 I4
Balakhta Rus. Fed. 88 G1
Balaklava Australia 137 B7
Balaklava Ukr. 112 D1
Balakleya Ukr. see Balakliya
Balakliya Ukr. 53 H6
Balakovo Rus. Fed. 53 J5
Bala Lake l. U.K. 59 D6
Balaman India 104 E4
Balambangan i. Malaysia 82 B5
Balan India 104 B4
Balancán Mex. 167 H5
Balanda Rus. Fed. see Kalininsk
Balanda r. Rus. Fed. 53 J6
Balan Dağı hill Turkey 69 M6
Balanga Luzon Phil. 82 C3
Balangir India see Bolangir
Balantak Sulawesi Indon. 83 B3
Balaözen r. Kazakh./Rus. Fed. see Malyy Uzen'
Balarampur India see Balrampur
Balase r. Indon. 83 B3
Balashov Rus. Fed. 53 I6
Balasore India see Baleshwar
Balaton, Lake Hungary 68 G1
Balatonboglár Hungary 68 G1
Balatonfüred Hungary 68 G1
Balauring Indon. 83 B5
Balbina Brazil 177 G4
Balbina, Represa de resr Brazil 177 G4
Balbriggan Ireland 61 F4
Balchik Bulg. 69 M3
Balclutha N.Z. 139 B8
Balcones Escarpment TX U.S.A. 161 C6
Bald Knob WV U.S.A. 164 E5
Bald Mountain NV U.S.A. 159 F3
Baldock Lake Canada 151 L3
Baldwin Canada 164 F1
Baldwin FL U.S.A. 163 D6
Baldwin MI U.S.A. 164 C2
Baldwin PA U.S.A. 164 F3
Baldwin Peninsula AK U.S.A. 148 G2
Baldy Mount Canada 156 D2
Baldy Mountain hill Canada 151 K5
Baldy Peak AZ U.S.A. 159 I5
Bal'dzhikan Rus. Fed. 95 G1
Bale Indon. 84 C3
Bâle Switz. see Basel
Baléa Mali 120 B3
Baleares is Spain see Balearic Islands
Baleares, Islas is Spain see Balearic Islands
Baleares Insulae is Spain see Balearic Islands
Balearic Islands is Spain 67 G4
Balears is Spain see Balearic Islands
Balears, Illes is Spain see Balearic Islands
Baleh r. Malaysia 85 F2
Baleia, Ponta da pt Brazil 179 D2
Bale Mountains National Park Eth. 122 D3
Baleno Masbate Phil. 82 C3
Baler Luzon Phil. 82 C3
Baler Bay Luzon Phil. 82 C3
Baleshwar India 105 F5
Balestrand Norway 55 E6
Baléyara Niger 120 D3
Balezino Rus. Fed. 51 Q4
Balfate Hond. 166 [inset] I6
Balfe's Creek Australia 136 D4
Balfour Downs Australia 134 C5
Balgatay Mongolia see Shilüüstey
Balgo Australia 134 D5
Balguntay China 98 D4
Bali India 104 C4
Bali i. Indon. 85 F5
Bali prov. Indon. 85 F5
Bali, Laut sea Indon. 85 F4
Bali, Selat sea chan. Indon. 85 F5
Balia India see Ballia
Baliangao Mindanao Phil. 82 C4
Baliapal India 105 F5
Bali Barat, Taman Nasional nat. park Bali Indon. 85 F5
Balige Sumatera Indon. 84 B2
Baliguda India 106 D1
Balihan China 95 I3
Balıkesir Turkey 69 L5
Balīkh r. Syria/Turkey 107 D2
Balikpapan Kalimantan Indon. 85 G3
Balikpapan, Teluk b. Indon. 85 G3
Balimila Reservoir India 106 D2
Balimo P.N.G. 81 K8
Balin China 95 J1
Baling Malaysia 84 C1
Balingen Germany 57 L6
Balingian Sarawak Malaysia 85 F2
Balingian r. Malaysia 85 F2
Balinqiao China see Bairin Qiao
Balintang Channel Phil. 82 C2
Balintore U.K. 60 F3
Bali Sea Indon. see Bali, Laut
Baliungan i. Phil. 82 C5
Balk Neth. 62 F2
Balkanabat Turkm. 110 D2
Balkan Mountains Bulg./Serbia 69 J3
Balkassar Pak. 111 I3
Balkhash Kazakh. 102 D2

▶Balkhash, Lake Kazakh. 102 D2
3rd largest lake in Asia.

Balkhash, Ozero l. Kazakh. see Balkhash, Lake
Balkuduk Kazakh. 53 J7
Ballachulish U.K. 60 D4
Balladonia Australia 135 C8
Balladoran Australia 138 D3
Ballaghaderreen Ireland 61 D4
Ballan Australia 138 B6
Ballangen Norway 54 J2
Ballantine MT U.S.A. 156 F3
Ballantrae U.K. 60 E5
Ballarat Australia 138 A6
Ballard, Lake salt flat Australia 135 C7
Ballarpur India 106 C2
Ballater U.K. 60 F3
Ballé Mali 120 C3
Ballena, Punta pt Chile 178 B3
Balleny Islands Antarctica 188 H2
Ballia India 105 F4
Ballina Australia 138 F2
Ballina Ireland 61 C3
Ballinafad Ireland 61 D3
Ballinalack Ireland 61 E4
Ballinamore Ireland 61 E3
Ballinasloe Ireland 61 D4
Ballindine Ireland 61 D4
Ballinger TX U.S.A. 161 D6
Ballinluig U.K. 60 F4
Ballinrobe Ireland 61 C4
Ballston Spa NY U.S.A. 165 I2
Ballybay Ireland 61 F3
Ballybunion Ireland 61 C5
Ballycanew Ireland 61 F5
Ballycastle Ireland 61 C3
Ballycastle U.K. 61 F2
Ballyclare U.K. 61 G3
Ballyconnell Ireland 61 E3
Ballygar Ireland 61 D4
Ballygawley U.K. 61 E3
Ballygorman Ireland 61 E2
Ballyhaunis Ireland 61 D4
Ballyheigue Ireland 61 C5
Ballykelly U.K. 61 E2
Ballylynan Ireland 61 E5
Ballymacmague Ireland 61 E5
Ballymahon Ireland 61 E4
Ballymena U.K. 61 F3
Ballymoney U.K. 61 F2
Ballymote Ireland 61 D3
Ballynahinch U.K. 61 G3
Ballyshannon Ireland 61 D3
Ballyteige Bay Ireland 61 F5
Ballyvaughan Ireland 61 C4
Ballyward U.K. 61 F3
Balmartin U.K. see Baile Mhartainn
Balmer India see Barmer
Balmertown Canada 151 M5
Balmorhea TX U.S.A. 161 C6
Baloa Sulawesi Indon. 83 B3
Balochistan prov. Pak. 111 G4
Balok, Teluk b. Indon. 85 D3
Balombo Angola 123 B5
Balonne r. Australia 138 D2
Balontohe i. Indon. 83 C2
Balotra India 104 C4
Balpyk Bi Kazakh. 98 B3
Balqash Kazakh. see Balkhash
Balqash Köli l. Kazakh. see Balkhash, Lake
Balrampur India 105 E4
Balranald Australia 138 A5
Balş Romania 69 K2
Balsam Lake Canada 165 F1
Balsas Brazil 177 I5
Balsas Mex. 167 F5
Balsas r. Mex. 166 E5
Balta Ukr. 53 F7
Baltasound U.K. 60 [inset]
Baltay Rus. Fed. 53 J5
Bălţi Moldova 53 E7
Baltic OH U.S.A. 164 E3
Baltic Sea g. Europe 55 J9
Balṭīm Egypt see Balṭīm
Balṭīm Egypt 112 C5
Baltimore S. Africa 125 I2
Baltimore MD U.S.A. 165 G4
Baltimore OH U.S.A. 164 D4
Baltinglass Ireland 61 F5
Baltistan reg. Pak. 104 C2
Baltiysk Rus. Fed. 55 K9
Balu India 96 B3
Baluarte, Arroyo watercourse TX U.S.A. 161 D7
Baluch Ab well Iran 110 E4
Balui r. Malaysia 85 F2
Balumundam Sumatera Indon. 84 B2
Baluran, Gunung mt. Indon. 85 F3
Baluran, Taman Nasional nat. park Indon. 85 F4
Balurghat India 105 G4
Balut i. Phil. 82 D5
Balve Germany 63 H3
Balvi Latvia 55 O8
Balya Turkey 69 L4
Balyaga Rus. Fed. 95 G1
Balykchy Kyrg. 102 E3
Balykshi Kazakh. 100 E2
Balyktyg-Khem r. Rus. Fed. 94 D1
Balyqshy Kazakh. see Balykshi
Bam Iran 110 E4
Bām Iran 110 E2
Bama China 96 E3

▶Bamako Mali 120 C3
Capital of Mali.

Bamba Mali 120 C3
Bambang Luzon Phil. 82 C2
Bambannan i. Phil. 82 C5
Bambari Cent. Afr. Rep. 122 C3
Bambel Sumatera Indon. 84 B2
Bamberg Germany 63 K5
Bamberg SC U.S.A. 163 D5
Bambili Dem. Rep. Congo 122 C3
Bambio Cent. Afr. Rep. 122 B3
Bamboesberg mts S. Africa 125 H6
Bamboo Creek Australia 134 C5
Bambouti Cent. Afr. Rep. 122 C3
Bambuí Brazil 179 B3
Bambulung Kalimantan Indon. 85 F3
Bamda China 96 C2
Bamenda Cameroon 120 E4
Bamiancheng China 95 K3
Bamiantong China see Muling
Bamingui Cent. Afr. Rep. 122 C3
Bamingui-Bangoran, Parc National du nat. park Cent. Afr. Rep. 122 B3
Bamkeri Papua Indon. 83 D3
Bâmnak Cambodia 87 D4
Bamnet Narong Thai. 86 C4
Bamoa Mex. 166 C3
Bamor India 104 D4
Bamori India 106 C1
Bamposht reg. Iran 111 F5
Bampton U.K. 59 D8
Bampūr Iran 111 F5
Bampūr watercourse Iran 111 E5
Bamrūd Iran 111 F3
Bam Tso l. China 105 G3
Bāmyān Afgh. 111 G3
Bamyili Australia 134 F3
Banaba i. Kiribati 133 G2
Banabuiu, Açude resr Brazil 177 K5
Bañados del Izozog swamp Bol. 176 F7
Banagher Ireland 61 E4
Banahao, Mount vol. Luzon Phil. 82 C3
Banalia Dem. Rep. Congo 122 C3
Banamana, Lagoa l. Moz. 125 K2
Banamba Mali 120 C3
Banámichi Mex. 166 C2
Banana Australia 136 E5
Bananal, Ilha do i. Brazil 177 H6
Bananga India 87 A6
Banapur India 106 E2
Banas r. India 104 D4
Banawaya i. Indon. 83 A4
Banaz Turkey 69 M5
Ban Ban Laos 86 C3
Banbar China 99 F7
Ban Bo Laos 86 C3
Banbridge U.K. 61 F3
Ban Bua Chum Thai. 86 C4
Ban Bua Yai Thai. 86 C4
Ban Bungxai Laos 86 D4
Banbury U.K. 59 F6
Ban Cang Vietnam 86 C2
Banc d'Arguin, Parc National du nat. park Mauritania 120 B2
Ban Channabot Thai. 86 C3
Banchory U.K. 60 G3
Bancoran i. Phil. 82 B5
Bancroft Canada 165 G1
Bancroft Zambia see Chililabombwe
Banda Dem. Rep. Congo 122 C3
Banda India 104 E4
Banda, Kepulauan is Maluku Indon. 83 D4
Banda, Laut sea Indon. 83 D4
Banda Aceh Sumatera Indon. 84 A1
Banda Banda, Mount Australia 138 F3
Banda Daud Shah Pak. 111 H3
Bandahara, Gunung mt. Indon. 84 B2
Bandama r. Côte d'Ivoire 120 C4
Bandaneira Maluku Indon. 83 D4
Bandān Kūh mts Iran 111 F4
Bandar India see Machilipatnam
Bandar Moz. 123 D5
Bandar Abbas Iran see Bandar-e 'Abbās
Bandaragung Sumatera Indon. 84 D4
Bandarban Bangl. 105 H5
Bandar-e 'Abbās Iran 110 E5
Bandar-e Anzalī Iran 110 C2
Bandar-e Deylam Iran 110 C4
Bandar-e Emām Khomeynī Iran 110 C4
Bandar-e Lengeh Iran 110 D5
Bandar-e Ma'shur Iran 110 C4
Bandar-e Nakhīlū Iran 110 D5
Bandar-e Pahlavī Iran see Bandar-e Anzalī
Bandar-e Shāh Iran see Bandar-e Torkeman
Bandar-e Shāhpūr Iran see Bandar-e Emām Khomeynī
Bandar-e Shīū' Iran 110 D5
Bandar-e Torkeman Iran 110 D2
Bandar Lampung Sumatera Indon. 84 D4
Bandarpunch mt. India 104 D3

▶Bandar Seri Begawan Brunei 85 F1
Capital of Brunei.

Banda Sea Indon. see Banda, Laut
Band-e Amīr l. Afgh. 111 G3
Band-e Amīr, Daryā-ye r. Afgh. 111 G2
Band-e Bābā, Silsilah-ye Kōh-e mts Afgh. 111 F3
Band-e Bamposht, Kūh-e mts Iran 111 F5
Bandeira Brazil 179 C1
Bandeirante Brazil 179 A1
Bandeiras, Pico de mt. Brazil 179 C3
Bandelierkop S. Africa 125 I2
Banderas Mex. 166 D2
Banderas, Bahía de b. Mex. 168 C4
Band-e Sar Qom Iran 110 D3
Bandhi Pak. 111 H5
Bandhogarh India 104 E5
Bandi r. India 104 C4
Bandiagara Mali 120 C3
Bandikui India 104 D4
Bandipur National Park India 106 C4
Bandırma Turkey 69 L4
Bandjarmasin Kalimantan Indon. see Banjarmasin
Bandon Ireland 61 D6
Bandon r. Ireland 61 D6
Ban Don Thai. see Surat Thani
Bandon OR U.S.A. 156 B4
Band Qīr Iran 110 C4
Bandra India 106 B2
Bandundu Dem. Rep. Congo 122 B4
Bandung Jawa Indon. 85 D4
Bandya Australia 135 C6
Bāneh Iran 110 B3
Banemo Halmahera Indon. 83 D2
Banera India 104 C4
Banes Cuba 169 I4
Banff Canada 150 H5
Banff U.K. 60 G3
Banff National Park Canada 150 G5
Banfora Burkina Faso 120 C3
Bang, Gunung mt. Indon. 85 F2
Banga Dem. Rep. Congo 123 C4
Banga Mindanao Phil. 82 D5
Banga r. Mindanao Phil. 82 D5
Bangai Point Mindanao Phil. 82 D5
Bangalore India 106 C3
Bangalow Australia 138 F2
Banganga r. India 99 B8
Bangaon India 105 G5
Bangar Brunei 85 F1
Bangar Luzon Phil. 82 C2
Bangassou Cent. Afr. Rep. 122 C3
Bangdag Co salt l. China 99 C6
Banggai Sulawesi Indon. 83 B3
Banggai i. Indon. 83 B3
Banggai, Kepulauan is Indon. 83 B3
Banggi i. Malaysia 85 G1
Banghāzī Libya see Benghazi
Banghiang, Xé r. Laos 86 D3
Bangil Jawa Indon. 85 F4
Bangka i. Indon. 83 C2
Bangka i. Indon. 84 D3
Bangka, Selat sea chan. Indon. 83 C2
Bangka, Selat sea chan. Indon. 84 D3
Bangka-Belitung prov. Indon. 84 D3
Bangkal Kalimantan Indon. 85 F3
Bangkala, Teluk b. Indon. 83 A4
Bangkalan Jawa Indon. 85 F4
Bangkalan i. Indon. 83 B3
Bangkaru i. Indon. 84 B2
Bangkinang Sumatera Indon. 84 C2
Bangkir Sulawesi Indon. 83 B2
Bangko Sumatera Indon. 84 C3
Bangkog Co salt l. China 99 E7

▶Bangkok Thai. 87 C4
Capital of Thailand.

Bangkok, Bight of b. Thai. 87 C4
Bangkor China 99 D7
Bangkuang Kalimantan Indon. 85 F3
Bangkulu i. Indon. 83 B3
Bangkulua Sumbawa Indon. 85 G5
Bangla state India see West Bengal

▶Bangladesh country Asia 105 G4
5th most populous country in Asia and 8th in the world.

Bang Lang, Ang Kep Nam Thai. 84 C1
Bangluo China 94 F5
Bangma Shan mts China 96 C4
Bang Mun Nak Thai. 86 C3
Ba Ngoi Vietnam 87 E5
Bangolo Côte d'Ivoire 120 C4
Bangong Co salt l. China/India 104 D2
Bangor Ireland 61 C3
Bangor Northern Ireland U.K. 61 G3
Bangor Wales U.K. 58 C5
Bangor ME U.S.A. 162 G2
Bangor MI U.S.A. 164 B2
Bangor PA U.S.A. 165 H3
Bangs, Mount AZ U.S.A. 159 G3
Bangsalsepulun Kalimantan Indon. 85 G3
Bang Saphan Yai Thai. 87 B5
Bangsund Norway 54 G4
Bangued Luzon Phil. 82 C2

▶Bangui Cent. Afr. Rep. 122 B3
Capital of the Central African Republic.

Bangui Luzon Phil. 82 C2
Bangunpurba Sumatera Indon. 84 B2
Bangweulu, Lake Zambia 123 C5
Banhā Egypt 112 C5
Banhine, Parque Nacional de nat. park Moz. 125 K2
Ban Hin Heup Laos 86 C3
Ban Houei Sai Laos see Huayxay
Ban Huai Khon Thai. 86 C3
Ban Huai Yang Thai. 87 B5
Bani Luzon Phil. 82 B2
Bani, Jbel ridge Morocco 64 C6
Bania Cent. Afr. Rep. 122 B3
Bani-Bangou Niger 120 D3
Banifing r. Mali 120 C3
Banī Forūr, Jazīreh-ye i. Iran 110 D5
Banihal Pass and Tunnel India 104 C2
Bani Point Luzon Phil. 82 B3
Banister r. VA U.S.A. 164 F5
Banī Suwayf Egypt 112 C5
Banī Walīd Libya 121 E1
Banī Wuṭayfān well Saudi Arabia 110 C5
Bāniyās Israel 107 B3
Bāniyās Syria 107 B2
Bani Yas reg. U.A.E. 110 D6
Banja Luka Bos.-Herz. 68 G2
Banjarmasin Kalimantan Indon. 85 F3
Banjës, Liqeni i resr Albania 69 I4
Banjiegou China 98 E4
Banjieta China 95 I3

▶Banjul Gambia 120 B3
Capital of The Gambia.

Banka India 105 F4
Banka Banka Australia 134 F4
Bankapur India 106 B3
Bankass Mali 120 C3
Ban Kèngkabao Laos 86 D3
Ban Khao Yoi Thai. 87 B4
Ban Khok Kloi Thai. 87 B5
Bankilaré Niger 120 D3
Bankobankoang i. Indon. 85 G4
Banks Island B.C. Canada 149 O5
Banks Island N.W.T. Canada 146 F2
Banks Islands Vanuatu 133 G3
Banks Lake Canada 151 M2
Banks Lake WA U.S.A. 156 D3
Banks Peninsula N.Z. 139 D6
Banks Strait Australia 137 [inset]
Bankura India 105 F5
Ban Lamduan Thai. 87 C4
Banlan China 97 F3
Ban Mae La Luang Thai. 86 B3
Banmaw Myanmar see Bhamo
Banmo Myanmar see Bhamo
Bann r. Ireland 61 F5
Bann r. U.K. 61 F2
Ban Nakham Laos 86 D3
Bannerman Town Bahamas 163 E7
Banning CA U.S.A. 158 E5
Banningville Dem. Rep. Congo see Bandundu
Ban Noi Myanmar 86 B3
Ban Nonghèt Laos 86 D3
Ban Nong Kung Thai. 86 D3
Bannu Pak. 111 H3
Bano India 105 F5
Bañolas Spain see Banyoles
Ban Phai Thai. 86 C3
Ban Phôn Laos see Lamam
Ban Phôn-Hông Laos 86 C3
Banqiao Gansu China 94 E4
Banqiao Yunnan China 96 C3
Banqiao Yunnan China 96 E3
Ban Sanam Chai Thai. 84 C1
Bansgaon India 99 C8
Bansi Bihar India 105 F4
Bansi Rajasthan India 104 C4
Bansi Uttar Prad. India 104 D4
Bansi Uttar Prad. India 105 E4
Bansihari India 105 G4
Banská Bystrica Slovakia 57 Q6
Banspani India 105 F5
Bansur India 104 D4
Ban Sut Ta Thai. 86 B3
Ban Suwan Wari Thai. 86 D4
Banswara India 104 C5
Banta i. Indon. 83 A5
Bantaeng Sulawesi Indon. 83 A4
Bantayan i. Phil. 82 C4
Banteer Ireland 61 D5
Banten prov. Indon. 84 D4
Ban Tha Song Yang Thai. 86 B3
Banthat mts Cambodia/Thai. see Cardamom Range
Ban Tha Tum Thai. 86 C4
Ban Thepha Thai. 84 C1
Ban Tôp Laos 86 D3
Bantry Ireland 61 C6
Bantry Bay Ireland 61 C6
Bantul Indon. 85 E4
Bantval India 106 B3
Ban Wang Chao Thai. 86 B3
Ban Woen Laos 86 C3
Ban Xepian Laos 86 D4
Banyak, Pulau-pulau is Indon. 84 B2
Ban Yang Yong Thai. 87 B4
Banyo Cameroon 120 E4
Banyoles Spain 67 H2
Banyuasin r. Indon. 84 D3
Banyuwangi Jawa Indon. 85 F5
Banzare Coast Antarctica 188 G2
Banzare Seamount sea feature Indian Ocean 185 N9
Banzart Tunisia see Bizerte
Banzkow Germany 63 L1
Banzyville Dem. Rep. Congo see Mobayi-Mbongo
Bao'an Guangdong China see Shenzhen
Bao'an Qinghai China 94 E5
Bao'an Shaanxi China see Zhidan
Baochang China 95 H3
Baocheng China 96 E1
Baodi China 95 I4
Baoding China 95 H4
Baofeng China 97 G1
Baohe China see Weixi
Baoji Shaanxi China 95 F5
Baoji Shaanxi China 95 F5
Baokang Hubei China 97 F2
Baokang Nei Mongol China 95 J2
Bao Lac Vietnam 86 D2
Baolin China 90 C3
Bao Lôc Vietnam 87 D5
Baoqing China 90 D3
Baoro Cent. Afr. Rep. 122 B3
Baoshan China 96 C3
Baotou China 95 G3
Baoulé r. Mali 120 C3
Baoxing China 96 D2
Baoying China 97 H1
Baoyou China see Ledong
Bap India 104 C4
Bapatla India 106 D3
Bapaume France 62 C4
Baptiste Lake Canada 165 F1
Bapu China see Meigu
Baq'ā' oasis Saudi Arabia 113 F6
Baqbaq Egypt see Buqbuq
Baqên Xizang China 99 F6
Baqên Xizang China 99 F7
Baqiu China 97 G3
Ba'qūbah Iraq 113 G4
Bar Montenegro 69 H3
Bar Rus. Fed. 95 F1
Bara Buru Indon. 83 C3
Bara Sudan 108 D7
Baraawe Somalia 122 E3
Barabai Kalimantan Indon. 85 F3
Barabanki India 104 E4
Bara Banki India see Barabanki
Baraboo WI U.S.A. 160 F3
Baracaju r. Brazil 179 A1
Baracaldo Spain see Barakaldo
Baracoa Cuba 169 J4
Baradá, Nahr r. Syria 107 C3
Baradine Australia 138 D3
Baradine r. Australia 138 D3
Baragarh India see Bargarh
Barahona Dom. Rep. 169 J5
Barahoti India 99 B7
Barail Range mts India 105 H4
Baraka watercourse Eritrea/Sudan 121 G3
Barakaldo Spain 67 E2
Barakī Barak Afgh. 111 H3
Baralaba Australia 136 E5
Bara Lacha Pass India 104 D2
Baralzon Lake Canada 151 L3
Baram India 105 F5
Baram r. Malaysia 85 F1
Baram, Tanjung pt Malaysia 85 F1
Baramati India 106 B2
Baramula India see Baramulla
Baramulla India 104 C2
Baran India 104 D4
Baran r. Pak. 111 H5
Bārān, Kūh-e mts Iran 111 F3
Barana Pak. 111 I4
Baranavichy Belarus 55 O10
Baṟang, Dasht-e des. Afgh. 111 F3
Baranikha Rus. Fed. 77 R3
Baranīs Egypt see Baranīs
Baranīs Egypt 108 E5
Barannda India 104 E4
Baranof AK U.S.A. 149 N4
Baranof Island AK U.S.A. 149 N4
Baranovichi Belarus see Baranavichy
Baranowicze Belarus see Baranavichy
Barouéli Mali 120 C3
Baraque de Fraiture hill Belgium 62 F4
Barasat India 105 G5
Barat Daya, Kepulauan is Maluku Indon. 83 C4
Barati Timor Indon. 83 B5
Baraut India 104 D3
Barbacena Brazil 179 C3
Barbados country West Indies 169 M6
Barbar, Gebel el mt. Egypt see Barbar, Jabal
Barbar, Jabal mt. Egypt 107 A5
Barbara Lake Canada 152 D4
Barbastro Spain 67 G2
Barbate Spain 67 D5
Barbaza Panay Phil. 82 C4
Barbechitos Mex. 166 D3
Barberton S. Africa 125 J3
Barberton OH U.S.A. 164 E3
Barbezieux-St-Hilaire France 66 D4
Barbour Bay Canada 151 M2
Barbourville KY U.S.A. 164 D5
Barbuda i. Antigua and Barbuda 169 L5
Barby (Elbe) Germany 63 L3
Barcaldine Australia 136 D4
Barce Libya see Al Marj
Barcelona Spain 67 H3
Barcelona Venez. 176 F1
Barcelonnette France 66 H4
Barcelos Brazil 176 F4
Barchfeld Germany 63 K4
Barcino Spain see Barcelona
Barclay de Tolly atoll Fr. Polynesia see Raroia
Barclayville Liberia 120 C4
Barcoo watercourse Australia 136 C5
Barcoo Creek watercourse Australia see Cooper Creek
Barcoo National Park Australia see Welford National Park
Barcs Hungary 68 G2
Bärdä Azer. 113 G2
Bardaï Chad 121 E2
Bárðarbunga mt. Iceland 54 [inset 1]
Bardāskan Iran 110 E3
Bardawīl, Khabrat al salt pan Saudi Arabia 107 D4
Bardawīl, Sabkhat al lag. Egypt 107 A4
Barddhaman India 105 F5
Bardejov Slovakia 53 D6
Bardera Somalia see Baardheere
Bardhaman India see Barddhaman
Bardsey Island U.K. 59 C6
Bardsīr Iran 110 E4
Barðsneshorn pt Iceland 50 D2
Bardstown KY U.S.A. 164 C5
Barduli Italy see Barletta
Bardwell KY U.S.A. 161 F4
Bareilly India 104 D3
Barellan Australia 138 C5
Barentin France 59 H9
Barentsburg Svalbard 76 C2
Barents Sea Arctic Ocean 52 I1
Barentu Eritrea 108 E6
Bareo Sarawak Malaysia 85 F2
Barfleur, Pointe de pt France 59 F9
Barga China 99 C7
Bārgāh Iran 110 E5
Bargarh India 105 E5
Barghamad Iran 110 E2
Bargrennan U.K. 60 E5
Bargteheide Germany 63 K1
Barguna Bangl. 105 G5
Barhaj India 105 E4
Barham Australia 138 B5
Bari Italy 68 G4
Bari Doab lowland Pak. 111 I4
Barika Alg. 64 F4
Barinas Venez. 176 D2
Baripada India 105 F5
Bariri Brazil 179 A3
Bari Sadri India 104 C4
Barisal Bangl. 105 G5
Barisan, Pegunungan mts Indon. 84 C3
Barito r. Indon. 85 F3
Barium Italy see Bari
Barkal Bangl. 105 H5
Barkam China 96 D2
Barkan, Ra's-e pt Iran 110 C4
Barkava Latvia 55 O8
Bark Lake Canada 165 G1
Barkly East S. Africa 125 H6
Barkly Homestead Australia 136 A3
Barkly-Oos S. Africa see Barkly East
Barkly Tableland reg. Australia 136 A3
Barkly-Wes S. Africa see Barkly West
Barkly West S. Africa 124 G5
Barkol China 94 C3
Barkol Hu salt l. China 94 C3
Barla Turkey 69 N5
Bârlad Romania 69 L1
Barlag Gol watercourse Mongolia 94 C2
Bar-le-Duc France 62 F6
Barlee, Lake salt flat Australia 135 B7
Barlee Range hills Australia 135 A5
Barletta Italy 68 G4
Barlow Canada 149 M3
Barlow Lake Canada 151 K2
Barmah Forest Australia 138 B5
Barmedman Australia 138 C5
Barmen-Elberfeld Germany see Wuppertal
Barmer India 104 B4
Barm Fīrūz, Kūh-e mt. Iran 110 C4
Barmouth U.K. 59 C6
Barnala India 104 C3
Barnard, Mount Canada/U.S.A. 149 M4
Barnard Castle U.K. 58 F4
Barnato Australia 138 B3
Barnaul Rus. Fed. 88 E2
Barnegat Bay NJ U.S.A. 165 H4
Barnes Icecap Canada 147 K2
Barnesville GA U.S.A. 163 D5
Barnesville MN U.S.A. 160 D2
Barneveld Neth. 62 F2
Barneville-Carteret France 59 F9
Barneys Lake imp. l. Australia 138 B4
Barney Top mt. UT U.S.A. 159 H3
Barnhart TX U.S.A. 167 E2
Barnsley U.K. 58 F5
Barnstable MA U.S.A. 165 J3
Barnstaple U.K. 59 C7
Barnstaple Bay U.K. 59 C7
Barnstorf Germany 63 I2
Barnum Bay Palau 82 [inset]
Baro Nigeria 120 D4
Baroda Gujarat India see Vadodara
Baroda Madh. Prad. India 104 D4
Barong China 96 C2
Barons Range hills Australia 135 D6
Barowghil, Kowtal-e Afgh. 111 I2
Barpathar India 96 B3
Barpeta India 105 G4
Bar Pla Soi Thai. see Chon Buri
Barques, Point Aux MI U.S.A. 164 D1
Barquisimeto Venez. 176 E1
Barra Brazil 177 J6
Barra i. U.K. 60 B4
Barra, Ponta da pt Moz. 125 L2
Barra, Sound of sea chan. U.K. 60 B3
Barraba Australia 138 E3
Barra Bonita Brazil 179 A3
Barracão do Barreto Brazil 177 G5
Barra de Navidad Mex. 166 D5
Barra do Bugres Brazil 177 G7
Barra do Corda Brazil 177 I5
Barra do Cuieté Brazil 179 C2
Barra do Garças Brazil 177 H7
Barra do Piraí Brazil 179 C3
Barra do São Manuel Brazil 177 G5
Barra do Turvo Brazil 179 A4
Barra Falsa, Ponta da pt Moz. 125 L2
Barraigh i. U.K. see Barra
Barra Kruta Hond. 166 [inset] J6
Barra Mansa Brazil 179 B3
Barranca Peru 176 C4

Barranca del Cobre, Parque Natural nature res. Mex. 166 D3
Barranqueras Arg. 178 E3
Barranquilla Col. 176 D1
Barre MA U.S.A. 165 I2
Barre VT U.S.A. 165 I1
Barre des Écrins mt. France 66 H4
Barreiras Brazil 177 J6
Barreirinha Brazil 177 G4
Barreirinhas Brazil 177 J4
Barreiro Port. 67 B4
Barreiros Brazil 177 K5
Barren Island India 87 A4
Barren Island Kiribati see Starbuck Island
Barren Islands AK U.S.A. 148 I4
Barren River Lake KY U.S.A. 164 B5
Barretos Brazil 179 A3
Barrett, Mount hill Australia 134 D4
Barrhead Canada 150 H4
Barrhead U.K. 60 E5
Barrie Canada 164 F1
Barrier Bay Antarctica 188 E2
Barrière Canada 150 F5
Barrier Range hills Australia 137 C6
Barrier Reef Belize 167 H5
Barrington Canada 153 I6
Barrington, Mount Australia 138 E4
Barrington Tops National Park Australia 138 E4
Barringun Australia 138 B2
Barro Alto Brazil 179 A1
Barrocão Brazil 179 C2
Barron WI U.S.A. 160 F2
Barroterán Mex. 167 E3
Barrow r. Ireland 61 F5
Barrow AK U.S.A. 148 H1
Barrow, Point pt AK U.S.A. 148 H1
Barrow Creek Australia 134 F5
Barrow-in-Furness U.K. 58 D4
Barrow Island Australia 134 A5
Barrow Range hills Australia 135 D6
Barrow Strait Canada 147 I2
Barr Smith Range hills Australia 135 C6
Barry U.K. 59 D7
Barrydale S. Africa 124 E7
Barry Mountains Australia 138 C6
Barrys Bay Canada 165 G1
Barryville NY U.S.A. 165 H3
Barsalpur India 104 C3
Barshatas Kazakh. 102 E2
Barshi India see Barsi
Barsi India 106 B2
Barsinghausen Germany 63 J2
Barstow CA U.S.A. 158 E4
Barsur India 106 D2
Bar-sur-Aube France 66 G2
Bartang Tajik. 111 H2
Barter Island AK U.S.A. 149 L1
Barth Germany 57 N3
Bartica Guyana 177 G2
Bartın Turkey 112 D2
Bartle Frere, Mount Australia 136 D3
Bartlett NE U.S.A. 160 D3
Bartlett Reservoir AZ U.S.A. 159 H5
Barton VT U.S.A. 165 I1
Barton-upon-Humber U.K. 58 G5
Bartoszyce Poland 57 R3
Bartow FL U.S.A. 163 D7
Barú, Volcán vol. Panama 169 H7
Barumun r. Indon. 84 C2
Barun China 94 D4
Barung i. Indon. 85 F5
Barunga Australia see Bamyili
Barun-Torey, Ozero l. Rus. Fed. 95 H1
Barus Sumatera Indon. 84 B2
Baruunbayan-Ulaan Mongolia 94 E2
Baruunbüren Mongolia 94 F1
Baruunharaa Mongolia see Bayangol
Baruunsuu Mongolia see Tsogttsetsiy
Baruunturuun Mongolia 94 C1
Baruun-Urt Mongolia 95 H2
Baruva India 106 E2
Barwani India 104 C5
Barwéli Mali see Baraouéli
Barwon r. Australia 138 C3
Barygaza India see Bharuch
Barykova, Mys hd Rus. Fed. 148 B3
Barysaw Belarus 55 P9
Barysh Rus. Fed. 53 J5
Basaga Turkm. 111 G2
Basăk, Tônlé r. Cambodia 87 D5
Basalt r. Australia 136 D3
Basalt Island H.K. China 97 [inset]
Basankusu Dem. Rep. Congo 122 B3
Basar India 106 C2
Basarabi Romania 69 M2
Basargechar Armenia see Vardenis
Basaseachic, Parque Nacional Cascada de nat. park Mex. 166 C2
Basay Negros Phil. 82 C4
Basco Phil. 82 C1
Bascuñán, Cabo c. Chile 178 B3
Basel Switz. 66 H3
Basey Samar Phil. 82 D4
Bāsh Ābdān Afgh. 111 H2
Bashākerd, Kūhhā-ye mts Iran 110 E5
Bashanta Rus. Fed. see Gorodovikovsk
Bashaw Canada 150 H4
Bashee r. S. Africa 125 I7
Bāshī Iran 110 C4
Bashi Channel Phil./Taiwan 81 G2
Bashkaus r. Rus. Fed. 98 D2
Bashmakovo Rus. Fed. 53 I5
Bāsht Iran 110 C4
Bashtanka Ukr. 53 G7
Basi Punjab India 104 D3
Basi Rajasthan India 104 D4
Basia India 105 F5
Basilan i. Phil. 82 C5
Basilan Strait Phil. 82 C5
Basildon U.K. 59 H7
Basile, Pico mt. Equat. Guinea 120 D4
Basin WY U.S.A. 156 F3
Basingstoke U.K. 59 F7
Basin Lake Canada 151 J4
Basirhat India 105 G5
Basīţ, Ra's al pt Syria 107 B2
Başkale Turkey 113 G3
Baskatong, Réservoir resr Canada 152 G5
Baskerville, Cape Australia 134 C4
Başkomutan Tarıhı Milli Parkı nat. park Turkey 69 N5
Başköy Turkey 107 A1
Baskunchak, Ozero l. Rus. Fed. 53 J6
Basle Switz. see Basel
Basmat India 106 C2
Baso i. Indon. 84 C3
Basoko Dem. Rep. Congo 122 C3
Basol r. Pak. 111 G5
Basra Iraq 113 G5
Bassano Canada 151 H5
Bassano del Grappa Italy 68 D2
Bassar Togo 120 D4
Bassas da India reef Indian Ocean 123 D6
Bassas de Pedro Padua Bank sea feature India 106 B3
Bassein Myanmar 86 A3
Bassein r. Myanmar 86 A3
Basse-Normandie admin. reg. France 59 F9
Bassenthwaite Lake U.K. 58 D4
Basse Santa Su Gambia 120 B3

▶Basse-Terre Guadeloupe 169 L5
Capital of Guadeloupe.

▶Basseterre St Kitts and Nevis 169 L5
Capital of St Kitts and Nevis.

Bassett NE U.S.A. 160 D3
Bassett VA U.S.A. 164 F5
Bassikounou Mauritania 120 C3
Bass Rock i. U.K. 60 G4
Bass Strait Australia 137 D8
Bassum Germany 63 I2
Basswood Lake Canada 152 C4
Båstad Sweden 55 H8
Bāstānābād Iran 110 B2
Bastheim Germany 63 K4
Basti India 105 E4
Bastia Corsica France 66 I5
Bastioes r. Brazil 177 K5
Bastogne Belgium 62 F4
Bastrop LA U.S.A. 161 F5
Bastrop TX U.S.A. 161 D6
Basu, Tanjung pt Indon. 84 C3
Basuo China see Dongfang
Basutoland country Africa see Lesotho
Başyayla Turkey 107 A1
Bata Equat. Guinea 120 D4
Bataan Peninsula Luzon Phil. 82 C3
Batabanó, Golfo de b. Cuba 169 H4
Batac Luzon Phil. 82 C2
Batagay Rus. Fed. 77 O3
Batakan Kalimantan Indon. 85 F4
Batala India 104 C3
Batalha Port. 67 B4
Batam i. Indon. 84 D2
Batamay Rus. Fed. 77 N3
Batamshinskiy Kazakh. 102 A1
Batamshy Kazakh. see Batamshinskiy
Batan Jiangsu China 97 I1
Batan Qinghai China 96 D1
Batan i. Phil. 82 C1
Batan i. Phil. 82 D3
Batang China 96 C2
Batang Jawa Indon. 85 E4
Batangafo Cent. Afr. Rep. 122 B3
Batang Ai National Park Malaysia 85 F2
Batangas Luzon Phil. 82 C3
Batanghari r. Indon. 84 D3
Batangpele i. Papua Indon. 83 D3
Batangtarang Kalimantan Indon. 85 E2
Batangtoru Sumatera Indon. 84 B2
Batan Islands Phil. 82 C1
Batanta i. Papua Indon. 83 D3
Batavia Jawa Indon. see Jakarta
Batavia NY U.S.A. 165 F2
Batavia OH U.S.A. 164 C4
Bataysk Rus. Fed. 53 H7
Batbatan i. Phil. 82 C4
Batchawana Mountain hill Canada 152 D5
Bătdâmbâng Cambodia 87 C4
Bateemeucica, Gunung mt. Indon. 84 A1
Batéké, Plateaux Congo 122 B4
Batemans Bay Australia 138 E5
Bates Range hills Australia 135 C6
Batesville AR U.S.A. 161 F5
Batesville IN U.S.A. 164 C4
Batesville MS U.S.A. 161 F5
Batetskiy Rus. Fed. 52 F4
Bath N.B. Canada 153 I5
Bath Ont. Canada 165 G1
Bath U.K. 59 E7
Bath ME U.S.A. 165 K2
Bath NY U.S.A. 165 G2
Bath PA U.S.A. 165 H3
Batha watercourse Chad 121 E3
Bathgate U.K. 60 F5
Bathinda India 104 C3
Bathurst Australia 138 D4
Bathurst Canada 153 I5
Bathurst Gambia see Banjul
Bathurst S. Africa 125 H7
Bathurst, Cape Canada 149 P1
Bathurst, Lake Australia 138 D5
Bathurst Inlet inlet Canada 146 H3
Bathurst Inlet (abandoned) Canada 146 H3
Bathurst Island Australia 134 E2
Bathurst Island Canada 147 I2
Bathyz Döwlet Gorugy nature res. Turkm. 111 F3
Batié Burkina Faso 120 C4
Batikala, Tanjung pt Indon. 83 B3
Batı Menteşe Dağları mts Turkey 69 L6
Batı Toroslar mts Turkey 69 N6
Batken Kyrg. 102 D4
Batkes Indon. 134 E1
Bāţlāq-e Gavkhūnī marsh Iran 110 D3
Batley U.K. 58 F5
Batlow Australia 138 D5
Batman Turkey 113 F3
Batna Alg. 64 F4
Batnorov Mongolia 95 G2
Batō Japan 93 G2
Batok, Bukit hill Sing. 87 [inset]
Bat-Öldziy Mongolia 94 E2
Batong, Ko i. Thai. 84 B1

▶Baton Rouge LA U.S.A. 161 F6
Capital of Louisiana.

Batopilas Mex. 166 D3
Batouri Cameroon 121 E4
Batrā' tourist site Jordan see Petra
Batrā', Jabal al mt. Jordan 107 B5
Batroûn Lebanon 107 B2
Båtsfjord Norway 54 P1
Batshireet Mongolia 95 G1
Batsümber Mongolia 94 F1
Battambang Cambodia see Bătdâmbâng
Batticaloa Sri Lanka 106 D5
Batti Malv i. India 87 A5
Battipaglia Italy 68 F4
Battle r. Canada 151 I4
Battle Creek MI U.S.A. 164 C2
Battleford Canada 151 I4
Battle Mountain NV U.S.A. 158 E1
Battle Mountain mt. NV U.S.A. 158 E1
Battsengel Mongolia 94 E2
Battura Glacier Pak. 104 C1
Batu mt. Eth. 122 D3
Batu, Bukit mt. Malaysia 85 F2
Batu, Pulau-pulau is Indon. 84 B3
Batu, Tanjung pt Indon. 85 G2
Batuata i. Indon. 83 B4
Batubetumbang Indon. 84 D3
Batu Bora, Bukit mt. Malaysia 85 F2
Batudaka i. Indon. 83 B3
Batu Gajah Malaysia 84 C1
Batuhitam, Tanjung pt Indon. 83 B3
Batui Sulawesi Indon. 83 B3
Batulaki Mindanao Phil. 82 D5
Batulicin Kalimantan Indon. 85 G3
Batulilangmebang, Gunung mt. Indon. 85 F2
Batum Georgia see Bat'umi
Bat'umi Georgia 113 F2
Batumonga Indon. 84 C3
Batu Pahat Malaysia 84 C2
Batu Putih, Gunung mt. Malaysia 84 C1
Baturaja Sumatera Indon. 84 D4
Baturetno Jawa Indon. 85 E5
Baturité Brazil 177 K4
Batusangkar Sumatera Indon. 84 C3
Batyrevo Rus. Fed. 53 J5
Batys Qazaqstan admin. div. Kazakh. see Zapadnyy Kazakhstan
Bau Sarawak Malaysia 85 E2
Baubau Sulawesi Indon. 83 B4
Baucau East Timor 83 C5
Bauchi Nigeria 120 D3
Bauda India see Boudh
Baudette MN U.S.A. 160 E1
Baudh India see Boudh
Baugé France 66 D3
Bauhinia Australia 136 E5
Baukau East Timor see Baucau
Baula Sulawesi Indon. 83 B4
Bauld, Cape Canada 153 L4
Baume-les-Dames France 66 H3
Baunach r. Germany 63 K5
Baundal India 104 C2
Baura Bangl. 105 G4
Bauru Brazil 179 A3
Bausendorf Germany 62 G4
Bauska Latvia 55 N8
Bautino Kazakh. 113 H1
Bautzen Germany 57 O5
Bavānāt Iran 110 D4
Bavaria land Germany see Bayern
Bavaria reg. Germany 63 L6
Bavda India 106 B2
Baviaanskloofberge mts S. Africa 124 F7
Bavispe Mex. 166 C2
Bavispe r. Mex. 166 C2
Bavla India 104 C5
Bavly Rus. Fed. 51 Q5
Baw Myanmar 86 A2
Bawal India 104 D3
Bawal i. Indon. 85 E3
Bawan Kalimantan Indon. 85 F3
Bawang, Tanjung pt Indon. 85 E3
Baw Baw National Park Australia 138 C6
Bawdeswell U.K. 59 I6
Bawdwin Myanmar 86 B2
Bawean i. Indon. 85 F4
Bawinkel Germany 63 H2
Bawlake Myanmar 86 B3
Bawolung China 96 D2
Baxi China 96 D1
Baxian China see Bazhou
Baxkorgan China 98 E5
Baxley GA U.S.A. 163 D6
Baxoi China 96 C2
Baxter Mountain CO U.S.A. 159 J2
Bay China see Baicheng
Bay, Laguna de lag. Luzon Phil. 82 C3
Bayamo Cuba 169 I4
Bayan Heilong. China 90 B3
Bayan Qinghai China 94 D5
Bayan Qinghai China see Hualong
Bayan Lombok Indon. 85 G5
Bayan Arhangay Mongolia see Hashaat
Bayan Govĭ-Altay Mongolia see Bayan-Uul
Bayan Töv Mongolia 95 F2
Bayana India 104 D4
Bayan-Adraga Mongolia 95 G1
Bayanauyl Kazakh. 102 E1
Bayanbulag Bayanhongor Mongolia see Bayantsagaan
Bayanbulag Bayanhongor Mongolia 94 D2
Bayanbulag Hentiy Mongolia see Ömnödelger
Bayanbulak Xinjiang China 98 D3
Bayanbulak Xinjiang China 98 D4
Bayanchandmanĭ Mongolia 94 F1
Bayandalay Mongolia 94 E3
Bayanday Rus. Fed. 88 J2
Bayandelger Sühbaatar Mongolia 95 H2
Bayandelger Töv Mongolia 95 G2
Bayandun Mongolia 95 H1
Bayang, Pegunungan mts Indon. 85 E2
Bayan Gol China see Dengkou
Bayangol Govĭ-Altay Mongolia see Bugat
Bayangol Selenge Mongolia 94 F1
Bayangol Rus. Fed. 94 E1
Bayan Har Shan mts China 94 C5
Bayan Har Shankou pass China 94 D5
Bayanhongor Mongolia 94 E2
Bayanhongor prov. Mongolia 94 D2
Bayan Hot China 94 F4
Bayanhushuu Mongolia see Galuut
Bayanjargalan Mongolia 95 F2
Bayan-Kol Rus. Fed. 94 D1
Bayan Kuang China 95 G3
Bayanlig Mongolia 94 E2
Bayan Mod China 94 F3
Bayanmönh Mongolia 95 G2
Bayan Nuru China 94 F3
Bayannuur Mongolia 94 F2
Bayan-Ölgiy prov. Mongolia 94 B1
Bayan-Öndör Mongolia 94 F2
Bayan-Önjüül Mongolia 94 F2
Bayan-Ovoo Govĭ-Altay Mongolia see Altay
Bayan-Ovoo Hentiy Mongolia see Dadal
Bayan-Ovoo Hentiy Mongolia 95 H2
Bayan-Ovoo Ömnögovĭ Mongolia 94 F3
Bayan Qagan Nei Mongol China 95 H3
Bayan Qagan Nei Mongol China 95 J2
Bayansayr Mongolia see Baatsagaan
Bayan Shan mt. China 94 D4
Bayansumküre China 98 D4
Bayan Tal China 95 I1
Bayanteeg Mongolia 94 E2
Bayan Tohoi China 95 I1
Bayantöhöm Mongolia see Büren
Bayantsagaan Bayanhongor Mongolia 94 D2
Bayantsagaan Töv Mongolia 95 F2
Bayan Ul Hot China 95 I2
Bayan Us China 95 G3
Bayan-Uul Dornod Mongolia 95 H1
Bayan-Uul Govĭ-Altay Mongolia 94 C2
Bayan Uul mts Mongolia 94 B1
Bayard NM U.S.A. 159 I5
Bayasgalant Mongolia see Mönhaan
Bayat Turkey 69 N5
Bayawan Negros Phil. 82 C4
Bayāz Iran 110 E4
Baybay Leyte Phil. 82 D4
Bayboro NC U.S.A. 163 E5
Bayburt Turkey 113 F2
Bay Canh, Hon i. Vietnam 87 D5
Bay City MI U.S.A. 164 D2
Bay City TX U.S.A. 161 D6
Baydaratskaya Guba Rus. Fed. 76 H3
Baydhabo Somalia 122 E3
Baydrag Mongolia see Dzag
Baydrag Gol r. Mongolia 94 D2
Bayerischer Wald mts Germany 57 N6
Bayerischer Wald, Nationalpark nat. park Germany 57 N6
Bayern land Germany 63 L6
Bayeux France 59 G9
Bayfield Canada 164 E2
Bayiji China 95 I5
Bayındır Turkey 69 L5
Bay Islands is Hond. see Bahía, Islas de la
Bayizhen China see Nyingchi
Bayjī Iraq 113 F4
Baykal-Amur Magistral Rus. Fed. 90 C1
Baykal Range mts Rus. Fed. see Baykal'skiy Khrebet
Baykal'sk Rus. Fed. 94 F1
Baykal'skiy Khrebet mts Rus. Fed. 89 J2
Baykal'skiy Zapovednik nature res. Rus. Fed. 94 F1
Baykan Turkey 113 F3
Bay-Khaak Rus. Fed. 102 H1
Baykibashevo Rus. Fed. 51 R4
Baykonur Kazakh. see Baykonyr
Baykonyr Kazakh. 102 B2
Baymak Rus. Fed. 76 G4
Bay Minette AL U.S.A. 163 C6
Baynūna'h reg. U.A.E. 110 D6
Bayombong Luzon Phil. 82 C2
Bayona Spain see Baiona
Bayonne France 66 D5
Bayonne NJ U.S.A. 165 H3
Bayo Point Panay Phil. 82 C4
Bay Point Phil. 82 B4
Bay Port MI U.S.A. 164 D2
Bayqongyr Kazakh. see Baykonyr
Bayram-Ali Turkm. see Baýramaly
Baýramaly Turkm. 111 F2
Bayramiç Turkey 69 L5
Bayreuth Germany 63 L5
Bayrüt Lebanon see Beirut
Bays, Lake of Canada 164 F1
Bayshore MI U.S.A. 164 C1
Bay Shore NY U.S.A. 165 I3
Bay Springs MS U.S.A. 161 F6
Bayston Hill U.K. 59 E6
Baysun Uzbek. see Boysun
Baytik Shan mts China 94 B2
Bayt Lahm West Bank see Bethlehem
Baytown TX U.S.A. 161 E6
Bayu Sulawesi Indon. 83 B3
Bayunglincir Sumatera Indon. 84 C3
Bay View N.Z. 139 F4
Bayy al Kabīr, Wādī watercourse Libya 121 E1
Baza Spain 67 E5
Baza, Sierra de mts Spain 67 E5
Bazar watercourse Kazakh. 98 C2
Bāzārak Afgh. 111 G3
Bazardüzü Dağı mt. Azer./Rus. Fed. see Bazardyuzyu, Gora
Bazardyuzyu, Gora mt. Azer./Rus. Fed. 113 G2
Bāzār-e Māsāl Iran 110 C2
Bazarnyy Karabulak Rus. Fed. 53 J5
Bazaruto, Ilha do i. Moz. 123 D6
Bazdar Pak. 111 G5
Bazhong China 96 E2
Bazhou Hebei China 95 I4
Bazhou Sichuan China see Bazhong
Bazin r. Canada 152 G5
Bazmān Iran 111 F5
Bazmān, Kūh-e mt. Iran 111 F4
Bcharré Lebanon 107 C2
Be, Sông r. Vietnam 87 D5
Beach ND U.S.A. 160 C2
Beachy Head hd U.K. 59 H8
Beacon NY U.S.A. 165 I3
Beacon Bay S. Africa 125 H7
Beaconsfield U.K. 59 G7
Beagle, Canal sea chan. Arg. 178 C8
Beagle Bank reef Australia 134 C3
Beagle Bay Australia 134 C4
Beagle Gulf Australia 134 E3
Bealanana Madag. 123 E5
Béal an Átha Ireland see Ballina
Béal an Mhuirthead Ireland 61 C3
Béal Átha na Sluaighe Ireland see Ballinasloe
Beale, Lake India 106 B2
Beaminster U.K. 59 E8
Bear r. ID U.S.A. 156 E4
Bearalváhki Norway see Berlevåg
Bear Cove Point Canada 151 O2
Beardmore Canada 152 D4
Beardmore Glacier Antarctica 188 H1
Bear Island Arctic Ocean see Bjørnøya
Bear Island Canada 152 E3
Bear Lake l. Canada 152 A3
Bear Lake MI U.S.A. 164 B1
Bear Lake l. ID U.S.A. 156 F4
Bearma r. India 104 D4
Bear Mountain SD U.S.A. 160 C3
Bearnaraigh i. U.K. see Berneray
Bear Paw Mountain MT U.S.A. 156 F2
Bearpaw Mountains MT U.S.A. 156 F2
Bearskin Lake Canada 151 N4
Beas Dam India 104 C3
Beata, Cabo c. Dom. Rep. 169 J5
Beatrice NE U.S.A. 160 D3
Beatrice, Cape Australia 136 B2
Beatton r. Canada 150 F3
Beatton River Canada 150 F3
Beatty NV U.S.A. 158 E3
Beattyville Canada 152 F4
Beattyville KY U.S.A. 164 D5
Beaucaire France 66 G5
Beauchene Island Falkland Is 178 E8
Beaufort Australia 138 A6
Beaufort Sabah Malaysia 85 F1
Beaufort NC U.S.A. 163 E5
Beaufort SC U.S.A. 163 D5
Beaufort Island H.K. China 97 [inset]
Beaufort Lagoon AK U.S.A. 149 L1
Beaufort Sea Canada/U.S.A. 146 D2
Beaufort West S. Africa 124 F7
Beaulieu r. Canada 151 H2
Beauly U.K. 60 E3
Beauly r. U.K. 60 E3
Beaumaris U.K. 58 C5
Beaumont Belgium 62 E4
Beaumont N.Z. 139 B7
Beaumont MS U.S.A. 161 F6
Beaumont TX U.S.A. 161 E6
Beaune France 66 G3
Beaupréau France 66 D3
Beauquesne France 62 C4
Beauraing Belgium 62 E4
Beauséjour Canada 151 L5
Beauvais France 62 C5
Beauval France 62 C4
Beaver r. Alba/Sask. Canada 151 J4
Beaver r. Ont. Canada 152 D3
Beaver r. Y.T. Canada 149 N3
Beaver r. Y.T. Canada 150 E3
Beaver AK U.S.A. 149 K2
Beaver OK U.S.A. 161 C4
Beaver PA U.S.A. 164 E3
Beaver UT U.S.A. 159 G2
Beaver r. UT U.S.A. 159 G2
Beaver Creek Canada 149 L3
Beavercreek OH U.S.A. 164 C4
Beaver Creek r. AK U.S.A. 149 K2
Beaver Creek r. MT U.S.A. 160 B1
Beaver Creek r. ND U.S.A. 160 C2
Beaver Dam KY U.S.A. 164 B5
Beaver Dam WI U.S.A. 160 F3
Beaver Falls PA U.S.A. 164 E3
Beaverhead Mountains MT U.S.A. 156 E3
Beaverhill Lake Alta Canada 151 H4
Beaver Hill Lake Man. Canada 151 M4
Beaverhill Lake N.W.T. Canada 151 J2
Beaver Island MI U.S.A. 162 C2
Beaverlodge Canada 150 G4
Beaver Mountains AK U.S.A. 148 H3
Beaverton Canada 164 F1
Beaverton MI U.S.A. 164 C2
Beaverton OR U.S.A. 156 C3
Beawar India 104 C4
Beazley Arg. 178 C4
Bebedouro Brazil 179 A3
Bebington U.K. 58 D5
Bebra Germany 63 J4
Bêca China 96 C2
Bécard, Lac l. Canada 153 G1
Beccles U.K. 59 I6
Bečej Serbia 69 I2
Becerreá Spain 67 C2
Béchar Alg. 64 D5
Becharof Lake AK U.S.A. 148 H4
Becharof National Wildlife Refuge nature res. AK U.S.A. 148 H4
Bechevin Bay AK U.S.A. 148 G5
Bechhofen Germany 63 K5
Bechuanaland country Africa see Botswana
Beckley WV U.S.A. 164 E5
Beckum Germany 63 I3
Becky Peak NV U.S.A. 159 F2
Beco East Timor 83 C5
Bečov nad Teplou Czech Rep. 63 M4
Bedale U.K. 58 F4
Bedburg Germany 62 G4
Bedel', Pereval pass China/Kyrg. see Bedel Pass
Bedelē Eth. 122 D3
Bedel Pass China/Kyrg. 98 B4
Bedford N.S. Canada 153 J5
Bedford Que. Canada 165 I1
Bedford E. Cape S. Africa 125 H7
Bedford KwaZulu-Natal S. Africa 125 J5
Bedford U.K. 59 G6
Bedford IN U.S.A. 164 B4
Bedford KY U.S.A. 164 C4
Bedford PA U.S.A. 165 F3
Bedford VA U.S.A. 164 F5
Bedford, Cape Australia 136 D2
Bedford Downs Australia 134 D4
Bedgerebong Australia 138 C4
Bedi India 104 B5
Bedinggong Indon. 84 D3
Bedla India 104 C4
Bedlington U.K. 58 F3
Bedok Sing. 87 [inset]
Bedok Jetty Sing. 87 [inset]
Bedok Reservoir Sing. 87 [inset]
Bedourie Australia 136 B5
Bedum Neth. 62 G1
Bedworth U.K. 59 F6
Beechworth Australia 138 C6
Beechy Canada 151 J5
Beecroft Peninsula Australia 138 E5
Beed India see Bid
Beelitz Germany 63 M2
Beenleigh Australia 138 F1
Beernem Belgium 62 D3
Beersheba Israel 107 B4
Be'ér Sheva' Israel see Beersheba
Be'ér Sheva' watercourse Israel 107 B4
Beervlei Dam S. Africa 124 F7
Beerwah Australia 138 F1
Beetaloo Australia 134 F4
Beethoven Peninsula Antarctica 188 L2
Beeville TX U.S.A. 161 D6
Befori Dem. Rep. Congo 122 C3
Beg, Lough l. U.K. 61 F3
Bega Australia 138 D6
Bega Maluku Indon. 83 C3
Begari r. Pak. 111 H4
Begicheva, Ostrov i. Rus. Fed. see Bol'shoy Begichev, Ostrov
Begur, Cap de c. Spain 67 H3
Begusarai India 105 F4
Behābād Iran 110 D4
Béhague, Pointe pt Fr. Guiana 177 H3
Behbehān Iran 110 C4
Behchokò Canada 150 G2
Behleg China 99 E5
Behrendt Mountains Antarctica 188 L2
Behrūsī Iran 110 D4
Behshahr Iran 110 D2
Bei'an China 90 B2
Bei'ao China see Dongtou
Beibei China 96 E2
Beichuan China 96 E2
Beida Libya see Al Bayḍā'
Beida Shan mts China 94 E4
Beigang Taiwan see Peikang
Beihai China 97 F4
Bei Hulsan Hu salt l. China 99 F5

▶Beijing China 95 I4
Capital of China.

Beijing mun. China 95 I3
Beik Myanmar see Myeik
Beilen Neth. 62 G2
Beiliu China 97 F4
Beilngries Germany 63 L5
Beilu He r. China 99 F6
Beiluheyan China 94 C5
Beining China see Beizhen
Beinn an Oir hill U.K. 60 D5
Beinn an Tuirc hill U.K. 60 D5
Beinn Bheigeir hill U.K. 60 C5
Beinn Bhreac hill U.K. 60 D4
Beinn Dearg mt. U.K. 60 E3
Beinn Heasgarnich mt. U.K. 60 E4
Beinn Mholach hill U.K. 60 C2
Beinn Mhòr hill U.K. 60 B3
Beinn na Faoghlia i. U.K. see Benbecula
Beipan Jiang r. China 96 E3
Beipiao China 95 J3
Beira Moz. 123 D5
Beiru He r. China 95 H5

▶Beirut Lebanon 107 B3
Capital of Lebanon.

Beishan China 94 D3
Bei Shan mts China 94 C3
Beitbridge Zimbabwe 123 C6
Beith U.K. 60 E5
Beit Jālā West Bank 107 B4
Beitun China 98 D3
Beizhen China 95 J3
Beja Port. 67 C4
Béja Tunisia 68 C6
Bejaïa Alg. 67 I5
Béjar Spain 67 D3
Beji r. Pak. 102 C6
Bejucos Mex. 167 E5
Bekaa valley Lebanon see El Béqaa
Bekasi Jawa Indon. 84 D4
Békés Hungary 69 I1
Békéscsaba Hungary 69 I1
Bekily Madag. 123 E6
Bekkai Japan 90 G4
Bēkma, Sadd dam Iraq 113 G3
Bekovo Rus. Fed. 53 I5
Bekwai Ghana 120 C4
Bela India 105 E4
Bela Pak. 111 G5
Belab r. Pak. 111 H4
Bela-Bela S. Africa 125 I3
Bélabo Cameroon 120 E4
Bela Crkva Serbia 69 I2
Belaga Sarawak Malaysia 85 F2
Bel'agash Kazakh. 98 C2
Bel Air MD U.S.A. 165 G4
Belalcázar Spain 67 D4
Bělá nad Radbuzou Czech Rep. 63 M5
Belang Sulawesi Indon. 83 C2
Belangbelang i. Maluku Indon. 83 C3
Belapur India 106 B2
Belarus country Europe 53 E5
Belau country N. Pacific Ocean see Palau
Bela Vista Brazil 178 E2
Bela Vista Moz. 125 K4
Bela Vista de Goiás Brazil 179 A2
Belawan Sumatera Indon. 84 B2
Belaya r. Rus. Fed. 77 S3
also known as Bila
Belaya, Gora mt. Rus. Fed. 148 A2
Belaya Glina Rus. Fed. 53 I7
Belaya Kalitva Rus. Fed. 53 I6
Belaya Kholunitsa Rus. Fed. 52 K4
Belayan r. Indon. 85 G3
Belayan, Gunung mt. Indon. 85 F2
Belaya Tserkva Ukr. see Bila Tserkva
Belbédji Niger 120 D3
Bełchatów Poland 57 Q5
Belcher KY U.S.A. 164 D5
Belcher Islands Canada 152 F2
Belchiragh Afgh. 111 G3
Belcoo U.K. 61 E3
Belden CA U.S.A. 158 C1
Belding MI U.S.A. 164 C2
Beleapani reef India see Cherbaniani Reef
Belebey Rus. Fed. 51 Q5
Beledweyne Somalia 122 E3
Belém Brazil 177 I4
Belém Novo Brazil 179 A5
Belén Arg. 178 C3
Belen Antalya Turkey 107 A1
Belen Hatay Turkey 107 C1
Belen NM U.S.A. 157 G6
Belep, Îles is New Caledonia 133 G3
Belev Rus. Fed. 53 H5

▶Belfast U.K. 61 G3
Capital of Northern Ireland.

Belfast ME U.S.A. 162 G2
Belfast Lough inlet U.K. 61 G3
Bēlfodiyo Eth. 122 D2
Belford U.K. 58 F3
Belfort France 66 H3
Belgaum India 106 B3
Belgern Germany 63 N3
Belgian Congo country Africa see Congo, Democratic Republic of the
België country Europe see Belgium
Belgique country Europe see Belgium
Belgium country Europe 62 E4

Belgorod Rus. Fed. 53 H6
Belgorod-Dnestrovskyy Ukr. see Bilhorod-Dnistrovs'kyy

▶Belgrade Serbia 69 I2
Capital of Serbia.

Belgrade ME U.S.A. 165 K1
Belgrade MT U.S.A. 156 F3
Belgrano II research station Antarctica 188 A1
Belice r. Sicily Italy 68 E6
Beliliou i. Palau see Peleliu
Belimbing Sumatera Indon. 84 D4
Belinskiy Rus. Fed. 53 I5
Belinyu Indon. 84 D3
Belitung i. Indon. 85 E3
Belize Angola 123 B4

▶Belize Belize 167 H5
Former capital of Belize.

Belize country Central America 167 H5
Beljak Austria see Villach
Belkina, Mys pt Rus. Fed. 90 E3
Belkofski AK U.S.A. 148 G5
Bel'kovskiy, Ostrov i. Rus. Fed. 77 O2
Bell Australia 138 E1
Bell r. Australia 138 D4
Bell r. Que. Canada 152 F4
Bell r. Y.T. Canada 149 M2
Bella Bella Canada 150 D4
Bellac France 66 E3
Bella Coola Canada 150 E4
Bellaire MI U.S.A. 164 C1
Bellaire TX U.S.A. 167 G2
Bellary India 106 C3
Bellata Australia 138 D2
Bella Unión Uruguay 178 E4
Bella Vista CA U.S.A. 158 B1
Bellbrook Australia 138 F3
Bell Cay reef Australia 136 E4
Belledonne mts France 66 G4
Bellefontaine OH U.S.A. 164 D3
Bellefonte PA U.S.A. 165 G3
Belle Fourche SD U.S.A. 160 C2
Belle Fourche r. SD U.S.A. 160 C2
Belle Glade FL U.S.A. 163 D7
Belle-Île i. France 66 C3
Belle Isle i. Canada 153 L4
Belle Isle, Strait of Canada 153 K4
Belleville Canada 165 G1
Belleville IL U.S.A. 160 F4
Belleville KS U.S.A. 160 D4
Bellevue IA U.S.A. 160 F3
Bellevue MI U.S.A. 164 C2
Bellevue OH U.S.A. 164 D3
Bellevue WA U.S.A. 156 C3
Bellin Canada see Kangirsuk
Bellingham U.K. 58 E3
Bellingham WA U.S.A. 156 C2
Bellingshausen research station Antarctica 188 A2
Bellingshausen Sea Antarctica 188 L2
Bellinzona Switz. 66 I3
Bellows Falls VT U.S.A. 165 I2
Bellpat Pak. 111 H4
Belluno Italy 68 E1
Bell Ville Arg. 178 D4
Bellville S. Africa 124 D7
Belm Germany 63 I2
Belmont Australia 138 E4
Belmont U.K. 60 [inset]
Belmont NY U.S.A. 165 F2
Belmonte Brazil 179 D1

▶Belmopan Belize 167 H5
Capital of Belize.

Belmore, Mount hill Australia 138 F2
Belo Madag. 123 E6
Belo Campo Brazil 179 C1
Belœil Belgium 62 D4
Belogorsk Rus. Fed. 90 C2
Belogorsk Ukr. see Bilohirs'k
Beloha Madag. 123 E6
Belo Horizonte Brazil 179 C2
Beloit KS U.S.A. 160 D4
Beloit WI U.S.A. 160 F3
Belokurikha Rus. Fed. 102 F1
Belo Monte Brazil 177 H4
Belomorsk Rus. Fed. 52 G2
Belonia India 105 G5
Belopa Sulawesi Indon. 83 B3
Belorechensk Rus. Fed. 113 E1
Belorechenskaya Rus. Fed. see Belorechensk
Belören Turkey 112 D3
Beloretsk Rus. Fed. 76 G4
Belorussia country Europe see Belarus
Belorusskaya S.S.R. country Europe see Belarus
Belostok Poland see Białystok
Belot, Lac l. Canada 149 P2
Belo Tsiribihina Madag. 123 E5
Belousovka Kazakh. 98 C2
Belovo Rus. Fed. 88 F2
Beloyarskiy Rus. Fed. 51 T3
Beloye, Ozero l. Rus. Fed. 52 H3
Beloye More sea Rus. Fed. see White Sea
Belozersk Rus. Fed. 52 H3
Belpre OH U.S.A. 164 E4
Beltana Australia 137 B6
Belted Range mts NV U.S.A. 158 E3
Beltes Gol r. Mongolia 94 D1
Belton TX U.S.A. 161 D6
Bel'ts' Moldova see Bălţi
Bel'tsy Moldova see Bălţi
Beluga Lake AK U.S.A. 149 J3
Belukha, Gora mt. Kazakh./Rus. Fed. 102 G2
Beluran Sabah Malaysia 85 G1
Belush'ye Rus. Fed. 52 J2
Belvidere IL U.S.A. 160 F3
Belvidere NJ U.S.A. 165 H3
Belyaka, Kosa spit Rus. Fed. 148 D2
Belyando r. Australia 136 D4
Belyayevka Ukr. see Bilyayivka
Belyy Rus. Fed. 52 G5
Belyy, Ostrov i. Rus. Fed. 76 I2
Belyy Bom Rus. Fed. 98 D2
Belzig Germany 63 M2
Belzoni MS U.S.A. 161 F5
Bemaraha, Plateau du Madag. 123 E5
Bembe Angola 123 B4
Bemidji MN U.S.A. 160 E2
Béna Burkina Faso 120 C3
Bena Dibele Dem. Rep. Congo 122 C4
Benagin Kalimantan Indon. 85 F3
Ben Alder mt. U.K. 60 E4
Benalla Australia 138 B6
Benares India see Varanasi
Ben Arous Tunisia 68 D6
Benavente Spain 67 D2
Ben Avon mt. U.K. 60 F3
Benbane Head hd U.K. 61 F2
Benbecula i. U.K. 60 B3
Ben Boyd National Park Australia 138 E6
Benburb U.K. 61 F3
Bencha China 97 I1
Bencheng China see Luannan
Ben Chonzie hill U.K. 60 F4
Ben Cleuch hill U.K. 60 F4
Ben Cruachan mt. U.K. 60 D4
Bend OR U.S.A. 156 C3
Bendearg mt. S. Africa 125 H6
Bendeleben, Mount AK U.S.A. 148 F2
Bendeleben Mountains AK U.S.A. 148 F2
Bender Moldova see Tighina
Bender-Bayla Somalia 122 F3
Bendery Moldova see Tighina
Bendigo Australia 138 B6
Bendoc Australia 138 D6
Bene Moz. 123 D5
Benedict, Mount hill Canada 153 K3
Benenitra Madag. 123 E6
Benešov Czech Rep. 57 O6
Bénestroff France 62 G6
Benevento Italy 68 F4
Beneventum Italy see Benevento
Benezette PA U.S.A. 165 F3
Beng, Nâm r. Laos 86 C3
Bengal, Bay of sea Indian Ocean 103 G8
Bengaluru India see Bangalore
Bengamisa Dem. Rep. Congo 122 C3
Bengbu China 97 H1
Benghazi Libya 121 F1
Beng He r. China 95 I5
Bengkalis Sumatera Indon. 84 C2
Bengkalis i. Indon. 84 C2
Bengkayang Kalimantan Indon. 85 E2
Bengkulu Sumatera Indon. 84 C3
Bengkulu prov. Indon. 84 C3
Bengkung Kalimantan Indon. 85 G3
Bengoi Seram Indon. 83 D3
Bengtsfors Sweden 55 H7
Benguela Angola 123 B5
Benha Egypt see Banhā
Ben Hiant hill U.K. 60 C4
Ben Hope hill U.K. 60 E2
Ben Horn hill U.K. 60 E2
Beni r. Bol. 176 E6
Beni Dem. Rep. Congo 122 C3
Beni Nepal 105 E3
Beni Abbès Alg. 64 D5
Beniah Lake Canada 151 H2
Benidorm Spain 67 F4
Beni Mellal Morocco 64 C5
Benin country Africa 120 D4
Benin, Bight of g. Africa 120 D4
Benin City Nigeria 120 D4
Beni Saf Alg. 67 F6
Beni Snassen, Monts des mts Morocco 67 E6
Beni Suef Egypt see Banī Suwayf
Benito, Islas is Mex. 166 B2
Benito Juárez Arg. 178 E5
Benito Juárez Mex. 159 F5
Benito Soliven Luzon Phil. 82 C2
Benjamim Constant Brazil 176 E4
Benjamin TX U.S.A. 161 D5
Benjamín Hill Mex. 166 C2
Benjina Indon. 81 I8
Benkelman NE U.S.A. 160 C3
Ben Klibreck hill U.K. 60 E2
Ben Lavin Nature Reserve S. Africa 125 I2
Ben Lawers mt. U.K. 60 E4
Ben Lomond mt. Australia 138 E3
Ben Lomond hill U.K. 60 E4
Ben Lomond National Park Australia 137 [inset]
Ben Macdui mt. U.K. 60 F3
Benmara Australia 136 B3
Ben More hill U.K. 60 C4
Ben More mt. U.K. 60 E4
Benmore, Lake N.Z. 139 C7
Ben More Assynt hill U.K. 60 E2
Bennetta, Ostrov i. Rus. Fed. 77 P2
Bennett Island Rus. Fed. see Bennetta, Ostrov
Bennett Lake Canada 149 N4
Bennettsville SC U.S.A. 163 E5
Ben Nevis mt. U.K. 60 D4
Bennington NH U.S.A. 165 J2
Bennington VT U.S.A. 165 I2
Benoni S. Africa 125 I4
Ben Rinnes hill U.K. 60 F3
Bensheim Germany 63 I5
Benson AZ U.S.A. 159 H6
Benson MN U.S.A. 160 E2
Benta Seberang Malaysia 84 C1
Benteng Sulawesi Indon. 83 B4
Bentinck Island Myanmar 87 B5
Bentiu South Sudan 108 C8
Bent Jbaïl Lebanon 107 B3
Bentley U.K. 58 F5
Bento Gonçalves Brazil 179 A5
Benton AR U.S.A. 161 E5
Benton CA U.S.A. 158 D3
Benton IL U.S.A. 160 F4
Benton KY U.S.A. 161 F4
Benton LA U.S.A. 161 E5
Benton MO U.S.A. 161 F4
Benton PA U.S.A. 165 G3
Bentong Malaysia see Bentung
Benton Harbor MI U.S.A. 164 B2
Bentonville AR U.S.A. 161 E4
Bên Tre Vietnam 87 D5
Bentung Malaysia 84 C2
Benua Sulawesi Indon. 83 B4
Benua i. Indon. 84 D2
Benuamartinus Kalimantan Indon. 85 F2
Benue r. Nigeria 120 D4
Benum, Gunung mt. Malaysia 84 C2
Ben Vorlich hill U.K. 60 E4
Benwee Head hd Ireland 61 C3
Benwood WV U.S.A. 164 E3
Ben Wyvis mt. U.K. 60 E3
Benxi Liaoning China 90 B4
Benxi Liaoning China 95 J3
Beo Sulawesi Indon. 83 C1
Beograd Serbia see Belgrade
Béoumi Côte d'Ivoire 120 C4
Bepagut, Gunung mt. Indon. 84 C4
Beppu Japan 91 C6
Béqaa valley Lebanon see El Béqaa
Bera, Tasik l. Malaysia 84 C2
Berach r. India 104 C4
Beraketa Madag. 123 E6
Berangas Kalimantan Indon. 85 G3
Bérard, Lac l. Canada 153 H2
Berasia India 104 D5
Berastagi Sumatera Indon. 84 B2
Berat Albania 69 H4
Beratus, Gunung mt. Indon. 85 G3
Berau r. Indon. 85 G2
Beravina Madag. 123 E5
Berbak, Taman Nasional nat. park Indon. 84 D3
Berber Sudan 108 D6
Berbera Somalia 122 E2
Berbérati Cent. Afr. Rep. 122 B3
Berchtesgaden, Nationalpark nat. park Germany 57 N7
Berck France 62 B4
Berdichev Ukr. see Berdychiv
Berdigestyakh Rus. Fed. 77 N3
Berdyans'k Ukr. 53 H7
Berdychiv Ukr. 53 F6
Berea KY U.S.A. 164 C5
Berea OH U.S.A. 164 E3
Berebere Maluku Indon. 83 D2
Beregovo Ukr. see Berehove
Beregovoy Rus. Fed. 90 B1
Berehove Ukr. 53 D6
Bereina P.N.G. 81 L8
Bere Island Ireland 61 C6
Bereket Turkm. 110 D2
Berekum Ghana 120 C4
Berel' Kazakh. 98 D2
Berenice Egypt see Baranīs
Berenice Libya see Benghazi
Berens r. Canada 151 L4
Berens Island Canada 151 L4
Berens River Canada 151 L4
Beresford SD U.S.A. 160 D3
Bereza Belarus see Byaroza
Berezino Belarus see Byerazino
Berezivka Ukr. 53 F7
Berezne Ukr. 53 E6
Bereznik Rus. Fed. 52 I3
Berezniki Rus. Fed. 51 R4
Berezov Rus. Fed. see Berezovo
Berezovka Rus. Fed. 90 B2
Berezovka Ukr. see Berezivka
Berezovo Rus. Fed. 51 T3
Berezovyy Rus. Fed. 90 D2
Berga Germany 63 L3
Berga Spain 67 G2
Bergama Turkey 69 L5
Bergamo Italy 68 C2
Bergby Sweden 55 J6
Bergen Mecklenburg-Vorpommern Germany 57 N3
Bergen Niedersachsen Germany 63 J2
Bergen Norway 55 D6
Bergen NY U.S.A. 165 G2
Bergen op Zoom Neth. 62 E3
Bergerac France 66 E4
Bergères-lès-Vertus France 62 E6
Bergheim (Erft) Germany 62 G4
Bergisches Land reg. Germany 63 H4
Bergisch Gladbach Germany 62 H4
Bergland Namibia 124 C2
Bergomum Italy see Bergamo
Bergoo WV U.S.A. 164 E4
Bergsjö Sweden 55 J6
Bergsviken Sweden 54 L4
Bergtheim Germany 63 K5
Bergues France 62 C4
Bergum Neth. see Burgum
Bergville S. Africa 125 I5
Berh Mongolia 95 G2
Berhala, Selat sea chan. Indon. 84 C3
Berhampur India see Baharampur
Berikat, Tanjung pt Indon. 84 D3
Beringa, Ostrov i. Rus. Fed. 77 R4
Beringen Belgium 62 F3
Bering Glacier AK U.S.A. 148 H4
Bering Glacier AK U.S.A. 149 L3
Bering Lake AK U.S.A. 149 K3
Bering Land Bridge National Preserve nature res. AK U.S.A. 148 F2
Beringovskiy Rus. Fed. 77 S3
Bering Sea N. Pacific Ocean 77 S4
Bering Strait Rus. Fed./U.S.A. 148 E2
Beris, Ra's pt Iran 111 F5
Berislav Ukr. see Beryslav
Berkåk Norway 54 G5
Berkane Morocco 67 E6
Berkel r. Neth. 62 G2
Berkeley CA U.S.A. 158 B3
Berkeley Springs WV U.S.A. 165 F4
Berkhout Neth. 62 F2
Berkner Island Antarctica 188 A1
Berkovitsa Bulg. 69 J3
Berkshire Downs hills U.K. 59 F7
Berkshire Hills MA U.S.A. 165 I2
Berland r. Canada 150 G4
Berlare Belgium 62 E3
Berlevåg Norway 54 P1

▶Berlin Germany 63 N2
Capital of Germany.

Berlin land Germany 63 N2
Berlin MD U.S.A. 165 H4
Berlin NH U.S.A. 165 J1
Berlin PA U.S.A. 165 F4
Berlin Lake OH U.S.A. 164 E3
Bermagui Australia 138 E6
Bermejíllo Mex. 166 E3
Bermejo r. Arg./Bol. 178 E3
Bermejo Bol. 176 F8
Bermen, Lac l. Canada 153 H3

▶Bermuda terr. N. Atlantic Ocean 169 L2
United Kingdom Overseas Territory.

Bermuda Rise sea feature N. Atlantic Ocean 184 D4

▶Bern Switz. 66 H3
Capital of Switzerland.

Bernalillo NM U.S.A. 157 G6
Bernardino de Campos Brazil 179 A3
Bernardo O'Higgins, Parque Nacional nat. park Chile 178 B7
Bernasconi Arg. 178 D5
Bernau Germany 63 N2
Bernburg (Saale) Germany 63 L3
Berne Germany 63 I1
Berne Switz. see Bern
Berne IN U.S.A. 164 C3
Berner Alpen mts Switz. 66 H3
Berneray i. Scotland U.K. 60 B3
Berneray i. Scotland U.K. 60 B4
Bernier Island Australia 135 A6
Bernina Pass Switz. 66 J3
Bernkastel-Kues Germany 62 H5
Beroea Greece see Veroia
Beroea Syria see Aleppo
Beroroha Madag. 123 E6
Beroun Czech Rep. 57 O6
Berounka r. Czech Rep. 57 O6
Berovina Madag. see Beravina
Berri Australia 137 C7
Berriane Alg. 64 E5
Berridale Australia 138 D6
Berriedale U.K. 60 F2
Berrigan Australia 138 B5
Berrima Australia 138 E5
Berrouaghia Alg. 67 H5
Berry Australia 138 E5
Berry KY U.S.A. 164 C4
Berryessa, Lake CA U.S.A. 158 B2
Berry Head hd U.K. 59 D8
Berry Islands Bahamas 163 E7
Berryville VA U.S.A. 165 G4
Berseba Namibia 124 C4
Bersenbrück Germany 63 H2
Berté, Lac l. Canada 153 H4
Berthoud Pass CO U.S.A. 156 G5
Bertolinía Brazil 177 J5
Bertoua Cameroon 120 E4
Bertraghboy Bay Ireland 61 C4
Beru atoll Kiribati 133 H2
Beruri Brazil 176 F4
Beruwala Sri Lanka 106 C5
Berwick Australia 138 B7
Berwick PA U.S.A. 165 G3
Berwick-upon-Tweed U.K. 58 E3
Berwyn hills U.K. 59 D6
Beryslav Ukr. 69 O1
Berytus Lebanon see Beirut
Besah Kalimantan Indon. 85 G2
Besalampy Madag. 123 E5
Besançon France 66 H3
Besar i. Indon. 83 B5
Besar, Gunung mt. Indon. 85 F3
Besar, Gunung mt. Malaysia 87 C7
Besbay Kazakh. 102 A2
Besboro Island AK U.S.A. 148 G2
Beserah Malaysia 84 C2
Beshkent Uzbek. 111 G2
Beshneh Iran 110 D4
Besikama Timor Indon. 83 C5
Besitang Sumatera Indon. 84 B1
Beskra Alg. see Biskra
Beslan Rus. Fed. 113 G2
Besnard Lake Canada 151 J4
Besni Turkey 112 E3
Besoba Kazakh. 98 A2
Besor watercourse Israel 107 B4
Beşparmak Dağları mts Cyprus see Pentadaktylos Range
Bessbrook U.K. 61 F3
Bessemer AL U.S.A. 163 C5
Besshoky, Gora hill Kazakh. 113 I1
Besskorbnaya Rus. Fed. 53 I7
Bessonovka Rus. Fed. 53 J5
Bestamak Kazakh. 98 B2
Betanzos Spain 67 B2
Betet i. Indon. 84 D3
Bethal S. Africa 125 I4
Bethanie Namibia 124 C4
Bethany MO U.S.A. 160 E3
Bethari Nepal 99 C8
Bethel AK U.S.A. 148 G3
Bethel ME U.S.A. 153 H5
Bethel Park PA U.S.A. 164 E3
Bethesda U.K. 58 C5
Bethesda MD U.S.A. 165 G4
Bethesda OH U.S.A. 164 E3
Bethlehem S. Africa 125 I5
Bethlehem PA U.S.A. 165 H3
Bethlehem West Bank 107 B4
Bethulie S. Africa 125 G6
Béthune France 62 C4
Beti Pak. 111 H4
Betim Brazil 179 B2
Betiri, Gunung mt. Indon. 85 F5
Bet Lehem West Bank see Bethlehem
Betma India 104 C5
Betong Sarawak Malaysia 85 E2
Betong Thai. 87 C6
Betoota Australia 136 C5
Betpakdala plain Kazakh. 102 D2
Betroka Madag. 123 E6
Bet She'an Israel 107 B3
Betsiamites Canada 153 H4
Betsiamites r. Canada 153 H4
Betsu-zan mt. Japan 92 C2
Bettiah India 105 F4
Bettles AK U.S.A. 149 J2
Bettyhill U.K. 60 E2
Bettystown Ireland 61 F4
Betul India 104 D5
Betun Timor Indon. 83 C5
Betung Kerihun, Taman Nasional Indon. 85 F2
Betwa r. India 104 D4
Betws-y-coed U.K. 59 D5
Betzdorf Germany 63 H4
Beulah Australia 137 C7
Beulah MI U.S.A. 164 B1
Beulah ND U.S.A. 160 C2
Beult r. U.K. 59 H7
Beuthen Poland see Bytom
Bever r. Germany 63 H2
Beverley U.K. 58 G5
Beverley, Lake AK U.S.A. 148 H4
Beverly MA U.S.A. 165 J2
Beverly OH U.S.A. 164 E4
Beverly Hills CA U.S.A. 158 D4
Beverly Lake Canada 151 K1
Beverstedt Germany 63 I1
Beverungen Germany 63 J3
Beverwijk Neth. 62 E2
Bewani P.N.G. 81 K7
Bexbach Germany 63 H5
Bexhill U.K. 59 H8
Bexley, Cape Canada 146 G3
Beyānlū Iran 110 B3
Beyce Turkey see Orhaneli
Bey Dağları mts Turkey 69 N6
Beykoz Turkey 69 M4
Beyla Guinea 120 C4
Beylagan Azer. see Beyläqan
Beyläqan Azer. 113 G3
Beyneu Kazakh. 100 E2
Beypazarı Turkey 69 N4
Beypınarı Turkey 112 E3
Beypore India 106 B4
Beyrouth Lebanon see Beirut
Beyşehir Turkey 112 C3
Beyşehir Gölü l. Turkey 112 C3
Beytonovo Rus. Fed. 90 B1
Beytüşşebap Turkey 113 F3
Bezameh Iran 110 E3
Bezbozhnik Rus. Fed. 52 K4
Bezhanitsy Rus. Fed. 52 F4
Bezhetsk Rus. Fed. 52 H4
Béziers France 66 F5
Bezmein Turkm. see Abadan
Bezwada India see Vijayawada
Bhabha India see Bhabhua
Bhabhar India 104 B4
Bhabhua India 105 E4
Bhabua India see Bhabhua
Bhachau India 104 B5
Bhachbhar India 104 B4
Bhadarwah India 99 A6
Bhadgaon Nepal see Bhaktapur
Bhadohi India 105 E4
Bhadra India 104 C3
Bhadrachalam Road Station India see Kottagudem
Bhadrak India 105 F5
Bhadrakh India see Bhadrak
Bhadravati India 106 B3
Bhag Pak. 111 G4
Bhaga r. India 99 B6
Bhagalpur India 105 F4
Bhainsa India 106 C2
Bhainsdehi India 104 D5
Bhairab Bazar Bangl. 105 G4
Bhairi Hol mt. Pak. 111 G5
Bhaktapur Nepal 105 F4
Bhalki India 106 C2
Bhamo Myanmar 86 B1
Bhamragarh India 106 D2
Bhandara India 104 D5
Bhanjanagar India 106 E2
Bhanrer Range hills India 104 D5
Bhaptiahi India 105 F4
Bharat country Asia see India
Bharatpur India 104 D4
Bhareli r. India 105 H4
Bharuch India 104 C5
Bhatapara India 105 E5
Bhatarsaigh i. U.K. see Vatersay
Bhatghar Lake India 106 B2
Bhatinda India see Bathinda
Bhatnair India see Hanumangarh
Bhatpara India 105 G5
Bhaunagar India see Bhavnagar
Bhavani r. India 106 C4
Bhavani Sagar l. India 106 C4
Bhavnagar India 104 C5
Bhawana Pak. 111 I4
Bhawanipatna India 106 D2
Bhearnaraigh, Eilean i. U.K. see Berneray
Bheemavaram India see Bhimavaram
Bhekuzulu S. Africa 125 J4
Bhera Pak. 111 I3
Bheri r. Nepal 99 C7
Bhigvan India 106 B2
Bhikhna Thori Nepal 105 F4
Bhilai India 104 E5
Bhildi India 104 C4
Bhilwara India 104 C4
Bhima r. India 106 C2
Bhimar India 104 B4
Bhimavaram India 106 D2
Bhimlath India 104 E5
Bhimphedi Nepal 99 D8
Bhind India 104 D4
Bhinga India 105 E4
Bhisho S. Africa 125 H7
Bhiwandi India 106 B2
Bhiwani India 104 D3
Bhogaipur India 104 D4
Bhojpur Nepal 105 F4
Bhola Bangl. 105 G5
Bhongweni S. Africa 125 I6
Bhopal India 104 D5
Bhopalpatnam India 106 D2
Bhrigukaccha India see Bharuch
Bhuban India 106 E1
Bhubaneshwar India 106 E1
Bhubaneswar India see Bhubaneshwar
Bhuj India 104 B5
Bhusawal India 104 C5
Bhutan country Asia 105 G4
Bhuttewala India 104 B4
Bia r. Ghana 120 C4
Bia, Phou mt. Laos 86 C3
Biābān mts Iran 110 E5
Biafo Glacier Pak. 104 C2
Biafra, Bight of g. Africa see Benin, Bight of
Biak Papua Indon. 81 J7
Biak Sulawesi Indon. 83 B3
Biak i. Indon. 81 J7
Biała Podlaska Poland 53 D5
Białogard Poland 57 O4
Białystok Poland 53 D5
Bianco, Monte mt. France/Italy see Mont Blanc
Biandangang Kou r. mouth China 95 J5
Bianzhao China 95 J2
Bianzhuang China see Cangshan
Biao Mindanao Phil. 82 D5
Biaora India 104 D5
Biaro i. Indon. 83 C2
Biarritz France 66 D5
Bi'ār Tabrāk well Saudi Arabia 110 B5
Bibai Japan 90 F4
Bibbenluke Australia 138 D6
Bibbiena Italy 68 D3
Bibby Island Canada 151 M2
Biberach an der Riß Germany 57 L6
Bibile Sri Lanka 106 D5
Biblis Germany 63 I5
Biblos Lebanon see Jbail
Bicas Brazil 179 C3
Biçer Turkey 69 N5
Bicester U.K. 59 F7
Bichabhera India 104 C4
Bicheng China see Bishan
Bichevaya Rus. Fed. 90 D3
Bichi r. Rus. Fed. 90 E1
Bichraltar Nepal 99 D8
Bichura Rus. Fed. 95 F1
Bickerton Island Australia 136 B2
Bickleigh U.K. 59 D8
Bicknell IN U.S.A. 164 B4
Bicoli Halmahera Indon. 83 D2
Bicuari, Parque Nacional do nat. park Angola 123 B5
Bid India 106 B2
Bida Nigeria 120 D4
Bidadari, Tanjung pt Malaysia 85 G1
Bidar India 106 C2
Biddeford ME U.S.A. 165 J2
Biddinghuizen Neth. 62 F2
Bidean nam Bian mt. U.K. 60 D4
Bideford U.K. 59 C7
Bideford Bay U.K. see Barnstaple Bay
Bīdokht Iran 110 E3
Bidzhan Rus. Fed. 90 C3
Bié Angola see Kuito
Bié, Planalto do Angola 123 B5
Biebrzański Park Narodowy nat. park Poland 55 M10
Biedenkopf Germany 63 I4
Biel Switz. 66 H3
Bielawa Poland 57 P5
Bielefeld Germany 63 I2
Bielitz Poland see Bielsko-Biała
Biella Italy 68 C2
Bielsko-Biała Poland 57 Q6
Bielstein hill Germany 63 J3
Bienenbüttel Germany 63 K1
Biên Hoa Vietnam 87 D5
Bienne Switz. see Biel
Bienville, Lac l. Canada 153 G3
Bierbank Australia 138 B1
Biesiesvlei S. Africa 125 G4
Bietigheim-Bissingen Germany 63 J6
Bièvre Belgium 62 F5
Bifoun Gabon 122 B4
Big r. Canada 153 K3
Big r. AK U.S.A. 148 I3
Biga Turkey 69 L4
Bigadiç Turkey 69 M5
Biga Yarımadası pen. Turkey 69 L5
Big Baldy Mountain MT U.S.A. 156 F3
Big Bar Creek Canada 150 F5
Big Bear Lake CA U.S.A. 158 E4
Big Belt Mountains MT U.S.A. 156 F3
Big Bend Swaziland 125 J4
Big Bend National Park TX U.S.A. 161 C6
Big Black r. MS U.S.A. 167 H1
Bigbury-on-Sea U.K. 59 D8
Big Canyon watercourse TX U.S.A. 161 C6
Big Delta AK U.S.A. 149 K2
Biger Mongolia 94 D2
Biger Nuur salt l. Mongolia 94 D2
Big Falls MN U.S.A. 160 E1
Big Fork r. MN U.S.A. 160 E1
Biggar Canada 151 J4
Biggar U.K. 60 F5
Biggar, Lac l. Canada 152 G4
Bigge Island Australia 134 D3
Biggenden Australia 137 F5
Bigger, Mount Canada 149 M4
Biggesee l. Germany 63 H3
Biggleswade U.K. 59 G6
Biggs CA U.S.A. 158 C2
Biggs OR U.S.A. 156 C3
Big Hole r. MT U.S.A. 156 E3
Bighorn r. MT/WY U.S.A. 156 G3
Bighorn Mountains WY U.S.A. 156 G3
Big Island Nunavut Canada 147 K3
Big Island N.W.T. Canada 150 G2
Big Island Ont. Canada 151 M5
Big Kalzas Lake Canada 149 N3
Big Koniuji Island AK U.S.A. 148 H5
Big Lake l. Canada 151 H1
Big Lake AK U.S.A. 149 J3
Big Lake TX U.S.A. 161 C6
Big Pine CA U.S.A. 158 D3
Big Pine Peak CA U.S.A. 158 D4
Big Raccoon r. IN U.S.A. 164 B4
Big Rapids MI U.S.A. 164 C2
Big River Canada 151 J4
Big Sable Point MI U.S.A. 164 B1
Big Salmon r. Canada 149 N3
Big Salmon (abandoned) Canada 149 N3
Big Sand Lake Canada 151 L3
Big Sandy r. WY U.S.A. 156 F4
Big Sandy Lake Canada 151 J4
Big Smokey Valley NV U.S.A. 158 E2
Big South Fork National River and Recreation Area park KY/TN U.S.A. 164 C5
Big Spring TX U.S.A. 161 C5
Big Stone Canada 151 I5
Big Stone Gap VA U.S.A. 164 D5
Bigstone Lake Canada 151 M4
Big Timber MT U.S.A. 156 F3
Big Trout Lake Canada 151 N4
Big Trout Lake l. Canada 151 N4
Big Valley Canada 151 H4
Big Water UT U.S.A. 159 H3
Bihać Bos.-Herz. 68 F2
Bihar state India 105 F4
Bihariganj India 105 F4
Bihar Sharif India 105 F4
Bihor, Vârful mt. Romania 69 J1
Bihoro Japan 90 G4
Bijagós, Arquipélago dos is Guinea-Bissau 120 B3
Bijainpur India 104 D4
Bijapur India 106 B2
Bījār Iran 110 B3
Bijbehara India 104 C2
Bijeljina Bos.-Herz. 69 H2
Bijelo Polje Montenegro 69 H3
Bijeraghogarh India 104 E5
Bijiang China see Zhiziluo
Bijie China 96 E3
Bijji India 106 D2
Bijnor India 104 D3
Bijnore India see Bijnor
Bijnot Pak. 111 H4
Bijrān well Saudi Arabia 110 C5
Bijrān, Khashm hill Saudi Arabia 110 C5
Bikampur India 104 C4
Bikaner India 104 C3

Bīkhūyeh Iran 110 D5
Bikin Rus. Fed. 90 D3
Bikin *r.* Rus. Fed. 90 D3
Bikini *atoll* Marshall Is 186 H5
Bikori Sudan 108 D7
Bikoro Dem. Rep. Congo 122 B4
Bikou China 96 E1
Bikramganj India 105 F4
Bilaa Point *Mindanao* Phil. 82 D4
Bilād Banī Bū 'Alī Oman 109 I5
Bilaigarh India 106 D1
Bilangbilangan *i.* Indon. 85 G2
Bilara India 104 C4
Bilaspur *Chhattisgarh* India 105 E5
Bilaspur *Hima. Prad.* India 104 D3
Biläsuvar Azer. 113 H3
Bila Tserkva Ukr. 53 F6
Bilauktaung Range *mts* Myanmar/Thai. 87 B4
Bilbao Spain 67 E2
Bilbays Egypt 112 C5
Bilbeis Egypt *see* **Bilbays**
Bilbo Spain *see* **Bilbao**
Bil'chir Rus. Fed. 95 G1
Bilecik Turkey 69 M4
Biłgoraj Poland 53 D6
Bilharamulo Tanz. 122 D4
Bilhaur India 104 E4
Bilhorod-Dnistrovs'kyy Ukr. 69 N1
Bili Dem. Rep. Congo 122 C3
Bilibino Rus. Fed. 77 R3
Bilin Myanmar 86 B3
Biliran *i.* Phil. 82 D4
Bilit *Sabah* Malaysia 85 G1
Bill *WY* U.S.A. 156 G4
Billabalong Australia 135 A6
Billabong Creek *r.* Australia *see* **Moulamein Creek**
Billericay U.K. 59 H7
Billiluna Australia 134 D4
Billingham U.K. 58 F4
Billings *MT* U.S.A. 156 F3
Billiton *i.* Indon. *see* **Belitung**
Bill Moores *AK* U.S.A. 148 G3
Bill of Portland *hd* U.K. 59 E8
Bill Williams *r.* *AZ* U.S.A. 159 F4
Bill Williams Mountain *AZ* U.S.A. 159 G4
Bilma Niger 120 E3
Bilo *r.* Rus. Fed. *see* **Belaya**
Biloela Australia 136 E5
Bilohirs'k Ukr. 112 D1
Bilohir"ya Ukr. 53 E6
Biloku Guyana 177 G3
Biloli India 106 C2
Bilovods'k Ukr. 53 H6
Biloxi *MS* U.S.A. 161 F6
Bilpa Morea Claypan *salt flat* Australia 136 B5
Bilston U.K. 60 F5
Biltine Chad 121 F3
Bilto Norway 54 L2
Bilugyun Island Myanmar 86 B3
Bilungala *Sulawesi* Indon. 83 B2
Bilwascarma Nicaragua 166 [inset] J6
Bilyayivka Ukr. 69 N1
Bilzen Belgium 62 F4
Bima *Sumbawa* Indon. 85 G5
Bima, Teluk *b.* *Sumbawa* Indon. 85 G5
Bimberi, Mount Australia 138 D5
Bimbo Cent. Afr. Rep. 121 E4
Bimini Islands Bahamas 163 E7
Bimlipatam India 106 D2
Bināb Iran 110 C2
Bina-Etawa India 104 D4
Binaija, Gunung *mt.* *Seram* Indon. 83 D3
Binalbagan *Negros* Phil. 82 C4
Bīnālūd, Reshteh Kūh-e *mts* Iran 110 E2
Binatang *Sarawak* Malaysia 85 E2
Binboğa Daği *mt.* Turkey 112 E3
Bincheng *Shandong* China 95 I4
Bincheng *Shandong* China *see* **Binzhou**
Binchuan China 96 D3
Bindebango Australia 138 C1
Binder Mongolia 95 G1
Bindle Australia 138 D1
Bindu Dem. Rep. Congo 123 B4
Bindura Zimbabwe 123 D5
Binéfar Spain 67 G3
Binga Zimbabwe 123 C5
Binga, Monte *mt.* Moz. 123 D5
Bingara Australia 138 E2
Bingaram *i.* India 106 B4
Bing Bong Australia 136 B2
Bingcaowan China 94 E4
Bingen am Rhein Germany 63 H5
Bingham *ME* U.S.A. 165 K1
Binghamton *NY* U.S.A. 165 H2
Bingmei China *see* **Congjiang**
Bingöl Turkey 113 F3
Bingol Daği *mt.* Turkey 113 F3
Bingxi China *see* **Yushan**
Bingzhongluo China 96 C2
Binh Gia Vietnam 86 D2
Binicuil *Negros* Phil. 82 C4
Binika India 105 E5
Binjai *Sumatera* Indon. 84 B2
Bin Mürkhan *well* U.A.E. 110 D5
Binnaway Australia 138 D3
Binongko *i.* Indon. 83 C4
Binpur India 105 F5
Bintan *i.* Indon. 84 D2
Bintang, Bukit *mts* Malaysia 84 C1
Bint Jbeil Lebanon *see* **Bent Jbaïl**
Bintuan Phil. 82 C3
Bintuhan *Sumatera* Indon. 84 C4
Bintulu *Sarawak* Malaysia 85 F2
Binubusan *Luzon* Phil. 82 C3
Binxian *Heilong.* China 90 B3
Binxian *Shaanxi* China 95 G5
Binxian *Shandong* China *see* **Bincheng**
Binya Australia 138 C5
Binyang China 97 F4
Bin-Yauri Nigeria 120 D3
Binzhou *Guangxi* China *see* **Binyang**
Binzhou *Heilong.* China *see* **Binxian**
Binzhou *Shandong* China 95 I4
Bioco *i.* Equat. Guinea 120 D4
Biograd na Moru Croatia 68 F3
Bioko *i.* Equat. Guinea *see* **Bioco**
Biokovo *mts* Croatia 68 G3
Bi Qu *r.* China 99 F6
Biquinhas Brazil 179 B2
Bir India *see* **Bid**
Bira Rus. Fed. 90 D2
Bi'r Abū Jady *oasis* Syria 107 D1
Birāk Libya 121 E2
Birakan Rus. Fed. 90 C2
Bi'r al 'Abd Egypt 107 A4
Bi'r al Ḩalbā *well* Syria 107 D2
Bi'r al Jifjāfah *well* Egypt 107 A4
Bi'r al Khamsah *well* Egypt 112 B5
Bi'r al Māliḩah *well* Egypt 107 A5
Bi'r al Mulūsi Iraq 113 F4
Bi'r al Munbaṭiḩ *well* Syria 107 D2
Bi'r al Qaṭrānī *well* Egypt 112 B5
Bi'r al Ubbayiḑ *well* Egypt 112 B6
Bi'r an Nuşf *well* Egypt *see* **Bi'r an Nuşş**
Bi'r an Nuşş *well* Egypt 112 B5
Bir Anzarane W. Sahara 120 B2
Birao Cent. Afr. Rep. 122 C2
Bi'r ar Rābiyah *well* Egypt 112 B5
Birata Turkm. 111 F1
Biratar Bulak *spring* China 98 E4
Biratnagar Nepal 105 F4
Bi'r aţ Ţarfāwī *well* Libya 112 B5
Bi'r Başīrī *well* Syria 107 C2
Bi'r Bayḑā' *well* Egypt 107 B4
Bi'r Baylī *well* Egypt 112 B5
Bir Beïda *well* Egypt *see* **Bi'r Bayḑā'**
Bi'r Buţaymān Syria 113 E3
Birch *r.* Canada 151 H3
Birch Creek *AK* U.S.A. 149 K2
Birch Creek *r.* *AK* U.S.A. 149 K2
Birches *AK* U.S.A. 148 I2
Birch Hills Canada 151 J4
Birch Island Canada 150 G5
Birch Lake *N.W.T.* Canada 150 G2
Birch Lake *Ont.* Canada 151 M5
Birch Lake *Sask.* Canada 151 I4
Birch Mountains Canada 150 H3
Birch River *WV* U.S.A. 164 E4
Birch Run *MI* U.S.A. 164 D2
Bircot Eth. 122 E3
Birdaard Neth. *see* **Burdaard**
Bîr Diqnâsh *well* Egypt *see* **Bi'r Diqnāsh**
Bi'r Diqnāsh *well* Egypt 112 B5
Bird Island N. Mariana Is *see* **Farallon de Medinilla**
Birdseye *UT* U.S.A. 159 H2
Birdsville Australia 137 B5
Birecik Turkey 112 E3
Bîr el 'Abd Egypt *see* **Bi'r al 'Abd**
Bir el Arbi *well* Alg. 67 I6
Bîr el Istabl *well* Egypt *see* **Bi'r Iştabl**
Bîr el Khamsa *well* Egypt *see* **Bi'r al Khamsah**
Bîr el Nuşş *well* Egypt *see* **Bi'r an Nuşş**
Bîr el Obeiyid *well* Egypt *see* **Bi'r al Ubbayiḑ**
Bîr el Qaṭrani *well* Egypt *see* **Bi'r al Qaṭrānī**
Bîr el Râbia *well* Egypt *see* **Bi'r ar Rābiyah**
Birendranagar Nepal *see* **Surkhet**
Bir en Natrûn *well* Sudan 108 C6
Bireun *Sumatera* Indon. 84 B1
Bi'r Fāḑil *well* Saudi Arabia 110 C6
Bi'r Fajr *well* Saudi Arabia 112 E5
Bi'r Fu'ād *well* Egypt 112 B5
Bīrg, Kūh-e *mts* Iran 111 F5
Birganj Nepal 99 D8
Bîr Gifgâfa *well* Egypt *see* **Bi'r al Jifjāfah**
Bi'r Ḩajal *well* Syria 107 D2
Birhan *mt.* Eth. 122 D2
Bi'r Ḩasanah *well* Egypt 107 A4
Bi'r Ḩayzān *well* Saudi Arabia 112 E6
Biri *i.* Phil. 82 D3
Bi'r Ibn Hirmās Saudi Arabia *see* **Al Bi'r**
Bir Ibn Juhayyim Saudi Arabia 110 C6
Birigüi Brazil 179 A3
Bīrīn Syria 107 C2
Bi'r Iştabl *well* Egypt 112 B5
Bīrjand Iran 110 E3
Bi'r Jubnī *well* Libya 112 B5
Birkát Hamad *well* Iraq 113 G5
Birkenfeld Germany 63 H5
Birkenhead U.K. 58 D5
Birkirkara Malta 68 F7
Birksgate Range *hills* Australia 135 E6
Bîrlad Romania *see* **Bârlad**
Bi'r Lahfān *well* Egypt 107 A4
Birlik *Zhambylskaya Oblast'* Kazakh. 98 A3
Birlik *Zhambylskaya Oblast'* Kazakh. 102 D3
Birmal *reg.* Afgh. 111 H3
Birmingham U.K. 59 F6
Birmingham *AL* U.S.A. 163 C5
Bîr Mogreïn Mauritania 120 B2
Bi'r Muḩaymid al Wazwaz *well* Syria 107 D2
Bi'r Nāḩid *oasis* Egypt 112 C5
Birnin-Gwari Nigeria 120 D3
Birnin-Kebbi Nigeria 120 D3
Birnin Konni Niger 120 D3
Birobidzhan Rus. Fed. 90 D2
Birong *Palawan* Phil. 82 B4
Bi'r Qaşīr as Sirr *well* Egypt 112 B5
Birr Ireland 61 E4
Bi'r Rawḑ Sālim *well* Egypt 107 A4
Birrie *r.* Australia 138 C2
Birrindudu Australia 134 E4
Bîr Rôḑ Sâlim *well* Egypt *see* **Bi'r Rawḑ Sālim**
Birsay U.K. 60 F1
Bi'r Shalatayn Egypt 108 E5
Bîr Shalatein Egypt *see* **Bi'r Shalatayn**
Birsk Rus. Fed. 51 R4
Birstall U.K. 59 F6
Birstein Germany 63 J4
Bir Ţalḩah *well* Saudi Arabia 110 B6
Birthday Mountain *hill* Australia 136 C2
Birtle Canada 151 K5
Biru China 99 F7
Birur India 106 B3
Bi'r Usaylīlah *well* Saudi Arabia 110 B6
Biržai Lith. 55 N8
Bisa India 86 A1
Bisa *i.* *Maluku* Indon. 83 C3
Bisai Japan 92 C3
Bisalpur India 104 D3
Bisau India 104 C3
Bisbee *AZ* U.S.A. 157 F7
Biscay, Bay of *sea* France/Spain 66 B4
Biscay Abyssal Plain *sea feature* N. Atlantic Ocean 184 H3
Biscayne National Park *FL* U.S.A. 163 D7
Biscoe Islands Antarctica 188 L2
Biscotasi Lake Canada 152 E5
Biscotasing Canada 152 E5
Bisezhai China 96 D4
Bishan China 96 E2
Bishbek Kyrg. *see* **Bishkek**
Bishenpur India *see* **Bishnupur**

▶**Bishkek** Kyrg. 102 D3
Capital of Kyrgyzstan.

Bishnath India 96 B3
Bishnupur *Manipur* India 105 H4
Bishnupur *W. Bengal* India 105 F5
Bishop *CA* U.S.A. 158 D3
Bishop Auckland U.K. 58 F4
Bishop Lake Canada 150 G1
Bishop's Stortford U.K. 59 H7
Bishopville *SC* U.S.A. 163 D5
Bishrī, Jabal *hills* Syria 107 D2
Bishui *Heilong.* China 90 A1
Bishui *Henan* China *see* **Biyang**
Biskra Alg. 64 F5
Bislig *Mindanao* Phil. 82 D4
Bislig Bay *Mindanao* Phil. 82 D4

▶**Bismarck** *ND* U.S.A. 160 C2
Capital of North Dakota.

Bismarck Archipelago *is* P.N.G. 81 L7
Bismarck Range *mts* P.N.G. 81 K7
Bismarck Sea P.N.G. 81 L7
Bismark (Altmark) Germany 63 L2
Bismil Turkey 113 F3
Bismo Norway 54 F6
Bison *SD* U.S.A. 160 C2
Bispgården Sweden 54 J5
Bispingen Germany 63 K1
Bissa, Djebel *mt.* Alg. 67 G5
Bissamcuttak India 106 D2

▶**Bissau** Guinea-Bissau 120 B3
Capital of Guinea-Bissau.

Bissaula Nigeria 120 E4
Bissett Canada 151 M5
Bistcho Lake Canada 150 G3
Bistriţa Romania 69 K1
Bistriţa *r.* Romania 69 L1
Bisucay *i.* Phil. 82 C4
Bitburg Germany 62 G5
Bitche France 63 H5
Bithur India 104 E4
Bithynia *reg.* Turkey 69 M4
Bitkine Chad 121 E3
Bitlis Turkey 113 F3
Bitola Macedonia 69 I4
Bitolj Macedonia *see* **Bitola**
Bitonto Italy 68 G4
Bitrān, Jabal *hill* Saudi Arabia 110 B6
Bitra Par *reef* India 106 B4
Bitter Creek *r.* *UT* U.S.A. 159 I2
Bitterfeld Germany 63 M3
Bitterfontein S. Africa 124 D6
Bitter Lakes Egypt 112 D5
Bitterroot *r.* *MT* U.S.A. 156 E3
Bitterroot Range *mts* *ID* U.S.A. 156 E3
Bitterwater *CA* U.S.A. 158 C3
Bittkau Germany 63 L2
Bitung *Sulawesi* Indon. 83 C2
Biu Nigeria 120 E3
Biwa-ko *l.* Japan 92 B3
Biwa-ko Kokutei-kōen *park* Japan 92 C3
Biwmaris U.K. *see* **Beaumaris**
Biyang China 97 G1
Bīye K'obē Eth. 122 E2
Biysk Rus. Fed. 88 F2
Bizana S. Africa 125 I6
Bizerta Tunisia *see* **Bizerte**
Bizerte Tunisia 68 C6
Bīzhanābād Iran 110 E5

▶**Bjargtangar** *hd* Iceland 54 [inset 1]
Most westerly point of Europe.

Bjästa Sweden 54 K5
Bjelovar Croatia 68 G2
Bjerkvik Norway 54 J2
Bjerringbro Denmark 55 F8
Bjørgan Norway 54 G5
Björkliden Sweden 54 K2
Björklinge Sweden 55 J6
Bjorli Norway 54 F5
Björna Sweden 54 K5
Björneborg Fin. *see* **Pori**

▶**Bjørnøya** *i.* Arctic Ocean 76 C2
Part of Norway.

Bjurholm Sweden 54 K5
Bla Mali 120 C3
Black *r.* *Man.* Canada 151 L5
Black *r.* *Ont.* Canada 152 E4
Black *r.* Canada/U.S.A. 149 K2
Black *AK* U.S.A. 148 F3
Black *r.* *AR* U.S.A. 161 F5
Black *r.* *AR* U.S.A. 161 F5
Black *r.* *AZ* U.S.A. 159 H5
Black *r.* Vietnam 86 D2
Blackadder Water *r.* U.K. 60 G5
Blackall Australia 136 D5
Blackbear *r.* Canada 151 N4
Black Birch Lake Canada 151 J3
Black Bourton U.K. 59 F7
Blackbull Australia 136 C3
Blackburn U.K. 58 E5
Blackburn, Mount *AK* U.S.A. 149 L3
Blackbutt Australia 138 F1
Black Butte *mt.* *CA* U.S.A. 158 B2
Black Butte Lake *CA* U.S.A. 158 B2
Black Canyon *gorge* *AZ* U.S.A. 159 F4
Black Canyon of the Gunnison National Park *CO* U.S.A. 159 J2
Black Combe *hill* U.K. 58 D4
Black Creek *watercourse* *AZ* U.S.A. 159 I4
Black Donald Lake Canada 165 G1
Blackdown Tableland National Park Australia 136 E4
Blackduck *MN* U.S.A. 160 E2
Blackfalds Canada 150 H4
Blackfoot *ID* U.S.A. 156 E4
Black Foot *r.* *MT* U.S.A. 156 E3
Black Forest *mts* Germany 57 L7
Black Hill *hill* U.K. 58 F5
Black Hills *SD* U.S.A. 154 G3
Black Hills *SD* U.S.A. 156 G3
Black Island Canada 151 L5
Black Lake Canada 151 J3
Black Lake *l.* Canada 151 J3
Black Lake *l.* *MI* U.S.A. 164 C1
Black Mesa *mt.* *AZ* U.S.A. 159 I5
Black Mesa *ridge* *AZ* U.S.A. 159 H3
Black Mountain Pak. 111 I3
Black Mountain *hill* U.K. 59 D7
Black Mountain *AK* U.S.A. 148 G1
Black Mountain *CA* U.S.A. 158 E4
Black Mountain *KY* U.S.A. 164 D5
Black Mountain *NM* U.S.A. 159 I5
Black Mountains *hills* U.K. 59 D7
Black Mountains *AZ* U.S.A. 159 F4
Black Nossob *watercourse* Namibia 124 D2
Black Pagoda India *see* **Konarka**
Blackpool U.K. 58 D5
Black Range *mts* *NM* U.S.A. 159 I5
Black Rapids *AK* U.S.A. 149 K3
Black River *MI* U.S.A. 164 D1
Black River *NY* U.S.A. 165 H1
Black River Falls *WI* U.S.A. 160 F2
Black Rock *hill* Jordan *see* **'Unāb, Jabal al**
Black Rock Desert *NV* U.S.A. 156 D4
Blacksburg *VA* U.S.A. 164 E5
Black Sea Asia/Europe 53 H8
Blacks Fork *r.* *WY* U.S.A. 156 F4
Blackshear *GA* U.S.A. 163 D6
Blacksod Bay Ireland 61 B3
Black Springs *NV* U.S.A. 158 D2
Blackstairs Mountains *hills* Ireland 61 F5
Blackstone *r.* Canada 149 M2
Blackstone *VA* U.S.A. 165 F5
Black Sugarloaf *mt.* Australia 138 E3
Black Tickle Canada 153 L3
Blackville Australia 138 E3
Blackwater Australia 136 E4
Blackwater Ireland 61 F5
Blackwater *r.* Ireland 61 E5
Blackwater *r.* Ireland/U.K. 61 F3
Blackwater *watercourse* *NM/TX* U.S.A. 161 C5
Blackwater Lake Canada 149 Q3
Blackwater Reservoir U.K. 60 E4
Blackwood *r.* Australia 135 A8
Blackwood National Park Australia 136 D4
Bladensburg National Park Australia 136 C4
Blaenavon U.K. 59 D7
Blagodarnyy Rus. Fed. 113 F1
Blagoevgrad Bulg. 69 J3
Blagoveshchensk *Amurskaya Oblast'* Rus. Fed. 90 B2
Blagoveshchensk *Respublika Bashkortostan* Rus. Fed. 51 R4
Blaikiston, Mount Canada 150 H5
Blaine Lake Canada 151 J4
Blair *NE* U.S.A. 160 D3
Blair Athol Australia 136 D4
Blair Atholl U.K. 60 F4
Blairgowrie U.K. 60 F4
Blairsden *CA* U.S.A. 158 C2
Blairsville *GA* U.S.A. 163 D5
Blakang Mati, Pulau *i.* Sing. *see* **Sentosa**
Blakely *GA* U.S.A. 163 C6
Blakeney U.K. 59 I6
Blambangan, Semenanjung *pen.* Indon. 85 F5
Blanca, Bahía *b.* Arg. 178 D5
Blanca, Sierra *mt.* *NM* U.S.A. 157 G6
Blanca Peak *CO* U.S.A. 157 G5
Blanche, Lake *salt flat* *S.A.* Australia 137 B6
Blanche, Lake *salt flat* *W.A.* Australia 134 C5
Blanchester *OH* U.S.A. 164 D4
Blanc Nez, Cap *c.* France 62 B4
Blanco *r.* Bol. 176 F6
Blanco *NM* U.S.A. 159 J3
Blanco, Cabo *c.* Costa Rica 166 [inset] I7
Blanco, Cape *OR* U.S.A. 156 B4
Blanc-Sablon Canada 153 K4
Bland *r.* Australia 138 C4
Bland *VA* U.S.A. 164 E5
Blanda *r.* Iceland 54 [inset 1]
Blandford Forum U.K. 59 E8
Blanding *UT* U.S.A. 159 I3
Blanes Spain 67 H3
Blangah, Telok Sing. 87 [inset]
Blangkejeren *Sumatera* Indon. 84 B2
Blangpidie *Sumatera* Indon. 84 B2
Blankenberge Belgium 62 D3
Blankenheim Germany 62 G4
Blanquilla, Isla *i.* Venez. 176 F1
Blansko Czech Rep. 57 P6
Blantyre Malawi 123 D5
Blarney Ireland 61 D6
Blau *Sulawesi* Indon. 83 B2
Blaufelden Germany 63 J5
Blåviksjön Sweden 54 K4
Blaye France 66 D4
Blayney Australia 138 D4
Blaze, Point Australia 134 E3
Bleckede Germany 63 K1
Blega *Jawa* Indon. 85 F4
Bleilochtalsperre *resr* Germany 63 L4
Blenheim Canada 164 E2
Blenheim N.Z. 139 D5
Blenheim Palace *tourist site* U.K. 59 F7
Blerick Neth. 62 G3
Blessington Lakes Ireland 61 F4
Bletchley U.K. 59 G6
Blida Alg. 67 H5
Blies *r.* Germany 63 H5
Bligh Water *b.* Fiji 133 H3
Blind River Canada 152 E5
Bliss *ID* U.S.A. 156 E4
Blissfield *MI* U.S.A. 164 D3
Blitar *Jawa* Indon. 85 F5
Blitta Togo 120 D4
Blocher *IN* U.S.A. 164 C4
Block Island *RI* U.S.A. 165 J3
Block Island Sound *sea chan.* *RI* U.S.A. 165 J3
Bloemfontein S. Africa 125 H5
Bloemhof S. Africa 125 G4
Bloemhof Dam S. Africa 125 G4
Bloemhof Dam Nature Reserve S. Africa 125 G4
Blomberg Germany 63 J3
Blönduós Iceland 54 [inset 1]
Blongas *Lombok* Indon. 85 G5
Bloods Range *mts* Australia 135 E6
Bloodsworth Island *MD* U.S.A. 165 G4
Bloodvein *r.* Canada 151 L5
Bloody *r.* Canada 149 Q2
Bloody Foreland *pt* Ireland 61 D2
Bloomer *WI* U.S.A. 160 F2
Bloomfield Canada 165 G2
Bloomfield *IA* U.S.A. 160 E3
Bloomfield *IN* U.S.A. 164 B4
Bloomfield *MO* U.S.A. 161 F4
Bloomfield *NM* U.S.A. 159 J3
Blooming Prairie *MN* U.S.A. 160 E3
Bloomington *IL* U.S.A. 160 F3
Bloomington *IN* U.S.A. 164 B4
Bloomington *MN* U.S.A. 160 E2
Bloomsburg *PA* U.S.A. 165 G3
Blora *Jawa* Indon. 85 E4
Blossburg *PA* U.S.A. 165 G3
Blosseville Kyst *coastal area* Greenland 147 P3
Blouberg S. Africa 125 I2
Blouberg Nature Reserve S. Africa 125 I2
Blountstown *FL* U.S.A. 163 C6
Blountville *TN* U.S.A. 164 D5
Blow *r.* Canada 149 M1
Bloxham U.K. 59 F6
Blue *r.* Canada 149 O4
Blue *watercourse* *AZ* U.S.A. 159 I5
Blue Bell Knoll *mt.* *UT* U.S.A. 159 H2
Blueberry *r.* Canada 150 F3
Blue Creek *r.* Mex. *see* **Azul**
Blue Diamond *NV* U.S.A. 159 F3
Blue Earth *MN* U.S.A. 160 E3
Bluefield *VA* U.S.A. 162 D4
Bluefield *WV* U.S.A. 164 E5
Bluefields Nicaragua 166 [inset] J6
Blue Hills Turks and Caicos Is 163 F8
Blue Knob *hill* *PA* U.S.A. 165 F3
Blue Mesa Reservoir *CO* U.S.A. 159 J2
Blue Mountain *hill* Canada 153 K4
Blue Mountain India 105 H5
Blue Mountain Lake *NY* U.S.A. 165 H2
Blue Mountain Pass Lesotho 125 H5
Blue Mountains Australia 138 D4
Blue Mountains *OR* U.S.A. 156 D3
Blue Mountains National Park Australia 138 E4
Blue Nile *r.* Eth./Sudan 108 D6
also known as Ābay Wenz (Ethiopia), Bahr el Azraq (Sudan)
Bluenose Lake Canada 149 R1
Blue Ridge *GA* U.S.A. 163 C5
Blue Ridge *VA* U.S.A. 164 F5
Blue Ridge *mts* *VA* U.S.A. 164 E5
Blue Stack *hill* Ireland 61 D3
Blue Stack Mountains *hills* Ireland 61 D3
Bluestone Lake *WV* U.S.A. 164 E5
Bluewater *NM* U.S.A. 159 J4
Bluff N.Z. 139 B8
Bluff *UT* U.S.A. 159 I3
Bluffdale *UT* U.S.A. 159 H1
Bluff Island H.K. China 97 [inset]
Bluff Knoll *mt.* Australia 135 B8
Bluffton *IN* U.S.A. 164 C3
Bluffton *OH* U.S.A. 164 D3
Blumenau Brazil 179 A4
Blustry Mountain Canada 156 C2
Blyde River Canyon Nature Reserve S. Africa 125 J3
Blying Sound *sea channel* *AK* U.S.A. 149 J4
Blyth Canada 164 E2
Blyth *England* U.K. 58 F3
Blyth *England* U.K. 58 F5
Blythe *CA* U.S.A. 159 F5
Blytheville *AR* U.S.A. 161 F5
Bø Norway 55 F7
Bo Sierra Leone 120 B4
Boac Phil. 82 C3
Boaco Nicaragua 166 [inset] I6
Boa Esperança Brazil 179 B3
Bo'ai *Henan* China 95 H5
Bo'ai *Yunnan* China 96 E4
Boali Cent. Afr. Rep. 122 B3
Boalsert Neth. *see* **Bolsward**
Boane Moz. 125 K4
Boano *i.* *Maluku* Indon. 83 C3
Boano, Selat *sea chan.* *Maluku* Indon. 83 C3
Boa Nova Brazil 179 C1
Boardman *OH* U.S.A. 164 E3
Boatlaname Botswana 125 G2
Boa Viagem Brazil 177 K5
Boa Vista Brazil 176 F3
Boa Vista *i.* Cape Verde 120 [inset]
Bobadah Australia 138 C4
Bobai China 97 F4
Bobaomby, Tanjona *c.* Madag. 123 E5
Bobbili India 106 D2
Bobcaygeon Canada 165 F1
Bobo-Dioulasso Burkina Faso 120 C3
Bobon *Samar* Phil. 82 D3
Bobotov Kuk *mt.* Montenegro *see* **Durmitor**
Bobriki Rus. Fed. *see* **Novomoskovsk**
Bobrinets Ukr. *see* **Bobrynets'**
Bobrov Rus. Fed. 53 I6
Bobrovitsa Ukr. *see* **Bobrovytsya**
Bobrovytsya Ukr. 53 F6
Bobruysk Belarus *see* **Babruysk**
Bobrynets' Ukr. 53 G6
Bobs Lake Canada 165 G1
Bobuk Sudan 108 D7
Bobures Venez. 176 D2
Boby *mt.* Madag. 123 E6
Boca del Río Mex. 167 F5
Boca de Macareo Venez. 176 F2
Boca do Acre Brazil 176 E5
Boca do Jari Brazil 177 H4
Bocaiúva Brazil 179 C2
Bocaranga Cent. Afr. Rep. 122 B3
Boca Raton *FL* U.S.A. 163 D7
Bocas del Toro Panama 166 [inset] J7
Bocas del Toro, Archipiélago de *is* Panama 166 [inset] J7
Bochnia Poland 57 R6
Bocholt Germany 62 G3
Bochum Germany 63 H3
Bockenem Germany 63 K2
Bocoio Angola 123 B5
Bocoyna Mex. 166 D3
Boda Cent. Afr. Rep. 122 B3
Bodalla Australia 138 E6
Bodallin Australia 135 B7
Bodaybo Rus. Fed. 77 M4
Boddam U.K. 60 H3
Bode *r.* Germany 63 L3
Bodega Head *hd* *CA* U.S.A. 158 B2
Bodélé *reg.* Chad 121 E3
Boden Sweden 54 L4
Bodenham U.K. 59 E6
Bodensee *l.* Germany/Switz. *see* **Constance, Lake**
Bodenteich Germany 63 K2
Bodenwerder Germany 63 J3
Bodie (abandoned) *CA* U.S.A. 158 D2
Bodinayakkanur India 106 C4
Bodmin U.K. 59 C8
Bodmin Moor *moorland* U.K. 59 C8
Bodø Norway 54 I3
Bodonchiyn Gol *watercourse* Mongolia 94 C2
Bodoquena Brazil 177 G7
Bodoquena, Serra da *hills* Brazil 178 E2
Bodrum Turkey 69 L6
Bodträskfors Sweden 54 L3
Boechout Belgium 62 E3
Boende Dem. Rep. Congo 121 F5
Bo Epinang *Sulawesi* Indon. 83 B4
Boerne *TX* U.S.A. 161 D6
Boeuf *r.* *LA* U.S.A. 161 F6
Boffa Guinea 120 B3
Bogalay Myanmar *see* **Bogale**
Bogale Myanmar 86 A3
Bogale *r.* Myanmar 86 A4
Bogalusa *LA* U.S.A. 161 F6
Bogan *r.* Australia 138 C2
Bogandé Burkina Faso 120 C3
Bogan Gate Australia 138 C4
Bogani Nani Wartabone, Taman Nasional *nat. park* Indon. 83 B2
Boğazlıyan Turkey 112 D3
Bogcang Zangbo *r.* China 99 D7
Bogd *Bayanhongor* Mongolia 94 E2
Bogd *Övörhangay* Mongolia 94 E2
Bogda Feng *mt.* China 98 E4
Bogda Shan *mts* China 94 B3
Bogen Kazakh. 102 B2
Boggabilla Australia 138 E2
Boggabri Australia 138 E3
Boggeragh Mountains *hills* Ireland 61 C5
Boghar Alg. 67 H6
Boghari Alg. *see* **Ksar el Boukhari**
Bognor Regis U.K. 59 G8
Bogo *Cebu* Phil. 82 D4
Bogodukhov Ukr. *see* **Bohodukhiv**
Bog of Allen *reg.* Ireland 61 E4
Bogong, Mount Australia 138 C6
Bogopol' Rus. Fed. 90 D3
Bogor *Jawa* Indon. 84 D4
Bogoroditsk Rus. Fed. 53 H5
Bogorodsk Rus. Fed. 52 I4
Bogorodskoye *Khabarovskiy Kray* Rus. Fed. 90 F1
Bogorodskoye *Kirovskaya Oblast'* Rus. Fed. 52 K4
Bogoslof Island *AK* U.S.A. 148 E5

▶**Bogotá** Col. 176 D3
Capital of Colombia. 5th most populous city in South America.

Bogotol Rus. Fed. 76 J4
Bogoyavlenskoye Rus. Fed. *see* **Pervomayskiy**
Bogra Bangl. 105 G4
Boguchany Rus. Fed. 77 K4
Boguchar Rus. Fed. 53 I6
Bogué Mauritania 120 B3
Boh *r.* Indon. 85 F2
Bo Hai *g.* China 95 I4
Bohai Haixia *sea chan.* China 95 J4
Bohain-en-Vermandois France 62 D5
Bohai Wan *b.* China 78 D4
Bohemian Forest *mts* Germany *see* **Böhmer Wald**
Böhlen Germany 63 M3
Bohlokong S. Africa 125 I5
Böhme *r.* Germany 63 J2
Böhmer Wald *mts* Germany 63 M5
Bohmte Germany 63 I2
Bohodukhiv Ukr. 53 G6
Bohol *i.* Phil. 82 D4
Bohol Sea Phil. 82 D4
Bohol Strait Phil. 82 C4
Bohu China 98 D4
Boiaçu Brazil 176 F4
Boiba China 96 C1
Boichoko S. Africa 124 F5
Boigu Island Australia 81 K8
Boikhutso S. Africa 125 H4
Boileau, Cape Australia 134 C4
Boim Brazil 177 G4
Boipeba, Ilha *i.* Brazil 179 D1
Bois *r.* Brazil 179 A2
Bois, Lac des *l.* Canada 149 P2
Bois Blanc Island *MI* U.S.A. 162 C2

▶**Boise** *ID* U.S.A. 156 D4
Capital of Idaho.

Boise City *OK* U.S.A. 161 C4
Boissevain Canada 151 K5
Boitumelong S. Africa 125 G4
Boizenburg Germany 63 K1
Bojd Iran 110 E3
Bojeador, Cape *Luzon* Phil. 82 C2
Bojnūrd Iran 110 E2
Bojonegoro *Jawa* Indon. 85 E4
Bojong *Jawa* Indon. 84 D4
Bokaak *atoll* Marshall Is *see* **Taongi**
Bokajan India 105 H4
Bokaro India 105 F5
Bokaro Reservoir India 105 F5
Bokat *Sulawesi* Indon. 83 B2
Bokatola Dem. Rep. Congo 122 B4
Boké Guinea 120 B3
Boke Kazakh. 98 C2
Bokele Dem. Rep. Congo 122 C4
Bokhara *r.* Australia 138 C2
Bo Kheo Cambodia *see* **Bâ Kêv**
Boknafjorden *sea chan.* Norway 55 D7
Bokoko Dem. Rep. Congo 122 C3
Bökönbaev Kyrg. 98 B4
Bokoro Chad 121 E3
Bokovskaya Rus. Fed. 53 I6
Bokspits S. Africa 124 E4
Boktor Rus. Fed. 90 E2
Bokurdak Turkm. 110 E2
Bol Chad 121 E3
Bolaang *Sulawesi* Indon. 83 B3
Bolaiti Dem. Rep. Congo 121 F5
Bolama Guinea-Bissau 120 B3
Bolangir India 106 D1
Bolan Pass Pak. 111 G4
Bolavén, Phouphieng *plat.* Laos 86 D4
Bolbec France 66 E2
Bole China 98 C3
Bole Ghana 120 C4
Boleko Dem. Rep. Congo 122 B4
Bolen Rus. Fed. 90 D2
Bolgar Rus. Fed. 53 K5
Bolgatanga Ghana 120 C3
Bolgrad Ukr. *see* **Bolhrad**
Bolhrad Ukr. 69 M2
Boli China 90 C3
Bolia Dem. Rep. Congo 122 B4
Boliden Sweden 54 L4
Bolikhamxai Laos 86 C3
Bolinao *Luzon* Phil. 82 B2
Bolingbrook *IL* U.S.A. 164 A3
Bolintin-Vale Romania 69 K2

Bolívar Peru 176 C5
Bolivar NY U.S.A. 165 F2
Bolivar TN U.S.A. 161 F5
Bolívar, Pico mt. Venez. 176 D2
Bolivia Cuba 163 E8

▶**Bolivia** country S. America 176 E7
5th largest country in South America.

Bolkhov Rus. Fed. 53 H5
Bollène France 66 G4
Bollnäs Sweden 55 J6
Bollon Australia 138 C2
Bollstabruk Sweden 54 J5
Bolmen l. Sweden 55 H8
Bolo Panay Phil. 82 C4
Bolobo Dem. Rep. Congo 122 B4
Bolod Islands Phil. 82 C5
Bologna Italy 68 D2
Bolognesi Peru 176 D5
Bologoye Rus. Fed. 52 G4
Bolokanang S. Africa 125 G5
Bolomba Dem. Rep. Congo 122 B3
Bolon' Rus. Fed. see **Achan**
Bolong Mindanao Phil. 82 C5
Bolpur India 105 F5
Bolsena, Lago di l. Italy 68 D3
Bol'shakovo Rus. Fed. 55 L9
Bol'shaya Chernigovka Rus. Fed. 51 Q5
Bol'shaya Glushitsa Rus. Fed. 53 K5
Bol'shaya Imandra, Ozero l. Rus. Fed. 54 R3
Bol'shaya Kovriga, Gora hill Rus. Fed. 52 K2
Bol'shaya Martynovka Rus. Fed. 53 I7
Bol'shaya Osinovaya r. Rus. Fed. 148 A2
Bol'shaya Tsarevshchina Rus. Fed. see **Volzhskiy**
Bol'shaya Vladimirovka Kazakh. 98 B2
Bol'shevik, Ostrov i. Rus. Fed. 77 L2
Bol'shezemel'skaya Tundra lowland Rus. Fed. 52 L2
Bol'shiye Barsuki, Peski des. Kazakh. 102 A2
Bol'shiye Chirki Rus. Fed. 52 J3
Bol'shiye Kozly Rus. Fed. 52 H2
Bol'shoy Begichev, Ostrov i. Rus. Fed. 189 E2
Bol'shoye Murashkino Rus. Fed. 52 J5
Bol'shoy Irgiz r. Rus. Fed. 53 J6
Bol'shoy Kamen' Rus. Fed. 90 D4
Bol'shoy Kavkaz mts Asia/Europe see **Caucasus**
Bol'shoy Kundysh r. Rus. Fed. 52 J4
Bol'shoy Lyakhovskiy, Ostrov i. Rus. Fed. 77 P2
Bol'shoy Tokmak Kyrg. see **Tokmok**
Bol'shoy Tokmak Ukr. see **Tokmak**
Bolsón de Mapimí des. Mex. 166 D3
Bolsward Neth. 62 F1
Bolton Canada 164 F2
Bolton Mindanao Phil. 82 D5
Bolton U.K. 58 E5
Bolu Turkey 69 N4
Boluntay China 99 F5
Boluo China 97 G4
Bolus Head hd Ireland 61 B6
Bolvadin Turkey 69 N5
Bolzano Italy 68 D1
Boma Dem. Rep. Congo 123 B4
Bomaderry Australia 138 E5
Bombala Australia 138 D6
Bombay India see **Mumbai**
Bombay Beach CA U.S.A. 159 F5
Bomberai, Semenanjung pen. Indon. 81 I7
Bömbögör Mongolia 94 D2
Bomboma Dem. Rep. Congo 122 B3
Bom Comércio Brazil 176 E5
Bomdila India 105 H4
Bomi China 99 F7
Bomili Dem. Rep. Congo 122 C3
Bom Jardim Brazil 179 D1
Bom Jardim de Goiás Brazil 179 A2
Bom Jesus Brazil 179 A5
Bom Jesus da Gurgueia, Serra do hills Brazil 177 J5
Bom Jesus da Lapa Brazil 179 C1
Bom Jesus do Norte Brazil 179 C3
Bømlo i. Norway 55 D7
Bomokandi r. Dem. Rep. Congo 122 C3
Bom Retiro Brazil 179 A4
Bom Sucesso Brazil 179 B3
Bon, Cap c. Tunisia 68 D6
Bon, Ko i. Thai. 87 B5
Bona Alg. see **Annaba**
Bona, Mount AK U.S.A. 149 L3
Bonāb Iran 110 B2
Bon Air VA U.S.A. 165 G5
Bonaire municipality West Indies 169 K6
Bonandolok Sumatera Indon. 84 B2
Bonanza Nicaragua 166 [inset] I6
Bonanza Peak WA U.S.A. 156 C2
Bonaparte Archipelago is Australia 134 D3
Bonaparte Lake Canada 150 F5
Bonar Bridge U.K. 60 E3
Bonasila Dome hill AK U.S.A. 148 G3
Bonavista Canada 153 L4
Bonavista Bay Canada 153 L4
Bonchester Bridge U.K. 60 G5
Bondo Dem. Rep. Congo 122 C3
Bondoc Peninsula Luzon Phil. 82 C3
Bondokodi Sumba Indon. 83 A5
Bondoukou Côte d'Ivoire 120 C4
Bondowoso Jawa Indon. 85 F4
Bonduel WI U.S.A. 164 A1
Bondyuzhskiy Rus. Fed. see **Mendeleyevsk**
Bône Alg. see **Annaba**
Bone Sulawesi Indon. 83 B4
Bone, Teluk b. Indon. 83 B4
Bonelipu Sulawesi Indon. 83 B4
Bönen Germany 63 H3
Bonerate Sulawesi Indon. 83 B4
Bonerate i. Indon. 83 B4
Bonerate, Kepulauan is Indon. 83 B4
Bo'ness U.K. 60 F4

▶**Bonete, Cerro** mt. Arg. 178 C3
3rd highest mountain in South America.

Bonga Eth. 122 D3
Bongabong Mindoro Phil. 82 C3
Bongaigaon India 105 G4
Bongandanga Dem. Rep. Congo 122 C3
Bongani S. Africa 124 F5
Bongao Phil. 82 B5
Bongba China 99 C6
Bong Co l. China 99 E7
Bongka r. Indon. 83 B3
Bongo i. Phil. 82 D5
Bongo, Massif des mts Cent. Afr. Rep. 122 C3
Bongo, Serra do mts Angola 123 B4
Bongolava mts Madag. 123 E5
Bongor Chad 121 E3
Bông Sơn Vietnam 87 E4
Bonham TX U.S.A. 161 D5
Bonheiden Belgium 62 E3
Boni Mali 120 C3
Bonifacio Corsica France 66 I6
Bonifacio, Bocche di strait France/Italy see **Bonifacio, Strait of**
Bonifacio, Bouches de strait France/Italy see **Bonifacio, Strait of**
Bonifacio, Strait of France/Italy 66 I6

▶**Bonin Islands** Japan 91 F8
Part of Japan.

Bonjol Sumatera Indon. 84 C2

▶**Bonn** Germany 62 H4
Former capital of Germany.

Bonna Germany see **Bonn**
Bonnåsjøen Norway 54 I3
Bonners Ferry ID U.S.A. 156 D2
Bonnet, Lac du resr Canada 151 M5
Bonnet Plume r. Canada 149 N2
Bonneville France 66 H3
Bonneville Salt Flats UT U.S.A. 159 G1
Bonnières-sur-Seine France 62 B5
Bonnie Rock Australia 135 B7
Bonnieville KY U.S.A. 164 C5
Bonnyrigg U.K. 60 F5
Bonnyville Canada 151 I4
Bonobono Palawan Phil. 82 B4
Bononia Italy see **Bologna**
Bonorva Sardinia Italy 68 C4
Bonshaw Australia 138 E2
Bontang Kalimantan Indon. 85 G2
Bontebok National Park S. Africa 124 E8
Bonthe Sierra Leone 120 B4
Bontoc Luzon Phil. 82 C2
Bontomatane Sulawesi Indon. 83 B4
Bontosunggu Sulawesi Indon. 83 A4
Bontrug S. Africa 125 G7
Bonvouloir Islands P.N.G. 136 E1
Bonwapitse Botswana 125 H2
Boo, Kepulauan is Papua Indon. 83 D3
Book Cliffs ridge UT U.S.A. 159 I2
Booker TX U.S.A. 161 C4
Boolba Australia 138 D2
Booligal Australia 138 B4
Boomer WV U.S.A. 164 E4
Boomi Australia 138 D2
Boon MI U.S.A. 164 C1
Boonah Australia 138 F1
Boone CO U.S.A. 157 G5
Boone IA U.S.A. 160 E3
Boone NC U.S.A. 162 D4
Boone Lake TN U.S.A. 164 D5
Boones Mill VA U.S.A. 164 F5
Booneville AR U.S.A. 161 E5
Booneville KY U.S.A. 164 D5
Booneville MS U.S.A. 161 F5
Böön Tsagaan Nuur salt l. Mongolia 94 D2
Boonville CA U.S.A. 158 B2
Boonville IN U.S.A. 164 B4
Boonville MO U.S.A. 160 E4
Boonville NY U.S.A. 165 H2
Boorabin National Park Australia 135 C7
Boorama Somalia 122 E3
Booroorban Australia 138 B5
Boorowa Australia 138 D5
Boort Australia 138 A6
Boothby, Cape Antarctica 188 D2
Boothia, Gulf of Canada 147 J3
Boothia Peninsula Canada 147 I2
Bootle U.K. 58 E5
Booué Gabon 122 B4
Boppard Germany 63 H4
Boqê China 99 E7
Boqueirão, Serra do hills Brazil 177 J6
Boquilla, Presa de la resr Mex. 166 D3
Boquillas del Carmen Mex. 166 E2
Bor Czech Rep. 63 M5
Bor Rus. Fed. 52 J4
Bor Serbia 69 J2
Bor South Sudan 121 G4
Bor Turkey 112 D3
Boraha, Nosy i. Madag. 123 F5
Borah Peak ID U.S.A. 156 E3
Borai India 106 D1
Borakalalo Nature Reserve S. Africa 125 H3
Boran Kazakh. see **Buran**
Boraphet, Bung l. Thai. 86 C4
Boraphet, Nong l. Thai. see **Boraphet, Bung**
Borås Sweden 55 H8
Borasambar India 106 D1
Borāzjān Iran 110 C4
Borba Brazil 177 G4
Borbon Cebu Phil. 82 D4
Borborema, Planalto da plat. Brazil 177 K5
Borchen Germany 63 I3
Borçka Turkey 113 F2
Bor Dağı mt. Turkey 69 M6
Bordeaux France 66 D4
Borden Island Canada 147 G2
Borden Peninsula Canada 147 J2
Border Ranges National Park Australia 138 F2
Borðeyri Iceland 54 [inset 1]
Bordj Bou Arréridj Alg. 67 I5
Bordj Bounaama Alg. 67 G6
Bordj Flye Ste-Marie Alg. 120 C2
Bordj Messaouda Alg. 64 F5
Bordj Mokhtar Alg. 120 D2
Bordj Omar Driss Alg. see **Bordj Omer Driss**
Bordj Omer Driss Alg. 120 D2
Bordu Kyrg. 98 A4
Boreas Abyssal Plain sea feature Arctic Ocean 189 H1
Borel r. Canada 153 H2
Borgå Fin. see **Porvoo**
Borgarfjörður Iceland 54 [inset 1]
Borgarnes Iceland 54 [inset 1]
Børgefjell Nasjonalpark nat. park Norway 54 H4
Borger TX U.S.A. 161 C5
Borgholm Sweden 55 J8
Borgne, Lake b. LA U.S.A. 161 F6
Borgo San Lorenzo Italy 68 D3
Bori India 106 C1
Bori r. India 104 C5
Borislav Ukr. see **Boryslav**
Borisoglebsk Rus. Fed. 53 I6
Borisov Belarus see **Barysaw**
Borisovka Rus. Fed. 53 H6
Borispol' Ukr. see **Boryspil'**
Bo River Post South Sudan 121 F4
Borja Peru 176 C4
Borken Germany 62 G3
Borkenes Norway 54 J2
Borkovskaya Rus. Fed. 52 K2
Borkum Germany 62 G1
Borkum i. Germany 62 G1
Borlänge Sweden 55 I6
Borlaug Norway 55 E6
Borlu Turkey 69 M5
Borna Germany 63 M3
Born-Berge hill Germany 63 K3
Borndiep sea chan. Neth. 62 F1
Borne Neth. 62 G2

▶**Borneo** i. Asia 80 E6
Largest island in Asia and 3rd in the world.

Bornholm county Denmark 189 H3
Bornholm i. Denmark 55 I9
Bornova Turkey 69 L5
Borobudur tourist site Indon. 85 E4
Borodino Rus. Fed. 76 J3
Borodinskoye Rus. Fed. 55 P6
Borogontsy Rus. Fed. 77 O3
Borohoro Shan mts China 98 C3
Boroko Sulawesi Indon. 83 B2
Borok-Sulezhskiy Rus. Fed. 52 H4
Boromo Burkina Faso 120 C3
Boron CA U.S.A. 158 E4
Borondi India 106 D2
Borongan Samar Phil. 82 D4
Boroughbridge U.K. 58 F4
Borovichi Rus. Fed. 52 G4
Borovoy Kirovskaya Oblast' Rus. Fed. 52 K4
Borovoy Respublika Kareliya Rus. Fed. 54 R4
Borovoy Respublika Komi Rus. Fed. 52 L3
Borpeta India see **Barpeta**
Borrisokane Ireland 61 D5
Borroloola Australia 136 B3
Børsa Norway 54 G5
Borşa Romania 53 E7
Borsakelmas sho'rxogi salt marsh Uzbek. 113 J2
Borshchiv Ukr. 53 E6
Borshchovochnyy Khrebet mts Rus. Fed. 95 G1
Bortala China see **Bole**
Bortala He r. China 98 C3
Borton IL U.S.A. 164 B4
Bor-Üdzüür Mongolia see **Altay**
Borūjen Iran 110 C4
Borūjerd Iran 110 C3
Bor Ul Shan mts China 94 D3
Borūn Iran 110 E3
Borve U.K. 60 C3
Boryslav Ukr. 53 D6
Boryspil' Ukr. 53 F6
Borzna Ukr. 53 G6
Borzya Rus. Fed. 95 I1
Borzya r. Rus. Fed. 95 H1
Bosaga Kazakh. 98 A3
Bosanska Dubica Bos.-Herz. 68 G2
Bosanska Gradiška Bos.-Herz. 68 G2
Bosanska Krupa Bos.-Herz. 68 G2
Bosanski Novi Bos.-Herz. 68 G2
Bosansko Grahovo Bos.-Herz. 68 G2
Boscawen Island Tonga see **Niuatoputapu**
Bose China see **Baise**
Bosencheve, Parque Nacional nat. park Mex. 167 E5
Boshof S. Africa 125 G5
Boshrūyeh Iran 110 E3
Bosna i Hercegovina country Europe see **Bosnia-Herzegovina**
Bosna Saray Bos.-Herz. see **Sarajevo**
Bosnia-Herzegovina country Europe 68 G2
Bosobogolo Pan salt pan Botswana 124 F3
Bosobolo Dem. Rep. Congo 122 B3
Bōsō-hantō pen. Japan 93 G3
Bosporus strait Turkey 69 M4
Bossaga Turkm. see **Basaga**
Bossangoa Cent. Afr. Rep. 122 B3
Bossembélé Cent. Afr. Rep. 122 B3
Bossier City LA U.S.A. 161 E5
Bossiesvlei Namibia 124 C3
Bossut, Cape Australia 134 C4
Bostan China 99 D5
Bostān Iran 110 B4
Bostan Pak. 111 G4
Bostāneh, Ra's-e pt Iran 110 D5
Bosten Hu l. China 98 D4
Boston U.K. 59 G6

▶**Boston** MA U.S.A. 165 J2
Capital of Massachusetts.

Boston Mountains AR U.S.A. 161 E5
Boston Spa U.K. 58 F5
Boswell IN U.S.A. 164 B3
Botad India 104 B5
Botany Bay Australia 138 E4
Botev mt. Bulg. 69 K3
Botevgrad Bulg. 69 J3
Bothaville S. Africa 125 H4
Bothnia, Gulf of Fin./Sweden 55 K6
Bothwell Canada 164 E2
Botkins OH U.S.A. 164 C3
Botlikh Rus. Fed. 113 G2
Botoşani Romania 53 E7
Botou China 95 I4
Bô Trach Vietnam 86 D3
Botshabelo S. Africa 125 H5
Botswana country Africa 123 C6
Botte Donato, Monte mt. Italy 68 G5
Bottesford U.K. 58 G5
Bottrop Germany 62 G3
Botucatu Brazil 179 A3
Botuporã Brazil 179 C1
Botwood Canada 153 L4
Bouaflé Côte d'Ivoire 120 C4
Bouaké Côte d'Ivoire 120 C4
Bouar Cent. Afr. Rep. 122 B3
Bouârfa Morocco 64 D5
Bouba Ndjida, Parc National de nat. park Cameroon 121 E4
Bouca Cent. Afr. Rep. 122 B3
Boucaut Bay Australia 134 F3
Bouchain France 62 D4
Bouctouche Canada 153 I5
Boudh India 106 E1
Bougaa Alg. 67 I5
Bougainville, Cape Australia 134 D3
Bougainville, Selat sea chan. Papua Indon. 83 D3
Bougainville Island P.N.G. 132 F2
Bougainville Reef Australia 136 D2
Boughessa Mali 120 D3
Bougie Alg. see **Bejaïa**
Bougouni Mali 120 C3
Bougtob Alg. 64 E5
Bouillon Belgium 62 F5
Bouira Alg. 67 H5
Bou Izakarn Morocco 120 C2
Boujdour W. Sahara 120 B2
Boulder Australia 135 C7
Boulder CO U.S.A. 156 G4
Boulder MT U.S.A. 156 E3
Boulder UT U.S.A. 159 H3
Boulder Canyon gorge NV U.S.A. 159 F3
Boulder City NV U.S.A. 159 F4
Boulevard CA U.S.A. 158 E5
Boulia Australia 136 B4
Boulogne France see **Boulogne-sur-Mer**
Boulogne-Billancourt France 62 C6
Boulogne-sur-Mer France 62 B4
Boumerdes Alg. 67 H5
Bouna Côte d'Ivoire 120 C4
Bou Naceur, Jbel mt. Morocco 64 D5
Boû Nâga Mauritania 120 B3
Boundary AK U.S.A. 149 L2
Boundary Mountains ME U.S.A. 165 J1
Boundary Peak NV U.S.A. 158 D3
Boundiali Côte d'Ivoire 120 C4
Boundji Congo 122 B4
Boun Nua Laos 86 C2
Bountiful UT U.S.A. 159 H1
Bounty Islands N.Z. 133 H6
Bounty Trough sea feature S. Pacific Ocean 186 H9
Bourail New Caledonia 133 G4
Bourbon reg. France see **Bourbonnais**
Bourbon terr. Indian Ocean see **Réunion**
Bourbon IN U.S.A. 164 B3
Bourbonnais reg. France 66 F3
Bourem Mali 120 C3
Bouressa Mali see **Boughessa**
Bourg-Achard France 59 H9
Bourganeuf France 66 E4
Bourg-en-Bresse France 66 G3
Bourges France 66 F3
Bourget Canada 165 H1
Bourgogne reg. France see **Burgundy**
Bourgogne, Canal de France 66 G3
Bourke Australia 138 B3
Bourne U.K. 59 G6
Bournemouth U.K. 59 F8
Bourtoutou Chad 121 F3
Bou Saâda Alg. 67 I6
Bou Salem Tunisia 68 C6
Bouse AZ U.S.A. 159 F5
Bouse Wash watercourse AZ U.S.A. 159 F4
Boussu Belgium 62 D4
Boutilimit Mauritania 120 B3
Bouvet Island terr. S. Atlantic Ocean see **Bouvetøya**

▶**Bouvetøya** terr. S. Atlantic Ocean 184 I9
Dependency of Norway.

Bouy France 62 E5
Bova Marina Italy 68 F6
Bovenden Germany 63 J3
Boven Kapuas Mountains Indon./Malaysia see **Kapuas Hulu, Pegunungan**
Bow r. Alta Canada 151 I5
Bow r. Alta Canada 156 F2
Bowa China see **Muli**
Bowbells ND U.S.A. 160 C1
Bowden WV U.S.A. 164 F4
Bowditch atoll Tokelau see **Fakaofo**
Bowen Australia 136 E4
Bowen, Mount Australia 138 D6
Bowenville Australia 138 E1
Bowers Ridge sea feature Bering Sea 186 H2
Bowie Australia 136 D4
Bowie AZ U.S.A. 159 I5
Bowie TX U.S.A. 161 D5
Bow Island Canada 151 I5
Bowling Green KY U.S.A. 164 B5
Bowling Green MO U.S.A. 160 F4
Bowling Green OH U.S.A. 164 D3
Bowling Green VA U.S.A. 165 G4
Bowling Green Bay National Park Australia 136 D3
Bowman ND U.S.A. 160 C2
Bowman, Mount Canada 156 C2
Bowman Island Antarctica 188 F2
Bowman Peninsula Antarctica 188 L2
Bowmore U.K. 60 C5
Bowo China see **Bomi**
Bowral Australia 138 E5
Bowser Lake Canada 149 O4
Boxberg Germany 63 J5
Box Elder SD U.S.A. 160 C2
Box Elder r. SD U.S.A. 160 C2
Boxing China 95 I4
Boxtel Neth. 62 F3
Boyabat Turkey 112 D2
Boyana tourist site Bulg. 69 J3
Boyang China see **Poyang**
Boyd r. Australia 138 F2
Boyd Lagoon salt flat Australia 135 D6
Boyd Lake Canada 151 K2
Boydton VA U.S.A. 165 F5
Boyers PA U.S.A. 164 F3
Boykins VA U.S.A. 165 G5
Boyle Canada 151 H4
Boyle Ireland 61 D4
Boyne r. Ireland 61 F4
Boyne City MI U.S.A. 164 C1
Boysen Reservoir WY U.S.A. 156 F4
Boysun Uzbek. 111 G2
Boyuibe Bol. 176 F8
Böyük Qafqaz mts Asia/Europe see **Caucasus**

▶**Bozcaada** i. Turkey 69 L5
Most westerly point of Asia.

Bozdağ mt. Turkey 69 L5
Bozdağ mt. Turkey 107 C1
Boz Dağları mts Turkey 69 L5
Bozdoğan Turkey 69 M6
Bozeat U.K. 59 G6
Bozeman MT U.S.A. 156 F3
Bozen Italy see **Bolzano**
Bozhou China 97 G1
Bozoum Cent. Afr. Rep. 122 B3
Bozova Turkey 112 E3
Bozqūsh, Kūh-e mts Iran 110 B2
Bozüyük Turkey 69 N5
Bozyazı Turkey 107 A1
Bozymbay Kazakh. 98 C2
Bra Italy 68 B2
Brač i. Croatia 68 G3
Bracadale U.K. 60 C3
Bracadale, Loch b. U.K. 60 C3
Bracara Port. see **Braga**
Bracciano, Lago di l. Italy 68 E3
Bracebridge Canada 164 F1
Bräcke Sweden 54 I5
Brackenheim Germany 63 J5
Brackettville TX U.S.A. 161 C6
Bracknell U.K. 59 G7
Bradano r. Italy 68 G4
Bradenton FL U.S.A. 163 D7

▶**Brades** Montserrat 169 L5
Temporary capital of Montserrat. Plymouth was abandoned in 1997 owing to volcanic activity.

Bradford Canada 164 F1
Bradford U.K. 58 F5
Bradford OH U.S.A. 164 C3
Bradford PA U.S.A. 165 F3
Bradley IL U.S.A. 164 B3
Brady TX U.S.A. 161 D6
Brady Glacier AK U.S.A. 150 B3
Brae U.K. 60 [inset]
Braemar U.K. 60 F3
Braga Port. 67 B3
Bragado Arg. 178 D5
Bragança Brazil 177 I4
Bragança Port. 67 C3
Bragança Paulista Brazil 179 B3
Brahin Belarus 53 F6
Brahlstorf Germany 63 K1
Brahmanbaria Bangl. 105 G5
Brahmapur India 106 E2
Brahmaputra r. Asia 105 H4
also known as Dihang (India) or Jamuna (Bangladesh) or Siang (India) or Yarlung Zangbo (China)
Brahmaur India 104 D2
Brăila Romania 69 L2
Braine France 62 D5
Braine-le-Comte Belgium 62 E4
Brainerd MN U.S.A. 160 E2
Braintree U.K. 59 H7
Braithwaite Point Australia 134 F2
Brak r. S. Africa 125 I2
Brakel Belgium 62 D4
Brakel Germany 63 J3
Brake (Unterweser) Germany 63 I1
Brakwater Namibia 124 C2
Bramfield Australia 135 F8
Bramming Denmark 55 F9
Brämön i. Sweden 54 J5
Brampton Canada 164 F2
Brampton England U.K. 58 E4
Brampton England U.K. 59 I6
Bramsche Germany 63 I2
Bramwell Australia 136 C2
Brancaster U.K. 59 H6
Branch Canada 153 L5
Branco r. Brazil 176 F4
Brandberg mt. Namibia 123 B6
Brandbu Norway 55 G6
Brande Denmark 55 F9
Brandenburg Germany 63 M2
Brandenburg land Germany 63 N2
Brandenburg KY U.S.A. 164 B5
Brandfort S. Africa 125 H5
Brandis Germany 63 N3
Brandon Canada 151 L5
Brandon U.K. 59 H6
Brandon MS U.S.A. 161 F5
Brandon VT U.S.A. 165 I2
Brandon Head hd Ireland 61 B5
Brandon Mountain hill Ireland 61 B5
Brandvlei S. Africa 124 E6
Braniewo Poland 57 Q3
Bransfield Strait Antarctica 188 L2
Branson CO U.S.A. 161 C4
Brantas r. Indon. 85 F4
Brantford Canada 164 E2
Branxton Australia 138 E4
Bras d'Or Lake Canada 153 J5
Brasil country S. America see **Brazil**
Brasileia Brazil 176 E6

▶**Brasília** Brazil 179 B1
Capital of Brazil.

Brasília de Minas Brazil 179 B2
Braslav Belarus see **Braslaw**
Braslaw Belarus 55 O9
Braşov Romania 69 K2
Brassey, Banjaran mts Malaysia 85 G1
Brassey, Mount Australia 135 F5
Brassey Range hills Australia 135 C6
Brasstown Bald mt. GA U.S.A. 163 D5

▶**Bratislava** Slovakia 57 P6
Capital of Slovakia.

Bratsk Rus. Fed. 88 I1
Bratskoye Vodokhranilishche resr Rus. Fed. 88 I1
Brattleboro VT U.S.A. 165 I2
Braulio Carrillo, Parque Nacional nat. park Costa Rica 166 [inset] J7
Braunau am Inn Austria 57 N6
Braunfels Germany 63 I4
Braunlage Germany 63 K3
Braunsbedra Germany 63 L3
Braunschweig Germany 63 K2
Brava i. Cape Verde 120 [inset]
Brave PA U.S.A. 164 E4
Bråviken inlet Sweden 55 J7
Bravo, Cerro mt. Bol. 176 F7
Bravo del Norte, Río r. Mex. 154 H6
Bravo del Norte, Río r. Mex./U.S.A. see **Rio Grande**
Brawley CA U.S.A. 159 F5
Bray Ireland 61 F4
Bray Island Canada 147 K3
Brazeau r. Canada 150 H4
Brazeau, Mount Canada 150 G4

▶**Brazil** country S. America 177 G5
Largest and most populous country in South America and 5th largest and 5th most populous in the world.

Brazil IN U.S.A. 164 B4
Brazil Basin sea feature S. Atlantic Ocean 184 G7
Brazilian Highlands plat. Brazil 177 J7
Brazos r. TX U.S.A. 161 E6

▶**Brazzaville** Congo 123 B4
Capital of Congo.

Brčko Bos.-Herz. 68 H2
Bré Ireland see **Bray**
Breadalbane Australia 136 B4
Breaksea Sound inlet N.Z. 139 A7
Bream Bay N.Z. 139 E2
Brebes Jawa Indon. 85 E4
Brebes, Tanjung pt Indon. 85 E4
Brechfa U.K. 59 C7
Brechin U.K. 60 G4
Brecht Belgium 62 E3
Breckenridge MI U.S.A. 164 C2
Breckenridge MN U.S.A. 160 D2
Breckenridge TX U.S.A. 161 D5
Břeclav Czech Rep. 57 P6
Brecon U.K. 59 D7
Brecon Beacons reg. U.K. 59 D7
Brecon Beacons National Park U.K. 59 D7
Breda Neth. 62 E3
Bredasdorp S. Africa 124 E8
Bredbo Australia 138 D5
Breddin Germany 63 M2
Bredevoort Neth. 62 G3
Bredviken Sweden 54 I3
Bree Belgium 62 F3
Breed WI U.S.A. 164 A1
Bregenz Austria 57 L7
Breiðafjörður b. Iceland 54 [inset 1]
Breiðdalsvík Iceland 54 [inset 1]
Breidenbach Germany 63 I4
Breien ND U.S.A. 160 C2
Breitenfelde Germany 63 K1
Breitengüßbach Germany 63 K5
Breiter Luzinsee l. Germany 63 N1
Breivikbotn Norway 54 M1
Breizh reg. France see **Brittany**
Brejo Velho Brazil 179 C1
Brekstad Norway 54 F5
Bremen Germany 63 I1
Bremen land Germany 63 I1
Bremen IN U.S.A. 164 B3
Bremen OH U.S.A. 164 D4
Bremer Bay Australia 135 B8
Bremerhaven Germany 63 I1
Bremer Range hills Australia 135 C8
Bremersdorp Swaziland see **Manzini**
Bremervörde Germany 63 J1
Bremm Germany 62 H4
Bremner r. AK U.S.A. 149 K3
Brenham TX U.S.A. 161 D6
Brenna Norway 54 H4
Brennero, Passo di pass Austria/Italy see **Brenner Pass**
Brenner Pass Austria/Italy 68 D1
Brennerpaß pass Austria/Italy see **Brenner Pass**
Brentwood U.K. 59 H7
Brescia Italy 68 D2
Breslau Poland see **Wrocław**
Bresle r. France 62 B4
Brésolles, Lac l. Canada 153 H3
Bressanone Italy 68 D1
Bressay i. U.K. 60 [inset]
Bressuire France 66 D3
Brest Belarus 55 M10
Brest France 66 B2
Brest-Litovsk Belarus see **Brest**
Bretagne reg. France see **Brittany**
Breteuil France 62 C5
Brétigny-sur-Orge France 62 C6
Breton Canada 150 H4
Breton Sound b. LA U.S.A. 161 F6
Brett, Cape N.Z. 139 E2
Bretten Germany 63 I5
Bretton U.K. 58 E5
Breueh, Pulau i. Indon. 84 A1
Brevard NC U.S.A. 163 D5
Breves Brazil 177 H4
Brevig Mission AK U.S.A. 148 F2
Brewarrina Australia 138 C2
Brewer ME U.S.A. 162 G2
Brewster NE U.S.A. 160 D3
Brewster OH U.S.A. 164 E3
Brewster, Kap c. Greenland see **Kangikajik**
Brewster, Lake imp. l. Australia 138 B4
Brewton AL U.S.A. 163 C6
Breyten S. Africa 125 I4
Breytovo Rus. Fed. 52 H4
Brezhnev Rus. Fed. see **Naberezhnyye Chelny**
Brezno Slovakia 57 Q6
Brezovo Bulg. 69 K3
Brezovo Polje hill Croatia 68 G2
Bria Cent. Afr. Rep. 122 C3
Briançon France 66 H4
Brian Head mt. UT U.S.A. 159 G3
Bribbaree Australia 138 C5
Bribie Island Australia 138 F1
Briceni Moldova 53 E6
Brichany Moldova see **Briceni**
Brichen' Moldova see **Briceni**
Bridgend U.K. 59 D7
Bridge of Orchy U.K. 60 E4
Bridgeport CA U.S.A. 158 D2
Bridgeport CT U.S.A. 165 I3
Bridgeport IL U.S.A. 164 B4
Bridgeport NE U.S.A. 160 C3
Bridgeport TX U.S.A. 167 F1
Bridger Peak WY U.S.A. 156 G4
Bridgeton NJ U.S.A. 165 H4
Bridgetown Australia 135 B8

▶**Bridgetown** Barbados 169 M6
Capital of Barbados.

Bridgetown Canada 153 I5
Bridgeville DE U.S.A. 165 H4
Bridgewater Canada 153 I5
Bridgewater NY U.S.A. 165 H2
Bridgnorth U.K. 59 E6
Bridgton ME U.S.A. 165 J1
Bridgwater U.K. 59 D7

Bridgwater Bay U.K. 59 D7
Bridlington U.K. 58 G4
Bridlington Bay U.K. 58 G4
Bridport Australia 137 [inset]
Bridport U.K. 59 E8
Brie reg. France 66 F2
Brie-Comte-Robert France 62 C6
Brieg Poland see Brzeg
Briery Knob mt. WV U.S.A. 164 E4
Brig Switz. 66 H3
Brigg U.K. 58 G5
Brigham City UT U.S.A. 156 E4
Brightlingsea U.K. 59 I7
Brighton Canada 165 G1
Brighton U.K. 59 G8
Brighton CO U.S.A. 156 G5
Brighton MI U.S.A. 164 D2
Brighton NY U.S.A. 165 G2
Brighton WV U.S.A. 164 D4
Brignoles France 66 H5
Brikama Gambia 120 B3
Brillion WI U.S.A. 164 A1
Brilon Germany 63 I3
Brindisi Italy 68 G4
Brinkley AR U.S.A. 161 F5
Brion, Île i. Canada 153 J5
Brioude France 66 F4
Brisay Canada 153 H3

▶Brisbane Australia 138 F1
Capital of Queensland. 3rd most populous city in Oceania.

Brisbane Ranges National Park Australia 138 B6
Bristol U.K. 59 E7
Bristol CT U.S.A. 165 I3
Bristol FL U.S.A. 163 C6
Bristol NH U.S.A. 165 J2
Bristol RI U.S.A. 165 J3
Bristol TN U.S.A. 164 D5
Bristol VT U.S.A. 165 I1
Bristol Bay AK U.S.A. 148 G4
Bristol Channel est. U.K. 59 C7
Bristol Lake CA U.S.A. 159 F4
Britannia Island New Caledonia see Maré
British Antarctic Territory reg. Antarctica 188 L2
British Columbia prov. Canada 150 F5
British Empire Range mts Canada 147 J1
British Guiana country S. America see Guyana
British Honduras country Central America see Belize

▶British Indian Ocean Territory terr. Indian Ocean 185 M6
United Kingdom Overseas Territory.

British Mountains Canada/U.S.A. 149 L1
British Solomon Islands country S. Pacific Ocean see Solomon Islands
Brito Godins Angola see Kiwaba N'zogi
Brits S. Africa 125 H3
Britstown S. Africa 124 F6
Brittany reg. France 66 C2
Britton SD U.S.A. 160 D2
Brive-la-Gaillarde France 66 E4
Briviesca Spain 67 E2
Brixham U.K. 59 D8
Brixia Italy see Brescia
Brlik Kazakh. see Birlik
Brno Czech Rep. 57 P6
Broach India see Bharuch
Broad r. SC U.S.A. 163 D5
Broadalbin NY U.S.A. 165 H2
Broad Arrow Australia 135 C7
Broadback r. Canada 152 F4
Broad Bay U.K. see Tuath, Loch a'
Broadford Australia 138 B6
Broadford Ireland 61 D5
Broadford U.K. 60 D3
Broad Law hill U.K. 60 F5
Broadmere Australia 136 A3
Broad Pass AK U.S.A. 149 J3
Broad Peak China/Pak. 111 J3
Broad Sound sea chan. Australia 136 E4
Broadstairs U.K. 59 I7
Broadus MT U.S.A. 156 G3
Broadview Canada 151 K5
Broadway VA U.S.A. 165 F4
Broadwood N.Z. 139 D2
Brochet Canada 151 K3
Brochet, Lac l. Canada 151 K3
Brochet, Lac au l. Canada 153 H4
Brock r. Canada 149 Q1
Brocken mt. Germany 63 K3
Brockman, Mount Australia 134 B5
Brockport NY U.S.A. 165 G2
Brockport PA U.S.A. 165 F3
Brockton MA U.S.A. 165 J2
Brockville Canada 165 H1
Brockway PA U.S.A. 165 F3
Brodeur Peninsula Canada 147 J2
Brodhead KY U.S.A. 164 C5
Brodick U.K. 60 D5
Brodnica Poland 57 Q4
Brody Ukr. 53 E6
Broken Arrow OK U.S.A. 161 E4
Broken Bay Australia 138 E4
Broken Bow NE U.S.A. 160 D3
Broken Bow OK U.S.A. 161 E5
Brokenhead r. Canada 151 L5
Broken Hill Australia 137 C6
Broken Hill Zambia see Kabwe
Broken Plateau sea feature Indian Ocean 185 O8
Brokopondo Suriname 177 G2
Brokopondo Stuwmeer resr Suriname see Professor van Blommestein Meer
Bromberg Poland see Bydgoszcz
Brome Germany 63 K2
Bromo Tengger Semeru, Taman Nasional nat. park Indon. 85 F4
Bromsgrove U.K. 59 E6
Brønderslev Denmark 55 F8
Brønnøysund Norway 54 H4
Bronson FL U.S.A. 163 D6
Bronson MI U.S.A. 164 C3
Brooke U.K. 59 I6
Brooke's Point Palawan Phil. 82 B4
Brookfield WI U.S.A. 164 A2
Brookhaven MS U.S.A. 161 F6
Brookings OR U.S.A. 156 B4
Brookings SD U.S.A. 160 D2
Brookline MA U.S.A. 165 J2
Brooklyn MI U.S.A. 164 C2
Brooklyn Park MN U.S.A. 160 E2
Brookneal VA U.S.A. 165 F5
Brooks Canada 151 I5
Brooks Brook Canada 149 N3
Brooks Mountain hill AK U.S.A. 148 F2
Brooks Range mts AK U.S.A. 149 K1
Brookston IN U.S.A. 164 B3
Brooksville FL U.S.A. 163 D6
Brooksville KY U.S.A. 164 C4
Brookton Australia 135 B8
Brookville IN U.S.A. 164 C4
Brookville PA U.S.A. 164 F3
Brookville Lake IN U.S.A. 164 C4
Broom, Loch inlet U.K. 60 D3
Broome Australia 134 C4
Brora U.K. 60 F2
Brora r. U.K. 60 F2
Brösarp Sweden 55 I9
Brosna r. Ireland 61 E4
Brosville VA U.S.A. 164 F5
Brothers is India 87 A5
Brough U.K. 58 E4
Brough Ness pt U.K. 60 G2
Broughshane U.K. 61 F3
Broughton Island Canada see Qikiqtarjuaq
Broughton Islands Australia 138 F4
Brovary Ukr. 53 F6
Brovinia Australia 137 E5
Brovst Denmark 55 F8
Brown City MI U.S.A. 164 D2
Brown Deer WI U.S.A. 164 B2
Browne Range hills Australia 135 D6
Brownfield TX U.S.A. 161 C5
Browning MT U.S.A. 156 E2
Brown Mountain CA U.S.A. 158 E4
Brownstown IN U.S.A. 164 B4
Brownsville KY U.S.A. 164 B5
Brownsville PA U.S.A. 164 F3
Brownsville TN U.S.A. 161 F5
Brownsville TX U.S.A. 161 D7
Brownwood TX U.S.A. 161 D6
Brownwood, Lake TX U.S.A. 167 F2
Browse Island Australia 134 C3
Bruay-la-Bussière France 62 C4
Bruce Peninsula Canada 164 E1
Bruce Peninsula National Park Canada 164 E1
Bruce Rock Australia 135 B7
Bruchsal Germany 63 I5
Brück Germany 63 M2
Bruck an der Mur Austria 57 O7
Brue r. U.K. 59 E7
Bruges Belgium see Brugge
Brugge Belgium 62 D3
Brühl Baden-Württemberg Germany 63 I5
Brühl Nordrhein-Westfalen Germany 62 G4
Bruin KY U.S.A. 164 D4
Bruin PA U.S.A. 164 F3
Bruin Point mt. UT U.S.A. 159 H2
Bruint India 105 I3
Brûk, Wâdi el watercourse Egypt see Burūk, Wādī al
Brukkaros Namibia 124 D3
Brûlé Canada 150 G4
Brûlé, Lac l. Canada 153 J3
Brûly Belgium 62 E5
Brumado Brazil 179 C1
Brumath France 63 H6
Brumunddal Norway 55 G6
Brunau Germany 63 L2
Brundisium Italy see Brindisi
Bruneau ID U.S.A. 156 E4
Brunei country Asia 85 F1
Brunei Brunei see Bandar Seri Begawan
Brunei Bay Malaysia 85 F1
Brunette Downs Australia 136 A3
Brunflo Sweden 54 I5
Brunico Italy 68 D1
Brünn Czech Rep. see Brno
Brunner, Lake N.Z. 139 C6
Bruno Canada 151 J4
Brunswick Germany see Braunschweig
Brunswick GA U.S.A. 163 D6
Brunswick MD U.S.A. 165 G4
Brunswick ME U.S.A. 165 K2
Brunswick, Península de pen. Chile 178 B8
Brunswick Bay Australia 134 D3
Brunswick Lake Canada 152 E4
Bruntál Czech Rep. 57 P6
Brunt Ice Shelf Antarctica 188 B2
Bruntville S. Africa 125 J5
Bruny Island Australia 137 [inset]
Brusa Turkey see Bursa
Brusenets Rus. Fed. 52 I3
Brushton NY U.S.A. 165 H1
Brusque Brazil 179 A4
Brussel Belgium see Brussels

▶Brussels Belgium 62 E4
Capital of Belgium.

Bruthen Australia 138 C6
Bruxelles Belgium see Brussels
Bruzual Venez. 176 E2
Bryan OH U.S.A. 164 C3
Bryan TX U.S.A. 161 D6
Bryan, Mount hill Australia 137 B7
Bryan Coast Antarctica 188 L2
Bryansk Bryanskaya Oblast' Rus. Fed. 53 G5
Bryansk Respublika Dagestan Rus. Fed. 113 G1
Bryant Pond ME U.S.A. 165 J1
Bryantsburg IN U.S.A. 164 C4
Bryce Canyon National Park UT U.S.A. 159 G3
Bryce Mountain AZ U.S.A. 159 I5
Brynbuga U.K. see Usk
Bryne Norway 55 D7
Bryukhovetskaya Rus. Fed. 53 H7
Brzeg Poland 57 P5
Brześć nad Bugiem Belarus see Brest
Bua r. Malawi 123 D5
Bu'aale Somalia 122 E3
Buala Solomon Is 133 F2
Buang i. Indon. 83 C2
Buatan Sumatera Indon. 84 C2
Bu'ayj well Saudi Arabia 110 C5
Būbīyān, Jazīrat Kuwait 110 C4
Bubuan i. Phil. 82 C5
Bucak Turkey 69 N6
Bucaramanga Col. 176 D2
Bucas Grande i. Phil. 82 D4
Buccaneer Archipelago is Australia 134 C4
Buchanan Liberia 120 B4
Buchanan MI U.S.A. 164 B3
Buchanan VA U.S.A. 164 F5
Buchanan, Lake salt flat Australia 136 D4
Buchanan, Lake TX U.S.A. 167 F2
Buchan Gulf Canada 147 K2

▶Bucharest Romania 69 L2
Capital of Romania.

Büchen Germany 63 K1
Buchen (Odenwald) Germany 63 J5
Buchholz Germany 63 M1
Bucholz in der Nordheide Germany 63 J1
Buchon, Point CA U.S.A. 158 C4
Buchy France 62 B5
Bucin, Pasul pass Romania 69 K1
Buckambool Mountain hill Australia 138 B3
Bückeburg Germany 63 J2
Bücken Germany 63 J2
Buckeye AZ U.S.A. 159 G5
Buckhannon WV U.S.A. 164 E4
Buckhaven U.K. 60 F4
Buckhorn Lake Canada 165 F1
Buckie U.K. 60 G3
Buckingham U.K. 59 G6
Buckingham VA U.S.A. 165 F5
Buckingham Bay Australia 79 F9
Buckland AK U.S.A. 148 G2
Buckland r. AK U.S.A. 148 G2
Buckland Tableland reg. Australia 136 E5
Buckleboo Australia 135 G8
Buckle Island Antarctica 188 H2
Buckley watercourse Australia 136 B4
Buckley Bay Antarctica 188 G2
Bucklin KS U.S.A. 160 D4
Buckskin Mountains AZ U.S.A. 159 G4
Bucks Mountain CA U.S.A. 158 C2
Bucksport ME U.S.A. 153 H5
Bückwitz Germany 63 M2
Bucureşti Romania see Bucharest
Bucyrus OH U.S.A. 164 D3
Buda-Kashalyova Belarus 53 F5
Budalin Myanmar 86 A2

▶Budapest Hungary 69 H1
Capital of Hungary.

Budaun India 104 D3
Budawang National Park Australia 138 E5
Budda Australia 138 B3
Budd Coast Antarctica 188 F2
Buddusò Sardinia Italy 68 C4
Bude U.K. 59 C8
Bude MS U.S.A. 161 F6
Budennovsk Rus. Fed. 113 G1
Buderim Australia 138 F1
Büding Iran 110 E5
Büdingen Germany 63 J4
Budīyah, Jabal hills Egypt 107 A5
Budongquan China 94 C5
Budoni Sardinia Italy 68 C4
Budū, Ḥadabat al plain Saudi Arabia 110 C6
Budū', Sabkhat al salt pan Saudi Arabia 110 C6
Budweis Czech Rep. see České Budějovice
Buenaventura Col. 176 C3
Buenaventura Mex. 166 D2
Buena Vista i. N. Mariana Is see Tinian
Buenavista Mindanao Phil. 82 D4
Buenavista Phil. 82 C3
Buena Vista CO U.S.A. 156 G5
Buena Vista VA U.S.A. 164 F5
Buendía, Embalse de resr Spain 67 E3

▶Buenos Aires Arg. 178 E4
Capital of Argentina. 2nd most populous city in South America.

Buenos Aires Costa Rica 166 [inset] J7
Buenos Aires, Lago l. Arg./Chile 178 B7
Buenos Aires National Wildlife Refuge nature res. AZ U.S.A. 166 C2
Buerarema Brazil 179 D1
Buet r. Canada 153 H1
Búfalo Mex. 166 D3
Buffalo r. Canada 150 H2
Buffalo KY U.S.A. 164 C5
Buffalo MO U.S.A. 160 E4
Buffalo NY U.S.A. 165 F2
Buffalo OK U.S.A. 161 D4
Buffalo SD U.S.A. 160 C2
Buffalo TX U.S.A. 161 D6
Buffalo WY U.S.A. 156 G3
Buffalo Head Hills Canada 150 G3
Buffalo Head Prairie Canada 150 G3
Buffalo Hump mt. ID U.S.A. 156 E3
Buffalo Lake Alta Canada 151 H4
Buffalo Lake N.W.T. Canada 150 H2
Buffalo Narrows Canada 151 I4
Buffels watercourse S. Africa 124 C5
Buffels Drift S. Africa 125 H2
Buftea Romania 69 K2
Bug r. Poland 57 S5
Buga Col. 176 C3
Buga Mongolia see Dörvöljin
Bugaldie Australia 138 D3
Bugant Mongolia 95 F1
Bugat Mongolia 94 C2
Bugdaýly Turkm. 110 D2
Bugel, Tanjung pt Indon. 85 E4
Buggenhout Belgium 62 E3
Bugojno Bos.-Herz. 68 G2
Bugrino Rus. Fed. 52 K1
Bugsuk i. Phil. 82 B4
Bugt China 95 J1
Buguey Luzon Phil. 82 C2
Bugul'ma Rus. Fed. 51 Q5
Bügür China see Luntai
Buguruslan Rus. Fed. 51 Q5
Buhera Zimbabwe 123 D5
Buh He r. China 94 D4
Buhi Luzon Phil. 82 C3
Bühl Germany 63 I6
Buhuşi Romania 69 L1
Buick Canada 150 F3
Builth Wells U.K. 59 D6
Bui National Park Ghana 120 C4
Buinsk Rus. Fed. 53 K5
Bu'in Zahrā Iran 110 C3
Buir Nur l. Mongolia 95 I2
Buitepos Namibia 124 D2
Bujanovac Serbia 69 I3

▶Bujumbura Burundi 122 C4
Capital of Burundi.

Bukachacha Rus. Fed. 89 L2
Bukadaban Feng mt. China 99 E5
Buka Island P.N.G. 132 F2
Būkān Iran 110 B2
Būkand Iran 110 D4
Bukavu Dem. Rep. Congo 122 C4
Bukhara Uzbek. see Buxoro
Bukhoro Uzbek. see Buxoro
Bukide i. Indon. 83 C2
Bukit Baka-Bukit Raya, Taman Nasional nat. park Indon. 85 F3
Bukitlidi Kalimantan Indon. 85 F3
Bukit Timah Sing. 87 [inset]
Bukittinggi Sumatera Indon. 84 C3
Bukkapatnam India 106 C3
Bukoba Tanz. 122 D4
Bükreş Romania see Bucharest
Buktyrma, Vodokhranilishche resr Kazakh. 98 D2
Buku, Tanjung pt Indon. 84 D3
Bukukun Rus. Fed. 95 G1
Būl, Kūh-e mt. Iran 110 D4
Bula Seram Indon. 83 D3
Bula P.N.G. 81 K8
Bülach Switz. 66 I3
Bulag Mongolia see Möngönmorit
Bulagtay Mongolia see Hüder
Bulalacao Mindoro Phil. 82 C3
Bulan i. Indon. 84 C2
Bulan Luzon Phil. 82 C3
Bulan i. Phil. 82 C5
Bulancak Turkey 112 E2
Bulandshahr India 104 D3
Bulanık Turkey 113 F3
Bulava Rus. Fed. 90 F2
Bulawa, Gunung mt. Indon. 83 B2
Bulawayo Zimbabwe 123 C6
Buldan Turkey 69 M5
Buldana India see Buldhana
Buldhana India 106 C1
Buldir Island AK U.S.A. 148 [inset] A5
Buldur India 99 B7
Buleda reg. Pak. 111 F5
Bulembu Swaziland 125 J3
Bulgan Bayan-Ölgiy Mongolia 94 B2
Bulgan Bulgan Mongolia 94 E1
Bulgan Dornod Mongolia 95 H1
Bulgan Hovd Mongolia 94 B2
Bulgan Hovd Mongolia see Darvi
Bulgan Hövsgöl Mongolia see Tsagaan-Üür
Bulgan Ömnögovĭ Mongolia 94 E2
Bulgan prov. Mongolia 94 E1
Bulgan Gol r. Mongolia 94 B2
Bulgar Rus. Fed. see Bolgar
Bulgaria country Europe 69 K3
Bŭlgariya country Europe see Bulgaria
Buli Halmahera Indon. 83 D2
Buli, Teluk b. Halmahera Indon. 83 D2
Buliluyan, Cape Palawan Phil. 82 B4
Bulkley Ranges mts Canada 149 O5
Bullawarra, Lake salt flat Australia 138 A1
Bullen r. Canada 151 K1
Bullen AK U.S.A. 149 K1
Buller r. N.Z. 139 C5
Buller, Mount Australia 138 C6
Bulleringa National Park Australia 136 C3
Bullfinch Australia 135 B7
Bullhead City AZ U.S.A. 159 F4
Bulli Australia 138 E5
Bullion Mountains CA U.S.A. 158 E4
Bullo r. Australia 134 E3
Bulloo Downs Australia 137 C6
Bulloo Lake salt flat Australia 137 C6
Büllsport Namibia 124 C3
Bully Choop Mountain CA U.S.A. 158 B1
Bulman Australia 134 F3
Bulman Gorge Australia 134 F3
Bulmer Lake Canada 150 F2
Buloh, Pulau i. Sing. 87 [inset]
Buloke, Lake dry lake Australia 138 A6
Bulolo P.N.G. 81 L8
Bulsar India see Valsad
Bultfontein S. Africa 125 H5
Bulu, Gunung mt. Indon. 85 G2
Buluan Mindanao Phil. 82 D5
Bulubulu Sulawesi Indon. 83 B4
Bulukumba Sulawesi Indon. 83 B4
Bulun Rus. Fed. 77 N2
Bulungu Dem. Rep. Congo 123 C4
Bulung'ur Uzbek. 111 G2
Bumba Dem. Rep. Congo 122 C3
Bümbah Libya 112 A4
Bumbah, Khalīj b. Libya 112 A4
Bumbat China 94 F3
Bumbat Mongolia see Bayan-Öndör
Bumhkang Myanmar 86 B1
Bumpha Bum mt. Myanmar 86 B1
Buna Dem. Rep. Congo 122 B4
Buna Kenya 122 D3
Bunayyān well Saudi Arabia 110 C6
Bunazi Tanz. 122 D4
Bunbury Australia 135 A8
Bunclody Ireland 61 F5
Buncrana Ireland 61 E2
Bunda Tanz. 122 D4
Bundaberg Australia 136 F5
Bundaleer Australia 138 C2
Bundarra Australia 138 E3
Bundi India 104 C4
Bundjalung National Park Australia 138 F2
Bundoran Ireland 61 D3
Bunduqiya South Sudan 121 G4
Buner reg. Pak. 111 I3
Bunga-dake mt. Japan 92 B3
Bungalaut, Selat sea chan. Indon. 84 B3
Bungay U.K. 59 I6
Bungendore Australia 138 D5
Bunger Hills Antarctica 188 F2
Bungi Sulawesi Indon. 83 B4
Bungku Sulawesi Indon. 83 B3
Bungle Bungle National Park Australia see Purnululu National Park
Bungona'og China 99 E6
Bungo-suidō sea chan. Japan 91 D6
Bunguran, Kepulauan is Indon. see Natuna, Kepulauan
Bunguran, Pulau i. Indon. see Natuna Besar
Buni, Ci r. Indon. 84 D4
Bunia Dem. Rep. Congo 122 D3
Buniangа Dem. Rep. Congo 122 C4
Buningonia well Australia 135 C7
Bunji Pak. 104 C2
Bunker Group atolls Australia 136 F4
Bunker Hill AK U.S.A. 148 F2
Bunkeya Dem. Rep. Congo 123 C5
Bunkie LA U.S.A. 167 G2
Bunnell FL U.S.A. 163 D6
Bünsum China 99 C7
Buntok Kalimantan Indon. 85 F3
Buntokecil Kalimantan Indon. 85 F3
Bunya Mountains National Park Australia 138 E1
Bünyan Turkey 112 D3
Bunyu i. Indon. 85 G2
Buôn Đôn Vietnam 87 D4
Buôn Ma Thuôt Vietnam 87 E4
Buor-Khaya, Guba b. Rus. Fed. 77 O2
Bup r. China 99 D7
Buqayq Saudi Arabia see Abqaiq
Buqbuq Egypt 112 B5
Bura Kenya 122 D4
Buraan Somalia 122 E2
Buram Sudan 121 F3
Buran Kazakh. 102 G2
Burang China 99 C7
Buranhaém Brazil 179 C2
Buranhaém r. Brazil 179 D2
Burāq Syria 107 C3
Burauen Leyte Phil. 82 D4
Buray r. India 104 C5
Buraydah Saudi Arabia 108 F4
Burbach Germany 63 I4
Burbank CA U.S.A. 158 D4
Burcher Australia 138 C4
Burco Somalia 122 E3
Bürd Mongolia 94 E2
Burdaard Neth. 62 F1
Burdalyk Turkm. 111 G2
Burdigala France see Bordeaux
Burdur Turkey 69 N6
Burdur Gölü l. Turkey 69 N6
Burdwan India see Barddhaman
Burē Eth. 122 D2
Bure r. U.K. 59 I6
Bureå Sweden 54 L4
Bureinskiy Khrebet mts Rus. Fed. 90 D2
Bureinskiy Zapovednik nature res. Rus. Fed. 90 D2
Büren Mongolia 94 F2
Bürentsogt Mongolia 95 G2
Burewala Pak. 111 I4
Bureya r. Rus. Fed. 90 C2
Bureya Range mts Rus. Fed. see Bureinskiy Khrebet
Burford Canada 164 E2
Burgaltay Mongolia see Baruunbüren
Burgas Bulg. 69 L3
Burgaw NC U.S.A. 163 E5
Burg bei Magdeburg Germany 63 L2
Burgbernheim Germany 63 K5
Burgdorf Germany 63 K2
Burgeo Canada 153 K5
Burgersdorp S. Africa 125 H6
Burgersfort S. Africa 125 J3
Burgess, Mount hill Australia 135 C7
Burgess, Mount Canada 149 M2
Burgess Hill U.K. 59 G8
Burghaun Germany 63 J4
Burghausen Germany 57 N6
Burghead U.K. 60 F3
Burgh-Haamstede Neth. 62 D3
Burgio, Serra di hill Sicily Italy 68 F6
Burglengenfeld Germany 63 M5
Burgos Mex. 167 F3
Burgos Spain 67 E2
Burgstädt Germany 63 M4
Burgsvik Sweden 55 K8
Burgum Neth. 62 G1
Burgundy reg. France 66 G3
Burhan Budai Shan mts China 94 C5
Burhaniye Turkey 69 L5
Burhanpur India 104 D5
Burhar-Dhanpuri India 105 E5
Burhi Gandak r. India 99 D8
Buri Brazil 179 A3
Buriai Indon. 84 C3
Burias i. Phil. 82 C3
Buriat-Mongol Republic aut. rep. Rus. Fed. see Buryatiya, Respublika
Burica, Punta pt Costa Rica 166 [inset] J7
Buri Gandak r. Nepal 99 C8
Burin Canada 153 L5
Burin Peninsula Canada 153 L5
Buriram Thai. 86 C4
Buritama Brazil 179 A3
Buriti Alegre Brazil 179 A2
Buriti Bravo Brazil 177 J5
Buritirama Brazil 177 J6
Buritis Brazil 179 B1
Burjay China 98 E4
Burj Aziz Khan Pak. 111 G4
Burkan-Suu r. Kyrg. 98 B4
Burke SD U.S.A. 160 D3
Burke Island Antarctica 188 K2
Burke Pass N.Z. see Burkes Pass
Burkes Pass N.Z. 139 C7
Burkesville KY U.S.A. 164 C5
Burketown Australia 136 B3
Burkeville VA U.S.A. 165 F5
Burkina country Africa see Burkina Faso
Burkina Faso country Africa 120 C3
Burkitty Kazakh. 98 B2
Burk's Falls Canada 152 F5
Burley ID U.S.A. 156 E4
Burlington Canada 164 F2
Burlington CO U.S.A. 160 C4
Burlington IA U.S.A. 160 F3
Burlington KS U.S.A. 160 E4
Burlington KY U.S.A. 164 C4
Burlington VT U.S.A. 165 I1
Burlington WI U.S.A. 164 A2
Burmantovo Rus. Fed. 51 S3
Burnaby Canada 150 F5
Burnet TX U.S.A. 161 D6
Burney CA U.S.A. 158 C1
Burney, Monte vol. Chile 178 B8
Burnham PA U.S.A. 165 G3
Burnie Australia 137 [inset]
Burniston U.K. 58 G4
Burnley U.K. 58 E5
Burns OR U.S.A. 156 D4
Burnside r. Canada 146 H3
Burnside KY U.S.A. 164 C5
Burnside, Lake salt flat Australia 135 C6
Burns Junction OR U.S.A. 156 D4
Burns Lake Canada 150 E4
Burntisland U.K. 60 F4
Burnt Lake Canada see Brûlé, Lac
Burntwood r. Canada 151 L4
Burog Co l. China 99 D6
Buron r. Canada 153 H2
Burovoy Uzbek. 111 F1
Burqin China 98 D3
Burqin He r. China 98 D3
Burqu' Jordan 107 D3
Burra Australia 137 B7
Burra i. U.K. 60 [inset]
Burravoe U.K. 60 [inset]
Burrel Albania 69 I4
Burrel CA U.S.A. 158 D3
Burren reg. Ireland 61 C4
Burrendong, Lake Australia 138 D4
Burren Junction Australia 138 D3
Burrewarra Point Australia 138 E5
Burrinjuck Australia 138 D5
Burrinjuck Reservoir Australia 138 D5
Burro, Serranías del mts Mex. 167 E2
Burr Oak Reservoir OH U.S.A. 164 D4
Burro Creek watercourse AZ U.S.A. 159 G4
Burro Peak NM U.S.A. 159 I5
Burrowa Pine Mountain National Park Australia 138 C6
Burrow Head hd U.K. 60 E6
Burrows IN U.S.A. 164 B3
Burrundie Australia 134 E3
Bursa Turkey 69 M4
Būr Safāga Egypt see Būr Safājah
Būr Safājah Egypt 108 D4
Būr Sa'īd Egypt see Port Said
Būr Sa'īd Egypt see Port Said
Būr Sa'īd governorate Egypt see Būr Sa'īd
Būr Sa'īd governorate Egypt 107 A4
Bursinskoye Vodokhranilishche resr Rus. Fed. 90 C2
Bürstadt Germany 63 I5
Būr Sudan Sudan see Port Sudan
Burt Lake MI U.S.A. 162 C2
Burton MI U.S.A. 164 D2
Burton, Lac l. Canada 152 F3
Burton upon Trent U.K. 59 F6
Burträsk Sweden 54 L4
Burt Well Australia 135 F5
Buru i. Maluku Indon. 83 C3
Burūk, Wādī al watercourse Egypt 107 A4
Burullus, Baḥra el lag. Egypt see Burullus, Lake
Burullus, Buḥayrat al lag. Egypt see Burullus, Lake
Burullus, Lake lag. Egypt 112 C5
Burultokay China see Fuhai
Burūn, Ra's pt Egypt 107 A4
Burundi country Africa 122 C4
Buruniy Rus. Fed. see Tsagan Aman
Bururi Burundi 122 C4
Burwash Landing Canada 149 M3
Burwick U.K. 60 G2
Buryatia aut. rep. Rus. Fed. see Buryatiya, Respublika
Buryatiya, Respublika aut. rep. Rus. Fed. 94 E1
Buryatskaya Mongolskaya A.S.S.R. aut. rep. Rus. Fed. see Buryatiya, Respublika
Burylbaytal Kazakh. 98 A3
Buryn' Ukr. 53 G6
Bury St Edmunds U.K. 59 H6
Burzil Pass Pak. 104 C2
Busan S. Korea see Pusan
Busan Bay Mindanao Phil. 82 C5
Busanga Dem. Rep. Congo 122 C4
Busby MT U.S.A. 156 G3
Buseire Syria see Al Buşayrah
Bush r. U.K. 61 F2
Būshehr Iran 110 C4
Bushêngcaka China 105 E2
Bushenyi Uganda 122 D4
Bushire Iran see Būshehr
Bushmills U.K. 61 F2
Bushnell FL U.S.A. 163 D6
Businga Dem. Rep. Congo 122 C3
Busobuso Maluku Indon. 83 D2
Buşrá ash Shām Syria 107 C3
Busse Rus. Fed. 90 B2
Busselton Australia 135 A8
Bussum Neth. 62 F2
Bustamante Mex. 167 E3
Bustillos, Lago l. Mex. 166 D2
Busto Arsizio Italy 68 C2
Busuanga i. Phil. 82 B3
Buta Dem. Rep. Congo 122 C3
Butare Rwanda 122 C4
Butaritari atoll Kiribati 186 H5
Bute Australia 137 B7
Bute i. U.K. 60 D5
Butedale Canada 150 D4
Butha Buthe Lesotho 125 I5
Butha Qi China see Zalantun
Buthidaung Myanmar 86 A2
Butler AL U.S.A. 161 F5
Butler GA U.S.A. 163 C5
Butler IN U.S.A. 164 C3
Butler KY U.S.A. 164 C4
Butler MO U.S.A. 160 E4
Butler PA U.S.A. 164 F3
Butlers Bridge Ireland 61 E3
Buton i. Indon. 83 B4
Buton, Selat sea chan. Indon. 83 B4
Bütow Germany 63 M1
Butte MT U.S.A. 156 E3
Butte NE U.S.A. 160 D3
Buttelstedt Germany 63 L3
Butterworth Malaysia 84 C1
Butterworth S. Africa 125 I7
Buttes, Sierra mt. CA U.S.A. 158 C2
Buttevant Ireland 61 D5
Butt of Lewis hd U.K. 60 C2
Button Bay Canada 151 M3
Butuan Mindanao Phil. 82 D4
Butuan Bay Mindanao Phil. 82 D4
Butuo China 96 D3
Buturlinovka Rus. Fed. 53 I6
Butwal Nepal 105 E4
Butzbach Germany 63 I4
Buulobarde Somalia 122 E3
Buur Gaabo Somalia 122 E4
Buurhabaka Somalia 122 E3
Buutsagaan Mongolia 94 D2
Buxar India 105 F4
Buxoro Uzbek. 111 G2
Buxtehude Germany 63 J1
Buxton U.K. 58 F5
Buy Rus. Fed. 52 I4
Buyant Bayanhongor Mongolia see Buutsagaan
Buyant Bayan-Ölgiy Mongolia 94 B1
Buyant Hentiy Mongolia see Galshar

Buyant Gol r. Mongolia 94 D2
Buyant Gol r. Mongolia 98 E2
Buyant-Ovoo Mongolia 95 F2
Buyant-Uhaa Mongolia 95 G2
Buynaksk Rus. Fed. 113 G2
Büyükçekmece Turkey 112 C2
Büyük Egri Dağ mt. Turkey 107 A1
Büyükmenderes r. Turkey 69 L6
Buyun Shan mt. China 95 J3
Buzancy France 62 E5
Buzău Romania 69 L2
Buzdyak Rus. Fed. 51 Q5
Búzi Moz. 123 D5
Büzmeýin Turkm. see Abadan
Buzuluk Rus. Fed. 51 Q5
Buzuluk r. Rus. Fed. 53 I6
Buzzards Bay MA U.S.A. 165 J3
Byakar Bhutan see Jakar
Byala Bulg. 69 K3
Byala Slatina Bulg. 69 J3
Byalynichy Belarus 53 F5
Byarezina r. Belarus 53 F5
Byaroza Belarus 55 N10
Byblos tourist site Lebanon 107 B2
Bydgoszcz Poland 57 Q4
Byelorussia country Europe see Belarus
Byerazino Belarus 53 F5
Byers CO U.S.A. 156 G5
Byeshankovichy Belarus 53 F5
Byesville OH U.S.A. 164 E4
Bygland Norway 55 E7
Bykhaw Belarus 53 F5
Bykhov Belarus see Bykhaw
Bykle Norway 55 E7
Bykovo Rus. Fed. 53 J6
Bylas AZ U.S.A. 159 H5
Bylkyldak Kazakh. 98 A2
Bylot Island Canada 147 K2
Byramgore Reef India 106 A4
Byrd Glacier Antarctica 188 H1
Byrdstown TN U.S.A. 164 C5
Byrka Rus. Fed. 95 I1
Byrkjelo Norway 55 E6
Byrock Australia 138 C3
Byron ME U.S.A. 165 J1
Byron, Cape Australia 138 F2
Byron Bay Australia 138 F2
Byron Island Kiribati see Nikunau
Byrranga, Gory mts Rus. Fed. 77 K2
Byske Sweden 54 L4
Byssa Rus. Fed. 90 C1
Byssa r. Rus. Fed. 90 C1
Bystrinskiy Golets, Gora mt. Rus. Fed. 95 G1
Bytom Poland 57 Q5
Bytów Poland 57 P3
Byurgyutli Turkm. 110 D2
Byzantium Turkey see İstanbul

C

Ca, Sông r. Vietnam 86 D3
Caacupé Para. 178 E3
Caatinga Brazil 179 B2
Caazapá Para. 178 E3
Cabaiguán Cuba 163 E8
Caballas Peru 176 C6
Caballococha Peru 176 D4
Caballo Reservoir NM U.S.A. 166 D1
Caballos Mesteños, Llano de los plain Mex. 166 D2
Cabanaconde Peru 176 D7
Cabanatuan Luzon Phil. 82 C3
Cabano Canada 153 H5
Cabarroguis Phil. 82 C2
Cabdul Qaadir Somalia 122 E2
Cabeceira Rio Manso Brazil 177 G7
Cabeceiras Brazil 179 B1
Cabeza del Buey Spain 67 D4
Cabeza Prieta National Wildlife Refuge nature res. AZ U.S.A. 166 B1
Cabezas Bol. 176 F7
Cabimas Venez. 176 D1
Cabinda Angola 123 B4
Cabinda prov. Angola 123 B5
Cabinet Inlet Antarctica 188 L2
Cabinet Mountains MT U.S.A. 156 E2
Cabingaan i. Phil. 82 C5
Cabistra Turkey see Ereğli
Cabo Frio Brazil 179 C3
Cabo Frio, Ilha do i. Brazil 179 C3
Cabonga, Réservoir resr Canada 152 F5
Cabool MO U.S.A. 161 E4
Caboolture Australia 138 F1
Cabo Orange, Parque Nacional de nat. park Brazil 177 H3
Cabo Pantoja Peru 176 C4
Cabora Bassa, Lake resr Moz. 123 D5
Cabo Raso Arg. 178 C6
Caborca Mex. 166 B2
Cabo San Lucas Mex. 166 C4
Cabot Head hd Canada 164 E1
Cabot Strait Canada 153 J5
Cabourg France 59 G9
Cabo Verde country N. Atlantic Ocean see Cape Verde
Cabo Verde, Ilhas do is N. Atlantic Ocean 120 [inset]
Cabo Yubi Morocco see Tarfaya
Cabra i. Phil. 82 C3
Cabral, Serra do mts Brazil 179 B2
Cäbrayıl Azer. 113 G3
Cabrera, Illa de i. Spain 67 H4
Cabri Canada 151 I5
Cabugao Luzon Phil. 82 C2
Cabulauan i. Phil. 82 C4
Cabullona Mex. 166 C2
Cabutunan Point Luzon Phil. 82 C2
Caçador Brazil 179 A4
Cacagoin China see Qagca
Cacahuatepec Mex. 167 F5
Čačak Serbia 69 I3
Caccia, Capo c. Sardinia Italy 68 C4
Çäçe Turkm. 111 F2
Cacequi Brazil 178 F3
Cáceres Brazil 177 G7
Cáceres Spain 67 C4
Cache Creek Canada 150 F5
Cache Peak ID U.S.A. 156 E4
Cacheu Guinea-Bissau 120 B3
Cachi, Nevados de mts Arg. 178 C2
Cachimbo, Serra do hills Brazil 177 H5
Cachoeira Brazil 179 D1
Cachoeira Alta Brazil 179 A2
Cachoeira de Goiás Brazil 179 A2
Cachoeira do Arari Brazil 177 I4
Cachoeiro de Itapemirim Brazil 179 C3
Cacine Guinea-Bissau 120 B3
Cacipore, Cabo c. Brazil 177 H3
Cacolo Angola 123 B5
Caconda Angola 123 B5
Cacongo Angola 123 B4
Cactus TX U.S.A. 161 C4
Caçu Brazil 179 A2
Caculé Brazil 179 C1
Čadca Slovakia 57 Q6
Caddo Lake TX U.S.A. 167 G1
Cadereyta Mex. 167 E3
Cadibarrawirracanna, Lake salt flat Australia 137 A6
Cadig Mountains Luzon Phil. 82 C3
Cadillac Canada 151 J5
Cadillac MI U.S.A. 164 C1
Cadiz Negros Phil. 82 C4
Cádiz Spain 67 C5
Cadiz IN U.S.A. 164 C4
Cadiz KY U.S.A. 162 C4
Cadiz OH U.S.A. 164 E3
Cádiz, Golfo de g. Spain 67 C5
Cadiz Lake CA U.S.A. 159 F4
Cadomin Canada 150 G4
Cadotte r. Canada 150 G3
Cadotte Lake Canada 150 G3
Caen France 66 D2
Caerdydd U.K. see Cardiff
Caerffili U.K. see Caerphilly
Caerfyrddin U.K. see Carmarthen
Caergybi U.K. see Holyhead
Caernarfon U.K. 59 C5
Caernarfon Bay U.K. 59 C5
Caernarvon U.K. see Caernarfon
Caerphilly U.K. 59 D7
Caesaraugusta Spain see Zaragoza
Caesarea Alg. see Cherchell
Caesarea Cappadociae Turkey see Kayseri
Caesarea Philippi Syria see Bāniyās
Caesarodunum France see Tours
Caesaromagus U.K. see Chelmsford
Caetité Brazil 179 C1
Cafayate Arg. 178 C3
Cafelândia Brazil 179 A3
Caffa Ukr. see Feodosiya
Cagayan i. Phil. 82 C4
Cagayan r. Luzon Phil. 82 C2
Cagayan de Oro Mindanao Phil. 82 D4
Cagayan de Tawi-Tawi i. Phil. 82 B5
Cagayan Islands Phil. 82 C4
Cagles Mill Lake IN U.S.A. 164 B4
Cagli Italy 68 E3
Cagliari Sardinia Italy 68 C5
Cagliari, Golfo di b. Sardinia Italy 68 C5
Cagua, Mount vol. Phil. 82 C2
Çagyl Turkm. 113 I2
Cahama Angola 123 B5
Caha Mountains hills Ireland 61 C6
Cahermore Ireland 61 B6
Cahersiveen Ireland see Cahirsiveen
Cahir Ireland 61 E5
Cahirsiveen Ireland 61 B6
Cahora Bassa, Lago de resr Moz. see Cabora Bassa, Lake
Cahore Point Ireland 61 F5
Cahors France 66 E4
Cahuapanas Peru 176 C5
Cahuita, Punta pt Costa Rica 166 [inset] J7
Cahul Moldova 69 M2
Caia Moz. 123 D5
Caiabis, Serra dos hills Brazil 177 G6
Caianda Angola 123 C5
Caiapó r. Brazil 179 A1
Caiapó, Serra do mts Brazil 179 A2
Caiapônia Brazil 179 A2
Caibarién Cuba 163 E8
Cai Bâu, Đao i. Vietnam 86 D2
Caicara Venez. 176 E2
Caicos Islands Turks and Caicos Is 169 J4
Caicos Passage Bahamas/Turks and Caicos Is 163 F8
Caidian China 97 G2
Caiguna Australia 135 D8
Caimanero, Laguna del lag. Mex. 166 D4
Caiman Point Luzon Phil. 82 B3
Caimodorro mt. Spain 67 F3
Cainnyigoin China 96 D1
Cains Store KY U.S.A. 164 C5
Caipe Arg. 178 C2
Caird Coast Antarctica 188 B1
Cairngorm Mountains U.K. 60 F3
Cairngorms National Park U.K. 60 F3
Cairn Mountain AK U.S.A. 148 I3
Cairnryan U.K. 60 D6
Cairns Australia 136 D3
Cairnsmore of Carsphairn hill U.K. 60 E5

▶Cairo Egypt 112 C5
Capital of Egypt. 2nd most populous city in Africa.

Cairo GA U.S.A. 163 C6
Caisleán an Bharraigh Ireland see Castlebar
Caiundo Angola 123 B5
Caiwarro (abandoned) Australia 138 B2
Caiyuanzhen China see Shengsi
Caizi Hu l. China 97 H2
Cajamarca Peru 176 C5
Cajati Brazil 179 A4
Cajidiocan Phil. 82 C3
Cajuru Brazil 179 B3
Caka China 94 D4
Caka'lho China see Yanjing
Čakovec Croatia 68 G1
Çal Turkey 69 M5
Çal Turkey see Çukurca
Cala S. Africa 125 H6
Calabar Nigeria 120 D4
Calabogie Canada 165 G1
Calabria, Parco Nazionale della nat. park Italy 68 G5
Calafat Romania 69 J3
Calagnaan i. Phil. 82 C4
Calagua Mex. 166 C3
Calagua Islands Phil. 82 C3
Calagurris Spain see Calahorra
Calahorra Spain 67 F2
Calai Angola 123 B5
Calais France 62 B4
Calais ME U.S.A. 153 I5
Calakmus tourist site Mex. 167 H5
Calalasteo, Sierra de mts Arg. 178 C3
Calama Brazil 176 F5
Calama Chile 178 C2
Calamajué Mex. 157 E7
Calamar Col. 176 D1
Calamian Group is Phil. 82 B4
Calamocha Spain 67 F3
Calandagan i. Phil. 82 C4
Calandula Angola 123 B4
Calang Sumatera Indon. 84 A1
Calapan Mindoro Phil. 82 C3
Călărași Romania 69 L2
Calatayud Spain 67 F3
Calauag Luzon Phil. 82 C3
Calauit i. Phil. 82 B3
Calavite Passage Phil. 82 C3
Calayan i. Phil. 82 C2
Calbayog Samar Phil. 82 D3
Calbe (Saale) Germany 63 L3
Calbiga Samar Phil. 82 D4
Calcasieu r. LA U.S.A. 167 G2
Calcasieu Lake LA U.S.A. 167 G2
Calçoene Brazil 177 H3
Calcutta India see Kolkata
Caldas da Rainha Port. 67 B4
Caldas Novas Brazil 177 I7
Calden Germany 63 J3
Calder r. Canada 150 G1
Caldera Chile 178 B3
Calderitas Mex. 167 H5
Caldervale Australia 136 D5
Caldew r. U.K. 58 E4
Caldwell ID U.S.A. 156 D4
Caldwell KS U.S.A. 161 D4
Caldwell OH U.S.A. 164 E4
Caldwell TX U.S.A. 161 D6
Caledon r. Lesotho/S. Africa 125 H6
Caledon S. Africa 124 D8
Caledon Bay Australia 136 B2
Caledonia Canada 164 F2
Caledonia admin. div. U.K. see Scotland
Caledonia NY U.S.A. 165 G2
Caleta el Cobre Chile 178 B2
Calexico CA U.S.A. 159 F5
Calf of Man i. Isle of Man 58 C4
Calgary Canada 150 H5
Calhoun KY U.S.A. 164 B5
Cali Col. 176 C3
Calicoan i. Phil. 82 D4
Calicut India see Kozhikode
Caliente NV U.S.A. 159 F3
California PA U.S.A. 164 F3
California state U.S.A. 157 C4
California, Golfo de g. Mex. 166 B2
California Aqueduct canal CA U.S.A. 158 C3
Cälilabad Azer. 113 H3
Calingasta Arg. 178 C4
Calipatria CA U.S.A. 159 F5
Calistoga CA U.S.A. 158 B2
Calkiní Mex. 167 H4
Callabonna, Lake salt flat Australia 137 C6
Callaghan, Mount NV U.S.A. 158 E2
Callan Ireland 61 E5
Callan r. U.K. 61 F3
Callander Canada 152 F5
Callander U.K. 60 E4
Callao Peru 176 C6
Callao UT U.S.A. 159 G2
Calles Mex. 167 F4
Callicoon NY U.S.A. 165 H3
Calling Lake Canada 150 H4
Callington U.K. 59 C8
Calliope Australia 136 E5
Callipolis Turkey see Gallipoli
Calmar IA U.S.A. 160 F3
Calobre Panama 166 [inset] J7
Caloosahatchee r. FL U.S.A. 163 D7
Calotmul Mex. 167 H4
Caloundra Australia 138 F1
Calpulálpan Mex. 167 F5
Caltagirone Sicily Italy 68 F6
Caltanissetta Sicily Italy 68 F6
Calucinga Angola 123 B5
Calulo Angola 123 B4
Calunga Angola 123 B5
Caluquembe Angola 123 B5
Calusa i. Phil. 82 C4
Caluula Somalia 122 F2
Caluula, Raas pt Somalia 122 F2
Caluya i. Phil. 82 C4
Calvert Hills Australia 136 B3
Calvert Island Canada 150 D5
Calvi Corsica France 66 I5
Calvià Spain 67 H4
Calvinia S. Africa 124 D6
Calvo, Monte mt. Italy 68 F4
Cam r. U.K. 59 H6
Camaçari Brazil 179 D1
Camache Reservoir CA U.S.A. 158 C2
Camachigama r. Canada 152 F5
Camacho Mex. 161 C7
Camacuio Angola 123 B5
Camacupa Angola 123 B5
Camagüey Cuba 169 I4
Camagüey, Archipiélago de is Cuba 169 I4
Camamu Brazil 179 D1
Camana Peru 176 D7
Camanongue Angola 123 C5
Camapuã Brazil 177 H7
Camaquã Brazil 178 F4
Çamardı Turkey 112 D3
Camargo Bol. 176 E8
Camargo Mex. 167 F3
Camargo, Parque Natural nature res. Mex. 167 F3
Camargue reg. France 66 G5
Camarillo CA U.S.A. 158 D4
Camarón, Cabo c. Hond. 166 [inset] I6
Camarones Arg. 178 C6
Camarones, Bahía b. Arg. 178 C6
Camas r. ID U.S.A. 156 E4
Ca Mau Vietnam 87 D5
Cambay India see Khambhat
Cambay, Gulf of India see Khambhat, Gulf of
Camberley U.K. 59 G7
Cambodia country Asia 87 D4
Camboriú Brazil 179 A4
Camborne U.K. 59 B8
Cambrai France 62 D4
Cambria admin. div. U.K. see Wales
Cambrian Mountains hills U.K. 59 D6
Cambridge Canada 164 E2
Cambridge N.Z. 139 E3
Cambridge U.K. 59 H6
Cambridge MA U.S.A. 165 J2
Cambridge MD U.S.A. 165 G4
Cambridge MN U.S.A. 160 E2
Cambridge NY U.S.A. 165 I2
Cambridge OH U.S.A. 164 E3
Cambridge Bay Canada 147 H3
Cambridge City IN U.S.A. 164 C4
Cambridge Springs PA U.S.A. 164 E3
Cambrien, Lac l. Canada 153 H2
Cambulo Angola 123 C4
Cambundi-Catembo Angola 123 B5
Cambuquira Brazil 179 B3
Cam Co l. China 99 C6
Camdeboo National Park S. Africa 124 G7
Camden AL U.S.A. 163 C5
Camden AR U.S.A. 161 E5
Camden NJ U.S.A. 165 H4
Camden NY U.S.A. 165 H2
Camden SC U.S.A. 163 D5
Camden Bay AK U.S.A. 149 K1
Camdenton MO U.S.A. 160 E4
Cameia Angola 123 C5
Cameia, Parque Nacional da nat. park Angola 123 C5
Cameron AZ U.S.A. 159 H4
Cameron LA U.S.A. 161 E6
Cameron MO U.S.A. 160 E4
Cameron TX U.S.A. 161 D6
Cameron Highlands mts Malaysia 84 C1
Cameron Hills Canada 150 G3
Cameron Island Canada 147 H2
Cameron Park CA U.S.A. 158 C2
Cameroon country Africa 120 E4
Cameroon, Mount vol. Cameroon see Cameroun, Mont
Cameroon Highlands slope Cameroon/Nigeria 120 E4
Caméroun country Africa see Cameroon
Cameroun, Mont vol. Cameroon 120 D4
Cametá Brazil 177 I4
Camiguin i. Phil. 82 C2
Camiguin i. Phil. 82 D4
Camiling Luzon Phil. 82 C3
Camiña Chile 176 E7
Camino Real de Tierra Adentro tourist site Mex. 161 B6
Camiri Bol. 176 F8
Camisea Peru 176 D6
Camocim Brazil 177 J4
Camooweal Australia 136 B3
Camooweal Caves National Park Australia 136 B4
Camorta i. India 103 H10
Camotes Sea g. Phil. 82 D4
Campamento Hond. 166 [inset] I6
Campana Mex. 166 E3
Campana, Isla i. Chile 178 A7
Campania Island Canada 150 D4
Campbell S. Africa 124 F5
Campbell, Cape N.Z. 139 E5
Campbell, Mount hill Australia 134 E5
Campbellford Canada 165 G1
Campbell Hill hill OH U.S.A. 164 D3
Campbell Island N.Z. 186 H9
Campbell Lake N.W.T. Canada 149 N1
Campbell Lake N.W.T. Canada 151 J2
Campbell Plateau sea feature S. Pacific Ocean 186 H9
Campbell Range hills Australia 134 D3
Campbell River Canada 150 E5
Campbellsville KY U.S.A. 164 C5
Campbellton Canada 153 I5
Campbelltown Australia 138 E5
Campbeltown U.K. 60 D5
Campeche Mex. 167 H5
Campeche state Mex. 167 H5
Campeche, Bahía de g. Mex. 168 F5
Camperdown Australia 138 A7
Câmpina Romania 69 K2
Campina Grande Brazil 177 K5
Campinas Brazil 179 B3
Campina Verde Brazil 179 A2
Camplong Timor Indon. 83 B5
Campo Cameroon 120 D4
Campobasso Italy 68 F4
Campo Belo Brazil 179 B3
Campo Belo do Sul Brazil 179 A4
Campo de Diauarum Brazil 177 H6
Campo Florido Brazil 179 A2
Campo Gallo Arg. 178 D3
Campo Grande Brazil 178 F2
Campo Largo Brazil 179 A4
Campo Maior Brazil 177 J4
Campo Maior Port. 67 C4
Campo Mourão Brazil 178 F2
Campos Brazil 179 C3
Campos Altos Brazil 179 B2
Campos Novos Brazil 179 A4
Campos Sales Brazil 177 J5
Campton KY U.S.A. 164 D5
Câmpulung Romania 69 K2
Câmpulung Moldovenesc Romania 69 K1
Camp Verde AZ U.S.A. 159 H4
Camrose Canada 151 H4
Camrose U.K. 59 B7
Camsell Lake Canada 151 I2
Camsell Portage Canada 151 I3
Camsell Range mts Canada 150 F2
Camulodunum U.K. see Colchester
Çan Turkey 69 L4
Ca Na, Mui hd Vietnam 87 E5
Canaan r. Canada 153 I5
Canaan CT U.S.A. 165 I2
Canaan Peak UT U.S.A. 159 H3
Canabrava Brazil 179 B2
Canabungan i. Phil. 82 B4
Canacona India 106 B3

▶Canada country N. America 146 H4
Largest country in North America and 2nd in the world. 3rd most populous country in North America.

Canada Basin sea feature Arctic Ocean 189 A1
Canadian TX U.S.A. 161 C5
Canadian r. U.S.A. 161 E5
Canadian Abyssal Plain sea feature Antarctica 189 A1
Cañadón Grande, Sierra mts Arg. 178 C7
Canaima, Parque Nacional nat. park Venez. 176 F2
Çanakkale Turkey 69 L4
Çanakkale Boğazı strait Turkey see Dardanelles
Canalejas Arg. 178 C5
Canal-Supe, Sacred City of tourist site Peru 176 C6
Cañamares Spain 67 E3
Canandaigua NY U.S.A. 165 G2
Cananea Mex. 166 C2
Cananéia Brazil 179 B4
Canápolis Brazil 179 A2
Cañar Ecuador 176 C4
Canarias terr. N. Atlantic Ocean see Canary Islands
Canárias, Ilha das i. Brazil 177 J4
Canarias, Islas terr. N. Atlantic Ocean see Canary Islands

▶Canary Islands terr. N. Atlantic Ocean 120 B2
Autonomous Community of Spain.

Canasayab Mex. 167 H5
Canaseraga NY U.S.A. 165 G2
Canastota NY U.S.A. 165 H2
Canastra, Serra da mts Goiás Brazil 179 A1
Canastra, Serra da mts Minas Gerais Brazil 179 B2
Canatiba Brazil 179 C1
Canatlán Mex. 161 B7
Canaveral, Cape FL U.S.A. 163 D6
Cañaveras Spain 67 E3
Canavieiras Brazil 179 D1
Cañazas Panama 166 [inset] J7
Canbelego Australia 138 C3

▶Canberra Australia 138 D5
Capital of Australia and Australian Capital Territory.

Cancún Mex. 167 I4
Çandar Turkey see Kastamonu
Çandarlı Turkey 69 L5
Candela Mex. 167 E3
Candela r. Mex. 161 C7
Candelaria Campeche Mex. 167 H5
Candelaria Chihuahua Mex. 166 D2
Candia Greece see Iraklion
Cândido de Abreu Brazil 179 A4
Çandır Turkey 112 D2
Candle AK U.S.A. 148 G2
Candle Lake Canada 151 J4
Candlewood, Lake CT U.S.A. 165 I3
Cando ND U.S.A. 160 D1
Candon Luzon Phil. 82 C2
Candon Point Luzon Phil. 82 C2
Cane r. Australia 134 A5
Canea Greece see Chania
Canela Brazil 179 A5
Canelones Uruguay 178 E4
Cane Valley KY U.S.A. 164 C5
Cangallo Peru 176 D6
Cangamba Angola 123 B5
Cangandala, Parque Nacional de nat. park Angola 123 B4
Canglun Malaysia see Changlun
Cango Caves S. Africa 124 F7
Cangola Angola 123 B4
Cangshan China 95 I5
Canguaretama Brazil 177 K5
Canguçu Brazil 178 F4
Canguçu, Serra do hills Brazil 178 F4
Cangwu China 97 F4
Cangzhou China 95 I4
Caniapiscau Canada 153 H3
Caniapiscau r. Canada 153 H2
Caniapiscau, Réservoir de l. Canada 153 H3
Caniçado Moz. see Guija
Canicattì Sicily Italy 68 E6
Canigao Channel Phil. 82 D4
Canim Lake Canada 150 F5
Canindé Brazil 177 K4
Canisteo NY U.S.A. 165 G2
Canisteo r. NY U.S.A. 165 G2
Canisteo Peninsula Antarctica 188 K2
Cañitas de Felipe Pescador Mex. 161 C8
Çankırı Turkey 112 D2
Canlaon Negros Phil. 82 C4
Canna Australia 135 A7
Canna i. U.K. 60 C3
Cannanore India see Kannur
Cannanore Islands India 106 B4
Cannelton IN U.S.A. 164 B5
Cannes France 66 H5
Canning r. AK U.S.A. 149 K1
Cannock U.K. 59 E6
Cannon Beach OR U.S.A. 156 C3
Cann River Australia 138 D6
Canoas Brazil 179 A5
Canõas, Rio das r. Brazil 179 A4
Canoeiros Brazil 179 B2
Canoe Lake Canada 151 I4
Canoe Lake l. Canada 151 I4
Canoinhas Brazil 179 A4
Canon City CO U.S.A. 157 G5
Cañón del Sumidero, Parque Nacional nat. park Mex. 167 G5
Cañon Largo watercourse NM U.S.A. 159 J3
Canoona Australia 136 E4
Canora Canada 151 K5
Canowindra Australia 138 D4
Canso Canada 153 J5
Canso, Cape Canada 153 J5
Cantabrian Mountains Spain see Cantábrica, Cordillera
Cantábrica, Cordillera mts Spain 67 D2
Cantábrico, Mar sea Spain 67 C2
Canterbury U.K. 59 I7
Canterbury Bight b. N.Z. 139 C7
Canterbury Plains N.Z. 139 C6
Cần Thơ Vietnam 87 D5
Cantil CA U.S.A. 158 E4
Cantilan Mindanao Phil. 82 D4
Canton GA U.S.A. 163 C5
Canton IL U.S.A. 160 F3
Canton MO U.S.A. 160 F3
Canton MS U.S.A. 161 F5
Canton NY U.S.A. 165 H1
Canton OH U.S.A. 164 E3
Canton PA U.S.A. 165 G3
Canton SD U.S.A. 160 D3
Canton TX U.S.A. 161 E5
Canton Island atoll Kiribati see Kanton
Cantuaria U.K. see Canterbury
Cantwell AK U.S.A. 149 J3
Canunda National Park Australia 137 C8
Canutama Brazil 176 F5
Canutillo Mex. 161 B7
Canvey Island U.K. 59 H7
Canwood Canada 151 J4
Cany-Barville France 59 H9
Canyon TX U.S.A. 161 C5
Canyon (abandoned) Canada 149 M3
Canyon City OR U.S.A. 156 D3
Canyondam CA U.S.A. 158 C1
Canyon de Chelly National Monument nat. park AZ U.S.A. 159 I3
Canyon Ferry Lake MT U.S.A. 156 F3
Canyon Lake AZ U.S.A. 159 H5
Canyonlands National Park UT U.S.A. 159 I2
Canyon Ranges mts Canada 149 P3
Canyons of the Ancients National Monument nat. park CO U.S.A. 159 I3
Canyonville OR U.S.A. 156 C4
Cao Băng Vietnam 86 D2
Caocheng China see Caoxian
Cao Daban China 94 E4
Caohai China see Weining
Caohe China see Qichun
Caohu Xinjiang China 98 D4
Caohu Xinjiang China 98 D4
Caojiahe China see Qichun
Caojian China 96 C3
Caoshi China 90 B4
Caoxian China 95 H5
Caozhou China see Heze
Cap i. Phil. 82 C5
Capac MI U.S.A. 164 D2
Çapakçur Turkey see Bingöl
Capalulu, Selat sea chan. Indon. 83 C3
Capanaparo r. Venez. 176 E2
Capanema Brazil 177 I4
Capão Bonito Brazil 179 A4
Caparaó, Serra do mts Brazil 179 C3
Capas Luzon Phil. 82 C3
Cap-aux-Meules Canada 153 J5
Cap-de-la-Madeleine Canada 153 G5
Cape r. Australia 136 D4
Cape Arid National Park Australia 135 C8
Cape Barren Island Australia 137 [inset]
Cape Basin sea feature S. Atlantic Ocean 184 I8
Cape Breton Highlands National Park Canada 153 J5
Cape Breton Island Canada 153 J5
Cape Charles Canada 153 L3
Cape Charles VA U.S.A. 165 G5
Cape Coast Ghana 120 C4
Cape Coast Castle Ghana see Cape Coast
Cape Cod Bay MA U.S.A. 165 J3
Cape Cod National Seashore nature res. MA U.S.A. 165 K3
Cape Coral FL U.S.A. 163 D7
Cape Crawford Australia 136 A3
Cape Dorset Canada 147 K3
Cape Fanshaw AK U.S.A. 149 N4
Cape Fear r. NC U.S.A. 163 E5
Cape George Canada 153 J5
Cape Girardeau MO U.S.A. 161 F4
Cape Johnson Depth sea feature N. Pacific Ocean 186 E5
Cape Juby Morocco see Tarfaya
Cape Krusenstern National Monument nat. park AK U.S.A. 148 G2
Capel Australia 135 A8
Cape Le Grand National Park Australia 135 C8
Capelinha Brazil 179 C2
Capella Australia 136 E4
Capelle aan de IJssel Neth. 62 E3
Capelongo Angola see Kuvango
Cape May NJ U.S.A. 165 H4
Cape May Court House NJ U.S.A. 165 H4
Cape May Point NJ U.S.A. 165 H4
Cape Melville National Park Australia 136 D2
Capenda-Camulemba Angola 123 B4
Cape Palmerston National Park Australia 136 E4
Cape Range National Park Australia 134 A5
Cape St George Canada 153 K4

▶Cape Town S. Africa 124 D7
Legislative capital of South Africa.

Cape Tribulation National Park Australia 136 D2
Cape Upstart National Park Australia 136 D3
Cape Verde country N. Atlantic Ocean 120 [inset]
Cape Verde Basin sea feature N. Atlantic Ocean 184 F5
Cape Verde Plateau sea feature N. Atlantic Ocean 184 F4
Cape Vincent NY U.S.A. 165 G1
Cape Yakataga AK U.S.A. 149 L3
Cape York Peninsula Australia 136 C2
Cap-Haïtien Haiti 169 J5
Capim r. Brazil 177 I4

▶Capitol Hill N. Mariana Is 81 L3
Capital of the Northern Mariana Islands, on Saipan.

Capitol Reef National Park UT U.S.A. 159 H2
Capivara, Represa resr Brazil 179 A3
Čapljina Bos.-Herz. 68 G3
Cappoquin Ireland 61 E5
Capraia, Isola di i. Italy 68 C3
Caprara, Punta pt Sardinia Italy 68 C4
Capri, Isola di i. Italy 68 F4
Capricorn Channel Australia 136 E4
Capricorn Group atolls Australia 136 F4
Caprivi Strip reg. Namibia 123 C5
Cap Rock Escarpment TX U.S.A. 161 C5
Capsa Tunisia see Gafsa
Captain Cook HI U.S.A. 157 [inset]
Captina r. OH U.S.A. 164 E4
Capuava Brazil 179 B4
Caquetá r. Col. 176 E4
Carabao i. Phil. 82 C3
Caracal Romania 69 K2

▶Caracas Venez. 176 E1
Capital of Venezuela.

Caraga Mindanao Phil. 82 D5
Caraguatatuba Brazil 179 B3
Caraí Brazil 179 C2
Carajás Brazil 177 H5
Carajás, Serra dos hills Brazil 177 H5
Carales Sardinia Italy see Cagliari
Caralis Sardinia Italy see Cagliari
Caramoan Peninsula Luzon Phil. 82 C3
Carandaí Brazil 179 C3
Caransebeş Romania 69 J2

Caraquet Canada **153** I5
Carat, Tanjung *pt* Indon. **84** D3
Caratasca Hond. **166** [inset] J6
Caratasca, Laguna de *lag.* Hond. **166** [inset] J6
Caratinga Brazil **179** C2
Carauari Brazil **176** E4
Caravaca de la Cruz Spain **67** F4
Caravelas Brazil **179** D2
Carberry Canada **151** L5
Carbó Mex. **166** C2
Carbon, Cap *hd* Alg. **67** F6

▶**Carbón, Laguna del** *l.* Arg. **178** C7
Lowest point in South America.

Carbonara, Capo *c. Sardinia* Italy **68** C5
Carbondale *CO* U.S.A. **159** J2
Carbondale *PA* U.S.A. **165** H3
Carboneras Mex. **161** D7
Carbonia *Sardinia* Italy **68** C5
Carbonita Brazil **179** C2
Carcaixent Spain **67** F4
Carcajou Canada **150** G3
Carcajou *r.* Canada **149** O2
Carcar *Cebu* Phil. **82** C4
Carcassonne France **66** F5
Carcross Canada **149** N3
Cardamomes, Chaîne des *mts* Cambodia/Thai. *see* **Cardamom Range**
Cardamom Hills India **106** C4
Cardamom Range *mts* Cambodia/Thai. **87** C4
Cárdenas Cuba **169** H4
Cárdenas *San Luis Potosí* Mex. **168** E4
Cárdenas *Tabasco* Mex. **167** G5
Cardenyabba *watercourse* Australia **138** A2
Çardi Turkey *see* **Harmancık**
Cardiel, Lago *l.* Arg. **178** B7

▶**Cardiff** U.K. **59** D7
Capital of Wales.

Cardiff *MD* U.S.A. **165** G4
Cardigan U.K. **59** C6
Cardigan Bay U.K. **59** C6
Cardinal Lake Canada **150** G3
Cardington *OH* U.S.A. **164** D3
Cardón, Cerro *hill* Mex. **166** B3
Cardoso Brazil **179** A3
Cardoso, Ilha do *i.* Brazil **179** B4
Cardston Canada **150** H5
Careen Lake Canada **151** I3
Carei Romania **69** J1
Carentan France **66** D2
Carey *OH* U.S.A. **164** D3
Carey, Lake *salt flat* Australia **135** C7
Carey Lake Canada **151** K2
Cargados Carajos Islands Mauritius **185** L7
Carhaix-Plouguer France **66** C2
Cariacica Brazil **179** C3
Cariamanga Ecuador **176** C4
Caribbean Sea N. Atlantic Ocean **169** H5
Cariboo Mountains Canada **150** F4
Caribou *r. Man.* Canada **151** M3
Caribou *r. N.W.T.* Canada **149** P3
Caribou *r. Y.T.* Canada **149** N2
Caribou *AK* U.S.A. **149** K2
Caribou *ME* U.S.A. **162** G2
Caribou Lake Canada **147** J4
Caribou Mountains Canada **150** H3
Carichic Mex. **166** D3
Carigara *Leyte* Phil. **82** D4
Carignan France **62** F5
Carinda Australia **138** C3
Cariñena Spain **67** F3
Carinhanha *r.* Brazil **179** C1
Carlabhagh U.K. *see* **Carloway**
Carleton *MI* U.S.A. **164** D2
Carleton, Mount *hill* Canada **153** I5
Carletonville S. Africa **125** H4
Carlin *NV* U.S.A. **158** E1
Carlingford Lough *inlet* Ireland/U.K. **61** F3
Carlinville *IL* U.S.A. **160** F4
Carlisle U.K. **58** E4
Carlisle *IN* U.S.A. **164** B4
Carlisle *KY* U.S.A. **164** C4
Carlisle *NY* U.S.A. **165** H2
Carlisle *PA* U.S.A. **165** G3
Carlisle Lakes *salt flat* Australia **135** D7
Carlit, Pic *mt.* France **66** E5
Carlos Chagas Brazil **179** C2
Carlow Ireland **61** F5
Carloway U.K. **60** C2
Carlsbad Czech Rep. *see* **Karlovy Vary**
Carlsbad *CA* U.S.A. **158** E5
Carlsbad *NM* U.S.A. **157** G6
Carlsbad *TX* U.S.A. **167** E2
Carlsbad Caverns National Park *NM* U.S.A. **157** G6
Carlsberg Ridge *sea feature* Indian Ocean **185** L5
Carlson Inlet Antarctica **188** L1
Carlton *MN* U.S.A. **160** E2
Carlton Hill Australia **134** E3
Carluke U.K. **60** F5
Carlyle Canada **151** K5
Carmacks Canada **149** M3
Carmagnola Italy **68** B2
Carman Canada **151** L5
Carmana Iran *see* **Kermān**
Carmarthen U.K. **59** C7
Carmarthen Bay U.K. **59** C7
Carmaux France **66** F4
Carmel *IN* U.S.A. **164** B4
Carmel *NY* U.S.A. **165** I3
Carmel, Mount *hill* Israel **107** B3
Carmel Head *hd* U.K. **58** C5
Carmelita Guat. **167** H5
Carmel Valley *CA* U.S.A. **158** C3
Carmen Mex. **167** E3
Carmen *r.* Mex. **166** D2
Carmen *Bohol* Phil. **82** D4
Carmen *AZ* U.S.A. **157** F7
Carmen, Isla *i.* Mex. **166** C3
Carmen, Isla del *i.* Mex. **167** H5
Carmen de Patagones Arg. **178** D6
Carmi *IL* U.S.A. **160** F4
Carmichael *CA* U.S.A. **158** C2
Carmo da Cachoeira Brazil **179** B3
Carmo do Paranaíba Brazil **179** B2
Carmona Angola *see* **Uíge**
Carmona Hond. **166** [inset] I7
Carmona Spain **67** D5
Carnac France **66** C3
Carnamah Australia **135** A7
Carnarvon Australia **135** A6
Carnarvon S. Africa **124** F6
Carnarvon National Park Australia **136** D5
Carnarvon Range *hills* Australia **135** C6
Carnarvon Range *mts* Australia **136** E5
Carn Dearg *hill* U.K. **60** E3
Carndonagh Ireland **61** E2
Carnegie Australia **135** C6
Carnegie, Lake *salt flat* Australia **135** C6
Carn Eige *mt.* U.K. **60** D3
Carnes Australia **135** F7
Carney Island Antarctica **188** J2
Carnforth U.K. **58** E4
Carn Glas-choire *hill* U.K. **60** F3
Car Nicobar *i.* India **87** A5
Carnlough U.K. **61** G3
Carn nan Gabhar *mt.* U.K. **60** F4
Carn Odhar *hill* U.K. **60** E3
Carnot Cent. Afr. Rep. **122** B3
Carnoustie U.K. **60** G4
Carnsore Point Ireland **61** F5
Carnwath *r.* Canada **149** O1
Carnwath U.K. **60** F5
Caro *AK* U.S.A. **149** J2
Caro *MI* U.S.A. **164** D2
Carola Cay *reef* Australia **136** F3
Carol City *FL* U.S.A. **163** D7
Carolina Brazil **177** I5
Carolina S. Africa **125** J4
Carolina Beach *NC* U.S.A. **163** E5
Caroline Canada **150** H4
Caroline Island *atoll* Kiribati **187** J6
Caroline Islands N. Pacific Ocean **81** K5
Caroline Peak N.Z. **139** A7
Caroline Range *hills* Australia **134** D4
Caroní *r.* Venez. **176** F2
Carp Canada **165** G1
Carpathian Mountains Europe **53** C6
Carpaţii *mts* Europe *see* **Carpathian Mountains**
Carpaţii Meridionali *mts* Romania *see* **Transylvanian Alps**
Carpaţii Occidentali *mts* Romania **69** J2
Carpentaria, Gulf of Australia **136** B2
Carpentras France **66** G4
Carpi Italy **68** D2
Carpinteria *CA* U.S.A. **158** D4
Carpio *ND* U.S.A. **160** C1
Carra, Lough *l.* Ireland **61** C4
Carraig na Siuire Ireland *see* **Carrick-on-Suir**
Carrantuohill *mt.* Ireland **61** C6
Carrara Italy **68** D2
Carrasco, Parque Nacional *nat. park* Bol. **176** F7
Carrathool Australia **138** B5
Carrhae Turkey *see* **Harran**
Carrickfergus U.K. **61** G3
Carrickmacross Ireland **61** F4
Carrick-on-Shannon Ireland **61** D4
Carrick-on-Suir Ireland **61** E5
Carrigallen Ireland **61** E4
Carrigtohill Ireland **61** D6
Carrillo Mex. **166** E3
Carrington *ND* U.S.A. **160** D2
Carrizal Mex. **166** D2
Carrizal Bajo Chile **178** B3
Carrizo *AZ* U.S.A. **159** H4
Carrizo Creek *r. TX* U.S.A. **161** C4
Carrizos Mex. **167** F3
Carrizo Springs *TX* U.S.A. **161** D6
Carrizo Wash *watercourse AZ/NM* U.S.A. **159** I4
Carrizozo *NM* U.S.A. **157** G6
Carroll *IA* U.S.A. **160** E3
Carrollton *AL* U.S.A. **161** F5
Carrollton *GA* U.S.A. **163** C5
Carrollton *IL* U.S.A. **160** F4
Carrollton *KY* U.S.A. **164** C4
Carrollton *MO* U.S.A. **160** E4
Carrollton *OH* U.S.A. **164** E3
Carrolltown *PA* U.S.A. **165** F3
Carron *r.* U.K. **60** E3
Carrot *r.* Canada **151** K4
Carrothers *OH* U.S.A. **164** D3
Carrot River Canada **151** K4
Carrowmore Lake Ireland **61** C3
Carrsville *VA* U.S.A. **165** G5
Carruthers Lake Canada **151** K2
Carruthersville *MO* U.S.A. **161** F4
Carry Falls Reservoir *NY* U.S.A. **165** H1
Çarşamba Turkey **112** E2
Carson *r. NV* U.S.A. **158** D2
Carson City *MI* U.S.A. **164** C2

▶**Carson City** *NV* U.S.A. **158** D2
Capital of Nevada.

Carson Escarpment Australia **134** D3
Carson Lake *NV* U.S.A. **158** D2
Carson Sink *l. NV* U.S.A. **158** D2
Carstensz Pyramid *mt.* Indon. *see* **Jaya, Puncak**
Carstensz-top *mt.* Indon. *see* **Jaya, Puncak**
Carswell Lake Canada **151** I3
Cartagena Col. **176** C1
Cartagena Spain **67** F5
Cartago Costa Rica **166** [inset] J7
Carteret Group *is* P.N.G. *see* **Kilinailau Islands**
Carteret Island Solomon Is *see* **Malaita**
Cartersville *GA* U.S.A. **163** C5
Carthage *tourist site* Tunisia **68** D6
Carthage *MO* U.S.A. **161** E4
Carthage *NC* U.S.A. **163** E5
Carthage *NY* U.S.A. **165** H2
Carthage *TX* U.S.A. **161** E5
Carthago *tourist site* Tunisia *see* **Carthage**
Carthago Nova Spain *see* **Cartagena**
Cartier Island Australia **134** C3
Cartmel U.K. **58** E4
Cartwright *Man.* Canada **151** L5
Cartwright *Nfld. and Lab.* Canada **153** K3
Caruarú Brazil **177** K5
Carúpano Venez. **176** F1
Carver *KY* U.S.A. **164** D5
Carvin France **62** C4
Cary *NC* U.S.A. **162** E5
Caryapundy Swamp Australia **137** C6
Casablanca Morocco **64** C5
Casa Branca Brazil **179** B3
Casa de Janos Mex. **166** C2
Casadepaga *AK* U.S.A. **148** F2
Casa de Piedra, Embalse *resr* Arg. **178** C5
Casa Grande *AZ* U.S.A. **159** H5
Casale Monferrato Italy **68** C2
Casalmaggiore Italy **68** D2
Casares Nicaragua **166** [inset] I7
Casas Grandes Mex. **166** D2
Casas Grandes *r.* Mex. **166** D2
Casca Brazil **179** A5
Cascade Australia **135** C8
Cascade *r.* N.Z. **139** B7
Cascade *ID* U.S.A. **156** D3
Cascade *MT* U.S.A. **156** F3
Cascade Point N.Z. **139** B7
Cascade Range *mts* Canada/U.S.A. **156** C4
Cascade Reservoir *ID* U.S.A. **156** D3
Cascais Port. **67** B4
Cascal, Paso del *pass* Nicaragua **166** [inset] I7
Cascavel Brazil **178** F2
Casco Bay *ME* U.S.A. **165** K2
Caserta Italy **68** F4
Casey *research station* Antarctica **188** F2
Casey Bay Antarctica **188** D2
Caseyr, Raas *c.* Somalia *see* **Gwardafuy, Gees**
Cashel Ireland **61** E5
Cashmere Australia **138** D1
Casiguran *Luzon* Phil. **82** C2
Casiguran Sound *sea chan. Luzon* Phil. **82** C2
Casino Australia **138** F2
Casiquiare, Canal *r.* Venez. **176** E3
Casita Mex. **157** F7
Casnewydd U.K. *see* **Newport**
Casogoran Bay Phil. **82** D4
Caspe Spain **67** F3
Casper *WY* U.S.A. **156** G4
Caspian Lowland Kazakh./Rus. Fed. **100** D2

▶**Caspian Sea** *l.* Asia/Europe **113** H1
Largest lake in the world and in Asia/Europe, and lowest point in Europe.

Cass *WV* U.S.A. **164** F4
Cass *r. MI* U.S.A. **164** D2
Cassacatiza Moz. **123** D5
Cassadaga *NY* U.S.A. **164** F2
Cassaigne Alg. *see* **Sidi Ali**
Cassamba Angola **123** C5
Cass City *MI* U.S.A. **164** D2
Cassel France **62** C4
Casselman Canada **165** H1
Cássia Brazil **179** B3
Cassiar Canada **149** O4
Cassiar Mountains Canada **149** O4
Cassilândia Brazil **179** A2
Cassilis Australia **138** D4
Cassino Italy **68** E4
Cassley *r.* U.K. **60** E3
Cassongue Angola **123** B5
Cassopolis *MI* U.S.A. **164** B3
Cassville *MO* U.S.A. **161** E4
Castanhal Brazil **177** I4
Castanho Brazil **176** F5
Castaños Mex. **167** E3
Castelfranco Veneto Italy **68** D2
Castell-nedd U.K. *see* **Neath**
Castell Newydd Emlyn U.K. *see* **Newcastle Emlyn**
Castellón Spain *see* **Castellón de la Plana**
Castellón de la Plana Spain **67** F4
Castelo Branco Port. **67** C4
Castelo de Vide Port. **67** C4
Casteltermini *Sicily* Italy **68** E6
Castelvetrano *Sicily* Italy **68** E6
Castiglione della Pescaia Italy **68** D3
Castignon, Lac *l.* Canada **153** H2
Castilla y León *reg.* Spain **66** B6
Castlebar Ireland **61** C4
Castlebay U.K. **60** B4
Castlebellingham Ireland **61** F4
Castleblayney Ireland **61** F3
Castlebridge Ireland **61** F5
Castle Carrock U.K. **58** E4
Castle Cary U.K. **59** E7
Castle Dale *UT* U.S.A. **159** H2
Castlederg U.K. **61** E3
Castledermot Ireland **61** F5
Castle Dome Mountains *AZ* U.S.A. **159** F5
Castle Donington U.K. **59** F6
Castle Douglas U.K. **60** F6
Castleford U.K. **58** F5
Castlegar Canada **150** G5
Castlegregory Ireland **61** B5
Castle Island Bahamas **163** F8
Castleisland Ireland **61** C5
Castlemaine Australia **138** B6
Castlemaine Ireland **61** C5
Castlemartyr Ireland **61** D6
Castle Mountain *Alta* Canada **150** H5
Castle Mountain *Y.T.* Canada **149** N2
Castle Mountain *CA* U.S.A. **158** C4
Castle Peak *hill* H.K. China **97** [inset]
Castle Peak Bay H.K. China **97** [inset]
Castlepoint N.Z. **139** F5
Castlepollard Ireland **61** E4
Castlerea Ireland **61** D4
Castlereagh *r.* Australia **138** C3
Castle Rock *CO* U.S.A. **156** G5
Castletown Ireland **61** E5
Castletown Isle of Man **58** C4
Castor Canada **151** I4
Castor *r. MO* U.S.A. **161** F4
Castor, Rivière du *r.* Canada **152** F3
Castra Regina Germany *see* **Regensburg**
Castres France **66** F5
Castricum Neth. **62** E2

▶**Castries** St Lucia **169** L6
Capital of St Lucia.

Castro Brazil **179** A4
Castro Chile **178** B6
Castro Alves Brazil **179** D1
Castro Verde Port. **67** B5
Castroville *CA* U.S.A. **158** C3
Cast Uul *mt.* Mongolia **94** B1
Caswell *AK* U.S.A. **149** J3
Çat Turkey **113** F3
Catacamas Hond. **166** [inset] I6
Catacaos Peru **176** B5
Cataguases Brazil **179** C3
Catahoula Lake *LA* U.S.A. **161** E6
Cataingan *Masbate* Phil. **82** C3
Çatak Turkey **113** F3
Catalão Brazil **179** B2
Çatalca Yarımadası *pen.* Turkey **69** M4
Catalina *AZ* U.S.A. **159** H5
Catalonia *aut. comm.* Spain *see* **Cataluña**
Cataluña *aut. comm.* Spain **67** G3
Catalunya *aut. comm.* Spain *see* **Cataluña**
Catamarca Arg. **178** C3
Catana *Sicily* Italy *see* **Catania**
Catanauan *Luzon* Phil. **82** C3
Catanduanes *i.* Phil. **82** D3
Catanduva Brazil **179** A3
Catania *Sicily* Italy **68** F6
Catanzaro Italy **68** G5
Cataract Creek *watercourse AZ* U.S.A. **159** G3
Catarina *TX* U.S.A. **161** D6
Catarino Rodríguez Mex. **167** E3
Catarman *Samar* Phil. **82** D3
Catarman Point *Mindanao* Phil. **82** D5
Catastrophe, Cape Australia **137** A7
Catawba *r. SC* U.S.A. **163** D5
Cataxa Moz. **123** D5
Cat Ba, Đao *i.* Vietnam **86** D2
Catbalogan *Samar* Phil. **82** D4
Cateel *Mindanao* Phil. **82** D5
Cateel Bay *Mindanao* Phil. **82** D5
Catemaco Mex. **167** G5
Catembe Moz. **125** K4
Catengue Angola **123** B5
Catete Angola **123** B4
Cathair Dónall Ireland **61** B6
Cathcart Australia **138** D6
Cathcart S. Africa **125** H7
Cathedral Peak S. Africa **125** I5
Cathedral Rock National Park Australia **138** F3
Catherine, Mount *UT* U.S.A. **159** G2
Catheys Valley *CA* U.S.A. **158** C3
Cathlamet *WA* U.S.A. **156** C3
Catió Guinea-Bissau **120** B3
Catisimiña Venez. **176** F3
Cat Island Bahamas **163** F7
Cat Lake Canada **151** N5
Catlettsburg *KY* U.S.A. **164** D4
Catoche, Cabo *c.* Mex. **167** I4
Cato Island and Bank *reef* Australia **136** F4
Catorce Mex. **167** E4
Catriló Arg. **178** D5
Cats, Mont des *hill* France **62** C4
Catskill *NY* U.S.A. **165** I2
Catskill Mountains *NY* U.S.A. **165** H2
Catuane Moz. **125** K4
Cauayan *Negros* Phil. **82** C4
Caubvick, Mount Canada **153** J2
Cauca *r.* Col. **169** J7
Caucaia Brazil **177** K4
Caucasia Col. **176** C2
Caucasus *mts* Asia/Europe **113** F2
Cauchon Lake Canada **151** L4
Caudry France **62** D4
Câu Giat Vietnam **86** D3
Cauit Point *Mindanao* Phil. **82** D4
Caulonia Italy **68** G5
Caungula Angola **123** B4
Cauquenes Chile **178** B5
Causapscal Canada **153** I4
Cavaglià Italy **68** C2
Cavalcante, Serra do *hills* Brazil **179** B1
Cavalier *ND* U.S.A. **160** D1
Cavan Ireland **61** E4
Çavdır Turkey **69** M6
Cave City *KY* U.S.A. **164** C5
Cave Creek *AZ* U.S.A. **159** H5
Caveira *r.* Brazil **179** C1
Cavern Island Myanmar **87** B5
Cave Run Lake *KY* U.S.A. **164** D4
Caviana, Ilha *i.* Brazil **177** H3
Cavili *rf* Phil. **82** C4
Cavite *Luzon* Phil. **82** C3
Cawdor U.K. **60** F3
Cawnpore India *see* **Kanpur**
Cawston U.K. **59** I6
Caxias Brazil **177** J4
Caxias do Sul Brazil **179** A5
Caxito Angola **123** B4
Çay Turkey **69** N5
Cayambe, Volcán *vol.* Ecuador **176** C3
Çaybaşı Turkey *see* **Çayeli**
Çaycuma Turkey **69** O4
Çayeli Turkey **113** F2

▶**Cayenne** Fr. Guiana **177** H3
Capital of French Guiana.

Cayeux-sur-Mer France **62** B4
Çayırhan Turkey **69** N4
Cayman Brac *i.* Cayman Is **169** I5

▶**Cayman Islands** *terr.* West Indies **169** H5
United Kingdom Overseas Territory.

Cayman Trench *sea feature* Caribbean Sea **184** C4
Caynabo Somalia **122** E3
Cay Sal *i.* Bahamas **163** D8
Cay Sal Bank *sea feature* Bahamas **163** D8
Cay Santa Domingo *i.* Bahamas **163** F8
Cayucos *CA* U.S.A. **158** C4
Cayuga Canada **164** F2
Cayuga Lake *NY* U.S.A. **165** G2
Cay Verde *i.* Bahamas **163** F8
Cazê China **99** D7
Cazenovia *NY* U.S.A. **165** H2
Cazombo Angola **123** C5
Ceadâr-Lunga Moldova *see* **Ciadîr-Lunga**
Ceanannus Mór Ireland *see* **Kells**
Ceann a Deas na Hearadh *pen.* U.K. *see* **South Harris**
Ceará Brazil *see* **Fortaleza**
Ceara Abyssal Plain *sea feature* S. Atlantic Ocean **184** F6
Ceatharlach Ireland *see* **Carlow**
Ceballos Mex. **166** D3
Ceboruco, Volcán *vol.* Mex. **166** D4
Cebu *Cebu* Phil. **82** C4
Cebu *i.* Phil. **82** C4
Čechy *reg.* Czech Rep. **57** N6
Cecil Plains Australia **138** E1
Cecil Rhodes, Mount *hill* Australia **135** C6
Cecina Italy **68** D3
Cedar *r. ND* U.S.A. **160** C2
Cedar *r. NE* U.S.A. **160** D3
Cedar City *UT* U.S.A. **159** G3
Cedar Creek Reservoir *TX* U.S.A. **167** F1
Cedaredge *CO* U.S.A. **159** J2
Cedar Falls *IA* U.S.A. **160** E3
Cedar Grove *WI* U.S.A. **164** B2
Cedar Hill *NM* U.S.A. **159** J3
Cedar Hill *TN* U.S.A. **164** B5
Cedar Island *VA* U.S.A. **165** H5
Cedar Lake Canada **151** K4
Cedar Point *OH* U.S.A. **164** D3
Cedar Rapids *IA* U.S.A. **160** F3
Cedar Run *NJ* U.S.A. **165** H4
Cedar Springs *MI* U.S.A. **164** C2
Cedartown *GA* U.S.A. **163** C5
Cedarville S. Africa **125** I6
Cedeño Hond. **166** [inset] I6
Cedral *Quintana Roo* Mex. **167** I4
Cedral *San Luis Potosí* Mex. **167** E4
Cedros Hond. **166** [inset] I6
Cedros *Sonora* Mex. **166** C3
Cedros *Zacatecas* Mex. **167** E3
Cedros, Cerro *mt.* Mex. **157** E7
Cedros, Isla *i.* Mex. **166** B2
Ceduna Australia **135** F8
Ceeldheere Somalia **122** E3
Ceerigaabo Somalia **122** E2
Cefalù *Sicily* Italy **68** F5
Cegléd Hungary **69** H1
Cêgnê China **99** F6
Ceheng China **96** E3
Çekerek Turkey **112** D2
Çekiçler Turkm. **110** D2
Celah, Gunung *mt.* Malaysia *see* **Mandi Angin, Gunung**
Celaque, Parque Nacional *nat. park* Hond. **167** H6
Celaya Mex. **168** D4
Celbridge Ireland **61** F4

▶**Celebes** *i.* Indon. **83** B3
4th largest island in Asia.

Celebes Basin *sea feature* Pacific Ocean **186** E5
Celebes Sea Indon./Phil. **81** G6
Celestún Mex. **167** H4
Celina *OH* U.S.A. **164** C3
Celina *TN* U.S.A. **164** C5
Celje Slovenia **68** F1
Celle Germany **63** K2
Celovec Austria *see* **Klagenfurt**
Celtic Sea Ireland/U.K. **56** D5
Celtic Shelf *sea feature* N. Atlantic Ocean **184** H2
Cemaru, Gunung *mt.* Indon. **85** F2
Çemenibit Turkm. **111** F3
Cempi, Teluk *b. Sumbawa* Indon. **85** G5
Cenderawasih, Teluk *b.* Indon. **81** J7
Çendir *r.* Turkm. **110** D2
Cenrana *Sulawesi Barat* Indon. **83** A3
Centane S. Africa *see* **Kentani**
Centenary Zimbabwe **123** D5
Center *NE* U.S.A. **160** D3
Center *TX* U.S.A. **161** E6
Centereach *NY* U.S.A. **165** I3
Center Point *AL* U.S.A. **163** C5
Centerville *IA* U.S.A. **160** E3
Centerville *MO* U.S.A. **161** F4
Centerville *TX* U.S.A. **161** E6
Centerville *WV* U.S.A. **164** E4
Centrafricaine, République *country* Africa *see* **Central African Republic**
Central *admin. dist.* Botswana **125** H2
Central *AK* U.S.A. **149** K2
Central *NM* U.S.A. **159** I5
Central, Cordillera *mts* Col. **176** C3
Central, Cordillera *mts* Panama **166** [inset] J7
Central, Cordillera *mts* Peru **176** C6
Central, Cordillera *mts Luzon* Phil. **82** C2
Central African Empire *country* Africa *see* **Central African Republic**
Central African Republic *country* Africa **122** B3
Central Brahui Range *mts* Pak. **111** G4
Central Butte Canada **156** G2
Central City *NE* U.S.A. **160** D3
Centralia *IL* U.S.A. **160** F4
Centralia *WA* U.S.A. **156** C3
Central Kalahari Game Reserve *nature res.* Botswana **124** F2
Central Kara Rise *sea feature* Arctic Ocean **189** F1
Central Makran Range *mts* Pak. **111** G5
Central Mount Stuart *hill* Australia **134** F5
Central Pacific Basin *sea feature* Pacific Ocean **186** H5
Central Provinces *state* India *see* **Madhya Pradesh**
Central Range *mts* P.N.G. **81** K7
Central Russian Upland *hills* Rus. Fed. **53** H5
Central Siberian Plateau Rus. Fed. **77** M3
Central Square *NY* U.S.A. **165** G2
Centre *AL* U.S.A. **163** C5
Centreville *AL* U.S.A. **163** C5
Centreville *MD* U.S.A. **165** G4
Cenxi China **97** F4
Cenyang China *see* **Hengfeng**
Ceos *i.* Greece *see* **Tzia**
Cephaloedium *Sicily* Italy *see* **Cefalù**
Cephalonia *i.* Greece **69** I5
Cepu *Jawa* Indon. **85** E4
Ceram *i. Maluku* Indon. *see* **Seram**
Ceram Sea Indon. *see* **Seram, Laut**
Cerbat Mountains *AZ* U.S.A. **159** F4
Čerchov *mt.* Czech Rep. **63** M5
Ceres Arg. **178** D3
Ceres Brazil **179** A1
Ceres S. Africa **124** D7
Ceres *CA* U.S.A. **158** C3
Céret France **66** F5
Cerezo de Abajo Spain **67** E3
Cêri China **99** D7
Cerignola Italy **68** F4
Cerigo *i.* Greece *see* **Kythira**
Cêringgolêb China *see* **Dongco**
Çerkeş Turkey **112** D2
Çerkeşli Turkey **69** M4
Çermik Turkey **113** E3
Cernăuţi Ukr. *see* **Chernivtsi**
Cernavodă Romania **69** M2
Cerralvo Mex. **167** F3
Cerralvo, Isla *i.* Mex. **166** C3
Cërrik Albania **69** H4
Cerritos Mex. **168** D4
Cerro Azul Brazil **179** A4
Cerro Azul Mex. **167** F4
Cerro de Pasco Peru **176** C6
Cerro Hoya, Parque Nacional *nat. park* Panama **166** [inset] J8
Cerro Prieto Mex. **166** D3
Cerros Colorados, Embalse *resr* Arg. **178** C5
Cervantes, Cerro *mt.* Arg. **178** B8
Cervati, Monte *mt.* Italy **68** F4
Cervione *Corsica* France **66** I5
Cervo Spain **67** C2
Cesena Italy **68** E2
Cēsis Latvia **55** N8
Česká Republika *country* Europe *see* **Czech Republic**
České Budějovice Czech Rep. **57** O6
Českomoravská vysočina *hills* Czech Rep. **57** O6
Český Krumlov Czech Rep. **57** O6
Český les *mts* Czech Rep./Germany **63** M5
Çeşme Turkey **69** L5
Cessnock Australia **138** E4
Cetaceo, Mount *Luzon* Phil. **82** C2
Cêtar China **94** E4
Cetatea Albă Ukr. *see* **Bilhorod-Dnistrovs'kyy**
Cetinje Montenegro **68** H3
Cetraro Italy **68** F5

▶**Ceuta** N. Africa **67** D6
Autonomous Community of Spain.

Ceva-i-Ra *reef* Fiji **133** H4
Cévennes *mts* France **66** F5
Cévennes, Parc National des *nat. park* France **66** F4
Cevizli Turkey **107** C1
Cevizlik Turkey *see* **Maçka**
Ceyhan Turkey **112** D3
Ceyhan *r.* Turkey **107** B1
Ceyhan Boğazı *r. mouth* Turkey **107** B1
Ceylanpınar Turkey **113** F3
Ceylon *country* Asia *see* **Sri Lanka**
Chābahār Iran **111** F5
Chablé Mex. **167** H5
Chabrol *i.* New Caledonia *see* **Lifou**
Chabug China **99** C6
Chabyêr Caka *salt l.* China **99** D7
Chachapoyas Peru **176** C5
Chacharan Pak. **111** H4
Chäche Turkm. *see* **Çäçe**
Chachoengsao Thai. **87** C4
Chachro Pak. **111** H5
Chaco *r. NM* U.S.A. **159** I3
Chaco Boreal *reg.* Para. **178** E2
Chaco Culture National Historical Park *nat. park NM* U.S.A. **159** J3
Chaco Mesa *plat. NM* U.S.A. **159** J4

▶**Chad** *country* Africa **121** E3
5th largest country in Africa.

Chad, Lake Africa **121** E3
Chadaasan Mongolia **94** E2
Chadan Rus. Fed. **102** H1
Chadibe Botswana **125** H2
Chadron *NE* U.S.A. **160** C3
Chadyr-Lunga Moldova *see* **Ciadîr-Lunga**
Chae Hom Thai. **86** B3
Chaek Kyrg. **98** A4
Chaeryŏng N. Korea **91** B5
Chae Son National Park Thai. **86** B3
Chagai Pak. **111** G4
Chagai Hills Afgh./Pak. **111** F4
Chaganuzun Rus. Fed. **98** E2
Chagdo Kangri *mt.* China **105** F2
Chaggur China **99** F6
Chaghcharān Afgh. **111** G3
Chagny France **66** G3
Chagoda Rus. Fed. **52** G4
Chagos Archipelago *is* B.I.O.T. **185** M6
Chagos-Laccadive Ridge *sea feature* Indian Ocean **185** M6
Chagos Trench *sea feature* Indian Ocean **185** M6
Chagoyan Rus. Fed. **90** C1
Chagrayskoye Plato *plat.* Kazakh. *see* **Shagyray, Plato**
Chagres, Parque Nacional *nat. park* Panama **166** [inset] K7
Chāh Ākhvor Iran **111** E3
Chāh 'Ali Akbar Iran **110** E3
Chahār Kent Afgh. **111** G2
Chahbounia Alg. **67** H6
Chahchaheh Turkm. **111** F2
Chāh-e Āb Afgh. **111** H2
Chāh-e Bāgh *well* Iran **110** D4
Chāh-e Bāzargānī Iran **110** D4
Chāh-e Dow Chāhī Iran **110** D4
Chāh-e Gonbad *well* Iran **110** D3
Chāh-e Kavīr *well* Iran **110** E3
Chāh-e Khorāsān *well* Iran **110** D3
Chāh-e Khoshāb Iran **110** E3
Chāh-e Malek *well* Iran **110** D3
Chāh-e Malek Mīrzā *well* Iran **110** D4
Chāh-e Mūjān *well* Iran **110** D3
Chāh-e Qeyşar *well* Iran **110** D4
Chāh-e Qobād *well* Iran **110** D3
Chāh-e Rāh Iran **110** D4
Chāh-e Raḥmān *well* Iran **111** E4
Chāh-e Shūr *well* Iran **110** D3
Chāh-e Tūnī *well* Iran **110** E3
Chāh Kūh Iran **110** D4
Chāh Lak Iran **110** E5
Chāh Pās *well* Iran **110** D3
Chah Sandan Pak. **111** F4
Chahuites Mex. **167** G5
Chaibasa India **105** F5
Chaigneau, Lac *l.* Canada **153** I3
Chaigoubu China *see* **Huai'an**
Chaihe China **95** J2
Chainat Thai. **86** C4
Chainjoin Co *l.* China **99** D6
Chai Prakan Thai. **86** B3
Chaitén Chile **178** B6
Chai Wan H.K. China **97** [inset]
Chaiwopu China **98** D4
Chaiya Thai. **87** B5
Chaiyaphum Thai. **86** C4
Chajarí Arg. **178** E4
Chakachamna Lake *AK* U.S.A. **148** I3
Chakai India **105** F4
Chak Amru Pak. **111** I3
Chakar *r.* Pak. **111** H4
Chakaria Bangl. **105** H5
Chakdarra Pak. **111** I3
Chakku Pak. **111** G5
Chakonipau, Lac *l.* Canada **153** H2
Chakoria Bangl. *see* **Chakaria**
Chakvi Georgia **113** F2
Chala Peru **176** D7
Chalatenango El Salvador **166** [inset] H6
Chaláua Moz. **123** D5
Chalaxung China **94** D5
Chalcedon Turkey *see* **Kadıköy**
Chalengkou China **99** F5
Chaleur Bay *inlet* Canada **153** I4

Chaleurs, Baie des inlet Canada see Chaleur Bay
Chali China 96 C2
Chaling China 97 G3
Chalisgaon India 106 B1
Chalki i. Greece 69 L6
Chalkida Greece 69 J5
Chalkyitsik AK U.S.A. 149 L2
Challakere India 106 C3
Challans France 66 D3
Challapata Bol. 176 E7

▶Challenger Deep sea feature N. Pacific Ocean 186 F5
Deepest point in the world (Mariana Trench).

Challenger Fracture Zone sea feature S. Pacific Ocean 186 M8
Challis ID U.S.A. 156 E3
Chalmette LA U.S.A. 161 F6
Châlons-en-Champagne France 62 E6
Châlons-sur-Marne France see Châlons-en-Champagne
Chalon-sur-Saône France 66 G3
Chaltan Pass Azer. 113 H2
Chālūs Iran 110 C2
Cham Germany 63 M5
Cham, Kūh-e hill Iran 110 C3
Chamah, Gunung mt. Malaysia 84 C1
Chamaico Arg. 178 D5
Chamais Bay Namibia 124 B4
Chaman Pak. 100 F3
Chaman Bīd Iran 110 E2
Chamao, Khao mt. Thai. 87 C4
Chamba India 104 D2
Chamba Tanz. 123 D5
Chambal r. India 104 D4
Chambas Cuba 163 E8
Chambeaux, Lac l. Canada 153 H3
Chamberlain r. Australia 134 D4
Chamberlain Canada 151 J5
Chamberlain SD U.S.A. 160 D3
Chamberlain Lake ME U.S.A. 162 G2
Chamberlin, Mount AK U.S.A. 149 K1
Chambers AZ U.S.A. 159 I4
Chambersburg PA U.S.A. 165 G4
Chambers Island WI U.S.A. 164 B1
Chambéry France 66 G4
Chambeshi r. Zambia 123 C5
Chambi, Jebel mt. Tunisia 68 C7
Chamda China 99 E7
Chamdo China see Qamdo
Chame Panama 166 [inset] K7
Chamechaude mt. France 66 G4
Chamela Mex. 166 D5
Chamis Bay Canada 150 E5
Chamoli India see Gopeshwar
Chamonix-Mont-Blanc France 66 H4
Champa India 105 E5
Champagne Canada 149 M3
Champagne-Ardenne admin. reg. France 62 E6
Champagne Castle mt. S. Africa 125 I5
Champagne Humide reg. France 66 G2
Champagne Pouilleuse reg. France 66 F2
Champagnole France 66 G3
Champagny Islands Australia 134 D3
Champaign IL U.S.A. 160 F3
Champasak Laos 86 D4
Champdoré, Lac l. Canada 153 I3
Champhai India 105 H5
Champion Canada 150 H5
Champlain VA U.S.A. 165 G4
Champlain, Lake Canada/U.S.A. 165 I1
Champotón Mex. 167 H5
Chamrajnagar India 106 C4
Chamu Co l. China 99 E6
Chamzinka Rus. Fed. 53 J5
Chana Thai. 87 C6
Chanak Turkey see Çanakkale
Chanal Mex. 167 G5
Chañaral Chile 178 B3
Chanchén Mex. 167 H5
Chanda India see Chandrapur
Chandalar AK U.S.A. 149 J2
Chandalar r. AK U.S.A. 149 K2
Chandalar, East Fork r. AK U.S.A. 149 K2
Chandalar, Middle Fork r. AK U.S.A. 149 J2
Chandalar, North Fork r. AK U.S.A. 149 J2
Chandalar Lake AK U.S.A. 149 J2
Chandausi India 104 D3
Chandbali India 105 F5
Chandeleur Islands LA U.S.A. 161 F6
Chanderi India 104 D4
Chandigarh India 104 D3
Chandil India 105 F5
Chandir Uzbek. 111 G2
Chandler Canada 153 I4
Chandler AZ U.S.A. 159 H5
Chandler IN U.S.A. 164 B4
Chandler OK U.S.A. 161 D5
Chandler r. AK U.S.A. 149 J1
Chandler Lake AK U.S.A. 148 I1
Chandmanī Dzavhan Mongolia see Yaruu
Chandmanī Govĭ-Altay Mongolia 94 D2
Chandod India 104 C5
Chandos Lake Canada 165 G1
Chandpur Bangl. 105 G5
Chandpur India 104 D3
Chandragiri India 106 C3
Chandrapur India 106 C2
Chandvad India 106 B1
Chang, Ko i. Thai. 87 C4
Chang'an China 95 G5
Changane r. Moz. 125 K3
Changbai China 90 C4
Changbai Shan mts China/N. Korea 90 B4
Chang Cheng research station Antarctica see Great Wall
Changcheng China 97 F5
Changchow Fujian China see Zhangzhou
Changchow Jiangsu China see Changzhou
Changchun China 90 B4
Changchunling China 90 B3
Changdao China 95 J4
Changde China 97 F2
Changgang China 97 G3
Changge China 95 H5
Changgi-ap pt S. Korea 91 C5
Changgo China 99 D7
Chang Hu l. China 97 G2
Changhua Taiwan 97 I3
Changhŭng S. Korea 91 B6
Changhwa Taiwan see Changhua
Changi Sing. 87 [inset]
Changji China 98 D4
Changjiang China 97 F5
Chang Jiang r. China 97 I2 see Yangtze
Changjiang Kou China see Mouth of the Yangtze
Changjin-ho resr N. Korea 91 B4
Changkiang China see Zhanjiang
Changlang India 105 H4
Changleng China see Xinjian
Changli China 95 I4
Changling China 95 J2
Changliushui China 94 F4
Changlun Malaysia 84 C1
Changlung India 109 M3
Changma China 94 D4
Changmar China 99 C6
Changning Jiangxi China see Xunwu
Changning Sichuan China 96 E2
Changnyŏn N. Korea 91 B5
Ch'ang-pai Shan mts China/N. Korea see Changbai Shan
Changping China 95 I3
Changpu China see Suining
Changp'yŏng S. Korea 91 C5
Changsan-got pt N. Korea 91 B5
Changsha China 97 G2
Changshan China 97 H2
Changshan Qundao is China 95 J4
Changshi China 96 E3
Changshou China 97 G2
Changshoujie China see Changshou
Changshu China 97 I2
Changtai China 97 H3
Changteh China see Changde
Changting Fujian China 97 H3
Changting Heilong. China 90 C3
Changuinola Panama 166 [inset] J7
Changweiliang China 99 F5
Ch'angwŏn S. Korea 91 C6
Changwu China 95 F5
Changxing China 97 H2
Changxing Dao i. China 95 J4
Changyang China 97 F2
Changyi China 95 I4
Changyŏn N. Korea 91 B5
Changyuan China 95 H5
Changzhi Shanxi China 95 H4
Changzhi Shanxi China 95 H5
Changzhou China 97 H2
Chañi, Nevado de mt. Arg. 178 C2
Chania Greece 69 K7
Chanion, Kolpos b. Greece 69 J7
Chankou China 94 F5
Channahon IL U.S.A. 164 A3
Channapatna India 106 C3
Channel Islands English Chan. 59 E9
Channel Islands CA U.S.A. 158 D5
Channel Islands National Park CA U.S.A. 158 D4
Channel-Port-aux-Basques Canada 153 K5
Channel Rock i. Bahamas 163 E8
Channel Tunnel France/U.K. 59 I7
Channing TX U.S.A. 161 C5
Chantada Spain 67 C2
Chantal'skiy mt. Rus. Fed. 148 B2
Chantal'vergyrgyn r. Rus. Fed. 148 C2
Chanthaburi Thai. 87 C4
Chantilly France 62 C5
Chanumla India 87 A5
Chanute KS U.S.A. 160 E4
Chanuwala Pak. 111 I3
Chany, Ozero salt l. Rus. Fed. 76 I4
Chaohu China 97 H2
Chao Hu l. China 97 H2
Chaor China 95 J1
Chaouèn Morocco 67 D6
Chaowula Shan mt. China 96 C1
Chaoyang Guangdong China 97 H4
Chaoyang Heilong. China see Jiayin
Chaoyang Liaoning China 95 J3
Chaoyangcun China 95 K1
Chaoyang Hu l. China 99 D6
Chaozhong China 95 J1
Chaozhou China 97 H4
Chapada Diamantina, Parque Nacional nat. park Brazil 179 C1
Chapada dos Veadeiros, Parque Nacional da nat. park Brazil 179 B1
Chapais Canada 152 G4
Chapak Gozār Afgh. 111 G2
Chapala Mex. 166 E4
Chapala, Laguna de l. Mex. 168 D4
Chāpārī, Kōtal-e Afgh. 111 G3
Chapayevo Kazakh. 100 E1
Chapayevsk Rus. Fed. 53 K5
Chapecó Brazil 178 F3
Chapecó r. Brazil 178 F3
Chapel-en-le-Frith U.K. 58 F5
Chapelle-lez-Herlaimont Belgium 62 E4
Chapeltown U.K. 58 F5
Chapleau Canada 152 E5
Chaplin Canada 151 J5
Chaplin Lake Canada 151 J5
Chaplino Rus. Fed. 148 D2
Chaplygin Rus. Fed. 53 H5
Chapman, Mount Canada 150 G5
Chapmanville WV U.S.A. 164 D5
Chappell NE U.S.A. 160 C3
Chappell Islands Australia 137 [inset]
Chapra Bihar India see Chhapra
Chapra Jharkhand India see Chatra
Chaqmaqtīn, Kōl-e Afgh. 111 I2
Charagua Bol. 176 F7
Charay Mex. 166 C3
Charcas Mex. 168 D4
Charcot Island Antarctica 188 L2
Chard Canada 151 I4
Chard U.K. 59 E8
Chardara Kazakh. see Shardara
Chardara, Step' plain Kazakh. 102 C3
Chardon OH U.S.A. 164 E3
Chardzhev Turkm. see Türkmenabat
Chardzhou Turkm. see Türkmenabat
Charef Alg. 67 H6
Charef, Oued watercourse Morocco 64 D5
Charente r. France 66 D4
Chari r. Cameroon/Chad 121 E3
Chārī Iran 110 E4
Chārīkār Afgh. 111 H3
Chariot AK U.S.A. 148 F1
Chariton IA U.S.A. 160 E3
Chärjew Turkm. see Türkmenabat
Charkayuvom Rus. Fed. 52 L2
Charkhlik China see Ruoqiang
Charleroi Belgium 62 E4
Charles, Cape VA U.S.A. 165 H5
Charlesbourg Canada 153 H5
Charles City IA U.S.A. 160 E3
Charles City VA U.S.A. 165 G5
Charles Hill Botswana 124 E2
Charles Island Galápagos Ecuador see Santa María, Isla
Charles Lake Canada 151 I3
Charles Point Australia 134 E3
Charleston N.Z. 139 C5
Charleston IL U.S.A. 160 F4
Charleston MO U.S.A. 161 F4
Charleston SC U.S.A. 163 E5

▶Charleston WV U.S.A. 164 E4
Capital of West Virginia.

Charleston Peak NV U.S.A. 159 F3
Charlestown Ireland 61 D4
Charlestown IN U.S.A. 164 C4
Charlestown NH U.S.A. 165 I2
Charlestown RI U.S.A. 165 J3
Charles Town WV U.S.A. 165 G4
Charleville Australia 137 D5
Charleville Ireland 61 D5
Charleville-Mézières France 62 E5
Charlevoix MI U.S.A. 164 C1
Charley r. AK U.S.A. 149 L2
Charlie Lake Canada 150 F3
Charlotte MI U.S.A. 164 C2
Charlotte NC U.S.A. 163 D5
Charlotte TN U.S.A. 164 B5

▶Charlotte Amalie Virgin Is (U.S.A.) 169 L5
Capital of the U.S. Virgin Islands.

Charlotte Bank sea feature S. China Sea 85 D1
Charlotte Harbor b. FL U.S.A. 163 D7
Charlotte Lake Canada 150 E4
Charlottesville VA U.S.A. 165 F4

▶Charlottetown Canada 153 J5
Capital of Prince Edward Island.

Charlton Australia 138 A6
Charlton Island Canada 152 F3
Charron Lake Canada 151 M4
Charsadda Pak. 111 H3
Charshanga Turkm. see Köýtendag
Charshangngy Turkm. see Köýtendag
Charters Towers Australia 136 D4
Chartres France 66 E2
Chas India 105 F5
Chase Canada 150 G5
Chase MI U.S.A. 164 C2
Chase City VA U.S.A. 165 F5
Chashmeh Nūrī Iran 110 E3
Chashmeh-ye Ab-e Garm spring Iran 110 E3
Chashmeh-ye Magu well Iran 110 E3
Chashmeh-ye Mūkīk spring Iran 110 E3
Chashmeh-ye Palasi Iran 110 D3
Chashmeh-ye Safīd spring Iran 110 E3
Chashmeh-ye Shotoran well Iran 110 D3
Chashniki Belarus 53 F5
Chaska MN U.S.A. 160 E2
Chaslands Mistake c. N.Z. 139 B8
Chasŏng N. Korea 90 B4
Chasseral mt. Switz. 57 K7
Chassiron, Pointe de pt France 66 D3
Chastab, Kūh-e mts Iran 110 D3
Chāt Iran 110 D2
Chatanika AK U.S.A. 149 K2
Chatanika r. AK U.S.A. 149 J2
Châteaubriant France 66 D3
Château-du-Loir France 66 E3
Châteaudun France 66 E2
Chateaugay NY U.S.A. 165 H1
Châteauguay Canada 165 I1
Châteauguay r. Canada 153 H2
Châteauguay, Lac l. Canada 153 H2
Châteaulin France 66 B2
Châteaumeillant France 66 F3
Châteauneuf-en-Thymerais France 62 B6
Châteauneuf-sur-Loire France 66 F3
Chateau Pond l. Canada 153 K3
Châteauroux France 66 E3
Château-Salins France 62 G6
Château-Thierry France 62 D5
Chateh Canada 150 G3
Châtelet Belgium 62 E4
Châtellerault France 66 E3
Chatfield MN U.S.A. 152 B6
Chatham Canada 164 D2
Chatham U.K. 59 H7
Chatham AK U.S.A. 149 N4
Chatham MA U.S.A. 165 K3
Chatham NY U.S.A. 165 I2
Chatham PA U.S.A. 165 H4
Chatham VA U.S.A. 164 F5
Chatham, Isla i. Chile 178 B8
Chatham Island Galápagos Ecuador see San Cristóbal, Isla
Chatham Island N.Z. 133 I6
Chatham Island Samoa see Savai'i
Chatham Islands N.Z. 133 I6
Chatham Rise sea feature S. Pacific Ocean 186 I8
Chatham Sound sea channel Canada 149 O5
Chatham Strait AK U.S.A. 149 N4
Châtillon-sur-Seine France 66 G3
Chatkal Range mts Kyrg./Uzbek. 102 D3
Chatom AL U.S.A. 161 F6
Chatra India 105 F4
Chatra Nepal 105 F4
Chatsworth Canada 164 E1
Chatsworth NJ U.S.A. 165 H4
Chattagam Bangl. see Chittagong
Chattanooga TN U.S.A. 163 C5
Chattarpur India see Chhatarpur
Chatteris U.K. 59 H6
Chattisgarh state India see Chhattisgarh
Chatturat Thai. 86 C4
Chatyr-Köl l. Kyrg. 98 A4
Chatyr-Tash Kyrg. 102 E3
Châu Đôc Vietnam 87 D5
Chauhtan India 104 B4
Chauk Myanmar 86 A2
Chauka r. India 99 C8
Chaukhamba mts India 99 B7
Chaumont France 66 G2
Chauncey OH U.S.A. 164 D4
Chaungzon Myanmar 86 B3
Chaunskaya Guba b. Rus. Fed. 77 R3
Chauny France 62 D5
Chau Phu Vietnam see Châu Đôc
Chausu-yama mt. Japan 92 D3
Chausy Belarus see Chavusy
Chautauqua, Lake NY U.S.A. 164 F2
Chauter Pak. 111 G4
Chauvin Canada 151 I4
Chavakachcheri Sri Lanka 106 D4
Chavakkad India 106 B4
Chaves Port. 67 C3
Chavigny, Lac l. Canada 152 G2
Chavusy Belarus 53 F5
Chawal r. Pak. 111 G4
Chay, Sông r. Vietnam 86 D2
Chayatyn, Khrebet ridge Rus. Fed. 90 E1
Chayevo Rus. Fed. 52 H4
Chaykovskiy Rus. Fed. 51 Q4
Chäyul China see Qayü
Chazhegovo Rus. Fed. 52 L3
Chazy NY U.S.A. 165 I1
Cheadle U.K. 59 F6
Cheaha Mountain hill AL U.S.A. 163 C5
Cheat r. WV U.S.A. 164 F4
Cheatham Lake TN U.S.A. 164 B5
Cheb Czech Rep. 63 M4
Chebba Tunisia 68 D7
Cheboksarskoye Vodokhranilishche resr Rus. Fed. 52 J5
Cheboksary Rus. Fed. 52 J4
Cheboygan MI U.S.A. 162 C2
Chechen Rus. Fed. 148 D2
Chechen', Ostrov i. Rus. Fed. 113 G2
Chech'ŏn S. Korea 91 C5
Chedabucto Bay Canada 153 J5
Chedao China 95 J4
Cheddar U.K. 59 E7
Cheduba Myanmar see Man-aung
Cheduba Island i. Myanmar see Man-aung Kyun
Chée r. France 62 E6
Cheektowaga NY U.S.A. 165 F2
Cheepie Australia 138 B1
Cheetham, Cape Antarctica 188 H2
Chefoo China see Yantai
Chefornak AK U.S.A. 148 F3
Chefu Moz. 125 K2
Chegdomyn Rus. Fed. 90 D2
Chegga Mauritania 120 C2
Chegitun' Rus. Fed. 148 E2
Chegitun' r. Rus. Fed. 148 E2
Chegutu Zimbabwe 123 D5
Chehalis WA U.S.A. 156 C3
Chehar Burj Iran 110 E2
Chehardeh Iran 110 E3
Chehel Chashmeh, Kūh-e hill Iran 110 B3
Chehel Dokhtarān, Kūh-e mt. Iran 111 F4
Chehel Pāyeh Iran 110 E4
Cheju S. Korea 91 B6
Cheju-do i. S. Korea 91 B6
Cheju-haehyŏp sea chan. S. Korea 91 B6
Chek Chue H.K. China see Stanley
Chekhov Moskovskaya Oblast' Rus. Fed. 53 H5
Chekhov Sakhalinskaya Oblast' Rus. Fed. 90 F3
Chekiang prov. China see Zhejiang
Chekichler Turkm. see Çekiçler
Chek Lap Kok reg. H.K. China 97 [inset]
Chek Mun Hoi Hap H.K. China see Tolo Channel
Chekunda Rus. Fed. 90 D2
Chela, Serra da mts Angola 123 B5
Chelan, Lake WA U.S.A. 156 C2
Chelatna Lake AK U.S.A. 149 J3
Cheleken Turkm. see Hazar
Cheline Moz. 125 L2
Chelkar Kazakh. see Shalkar
Chełm Poland 53 D6
Chelmer r. U.K. 59 H7
Chełmno Poland 57 Q4
Chelmsford U.K. 59 H7
Chelsea MI U.S.A. 164 C2
Chelsea VT U.S.A. 165 I2
Cheltenham U.K. 59 E7
Chelva Spain 67 F4
Chelyabinsk Rus. Fed. 76 H4
Chemax Mex. 167 I4
Chemba Moz. 123 D5
Chêm Co l. China 99 B6
Chemnitz Germany 63 M4
Chemulpo S. Korea see Inch'ŏn
Chemyndy Kyrg. 98 A4
Chena r. AK U.S.A. 149 K2
Chenab r. India/Pak. 104 B3
Chenachane, Oued watercourse Alg. 120 C2
Chena Hot Springs AK U.S.A. 149 K2
Chenārān Iran 110 E2
Chenderoh, Tasik resr Malaysia 84 C1
Chendir r. Turkm. see Çendir
Chenega (abandoned) AK U.S.A. 149 J3
Cheney WA U.S.A. 156 D3
Cheney Reservoir KS U.S.A. 160 D4
Chengalpattu India 106 D3
Cheng'an China 95 H4
Chengbu China 97 F3
Chengcheng China 95 G5
Chengchow China see Zhengzhou
Chengde Hebei China 95 I3
Chengde Hebei China 95 I3
Chengdu China 96 E2
Chengele India 96 C2
Chenggong China 96 D3
Chenghai China 97 H4
Cheng Hai l. China 96 D3
Chengjiang China see Taihe
Chengmai China 97 F5
Chengqian China 95 I5
Chengshan China 95 J4
Chengtu China see Chengdu
Chengwu China 95 H5
Chengxian China 96 E1
Chengxiang Chongqing China see Wuxi
Chengxiang Jiangxi China see Quannan
Chengyang China see Juxian
Chengzhong China see Ningming
Cheniu Shan i. China 95 I5
Chenkaladi Sri Lanka 106 D5
Chennai India 106 D3
Chenqian Shan i. China 97 I2
Chenqing China 90 B2
Chenqingqiao China see Chenqing
Chenstokhov Poland see Częstochowa
Chentejn Nuruu mts Mongolia 95 F1
Chenxi China 97 F3
Chenyang China see Chenxi
Chenying China see Wannian
Chenzhou China 97 G3
Chenzhuang China 95 H4
Chepén Peru 176 C5
Chepes Arg. 178 C4
Chepo Panama 166 [inset] K7
Chepstow U.K. 59 E7
Cheptsa r. Rus. Fed. 52 K4
Chequamegon Bay WI U.S.A. 160 F2
Cher r. France 66 E3
Chera state India see Kerala
Cherán Mex. 167 E5
Cheraw SC U.S.A. 163 E5
Cherbaniani Reef India 106 A3
Cherbourg-Octeville France 66 D2
Cherchell Alg. 67 H5
Cherchen China see Qiemo
Cherdakly Rus. Fed. 53 K5
Cherdyn' Rus. Fed. 51 R3
Chereapani reef India see Byramgore Reef
Cheremkhovo Rus. Fed. 88 I2
Cheremshany Rus. Fed. 90 D3
Cheremukhovka Rus. Fed. 52 K4
Cherepanovo Rus. Fed. 88 E2
Cherepovets Rus. Fed. 52 H4
Cherevkovo Rus. Fed. 52 J3
Chergui, Chott ech imp. l. Alg. 64 D5
Chéria Alg. 68 B7
Cheriton VA U.S.A. 165 H5
Cheriyam atoll India 106 B4
Cherkassy Ukr. see Cherkasy
Cherkasy Ukr. 53 G6
Cherkessk Rus. Fed. 113 F1
Cherla India 106 D2
Chernabura Island AK U.S.A. 148 H5
Chernaya Rus. Fed. 52 M1
Chernaya r. Rus. Fed. 52 M1
Chernigov Ukr. see Chernihiv
Chernigovka Rus. Fed. 90 D3
Chernihiv Ukr. 53 F6
Cherninivka Ukr. 53 H7
Chernivtsi Ukr. 53 E6
Chernobyl' Ukr. see Chornobyl'
Chernogorsk Rus. Fed. 88 G2
Chernovtsy Ukr. see Chernivtsi
Chernoye More sea Asia/Europe see Black Sea
Chernushka Rus. Fed. 51 R4
Chernyakhiv Ukr. 53 F6
Chernyakhovsk Rus. Fed. 55 L9
Chernyanka Rus. Fed. 53 H6
Chernyayevo Rus. Fed. 90 B1
Chernyshevsk Rus. Fed. 89 L2
Chernyshevskiy Rus. Fed. 77 M3
Chernyshkovskiy Rus. Fed. 53 I6
Chernyye Zemli reg. Rus. Fed. 53 J7
Chernyy Irtysh r. China/Kazakh. see Ertix He
Chernyy Porog Rus. Fed. 52 G3
Chernyy Yar Rus. Fed. 53 J6
Cherokee IA U.S.A. 160 E3
Cherokee Sound Bahamas 163 E7

▶Cherrapunji India 105 G4
Highest recorded annual rainfall in the world.

Cherry Creek r. SD U.S.A. 160 C2
Cherry Creek Mountains NV U.S.A. 159 F1
Cherry Hill NJ U.S.A. 165 H4
Cherry Island Solomon Is 133 G3
Cherry Lake CA U.S.A. 158 D2
Cherskiy Rus. Fed. 189 C2
Cherskiy Range mts Rus. Fed. see Cherskogo, Khrebet
Cherskogo, Khrebet mts Rus. Fed. 95 G1
Cherskogo, Khrebet mts Rus. Fed. 77 P3
Chertkov Ukr. see Chortkiv
Chertkovo Rus. Fed. 53 I6
Cherven Bryag Bulg. 69 K3
Chervonoarmeyskoye Ukr. see Vil'nyans'k
Chervonoarmiys'k Donets'ka Oblast' Ukr. see Krasnoarmiys'k
Chervonoarmiys'k Rivnens'ka Oblast' Ukr. see Radyvyliv
Chervonograd Ukr. see Chervonohrad
Chervonohrad Ukr. 53 E6
Chervyen' Belarus 53 F5
Cherwell r. U.K. 59 F7
Cherykaw Belarus 53 F5
Chesapeake VA U.S.A. 165 G5
Chesapeake Bay MD/VA U.S.A. 165 G4
Chesham U.K. 59 G7
Cheshire Plain U.K. 58 E5
Cheshme Vtoroy Turkm. 111 F2
Cheshskaya Guba b. Rus. Fed. 52 J2
Cheshtebe Tajik. 111 I2
Cheshunt U.K. 59 G7
Chesnokovka Rus. Fed. see Novoaltaysk
Chester Canada 153 I5
Chester U.K. 58 E5
Chester CA U.S.A. 158 C1
Chester IL U.S.A. 160 F4
Chester MT U.S.A. 156 F2
Chester OH U.S.A. 164 E4
Chester SC U.S.A. 163 D5
Chester r. MD U.S.A. 165 G4
Chesterfield U.K. 58 F5
Chesterfield VA U.S.A. 165 G5
Chesterfield, Îles is New Caledonia 133 F3
Chesterfield Inlet Canada 151 N2
Chesterfield Inlet inlet Canada 151 M2
Chester-le-Street U.K. 58 F4
Chestertown MD U.S.A. 165 G4
Chestertown NY U.S.A. 165 I2
Chesterville Canada 165 H1
Chestnut Ridge PA U.S.A. 164 F3
Chesuncook Lake ME U.S.A. 162 G2
Chetaïbi Alg. 68 B6
Chéticamp Canada 153 J5
Chetlat i. India 106 B4
Chetumal Mex. 167 H5
Chetwynd Canada 150 F4
Cheung Chau H.K. China 97 [inset]
Chevak AK U.S.A. 148 F3
Chevelon Creek r. AZ U.S.A. 159 H4
Cheviot N.Z. 139 D6
Cheviot Hills U.K. 58 E3
Cheviot Range hills Australia 136 C5
Chevreulx r. Canada 152 G3
Cheyenne OK U.S.A. 161 D5

▶Cheyenne WY U.S.A. 156 G4
Capital of Wyoming.

Cheyenne r. SD U.S.A. 160 C2
Cheyenne Wells CO U.S.A. 160 C4
Cheyne Bay Australia 135 B8
Cheyur India 106 D3
Chezacut Canada 150 E4
Chhapra India 105 F4
Chhata India 104 D4
Chhatak Bangl. 105 G4
Chhatarpur Jharkhand India 105 F4
Chhatarpur Madh. Prad. India 104 D4
Chhatr Pak. 111 H4
Chhatrapur India 106 E2
Chhattisgarh state India 105 E5
Chhay Arêng, Stœ̆ng r. Cambodia 87 C5
Chhindwara India 104 D5
Chhitkul India 104 D3
Chhukha Bhutan 105 G4
Chi, Lam r. Thai. 87 C4
Chi, Mae Nam r. Thai. 86 D4
Chiai Taiwan 97 I4
Chiamboni Somalia 122 E4
Chiange Angola 123 B5
Chiang Kham Thai. 86 C3
Chiang Khan Thai. 86 C3
Chiang Mai Thai. 86 B3
Chiang Rai Thai. 86 B3
Chiang Saen Thai. 86 C2
Chiapa Mex. 167 G5
Chiapas state Mex. 167 G5
Chiapilla Mex. 167 G5
Chiari Italy 68 C2
Chiautla Mex. 168 E5
Chiavenna Italy 68 C1
Chiayi Taiwan see Chiai
Chiba Japan 93 G3
Chiba pref. Japan 93 G3
Chibi China 97 G2
Chibia Angola 123 B5
Chibit Rus. Fed. 98 D2
Chibizovka Rus. Fed. see Zherdevka
Chiboma Moz. 123 D6
Chibougamau Canada 152 G4
Chibougamau, Lac l. Canada 152 G4
Chibuto Moz. 125 K3
Chibuzhang Co l. China 99 E6
Chicacole India see Srikakulam

▶Chicago IL U.S.A. 164 B3
4th most populous city in North America.

Chic-Chocs, Monts mts Canada 153 I4
Chichagof AK U.S.A. 149 M4
Chichagof Island AK U.S.A. 149 N4
Chichak r. Pak. 111 G5
Chichaoua Morocco 64 C5
Chichatka Rus. Fed. 90 A1
Chicheng Hebei China 95 H3
Chicheng Sichuan China see Pengxi
Chichén Itzá tourist site Mex. 167 H4
Chichester U.K. 59 G8
Chichester Range mts Australia 134 B5
Chichgarh India 106 D1
Chichibu Japan 93 F3
Chichibu-gawa r. Japan 93 F2
Chichibu-Tama Kokuritsu-kōen nat. park Japan 93 E3
Chichijima-rettō is Japan 91 F8
Chickaloon AK U.S.A. 149 J3
Chickasawhay r. MS U.S.A. 167 H2
Chickasha OK U.S.A. 161 D5
Chicken AK U.S.A. 149 L2
Chiclana de la Frontera Spain 67 C5
Chiclayo Peru 176 C5
Chico r. Arg. 178 C6
Chico CA U.S.A. 158 C2
Chicomo Moz. 125 L3
Chicomucelo Mex. 167 G6
Chicopee MA U.S.A. 165 I2
Chico Sapocoy, Mount Luzon Phil. 82 C2
Chicoutimi Canada 153 H4
Chicualacuala Moz. 125 J2
Chidambaram India 106 C4
Chidenguele Moz. 125 L3
Chidley, Cape Canada 147 L3
Chido China see Sêndo
Chido S. Korea 91 B6
Chiducuane Moz. 125 L3
Chiefland FL U.S.A. 163 D6
Chiemsee l. Germany 57 N7
Chiengmai Thai. see Chiang Mai
Chiers r. France 62 F5
Chieti Italy 68 F3
Chifeng China 95 I3
Chifre, Serra do mts Brazil 179 C2
Chiganak Kazakh. 102 D2
Chigasaki Japan 93 F3
Chiginagak Volcano, Mount AK U.S.A. 146 C4
Chigmit Mountains AK U.S.A. 148 I3
Chignik AK U.S.A. 148 H4
Chignik Bay AK U.S.A. 148 H4
Chignik Lagoon AK U.S.A. 148 H4
Chignik Lake AK U.S.A. 148 H4
Chigu China 99 E7
Chigubo Moz. 125 K2
Chigu Co l. China 99 E7
Chihil Abdālān, Kōh-e mts Afgh. 111 G3
Chihuahua Mex. 166 D2
Chihuahua state Mex. 166 D2
Chiili Kazakh. 102 C3
Chijinpu China 94 D3
Chikalda India 104 D5
Chikan China 97 F4
Chikaskia r. KS U.S.A. 161 D4
Chikhali Kalan Parasia India 104 D5
Chikhli India 106 C1
Chikishlyar Turkm. see Çekiçler
Chikmagalur India 106 B3
Chikodi India 106 B2
Chikoy Rus. Fed. 94 F1
Chikoy r. Rus. Fed. 95 F1
Chikuma-gawa r. Japan 93 E1
Chikuminuk Lake AK U.S.A. 148 H3
Chikura Japan 93 F4
Chilanko r. Canada 150 F4
Chilapa Mex. 167 F5
Chilas Pak. 104 C2
Chilaw Sri Lanka 106 C5
Chilcotin r. Canada 150 F5
Childers Australia 136 F5
Childress TX U.S.A. 161 C5
Chile country S. America 178 B4
Chile Basin sea feature S. Pacific Ocean 187 O8
Chile Chico Chile 178 B7
Chile Rise sea feature S. Pacific Ocean 187 O8
Chilgir Rus. Fed. 53 J7
Chilhowie VA U.S.A. 164 E5

Chilia-Nouă Ukr. see Kiliya
Chilik Kazakh. 102 E3
Chilika Lake India 106 E2
Chililabombwe Zambia 123 C5
Chilko r. Canada 150 F4
Chilko Lake Canada 150 E5
Chilkoot Pass Canada/U.S.A. 149 N4
Chilkoot Trail National Historic Site nat. park Canada 149 N4
Chillán Chile 178 B5
Chillicothe MO U.S.A. 160 E4
Chillicothe OH U.S.A. 164 D4
Chilliwack Canada 150 F5
Chilo India 104 C4
Chiloé, Isla de i. Chile 178 B6
Chiloé, Isla Grande de i. Chile see Chiloé, Isla de
Chilpancingo Mex. 168 E5
Chilpancingo de los Bravos Mex. see Chilpancingo
Chilpi Pak. 104 C1
Chiltern Hills U.K. 59 G7
Chilton WI U.S.A. 164 A1
Chiluage Angola 123 C4
Chilubi Zambia 123 C5
Chilung Taiwan 97 I3
Chilwa, Lake Malawi 123 D5
Chimala Tanz. 123 D4
Chimalapa Mex. 167 G5
Chimaltenango Guat. 167 H6
Chimán Panama 166 [inset] K7
Chi Ma Wan H.K. China 97 [inset]
Chimay Belgium 62 E4
Chimbas Arg. 178 C4
Chimbay Uzbek. see Chimboy
Chimborazo mt. Ecuador 176 C4
Chimbote Peru 176 C5
Chimboy Uzbek. 102 A3
Chimchineykuyim, Laguna lag. Rus. Fed. 148 B3
Chimishliya Moldova see Cimişlia
Chimkent Kazakh. see Shymkent
Chimney Rock CO U.S.A. 159 J3
Chimoio Moz. 123 D5
Chimtargha, Qullai mt. Tajik. 111 H2
Chimtorga, Gora mt. Tajik. see Chimtargha, Qullai

▶China country Asia 88 H5
Most populous country in Asia and the world. 2nd largest country in Asia and 4th largest in the world.

China Mex. 167 F3
China, Republic of country Asia see Taiwan
China Bakir r. Myanmar see To
Chinacates Mex. 166 D3
Chinajá Guat. 167 H5
China Lake CA U.S.A. 158 E4
China Lake ME U.S.A. 165 K1
Chinandega Nicaragua 166 [inset] I6
China Point CA U.S.A. 158 D5
Chinati Peak TX U.S.A. 161 B6
Chincha Alta Peru 176 C6
Chinchaga r. Canada 150 G3
Chinchilla Australia 138 E1
Chincholi India 106 C2
Chinchorro, Banco sea feature Mex. 167 I5
Chincoteague Bay MD/VA U.S.A. 165 H5
Chinde Moz. 123 D5
Chindo S. Korea 91 B6
Chin-do i. S. Korea 91 B6
Chindwin r. Myanmar 86 A2
Chinese Turkestan aut. reg. China see Xinjiang Uygur Zizhiqu
Chinghai prov. China see Qinghai
Chingleput India see Chengalpattu
Chingola Zambia 123 C5
Chinguar Angola 123 B5
Chinguețți Mauritania 120 B2
Chinhae S. Korea 91 C6
Chinhoyi Zimbabwe 123 D5
Chini India see Kalpa
Chiniak AK U.S.A. 148 I4
Chiniak, Cape AK U.S.A. 148 I4
Chining China see Jining
Chiniot Pak. 111 I4
Chinipas Mex. 166 C3
Chinit, Stœng r. Cambodia 87 D4
Chinju S. Korea 91 C6
Chinle AZ U.S.A. 159 I3
Chinmen Taiwan 97 H3
Chinmen Tao i. Taiwan 97 H3
Chinnamp'o N. Korea see Namp'o
Chinnur India 106 C2
Chino Japan 93 E3
Chino Creek watercourse AZ U.S.A. 159 G4
Chinon France 66 E3
Chinook MT U.S.A. 156 F2
Chinook Trough sea feature N. Pacific Ocean 186 I3
Chino Valley AZ U.S.A. 159 G4
Chin-shan China see Zhujing
Chintamani India 106 C3
Chioggia Italy 68 E2
Chios Greece 69 L5
Chios i. Greece 69 K5
Chipam Guat. 167 H6
Chipata Zambia 123 D5
Chip Chap r. China/India 99 B6
Chipchihua, Sierra de mts Arg. 178 C6
Chiphu Cambodia 87 D5
Chipindo Angola 123 B5
Chiping China 95 I4
Chipinga Zimbabwe see Chipinge
Chipinge Zimbabwe 123 D6
Chipley FL U.S.A. 163 C6
Chipman Canada 153 I5
Chippenham U.K. 59 E7
Chippewa, Lake WI U.S.A. 160 F2
Chippewa Falls WI U.S.A. 160 F2
Chipping Norton U.K. 59 F7
Chipping Sodbury U.K. 59 E7
Chipurupalle Andhra Prad. India 106 D2
Chipurupalle Andhra Prad. India 106 D2
Chiquibul National Park Belize 167 H5
Chiquilá Mex. 167 I4
Chiquimula Guat. 167 H6
Chiquinquira Col. 176 D2
Chir r. Rus. Fed. 53 I6
Chirada India 106 D3
Chirala India 106 D3
Chīras Afgh. 111 G3
Chirchiq Uzbek. 102 C3
Chiredzi Zimbabwe 123 D6
Chirfa Niger 120 E2
Chiricahua National Monument nat. park AZ U.S.A. 159 I5
Chiricahua Peak AZ U.S.A. 159 I6
Chirikof Island AK U.S.A. 148 I5
Chiriquí, Golfo de b. Panama 166 [inset] J7
Chiriquí, Laguna de b. Panama 166 [inset] J7
Chiriquí, Volcán de vol. Panama see Barú, Volcán
Chiriquí Grande Panama 166 [inset] J7
Chiri-san mt. S. Korea 91 B6
Chirk U.K. 59 D6
Chirnside U.K. 60 G5
Chirripó mt. Costa Rica 169 H7
Chirripó, Parque Nacional nat. park Costa Rica 166 [inset] J7
Chiryū Japan 92 D3
Chisamba Zambia 123 C5
Chisana AK U.S.A. 149 L3
Chisana r. AK U.S.A. 149 L3
Chisana Glacier AK U.S.A. 149 J3
Chisasibi Canada 152 F3
Chisec Guat. 167 H6
Chishima-retto is Rus. Fed. see Kuril Islands
Chisholm Canada 150 H4
Chishtian Pak. 111 I4
Chishui Guizhou China 96 E2
Chishui Sichuan China 96 E3
Chisimaio Somalia see Kismaayo

▶Chişinău Moldova 69 M1
Capital of Moldova.

Chistochina AK U.S.A. 149 K3
Chistopol' Rus. Fed. 52 K5
Chita Japan 92 C4
Chita Rus. Fed. 89 K2
Chitado Angola 123 B5
Chita-hantō pen. Japan 92 C4
Chitaldrug India see Chitradurga
Chitalwana India 104 B4
Chitambo Zambia 123 D5
Chitanana r. AK U.S.A. 149 J2
Chitanga Rus. Fed. 95 G1
Chitato Angola 123 C4
Chita-wan b. Japan 92 C4
Chitek Lake Canada 151 J4
Chitek Lake l. Canada 151 L4
Chitembo Angola 123 B5
Chitina AK U.S.A. 149 K3
Chitina r. AK U.S.A. 149 K3
Chitipa Malawi 123 D4
Chitkul India see Chhitkul
Chitobe Moz. 123 D6
Chitoor India see Chittoor
Chitor India see Chittaurgarh
Chitose Japan 90 F4
Chitradurga India 106 C3
Chitrakoot India 104 E4
Chitrakut India see Chitrakoot
Chitral Pak. 111 H3
Chitral r. Pak. 111 H3
Chitravati r. India 106 C3
Chitré Panama 166 [inset] J8
Chitrod India 104 B5
Chittagong Bangl. 105 G5
Chittaurgarh India 104 C4
Chittoor India 106 C3
Chittor India see Chittoor
Chittorgarh India see Chittaurgarh
Chittur India 106 C4
Chitungwiza Zimbabwe 123 D5
Chiu Lung H.K. China see Kowloon
Chiume Angola 123 C5
Chivasso Italy 68 B2
Chívato, Punta pt Mex. 166 C3
Chivela Mex. 167 G5
Chivhu Zimbabwe 123 D5
Chixi China 97 G4
Chiyoda Gunma Japan 93 F2
Chiyoda Ibaraki Japan 93 G2
Chiyogawa Japan 93 F2
Chizarira National Park Zimbabwe 123 C5
Chizhou China 97 H2
Chizu Japan 91 D6
Chkalov Rus. Fed. see Orenburg
Chkalovsk Rus. Fed. 52 I4
Chkalovskoye Rus. Fed. 90 D3
Chlef Alg. 67 G5
Chlef, Oued r. Alg. 67 G5
Chloride AZ U.S.A. 159 F4
Chlya, Ozero l. Rus. Fed. 90 F1
Choa Chu Kang Sing. 87 [inset]
Choa Chu Kang hill Sing. 87 [inset]
Chobe National Park Botswana 123 C5
Chodov Czech Rep. 63 M4
Chodro Rus. Fed. 98 E2
Choele Choel Arg. 178 C5
Chōfu Japan 93 F3
Chogar r. Rus. Fed. 90 D1
Chogo Lungma Glacier Pak. 99 A6
Chogori Feng mt. China/Pak. see K2
Chograyskoye Vodokhranilishche resr Rus. Fed. 53 J7
Choiseul i. Solomon Is 133 F2
Choix Mex. 166 C3
Chojnice Poland 57 P4
Chōkai-san vol. Japan 91 F5
Ch'ok'ē mts Eth. 122 D2
Ch'ok'ē Mountains Eth. see Ch'ok'ē
Chokola mt. China 104 E3
Choksum China 105 F3
Chok-Tal Kyrg. 98 B4
Chokue Moz. see Chókwé
Chokurdakh Rus. Fed. 77 P2
Chókwé Moz. 125 K3
Cho La pass China 96 C2
Cholame CA U.S.A. 158 C4
Cholet France 66 D3
Choloma Hond. 166 [inset] I6
Cholpon Kyrg. 98 A4
Cholpon-Ata Kyrg. 102 E3
Cholula Mex. 167 F5
Choluteca Hond. 166 [inset] I6
Choma Zambia 123 C5
Chomo Ganggar mt. China 99 E7
Chơ Moi Vietnam 86 D2
Chomo Lhari mt. China/Bhutan 105 G4
Chom Thong Thai. 86 B3
Chomun India 99 A8
Chomutov Czech Rep. 57 N5
Chōnan Japan 93 G3
Ch'ŏnan S. Korea 91 B5
Chon Buri Thai. 87 C4
Ch'ŏnch'ŏn N. Korea 90 B4
Chone Ecuador 176 B4
Ch'ŏngch'ŏn-gang r. N. Korea 91 B5
Ch'ongdo S. Korea 91 C6
Chonggye China see Qonggyai
Ch'ŏngjin N. Korea 90 C4
Ch'ŏngju S. Korea 91 B5
Chŏng Kal Cambodia 87 C4
Chongkü China 96 C2
Chongli China 95 H3
Chonglong China see Zizhong
Chongming Dao i. China 97 I2
Chongoroi Angola 123 B5
Chŏngp'yŏng N. Korea 91 B5
Chongqing China 96 E2
Chongqing municipality China 96 E2
Chonguene Moz. 125 K3
Chŏngŭp S. Korea 91 B6
Chongyang China 97 G2
Chongyi China 97 G3
Chongzuo China 96 E4
Chŏnju S. Korea 91 B6
Chonogol Mongolia see Erdenetsagaan
Chontalpa Mex. 167 G5

▶Cho Oyu mt. China/Nepal 105 F3
6th highest mountain in Asia and the world.

Chopda India 104 C5
Chor Pak. 111 H5
Chora Sfakion Greece 69 K7
Chorley U.K. 58 E5
Chornobyl' Ukr. 53 F6
Chornomors'ke Ukr. 69 O2
Chortkiv Ukr. 53 E6
Ch'osan N. Korea 90 B4
Chōshi Japan 93 G3
Chosŏn country Asia see South Korea
Chosŏn-minjujuŭi-inmin-konghwaguk country Asia see North Korea
Choszczno Poland 57 O4
Chota Peru 176 C5
Chota Sinchula hill India 105 G4
Choteau MT U.S.A. 156 E3
Choti Pak. 111 H4
Choûm Mauritania 120 B2
Chowchilla CA U.S.A. 158 C3
Chown, Mount Canada 150 G4
Choybalsan Mongolia 95 H2
Choyr Mongolia 95 G2
Chrétiens, Île aux i. Canada see Christian Island
Chřiby hills Czech Rep. 57 P6
Chrisman IL U.S.A. 164 B4
Chrissiesmeer S. Africa 125 J4
Christchurch N.Z. 139 D6
Christchurch U.K. 59 F8
Christian AK U.S.A. 149 K2
Christian r. AK U.S.A. 149 K2
Christian, Cape Canada 147 L2
Christiana S. Africa 125 G4
Christiania Norway see Oslo
Christian Island Canada 164 E1
Christiansburg VA U.S.A. 164 E5
Christianshåb Greenland see Qasigiannguit
Christie Bay Canada 151 I2
Christie Island Myanmar 87 B5
Christina r. Canada 151 I3
Christina, Mount N.Z. 139 B7

▶Christmas Island terr. Indian Ocean 80 D9
Australian External Territory.

Christopher, Lake salt flat Australia 135 D6
Chrudim Czech Rep. 57 O6
Chrysi i. Greece see Gaïdouronisi
Chrysochou Bay Cyprus 107 A2
Chrysochous, Kolpos b. Cyprus see Chrysochou Bay
Chu Kazakh. see Shu
Chu r. Kazakh./Kyrg. 102 C3
Chuadanga Bangl. 105 G5
Chuali, Lago l. Moz. 125 K3
Chuanhui China see Zhoukou
Chuansha China 97 I2
Chuathbaluk AK U.S.A. 148 H3
Chubalung China 96 C2
Chubarovka Ukr. see Polohy
Chubartau Kazakh. see Barshatas
Chūbu airport Japan 92 C4
Chūbu-Sangaku Kokuritsu-kōen nat. park Japan 92 D2
Chubxi China 94 D5
Chu-ching China see Zhujing
Chuchkovo Rus. Fed. 53 I5
Chuckwalla Mountains CA U.S.A. 159 F5
Chucunaque r. Panama 166 [inset] K7
Chudniv Ukr. 53 F6
Chudovo Rus. Fed. 52 F4
Chudskoye, Ozero l. Estonia/Rus. Fed. see Peipus, Lake
Chugach Mountains AK U.S.A. 149 K3
Chuginadak Island AK U.S.A. 148 E5
Chūgoku-sanchi mts Japan 91 D6
Chugqênsumdo China see Jigzhi
Chuguchak China see Tacheng
Chuguyev Ukr. see Chuhuyiv
Chuguyevka Rus. Fed. 90 D3
Chugwater WY U.S.A. 156 G4
Chuhai China see Zhuhai
Chuhuyiv Ukr. 53 H6
Chuimatan China see Jishishan
Chujiang China see Shimen
Chukai Malaysia see Cukai
Chukchagirskoye, Ozero l. Rus. Fed. 90 E1
Chukchi Abyssal Plain sea feature Arctic Ocean 189 B1
Chukchi Plateau sea feature Arctic Ocean 189 B1
Chukchi Sea Rus. Fed./U.S.A. 148 E1
Chukhloma Rus. Fed. 52 I4
Chukotskiy, Mys c. Rus. Fed. 148 D2
Chukotskiy Khrebet mts Rus. Fed. 148 B2
Chukotskiy Poluostrov pen. Rus. Fed. 148 D2
Chulakkurgan Kazakh. see Sholakkorgan
Chulaktau Kazakh. see Karatau
Chulasa Rus. Fed. 52 J2
Chula Vista CA U.S.A. 158 E5
Chulitna AK U.S.A. 149 J3
Chuloonawick AK U.S.A. 148 F3
Chulucanas Peru 176 B5
Chulung Pass Pak. 104 D2
Chuluut Gol r. Mongolia 94 E1
Chulym Rus. Fed. 76 J4
Chulyshman r. Rus. Fed. 98 D2
Chumar India 104 D2
Chumbicha Arg. 178 C3
Chumda China 96 C1
Chumek Kazakh. 98 D2
Chumikan Rus. Fed. 77 O4
Chum Phae Thai. 86 C3
Chumphon Thai. 87 B5
Chum Saeng Thai. 86 C4
Chunar India 105 E4
Ch'unch'ŏn S. Korea 91 B5
Chundzha Kazakh. 102 E3
Chunga Zambia 123 C5
Chung-hua Jen-min Kung-ho-kuo country Asia see China
Chung-hua Min-kuo country Asia see Taiwan
Ch'ungju S. Korea 91 B5
Chungking China see Chongqing
Ch'ungmu S. Korea see T'ongyŏng
Chŭngsan N. Korea 91 B5
Chungyang Shanmo mts Taiwan 97 I4
Chunhua China 95 G5
Chunhuhux Mex. 167 H5
Chunian Pak. 111 I4
Chunskiy Rus. Fed. 88 H1
Chunya r. Rus. Fed. 77 K3
Chuôi, Hon i. Vietnam 87 D5
Chuosijia China see Guanyinqiao
Chupa Rus. Fed. 54 R3
Chūplū Iran 110 B2
Chuquicamata Chile 178 C2
Chur Switz. 66 I3
Churachandpur India 105 H4
Chūrān Iran 110 D4
Churapcha Rus. Fed. 77 O3
Churchill Canada 151 M3
Churchill r. Man. Canada 151 M3
Churchill r. Nfld. and Lab. Canada 153 J3
Churchill, Cape Canada 151 M3
Churchill Falls Canada 153 I3
Churchill Lake Canada 151 I4
Churchill Mountains Antarctica 188 H1
Churchill Sound sea chan. Canada 152 F2
Churchs Ferry ND U.S.A. 160 D1
Churchville VA U.S.A. 164 F4
Churek-Dag, Gora mt. Rus. Fed. 94 B1
Churia Ghati Hills Nepal 105 F4
Churu India 104 C3
Churubusco IN U.S.A. 164 C3
Churumuco Mex. 167 E5
Churún-Merú waterfall Venez. see Angel Falls
Chushul India 104 D2
Chuska Mountains NM U.S.A. 159 I3
Chusovaya r. Rus. Fed. 51 R4
Chusovoy Rus. Fed. 51 R4
Chust Ukr. see Khust
Chute-des-Passes Canada 153 H4
Chutia Assam India 105 H4
Chutia Jharkhand India 105 F5
Chutung Taiwan 97 I3
Chuuk is Micronesia 186 G5
Chuxiong China 96 D3
Chüy r. Kazakh./Kyrg. see Chu
Chüy admin. div. Kyrg. 98 A4
Chư Yang Sin mt. Vietnam 87 E4
Chūzenji-ko l. Japan 93 F2
Chuzhou Anhui China 97 H1
Chuzhou Jiangsu China 97 H1
Chūzu Japan 92 C3
Chymyshliya Moldova see Cimişlia
Chyulu Hills National Park Kenya 122 D4
Ciadâr-Lunga Moldova see Ciadîr-Lunga
Ciadîr-Lunga Moldova 69 M1
Ciamis Jawa Indon. 85 E4
Cianjur Jawa Indon. 84 D4
Cianorte Brazil 178 F2
Cibadak Jawa Indon. 84 D4
Cibatu Jawa Indon. 85 E4
Cibecue AZ U.S.A. 159 H4
Cibinong Jawa Indon. 84 D4
Cibolo Creek r. TX U.S.A. 161 D6
Cibuta Mex. 166 C2
Cibuta, Sierra mt. Mex. 166 C2
Čičarija mts Croatia 68 E2
Cicero IL U.S.A. 164 B3
Cidade Velha Cape Verde 120 [inset]
Cidaun Jawa Indon. 84 D4
Cide Turkey 112 D2
Ciechanów Poland 57 R4
Ciego de Ávila Cuba 169 I4
Ciénaga Col. 176 D1
Ciénega Mex. 167 E3
Ciénega de Flores Mex. 161 C7
Cieneguillas Mex. 166 D3
Cienfuegos Cuba 169 H4
Cieza Spain 67 F4
Çiftlik Turkey see Kelkit
Cifuentes Spain 67 E3
Cigeulis Jawa Indon. 84 D4
Cigüela r. Spain 67 E4
Cihanbeyli Turkey 112 D3
Cihuatlán Mex. 166 D5
Cíjara, Embalse de resr Spain 67 D4
Cikalong Jawa Indon. 85 E4
Cilacap Jawa Indon. 85 E4
Cilangkahan Jawa Indon. 84 D4
Çıldır Turkey 113 F2
Çıldır Gölü l. Turkey 113 F2
Çıldıroba Turkey 107 C1
Ciledug Jawa Indon. 85 E4
Cilento e del Vallo di Diano, Parco Nazionale del nat. park Italy 68 F4
Cili China 97 F2
Cilician Gates pass Turkey see Gülek Boğazı
Cill Airne Ireland see Killarney
Cill Chainnigh Ireland see Kilkenny
Cill Mhantáin Ireland see Wicklow
Çilmämmetgum des. Turkm. 110 D1
Cilo Dağı mt. Turkey 113 G3
Çiloy Adası i. Azer. 113 H2
Cimahi Jawa Indon. 84 D4
Cimarron CO U.S.A. 159 J2
Cimarron KS U.S.A. 160 C4
Cimarron NM U.S.A. 157 G5
Cimarron r. OK U.S.A. 161 D4
Cimişlia Moldova 69 M1
Cimone, Monte mt. Italy 68 D2
Cîmpina Romania see Câmpina
Cîmpulung Romania see Câmpulung
Cîmpulung Moldovenesc Romania see Câmpulung Moldovenesc
Cina, Tanjung c. Indon. 84 D4
Çınar Turkey 113 F3
Cinca r. Spain 67 G3
Cincinnati OH U.S.A. 164 C4
Cinco de Outubro Angola see Xá-Muteba
Cinderford U.K. 59 E7
Çine Turkey 69 M6
Ciney Belgium 62 F4
Cintalapa Mex. 168 F5
Cinto, Monte mt. France 66 I5
Cipatuja Jawa Indon. 85 E4
Ciping China 97 G3
Cirata, Waduk resr Jawa Indon. 84 D4
Circeo, Parco Nazionale del nat. park Italy 68 E4
Circle AK U.S.A. 149 K2
Circle MT U.S.A. 156 G3
Circle Hot Springs AK U.S.A. 149 K2
Circleville OH U.S.A. 164 D4
Circleville UT U.S.A. 159 G2
Cirebon Jawa Indon. 85 E4
Cirencester U.K. 59 F7
Cirenti Sumatera Indon. 84 C3
Cirò Marina Italy 68 G5
Cirta Alg. see Constantine
Cisco UT U.S.A. 159 I2
Cisne, Islas del is Caribbean Sea 169 H5
Citlaltépetl vol. Mex. see Orizaba, Pico de
Čitluk Bos.-Herz. 68 G3
Citronelle AL U.S.A. 161 F6
Citrus Heights CA U.S.A. 158 C2
Città di Castello Italy 68 E3
Ciucaş, Vârful mt. Romania 69 K2
Ciudad Acuña Mex. 167 E2
Ciudad Altamirano Mex. 168 D5
Ciudad Bolívar Venez. 176 F2
Ciudad Camargo Mex. 166 D3
Ciudad Constitución Mex. 166 C3
Ciudad Cuauhtémoc Mex. 167 H6
Ciudad del Carmen Mex. 167 H5
Ciudad Delicias Mex. 166 D2
Ciudad del Maíz Mex. 167 F4
Ciudad de Panamá Panama see Panama City
Ciudad de Valles Mex. 168 E4
Ciudad Guayana Venez. 176 F2
Ciudad Guerrero Mex. 157 G7
Ciudad Guzmán Mex. 168 D5
Ciudad Hidalgo Mex. 167 E5
Ciudad Ixtepec Mex. 167 G5
Ciudad Juárez Mex. 166 D2
Ciudad Lerdo Mex. 166 E3
Ciudad Madero Mex. 167 F4
Ciudad Mante Mex. 168 E4
Ciudad Manuel Doblado Mex. 167 E4
Ciudad Mendoza Mex. 167 F5
Ciudad Mier Mex. 167 F3
Ciudad Obregón Mex. 166 C3
Ciudad Real Spain 67 E4
Ciudad Río Bravo Mex. 167 F3
Ciudad Rodrigo Spain 67 C3
Ciudad Tecún Uman Guat. 167 G6
Ciudad Trujillo Dom. Rep. see Santo Domingo
Ciudad Victoria Mex. 161 D8
Ciutadella Spain 67 H3
Civa Burnu pt Turkey 112 E2
Cividale del Friuli Italy 68 E1
Civitanova Marche Italy 68 E3
Civitavecchia Italy 68 D3
Çivril Turkey 69 M5
Cixi China 97 I2
Cixian China 95 H4
Ciyao China 95 I5
Cizhou China see Cixian
Cizre Turkey 113 F3
Clacton-on-Sea U.K. 59 I7
Clady U.K. 61 E3
Claire, Lake Canada 151 H3
Clairfontaine Alg. see El Aouinet
Clamecy France 66 F3
Clam Gulch AK U.S.A. 149 J3
Clane Ireland 61 F4
Clanton AL U.S.A. 163 C5
Clanwilliam Dam S. Africa 124 D7
Clara Ireland 61 E4
Clara Island Myanmar 87 B5
Claraville Australia 136 C3
Clare N.S.W. Australia 138 A4
Clare S.A. Australia 137 B7
Clare r. Ireland 61 C4
Clare MI U.S.A. 164 C2
Clarecastle Ireland 61 D5
Clare Island Ireland 61 B4
Claremont NH U.S.A. 165 I2
Claremore OK U.S.A. 161 E4
Claremorris Ireland 61 D4
Clarence r. Australia 138 F2
Clarence N.Z. 139 D6
Clarence Island Antarctica 188 A2
Clarence Strait Iran see Khūran
Clarence Strait AK U.S.A. 149 N4
Clarence Town Bahamas 163 F8
Clarendon AR U.S.A. 161 F5
Clarendon PA U.S.A. 164 F3
Clarendon TX U.S.A. 161 C5
Clarenville Canada 153 L4
Claresholm Canada 150 H5
Clarie Coast Antarctica see Wilkes Coast
Clarington OH U.S.A. 164 E4
Clarion IA U.S.A. 160 E3
Clarion PA U.S.A. 164 F3
Clarion r. PA U.S.A. 164 F3
Clarión, Isla i. Mex. 168 B5
Clark SD U.S.A. 160 D2
Clark, Lake AK U.S.A. 148 I3
Clark, Mount Canada 149 Q2
Clarkdale AZ U.S.A. 159 G4
Clarkebury S. Africa 125 I6
Clarke Range mts Australia 136 D4
Clarke River Australia 136 D3
Clarke's Head Canada 153 L4
Clark Mountain CA U.S.A. 159 F4
Clark Point Canada 164 E1
Clarksburg WV U.S.A. 164 E4
Clarksdale MS U.S.A. 161 F5
Clarks Hill IN U.S.A. 164 B3
Clarks Point AK U.S.A. 148 H4
Clarksville AR U.S.A. 161 E5
Clarksville TN U.S.A. 164 B5
Clarksville TX U.S.A. 161 E5
Clarksville VA U.S.A. 165 F5
Claro r. Goiás Brazil 179 A2
Claro r. Mato Grosso Brazil 179 A1
Clashmore Ireland 61 E5
Claude TX U.S.A. 161 C5
Claudy U.K. 61 E3
Claveria Luzon Phil. 82 C2
Clavier Belgium 62 F4
Claxton GA U.S.A. 163 D5
Clay WV U.S.A. 164 E4
Clayburg NY U.S.A. 165 I1
Clay Center KS U.S.A. 160 D4
Clay Center NE U.S.A. 160 D3
Clay City IN U.S.A. 164 B4
Clay City KY U.S.A. 164 D5
Clayhole Wash watercourse AZ U.S.A. 159 G3
Claypool AZ U.S.A. 159 H5
Clay Springs AZ U.S.A. 159 H4
Clayton DE U.S.A. 165 H4
Clayton GA U.S.A. 163 D5
Clayton MI U.S.A. 164 C3
Clayton MO U.S.A. 160 F4
Clayton NM U.S.A. 161 C4
Clayton NY U.S.A. 165 G1
Claytor Lake VA U.S.A. 164 E5
Clay Village KY U.S.A. 164 C4
Clear, Cape Ireland 61 C6
Clearco WV U.S.A. 164 E4
Clear Creek Canada 164 E2
Clear Creek r. AZ U.S.A. 159 H4
Cleare, Cape AK U.S.A. 146 D4
Clearfield PA U.S.A. 165 F3
Clearfield UT U.S.A. 156 E4
Clear Fork Brazos r. TX U.S.A. 161 D5
Clear Hills Canada 150 G3
Clear Island Ireland 61 C6
Clear Lake IA U.S.A. 160 E3
Clear Lake SD U.S.A. 160 D2
Clear Lake l. CA U.S.A. 158 B2
Clear Lake l. UT U.S.A. 159 G2
Clearmont WY U.S.A. 156 G3
Clearwater Canada 150 G5
Clearwater r. Alba/Sask. Canada 151 I3
Clearwater r. Alta Canada 150 H4
Clearwater FL U.S.A. 163 D7
Clearwater Lake Canada 151 K4
Clearwater Mountains ID U.S.A. 156 E3
Cleaton KY U.S.A. 164 B5
Cleburne TX U.S.A. 161 D5
Cleethorpes U.K. 58 G5
Clementi Sing. 87 [inset]
Clendenin WV U.S.A. 164 E4
Clendening Lake OH U.S.A. 164 E3
Cleopatra Needle mt. Palawan Phil. 82 B4
Clères France 62 B5
Clerf Lux. see Clervaux
Clerke Reef Australia 134 B4
Clermont Australia 136 D4
Clermont France 62 C5
Clermont-en-Argonne France 62 F5
Clermont-Ferrand France 66 F4
Clervaux Lux. 62 G4
Cles Italy 68 D1
Clevedon U.K. 59 E7
Cleveland MS U.S.A. 161 F5
Cleveland OH U.S.A. 164 E3
Cleveland TN U.S.A. 163 C5
Cleveland TX U.S.A. 167 G2
Cleveland UT U.S.A. 159 H2
Cleveland WI U.S.A. 164 B2
Cleveland, Cape Australia 136 D3
Cleveland, Mount MT U.S.A. 156 E2
Cleveland Heights OH U.S.A. 164 E3
Cleveland Hills U.K. 58 F4
Cleveleys U.K. 58 D5
Cleves Germany see Kleve
Clew Bay Ireland 61 C4
Clifden Ireland 61 B4
Cliff NM U.S.A. 159 I5
Cliffoney Ireland 61 D3
Clifton Australia 138 E1
Clifton AZ U.S.A. 159 I5
Clifton Beach Australia 136 D3
Clifton Forge VA U.S.A. 164 F5
Clifton Park NY U.S.A. 165 I2
Climax Canada 151 I5
Climax MI U.S.A. 164 C2
Clinch Mountain mts TN/VA U.S.A. 164 D5
Cline River Canada 150 G4
Clinton B.C. Canada 150 F5
Clinton Ont. Canada 164 E2
Clinton IA U.S.A. 160 F3
Clinton IL U.S.A. 160 F3
Clinton IN U.S.A. 164 B4
Clinton KY U.S.A. 161 F4
Clinton MI U.S.A. 164 D2
Clinton MO U.S.A. 160 E4
Clinton MS U.S.A. 161 F5
Clinton NC U.S.A. 163 E5
Clinton OK U.S.A. 161 D5
Clinton-Colden Lake Canada 151 J1
Clinton Creek (abandoned) Canada 149 L2
Clintwood VA U.S.A. 164 D5

▶Clipperton, Île terr. N. Pacific Ocean 187 M5
Part of France. Most easterly point of Oceania.

Clisham hill U.K. 60 C3
Clitheroe U.K. 58 E5
Clive Lake Canada 150 G2
Cliza Bol. 176 E7
Clocolan S. Africa 125 H5
Cloghan Ireland 61 E4
Clonakilty Ireland 61 D6
Clonbern Ireland 61 D4
Cloncurry Australia 136 C4
Cloncurry r. Australia 136 C3
Clones Ireland 61 E3
Clonmel Ireland 61 E5
Clonygowan Ireland 61 E4
Cloonbannin Ireland 61 C5
Clooneagh Ireland 61 E4
Cloppenburg Germany 63 I2
Cloquet MN U.S.A. 160 E2
Cloquet r. MN U.S.A. 160 E2
Cloud Peak WY U.S.A. 154 F3
Cloud Peak WY U.S.A. 156 G3
Clova Canada 152 G4
Clover UT U.S.A. 159 G1
Cloverdale CA U.S.A. 158 B2
Cloverdale IN U.S.A. 164 B4
Cloverport KY U.S.A. 164 B5
Clovis CA U.S.A. 158 D3
Clovis NM U.S.A. 161 C5
Cloyne Canada 165 G1
Cluain Meala Ireland see Clonmel
Cluanie, Loch l. U.K. 60 D3
Cluff Lake Mine Canada 151 I3
Cluj-Napoca Romania 69 J1

Clun U.K. 59 D6
Clunes Australia 138 A6
Cluny Australia 136 B5
Cluses France 66 H3
Cluster Springs VA U.S.A. 165 F5
Clut Lake Canada 150 G1
Clutterbuck Head hd Canada 153 H1
Clutterbuck Hills hill Australia 135 D6
Clwydian Range hills U.K. 58 D5
Clyde Canada 150 H4
Clyde r. U.K. 60 E5
Clyde NY U.S.A. 165 G2
Clyde OH U.S.A. 164 D3
Clyde, Firth of est. U.K. 60 E5
Clydebank U.K. 60 E5
Clyde River Canada 147 L2
Côa r. Port. 67 C3
Coachella CA U.S.A. 158 E5
Coahuayutla de Guerrero Mex. 167 E5
Coahuila state Mex. 166 E3
Coal r. Canada 149 P4
Coal City IL U.S.A. 164 A3
Coalcomán Mex. 166 E5
Coaldale NV U.S.A. 158 E2
Coalgate OK U.S.A. 161 D5
Coal Harbour Canada 150 E5
Coalinga CA U.S.A. 158 C3
Coalport PA U.S.A. 165 F3
Coal River Canada 149 P4
Coal Valley NV U.S.A. 159 F3
Coalville U.K. 59 F6
Coalville UT U.S.A. 159 H1
Coari Brazil 176 F4
Coari r. Brazil 176 F4
Coarsegold CA U.S.A. 158 D3
Coastal Plain U.S.A. 161 E6
Coast Mountains Canada 150 E4
Coast Range hills Australia 137 E5
Coast Ranges mts CA U.S.A. 158 B1
Coatbridge U.K. 60 E5
Coatepec Mex. 167 F5
Coatepeque Guat. 167 H6
Coatesville PA U.S.A. 165 H4
Coaticook Canada 165 J1
Coatlán Mex. 167 F5
Coats Island Canada 147 J3
Coats Land reg. Antarctica 188 A1
Coatzacoalcos Mex. 168 F5
Cobán Guat. 167 H6
Cobar Australia 138 B3
Cobargo Australia 138 D6
Cobden Australia 138 A7
Cobh Ireland 61 D6
Cobham r. Canada 151 M4
Cobija Bol. 176 E6
Coblenz Germany see Koblenz
Cobleskill NY U.S.A. 165 H2
Cobos Mex. 167 F4
Cobourg Peninsula Australia 134 F2
Cobra Australia 135 B6
Cobram Australia 138 B5
Coburg Germany 63 K4
Coburg Island Canada 147 K2
Coca Ecuador 176 C4
Coca Spain 67 D3
Cocalinho Brazil 179 A1
Cocanada India see Kakinada
Cochabamba Bol. 176 E7
Cochem Germany 63 H4
Cochin India see Kochi
Cochin reg. Vietnam 87 D5
Cochinos, Bahía de b. Cuba see Pigs, Bay of
Cochise AZ U.S.A. 159 I5
Cochise Head mt. AZ U.S.A. 159 I5
Cochrane Alta Canada 150 H5
Cochrane Ont. Canada 152 E4
Cochrane r. Canada 151 K3
Cockburn Australia 137 C7
Cockburnspath U.K. 60 G5
Cockburn Town Bahamas 163 F7
Cockburn Town Turks and Caicos Is see Grand Turk
Cockermouth U.K. 58 D4
Cocklebiddy Australia 135 D8
Cockscomb mt. S. Africa 124 G7
Coclé del Norte Panama 166 [inset] J7
Coco r. Hond./Nicaragua 166 [inset] J6
Coco, Cayo i. Cuba 163 E8
Coco, Isla de i. N. Pacific Ocean 169 G7
Cocobeach Gabon 122 A3
Coco Channel India 87 A4
Cocomórachic Mex. 166 D2
Coconino Plateau AZ U.S.A. 159 G4
Cocopara National Park Australia 138 C5
Cocoro i. Phil. 82 C4
Cocos Brazil 179 B1
Cocos Basin sea feature Indian Ocean 185 O5

▶Cocos Islands terr. Indian Ocean 80 B9
Australian External Territory.

Cocos Ridge sea feature N. Pacific Ocean 187 O5
Cocula Mex. 166 E4
Cocuy, Sierra Nevada del mt. Col. 176 D2
Cod, Cape MA U.S.A. 165 J3
Codajás Brazil 176 F4
Coderre Canada 151 J5
Codfish Island N.Z. 139 A8
Codigoro Italy 68 E2
Cod Island Canada 153 J2
Codlea Romania 69 K2
Codó Brazil 177 J4
Codsall U.K. 59 E6
Cod's Head hd Ireland 61 B6
Cody WY U.S.A. 156 F3
Coeburn VA U.S.A. 164 D5
Coen Australia 136 C2
Coesfeld Germany 63 H3
Coeur d'Alene ID U.S.A. 156 D3
Coeur d'Alene Lake ID U.S.A. 156 D3
Coevorden Neth. 62 G2
Coffee Bay S. Africa 125 I6
Coffee Cultural Landscape of Colombia tourist site Col. 176 C2
Coffeyville KS U.S.A. 161 E4
Coffin Bay Australia 137 A7
Coffin Bay National Park Australia 137 A7
Coffs Harbour Australia 138 F3
Cofimvaba S. Africa 125 H7
Cofradía Hond. 166 [inset] H6
Cofre de Perote, Parque Nacional nat. park Mex. 167 F5
Cognac France 66 D4
Cogo Equat. Guinea 120 D4
Coguno Moz. 125 L3
Cohoes NY U.S.A. 165 I2
Cohuna Australia 138 B5
Coiba, Isla de i. Panama 166 [inset] J8
Coigeach, Rubha pt U.K. 60 D2
Coihaique Chile 178 B7
Coimbatore India 106 C4
Coimbra Port. 67 B3
Coipasa, Salar de salt flat Bol. 176 E7
Coire Switz. see Chur
Colac Australia 138 A7
Colair Lake India see Kolleru Lake
Colatina Brazil 179 C2
Colbitz Germany 63 L2
Colborne Canada 165 G2
Colby KS U.S.A. 160 C4
Colchester U.K. 59 H7
Colchester CT U.S.A. 165 I3
Cold Bay AK U.S.A. 148 G5
Cold Bay AK U.S.A. 148 G5
Coldfoot AK U.S.A. 149 J2
Coldingham U.K. 60 G5
Colditz Germany 63 M3
Cold Lake Canada 151 I4
Cold Lake l. Canada 151 I4
Coldspring TX U.S.A. 161 E6
Coldstream Canada 150 G5
Coldstream U.K. 60 G5
Coldwater Canada 164 F1
Coldwater KS U.S.A. 161 D4
Coldwater MI U.S.A. 164 C3
Coldwater r. MS U.S.A. 161 F5
Coleambally Australia 138 B5
Colebrook NH U.S.A. 165 J1
Coleen r. AK U.S.A. 149 L2
Coleman r. Australia 136 C2
Coleman TX U.S.A. 161 D6
Çölemerik Turkey see Hakkâri
Colenso S. Africa 125 I5
Cole Peninsula Antarctica 188 L2
Coleraine Australia 137 C8
Coleraine U.K. 61 F2
Coles, Punta de pt Peru 176 D7
Coles Bay Australia 137 [inset]
Colesberg S. Africa 125 G6
Coleville Canada 151 I5
Colfax CA U.S.A. 158 C2
Colfax LA U.S.A. 161 E6
Colfax WA U.S.A. 156 D3
Colhué Huapí, Lago l. Arg. 178 C7
Coligny S. Africa 125 H4
Colima Mex. 168 D5
Colima state Mex. 166 E5
Colima, Nevado de vol. Mex. 168 D5
Coll i. U.K. 60 C4
Collado Villalba Spain 67 E3
Collarenebri Australia 138 D2
College AK U.S.A. 149 K2
College Station TX U.S.A. 161 D6
Collerina Australia 138 C2
Collie N.S.W. Australia 138 D3
Collie W.A. Australia 135 B8
Collier Bay Australia 134 D4
Collier Range National Park Australia 135 B6
Collingwood Canada 164 E1
Collingwood N.Z. 139 D5
Collins MS U.S.A. 161 F6
Collins Glacier Antarctica 188 E2
Collinson Peninsula Canada 147 H2
Collipulli Chile 178 B5
Collmberg hill Germany 63 N3
Collooney Ireland 61 D3
Colmar France 66 H2
Colmenar Viejo Spain 67 E3
Colmonell U.K. 60 E5
Colne r. U.K. 59 H7
Cologne Germany 62 G4
Coloma MI U.S.A. 164 B2
Colomb-Béchar Alg. see Béchar
Colômbia Brazil 179 A3
Colombia Mex. 167 F3

▶Colombia country S. America 176 D3
2nd most populous and 4th largest country in South America.

Colombian Basin sea feature S. Atlantic Ocean 184 C5

▶Colombo Sri Lanka 106 C5
Former capital of Sri Lanka.

Colomiers France 66 E5
Colón Buenos Aires Arg. 178 D4
Colón Entre Ríos Arg. 178 E4
Colón Cuba 163 D8
Colón Panama 166 [inset] K7
Colon MI U.S.A. 164 C3
Colón, Archipiélago de is Ecuador see Galapagos Islands
Colón, Isla de i. Panama 166 [inset] J7
Colona Australia 135 F7
Colonelganj India 105 E4
Colonel Hill Bahamas 163 F8
Colonet, Cabo c. Mex. 166 A2
Colônia r. Brazil 179 D1
Colonia Micronesia 81 J5
Colonia Agrippina Germany see Cologne
Colonia Díaz Mex. 166 C2
Colonia Julia Fenestris Italy see Fano
Colonia Las Heras Arg. 178 C7
Colonial Heights VA U.S.A. 165 G5
Colonna, Capo c. Italy 68 G5
Colonsay i. U.K. 60 C4
Colorado r. Arg. 178 D5
Colorado r. Mex./U.S.A. 157 E7
Colorado r. TX U.S.A. 161 D6
Colorado state U.S.A. 156 G5
Colorado City AZ U.S.A. 159 G3
Colorado City TX U.S.A. 161 C5
Colorado Desert CA U.S.A. 158 E5
Colorado National Monument nat. park CO U.S.A. 159 I2
Colorado Plateau CO U.S.A. 159 I3
Colorado River Aqueduct canal CA U.S.A. 159 F4
Colorado Springs CO U.S.A. 156 G5
Colossae Turkey see Honaz
Colotlán Mex. 168 D4
Cölpin Germany 63 N1
Colquiri Bol. 176 E7
Colquitt GA U.S.A. 163 C6
Colson KY U.S.A. 164 D5
Colsterworth U.K. 59 G6
Colstrip MT U.S.A. 156 G3
Coltishall U.K. 59 I6
Colton CA U.S.A. 158 E4
Colton NY U.S.A. 165 H1
Colton UT U.S.A. 159 H2
Columbia KY U.S.A. 164 C5
Columbia LA U.S.A. 161 E5
Columbia MD U.S.A. 165 G4
Columbia MO U.S.A. 160 E4
Columbia MS U.S.A. 161 F6
Columbia NC U.S.A. 162 E5
Columbia PA U.S.A. 165 G3

▶Columbia SC U.S.A. 163 D5
Capital of South Carolina.

Columbia TN U.S.A. 162 C5
Columbia r. WA U.S.A. 156 C3
Columbia, District of admin. dist. U.S.A. 165 G4
Columbia, Mount Canada 150 G4
Columbia, Sierra mts Mex. 166 B2
Columbia City IN U.S.A. 164 C3
Columbia Lake Canada 150 H5
Columbia Mountains Canada 150 F4
Columbia Plateau U.S.A. 156 D3
Columbine, Cape S. Africa 124 C7
Columbus GA U.S.A. 163 C5
Columbus IN U.S.A. 164 C4
Columbus MS U.S.A. 161 F5
Columbus MT U.S.A. 156 F3
Columbus NC U.S.A. 163 D5
Columbus NE U.S.A. 160 D3
Columbus NM U.S.A. 157 G7

▶Columbus OH U.S.A. 164 D4
Capital of Ohio.

Columbus TX U.S.A. 161 D6
Columbus Grove OH U.S.A. 164 C3
Columbus Salt Marsh NV U.S.A. 158 D2
Colusa CA U.S.A. 158 B2
Colville N.Z. 139 E3
Colville WA U.S.A. 156 D2
Colville r. AK U.S.A. 149 J1
Colville Channel N.Z. 139 E3
Colville Lake Canada 149 P2
Colville Lake l. Canada 149 P2
Colwyn Bay U.K. 58 D5
Comacchio Italy 68 E2
Comacchio, Valli di lag. Italy 68 E2
Comai China 99 E7
Comalcalco Mex. 167 G5
Comanche TX U.S.A. 161 D6
Comandante Ferraz research station Antarctica 188 A2
Comandante Salas Arg. 178 C4
Comănești Romania 69 L1
Comayagua Hond. 166 [inset] I6
Combahee r. SC U.S.A. 163 D5
Combarbalá Chile 178 B4
Comber U.K. 61 G3
Combermere Bay Myanmar 86 A3
Combles France 62 C4
Combol i. Indon. 84 C2
Combomune Moz. 125 K2
Comboyne Australia 138 F3
Comencho, Lac l. Canada 152 G4
Comendador Dom. Rep. see Elías Piña
Comendador Gomes Brazil 179 A2
Comeragh Mountains hills Ireland 61 E5
Comercinho Brazil 179 C2
Cometela Moz. 125 L1
Comfort TX U.S.A. 161 D6
Comilla Bangl. 105 G5
Comines Belgium 62 C4
Comino, Capo c. Sardinia Italy 68 C4
Comitán de Domínguez Mex. 167 G5
Commack NY U.S.A. 165 I3
Commentry France 66 F3
Committee Bay Canada 147 J3
Commonwealth Territory admin. div. Australia see Jervis Bay Territory
Como Italy 68 C2
Como, Lago di Italy see Como, Lake
Como, Lake Italy 68 C2
Como Chamling l. China 99 E7
Comodoro Rivadavia Arg. 178 C7
Comonfort Mex. 167 E4
Comores country Africa see Comoros
Comorin, Cape India 106 C4
Comoro Islands country Africa see Comoros
Comoros country Africa 123 E5
Compiègne France 62 C5
Compostela Mex. 166 D4
Compostela Mindanao Phil. 82 D5
Comprida, Ilha i. Brazil 179 B4
Comrat Moldova 69 M1
Comrie U.K. 60 F4
Comstock TX U.S.A. 161 C6
Cơn, Sông r. Vietnam 87 E4
Cona China 99 E8

▶Conakry Guinea 120 B4
Capital of Guinea.

Cona Niyeo Arg. 178 C6
Conceição r. Brazil 179 B2
Conceição da Barra Brazil 179 D2
Conceição do Araguaia Brazil 177 I5
Conceição do Mato Dentro Brazil 179 C2
Concepción Chile 178 B5
Concepción Mex. 161 C7
Concepción r. Mex. 166 B2
Concepción Para. 178 E2
Concepción, Punta pt Mex. 166 C3
Concepción de la Vega Dom. Rep. see La Vega
Conception, Point CA U.S.A. 158 C4
Conception Island Bahamas 163 F8
Concha Mex. 166 D4
Conchas NM U.S.A. 157 G6
Conchas Lake NM U.S.A. 157 G6
Concho Mex. 166 D3
Concho AZ U.S.A. 159 I4
Conchos r. Chihuahua Mex. 166 D2
Conchos r. Nuevo León/Tamaulipas Mex. 167 F3
Concord CA U.S.A. 158 B3
Concord NC U.S.A. 163 D5

▶Concord NH U.S.A. 165 J2
Capital of New Hampshire.

Concord VT U.S.A. 165 J1
Concordia research stn Antarctica 188 G2
Concordia Arg. 178 E4
Concordia Mex. 161 B8
Concordia Peru 176 D4
Concordia S. Africa 124 C5
Concordia KS U.S.A. 160 D4
Concordia KY U.S.A. 164 B4
Concord Peak Afgh. 111 I2
Con Cuông Vietnam 86 D3
Condamine Australia 138 E1
Condamine r. Australia 138 D1
Côn Đao Vietnam 87 D5
Condega Nicaragua 166 [inset] I6
Condeúba Brazil 179 C1
Condobolin Australia 138 C4
Condom France 66 E5
Condon OR U.S.A. 156 C3
Condor, Cordillera del mts Ecuador/Peru 176 C4
Condroz reg. Belgium 62 E4
Conecuh r. AL U.S.A. 163 C6
Conegliano Italy 68 E2
Conejos Mex. 166 E3
Conejos CO U.S.A. 157 G5
Conemaugh r. PA U.S.A. 164 F3
Cone Mountain AK U.S.A. 148 H2
Conestogo Lake Canada 164 E2
Conesus Lake NY U.S.A. 165 G2
Conflict Group is P.N.G. 136 E1
Confoederatio Helvetica country Europe see Switzerland
Confusion Range mts UT U.S.A. 159 G2
Congdü China 99 D7
Conghua China 97 G4
Congjiang China 97 F3
Congleton U.K. 58 E5
Congo country Africa 122 B4

▶Congo r. Congo/Dem. Rep. Congo 122 B4
2nd longest river in Africa and 8th in the world. Formerly known as Zaïre.

▶Congo, Democratic Republic of the country Africa 122 C4
2nd largest and 4th most populous country in Africa.

Congo, Republic of country Africa see Congo
Congo Basin Dem. Rep. Congo 122 C4
Congo (Brazzaville) country Africa see Congo
Congo Cone sea feature S. Atlantic Ocean 184 I6
Congo Free State country Africa see Congo, Democratic Republic of the
Congo (Kinshasa) country Africa see Congo, Democratic Republic of the
Congonhas Brazil 179 C3
Congress AZ U.S.A. 159 G4
Conhuas Mex. 167 H5
Conimbla National Park Australia 138 D4
Coningsby U.K. 59 G5
Coniston Canada 152 E5
Coniston U.K. 58 D4
Conjuboy Australia 136 D3
Conkal Mex. 167 H4
Conklin Canada 151 I4
Conn r. Canada 152 F3
Conn, Lough l. Ireland 61 C3
Connacht reg. Ireland see Connaught
Connaught reg. Ireland 61 C4
Conneaut OH U.S.A. 164 E3
Connecticut state U.S.A. 165 I3
Connemara reg. Ireland 61 C4
Connemara National Park Ireland 61 C4
Connersville IN U.S.A. 164 C4
Connolly, Mount Canada 149 N3
Connors Range hills Australia 136 E4
Conoble Australia 138 B4
Conquista Brazil 179 B2
Conrad MT U.S.A. 156 F2
Conrad Rise sea feature Southern Ocean 185 K9
Conroe TX U.S.A. 161 E6
Conroe, Lake TX U.S.A. 167 G2
Consejo Belize 167 H5
Conselheiro Lafaiete Brazil 179 C3
Consett U.K. 58 F4
Consolación del Sur Cuba 163 D8
Côn Sơn, Đao i. Vietnam 87 D5
Consort Canada 151 I4
Constance Germany see Konstanz
Constance, Lake Germany/Switz. 57 L7
Constância dos Baetas Brazil 176 F5
Constanța Romania 69 M2
Constantia tourist site Cyprus see Salamis
Constantia Germany see Konstanz
Constantina Spain 67 D5
Constantine Alg. 64 F4
Constantine, Cape AK U.S.A. 148 H4
Constantine Harbor AK U.S.A. 148 [inset] B6
Constantinople Turkey see İstanbul
Constitución de 1857, Parque Nacional nat. park Mex. 166 B1
Consul Canada 151 I5
Contact NV U.S.A. 156 E4
Contagalo Brazil 179 C3
Contamana Peru 176 C5
Contas r. Brazil 179 D1
Contoy, Isla i. Mex. 167 I4
Contria Brazil 179 B2
Contwoyto Lake Canada 151 I1
Convención Col. 176 D2
Convent LA U.S.A. 161 F6
Conway U.K. see Conwy
Conway AR U.S.A. 161 E5
Conway ND U.S.A. 160 D1
Conway NH U.S.A. 165 J2
Conway SC U.S.A. 163 E5
Conway, Cape Australia 136 E4
Conway, Lake salt flat Australia 137 A6
Conway National Park Australia 136 E4
Conway Reef Fiji see Ceva-i-Ra
Conwy U.K. 58 D5
Conwy r. U.K. 59 D5
Coober Pedy Australia 135 F7
Coochbehar India see Koch Bihar
Cooch Behar India see Koch Bihar
Cook Australia 135 E7
Cook, Cape Canada 150 E5
Cook, Grand Récif de reef New Caledonia 133 G3
Cook, Mount Canada/U.S.A. 149 M3
Cook, Mount N.Z. see Aoraki
Cookes Peak NM U.S.A. 157 G6
Cookeville TN U.S.A. 162 C4
Cookhouse S. Africa 125 G7
Cook Ice Shelf Antarctica 188 H2
Cook Inlet sea channel AK U.S.A. 148 I3

▶Cook Islands terr. S. Pacific Ocean 186 J7
Self-governing New Zealand territory.

Cooksburg NY U.S.A. 165 H2
Cooks Passage Australia 136 D2
Cookstown U.K. 61 F3
Cook Strait N.Z. 139 E5
Cooktown Australia 136 D2
Coolabah Australia 138 C3
Cooladdi Australia 138 B1
Coolah Australia 138 D3
Coolamon Australia 138 C5
Coolgardie Australia 135 C7
Coolibah Australia 134 E3
Coolidge AZ U.S.A. 159 H5
Cooloola National Park Australia 137 F5
Coolum Beach Australia 137 F5
Cooma Australia 138 D6
Coombah Australia 137 C7
Coonabarabran Australia 138 D3
Coonamble Australia 138 D3
Coondambo Australia 137 A6
Coondapoor India see Kundapura
Coongoola Australia 138 B1
Coon Rapids MN U.S.A. 160 E2
Cooper Creek watercourse Australia 137 B6
Cooper Mountain Canada 150 G5
Coopernook Australia 138 F3
Cooper's Town Bahamas 163 E7
Cooperstown ND U.S.A. 160 D2
Cooperstown NY U.S.A. 165 H2
Coopracambra National Park Australia 138 D6
Coorabie Australia 135 F7
Coorong National Park Australia 137 B8
Coorow Australia 135 B7
Coosa r. AL U.S.A. 163 C5
Coos Bay OR U.S.A. 156 B4
Coos Bay b. OR U.S.A. 156 B4
Cootamundra Australia 138 D5
Cootehill Ireland 61 E3
Cooyar Australia 138 E1
Copainalá Mex. 167 G5
Copala Mex. 168 E5
Copán tourist site Hond. 166 [inset] H6
Cope CO U.S.A. 160 C4
Copemish MI U.S.A. 164 C1

▶Copenhagen Denmark 55 H9
Capital of Denmark.

Copenhagen NY U.S.A. 165 H2
Copertino Italy 68 H4
Copeton Reservoir Australia 138 E2
Cô Pi, Phou mt. Laos/Vietnam 86 D3
Copiapó Chile 178 B3
Copley Australia 137 B6
Copparo Italy 68 D2
Copper r. AK U.S.A. 149 K3
Copper Cliff Canada 152 E5
Copper Harbor MI U.S.A. 162 C2
Coppermine Canada see Kugluktuk
Coppermine r. Canada 150 H1
Coppermine Point Canada 152 D5
Copperton S. Africa 124 F5
Copp Lake Canada 150 H2
Coqên Xizang China 99 D7
Coqên Xizang China 99 D7
Coquilhatville Dem. Rep. Congo see Mbandaka
Coquille i. Micronesia see Pikelot
Coquille OR U.S.A. 156 B4
Coquimbo Chile 178 B3
Coquitlam Canada 150 F5
Corabia Romania 69 K3
Coração de Jesus Brazil 179 B2
Coracesium Turkey see Alanya
Coraki Australia 138 F2
Coral Bay Australia 135 A5
Coral Bay Palawan Phil. 82 B4
Coral Harbour Canada 147 J3
Coral Sea S. Pacific Ocean 132 F3
Coral Sea Basin S. Pacific Ocean 186 G6

▶Coral Sea Islands Territory terr. Australia 132 F3
Australian External Territory.

Corangamite, Lake Australia 138 A7
Corat Azer. 113 H2
Corbeny France 62 D5
Corbett Inlet Canada 151 M2
Corbett National Park India 104 D3
Corbie France 62 C5
Corbin KY U.S.A. 164 C5
Corby U.K. 59 G6
Corcaigh Ireland see Cork
Corcoran CA U.S.A. 158 D3
Corcovado, Golfo de sea chan. Chile 178 B6
Corcovado, Parque Nacional nat. park Costa Rica 166 [inset] J7
Corcyra i. Greece see Corfu
Cordele GA U.S.A. 163 D6
Cordelia CA U.S.A. 158 B2
Cordell OK U.S.A. 161 D5
Cordilheiras, Serra das hills Brazil 177 I5
Cordillera Azul, Parque Nacional nat. park Peru 176 C5
Cordillera de los Picachos, Parque Nacional nat. park Col. 176 D3
Cordilleras Range mts Panay Phil. 82 C4
Cordillo Downs Australia 137 C5
Cordisburgo Brazil 179 B2
Córdoba Arg. 178 D4
Córdoba Durango Mex. 166 E3
Córdoba Veracruz Mex. 168 E5
Córdoba Spain 67 D5
Córdoba, Sierras de mts Arg. 178 D4
Cordova Spain see Córdoba
Cordova AK U.S.A. 149 K3
Cordova Peak AK U.S.A. 149 K3
Corduba Spain see Córdoba
Corfu i. Greece 69 H5
Coria Spain 67 C4
Coribe Brazil 179 B1
Coricudgy mt. Australia 138 E4
Corigliano Calabro Italy 68 G5
Coringa Islands Australia 136 E3
Corinium U.K. see Cirencester
Corinth Greece 69 J6
Corinth KY U.S.A. 164 C4
Corinth MS U.S.A. 161 F5
Corinth NY U.S.A. 165 I2
Corinth, Gulf of sea chan. Greece 69 J5
Corinthus Greece see Corinth
Corinto Brazil 179 B2
Corinto Nicaragua 166 [inset] I6
Cork Ireland 61 D6
Corleone Sicily Italy 68 E6
Çorlu Turkey 69 L4
Cormeilles France 59 H9
Cormoran Reef Palau 82 [inset]
Cornelia S. Africa 125 I4
Cornélio Procópio Brazil 179 A3
Cornélios Brazil 179 A5
Cornell WI U.S.A. 160 F2
Corner Brook Canada 153 K4
Corner Inlet b. Australia 138 C7
Corner Seamounts sea feature N. Atlantic Ocean 184 E3
Corneto Italy see Tarquinia
Cornillet, Mont hill France 62 E5
Corning AR U.S.A. 161 F4
Corning CA U.S.A. 158 B2
Corning NY U.S.A. 165 G2
Cornish watercourse Australia 136 D4
Corn Islands is Nicaragua see Maíz, Islas del
Corno di Campo mt. Italy/Switz. 66 J3
Corno Grande mt. Italy 68 E3
Cornwall Canada 165 H1
Cornwallis Island Canada 147 I2
Cornwall Island Canada 147 I2
Coro Venez. 176 E1
Coroaci Brazil 179 C2
Coroatá Brazil 177 J4
Corofin Ireland 61 C5
Coromandel Brazil 179 B2
Coromandel Coast India 106 D4
Coromandel Peninsula N.Z. 139 E3
Coromandel Range hills N.Z. 139 E3
Coron Phil. 82 C3
Corona CA U.S.A. 158 E5
Corona NM U.S.A. 157 G6
Coronado CA U.S.A. 158 E5
Coronado, Bahía de b. Costa Rica 166 [inset] J7
Coronado Bay Mindanao Phil. 82 C5
Coronation Canada 151 I4
Coronation Gulf Canada 146 G3
Coronation Island S. Atlantic Ocean 188 A2
Coronation Island AK U.S.A. 149 N5
Coron Bay Phil. 82 C4
Coronda Arg. 178 D4
Coronel Fabriciano Brazil 179 C2
Coronel Oviedo Para. 178 E3
Coronel Pringles Arg. 178 D5
Coronel Suárez Arg. 178 D5
Çorovodë Albania 69 I4
Corowa Australia 138 C5
Corozal Belize 167 H5
Corpus Christi TX U.S.A. 161 D7
Corpus Christi, Lake TX U.S.A. 167 F2
Corque Bol. 176 E7
Corral de Cantos mt. Spain 67 D4
Corrales Mex. 161 B7
Corralilla Cuba 163 D8
Corrandibby Range hills Australia 135 A6
Corrente Brazil 177 I6
Corrente r. Bahia Brazil 179 C1
Corrente r. Minas Gerais Brazil 179 A2
Correntes Brazil 177 H7
Correntina Brazil 179 B1
Correntina r. Brazil see Éguas
Corrib, Lough l. Ireland 61 C4
Corrientes Arg. 178 E3
Corrientes, Cabo c. Col. 176 C2
Corrientes, Cabo c. Cuba 163 C8
Corrientes, Cabo c. Mex. 168 C4
Corrigan TX U.S.A. 167 G2
Corrigin Australia 135 B8
Corris U.K. 59 D6
Corry PA U.S.A. 164 F3
Corse i. France see Corsica
Corse, Cap c. Corsica France 66 I5
Corsham U.K. 59 E7
Corsica i. France 66 I5
Corsicana TX U.S.A. 161 D5
Corte Corsica France 66 I5
Cortegana Spain 67 C5
Cortes, Sea of g. Mex. see California, Golfo de
Cortez CO U.S.A. 159 I3
Cortina d'Ampezzo Italy 68 E1
Cortland NY U.S.A. 165 G2
Corton U.K. 59 I6
Cortona Italy 68 D3
Coruche Port. 67 B4
Çoruh Turkey see Artvin
Çoruh r. Turkey 113 F2
Çorum Turkey 112 D2
Corumbá Brazil 177 G7
Corumbá r. Brazil 179 A2
Corumbá de Goiás Brazil 179 A1
Corumbaíba Brazil 179 A2
Corumbaú, Ponta pt Brazil 179 D2
Corunna Spain see A Coruña
Corunna MI U.S.A. 164 C2
Corvallis OR U.S.A. 156 C3
Corwen U.K. 59 D6
Corydon IA U.S.A. 160 E3
Corydon IN U.S.A. 164 B4
Coryville PA U.S.A. 165 F3
Cos i. Greece see Kos
Cosalá Mex. 166 D3
Cosamaloapan Mex. 167 G5
Cosentia Italy see Cosenza
Cosenza Italy 68 G5
Coshocton OH U.S.A. 164 E3
Cosne-Cours-sur-Loire France 66 F3
Costa Blanca coastal area Spain 67 F4
Costa Brava coastal area Spain 67 H3
Costa de la Luz coastal area Spain 67 C5
Costa del Sol coastal area Spain 67 D5
Costa de Mosquitos coastal area Nicaragua 166 [inset] J6
Costa Marques Brazil 176 F6
Costa Rica Brazil 177 H7
Costa Rica country Central America 169 H6
Costa Rica Mex. 166 D3
Costa Verde coastal area Spain 67 C2
Costermansville Dem. Rep. Congo see Bukavu
Costești Romania 69 K2

Costigan Lake Canada 151 J3
Coswig Germany 63 M3
Cotabato Mindanao Phil. 82 D5
Cotagaita Bol. 176 E8
Cotahuasi Peru 176 D7
Cote, Mount AK U.S.A. 149 O4
Coteau des Prairies slope SD U.S.A. 160 D2
Coteau du Missouri slope ND U.S.A. 160 C1
Coteau du Missouri slope SD U.S.A. 160 C2
Côte d'Azur coastal area France 66 H5
Côte d'Ivoire country Africa 120 C4
Côte Française de Somalis country Africa see Djibouti
Cotentin pen. France 59 F9
Côtes de Meuse ridge France 62 E5
Cothi r. U.K. 59 C7
Cotiaeum Turkey see Kütahya
Cotiella mt. Spain 67 G2
Cotonou Benin 120 D4
Cotopaxi, Volcán vol. Ecuador 176 C4
Cotswold Hills U.K. 59 E7
Cottage Grove OR U.S.A. 156 C4
Cottbus Germany 57 O5
Cottenham U.K. 59 H6
Cottian Alps mts France/Italy 66 H4
Cottica Suriname 177 H3
Cottiennes, Alpes mts France/Italy see Cottian Alps
Cottonwood AZ U.S.A. 159 G4
Cottonwood CA U.S.A. 158 B1
Cottonwood r. KS U.S.A. 160 D4
Cottonwood Falls KS U.S.A. 160 D4
Cotulla TX U.S.A. 161 D6
Coudersport PA U.S.A. 165 F3
Couedic, Cape du Australia 137 B8
Coulee City WA U.S.A. 156 D3
Coulee Dam WA U.S.A. 156 D3
Coulman Island Antarctica 188 H2
Coulogne France 62 B4
Coulommiers France 62 D6
Coulonge r. Canada 152 F5
Coulterville CA U.S.A. 158 C3
Council AK U.S.A. 148 G2
Council ID U.S.A. 156 D3
Council Bluffs IA U.S.A. 160 E3
Council Grove KS U.S.A. 160 D4
Councillor Island Australia 137 [inset]
Counselor NM U.S.A. 159 J3
Coupeville WA U.S.A. 156 C2
Courageous Lake Canada 151 I1
Courland Lagoon b. Lith./Rus. Fed. 55 L9
Courtenay Canada 150 E5
Courtland VA U.S.A. 165 G5
Courtmacsherry Ireland 61 D6
Courtmacsherry Bay Ireland 61 D6
Courtown Ireland 61 F5
Courtrai Belgium see Kortrijk
Coushatta LA U.S.A. 161 E5
Coutances France 66 D2
Coutts Canada 151 I5
Couture, Lac l. Canada 152 G2
Couvin Belgium 62 E4
Cove Fort UT U.S.A. 159 G2
Cove Island Canada 164 E1
Cove Mountains hills PA U.S.A. 165 F4
Coventry U.K. 59 F6
Covered Wells AZ U.S.A. 159 G5
Covesville VA U.S.A. 165 F5
Covilhã Port. 67 C3
Coville, Lake AK U.S.A. 148 I4
Covington GA U.S.A. 163 D5
Covington IN U.S.A. 164 B3
Covington KY U.S.A. 164 C4
Covington LA U.S.A. 161 F6
Covington MI U.S.A. 160 F2
Covington TN U.S.A. 161 F5
Covington VA U.S.A. 164 E5
Cowal, Lake dry lake Australia 138 C4
Cowan, Lake salt flat Australia 135 C7
Cowansville Canada 165 I1
Cowargarzê China 96 C1
Cowcowing Lakes salt flat Australia 135 B7
Cowdenbeath U.K. 60 F4
Cowell Australia 137 B7
Cowes U.K. 59 F8
Cowichan Lake Canada 150 E5
Cowley Australia 138 B1
Cowper Point Canada 147 G2
Cowra Australia 138 D4
Cox r. Australia 136 A2
Coxá r. Brazil 179 B1
Coxen Hole Hond. see Roatán
Coxilha de Santana hills Brazil/Uruguay 178 E4
Coxilha Grande hills Brazil 178 F3
Coxim Brazil 177 H7
Cox's Bazar Bangl. 105 G5
Coyame Mex. 161 B6
Coyhaique Chile see Coihaique
Coyote, Punta pt Mex. 166 C3
Coyote Lake CA U.S.A. 158 E4
Coyote Peak hill AZ U.S.A. 159 F5
Coyotitán Mex. 166 D4
Coyuca de Benítez Mex. 167 E5
Cozhê China 105 F2
Cozie, Alpi mts France/Italy see Cottian Alps
Cozumel Mex. 167 I4
Cozumel, Isla de i. Mex. 167 I4
Craboon Australia 138 D4
Cracovia Poland see Kraków
Cracow Australia 136 E5
Cracow Poland see Kraków
Cradle Mountain Lake St Clair National Park Australia 137 [inset]
Cradock S. Africa 125 G7
Craig U.K. 60 D3
Craig AK U.S.A. 149 N5
Craig CO U.S.A. 159 J1
Craigavon U.K. 61 F3
Craigieburn Australia 138 B6
Craig Island Taiwan see Mienhua Yü
Craignure U.K. 60 D4
Craigsville WV U.S.A. 164 E4
Crail U.K. 60 G4
Crailsheim Germany 63 K5
Craiova Romania 69 J2
Cramlington U.K. 58 F3
Cranberry Junction Canada 149 O5
Cranberry Lake NY U.S.A. 165 H1
Cranberry Portage Canada 151 K4
Cranborne Chase for. U.K. 59 E8
Cranbourne Australia 138 B7
Cranbrook Canada 150 H5
Crandon WI U.S.A. 160 F2
Crane TX U.S.A. 166 E2
Crane Lake Canada 151 I5
Cranston KY U.S.A. 164 D4
Cranston RI U.S.A. 165 J3
Cranz Rus. Fed. see Zelenogradsk
Crary Ice Rise Antarctica 188 I1
Crary Mountains Antarctica 188 J1
Crater Lake National Park OR U.S.A. 156 C4
Crater Peak CA U.S.A. 158 C1
Craters of the Moon National Monument nat. park ID U.S.A. 156 E4
Crateús Brazil 177 J5
Crato Brazil 177 K5
Crawford CO U.S.A. 159 J2
Crawford NE U.S.A. 160 C3
Crawford Point Palawan Phil. 82 B4
Crawfordsville IN U.S.A. 164 B3
Crawfordville FL U.S.A. 163 C6
Crawfordville GA U.S.A. 163 D5
Crawley U.K. 59 G7
Crazy Mountains AK U.S.A. 149 K2
Crazy Mountains MT U.S.A. 156 F3
Creag Meagaidh mt. U.K. 60 E4
Crécy-en-Ponthieu France 62 B4
Credenhill U.K. 59 E6
Crediton U.K. 59 D8
Cree r. Canada 151 J3
Creel Mex. 157 G8
Cree Lake Canada 151 J3
Creemore Canada 164 E1
Creighton Canada 151 K4
Creil France 62 C5
Creil Neth. 62 F2
Crema Italy 68 C2
Cremlingen Germany 63 K2
Cremona Canada 150 H5
Cremona Italy 68 D2
Crépy-en-Valois France 62 C5
Cres i. Croatia 68 F2
Crescent OR U.S.A. 156 C4
Crescent City CA U.S.A. 156 B4
Crescent City FL U.S.A. 163 D6
Crescent Group is Paracel Is 80 E3
Crescent Head Australia 138 F3
Crescent Junction UT U.S.A. 159 I2
Crescent Valley NV U.S.A. 158 E1
Cressy Australia 138 A7
Cresta, Mount Phil. 82 C2
Crest Hill hill H.K. China 97 [inset]
Crestline OH U.S.A. 164 D3
Creston Canada 150 G5
Creston IA U.S.A. 160 E3
Creston WY U.S.A. 156 G4
Crestview FL U.S.A. 163 C6
Creswick Australia 138 A6
Creta i. Greece see Crete
Crete i. Greece 69 K7
Crete NE U.S.A. 160 D3
Creus, Cabo de c. Spain 67 H2
Creuse r. France 66 E3
Creußen Germany 63 L5
Creutzwald France 62 G5
Creuzburg Germany 63 K3
Crevasse Valley Glacier Antarctica 188 J1
Crewe U.K. 59 E5
Crewe VA U.S.A. 165 F5
Crewkerne U.K. 59 E8
Crianlarich U.K. 60 E4
Criccieth U.K. 59 C6
Criciúma Brazil 179 A5
Crieff U.K. 60 F4
Criffel hill U.K. 60 F6
Criffell hill U.K. see Criffel
Crikvenica Croatia 68 F2
Crillon, Mount AK U.S.A. 149 M4
Crimea pen. Ukr. 112 D1
Crimmitschau Germany 63 M4
Crimond U.K. 60 H3
Cripple Landing AK U.S.A. 148 H3
Crisfield MD U.S.A. 165 H5
Cristalândia Brazil 177 I6
Cristalina Brazil 179 B2
Cristalino r. Brazil see Mariembero
Cristóbal Colón, Pico mt. Col. 176 D1
Crixás Brazil 179 A1
Crixás Açu r. Brazil 179 A1
Crixás Mirim r. Brazil 179 A1
Crna Gora country Europe see Montenegro
Crni Vrh mt. Serbia 69 J2
Črnomelj Slovenia 68 F2
Croagh Patrick hill Ireland 61 C4
Croajingolong National Park Australia 138 D6
Croatia country Europe 68 G2
Crocker, Banjaran mts Malaysia 85 F1
Crocker Range National Park Malaysia 85 G1
Crockett TX U.S.A. 161 E6
Crofton KY U.S.A. 164 B5
Crofton NE U.S.A. 160 D3
Croghan NY U.S.A. 165 H2
Croisilles France 62 C4
Croker r. Canada 149 R1
Croker, Cape Canada 164 E1
Croker Island Australia 134 F2
Cromarty U.K. 60 E3
Cromarty Firth est. U.K. 60 E3
Cromer U.K. 59 I6
Cromwell N.Z. 139 B7
Crook U.K. 58 F4
Crooked Creek AK U.S.A. 148 H3
Crooked Creek AK U.S.A. 149 L2
Crooked Harbour b. H.K. China 97 [inset]
Crooked Island Bahamas 163 F8
Crooked Island H.K. China 97 [inset]
Crooked Island Passage Bahamas 163 F8
Crookston MN U.S.A. 160 D2
Crooksville OH U.S.A. 164 D4
Crookwell Australia 138 D5
Croom Ireland 61 D5
Croppa Creek Australia 138 E2
Crosby U.K. 58 D5
Crosby MN U.S.A. 160 E2
Crosby ND U.S.A. 160 C1
Crosbyton TX U.S.A. 161 C5
Cross Bay Canada 151 M2
Cross City FL U.S.A. 163 D6
Cross Fell hill U.K. 58 E4
Crossfield Canada 150 H5
Crossgar U.K. 61 G3
Crosshaven Ireland 61 D6
Cross Inn U.K. 59 C6
Cross Lake Canada 151 L4
Cross Lake l. Canada 151 L4
Cross Lake l. NY U.S.A. 165 G2
Crossley Lakes Canada 149 O1
Crossmaglen U.K. 61 F3
Crossman Peak AZ U.S.A. 159 F4
Cross Sound sea channel AK U.S.A. 149 M4
Crossville TN U.S.A. 162 C5
Crotch Lake Canada 165 G1
Croton Italy see Crotone
Crotone Italy 68 G5
Crouch r. U.K. 59 H7
Crow r. Canada 150 E3
Crow Agency MT U.S.A. 156 G3
Crowal watercourse Australia 138 C3
Crowborough U.K. 59 H7
Crowdy Bay National Park Australia 138 F3
Crowell TX U.S.A. 161 D5
Crowland U.K. 59 G6
Crowley LA U.S.A. 161 E6
Crowley, Lake CA U.S.A. 158 D3
Crown Point IN U.S.A. 164 B3
Crownpoint NM U.S.A. 159 I4
Crown Point NY U.S.A. 165 I2
Crown Prince Olav Coast Antarctica 188 D2
Crown Princess Martha Coast Antarctica 188 B1
Crows Nest Australia 138 F1
Crowsnest Pass Canada 150 H5
Crowsnest Pass pass Canada 150 H5
Crow Wing r. MN U.S.A. 160 E2
Croydon Australia 136 C3
Crozet VA U.S.A. 165 F4
Crozet, Îles is Indian Ocean 185 L9
Crozet Basin sea feature Indian Ocean 185 M8
Crozet Plateau sea feature Indian Ocean 185 K8
Crozon France 66 B2
Cruces Cuba 163 D8
Cruden Bay U.K. 60 H3
Cruillas Mex. 161 D7
Crum WV U.S.A. 164 D5
Crumlin U.K. 61 F3
Crusheen Ireland 61 D5
Cruz Alta Brazil 178 F3
Cruz del Eje Arg. 178 D4
Cruzeiro Brazil 179 B3
Cruzeiro do Sul Brazil 176 D5
Cruz Grande Mex. 167 F5
Cry Lake Canada 149 O4
Crysdale, Mount Canada 150 F4
Crystal NM U.S.A. 159 I3
Crystal City Canada 151 L5
Crystal City TX U.S.A. 161 D6
Crystal Falls MI U.S.A. 160 F2
Crystal Lake IL U.S.A. 164 A2
Crystal River FL U.S.A. 163 D6
Csongrád Hungary 69 I1
Cửa Lớn, Sông r. Vietnam 87 D5
Cuamba Moz. 123 D5
Cuando r. Angola/Zambia 123 C5
Cuangar Angola 123 B5
Cuango Angola 123 B4
Cuanza r. Angola 123 B4
Cuatro Ciénegas Mex. 166 E3
Cuauhtémoc Mex. 166 D2
Cuautla Mex. 167 F5
Cuba NM U.S.A. 157 G5
Cuba NY U.S.A. 165 F2

▶Cuba country West Indies 169 H4
5th largest island and 5th most populous country in North America.

Cubal Angola 123 B5
Cubango r. Angola/Namibia 123 C5
Cubatão Brazil 179 B3
Cub Hills Canada 151 J4
Çubuk Turkey 112 D2
Cubulco Guat. 167 H6
Cucapa, Sierra mts Mex. 159 F5
Cuchi Angola 123 B5
Cuchilla Grande hills Uruguay 178 E4
Cucuí Brazil 176 E3
Cucurpe Mex. 166 C2
Cúcuta Col. 176 D2
Cudal Australia 138 D4
Cuddalore India 106 C4
Cuddapah India 106 C3
Cuddeback Lake CA U.S.A. 158 E4
Cue Australia 135 B6
Cuéllar Spain 67 D3
Cuemba Angola 123 B5
Cuenca Ecuador 176 C4
Cuenca Luzon Phil. 82 C3
Cuenca Spain 67 E3
Cuenca, Serranía de mts Spain 67 E3
Cuencamé Mex. 166 E3
Cuernavaca Mex. 168 E5
Cuero TX U.S.A. 161 D6
Cuervos Mex. 159 F5
Cugir Romania 69 J2
Cuiabá Amazonas Brazil 177 G5
Cuiabá Mato Grosso Brazil 177 G7
Cuiabá r. Brazil 177 G7
Cuicatlan Mex. 167 F5
Cuihua China see Daguan
Cuijiang China see Ninghua
Cuijk Neth. 62 F3
Cuilapa Guat. 167 H6
Cuilcagh hill Ireland/U.K. 61 E3
Cuillin Hills U.K. 60 C3
Cuillin Sound sea chan. U.K. 60 C3
Cuilo Angola 123 B4
Cuiluan China 90 C3
Cuité r. Brazil 179 C2
Cuitláhuac Mex. 167 F5
Cuito r. Angola 123 C5
Cuito Cuanavale Angola 123 B5
Cuitzeo, Laguna de l. Mex. 167 E5
Cujangan i. Phil. 82 C5
Cukai Malaysia 84 C1
Çukurca Turkey 110 A2
Çukurova plat. Turkey 107 B1
Culai Shan mt. China 95 I4
Cu Lao Cham i. Vietnam 86 E4
Cu Lao Xanh i. Vietnam 87 E4
Culasi Panay Phil. 82 C4
Culcairn Australia 138 C5
Culfa Azer. 113 G3
Culgoa r. Australia 138 C2
Culiacán Mex. 166 D3
Culion Phil. 82 B4
Culion i. Phil. 82 B4
Cullen U.K. 60 G3
Cullen Point Australia 136 C1
Cullera Spain 67 F4
Cullivoe U.K. 60 [inset]
Cullman AL U.S.A. 163 C5
Cullybackey U.K. 61 F3
Cul Mòr hill U.K. 60 D2
Culpeper VA U.S.A. 165 G4
Culuene r. Brazil 177 H6
Culver, Point Australia 135 D8
Culverden N.Z. 139 D6
Cumaná Venez. 176 F1
Cumari Brazil 179 A2
Cumbal, Nevado de vol. Col. 176 C3
Cumberland KY U.S.A. 164 D5
Cumberland MD U.S.A. 165 F4
Cumberland VA U.S.A. 165 F5
Cumberland r. KY U.S.A. 162 C4
Cumberland, Lake KY U.S.A. 164 C5
Cumberland Lake Canada 151 K4
Cumberland Mountains KY/TN U.S.A. 164 D5
Cumberland Peninsula Canada 147 L3
Cumberland Plateau KY/TN U.S.A. 162 C5
Cumberland Point MI U.S.A. 160 F2
Cumberland Sound sea chan. Canada 147 L3
Cumbernauld U.K. 60 F5
Cumbres de Majalca, Parque Nacional nat. park Mex. 166 D2
Cumbres de Monterey, Parque Nacional nat. park Mex. 167 E3
Cumbum India 106 C3
Cumlosen Germany 63 L1
Cummings CA U.S.A. 158 B2
Cummins Australia 137 A7
Cummins Range hills Australia 134 D4
Cumnock Australia 138 D4
Cumnock U.K. 60 E5
Cumpas Mex. 166 C2
Çumra Turkey 112 D3
Cumuripa Mex. 166 C2
Cumuruxatiba Brazil 179 D2
Cunagua Cuba see Bolivia
Cunderdin Australia 135 B7
Cunén Guat. 167 H6
Cunene r. Angola 123 B5
also known as Kunene
Cuneo Italy 68 B2
Cung Sơn Vietnam 87 E4
Cunnamulla Australia 138 B2
Cunningsburgh U.K. 60 [inset]
Cupar U.K. 60 F4
Cupica, Golfo de b. Col. 176 C2
Cupula, Pico mt. Mex. 166 C3
Curaçá Brazil 177 K5
Curaçá r. Brazil 176 D4

▶Curaçao terr. West Indies 169 K6
Self-governing Netherlands territory.

Curaray r. Ecuador 176 D4
Curdlawidny Lagoon salt flat Australia 137 B6
Curia Switz. see Chur
Curicó Chile 178 B4
Curitiba Brazil 179 A4
Curitibanos Brazil 179 A4
Curlewis Australia 138 E3
Curlew Lake AK U.S.A. 148 G3
Curnamona Australia 137 B6
Currabubula Australia 138 E3
Currais Novos Brazil 177 K5
Curran MI U.S.A. 164 D1
Currane, Lough l. Ireland 61 B6
Currant NV U.S.A. 159 F2
Curranyalpa Australia 138 B3
Currawilla Australia 136 C5
Currawinya National Park Australia 138 B2
Currie Australia 132 E5
Currie NV U.S.A. 159 F1
Currituck NC U.S.A. 165 G5
Currockbilly, Mount Australia 138 E5
Curry AK U.S.A. 149 J3
Curtis Channel Australia 136 F5
Curtis Island Australia 136 E4
Curtis Island N.Z. 133 I5
Curuá r. Brazil 177 H5
Curup Sumatera Indon. 84 C3
Curupira, Serra mts Brazil/Venez. 176 F3
Cururupu Brazil 177 J4
Curvelo Brazil 179 B2
Curwood, Mount hill MI U.S.A. 160 F2
Cusco Peru 176 D6
Cushendall U.K. 61 F2
Cushendun U.K. 61 F2
Cushing OK U.S.A. 161 D4
Cusseta GA U.S.A. 163 C5
Custer MT U.S.A. 156 G3
Custer SD U.S.A. 160 C3
Cut Bank MT U.S.A. 156 E2
Cuthbert GA U.S.A. 163 C6
Cuthbertson Falls Australia 134 F3
Cut Knife Canada 151 I4
Cutler Ridge FL U.S.A. 163 D7
Cut Off LA U.S.A. 167 H2
Cuttaburra Creek r. Australia 138 B2
Cuttack India 106 E1
Cuvelai Angola 123 B5
Cuxhaven Germany 57 L4
Cuya Chile 176 D7
Cuyahoga Falls OH U.S.A. 164 E3
Cuyama CA U.S.A. 158 D4
Cuyama r. CA U.S.A. 158 C4
Cuyapo Luzon Phil. 82 C3
Cuyo Phil. 82 C4
Cuyo i. Phil. 82 C4
Cuyo East Passage Phil. 82 C4
Cuyo Islands Phil. 82 C4
Cuyo West Passage Phil. 82 C4
Cuyuni r. Guyana 177 G2
Cuyutingni Nicaragua see Kuyu Tingni
Cuzco Peru see Cusco
Cwmbrân U.K. 59 D7
Cyangugu Rwanda 122 C4
Cyclades is Greece 69 K6
Cydonia Greece see Chania
Cygnet OH U.S.A. 164 D3
Cymru admin. div. U.K. see Wales
Cynthiana KY U.S.A. 164 C4
Cypress Hills Canada 151 I5
Cyprus country Asia 107 A2
Cyrenaica reg. Libya 121 F2
Cythera i. Greece see Kythira
Czar Canada 151 I4
Czechia country Europe see Czech Republic

▶Czechoslovakia
Divided in 1993 into the Czech Republic and Slovakia.

Czech Republic country Europe 57 O6
Czernowitz Ukr. see Chernivtsi
Czersk Poland 57 P4
Częstochowa Poland 57 Q5

D

Đa, Sông r. Vietnam see Black
Da'an China 95 K2
Daanbantayan Phil. 82 C4
Daba China 99 B7
Ḑabāb, Jabal aḑ mt. Jordan 107 B4
Dabakala Côte d'Ivoire 120 C4
Daban China 95 I3
Daban Shan mts China 94 E4
Dabao China 96 D2
Daba Shan mts China 97 F1
Dabba China see Daocheng
Dabein Myanmar 86 B3
Dabhoi India 104 C5
Ḑab'ī, Wādī aḑ watercourse Jordan 107 C4
Dabiegai China 94 C4
Dabie Shan mts China 97 G2
Dablana India 104 C4
Dabola Guinea 120 B3
Dabqig China 95 G4
Dąbrowa Górnicza Poland 57 Q5
Dabsan China 94 C4
Dabs Nur l. China 90 A3
Dabu Guangdong China 97 H3
Dabu Guangxi China see Liucheng
Dabusu Pao l. China see Dabs Nur
Dacca Bangl. see Dhaka
Dachau Germany 57 M6
Dachechang China 94 E4
Dachengzi China 95 I3
Dachuan China see Dazhou
Dacre Canada 165 G1
Dadal Mongolia 95 G1
Daday Turkey 112 D2
Dade City FL U.S.A. 163 D6
Dadeville AL U.S.A. 163 C5
Dādkān Iran 111 F5
Dadong China see Donggang
Dadra India see Achalpur
Dadu Pak. 111 G5
Daegu S. Korea see Taegu
Daejŏn S. Korea see Taejŏn
Daet Luzon Phil. 82 C3
Dafang China 96 E3
Dafeng China 97 I1
Dafla Hills India 105 H4
Dafoe Canada 151 J5
Dafoe r. Canada 151 M4
Dagana Senegal 120 B3
Dagasuli i. Maluku Indon. 83 C2
Dagcagoin China see Zoigê
Dagcanglhamo China 94 E5
Dage China see Fengning
Dagezhen China see Fengning
Daghmar Oman 110 E6
Dağlıq Qarabağ terr. Azer. see Nagorno-Karabakh
Daglung China 99 E7
Dagma China 99 F7
Dagö i. Estonia see Hiiumaa
Dagon Myanmar see Rangoon
Dagrag Zangbo r. China 99 D7
Dagu China 95 I4
Daguan China 96 D3
Daguokui Shan hill China 90 C3
Dagupan Luzon Phil. 82 C2
Dagur China 94 C4
Dagxoi Sichuan China see Yidun
Dagxoi Sichuan China see Sowa
Dagzê China 99 E7
Dagzê Co salt l. China 99 D7
Dagzhuka China 99 E7
Dahadinni r. Canada 149 P3
Dahalach, Isole is Eritrea see Dahlak Archipelago
Dahana des. Saudi Arabia see Ad Dahnā'
Dahe China see Ziyuan
Daheba China 94 D5
Daheiding Shan mt. China 90 C3
Dahei Shan mt. China 94 C3
Dahei Shan mts China 90 B4
Dahej India 104 C5
Daheyan China see Turpan Zhan
Da Hinggan Ling mts China 95 I3
Dahlak Archipelago is Eritrea 108 F6
Dahlak Marine National Park Eritrea 108 F6
Daḩl al Furayy well Saudi Arabia 110 B5
Dahlem Germany 62 G4
Dahlenburg Germany 63 K1
Dahm, Ramlat des. Saudi Arabia/Yemen 108 G6
Dahmani Tunisia 68 C7
Dahme Germany 63 N3
Dahn Germany 63 H5
Dahnā' plain Saudi Arabia 110 B5
Dahod India 104 C5
Dahomey country Africa see Benin
Dahongliutan Aksai Chin 99 B6
Dahra Senegal see Dara
Dähre Germany 63 K2
Dahūk Iraq 113 F3
Dai i. Maluku Indon. 83 D4
Daibosatsu-rei mt. Japan 93 E3
Daicheng China 95 I4
Daigo Japan 93 G2
Daik Indon. 84 D3
Daik-U Myanmar 86 B3
Đai Lanh, Mui pt Vietnam 87 E4
Dailekh Nepal 105 E3
Dailly U.K. 60 E5
Daimiel Spain 67 E4
Daimon Japan 92 D2
Daimon-tōge pass Japan 93 E2
Daimugen-zan mt. Japan 93 E3
Dainichiga-take vol. Japan 92 C2
Dainichi-gawa r. Japan 92 C2
Dainichi-zan mt. Japan 92 C2
Dainkognubma China 96 C1
Daintree National Park Australia 136 D3
Daiō Japan 92 C4
Daiō-zaki pt Japan 92 C4
Dair, Jebel ed mt. Sudan 108 D7
Dairen China see Dalian
Dai-sen vol. Japan 91 D6
Daisetsu-zan Kokuritsu-kōen Japan 90 F4
Daishan China 97 I2
Daitō Ōsaka Japan 92 B4
Daitō Shizuoka Japan 93 E4
Daiya-gawa r. Japan 93 F2
Daiyue China see Shanyin
Daiyun Shan mts China 97 H3
Dajan Japan 92 C3
Dajarra Australia 136 B4
Dajin Chuan r. China 96 D2
Dajing China 94 E4
Da Juh China 94 C4

▶Dakar Senegal 120 B3
Capital of Senegal.

Dākhilah, Wāḩāt ad oasis Egypt 108 C4
Dakhla W. Sahara see Ad Dakhla
Dakhla Oasis oasis Egypt see Dākhilah, Wāḩāt ad
Dakituy Rus. Fed. 95 G1
Đắk Lắk, Cao Nguyên plat. Vietnam 87 E4
Dakoank India 87 A6
Dakol'ka r. Belarus 53 F5
Dakor India 104 C5
Dakoro Niger 120 D3
Dakota City IA U.S.A. 160 E3
Dakota City NE U.S.A. 160 D3
Đakovica Kosovo see Gjakovë
Đakovo Croatia 68 H2
Daktuy Rus. Fed. 90 B1
Dala Angola 123 C5
Dalaba Guinea 120 B3
Dalad Qi China see Shulinzhao
Dalai China see Da'an
Dalain Hob China 94 E3
Dalai Nur l. China 95 I3
Dālakī Iran 110 C4
Dalälven r. Sweden 55 J6
Dalamamiao China 95 H3
Dalaman Turkey 69 M6
Dalandzadgad Mongolia 94 F3
Dalanganem Islands Phil. 82 C4
Dalap-Uliga-Darrit Marshall Is see Delap-Uliga-Djarrit
Dalat Sarawak Malaysia 85 E2
Đa Lat Vietnam 87 E5
Dalatando Angola see N'dalatando
Dalaud India 104 C5
Dalauda India 104 C5
Dalay Mongolia see Bayandalay
Dalbandin Pak. 111 G4
Dalbeattie U.K. 60 F6
Dalbeg Australia 136 D4
Dalby Australia 138 E1
Dalby Isle of Man 58 C4
Dale Hordaland Norway 55 D6
Dale Sogn og Fjordane Norway 55 D6
Dale City VA U.S.A. 165 G4
Dale Hollow Lake TN U.S.A. 164 C5
Dalen Neth. 62 G2
Dalet Myanmar 86 A3
Daletme Myanmar 86 A2
Dalfors Sweden 55 I6
Dalgān Iran 110 E5
Dalgety Australia 138 D6
Dalgety r. Australia 135 A6
Dalhart TX U.S.A. 161 C4
Dalhousie Canada 153 I4
Dalhousie, Cape Canada 149 O1
Dali Shaanxi China 95 G5
Dali Yunnan China 96 D3
Dalian China 95 J4
Daliang Guangdong China see Shunde
Daliang Qinghai China 94 E4
Daliang Shan mts China 96 D2
Dalian Wan b. China 95 J4
Dali He r. China 95 G4
Dalin China 95 J3
Dalinghe China see Linghai
Daling He r. China 95 J3
Dalizi China 90 B4
Dalkeith U.K. 60 F5
Dall, Mount AK U.S.A. 148 I3
Dallas OR U.S.A. 156 C3
Dallas TX U.S.A. 161 D5
Dalles City OR U.S.A. see The Dalles
Dall Island AK U.S.A. 149 N5
Dall Lake AK U.S.A. 148 G3
Dall Mountain AK U.S.A. 149 J2
Dalmā i. U.A.E. 110 D5
Dalmacija reg. Bos.-Herz./Croatia see Dalmatia
Dalmas, Lac l. Canada 153 H3
Dalmatia reg. Bos.-Herz./Croatia 100 A2
Dalmau India 104 E4
Dalmellington U.K. 60 E5
Dalmeny Canada 151 J4
Dalmi India 105 F5
Dal'negorsk Rus. Fed. 90 D3
Dal'nerechensk Rus. Fed. 90 D3
Dal'niye Zelentsy Rus. Fed. 52 H1
Dalny China see Dalian
Daloa Côte d'Ivoire 120 C4

▶Dalol Eth. 108 F7
Highest recorded annual mean temperature in the world.

Daloloia Group is P.N.G. 136 E1
Dalou Shan mts China 96 E3
Dalqān well Saudi Arabia 110 B5
Dalry U.K. 60 E5
Dalrymple U.K. 60 E5
Dalrymple, Lake Australia 136 D4
Daltenganj India 105 F4
Dalton Canada 152 D4
Dalton S. Africa 125 J5
Dalton GA U.S.A. 163 C5
Dalton MA U.S.A. 165 I2
Dalton PA U.S.A. 165 H3
Daltonganj India see Daltenganj
Dalton-in-Furness U.K. 58 D4
Daludalu Sumatera Indon. 84 C2
Daluo China 96 D4
Dalupiri i. Phil. 82 C2
Daly r. Australia 134 E3
Daly City CA U.S.A. 158 B3
Daly River Australia 134 E3
Daly Waters Australia 134 F4
Damagaram Takaya Niger 120 D3
Daman India 106 B1
Daman and Diu union terr. India 106 A1
Damanhûr Egypt see Damanhūr
Damanhūr Egypt 112 C5
Damant Lake Canada 151 J2
Damão India see Daman
Damaqun Shan mts China 95 H3

Damar Sulawesi Indon. 83 C2
Damar i. Maluku Indon. 83 D3
Damar i. Maluku Indon. 83 D4
Damara Cent. Afr. Rep. 122 B3
Damaraland reg. Namibia 123 B6
Damas Syria see Damascus

▶Damascus Syria 107 C3
Capital of Syria.

Damascus VA U.S.A. 164 E5
Damaturu Nigeria 120 E3
Damāvand Iran 110 D3
Damāvand, Qolleh-ye mt. Iran 110 D3
Dambulla Sri Lanka 106 D5
Damdy Kazakh. 102 B1
Dāmghān Iran 110 D2
Damianópolis Brazil 179 B1
Damietta Egypt see Dumyāṭ
Daming China 95 H4
Daming Shan mt. China 97 F4
Dāmiyā Jordan 107 B3
Damjong China 96 B1
Damlasu Turkey 107 D1
Dammam Saudi Arabia 108 H4
Damme Belgium 62 D3
Damme Germany 63 I2
Damoh India 104 D5
Damour Lebanon 107 B3
Dampar, Tasik l. Malaysia 84 C2
Dampelas, Tanjung pt Indon. 83 A2
Dampier Archipelago is Australia 134 B5
Dampier Island P.N.G. see Karkar Island
Dampier Land reg. Australia 134 C4
Dampier Strait P.N.G. 81 L8
Dampir, Selat sea chan. Papua Indon. 83 D3
Damqoq Zangbo r. China see Maquan He
Dam Qu r. China 99 F6
Dâmrei, Chuŏr Phnum mts Cambodia 87 D5
Damroh India 96 B2
Damwâld Neth. see Damwoude
Damwoude Neth. 62 G1
Damxoi China see Comai
Damxung China 99 E7
Dana i. Indon. 83 B5
Ḍānā Jordan 107 B4
Dana Nepal 105 E3
Danakil reg. Africa see Denakil
Danané Côte d'Ivoire 120 C4
Đa Nâng Vietnam 86 E3
Đa Nâng, Vung b. Vietnam 86 E3
Danao Cebu Phil. 82 D4
Danata Turkm. 110 D2
Danau Sentarum, Taman Nasional nature res. Kalimantan Indon. 85 F2
Danba Shaanxi China 95 G4
Danba Sichuan China 96 D2
Danbury CT U.S.A. 165 I3
Danbury NC U.S.A. 162 D4
Danby VT U.S.A. 165 I2
Danby Lake CA U.S.A. 159 F4
Dancheng China 95 H5
Dandaragan Australia 135 A7
Dande Eth. 122 D3
Dandeldhura Nepal 104 E3
Dandeli India 106 B3
Dandong China 91 B4
Dando-san mt. Japan 92 D3
Dandot Pak. 111 I3
Dandridge TN U.S.A. 162 D4
Dane r. U.K. 58 E5
Daneborg Greenland 189 I2
Danese WV U.S.A. 164 E5
Danfeng China see Shizong
Dangan Liedao i. China 97 G4
Dangara Tajik. see Danghara
Dangbi Rus. Fed. 90 C3
Dangchang China 94 F5
Dangchengwan China see Subei
Danger Islands atoll Cook Is see Pukapuka
Danger Point S. Africa 124 D8
Danghara Tajik. 111 H2
Dang He r. China 94 C3
Danghe Nanshan mts China 94 C4
Dangjin Shankou pass China 98 F5
Dangla Shan mts China see Tanggula Shan
Dangqên China 99 E7
Dângrêk, Chuŏr Phnum mts Cambodia/Thai. see Phanom Dong Rak, Thiu Khao
Dangriga Belize 167 H5
Dangshan China 95 I5
Dangtu China 97 H2
Daniel's Harbour Canada 153 K4
Danielskuil S. Africa 124 F5
Danilov Rus. Fed. 52 I4
Danilovka Rus. Fed. 53 J6
Danilovskaya Vozvyshennost' hills Rus. Fed. 52 H4
Daning China 95 G4
Danjiang China see Leishan
Danjiangkou China 97 F1
Danjiangkou Shuiku resr China 97 F1
Danjo-guntō is Japan 91 C6
Ḍank Oman 110 E6
Dankhar India 104 D2
Dankov Rus. Fed. 53 H5
Dan'kova, Pik mt. Kyrg. 98 B4
Danlí Hond. 166 [inset] I6
Danmark country Europe see Denmark
Dannebrog Ø i. Greenland see Qillak
Dannenberg (Elbe) Germany 63 L1
Dannenwalde Germany 63 N1
Dannevirke N.Z. 139 F5
Dannhauser S. Africa 125 J5
Dano Burkina Faso 120 C3
Danshui Taiwan see Tanshui
Dansville NY U.S.A. 165 G2
Danta India 104 C4
Dantan India 105 F5
Dantevada India see Dantewara
Dantewada India see Dantewara
Dantewara India 106 D2
Dantu China see Zhenjiang

▶Danube r. Europe 57 P6
2nd longest river in Europe.
Also spelt Donau (Austria/Germany) or Duna (Hungary) or Dunaj (Slovakia) or Dunărea (Romania) or Dunav (Bulgaria/Croatia/Serbia) or Dunay (Ukraine).

Danube Delta Romania/Ukr. 69 M2
Danubyu Myanmar 86 A3
Danumparai Kalimantan Indon. 85 F2
Danum Valley Conservation Area nature res. Malaysia 85 G1
Danville IL U.S.A. 164 B3
Danville IN U.S.A. 164 B4
Danville KY U.S.A. 164 C5
Danville OH U.S.A. 164 D3
Danville PA U.S.A. 165 G3
Danville VA U.S.A. 164 F5
Danville VT U.S.A. 165 I1
Danxian China see Danzhou
Danzhai China 96 E3
Danzhou Guangxi China 97 F3
Danzhou Hainan China 97 F5
Danzhou Shaanxi China see Yichuan
Danzig Poland see Gdańsk
Danzig, Gulf of Poland/Rus. Fed. see Gdańsk, Gulf of
Daocheng China 96 D2
Daokou China see Huaxian
Daotanghe China 94 E4
Dao Tay Sa is S. China Sea see Paracel Islands
Daoud Alg. see Aïn Beïda
Daoukro Côte d'Ivoire 120 C4
Daozhen China 96 E2
Dapa Phil. 82 D4
Dapaong Togo 120 D3
Dapeng Wan b. H.K. China see Mirs Bay
Daphabum mt. India 105 I4
Dapiak, Mount Mindanao Phil. 82 C4
Dapitan Mindanao Phil. 82 C4
Daporijo India 105 H4
Dapu China see Liucheng
Da Qaidam China 99 F5
Daqiao China 96 D3
Daqing China 90 B3
Daqinghe China 95 I4
Daqing Shan mts China 95 G3
Daqin Tal China 95 J3
Daqiu China 97 H3
Dāq Mashī Iran 110 E3
Daqq-e Patargān salt flat Iran 111 F3
Daquan China 98 F4
Daquanwan China 94 C3
Daqu Shan i. China 97 I2
Dara Senegal 120 B3
Dar'ā Syria 107 C3
Dâra, Gebel mt. Egypt see Dārah, Jabal
Dārāb Iran 110 D4
Daraga Luzon Phil. 82 C3
Darāgāh Iran 110 D4
Dārah, Jabal mt. Egypt 112 D6
Daraj Libya 120 E1
Dārākūyeh Iran 110 D4
Dārān Iran 110 C3
Daraut-Korgon Kyrg. 111 I2
Darazo Nigeria 120 E3
Darband, Kūh-e mt. Iran 110 E4
Darband-e Hajjī Boland Turkm. 111 F2
Darbhanga India 105 F4
Darby, Cape AK U.S.A. 148 G2
Darby Mountains AK U.S.A. 148 G2
Darcang China 96 C1
Dardanelle AR U.S.A. 161 E5
Dardanelles strait Turkey 69 L4
Dardania prov. Europe see Kosovo
Dardesheim Germany 63 K3
Dardo China see Kangding
Dar el Beida Morocco see Casablanca
Darende Turkey 112 E3

▶Dar es Salaam Tanz. 123 D4
Former capital of Tanzania.

Dāreyn, Kūh-e mt. Iran 110 E3
Darfo Boario Terme Italy 68 D2
Dargai Pak. 111 H3
Dargaville N.Z. 139 D2
Dargo Australia 138 C6
Dargo Zangbo r. China 105 F3
Darhan Mongolia 94 F1
Darhan Muminggan Lianheqi China see Bailingmiao
Darien GA U.S.A. 163 D6
Darién, Golfo del g. Col. 176 C2
Darién, Parque Nacional de nat. park Panama 166 [inset] K8
Darién, Serranía del mts Panama 166 [inset] K7
Dariga Pak. 111 G5
Dariganga Mongolia 95 H2
Darío Nicaragua 166 [inset] I6
Dariya Kazakh. 98 A2
Darjeeling India see Darjiling
Darjiling India 105 G4
Darkhazīneh Iran 110 C4
Darlag China 96 C1

▶Darling r. Australia 138 B3
2nd longest river in Oceania, and a major part of the longest (Murray-Darling)

Darling Downs hills Australia 138 D1
Darling Range hills Australia 135 A8
Darlington U.K. 58 F4
Darlington WI U.S.A. 160 F3
Darlington Point Australia 138 C5
Darlot, Lake salt flat Australia 135 C6
Darłowo Poland 57 P3
Darma Pass China/India 99 C7
Darmstadt Germany 63 I5
Darnah Libya 112 A4
Darnall S. Africa 125 J5
Darnick Australia 138 A4
Darnley, Cape Antarctica 188 E2
Darnley Bay Canada 149 P1
Daroca Spain 67 F3
Darong China 97 H3
Daroot-Korgon Kyrg. see Daraut-Korgon
Darovskoy Rus. Fed. 52 J4
Darr watercourse Australia 136 C4
Darreh Bīd Iran 110 E3
Darreh-ye Bāhābād Iran 110 D4
Darreh-ye Shahr Iran 110 B3
Darsi India 106 C3
Dart r. U.K. 59 D8
Dartang China see Baqên
Dartford U.K. 59 H7
Dartmoor Australia 137 C8
Dartmoor hills U.K. 59 C8
Dartmoor National Park U.K. 59 D8
Dartmouth Canada 153 J5
Dartmouth U.K. 59 D8
Dartmouth, Lake salt flat Australia 137 D5
Dartmouth Reservoir Australia 138 C6
Darton U.K. 58 F5
Daru P.N.G. 81 K8
Daru Sierra Leone 120 B4
Daruba Maluku Indon. 83 D2
Daruga-mine mt. Japan 92 A3
Darvaza Turkm. see Derweze
Darvi Govĭ-Altay Mongolia 94 C2
Darvi Hovd Mongolia 94 C2
Darvoz, Qatorkŭhi mts Tajik. 111 H2
Darwāzahgēy Afgh. 111 G4
Darwen U.K. 58 E5

▶Darwin Australia 134 E3
Capital of Northern Territory.

Darwin, Monte mt. Chile 178 C8
Daryācheh-ye Orūmīyeh salt l. Iran see Urmia, Lake
Dar'yalyktakyr, Ravnina plain Kazakh. 102 B2
Dar"yoi Amu r. Asia see Amudar'ya
Darz Āb Afgh. 111 G3
Darzhuo China 99 E6
Dārzīn Iran 110 E4
Dās i. U.A.E. 110 D5
Dasada India 104 B5
Dashbalbar Mongolia 95 H1
Dashennongjia mt. China see Shennong Ding
Dashetai China 95 G3
Dashhowuz Turkm. see Daşoguz
Dashiqiao China 95 J3
Dashitou China 94 B3
Dashizhai China 95 J2
Dashkesan Azer. see Daşkäsän
Dashkhovuz Turkm. see Daşoguz
Dashköpri Turkm. see Daşköpri
Dashoguz Turkm. see Daşoguz
Dasht Iran 110 E2
Dashtiari Iran 111 F5
Dashuikeng China 94 F4
Dashuiqiao China 94 D4
Dashuitou China 94 F4
Daska Pak. 111 I3
Daşkäsän Azer. 113 G2
Daşköpri Turkm. 111 F2
Daşoguz Turkm. 109 I1
Daşoguz Turkm. see Daşoguz
Daspar mt. Pak. 111 I2
Dassalan i. Phil. 82 C5
Dassel Germany 63 J3
Dastgerdān Iran 110 E3
Datadian Kalimantan Indon. 85 F2
Datça Turkey 69 L6
Date Japan 90 F4
Date Creek watercourse AZ U.S.A. 159 G4
Dateland AZ U.S.A. 159 G5
Datha India 104 C5
Datia India 104 D4
Datian China 97 H3
Datian Ding mt. China 97 F4
Datil NM U.S.A. 159 J4
Datong Anhui China 97 H2
Datong Heilong. China 90 B3
Datong Qinghai China 94 E4
Datong Shanxi China 95 H3
Datong He r. China 94 E4
Datong Shan mts China 94 D4
Dattapur India 106 C1
Datu i. Indon. 85 E2
Datu, Tanjung c. Indon./Malaysia 85 E2
Datuk, Tanjung pt Indon. 84 C3
Datu Piang Mindanao Phil. 82 D5
Daudkandi Bangl. 105 G5
Daugava r. Latvia 55 N8
Daugavpils Latvia 55 O9
Daulatabad India 106 B2
Daulatabad Iran see Malāyer
Daulatpur Bangl. 105 G5
Daun Germany 62 G4
Daungyu r. Myanmar 86 A2
Dauphin Canada 151 K5
Dauphiné reg. France 66 G4
Dauphiné, Alpes du mts France 66 G4
Dauphin Island AL U.S.A. 167 H2
Dauphin Lake Canada 151 L5
Daurie Creek r. Australia 135 A6
Dauriya Rus. Fed. 95 I1
Daurskiy Khrebet mts Rus. Fed. 95 G1
Dausa India 104 D4
Dầu Tiêng, Hô resr Vietnam 87 D5
Dava U.K. 60 F3
Däväçi Azer. 113 H2
Davanagere India see Davangere
Davangere India 106 B3
Davao Mindanao Phil. 82 D5
Davao Gulf Mindanao Phil. 82 D5
Dāvarī Iran 110 E5
Dāvarzan Iran 110 E2
Davel S. Africa 125 I4
Davenport IA U.S.A. 160 F3
Davenport WA U.S.A. 156 D3
Davenport Downs Australia 136 C5
Davenport Range hills Australia 134 F5
Daventry U.K. 59 F6
Daveyton S. Africa 125 I4
David Panama 166 [inset] J7
David City NE U.S.A. 160 D3
Davidson Canada 151 J5
Davidson, Mount hill Australia 134 E5
Davidson Mountains AK U.S.A. 149 L1
Davis research station Antarctica 188 E2
Davis r. Australia 134 C5
Davis i. Myanmar see Than Kyun
Davis CA U.S.A. 158 C2
Davis WV U.S.A. 164 F4
Davis, Mount hill PA U.S.A. 164 F4
Davis Bay Antarctica 188 G2
Davis Dam AZ U.S.A. 159 F4
Davis Inlet (abandoned) Canada 153 J3
Davis Sea Antarctica 188 F2
Davis Strait Canada/Greenland 147 M3
Davlekanovo Rus. Fed. 51 Q5
Davos Switz. 66 I3
Davy Lake Canada 151 I3
Dawa China 95 J3
Dawa Co l. China 99 D7
Dawa Wenz r. Eth. 122 E3
Dawaxung China 99 D7
Dawê China 96 D2
Dawei Myanmar see Tavoy
Dawei r. mouth Myanmar see Tavoy
Daweloor i. Maluku Indon. 83 D4
Dawera i. Maluku Indon. 83 D4
Dawna Range mts Myanmar/Thai. 86 B3
Dawna Taungdan mts Myanmar/Thai. see Dawna Range
Dawo China see Maqên
Dawqah Oman 109 H6
Dawson r. Australia 136 E4
Dawson Canada 149 M2
Dawson GA U.S.A. 163 C6
Dawson ND U.S.A. 160 D2
Dawson, Mount Canada 150 G5
Dawson Bay Canada 151 K4
Dawson Creek Canada 150 F4
Dawson Inlet Canada 151 M2
Dawson Range mts Canada 149 L3
Dawsons Landing Canada 150 E5
Dawu China 97 G2
Dawu Taiwan see Tawu
Dawukou China see Shizuishan
Dawu Shan hill China 97 G2
Dawusi China 99 E5
Dax France 66 D5
Daxian China see Dazhou
Daxiang Ling mts China 96 D2
Daxihaizi Shuiku resr China 98 D4
Daxin China 96 E4
Daxing Yunnan China see Ninglang
Daxing Yunnan China see Lüchun
Daxue Shan mt. China 94 D4
Da Xueshan mts China 96 D2
Dayan China see Lijiang
Dayang r. India 99 F8
Dayangshu China 95 K1
Dayan Nuur l. Mongolia 94 B1
Dayao China 96 D3
Dayao Shan mts China 97 F4
Daye China 97 G2
Daying China 96 E2
Daying Jiang r. China 96 C3
Dayishan China see Guanyun
Daylesford Australia 138 B6
Daylight Pass NV U.S.A. 158 E3
Dayong China see Zhangjiajie
Dayr Abū Sa'īd Jordan 107 B3
Dayr az Zawr Syria 113 F4
Dayr Ḥāfir Syria 107 C1
Daysland Canada 151 H4
Dayton OH U.S.A. 164 C4
Dayton TN U.S.A. 162 C5
Dayton TX U.S.A. 167 G2
Dayton VA U.S.A. 165 F4
Dayton WA U.S.A. 156 D3
Daytona Beach FL U.S.A. 163 D6
Dayu Kalimantan Indon. 85 F3
Dayu Ling mts China 97 G3
Da Yunhe canal China 95 I5
Dayyer Iran 110 C5
Dayyīna i. U.A.E. 110 D5
Dazhai China 95 H4
Dazhongji China see Dafeng
Dazhou China 96 E2
Dazhou Dao i. China 97 F5
Dazhu China 96 E2
Dazigou China 94 C3
Dazu China 96 E2
Dazu Rock Carvings tourist site China 96 E2
Ddhaw Gro Habitat Protection Area nature res. Canada 149 N3
De Aar S. Africa 124 G6
Dead r. Ireland 61 D5
Deadhorse AK U.S.A. 149 J1
Deadman Lake CA U.S.A. 158 E4
Deadman's Cay Bahamas 163 F8
Dead Mountains NV U.S.A. 159 F4

▶Dead Sea salt l. Asia 107 B4
Lowest point in the world and in Asia.

Deadwood SD U.S.A. 160 C2
Deakin Australia 135 E7
Deal U.K. 59 I7
Dealesville S. Africa 125 G5
De'an China 97 G2
Dean, Forest of U.K. 59 E7
Deán Funes Arg. 178 D4
Deanuvuotna inlet Norway see Tanafjorden
Dearborn MI U.S.A. 164 D2
Dearne r. U.K. 58 F5
Deary ID U.S.A. 156 D3
Dease r. Canada 149 O4
Dease Arm b. Canada 149 Q2
Dease Inlet AK U.S.A. 148 I1
Dease Lake Canada 149 O4
Dease Lake Canada 149 O4
Dease Strait Canada 146 H3

▶Death Valley depr. CA U.S.A. 158 E3
Lowest point in the Americas.

Death Valley Junction CA U.S.A. 158 E3
Death Valley National Park CA U.S.A. 158 E3
Deauville France 66 E2
Deaver WY U.S.A. 156 F3
De Baai S. Africa see Port Elizabeth
Debak Sarawak Malaysia 85 E2
Debao China 96 E4
Debar Macedonia 69 I4
Debauch Mountain AK U.S.A. 148 H2
Debden Canada 151 J4
Debenham U.K. 59 I6
De Beque CO U.S.A. 159 I2
De Biesbosch, Nationaal Park nat. park Neth. 62 E3
Débo, Lac l. Mali 120 C3
Deborah, Mount AK U.S.A. 149 K3
Deborah East, Lake salt flat Australia 135 B7
Deborah West, Lake salt flat Australia 135 B7
Debrecen Hungary 69 I1
Debre Markos Eth. 108 E7
Debre Tabor Eth. 108 E7
Debre Zeyit Eth. 122 D3
Decatur AL U.S.A. 163 C5
Decatur GA U.S.A. 163 C5
Decatur IL U.S.A. 160 F4
Decatur IN U.S.A. 164 C3
Decatur MI U.S.A. 164 C2
Decatur MS U.S.A. 161 F5
Decatur TX U.S.A. 161 D5

▶Deccan plat. India 106 C2
Plateau making up most of southern and central India.

Deception Bay Australia 138 F1
Dechang China 96 D3
Děčín Czech Rep. 57 O5
Decker MT U.S.A. 156 G3
Decorah IA U.S.A. 160 F3
Dedap i. Indon. see Penasi, Pulau
Dedaye Myanmar 86 A3
Deddington U.K. 59 F7
Dedegöl Dağları mts Turkey 69 N6
Dedeleben Germany 63 K2
Dedelstorf Germany 63 K2
Dedemsvaart Neth. 62 G2
Dedo de Deus mt. Brazil 179 B4
Dédougou Burkina Faso 120 C3
Dedovichi Rus. Fed. 52 F4
Dedu China see Wudalianchi
Dee r. Ireland 61 F4
Dee est. U.K. 58 D5
Dee r. England/Wales U.K. 59 D5
Dee r. Scotland U.K. 60 G3
Deel r. Cork/Limerick Ireland 61 D5
Deel r. Meath/Westmeath Ireland 61 F4
Deep Bay H.K. China 97 [inset]
Deep Creek Lake MD U.S.A. 164 F4
Deep Creek Range mts UT U.S.A. 159 G2
Deep River Canada 152 F5
Deepwater Australia 138 E2
Deeri Somalia 122 E3
Deering AK U.S.A. 148 G2
Deering, Mount Australia 135 E6
Deer Island AK U.S.A. 148 G5
Deer Lake Canada 151 M4
Deer Lake l. Canada 151 M4
Deer Lodge MT U.S.A. 156 E3
Deerpass Bay Canada 149 Q2
Deesa India see Disa
Deeth NV U.S.A. 156 E4
Defeng China see Liping
Defensores del Chaco, Parque Nacional nat. park Para. 178 D2
Defiance OH U.S.A. 164 C3
Defiance Plateau AZ U.S.A. 159 I4
De Funiak Springs FL U.S.A. 167 I2
Degana India 104 C4
Degeh Bur Eth. 122 E3
Degema Nigeria 120 D4
Deggendorf Germany 63 M6
Degh r. Pak. 111 I4
De Grey r. Australia 134 B5
De Groote Peel, Nationaal Park nat. park Neth. 62 F3
Degtevo Rus. Fed. 53 I6
De Haan Belgium 62 D3
Dē Ḥadē Ghar Afgh. 111 G4
Dehak Iran 111 F4
De Hamert, Nationaal Park nat. park Neth. 62 G3
Dehaq Iran 110 C3
Deh-Dasht Iran 110 C4
Deh-e Shū Afgh. 111 F4
Dehestān Iran 110 D4
Deh Golān Iran 110 B3
Dehgon Afgh. 111 F3
Dehī Afgh. 111 G3
Dehkūyeh Iran 110 D5
Dehlorān Iran 110 B3
De Hoge Veluwe, Nationaal Park nat. park Neth. 62 F2
De Hoop Nature Reserve S. Africa 124 E8
Dehqonobod Uzbek. 111 G2
Dehradun India see Dehra Dun
Dehra Dun India 104 D3
Dehri India 105 F4
Deim Zubeir South Sudan 121 F4
Deinze Belgium 62 D4
Deir-ez-Zor Syria see Dayr az Zawr
Dej Romania 69 J1
Deji China see Rinbung
Dejiang China 97 F2
De Jouwer Neth. see Joure
De Kalb IL U.S.A. 160 F3
De Kalb MS U.S.A. 161 F5
De Kalb TX U.S.A. 161 E5
De Kalb Junction NY U.S.A. 165 H1
De-Kastri Rus. Fed. 90 F2
Dekemhare Eritrea 108 E6
Dekhkanabad Uzbek. see Dehqonobod
Dekina Nigeria 120 D4
Dékoa Cent. Afr. Rep. 122 B3
De Koog Neth. 62 E1
De Kooy Neth. 62 E2
Delaki Indon. 83 C5
Delamar Lake NV U.S.A. 159 F3
De Land FL U.S.A. 163 D6
Delano CA U.S.A. 158 D4
Delano Peak UT U.S.A. 159 G2

▶Delap-Uliga-Djarrit Marshall Is 186 H5
Capital of the Marshall Islands, on Majuro atoll.

Delareyville S. Africa 125 G4
Delarof Islands AK U.S.A. 148 [inset] C6
Delaronde Lake Canada 151 J4
Delavan WI U.S.A. 152 C6
Delaware OH U.S.A. 164 D3
Delaware r. NJ/PA U.S.A. 165 H4
Delaware state U.S.A. 165 H4
Delaware, East Branch r. NY U.S.A. 165 H3
Delaware Bay DE/NJ U.S.A. 165 H4
Delaware Lake OH U.S.A. 164 D3
Delaware Water Gap National Recreational Area park NJ/PA U.S.A. 165 H3
Delay r. Canada 153 H2
Delbarton WV U.S.A. 164 D5
Delbrück Germany 63 I3
Delburne Canada 150 H4
Dêlêg China 99 D7
Delegate Australia 138 D6
De Lemmer Neth. see Lemmer
Delémont Switz. 66 H3
Delevan CA U.S.A. 158 B2
Delevan NY U.S.A. 165 F2
Delfinópolis Brazil 179 B3
Delft Neth. 62 E2
Delfzijl Neth. 62 G1
Delgada, Point CA U.S.A. 158 A1
Delgado, Cabo c. Moz. 123 E5
Delger Mongolia 94 D2
Delgerhaan Mongolia 94 F2
Delgerhangay Mongolia 94 F2
Delgermörön Mongolia see Hüreemaral
Delger Mörön r. Mongolia 94 E1
Delgertsogt Mongolia 94 F2
Delhi Canada 164 E2
Delhi China 94 D4

▶Delhi India 104 D3
2nd most populous city in Asia and the world.

Delhi admin. div. India 99 B7
Delhi CO U.S.A. 157 G5
Delhi LA U.S.A. 161 F5
Delhi NY U.S.A. 165 H2
Deli i. Indon. 84 D4
Delice Turkey 112 D3
Delice r. Turkey 112 D2
Delījān Iran 110 C3
Déline Canada 149 Q2
Delingha China see Delhi
Delisle Canada 151 J5
Delitua Sumatera Indon. 84 B2
Delitzsch Germany 63 M3
Delligsen Germany 63 J3
Dell Rapids SD U.S.A. 160 D3
Dellys Alg. 67 H5
Del Mar CA U.S.A. 158 E5
Delmenhorst Germany 63 I1
Delnice Croatia 68 F2
Del Norte CO U.S.A. 157 G5
Delong China see Ande
De-Longa, Ostrova is Rus. Fed. 77 Q2
De Long Islands Rus. Fed. see De-Longa, Ostrova
De Long Mountains AK U.S.A. 148 G1
De Long Strait Rus. Fed. see Longa, Proliv
Deloraine Canada 151 K5
Delphi IN U.S.A. 164 B3
Delphos OH U.S.A. 164 C3
Delportshoop S. Africa 124 G5
Delray Beach FL U.S.A. 163 D7
Delrey IL U.S.A. 164 A3
Del Río Mex. 166 C2
Del Rio TX U.S.A. 161 C6
Delsbo Sweden 55 J6
Delta CO U.S.A. 159 I2
Delta OH U.S.A. 164 C3
Delta UT U.S.A. 159 G2
Delta r. AK U.S.A. 149 K2
Delta Downs Australia 136 C3
Delta Junction AK U.S.A. 149 K2
Deltona FL U.S.A. 163 D6
Delungra Australia 138 E2
Delüün Mongolia 94 B2
Delvin Ireland 61 E4
Delvinë Albania 69 I5
Delwara India 104 C4
Demak Jawa Indon. 85 E4
Demarcation Point pt AK U.S.A. 149 L1
Demavend mt. Iran see Damāvand, Qolleh-ye
Demba Dem. Rep. Congo 123 C4
Dembī Dolo Eth. 108 D8
Demerara Guyana see Georgetown
Demerara Abyssal Plain sea feature S. Atlantic Ocean 184 E5
Demidov Rus. Fed. 53 F5
Deming NM U.S.A. 157 G6
Demirci Turkey 69 M5
Demirköy Turkey 69 L4
Demirtaş Turkey 107 A1
Demmin Germany 57 N4
Demopolis AL U.S.A. 163 C5
Demotte IN U.S.A. 164 B3
Dempo, Gunung vol. Indon. 84 C4
Dempster Highway Canada 149 M2
Dêmqog China 104 D2
Demta Indon. 81 K7
Dē Mūsá Qal'ah Rōd r. Afgh. 111 G3
Dem'yanovo Rus. Fed. 52 J3
De Naawte S. Africa 124 E6
Denakil reg. Africa 122 E2
Denali AK U.S.A. 149 K3
Denali AK U.S.A. see McKinley, Mount
Denali Highway AK U.S.A. 149 K3
Denali National Park and Preserve AK U.S.A. 149 J3
Denan Eth. 122 E3
Denbigh Canada 165 G1
Denbigh U.K. 58 D5
Denbigh, Cape AK U.S.A. 148 G2
Den Bosch Neth. see 's-Hertogenbosch
Den Burg Neth. 62 E1
Den Chai Thai. 86 C3
Dendang Indon. 85 D3
Dendâra Mauritania 120 C3
Dendermonde Belgium 62 E3
Dendi mt. Eth. 122 D3
Dendre r. Belgium 62 E3
Dendron S. Africa see Mogwadi
Denezhkin Kamen', Gora mt. Rus. Fed. 51 R3
Denges Passage Palau 82 [inset]
Dengfeng China 95 H5
Dênggar China 99 D7
Dêngka China see Têwo
Dêngkagoin China see Têwo
Dengkou China 95 F3
Dêngqên China 99 F7
Dengta China 97 G4
Dengxian China see Dengzhou
Dêngzê China 99 C6
Dengzhou Henan China 97 G1
Dengzhou Shandong China see Penglai
Den Haag Neth. see The Hague
Denham Australia 135 A6
Denham r. Australia 134 E3
Den Ham Neth. 62 G2
Denham Range mts Australia 136 E4
Den Helder Neth. 62 E2
Denholm Canada 151 I4
Dénia Spain 67 G4
Denial Bay Australia 137 A7
Deniliquin Australia 138 B5
Denio NV U.S.A. 156 D4
Denison IA U.S.A. 160 E3
Denison TX U.S.A. 161 D5
Denison, Cape Antarctica 188 G2
Denison Plains Australia 134 E4
Deniyaya Sri Lanka 106 D5
Denizli Turkey 69 M6
Denman Australia 138 E4
Denman Glacier Antarctica 188 F2
Denmark Australia 132 B5
Denmark country Europe 55 G8
Denmark WI U.S.A. 164 B1
Denmark Strait Greenland/Iceland 50 A2
Dennis, Lake salt flat Australia 134 E5
Dennison IL U.S.A. 164 B4
Dennison OH U.S.A. 164 E3
Denny U.K. 60 F4
Denov Uzbek. 111 G2
Denow Uzbek. see Denov
Denpasar Bali Indon. 85 F5
Densongi Sulawesi Indon. 83 B3
Denton MD U.S.A. 165 H4

Denton *TX* U.S.A. **161** D5
D'Entrecasteaux, Point Australia **135** A8
D'Entrecasteaux, Récifs *reef* New Caledonia **133** G3
D'Entrecasteaux Islands P.N.G. **132** F2
D'Entrecasteaux National Park Australia **135** A8

▶**Denver** *CO* U.S.A. **156** G5
Capital of Colorado.

Denver *PA* U.S.A. **165** G3
Denys *r.* Canada **152** F3
Deo India **105** F4
Deoband India **104** D3
Deogarh *Jharkhand* India *see* **Deoghar**
Deogarh *Odisha* India **105** F5
Deogarh *Rajasthan* India **104** C4
Deogarh *Uttar Prad.* India **104** D4
Deogarh *mt.* India **105** E5
Deoghar India **105** F4
Deolali India **106** B2
Deoli India **105** F5
Deori India **104** D5
Deoria India **105** E4
Deosai, Plains of Pak. **104** C2
Deosil India **105** E5
Deothang Bhutan **105** G4
De Panne Belgium **62** C3
De Pere *WI* U.S.A. **164** A1
Deposit *NY* U.S.A. **165** H2
Depsang Point *hill* Aksai Chin **99** B6
Deputatskiy Rus. Fed. **77** O3
Dêqên *Xizang* China **99** E7
Dêqên *Xizang* China **99** E7
Dêqên *Xizang* China *see* **Dagzê**
De Queen *AR* U.S.A. **161** E5
De Quincy *LA* U.S.A. **167** G2
Dera Ghazi Khan Pak. **111** H4
Dera Ismail Khan Pak. **111** H4
Derajat *reg.* Pak. **111** H4
Derawar Fort Pak. **111** H4
Derbent Rus. Fed. **113** H2
Derbesiye Turkey *see* **Şenyurt**
Derbur China **90** A2
Derby Australia **134** C4
Derby U.K. **59** F6
Derby *CT* U.S.A. **165** I3
Derby *KS* U.S.A. **161** D4
Derby *NY* U.S.A. **165** F2
Đerdap, Nacionalni Park *nat. park* Serbia **69** J2
Dereham U.K. **59** H6
Derg *r.* Ireland/U.K. **61** E3
Derg, Lough *l.* Ireland **61** D5
Dergachi Rus. Fed. **53** K6
Dergachi Ukr. *see* **Derhachi**
Derhachi Ukr. **53** H6
De Ridder *LA* U.S.A. **161** E6
Derik Turkey **113** F3
Derm Namibia **124** D2
Derna Libya *see* **Darnah**
Dernberg, Cape Namibia **124** B4
Dêrong China **96** C2
Derravaragh, Lough *l.* Ireland **61** E4
Derry U.K. *see* **Londonderry**
Derry *NH* U.S.A. **165** J2
Derryveagh Mountains *hills* Ireland **61** D3
Derst China **95** H3
Derstei China **94** E3
Dêrub China **99** B6
Derudeb Sudan **108** E6
De Rust S. Africa **124** F7
Derventa Bos.-Herz. **68** G2
Derwent *r. England* U.K. **58** F6
Derwent *r. England* U.K. **58** G5
Derwent Water *l.* U.K. **58** D4
Derweze Turkm. **110** E1
Derzhavinsk Kazakh. **102** C1
Derzhavinskiy Kazakh. *see* **Derzhavinsk**
Desaguadero *r.* Arg. **178** C4
Désappointement, Îles du *is* Fr. Polynesia **187** K6
Desatoya Mountains *NV* U.S.A. **158** E2
Deschambault Lake Canada **151** K4
Deschutes *r. OR* U.S.A. **156** C3
Desē Eth. **122** D2
Deseado Arg. **178** C7
Deseado *r.* Arg. **178** C7
Desemboque Mex. **166** B2
Desengaño, Punta *pt* Arg. **178** C7
Deseret *UT* U.S.A. **159** G2
Deseret Peak *UT* U.S.A. **159** G1
Deseronto Canada **165** G1
Desert Canal Pak. **111** H4
Desert Center *CA* U.S.A. **159** F5
Desert Lake *NV* U.S.A. **159** F3
Desert View *AZ* U.S.A. **159** H3
Deshler *OH* U.S.A. **164** D3
Desierto Central de Baja California, Parque Natural del *nature res.* Mex. **166** B2
De Smet *SD* U.S.A. **160** D2

▶**Des Moines** *IA* U.S.A. **160** E3
Capital of Iowa.

Des Moines *NM* U.S.A. **161** C4
Des Moines *r. IA* U.S.A. **160** F3
Desna *r.* Rus. Fed./Ukr. **53** F6
Desnogorsk Rus. Fed. **53** G5
Desolación, Isla *i.* Chile **178** B8
Desolation Point Phil. **82** D4
Despen Rus. Fed. **94** C1
Des Plaines *IL* U.S.A. **164** B2
Dessau Germany **63** M3
Dessye Eth. *see* **Desē**
Destelbergen Belgium **62** D3
Destruction Bay Canada **189** A2
Desventuradas, Islas *is* S. Pacific Ocean **187** O7
Desvres France **62** B4
Detah Canada **150** H2
Dete Zimbabwe **123** C5
Detmold Germany **63** I3
Detrital Wash *watercourse AZ* U.S.A. **159** F3
Detroit *MI* U.S.A. **164** D2
Detroit Lakes *MN* U.S.A. **160** E2
Dett Zimbabwe *see* **Dete**
Deua National Park Australia **138** D5
Deuben Germany **63** M3
Deurne Neth. **62** F3
Deutschland *country* Europe *see* **Germany**
Deutschlandsberg Austria **57** O7
Deutzen Germany **63** M3
Deva Romania **69** J2
Deva U.K. *see* **Chester**
Devana U.K. *see* **Aberdeen**
Devangere India *see* **Davangere**
Devanhalli India **106** C3
Deve Bair *pass* Bulg./Macedonia *see* **Velbŭzhdki Prokhod**
Develi Turkey **112** D3
Deventer Neth. **62** G2
Deveron *r.* U.K. **60** G3
Devét skal *hill* Czech Rep. **57** P6
Devgarh India **106** B2
Devghar India *see* **Deoghar**
Devikot India **104** B4
Devil Mountain *hill AK* U.S.A. **148** F2
Devil's Bridge U.K. **59** D6
Devil's Gate *pass CA* U.S.A. **158** D2
Devil's Lake *ND* U.S.A. **160** D1
Devil's Lake *l. TX* U.S.A. **167** E2
Devil's Paw *mt. AK* U.S.A. **149** N4
Devil's Peak *CA* U.S.A. **158** D3
Devil's Point Bahamas **163** F7
Devil's Thumb *mt.* Canada/U.S.A. **149** N4
Devine *TX* U.S.A. **161** D6
Devizes U.K. **59** F7
Devli India **104** C4
Devnya Bulg. **69** L3
Devon *r.* U.K. **60** F4
Devon Island Canada **147** I2
Devonport Australia **137** [inset]
Devrek Turkey **69** N4
Devrukh India **106** B2
Dewa, Tanjung *pt* Indon. **84** A2
Dewakang Besar *i.* Indon. **85** G4
Dewas India **104** D5
De Weerribben, Nationaal Park *nat. park* Neth. **62** G2
Dewetsdorp S. Africa **125** H5
De Witt *AR* U.S.A. **161** F5
De Witt *IA* U.S.A. **160** F3
Dewsbury U.K. **58** F5
Dexing China **97** H2
Dêxing China **99** F7
Dexter *ME* U.S.A. **165** K1
Dexter *MI* U.S.A. **164** D2
Dexter *MO* U.S.A. **161** F4
Dexter *NM* U.S.A. **157** G6
Dexter *NY* U.S.A. **165** G1
Deyang China **96** E2
Dey-Dey Lake *salt flat* Australia **135** E7
Deyhūk Iran **110** E3
Deyong, Tanjung *pt* Indon. **81** J8
Dez *r.* Iran **108** G3
Dezadeash Lake Canada **149** M3
Dezfūl Iran **110** C3

▶**Dezhneva, Mys** *c.* Rus. Fed. **148** E2
Most easterly point of Asia.

Dezhou *Shandong* China **95** I4
Dezhou *Sichuan* China *see* **Dechang**
Dezh Shāhpūr Iran *see* **Marīvān**
Dhabarau India **105** E4
Dhahab, Wādī adh *r.* Syria **107** B3
Dhāhiriya West Bank **107** B4
Dhahran Saudi Arabia **110** C5

▶**Dhaka** Bangl. **105** G5
Capital of Bangladesh. 9th most populous city in the world.

Dhalbhum *reg.* India **105** F5
Dhalgaon India **106** B2
Dhamār Yemen **108** F7
Dhamoni India **104** D4
Dhamtari India **106** D1
Dhana Pak. **111** H5
Dhana Sar Pak. **111** H4
Dhanbad India **105** F5
Dhanera India **104** C4
Dhang Range *mts* Nepal **105** E3
Dhankuta Nepal **105** F4
Dhansia India **104** C3
Dhar India **104** C5
Dhar Adrar *hills* Mauritania **120** B3
Dharampur India **106** B1
Dharan Bazar Nepal **105** F4
Dharashiv India *see* **Osmanabad**
Dhari India **104** B5
Dharmapuri India **106** C3
Dharmavaram India **106** C3
Dharmshala *Hima. Prad.* India *see* **Dharmshala**
Dharmsala *Odisha* India **105** F5
Dharmshala India **104** D2
Dharnaoda India **104** D4
Ḍhar Oualâta *hills* Mauritania **120** C3
Ḍhar Tîchît *hills* Mauritania **120** C3
Dharug National Park Australia **138** E4
Dharur India **106** C2
Dharwad India **106** B3
Dharwar India *see* **Dharwad**
Dharwas India **104** D2
Dhasan *r.* India **104** D4
Dhāt al Ḥājj Saudi Arabia **112** E5

▶**Dhaulagiri** *mt.* Nepal **105** E3
7th highest mountain in Asia and the world.

Dhaulpur India *see* **Dholpur**
Dhaura India **104** D4
Dhaurahra India **104** E4
Dhawlagiri *mt.* Nepal *see* **Dhaulagiri**
Dhebar Lake India *see* **Jaisamand Lake**
Dhekelia Sovereign Base Area *military base* Cyprus **107** A2
Dhemaji India **105** H4
Dhenkanal India **106** E1
Dhībān Jordan **107** B4
Dhidhimótikhon Greece *see* **Didymoteicho**
Dhing India **105** H4
Dhirwah, Wādī adh *watercourse* Jordan **107** C4
Dhodhekánisos *is* Greece *see* **Dodecanese**
Dhola India **104** B5
Dholera India **104** C5
Dholpur India **104** D4
Dhomokós Greece *see* **Domokos**
Dhone India **106** C3
Dhoraji India **104** B5
Dhori India **104** B5
Dhrangadhra India **104** B5
Dhubāb Yemen **108** F7
Dhubri India **105** G4
Dhuburi India *see* **Dhubri**
Dhudial Pak. **111** I3
Dhule India **106** B1
Dhulia India *see* **Dhule**
Dhulian India **105** F4
Dhulian Pak. **111** I3
Dhuma India **104** D5
Dhund *r.* India **104** D4
Dhurwai India **104** D4
Dhuusa Marreeb Somalia **122** E3
Dia *i.* Greece **69** K7
Diablo, Mount *CA* U.S.A. **158** C3
Diablo, Picacho del *mt.* Mex. **166** B2
Diablo Range *mts CA* U.S.A. **158** C3
Diagbe Dem. Rep. Congo **122** C3
Diamante Arg. **178** D4
Diamantina *watercourse* Australia **136** B5
Diamantina Brazil **179** C2
Diamantina, Chapada *plat.* Brazil **179** C1
Diamantina Deep *sea feature* Indian Ocean **185** O8
Diamantina Gates National Park Australia **136** C4
Diamantino Brazil **177** G6
Diamond Islets Australia **136** E3
Diamond Peak *NV* U.S.A. **159** F2
Dianbai China **97** F4
Diancang Shan *mt.* China **96** D3
Dian Chi *l.* China **96** D3
Diandioumé Mali **120** C3
Diane Bank *sea feature* Australia **136** E2
Dianjiang China **96** E2
Dianópolis Brazil **177** I6
Dianyang China *see* **Shidian**
Diaobingshan China **95** J3
Diaokou China **95** I4
Diaoling China **90** C3
Diapaga Burkina Faso **120** D3
Diarizos *r.* Cyprus **107** A2
Diavolo, Mount *hill* India **87** A4
Diaz Point Namibia **124** B4
Dibaya Dem. Rep. Congo **123** C4
Dibella *well* Niger **120** E3
Dibeng S. Africa **124** F4
Dibete Botswana **125** H2
Dibrugarh India **105** H4
Dibse Syria *see* **Dibsī**
Dibsī Syria **107** D2
Dickens *TX* U.S.A. **161** C5
Dickinson *ND* U.S.A. **160** C2
Dicle *r.* Asia **113** F3 *see* **Tigris**
Didēsa Wenz *r.* Eth. **122** D3
Didicas *i.* Phil. **82** C2
Didiéni Mali **120** C3
Didsbury Canada **150** H5
Didwana India **104** C4
Didymoteicho Greece **69** L4
Die France **66** G4
Dieblich Germany **63** H4
Diébougou Burkina Faso **120** C3
Dieburg Germany **63** I5
Diedenhofen France *see* **Thionville**
Diefenbaker, Lake Canada **151** I5
Diego de Almagro, Isla *i.* Chile **178** A8
Diégo Suarez Madag. *see* **Antsirañana**
Diekirch Lux. **62** G5
Diéma Mali **120** C3
Diemel *r.* Germany **63** J3
Điện Biên Vietnam *see* **Điện Biên Phu**
Điện Biên Phu Vietnam **86** C2
Diên Châu Vietnam **86** D3
Diên Khanh Vietnam **87** E4
Diepholz Germany **63** I2
Dieppe France **62** B5
Dierks *AR* U.S.A. **161** E5
Di'er Songhua Jiang *r.* China **90** B3
Diessen Neth. **62** F3
Diest Belgium **62** F4
Dietikon Switz. **66** I3
Dietrich Camp *AK* U.S.A. **149** J2
Diez Germany **63** I4
Diffa Niger **120** E3
Digby Canada **153** I5
Diggi India **104** C4
Diglur India **106** C2
Digne France *see* **Digne-les-Bains**
Digne-les-Bains France **66** H4
Digoin France **66** F3
Digollorin Point *Luzon* Phil. **82** C2
Digos *Mindanao* Phil. **82** D5
Digras India **106** C1
Digri Pak. **111** H5
Digul *r.* Indon. **81** K8
Diguojiadan China **99** D4
Digya National Park Ghana **120** C4
Dihang *r.* India **105** H4 *see* **Brahmaputra**
Dihōk Iraq *see* **Dahūk**
Dihourse, Lac *l.* Canada **153** I2
Diinsoor Somalia **122** E3
Dijon France **66** G3
Dik Chad **121** E4
Diken India **104** C4
Dikhil Djibouti **108** F7
Dikho *r.* India **99** F8
Dikili Turkey **69** L5
Diklosmta *mt.* Rus. Fed. **53** J8
Diksmuide Belgium **62** C3
Dikson Rus. Fed. **76** J2
Dīla Eth. **122** D3
Dilārām Afgh. **111** F3
Dilaram Iran **110** E4

▶**Dili** East Timor **83** C5
Capital of East Timor (Timor-Leste).

Di Linh Vietnam **87** E5
Dillenburg Germany **63** I4
Dilley *TX* U.S.A. **161** D6
Dillingen an der Donau Germany **57** M6
Dillingen (Saar) Germany **62** G5
Dillingham *AK* U.S.A. **148** H4
Dillon *r.* Canada **151** I4
Dillon *MT* U.S.A. **156** E3
Dillon *SC* U.S.A. **163** E5
Dillwyn *VA* U.S.A. **165** F5
Dilolo Dem. Rep. Congo **123** C5
Dilsen Belgium **62** F3
Dimapur India **105** H4
Dimas Mex. **166** D4
Dimashq Syria *see* **Damascus**
Dimbokro Côte d'Ivoire **120** C4
Dimboola Australia **137** C8
Dime Landing *AK* U.S.A. **148** G2
Dimitrov Ukr. *see* **Dymytrov**
Dimitrovgrad Bulg. **69** K3
Dimitrovgrad Rus. Fed. **53** K5
Dimitrovo Bulg. *see* **Pernik**
Dimmitt *TX* U.S.A. **161** C5
Dīmona Israel **107** B4
Dimpho Pan *salt pan* Botswana **124** E3
Dinagat *i.* Phil. **82** D4
Dinajpur Bangl. **105** G4
Dinan France **66** C2
Dinant Belgium **62** E4
Dinapur India **105** F4
Dinar Turkey **69** N5
Dīnār, Kūh-e *mt.* Iran **110** C4
Dinara Planina *mts* Bos.-Herz./Croatia *see* **Dinaric Alps**
Dinaric Alps *mts* Bos.-Herz./Croatia **68** G2
Dinbych U.K. *see* **Denbigh**
Dinbych-y-pysgod U.K. *see* **Tenby**
Dinder National Park Sudan **121** G3
Dindi *r.* India **106** C2
Dindigul India **106** C4
Dindima Nigeria **120** E3
Dindiza Moz. **125** K2
Dindori India **104** E5
Dingalan Bay *Luzon* Phil. **82** C3
Dingbian China **95** F4
Dingcheng China *see* **Dingyuan**
Dingelstädt Germany **63** K3
Dinggo China **99** D6
Dingin, Bukit *mt.* Indon. **84** C3
Dingla Nepal **105** F4
Dingle Bay Ireland **61** B5
Dingnan China **97** G3
Dingo Australia **136** E4
Dingolfing Germany **63** M6
Dingping China *see* **Linshui**
Dingras *Luzon* Phil. **82** C2
Dingshan China **98** D3
Dingtao China **95** H5
Dinguiraye Guinea **120** B3
Dingwall U.K. **60** E3
Dingxi China **94** F5
Dingxian China *see* **Dingzhou**
Dingxin China **94** D3
Dingxing China **95** H4
Dingyuan China **97** H1
Dingzhou China **95** H4
Dingzi Gang *b.* China **95** J4
Dingzikou China **98** F5
Dinh Lâp Vietnam **86** D2
Dinkelsbühl Germany **63** K5
Dinngyê China **99** D7
Dinokwe Botswana **125** H2
Dinosaur *CO* U.S.A. **159** I1
Dinosaur National Monument *nat. park CO* U.S.A. **159** I1
Dinslaken Germany **62** G3
Dintiteladas *Sumatera* Indon. **84** D4
Dinwiddie *VA* U.S.A. **165** G5
Dioïla Mali **120** C3
Diomede *AK* U.S.A. **148** E2
Diomede Islands Rus. Fed./U.S.A. **148** E2
Dionísio Cerqueira Brazil **178** F3
Diorama Brazil **179** A2
Dioscurias Georgia *see* **Sokhumi**
Diouloulou Senegal **120** B3
Diourbel Senegal **120** B3
Dipayal Nepal **104** E3
Diphu India **105** H4
Dipkarpaz Cyprus *see* **Rizokarpason**
Diplo Pak. **111** H5
Dipolog *Mindanao* Phil. **82** C4
Dipperu National Park Australia **136** E4
Dipu China *see* **Anji**
Dir *reg.* Pak. **111** I3
Dirang India **105** H4
Diré Mali **120** C3
Direction, Cape Australia **136** C2
Dirē Dawa Eth. **122** E3
Diriamba Nicaragua **166** [inset] I7
Dirico Angola **123** C5
Dirk Hartog Island Australia **135** A6
Dirranbandi Australia **138** D2
Ḑirs Saudi Arabia **122** E2
Dirschau Poland *see* **Tczew**
Dirty Devil *r. UT* U.S.A. **159** H3
Disa India **104** C4
Disang *r.* India **105** H4
Disappointment, Cape S. Georgia **178** I8
Disappointment, Cape *WA* U.S.A. **156** B3
Disappointment, Lake *salt flat* Australia **135** C5
Disappointment Islands Fr. Polynesia *see* **Désappointement, Îles du**
Disappointment Lake Canada **153** J3
Disaster Bay Australia **138** D6
Discovery Bay Australia **137** C8
Dishna *r. AK* U.S.A. **148** H3
Disko *i.* Greenland *see* **Qeqertarsuaq**
Disko Bugt *b.* Greenland *see* **Qeqertarsuup Tunua**
Dismal Swamp *VA* U.S.A. **162** E4
Dispur India **105** G4
Disputanta *VA* U.S.A. **165** G5
Disraëli Canada **153** H5
Diss U.K. **59** I6
Distrito Federal *admin. dist.* Brazil **179** B1
Distrito Federal *admin. dist.* Mex. **167** F5
Disūq Egypt **112** C5
Dit *i.* Phil. **82** C4
Ditloung S. Africa **124** F5
Dittaino *r. Sicily* Italy **68** F6
Diu India **106** A1
Diuata Mountains *Mindanao* Phil. **82** D4
Diuata Point *Mindanao* Phil. **82** D4
Dīvān Darreh Iran **110** B3
Divehi *country* Indian Ocean *see* **Maldives**
Divi, Point India **106** D3
Divichi Azer. *see* **Dāvāçi**
Divide Mountain *AK* U.S.A. **149** L3
Divilican Bay *Luzon* Phil. **82** C2
Divinópolis Brazil **179** B3
Divnoye Rus. Fed. **53** I7
Divo Côte d'Ivoire **120** C4
Divriği Turkey **112** E3
Diwana Pak. **111** G5
Dīwanīyah Iraq *see* **Ad Dīwānīyah**
Dixfield *ME* U.S.A. **165** J1
Dixon *CA* U.S.A. **158** C2
Dixon *IL* U.S.A. **160** F3
Dixon *KY* U.S.A. **164** B5
Dixon *MT* U.S.A. **156** E3
Dixon Entrance *sea channel* Canada/U.S.A. **149** N5
Dixonville Canada **150** G3
Dixville Canada **165** J1
Diyadin Turkey **113** F3
Diyarbakır Turkey **113** F3
Diz Pak. **111** F5
Diz Chah Iran **110** D3
Dize Turkey *see* **Yüksekova**
Dizney *KY* U.S.A. **164** D5
Djado Niger **120** E2
Djado, Plateau du Niger **120** E2
Djaja, Puntjak *mt.* Indon. *see* **Jaya, Puncak**
Djakarta *Jawa* Indon. *see* **Jakarta**
Djakovica Kosovo *see* **Gjakovë**
Djakovo Croatia *see* **Đakovo**
Djambala Congo **122** B4
Djanet Alg. **120** D2
Djarrit-Uliga-Dalap Marshall Is *see* **Delap-Uliga-Djarrit**
Djelfa Alg. **67** H6
Djéma Cent. Afr. Rep. **122** C3
Djenné Mali **120** C3
Djibo Burkina Faso **120** C3
Djibouti *country* Africa **108** F7

▶**Djibouti** Djibouti **108** F7
Capital of Djibouti.

Djidjelli Alg. *see* **Jijel**
Djizak Uzbek. *see* **Jizzax**
Djougou Benin **120** D4
Djoum Cameroon **120** E4
Djourab, Erg du *des.* Chad **121** E3
Djúpivogur Iceland **54** [inset 1]
Djurås Sweden **55** I6
Djurdjura, Parc National du Alg. **67** I5
Dmitriya Lapteva, Proliv *sea chan.* Rus. Fed. **77** P2
Dmitriyev-L'govskiy Rus. Fed. **53** G5
Dmitriyevsk Ukr. *see* **Makiyivka**
Dmitrov Rus. Fed. **52** H4
Dmytriyevs'k Ukr. *see* **Makiyivka**
Dnepr *r.* Europe **53** F5 *see* **Dnieper**
Dneprodzerzhinsk Ukr. *see* **Dniprodzerzhyns'k**
Dnepropetrovsk Ukr. *see* **Dnipropetrovs'k**

▶**Dnieper** *r.* Europe **53** G7
3rd longest river in Europe.
Also spelt Dnepr (Rus. Fed.) or Dnipro (Ukraine) or Dnyapro (Belarus).

Dniester *r.* Ukr. **53** F6
also spelt Dnister (Ukraine) or Nistru (Moldova)
Dnipro *r.* Europe **53** G7 *see* **Dnieper**
Dniprodzerzhyns'k Ukr. **53** G6
Dnipropetrovs'k Ukr. **53** G6
Dnister *r.* Ukr. **53** F6 *see* **Dniester**
Dno Rus. Fed. **52** F4
Dnyapro *r.* Europe **53** F6 *see* **Dnieper**
Doaba Pak. **111** H3
Doangdoangan Besar *i.* Indon. **85** G4
Doangdoangan Kecil *i.* Indon. **85** G4
Đoan Hung Vietnam **86** D2
Doba Chad **121** E4
Dobdain China **94** E5
Dobele Latvia **55** M8
Döbeln Germany **63** N3
Doberai, Jazirah *pen.* Indon. **81** I7
Doberai Peninsula Indon. *see* **Doberai, Jazirah**
Dobo Indon. **81** I8
Doboj Bos.-Herz. **68** H2
Do Borjī Iran **110** D4
Döbraberg *hill* Germany **63** L4
Dobrich Bulg. **69** L3
Dobrinka Rus. Fed. **53** I5
Dobroye Rus. Fed. **53** H5
Dobrudja *reg.* Romania *see* **Dobruja**
Dobruja *reg.* Romania **69** L3
Dobrush Belarus **53** F5
Dobryanka Rus. Fed. **51** R4
Dobyn Kazakh. **98** C4
Dobzha China **99** E7
Doc Can *rf* Phil. **82** B5
Doce *r.* Brazil **179** D2
Dochart *r.* U.K. **60** E4
Docking U.K. **59** H6
Doctor Arroyo Mex. **167** E4
Doctor Belisario Domínguez Mex. **166** D2
Doctor Hicks Range *hills* Australia **135** D7
Doctor Pedro P. Peña Para. **178** D2
Doda India **104** C2
Doda Betta *mt.* India **106** C4
Dod Ballapur India **106** C3
Dodē China **99** E7
Dodecanese *is* Greece **69** L7
Dodekanisa *is* Greece *see* **Dodecanese**
Dodekanisos *is* Greece *see* **Dodecanese**
Dodge City *KS* U.S.A. **160** C4
Dodgeville *WI* U.S.A. **160** F3
Dodman Point U.K. **59** C8

▶**Dodoma** Tanz. **123** D4
Capital of Tanzania.

Dodsonville *OH* U.S.A. **164** D4
Doetinchem Neth. **62** G3
Dofa *Maluku* Indon. **83** C3
Dog *r.* Canada **152** C4
Dogai Coring *salt l.* China **99** E6
Dogaicoring Qangco *salt l.* China **99** E6
Doğanşehir Turkey **112** E3
Dogên Co *l.* China **99** E7
Dōgen-ko *l.* Japan **93** F7
Doghārūn Iran **111** F3
Dog Island Canada **153** J2
Dog Lake *Man.* Canada **151** L5
Dog Lake *Ont.* Canada **152** C4
Dog Lake *Ont.* Canada **152** D4
Dōgo *i.* Japan **91** D5
Dogondoutchi Niger **120** D3
Dog Rocks *is* Bahamas **163** E7
Doğubeyazıt Turkey **113** G3
Doğu Menteşe Dağları *mts* Turkey **69** M6
Dogxung Zangbo *r.* China **99** D7
Do'gyaling China **105** G3

▶**Doha** Qatar **110** C5
Capital of Qatar.

Dohad India *see* **Dahod**
Dohazari Bangl. **105** H5
Dohrighat India **99** C8
Doi *i.* Fiji **133** I4
Doi *i. Maluku* Indon. **83** C2
Doi Inthanon National Park Thai. **86** B3
Doijang China **99** E7
Doi Luang National Park Thai. **86** B3
Doire U.K. *see* **Londonderry**
Doi Saket Thai. **86** B3
Dois Irmãos, Serra dos *hills* Brazil **177** J5
Dokan, Sadd Iraq **113** G4
Dok-dō *i.* N. Pacific Ocean *see* **Liancourt Rocks**
Dokhara, Dunes de *des.* Alg. **64** F5
Dokka Norway **55** G6
Dokkum Neth. **62** F1
Dokog He *r.* China **96** D2
Dokri Pak. **111** H5
Dokshukino Rus. Fed. *see* **Nartkala**
Dokshytsy Belarus **55** O9
Dokuchayeva, Mys *c.* Rus. Fed. **90** G3
Dokuchayevka Kazakh. *see* **Karamendy**
Dokuchayevs'k Ukr. **53** H7
Dolbenmaen U.K. **59** C6
Dol-de-Bretagne France **66** D2
Dole France **66** G3
Dolgellau U.K. **59** D6
Dolgen Germany **63** N1
Dolgiy, Ostrov *i.* Rus. Fed. **52** L1
Dolgorukovo Rus. Fed. **53** H5
Dolina Ukr. *see* **Dolyna**
Dolinsk Rus. Fed. **90** F3
Dolisie Congo *see* **Loubomo**
Dolit *Halmahera* Indon. **83** C3
Dolleman Island Antarctica **188** L2
Dollnstein Germany **63** L6
Dolo *Sulawesi* Indon. **83** A3
Dolok, Pulau *i.* Indon. **81** J8
Dolomites *mts* Italy **68** D2
Dolomiti *mts* Italy *see* **Dolomites**
Dolomiti Bellunesi, Parco Nazionale delle *nat. park* Italy **68** D1
Dolomitiche, Alpi *mts* Italy *see* **Dolomites**
Dolon Ashuusu *pass* Kyrg. **98** A4
Dolonnur China **95** I3
Dolo Odo Eth. **122** E3
Doloon Mongolia *see* **Tsogt-Ovoo**
Dolores Arg. **178** E5
Dolores Guat. **167** H5
Dolores Mex. **166** C3
Dolores Uruguay **178** E4
Dolores *CO* U.S.A. **159** I3
Dolores Hidalgo Mex. **167** E4
Dolphin and Union Strait Canada **146** G3
Dolphin Head *hd* Namibia **124** B3
Đô Lương Vietnam **86** D3
Dolyna Ukr. **53** D6
Domaila India **104** D3
Domaniç Turkey **69** M5
Domar Bangl. **99** E8
Domar China **99** C6
Domartang China **99** F7
Domažlice Czech Rep. **63** M5
Domba China **99** F6
Dom Bākh Iran **110** B3
Dombås Norway **54** F5
Dombóvár Hungary **68** H1
Dombrau Poland *see* **Dąbrowa Górnicza**
Dombrovitsa Ukr. *see* **Dubrovytsya**
Dombrowa Poland *see* **Dąbrowa Górnicza**
Domda China *see* **Qingshuihe**
Dome Argus *ice feature* Antarctica **188** E1
Dome Charlie *ice feature* Antarctica **188** F2
Dome Creek Canada **150** F4
Dome Rock Mountains *AZ* U.S.A. **159** F5
Domeyko Chile **178** B3
Domfront France **66** D2
Dominica *country* West Indies **169** L5
Dominicana, República *country* West Indies *see* **Dominican Republic**
Dominican Republic *country* West Indies **169** J5
Dominion, Cape Canada **147** K3
Dominique *i.* Fr. Polynesia *see* **Hiva Oa**
Dömitz Germany **63** L1
Dom Joaquim Brazil **179** C2
Dommel *r.* Neth. **62** F3
Domo Eth. **122** E3
Domokos Greece **69** J5
Dompu *Sumbawa* Indon. **85** G5
Domuyo, Volcán *vol.* Arg. **178** B5
Domville, Mount *hill* Australia **138** E2
Don Mex. **166** C3

▶**Don** *r.* Rus. Fed. **53** H7
5th longest river in Europe.

Don *r.* U.K. **60** G3
Don, Xé *r.* Laos **86** D4
Donaghadee U.K. **61** G3
Donaghmore U.K. **61** F3
Donald Australia **138** A6
Donaldsonville *LA* U.S.A. **161** F6
Donalsonville *GA* U.S.A. **163** C6
Doñana, Parque Nacional de *nat. park* Spain **67** C5
Donau *r.* Europe **57** P6 *see* **Danube**
Donauwörth Germany **63** K6
Don Benito Spain **67** D4
Doncaster U.K. **58** F5
Dondo Angola **123** B4
Dondo Moz. **123** D5
Dondo, Tanjung *pt* Indon. **83** B2
Dondo, Teluk *b.* Indon. **83** B2
Dondonay *i.* Phil. **82** C4
Dondra Head *hd* Sri Lanka **106** D5
Donegal Ireland **61** D3
Donegal Bay Ireland **61** D3
Donenbay Kazakh. **98** C2
Donets'k Ukr. **53** H7
Donetsko-Amrovsiyevka Ukr. *see* **Amvrosiyivka**
Donets'kyy Kryazh *hills* Rus. Fed./Ukr. **53** H6
Donga *r.* Cameroon/Nigeria **120** D4
Dong'an China **97** F3
Dongane, Lagoa *lag.* Moz. **125** L3
Dongara Australia **135** A7
Dongbatu China **98** F4
Dongbei Pingyuan *plain* China **95** J3
Dongbo China *see* **Mêdog**
Dongchuan *Yunnan* China *see* **Yao'an**
Dongchuan *Yunnan* China **96** D3
Dongco China **99** D6
Dong Co *l.* China **99** D6
Dongcun *Shandong* China *see* **Haiyang**
Dongcun *Shanxi* China *see* **Lanxian**
Dong Dabsan Hu *salt l.* China **99** F5
Dong'e China **95** I4
Dongfang China **97** F5
Dongfanghong China **90** D3
Donggala *Sulawesi* Indon. **83** A3
Donggang *Liaoning* China **91** B5
Donggang *Shandong* China **95** I5
Donggi Conag *l.* China **94** D5
Donggou *Liaoning* China *see* **Donggang**
Donggou *Qinghai* China **94** E5
Donggu China **97** G3

Dongguan China 97 G4
Donghai China 95 I5
Dong Hai sea N. Pacific Ocean see East China Sea
Donghaiba China 94 F4
Đông Hơi Vietnam 86 D3
Donghuachi China 95 G4
Donghuang China see Xishui
Dongjiang Shuiku resr China 97 G3
Dongjug China 96 B2
Dongkait, Tanjung pt Indon. 83 A3
Dongkar China 99 E7
Dongkou China 97 F3
Donglai China 95 J4
Donglan China 96 E3
Dongle China 94 E4
Dongliao He r. China 95 J3
Donglük China 98 E5
Dongmen China see Luocheng
Dongming China 95 H5
Dongminzhutun China 90 A3
Dongning China 90 C3
Dongo Angola 123 B5
Dongo Dem. Rep. Congo 122 B3
Dongola Sudan 108 D6
Dongou Congo 122 B3
Dong Phraya Yen esc. Thai. 86 C4
Dongping Guangdong China 97 G4
Dongping Hunan China see Anhua
Dongping Hu l. China 95 I4
Dongpo China see Meishan
Dongqiao China 99 E7
Dongqinghu China 94 F4
Dong Qu r. China 99 F6
Dongquan China 94 C3
Dongshan Fujian China 97 H4
Dongshan Jiangsu China 97 I2
Dongshan Jiangxi China see Shangyou
Dongshao China 97 G3
Dongsha Qundao is China 80 F2
Dongsheng Nei Mongol China see Ordos
Dongsheng Sichuan China see Shuangliu
Dongshuan China see Tangdan
Dongtai China 97 I1
Dong Taijnar Hu l. China 99 F5
Dongting Hu l. China 97 G2
Dongtou China 97 I3
Đông Triêu Vietnam 86 D2
Dong Ujimqin Qi China see Uliastai
Đông Văn Vietnam 86 D2
Dongxiang China 97 H2
Dongxiangzu China 94 E5
Dongxi Liandao i. China 97 H1
Dongxing Guangxi China 96 E4
Dongxing Heilong. China 90 B3
Dongxing Heilong. China 90 D3
Dongyang China 97 I2
Dongying China 95 I4
Dongzhen China 94 E4
Dongzhi China 97 H2
Donkerbroek Neth. 62 G1
Donnacona Canada 153 H5
Donnelly AK U.S.A. 149 K3
Donnellys Crossing N.Z. 139 D2
Donner Pass CA U.S.A. 158 C2
Donnersberg hill Germany 63 H5
Donostia Spain see San Sebastián
Donousa i. Greece 69 K6
Donoussa i. Greece see Donousa
Donskoye Rus. Fed. 53 I7
Donsol Luzon Phil. 82 C3
Donyztau, Sor dry lake Kazakh. 102 A2
Dooagh Ireland 61 B4
Doomadgee Australia 136 B3
Doon r. U.K. 60 E5
Doon, Loch l. U.K. 60 E5
Doonbeg r. Ireland 61 C5
Doonerak, Mount AK U.S.A. 149 J2
Doorn Neth. 62 F2
Door Peninsula WI U.S.A. 164 B1
Doorwerth Neth. 62 F3
Dooxo Nugaaleed valley Somalia 122 E3
Doqêmo China 99 F7
Doqoi China 99 E7
Do Qu r. China 94 D5
Dor watercourse Afgh. 111 F4
Dor Israel 107 B3
Dora NM U.S.A. 161 C5
Dora, Lake salt flat Australia 134 C5
Dorado Mex. 166 D3
Dorah Pass Pak. 111 H2
Dorānī reg. Afgh. 111 G4
Doran Lake Canada 151 I2
Ḏoray r. Afgh. 111 G4
Dorbiljin China see Emin
Dorbod China see Taikang
Dorbod Qi China see Ulan Hua
Dorchester U.K. 59 E8
Dordabis Namibia 124 C2
Dordogne r. France 66 D4
Dordrecht Neth. 62 E3
Dordrecht S. Africa 125 H6
Doreenville Namibia 124 D2
Doré Lake Canada 151 J4
Doré Lake l. Canada 151 J4
Dores do Indaiá Brazil 179 B2
Dorgê Co l. China 94 C5
Dörgön Mongolia 94 C1
Dori Burkina Faso 120 C3
Doring r. S. Africa 124 D6
Dorisvale Australia 134 E3
Dorking U.K. 59 G7
Dormagen Germany 62 G3
Dormans France 62 D5
Dormidontovka Rus. Fed. 90 D3
Dornoch U.K. 60 E3
Dornoch Firth est. U.K. 60 E3
Dornod prov. Mongolia 95 H1
Dornogovĭ prov. Mongolia 95 G2
Dornum Germany 63 H1
Doro Mali 120 C3
Dorogobuzh Rus. Fed. 53 G5
Dorogorskoye Rus. Fed. 52 J2
Doroḩ Iran 111 F3
Dorohoi Romania 53 E7
Doroninskoye Rus. Fed. 95 H1
Döröö Nuur salt l. Mongolia 94 C2
Dorostol Bulg. see Silistra
Dorotea Sweden 54 J4
Dorpat Estonia see Tartu
Dorre Island Australia 135 A6
Dorrigo Australia 138 F3
Dorris CA U.S.A. 156 C4
Dorset Canada 165 F1
Dorset & East Devon Coast tourist site U.K. 59 D8
Dorsoidong Co l. China 99 E6
Dortmund Germany 63 H3
Dörtyol Turkey 107 C1
Dorūd Iran 110 C3
Dorum Germany 63 I1
Doruma Dem. Rep. Congo 122 C3
Dorūneh, Kūh-e mts Iran 110 E3
Dörverden Germany 63 J2
Dörvöljin Mongolia 94 C2
Dorylaeum Turkey see Eskişehir
Dos Bahías, Cabo c. Arg. 178 C6
Dos de Mayo Peru 176 C5
Doshakh, Koh-i- mt. Afgh. see Do Shākh, Kūh-e
Do Shākh, Kūh-e mt. Afgh. 111 F3
Dōshi Japan 93 F3
Dos Lagunos Guat. 167 H5
Đô Sơn Vietnam 86 D2
Dos Palos CA U.S.A. 158 C3
Dosse r. Germany 63 M2
Dosso Niger 120 D3
Dostyk Kazakh. 98 C3
Dothan AL U.S.A. 163 C6
Dot Lake AK U.S.A. 149 K3
Dotsero CO U.S.A. 159 J2
Douai France 62 D4
Douala Cameroon 120 D4
Douarnenez France 66 B2
Double Headed Shot Cays is Bahamas 163 D8
Double Island H.K. China 97 [inset]
Double Island Point Australia 137 F5
Double Mountain Fork r. TX U.S.A. 161 C5
Double Peak AK U.S.A. 148 I3
Double Peak CA U.S.A. 158 D4
Double Point Australia 136 D3
Double Springs AL U.S.A. 163 C5
Doubs r. France/Switz. 66 G3
Doubtful Sound inlet N.Z. 139 A7
Doubtless Bay N.Z. 139 D2
Doucan China see Fuping
Douentza Mali 120 C3
Dougga tourist site Tunisia 68 C6

▶Douglas Isle of Man 58 C4
Capital of the Isle of Man.

Douglas S. Africa 124 F5
Douglas U.K. 60 F5
Douglas AZ U.S.A. 157 F7
Douglas GA U.S.A. 163 D6
Douglas WY U.S.A. 156 G4
Douglas, Cape AK U.S.A. 148 I4
Douglas Reef i. Japan see Okino-Tori-shima
Douglasville GA U.S.A. 163 C5
Douhudi China see Gong'an
Doulatpur Bangl. see Daulatpur
Douliu Taiwan see Touliu
Doullens France 62 C4
Douna Mali 120 C3
Doune U.K. 60 E4
Doupovské hory mts Czech Rep. 63 N4
Dourada, Serra hills Brazil 179 A2
Dourada, Serra mts Brazil 179 A1
Dourados Brazil 178 F2
Douro r. Port. 67 B3
also known as Duero (Spain)
Doushi China see Gong'an
Doushui Shuiku resr China 97 G3
Douve r. France 59 F9
Douzy France 62 F5
Dove r. U.K. 59 F6
Dove Brook Canada 153 K3
Dove Creek CO U.S.A. 159 I3
Dover U.K. 59 I7

▶Dover DE U.S.A. 165 H4
Capital of Delaware.

Dover NH U.S.A. 165 J2
Dover NJ U.S.A. 165 H3
Dover OH U.S.A. 164 E3
Dover TN U.S.A. 162 C4
Dover, Strait of France/U.K. 66 E1
Dover-Foxcroft ME U.S.A. 165 K1
Dovey r. U.K. 59 D6
Dovrefjell Nasjonalpark nat. park Norway 54 F5
Dowagiac MI U.S.A. 164 B3
Dowi, Tanjung pt Indon. 84 B2
Dowlaiswaram India 106 D2
Dowlatābād Afgh. 111 F3
Dowlatābād Fārs Iran 110 C4
Dowlatābād Fārs Iran 110 D4
Dowlatābād Khorāsān-e Razavī Iran 110 E2
Dowlatābād Khorāsān-e Razavī Iran 111 F2
Dowlat Khān Afgh. 111 H3
Dowlat Yār Afgh. 111 G3
Downieville CA U.S.A. 158 C2
Downpatrick U.K. 61 G3
Downsville NY U.S.A. 165 H2
Doxong China 99 F7
Doyle CA U.S.A. 158 C1
Doylestown PA U.S.A. 165 H3
Dozdān r. Iran 110 E5
Dōzen is Japan 91 D5
Dozois, Réservoir resr Canada 152 F5
Dozulé France 59 G9
Drâa, Hamada du plat. Alg. 64 C6
Dracena Brazil 179 A3
Drachten Neth. 62 G1
Drăgănești-Olt Romania 69 K2
Drăgășani Romania 69 K2
Dragonera, Isla i. Spain see Sa Dragonera
Dragoon AZ U.S.A. 159 H5
Dragsfjärd Fin. 55 M6
Draguignan France 66 H5
Drahichyn Belarus 55 N10
Drake Australia 138 F2
Drake ND U.S.A. 160 C2
Drakensberg mts S. Africa 125 I3
Drake Passage S. Atlantic Ocean 184 D9
Drakes Bay CA U.S.A. 158 B3
Drama Greece 69 K4
Drammen Norway 55 G7
Drang, Ia r. Cambodia 87 D4
Drangedal Norway 55 F7
Drangme Chhu r. Bhutan 99 E8
Dransfeld Germany 63 J3
Draper, Mount AK U.S.A. 149 M4
Draperstown U.K. 61 F3
Drapsaca Afgh. see Kunduz
Dras India 104 C2
Drasan Pak. 111 I2
Drau r. Europe 57 O7 see Drava
Drava r. Europe 68 H2
also known as Drau (Austria), Drave or Drava (Slovenia and Croatia), Dráva (Hungary)
Dráva r. Europe see Drava
Drave r. Europe see Drava
Drayton Valley Canada 150 H4
Drazinda Pak. 111 H4
Dréan Alg. 68 B6
Dreistelzberge hill Germany 63 J4
Drentse Hoofdvaart canal Neth. 62 G2
Drepano, Akra pt Greece see Laimos, Akrotirio
Dresden Canada 164 D2
Dresden Germany 57 N5
Dreux France 62 B6
Drevsjø Norway 55 H6
Drewryville VA U.S.A. 165 G5
Dri China 96 C2
Driffield U.K. 58 G4
Driftwood PA U.S.A. 165 F3
Driggs ID U.S.A. 156 F4
Drillham Australia 138 E1
Drimoleague Ireland 61 C6
Drina r. Bos.-Herz./Serbia 69 H2
Driscoll Island Antarctica 188 J1
Drissa Belarus see Vyerkhnyadzvinsk
Drniš Croatia 68 G3
Drobeta-Turnu Severin Romania 69 J2
Drochtersen Germany 63 J1
Drogheda Ireland 61 F4
Drogichin Belarus see Drahichyn
Drogobych Ukr. see Drohobych
Drohobych Ukr. 53 D6
Droichead Átha Ireland see Drogheda
Droichead Nua Ireland see Newbridge
Droitwich U.K. see Droitwich Spa
Droitwich Spa U.K. 59 E6
Dromedary, Cape Australia 138 E6
Dromod Ireland 61 E4
Dromore Northern Ireland U.K. 61 E3
Dromore Northern Ireland U.K. 61 F3
Dronfield U.K. 58 F5
Dronning Louise Land reg. Greenland 189 I1
Dronning Maud Land reg. Antarctica see Queen Maud Land
Dronten Neth. 62 F2
Drovyanaya Rus. Fed. 95 H1
Druk-Yul country Asia see Bhutan
Drumheller Canada 151 H5
Drummond atoll Kiribati see Tabiteuea
Drummond MT U.S.A. 156 E3
Drummond, Lake VA U.S.A. 165 G5
Drummond Island Kiribati see McKean
Drummond Range hills Australia 136 D5
Drummondville Canada 153 G5
Drummore U.K. 60 E6
Drury Lake Canada 150 C2
Druskieniki Lith. see Druskininkai
Druskininkai Lith. 55 N10
Druzhina Rus. Fed. 77 P3
Druzhnaya Gorka Rus. Fed. 55 Q7
Dry r. Australia 134 F3
Dryanovo Bulg. 69 K3
Dryberry Lake Canada 151 M5
Dry Creek AK U.S.A. 149 K3
Dryden Canada 151 M5
Dryden NY U.S.A. 165 G2
Dry Fork r. WY U.S.A. 156 G4
Drygalski Ice Tongue Antarctica 188 H1
Drygalski Island Antarctica 188 F2
Dry Lake NV U.S.A. 159 F3
Dry Lake l. ND U.S.A. 160 D1
Drymen U.K. 60 E4
Dry Ridge KY U.S.A. 164 C4
Drysdale r. Australia 134 D3
Drysdale River National Park Australia 134 D3
Dry Tortugas is FL U.S.A. 163 D7
Du'an China 97 F4
Duancun China see Wuxiang
Duaringa Australia 136 E4
Duars reg. India 99 E8
Duarte, Pico mt. Dom. Rep. 169 J5
Duartina Brazil 179 A3
Ḑubā Saudi Arabia 108 E4
Dubai U.A.E. 110 D5
Dubakella Mountain CA U.S.A. 158 B1
Dubawnt r. Canada 151 L2
Dubawnt Lake Canada 151 K2
Dubayy U.A.E. see Dubai
Dubbo Australia 138 D4
Dublán Mex. 166 D2

▶Dublin Ireland 61 F4
Capital of Ireland.

Dublin GA U.S.A. 163 D5
Dubna Rus. Fed. 52 H4
Dubno Ukr. 53 E6
Dubois ID U.S.A. 156 E3
Dubois IN U.S.A. 164 B4
Du Bois PA U.S.A. 165 F3
Dubovka Rus. Fed. 53 J6
Dubovskoye Rus. Fed. 53 I7
Dubréka Guinea 120 B4
Dubris U.K. see Dover
Dubrovnik Croatia 68 H3
Dubrovytsya Ukr. 53 E6
Dubuque IA U.S.A. 160 F3
Dubysa r. Lith. 55 M9
Đức Bôn Vietnam 87 D5
Duc de Gloucester, Îles du is Fr. Polynesia 187 K7
Duchang China 97 H2
Ducheng China see Yunan
Duchesne UT U.S.A. 159 H1
Duchesne r. UT U.S.A. 159 I1
Duchess Australia 136 B4
Duchess Canada 151 I5
Ducie Island atoll Pitcairn Is 187 L7
Duck Bay Canada 151 K4
Duck Creek r. Australia 134 B5
Duck Lake Canada 151 J4
Duckwater Peak NV U.S.A. 159 F2
Duc Tho Vietnam 86 D3
Ducun China see Fuping
Dudelange Lux. 62 G5
Duderstadt Germany 63 K3
Dudhi India 105 E4
Dudhwa India 104 E3
Dudinka Rus. Fed. 76 J3
Dudley U.K. 59 E6
Dudleyville AZ U.S.A. 159 H5
Dudna r. India 106 C2
Dudu India 104 C4
Duékoué Côte d'Ivoire 120 C4
Duen, Bukit vol. Indon. 84 C3
Duero r. Spain 67 C3
also known as Douro (Portugal)
Duffel Belgium 62 E3
Dufferin, Cape Canada 152 F2
Duffer Peak NV U.S.A. 156 D4
Duff Islands Solomon Is 133 G2
Duffreboy, Lac l. Canada 153 H2
Dufftown U.K. 60 F3
Dufourspitze mt. Italy/Switz. 66 H4
Dufrost, Pointe pt Canada 152 F1
Dugi Otok i. Croatia 68 F2
Dugi Rat Croatia 68 G3
Dugui Qarag China 95 G4
Du He r. China 97 F1
Duida-Marahuaca, Parque Nacional nat. park Venez. 176 E3
Duisburg Germany 62 G3
Duiwelskloof S. Africa 125 J2
Dujiangyan China 96 D2
Dukathole S. Africa 125 H6
Duke Island AK U.S.A. 149 O5
Duke of Clarence atoll Tokelau see Nukunonu
Duke of Gloucester Islands Fr. Polynesia see Duc de Gloucester, Îles du
Duke of York atoll Tokelau see Atafu
Duk Fadiat South Sudan 121 G4
Dukhovnitskoye Rus. Fed. 53 K5
Duki Pak. 111 H4
Duki Rus. Fed. 90 D2
Duki r. Rus. Fed. 90 D2
Dukou China see Panzhihua
Dūkštas Lith. 55 O9
Dulaanhaan Mongolia 94 F1
Dulac LA U.S.A. 161 F6
Dulan China 94 D4
Dulawan Mindanao Phil. see Datu Piang
Dulbi r. AK U.S.A. 148 H2
Dulce r. Arg. 178 D4
Dulce NM U.S.A. 157 G5
Dulce, Golfo b. Costa Rica 166 [inset] J7
Dulce Nombre de Culmí Hond. 166 [inset] I6
Dul'durga Rus. Fed. 95 H1
Dulhunty r. Australia 136 C1
Dulishi Hu salt l. China 99 C6
Dulit, Pegunungan mts Malaysia 85 F2
Duliu Jiang r. China 97 F3
Dullewala Pak. 111 H4
Dullstroom S. Africa 125 J3
Dülmen Germany 63 H3
Dulmera India 104 C3
Dulovo Bulg. 69 L3
Duluth MN U.S.A. 160 E2
Dulverton U.K. 59 D7
Dūmā Syria 107 C3
Dumaguete Negros Phil. 82 C4
Dumai Sumatera Indon. 84 C2
Dumanquilas Bay Mindanao Phil. 82 C5
Dumaran i. Phil. 82 C4
Dumarchen i. Indon. 83 C1
Dumaresq r. Australia 138 E2
Dumas TX U.S.A. 161 C5
Dumat al Jandal Saudi Arabia 113 E5
Ḑumayr Syria 107 C3
Ḑumayr, Jabal mts Syria 107 C3
Dumbakh Iran see Dom Bākh
Dumbarton U.K. 60 E5
Dumbe S. Africa 125 J4
Ďumbier mt. Slovakia 57 Q6
Dumchele India 104 D2
Dumdum i. Indon. 84 D2
Dum Duma India 105 H4
Dumfries U.K. 60 F5
Dumka India 105 F4
Dumoga Sulawesi Indon. 83 C2
Dumont d'Urville research station Antarctica 188 G2
Dumont d'Urville Sea Antarctica 188 G2
Dümpelfeld Germany 62 G4
Dumyāţ Egypt 112 C5
Dumyât Egypt see Dumyāţ
Duna r. Europe 68 H2 see Danube
Dünaburg Latvia see Daugavpils
Dunaj r. Europe see Danube
Dunajská Streda Slovakia 57 P7
Dunakeszi Hungary 69 H1
Dunany Point Ireland 61 F4
Dunărea r. Europe see Danube
Dunării, Delta Romania/Ukr. see Danube Delta
Dunaújváros Hungary 68 H1
Dunav r. Europe see Danube
Dunay r. Europe see Danube
Dunayivtsi Ukr. 53 E6
Dunbar Australia 136 C3
Dunbar U.K. 60 G4
Dunbar AK U.S.A. 149 J2
Dunblane U.K. 60 F4
Dunboyne Ireland 61 F4
Duncan Canada 150 F5
Duncan AZ U.S.A. 159 I5
Duncan OK U.S.A. 161 D5
Duncan, Cape Canada 152 E3
Duncan, Lac l. Canada 152 F3
Duncan Lake Canada 150 H2
Duncan Passage India 87 A5
Duncansby Head hd U.K. 60 F2
Duncan Town Bahamas 163 F8
Duncormick Ireland 61 F5
Dundaga Latvia 55 M8
Dundalk Ireland 61 F3
Dundalk MD U.S.A. 165 G4
Dundalk Bay Ireland 61 F4
Dundas Canada 164 F2
Dundas Greenland 147 L2
Dundas, Lake salt flat Australia 135 C8
Dundas Island Canada 149 O5
Dundas Strait Australia 134 E2
Dundbürd Mongolia see Batnorov
Dún Dealgan Ireland see Dundalk
Dundee S. Africa 125 J5
Dundee U.K. 60 G4
Dundee MI U.S.A. 164 D3
Dundee NY U.S.A. 165 G2
Dundgovĭ prov. Mongolia 94 F2
Dund Hot China 95 I3
Dundonald U.K. 61 G3
Dundoo Australia 138 B1
Dundrennan U.K. 60 F6
Dundrum U.K. 61 G3
Dundrum Bay U.K. 61 G3
Dundwa Range mts India/Nepal 105 E4
Dune, Lac l. Canada 152 G2
Dunedin N.Z. 139 C7
Dunedin FL U.S.A. 163 D6
Dunfermline U.K. 60 F4
Dungannon U.K. 61 F3
Dún Garbhán Ireland see Dungarvan
Dungarpur India 104 C5
Dungarvan Ireland 61 E5
Dung Co l. China 99 E7
Dungeness hd U.K. 59 H8
Dungeness, Punta pt Arg. 178 C8
Düngenheim Germany 63 H4
Dungiven U.K. 61 F3
Dungog Australia 138 E4
Dungu Dem. Rep. Congo 122 C3
Dungun Malaysia 84 C1
Dungunab Sudan 108 E5
Dunhua China 90 C4
Dunhuang China 98 F4
Dunkeld Australia 138 D1
Dunkeld U.K. 60 F4
Dunkellin r. Ireland 61 D4
Dunkerque France see Dunkirk
Dunkery Hill hill U.K. 59 D7
Dunkirk France 62 C3
Dunkirk NY U.S.A. 164 F2
Dún Laoghaire Ireland 61 F4
Dunlap IA U.S.A. 160 E3
Dunlap TN U.S.A. 162 C5
Dunlavin Ireland 61 F4
Dunleer Ireland 61 F4
Dunloy U.K. 61 F2
Dunmanway Ireland 61 C6
Dunmarra Australia 134 F4
Dunmor KY U.S.A. 164 B5
Dunmore Ireland 61 D4
Dunmore PA U.S.A. 165 H3
Dunmore Town Bahamas 163 E7
Dunmurry U.K. 61 G3
Dunnet Head hd U.K. 60 F2
Dunnigan CA U.S.A. 158 C2
Dunning NE U.S.A. 160 C3
Dunnville Canada 164 F2
Dunnville KY U.S.A. 164 C5
Dunolly Australia 138 A6
Dunoon U.K. 60 E5
Dunphy NV U.S.A. 158 E1
Duns U.K. 60 G5
Dunseith ND U.S.A. 160 C1
Dunstable U.K. 59 G7
Dunstan Mountains N.Z. 139 B7
Dun-sur-Meuse France 62 F5
Duntroon N.Z. 139 C7
Dunvegan Lake Canada 151 J2
Dunyapur Pak. 111 H4
Duobukur He r. China 95 K1
Duolun China see Dolonnur
Duomula China 99 C6
Dupang Ling mts China 97 F3
Duperré Alg. see Aïn Defla
Dupnitsa Bulg. 69 J3
Dupree SD U.S.A. 160 C2
Duque de Bragança Angola see Calandula
Dūrā West Bank 107 B4
Durack r. Australia 134 D3
Durack Range hills Australia 134 D4
Dura Europos Syria see Aş Şāliḩīyah
Durağan Turkey 112 D2
Durance r. France 66 G5
Durand WI U.S.A. 160 F2
Durango Mex. 161 B7
Durango state Mex. 161 B7
Durango Spain 67 E2
Durango CO U.S.A. 159 J3
Durant OK U.S.A. 161 D5
Durazno Uruguay 178 E4
Durazzo Albania see Durrës
Durban S. Africa 125 J5
Durban-Corbières France 66 F5
Durbanville S. Africa 124 D7
Durbin WV U.S.A. 164 F4
Durbun Pak. 111 G4
Durbuy Belgium 62 F4
Düre China 98 E3
Düren Germany 62 G4
Düren Iran 110 E3
Durg India 104 E5
Durgapur Bangl. 105 G4
Durgapur India 105 F5
Durham Canada 164 E1
Durham U.K. 58 F4
Durham NC U.S.A. 162 E5
Durham Downs Australia 137 C5
Duri Sumatera Indon. 84 C2
Duriansebatang Kalimantan Indon. 85 E3
Durlas Ireland see Thurles
Durlești Moldova 69 M1
Durmersheim Germany 63 I6
Durmitor mt. Montenegro 69 H3
Durmitor, Nacionalni Park nat. park Montenegro 68 H3
Durness U.K. 60 E2
Durocortorum France see Reims
Durong South Australia 137 E5
Durostorum Bulg. see Silistra
Durour Island P.N.G. see Aua Island
Durovernum U.K. see Canterbury
Durrës Albania 69 H4
Durrie Australia 136 C5
Durrington U.K. 59 F7
Dursey Island Ireland 61 B6
Dursunbey Turkey 69 M5
Duru China see Wuchuan
Durukhsi Somalia 122 E3
Durusu Gölü l. Turkey 69 M4
Durūz, Jabal ad mt. Syria 107 C3
D'Urville, Tanjung pt Indon. 81 J7
D'Urville Island N.Z. 139 D5
Duşak Turkm. 111 E2
Dushai Pak. 111 G4
Dushan China 96 E3

▶Dushanbe Tajik. 111 H2
Capital of Tajikistan.

Dushanzi China 98 D3
Dusheti Georgia 113 G2
Dushikou China 95 H3
Dushore PA U.S.A. 165 G3
Dusse-Alin', Khrebet mts Rus. Fed. 90 D2
Düsseldorf Germany 62 G3
Dusty NM U.S.A. 159 J5
Dusty WA U.S.A. 156 D3
Dutch East Indies country Asia see Indonesia
Dutch Guiana country S. America see Suriname
Dutch Mountain UT U.S.A. 159 G1
Dutlwe Botswana 124 F2
Dutse Nigeria 120 D3
Dutsin-Ma Nigeria 120 D3
Dutton r. Australia 136 C4
Dutton Canada 164 E2
Dutton MT U.S.A. 156 F3
Dutton, Lake salt flat Australia 137 B6
Dutton, Mount UT U.S.A. 159 G2
Duval Canada 151 J5
Duvert, Lac l. Canada 153 H2
Duvno Bos.-Herz. see Tomislavgrad
Duwa China 99 B5
Duwin Iraq 113 G3
Düxanbibazar China 99 C5
Duyun China 96 E3
Duzab Pak. 111 F5
Düzce Turkey 69 N4
Duzdab Iran see Zāhedān
Dvina r. Europe see Zapadnaya Dvina
Dvina r. Rus. Fed. see Severnaya Dvina
Dvinsk Latvia see Daugavpils
Dvinskaya Guba g. Rus. Fed. 52 H2
Dwarka India 104 B5
Dwarsberg S. Africa 125 H3
Dwingelderveld, Nationaal Park nat. park Neth. 62 G2
Dworshak Reservoir ID U.S.A. 156 E3
Dwyka S. Africa 124 E7
Dyat'kovo Rus. Fed. 53 G5
Dyce U.K. 60 G3
Dyer, Cape Canada 147 L3
Dyer Bay Canada 164 E1
Dyersburg TN U.S.A. 161 F4
Dyffryn U.K. see Valley
Dyfi r. U.K. see Dovey
Dyfrdwy r. U.K. see Dee
Dyje r. Austria/Czech Rep. 57 P6
Dyke U.K. 60 F3

▶Dykh-Tau, Gora mt. Rus. Fed. 113 F2
2nd highest mountain in Europe.

Dyle r. Belgium 62 E4
Dyleň hill Czech Rep. 63 M5
Dylewska Góra hill Poland 57 Q4
Dymytrov Ukr. 53 H6
Dynevor Downs Australia 138 B2
Dyoki S. Africa 125 I6
Dyrrhachium Albania see Durrës
Dysart Australia 136 E4
Dysselsdorp S. Africa 124 F7
Dyurtyuli Rus. Fed. 51 Q4
Dzaanhushuu Mongolia see Ihtamir
Dzadgay Mongolia see Bömbögör
Dzadrān reg. Afgh. 111 H3
Dzag Mongolia 94 D2
Dzag Gol r. Mongolia 94 D2
Dzalaa Mongolia see Shinejinst
Dzamīn Üüd Mongolia 95 G3
Dzanga-Ndoki, Parc National de nat. park Cent. Afr. Rep. 122 B3

▶Dzaoudzi Mayotte 123 E5
Capital of Mayotte.

Dzaudzhikau Rus. Fed. see Vladikavkaz
Dzavhan Mongolia 94 C1
Dzavhan prov. Mongolia 94 C1
Dzavhan Gol r. Mongolia 94 C1
Dzavhanmandal Mongolia 94 C1
Dzegstey Mongolia see Ögiynuur
Dzelter Mongolia 94 F1
Dzerzhinsk Belarus see Dzyarzhynsk
Dzerzhinsk Rus. Fed. 52 I4
Dzhagdy, Khrebet mts Rus. Fed. 90 C1
Dzhaki-Unakhta Yakbyyana, Khrebet mts Rus. Fed. 90 D2
Dzhalalabad Azer. see Cälilabad
Dzhalal-Abad Kyrg. see Jalal-Abad
Dzhalil' Rus. Fed. 51 Q4
Dzhalinda Rus. Fed. 90 A1
Dzhaltyr Kazakh. see Zhaltyr
Dzhambeyty Kazakh. see Zhympity
Dzhambul Kazakh. see Taraz
Dzhangala Kazakh. 51 Q6
Dzhankoy Ukr. 53 G7
Dzhanybek Kazakh. see Zhanibek
Dzharkent Kazakh. see Zharkent
Dzhava Georgia see Java
Dzhetygara Kazakh. see Zhitikara
Dzhezkazgan Kazakh. see Zhezkazgan
Dzhida Rus. Fed. 94 F1
Dzhida r. Rus. Fed. 94 F1
Dzhidinskiy Khrebet mts Mongolia/Rus. Fed. 94 E1
Dzhirgatal' Tajik. see Jirgatol
Dzhizak Uzbek. see Jizzax
Dzhokhar Ghala Rus. Fed. see Groznyy
Dzhubga Rus. Fed. 112 E1
Dzhugdzhur, Khrebet mts Rus. Fed. 77 O4
Dzhul'fa Azer. see Culfa
Dzhuma Uzbek. see Juma
Dzhungarskiye Vorota val. Kazakh. 98 C3
Dzhungarskiye Vorota val. Kazakh. 98 C3
Dzhusaly Kyzylordinskaya Oblast' Kazakh. 102 B2
Dzhusaly Pavlodarskaya Oblast' Kazakh. 98 B2
Działdowo Poland 57 R4
Dzibalchén Mex. 167 H5
Dzilam de Bravo Mex. 167 H4
Dzitás Mex. 167 H4
Dzogsool Mongolia see Bayantsagaan
Dzöölön Mongolia see Renchinlhümbe
Dzūkija nat. park Lith. 55 N9
Dzungarian Basin China see Junggar Pendi
Dzungarian Gate pass China/Kazakh. 102 F2
Dzur Mongolia see Tes
Dzüünbayan Mongolia 95 G2
Dzüünharaa Mongolia 94 F1
Dzuunmod Mongolia 94 F2
Dzüyl Mongolia see Tonhil
Dzyaniskavichy Belarus 55 O10
Dzyarzhynsk Belarus 55 O10
Dzyatlavichy Belarus 55 O10

E

Eabamet Lake Canada 152 D4
Eads CO U.S.A. 160 C4
Eagar AZ U.S.A. 159 I4
Eagle r. Nfld. and Lab. Canada 153 K3
Eagle r. Y.T. Canada 149 M2
Eagle AK U.S.A. 146 D3

Eagle CO U.S.A. 156 G5
Eagle Cap mt. OR U.S.A. 156 D3
Eagle Crags mt. CA U.S.A. 158 E4
Eagle Creek r. Canada 151 J4
Eagle Lake Canada 151 M5
Eagle Lake CA U.S.A. 158 C1
Eagle Lake ME U.S.A. 162 G2
Eagle Mountain CA U.S.A. 159 F5
Eagle Mountain hill MN U.S.A. 160 F2
Eagle Mountain Lake TX U.S.A. 167 F1
Eagle Pass TX U.S.A. 161 C6
Eagle Peak TX U.S.A. 157 G7
Eagle Plain Canada 149 M2
Eagle Plains Canada 149 M2
Eagle River AK U.S.A. 149 J3
Eagle River WI U.S.A. 160 F2
Eagle Rock VA U.S.A. 164 F5
Eaglesham Canada 150 G4
Eagle Summit pass AK U.S.A. 149 K2
Eagle Village AK U.S.A. 149 L2
Eap i. Micronesia see Yap
Ear Falls Canada 151 M5
Earlimart CA U.S.A. 158 D4
Earl's Seat hill U.K. 60 E4
Earlston U.K. 60 G5
Earn r. U.K. 60 F4
Earn, Loch l. U.K. 60 E4
Earn Lake Canada 149 N3
Earp CA U.S.A. 159 F4
Earth TX U.S.A. 161 C5
Easington U.K. 58 H5
Easley SC U.S.A. 163 D5
East Alligator r. Australia 134 F3
East Antarctica reg. Antarctica 188 F1
East Ararat PA U.S.A. 165 H3
East Aurora NY U.S.A. 165 F2
East Bay LA U.S.A. 167 H2
East Bay inlet FL U.S.A. 163 C6
East Bengal country Asia see Bangladesh
Eastbourne U.K. 59 H8
East Branch Clarion River Reservoir PA U.S.A. 165 F3
East Caicos i. Turks and Caicos Is 163 G8
East Cape N.Z. 139 G3
East Cape AK U.S.A. 148 [inset] B6
East Carbon City UT U.S.A. 159 H2
East Caroline Basin sea feature N. Pacific Ocean 186 F5
East Channel watercourse Canada 149 N1
East China Sea N. Pacific Ocean 89 N6
East Coast Bays N.Z. 139 E3
East Dereham U.K. see Dereham
Eastend Canada 151 I5
East Entrance sea chan. Palau 82 [inset]

▶Easter Island S. Pacific Ocean 187 M7
Part of Chile.

Eastern Cape prov. S. Africa 125 H6
Eastern Desert Egypt 108 D4
Eastern Fields reef Australia 136 D1
Eastern Ghats mts India 106 C4

▶Eastern Island HI U.S.A. 186 I4
Most northerly point of Oceania.

Eastern Nara canal Pak. 111 H5
Eastern Samoa terr. S. Pacific Ocean see American Samoa
Eastern Sayan Mountains Rus. Fed. see Vostochnyy Sayan
Eastern Taurus plat. Turkey see Güneydoğu Toroslar
Eastern Transvaal prov. S. Africa see Mpumalanga
Easterville Canada 151 L4
Easterwâlde Neth. see Oosterwolde
East Falkland i. Falkland Is 178 E8
East Falmouth MA U.S.A. 165 J3
East Frisian Islands Germany 57 K4
Eastgate NV U.S.A. 158 E2
East Greenwich RI U.S.A. 165 J3
East Grinstead U.K. 59 G7
Easthampton MA U.S.A. 165 I2
East Hampton NY U.S.A. 165 I3
East Hartford CT U.S.A. 165 I3
East Indiaman Ridge sea feature Indian Ocean 185 O7
East Jordan MI U.S.A. 164 C1
East Kilbride U.K. 60 E5
Eastlake OH U.S.A. 164 E3
East Lamma Channel H.K. China 97 [inset]
Eastland TX U.S.A. 161 D5
East Lansing MI U.S.A. 164 C2
Eastleigh U.K. 59 F8
East Liverpool OH U.S.A. 164 E3
East London S. Africa 125 H7
East Lynn Lake WV U.S.A. 164 D4
Eastmain Canada 152 F3
Eastmain r. Canada 152 F3
Eastman GA U.S.A. 163 D5
East Mariana Basin sea feature N. Pacific Ocean 186 G5
Eastmere Australia 136 D4
East Naples FL U.S.A. 163 D7
Easton MD U.S.A. 165 G4
Easton PA U.S.A. 165 H3
East Orange NJ U.S.A. 165 H3
East Pacific Rise sea feature N. Pacific Ocean 187 M4
East Pakistan country Asia see Bangladesh
East Palestine OH U.S.A. 164 E3
East Park Reservoir CA U.S.A. 158 B2
East Point Canada 153 J5
East Porcupine r. Canada 149 M2
Eastport ME U.S.A. 162 H2
East Providence RI U.S.A. 165 J3
East Range mts NV U.S.A. 158 E1
East Retford U.K. see Retford
East St Louis IL U.S.A. 160 F4
East Sea N. Pacific Ocean see Japan, Sea of
East Shoal Lake Canada 151 L5
East Siberian Sea Rus. Fed. 77 P2
East Side Canal r. CA U.S.A. 158 D4
East Stroudsburg PA U.S.A. 165 H3
East Tavaputs Plateau UT U.S.A. 159 I2

▶East Timor country Asia 83 C5
Former Portuguese territory. Gained independence from Indonesia in 2002.

East Tons r. India 99 D8
East Toorale Australia 138 B3
East Troy WI U.S.A. 164 A2
East Verde r. AZ U.S.A. 159 H4
Eastville VA U.S.A. 165 H5
East-Vlylân Neth. see Oost-Vlieland
East York Canada 164 F2
Eaton OH U.S.A. 164 C4
Eatonia Canada 151 I5
Eaton Rapids MI U.S.A. 164 C2
Eatonton GA U.S.A. 163 D5
Eau Claire WI U.S.A. 160 F2
Eauripik atoll Micronesia 81 K5
Eauripik Rise-New Guinea Rise sea feature N. Pacific Ocean 186 F5
Eaurypyg atoll Micronesia see Eauripik
Ebano Mex. 167 F4
Ebbw Vale U.K. 59 D7
Ebebiyin Equat. Guinea 120 E4
Ebenerde Namibia 124 C3
Ebensburg PA U.S.A. 165 F3
Eber Gölü l. Turkey 69 N5
Ebergötzen Germany 63 K3
Eberswalde-Finow Germany 57 N4
Ebetsu Japan 90 F4
Ebian China 96 D2
Ebina Japan 93 F3
Ebi Nor salt l. China see Ebinur Hu
Ebinur Hu salt l. China 98 C3
Eboli Italy 68 F4
Ebolowa Cameroon 120 E4
Ebony Namibia 124 B2
Ebre r. Spain see Ebro
Ebro r. Spain 67 G3
Ebstorf Germany 63 K1
Eburacum U.K. see York
Ebusus i. Spain see Ibiza
Ecbatana Iran see Hamadān
Eceabat Turkey 69 L4
Echague Luzon Phil. 82 C2
Ech Chélif Alg. see Chlef
Echegárate, Puerto pass Spain 67 E2
Echeng China see Ezhou
Echeverria, Pico mt. Mex. 166 B2
Echigawa Japan 92 C3
Echigo-Sanzan-Tadami Kokutei-kōen park Japan 93 F1
Echizen Japan 92 C3
Echizen-dake mt. Japan 93 E3
Echizen-Kaga-kaigan Kokutei-kōen park Japan 92 C2
Echizen-misaki pt Japan 92 B3
Echmiadzin Armenia see Ejmiatsin
Echo OR U.S.A. 156 D3
Echo Bay N.W.T. Canada 150 G1
Echo Bay Ont. Canada 152 D5
Echo Cliffs AZ U.S.A. 159 H3
Echoing r. Canada 151 M4
Echt Neth. 62 F3
Echternach Lux. 62 G5
Echuca Australia 138 B6
Écija Spain 67 D5
Eckental Germany 63 L5
Eckernförde Germany 57 L3
Eclipse Sound sea chan. Canada 147 J2
Écrins, Parc National des nat. park France 66 H4
Ecuador country S. America 176 C4
Écueils, Pointe aux pt Canada 152 F2
Ed Eritrea 108 F7
Ed Sweden 55 G7
Edam Neth. 62 F2
Eday i. U.K. 60 G1
Ed Da'ein Sudan 121 F3
Ed Damazin Sudan 108 D7
Ed Damer Sudan 108 D6
Ed Debba Sudan 108 D6
Eddies Cove Canada 153 K4
Ed Dueim Sudan 108 D7
Eddystone Point Australia 137 [inset]
Eddyville KY U.S.A. 161 F4
Ede Neth. 62 F2
Edéa Cameroon 120 E4
Edehon Lake Canada 151 L2
Edéia Brazil 179 A2
Eden Australia 138 D6
Eden r. U.K. 58 D4
Eden NC U.S.A. 164 F5
Eden TX U.S.A. 161 D6
Eden, Tanjung pt Maluku Indon. 83 C4
Edenburg S. Africa 125 G5
Edendale N.Z. 139 B8
Edenderry Ireland 61 E4
Edenton NC U.S.A. 162 E4
Edenville S. Africa 125 H4
Eder r. Germany 63 J3
Eder-Stausee resr Germany 63 I3
Edessa Greece 69 J4
Edessa Turkey see Şanlıurfa
Edewecht Germany 63 H1
Edfu Egypt see Idfū
Edgar Ranges hills Australia 134 C4
Edgartown MA U.S.A. 165 J3
Edgecumbe Island Solomon Is see Utupua
Edgefield SC U.S.A. 163 D5
Edge Island Svalbard see Edgeøya
Edgemont SD U.S.A. 160 C3
Edgeøya i. Svalbard 76 D2
Edgerton Canada 151 I4
Edgerton OH U.S.A. 164 C3
Edgeworthstown Ireland 61 E4
Édhessa Greece see Edessa
Edina MO U.S.A. 160 E3
Edinboro PA U.S.A. 164 E3
Edinburg TX U.S.A. 161 D7
Edinburg VA U.S.A. 165 F4

▶Edinburgh U.K. 60 F5
Capital of Scotland.

Edirne Turkey 69 L4
Edith, Mount MT U.S.A. 156 F3
Edith Cavell, Mount Canada 150 G4
Edith Ronne Land ice feature Antarctica see Ronne Ice Shelf
Edjeleh Libya 120 D2
Edjudina Australia 135 C7
Edku Egypt see Idkū
Edmond OK U.S.A. 161 D5
Edmonds WA U.S.A. 156 C3

▶Edmonton Canada 150 H4
Capital of Alberta.

Edmonton KY U.S.A. 164 C5
Edmore MI U.S.A. 164 C2
Edmore ND U.S.A. 160 D1
Edmund Lake Canada 151 M4
Edmundston Canada 153 H5
Edna TX U.S.A. 161 D6
Edna Bay AK U.S.A. 149 N5
Edo Japan see Tōkyō
Edo-gawa r. Japan 93 F3
Edom reg. Israel/Jordan 107 B4
Edosaki Japan 93 G3
Édouard, Lac l. Dem. Rep. Congo/Uganda see Edward, Lake
Edremit Turkey 69 L5
Edremit Körfezi b. Turkey 69 L5
Edrengiyn Nuruu mts Mongolia 94 D2
Edsbyn Sweden 55 I6
Edson Canada 150 G4
Eduni, Mount Canada 149 O2
Edward r. N.S.W. Australia 138 B5
Edward r. Qld Australia 136 C2
Edward, Lake Dem. Rep. Congo/Uganda 122 C4
Edward, Mount Antarctica 188 L1
Edwardesabad Pak. see Bannu
Edwards NY U.S.A. 165 H1
Edward's Creek Australia 137 A6
Edwards Plateau TX U.S.A. 161 C6
Edwardsville IL U.S.A. 160 F4
Edward VII Peninsula Antarctica 188 I1
Edziza, Mount Canada 149 O4
Eek AK U.S.A. 148 G3
Eek r. AK U.S.A. 148 G3
Eeklo Belgium 62 D3
Eel r. CA U.S.A. 158 A1
Eel, South Fork r. CA U.S.A. 158 B1
Eem r. Neth. 62 F2
Eemshaven pt Neth. 62 G1
Eenrum Neth. 62 G1
Eenzamheid Pan salt pan S. Africa 124 E4
Eesti country Europe see Estonia
Éfaté i. Vanuatu 133 G3
Effingham IL U.S.A. 160 F4
Efsus Turkey see Afşin
Eg Mongolia see Batshireet
Egadi, Isole is Sicily Italy 68 D5
Egan Range mts NV U.S.A. 159 F2
Eganville Canada 165 G1
Egavik AK U.S.A. 148 G2
Egedesminde Greenland see Aasiaat
Egegik Bay AK U.S.A. 148 H4
Eger r. Germany 63 M4
Eger Hungary 57 R7
Egersund Norway 55 E7
Egerton, Mount hill Australia 135 B6
Eggegebirge hills Germany 63 I3
Egg Island AK U.S.A. 148 G3
Egg Lake Canada 151 J4
Eggolsheim Germany 63 L5
Eghezée Belgium 62 E4
Egilsstaðir Iceland 54 [inset 1]
Eğin Turkey see Kemaliye
Eğirdir Turkey 69 N6
Eğirdir Gölü l. Turkey 69 N6
Egiyn Gol r. Mongolia 94 E1
Eglinton U.K. 61 E2
Egmond aan Zee Neth. 62 E2
Egmont, Cape N.Z. 139 D4
Egmont, Mount vol. N.Z. see Taranaki, Mount
Egmont National Park N.Z. 139 E4
eGoli S. Africa see Johannesburg
Eğrigöz Dağı mts Turkey 69 M5
Egton U.K. 58 G4
Éguas r. Brazil 179 B1
Egvekinot Rus. Fed. 148 C2

▶Egypt country Africa 108 C4
3rd most populous country in Africa.

Ehden Lebanon 107 B2
Ehen Hudag China 94 E4
Ehingen (Donau) Germany 57 L6
Ehle r. Germany 63 L2
Ehra-Lessien Germany 63 K2
Ehrenberg AZ U.S.A. 159 F5
Ehrenberg Range hills Australia 135 E5
Eibelstadt Germany 63 K5
Eibergen Neth. 62 G2
Eichenzell Germany 63 J4
Eichstätt Germany 63 L6
Eidfjord Norway 55 E6
Eidsvold Australia 136 E5
Eidsvoll Norway 55 G6
Eifel hills Germany 62 G4
Eigenji Japan 92 C3
Eigg i. U.K. 60 C4
Eight Degree Channel India/Maldives 106 B5
Eights Coast Antarctica 188 K2
Eighty Mile Beach Australia 134 C4
Eiheiji Japan 92 C2
Eilat Israel 107 B5
Eildon Australia 138 B6
Eildon, Lake Australia 138 C6
Eileen Lake Canada 151 J2
Eilenburg Germany 63 M3
Eil Malk i. Palau 82 [inset]
Eimke Germany 63 K2
Einasleigh Australia 136 D3
Einasleigh r. Australia 136 C3
Einbeck Germany 63 J3
Eindhoven Neth. 62 F3
Einme Myanmar 86 A3
Einsiedeln Switz. 66 I3
Éire country Europe see Ireland
Eirik Ridge sea feature N. Atlantic Ocean 184 F2
Eiriosgaigh i. U.K. see Eriskay
Eirunepé Brazil 176 E5
Eisberg hill Germany 63 J3
Eiseb watercourse Namibia 123 C5
Eisenach Germany 63 K4
Eisenberg Germany 63 L4
Eisenhower, Mount Canada see Castle Mountain
Eisenhüttenstadt Germany 57 O4
Eisenstadt Austria 57 P7
Eisfeld Germany 63 K4
Eisleben Lutherstadt Germany 63 L3
Eite, Loch inlet U.K. see Etive, Loch
Eiterfeld Germany 63 J4
Eivissa Spain see Ibiza
Eivissa i. Spain see Ibiza
Ejea de los Caballeros Spain 67 F2
Ejeda Madag. 123 E6
Ejin Horo Qi China see Altan Shiret
Ejin Qi China see Dalain Hob
Ejmiadzin Armenia see Ejmiatsin
Ejmiatsin Armenia 113 G2
Ejutla Mex. 167 F5
Ekalaka MT U.S.A. 156 G3
Ekenäs Fin. 55 M7
Ekerem Turkm. 110 D2
Ekeren Belgium 62 E3
Eketahuna N.Z. 139 E5
Ekimchan Rus. Fed. 90 D1
Ekinyazı Turkey 107 D1
Ekityki, Ozero l. Rus. Fed. 148 B2
Ekka Island Canada 149 Q2
Ekonda Rus. Fed. 77 L3
Ekostrovskaya Imandra, Ozero l. Rus. Fed. 54 R3
Ekshärad Sweden 55 H6
Eksjö Sweden 55 I8
Eksteenfontein S. Africa 124 C5
Ekström Ice Shelf Antarctica 188 B2
Ekuk AK U.S.A. 148 H4
Ekwan r. Canada 152 E3
Ekwan Point Canada 152 E3
Ekwok AK U.S.A. 148 H4
Ela Myanmar 86 B3
El Aaiún W. Sahara see Laâyoune
Elafonisou, Steno sea chan. Greece 69 J6
El 'Agrûd well Egypt see Al 'Ajrūd
Elaia, Cape Cyprus 107 B2
El 'Alamein Egypt see Al 'Alamayn
El Alamo Mex. 166 A2
El 'Âmirîya Egypt see Al 'Āmirīyah
Elands r. S. Africa 125 I3
Elandsdoorn S. Africa 125 I3
El Aouinet Alg. 68 B7
Elar Armenia see Abovyan
El Araïche Morocco see Larache
El Arco Mex. 166 B2
El Ariana Tunisia see L'Ariana
El Aricha Alg. 64 D5
El 'Arîsh Egypt see Al 'Arīsh
El Arrouch Alg. 68 B6
El Ashmûnein Egypt see Al Ashmūnayn
El Asnam Alg. see Chlef
Elassona Greece 69 J5
Elat Israel see Eilat
Elato atoll Micronesia 81 L5
Elazığ Turkey 113 E3
Elba AL U.S.A. 163 C6
Elba, Isola d' i. Italy 68 D3
El'ban Rus. Fed. 90 E2
El Barco de Valdeorras Spain see O Barco
El Barreal salt l. Mex. 166 D2
Elbasan Albania 69 I4
El Batroun Lebanon see Batroûn
El Baúl Venez. 176 E2
El Bawîti Egypt see Al Bawīṭī
El Bayadh Alg. 64 E5
Elbe r. Germany 63 J1
also known as Labe (Czech Republic)
Elbe-Havel-Kanal canal Germany 63 L2
El Béqaa valley Lebanon 107 C2
Elbert, Mount CO U.S.A. 156 G5
Elberta UT U.S.A. 159 H2
Elberton GA U.S.A. 163 D5
Elbeuf France 66 E2
Elbeyli Turkey 107 C1
El Billete, Cerro mt. Mex. 167 E5
Elbing Poland see Elbląg
Elbistan Turkey 112 E3
Elbląg Poland 57 Q3
El Bluff Nicaragua 166 [inset] J6
El Boulaïda Alg. see Blida
Elbow Canada 151 J5
Elbow Lake MN U.S.A. 160 D2
El Bozal Mex. 161 C8
El Brasil Mex. 167 E3

▶El'brus mt. Rus. Fed. 113 F2
Highest mountain in Europe.

Elburg Neth. 62 F2
El Burgo de Osma Spain 67 E3
Elburz Mountains Iran 110 C2
El Cajon CA U.S.A. 158 E5
El Cajón, Represa dam Hond. 166 [inset] I6
El Callao Venez. 176 F2
El Campo TX U.S.A. 161 D6
El Capitan Mountain NM U.S.A. 157 G6
El Capulín r. Mex. 161 C7
El Casco Mex. 166 D3
El Cebú, Cerro mt. Mex. 167 G6
El Centro CA U.S.A. 159 F5
El Cerro Bol. 176 F7
Elche Spain see Elche-Elx
Elche-Elx Spain 67 F4
El Chichónal vol. Mex. 167 G5
El Chilicote Mex. 166 D2
Elcho Island Australia 136 A1
El Coca Ecuador see Coca
El Cocuy, Parque Nacional nat. park Col. 176 D2
El Cuyo Mex. 167 I4
Elda Spain 67 F4
El Dátil Mex. 166 B2
El Desemboque Mex. 157 E7
El Diamante Mex. 166 E2
El'dikan Rus. Fed. 77 O3
El Djezair country Africa see Algeria
El Djezair Alg. see Algiers
El Doctor Mex. 166 B2
Eldon MO U.S.A. 160 E4
Eldorado Arg. 178 F3
Eldorado Brazil 179 A4
El Dorado Col. 176 D3
El Dorado Mex. 166 D3
El Dorado AR U.S.A. 161 E5
El Dorado KS U.S.A. 160 D4
Eldorado TX U.S.A. 161 C6
El Dorado Venez. 176 F2
Eldorado Mountains NV U.S.A. 159 F4
Eldoret Kenya 122 D3
Eldridge, Mount AK U.S.A. 149 L2
Elea, Cape Cyprus see Elaia, Cape
Eleanor WV U.S.A. 164 E4
Electric Peak MT U.S.A. 156 F3
Elefantes r. Moz./S. Africa see Olifants
El Eglab plat. Alg. 120 C2
El Ejido Spain 67 E5
El Encanto Col. 176 D4
Elend Germany 63 K3
Elephanta Caves tourist site India 106 B2
Elephant Butte Reservoir NM U.S.A. 157 G6
Elephant Island Antarctica 188 A2
Elephant Pass Sri Lanka 106 D4
Elephant Point Bangl. 105 H5
Elephant Point AK U.S.A. 148 G2
Eleşkirt Turkey 113 F3
El Estor Guat. 167 H6
El Eulma Alg. 64 F4
Eleuthera i. Bahamas 163 E7
Eleven Point r. MO U.S.A. 161 F4
El Fahs Tunisia 68 C6
El Faiyûm Egypt see Al Fayyūm
El Fasher Sudan 121 F3
El Ferrol Spain see Ferrol
El Ferrol del Caudillo Spain see Ferrol
Elfershausen Germany 63 J4
El Fud Eth. 122 E3
El Fuerte Mex. 166 C3
El Gara Egypt see Qārah
El Geneina Sudan 121 F3
El Geteina Sudan 108 D7
El Ghardaqa Egypt see Al Ghurdaqah
El Ghor plain Jordan/West Bank see Al Ghawr
Elgin U.K. 60 F3
Elgin IL U.S.A. 160 F3
Elgin ND U.S.A. 160 C2
Elgin NV U.S.A. 159 F3
Elgin TX U.S.A. 161 D6
El'ginskiy Rus. Fed. 77 P3
El Gîza Egypt see Giza
El Goléa Alg. 64 E5
El Golfo de Santa Clara Mex. 166 B2
Elgon, Mount Kenya/Uganda 100 C6
El Grullo Mex. 167 F3
El Guante Mex. 166 D2
El Hadjar Alg. 68 B6
El Ḥammâm Egypt see Al Ḥammām
El Ḥammâmi reg. Mauritania 120 B2
El Ḥank esc. Mali/Mauritania 120 C2
El Ḥarra Egypt see Al Ḥarrah
El Hazim Jordan see Al Hazīm
El Ḥeiz Egypt see Al Ḥayz
El Hierro i. Canary Is 120 B2
El Higo Mex. 167 F4
El Homr Alg. 64 E6
El Homra Sudan 108 D7
Eliase Maluku Indon. 83 D5
Elías Piña Dom. Rep. 169 J5
Elichpur India see Achalpur
Elida OH U.S.A. 164 C3
Elie U.K. 60 G4
Elila r. Dem. Rep. Congo 122 C4
Elim AK U.S.A. 148 G2
Elimberrum France see Auch
Eling China see Yinjiang
Elingampangu Dem. Rep. Congo 122 C4
Eliot, Mount Canada 153 J2
Élisabethville Dem. Rep. Congo see Lubumbashi
Eliseu Martins Brazil 177 J5
El Iskandarîya Egypt see Alexandria
Elista Rus. Fed. 53 J7
Elixku China 98 B5
Elizabeth NJ U.S.A. 165 H3
Elizabeth WV U.S.A. 164 E4
Elizabeth, Mount hill Australia 134 D4
Elizabeth Bay Namibia 124 B4
Elizabeth City NC U.S.A. 162 E4
Elizabeth Island Pitcairn Is see Henderson Island
Elizabeth Point Namibia 124 B4
Elizabethton TN U.S.A. 162 D4
Elizabethtown IL U.S.A. 160 F4
Elizabethtown KY U.S.A. 164 C5
Elizabethtown NC U.S.A. 163 E5
Elizabethtown NY U.S.A. 165 I1
El Jadida Morocco 64 C5
El Jaralito Mex. 166 D3
El Jem Tunisia 68 D7
El Jicaro Nicaragua 166 [inset] I6
El Juile Mex. 167 G5
Elk r. Canada 150 H5
Ełk Poland 57 S4
Elk r. MD U.S.A. 165 H4
El Kaa Lebanon see Qaa
El Kab Sudan 108 D6
Elkader IA U.S.A. 160 F3
El Kala Alg. 68 C6
Elk City OK U.S.A. 161 D5
Elkedra Australia 136 A4
Elkedra watercourse Australia 136 B4
El Kef Tunisia see Le Kef
El Kelaâ des Srarhna Morocco 64 C5
Elkford Canada 150 H5
Elk Grove CA U.S.A. 158 C2
El Khalil West Bank see Hebron
El Khandaq Sudan 108 D6
El Khârga Egypt see Al Khārijah
El Kharrûba Egypt see Al Kharrūbah
Elkhart IN U.S.A. 164 C3
Elkhart KS U.S.A. 161 C4
El Khartûm Sudan see Khartoum
El Khenachich esc. Mali see El Khnâchîch
El Khnâchîch esc. Mali 120 C2
Elkhorn WI U.S.A. 160 F3
Elkhorn City KY U.S.A. 164 D5
Elkhovo Bulg. 69 L3
Elki Turkey see Beytüşşebap
Elkin NC U.S.A. 162 D4
Elkins WV U.S.A. 164 F4
Elk Island National Park Canada 151 H4
Elk Lake Canada 152 E5
Elk Lake l. MI U.S.A. 164 C1
Elkland PA U.S.A. 165 G3
Elk Mountain WY U.S.A. 156 G4
Elk Mountains CO U.S.A. 159 J2
Elko Canada 150 H5
Elko NV U.S.A. 159 F1
Elk Point Canada 151 I4
Elk Point SD U.S.A. 160 D3
Elk Springs CO U.S.A. 159 I1
Elkton MD U.S.A. 165 H4
Elkton VA U.S.A. 165 F4
El Kûbri Egypt see Al Kūbrī
El Kuntilla Egypt see Al Kuntillah
Elkview WV U.S.A. 164 E4
Ellas country Europe see Greece
Ellaville GA U.S.A. 163 C5
Ell Bay Canada 151 O1
Ellef Ringnes Island Canada 147 H2
Ellen, Mount UT U.S.A. 159 H2
Ellenburg Depot NY U.S.A. 165 I1
Ellendale ND U.S.A. 160 D2
Ellensburg WA U.S.A. 156 C3
Ellenville NY U.S.A. 165 H3
El León, Cerro mt. Mex. 161 B7
Ellesmere, Lake N.Z. 139 D6

▶Ellesmere Island Canada 147 J2
4th largest island in North America and 10th in the world.

Ellesmere Island National Park Reserve Canada see Quttinirpaaq National Park
Ellesmere Port U.K. 58 E5
Ellettsville IN U.S.A. 164 B4
Ellice r. Canada 151 K1
Ellice Island Canada 149 N1
Ellice Island atoll Tuvalu see Funafuti
Ellice Islands country S. Pacific Ocean see Tuvalu
Ellicott City MD U.S.A. 165 G4
Ellijay GA U.S.A. 163 C5
El Limón Mex. 167 F4
Ellingen Germany 63 K5
Elliot S. Africa 125 H6
Elliot, Mount Australia 136 D3
Elliotdale S. Africa 125 I6
Elliot Knob mt. VA U.S.A. 164 F4
Elliot Lake Canada 152 E5
Elliott Australia 134 F4
Elliott Highway AK U.S.A. 149 J2
Elliston VA U.S.A. 164 E5
Ellon U.K. 60 G3
Ellora Caves tourist site India 106 B1
Ellsworth KS U.S.A. 160 D4
Ellsworth ME U.S.A. 162 G2
Ellsworth NE U.S.A. 160 C3
Ellsworth WI U.S.A. 160 E2
Ellsworth Land reg. Antarctica 188 K1
Ellsworth Mountains Antarctica 188 L1
Ellwangen (Jagst) Germany 63 K6
El Maghreb country Africa see Morocco
Elmakuz Dağı mt. Turkey 107 A1
Elmalı Turkey 69 M6
El Malpais National Monument nat. park NM U.S.A. 159 J4
El Manṣûra Egypt see Al Manṣūrah
El Maṭarîya Egypt see Al Maṭarīyah
El Mazâr Egypt see Al Mazār
El Médano Mex. 166 C3
El Meghaïer Alg. 64 F5
El Milia Alg. 64 F4
El Minya Egypt see Al Minyā
Elmira Ont. Canada 164 E2
Elmira P.E.I. Canada 153 J5
Elmira MI U.S.A. 164 C1
Elmira NY U.S.A. 165 G2
El Mirage AZ U.S.A. 159 G5
El Moral Mex. 167 E2
El Moral Spain 67 E5
Elmore Australia 138 B6
El Mreyyé reg. Mauritania 120 C3
Elmshorn Germany 63 J1
El Muglad Sudan 108 C7
Elmvale Canada 164 F1
Elnesvågen Norway 54 E5
El Nevado, Cerro mt. Col. 176 D3
El Nido Palawan Phil. 82 B4
El Oasis Mex. 159 F5
El Obeid Sudan 108 D7
El Ocote, Parque Natural nature res. Mex. 167 G5
El Odaiya Sudan 108 C7
El Oro Mex. 166 E3
Elorza Venez. 176 E2
Elota Mex. 166 D4
El Oued Alg. 64 F5
Eloy AZ U.S.A. 159 H5
El Palmito Mex. 166 D3
Elpaputih, Teluk b. Seram Indon. 83 D3
El Paso IL U.S.A. 160 F3
El Paso KS U.S.A. see Derby
El Paso TX U.S.A. 157 G7
El Peñasco Mex. 167 E4
Elphin U.K. 60 D2
Elphinstone i. Myanmar see Thayawthadangyi Kyun
El Pino, Sierra mts Mex. 166 E2
El Portal CA U.S.A. 158 D3
El Porvenir Mex. 166 D2
El Porvenir Panama 166 [inset] K7
El Prat de Llobregat Spain 67 H3
El Progreso Guat. see Guastatoya
El Progreso Hond. 166 [inset] I6
El Puente Nicaragua 166 [inset] I6
El Puerto de Santa María Spain 67 C5
El Qâhira Egypt see Cairo
El Qasimiye r. Lebanon 107 B3
El Quds Israel/West Bank see Jerusalem
El Quṣeima Egypt see Al Quṣaymah
El Quṣeir Egypt see Al Quṣayr
El Qûṣîya Egypt see Al Qūṣīyah
El Real Panama 166 [inset] K7
El Regocijo Mex. 161 B8
El Reno OK U.S.A. 161 D5
El Retorno Mex. 167 E4
Elrose Canada 151 I5
El Rucio Mex. 166 E4
Elsa Canada 149 N3
El Sabinal, Parque Nacional nat. park Mex. 167 F3
El Ṣaff Egypt see Aṣ Ṣaff
El Sahuaro Mex. 166 B2
El Salado Mex. 161 C7
El Salto Mex. 161 B8
El Salvador country Central America 167 H6
El Salvador Chile 178 C3
El Salvador Mex. 161 C7
Elsass reg. France see Alsace
El Sauz Mex. 166 D2
Else r. Germany 63 I2
El Sellûm Egypt see As Sallūm
Elsey Australia 134 F3
El Shallûfa Egypt see Ash Shallūfah
El Sharana Australia 134 F3
El Shaṭṭ Egypt see Ash Shaṭṭ
Elsie MI U.S.A. 164 C2
Elsinore Denmark see Helsingør
Elsinore CA U.S.A. 158 E5
Elsinore UT U.S.A. 159 G2
Elsinore Lake CA U.S.A. 158 E5
El Socorro Mex. 166 E3
Elson Lagoon AK U.S.A. 148 H1
El Sueco Mex. 166 D2
El Suweis Egypt see Suez
El Suweis governorate Egypt see As Suways
El Tajín tourist site Mex. 167 F4
El Tama, Parque Nacional nat. park Venez. 176 D2
El Tarf Alg. 68 C6

El Teleno *mt.* Spain 67 C2
El Temascal Mex. 161 D7
El Thamad Egypt *see* Ath Thamad
El Tigre Venez. 176 F2
El Tigre, Parque Nacional *nat. park* Guat. 167 H5
Eltmann Germany 63 K5
El'ton Rus. Fed. 53 J6
El'ton, Ozero *l.* Rus. Fed. 53 J6
El Tren Mex. 166 B2
El Triunfo Mex. 166 C4
El Tuparro, Parque Nacional *nat. park* Col. 176 E2
El Ṭûr Egypt *see* Aṭ Ṭūr
El Turbio Arg. 178 B8
El Uqṣur Egypt *see* Luxor
Eluru India 106 D2
Elva Estonia 55 O7
El Vallecillo Mex. 166 C2
Elvanfoot U.K. 60 F5
Elvas Port. 67 C4
Elverum Norway 55 G6
El Vigía, Cerro *mt.* Mex. 166 D4
Elvira Brazil 176 D5
El Wak Kenya 122 E3
El Wâtya *well* Egypt *see* Al Wāṭiyah
Elwood *IN* U.S.A. 164 C3
Elwood *NE* U.S.A. 160 D3
El Wuz Sudan 108 D7
Elx Spain *see* Elche-Elx
Elxleben Germany 63 K3
Ely U.K. 59 H6
Ely *MN* U.S.A. 160 F2
Ely *NV* U.S.A. 159 F2
Elyria *OH* U.S.A. 164 D3
Elz Germany 63 I4
El Zacatón, Cerro *mt.* Mex. 167 F5
El Zagâzîg Egypt *see* Az Zaqāzīq
El Zape Mex. 166 D3
Elze Germany 63 J2
Émaé *i.* Vanuatu 133 G3
eMakhazeni S. Africa 125 J3
Emāmrūd Iran 110 D2
Emām Taqī Iran 110 E2
Emån *r.* Sweden 55 J8
E. Martínez Mex. *see* Emiliano Martínez
Emas, Parque Nacional das *nat. park* Brazil 177 H7
Emazar Kazakh. 98 C3
Emba Kazakh. 102 A2
Embalenhle S. Africa 125 I4
Embarcación Arg. 178 D2
Embarras Portage Canada 151 I3
Embi Kazakh. *see* Emba
Embira *r.* Brazil *see* Envira
Emborcação, Represa de *resr* Brazil 179 B2
Embrun Canada 165 H1
Embu Kenya 122 D4
Emden Germany 63 H1
Emden Deep *sea feature* N. Pacific Ocean *see* Cape Johnson Depth
Emei China *see* Emeishan
Emeishan China 96 D2
Emei Shan *mt.* China 96 D2
Emerald Australia 136 E4
Emeril Canada 153 I3
Emerita Augusta Spain *see* Mérida
Emerson Canada 151 L5
Emerson *KY* U.S.A. 164 D4
Emery *UT* U.S.A. 159 H2
Emesa Syria *see* Homs
Emet Turkey 69 M5
Emgwenya S. Africa 125 J3
eMgwenya S. Africa 125 J3
Emigrant Pass *NV* U.S.A. 158 E1
Emigrant Valley *NV* U.S.A. 159 F3
Emi Koussi *mt.* Chad 121 E3
Emile *r.* Canada 150 G2
Emiliano Martínez Mex. 166 D3
Emiliano Zapata Mex. 167 H5
Emin China 98 C3
Emine, Nos *pt* Bulg. 69 L3
Eminence *KY* U.S.A. 164 C4
Emin He *r.* China 98 C3
Eminska Planina *hills* Bulg. 69 L3
Emirdağ Turkey 69 N5
Emir Dağı *mt.* Turkey 69 N5
Emir Dağları *mts* Turkey 69 N5
eMjindini S. Africa 125 J3
eMkhondo S. Africa 125 J4
Emmaboda Sweden 55 I8
Emmahaven *Sumatera* Indon. *see* Telukbayur
Emmaste Estonia 55 M7
Emmaville Australia 138 E2
Emmeloord Neth. 62 F2
Emmelshausen Germany 63 H4
Emmen Neth. 62 G2
Emmen Switz. 66 I3
Emmerich Germany 62 G3
Emmet Australia 136 D5
Emmetsburg *IA* U.S.A. 160 E3
Emmett *ID* U.S.A. 156 D4
Emmiganuru India 106 C3
Emmonak *AK* U.S.A. 148 F3
Emo Canada 151 M5
Emona Slovenia *see* Ljubljana
Emory Peak *TX* U.S.A. 161 C6
Empalme Mex. 166 C3
Empangeni S. Africa 125 J5
Emperor Seamount Chain *sea feature* N. Pacific Ocean 186 H2
Emperor Trough *sea feature* N. Pacific Ocean 186 H2
Empingham Reservoir U.K. *see* Rutland Water
Emplawas *Maluku* Indon. 83 D5
Empoli Italy 68 D3
Emporia *KS* U.S.A. 160 D4
Emporia *VA* U.S.A. 165 G5
Emporium *PA* U.S.A. 165 F3
Empress Canada 151 I5
Empty Quarter *des.* Saudi Arabia *see* Rub' al Khālī
Ems *r.* Germany 63 H1
Emsdale Canada 164 F1
Emsdetten Germany 63 H2
Ems-Jade-Kanal *canal* Germany 63 H1
eMzinoni S. Africa 125 I4
Ena Japan 92 D3
Enafors Sweden 54 H5
Ena-san *mt.* Japan 92 D3
Encantadas, Serra das *hills* Brazil 178 F4
Encanto, Cape *Luzon* Phil. 82 C3
Encarnación Mex. 166 E4
Encarnación Para. 178 E3
Enchi Ghana 120 C4
Encinal *TX* U.S.A. 161 D6
Encinitas *CA* U.S.A. 158 E5
Encino *NM* U.S.A. 157 G6
Encruzilhada Brazil 179 C1
Endako Canada 150 E4
Endau *r.* Malaysia 84 C2
Endau-Rompin National Park *nat. park* Malaysia 87 C7
Ende *Flores* Indon. 83 B5
Ende *i.* Indon. 83 B5
Endeavour Strait Australia 136 C1
Enderby Canada 150 G5
Enderby *atoll* Micronesia *see* Puluwat
Enderby Land *reg.* Antarctica 188 D2
Endicott *NY* U.S.A. 165 G2
Endicott Mountains *AK* U.S.A. 148 I2
EnenKio *terr.* N. Pacific Ocean *see* Wake Island
Energodar Ukr. *see* Enerhodar
Enerhodar Ukr. 53 G7
Enewetak *atoll* Marshall Is 186 G5
Enez Turkey 69 L4
Enfe Lebanon 107 B2
Enfião, Ponta do *pt* Angola 123 B5
Enfidaville Tunisia 68 D6
Enfield *NC* U.S.A. 162 E4
Engan Norway 54 F5
Engaru Japan 90 F3
Engcobo S. Africa 125 H6
En Gedi Israel 107 B4
Engelhard *NC* U.S.A. 162 F5
Engel's Rus. Fed. 53 J6
Engelschmangat *sea chan.* Neth. 62 E1
Enggano *i.* Indon. 84 C4
Enghien Belgium 62 E4
England *admin. div.* U.K. 59 E6
Englee Canada 153 L4
Englehart Canada 152 F5
Englewood *FL* U.S.A. 163 D7
Englewood *OH* U.S.A. 164 C4
English *r.* Canada 151 M5
English *IN* U.S.A. 164 B4
English Bazar India *see* Ingraj Bazar
English Channel France/U.K. 59 F9
English Coast Antarctica 188 L2
Engozero Rus. Fed. 52 G2
Enhlalakahle S. Africa 125 J5
Enid *OK* U.S.A. 161 D4
Eniwa Japan 90 F4
Eniwetok *atoll* Marshall Is *see* Enewetak
Enjiang China *see* Yongfeng
Enkeldoorn Zimbabwe *see* Chivhu
Enkhuizen Neth. 62 F2
Enköping Sweden 55 J7
Enmelen Rus. Fed. 148 D2
Enna *Sicily* Italy 68 F6
Ennadai Lake Canada 151 K2
En Nahud Sudan 108 C7
Ennedi, Massif *mts* Chad 121 F3
Ennell, Lough *l.* Ireland 61 E4
Enngonia Australia 138 B2
Enning *SD* U.S.A. 160 C2
Ennis Ireland 61 D5
Ennis *MT* U.S.A. 156 F3
Ennis *TX* U.S.A. 161 D5
Enniscorthy Ireland 61 F5
Enniskillen U.K. 61 E3
Ennistymon Ireland 61 C5
Enn Nâqoûra Lebanon 107 B3
Enns *r.* Austria 57 O6
Eno Fin. 54 Q5
Enoch *UT* U.S.A. 159 G3
Enok *Sumatera* Indon. 84 C3
Enontekiö Fin. 54 M2
Enosburg Falls *VT* U.S.A. 165 I1
Enosville *IN* U.S.A. 164 B4
Enping China 97 G4
Enrekang *Sulawesi* Indon. 83 A3
Enrile *Luzon* Phil. 82 C2
Ens Neth. 62 F2
Ensay Australia 138 C6
Enschede Neth. 62 G2
Ense Germany 63 I3
Ensenada *Baja California* Mex. 166 A2
Ensenada *Baja California Sur* Mex. 166 C4
Enshi China 97 F2
Enshū-nada *g.* Japan 92 D4
Ensley *FL* U.S.A. 163 C6
Entebbe Uganda 122 D3
Enterprise Canada 150 G2
Enterprise *AL* U.S.A. 163 C6
Enterprise *OR* U.S.A. 156 D3
Enterprise *UT* U.S.A. 159 G3
Enterprise Point *Palawan* Phil. 82 B4
Entimau, Bukit *hill* Malaysia 85 F2
Entre Ríos Bol. 176 F8
Entre Rios Brazil 177 H5
Entre Rios de Minas Brazil 179 B3
Entroncamento Port. 67 B4
Enugu Nigeria 120 D4
Enurmino Rus. Fed. 148 E2
Envira Brazil 176 D5
Envira *r.* Brazil 176 D5
'En Yahav Israel 107 B4
Enyamba Dem. Rep. Congo 122 C4
Enzan Japan 93 E3
Eochaill Ireland *see* Youghal
Epe Neth. 62 F2
Epéna Congo 122 B3
Épernay France 62 D5
Ephraim *UT* U.S.A. 159 H2
Ephrata *PA* U.S.A. 165 G3
Epi *i.* Vanuatu 133 G3
Epidamnus Albania *see* Durrës
Épinal France 66 H2
Episkopi Bay Cyprus 107 A2
Episkopis, Kolpos *b.* Cyprus *see* Episkopi Bay
ePitoli S. Africa *see* Pretoria
Epomeo, Monte *hill* Italy 68 E4
Epping U.K. 59 H7
Epping Forest National Park Australia 136 D4
Eppstein Germany 63 I4
Eppynt, Mynydd *hills* U.K. 59 D6
Epsom U.K. 59 G7
Epte *r.* France 62 B5
Eqlīd Iran 110 D4
Equatorial Guinea *country* Africa 120 D4
Équeurdreville-Hainneville France 59 F9
Erac Creek *watercourse* Australia 138 B1
Eran Bay *Palawan* Phil. 82 B4
Erandol India 106 B1
Erawadi *r.* Myanmar *see* Irrawaddy
Erawan National Park Thai. 87 B4
Erbaa Turkey 112 E2
Erbendorf Germany 63 M5
Erbeskopf *hill* Germany 62 H5
Ercan *airport* Cyprus 107 A2
Erciş Turkey 113 F3
Erciyes Dağı *mt.* Turkey 112 D3
Érd Hungary 68 H1
Erdaobaihe China *see* Baihe
Erdaogou Bingzhan China 94 C5
Erdao Jiang *r.* China 90 B4
Erdek Turkey 69 L4
Erdemli Turkey 107 B1
Erdene Mongolia 95 G2
Erdenedalay Mongolia 94 F2
Erdenemandal Mongolia 94 E1
Erdenesant Mongolia 94 F2
Erdenet *Hövsgöl* Mongolia *see* Shine-Ider
Erdenet *Orhon* Mongolia 94 F1
Erdenetsagaan Mongolia 95 H2
Erdenetsogt *Bayanhongor* Mongolia 94 E2
Erdenetsogt *Ömnögovĭ* Mongolia *see* Bayan-Ovoo
Erdi *reg.* Chad 121 F3
Erdniyevskiy Rus. Fed. 53 J7

▶Erebus, Mount *vol.* Antarctica 188 H1
Highest active volcano in Antarctica.

Erechim Brazil 178 F3
Ereentsav Mongolia 95 H1
Ereğli *Konya* Turkey 112 D3
Ereğli *Zonguldak* Turkey 69 N4
Erego Moz. *see* Errego
Erei, Monti *mts Sicily* Italy 68 F6
Ereke *Sulawesi* Indon. 83 B4
Erementaū Kazakh. *see* Yereymentau
Eréndira Mex. 167 E5
Eren Habirga Shan *mts* China 98 D4
Erenhot China 95 H3
Erepucu, Lago de *l.* Brazil 177 G4
Erevan Armenia *see* Yerevan
Erfurt Germany 63 L4
Erfurt *airport* Germany 63 K4
Ergani Turkey 113 E3
'Erg Chech *des.* Alg./Mali 120 C2
Ergel Mongolia *see* Hatanbulag
Ergene *r.* Turkey 69 L4
Ērgļi Latvia 55 N8
Ergu China 90 C3
Ergun China 95 J1
Ergun He *r.* China/Rus. Fed. *see* Argun'
Ergun Youqi China *see* Yongfeng
Ergun Zuoqi China *see* Gegen Gol
Erguveyem *r.* Rus. Fed. 148 C2
Er Hai *l.* China 96 D3
Erhulai China 90 B4
Eriboll, Loch *inlet* U.K. 60 E2
Ericht *r.* U.K. 60 F4
Ericht, Loch *l.* U.K. 60 E4
Erickson Canada 151 L5
Erie *KS* U.S.A. 161 E4
Erie *PA* U.S.A. 164 E2
Erie, Lake Canada/U.S.A. 164 E2
'Erîgât *des.* Mali 120 C3
Erik Eriksenstretet *sea chan.* Svalbard 76 D2
Eriksdale Canada 151 L5
Erimo-misaki *c.* Japan 90 F4
Erin Canada 164 E2
Erinpura Road India 104 C4
Eriskay *i.* U.K. 60 B3
Eritrea *country* Africa 108 E6
Erlangen Germany 63 L5
Erlangping China 97 F1
Erldunda Australia 135 F6
Erlistoun *watercourse* Australia 135 C6
Erlong Shan *mt.* China 90 C4
Erlongshan Shuiku *resr* China 90 B4
Ermak Kazakh. *see* Aksu
Ermana, Khrebet *mts* Rus. Fed. 95 H1
Ermelo Neth. 62 F2
Ermelo S. Africa 125 I4
Ermenek Turkey 107 A1
Ermenek *r.* Turkey 107 A1
Ermont Egypt *see* Armant
Ermoupoli Greece 69 K6
Ernakulam India 106 C4
Erne *r.* Ireland/U.K. 61 D3
Ernest Giles Range *hills* Australia 135 C6
Erode India 106 C4
Eromanga Australia 137 C5
Erongo *admin. reg.* Namibia 124 B1
Erp Neth. 62 F3
Erpu China 94 C3
Erqu China *see* Zhouzhi
Errabiddy Hills Australia 135 A6
Er Rachidia Morocco 64 D5
Errego Moz. 123 D5
Er Remla Tunisia 68 D7
Er Renk South Sudan 108 D7
Errigal *hill* Ireland 61 D2
Errinundra National Park Australia 138 D6
Erris Head *hd* Ireland 61 B3
Errol *NH* U.S.A. 165 J1
Erromango *i.* Vanuatu 133 G3
Erronan *i.* Vanuatu *see* Futuna
Erseka Albania *see* Ersekë
Ersekë Albania 69 I4
Erskine *MN* U.S.A. 160 D2
Ersmark Sweden 54 L5
Ertai China 94 B2
Ertil' Rus. Fed. 53 I6
Ertis *r.* Kazakh./Rus. Fed. *see* Irtysh
Ertix He *r.* China/Kazakh. 102 G2
Ērtra *country* Africa *see* Eritrea
Eruh Turkey 113 F3
Erwin *TN* U.S.A. 162 D4
Erwitte Germany 63 I3
Erxleben *Sachsen-Anhalt* Germany 63 L2
Erxleben *Sachsen-Anhalt* Germany 63 L2
Eryuan China 96 C3
Erzerum Turkey *see* Erzurum
Erzgebirge *mts* Czech Rep./Germany 63 N4
Erzhan China 90 B2
Erzin Rus. Fed. 94 C1
Erzin Turkey 107 C1
Erzincan Turkey 113 E3
Erzurum Turkey 113 F3
Esa-ala P.N.G. 136 E1
Esan-misaki *pt* Japan 90 F4
Esashi Japan 90 F3
Esbjerg Denmark 55 F9
Esbo Fin. *see* Espoo
Escalante *Negros* Phil. 82 C4
Escalante *UT* U.S.A. 159 H3
Escalante *r. UT* U.S.A. 159 H3
Escalante Desert *UT* U.S.A. 159 G3
Escalón Mex. 166 D3
Escambia *r. FL* U.S.A. 163 C6
Escanaba *MI* U.S.A. 162 C2
Escárcega Mex. 167 H5
Escarpada Point *Luzon* Phil. 82 C2
Escatrón Spain 67 F3
Escaut *r.* Belgium 62 D4
Esch Neth. 62 F3
Eschede Germany 63 K2
Eschscholtz *atoll* Marshall Is *see* Bikini
Eschscholtz Bay *AK* U.S.A. 148 G2
Esch-sur-Alzette Lux. 62 F5
Eschwege Germany 63 K3
Eschweiler Germany 62 G4
Escondido *r.* Mex. 161 C6
Escondido *r.* Nicaragua 166 [inset] J6
Escondido *CA* U.S.A. 158 E5
Escudilla *mt. AZ* U.S.A. 159 I5
Escuinapa Mex. 168 C4
Escuintla Guat. 167 H6
Escuintla Mex. 167 G6
Eséka Cameroon 120 E4
Eşen Turkey 69 M6
Esenguly Turkm. 110 D2
Esenguly Döwlet Gorugy *nature res.* Turkm. 110 D2
Esens Germany 63 H1
Eşfahān Iran 110 C3
Esfarayen, Reshteh-ye *mts* Iran 110 E2
Esfedān Iran 111 E3
Eshan China 96 D3
Eshkanān Iran 110 D5
Eshowe S. Africa 125 J5
'Eshqābād Iran 110 E3
Esikhawini S. Africa 125 K5
Esil Kazakh. *see* Yesil'
Esil *r.* Kazakh./Rus. Fed. *see* Ishim
Esk Australia 138 F1
Esk *r.* Australia 137 [inset]
Esk *r.* U.K. 58 D4
Eskdalemuir U.K. 60 F5
Esker Canada 153 I3
Eskifjörður Iceland 54 [inset 1]
Eski Gediz Turkey 69 M5
Eskilstuna Sweden 55 J7
Eskimo Lakes Canada 149 O1
Eskimo Point Canada *see* Arviat
Eskipazar Turkey 112 D2
Eskişehir Turkey 69 N5
Eski-Yakkabog' Uzbek. 111 G2
Esla *r.* Spain 67 C3
Eslāmābād-e Gharb Iran 110 B3
Esler Dağı *mt.* Turkey 69 M6
Eslohe (Sauerland) Germany 63 I3
Eslöv Sweden 55 H9
Esmā'īlī-ye Soflá Iran 110 E4
Eşme Turkey 69 M5
Esmeraldas Ecuador 176 C3
Esmont *VA* U.S.A. 165 F5
Esnagami Lake Canada 152 D4
Esnes France 62 D4
Espakeh Iran 111 F5
Espalion France 66 F4
España *country* Europe *see* Spain
Espanola Canada 152 E5
Espanola *NM* U.S.A. 161 B4
Esparta Hond. 166 [inset] I6
Espelkamp Germany 63 I2
Espenberg, Cape *AK* U.S.A. 148 G2
Esperance Australia 135 C8
Esperance Bay Australia 135 C8
Esperanza *research station* Antarctica 188 A2
Esperanza Arg. 178 B8
Esperanza Mex. 166 C3
Esperanza *Masbate* Phil. 82 D4
Esperanza, Sierra de la *mts* Hond. 166 [inset] I6
Espichel, Cabo *c.* Port. 67 B4
Espigão, Serra do *mts* Brazil 179 A4
Espigüete *mt.* Spain 67 D2
Espinazo Mex. 167 E3
Espinhaço, Serra do *mts* Brazil 179 C2
Espinosa Brazil 179 C1
Espírito Santo Brazil *see* Vila Velha
Espírito Santo *state* Brazil 179 C2
Espiritu *Luzon* Phil. 82 C2
Espiritu Santo *i.* Vanuatu 133 G3
Espíritu Santo, Isla *i.* Mex. 166 C3
Espita Mex. 167 H4
Espoo Fin. 55 N6
Espuña *mt.* Spain 67 F5
Esqueda Mex. 166 C2
Esquel Arg. 178 B6
Esquimalt Canada 150 F5
Essang *Sulawesi* Indon. 83 C1
Essaouira Morocco 120 C1
Es Semara W. Sahara 120 B2
Essen Belgium 62 E3
Essen Germany 62 H3
Essen (Oldenburg) Germany 63 H2
Essequibo *r.* Guyana 177 G2
Essex Canada 164 D2
Essex *CA* U.S.A. 159 F4
Essex *MD* U.S.A. 165 G4
Essex *NY* U.S.A. 165 I1
Essexville *MI* U.S.A. 164 D2
Esslingen am Neckar Germany 63 J6
Esso Rus. Fed. 77 Q4
Essoyla Rus. Fed. 52 G3
Estación Marítima Antártica *research station* Chile 188 A2
Estagno Point *Luzon* Phil. 82 C2
Eşţahbān Iran 110 D4
Estância Brazil 177 K6
Estancia *NM* U.S.A. 157 G6
Estand, Kūh-e *mt.* Iran 111 F4
Estats, Pic d' *mt.* France/Spain 66 E5
Estcourt S. Africa 125 I5
Este *r.* Germany 63 J1
Estelí Nicaragua 166 [inset] I6
Estella Spain 67 E2
Estepa Spain 67 D5
Estepona Spain 67 D5
Ester *AK* U.S.A. 149 K2
Esteras de Medinaceli Spain 67 E3
Esterhazy Canada 151 K5
Estero Bay *CA* U.S.A. 158 C4
Esteros Mex. 167 F4
Esteros Para. 178 D2
Este Sudeste, Cayos del *is* Col. 166 [inset] J6
Estevan Canada 151 K5
Estevan Group *is* Canada 150 D4
Estherville *IA* U.S.A. 160 E3
Estill *SC* U.S.A. 163 D5
Eston Canada 151 I5
Estonia *country* Europe 55 N7
Estonskaya S.S.R. *country* Europe *see* Estonia
Estrées-St-Denis France 62 C5
Estrela Brazil 179 A5
Estrela, Serra da *mts* Port. 67 C3
Estrela do Sul Brazil 179 B2
Estrella *mt.* Spain 67 E4
Estrella, Punta *pt* Mex. 166 B2
Estremoz Port. 67 C4
Estrondo, Serra *hills* Brazil 177 I5
Etadunna Australia 137 B6
Etah India 104 D4
Étain France 62 F5
Étamamiou Canada 153 K4
Étampes France 66 F2
Étaples France 62 B4
Etawah *Rajasthan* India 104 D4
Etawah *Uttar Prad.* India 104 D4
Etchojoa Mex. 166 C3
Ethandakukhanya S. Africa 125 J4
Ethelbert Canada 151 K5
Ethel Creek Australia 135 C5
E'Thembini S. Africa 124 F5

▶Ethiopia *country* Africa 122 D3
2nd most populous country in Africa.

Etimesğut Turkey 112 D3
Etive, Loch *inlet* U.K. 60 D4
Etivluk *r. AK* U.S.A. 148 H1

▶Etna, Mount *vol. Sicily* Italy 68 F6
Highest active volcano in Europe.

Etne Norway 55 D7
Etobicoke Canada 164 F2
Etolin Strait *AK* U.S.A. 148 F3
Etorofu-tō *i.* Rus. Fed. *see* Iturup, Ostrov
Etosha National Park Namibia 123 B5
Etosha Pan *salt pan* Namibia 123 B5
Etoumbi Congo 122 B3
Etrek *r.* Iran/Turkm. *see* Atrek
Etrek Turkm. 110 D2
Étrépagny France 62 B5
Étretat France 59 H9
Ettelbruck Lux. 62 G5
Etten-Leur Neth. 62 E3
Ettlingen Germany 63 I6
Ettrick Water *r.* U.K. 60 F5
Etzatlán Mex. 166 D4
Euabalong Australia 138 C4
Euboea *i.* Greece *see* Evvoia
Eucla Australia 135 E7
Euclid *OH* U.S.A. 164 E3
Euclides da Cunha Brazil 177 K6
Eucumbene, Lake Australia 138 D6
Eudistes, Lac des *l.* Canada 153 I4
Eudora *AR* U.S.A. 161 F5
Eudunda Australia 137 B7
Eufaula *AL* U.S.A. 163 C6
Eufaula *OK* U.S.A. 161 E5
Eufaula Lake *resr OK* U.S.A. 161 E5
Eugene *OR* U.S.A. 156 C3
Eugenia, Punta *pt* Mex. 166 B3
Eugowra Australia 138 D4
Eulo Australia 138 B2
Eumungerie Australia 138 D3
Eungella Australia 136 E4
Eungella National Park Australia 136 E4
Eunice *LA* U.S.A. 161 E6
Eunice *NM* U.S.A. 161 C5
Eupen Belgium 62 G4

▶Euphrates *r.* Asia 113 G5
Longest river in western Asia.
Also known as Al Furāt (Iraq/Syria) or Firat (Turkey).

Eura Fin. 55 M6
Eure *r.* France 62 B5
Eureka *AK* U.S.A. 149 J2
Eureka *CA* U.S.A. 156 B4
Eureka *KS* U.S.A. 160 D4
Eureka *MT* U.S.A. 156 E2
Eureka *NV* U.S.A. 159 F2
Eureka *OH* U.S.A. 164 D4
Eureka *SD* U.S.A. 160 D2
Eureka *UT* U.S.A. 159 G2
Eureka Roadhouse *AK* U.S.A. 149 K3
Eureka Sound *sea chan.* Canada 147 J2
Eureka Springs *AR* U.S.A. 161 E4
Eureka Valley *CA* U.S.A. 158 E3
Euriowie Australia 137 C6
Euroa Australia 138 B6
Eurombah Australia 137 E5
Eurombah Creek *r.* Australia 137 E5
Europa, Île *i.* Indian Ocean 123 E6
Europa, Punta de *pt* Gibraltar *see* Europa Point
Europa Point Gibraltar 67 D5
Euskirchen Germany 62 G4
Eutaw *AL* U.S.A. 163 C5
Eutsuk Lake Canada 150 E4
Eutzsch Germany 63 M3
Eva Downs Australia 134 F4
Evans, Lac *l.* Canada 152 F4
Evans, Mount *CO* U.S.A. 156 G5
Evansburg Canada 150 H4
Evans City *PA* U.S.A. 164 E3
Evans Head Australia 138 F2
Evans Head *hd* Australia 138 F2
Evans Ice Stream Antarctica 188 L1
Evans Strait Canada 151 P2
Evanston *IL* U.S.A. 164 B2
Evanston *WY* U.S.A. 156 F4
Evansville Canada 152 E5
Evansville *AK* U.S.A. 149 J2
Evansville *IN* U.S.A. 164 B5
Evansville *WY* U.S.A. 156 G4
Evant *TX* U.S.A. 161 D6
Eva Perón Arg. *see* La Plata
Evart *MI* U.S.A. 164 C2
Evaton S. Africa 125 H4
Evaz Iran 110 D5
Evening Shade *AR* U.S.A. 161 F4
Evensk Rus. Fed. 77 Q3
Everard, Lake *salt flat* Australia 137 A6
Everard, Mount Australia 135 F5
Everard Range *hills* Australia 135 F6
Everdingen Neth. 62 F3
Everek Turkey *see* Develi

▶Everest, Mount China/Nepal 105 F4
Highest mountain in Asia and the world.

Everett *PA* U.S.A. 165 F3
Everett *WA* U.S.A. 156 C3
Evergem Belgium 62 D3
Everglades *swamp FL* U.S.A. 163 D7
Everglades National Park *FL* U.S.A. 163 D7
Evergreen *AL* U.S.A. 163 C6
Evesham Australia 136 C4
Evesham U.K. 59 F6
Evesham, Vale of *valley* U.K. 59 F6
Evijärvi Fin. 54 M5
Evje Norway 55 E7
Évora Port. 67 C4
Evoron, Ozero *l.* Rus. Fed. 90 E2
Évreux France 62 B5
Evros *r.* Bulg. *see* Maritsa
Evros *r.* Turkey *see* Meriç
Evrotas *r.* Greece 69 J6
Évry France 62 C6
Evrychou Cyprus 107 A2
Evrykhou Cyprus *see* Evrychou
Evvoia *i.* Greece 69 K5
Ewan Australia 136 D3
Ewaso Ngiro *r.* Kenya 122 E3
Ewe, Loch *b.* U.K. 60 D3
Ewenkizu Zizhiqi China *see* Bayan Tohoi
Ewing *VA* U.S.A. 164 D5
Ewirgol China 98 D4
Ewo Congo 122 B4
Exaltación Bol. 176 E6
Excelsior S. Africa 125 H5
Excelsior Mountain *CA* U.S.A. 158 D2
Excelsior Mountains *NV* U.S.A. 158 D2
Exe *r.* U.K. 59 D8
Exeter Australia 138 E5
Exeter Canada 164 E2
Exeter U.K. 59 D8
Exeter *CA* U.S.A. 158 D3
Exeter *NH* U.S.A. 165 J2
Exeter Lake Canada 151 I1
Exloo Neth. 62 G2
Exminster U.K. 59 D8
Exmoor *hills* U.K. 59 D7
Exmoor National Park U.K. 59 D7
Exmore *VA* U.S.A. 165 H5
Exmouth Australia 134 A5
Exmouth U.K. 59 D8
Exmouth, Mount Australia 138 D3
Exmouth Gulf Australia 134 A5
Exmouth Lake Canada 150 H1
Exmouth Plateau *sea feature* Indian Ocean 185 P7
Expedition National Park Australia 136 E5
Expedition Range *mts* Australia 136 E5
Exploits *r.* Canada 153 L4
Exton *PA* U.S.A. 165 H3
Extremadura *aut. comm.* Spain 67 D4
Exuma Cays *is* Bahamas 163 E7
Exuma Sound *sea chan.* Bahamas 163 F7
Eyasi, Lake *salt l.* Tanz. 122 D4
Eyawadi *r.* Myanmar *see* Irrawaddy
Eye U.K. 59 I6
Eyeberry Lake Canada 151 J2
Eyelenoborsk Rus. Fed. 51 S3
Eyemouth U.K. 60 G5
Eyjafjörður *inlet* Iceland 54 [inset 1]
Eyl Somalia 122 E3
Eylau Rus. Fed. *see* Bagrationovsk
Eynsham U.K. 59 F7

▶Eyre, Lake Australia 137 B6
Largest lake in Oceania and lowest point.

Eyre Creek *watercourse* Australia 136 B5
Eyre Mountains N.Z. 139 B7
Eyre (North), Lake Australia 137 B6
Eyre Peninsula Australia 137 A7
Eyre (South), Lake Australia 137 B6
Eystrup Germany 63 J2
Eysturoy *i.* Faroe Is 54 [inset 2]
Ezakheni S. Africa 125 J5
Ezel *KY* U.S.A. 164 D5
Ezenzeleni S. Africa 125 I4
Ezequiel Ramos Mexía, Embalse *resr* Arg. 178 C5
Ezhou China 97 G2
Ezhva Rus. Fed. 52 K3
Ezine Turkey 69 L5
Ezo *i.* Japan *see* Hokkaidō
Ezousa *r.* Cyprus 107 A2

F

Faaborg Denmark 55 G9
Faadhippolhu Atoll Maldives 106 B5
Faafxadhuun Somalia 122 E3
Fabens *TX* U.S.A. 157 G7
Faber, Mount *hill* Sing. 87 [inset]
Faber Lake Canada 150 G2
Fåborg Denmark *see* Faaborg
Fabriano Italy 68 E3
Faches-Thumesnil France 62 D4
Fachi Niger 120 E3
Fada Chad 121 F3
Fada-N'Gourma Burkina Faso 120 D3
Fadghāmī Syria 113 F4
Fadiffolu Atoll Maldives *see* Faadhippolhu Atoll
Fadippolu Atoll Maldives *see* Faadhippolhu Atoll
Faenza Italy 68 D2
Færoerne *terr.* N. Atlantic Ocean *see* Faroe Islands
Faeroes *terr.* N. Atlantic Ocean *see* Faroe Islands
Fafanlap *Papua* Indon. 83 D3
Făgăraş Romania 69 K2

▶Fagatogo American Samoa 133 I3
Capital of American Samoa.

Fagersta Sweden 55 I7
Fagita *Papua* Indon. 83 D3
Fagne *reg.* Belgium 62 E4
Fagurhólsmýri Iceland 54 [inset 1]
Fagwir South Sudan 108 D8
Fahraj Iran 110 D4
Fā'id Egypt 112 D5
Fairbanks *AK* U.S.A. 149 K2
Fairborn *OH* U.S.A. 164 C4

Fairbury *NE* U.S.A. **160** D3
Fairchance *PA* U.S.A. **164** F4
Fairfax *VA* U.S.A. **165** G4
Fairfield *CA* U.S.A. **158** B2
Fairfield *IA* U.S.A. **160** F3
Fairfield *ID* U.S.A. **156** E4
Fairfield *IL* U.S.A. **160** F4
Fairfield *OH* U.S.A. **164** C4
Fairfield *TX* U.S.A. **161** D6
Fair Haven *VT* U.S.A. **165** I2
Fair Head *hd* U.K. **61** F2
Fairie Queen Shoal *sea feature* Phil. **82** B4
Fair Isle *i.* U.K. **60** H1
Fairlee *VT* U.S.A. **165** I2
Fairlie N.Z. **139** C7
Fairmont *MN* U.S.A. **160** E3
Fairmont *WV* U.S.A. **164** E4
Fair Oaks *IN* U.S.A. **164** B3
Fairplay, Mount *AK* U.S.A. **149** L3
Fairview Australia **136** D2
Fairview Canada **150** G3
Fairview *MI* U.S.A. **164** C1
Fairview *OK* U.S.A. **161** D4
Fairview *PA* U.S.A. **164** E2
Fairview *UT* U.S.A. **159** H2
Fairview Park *H.K.* China **97** [inset]
Fairweather, Cape *AK* U.S.A. **149** M4
Fairweather, Mount Canada/U.S.A. **149** M4
Fais *i.* Micronesia **81** K5
Faisalabad Pak. **111** I4
Faissault France **62** E5
Faith *SD* U.S.A. **160** C2
Faizabad Afgh. *see* **Feyzābād**
Faizabad India **105** E4
Fakaofo *atoll* Tokelau **133** I2
Fakaofu *atoll* Tokelau *see* **Fakaofo**
Fakenham U.K. **59** H6
Fåker Sweden **54** I5
Fakfak Indon. **81** I7
Fakhrābād Iran **110** D4
Fakiragram India **105** G4
Fako *vol.* Cameroon *see* **Cameroun, Mont**
Faku China **95** J3
Fal *r.* U.K. **59** C8
Falaba Sierra Leone **120** B4
Falaise Lake Canada **150** G2
Falam Myanmar **86** A2
Falcon Lake Canada **151** M5
Falcon Lake *l.* Mex./U.S.A. **167** F3
Falenki Rus. Fed. **52** K4
Falfurrias *TX* U.S.A. **161** D7
Falher Canada **150** G4
Falkenberg Germany **63** N3
Falkenberg Sweden **55** H8
Falkenhagen Germany **63** M1
Falkenhain Germany **63** M3
Falkensee Germany **63** N2
Falkenstein Germany **63** M5
Falkirk U.K. **60** F5
Falkland U.K. **60** F4
Falkland Escarpment *sea feature* S. Atlantic Ocean **184** E9

▶**Falkland Islands** *terr.* S. Atlantic Ocean **178** E8
United Kingdom Overseas Territory.

Falkland Plateau *sea feature* S. Atlantic Ocean **184** E9
Falkland Sound *sea chan.* Falkland Is **178** D8
Falköping Sweden **55** H7
Fallbrook *CA* U.S.A. **158** E5
Fallieres Coast Antarctica **188** L2
Fallingbostel Germany **63** J2
Fallon *NV* U.S.A. **158** D2
Fall River *MA* U.S.A. **165** J3
Fall River Pass *CO* U.S.A. **156** G4
Falls City *NE* U.S.A. **160** E3
Falmouth U.K. **59** B8
Falmouth *KY* U.S.A. **164** C4
Falmouth *VA* U.S.A. **165** G4
False *r.* Canada **153** H2
False Bay S. Africa **124** D8
False Pass *AK* U.S.A. **148** G5
False Point India **105** F5
Falso, Cabo *c.* Hond. **166** [inset] J6
Falster *i.* Denmark **55** G9
Fălticeni Romania **53** E7
Falun Sweden **55** I6
Fam, Kepulauan *is Papua* Indon. **83** D3
Famagusta Cyprus **107** A2
Famagusta Bay Cyprus *see* **Ammochostos Bay**
Fameck France **62** G5
Famenin Iran **110** C3
Fame Range *hills* Australia **135** C6
Family Lake Canada **151** M5
Family Well Australia **134** D5
Fāmūr, Daryācheh-ye *l.* Iran **110** C4
Fana Mali **120** C3
Fanad Head *hd* Ireland **61** E2
Fandriana Madag. **123** E6
Fane *r.* Ireland **61** F4
Fang Thai. **86** B3
Fangcheng *Guangxi* China *see* **Fangchenggang**
Fangcheng *Henan* China **97** G1
Fangchenggang China **97** F4
Fangdou Shan *mts* China **97** F2
Fangliao Taiwan **97** I4
Fangshan Taiwan **97** I4
Fangxian China **97** F1
Fangzheng China **90** C3
Fankuai China **97** F2
Fankuaidian China *see* **Fankuai**
Fanling *H.K.* China **97** [inset]
Fannich, Loch *l.* U.K. **60** D3
Fannūj Iran **111** E5
Fano Italy **68** E3
Fanshan *Anhui* China **97** H2
Fanshan *Zhejiang* China **97** I3
Fanshi China **95** H4
Fanum Fortunae Italy *see* **Fano**
Faqīh Aḩmadān Iran **110** C4
Farab Turkm. *see* **Farap**
Faraba Mali **120** B3
Faradofay Madag. *see* **Tôlañaro**
Farafangana Madag. **123** E6
Farāfirah, Wāḩāt al *oasis* Egypt **108** C4
Farafra Oasis *oasis* Egypt *see* **Farāfirah, Wāḩāt al**
Farāh Afgh. **111** F3
Faraḩābād Iran *see* **Khezerābād**
Farallon de Medinilla *i.* N. Mariana Is **81** L3
Farallon de Pajaros *vol.* N. Mariana Is **81** K2
Farallones de Cali, Parque Nacional *nat. park* Col. **176** C3
Faranah Guinea **120** B3
Farap Turkm. **111** F2
Fararah Oman **109** I6
Farasān, Jazā'ir *is* Saudi Arabia **108** F6
Faraulep *atoll* Micronesia **81** K5
Fareham U.K. **59** F8
Farewell *AK* U.S.A. **148** I3
Farewell, Cape Greenland **147** N3
Farewell, Cape N.Z. **139** D5
Farewell Spit N.Z. **139** D5
Färgelanda Sweden **55** H7
Farghona Uzbek. *see* **Farg'ona**
Fargo *ND* U.S.A. **160** D2
Farg'ona Uzbek. **109** L1
Faribault *MN* U.S.A. **160** E2
Faribault, Lac *l.* Canada **153** H2
Faridabad India **104** D3
Faridkot India **104** C3
Faridpur Bangl. **105** G5
Farīmān Iran **111** E3
Farkhar Afgh. *see* **Farkhato**
Farkhato Afgh. **111** H2
Farkhor Tajik. **111** H2
Farmahīn Iran **110** C3
Farmer Island Canada **152** E2
Farmerville *LA* U.S.A. **161** E5
Farmington Canada **150** F4
Farmington *ME* U.S.A. **165** J1
Farmington *MO* U.S.A. **160** F4
Farmington *NH* U.S.A. **165** J2
Farmington *NM* U.S.A. **159** I3
Farmington Hills *MI* U.S.A. **164** D2
Far Mountain Canada **150** E4
Farmville *VA* U.S.A. **165** F5
Farnborough U.K. **59** G7
Farne Islands U.K. **58** F3
Farnham U.K. **59** G7
Farnham, Lake *salt flat* Australia **135** D6
Farnham, Mount Canada **150** G5
Faro Brazil **177** G4
Faro Canada **149** N3
Faro Port. **67** C5
Fårö *i.* Sweden **55** K8
Faroe - Iceland Ridge *sea feature* Arctic Ocean **189** I2

▶**Faroe Islands** *terr.* N. Atlantic Ocean **54** [inset 2]
Self-governing Danish territory.

Fårösund Sweden **55** K8
Farquhar Group *is* Seychelles **123** F5
Farquharson Tableland *hills* Australia **135** C6
Farrāshband Iran **110** D4
Farr Bay Antarctica **188** F2
Farristown *KY* U.S.A. **164** C5
Farrukhabad India *see* **Fatehgarh**
Farsund Norway **55** E7
Fārūj Iran **110** E2
Farwell *MI* U.S.A. **164** C2
Farwell *TX* U.S.A. **161** C5
Fasā Iran **110** D4
Fasano Italy **68** G4
Faşikan Geçidi *pass* Turkey **107** A1
Faßberg Germany **63** K2
Fastiv Ukr. **53** F6
Fastov Ukr. *see* **Fastiv**
Fatehabad India **104** C3
Fatehgarh India **104** D4
Fatehpur *Rajasthan* India **104** C4
Fatehpur *Uttar Prad.* India **104** E4
Fatick Senegal **120** B3
Fattoilep *atoll* Micronesia *see* **Faraulep**
Faughan *r.* U.K. **61** E2
Faulkton *SD* U.S.A. **160** D2
Faulquemont France **62** G5
Fauresmith S. Africa **125** G5
Fauske Norway **54** I3
Faust Canada **150** H4
Fawcett Canada **150** H4
Fawley U.K. **59** F8
Fawn *r.* Canada **151** N4
Faxaflói *b.* Iceland **54** [inset 1]
Faxälven *r.* Sweden **54** J5
Faya Chad **121** E3
Fayette *AL* U.S.A. **163** C5
Fayette *MO* U.S.A. **160** E4
Fayette *MS* U.S.A. **161** F6
Fayette *OH* U.S.A. **164** C3
Fayetteville *AR* U.S.A. **161** E4
Fayetteville *NC* U.S.A. **163** E5
Fayetteville *TN* U.S.A. **163** C5
Fayetteville *WV* U.S.A. **164** E4
Fâyid Egypt *see* **Fā'id**
Faylakah *i.* Kuwait **110** C4
Fazao Malfakassa, Parc National de *nat. park* Togo **120** D4
Fazilka India **104** C3
Fazrān, Jabal *hill* Saudi Arabia **110** C5
Fdérik Mauritania **120** B2
Fead Group *is* P.N.G. *see* **Nuguria Islands**
Feale *r.* Ireland **61** C5
Fear, Cape *NC* U.S.A. **163** E5
Featherston N.Z. **139** E5
Feathertop, Mount Australia **138** C6
Fécamp France **66** E2
Federal District *admin. dist.* Brazil *see* **Distrito Federal**
Federalsburg *MD* U.S.A. **165** H4
Federated Malay States *country* Asia *see* **Malaysia**
Fedusar India **104** C4
Fehet Lake Canada **151** M1
Fehmarn *i.* Germany **57** M3
Fehrbellin Germany **63** M2
Feia, Lagoa *lag.* Brazil **179** C3
Feicheng China *see* **Feixian**
Feijó Brazil **176** D5
Feilding N.Z. **139** E5
Fei Ngo Shan *hill H.K.* China *see* **Kowloon Peak**
Feio *r.* Brazil *see* **Aguapeí**
Feira de Santana Brazil **179** D1
Feixi China **97** H2
Feixian China **95** I5
Feixiang China **95** H4
Fejd el Abiod *pass* Alg. **68** B6
Feke Turkey **112** D3
Felanitx Spain **67** H4
Felāvarjān Iran **110** C3
Feldberg Germany **63** N1
Feldberg *mt.* Germany **57** L7
Feldkirch Austria **57** L7
Feldkirchen in Kärnten Austria **57** O7
Felidhu Atoll Maldives **103** D11
Felidu Atoll Maldives *see* **Felidhu Atoll**
Felipe C. Puerto Mex. **167** H5
Felixlândia Brazil **179** B2
Felixstowe U.K. **59** I7
Felixton S. Africa **125** J5
Fellowsville *WV* U.S.A. **164** F4
Felsina Italy *see* **Bologna**
Felton *DE* U.S.A. **165** H4
Feltre Italy **68** D1
Femunden *l.* Norway **54** G5
Femundsmarka Nasjonalpark *nat. park* Norway **54** H5
Fenaio, Punta del *pt* Italy **68** D3
Fence Lake *NM* U.S.A. **159** I4
Fener Burnu *hd* Turkey **107** B1
Fénérive Madag. *see* **Fenoarivo Atsinanana**
Fengari *mt.* Greece **69** K4
Fengcheng *Fujian* China *see* **Lianjiang**
Fengcheng *Fujian* China *see* **Anxi**
Fengcheng *Fujian* China *see* **Yongding**
Fengcheng *Guangdong* China *see* **Xinfeng**
Fengcheng *Guangxi* China *see* **Fengshan**
Fengcheng *Guizhou* China *see* **Tianzhu**
Fengcheng *Jiangxi* China **97** G2
Fenggang *Fujian* China *see* **Shaxian**
Fenggang *Guizhou* China **96** E3
Fenggang *Jiangxi* China *see* **Yihuang**
Fenggeling China **94** F5
Fengguang China **90** B3
Fenghuang China **97** F3
Fengjiaba China *see* **Wangcang**
Fengjie China **97** F2
Fengkai China **97** F4
Fenglin Taiwan **97** I4
Fengman China **90** B4
Fengming *Shaanxi* China *see* **Qishan**
Fengming *Sichuan* China *see* **Pengshan**
Fengnan China **95** I4
Fengning China **95** I3
Fengqi China *see* **Luochuan**
Fengqing China **96** C3
Fengqiu China **95** H5
Fengrun China **95** I4
Fengshan *Fujian* China *see* **Luoyuan**
Fengshan *Guangxi* China **96** E3
Fengshan *Hubei* China *see* **Luotian**
Fengshan *Yunnan* China *see* **Fengqing**
Fengshuba Shuiku *resr* China **97** G3
Fengtongzhai Giant Panda Reserve *nature res.* China **96** D2
Fengxian *Jiangsu* China **95** I5
Fengxian *Shaanxi* China **96** E1
Fengxiang *Heilong.* China *see* **Luobei**
Fengxiang *Shaanxi* China **95** F5
Fengxiang *Yunnan* China *see* **Lincang**
Fengyang China **97** H1
Fengyuan China **95** G5
Fengyüan Taiwan **97** I3
Fengzhen China **95** H3
Feni Bangl. **105** G5
Feniak Lake *AK* U.S.A. **148** H1
Feni Islands P.N.G. **132** F2
Fenimore Pass *sea channel AK* U.S.A. **148** [inset] D5
Fennville *MI* U.S.A. **164** B2
Feno, Capo di *c. Corsica* France **66** I6
Fenoarivo Atsinanana Madag. **123** E5
Fenshui Guan *pass* China **97** H3
Fenton *MI* U.S.A. **164** D2
Fenua Ura *atoll* Fr. Polynesia *see* **Manuae**
Fenyang China **95** G4
Fenyi China **97** G3
Feodosiya Ukr. **112** D1
Fer, Cap de *c.* Alg. **68** B6
Férai Greece *see* **Feres**
Ferdows Iran **110** E3
Fère-Champenoise France **62** D6
Feres Greece **69** L4
Fergus Canada **164** E2
Fergus Falls *MN* U.S.A. **160** D2
Ferguson Lake Canada **151** L2
Fergusson Island P.N.G. **132** F2
Fériana Tunisia **68** C7
Ferizaj Kosovo **69** I3
Ferkessédougou Côte d'Ivoire **120** C4
Fermo Italy **68** E3
Fermont Canada **153** I3
Fermoselle Spain **67** C3
Fermoy Ireland **61** D5
Fernandina, Isla *i. Galápagos* Ecuador **176** [inset]
Fernandina Beach *FL* U.S.A. **163** D6
Fernando de Magallanes, Parque Nacional *nat. park* Chile **178** B8
Fernando de Noronha *i.* Brazil **184** F6
Fernandópolis Brazil **179** A3
Fernando Poó *i.* Equat. Guinea *see* **Bioco**
Fernão Dias Brazil **179** B2
Ferndale *CA* U.S.A. **158** A1
Ferndown U.K. **59** F8
Fernlee Australia **138** C2
Fernley *NV* U.S.A. **158** D2
Ferns Ireland **61** F5
Ferozepore India *see* **Firozpur**
Ferrara Italy **68** D2
Ferreira-Gomes Brazil **177** H3
Ferriday *LA* U.S.A. **167** H2
Ferro, Capo *c. Sardinia* Italy **68** C4
Ferrol Spain **67** B2
Ferron *UT* U.S.A. **159** H2
Ferros Brazil **179** C2
Ferry *AK* U.S.A. **149** J2
Ferryland Canada **153** L5
Ferryville Tunisia *see* **Menzel Bourguiba**
Fertő-tavi *nat. park* Hungary **68** G1
Ferwerd Neth. *see* **Ferwert**
Ferwert Neth. **62** F1
Fès Morocco **64** D5
Feshi Dem. Rep. Congo **123** B4
Fessenden *ND* U.S.A. **160** D2
Festus *MO* U.S.A. **160** F4
Fet Dom, Tanjung *pt Papua* Indon. **83** D3
Fété Bowé Senegal **120** B3
Fethard Ireland **61** E5
Fethiye *Malatya* Turkey *see* **Yazıhan**
Fethiye *Muğla* Turkey **69** M6
Fethiye Körfezi *b.* Turkey **69** M6
Fetisovo Kazakh. **113** I2
Fetlar *i.* U.K. **60** [inset]
Fettercairn U.K. **60** G4
Feucht Germany **63** L5
Feuchtwangen Germany **63** K5
Feuilles, Rivière aux *r.* Canada **153** H2
Fevral'sk Rus. Fed. **90** C1
Fevzipaşa Turkey **112** E3
Feyzābād Afgh. **111** H2
Feyẕābād *Kermān* Iran **110** D4
Feyẕābād *Khorāsān-e Raẕavī* Iran **110** E3
Fez Morocco *see* **Fès**
Ffestiniog U.K. **59** D6
Fianarantsoa Madag. **123** E6
Fichē Eth. **122** D3
Fichtelgebirge *hills* Germany **63** M4
Field *KY* U.S.A. **164** D5
Fier Albania **69** H4
Fiery Creek *r.* Australia **136** B3
Fife Lake *MI* U.S.A. **164** C1
Fife Ness *pt* U.K. **60** G4
Fifield Australia **138** C4
Fifth Meridian Canada **150** H3
Figeac France **66** F4
Figueira da Foz Port. **67** B3
Figueras Spain *see* **Figueres**
Figueres Spain **67** H2
Figuig Morocco **64** D5
Figuil Cameroon **121** E4

▶**Fiji** *country* S. Pacific Ocean **133** H3
4th most populous and 5th largest country in Oceania.

Fīk' Eth. **122** E3
Filadelfia Para. **178** D2
Filchner Ice Shelf Antarctica **188** A1
Filey U.K. **58** G4
Filibe Bulg. *see* **Plovdiv**
Filingué Niger **120** D3
Filipinas *country* Asia *see* **Philippines**
Filippiada Greece **69** I5
Filipstad Sweden **55** I7
Fillan Norway **54** F5
Fillmore *CA* U.S.A. **158** D4
Fillmore *UT* U.S.A. **159** G2
Fils *r.* Germany **63** J6
Fīltu Eth. **122** E3
Fimbul Ice Shelf Antarctica **188** C2
Fīn Iran **110** C3
Finch Canada **165** H1
Findhorn *r.* U.K. **60** F3
Fındık Turkey **110** A2
Findlay *OH* U.S.A. **164** D3
Fine *NY* U.S.A. **165** H1
Finger Lake Canada **151** M4
Finger Lakes *NY* U.S.A. **165** G2
Finike Turkey **69** N6
Finike Körfezi *b.* Turkey **69** N6
Finisterre Spain *see* **Fisterra**
Finisterre, Cabo *c.* Spain *see* **Finisterre, Cape**
Finisterre, Cape Spain **67** B2
Fink Creek *AK* U.S.A. **148** G2
Finke *watercourse* Australia **136** A5
Finke, Mount *hill* Australia **135** F7
Finke Bay Australia **134** E3
Finke Gorge National Park Australia **135** F6
Finland *country* Europe **54** O5
Finland, Gulf of Europe **55** M7

▶**Finlay** *r.* Canada **150** E3
Part of the Mackenzie-Peace-Finlay, the 2nd longest river in North America.

Finlay, Mount Canada **150** E3
Finlay Forks Canada **150** F4
Finley *ND* U.S.A. **160** D2
Finn *r.* Ireland **61** E3
Finne *ridge* Germany **63** L3
Finnigan, Mount Australia **136** D2
Finniss, Cape Australia **135** F8
Finnmarksvidda *reg.* Norway **54** H2
Finnsnes Norway **54** J2
Fins Oman **110** E6
Finschhafen P.N.G. **81** L8
Finspång Sweden **55** I7
Fintona U.K. **61** E3
Finucane Range *hills* Australia **136** C4
Fionn Loch *l.* U.K. **60** D3
Fionnphort U.K. **60** C4
Fiordland National Park N.Z. **139** A7
Fir *reg.* Saudi Arabia **110** B4
Fırat *r.* Asia **112** E3 *see* **Euphrates**
Firebaugh *CA* U.S.A. **158** C3
Firedrake Lake Canada **151** J2
Fire Island *AK* U.S.A. **149** J3
Firenze Italy *see* **Florence**
Fireside Canada **149** P4
Firk, Sha'īb *watercourse* Iraq **113** G5
Firmat Arg. **178** D4
Firminy France **66** G4
Firmum Italy *see* **Fermo**
Firmum Picenum Italy *see* **Fermo**
Firovo Rus. Fed. **52** G4
Firozabad India **104** D4
Firozkoh *reg.* Afgh. **111** G3
Firozpur *Haryana* India **99** B8
Firozpur *Punjab* India **104** C3
Firth *r.* Canada **149** M1
Fīrūzābād Iran **110** D4
Fīrūz Kūh Iran **110** D3
Firyuza Turkm. *see* **Pöwrize**
Fischbach Germany **63** H5
Fischersbrunn Namibia **124** B3
Fish *watercourse* Namibia **124** C5
Fisher (abandoned) Australia **135** E7
Fisher Bay Antarctica **188** G2
Fisher Glacier Antarctica **188** E2
Fisher River Canada **151** L5
Fishers *IN* U.S.A. **164** B4
Fishers Island *NY* U.S.A. **165** J3
Fisher Strait Canada **147** J3
Fishguard U.K. **59** C7
Fishing Branch Game Reserve *nature res.* Canada **149** M2
Fishing Creek *MD* U.S.A. **165** G4
Fishing Lake Canada **151** M4
Fish Lake Canada **150** F2
Fish Lake *AK* U.S.A. **149** J2
Fish Point *MI* U.S.A. **164** D2
Fish Ponds *H.K.* China **97** [inset]
Fiske, Cape Antarctica **188** L2
Fiskenæsset Greenland *see* **Qeqertarsuatsiaat**
Fismes France **62** D5
Fisterra Spain **67** B2
Fisterra, Cabo *c.* Spain *see* **Finisterre, Cape**
Fitchburg *WI* U.S.A. **160** F3
Fitri, Lac *l.* Chad **121** E3
Fitton, Mount Canada **149** M1
Fitzgerald Canada **151** I3
Fitzgerald *GA* U.S.A. **163** D6
Fitzgerald River National Park Australia **135** B8
Fitz Hugh Sound *sea chan.* Canada **150** D5
Fitz Roy Arg. **178** C7
Fitzroy *r.* Australia **134** C4
Fitz Roy, Cerro *mt.* Arg. **178** B7
Fitzroy Crossing Australia **134** D4
Fitzwilliam Island Canada **164** E1
Fiume Croatia *see* **Rijeka**
Fivemiletown U.K. **61** E3
Five Points *CA* U.S.A. **158** C3
Fizi Dem. Rep. Congo **123** C4
Fizuli Azer. *see* **Füzuli**
Flå Norway **55** F6
Flagstaff S. Africa **125** I6
Flagstaff *AZ* U.S.A. **159** H4
Flagstaff Lake *ME* U.S.A. **162** G2
Flaherty Island Canada **152** F2
Flambeau *r. WI* U.S.A. **160** F2
Flamborough Head *hd* U.K. **58** G4
Fläming *hills* Germany **63** M2
Flaming Gorge Reservoir *WY* U.S.A. **156** F4
Flaminksvlei *salt pan* S. Africa **124** E6
Flanagan *r.* Canada **151** M4
Flandre *reg.* France **62** C4
Flannagan Lake *VA* U.S.A. **164** D5
Flannan Isles U.K. **60** B2
Flåsjön *l.* Sweden **54** I4
Flat *r.* Canada **149** P3
Flat *AK* U.S.A. **148** H3
Flat *r. MI* U.S.A. **164** C2
Flat Creek Canada **149** M3
Flathead *r. MT* U.S.A. **154** E2
Flathead Lake *MT* U.S.A. **156** E3
Flatiron *mt. ID* U.S.A. **156** E3
Flat Island S. China Sea **80** F4
Flat Lick *KY* U.S.A. **164** D5
Flattery, Cape Australia **136** D2
Flattery, Cape *WA* U.S.A. **156** B2
Flat Top *mt.* Canada **149** M3
Flatwillow Creek *r. MT* U.S.A. **156** G3
Flatwoods *WV* U.S.A. **164** E4
Fleetmark Germany **63** L2
Fleetwood Australia **136** D4
Fleetwood U.K. **58** D5
Fleetwood *PA* U.S.A. **165** H3
Flekkefjord Norway **55** E7
Flemingsburg *KY* U.S.A. **164** D4
Flemington *NJ* U.S.A. **165** H3
Flen Sweden **55** J7
Flensburg Germany **57** L3
Flers France **66** D2
Flesherton Canada **164** E1
Flesko, Tanjung *pt* Indon. **83** C2
Fletcher Lake Canada **151** I2
Fletcher Peninsula Antarctica **188** L2
Fleur de Lys Canada **153** K4
Fleur-de-May, Lac *l.* Canada **153** I4
Flinders *r.* Australia **136** C3
Flinders Chase National Park Australia **137** B7
Flinders Group National Park Australia **136** D2
Flinders Island Australia **137** [inset]
Flinders Passage Australia **136** E3
Flinders Ranges *mts* Australia **137** B7
Flinders Ranges National Park Australia **137** B6
Flinders Reefs Australia **136** E3
Flin Flon Canada **151** K4
Flint U.K. **58** D5
Flint *MI* U.S.A. **164** D2
Flint *r. GA* U.S.A. **163** C6
Flint Island Kiribati **187** J6
Flinton Australia **138** D1
Flisa Norway **55** H6

▶**Flissingskiy, Mys** *c.* Rus. Fed. **76** H2
Most easterly point of Europe.

Flixecourt France **62** C4
Flodden U.K. **58** E3
Flöha Germany **63** N4
Flood Range *mts* Antarctica **188** J1
Flora *r.* Australia **134** E3
Flora *IN* U.S.A. **164** B3
Florac France **66** F4
Florala *AL* U.S.A. **163** C6
Florange France **62** G5
Flora Reef Australia **136** D3
Florence Italy **68** D3
Florence *AL* U.S.A. **163** C5
Florence *AZ* U.S.A. **159** H5
Florence *CO* U.S.A. **157** G5
Florence *OR* U.S.A. **156** B4
Florence *SC* U.S.A. **163** E5
Florence *WI* U.S.A. **160** F2
Florence Junction *AZ* U.S.A. **159** H5
Florencia Col. **176** C3
Florennes Belgium **62** E4
Florentia Italy *see* **Florence**
Florentino Ameghino, Embalse *resr* Arg. **178** C6
Flores *r.* Arg. **178** E5
Flores Guat. **167** H5
Flores *i.* Indon. **83** B5
Flores, Laut *sea* Indon. **83** A4
Flores Island Canada **150** E5
Flores Sea Indon. *see* **Flores, Laut**
Floresta Brazil **177** K5
Floresville *TX* U.S.A. **161** D6
Floriano Brazil **177** J5
Florianópolis Brazil **179** A4
Florida Uruguay **178** E4
Florida *state* U.S.A. **163** D6
Florida, Straits of Bahamas/U.S.A. **163** D8
Florida Bay *FL* U.S.A. **163** D7
Florida City *FL* U.S.A. **163** D7
Florida Islands Solomon Is **133** G2
Florida Keys *is FL* U.S.A. **163** D7
Florin *CA* U.S.A. **158** C2
Florina Greece **69** I4
Florissant *MO* U.S.A. **160** F4
Florø Norway **55** D6
Flour Lake Canada **153** I3
Floyd *VA* U.S.A. **164** E5
Floyd, Mount *AZ* U.S.A. **159** G4
Floydada *TX* U.S.A. **161** C5
Fluessen *l.* Neth. **62** F2
Fluk *Maluku* Indon. **83** C3
Flushing Neth. *see* **Vlissingen**
Fly *r.* P.N.G. **81** K8
Flying Fish, Cape Antarctica **188** K2
Flying Mountain *NM* U.S.A. **159** I6
Flylân *i.* Neth. *see* **Vlieland**
Foam Lake Canada **151** K5
Foča Bos.-Herz. **68** H3
Foça Turkey **69** L5
Fochabers U.K. **60** F3
Focşani Romania **69** L2
Fogang China **97** G4
Foggia Italy **68** F4
Fogi *Buru* Indon. **83** C3
Fogo *i.* Cape Verde **120** [inset]
Fogo Island Canada **153** L4
Foinaven *hill* U.K. **60** E2
Foix France **66** E5
Folda *sea chan.* Norway **54** I3
Foldereid Norway **54** H4
Foldfjorden *sea chan.* Norway **54** G4
Folegandros *i.* Greece **69** K6
Foleyet Canada **152** E4
Foley Island Canada **147** K3
Folger *AK* U.S.A. **148** H3
Foligno Italy **68** E3
Folkestone U.K. **59** I7
Folkingham U.K. **59** G6
Folkston *GA* U.S.A. **163** D6
Folldal Norway **54** G5
Follonica Italy **68** D3
Folsom Lake *CA* U.S.A. **158** C2
Fomboni Comoros **123** E5
Fomento Cuba **163** E8
Fomin Rus. Fed. **53** I7
Fominskaya Rus. Fed. **52** K2
Fominskoye Rus. Fed. **52** I4
Fonda *NY* U.S.A. **165** H2
Fond-du-Lac Canada **151** J3
Fond du Lac *r.* Canada **151** J3
Fond du Lac *WI* U.S.A. **164** A2
Fondevila Spain **67** B3
Fondi Italy **68** E4
Fonni *Sardinia* Italy **68** C4
Fonsagrada Spain *see* **A Fonsagrada**
Fonseca, Golfo do *b.* Central America **168** G6
Fontaine Lake Canada **151** J3
Fontanges Canada **153** H3
Fontas Canada **150** F3
Fontas *r.* Canada **150** F3
Fonte Boa Brazil **176** E4
Fonteneau, Lac *l.* Canada **153** J4
Fontur *pt* Iceland **54** [inset 1]
Foochow China *see* **Fuzhou**
Foot's Bay Canada **164** F1
Foping China **97** F1
Foraker, Mount *AK* U.S.A. **149** J3
Foraulep *atoll* Micronesia *see* **Faraulep**
Forbes Australia **138** D4
Forbes, Mount Canada **150** G4
Forchheim Germany **63** L5
Ford *r. MI* U.S.A. **162** C2
Ford City *CA* U.S.A. **158** D4
Førde Norway **55** D6
Forde Lake Canada **151** L2
Fordham U.K. **59** H6
Fordingbridge U.K. **59** F8
Ford Range *mts* Antarctica **188** J1
Fords Bridge Australia **138** B2
Fordsville *KY* U.S.A. **164** B5
Fordyce *AR* U.S.A. **161** E5
Forécariah Guinea **120** B4
Forel, Mont *mt.* Greenland **147** O3
Foreland *hd* U.K. **59** F8
Foreland Point U.K. **59** D7
Foremost Canada **156** F2
Foresight Mountain Canada **150** E4
Forest Canada **164** E2
Forest *MS* U.S.A. **161** F5
Forest *OH* U.S.A. **164** D3
Forestburg Canada **151** H4
Forest Creek *r.* Australia **136** C3
Forest Hill Australia **138** C5
Forest Ranch *CA* U.S.A. **158** C2
Forestville Canada **153** H4
Forestville *CA* U.S.A. **158** B2
Forestville *MI* U.S.A. **164** D2
Forfar U.K. **60** G4
Forgan *OK* U.S.A. **161** C4
Forges-les-Eaux France **62** B5
Forillon, Parc National de *nat. park* Canada **153** I4
Forked River *NJ* U.S.A. **165** H4
Forks *WA* U.S.A. **156** B3
Fork Union *VA* U.S.A. **165** F5
Forlì Italy **68** E2
Forman *ND* U.S.A. **160** D2
Formby U.K. **58** D5
Formentera *i.* Spain **67** G4
Formentor, Cap de *c.* Spain **67** H4
Formerie France **62** B5
Former Yugoslav Republic of Macedonia *country* Europe *see* **Macedonia**
Formiga Brazil **179** B3
Formosa Arg. **178** E3
Formosa *country* Asia *see* **Taiwan**
Formosa Brazil **179** B1
Formosa, Serra *hills* Brazil **177** G6
Formosa Bay Kenya *see* **Ungwana Bay**
Formosa Strait China/Taiwan *see* **Taiwan Strait**
Formoso *r. Bahia* Brazil **179** B1
Formoso *r. Tocantins* Brazil **179** A1
Fornos Moz. **125** L2
Forres U.K. **60** F3
Forrest *Vic.* Australia **138** A7
Forrest *W.A.* Australia **135** E7
Forrestal Range *mts* Antarctica **188** A1
Forrest City *AR* U.S.A. **161** F5
Forrester Island *AK* U.S.A. **149** N5
Forrest Lake Canada **151** I3
Forrest Lakes *salt flat* Australia **135** E7
Fors Sweden **54** J5
Forsayth Australia **136** C3
Forsnäs Sweden **54** M3
Forssa Fin. **55** M6
Forster Australia **138** F4
Forsyth *GA* U.S.A. **163** D5
Forsyth *MT* U.S.A. **156** G3
Forsyth Range *hills* Australia **136** C4
Fort Abbas Pak. **111** I4
Fort Albany Canada **152** E3
Fortaleza Brazil **177** K4
Fort Amsterdam *NY* U.S.A. *see* **New York**
Fort Archambault Chad *see* **Sarh**
Fort Ashby *WV* U.S.A. **165** F4
Fort Assiniboine Canada **150** H4
Fort Augustus U.K. **60** E3
Fort Beaufort S. Africa **125** H7
Fort Benton *MT* U.S.A. **156** F3
Fort Bragg *CA* U.S.A. **158** B2
Fort Branch *IN* U.S.A. **164** B4

Fort Carillon NY U.S.A. see Ticonderoga
Fort Charlet Alg. see Djanet
Fort Chimo Canada see Kuujjuaq
Fort Chipewyan Canada 151 I3
Fort Collins CO U.S.A. 156 G4
Fort-Coulonge Canada 152 F5
Fort Crampel Cent. Afr. Rep. see Kaga Bandoro
Fort-Dauphin Madag. see Tôlañaro
Fort Davis TX U.S.A. 161 C6

▶Fort-de-France Martinique 169 L6
Capital of Martinique.

Fort de Kock Sumatera Indon. see Bukittinggi
Fort de Polignac Alg. see Illizi
Fort Deposit AL U.S.A. 167 I1
Fort Dodge IA U.S.A. 160 E3
Fort Duchesne UT U.S.A. 159 I1
Fort Edward NY U.S.A. 165 I2
Fortescue r. Australia 134 B5
Forte Veneza Brazil 177 H5
Fort Flatters Alg. see Bordj Omer Driss
Fort Foureau Cameroon see Kousséri
Fort Franklin Canada see Déljne
Fort Gardel Alg. see Zaouatallaz
Fort Gay WV U.S.A. 164 D4
Fort George Canada see Chisasibi
Fort Glenn AK U.S.A. 148 F5
Fort Good Hope Canada 149 O2
Fort Gouraud Mauritania see Fdérik
Forth r. U.K. 60 F4
Forth, Firth of est. U.K. 60 F4
Fort Hancock TX U.S.A. 166 D2
Fort Hertz Myanmar see Putao
Fortification Range mts NV U.S.A. 159 F2
Fortín General Mendoza Para. 178 D2
Fortín Leonida Escobar Para. 178 D2
Fortín Madrejón Para. 178 E2
Fortín Pilcomayo Arg. 178 D2
Fortín Ravelo Bol. 176 F7
Fortín Sargento Primero Leyes Arg. 178 E2
Fortín Suárez Arana Bol. 176 F7
Fortín Teniente Juan Echauri López Para. 178 D2
Fort Jameson Zambia see Chipata
Fort Johnston Malawi see Mangochi
Fort Kent ME U.S.A. 162 G2
Fort Lamy Chad see Ndjamena
Fort Laperrine Alg. see Tamanrasset
Fort Laramie WY U.S.A. 156 G4
Fort Lauderdale FL U.S.A. 163 D7
Fort Liard Canada 150 F2
Fort Mackay Canada 151 I3
Fort Macleod Canada 150 H5
Fort Madison IA U.S.A. 160 F3
Fort Manning Malawi see Mchinji
Fort McMurray Canada 151 I3
Fort McPherson Canada 149 N2
Fort Meyers Beach FL U.S.A. 163 D7
Fort Morgan CO U.S.A. 160 C3
Fort Munro Pak. 111 H4
Fort Myers FL U.S.A. 163 D7
Fort Nelson Canada 150 F3
Fort Nelson r. Canada 150 F3
Fort Norman Canada see Tulita
Fort Orange NY U.S.A. see Albany
Fort Payne AL U.S.A. 163 C5
Fort Peck MT U.S.A. 156 G2
Fort Peck Reservoir MT U.S.A. 156 G3
Fort Pierce FL U.S.A. 163 D7
Fort Portal Uganda 122 D3
Fort Providence Canada 150 G2
Fort Resolution Canada 150 H2
Fortrose N.Z. 139 B8
Fortrose U.K. 60 E3
Fort Rosebery Zambia see Mansa
Fort Rousset Congo see Owando
Fort Rupert Canada see Waskaganish
Fort St James Canada 150 E4
Fort St John Canada 150 F3
Fort Sandeman Pak. see Zhob
Fort Saskatchewan Canada 150 H4
Fort Scott KS U.S.A. 160 E4
Fort Severn Canada 152 D2
Fort-Shevchenko Kazakh. 100 E2
Fort Simpson Canada 150 F2
Fort Smith Canada 151 H2
Fort Smith AR U.S.A. 161 E5
Fort Stockton TX U.S.A. 161 C6
Fort Sumner NM U.S.A. 157 G6
Fort Supply OK U.S.A. 161 D4
Fort Thomas AZ U.S.A. 159 I5
Fort Trinquet Mauritania see Bîr Mogreïn
Fortuna ND U.S.A. 160 C1
Fortune Bay Canada 153 L5
Fort Valley GA U.S.A. 163 D5
Fort Vermilion Canada 150 G3
Fort Victoria Zimbabwe see Masvingo
Fort Walton Beach FL U.S.A. 167 I2
Fort Ware Canada see Ware
Fort Wayne IN U.S.A. 164 C3
Fort William U.K. 60 D4
Fort Worth TX U.S.A. 161 D5
Fort Yates ND U.S.A. 160 C2
Fortymile r. Canada/U.S.A. 149 L2
Fortymile, Middle Fork r. AK U.S.A. 149 L2
Fortymile, West Fork r. AK U.S.A. 149 L2
Fort Yukon AK U.S.A. 149 K2
Forum Iulii France see Fréjus
Forūr, Jazīreh-ye i. Iran 110 D5
Forvik Norway 54 H4
Foshan China 97 G4
Fo Shek Chau H.K. China see Basalt Island
Fossano Italy 68 B2
Fossil OR U.S.A. 156 C3
Fossil Downs Australia 134 D4
Foster Australia 138 C7
Foster KY U.S.A. 164 C4
Foster, Mount Canada/U.S.A. 149 N4
Foster Lakes Canada 151 J3
Fostoria OH U.S.A. 164 D3
Fotadrevo Madag. 123 E6
Fotherby U.K. 58 G5
Fotokol Cameroon 121 E3
Fotuna i. Vanuatu see Futuna
Fougères France 66 D2
Foula i. U.K. 60 [inset]
Foul Island Myanmar 86 A3
Foulness Point U.K. 59 H7
Foul Point Sri Lanka 106 D4
Foumban Cameroon 120 E4
Foundation Ice Stream glacier Antarctica 188 L1
Fount KY U.S.A. 164 D5
Fountains Abbey and Royal Water Garden (NT) tourist site U.K. 58 F4
Fourches, Mont des hill France 66 G2
Four Corners CA U.S.A. 158 E4
Fouriesburg S. Africa 125 I5
Fourmies France 62 E4
Four Mountains, Islands of the AK U.S.A. 148 E5
Fournier, Lac l. Canada 153 I4
Fournoi i. Greece 69 L6
Fourpeaked Mountain AK U.S.A. 148 I4
Fouta Djallon reg. Guinea 120 B3
Foveaux Strait N.Z. 139 A8
Fowey r. U.K. 59 C8
Fowler CO U.S.A. 157 G5
Fowler IN U.S.A. 164 B3
Fowler Ice Rise Antarctica 188 L1
Fowlers Bay Australia 132 D5
Fowlers Bay b. Australia 135 F8
Fowlerville MI U.S.A. 164 C2
Fox r. B.C. Canada 150 E3
Fox r. Man. Canada 151 M3
Fox r. WI U.S.A. 160 F3
Fox Creek Canada 150 G4
Fox Creek KY U.S.A. 164 C5
Foxdale Isle of Man 58 C4
Foxe Basin g. Canada 147 K3
Foxe Channel Canada 147 J3
Foxe Peninsula Canada 147 K3
Fox Glacier N.Z. 139 C6
Fox Islands AK U.S.A. 148 E5
Fox Lake Canada 150 H3
Fox Mountain Canada 149 N3
Fox Valley Canada 151 I5
Foyers U.K. 60 E3
Foyle r. Ireland/U.K. 61 E3
Foyle, Lough b. Ireland/U.K. 61 E2
Foynes Ireland 61 C5
Foz de Areia, Represa de resr Brazil 179 A4
Foz do Cunene Angola 123 B5
Foz do Iguaçu Brazil 178 F3
Fraga Spain 67 G3
Frakes, Mount Antarctica 188 K1
Framingham MA U.S.A. 165 J2
Framnes Mountains Antarctica 188 E2
Franca Brazil 179 B3
Français, Récif des reef New Caledonia 133 G3
Francavilla Fontana Italy 68 G4

▶France country Europe 66 F3
3rd largest and 3rd most populous country in Europe.

Frances Australia 137 C8
Frances r. Canada 149 O3
Frances Lake Canada 150 D2
Frances Lake Canada 149 O3
Franceville Gabon 122 B4
Francis Canada 151 K5
Francis atoll Kiribati see Beru
Francis, Lake NH U.S.A. 165 J1
Francisco de Orellana Ecuador see Coca
Francisco I. Madero Coahuila Mex. 166 E3
Francisco I. Madero Durango Mex. 161 B7
Francisco Zarco Mex. 166 A1
Francistown Botswana 123 C6
Francois Canada 153 K5
François Lake Canada 150 E4
Francois Peron National Park Australia 135 A6
Francs Peak WY U.S.A. 156 F4
Franeker Neth. 62 F1
Frankenberg Germany 63 N4
Frankenberg (Eder) Germany 63 I3
Frankenhöhe hills Germany 57 M6
Frankenmuth MI U.S.A. 164 D2
Frankenthal (Pfalz) Germany 63 I5
Frankenwald mts Germany 63 L4
Frankford Canada 165 G1
Frankfort IN U.S.A. 164 B3

▶Frankfort KY U.S.A. 164 C4
Capital of Kentucky.

Frankfort MI U.S.A. 164 B1
Frankfort OH U.S.A. 164 D4
Frankfurt Germany see Frankfurt am Main
Frankfurt am Main Germany 63 I4
Frankfurt an der Oder Germany 57 O4
Frank Hann National Park Australia 135 C8
Frankin Lake NV U.S.A. 159 F1
Fränkische Alb hills Germany 63 K6
Fränkische Schweiz reg. Germany 63 L5
Frankland, Cape Australia 137 [inset]
Franklin AZ U.S.A. 159 I5
Franklin GA U.S.A. 163 C5
Franklin IN U.S.A. 164 B4
Franklin KY U.S.A. 164 B5
Franklin LA U.S.A. 161 F6
Franklin MA U.S.A. 165 J2
Franklin NC U.S.A. 163 D5
Franklin NE U.S.A. 160 D3
Franklin NH U.S.A. 165 J2
Franklin PA U.S.A. 164 F3
Franklin TN U.S.A. 162 C5
Franklin TX U.S.A. 161 D6
Franklin VA U.S.A. 165 G5
Franklin WV U.S.A. 164 F4
Franklin, Point pt AK U.S.A. 148 H1
Franklin Bay Canada 149 P1
Franklin D. Roosevelt Lake resr WA U.S.A. 156 D2
Franklin Furnace OH U.S.A. 164 D4
Franklin-Gordon National Park Australia 137 [inset]
Franklin Island Antarctica 188 H1
Franklin Mountains Canada 149 Q3
Franklin Mountains AK U.S.A. 149 K1
Franklin Strait Canada 147 I2
Franklinton LA U.S.A. 161 F6
Franklinville NY U.S.A. 165 F2
Frankston Australia 138 B7
Fränsta Sweden 54 J5
Frantsa-Iosifa, Zemlya is Rus. Fed. 76 G2
Franz Canada 152 D4
Franz Josef Glacier N.Z. 139 C6
Frasca, Capo della c. Sardinia Italy 68 C5
Frascati Italy 68 E4
Fraser r. Australia 134 C4
Fraser r. B.C. Canada 150 F5
Fraser r. Nfld. and Lab. Canada 153 J2
Fraser, Mount hill Australia 135 B6
Fraserburg S. Africa 124 E6
Fraserburgh U.K. 60 G3
Fraserdale Canada 152 E4
Fraser Island Australia 136 F5
Fraser Island National Park Australia 136 F5
Fraser Lake Canada 150 E4
Fraser National Park Australia 138 B6
Fraser Plateau Canada 150 E4
Fraser Range hills Australia 135 C8
Frauenfeld Switz. 66 I3
Fray Bentos Uruguay 178 E4
Frazeysburg OH U.S.A. 164 D3
Frechen Germany 62 G4
Freckleton U.K. 58 E5
Frederic MI U.S.A. 164 C1
Frederica DE U.S.A. 165 H4
Fredericia Denmark 55 F9
Frederick MD U.S.A. 165 G4
Frederick OK U.S.A. 161 D5
Frederick Reef Australia 136 F4
Fredericksburg TX U.S.A. 161 D6
Fredericksburg VA U.S.A. 165 G4
Frederick Sound sea channel AK U.S.A. 149 N4
Fredericktown MO U.S.A. 160 F4

▶Fredericton Canada 153 I5
Capital of New Brunswick.

Frederikshåb Greenland see Paamiut
Frederikshavn Denmark 55 G8
Frederiksværk Denmark 55 H9
Fredonia AZ U.S.A. 159 G3
Fredonia KS U.S.A. 161 E4
Fredonia NY U.S.A. 164 F2
Fredonia WI U.S.A. 164 B2
Fredrika Sweden 54 K4
Fredrikshamn Fin. see Hamina
Fredrikstad Norway 55 G7
Freedonyer Peak CA U.S.A. 158 C1
Freehold NJ U.S.A. 165 H3
Freeland PA U.S.A. 165 H3
Freeling Heights hill Australia 137 B6
Freel Peak CA U.S.A. 158 D2
Freels, Cape Canada 153 L4
Freeman SD U.S.A. 160 D3
Freeman, Lake IN U.S.A. 164 B3
Freeport FL U.S.A. 163 C6
Freeport IL U.S.A. 160 F3
Freeport TX U.S.A. 161 E6
Freeport City Bahamas 163 E7
Freer TX U.S.A. 161 D7
Freesoil MI U.S.A. 164 B1
Free State prov. S. Africa 125 H5

▶Freetown Sierra Leone 120 B4
Capital of Sierra Leone.

Fregenal de la Sierra Spain 67 C4
Fregon Australia 135 F6
Fréhel, Cap c. France 66 C2
Freiberg Germany 63 N4
Freiburg Switz. see Fribourg
Freiburg im Breisgau Germany 57 K6
Frei (Chile) research station Antarctica 188 A2
Freisen Germany 63 H5
Freising Germany 57 M6
Freistadt Austria 57 O6
Fréjus France 66 H5
Fremantle Australia 135 A8
Fremont CA U.S.A. 158 C3
Fremont IN U.S.A. 164 C3
Fremont MI U.S.A. 164 C2
Fremont NE U.S.A. 160 D3
Fremont OH U.S.A. 164 D3
Fremont r. UT U.S.A. 159 H2
Fremont Junction UT U.S.A. 159 H2
Frenchburg KY U.S.A. 164 D5
French Cay i. Turks and Caicos Is 163 F8
French Congo country Africa see Congo

▶French Guiana terr. S. America 177 H3
French Overseas Department.

French Guinea country Africa see Guinea
French Island Australia 138 B7
French Lick IN U.S.A. 164 B4
Frenchman r. MT U.S.A. 156 G2
Frenchman Lake CA U.S.A. 158 C2
Frenchman Lake NV U.S.A. 159 F3
Frenchpark Ireland 61 D4
French Pass N.Z. 139 D5

▶French Polynesia terr. S. Pacific Ocean 187 K7
French Overseas Country.

French Somaliland country Africa see Djibouti

▶French Southern and Antarctic Lands terr. Indian Ocean 185 M8
French Overseas Territory.

French Sudan country Africa see Mali
French Territory of the Afars and Issas country Africa see Djibouti
Frenda Alg. 67 G6
Frentsjer Neth. see Franeker
Freren Germany 63 H2
Fresco r. Brazil 177 H5
Freshford Ireland 61 E5
Fresnillo Mex. 168 D4
Fresno CA U.S.A. 158 D3
Fresno r. CA U.S.A. 158 C3
Fresno Reservoir MT U.S.A. 156 F2
Fressel, Lac l. Canada 152 G3
Freu, Cap des c. Spain 67 H4
Freudenberg Germany 63 H4
Freudenstadt Germany 57 L6
Frévent France 62 C4
Frew watercourse Australia 136 A4
Frewena Australia 136 A3
Freycinet Estuary inlet Australia 135 A6
Freycinet Peninsula Australia 137 [inset]
Freyenstein Germany 63 M1
Freyming-Merlebach France 62 G5
Fria Guinea 120 B3
Fria, Cape Namibia 123 B5
Friant CA U.S.A. 158 D3
Frias Arg. 178 C3
Fribourg Switz. 66 H3
Friday Harbor WA U.S.A. 156 C2
Friedeburg Germany 63 H1
Friedens PA U.S.A. 165 F3
Friedland Rus. Fed. see Pravdinsk
Friedrichshafen Germany 57 L7
Friedrichskanal canal Germany 63 L2
Friend NE U.S.A. 160 D3
Friendly Islands country S. Pacific Ocean see Tonga
Friendship WI U.S.A. 160 F3
Friesack Germany 63 M2
Friese Wad tidal flat Neth. 62 F1
Friesoythe Germany 63 H1
Frinton-on-Sea U.K. 59 I7
Frio r. TX U.S.A. 161 D6
Frio watercourse NM/TX U.S.A. 161 C5
Frisco Mountain UT U.S.A. 159 G2
Frissell, Mount hill CT U.S.A. 165 I2
Fritzlar Germany 63 J3
Frjentsjer Neth. see Franeker
Frobisher Bay Canada see Iqaluit
Frobisher Bay b. Canada 147 L3
Frobisher Lake Canada 151 I3
Frohavet b. Norway 54 F5
Frohburg Germany 63 M3
Froissy France 62 C5
Frolovo Rus. Fed. 53 I6
Frome watercourse Australia 137 B6
Frome U.K. 59 E7
Frome r. U.K. 59 E8
Frome, Lake salt flat Australia 137 B6
Frome Downs Australia 137 B6
Fröndenberg Germany 63 H3
Frontera Coahuila Mex. 167 E3
Frontera Tabasco Mex. 167 G5
Frontera, Punta pt Mex. 167 G5
Fronteras Mex. 166 C2
Front Royal VA U.S.A. 165 F4
Frosinone Italy 68 E4
Frostburg MD U.S.A. 165 F4
Frøya i. Norway 54 F5
Fruges France 62 C4
Fruita CO U.S.A. 159 I2
Fruitland UT U.S.A. 159 H1
Fruitvale CO U.S.A. 159 I2
Frunze Kyrg. see Bishkek
Frusino Italy see Frosinone
Fruška Gora, Nacionalni Park nat. park Serbia 69 H2
Frýdek-Místek Czech Rep. 57 Q6
Fu'an China 97 H3
Fucheng Anhui China see Fengyang
Fucheng Shaanxi China see Fuxian
Fuchū Tōkyō Japan 93 F3
Fuchū Toyama Japan 92 D2
Fuchuan China 97 F3
Fuchun Jiang r. China 97 I2
Fude China 97 H3
Fuding China 97 I3
Fudul reg. Saudi Arabia 110 B6
Fuenlabrada Spain 67 E3
Fuerte r. Mex. 157 F8
Fuerte Olimpo Para. 178 E2
Fuerteventura i. Canary Is 120 B2
Fufeng China 96 E1
Fuga i. Phil. 82 C2
Fugong China 96 C3
Fugou China 97 G1
Fugu China 95 G4
Fuguo China see Zhanhua
Fuhai China 98 D3
Fuhai Linchang China 98 E3
Fuḩaymī Iraq 113 F4
Fujairah U.A.E. 110 E5
Fujeira U.A.E. see Fujairah
Fuji Japan 93 E3
Fujian prov. China 97 H3
Fujieda Japan 93 E4
Fuji-Hakone-Izu Kokuritsu-kōen nat. park Japan 93 F4
Fujihashi Japan 92 C3
Fujiidera Japan 92 B4
Fujikawa Japan 93 E3
Fuji-kawa r. Japan 93 E3
Fujimi Nagano Japan 93 E3
Fujimi Saitama Japan 93 F3
Fujin China 90 C3
Fujino Japan 93 F3
Fujinomiya Japan 93 E3
Fujioka Aichi Japan 92 D3
Fujioka Gunma Japan 93 F2
Fujioka Tochigi Japan 93 F2
Fuji-san vol. Japan 93 E3
Fujisawa Japan 93 F3
Fujishiro Japan 93 G3
Fujiwara Mie Japan 92 C3
Fujiwara Tochigi Japan 93 F2
Fujiyoshida Japan 93 E3
Fūka Egypt see Fūkah
Fūkah Egypt 112 B5
Fukang China 98 D3
Fukaya Japan 93 F2
Fukiage Japan 93 F2
Fukien prov. China see Fujian
Fukuchiyama Japan 92 B3
Fukude Japan 93 D4
Fukue-jima i. Japan 91 C6
Fukui Japan 92 C2
Fukui pref. Japan 92 C3
Fukumitsu Japan 92 C2
Fukuno Japan 92 C2
Fukuoka Fukuoka Japan 91 C6
Fukuoka Gifu Japan 92 D3
Fukuoka Toyama Japan 92 C2
Fukuroi Japan 93 D4
Fukusaki Japan 92 A4
Fukushima Japan 91 F5
Fukuyama Japan 91 C7
Fūl, Gebel hill Egypt see Fūl, Jabal
Fūl, Jabal hill Egypt 107 A5
Fulchhari Bangl. 105 G4
Fulda Germany 63 J4
Fulda r. Germany 63 J3
Fulham U.K. 59 G7
Fuli Anhui China 97 H1
Fuli Heilong. China see Jixian
Fuling China 96 E2
Fulitun China see Jixian
Fullerton CA U.S.A. 158 E5
Fullerton NE U.S.A. 160 D3
Fullerton, Cape Canada 151 N2
Fulton IN U.S.A. 164 B3
Fulton MO U.S.A. 160 F4
Fulton MS U.S.A. 161 F5
Fulton NY U.S.A. 165 G2
Fumane Moz. 125 K3
Fumay France 62 E5
Fumin China 96 D3
Funabashi Chiba Japan 93 F3
Funabashi Toyama Japan 92 D2
Funafuti atoll Tuvalu 133 H2
Funan China 97 G1

▶Funchal Madeira 120 B1
Capital of Madeira.

Fundão Brazil 179 C2
Fundão Port. 67 C3
Fundi Italy see Fondi
Fundición Mex. 166 C3
Fundy, Bay of g. Canada 153 I5
Fundy National Park Canada 153 I5
Fünen i. Denmark see Fyn
Funeral Peak CA U.S.A. 158 E3
Fünfkirchen Hungary see Pécs
Fung Wong Shan hill H.K. China see Lantau Peak
Funhalouro Moz. 125 L2
Funing Jiangsu China 97 H1
Funing Yunnan China 96 E4
Funiu Shan mts China 97 F1
Funtua Nigeria 120 D3
Funzie U.K. 60 [inset]
Fuping Hebei China 95 H4
Fuping Shaanxi China 95 G5
Fuqing China 97 H3
Fürgun, Kūh-e mt. Iran 110 E5
Furmanov Rus. Fed. 52 I4
Furmanovka Kazakh. see Moyynkum
Furmanovo Kazakh. see Zhalpaktal
Furnás hill Spain 67 G4
Furnas, Represa resr Brazil 179 B3
Furneaux Group is Australia 137 [inset]
Furnes Belgium see Veurne
Furong China see Wan'an
Fürstenau Germany 63 H2
Fürstenberg Germany 63 N1
Fürstenwalde Germany 57 O4
Fürth Germany 63 K5
Furth im Wald Germany 63 M5
Furudono Japan 93 G1
Furukawa Gifu Japan 92 D2
Furukawa Miyagi Japan 91 F5
Fury and Hecla Strait Canada 147 J3
Fusan S. Korea see Pusan
Fushan Shandong China 95 J4
Fushan Shanxi China 95 G5
Fushimi Japan 92 B4
Fushun China 95 J3
Fushuncheng China see Shuncheng
Fuso Japan 92 C3
Fusong China 90 B4
Fussa Japan 93 F3
Futaba Japan 93 E3
Futagawa Japan 92 D4
Futago-yama mt. Japan 93 E2
Futami Japan 92 C4
Fu Tau Pun Chau i. H.K. China 97 [inset]
Futtsu Japan 93 F3
Futtsu-misaki pt Japan 93 F3
Futuna i. Vanuatu 133 H3
Futuna Islands Wallis and Futuna Is see Hoorn, Îles de
Fuxian Liaoning China see Wafangdian
Fuxian Shaanxi China 95 G5
Fuxian Hu l. China 96 D3
Fuxin Liaoning China 95 J3
Fuxin Liaoning China 95 J3
Fuxing China see Wangmo
Fuxinzhen China see Fuxin
Fuyang Anhui China 97 G1
Fuyang Guangxi China see Fuchuan
Fuyang Zhejiang China 97 H2
Fuyang He r. China 95 I4
Fuying Dao i. China 97 I3
Fuyu Anhui China see Susong
Fuyu Heilong. China 95 K2
Fuyu Jilin China 90 B3
Fuyu Jilin China see Songyuan
Fuyuan Heilong. China 90 D2
Fuyuan Yunnan China 96 E3
Fuyun China 94 B2
Fuzhou Fujian China 97 H3
Fuzhou Jiangxi China 97 H3
Füzuli Azer. 113 G3
Fyn i. Denmark 55 G9
Fyne, Loch inlet U.K. 60 D5

G

Gaaf Atoll Maldives see Huvadhu Atoll
Gaâfour Tunisia 68 C6
Gaalkacyo Somalia 122 E3
Gaat r. Malaysia 85 F2
Gabakly Turkm. 111 F2
Gabasumdo China see Tongde
Gabbs NV U.S.A. 158 E2
Gabbs Valley Range mts NV U.S.A. 158 D2
Gabd Pak. 111 F5
Gabela Angola 123 B5
Gaberones Botswana see Gaborone
Gabès Tunisia 64 G5
Gabès, Golfe de g. Tunisia 64 G5
Gabiden Mustafin Kazakh. 98 A2
Gabo Island Australia 138 D6
Gabon country Africa 122 B4

▶Gaborone Botswana 125 G3
Capital of Botswana.

Gābrīk Iran 110 E5
Gabrovo Bulg. 69 K3
Gabú Guinea-Bissau 120 B3
Gadag India 106 B3
Gadaisu P.N.G. 136 E1
Gadap Pak. 111 G5
Gadchiroli India 106 D1
Gäddede Sweden 54 I4
Gadê China 96 C1
Gades Spain see Cádiz
Gadhka India 111 H6
Gadhra India 104 B5
Gadra Pak. 111 H5
Gadsden AL U.S.A. 163 C5
Gadsden AZ U.S.A. 166 B1
Gadwal India 106 C2
Gadyach Ukr. see Hadyach
Gaer U.K. 59 D7
Găeşti Romania 69 K2
Gaeta Italy 68 E4
Gaeta, Golfo di g. Italy 68 E4
Gaferut i. Micronesia 81 L5
Gaffney SC U.S.A. 163 D5
Gafsa Tunisia 68 C7
Gag i. Papua Indon. 83 D3
Gagarin Rus. Fed. 53 G5
Gagnoa Côte d'Ivoire 120 C4
Gagnon Canada 153 H4
Gago Coutinho Angola see Lumbala N'guimbo
Gagra Georgia 53 I8
Gahai China 94 D4
Gaiab watercourse Namibia 124 D5
Gaibanda Bangl. see Gaibandha
Gaibandha Bangl. 105 G4
Gaïdouronisi i. Greece 69 K7
Gaifi, Wâdi el watercourse Egypt see Jayfi, Wādī al
Gail TX U.S.A. 161 C5
Gaildorf Germany 63 J6
Gaillac France 66 E5
Gaillimh Ireland see Galway
Gaillon France 62 B5
Gaindainqoinkor China 99 E7
Gainesboro TN U.S.A. 164 C5
Gainesville FL U.S.A. 163 D6
Gainesville GA U.S.A. 163 D5
Gainesville MO U.S.A. 161 E4
Gainesville TX U.S.A. 161 D5
Gainsborough U.K. 58 G5
Gairdner, Lake salt flat Australia 137 A6
Gairloch U.K. 60 D3
Gair Loch b. U.K. 60 D3
Gaixian China see Gaizhou
Gaizhou China 95 J3
Gajah Hutan, Bukit hill Malaysia 84 C1
Gajipur India see Ghazipur
Gajol India 105 G4
Gakarosa mt. S. Africa 124 F4
Gakona AK U.S.A. 149 K3
Gala China 99 E7
Galaasiya Uzbek. see Galaosiyo
Gala Co l. China 99 E7
Galâla el Baḥarîya, Gebel el plat. Egypt see Jalālah al Baḥrīyah, Jabal
Galana r. Kenya 122 E4
Galang Besar i. Indon. 84 D2
Galanta Slovakia 57 P6
Galaosiyo Uzbek. 111 G2
Galápagos, Parque Nacional nat. Park Ecuador 176 [inset]

▶Galapagos Islands is Ecuador 187 O6
Part of Ecuador. Most westerly point of South America.

Galapagos Rise sea feature Pacific Ocean 187 N6
Galashiels U.K. 60 G5
Galaţi Romania 69 M2
Galatina Italy 68 H4
Gala Water r. U.K. 60 G5
Galax VA U.S.A. 164 E5
Galaýmor Turkm. 111 F3
Galaymor Turkm. see Galaýmor
Galbally Ireland 61 D5
Galdhøpiggen mt. Norway 55 F6
Galeana Chihuahua Mex. 166 D2
Galeana Nuevo León Mex. 167 E3
Galela Halmahera Indon. 83 C2
Galena AK U.S.A. 148 H2
Galena IL U.S.A. 160 F3
Galena MD U.S.A. 165 H4
Galena MO U.S.A. 161 E4
Galera, Punta pt Chile 178 B6
Galera, Punta pt Mex. 167 F6
Galesburg IL U.S.A. 160 F3
Galesburg MI U.S.A. 164 C2
Galeshewe S. Africa 124 G5
Galeton PA U.S.A. 165 G3
Galey r. Ireland 61 C5
Galheirão r. Brazil 179 B1
Galiano Island Canada 150 F5
Galich Rus. Fed. 52 I4
Galichskaya Vozvyshennost' hills Rus. Fed. 52 I4
Galicia aut. comm. Spain 67 C2
Galičica nat. park Macedonia 69 I4
Galilee, Lake salt flat Australia 136 D4
Galilee, Sea of l. Israel 107 B3
Galion OH U.S.A. 164 D3
Galiuro Mountains AZ U.S.A. 159 H5
Galizia aut. comm. Spain see Galicia
Gallabat Sudan 108 E7
G'allaorol Uzbek. 111 G1
Gallatin MO U.S.A. 160 E4
Gallatin TN U.S.A. 164 B5
Galle Sri Lanka 106 D5
Gallego Rise sea feature Pacific Ocean 187 M6
Gallegos r. Arg. 178 C8
Gallia country Europe see France

▶Gallinas, Punta pt Col. 176 D1
Most northerly point of South America.

Gallipoli Italy 68 H4
Gallipoli Turkey 69 L4
Gallipolis OH U.S.A. 164 D4
Gällivare Sweden 54 L3
Gällö Sweden 54 I5
Gallo Island NY U.S.A. 165 G2
Gallo Mountains NM U.S.A. 159 I4
Gallup NM U.S.A. 159 I4
Galmisdale U.K. 60 C4
Galmudug reg. Somalia 122 E3
Galong Australia 138 D5
Galoya Sri Lanka 106 D4
Gal Oya National Park Sri Lanka 106 D5
Galshar Mongolia 95 G2
Galston U.K. 60 E5
Galt Mongolia 94 D1
Galt CA U.S.A. 158 C2
Galtat Zemmour W. Sahara 120 B2
Galtee Mountains hills Ireland 61 D5
Galtymore hill Ireland 56 C4
Galūgāh, Kūh-e mts Iran 110 D4
Galuut Mongolia 94 E2
Galveston IN U.S.A. 164 B3
Galveston TX U.S.A. 161 E6
Galveston Bay TX U.S.A. 161 E6
Galwa Nepal 105 E3
Galway Ireland 61 C4
Galway Bay Ireland 61 C4
Gam i. Papua Indon. 83 D3
Gâm, Sông r. Vietnam 86 D2
Gamagōri Japan 92 D4
Gamalakhe S. Africa 125 J6

Gamalama vol. Maluku Indon. 83 C2
Gamay Bay Samar Phil. 82 D3
Gamba China see Gongbalou
Gamba Gabon 122 A4
Gambēla Eth. 122 D3
Gambēla National Park Eth. 122 D3
Gambell AK U.S.A. 148 E3
Gambella Eth. see Gambēla
Gambia, The country Africa 120 B3
Gambier, Îles is Fr. Polynesia 187 L7
Gambier Islands Australia 137 B7
Gambier Islands Fr. Polynesia see Gambier, Îles
Gambo Canada 153 L4
Gamboma Congo 122 B4
Gamboola Australia 136 C3
Gamboula Cent. Afr. Rep. 122 B3
Gamda China see Zamtang
Gamêtì Canada 149 R2
Gamkunoro, Gunung vol. Halmahera Indon. 83 C2
Gamlakarleby Fin. see Kokkola
Gamleby Sweden 55 J8
Gammelstaden Sweden 54 M4
Gammon Ranges National Park Australia 137 B6
Gamō Japan 92 C3
Gamova, Mys pt Rus. Fed. 90 C4
Gamshadzai Kūh mts Iran 111 F4
Gamtog China 96 C2
Gamud mt. Eth. 122 D3
Gana China 96 D1
Ganado AZ U.S.A. 159 I4
Gananoque Canada 165 G1
Gäncä Azer. 113 G2
Gancaohu China 98 E4
Gancheng China 97 F5
Ganda Angola 123 B5
Ganda China 99 F7
Gandadiwata, Bukit mt. Indon. 83 A3
Gandaingoin China 105 G3
Gandajika Dem. Rep. Congo 123 C4
Gandak Barrage Nepal 105 E4
Gandari Mountain Pak. 111 H4
Gandava Pak. 111 G4
Gander Canada 153 L4
Ganderkesee Germany 63 I1
Gandesa Spain 67 G3
Gandhidham India 104 B5
Gandhinagar India 104 C5
Gandhi Sagar resr India 104 C4
Gandia Spain 67 F4
Gandu China 94 E5
Gandzha Azer. see Gäncä
Ganes Creek AK U.S.A. 148 H3
Ganga r. Bangl./India 105 G5 see Ganges
Ganga Cone sea feature Indian Ocean see Ganges Cone
Gangán Arg. 178 C6
Ganganagar India 104 C3
Gangapur India 104 D4
Ganga Sera India 104 B4
Gangaw Myanmar 86 A2
Gangawati India 106 C3
Gangaw Range mts Myanmar 86 B2
Gangca China 94 E4
Gangdisê Shan mts China 99 C7
Ganges r. Bangl./India 105 G5 also known as Ganga
Ganges France 66 F5
Ganges, Mouths of the Bangl./India 105 G5
Ganges Cone sea feature Indian Ocean 185 N4
Gangou China 94 D4
Gangouyi China 94 F5
Gangra Turkey see Çankırı
Gangtok India 105 G4
Gangu China 94 F5
Gangziyao China 95 H4
Gan He r. China 95 K1
Ganhezi China 98 E3
Gani Halmahera Indon. 83 D3
Ganjig China 95 J3
Ganjing China 95 G5
Ganjur Sum China 95 H2
Ganluo China 96 D2
Ganmain Australia 138 C5
Gannan China 95 J2
Gannat France 66 F3
Gannett Peak WY U.S.A. 156 F4
Ganq China 99 F5
Ganquan China 95 G4
Ganshui China 96 E2
Gansu prov. China 94 D3
Gantang China 94 F4
Gantheaume Point Australia 134 C4
Ganting China see Huxian
Gantsevichi Belarus see Hantsavichy
Gantung Indon. 85 E3
Ganxian China 97 G3
Ganye Nigeria 120 E4
Ganyu China 95 I5
Ganyushkino Kazakh. 51 P6
Ganzhou China 97 G3
Ganzi South Sudan 121 G4
Gao Mali 120 C3
Gaoba China 94 E4
Gaocheng Hebei China 95 H4
Gaocheng Sichuan China see Litang
Gaocun China see Mayang
Gaohe China see Huaining
Gaohebu China see Huaining
Gaolan China 94 E4
Gaoleshan China see Xianfeng
Gaoliangjian China see Hongze
Gaoling China 95 G5
Gaomi China 95 I4
Gaomudang China 97 F3
Gaoping China 95 H5
Gaoqing China 95 I4
Gaotai China 94 D4
Gaotang China 95 I4
Gaoth Dobhair Ireland 61 D2
Gaoting China see Daishan
Gaotingzhen China see Daishan
Gaotouyao China 95 G4
Gaoua Burkina Faso 120 C3
Gaoual Guinea 120 B3
Gaoxiong Taiwan see Kaohsiung
Gaoyang China 95 H4
Gaoyao China see Zhaoqing
Gaoyi China 95 H4
Gaoyou China 97 H1
Gaoyou Hu l. China 97 H1
Gap France 66 H4
Gapan Luzon Phil. 82 C3
Gapuwiyak Australia 136 A2
Gaqoi China 99 C7
Gaqung China 99 D7
Gar China 104 E2
Gar Pak. 111 F5
Gar' r. Rus. Fed. 90 C1
Gara, Lough l. Ireland 61 D4
Garabekevyul Turkm. see Garabekewül
Garabekewül Turkm. 111 G2
Garabil Belentligi hills Turkm. 111 F2
Garabogaz Turkm. 113 I2
Garabogaz Aylagy b. Turkm. see Garabogazköl Aýlagy
Garabogazköl Aylagy b. Turkm. see Garabogazköl Aýlagy
Garabogazköl Aýlagy b. Turkm. 113 I2
Garabogazköl Bogazy sea chan. Turkm. 113 I2
Garachiné Panama 166 [inset] K7
Garachiné, Punta pt Panama 166 [inset] K7
Garāgheh Iran 111 F4
Garagum des. Turkm. see Karakum Desert
Garagum Kanaly canal Turkm. 111 F2
Garah Australia 138 D2
Garalo Mali 120 C3
Garamätnyýaz Turkm. 111 G2
Garamätnyyaz Turkm. see Garamätnyýaz
Garamba r. Dem. Rep. Congo 122 C3
Garang China 94 E4
Garanhuns Brazil 177 K5
Ga-Rankuwa S. Africa 125 H3
Garapuava Brazil 179 B2
Gárasavvon Sweden see Karesuando
Garautha India 104 D4
Garba China see Jiulong
Garbahaarrey Somalia 122 E3
Garba Tula Kenya 122 D3
Garberville CA U.S.A. 158 B1
Garbsen Germany 63 J2
Garça Brazil 179 A3
Garco China 105 G2
Garda, Lago di Italy see Garda, Lake
Garda, Lake Italy 68 D2
Garde, Cap de c. Alg. 68 B6
Gardelegen Germany 63 L2
Garden City KS U.S.A. 160 C4
Garden Hill Canada 151 M4
Garden Mountain VA U.S.A. 164 E5
Garden Route National Park nat. park S. Africa 124 F7
Gardeyz Afgh. see Gardēz
Gardēz Afgh. 111 H3
Gardinas Belarus see Hrodna
Gardiner ME U.S.A. 165 K1
Gardiner, Mount Australia 134 F5
Gardiner Range hills Australia 134 E4
Gardiners Island NY U.S.A. 165 I3
Gardīz Afgh. see Gardēz
Gardner atoll Micronesia see Faraulep
Gardner MA U.S.A. 165 J2
Gardner Inlet Antarctica 188 L1
Gardner Island atoll Kiribati see Nikumaroro
Gardner Pinnacles is HI U.S.A. 186 I4
Gáregasnjárga Fin. see Karigasniemi
Garelochhead U.K. 60 E4
Gareloi Island AK U.S.A. 148 [inset] C6
Garet el Djenoun mt. Alg. 120 D2
Gargano, Parco Nazionale del nat. park Italy 68 F4
Gargantua, Cape Canada 152 D5
Gargunsa China see Gar
Gargždai Lith. 55 L9
Garhchiroli India see Gadchiroli
Garhi Madh. Prad. India 106 C1
Garhi Rajasthan India 104 C5
Garhi Khairo Pak. 111 G4
Garhmuktesar India 99 B7
Garhwa India 105 E4
Gari Rus. Fed. 51 S4
Gariau Indon. 81 I7
Garibaldi, Mount Canada 150 F5
Gariep Dam resr S. Africa 125 G6
Garies S. Africa 124 C6
Garigliano r. Italy 68 E4
Garissa Kenya 122 D4
Garkalne Latvia 55 N8
Garkung Caka l. China 99 D6
Garland TX U.S.A. 161 D5
Garm Tajik. see Gharm
Garmāb Khorāsān-e Jonūbī Iran 111 E3
Garmāb Semnān Iran 110 E3
Garm Āb, Chashmeh-ye spring Iran 110 E3
Garmī Iran 110 C2
Garmsār Iran 110 D3
Garmsel reg. Afgh. 111 F4
Garner IA U.S.A. 160 E3
Garner KY U.S.A. 164 D5
Garnett KS U.S.A. 160 E4
Garnpung Lake imp. l. Australia 138 A4
Garo Hills India 105 G4
Garonne r. France 66 D4
Garoowe Somalia 122 E3
Garopaba Brazil 179 A5
Garoua Cameroon 120 E4
Garoua Boulai Cameroon 121 E4
Gar Qu r. China 99 F6
Garqu Yan China 99 F6
Garré Arg. 178 D5
Garrett IN U.S.A. 164 C3
Garrison MN U.S.A. 160 E2
Garruk Pak. 111 G4
Garry r. U.K. 60 E3
Garrychyrla Turkm. see Garryçyrla
Garryçyrla Turkm. 111 F2
Garry Island Canada 149 N1
Garry Lake Canada 151 K1
Garrynahine U.K. 60 C2
Garsen Kenya 122 E4
Garshy Turkm. see Garşy
Garsila Sudan 121 F3
Garşy Turkm. 113 I2
Gartar China see Qianning
Garth U.K. 59 D6
Gartog China see Markam
Gartok China see Garyarsa
Gartow Germany 63 L1
Garub Namibia 124 C4
Garusuun Palau 82 [inset]
Garut Jawa Indon. 85 D4
Garvagh U.K. 61 F3
Garve U.K. 60 E3
Garwa India see Garhwa
Garwha India see Garhwa
Gar Xincun China 99 C6
Gary IN U.S.A. 164 B3
Gary WV U.S.A. 164 E5
Garyarsa China 99 C7
Garyi China 96 C2
Garyū-zan mt. Japan 91 D6
Garza García Mex. 161 C7
Gar Zangbo r. China 99 B6
Garzê China 96 C2
Gasan-Kuli Turkm. see Esenguly
Gas City IN U.S.A. 164 C3
Gascogne reg. France see Gascony
Gascogne, Golfe de g. France see Gascony, Gulf of
Gascony reg. France 66 D5
Gascony, Gulf of France 66 C5
Gascoyne r. Australia 135 A6
Gascoyne Junction Australia 135 A6
Gase China 99 D7
Gasherbrum I mt. China/Pak. 104 D2
Gas Hu salt l. China 99 E5
Gashua Nigeria 120 E3
Gask Iran 111 E3
Gaspar Cuba 163 E8
Gaspar, Selat sea chan. Indon. 84 D3
Gaspé Canada 153 I4
Gaspé, Cap c. Canada 153 I4
Gaspésie, Péninsule de la pen. Canada 153 I4
Gassan vol. Japan 91 F5
Gassaway WV U.S.A. 164 E4
Gasselte Neth. 62 G2
Gasteiz Spain see Vitoria-Gasteiz
Gastello Rus. Fed. 90 F2
Gaston NC U.S.A. 165 G5
Gaston, Lake NC U.S.A. 165 G5
Gastonia NC U.S.A. 163 D5
Gata, Cabo de c. Spain 67 E5
Gata, Cape Cyprus 107 A2
Gata, Sierra de mts Spain 67 C3
Gataga r. Canada 149 P4
Gatas, Akra c. Cyprus see Gata, Cape
Gatchina Rus. Fed. 55 Q7
Gate City VA U.S.A. 164 D5
Gatehouse of Fleet U.K. 60 E6
Gatentiri Indon. 81 K8
Gateshead U.K. 58 F4
Gates of the Arctic National Park and Preserve AK U.S.A. 148 I2
Gatesville TX U.S.A. 161 D6
Gateway CO U.S.A. 159 I2
Gatineau Canada 165 H1
Gatineau r. Canada 152 G5
Gatong China see Jomda
Gatooma Zimbabwe see Kadoma
Gatton Australia 138 F1
Gatvand Iran 110 C3
Gatyana S. Africa see Willowvale
Gau i. Fiji 133 H3
Gauer Lake Canada 151 L3
Gauhati India see Guwahati
Gaujas nacionālais parks nat. park Latvia 55 N8
Gaul country Europe see France
Gaula r. Norway 54 G5
Gaume reg. Belgium 62 F5
Gaurama Brazil 179 A4
Gauribidanur India 106 C3
Gauteng prov. S. Africa 125 I4
Gavarr Armenia 113 G2
Gāvbandī Iran 110 D5
Gāvbūs, Kūh-e mts Iran 110 D5
▶Gavdos i. Greece 69 K7
Most southerly point of Europe.
Gavião r. Brazil 179 C1
Gavīleh Iran 110 B3
Gav Khūnī Iran 110 D3
Gävle Sweden 55 J6
Gavrilovka Vtoraya Rus. Fed. 53 I5
Gavrilov-Yam Rus. Fed. 52 H4
Gawachab Namibia 124 C4
Gawai Myanmar 96 C3
Gawan India 105 F4
Gawilgarh Hills India 104 D5
Gawler Australia 137 B7
Gawler Ranges hills Australia 137 A7
Gaxun Nur salt l. China 94 E3
Gaya India 105 F4
Gaya i. Malaysia 85 G1
Gaya i. Malaysia 85 G1
Gaya Niger 120 D3
Gaya He r. China 90 C4
Gayam Jawa Indon. 85 F4
Gayéri Burkina Faso 120 D3
Gaylord MI U.S.A. 164 C1
Gayndah Australia 137 E5
Gayny Rus. Fed. 52 L3
Gaysin Ukr. see Haysyn
Gayutino Rus. Fed. 52 H4
Gaz Iran 110 C3
▶Gaza terr. Asia 107 B4
Disputed Territory
▶Gaza Gaza 107 B4
Capital of Gaza.
Gaza prov. Moz. 125 K2
Gazan Pak. 111 G4
Gazandzhyk Turkm. see Bereket
Gazanjyk Turkm. see Bereket
Gaza Strip terr. Asia see Gaza
Gaziantep Turkey 112 E3
Gaziantep prov. Turkey 107 C1
Gazibenli Turkey see Yahyalı
Gazīk Iran 111 F3
Gazimağusa Cyprus see Famagusta
Gazimuro-Ononskiy Khrebet mts Rus. Fed. 95 G1
Gazimurskiy Khrebet mts Rus. Fed. 89 L2
Gazimurskiy Zavod Rus. Fed. 89 L2
Gazipaşa Turkey 107 A1
Gazli Uzbek. 111 F1
Gaz Māhū Iran 110 E5
Gbarnga Liberia 120 C4
Gboko Nigeria 120 D4
Gcuwa S. Africa see Butterworth
Gdańsk Poland 57 Q3
Gdańsk, Gulf of Poland/Rus. Fed. 57 Q3
Gdańska, Zatoka g. Poland/Rus. Fed. see Gdańsk, Gulf of
Gdingen Poland see Gdynia
Gdov Rus. Fed. 55 O7
Gdynia Poland 57 Q3
Geaidnovuohppi Norway 54 M2
Gearhart Mountain OR U.S.A. 156 C4
Gearraidh na h-Aibhne U.K. see Garrynahine
Gebe i. Maluku Indon. 83 D2
Gebesee Germany 63 K3
Geçitkale Cyprus see Lefkonikon
Gedang, Gunung mt. Indon. 84 C3
Gedaref Sudan 108 E7
Gedern Germany 63 J4
Gedinne Belgium 62 E5
Gediz r. Turkey 69 L5
Gedney Drove End U.K. 59 H6
Gedong Sarawak Malaysia 85 E2
Gedong, Tanjong pt Sing. 87 [inset]
Gedser Denmark 55 G9
Gedungpakuan Sumatera Indon. 84 D4
Geel Belgium 62 F3
Geelong Australia 138 B7
Geelvink Channel Australia 135 A7
Geel Vloer salt pan S. Africa 124 E5
Gees Gwardafuy c. Somalia see Gwardafuy, Gees
Geeste Germany 63 H2
Geesthacht Germany 63 K1
Gegen Gol China 90 A2
Gegen He r. China 95 I1
Gê'gyai China 99 C6
Ge Hu l. China 97 H2
Geidam Nigeria 120 E3
Geiersberg hill Germany 63 J5
Geikie r. Canada 151 K3
Geilenkirchen Germany 62 G4
Geilo Norway 55 F6
Geinō Japan 92 C4
Geiranger Norway 54 E5
Geislingen an der Steige Germany 63 J6
Geisūm, Gezā'ir is Egypt see Qaysūm, Juzur
Geita Tanz. 122 D4
Geithain Germany 63 M3
Gejiu China 96 D4
Geka, Mys hd Rus. Fed. 148 B2
Geka, Mys hd Rus. Fed. 148 B2
Gëkdepe Turkm. 110 E2
Gela Sicily Italy 68 F6
Gëladaindong mt. China 99 E6
Geladī Eth. 122 E3
Gelam i. Indon. 85 E3
Gelang, Tanjung pt Malaysia 87 C7
Geldern Germany 62 G3
Gelendzhik Rus. Fed. 112 E1
Gelibolu Turkey see Gallipoli
Gelidonya Burnu pt Turkey see Yardımcı Burnu
Gelincik Dağı mt. Turkey 69 N5
Gelmord Iran 110 E3
Gelnhausen Germany 63 J4
Gelsenkirchen Germany 62 H3
Gelumbang Sumatera Indon. 84 D3
Gemas Malaysia 84 C2
Gemena Dem. Rep. Congo 122 B3
Geminokağı Cyprus see Karavostasi
Gemlik Turkey 69 M4
Gemona del Friuli Italy 68 E1
Gemsa Egypt see Jamsah
Gemsbok National Park Botswana 124 E3
Gemsbokplein well S. Africa 124 E4
Gemuk Mountain AK U.S.A. 148 H3
Genalē Wenz r. Eth. 122 E3
Genappe Belgium 62 E4
Genäveh Iran 110 C4
General Acha Arg. 178 D5
General Alvear Arg. 178 C5
General Belgrano II research station Antarctica see Belgrano II
General Bravo Mex. 161 D7
▶General Carrera, Lago l. Arg./Chile 178 B7
Deepest lake in South America.
General Conesa Arg. 178 D6
General Escobeda Mex. 167 E3
General Freire Angola see Muxaluando
General Juan Madariaga Arg. 178 E5
General La Madrid Arg. 178 D5
General Luna Phil. 82 D4
General MacArthur Samar Phil. 82 D4
General Machado Angola see Camacupa
General Pico Arg. 178 D5
General Pinedo Arg. 178 D3
General Roca Arg. 178 C5
General Salgado Brazil 179 A3
General San Martín research station Antarctica see San Martín
General Santos Mindanao Phil. 82 D5
General Simón Bolívar Mex. 161 C7
General Terán Mex. 167 F3
General Trías Mex. 166 D2
General Villegas Arg. 178 D5
Genesee PA U.S.A. 165 G3
Geneseo NY U.S.A. 165 G2
Geneva S. Africa 125 H4
Geneva Switz. 66 H3
Geneva AL U.S.A. 163 C6
Geneva IL U.S.A. 164 A3
Geneva NE U.S.A. 160 D3
Geneva NY U.S.A. 165 G2
Geneva OH U.S.A. 164 E3
Geneva, Lake France/Switz. 66 H3
Genève Switz. see Geneva
Genf Switz. see Geneva
Gengda China see Gana
Genglou China 97 H2
Gengma China 96 C4
Gengxuan China see Gengma
Genhe China see Gegen Gol
Genichesk Ukr. see Heniches'k
Genji India 104 C5
Genk Belgium 62 F4
Genkanyy, Khrebet ridge Rus. Fed. 148 D2
Gennep Neth. 62 F3
Genoa Australia 138 D6
Genoa Italy 68 C2
Genoa, Gulf of Italy 68 C2
Genova Italy see Genoa
Genova, Golfo di Italy see Genoa, Gulf of
Gent Belgium see Ghent
Genteng Jawa Indon. 84 D4
Genteng i. Indon. 85 F4
Genthin Germany 63 M2
Genting Highlands Malaysia 84 C2
Gentioux, Plateau de France 66 F4
Genua Italy see Genoa
Geographe Bay Australia 135 A8
Geographical Society Ø i. Greenland 147 P2
Geok-Tepe Turkm. see Gëkdepe
Georga, Zemlya i. Rus. Fed. 76 F1
George r. Canada 153 I2
George S. Africa 124 F7
George, Lake Australia 138 D5
George, Lake AK U.S.A. 149 K3
George, Lake FL U.S.A. 163 D6
George, Lake NY U.S.A. 165 I2
George Land i. Rus. Fed. see Georga, Zemlya
Georges Mills NH U.S.A. 165 I2
George Sound inlet N.Z. 139 A7
Georgetown Australia 136 C3
▶George Town Cayman Is 169 H5
Capital of the Cayman Islands.
Georgetown Gambia 120 B3
▶Georgetown Guyana 177 G2
Capital of Guyana.
George Town Malaysia 84 C1
Georgetown AK U.S.A. 148 H3
Georgetown DE U.S.A. 165 H4
Georgetown GA U.S.A. 163 C6
Georgetown IL U.S.A. 164 B4
Georgetown KY U.S.A. 164 C4
Georgetown OH U.S.A. 164 D4
Georgetown SC U.S.A. 163 E5
Georgetown TX U.S.A. 161 D6
George VI Sound sea chan. Antarctica 188 L2
George V Land reg. Antarctica 188 G2
George West TX U.S.A. 161 D6
Georgia country Asia 113 F2
Georgia state U.S.A. 163 D5
Georgia, Strait of Canada 150 E5
Georgiana AL U.S.A. 161 G6
Georgian Bay Canada 164 E1
Georgian Bay Islands National Park Canada 164 F1
Georgienne, Baie b. Canada see Georgian Bay
Georgina watercourse Australia 136 B5
Georgiu-Dezh Rus. Fed. see Liski
Georgiyevka Vostochnyy Kazakhstan Kazakh. 102 F2
Georgiyevka Zhambylskaya Oblast' Kazakh. see Korday
Georgiyevsk Rus. Fed. 113 F1
Georgiyevskoye Rus. Fed. 52 J4
Georg von Neumayer research station Antarctica see Neumayer III
Gera Germany 63 M4
Geraardsbergen Belgium 62 D4
Geral, Serra mts Brazil 179 A4
Geral de Goiás, Serra hills Brazil 179 B1
Geraldine N.Z. 139 C7
Geral do Paraná, Serra hills Brazil 179 B1
Geraldton Australia 135 A7
Gerama i. Indon. 83 C1
Gerar watercourse Israel 107 B4
Gerber CA U.S.A. 158 B1
Gercüş Turkey 113 F3
Gerdine, Mount AK U.S.A. 148 I3
Gerede Turkey 112 D2
Gerik Malaysia 84 C1
Gerlach NV U.S.A. 158 D1
Gerlachovský štít mt. Slovakia 57 R6
Germaine, Lac l. Canada 153 I3
Germania country Europe see Germany
Germanicea Turkey see Kahramanmaraş
Germansen Landing Canada 150 E4
German South-West Africa country Africa see Namibia
Germantown OH U.S.A. 164 C4
Germantown WI U.S.A. 164 A2
▶Germany country Europe 57 L5
2nd most populous country in Europe.
Germersheim Germany 63 I5
Gernsheim Germany 63 I5
Gero Japan 92 D3
Gerolstein Germany 62 G4
Gerolzhofen Germany 63 K5
Gerona Spain see Girona
Gerrit Denys is P.N.G. see Lihir Group
Gers r. France 66 E4
Gersfeld (Rhön) Germany 63 J4
Gersoppa India 106 B3
Gerstungen Germany 63 K4
Gerwisch Germany 63 L2
Gêryville Alg. see El Bayadh
Gêrzê China 99 D6
Gerze Turkey 112 D2
Gescher Germany 62 H3
Gesoriacum France see Boulogne-sur-Mer
Gessie IN U.S.A. 164 B3
Getai China 95 G5
Gete r. Belgium 62 F4
Gettysburg PA U.S.A. 165 G4
Gettysburg SD U.S.A. 160 D2
Gettysburg National Military Park nat. park PA U.S.A. 165 G4
Getz Ice Shelf Antarctica 188 J2
Geumapang r. Indon. 84 B2
Geumpang Sumatera Indon. 84 B1
Geureudong, Gunung vol. Indon. 84 B1
Geurie Australia 138 D4
Gevaş Turkey 113 F3
Gevgelija Macedonia 69 J4
Gēwārām Band Afgh. 111 G4
Gexianzhuang China see Qinghe
Gexto Spain see Algorta
Gey Iran see Nīkshahr
Geyikli Turkey 69 L5
Geylegphug Bhutan 105 G4
Geysdorp S. Africa 125 G4
Geyserville CA U.S.A. 158 B2
Geyve Turkey 69 N4
Gezidong China 94 E4
Gezīr Iran 110 D5
Ghaap Plateau S. Africa 124 F4
Ghāb, Wādī al r. Syria 107 C2
Ghabāghib Syria 107 C3
Ghabeish Sudan 108 C7
Ghadaf, Wādī al watercourse Jordan 107 C4
Ghadamés Libya see Ghadāmis
Ghadāmis Libya 120 D1
Gha'em Shahr Iran 110 D2
Ghaghara r. India 105 F4
Ghaibi Dero Pak. 111 G5
Ghalend Iran 111 F4
Ghallaorol Uzbek. see G'allaorol
Ghana country Africa 120 C4
Ghanādah, Rās pt U.A.E. 110 D5
Ghantila India 104 B5
Ghanwā Saudi Arabia 108 G4
Ghanzi Botswana 123 C6
Ghanzi admin. dist. Botswana 124 F2
Ghap'an Armenia see Kapan
Ghār, Ras al pt Saudi Arabia 110 C5
Ghardaïa Alg. 64 E5
Gharghoda India 106 D1
Ghārib, Gebel mt. Egypt see Ghārib, Jabal
Ghārib, Jabal mt. Egypt 112 D5
Gharm Tajik. 111 H2
Gharq Ābād Iran 110 C3
Gharwa India see Garhwa
Gharyān Libya 121 E1
Ghāt Libya 120 E2
Ghatgan India 105 F5
Ghatol India 104 C5
Ghawdex i. Malta see Gozo
Ghazal, Bahr el watercourse Chad 121 E3
Ghazaouet Alg. 67 F6
Ghaziabad India 104 D3
Ghazi Ghat Pak. 111 H4
Ghazipur India 105 E4
Ghazna Afgh. see Ghaznī
Ghaznī Afgh. 111 H3
Ghaznī Rōd r. Afgh. 111 G3
Ghazzah Gaza see Gaza
Ghebar Gumbad Iran 110 E3
Ghent Belgium 62 D3
Gheorghe Gheorghiu-Dej Romania see Onești
Gheorgheni Romania 69 K1
Gherla Romania 69 J1
Ghijduwon Uzbek. see G'ijduvon
Ghilzai reg. Afgh. 111 G4
Ghīnah, Wādī al watercourse Saudi Arabia 107 D4
Ghisonaccia Corsica France 66 I5
Ghōrak Afgh. 111 G3
Ghost Lake Canada 150 H2
Ghotaru India 104 B4
Ghotki Pak. 111 H5
Ghudamis Libya see Ghadāmis
Ghugri r. India 105 F4
Ghurayfah hill Saudi Arabia 107 C4
Ghūrī Iran 110 D4
Ghūriān Afgh. 111 F3
Ghurrab, Jabal hill Saudi Arabia 110 B5
Ghuzor Uzbek. see G'uzor
Ghyvelde France 62 C3
Giaginskaya Rus. Fed. 113 F1
Gialias r. Cyprus 107 A2
Gia Nghia Vietnam 87 D4
Gianisada i. Greece 69 L7
Giannitsa Greece 69 J4
Giant's Castle mt. S. Africa 125 I5
Giant's Causeway lava field U.K. 61 F2
Gianysada i. Greece see Gianisada
Gia Rai Vietnam 87 D5
Giarre Sicily Italy 68 F6
Gibb r. Australia 134 D3
Gibbonsville ID U.S.A. 156 E3
Gibeon Namibia 124 C3
Gibraltar terr. Europe 67 D5
▶Gibraltar Gibraltar 184 H3
United Kingdom Overseas Territory.
Gibraltar, Strait of Morocco/Spain 67 C6
Gibraltar Range National Park Australia 138 F2
Gibson Australia 135 C8
Gibson City IL U.S.A. 164 A3
Gibson Desert Australia 135 C6
Gichgeniyn Nuruu mts Mongolia 94 C2
Gidar Pak. 111 G4
Giddalur India 106 C3
Giddi, Gebel el hill Egypt see Jiddī, Jabal al
Giddings TX U.S.A. 161 D6
Gīdolē Eth. 121 G4
Gien France 66 F3
Gießen Germany 63 I4
Gīfan Iran 110 E2
Gifford r. Canada 147 J2
Gifhorn Germany 63 K2
Gift Lake Canada 150 H4
Gifu Japan 92 C3
Gifu pref. Japan 92 C3
Giganta, Cerro mt. Mex. 166 C3
Gigha i. U.K. 60 D5
Gīgīga Eth. see Jijiga
G'ijduvon Uzbek. 111 G1
Gijón Spain see Gijón-Xixón
Gijón-Xixón Spain 67 D2
Gila r. AZ U.S.A. 159 F5
Gila, Tanjung pt Maluku Indon. 83 D2
Gila Bend AZ U.S.A. 159 G5
Gila Bend Mountains AZ U.S.A. 159 G5
Gīlān-e Gharb Iran 110 B3
Gilbert r. Australia 136 C3
Gilbert AZ U.S.A. 159 H5
Gilbert WV U.S.A. 164 E5
Gilbert, Mount AK U.S.A. 149 J3
Gilbert Islands Kiribati 186 H5
Gilbert Islands country Pacific Ocean see Kiribati
Gilbert Peak UT U.S.A. 159 H1
Gilbert Ridge sea feature Pacific Ocean 186 H6
Gilbert River Australia 136 C3
Gilbués Brazil 177 I5
Gil Chashmeh Iran 110 E3
Gilé Moz. 123 D5
Giles Creek r. Australia 134 E4
Gilford Island Canada 150 E5
Gilgai Australia 138 E2
Gilgandra Australia 138 D3
Gil Gil Creek r. Australia 138 D2
Gilgit Pak. 104 C2
Gilgit r. Pak. 109 L2
Gilgit-Baltistan admin. div. Pak. 111 I2
Gilgunnia Australia 138 C4
Gili Iyang i. Indon. 85 F4
Gilimanuk Bali Indon. 85 F5
Gılındire Turkey see Aydıncık
Gillam Canada 151 M3
Gillen, Lake salt flat Australia 135 D6
Gilles, Lake salt flat Australia 137 B7
Gillett PA U.S.A. 165 G3
Gillette WY U.S.A. 156 G3
Gilliat Australia 136 C4
Gillingham England U.K. 59 E7
Gillingham England U.K. 59 H7
Gilling West U.K. 58 F4
Gillon Point pt AK U.S.A. 148 [inset] A5
Gilman IL U.S.A. 164 B3
Gilmer TX U.S.A. 161 E5
Gilmour Island Canada 152 F2

Gilroy CA U.S.A. 158 C3
Gīmbī Eth. 122 D3
Gimhae S. Korea see Kimhae
Gimli Canada 151 L5
Gimol'skoye, Ozero l. Rus. Fed. 52 G3
Ginebra, Laguna l. Bol. 176 E6
Gineifa Egypt see Junayfah
Gin Gin Australia 136 E5
Gingin Australia 135 A7
Gingolx Canada 150 D4
Gingoog Mindanao Phil. 82 D4
Gīnīr Eth. 122 E3
Ginosa Italy 68 G4
Ginzo de Limia Spain see Xinzo de Limia
Gioia del Colle Italy 68 G4
Gipouloux r. Canada 152 G3
Gippsland reg. Australia 138 B7
Girā, Wâdi watercourse Egypt see Jirā', Wādī
Girān Rīg mt. Iran 110 E4
Girard PA U.S.A. 164 E2
Girardin, Lac l. Canada 153 I2
Girdab Iran 110 E3
Girdwood AK U.S.A. 149 J3
Giresun Turkey 112 E2
Girgenti Sicily Italy see Agrigento
Giridh India see Giridih
Giridih India 105 F4
Girilambone Australia 138 C3
Girishk Afgh. 111 G4
Girna r. India 104 C5
Gir National Park India 104 B5
Girne Cyprus see Kyrenia
Girón Ecuador 176 C4
Giron Sweden see Kiruna
Girona Spain 67 H3
Gironde est. France 66 D4
Girot Pak. 111 I3
Girral Australia 138 C4
Girraween National Park Australia 138 E2
Girvan U.K. 60 E5
Girvas Rus. Fed. 52 G3
Gisasa r. AK U.S.A. 148 H2
Gisborne N.Z. 139 G4
Giscome Canada 150 F4
Gislaved Sweden 55 H8
Gisors France 62 B5
Gissar Tajik. see Hisor
Gissar Range mts Tajik./Uzbek. 111 G2
Gissarskiy Khrebet mts Tajik./Uzbek. see Gissar Range
Gitarama Rwanda 122 C4
Gitega Burundi 122 C4
Giuba r. Somalia see Jubba
Giulianova Italy 68 E3
Giurgiu Romania 69 K3
Giuvala, Pasul pass Romania 69 K2
Givar Iran 110 E2
Givet France 62 E4
Givors France 66 G4
Givry-en-Argonne France 62 E6
Giyani S. Africa 125 J2
Giza Egypt 112 C5
Gizhiga Rus. Fed. 77 R3
Gjakovë Kosovo 69 I3
Gjilan Kosovo 69 I3
Gjirokastër Albania 69 I4
Gjirokastra Albania see Gjirokastër
Gjoa Haven Canada 147 I3
Gjøra Norway 54 F5
Gjøvik Norway 55 G6
Gkinas, Akrotirio pt Greece 69 M6
Glace Bay Canada 153 K5
Glacier Bay AK U.S.A. 149 N4
Glacier Bay National Park and Preserve AK U.S.A. 149 M4
Glacier National Park Canada 150 G5
Glacier National Park MT U.S.A. 156 E2
Glacier Peak vol. WA U.S.A. 156 C2
Gladstad Norway 54 G4
Gladstone Australia 136 E4
Gladstone Canada 151 L5
Gladwin MI U.S.A. 164 C2
Gladys VA U.S.A. 164 F5
Gladys Lake Canada 150 C3
Glamis U.K. 60 F4
Glamis CA U.S.A. 159 F5
Glamoč Bos.-Herz. 68 G2
Glan r. Germany 63 H5
Glan Mindanao Phil. 82 D5
Glandorf Germany 63 I2
Glanton U.K. 58 F3
Glasgow U.K. 60 E5
Glasgow KY U.S.A. 164 C5
Glasgow MT U.S.A. 156 G2
Glasgow VA U.S.A. 164 F5
Glaslyn Canada 151 I4
Glass, Loch l. U.K. 60 E3
Glass Mountain CA U.S.A. 158 D3
Glass Peninsula AK U.S.A. 149 N4
Glastonbury U.K. 59 E7
Glauchau Germany 63 M4
Glazov Rus. Fed. 52 L4
Gleiwitz Poland see Gliwice
Glen NH U.S.A. 165 J1
Glen Allen VA U.S.A. 165 G5
Glen Alpine Dam S. Africa 125 I2
Glenamaddy Ireland 61 D4
Glenamoy r. Ireland 61 C3
Glen Arbor MI U.S.A. 164 C1
Glenbawn, Lake Australia 138 E4
Glenboro Canada 151 L5
Glen Canyon gorge UT U.S.A. 159 H3
Glen Canyon Dam AZ U.S.A. 159 H3
Glencoe Canada 164 E2
Glencoe S. Africa 125 J5
Glencoe MN U.S.A. 160 E2
Glendale AZ U.S.A. 159 G5
Glendale CA U.S.A. 158 D4
Glendale UT U.S.A. 159 G3
Glendale Lake PA U.S.A. 165 F3
Glen Davis Australia 138 E4
Glenden Australia 136 E4
Glendive MT U.S.A. 156 G3
Glendon Canada 151 I4
Glendo Reservoir WY U.S.A. 156 G4
Glenfield NY U.S.A. 165 H2
Glengavlen Ireland 61 E3
Glengyle Australia 136 B5
Glen Innes Australia 138 E2
Glenluce U.K. 60 E6
Glen Lyon PA U.S.A. 165 G3
Glenlyon Peak Canada 149 N3
Glen More valley U.K. 60 E3
Glenmorgan Australia 138 D1
Glenn CA U.S.A. 158 B2
Glennallen AK U.S.A. 149 K3
Glenn Highway AK U.S.A. 149 K3
Glennie MI U.S.A. 164 D1
Glenns Ferry ID U.S.A. 156 E4
Glenora Canada 149 O4
Glenore Australia 136 C3
Glenormiston Australia 136 B4
Glenreagh Australia 138 F3
Glen Rose TX U.S.A. 161 D5
Glenrothes U.K. 60 F4
Glens Falls NY U.S.A. 165 I2
Glen Shee valley U.K. 60 F4
Glenties Ireland 61 D3
Glenveagh National Park Ireland 61 E2
Glenville WV U.S.A. 164 E4
Glenwood AR U.S.A. 161 E5
Glenwood IA U.S.A. 160 E3
Glenwood MN U.S.A. 160 E2
Glenwood NM U.S.A. 159 I5
Glenwood Springs CO U.S.A. 159 J2
Glevum U.K. see Gloucester
Glinde Germany 63 K1
Glittertinden mt. Norway 55 F6
Gliwice Poland 57 Q5
Globe AZ U.S.A. 159 H5
Glogau Poland see Głogów
Głogów Poland 57 P5
Glomfjord Norway 54 H3
Glomma r. Norway 54 G7
Glommersträsk Sweden 54 K4
Glorieuses, Îles is Indian Ocean 123 E5
Glorioso Islands Indian Ocean see Glorieuses, Îles
Glory of Russia Cape AK U.S.A. 148 D3
Gloster MS U.S.A. 161 F6
Gloucester Australia 138 E3
Gloucester U.K. 59 E7
Gloucester MA U.S.A. 165 J2
Gloucester VA U.S.A. 165 G5
Glover Reef Belize 167 I5
Gloversville NY U.S.A. 165 H2
Glovertown Canada 153 L4
Glöwen Germany 63 M2
Glubinnoye Rus. Fed. 90 D3
Glubokiy Krasnoyarskiy Kray Rus. Fed. 88 H2
Glubokiy Rostovskaya Oblast' Rus. Fed. 53 I6
Glubokoye Belarus see Hlybokaye
Glubokoye Kazakh. 102 F1
Gluggarnir hill Faroe Is 54 [inset 2]
Glukhov Ukr. see Hlukhiv
Glusburn U.K. 58 F5
Glynebwy U.K. see Ebbw Vale
Gmelinka Rus. Fed. 53 J6
Gmünd Austria 57 O6
Gmunden Austria 57 N7
Gnarp Sweden 55 J5
Gnarrenburg Germany 63 J1
Gnesen Poland see Gniezno
Gniezno Poland 57 P4
Gnjilane Kosovo see Gjilan
Gnowangerup Australia 135 B8
Gnows Nest Range hills Australia 135 B7
Goa India 106 B3
Goa state India 106 B3
Goageb Namibia 124 C4
Goalen Head hd Australia 138 E6
Goalpara India 105 G4
Goang Flores Indon. 83 A5
Goat Fell hill U.K. 60 D5
Goba Eth. 122 E3
Gobabis Namibia 124 D2
Gobannium U.K. see Abergavenny
Gobas Namibia 124 D4
Gobi Desert des. China/Mongolia 88 J4
Gobindpur India 105 F5
Gobles MI U.S.A. 164 C2
Gobō Japan 92 B5
Goch Germany 62 G3
Gochas Namibia 124 D3
Go Công Vietnam 87 D5
Godalming U.K. 59 G7
Godavari r. India 106 D2
Godavari, Cape India 106 D2
Godda India 105 F4
Godē Eth. 122 E3
Godere Eth. 122 E3
Goderich Canada 164 E2
Goderville France 59 H9
Godhavn Greenland see Qeqertarsuaq
Godhra India 104 C5
Godia Creek b. India 111 H6
Gōdo Japan 92 C3
Godo, Gunung mt. Indon. 83 C3
Gods r. Canada 151 M3
Gods Lake Canada 151 M4
God's Mercy, Bay of Canada 151 O2
Godthåb Greenland see Nuuk
Godwin-Austen, Mount China/Pak. see K2
Goedereede Neth. 62 D3
Goedgegun Swaziland see Nhlangano
Goegap Nature Reserve S. Africa 124 D5
Goélands, Lac aux l. Canada 153 J3
Goes Neth. 62 D3
Gogama Canada 152 E5
Gogebic Range hills MI U.S.A. 160 F2
Gogra r. India see Ghaghara
Goiana Brazil 177 L5
Goiandira Brazil 179 A2
Goianésia Brazil 179 A1
Goiânia Brazil 179 A2
Goiás Brazil 179 A1
Goiás state Brazil 179 A2
Goicangmai China 99 C6
Goikul Palau 82 [inset]
Goincang China 94 E5
Goinsargoin China 96 C2
Goio-Erê Brazil 178 F2
Gojō Japan 92 B4
Gojra Pak. 111 I4
Goka Japan 93 F2
Gokak India 106 B2
Gokarn India 106 B3
Gök Çay r. Turkey 107 A1
Gökçeada i. Turkey 69 K4
Gökdepe Turkm. see Gëkdepe
Gökdere r. Turkey 107 A1
Goklenkuy, Solonchak salt l. Turkm. 110 E1
Gökova Körfezi b. Turkey 69 L6
Gokprosh Hills Pak. 111 F5
Göksun Turkey 112 E3
Göksu Parkı Turkey 107 A1
Gokteik Myanmar 86 B2
Gokwe Zimbabwe 123 C5
Gol Norway 55 F6
Golaghat India 105 H4
Golbāf Iran 110 E4
Gölbaşı Turkey 112 E3
Golconda NV U.S.A. 158 E1
Gölcük Turkey 69 M4
Gold PA U.S.A. 165 G3
Gołdap Poland 57 S3
Gold Beach OR U.S.A. 156 B4
Goldberg Germany 63 M1
Gold Coast country Africa see Ghana
Gold Coast Australia 138 F2
Gold Creek AK U.S.A. 149 J3
Golden CO U.S.A. 156 G5
Golden Bay N.Z. 139 D5
Goldendale WA U.S.A. 156 C3
Goldene Aue reg. Germany 63 K3
Golden Gate Highlands National Park S. Africa 125 I5
Golden Hinde mt. Canada 150 E5
Golden Lake Canada 165 G1
Golden Meadow LA U.S.A. 167 H2
Golden Prairie Canada 151 I5
Goldenstedt Germany 63 I2
Goldfield NV U.S.A. 158 E3
Goldsand Lake Canada 151 K3
Goldsboro NC U.S.A. 163 E5
Goldstone Lake CA U.S.A. 158 E4
Goldsworthy (abandoned) Australia 134 B5
Goldthwaite TX U.S.A. 161 D6
Goldvein VA U.S.A. 165 G4
Göle Turkey 113 F2
Goleta CA U.S.A. 158 D4
Golets-Davydov, Gora mt. Rus. Fed. 89 J2
Golfito Costa Rica 166 [inset] J7
Golfo di Orosei Gennargentu e Asinara, Parco Nazionale del nat. park Sardinia Italy 68 C4
Gölgeli Dağları mts Turkey 69 M6
Goliad TX U.S.A. 161 D6
Golin Baixing China 95 J2
Gölköy Turkey 112 E2
Gollel Swaziland see Lavumisa
Golm Germany 63 M2
Golmberg hill Germany 63 N2
Golmud China 94 C4
Golmud He r. China 94 C4
Golovin AK U.S.A. 148 G2
Golovin Bay AK U.S.A. 148 G2
Golovnino Rus. Fed. 90 G4
Golpāyegān Iran 110 C3
Gölpazarı Turkey 69 N4
Golsovia AK U.S.A. 148 G3
Golspie U.K. 60 F3
Golyama Syutkya mt. Bulg. 69 K4
Golyam Persenk mt. Bulg. 69 K4
Golyshi Rus. Fed. see Vetluzhskiy
Golzow Germany 63 M2
Goma Dem. Rep. Congo 122 C4
Gomal Kēlay Afgh. 111 H3
Gomang Co salt l. China 99 E7
Gomangxung China 94 E5
Gomati r. India 109 N4
Gombak, Bukit hill Sing. 87 [inset]
Gombe Nigeria 120 E3
Gombe r. Tanz. 123 D4
Gombi Nigeria 120 E3
Gombroon Iran see Bandar-e 'Abbās
Gomel' Belarus see Homyel'
Gómez Palacio Mex. 166 E3
Gomīshān Iran 110 D2
Gommern Germany 63 L2
Gomo China 99 D6
Gomo Co salt l. China 99 D6
Gomumu i. Maluku Indon. 83 C3
Gonābād Iran 110 E2
Gonaïves Haiti 169 J5
Gonarezhou National Park Zimbabwe 123 D6
Gonbad-e Kāvūs Iran 110 D2
Gonda India 105 E4
Gondal India 104 B5
Gondar Eth. see Gonder
Gonder Eth. 122 D2
Gondia India 104 E5
Gondiya India see Gondia
Gönen Turkey 69 L4
Gonfreville-l'Orcher France 59 H9
Gong'an China 97 G2
Gongbalou China 99 E7
Gongbo'gyamda China 99 F7
Gongchakou China 94 D4
Gongchang China see Longxi
Gongcheng China 97 F3
Gonggar China 99 E7
Gongga Shan mt. China 96 D2
Gonghe Qinghai China 94 E4
Gonghe Yunnan China see Mouding
Gonghui China 95 H3
Gongjiang China see Yudu
Gongliu China 98 C4
Gongogi r. Brazil 179 D1
Gongolgon Australia 138 C3
Gongquan China 96 E2
Gongwang Shan mts China 96 D3
Gongxian Henan China see Gongyi
Gongxian Sichuan China see Gongquan
Gongyi China 95 H5
Gonjo China see Kasha
Gonzáles Mex. 167 F4
Gonzales CA U.S.A. 158 C3
Gonzales TX U.S.A. 161 D6
Gonzha Rus. Fed. 90 B1
Goochland VA U.S.A. 165 G5
Goodenough, Cape Antarctica 188 G2
Goodenough, Mount hill Canada 149 N2
Goodenough Island P.N.G. 132 F2
Gooderham Canada 165 F1
Good Hope, Cape of S. Africa 124 D8
Goodhope Bay AK U.S.A. 148 G2
Good Hope Mountain Canada 156 B2
Gooding ID U.S.A. 156 E4
Goodland IN U.S.A. 164 B3
Goodland KS U.S.A. 160 C4
Goodlettsville TN U.S.A. 164 B5
Goodnews Bay AK U.S.A. 148 G4
Goodnews Bay b. AK U.S.A. 148 G4
Goodooga Australia 138 C2
Goodpaster r. AK U.S.A. 149 K2
Goodspeed Nunataks Antarctica 188 E2
Goole U.K. 58 G5
Goolgowi Australia 138 B5
Goolma Australia 138 D4
Gooloogong Australia 138 D4
Goomalling Australia 135 B7
Goombalie Australia 138 B2
Goondiwindi Australia 138 E2
Goongarrie, Lake salt flat Australia 135 C7
Goongarrie National Park Australia 135 C7
Goonyella Australia 136 D4
Goorly, Lake salt flat Australia 135 B7
Goose Bay Canada see Happy Valley-Goose Bay
Goose Creek SC U.S.A. 163 D5
Goose Lake CA U.S.A. 156 C4
Gooty India 106 C3
Gopalganj Bangl. 105 G5
Gopalganj India 105 F4
Gopeshwar India 104 D3
Göppingen Germany 63 J6
Gorakhpur India 105 E4
Goražde Bos.-Herz. 68 H3
Gorbernador NM U.S.A. 159 J3
Gorczański Park Narodowy nat. park Poland 57 R6
Gorda, Punta pt Nicaragua 166 [inset] J6
Gorda, Punta pt CA U.S.A. 158 A1
Gördes Turkey 69 M5
Gordil Cent. Afr. Rep. 122 C3
Gordon r. Canada 151 O1
Gordon U.K. 60 G5
Gordon AK U.S.A. 149 L1
Gordon NE U.S.A. 160 C3
Gordon, Lake Australia 137 [inset]
Gordon Downs (abandoned) Australia 134 E4
Gordon Lake Canada 151 I3
Gordon Lake PA U.S.A. 165 F4
Gordonsville VA U.S.A. 165 F4
Goré Chad 121 E4
Gorē Eth. 122 D3
Gore N.Z. 139 B8
Gore VA U.S.A. 165 F4
Gorebridge U.K. 60 F5
Gore Point pt AK U.S.A. 149 J4
Gorey Ireland 61 F5
Gorg Iran 111 E4
Gorgān Iran 110 D2
Gorgān, Khalīj-e Iran 110 D2
Gorge Range hills Australia 134 B5
Gorgona, Isla i. Col. 176 C3
Gorham NH U.S.A. 165 J1
Gori Georgia 108 F1
Gorinchem Neth. 62 E3
Goris Armenia 113 G3
Gorizia Italy 68 E2
Gorki Belarus see Horki
Gor'kiy Rus. Fed. see Nizhniy Novgorod
Gor'kovskoye Vodokhranilishche resr Rus. Fed. 52 I4
Gorlice Poland 53 D6
Görlitz Germany 57 O5
Gorlovka Ukr. see Horlivka
Gorna Dzhumaya Bulg. see Blagoevgrad
Gorna Oryakhovitsa Bulg. 69 K3
Gornji Milanovac Serbia 69 I2
Gornji Vakuf Bos.-Herz. 68 G3
Gorno-Altaysk Rus. Fed. 102 G1
Gorno-Altayskaya Avtonomnaya Oblast' aut. rep. Rus. Fed. see Altay, Respublika
Gornotrakiyska Nizina lowland Bulg. 69 K3
Gornozavodsk Permskiy Kray Rus. Fed. 51 R4
Gornozavodsk Sakhalinskaya Oblast' Rus. Fed. 90 F3
Gornyak Rus. Fed. 98 C2
Gornyy Rus. Fed. 53 K6
Gornyy Altay aut. rep. Rus. Fed. see Altay, Respublika
Gornyye Klyuchi Rus. Fed. 90 D3
Goro i. Fiji see Koro
Gorodenka Ukr. see Horodenka
Gorodets Rus. Fed. 52 I4
Gorodishche Penzenskaya Oblast' Rus. Fed. 53 J5
Gorodishche Volgogradskaya Oblast' Rus. Fed. 53 J6
Gorodok Belarus see Haradok
Gorodok Rus. Fed. see Zakamensk
Gorodok Khmel'nyts'ka Oblast' Ukr. see Horodok
Gorodok L'vivs'ka Oblast' Ukr. see Horodok
Gorodovikovsk Rus. Fed. 53 I7
Goroka P.N.G. 81 L8
Gorokhovets Rus. Fed. 52 I4
Gorom Gorom Burkina Faso 120 C3
Gorong, Kepulauan is Indon. 81 I7
Gorongosa mt. Moz. 123 D5
Gorongosa, Parque Nacional da nat. park Moz. 123 D5
Gorontalo Sulawesi Indon. 83 B2
Gorontalo prov. Indon. 83 B2
Gorshechnoye Rus. Fed. 53 H6
Gort Ireland 61 D4
Gort an Choirce Ireland 61 D2
Gorutuba r. Brazil 179 C1
Gorveh Iran 110 E4
Goryachiy Klyuch Rus. Fed. 113 E1
Görzke Germany 63 M2
Gorzów Wielkopolski Poland 57 O4
Gosainthan mt. China see Xixabangma Feng
Gose Japan 92 B4
Gosforth U.K. 58 F3
Goshen CA U.S.A. 158 D3
Goshen IN U.S.A. 164 C3
Goshen NH U.S.A. 165 I2
Goshen NY U.S.A. 165 H3
Goshen VA U.S.A. 164 F5
Goshiki Japan 92 A4
Goshoba Turkm. see Goşoba
Goslar Germany 63 K3
Goşoba Turkm. 113 I2
Gospić Croatia 68 F2
Gosport U.K. 59 F8
Gossi Mali 120 C3
Gostivar Macedonia 69 I4
Gosu China 96 C1
Göteborg Sweden see Gothenburg
Gotemba Japan see Gotenba
Gotenba Japan 93 E3
Götene Sweden 55 H7
Gotenhafen Poland see Gdynia
Gotha Germany 63 K4
Gothenburg Sweden 55 G8
Gothenburg NE U.S.A. 160 C3
Gotland i. Sweden 55 K8
Gotō-rettō is Japan 91 C6
Gotse Delchev Bulg. 69 J4
Gotska Sandön i. Sweden 55 K7
Gōtsu Japan 91 D6
Göttingen Germany 63 J3
Gott Peak Canada 150 F5
Gottwaldow Czech Rep. see Zlín
Gouda Neth. 62 E2
Goudiri Senegal 120 B3
Goudoumaria Niger 120 E3
Goûgaram Niger 120 D3
▶Gough Island S. Atlantic Ocean 184 H8
Dependency of Tristan da Cunha.
Gouin, Réservoir resr Canada 152 G4
Goulburn Australia 138 D5
Goulburn r. N.S.W. Australia 138 E4
Goulburn r. Vic. Australia 138 B6
Goulburn Islands Australia 134 F2
Goulburn River National Park Australia 138 E4
Gould Coast Antarctica 188 J1
Goulou atoll Micronesia see Ngulu
Goundam Mali 120 C3
Goundi Chad 121 E4
Goupil, Lac l. Canada 153 H3
Gouraya Alg. 67 G5
Gourcy Burkina Faso 120 C3
Gourdon France 66 E4
Gouré Niger 120 E3
Gouripur Bangl. 105 G4
Gourits r. S. Africa 124 E8
Gourma-Rharous Mali 120 C3
Gournay-en-Bray France 62 B5
Goussainville France 62 C5
Gouverneur NY U.S.A. 165 H1
Governador Valadares Brazil 179 C2
Governor Generoso Mindanao Phil. 82 D5
Governor's Harbour Bahamas 163 E7
Govĭ-Altay prov. Mongolia 94 C2
Govĭ Altayn Nuruu mts Mongolia 94 D2
Govind Ballash Pant Sagar resr India 105 E4
Govind Sagar resr India 99 B7
Govĭ-Ugtaal Mongolia 95 F2
Gowanda NY U.S.A. 165 F2
Gowan Range hills Australia 136 D5
Gowaqungo China 99 D7
Gowd-e Mokh l. Iran 110 D4
Gowna, Lough l. Ireland 61 E4
Goya Arg. 178 E3
Göyçay Azer. 113 G2
Goyder watercourse Australia 135 F6
Göygöl Azer. 113 G2
Goýmatdag hills Turkm. 110 D1
Goymatdag hills Turkm. see Goýmatdag
Göynük Turkey 69 N4
Goyoum Cameroon 120 E4
Gozareh Afgh. 111 F3
Goz-Beïda Chad 121 F3
Gozen-yama Japan 93 G2
Gozha Co salt l. China 99 C6
Gözkaya Turkey 107 C1
Gozo i. Malta 68 F6
Graaff-Reinet S. Africa 124 G7
Grabfeld plain Germany 63 K4
Grabo Côte d'Ivoire 120 C4
Grabouw S. Africa 124 D8
Grabow Germany 63 L1
Gračac Croatia 68 F2
Gracefield Canada 152 F5
Gracey KY U.S.A. 164 B5
Grachi (abandoned) Kazakh. 98 B2
Gracias Hond. 166 [inset] H6
Gradaús, Serra dos hills Brazil 177 H5
Gradiška Bos.-Herz. see Bosanska Gradiška
Grady NM U.S.A. 161 C5
Gräfenhainichen Germany 63 M3
Grafenwöhr Germany 63 L5
Grafton Australia 138 F2
Grafton ND U.S.A. 160 D1
Grafton WI U.S.A. 164 B2
Grafton WV U.S.A. 164 E4
Grafton, Cape Australia 136 D3
Grafton, Mount NV U.S.A. 159 F2
Grafton Passage Australia 136 D3
Graham NC U.S.A. 162 E4
Graham TX U.S.A. 161 D5
Graham, Mount AZ U.S.A. 159 I5
Graham Bell Island Rus. Fed. see Greem-Bell, Ostrov
Graham Island B.C. Canada 149 N5
Graham Island Nunavut Canada 147 I2
Graham Land reg. Antarctica 188 L2
Grahamstown S. Africa 125 H7
Grahovo Bos.-Herz. see Bosansko Grahovo
Graigue Ireland 61 F5
Grajagan Jawa Indon. 85 F5
Grajaú Brazil 177 I5
Grajaú r. Brazil 177 J4
Grammont Belgium see Geraardsbergen
Grammos mt. Greece 69 I4
Grampian Mountains U.K. 60 E4
Grampians National Park Australia 137 C8
Granada Nicaragua 166 [inset] I7
Granada Spain 67 E5
Granada CO U.S.A. 160 C4
Granard Ireland 61 E4
Granbury TX U.S.A. 161 D5
Granby Canada 153 G5
Gran Canaria i. Canary Is 120 B2
Gran Chaco reg. Arg./Para. 178 D3
Grand r. MO U.S.A. 164 B2
Grand r. SD U.S.A. 160 C2
Grand Atlas mts Morocco see Haut Atlas
Grand Bahama i. Bahamas 163 E7
Grand Ballon mt. France 57 K7
Grand Bank Canada 153 L5
Grand Banks of Newfoundland sea feature N. Atlantic Ocean 184 E3
Grand-Bassam Côte d'Ivoire 120 C4
Grand Bay-Westfield Canada 153 I5
Grand Bend Canada 164 E2
Grand Blanc MI U.S.A. 164 D2
Grand Canal Ireland 61 E4
Grand Canary i. Canary Is see Gran Canaria
Grand Canyon AZ U.S.A. 159 G3
Grand Canyon gorge AZ U.S.A. 159 G3
Grand Canyon National Park AZ U.S.A. 159 G3
Grand Canyon - Parashant National Monument nat. park AZ U.S.A. 159 G3
Grand Cayman i. Cayman Is 169 H5
Grand Drumont mt. France 57 K7
Grande r. Bahia Brazil 179 B1
Grande r. São Paulo Brazil 179 A3
Grande r. Nicaragua 166 [inset] J6
Grande, Bahía b. Arg. 178 C8
Grande, Cerro mt. Mex. 167 F5
Grande, Ilha i. Brazil 179 B3
Grande Cache Canada 150 G4
Grande Comore i. Comoros see Ngazidja
Grande Prairie Canada 150 G4
Grand Erg de Bilma des. Niger 120 E3
Grand Erg Occidental des. Alg. 64 D5
Grand Erg Oriental des. Alg. 64 F6
Grande-Rivière Canada 153 I4
Grandes, Salinas salt marsh Arg. 178 C4
Gran Desierto del Pinacate, Parque Natural del nature res. Mex. 166 B2
Grande-Vallée Canada 153 I4
Grand Falls Canada 153 I5
Grand Falls-Windsor Canada 153 L4
Grand Forks Canada 150 G5
Grand Forks ND U.S.A. 160 D2
Grand Gorge NY U.S.A. 165 H2
Grand Haven MI U.S.A. 164 B2
Grandin, Lac l. Canada 150 G1
Grandioznyy, Pik mt. Rus. Fed. 88 H2
Grand Island NE U.S.A. 160 D3
Grand Isle LA U.S.A. 161 F6
Grand Junction CO U.S.A. 159 I2
Grand Lac Germain l. Canada 153 I4
Grand-Lahou Côte d'Ivoire 120 C4
Grand Lake N.B. Canada 153 I5
Grand Lake Nfld. and Lab. Canada 153 J3
Grand Lake Nfld. and Lab. Canada 153 K4
Grand Lake LA U.S.A. 161 E6
Grand Lake MI U.S.A. 164 D1
Grand Lake St Marys OH U.S.A. 164 C3
Grand Ledge MI U.S.A. 164 C2
Grand Manan Island Canada 153 I5
Grand Marais MI U.S.A. 162 C2
Grand Marais MN U.S.A. 160 F2
Grand-Mère Canada 153 G5
Grand Mesa CO U.S.A. 159 J2
Grândola Port. 67 B4
Grand Passage New Caledonia 133 G3
Grand Rapids Canada 151 L4
Grand Rapids MI U.S.A. 164 C2
Grand Rapids MN U.S.A. 160 E2
Grand-Sault Canada see Grand Falls
Grand St-Bernard, Col du pass Italy/Switz. see Great St Bernard Pass
Grand Teton mt. WY U.S.A. 156 F4
Grand Teton National Park WY U.S.A. 156 F4
Grand Traverse Bay MI U.S.A. 164 C1
▶Grand Turk Turks and Caicos Is 169 J4
Capital of the Turks and Caicos Islands.
Grandville MI U.S.A. 164 C2
Grandvilliers France 62 B5
Grand Wash Cliffs mts AZ U.S.A. 159 F4
Grange Ireland 61 E6
Grängesberg Sweden 55 I6
Grangeville ID U.S.A. 156 D3
Granisle Canada 150 E4
Granite Falls MN U.S.A. 160 E2
Granite Mountain hill AK U.S.A. 148 G2
Granite Mountain hill AK U.S.A. 148 H3
Granite Mountain NV U.S.A. 158 E1
Granite Mountains CA U.S.A. 159 F4
Granite Mountains CA U.S.A. 159 F5
Granite Peak MT U.S.A. 156 F3
Granite Peak UT U.S.A. 159 G1
Granite Range mts AK U.S.A. 149 K4
Granite Range mts NV U.S.A. 158 D1
Granitola, Capo c. Sicily Italy 68 E6
Granja Brazil 177 J4
Gran Laguna Salada l. Arg. 178 C6
Gränna Sweden 55 I7
Gran Paradiso mt. Italy 68 B2
Gran Paradiso, Parco Nazionale del nat. park Italy 68 B2
Gran Pilastro mt. Austria/Italy 57 M7
Gran San Bernardo, Colle del pass Italy/Switz. see Great St Bernard Pass
Gran Sasso e Monti della Laga, Parco Nazionale del nat. park Italy 68 E3
Granschütz Germany 63 M3
Gransee Germany 63 N1
Grant NE U.S.A. 160 C3
Grant, Mount NV U.S.A. 158 E2
Grant Creek AK U.S.A. 148 I2
Grantham U.K. 59 G6
Grant Island Antarctica 188 J2
Grant Lake Canada 150 G1
Grantown-on-Spey U.K. 60 F3
Grant Range mts NV U.S.A. 159 F2
Grants NM U.S.A. 159 J4
Grants Pass OR U.S.A. 156 C4
Grantsville UT U.S.A. 159 G1
Grantsville WV U.S.A. 164 E4
Granville France 66 D2
Granville AZ U.S.A. 159 I5
Granville NY U.S.A. 165 I2
Granville TN U.S.A. 164 C5
Granville (abandoned) Canada 149 M3
Granville Lake Canada 151 K3
Grão Mogol Brazil 179 C2
Grapevine Mountains NV U.S.A. 158 E3
Gras, Lac de l. Canada 151 I1
Graskop S. Africa 125 J3
Grasplatz Namibia 124 B4
Grass r. Canada 151 L3
Grass r. NY U.S.A. 165 H1
Grasse France 66 H5
Grassflat PA U.S.A. 165 F3
Grassington U.K. 58 F4
Grasslands National Park Canada 151 J5
Grassrange MT U.S.A. 156 F3
Grass Valley CA U.S.A. 158 C2
Grassy Butte ND U.S.A. 160 C2
Grästorp Sweden 55 H7
Gratz KY U.S.A. 164 C4
Graudenz Poland see Grudziądz
Graus Spain 67 G2
Gravataí Brazil 179 A5
Grave, Pointe de pt France 66 D4
Gravelbourg Canada 151 J5
Gravel Hill Lake Canada 151 K2
Gravelines France 62 C4
Gravelotte S. Africa 125 J2
Gravenhurst Canada 164 F1
Grave Peak ID U.S.A. 156 E3
Gravesend Australia 138 E2
Gravesend U.K. 59 H7
Gravina in Puglia Italy 68 G4
Grawn MI U.S.A. 164 C1
Gray France 66 G3
Gray GA U.S.A. 163 D5
Gray KY U.S.A. 164 C5
Gray ME U.S.A. 165 J2
Grayback Mountain OR U.S.A. 156 C4
Gray Lake Canada 151 I2

Gushan China 91 A5
Gushgy Turkm. see Serhetabat
Gushi China 97 G1
Gusino Rus. Fed. 53 F5
Gusinoozersk Rus. Fed. 94 F1
Gusinoye, Ozero l. Rus. Fed. 94 F1
Gus'-Khrustal'nyy Rus. Fed. 52 I5
Guspini Sardinia Italy 68 C5
Gustav Holm, Kap c. Greenland see Tasiilap Karra
Gustavo Sotelo Mex. 166 B2
Gustavus AK U.S.A. 149 N4
Güsten Germany 63 L3
Gustine CA U.S.A. 158 C3
Güstrow Germany 57 N4
Gutang China 99 F7
Güterfelde Germany 63 N2
Gütersloh Germany 63 I3
Guthrie AZ U.S.A. 159 I5
Guthrie KY U.S.A. 164 B5
Guthrie OK U.S.A. 161 D5
Guthrie TX U.S.A. 161 C5
Guting China see Yutai
Gutsuo China 105 F3
Guwahati India 105 G4
Guwēr Iraq 113 F3
Guwlumayak Turkm. see Guwlumaýak
Guwlumaýak Turkm. 110 D1
Guxhagen Germany 63 J3
Guxian China 97 G3
Guyana country S. America 177 G2
Guyane Française terr. S. America see French Guiana
Guyang Hunan China see Guzhang
Guyang Nei Mongol China 95 G3
Guyenne reg. France 66 C4
Guy Fawkes River National Park Australia 138 F3
Guyi China see Sanjiang
Guymon OK U.S.A. 161 C4
Guyot Glacier Canada/U.S.A. 149 L3
Guyra Australia 138 E3
Guyuan Hebei China 95 H4
Guyuan Ningxia China 94 F5
Güzeloluk Turkey 107 B1
Guzhang China 97 F7
Guzhen China 97 H1
Guzhou China see Rongjiang
Guzmán Mex. 166 D2
Guzmán, Lago l. Mex. 166 D2
G'uzor Uzbek. 111 G2
Gvardeysk Rus. Fed. 55 L9
Gvasyugi Rus. Fed. 90 E3
Gwa Myanmar 86 A3
Gwabegar Australia 138 D3
Gwadar West Bay Pak. 111 F5
Gwaii Haanas Canada 149 N5
Gwaii Haanas National Park Reserve and Haida Heritage Site Canada 150 D4
Gwaldam India 99 B7
Gwal Haidarzai Pak. 111 H4
Gwalior India 104 D4
Gwanda Zimbabwe 123 C6
Gwane Dem. Rep. Congo 122 C3
Gwardafuy, Gees c. Somalia 122 F2
Gwash Pak. 111 G4
Gwatar Bay Pak. 111 F5
Gwedaukkon Myanmar 86 A1
Gweebarra Bay Ireland 61 D3
Gwelo Zimbabwe see Gweru
Gweru Zimbabwe 123 C5
Gweta Botswana 123 C6
Gwinner ND U.S.A. 160 D2
Gwoza Nigeria 120 E3
Gwydir r. Australia 138 D2
Gyablung China 99 F7
Gyaca China 99 F7
Gyaco China 99 F7
Gyagartang China 96 D1
Gyaijêpozhanggê China see Zhidoi
Gyai Qu r. China 99 F7
Gyaisi China see Jiulong
Gyali i. Greece 69 L6
Gyamug China 99 D7
Gyandzha Azer. see Gäncä
Gyangnyi Caka salt l. China 99 D6
Gyangrang China 99 D7
Gyangtse China see Gyangzê
Gyangzê China 99 E7
Gya'nyima China 99 C7
Gyaring China 94 D3
Gyaring Co l. China 99 E7
Gyaring Hu l. China 94 D5
Gyarishing India 96 B2
Gyaros i. Greece 69 K6
Gyarubtang China 96 B2
Gydan, Khrebet mts Rus. Fed. see Kolymskiy, Khrebet
Gydan Peninsula Rus. Fed. 76 I2
Gydanskiy Poluostrov pen. Rus. Fed. see Gydan Peninsula
Gyêgu China see Yushu
Gyêmdong China 99 F7
Gyêsar Co l. China 99 D7
Gyêwa China see Zabqung
Gyigang China 96 C2
Gyimda China 99 F7
Gyipug China 99 C6
Gyirong Xizang China 99 D7
Gyirong Xizang China 99 D7
Gyixong China see Gonggar
Gyiza China 99 F6
Gyldenløve Fjord inlet Greenland see Umiiviip Kangertiva
Gympie Australia 137 F5
Gyobingauk Myanmar 86 A3
Gyôda Japan 93 F3
Gyöngyös Hungary 57 Q7
Győr Hungary 68 G1
Gypsum Point Canada 150 H2
Gypsumville Canada 151 L5
Gyrfalcon Islands Canada 153 H2
Gytheio Greece 69 J6
Gyula Hungary 69 I1
Gyulafehérvár Romania see Alba Iulia
Gyümai China see Darlag
Gyumri Armenia 113 F2
Gyungcang China 99 B6
Gyzylarbat Turkm. see Serdar

Gyzylbaýdak Turkm. 111 F2
Gyzylbaýdak Turkm. see Gyzylbaýdak
Gzhatsk Rus. Fed. see Gagarin

Ha Bhutan 105 G4
Haa-Alif Atoll Maldives see Ihavandhippolhu Atoll
Haanhöhiy Uul mts Mongolia 94 C1
Ha'apai Group is Tonga 133 I3
Haapajärvi Fin. 54 N5
Haapavesi Fin. 54 N4
Haapsalu Estonia 55 M7
Ha 'Arava watercourse Israel/Jordan see 'Arabah, Wādī al
Ha'Arava, Naḥal watercourse Israel/Jordan see Jayb, Wādī al
Haarlem Neth. 62 E2
Haarlem S. Africa 124 F7
Haarstrang ridge Germany 63 H3
Hab r. Pak. 111 G5
Habahe China 98 D2
Habana Cuba see Havana
Habarane Sri Lanka 106 D4
Habarōn well Saudi Arabia 110 C6
Habaswein Kenya 122 D3
Habay Canada 150 G3
Habbān Yemen 108 G7
Ḥabbānīyah, Hawr al l. Iraq 113 F4
Hab Chauki Pak. 111 G5
Habiganj Bangl. 105 G4
Habikino Japan 92 B4
Habirag China 95 H3
Habra India 105 G5
Hachibuse-yama mt. Japan 93 E2
Hachijō-jima i. Japan 91 E6
Hachiman Japan 92 C3
Hachiman-misaki c. Japan 93 G3
Hachimori-yama mt. Japan 92 D2
Hachinohe Japan 90 F4
Hachiōji Japan 93 F3
Hachita NM U.S.A. 159 I6
Hacıköy Turkey see Çekerek
Hack, Mount Australia 137 B6
Hackberry AZ U.S.A. 159 G4
Hackensack NJ U.S.A. 165 H3
Hacufera Moz. 123 D6
Ḥaḍabat al Jilf al Kabīr plat. Egypt see Jilf al Kabīr, Haḍabat al
Hadadong China 98 C4
Hadagalli India 106 B3
Hadano Japan 93 F3
Hadapu China 94 F5
Hadat China 95 I1
Hadayang China 95 K1
Ḥadd, Ra's al pt Oman 111 E6
Haddington U.K. 60 G5
Haddumati Atoll Maldives see Hadhdhunmathi Atoll
Haddunmati Atoll Maldives see Hadhdhunmathi Atoll
Hadejia Nigeria 120 E3
Hadera r. Israel 107 B3
Haderslev Denmark 55 F9
Hadhdhunmathi Atoll Maldives 103 D11
Hadhramaut reg. Yemen see Ḥaḍramawt
Ḥāḍī, Jabal al imt. Jordan 107 C4
Hadilik China 99 D5
Ḥadīm Turkey 112 D3
Hadleigh U.K. 59 H6
Hadong S. Korea 91 B6
Ḥadraj, Wādī watercourse Saudi Arabia 107 C4
Ḥaḍramawt reg. Yemen 122 E2
Hadranum Sicily Italy see Adrano
Hadrian's Wall tourist site U.K. 58 E3
Hadrumetum Tunisia see Sousse
Hadsund Denmark 55 G8
Hadweenzic r. AK U.S.A. 149 K2
Haeju N. Korea 91 B5
Haeju-man b. N. Korea 91 B5
Haenam S. Korea 91 B6
Haenertsburg S. Africa 125 I2
Ha'erbin China see Harbin
Ḥafar al 'Atk well Saudi Arabia 110 B5
Ḥafar al Bāṭin Saudi Arabia 108 G4
Hafford Canada 151 J4
Hafik Turkey 112 E3
Ḥafīrah, Qā' al salt pan Jordan 107 C4
Hafizabad Pak. 111 I3
Haflong India 105 H4
Hafnarfjörður Iceland 54 [inset 1]
Hafren r. U.K. see Severn
Haft Gel Iran 110 C4
Hafursfjörður b. Iceland 54 [inset 1]
Haga Myanmar see Haka
Hagachi-zaki pt Japan 93 F3
Hagar Nish Plateau Eritrea 108 E6

▶Hagåtña Guam 81 K4
Capital of Guam.

Hagelberg hill Germany 63 M2
Hagemeister Island AK U.S.A. 148 G4
Hagemeister Strait AK U.S.A. 148 G4
Hagen Germany 63 H3
Hagenow Germany 63 L1
Hagerhill KY U.S.A. 164 D5
Hagerstown MD U.S.A. 165 G4
Hagfors Sweden 55 H6
Haggin, Mount MT U.S.A. 156 E3
Hagi Japan 91 C6
Ha Giang Vietnam 86 D2
Hagiwara Japan 92 D3
Hagley U.K. 59 E6
Hag's Head hd Ireland 61 C5
Hague NY U.S.A. 165 I2
Hague U.K. 59 E6
Haguenau France 63 H6
Hahajima-rettō is Japan 91 F8
Hahoe tourist site S. Korea 91 C5
Hai Tanz. 121 G5
Hai, Ko i. Thai. 84 B1
Hai'an China 97 I4
Haib watercourse Namibia 124 C5
Haibara Nara Japan 92 B4
Haibara Shizuoka Japan 93 E4
Haibowan China see Wuhai
Haicheng Guangdong China see Haifeng

Haicheng Liaoning China 95 J3
Haicheng Ningxia China see Haiyuan
Haida Gwaii Canada 149 N5
Haiding Hu salt l. China 94 C5
Hai Dương Vietnam 86 D2
Haifa Israel 107 B3
Haifa, Bay of Israel 107 B3
Haifeng China 97 G4
Haig Australia 135 D7
Haiger Germany 63 I4
Haihu China 94 E4
Haikakan country Asia see Armenia
Haikang China see Leizhou
Haikou China 97 F5
Hailar China see Hulun Buir
Hailin China 90 C3
Hailong China see Meihekou
Hails China 95 I3
Hailsham U.K. 59 H8
Hailun China 90 B3
Hailuoto Fin. 54 N4
Hainan prov. China 97 F5
Hainan Dao i. China 97 F5
Hainan Strait China 97 F5
Hainaut reg. France 62 D4
Haines AK U.S.A. 149 N4
Haines Junction Canada 149 M3
Haines Road Canada/U.S.A. 149 M3
Hainichen Germany 63 N4
Hainleite ridge Germany 63 K3
Hai Phong Vietnam 86 D2
Haiphong Vietnam see Hai Phong
Haiqing China 90 D3
Hairag China 94 E4
Haitan China see Sanmen
Haitan Dao i. China 97 H3
Haitangwan China 97 F5
Haiti country West Indies 169 J5
Haitou China 97 F5
Hai Triều Vietnam 86 D2
Haiwee Reservoir CA U.S.A. 158 E3
Haiya Sudan 108 F6
Haiyan Qinghai China 94 E4
Haiyan Zhejiang China 97 I2
Haiyang Anhui China see Xiuning
Haiyang Shandong China 95 J4
Haiyang Dao i. China 91 A5
Haiyou China see Sanmen
Haiyuan China 94 F4
Haizhou Wan b. China 95 I5
Hajdúböszörmény Hungary 69 I1
Hajeb El Ayoun Tunisia 68 C7
Hajhir mt. Yemen 109 H7
Haji Mahesar Pak. 111 G4
Hajipur India 105 F4
Hajir reg. Saudi Arabia 110 C5
Ḥājj 'Alī Qolī, Kavīr-e salt l. Iran 110 D3
Ḥājjīābād Fārs Iran 110 D4
Ḥājjīābād Hormozgān Iran 110 D4
Ḥājjīābād Yazd Iran 110 D3
Haju China 94 D3
Hajuu-Us Mongolia see Govĭ-Ugtaal
Haka Myanmar 86 A2
Hakha Myanmar see Haka
Hakkâri Turkey 113 F3
Hakkas Sweden 54 L3
Hakken-zan mt. Japan 92 B4
Hakkō-san hill Japan 92 C2
Hako-dake mt. Japan 90 F3
Hakodate Japan 90 F4
Hakone Japan 93 F3
Hakone-tōge pass Japan 93 F3
Hakos Mountains Namibia 124 C2
Hakseen Pan salt pan S. Africa 124 E4
Hakuba Japan 93 D2
Hakui Japan 92 C2
Hakusan Japan 92 C2
Haku-san vol. Japan 92 C2
Haku-san Kokuritsu-kōen nat. park Japan 92 C2
Hakushū Japan 93 E3
Hal Belgium see Halle
Hala Pak. 111 H5
Halab Syria see Aleppo
Halabja Iraq 113 G4
Halaç Turkm. see Halaç
Halaç Turkm. 111 G2
Halachó Mex. 167 H4
Halahai China 90 B3
Halaib Sudan 108 E5
Halaib Triangle terr. Egypt 108 E5
Halāl, Gebel hill Egypt see Hilāl, Jabal
Ha Lam Vietnam 86 E4
Hālaniyāt, Juzur al is Oman 109 I6
Hālawa HI U.S.A. 157 [inset]
Halba Lebanon 107 C2
Halban Mongolia see Tsetserleg
Halberstadt Germany 63 L3
Halcon, Mount Mindoro Phil. 82 C3
Haldane r. Canada 150 G1
Halden Norway 55 G7
Haldensleben Germany 63 L2
Haldwani India 104 D3
Hale watercourse Australia 136 A4
Hale China 95 G3
Hale MT U.S.A. 164 D2
Hāleh Iran 110 D5
Haleparki Deresi r. Syria/Turkey see Quwayq, Nahr
Halesowen U.K. 59 E6
Halesworth U.K. 59 I6
Half Assini Ghana 120 C4
Halfmoon Bay N.Z. 139 B8
Halfway r. Canada 150 F3
Halfway Ireland 61 D6
Halfway Mountain hill AK U.S.A. 148 I3
Halfweg Neth. 62 E2
Halhgol Dornod Mongolia 95 I2
Halhgol Dornod Mongolia 95 I2
Halia India 105 E4
Ḥalībīyah Syria 113 E4
Haliburton Canada 165 F1
Haliburton Highlands hills Canada 165 F1
Halicarnassus Turkey see Bodrum

▶Halifax Canada 153 J5
Capital of Nova Scotia.

Halifax U.K. 58 F5
Halifax NC U.S.A. 162 E4
Halifax VA U.S.A. 165 F5
Halifax, Mount Australia 136 D3
Halik Shan mts China 98 C4
Halilulik Timor Indon. 83 C5
Ḥalīmah, mt. Lebanon/Syria 107 C2
Haliut China 95 G3
Halkett, Cape AK U.S.A. 148 I1
Halkirk U.K. 60 F2
Hall KY U.S.A. 164 C5
Hall r. China 90 E3
Hälla Sweden 54 J5
Halladale r. U.K. 60 F2
Halla-san National Park S. Korea 91 B6
Hall Beach Canada 147 J3
Halle Belgium 62 E4
Halle Neth. 62 G3
Halleck NV U.S.A. 159 F1
Hällefors Sweden 55 I7
Hallein Austria 57 N7
Halle-Neustadt Germany 63 L3
Halle (Saale) Germany 63 L3
Hallett, Cape Antarctica 188 H2
Hallettsville TX U.S.A. 161 D6
Halley research station Antarctica 188 B1
Hallgreen, Mount Antarctica 188 B2
Halliday ND U.S.A. 160 C2
Halliday Lake Canada 151 I2
Hall Island AK U.S.A. 148 D3
Hall Islands Micronesia 186 G5
Hällnäs Sweden 54 K4
Hallock MN U.S.A. 160 D1
Hall Peninsula Canada 147 L3
Halls Creek Australia 134 D4
Halls Lake Canada 165 F1
Hallstead PA U.S.A. 165 H3
Halluin Belgium 62 D4
Hallviken Sweden 54 I5
Halmahera i. Maluku Indon. 83 D2
Halmahera, Laut sea Maluku Indon. 83 D3
Halmahera Sea Maluku Indon. see Halmahera, Laut
Halmstad Sweden 55 H8
Ha Long Vietnam 86 D2
Hals Denmark 55 G8
Hälsingborg Sweden see Helsingborg
Halsua Fin. 54 N5
Haltang He r. China 94 C4
Haltern Germany 63 H3
Haltunchén Mex. 167 H5
Haltwhistle U.K. 58 E4
Ḥālūl i. Qatar 110 D5
Halura i. Indon. 83 B5
Halvān Iran 110 E3
Halver Germany 63 H3
Haly, Mount hill Australia 138 E1
Ham France 62 D5
Hama Japan 91 D6
Hamada El Haricha des. Mali 120 C2
Hamadān Iran 110 C3
Ḥamādat Murzuq plat. Libya 122 B1
Ḥamāh Syria 107 C2
Hamajima Japan 92 C4
Hamakita Japan 93 D4
Hamam Turkey 107 C1
Hamamatsu Japan 92 D4
Hamana-ko l. Japan 92 D4
Hamaoka Japan 93 E4
Hamar Norway 55 G6
Hamaröy Norway 54 I2
Ḥamāta, Gebel mt. Egypt see Ḥamāṭah, Jabal
Ḥamāṭah, Jabal mt. Egypt 108 D5
Hamatonbetsu Japan 90 F3
Hambantota Sri Lanka 106 D5
Hambergen Germany 63 I1
Hambleton U.K. 58 F4
Hamburg Germany 63 J1
Hamburg S. Africa 125 H7
Hamburg AR U.S.A. 161 F5
Hamburg NY U.S.A. 165 F2
Hamburgisches Wattenmeer, Nationalpark nat. park Germany 63 I1
Ḥamḍ, Wādī al watercourse Saudi Arabia 108 E4
Hamden CT U.S.A. 165 I3
Hāmeenlinna Fin. 55 N6
HaMelaḥ, Yam salt l. Asia see Dead Sea
Hamelin Australia 135 A6
Hameln Germany 63 J2
Hamersley Lakes salt flat Australia 135 B7
Hamersley Range mts Australia 134 B5
Hamhŭng N. Korea 91 B5
Hami China 94 D3
Hamid Sudan 108 D5
Hamilton Australia 136 C4
Hamilton Qld Australia 137 A5
Hamilton S.A. Australia 137 A5
Hamilton Vic. Australia 136 C4
Hamilton watercourse Qld Australia 136 B4
Hamilton watercourse S.A. Australia 137 A5

▶Hamilton Bermuda 169 L2
Capital of Bermuda.

Hamilton Canada 164 F2
Hamilton r. Canada see Churchill
Hamilton N.Z. 139 E3
Hamilton U.K. 60 E5
Hamilton AL U.S.A. 163 C5
Hamilton CO U.S.A. 159 J1
Hamilton MI U.S.A. 164 B2
Hamilton MT U.S.A. 156 E3
Hamilton NY U.S.A. 165 H2
Hamilton OH U.S.A. 164 C4
Hamilton TX U.S.A. 161 D6
Hamilton, Mount AK U.S.A. 148 H3
Hamilton, Mount CA U.S.A. 158 C3
Hamilton, Mount NV U.S.A. 159 F2
Hamilton City CA U.S.A. 158 B2
Hamilton Inlet Canada 153 K3
Hamilton Mountain hill NY U.S.A. 165 H2
Hamīm, Wādī al watercourse Libya 65 I5
Hamina Fin. 55 N6
Hamirpur Hima. Prad. India 104 D3
Hamirpur Uttar Prad. India 104 E4
Hamitabat Turkey see Isparta
Hamju N. Korea 91 B5
Hamlet NC U.S.A. 163 E5
Hamlin TX U.S.A. 161 C5
Hamlin WV U.S.A. 164 D4
Hamm Germany 63 H3
Hammām al 'Alīl Iraq 113 F3

Hammam Boughrara Alg. 67 F6
Hammamet Tunisia 68 D6
Hammamet, Golfe de g. Tunisia 68 D6
Ḥammār, Hawr al imp. l. Iraq 113 G5
Hammarstrand Sweden 54 J5
Hammelburg Germany 63 J4
Hammerdal Sweden 54 I5
Hammerfest Norway 54 M1
Hamminkeln Germany 62 G3
Hammond IN U.S.A. 164 B3
Hammond LA U.S.A. 161 F6
Hammond NJ U.S.A. 165 H4
Hammondsport NY U.S.A. 165 G2
Hammone, Lac l. Canada 153 K4
Hamoir Belgium 62 F4
Hampden Sydney VA U.S.A. 165 F5
Hampshire Downs hills U.K. 59 F7
Hampton AR U.S.A. 161 E5
Hampton IA U.S.A. 160 E3
Hampton NH U.S.A. 165 J2
Hampton SC U.S.A. 163 D5
Hampton VA U.S.A. 165 G5
Hampton Tableland reg. Australia 135 D8
Ḥamrā, Birkat al well Saudi Arabia 113 F5
Hamra, Vādīi watercourse Syria/Turkey see Ḥimār, Wādī al
Hamrā jūdah plat. Saudi Arabia 110 C5
Ḥamrat esh Sheikh Sudan 108 C7
Hamta Pass India 104 D3
Hāmūn-e Jaz Mūriān salt marsh Iran 110 E5
Hāmūn-e Lowrah dry lake Afgh./Pak. see Hamun-i-Lora
Hāmūn-e Ṣāberī marsh Afgh./Iran 111 F3
Hamun-i-Lora dry lake Afgh./Pak. 111 F4
Hamun-i-Mashkel salt flat Pak. 111 F4
Hamunt Kūh hill Iran 111 F5
Hamura Japan 93 F3
Hamur Turkey 113 F3
Han r. China see Southampton
Hāna HI U.S.A. 157 [inset]
Hanábana r. Cuba 163 D8
Hanahai watercourse Botswana/Namibia 124 E2
Ḥanak Saudi Arabia 108 E4
Hanakpınar Turkey see Çınar
Hanalei HI U.S.A. 157 [inset]
Hanamaki Japan 91 F5
Hanamigawa Japan 93 G3
Hanang mt. Tanz. 123 D4
Hanau Germany 63 I4
Hanawa Japan 93 G2
Hanbin China see Ankang
Hanbogd Mongolia 95 G3
Hanchang China see Pingjiang
Hancheng China 95 G5
Hanchuan China 97 G2
Hancock MD U.S.A. 165 F4
Hancock NY U.S.A. 165 H3
Handa Japan 92 D4
Handa Island U.K. 60 D2
Handan China 95 H4
Handeni Tanz. 123 D4
Handian China see Changzhi
Haneda airport Japan 93 F3
HaNegev des. Israel see Negev
HaNeqarot watercourse Israel 107 B4
Hanfeng China see Kaixian
Hanford CA U.S.A. 158 D3
Hangan Myanmar 86 B4
Hangayn Nuruu mts Mongolia 94 D1
Hangchow China see Hangzhou
Hangchuan China see Guangze
Hanggin Houqi China see Xamba
Hanggin Qi China see Xin
Hangö Fin. see Hanko
Hangu China 95 I4
Hanguang China 97 G3
Hangya China 94 D4
Hangzhou China 97 I2
Hangzhou Wan b. China 97 I2
Hani Turkey 113 F3
Hanish Kabir i. Yemen see Suyūl Ḥanīsh
Hanji China see Linxia
Hanjia China see Pengshui
Hanjiaoshui China 94 F4
Hankensbüttel Germany 63 K2
Hankey S. Africa 124 G7
Hanko Fin. 55 M7
Hanksville UT U.S.A. 159 H2
Hanle India 104 D2
Hanley Canada 151 J5
Hann, Mount hill Australia 134 D3
Hanna Canada 151 I5
Hannagan Meadow AZ U.S.A. 159 I5
Hannah Bay Canada 152 E4
Hannibal MO U.S.A. 160 F4
Hannibal NY U.S.A. 165 G2
Hannô Japan 93 F3
Hannover Germany 63 J2
Hanover Germany see Hannover
Hanover S. Africa 124 G6
Hanover NH U.S.A. 165 I2
Hanover PA U.S.A. 165 G4
Hanover VA U.S.A. 165 G5
Hansen Mountains Antarctica 188 D2
Hanshou China 97 F2
Han Shui r. China 97 G2
Hansi India 104 D3
Hansnes Norway 54 K2
Hanstholm Denmark 55 F8
Han Sum China 95 I2
Han-sur-Nied France 62 G6
Hantsavichy Belarus 55 O10
Hanumangarh India 104 C3
Hanwood Australia 138 C5
Hanxia China 94 D4
Hanyang China see Caidian
Hanyang Feng mt. China 97 G2
Hanyin China 97 F1
Hanyü Japan 93 F3
Hanzhong China 96 E1
Hao atoll Fr. Polynesia 187 K7

Haomen China see Menyuan
Haora India 105 G5
Haparanda Sweden 54 N4
Happy Jack AZ U.S.A. 159 H4
Happy Valley-Goose Bay Canada 153 J3
Hapur India 99 B7
Ḥaql Saudi Arabia 107 B5
Haqshah well Saudi Arabia 110 C6
Ḥaraḍ well Saudi Arabia 110 C5
Ḥarad, Jabal al mt. Jordan 107 B5
Ḥaraḍh Saudi Arabia 108 G5
Haradok Belarus 53 F5
Haramachi Japan 91 F5
Haramgai China 98 D3
Haramukh mt. India 104 C2
Haran Turkey see Harran
Harappa Road Pak. 111 I4
Harar Eth. see Härer

▶Harare Zimbabwe 123 D5
Capital of Zimbabwe.

Ḥarāsīs, Jiddat al des. Oman 109 I6
Harāt Iran 110 D4
Har-Ayrag Mongolia 95 G2
Haraze-Mangueigne Chad 121 F3
Harb, Jabal mt. Saudi Arabia 112 D6
Harbin China 90 B3
Harboi Hills Pak. 111 G4
Harbor Beach MI U.S.A. 164 D2
Harchoka India 105 E5
Harda India 104 D5
Harda Khas India see Harda
Hardangerfjorden sea chan. Norway 55 D6
Hardangervidda plat. Norway 55 E6
Hardangervidda Nasjonalpark nat. park Norway 55 E6
Hardap admin. reg. Namibia 124 C3
Hardap nature res. Namibia 124 C3
Hardap Dam Namibia 124 C3
Harden, Bukit mt. Indon. 85 F1
Hardenberg Neth. 62 G2
Harderwijk Neth. 62 F2
Hardeveld mts S. Africa 124 D6
Hardin MT U.S.A. 156 G3
Harding S. Africa 125 I6
Harding Ice Field AK U.S.A. 149 J3
Harding Range hills Australia 135 B6
Hardinsburg IN U.S.A. 164 B4
Hardinsburg KY U.S.A. 164 B5
Hardoi India 104 E4
Hardwar India see Haridwar
Hardwick VT U.S.A. 165 I1
Hardy AR U.S.A. 161 F4
Hardy Reservoir MI U.S.A. 164 C2
Hare Bay Canada 153 L4
Ḥareidīn, Wādī watercourse Egypt see Ḥuraydīn, Wādī
Hare Indian r. Canada 149 O2
Harelbeke Belgium 62 D4
Haren Neth. 62 G1
Haren (Ems) Germany 63 H2
Härer Eth. 122 E3
Harf el Mreffi mt. Lebanon 107 B3
Hargant China 95 I1
Hargeisa Somalia see Hargeysa
Hargele Eth. 122 E3

▶Hargeysa Somalia 122 E3
Capital of Somaliland.

Harghita-Mădăraş, Vârful mt. Romania 69 K1
Harhatan China 95 F4
Harhorin Mongolia 94 E2
Har Hu l. China 94 D4
Haridwar India 104 D3
Ḥarif, Har mt. Israel 107 B4
Harihar India 106 B3
Harihari N.Z. 139 C6
Ḥārim Syria 107 C1
Ḥarīm, Jabal al mt. Oman 110 E5
Harima Japan 92 A4
Harima-nada b. Japan 92 A4
Haringhat r. Bangl. 105 G5
Haringvliet est. Neth. 62 E3
Harinoki-dake mt. Japan 92 D2
Ḥarīr, Wādī adh r. Syria 107 C3
Harī Rūd r. Afgh./Iran 111 F3
Harjavalta Fin. 55 M6
Harlan IA U.S.A. 160 E3
Harlan KY U.S.A. 164 D5
Harlan County Lake NE U.S.A. 160 D3
Harlech U.K. 59 C6
Harleston U.K. 59 I6
Harlingen Neth. 62 F1
Harlingen TX U.S.A. 161 D7
Harlow U.K. 59 H7
Harlowton MT U.S.A. 156 F3
Harly France 62 D5
Harman WV U.S.A. 164 F4
Harmancık Turkey 69 M5
Harmony ME U.S.A. 165 K1
Harmsdorf Germany 63 K1
Harnai India 106 B2
Harnai Pak. 111 G4
Harnes France 62 C4
Harney Basin OR U.S.A. 156 D4
Harney Lake OR U.S.A. 156 D4
Härnösand Sweden 54 J5
Harns Neth. see Harlingen
Har Nuden China 95 I1
Har Nuur l. Mongolia 94 C1
Har Nuur l. Mongolia 94 D1
Haroldswick U.K. 60 [inset]
Harper Liberia 120 C4
Harper KS U.S.A. 161 D4
Harper, Mount Canada 149 M2
Harper, Mount AK U.S.A. 149 L2
Harper Bend Canada 150 D3
Harper Creek r. Canada 150 H3
Harper Lake CA U.S.A. 158 E4
Harp Lake Canada 153 J3
Harqin Qi China see Jinshan
Harqin Zuoqi Mongolzu Zizhixian China see Dachengzi
Harquahala Mountains AZ U.S.A. 157 E6
Harrai India 104 D5
Harran Turkey 107 D1
Harrand Pak. 111 H4

Harricana, Rivière d' r. Canada 152 F4
Harrington Australia 138 F3
Harrington DE U.S.A. 165 H4
Harris, Lake salt flat Australia 137 A6
Harris, Mount Australia 135 E6
Harris, Sound of sea chan. U.K. 60 B3
Harrisburg AR U.S.A. 161 F5
Harrisburg IL U.S.A. 160 F4
Harrisburg NE U.S.A. 160 C3
▶Harrisburg PA U.S.A. 165 G3
Capital of Pennsylvania.
Harrismith Australia 135 B8
Harrison AR U.S.A. 161 E4
Harrison MI U.S.A. 164 C1
Harrison NE U.S.A. 160 C3
Harrison OH U.S.A. 164 C4
Harrison, Cape Canada 153 K3
Harrison Bay AK U.S.A. 149 J1
Harrisonburg LA U.S.A. 161 F6
Harrisonburg VA U.S.A. 165 F4
Harrisonville MO U.S.A. 160 E4
Harriston Canada 164 E2
Harrisville MI U.S.A. 164 D1
Harrisville NY U.S.A. 165 H1
Harrisville PA U.S.A. 164 E3
Harrisville WV U.S.A. 164 E4
Harrodsburg IN U.S.A. 164 B4
Harrodsburg KY U.S.A. 164 C5
Harrodsville N.Z. see Otorohanga
Harrogate U.K. 58 F5
Harrowsmith Canada 165 G1
Harry S. Truman Reservoir MO U.S.A. 160 E4
Har Sai Shan mt. China 94 D5
Harsefeld Germany 63 J1
Harsīn Iran 110 B3
Harşit r. Turkey 112 E2
Hârşova Romania 69 L2
Harstad Norway 54 J2
Harsud India 104 D5
Harsum Germany 63 J2
Hart r. Canada 146 E3
Hart MI U.S.A. 164 B2
Hartao China 95 J3
Hartbees watercourse S. Africa 124 E5
Hartberg Austria 57 O7
Harteigan mt. Norway 55 E6
Haute-Normandie admin. reg. France
Harter Fell hill U.K. 58 E4
▶Hartford CT U.S.A. 165 I3
Capital of Connecticut.
Hartford KY U.S.A. 164 B5
Hartford MI U.S.A. 164 B2
Hartford City IN U.S.A. 164 C3
Hartland U.K. 59 C8
Hartland ME U.S.A. 165 K1
Hartland Point U.K. 59 C7
Hartlepool U.K. 58 F4
Hartley TX U.S.A. 161 C5
Hartley Zimbabwe see Chegutu
Hartley Bay Canada 150 D4
Hartola Fin. 55 O6
Harts r. S. Africa 125 G5
Härtsfeld hills Germany 63 K6
Harts Range mts Australia 135 F5
Hartsville TN U.S.A. 164 B5
Hartswater S. Africa 124 G4
Hartville MO U.S.A. 161 E4
Hartwell GA U.S.A. 163 D5
Harue Japan 92 C2
Haruku i. Maluku Indon. 83 D3
Haruna Japan 93 E2
Haruno Japan 93 D3
Har Us Nuur l. Mongolia 94 C2
Har Us Nuur salt l. Mongolia 94 C1
Hārūt r. Afgh. 111 F3
Haruuhin Gol r. Mongolia 94 F1
Harūz-e Bālā Iran 110 E4
Harvard, Mount CO U.S.A. 156 G5
Harvey Australia 135 A8
Harvey ND U.S.A. 160 C2
Harvey Mountain CA U.S.A. 158 C1
Harwich U.K. 59 I7
Haryana state India 104 D3
Harz hills Germany 57 M5
Har Zin Israel 107 B4
Ḩaşāh, Wādī al watercourse Jordan 107 B4
Ḩaşāh, Wādī al watercourse Jordan/Saudi Arabia 107 C4
Hasalbag China 99 B5
Ḩasanah, Wādī watercourse Egypt 107 A4
Hasan Dağı mts Turkey 112 D3
Hasan Guli Turkm. see Esenguly
Hasankeyf Turkey 113 F3
Ḩasan Kūlah Afgh. 111 F3
Hasanur India 106 C4
Hasardag mt. Turkm. 110 E2
Hasbaïya Lebanon 107 B3
Hasbaya Lebanon see Hasbaïya
Hase r. Germany 63 H2
Hase Japan 93 E3
Haselünne Germany 63 H2
Hashaat Arhangay Mongolia 94 E2
Hashaat Dundgovĭ Mongolia see Delgerhangay
HaSharon plain Israel 107 B3
Hashima Japan 92 C3
Hashimoto Japan 92 B4
Hashtgerd Iran 110 C3
Hashtpar Iran 110 C2
Hashtrud Iran 110 B2
Haskell TX U.S.A. 161 D5
Haslemere U.K. 59 G7
Hăşmaşul Mare mt. Romania 69 K1
Ḩaşş, Jabal al hills Syria 107 C1
Hassan India 106 C3
Hassayampa watercourse AZ U.S.A. 159 G5
Haßberge hills Germany 63 K4
Hasselt Belgium 62 F4
Hasselt Neth. 62 G2
Hassi Bel Guebbour Alg. 120 D2
Hassi Messaoud Alg. 64 F5
Hässleholm Sweden 55 H8
Hastings Australia 138 B7
Hastings r. Australia 138 F3
Hastings Canada 165 G1
Hastings N.Z. 139 F4
Hastings U.K. 59 H8
Hastings MI U.S.A. 164 C2
Hastings MN U.S.A. 160 E2
Hastings NE U.S.A. 160 D3
Hasuda Japan 93 F3
Hasunuma Japan 93 G3
Hata India 105 E4
Hata Japan 93 D2
Hatanbulag Mongolia 95 G3
Hatansuudal Mongolia see Bayanlig
Hatashō Japan 92 C3
Hatay Turkey see Antakya
Hatay prov. Turkey 107 C1
Hatch UT U.S.A. 159 G3
Hatches Creek (abandoned) Australia 136 A4
Hatchet Lake Canada 151 K3
Hatfield Australia 138 A4
Hatfield U.K. 58 G5
Hatgal Mongolia 94 E1
Hath India 106 D1
Hat Head National Park Australia 138 F3
Hathras India 104 D4
Ha Tiên Vietnam 87 D5
Ha Tinh Vietnam 86 D3
Hatisar Bhutan see Geylegphug
Hatod India 104 C5
Hato Hud East Timor see Hatudo
Hatra Iraq 113 F4
Hatsu-shima i. Japan 93 F3
Hattah Australia 137 C7
Hattah Kulkyne National Park Australia 137 C7
Hatteras, Cape NC U.S.A. 163 F5
Hatteras Abyssal Plain sea feature S. Atlantic Ocean 184 D4
Hattfjelldal Norway 54 H4
Hattiesburg MS U.S.A. 161 F6
Hattingen Germany 63 H3
Hatton, Gunung hill Malaysia 85 G1
Hattori-gawa r. Japan 92 C4
Hattras Passage Myanmar 87 B4
Hatudo East Timor 83 C5
Hat Yai Thai. 87 C6
Hau Bon Vietnam see A Yun Pa
Haubstadt IN U.S.A. 164 B4
Haud reg. Eth. 122 E3
Hauge Norway 55 E7
Haugesund Norway 55 D7
Haukeligrend Norway 55 E7
Haukipudas Fin. 54 N4
Haukivesi l. Fin. 54 P5
Haultain r. Canada 151 J4
Hauraki Gulf N.Z. 139 E3
Haut Atlas mts Morocco 64 C5
Haute-Normandie admin. reg. France 62 B5
Haute-Volta country Africa see Burkina Faso
Haut-Folin hill France 66 G3
Hauts Plateaux Alg. 64 D5
▶Havana Cuba 169 H4
Capital of Cuba.
Havana IL U.S.A. 160 F3
Havant U.K. 59 G8
Havasu, Lake AZ/CA U.S.A. 159 F4
Havel r. Germany 63 L2
Havelange Belgium 62 F4
Havelberg Germany 63 M2
Havelock Canada 165 G1
Havelock N.Z. 139 D5
Havelock Swaziland see Bulembu
Havelock NC U.S.A. 163 E5
Havelock Falls Australia 134 F3
Havelock Island India 87 A5
Havelock North N.Z. 139 F4
Haverfordwest U.K. 59 C7
Haverhill MA U.S.A. 165 J2
Haveri India 106 B3
Haversin Belgium 62 F4
Havixbeck Germany 63 H3
Havlíčkův Brod Czech Rep. 57 O6
Havøysund Norway 54 N1
Havran Turkey 69 L5
Havre MT U.S.A. 156 F2
Havre Aubert, Île du i. Canada 153 J5
Havre Rock i. Kermadec Is 133 I5
Havre-St-Pierre Canada 153 J4
Havza Turkey 112 D2
Hawai'i i. HI U.S.A. 157 [inset]
Hawai'ian Islands N. Pacific Ocean 186 I4
Hawaiian Ridge sea feature N. Pacific Ocean 186 I4
Hawai'i Volcanoes National Park HI U.S.A. 157 [inset]
Ḩawallī Kuwait 110 C4
Hawar i. Bahrain see Ḩuwār
Hawarden U.K. 58 D5
Hawea, Lake N.Z. 139 B7
Hawera N.Z. 139 E4
Hawes U.K. 58 E4
Hawesville KY U.S.A. 164 B5
Hāwī HI U.S.A. 157 [inset]
Hawick U.K. 60 G5
Ḩawīzah, Hawr al imp. l. Iraq 113 G5
Hawkdun Range mts N.Z. 139 B7
Hawke Bay N.Z. 139 F4
Hawkes Bay Canada 153 K4
Hawkins Peak UT U.S.A. 159 G3
Hawlêr Iraq see Arbīl
Hawley PA U.S.A. 165 H3
Hawng Luk Myanmar 86 B2
Ḩawrān, Wādī watercourse Iraq 113 F4
Ḩawshah, Jibāl al mts Saudi Arabia 110 B6
Hawston S. Africa 124 D8
Hawthorne NV U.S.A. 158 D2
Haxat China 90 B3
Haxat Hudag China 95 H2
Haxby U.K. 58 F4
Hay Australia 138 B5
Hay watercourse Australia 136 B5
Hay r. Canada 150 H2
Haya Seram Indon. 83 D3
Hayachine-san mt. Japan 91 F5
Haya-gawa r. Japan 93 D1
Hayakawa Japan 93 E3
Haya-kawa r. Japan 93 E3
Hayama Japan 93 F3
Hayastan country Asia see Armenia
Haycock AK U.S.A. 148 G2
Haydān, Wādī al r. Jordan 107 B4
Hayden AZ U.S.A. 159 H5
Hayden CO U.S.A. 159 J1
Hayden IN U.S.A. 164 C4
Hayes r. Man. Canada 151 M3
Hayes r. Nunavut Canada 147 I3
Hayes, Mount AK U.S.A. 149 K3
Hayes Halvø pen. Greenland 147 L2
Hayfield Reservoir CA U.S.A. 159 F5
Hayfork CA U.S.A. 158 B1
Hayl, Wādī watercourse Syria 107 C3
Hayl, Wādī al watercourse Syria 107 D2
Haylaastay Mongolia see Sühbaatar
Hayle U.K. 59 B8
Haymā' Oman 109 I6
Haymana Turkey 112 D3
Haymarket VA U.S.A. 165 G4
Hay-on-Wye U.K. 59 D6
Hayrabolu Turkey 69 L4
Hayrhandulaan Mongolia 94 E2
Hay River Canada 146 G3
Hay River Reserve Canada 150 H2
Hays KS U.S.A. 160 D4
Hays MT U.S.A. 156 F2
Ḩays Yemen 108 F7
Haysville KS U.S.A. 161 D4
Haysyn Ukr. 53 F6
Ḩaytān, Jabal hill Egypt 107 A4
Hayward CA U.S.A. 158 B3
Hayward WI U.S.A. 160 F2
Haywards Heath U.K. 59 G8
Hazar Turkm. 110 D2
Hazārah Jāt reg. Afgh. 111 G3
Hazard KY U.S.A. 164 D5
Hazaribag India see Hazaribagh
Hazaribagh India 105 F5
Hazaribagh Range mts India 105 E5
Hazār Masjed, Kūh-e mts Iran 110 E2
Hazebrouck France 62 C4
Hazelton Canada 150 E4
Hazen Bay AK U.S.A. 148 F3
Hazen Strait Canada 147 G2
Hazerswoude-Rijndijk Neth. 62 E2
Hazhdanahr reg. Afgh. 111 G2
Hazlehurst MS U.S.A. 167 H2
Hazleton IN U.S.A. 164 B4
Hazleton PA U.S.A. 165 H3
Hazlett, Lake salt flat Australia 134 E5
Ḩazrat-e Sulţān Afgh. 111 G2
Hazu Japan 92 D4
Hazumi-saki pt Japan 92 C4
H. Bouchard Arg. 178 D4
Headford Ireland 61 C4
Headingly Australia 136 B4
Head of Bight b. Australia 135 E7
Healdsburg CA U.S.A. 158 B2
Healesville Australia 138 B6
Healy AK U.S.A. 149 J3
Healy Lake AK U.S.A. 149 K3
Heanor U.K. 59 F5
Heard Island Indian Ocean 185 M9
▶Heard Island and McDonald Islands terr. Indian Ocean 185 M9
Australian External Territory.
Hearne TX U.S.A. 161 D6
Hearne Lake Canada 151 H2
Hearrenfean Neth. see Heerenveen
Hearst Canada 152 E4
Hearst Island Antarctica 188 L2
Heart r. ND U.S.A. 160 C2
Heart of Neolithic Orkney tourist site U.K. 60 F1
Heathcote Australia 138 B6
Heathfield U.K. 59 H8
Heathsville VA U.S.A. 165 G5
Hebbardsville KY U.S.A. 164 B5
Hebbronville TX U.S.A. 161 D7
Hebei prov. China 95 H4
Hebel Australia 138 C2
Heber AZ U.S.A. 159 H4
Heber City UT U.S.A. 159 H1
Heber Springs AR U.S.A. 161 E5
Hebi China 95 H5
Hebian China 95 H4
Hebron Canada 153 J2
Hebron NE U.S.A. 160 D3
Hebron West Bank 107 B4
Hecate Strait Canada 149 O5
Hecelchakán Mex. 167 H4
Hecheng Jiangxi China see Zixi
Hecheng Zhejiang China see Qingtian
Hechi China 97 F3
Hechuan Chongqing China 96 E2
Hechuan Jiangxi China see Yongxin
Hecla Island Canada 151 L5
Heda Japan 93 E4
Hede China see Sheyang
Hede Sweden 54 H5
Hedemora Sweden 55 I6
He Devil Mountain ID U.S.A. 156 D3
Hedionda Grande Mex. 167 E3
Hedi Shuiku resr China 97 F4
Heech Neth. see Heeg
Heeg Neth. 62 F2
Heek Germany 62 H2
Heer Belgium 62 E4
Heerde Neth. 62 G2
Heerenveen Neth. 62 F2
Heerhugowaard Neth. 62 E2
Heerlen Neth. 62 F4
Ḩefa Israel see Haifa
Ḩefa, Mifraz Israel see Haifa, Bay of
Hefei China 97 H2
Hefeng China 97 F2
Heflin AL U.S.A. 163 C5
Hegang China 90 C3
Heho Myanmar 86 B2
Heidan r. Jordan see Haydān, Wādī al
Heidberg hill Germany 63 L3
Heide Germany 57 L3
Heide Namibia 124 C2
Heidelberg Germany 63 I5
Heidelberg S. Africa 125 I4
Heidenheim an der Brenz Germany 63 K6
Heihe China 90 B2
Heilbron S. Africa 125 H4
Heilbronn Germany 63 J5
Heiligenhafen Germany 57 M3
Hei Ling Chau i. H.K. China 97 [inset]
Heilongjiang prov. China 95 J2
Heilong Jiang r. China/Rus. Fed. 90 D2
also known as Amur (Rus. Fed.)
Heilong Jiang r. Rus. Fed. see Amur
Heilsbronn Germany 63 K5
Heilungkiang prov. China see Heilongjiang
Heimahe China 94 D4
Heinola Fin. 55 O6
Heinze Islands Myanmar 87 B4
Heiquan China 94 D4
Heirnkut Myanmar 86 A1
Heishan China 95 J3
Heishantou Nei Mongol China 95 I1
Heishantou Xinjiang China 94 B2
Heishi Beihu l. China 99 C6
Heishui China 96 D1
Heisker Islands U.K. see Monach Islands
Heist-op-den-Berg Belgium 62 E3
Ḩeiţān, Gebel hill Egypt see Ḩaytān, Jabal
Heituo Shan mt. China 95 H4
Hejaz reg. Saudi Arabia see Hijaz
Hejian China 95 I4
Hejiang China 96 E2
He Jiang r. China 97 F4
Hejiao China 95 G3
Hejin China 95 G5
Hejing China 98 D4
Hekimhan Turkey 112 E3
Hekinan Japan 92 C4
Hekla vol. Iceland 54 [inset 1]
Heko-san mt. Japan 92 C3
Hekou Gansu China 94 E4
Hekou Hubei China 97 G2
Hekou Jiangxi China see Yanshan
Hekou Sichuan China see Yajiang
Hekou Yunnan China 96 D4
Helagsfjället mt. Sweden 54 H5
Helam India 96 B3
Helan Shan mts China 94 F4
Helbra Germany 63 L3
Helen atoll Palau 81 I6
Helena AR U.S.A. 161 F5
▶Helena MT U.S.A. 156 E3
Capital of Montana.
Helen Reef Palau 81 I6
Helensburgh U.K. 60 E4
Helen Springs Australia 134 F4
Ḩelez Israel 107 B4
Helgoland i. Germany 57 K3
Helgoländer Bucht g. Germany 57 L3
Heligoland i. Germany see Helgoland
Heligoland Bight g. Germany see Helgoländer Bucht
Heliopolis Lebanon see Ba'albek
Helixi China see Ningguo
Hella Iceland 54 [inset 1]
Helland Norway 54 J2
Hellas country Europe see Greece
Helleh r. Iran 110 C4
Hellespont strait Turkey see Dardanelles
Hellevoetsluis Neth. 62 E3
Hellhole Gorge National Park Australia 136 D5
Hellín Spain 67 F4
Hellinikon tourist site Greece 112 A3
Hells Canyon gorge ID/OR U.S.A. 156 D3
Hell-Ville Madag. see Andoany
Helmand r. Afgh. 111 F4
Helmantica Spain see Salamanca
Helmbrechts Germany 63 L4
Helme r. Germany 63 L3
Helmeringhausen Namibia 124 C3
Helmet Mountain AK U.S.A. 149 K2
Helmond Neth. 62 F3
Helmsdale U.K. 60 F2
Helmsdale r. U.K. 60 F2
Helmstedt Germany 63 L2
Helong China 90 C4
Helper UT U.S.A. 159 H2
Helpter Berge hills Germany 63 N1
Helsingborg Sweden 55 H8
Helsingfors Fin. see Helsinki
Helsingør Denmark 55 H8
▶Helsinki Fin. 55 N6
Capital of Finland.
Helston U.K. 59 B8
Helvécia Brazil 179 D2
Helvetic Republic country Europe see Switzerland
Ḩelwân Egypt see Ḩulwān
Hemel Hempstead U.K. 59 G7
Hemet CA U.S.A. 158 E5
Hemingford NE U.S.A. 160 C3
Hemlock Lake NY U.S.A. 165 G2
Hemmingen Germany 63 J2
Hemmingford Canada 165 I1
Hemmoor Germany 63 J1
Hempstead TX U.S.A. 161 D6
Hemsby U.K. 59 I6
Hemse Sweden 55 K8
Henan China 94 E5
Henan prov. China 97 G1
Henares r. Spain 67 E3
Henashi-zaki pt Japan 91 E4
Henbury Australia 135 F6
Hendek Turkey 69 N4
Henderson KY U.S.A. 164 B5
Henderson NC U.S.A. 162 E4
Henderson NV U.S.A. 159 F3
Henderson NY U.S.A. 165 G2
Henderson TN U.S.A. 161 F5
Henderson TX U.S.A. 161 E5
Henderson Island Pitcairn Is 187 L7
Hendersonville NC U.S.A. 163 D5
Hendersonville TN U.S.A. 164 B5
Henderville atoll Kiribati see Aranuka
Hendon U.K. 59 G7
Hendorābī i. Iran 110 D5
Hendy-Gwyn U.K. see Whitland
Hengām Iran 111 E5
Hengduan Shan mts China 96 C2
Hengelo Neth. 62 G2
Hengfeng China 97 H2
Hengnan China see Hengyang
Hengshan Heilong. China 90 C3
Hengshan Shaanxi China 95 G4
Heng Shan mt. China 97 G3
Heng Shan mts China 95 H4
Hengshui Hebei China 95 H4
Hengshui Jiangxi China see Chongyi
Hengxian China 97 F4
Hengyang Hunan China 97 G3
Hengyang Hunan China 97 G3
Hengzhou China see Hengxian
Heniches'k Ukr. 53 G7
Henley N.Z. 139 C7
Henley-on-Thames U.K. 59 G7
Henlopen, Cape DE U.S.A. 165 H4
Hennef (Sieg) Germany 63 H4
Hennenman S. Africa 125 H4
Hennepin IL U.S.A. 160 F3
Hennessey OK U.S.A. 161 D4
Hennigsdorf Berlin Germany 63 N2
Henniker NH U.S.A. 165 J2
Henning IL U.S.A. 164 B3
Henrietta TX U.S.A. 161 D5
Henrietta Maria, Cape Canada 152 E3
Henrieville UT U.S.A. 159 H3
Henrique de Carvalho Angola see Saurimo
Henry, Cape NC U.S.A. 165 G5
Henry Ice Rise Antarctica 188 A1
Henryk Arctowski research station Antarctica see Arctowski
Henry Kater, Cape Canada 147 L3
Henry Mountains UT U.S.A. 159 H2
Hensall Canada 164 E2
Henshaw, Lake CA U.S.A. 158 E5
Hentiesbaai Namibia 124 B2
Hentiy prov. Mongolia 95 G2
Henty Australia 138 C5
Henzada Myanmar see Hinthada
Heping Guangdong China 97 G3
Heping Guizhou China see Huishui
Heping Guizhou China see Yanhe
Hepo China see Jiexi
Heppner OR U.S.A. 156 D3
Heptanesus is Greece see Ionian Islands
Hepu China 97 F4
Heqiao China 94 E4
Heqing China 96 D3
Hequ China 95 G4
Heraclea Turkey see Ereğli
Heraclea Pontica Turkey see Ereğli
Heraklion Greece see Iraklion
Herald Cays atolls Australia 136 E3
Herāt Afgh. 111 F3
Hérault r. France 66 F5
Herbertabad India 87 A5
Herbert Downs Australia 136 B4
Herbert Island AK U.S.A. 148 E5
Herbert River Falls National Park Australia 136 D3
Herbert Wash salt flat Australia 135 D6
Herborn Germany 63 I4
Herbstein Germany 63 J4
Hercules Dome ice feature Antarctica 188 K1
Herdecke Germany 63 H3
Herdorf Germany 63 H4
Heredia Costa Rica 166 [inset] I7
Hereford U.K. 59 E6
Hereford TX U.S.A. 161 C5
Héréhérétué atoll Fr. Polynesia 187 K7
Herent Belgium 62 E4
Herford Germany 63 I2
Heringen (Werra) Germany 63 K4
Herington KS U.S.A. 160 D4
Herīs Iran 110 B2
Herisau Switz. 66 I3
Herkimer NY U.S.A. 165 H2
Herlen Mongolia 95 G2
Herlen Gol r. China/Mongolia 89 L3
Herlen He r. China/Mongolia see Herlen Gol
Herleshausen Germany 63 K3
Herlong CA U.S.A. 158 C1
Herm i. Channel Is 59 E9
Hermanas Mex. 167 E3
Herma Ness hd U.K. 60 [inset]
Hermann MO U.S.A. 160 F4
Hermannsburg Germany 63 K2
Hermanus S. Africa 124 D8
Hermel Lebanon 107 C2
Hermes, Cape S. Africa 125 I6
Hermidale Australia 138 C3
Hermiston OR U.S.A. 156 D3
Hermitage MO U.S.A. 160 E4
Hermitage PA U.S.A. 164 E3
Hermitage Bay Canada 153 K5
Hermite, Islas is Chile 178 C9
Hermit Islands P.N.G. 81 L7
Hermon, Mount Lebanon/Syria 107 B3
Hermonthis Egypt see Armant
Hermopolis Magna Egypt see Al Ashmūnayn
Hermosa CO U.S.A. 159 J3
Hermosillo Mex. 166 C2
Hernandarias Para. 178 F3
Hernando MS U.S.A. 161 F5
Herndon CA U.S.A. 158 D3
Herndon PA U.S.A. 165 G3
Herndon WV U.S.A. 164 E5
Herne Germany 63 H3
Herne Bay U.K. 59 I7
Herning Denmark 55 F8
Heroica Nogales Mex. see Nogales
Heroica Puebla de Zaragoza Mex. see Puebla
Hérouville-St-Clair France 59 G9
Herowābād Iran see Khalkhāl
Herradura Mex. 167 E4
Herrera del Duque Spain 67 D4
Herrero, Punta pt Mex. 167 I5
Herrieden Germany 63 K5
Herschel Canada 149 M1
Herschel Island Canada 149 M1
Hershey PA U.S.A. 165 G3
Hertford U.K. 59 G7
Hertzogville S. Africa 125 G5
Herve Belgium 62 F4
Hervé, Lac l. Canada 153 H3
Hervey Islands Cook Is 187 J7
Herzberg Brandenburg Germany 63 M2
Herzberg Brandenburg Germany 63 N3
Herzlake Germany 63 H2
Herzliyya Israel 107 B3
Herzogenaurach Germany 63 K5
Herzsprung Germany 63 M1
Ḩeşār Būshehr Iran 110 C4
Ḩeşār Hormozgān Iran 110 E5
Hesdin France 62 C4
Hesel Germany 63 H1
Heshan China 97 F4
Heshengqiao China 97 G2
Heshui China 95 G5
Heshun China 95 H4
Hesperia CA U.S.A. 158 E4
Hesperus CO U.S.A. 159 I3
Hesperus, Mount AK U.S.A. 148 I3
Hesperus Peak CO U.S.A. 159 I3
Hesquiat Canada 150 E5
Hess r. Canada 149 N3
Hess Creek r. AK U.S.A. 149 J2
Heßdorf Germany 63 K5
Hesse land Germany see Hessen
Hesselberg hill Germany 63 K5
Hessen land Germany 63 J4
Hessisch Lichtenau Germany 63 J3
Hess Mountains Canada 149 N3
Het r. Laos 86 D2
Hetauda Nepal 105 F4
Heteren Neth. 62 F3
Hetou China 97 F4
Hettinger ND U.S.A. 160 C2
Hetton U.K. 58 E4
Hettstedt Germany 63 L3
Heung Kong Tsai H.K. China see Aberdeen
Ḩevron West Bank see Hebron
Hexham U.K. 58 E4
Hexian Anhui China 97 H2
Hexian Guangxi China see Hezhou
Hexigten Qi China see Jingpeng
Hexipu China 94 E4
Heyang China 95 G5
Ḩeydarābād Āzarbāyjān-e Gharbī Iran 110 B2
Ḩeydarābād Khorāsān-e Jonūbī Iran 111 F4
Heydebreck Poland see Kędzierzyn-Koźle
Heyin China see Guide
Heysham U.K. 58 E4
Heyshope Dam S. Africa 125 J4
Heyuan China 97 G4
Heywood U.K. 58 E5
Heze China 95 H5
Hezhang China 96 E3
Hezheng China 94 E5
Hezhou China 97 F3
Hezuo China 94 E5
Hialeah FL U.S.A. 163 D7
Hiawassee GA U.S.A. 163 D5
Hiawatha KS U.S.A. 160 E4
Hibbing MN U.S.A. 160 E2
Hibbs, Point Australia 137 [inset]
Hibernia Reef Australia 134 C3
Hīchān Iran 111 F5
Hichisō Japan 92 D3
Hicks, Point Australia 138 D6
Hicks Bay N.Z. 139 G3
Hicks Cayes is Belize 167 H5
Hicks Lake Canada 151 K2
Hicksville OH U.S.A. 164 C3
Hico TX U.S.A. 161 D5
Hida-gawa r. Japan 92 D3
Hidaka Hyōgo Japan 92 A3
Hidaka Saitama Japan 93 F3
Hidaka Wakayama Japan 92 B5
Hidaka-gawa r. Japan 92 B5
Hidaka-sanmyaku mts Japan 90 F4
Hida-Kiso-gawa Kokutei-kōen park Japan 92 D3
Hida-kōchi plat. Japan 92 C2
Hidalgo Coahuila Mex. 167 F3
Hidalgo Tamaulipas Mex. 161 D7
Hidalgo state Mex. 167 F4
Hidalgo del Parral Mex. 166 D3
Hidalgotitlán Mex. 167 G5
Hida-sanmyaku mts Japan 92 D2
Hidrolândia Brazil 179 A2
Hierosolyma Israel/West Bank see Jerusalem
Higashi Japan 93 G1
Higashiizu Japan 93 F4
Higashi-Matsuyama Japan 93 F2
Higashimurayama Japan 93 F3
Higashi-Ōsaka Japan 92 B4
Higashi-Shirakawa Japan 92 D3
Higashi-suidō sea chan. Japan 91 C6
Higashiura Aichi Japan 92 C4
Higashiura Hyōgo Japan 92 A4
Higashi-yama mt. Japan 93 D2
Higgins TX U.S.A. 161 C4
Higgins Bay NY U.S.A. 165 H2
Higgins Lake MI U.S.A. 164 C1
High Atlas mts Morocco see Haut Atlas
High Desert OR U.S.A. 156 C4
High Island i. H.K. China 97 [inset]
High Island TX U.S.A. 161 E6
High Island Reservoir H.K. China 97 [inset]
Highland Peak CA U.S.A. 158 D2
Highland Peak NV U.S.A. 159 F3
Highlands NJ U.S.A. 165 I3
Highland Springs VA U.S.A. 165 G5
High Level Canada 150 G3
Highmore SD U.S.A. 160 D2
High Point NC U.S.A. 162 E5
High Point hill NJ U.S.A. 165 H3
High Prairie Canada 150 G4
High River Canada 150 H5
Highrock Lake Man. Canada 151 K4
Highrock Lake Sask. Canada 151 J3
High Springs FL U.S.A. 163 D6
High Tatras mts Poland/Slovakia see Tatra Mountains
High Wycombe U.K. 59 G7
Higuera de Abuya Mex. 166 D3
Higuera de Zaragoza Mex. 166 C3
Higüey Dom. Rep. 169 K5
Higuri-gawa r. Japan 93 F3
Hiiumaa i. Estonia 55 M7
Hijānah, Buḩayrat al imp. l. Syria 107 C3
Hijau, Gunung mt. Indon. 84 C3
Hijaz reg. Saudi Arabia 108 E4
Hijiri-dake mt. Japan 93 E3
Hikabo-yama mt. Japan 93 E2
Hikami Japan 92 B3
Hikata Japan 93 G3
Hiki-gawa r. Japan 92 B5
Ḩikmah, Ra's al pt Egypt 112 B5
Hiko NV U.S.A. 159 F3
Hikone Japan 92 C3
Hikurangi mt. N.Z. 139 G3
Hila Maluku Indon. 83 C4
Hilahila Sulawesi Indon. 83 B4
Hilāl, Jabal hill Egypt 107 A4
Hilāl, Ra's al pt Libya 108 B3
Hilary Coast Antarctica 188 H1
Hildale UT U.S.A. 159 G3
Hildburghausen Germany 63 K4
Hilders Germany 63 K4
Hildesheim Germany 63 J2
Hillah Iraq 113 G4
Hill Bank Belize 167 H5
Hill City KS U.S.A. 160 D4
Hillegom Neth. 62 E2
Hill End Australia 138 D4
Hillerød Denmark 55 H9
Hillgrove Australia 136 D3
Hill Island Lake Canada 151 I2
Hillman MI U.S.A. 164 D1
Hillsboro ND U.S.A. 160 D2
Hillsboro NM U.S.A. 157 G6
Hillsboro OH U.S.A. 164 D4
Hillsboro OR U.S.A. 156 C3
Hillsboro TX U.S.A. 161 D5
Hillsdale IN U.S.A. 164 B4
Hillsdale MI U.S.A. 164 C3
Hillside Australia 134 B5
Hillston Australia 138 B4
Hillsville VA U.S.A. 164 E5

Hilo HI U.S.A. 157 [inset]
Hilton Australia 136 B4
Hilton S. Africa 125 J5
Hilton NY U.S.A. 165 G2
Hilton Head Island SC U.S.A. 163 D5
Hilvan Turkey 112 E3
Hilversum Neth. 62 F2
Himachal Pradesh state India 104 D3
Himaga-shima i. Japan 92 D4
Himalaya mts Asia 104 D2
Himalchul mt. Nepal 105 F3
Himanka Fin. 54 M4
Ḥimār, Wādī al watercourse Syria/Turkey 107 D1
Himarë Albania 69 H4
Himatnagar India 104 C5
Hime-gawa r. Japan 93 D1
Himeji Japan 92 A4
Himi Japan 92 C2
Ḥimş Syria see Homs
Ḥimş, Baḥrat resr Syria see Qaṭṭīnah, Buḥayrat
Hinako i. Indon. 84 B2
Hinatuan Mindanao Phil. 82 D4
Hinatuan Passage Phil. 82 D4
Hinchinbrook Entrance sea channel AK U.S.A. 149 K3
Hinchinbrook Island Australia 136 D3
Hinchinbrook Island AK U.S.A. 149 K3
Hinckley U.K. 59 F6
Hinckley MN U.S.A. 160 E2
Hinckley UT U.S.A. 159 G2
Hinckley Reservoir NY U.S.A. 165 H2
Hindan r. India 99 B7
Hindaun India 104 D4
Hinderwell U.K. 58 G4
Hindley U.K. 58 E5
Hindman KY U.S.A. 164 D5
Hindmarsh, Lake dry lake Australia 137 C8
Hindu Kush mts Afgh./Pak. 111 G3
Hindupur India 106 C3
Hines Creek Canada 150 G3
Hinesville GA U.S.A. 163 D6
Hinganghat India 106 C1
Hingoli India 106 C2
Hınıs Turkey 113 F3
Hinnøya i. Norway 54 I2
Hino Shiga Japan 92 C3
Hino Tōkyō Japan 93 F3
Hinoba-an Negros Phil. 82 C4
Hinoemata Japan 93 F1
Hino-gawa r. Japan 92 C2
Hino-gawa r. Japan 92 C3
Hinojosa del Duque Spain 67 D4
Hino-misaki pt Japan 92 B5
Hinsdale NH U.S.A. 165 I2
Hinte Germany 63 H1
Hinthada Myanmar 86 A3
Hinton Canada 150 G4
Hinton WV U.S.A. 164 E5
Hi-numa l. Japan 93 G2
Hiort i. U.K. see St Kilda
Hippolytushoef Neth. 62 E2
Hipponium Italy see Vibo Valentia
Hippo Regius Alg. see Annaba
Hippo Zarytus Tunisia see Bizerte
Hirabit Dağ mt. Turkey 113 G3
Hiraga-take mt. Japan 93 F1
Hiraizumi tourist site Japan 91 F5
Hirakata Japan 92 B4
Hirakud Dam India 105 E5
Hirakud Reservoir India 105 E5
Hirapur India 104 D4
Hiratsuka Japan 93 F3
Hiraya Japan 92 D3
Hiriyur India 106 C3
Hirokawa Japan 92 B4
Hirosaki Japan 90 F4
Hiroshima Japan 91 D6
Hirschaid Germany 63 L5
Hirschberg Germany 63 L4
Hirschberg mt. Germany 57 M7
Hirschberg Poland see Jelenia Góra
Hirschenstein mt. Germany 63 M6
Hirson France 62 E5
Hîrşova Romania see Hârşova
Hirta is U.K. see St Kilda
Hirtshals Denmark 55 F8
Hiruga-take mt. Japan 93 F3
Hirukawa Japan 92 D3
Hisai Japan 92 C4
Hisar India 104 C3
Hisar Iran 110 C2
Hisarköy Turkey see Domaniç
Hisarönü Turkey 69 O4
Ḥisb, Sha'īb watercourse Iraq 113 G5
Ḥisbān Jordan 107 B4
Hishig-Öndör Mongolia 94 E1
Hisiu P.N.G. 81 L8
Hisor Tajik. 111 H2
Hisor Tizmasi mts Tajik./Uzbek. see Gissar Range
Hispalis Spain see Seville
Hispania country Europe see Spain

▶Hispaniola i. Caribbean Sea 169 J4
Consists of the Dominican Republic and Haiti.

Hispur Glacier Pak. 104 C1
Hissar India see Hisar
Hisua India 105 F4
Ḥisyah Syria 107 C2
Hīt Iraq 113 F4
Hitachi Japan 93 G2
Hitachinaka Japan 93 G2
Hitachi-Ōta Japan 93 G2
Hitra i. Norway 54 F5
Hitzacker Germany 63 L1
Hiuchiga-take vol. Japan 93 F2
Hiva Oa i. Fr. Polynesia 187 K6
Hixon Canada 150 F4
Hixson Cay reef Australia 136 F4
Hiyoshi Kyōto Japan 92 B3
Hiyoshi Nagano Japan 92 D3
Hiyyon watercourse Israel 107 B4
Hizan Turkey 113 F3
Hjälmaren l. Sweden 55 I7
Hjerkinn Norway 54 F5
Hjo Sweden 55 I7
Hjørring Denmark 55 G8
Hkakabo Razi mt. China/Myanmar 96 C2
Hlaingdet Myanmar 86 B2
Hlako Kangri mt. China see Lhagoi Kangri
Hlane Royal National Park Swaziland 125 J4
Hlatikulu Swaziland 125 J4
Hlegu Myanmar 86 B3
Hlohlowane S. Africa 125 H5
Hlotse Lesotho 125 I5
Hluhluwe-Umfolozi Park nature res. S. Africa 125 J5
Hlukhiv Ukr. 53 G6
Hlung-Tan Myanmar 86 B2
Hlusha Belarus 53 F5
Hlybokaye Belarus 55 O9
Ho Ghana 120 D4
Hoa Binh Hoa Binh Vietnam 86 D2
Hoa Binh Nghê An Vietnam 86 D3
Hoachanas Namibia 124 D2
Hoagland IN U.S.A. 164 C3
Hoang Liên Sơn mts Vietnam 86 C2
Hoang Sa is S. China Sea see Paracel Islands

▶Hobart Australia 137 [inset]
Capital of Tasmania.

Hobart OK U.S.A. 161 D5
Hobbs NM U.S.A. 161 C5
Hobbs Coast Antarctica 188 J1
Hobe Sound FL U.S.A. 163 D7
Hobiganj Bangl. see Habiganj
Hoboksar China 98 D3
Hobor China 95 H3
Hobro Denmark 55 F8
Hobyo Somalia 122 E3
Hoceima, Baie d'Al b. Morocco 67 E6
Hochandochtla Mountain hill AK U.S.A. 148 I2
Höchberg Germany 63 J5
Hochfeiler mt. Austria/Italy see Gran Pilastro
Hochfeld Namibia 123 B6
Hochharz, Nationalpark nat. park Germany 63 K3
Hô Chi Minh Vietnam see Ho Chi Minh City
Ho Chi Minh City Vietnam 87 D5
Hochschwab mt. Austria 57 O7
Hochschwab mts Austria 57 O7
Hockenheim Germany 63 I5
Ḥôḍ reg. Mauritania 120 C3
Hodal India 99 B8
Hōdatsu-san hill Japan 92 C2
Hoddesdon U.K. 59 G7
Hodeidah Yemen 108 F7
Hodgenville KY U.S.A. 164 C5
Hodgson Downs Australia 134 F3
Hódmezővásárhely Hungary 69 I1
Hodna, Chott el salt l. Alg. 67 I6
Hodo-dan pt N. Korea 91 B5
Hödrögö Mongolia see Nömrög
Ho Dynasty Citadel tourist site Vietnam 86 D2
Hodzana r. AK U.S.A. 149 K2
Hoek van Holland Neth. see Hook of Holland
Hoensbroek Neth. 62 F4
Hoeryŏng N. Korea 90 C4
Hof Germany 63 L4
Hoffman Mountain NY U.S.A. 165 I2
Hofheim in Unterfranken Germany 63 K4
Hofmeyr S. Africa 125 G6
Höfn Iceland 54 [inset 1]
Hofors Sweden 55 J6
Hofsjökull ice cap Iceland 54 [inset 1]
Hofsós Iceland 54 [inset 1]
Hōfu Japan 91 C6
Hofūf Saudi Arabia 108 G4
Höganäs Sweden 55 H8
Hogan Group is Australia 138 C7
Hogansburg NY U.S.A. 165 H1
Hogatza AK U.S.A. 148 I2
Hogatza r. AK U.S.A. 148 I2
Hogback Mountain NE U.S.A. 160 C3
Hoge Vaart canal Neth. 62 F2
Hogg, Mount Canada 149 N3
Hoggar plat. Alg. see Ahaggar
Hog Island VA U.S.A. 165 H5
Högsby Sweden 55 J8
Hohenloher Ebene plain Germany 63 J5
Hohenmölsen Germany 63 M3
Hohennauen Germany 63 M2
Hohensalza Poland see Inowrocław
Hohenwald TN U.S.A. 162 C5
Hohenwartetalsperre resr Germany 63 L4
Hoher Dachstein mt. Austria 57 N7
Hoh Ereg China see Wuchuan
Hohe Rhön mts Germany 63 J4
Hohe Tauern mts Austria 57 N7
Hohe Venn moorland Belgium 62 G4
Hohhot China 95 G3
Höhmorït Mongolia 94 C2
Hohneck mt. France 66 H2
Hoholitna r. AK U.S.A. 148 H3
Hoh Sai Hu l. China 94 C5
Hoh Xil Hu salt l. China 99 E6
Hoh Xil Shan mts China 99 E6
Hoh Yanhu salt l. China 94 D4
Hôi An Vietnam 86 E4
Hoika China 94 D5
Hoima Uganda 122 D3
Hoit Taria China 94 D4
Hojagala Turkm. 110 E2
Hojai India 105 H4
Hojambaz Turkm. 111 G2
Højryggen mts Greenland 147 M2
Hōki-gawa r. Japan 93 G2
Hokitika N.Z. 139 C6
Hokkaidō i. Japan 90 F4
Hokksund Norway 55 F7
Hokota Japan 93 G2
Hokudan Japan 92 A4
Hokunō Japan 92 C3
Hokusei Japan 92 C3
Hol Norway 55 F6
Holbæk Denmark 55 G9
Holbeach U.K. 59 H6
Holbrook Australia 138 C5
Holbrook AZ U.S.A. 159 H4
Holden UT U.S.A. 159 G2
Holdenville OK U.S.A. 161 D5
Holdrege NE U.S.A. 160 D3
Holgate OH U.S.A. 164 C3
Holguín Cuba 169 I4
Holikachuk AK U.S.A. 148 H3
Holitna r. AK U.S.A. 148 H3
Höljes Sweden 55 H6
Holland country Europe see Netherlands
Holland MI U.S.A. 164 B2
Holland NY U.S.A. 165 F2
Hollandia Indon. see Jayapura
Hollick-Kenyon Peninsula Antarctica 188 L2
Hollick-Kenyon Plateau Antarctica 188 K1
Hollidaysburg PA U.S.A. 165 F3
Hollis AK U.S.A. 149 N5
Hollis OK U.S.A. 161 D5
Hollister CA U.S.A. 158 C3
Holly MI U.S.A. 164 D2
Hollyhill KY U.S.A. 164 C5
Holly Springs MS U.S.A. 161 F5
Hollywood CA U.S.A. 159 D4
Hollywood FL U.S.A. 163 D7
Holm Norway 54 H4
Holmes Reef Australia 136 D3
Holmestrand Norway 55 G7
Holmgard Rus. Fed. see Velikiy Novgorod
Holm Ø i. Greenland see Kiatassuaq
Holmön i. Sweden 54 L5
Holmsund Sweden 54 L5
Holokuk Mountain hill AK U.S.A. 148 H3
Ḥolon Israel 107 B3
Holoog Namibia 124 C4
Holothuria Banks reef Australia 134 D3
Holroyd r. Australia 136 C2
Holstebro Denmark 55 F8
Holstein IA U.S.A. 160 E3
Holsteinsborg Greenland see Sisimiut
Holston r. TN U.S.A. 162 D4
Holsworthy U.K. 59 C8
Holt U.K. 59 I6
Holt MI U.S.A. 164 C2
Holton MI U.S.A. 164 B2
Holwerd Neth. 62 F1
Holwert Neth. see Holwerd
Holycross Ireland 61 E5
Holy Cross AK U.S.A. 148 H3
Holy Cross, Mount of the CO U.S.A. 156 G5
Holyhead U.K. 58 C5
Holyhead Bay U.K. 58 C5
Holy Island England U.K. 58 F3
Holy Island Wales U.K. 58 C5
Holyoke CO U.S.A. 160 C3
Holy See Europe see Vatican City
Holywell U.K. 58 D5
Holzhausen Germany 63 M3
Holzkirchen Germany 57 M7
Holzminden Germany 63 J3
Homand Iran 111 E3
Homāyūnshahr Iran see Khomeynīshahr
Homberg (Efze) Germany 63 J3
Hombori Mali 120 C3
Homburg Germany 63 H5
Home Bay Canada 147 L3
Homécourt France 62 F5
Homer AK U.S.A. 149 J4
Homer GA U.S.A. 163 D5
Homer LA U.S.A. 161 E5
Homer MI U.S.A. 164 C2
Homer NY U.S.A. 165 G2
Homerville GA U.S.A. 163 D6
Homestead Australia 136 D4
Homnabad India 106 C2
Homoine Moz. 125 L2
Homs Libya see Al Khums
Homs Syria 107 C2
Homyel' Belarus 53 F5
Honan prov. China see Henan
Honavar India 106 B3
Honawad India 106 B2
Honaz Turkey 69 M6
Hon Chông Vietnam 87 D5
Honda Bay Palawan Phil. 82 B4
Hondeklipbaai S. Africa 124 C6
Hondo r. Belize/Mex. 167 H5
Hondo TX U.S.A. 161 D6
Hondsrug reg. Neth. 62 G1

▶Honduras country Central America 169 G6
5th largest country in North America.

Honduras, Gulf of Belize/Hond. 166 [inset] I5
Hønefoss Norway 55 G6
Honesdale PA U.S.A. 165 H3
Honey Mex. 167 F4
Honey Lake salt l. CA U.S.A. 158 C1
Honeyoye Lake NY U.S.A. 165 G2
Honfleur France 66 E2
Hong, Mouths of the Vietnam see Red River, Mouths of the
Hông, Sông r. Vietnam see Red
Hongchengzi China 94 E4
Hongchuan China see Hongya
Hongde China 95 F4
Honggor China 95 H2
Honggouzi China 98 E5
Honggu China 94 E4
Hongguo China see Panxian
Honghai Wan b. China 97 G4
Honghe China 96 D4
Hong He r. China 97 G1
Honghu China 97 G2
Hongjialou China see Licheng
Hongjiang Hunan China 97 F3
Hongjiang Sichuan China see Wangcang
Hong Kong H.K. China 97 [inset]
Hong Kong aut. reg. China 97 [inset]
Hong Kong Harbour sea chan. H.K. China 97 [inset]
Hong Kong Island H.K. China 97 [inset]
Hongliu Daquan well China 94 D3
Hongliuhe China 94 C3
Hongliu He r. China 95 G4
Hongliuquan China 98 E5
Hongliuwan China see Aksay
Hongliuyuan Gansu China 94 E4
Hongliuyuan Gansu China 98 F4
Hongor Mongolia see Naran
Hongqiao China see Qidong
Hongqicun China 94 C3
Hongqizhen China see Wuzhishan
Hongshan China 97 G2
Hongshansi China 94 F4
Hongshilazi China 90 B4
Hongshui He r. China 96 F4
Hongtong China 95 G4
Honguedo, Détroit d' sea chan. Canada 153 I4
Hongwansi China see Sunan
Hongwŏn N. Korea 91 B4
Hongxing China 95 J2
Hongya China 96 D2
Hongyashan Shuiku resr China 94 E4
Hongyuan China 96 D1
Hongze China 97 H1
Hongze Hu l. China 97 H1

▶Honiara Solomon Is 133 F2
Capital of the Solomon Islands.

Honiton U.K. 59 D8
Honjō Akita Japan 91 F5
Honjo Japan 93 D2
Honjō Saitama Japan 93 F2
Honkajoki Fin. 55 M6
Honkawane Japan 93 E3
Honningsvåg Norway 54 N1
Honoka'a HI U.S.A. 157 [inset]

▶Honolulu HI U.S.A. 157 [inset]
Capital of Hawaii.

▶Honshū i. Japan 91 E6
Largest island in Japan, 3rd largest in Asia and 7th in the world.

Hood, Mount vol. OR U.S.A. 156 C3
Hood Bay AK U.S.A. 149 N4
Hood Point Australia 135 B8
Hood Point P.N.G. 136 D1
Hood River OR U.S.A. 156 C3
Hoogeveen Neth. 62 G2
Hoogezand-Sappemeer Neth. 62 G1
Hooghly r. mouth India see Hugli
Hooker OK U.S.A. 161 C4
Hook Head hd Ireland 61 F5
Hook of Holland Neth. 62 E3
Hook Reef Australia 136 E3
Hoolt Mongolia see Tögrög
Hoonah AK U.S.A. 149 N4
Hooper Bay AK U.S.A. 148 F3
Hooper Bay b. AK U.S.A. 148 F3
Hooper Island MD U.S.A. 165 G4
Hoopeston IL U.S.A. 164 B3
Hoopstad S. Africa 125 G4
Höör Sweden 55 H9
Hoorn Neth. 62 F2
Hoorn, Îles de is Wallis and Futuna Is 133 I3
Höö-san mt. Japan 93 E3
Hoosick NY U.S.A. 165 I2
Hoover Dam AZ/NAU.S.A. 159 F3
Hoover Memorial Reservoir OH U.S.A. 164 D3
Höövör Mongolia see Baruunbayan-Ulaan
Hopa Turkey 113 F2
Hope Canada 150 F5
Hope r. N.Z. 139 D6
Hope AK U.S.A. 149 J3
Hope AR U.S.A. 161 E5
Hope IN U.S.A. 164 C4
Hope, Lake salt flat Australia 135 C8
Hope, Point pt AK U.S.A. 148 F1
Hopedale Canada 153 J3
Hopefield S. Africa 124 D7
Hopei prov. China see Hebei
Hopelchén Mex. 167 H5
Hope Mountains Canada 153 J3
Hope Saddle pass N.Z. 139 D5
Hopes Advance, Baie b. Canada 153 H2
Hopes Advance, Cap c. Canada 147 L3
Hopes Advance Bay Canada see Aupaluk
Hopetoun Australia 137 C7
Hopetown S. Africa 124 G5
Hopewell VA U.S.A. 165 G5
Hopewell Islands Canada 152 F2
Hopin Myanmar 86 B1
Hopkins r. Australia 137 C8
Hopkins, Lake salt flat Australia 135 E6
Hopkinsville KY U.S.A. 164 B5
Hopland CA U.S.A. 158 B2
Hoquiam WA U.S.A. 156 C3
Hor Qinghai China 94 E5
Hor Xizang China 99 C7
Horace Mountain AK U.S.A. 149 J2
Horado Japan 92 C3
Hōrai Japan 92 D4
Hōraiji-san hill Japan 92 D4
Horasan Turkey 113 F2
Hörby Sweden 55 H9
Horcasitas Mex. 166 D2
Horgo Mongolia see Tariat
Hörh Uul mts Mongolia 94 F3
Horigane Japan 93 D2
Horinger China 95 G3
Horiult Mongolia see Bogd

▶Horizon Deep sea feature S. Pacific Ocean 186 I7
Deepest point in the Tonga Trench (2nd in the world).

Horki Belarus 53 F5
Horlick Mountains Antarctica 188 K1
Horlivka Ukr. 53 H6
Hormoz i. Iran 110 E5
Hormoz, Kūh-e mt. Iran 110 D5
Hormuz, Strait of Iran/Oman 110 E5
Horn Austria 57 O6
Horn r. Canada 150 G2
Horn c. Iceland 54 [inset 1]

▶Horn, Cape Chile 178 C9
Most southerly point of South America.

Hornaday r. Canada 149 Q1
Hornavan l. Sweden 54 J3
Hornbeck LA U.S.A. 167 G2
Hornbrook CA U.S.A. 156 C4
Hornburg Germany 63 K2
Horncastle U.K. 58 G5
Horndal Sweden 55 J6
Horne, Îles de is Wallis and Futuna Is see Hoorn, Îles de
Horneburg Germany 63 J1
Hörnefors Sweden 54 K5
Hornell NY U.S.A. 165 G2
Hornepayne Canada 152 D4
Hornillos Mex. 166 C3
Hornisgrinde mt. Germany 57 L6
Horn Island MS U.S.A. 167 H2
Hornkranz Namibia 124 C2
Horn Mountains Canada 150 F2
Horn Mountains AK U.S.A. 148 H3
Hornos, Cabo de Chile see Horn, Cape
Hornoy-le-Bourg France 62 B5
Horn Peak Canada 149 O3
Hornsby Australia 138 E4
Hornsea U.K. 58 G5
Hornslandet pen. Sweden 55 J6
Horodenka Ukr. 53 E6
Horodnya Ukr. 53 F6
Horodok Khmel'nyts'ka Oblast' Ukr. 53 E6
Horodok L'vivs'ka Oblast' Ukr. 53 D6
Horokanai Japan 90 F3
Horo Shan mts China 98 C4
Horoshiri-dake mt. Japan 90 F4
Horqin Shadi reg. China 95 J3
Horqin Youyi Qianqi China see Ulanhot
Horqin Zuoyi Houqi China see Ganjig
Horqin Zuoyi Zhongqi China see Baokang
Horrabridge U.K. 59 C8
Horrocks Australia 135 A7
Horru China 99 E7
Horse Cave KY U.S.A. 164 C5
Horsefly Canada 150 F4
Horseheads NY U.S.A. 165 G2
Horse Islands Canada 153 L4
Horseleap Ireland 61 D4
Horsens Denmark 55 F9
Horseshoe Bend Australia 135 F6
Horseshoe Reservoir AZ U.S.A. 159 H4
Horseshoe Seamounts sea feature N. Atlantic Ocean 184 G3
Horsham Australia 137 C8
Horsham U.K. 59 G7
Horšovský Týn Czech Rep. 63 M5
Horst hill Germany 63 J4
Hörstel Germany 63 H2
Horten Norway 55 G7
Hortobágyi nat. park Hungary 69 I1
Horton r. Canada 149 P1
Horwood Lake Canada 152 E4
Hōryūji tourist site Japan 92 B4
Hösbach Germany 63 J4
Hose, Pegunungan mts Malaysia 85 F2
Ḥoseynābād Iran 110 B3
Ḥoseynīyeh Iran 110 C4
Hoshab Pak. 111 F5
Hoshangabad India 104 D5
Hoshiarpur India 104 C3
Höshööt Arhangay Mongolia see Öldziyt
Höshööt Bayan-Ölgiy Mongolia see Tsengel
Hosoe Japan 92 D4
Hospet India 106 C3
Hospital Ireland 61 D5
Hosséré Vokre mt. Cameroon 120 E4
Hosta Butte mt. NM U.S.A. 159 I4
Hotagen r. Sweden 54 I5
Hotahudo East Timor see Hatudo
Hotaka Japan 93 D2
Hotaka-dake mt. Japan 92 D2
Hotaka-yama mt. Japan 93 F2
Hotan China 99 C5
Hotan He watercourse China 98 C4
Hotazel S. Africa 124 F4
Hot Creek Range mts NV U.S.A. 158 E2
Hotgi India 106 C2
Hotham r. Australia 135 B8
Hotham Inlet AK U.S.A. 148 G2
Hoti Seram Indon. 83 D3
Hoting Sweden 54 J4
Hot Springs AR U.S.A. 161 E5
Hot Springs NM U.S.A. see Truth or Consequences
Hot Springs SD U.S.A. 160 C3
Hot Sulphur Springs CO U.S.A. 156 G4
Hottah Lake Canada 150 G1
Hottentots Bay Namibia 124 B4
Hottentots Point Namibia 124 B4
Houdan France 62 B6
Houffalize Belgium 62 F4
Hougang Sing. 87 [inset]
Houghton MI U.S.A. 160 F2
Houghton NY U.S.A. 165 F2
Houghton Lake MI U.S.A. 164 C1
Houghton Lake l. MI U.S.A. 164 C1
Houghton le Spring U.K. 58 F4
Houie Moc, Phou mt. Laos 86 C2
Houlton ME U.S.A. 162 H2
Houma China 95 G5
Houma LA U.S.A. 161 F6
Houmen China 97 G4
Houri China 94 D4
House Range mts UT U.S.A. 159 G2
Houston Canada 150 E4
Houston AK U.S.A. 149 J3
Houston MO U.S.A. 161 F4
Houston MS U.S.A. 161 F5
Houston TX U.S.A. 161 E6
Hout r. S. Africa 125 I2
Houtman Abrolhos is Australia 135 A7
Houton U.K. 60 F2
Houwater S. Africa 124 F6
Houxia China 98 D4
Houzihe China 94 E4
Hovd Hovd Mongolia 94 B2
Hovd Övörhangay Mongolia see Bogd
Hovd prov. Mongolia 94 C2
Hovd Gol r. Mongolia 94 C1
Hove U.K. 59 G8
Hoveton U.K. 59 I6
Hovmantorp Sweden 55 I8
Hövsgöl Mongolia 95 G3
Hövsgöl prov. Mongolia 94 E1
Hövsgöl Nuur l. Mongolia 94 E1
Hövüün Mongolia see Noyon
Howar, Wadi watercourse Sudan 108 C6
Howard Australia 136 F5
Howard PA U.S.A. 165 G3
Howard SD U.S.A. 160 D2
Howard WI U.S.A. 164 A1
Howard City MI U.S.A. 164 C2
Howard Lake Canada 151 J2
Howard Pass AK U.S.A. 148 H1
Howden U.K. 58 G5
Howe, Cape Australia 138 D6
Howe, Mount Antarctica 188 J1
Howell MI U.S.A. 164 D2
Howick Canada 165 I1
Howick S. Africa 125 J5
Howland ME U.S.A. 162 G2

▶Howland Island terr. N. Pacific Ocean 133 I1
United States Unincorporated Territory.

Howlong Australia 138 C5
Howrah India see Haora
Howth Ireland 61 F4
Ḥowz well Iran 110 E3
Ḥowz-e Khān well Iran 110 E3
Ḥowz-e Panj Iran 110 E4
Ḥowz-e Panj waterhole Iran 110 D3
Howz i-Mian i-Tak Iran 110 D3
Hô Xa Vietnam 86 D3
Höxter Germany 63 J3
Hoxtolgay China 98 D3
Hoxud China 98 D4
Hoy i. U.K. 60 F2
Hoya Germany 63 J2
Höya Japan 93 F3
Høyanger Norway 55 E6
Hoyerswerda Germany 57 O5
Høylandet Norway 54 H4
Hoym Germany 63 L3
Hoyor Amt China 94 F3
Höytiäinen l. Fin. 54 P5
Hoyt Peak UT U.S.A. 159 H1
Hozu-gawa r. Japan 92 B3
Hpa-an Myanmar 86 B3
Hpapun Myanmar 86 B3
Hradec Králové Czech Rep. 57 O5
Hradiště hill Czech Rep. 63 N4
Hrasnica Bos.-Herz. 68 H3
Hrazdan Armenia 113 G2
Hrebinka Ukr. 53 G6
Hrodna Belarus 55 M10
Hrvatska country Europe see Croatia
Hrvatsko Grahovo Bos.-Herz. see Bosansko Grahovo
Hsenwi Myanmar 86 B2
Hsiang Chang i. H.K. China see Hong Kong Island
Hsiang Kang H.K. China see Hong Kong
Hsi-hseng Myanmar 86 B2
Hsin-chia-p'o country Asia see Singapore
Hsin-chia-p'o Sing. see Singapore
Hsinchu Taiwan 97 I3
Hsinking China see Changchun
Hsinying Taiwan 97 I4
Hsipaw Myanmar 86 B2
Hsi-sha Ch'ün-tao is S. China Sea see Paracel Islands
Hsiyüp'ing Yü i. Taiwan 97 H4
Hsüeh Shan mt. Taiwan 97 I3
Huab watercourse Namibia 123 B6
Huabei Pingyuan plain China 95 H4
Huachi China 95 G4
Huachinera Mex. 166 C2
Huacho Peru 176 C6
Huachuan China 90 C3
Huade China 95 H3
Huadian China 90 B4
Huadu China 97 G4
Huahai China 94 D3
Huahaizi China 98 F5
Hua Hin Thai. 87 B4
Huai'an Hebei China 95 H3
Huai'an Jiangsu China 97 H1
Huai'an Jiangsu China see Chuzhou
Huai'an Jiangsu China 97 H1
Huaibei China 97 H1
Huaibin China 97 G1
Huaicheng Guangdong China see Huaiji
Huaicheng Jiangsu China see Chuzhou
Huaide China 90 B4
Huaidian China see Shenqiu
Huai Had National Park Thai. 86 D3
Huaihua China 97 F3
Huaiji China 97 G4
Huai Kha Khaeng Wildlife Reserve nature res. Thai. 86 B4
Huailai China 95 H3
Huailillas mt. Peru 176 C5
Huainan China 97 H1
Huaining Anhui China see Shipai
Huaining Anhui China 97 H2
Huairen China 95 H4
Huairou China 95 I3
Huaiyang China 97 G1
Huaiyin Jiangsu China see Huai'an
Huaiyin Jiangsu China see Huai'an
Huaiyuan China 97 H1
Huajialing China 94 F5
Huajuápan de León Mex. 168 E5
Huaki Maluku Indon. 83 C4
Hualahuises Mex. 167 F3
Hualapai Peak AZ U.S.A. 159 G4
Hualian Taiwan see Hualien
Hualien Taiwan 97 I3
Huallaga r. Peru 176 C5
Hualong China 94 E4
Huambo Angola 123 B5
Huanan China 90 C3
Huancane Peru 176 E7
Huancavelica Peru 176 C6
Huancayo Peru 176 C6
Huancheng China see Huanxian
Huangbei China 97 G3
Huangcaoba China see Xingyi
Huangcheng China 94 E4
Huang-chou China see Huanggang
Huangchuan China 97 G1
Huanggang China 97 G2
Huang Hai sea N. Pacific Ocean see Yellow Sea
Huang He r. China see Yellow River
Huanghe Kou r. mouth China 95 I4
Huanghua China 95 I4
Huangjian China 97 I1
Huang-kang China see Huanggang
Huangling China 95 G5
Huangliu China 97 F5
Huanglong China 95 G5
Huanglongsi China 95 H5
Huangmao Jian mt. China 97 H3
Huangmei China 97 G2
Huangpu China 97 G4
Huangqi China 97 H3
Huangshan China 97 H2
Huangshi China 97 G2
Huangtu Gaoyuan plat. China 95 F4
Huangxian China see Donglai
Huangyan China 97 I2
Huangyang China 94 E4
Huangyuan China 94 E4
Huangzhong China 94 E4
Huangzhou China see Huanggang
Huaning China 96 D3
Huaniushan China 94 C3
Huanjiang China 97 F3
Huanren China 90 B4
Huanshan China see Yuhuan
Huantai China 95 I4
Huánuco Peru 176 C5
Huanxian China 95 F4
Huaping China 96 D3
Huap'ing Yü i. Taiwan 97 I3
Huaqiao China 96 E2
Huaqiaozhen China see Huaqiao
Huaráz Peru 176 C5
Huarmey Peru 176 C6
Huarong China 97 G2
Huascarán, Nevado de mt. Peru 176 C5
Huasco Chile 178 B3
Hua Shan mt. China 95 G5

Huashaoying China **95** H3
Huashixia China **94** D5
Huashugou China *see* **Jingtieshan**
Huashulinzi China **90** B4
Huatabampo Mex. **166** C3
Huatong China **95** J3
Huatusco Mex. **167** F5
Huauchinango Mex. **167** F4
Huaxian *Guangdong* China *see* **Huadu**
Huaxian *Henan* China **95** H5
Huaxian *Shaanxi* China **95** G5
Huayacocotla Mex. **167** F4
Huayang China *see* **Jixi**
Huayin China **97** F1
Huayuan China **97** F2
Huayxay Laos **86** C2
Huazangsi China *see* **Tianzhu**
Huazhaizi China **94** E4
Hubballi India *see* **Hubli**
Hubbard, Mount Canada/U.S.A. **149** M3
Hubbard, Pointe *pt* Canada **153** I2
Hubbard Lake *MI* U.S.A. **164** D1
Hubbart Point Canada **151** M3
Hubei *prov.* China **97** G2
Hubli India **106** B3
Hückelhoven Germany **62** G3
Hucknall U.K. **59** F5
Huddersfield U.K. **58** F5
Huder China **95** J1
Hüder Mongolia **95** F1
Hudiksvall Sweden **55** J6
Hudson *MA* U.S.A. **165** J2
Hudson *MD* U.S.A. **165** G4
Hudson *MI* U.S.A. **164** C3
Hudson *NH* U.S.A. **165** J2
Hudson *NY* U.S.A. **165** I2
Hudson *r. NY* U.S.A. **165** I3
Hudson, Baie d' *sea* Canada *see* **Hudson Bay**
Hudson, Détroit d' *strait* Canada *see* **Hudson Strait**
Hudson Bay Canada **151** K4
Hudson Bay *sea* Canada **147** J4
Hudson Falls *NY* U.S.A. **165** I2
Hudson Island Tuvalu *see* **Nanumanga**
Hudson Mountains Antarctica **188** K2
Hudson's Hope Canada **150** F3
Hudson Strait Canada **147** K3
Huê Vietnam **86** D3
Huehuetán Mex. **167** G6
Huehuetenango Guat. **167** H6
Huehueto, Cerro *mt.* Mex. **161** B7
Huejuqilla Mex. **166** E4
Huejutla Mex. **167** F4
Huelva Spain **67** C5
Huentelauquén Chile **178** B4
Huépac Mex. **166** C2
Huércal-Overa Spain **67** F5
Huertecillas Mex. **161** C7
Huesca Spain **67** F2
Huéscar Spain **67** E5
Huétamo Mex. **167** E5
Huggins Island *AK* U.S.A. **148** I2
Hughenden Australia **136** D4
Hughes *r.* Canada **151** K3
Hughes *AK* U.S.A. **148** I2
Hughes (abandoned) Australia **135** E7
Hughson *CA* U.S.A. **158** C3
Hugli *r. mouth* India **105** F5
Hugli-Chinsurah India **105** G5
Hugo *CO* U.S.A. **160** C4
Hugo *OK* U.S.A. **161** E5
Hugo Lake *OK* U.S.A. **161** E5
Hugoton *KS* U.S.A. **161** C4
Huhehot China *see* **Hohhot**
Huhhot China *see* **Hohhot**
Huhudi S. Africa **124** G4
Hui'an China **97** H3
Hui'anpu China **94** F4
Huiarau Range *mts* N.Z. **139** F4
Huib-Hoch Plateau Namibia **124** C4
Huichang China **97** G3
Huicheng *Anhui* China *see* **Shexian**
Huicheng *Guangdong* China *see* **Huilai**
Huicholes, Sierra de los *mts* Mex. **166** D4
Huidong China **96** D3
Huihe China **95** I1
Huijbergen Neth. **62** E3
Huiji He *r.* China **95** H5
Huila, Nevado de *vol.* Col. **176** C3
Huíla, Planalto da Angola **123** B5
Huilai China **97** H4
Huili China **96** D3
Huimanguillo Mex. **167** G5
Huimin China **95** I4
Huinan China *see* **Nanhui**
Huining China **94** F5
Huinong China **94** F4
Huishi China *see* **Huining**
Huishui China **96** E3
Huiten Nur *l.* China **94** B5
Huitong China **97** F3
Huittinen Fin. **55** M6
Huitupan Mex. **167** G5
Huixian *Gansu* China **96** E1
Huixian *Henan* China **95** H5
Huixtla Mex. **167** G6
Huiyang China *see* **Huizhou**
Huize China **96** D3
Huizhou China **97** G4
Hujirt *Arhangay* Mongolia *see* **Tsetserleg**
Hujirt *Övörhangay* Mongolia **94** E2
Hujirt *Töv* Mongolia *see* **Delgerhaan**
Hujr Saudi Arabia **108** F4
Hukawng Valley Myanmar **86** B1
Hukuntsi Botswana **124** E2
Hulahula *r. AK* U.S.A. **149** K1
Hulan China **90** B3
Hulan Ergi China **95** J2
Ḩulayfah Saudi Arabia **108** F4
Ḩulayḩilah *well* Syria **107** D2
Huliao China *see* **Dabu**
Hulilan Iran **110** B3
Hulin China **90** D3
Hulingol China **95** J2
Hulin Gol *r.* China **90** B3
Hull Canada **165** H1
Hull U.K. *see* **Kingston upon Hull**
Hull Island *atoll* Kiribati *see* **Orona**
Hultsfred Sweden **55** I8
Huludao China **95** J3
Hulu Hu *salt l.* China **99** E6
Hulun Buir China **95** I1
Hulun Nur *l.* China **95** I1
Ḩulwān Egypt **112** C5
Huma China **90** B2
Humahuaca Arg. **178** C2
Humaitá Brazil **176** F5
Humaya *r.* Mex. **157** G8
Humaym *well* U.A.E. **110** D6
Humayyān, Jabal *hill* Saudi Arabia **110** B5
Humber, Mouth of the U.K. **58** H5
Humboldt Canada **151** J4
Humboldt *AZ* U.S.A. **159** G4
Humboldt *NE* U.S.A. **160** E3
Humboldt *NV* U.S.A. **158** D1
Humboldt *r. NV* U.S.A. **158** D1
Humboldt Bay *CA* U.S.A. **156** B4
Humboldt Range *mts NV* U.S.A. **158** D1
Humbolt Salt Marsh *NV* U.S.A. **158** E2
Hume *r.* Canada **149** O2
Humeburn Australia **138** B1
Hu Men *sea chan.* China **97** G4
Hume Reservoir Australia **138** C5
Humphrey Island *atoll* Cook Is *see* **Manihiki**
Humphreys, Mount *CA* U.S.A. **158** D3
Humphreys Peak *AZ* U.S.A. **159** H4
Hūn Libya **121** E2
Húnaflói *b.* Iceland **54** [inset 1]
Hunan *prov.* China **97** F3
Hundeluft Germany **63** M3
Hunedoara Romania **69** J2
Hünfeld Germany **63** J4
Hungary *country* Europe **65** H2
Hungerford Australia **138** B2
Hung Fa Leng *hill H.K.* China *see* **Robin's Nest**
Hüngiy Gol *r.* Mongolia **94** C1
Hŭngnam N. Korea **91** B5
Hung Shui Kiu *H.K.* China **97** [inset]
Hưng Yên Vietnam **86** D2
Hun He *r.* China **95** J3
Hunjiang China *see* **Baishan**
Huns Mountains Namibia **124** C4
Hunstanton U.K. **59** H6
Hunte *r.* Germany **63** I1
Hunter *r.* Australia **138** E4
Hunter, Mount *AK* U.S.A. **149** J3
Hunter Island Australia **137** [inset]
Hunter Island Canada **150** D5
Hunter Island S. Pacific Ocean **133** H4
Hunter Islands Australia **137** [inset]
Huntingburg *IN* U.S.A. **164** B4
Huntingdon Canada **165** H1
Huntingdon U.K. **59** G6
Huntingdon *PA* U.S.A. **165** G3
Huntingdon *TN* U.S.A. **161** F4
Huntington *IN* U.S.A. **164** C3
Huntington *OR* U.S.A. **156** D3
Huntington *WV* U.S.A. **164** D4
Huntington Beach *CA* U.S.A. **158** D5
Huntington Creek *r. NV* U.S.A. **159** F1
Huntly N.Z. **139** E3
Huntly U.K. **60** G3
Hunt Mountain *WY* U.S.A. **156** G3
Huntsville Canada **164** F1
Huntsville *AL* U.S.A. **163** C5
Huntsville *AR* U.S.A. **161** E4
Huntsville *TN* U.S.A. **164** C5
Huntsville *TX* U.S.A. **161** E6
Hunucmá Mex. **167** H4
Hunyuan China **95** H4
Hunza *r.* Pak. **99** A6
Hunza *reg.* Pak. **104** C1
Huocheng China **98** C3
Huoer China *see* **Hor**
Huojia China **95** H5
Huolin He *r.* China *see* **Hulin Gol**
Huolongmen China **90** B2
Huolu China *see* **Luquan**
Hương Khê Vietnam **86** D3
Huonville Australia **137** [inset]
Huoqiu China **97** H1
Huoshan China **97** H2
Huo Shan *mt.* China *see* **Baima Jian**
Huoshao Tao *i.* Taiwan *see* **Lü Tao**
Huoxian China *see* **Huozhou**
Huozhou China **95** G4
Hupeh *prov.* China *see* **Hubei**
Hupnik *r.* Turkey **107** C1
Hupu India **96** B2
Ḩūr Iran **110** E4
Hurault, Lac *l.* Canada **153** H3
Ḩuraydīn, Wādī *watercourse* Egypt **107** A4
Huraysān *reg.* Saudi Arabia **110** B6
Hurd, Cape Canada **164** E1
Hurd Island Kiribati *see* **Arorae**
Hure China **95** J3
Hüreemaral Mongolia **94** D2
Hüremt Mongolia *see* **Sayhan**
Hürent Mongolia *see* **Taragt**
Hure Qi China *see* **Hure**
Hurghada Egypt *see* **Al Ghurdaqah**
Hurleg China **94** D4
Hurleg Hu *l.* China **94** D4
Hurler's Cross Ireland **61** D5
Hurley *NM* U.S.A. **159** I5
Hurley *WI* U.S.A. **160** F2
Hurmagai Pak. **111** G4
Huron *CA* U.S.A. **158** C3
Huron *SD* U.S.A. **160** D2

▶**Huron, Lake** Canada/U.S.A. **164** D1
2nd largest lake in North America and 4th in the world.

Hurricane *UT* U.S.A. **159** G3
Hursley U.K. **59** F7
Hurst Green U.K. **59** H7
Hurung, Gunung *mt.* Indon. **85** F2
Husain Nika Pak. **111** H4
Húsavík *Norðurland eystra* Iceland **54** [inset 1]
Húsavík *Vestfirðir* Iceland **54** [inset 1]
Huseyinabat Turkey *see* **Alaca**
Huseyınli Turkey *see* **Kızılırmak**
Hūshak Iran **111** F5
Hushan *Zhejiang* China **97** H2
Hushan *Zhejiang* China *see* **Wuyi**
Hushan *Zhejiang* China *see* **Cixi**
Huşi Romania **69** M1
Huskvarna Sweden **55** I8
Huslia *AK* U.S.A. **148** H2
Huslia *r. AK* U.S.A. **148** H2
Husn Jordan *see* **Al Ḩişn**
Ḩusn Āl 'Abr Yemen **108** G6
Husnes Norway **55** D7
Husum Germany **57** L3
Husum Sweden **54** K5
Hutag Mongolia *see* **Hutag-Öndör**
Hutag-Öndör Mongolia **94** E1
Hutanopan *Sumatera* Indon. **84** B2
Hutchinson *KS* U.S.A. **160** D4
Hutchinson *MN* U.S.A. **160** E2
Hutch Mountain *AZ* U.S.A. **159** H4
Hutou China **90** D3
Hutsonville *IL* U.S.A. **164** B4
Hutton, Mount *hill* Australia **137** E5
Hutton Range *hills* Australia **135** C6
Hutubi China **98** D3
Hutubi He *r.* China **98** D3
Hutuo He *r.* China **95** I4
Huvadhu Atoll Maldives **103** D11
Hüvek Turkey *see* **Bozova**
Hūvīān, Kūh-e *mts* Iran **111** E5
Ḩuwār *i.* Bahrain **110** C5
Huwaytat *reg.* Saudi Arabia **107** C5
Huxi China **97** G3
Huxian China **95** G5
Huzhong China **90** A2
Huzhou China **97** I2
Huzhu China **94** E4
Hvannadalshnúkur *vol.* Iceland **54** [inset 1]
Hvar *i.* Croatia **68** G3
Hvide Sande Denmark **55** F8
Hvíta *r.* Iceland **54** [inset 1]
Hwange Zimbabwe **123** C5
Hwange National Park Zimbabwe **123** C5
Hwang Ho *r.* China *see* **Yellow River**
Hwedza Zimbabwe **123** D5
Hwlffordd U.K. *see* **Haverfordwest**
Hyakuriga-take *hill* Japan **92** B3
Hyannis *MA* U.S.A. **165** J3
Hyannis *NE* U.S.A. **160** C3
Hyargas Nuur *salt l.* Mongolia **94** C1
Hyco Lake *NC* U.S.A. **164** F5
Hyde N.Z. **139** C7
Hyden Australia **135** B8
Hyden *KY* U.S.A. **164** D5
Hyde Park *VT* U.S.A. **165** I1
Hyder *AK* U.S.A. **149** O5
Hyderabad India **106** C2
Hyderabad Pak. **111** H5
Hydra *i.* Greece *see* **Ydra**
Hyères France **66** H5
Hyères, Îles d' *is* France **66** H5
Hyesan N. Korea **90** C4
Hyland *r.* Canada **149** O4
Hyland, Mount Australia **138** F3
Hyland Post Canada **150** D3
Hyllestad Norway **55** D6
Hyltebruk Sweden **55** H8
Hyndman Peak *ID* U.S.A. **156** E4
Hyōgo *pref.* Japan **92** A3
Hyōno-sen *mt.* Japan **91** D6
Hyrcania Iran *see* **Gorgān**
Hyrynsalmi Fin. **54** P4
Hysham *MT* U.S.A. **156** G3
Hythe Canada **150** G4
Hythe U.K. **59** I7
Hyūga Japan **91** C6
Hyvinkää Fin. **55** N6

I

Iaciara Brazil **179** B1
Iaco *r.* Brazil **176** E5
Iaçu Brazil **179** C1
Iadera Croatia *see* **Zadar**
Iaeger *WV* U.S.A. **164** E5
Iakora Madag. **123** E6
Ialomiţa *r.* Romania **69** L2
Ianca Romania **69** L2
Iaşi Romania **69** L1
Iba *Luzon* Phil. **82** B3
Ibadan Nigeria **120** D4
Ibagué Col. **176** C3
Ibaiti Brazil **179** A3
Ibapah *UT* U.S.A. **159** G1
Ibaraki *Ibaraki* Japan **93** G2
Ibaraki *Ōsaka* Japan **92** B4
Ibaraki *pref.* Japan **93** G2
Ibarra Ecuador **176** C3
Ibb Yemen **108** F7
Ibbenbüren Germany **63** H2
Iberá, Esteros del *marsh* Arg. **178** E3
Iberia Peru **176** E6

▶**Iberian Peninsula** Europe **67**
Consists of Portugal, Spain and Gibraltar.

Iberville, Lac d' *l.* Canada **153** G3
Ibeto Nigeria **120** D3
iBhayi S. Africa *see* **Port Elizabeth**
Ibi *Sumatera* Indon. **84** B1
Ibi Nigeria **120** D4
Ibiá Brazil **179** B2
Ibiaí Brazil **179** B2
Ibiapaba, Serra da *hills* Brazil **177** J4
Ibiassucê Brazil **179** C1
Ibicaraí Brazil **179** D1
Ibigawa Japan **92** C3
Ibi-gawa *r.* Japan **92** C3
Ibiquera Brazil **179** C1
Ibirama Brazil **179** A4
Ibiranhém Brazil **179** C2
Ibi-Sekigahara-Yōrō Kokutei-kōen *park* Japan **92** C3
Ibitinga Brazil **179** A3
Ibiza Spain **67** G4
Ibiza *i.* Spain **67** G4
Iblei, Monti *mts Sicily* Italy **68** F6
Ibn Buşayyiş *well* Saudi Arabia **110** B5
Ibotirama Brazil **177** J6
Iboundji, Mont *hill* Gabon **122** B4
Ibrā' Oman **110** E6
İbradı Turkey **112** C3
Ibrī Oman **110** E6
Ibu *Halmahera* Indon. **83** C2
Ibuhos *i.* Phil. **82** C1
Ibuki Japan **92** C3
Ibuki-sanchi *mts* Japan **92** C3
Ibuki-yama *mt.* Japan **92** C3
Ica *r.* Col. *see* **Putumayo**
Ica Peru **176** C6
Icaiché Mex. **167** H5
Içana Brazil **176** E3
Içana *r.* Brazil **176** E3
Icaria *i.* Greece *see* **Ikaria**
Icatu Brazil **177** J4
Iceberg Canyon *gorge NV* U.S.A. **159** F3
İçel Turkey *see* **Mersin**

▶**Iceland** *country* Europe **54** [inset 1]
2nd largest island in Europe.

Iceland Basin *sea feature* N. Atlantic Ocean **184** G2
Icelandic Plateau *sea feature* N. Atlantic Ocean **189** I2
Ichalkaranji India **106** B2
Ichifusa-yama *mt.* Japan **91** C6
Ichihara Japan **93** G3
Ichikai Japan **93** G2
Ichikawa *Chiba* Japan **93** F3
Ichikawa *Hyōgo* Japan **92** A3
Ichi-kawa *r.* Japan **92** A4
Ichikawadaimon Japan **93** E3
Ichinomiya *Aichi* Japan **92** C3
Ichinomiya *Aichi* Japan **92** D4
Ichinomiya *Chiba* Japan **93** G3
Ichinomiya *Hyōgo* Japan **92** A4
Ichinomiya *Yamanashi* Japan **93** E3
Ichinoseki Japan **91** F5
Ichinskaya Sopka, Vulkan *vol.* Rus. Fed. **77** Q4
Ichishi Japan **92** C4
Ichkeul, Parc National de l' Tunisia **68** C6
Ichnya Ukr. **53** G6
Ichtegem Belgium **62** D3
Ichtershausen Germany **63** K4
Icó Brazil **177** K5
Iconha Brazil **179** C3
Iconium Turkey *see* **Konya**
Icosium Alg. *see* **Algiers**
Iculisma France *see* **Angoulême**
Icy Bay *AK* U.S.A. **149** K4
Icy Bay *AK* U.S.A. **149** L4
Icy Cape *AK* U.S.A. **148** G1
Icy Strait *AK* U.S.A. **149** N4
İd Turkey *see* **Narman**
Idabel *OK* U.S.A. **161** E5
Ida Grove *IA* U.S.A. **160** E3
Idah Nigeria **120** D4
Idaho *state* U.S.A. **156** E3
Idaho City *ID* U.S.A. **156** E4
Idaho Falls *ID* U.S.A. **156** E4
Idalia National Park Australia **136** D5
Idar India **104** C5
Idar-Oberstein Germany **63** H5
Ide Japan **92** B4
Ider Mongolia *see* **Galt**
Ideriyn Gol *r.* Mongolia **94** E1
Idfū Egypt **108** D5
Idhān Awbārī *des.* Libya **120** E2
Idhān Murzūq *des.* Libya **120** E2
Idhra *i.* Greece *see* **Ydra**
Idi Amin Dada, Lake Dem. Rep. Congo/Uganda *see* **Edward, Lake**
Idiofa Dem. Rep. Congo **123** B4
Iditarod *AK* U.S.A. **148** H3
Iditarod *r. AK* U.S.A. **148** H3
Idivuoma Sweden **54** M2
Idkū Egypt **112** C5
Idle *r.* U.K. **58** G5
Idlewild *airport NY* U.S.A. *see* **John F. Kennedy**
Idlib Syria **107** C2
Idra *i.* Greece *see* **Ydra**
Idre Sweden **55** H6
Idstein Germany **63** I4
Idutywa S. Africa **125** I7
Idzhevan Armenia *see* **Ijevan**
Iecava Latvia **55** N8
Iepê Brazil **179** A3
Ieper Belgium **62** C4
Ierapetra Greece **69** K7
Ierissou, Kolpos *b.* Greece **69** J4
Iešjávri *l.* Norway **54** N2
Ifakara Tanz. **123** D4
Ifalik *atoll* Micronesia **81** K5
Ifaluk *atoll* Micronesia *see* **Ifalik**
Ifanadiana Madag. **123** E6
Ife Nigeria **120** D4
Ifenat Chad **121** E3
Iferouâne Niger **120** D3
Iffley Australia **136** C3
Ifjord Norway **54** O1
Ifôghas, Adrar des *hills* Mali **120** D3
Iforas, Adrar des *hills* Mali *see* **Ifôghas, Adrar des**
Iga Japan **92** C4
Igan *Sarawak* Malaysia **85** E2
Igan *r.* Malaysia **85** E2
Iganga Uganda **121** G4
Igarapava Brazil **179** B3
Igarka Rus. Fed. **76** J3
Igatpuri India **106** B2
Igbeti Nigeria *see* **Igbetti**
Igbetti Nigeria **120** D4
Igdir Iran **110** B2
Iğdır Turkey **113** G3
Igel'veyem *r.* Rus. Fed. **148** D2
Iggesund Sweden **55** J6
Igikpak, Mount *AK* U.S.A. **148** I2
Igiugig *AK* U.S.A. **148** I4
Igizyar China **111** J2
Iglesias *Sardinia* Italy **68** C5
Iglesiente *reg. Sardinia* Italy **68** C5
Igloolik Canada **147** J3
Igluligaarjuk Canada *see* **Chesterfield Inlet**
Ignace Canada **151** N5
Ignacio Zaragosa Mex. **166** D2
Ignacio Zaragoza *Tamaulipas* Mex. **167** F4
Ignacio Zaragoza *Zacatecas* Mex. **161** C8
Ignalina Lith. **55** O9
İğneada Turkey **69** L4
İğneada Burnu *pt* Turkey **69** M4
Ignoitijala India **87** A5
iGoli S. Africa *see* **Johannesburg**
Igom *Papua* Indon. **83** D3
Igoumenitsa Greece **69** I5
Igra Rus. Fed. **51** Q4
Igrim Rus. Fed. **51** S3
Iguaçu *r.* Brazil **179** A4
Iguaçu, Saltos do *waterfall* Arg./Brazil *see* **Iguaçu Falls**
Iguaçu Falls Arg./Brazil **178** F3
Iguaí Brazil **179** C1
Iguala Mex. **168** E5
Igualada Spain **67** G3
Iguape Brazil **179** B4
Iguaraçu Brazil **179** A3
Iguatama Brazil **179** B3
Iguatemi Brazil **178** F2
Iguatu Brazil **177** K5
Iguazú, Cataratas do *waterfall* Arg./Brazil *see* **Iguaçu Falls**
Iguéla Gabon **122** A4
Iguidi, Erg *des.* Alg./Mauritania **120** C2
Igunga Tanz. **123** D4
Iharaña Madag. **123** E5
Ihavandhippolhu Atoll Maldives **106** B5
Ihavandiffulu Atoll Maldives *see* **Ihavandhippolhu Atoll**
Ih Bogd Uul *mt.* Mongolia **102** J3
Ihbulag Mongolia *see* **Hanbogd**
Ihhayrhan Mongolia *see* **Bayan-Önjüül**
Ihosy Madag. **123** E6
Ih Tal China **95** J3
Ihtamir Mongolia **94** E2
Ih Tol Gol China **95** J1
Ih-Uul Mongolia **94** E1
Iida Japan **93** D3
Iide-san *mt.* Japan **91** E5
Iijärvi *l.* Fin. **54** O2
Iijima Japan **93** D3
Iijoki *r.* Fin. **54** N4
Iinan Japan **92** C4
Iioka Japan **93** G3
Iisalmi Fin. **54** O5
Iitaka Japan **92** C4
Iiyama Japan **93** E2
Iizuka Japan **91** C6
Ijebu-Ode Nigeria **120** D4
Ijen-Merapi-Maelang, Cagar Alam *nature res. Jawa* Indon. **85** F5
Ijevan Armenia **113** G2
IJmuiden Neth. **62** E2
IJssel *r.* Neth. **62** F2
IJsselmeer *l.* Neth. **62** F2
IJzer *r.* France *see* **Yser**
Ikaahuk Canada *see* **Sachs Harbour**
Ikaalinen Fin. **55** M6
Ikageleng S. Africa **125** H3
Ikageng S. Africa **125** H4
Ikaho Japan **93** E2
iKapa S. Africa *see* **Cape Town**
Ikare Nigeria **120** D4
Ikaria *i.* Greece **69** L6
Ikaruga Japan **92** B4
Ikast Denmark **55** F8
Ikawa Japan **93** E3
Ikeda *Fukui* Japan **92** C3
Ikeda *Hokkaidō* Japan **90** F4
Ikeda *Nagano* Japan **93** D2
Ikeda *Ōsaka* Japan **92** B3
Ikegoya-yama *mt.* Japan **92** C4
Ikela Dem. Rep. Congo **122** C4
Ikhtiman Bulg. **69** J3
Ikhutseng S. Africa **124** G5
Iki-Burul Rus. Fed. **53** J7
Ikom Nigeria **120** D4
Ikoma Japan **92** B4
Ikpikpuk *r. AK* U.S.A. **148** I1
Iksan S. Korea **91** B6
Ikuji-hana *pt* Japan **92** D2
Ikungu Tanz. **123** D4
Ikuno Japan **92** A3
Ikusaka Japan **93** D2
Ilagan *Luzon* Phil. **82** C2
Ilaisamis Kenya **122** D3
Īlām Iran **110** B3
Ilam Nepal **105** F4
Ilan Taiwan **97** I3
Ilave Peru **176** E7
Iława Poland **57** Q4
Ilazārān, Kūh-e *mt.* Iran **110** E4
Il Bogd Uul *mts* Mongolia **94** D2
Île-à-la-Crosse Canada **151** J4
Île-à-la-Crosse, Lac *l.* Canada **151** J4
Ilebo Dem. Rep. Congo **123** C4
Île-de-France *admin. reg.* France **62** C6
Île Europa *i.* Indian Ocean *see* **Europa, Île**
Ilek Kazakh. **51** Q5
Ilemi Triangle *terr.* Africa **122** D3
Ilen *r.* Ireland **61** C6
Ileret Kenya **122** D3
Ileza Rus. Fed. **52** I3
Ilfeld Germany **63** K3
Ilford Canada **151** M3
Ilford U.K. **59** H7
Ilfracombe Australia **136** D4
Ilfracombe U.K. **59** C7
Ilgaz Turkey **112** D2
Ilgın Turkey **112** C3
Ilha Grande, Represa *resr* Brazil **178** F2
Ilha Solteíra, Represa *resr* Brazil **179** A3
Ílhavo Port. **67** B3
Ilhéus Brazil **179** D1
Ili *r.* China/Kazakh. **98** B3
Ili Kazakh. *see* **Kapchagay**
Iliamna *AK* U.S.A. **148** I4
Iliamna Lake *AK* U.S.A. **148** I4
Iliamna Volcano *AK* U.S.A. **148** I3
İliç Turkey **112** E3
Il'ichevsk Azer. *see* **Şərur**
Il'ichevsk Ukr. *see* **Illichivs'k**
Ilici Spain *see* **Elche-Elx**
Iligan *Mindanao* Phil. **82** D4
Iligan Bay *Mindanao* Phil. **82** D4
Iligan Point *Luzon* Phil. **82** C2
Ilimananngip Nunaa *i.* Greenland **147** P2
Il'inka *Astrakhanskaya Oblast'* Rus. Fed. **53** J7
Il'inka *Respublika Tyva* Rus. Fed. **94** C1
Il'inskiy *Permskiy Kray* Rus. Fed. **51** R4
Il'inskiy *Sakhalinskaya Oblast'* Rus. Fed. **90** F3
Il'insko-Podomskoye Rus. Fed. **52** J3
Ilin Strait Phil. **82** C3
Iliomar East Timor **83** C5
Ilion *NY* U.S.A. **165** H2
Ilium *tourist site* Turkey *see* **Troy**
Ilivit Mountains *AK* U.S.A. **148** G3
Iliysk Kazakh. *see* **Kapchagay**
Ilkal India **106** C3
Ilkeston U.K. **59** F6
Ilkley U.K. **58** F5
Illana Bay *Mindanao* Phil. **82** C5
Illapel Chile **178** B4
Illéla Niger **120** D3
Iller *r.* Germany **57** L6
Illichivs'k Ukr. **69** N1
Illimani, Nevado de *mt.* Bol. **176** E7
Illinois *r. IL* U.S.A. **160** F4
Illinois *state* U.S.A. **164** A3
Illizi Alg. **120** D2
Illogwa *watercourse* Australia **136** A5
Ilm *r.* Germany **63** L3
Ilmajoki Fin. **54** M5
Il'men', Ozero *l.* Rus. Fed. **52** F4
Ilmenau Germany **63** K4
Ilmenau *r.* Germany **63** K1
Ilminster U.K. **59** E8
Ilnik *AK* U.S.A. **148** H4
Ilo Peru **176** D7
Iloc *i.* Phil. **82** B4
Iloilo *Panay* Phil. **82** C4
Iloilo Strait Phil. **82** C4
Ilomantsi Fin. **54** Q5
Ilong India **96** B3
Ilorin Nigeria **120** D4
Ilovlya Rus. Fed. **53** I6
Ilsede Germany **63** K2
Iluka Australia **138** F2
Ilulissat Greenland **147** M3
Iluppur India **106** C4
Ilva *i.* Italy *see* **Elba, Isola d'**
Imabari Japan **91** D6
Imadate Japan **92** C3
Imaichi Japan **93** F2
Imajō Japan **92** C3
Imala Moz. **123** D5
Imam-baba Turkm. **111** F2
İmamoğlu Turkey **112** D3
Imām Şāḩib Afgh. **111** H2
Iman Rus. Fed. *see* **Dal'nerechensk**
Iman *r.* Rus. Fed. **90** D3
Imari Japan **91** C6
Imaruí Brazil **179** A5
Imataca, Serranía de *mts* Venez. **176** F2
Imatra Fin. **55** P6
Imazu Japan **92** C3
Imba-numa *l.* Japan *see* **Inba-numa**
Imbituva Brazil **179** A4
imeni 26 Bakinskikh Komissarov Azer. *see* **Uzboy**
imeni Babushkina Rus. Fed. **52** I4
imeni Chapayevka Turkm. *see* **S. A. Nyýazow Adyndaky**
imeni Kalinina Tajik. *see* **Cheshtebe**
imeni Kirova Kazakh. *see* **Kopbirlik**
imeni Petra Stuchki Latvia *see* **Aizkraukle**
imeni Poliny Osipenko Rus. Fed. **90** E1
imeni Tel'mana Rus. Fed. **90** D2
Īmī Eth. **122** E3
Imishli Azer. *see* **İmişli**
İmişli Azer. **113** H3
Imit Pak. **104** C1
Imja-do *i.* S. Korea **91** B6
Imlay *NV* U.S.A. **158** D1
Imlay City *MI* U.S.A. **164** D2
Imola Italy **68** D2
iMonti S. Africa *see* **East London**
Impendle S. Africa **125** I5
Imperatriz Brazil **177** I5
Imperia Italy **68** C3
Imperial *CA* U.S.A. **159** F5
Imperial *NE* U.S.A. **160** C3
Imperial Beach *CA* U.S.A. **158** E5
Imperial Dam *AZ/CA* U.S.A. **159** F5
Imperial Valley *plain CA* U.S.A. **159** F5
Imperieuse Reef Australia **134** B4
Impfondo Congo **122** B3
Imphal India **105** H4
İmralı Adası *i.* Turkey **69** M4
İmroz Turkey **69** K4
İmroz *i.* Turkey *see* **Gökçeada**
Imtān Syria **107** C3
Imuris Mex. **166** C2
Imuruan Bay *Palawan* Phil. **82** B4
Imuruk Basin *l. AK* U.S.A. **148** F2
Imuruk Lake *AK* U.S.A. **148** G2
In *r.* Rus. Fed. **90** D2
Ina *Ibaraki* Japan **93** G3
Ina *Nagano* Japan **93** D3
Inabe Japan **92** C3
Inabu Japan **92** D3
Inae Japan **92** C3
Inagauan *Palawan* Phil. **82** B4
Inagawa Japan **92** B4
Ina-gawa *r.* Japan **92** B4
Inage Japan **93** G3
Inagi Japan **93** F3
Inalik *AK* U.S.A. *see* **Diomede**
Inambari *r.* Peru **176** E6
Inami *Hyōgo* Japan **92** A4
Inami *Toyama* Japan **92** C2
Inanam *Sabah* Malaysia **85** G1
Inanudak Bay *AK* U.S.A. **148** E5
Inari Fin. **54** O2
Inarijärvi *l.* Fin. **54** O2
Inarijoki *r.* Fin./Norway **54** N2
Inasa Japan **92** D4
Inazawa Japan **92** C3
Inba Japan **93** G3
Inba-numa *l.* Japan **93** G3
Inca Spain **67** H4
İnce Burnu *pt* Turkey **69** L4
İnce Burun *pt* Turkey **112** D2
Inch Ireland **61** F5
Inchard, Loch *b.* U.K. **60** D2
Incheon S. Korea *see* **Inch'ŏn**
Inchicronan Lough *l.* Ireland **61** D5
Inch'ŏn S. Korea **91** B5
Inchoun Rus. Fed. **148** E2
Incirli Turkey *see* **Karasu**
Indaal, Loch *b.* U.K. **60** C5
Indalsälven *r.* Sweden **54** J5
Indalstø Norway **55** D6
Inda Silasē Eth. **122** D2
Indaw Myanmar **86** A2
Indawgyi, Lake Myanmar **96** C3
Indé Mex. **166** D3
Indefatigable Island *Galápagos* Ecuador *see* **Santa Cruz, Isla**
Independence *CA* U.S.A. **158** D3
Independence *IA* U.S.A. **160** F3
Independence *KS* U.S.A. **161** E4
Independence *KY* U.S.A. **164** C4
Independence *MO* U.S.A. **160** E4
Independence *VA* U.S.A. **164** E5
Independence Mountains *NV* U.S.A. **156** D4
Inder China **95** J2
Inderbor Kazakh. **100** E2
Indi India **106** C2

▶**India** *country* Asia **103** E7
2nd most populous country in Asia and the world. 3rd largest country in Asia and 7th in the world.

Indian *r.* Canada **149** M3
Indiana *PA* U.S.A. **164** F3
Indiana *state* U.S.A. **164** B3
Indian-Antarctic Ridge *sea feature* Southern Ocean **186** D9

Jagatsinghapur India see Jagatsinghpur
Jagatsinghpur India 105 F5
Jagdalpur India 106 D2
Jagdaqi China 95 K1
Jagersfontein S. Africa 125 G5
Jaggang China 99 B6
Jaggayyapeta India 106 D2
Jaghīn Iran 110 E5
Jagok Tso salt l. China see Urru Co
Jagsamka China see Luding
Jagst r. Germany 63 J5
Jagtial India 106 C2
Jaguariaíva Brazil 179 A4
Jaguaripe Brazil 179 D1
Jagüey Grande Cuba 163 D8
Jahām, 'Irq des. Saudi Arabia 110 B5
Jahanabad India see Jehanabad
Jahmah well Iraq 113 G5
Jahrom Iran 110 D4
Jaicós Brazil 177 J5
Jaigarh India 106 B2
Jailolo Halmahera Indon. 83 C2
Jailolo, Selat sea chan. Maluku Indon. 83 D3
Jailolo Gilolo i. Maluku Indon. see Halmahera
Jainca China 94 E5
Jainpur India 105 E4
Jaintapur Bangl. see Jaintiapur
Jaintiapur Bangl. 105 H4
Jainzhug China see Gutang
Jaipur India 104 C4
Jaipurhat Bangl. see Joypurhat
Jais India 105 E4
Jaisalmer India 104 B4
Jaisamand Lake India 104 C4
Jaitaran India 104 C4
Jaitgarh hill India 106 C1
Jajapur India see Jajpur
Jajarkot Nepal 109 N4
Jajce Bos.-Herz. 68 G2
Jajnagar state India see Odisha
Jajpur India 105 F5
Jakān mt. Afgh. 111 G4
Jakar Bhutan 105 G4

▶Jakarta Jawa Indon. 84 D4
Capital of Indonesia.

Jakes Corner Canada 149 N3
Jakhau India 104 B5
Jakkī Kowr Iran 111 F5
Jäkkvik Sweden 54 J3
Jakliat India 104 C3
Jako i. East Timor see Jaco
Jakobshavn Greenland see Ilulissat
Jakobstad Fin. 54 M5
Jal NM U.S.A. 161 C5
Jalaid China see Inder
Jalājil Saudi Arabia 110 B5
Jalālābād Afgh. 111 H3
Jalalabad India 99 B8
Jalal-Abad Kyrg. 102 D3
Jalal-Abad admin. div. Kyrg. 98 A4
Jalālah al Baḩrīyah, Jabal plat. Egypt 112 C5
Jalalpur Pirwala Pak. 111 H4
Jalāmid, Ḩazm al ridge Saudi Arabia 113 E5
Jalandhar India 104 C3
Jalapa Guat. 167 H6
Jalapa Tabasco Mex. 167 G5
Jalapa Veracruz Mex. see Xalapa
Jalapa Nicaragua 166 [inset] I6
Jalapa Enríquez Mex. see Xalapa
Jalasjärvi Fin. 54 M5
Jalaun India 104 D4
Jalawlā' Iraq 113 G4
Jaldhaka r. Bangl. 99 E8
Jaldrug India 106 C2
Jales Brazil 179 A3
Jalesar India 104 D4
Jalgaon India 104 C5
Jalībah Iraq 113 G5
Jalingo Nigeria 120 E4
Jalisco state Mex. 166 D5
Jallābī Iran 110 E5
Jalna India 106 B2
Jālo Iran 111 F5
Jalón r. Spain 67 F3
Jalor India see Jalore
Jalore India 104 C4
Jalostotitlán Mex. 166 E4
Jalpa Guanajuato Mex. 167 E4
Jalpa Zacatecas Mex. 168 D4
Jalpaiguri India 105 G4
Jalpan Mex. 167 F4
Jālū Libya 121 F2
Jalūlā Iraq see Jalawlā'
Jām reg. Iran 111 F3
Jamaica country West Indies 169 I5
Jamaica Channel Haiti/Jamaica 169 I5
Jamalpur Bangl. 105 G4
Jamalpur India 105 F4
Jamanxim r. Brazil 177 G4
Jamati China 98 C3
Jambi Sumatera Indon. 84 C3
Jambi prov. Indon. 84 C3
Jambin Australia 136 E5
Jambo India 104 C4
Jamboaye r. Indon. 84 B1
Jambongan i. Malaysia 85 G1
Jambu Kalimantan Indon. 85 G3
Jambuair, Tanjung pt Indon. 84 B1
Jamda India 105 F5
Jamekunte India 106 C2
James r. N. Dakota/S. Dakota U.S.A. 160 D3
James r. VA U.S.A. 165 G5
James, Baie b. Canada see James Bay
Jamesabad Pak. 111 H5
James Bay Canada 152 E3
Jamesburg NJ U.S.A. 165 H3
James Island Galápagos Ecuador see San Salvador, Isla
Jameson Land reg. Greenland 147 P2
James Peak N.Z. 139 B7
James Ranges mts Australia 135 F6
James Ross Island Antarctica 188 A2
James Ross Strait Canada 147 I3
Jamestown Australia 137 B7
Jamestown Canada see Wawa
Jamestown S. Africa 125 H6

▶Jamestown St Helena 184 H7
Capital of St Helena.

Jamestown ND U.S.A. 160 D2
Jamestown NY U.S.A. 164 F2
Jamestown TN U.S.A. 164 C5
Jamkhed India 106 B2
Jammu India 104 C2
Jammu and Kashmir terr. Asia 104 D2
Jamnagar India 104 B5
Jampang Kulon Jawa Indon. 84 D4
Jampur Pak. 111 H4
Jamrud Pak. 111 H3
Jämsä Fin. 55 N6
Jamsah Egypt 112 D6
Jämsänkoski Fin. 54 N6
Jamshedpur India 105 F5
Jamtai China 98 C4
Jamtari Nigeria 120 E4
Jamui India 105 F4
Jamuk, Gunung mt. Indon. 85 G2
Jamuna r. Bangl. see Raimangal
Jamuna r. India 99 F8
Jamuna r. India see Yamuna
Janā i. Saudi Arabia 110 C5
Janāb, Wādī al watercourse Jordan 107 C4
Janakpur India 105 E5
Janaúba Brazil 179 C1
Jand Pak. 111 I3
Jandaia Brazil 179 A2
Jandaq Iran 110 D3
Jandola Pak. 111 H3
Jandowae Australia 138 E1
Janesville CA U.S.A. 158 C1
Janesville WI U.S.A. 160 F3
Jang, Tanjung pt Indon. 84 D3
Jangada Brazil 179 A4
Jangal Iran 110 E3
Jangamo Moz. 125 L3
Jangaon India 106 C2
Jangco China 99 E7
Jangipur India 105 G4
Jangnga Turkm. see Jaňňa
Jangngai Ri mts China 99 D6
Jangngai Zangbo r. China 99 D6
Jänickendorf Germany 63 N2
Jani Khel Pak. 111 H3

▶Jan Mayen terr. Arctic Ocean 189 I2
Part of Norway.

Jan Mayen Fracture Zone sea feature Arctic Ocean 189 I2
Jaňňa Turkm. 110 D1
Janos Mex. 166 C2
Jans Bay Canada 151 I4
Jansenville S. Africa 124 G7
Januária Brazil 179 B1
Janûb Sînâ' governorate Egypt see Janūb Sīnā'
Janūb Sīnā' governorate Egypt 107 A5
Janzar mt. Pak. 111 F5
Jaodar Pak. 111 F5

▶Japan country Asia 91 D5
10th most populous country in the world.

Japan, Sea of N. Pacific Ocean 91 D5
Japan Alps National Park Japan see Chūbu-Sangaku Kokuritsu-kōen
Japan Trench sea feature N. Pacific Ocean 186 F3
Japiim Brazil 176 D5
Japón Hond. 166 [inset] I6
Japurá r. Brazil 176 F4
Japvo Mount India 105 H4
Jaqué Panama 166 [inset] K8
Jarābulus Syria 107 D1
Jaraguá Brazil 179 A1
Jaraguá, Serra mts Brazil 179 A4
Jaraguá do Sul Brazil 179 A4
Jarantai China 94 F4
Jarantai Yanchi salt l. China 94 F4
Jarash Jordan 107 B3
Jarboesville MD U.S.A. see Lexington Park
Jardine River National Park Australia 136 C1
Jardinésia Brazil 179 A2
Jardinópolis Brazil 179 B3
Jargalang China 90 A4
Jargalant Arhangay Mongolia see Battsengel
Jargalant Bayanhongor Mongolia 94 D2
Jargalant Bayan-Ölgiy Mongolia see Bulgan
Jargalant Dornod Mongolia see Matad
Jargalant Govĭ-Altay Mongolia see Biger
Jargalant Hovd Mongolia see Hovd
Jargalant Hövsgöl Mongolia 94 D1
Jargalant Töv Mongolia 94 F1
Jargalant Hayrhan mt. Mongolia 94 C2
Jargalthaan Mongolia 95 G2
Jari r. Brazil 177 H4
Jarm Afgh. 111 H2
Järna Sweden 55 J7
Jarocin Poland 57 P5
Jarosław Poland 53 D6
Järpen Sweden 54 H5
Jarqo'rg'on Uzbek. 111 G2
Jarqŭrghon Uzbek. see Jarqo'rg'on
Jarrettsville MD U.S.A. 165 G4
Jarú Brazil 176 F6
Jarud China see Lubei
Järvakandi Estonia 55 N7
Järvenpää Fin. 55 N6

▶Jarvis Island terr. S. Pacific Ocean 186 J6
United States Unincorporated Territory.

Jarwa India 105 E4
Jashpurnagar India 105 F5
Jāsk Iran 110 E5
Jāsk-e Kohneh Iran 110 E5
Jasliq Uzbek. 113 J2
Jasło Poland 53 D6
Jasol India 104 C4
Jason Islands Falkland Is 178 D8
Jason Peninsula Antarctica 188 L2
Jasonville IN U.S.A. 164 B4
Jasper Canada 150 G4
Jasper AL U.S.A. 163 C5
Jasper FL U.S.A. 163 D6
Jasper GA U.S.A. 163 C5
Jasper IN U.S.A. 164 B4
Jasper NY U.S.A. 165 G2
Jasper TN U.S.A. 163 C5
Jasper TX U.S.A. 161 E6
Jasper National Park Canada 150 G4
Jasrasar India 104 C4
Jaşşān Iraq 113 G4
Jassy Romania see Iaşi
Jastrzębie-Zdrój Poland 57 Q6
Jaswantpura India 104 C4
Jászberény Hungary 69 H1
Jataí Brazil 179 A2
Jatapu r. Brazil 177 G4
Jath India 106 B2
Jati Pak. 111 H5
Jatibarang Jawa Indon. 85 E4
Jatibonico Cuba 163 E8
Jatiluhur, Waduk resr Jawa Indon. 84 D4
Játiva Spain see Xàtiva
Jatiwangi Jawa Indon. 85 E4
Jatoi Janubi Pak. 111 H4
Jaú Brazil 179 A3
Jaú r. Brazil 176 F4
Jaú, Parque Nacional do nat. park Brazil 176 F4
Jaua-Sarisariñama, Parque Nacional nat. park Venez. 176 F3
Jauja Peru 176 C6
Jaumave Mex. 167 F4
Jaunlutriņi Latvia 55 M8
Jaunpiebalga Latvia 55 O8
Jaunpur India 105 E4
Jauri Iran 111 F4
Java Georgia 113 F2

▶Java i. Indon. 85 E4
5th largest island in Asia.

Javaés r. Brazil see Formoso
Javari r. Brazil/Peru see Yavari
Java Ridge sea feature Indian Ocean 185 P6
Javarthushuu Mongolia see Bayan-Uul
Java Sea Indon. see Jawa, Laut

▶Java Trench sea feature Indian Ocean 185 P6
Deepest point in the Indian Ocean.

Jävenitz Germany 63 L2
Jävre Sweden 54 L4
Jawa i. Indon. see Java
Jawa, Laut sea Indon. 85 E4
Jawa Barat prov. Indon. 84 D4
Jawa Tengah prov. Indon. 85 E4
Jawa Timur prov. Indon. 85 F4
Jawhar India 106 B2
Jawhar Somalia 122 E3
Jawor Poland 57 P5
Jay OK U.S.A. 161 E4

▶Jaya, Puncak mt. Indon. 81 J7
Highest mountain in Oceania.

Jayakusumu mt. Indon. see Jaya, Puncak
Jayakwadi Sagar l. India 106 B2
Jayantiapur Bangl. see Jaintiapur
Jayapura Indon. 81 K7
Jayawijaya, Pegunungan mts Indon. 81 J7
Jayb, Wādī al watercourse Israel/Jordan 107 B4
Jayfī, Wādī al watercourse Egypt 107 B4
Jaypur India 106 D2
Jayrūd Syria 107 C3
Jayton TX U.S.A. 161 C5
Jazīreh-ye Shīf Iran 110 C4
Jazminal Mex. 167 E3
Jbail Lebanon 107 B2
J. C. Murphey Lake IN U.S.A. 164 B3
Jean NV U.S.A. 159 F4
Jean Marie River Canada 150 F2
Jeannin, Lac l. Canada 153 I2
Jebāl Bārez, Kūh-e mts Iran 110 E4
Jebel, Bahr el r. Africa see White Nile
Jebel Abyad Plateau Sudan 108 C6
Jebus Indon. 84 D3
Jech Doab lowland Pak. 111 I4
Jedburgh U.K. 60 G5
Jeddah Saudi Arabia 108 E5
Jedeida Tunisia 68 C6
Jeetze r. Germany 63 L1
Jefferson IA U.S.A. 160 E3
Jefferson NC U.S.A. 162 D4
Jefferson OH U.S.A. 164 E3
Jefferson TX U.S.A. 161 E5
Jefferson, Mount NV U.S.A. 158 E2
Jefferson, Mount vol. OR U.S.A. 156 C3

▶Jefferson City MO U.S.A. 160 E4
Capital of Missouri.

Jeffersonville GA U.S.A. 163 D5
Jeffersonville IN U.S.A. 164 C4
Jeffersonville OH U.S.A. 164 D4
Jeffreys Bay S. Africa 124 G8
Jehanabad India 105 F4
Jeju S. Korea see Cheju
Jejuí Guazú r. Para. 178 E2
Jēkabpils Latvia 55 N8
Jelbart Ice Shelf Antarctica 188 B2
Jelenia Góra Poland 57 O5
Jelep La pass China/India 99 E8
Jelgava Latvia 55 M8
Jellico TN U.S.A. 164 C5
Jellicoe Canada 152 D4
Jelloway OH U.S.A. 164 D3
Jemaja i. Indon. 84 D2
Jember Jawa Indon. 85 F5
Jeminay China 98 D3
Jeminay Kazakh. 98 D3
Jempang, Danau l. Indon. 85 G3
Jena Germany 63 L4
Jena LA U.S.A. 161 E6
Jendouba Tunisia 68 C6
Jengish Chokusu mt. China/Kyrg. see Pobeda Peak
Jenīn West Bank 107 B3
Jenkins KY U.S.A. 164 D5
Jênlung China 99 D7
Jenne Mali see Djenné
Jenner Canada 151 I5
Jennings r. Canada 149 N4
Jennings LA U.S.A. 161 E6
Jenolan Caves Australia 138 E4
Jenpeg Canada 151 L4
Jensen UT U.S.A. 159 I1
Jens Munk Island Canada 147 K3
Jepara Jawa Indon. 85 E4
Jeparit Australia 137 C8
Jequié Brazil 179 C1
Jequitaí r. Brazil 179 B2
Jequitinhonha Brazil 179 C2
Jequitinhonha r. Brazil 179 D1
Jerantut Malaysia 84 C2
Jerba, Île de i. Tunisia 64 G5
Jerbar South Sudan 121 G4
Jereh Iran 110 C4
Jérémie Haiti 169 J5
Jerez Mex. 168 D4
Jerez de la Frontera Spain 67 C5
Jergol Norway 54 N2
Jergucat Albania 69 I5
Jericho Australia 136 D4
Jericho West Bank 107 B4
Jerichow Germany 63 M2
Jerid, Chott el salt l. Tunisia 64 F5
Jerijeh, Tanjung pt Malaysia 85 E2
Jerilderie Australia 138 B5
Jerimoth Hill hill RI U.S.A. 165 J3
Jeroaquara Brazil 179 A1
Jerome ID U.S.A. 156 E4
Jerruck Pak. 111 H5

▶Jersey terr. Channel Is 59 E9
United Kingdom Crown Dependency.

Jersey City NJ U.S.A. 165 H3
Jersey Shore PA U.S.A. 165 G3
Jerseyville IL U.S.A. 160 F4
Jerumenha Brazil 177 J5

▶Jerusalem Israel/West Bank 107 B4
De facto capital of Israel, disputed.

Jervis Bay Australia 138 E5
Jervis Bay b. Australia 138 E5
Jervis Bay Territory admin. div. Australia 138 E5
Jesenice Slovenia 68 F1
Jesenice, Vodní nádrž resr Czech Rep. 63 M4
Jesi Italy 68 E3
Jesselton Sabah Malaysia see Kota Kinabalu
Jessen Germany 63 M3
Jessheim Norway 55 G6
Jessore Bangl. 105 G5
Jesteburg Germany 63 J1
Jesu Maria Island P.N.G. see Rambutyo Island
Jesup GA U.S.A. 163 D6
Jesús Carranza Mex. 167 G5
Jesús María, Barra spit Mex. 161 D7
Jeti-Ögüz Kyrg. 98 B4
Jetmore KS U.S.A. 160 D4
Jetpur India 104 B5
Jever Germany 63 H1
Jewell Ridge VA U.S.A. 164 E5
Jewish Autonomous Oblast admin. div. Rus. Fed. see Yevreyskaya Avtonomnaya Oblast'
Jeypur India see Jaypur
Jezzine Lebanon 107 B3
Jhabua India 104 C5
Jhajhar India see Jhajjar
Jhajjar India 104 D3
Jhal Pak. 111 G4
Jhalawar India 104 D4
Jhal Jhao Pak. 111 G5
Jhang Pak. 111 I4
Jhansi India 104 D4
Jhanzi r. India 86 A1
Jhapa Nepal 105 F4
Jharia India 105 F5
Jharkhand state India 105 F5
Jharsuguda India 105 F5
Jhawani Nepal 105 F4
Jhelum r. India/Pak. 111 I4
Jhelum Pak. 111 I3
Jhenaidah Bangl. 105 G5
Jhenaidaha Bangl. see Jhenaidah
Jhenida Bangl. see Jhenaidah
Jhimpir Pak. 111 H5
Jhudo Pak. 111 H5
Jhumritilaiya India 105 F4
Jhund India 104 B5
Jhunjhunun India 104 C3
Jiachuan China 96 E1
Jiachuanzhen China see Jiachuan
Jiading Jiangxi China see Xinfeng
Jiading Shanghai China 97 I2
Jiahe China 97 G3
Jiajiang China 96 D2
Jialing Jiang r. China 94 F6
Jialu China see Jiaxian
Jialu He r. China 95 H5
Jiamusi China 90 C3
Ji'an Jiangxi China 97 G3
Ji'an Jilin China 90 B4
Jianchang China 95 I3
Jianchuan China 96 C3
Jiande China 97 H2
Jiangbei China see Yubei
Jiangbiancun China 97 G3
Jiangcheng China 96 D4
Jiangcun China 97 F3
Jiangdu China 97 H1
Jiange China see Pu'an
Jianghong China 97 F4
Jiangjiapo China 95 J4
Jiangjin China 96 E2
Jiangjunmiao China 94 B2
Jiangjunmu China 95 H4
Jiangjuntai China 94 D3
Jiangkou Guangdong China see Fengkai
Jiangkou Guizhou China 97 F3
Jiangkou Shaanxi China 96 E1
Jiangling China see Jingzhou
Jiangluozhen China 96 E1
Jiangmen China 97 G4
Jiangna China see Yanshan
Jiangshan China 97 H2
Jiangsi China see Dejiang
Jiangsu prov. China 97 H1
Jiangtai China 94 F5
Jiangxi prov. China 97 G3
Jiangxia China 97 G2
Jiangxian China 95 G5
Jiangxigou China 94 E4
Jiangyan China 97 I1
Jiangyin China 97 I2
Jiangyou China 96 E2
Jiangyu China 95 I4
Jiangzhesongrong China 99 D7
Jianhu China 95 I5
Jianjun China see Yongshou
Jiankang China 96 D3
Jianli China 97 G2
Jian'ou China 97 H3
Jianping Anhui China see Langxi
Jianping Liaoning China 95 I3
Jianping Liaoning China 95 I3
Jianqiao China 95 I4
Jianshe Qinghai China 94 D5
Jianshe Sichuan China see Baiyü
Jianshi China 97 F2
Jianshui China 96 D4
Jianshui Hu l. China 99 C6
Jianxing China 96 E2
Jianyang Fujian China 97 H3
Jianyang Sichuan China 96 E2
Jiaochang China 96 D1
Jiaochangba China see Jiaochang
Jiaocheng Guangdong China see Jiaoling
Jiaocheng Shanxi China 95 H4
Jiaohe Hebei China 95 I4
Jiaohe Jilin China 90 B4
Jiaojiang China see Taizhou
Jiaokou China 95 G4
Jiaokui China see Yiliang
Jiaolai He r. China 95 J3
Jiaoling China 97 H3
Jiaonan China 95 I5
Jiaopingdu China 96 D3
Jiaowei China 97 H3
Jiaozhou China 95 J4
Jiaozuo China 95 H5
Jiarsu China 94 C4
Jiasa China 96 D3
Jiashan China see Mingguang
Jiashi China 98 B5
Jia Tsuo La pass China 99 D7
Jiawang China 97 H1
Jiaxian Henan China 97 G1
Jiaxian Shaanxi China 95 G4
Jiaxing China 97 I2
Jiayi Taiwan see Chiai
Jiayin China 90 C2
Jiayuguan China 94 D4
Jiazi China 97 H4
Jibūtī country Africa see Djibouti
Jibuti Djibouti see Djibouti
Jiddah Saudi Arabia see Jeddah
Jiddī, Jabal al hill Egypt 107 A4
Jidong China 90 C3
Jiehkkevárri mt. Norway 54 K2
Jiehu China see Yinan
Jieshi China 97 G4
Jieshipu China 94 F5
Jieshi Wan b. China 97 G4
Jiexi China 97 G4
Jiexiu China 95 G4
Jieyang China 97 H4
Jieznas Lith. 55 N9
Jigzhi China 96 D1
Jiḩār, Wādī al watercourse Syria 107 C2
Jih-chao China see Donggang
Jihlava Czech Rep. 57 O6
Jījah Afgh. 111 F3
Jijel Alg. 64 F4
Jijiga Eth. 122 E3
Jījīrud Iran 110 C3
Jijitai China 94 D3
Jijü China 96 D2
Jil'ād reg. Jordan 107 B3
Jilf al Kabīr, Haḑabat al plat. Egypt 108 C5
Jilh al 'Ishār plain Saudi Arabia 110 B5
Jilib Somalia 122 E3
Jili Hu l. China 98 D3
Jilin China 90 B4
Jilin prov. China 95 K3
Jiling China 94 E4
Jilin Hada Ling mts China 90 B4
Jiliu He r. China 90 A2
Jilo India 104 C4
Jilong Taiwan see Chilung
Jīma Eth. 122 D3
Jimda China see Zindo
Jiménez Chihuahua Mex. 166 D3
Jiménez Coahuila Mex. 167 E2
Jiménez Tamaulipas Mex. 161 D7
Jimía, Cerro mt. Hond. 168 G5
Jimo China 95 J4
Jimokuji Japan 92 C3
Jimsar China 98 E4
Jim Thorpe PA U.S.A. 165 H3
Jinan China 95 I4
Jin'an China see Songpan
Jinbi China see Dayao
Jinchang China 94 E4
Jincheng Shanxi China 95 H5
Jincheng Sichuan China see Yilong
Jincheng Yunnan China see Wuding
Jinchengjiang China see Hechi
Jinchuan Gansu China see Jinchang
Jinchuan Jiangxi China see Xingan
Jind India 104 D3
Jinding China see Lanping
Jindřichův Hradec Czech Rep. 57 O6
Jin'e China see Longchang
Jinfosi China 94 D4
Jing China see Jinghe
Jingbian China 95 G4
Jingchuan China 95 F5
Jingde China 97 H2
Jingdezhen China 97 H2
Jingellic Australia 138 C5
Jinggangshan China see Ciping
Jinggang Shan hill China 97 G3
Jinggongqiao China 97 H2
Jinggu Gansu China 94 E5
Jinggu Yunnan China 96 D4
Jinghai China 95 I4
Jinghe China 98 C3
Jing He r. China 95 G5
Jinghong China 96 D4
Jingle China 95 H4
Jingmen China 97 G2
Jingning China 94 F5
Jingpeng China 95 I3
Jingpo China 90 C4
Jingpo Hu resr China 90 C4
Jingsha China see Jingzhou
Jingtai China 94 E4
Jingtieshan China 94 D4
Jingxi China 96 E4
Jingxian Anhui China 97 H2
Jingxian Hunan China see Jingzhou
Jingyang China see Jingde
Jingyu China 90 B4
Jingyuan China 94 F4
Jingzhou Hubei China 97 G2
Jingzhou Hubei China 97 G2
Jingzhou Hunan China 97 F3
Jinhe Nei Mongol China 90 A2
Jinhe Yunnan China see Jinping
Jinhu China 97 H1
Jinhua Yunnan China see Jianchuan
Jinhua Zhejiang China 97 H2
Jining Nei Mongol China 95 H3
Jining Shandong China 95 I5
Jinja Uganda 122 D3
Jinjiang Hainan China see Chengmai
Jinjiang Yunnan China 96 D3
Jin Jiang r. China 97 G2
Jinka Eth. 122 D3
Jinmen Taiwan see Chinmen
Jinmen Dao i. Taiwan see Chinmen Tao
Jinmu Jiao pt China 97 F5
Jinning China 96 D3
Jinotega Nicaragua 166 [inset] I6
Jinotepe Nicaragua 166 [inset] I7
Jinping Guizhou China 97 F3
Jinping Yunnan China 96 D4
Jinping Yunnan China see Qiubei
Jinping Shan mts China 96 D3
Jinsen S. Korea see Inch'ŏn
Jinsha China 96 E3
Jinsha Jiang r. China 96 C2 see Yangtze
Jinshan Nei Mongol China see Guyang
Jinshan Nei Mongol China 95 I3
Jinshan Shanghai China see Zhujing
Jinshan Yunnan China see Lufeng
Jinshi Hunan China 97 F2
Jinshi Hunan China see Xinning
Jinta China 94 D4
Jintotolo i. Phil. 82 C4
Jintotolo Channel Phil. 82 C4
Jintur India 106 C2
Jinxi Anhui China see Taihu
Jinxi Jiangxi China 97 H3
Jinxi Liaoning China see Lianshan
Jin Xi r. China 97 H3
Jinxian Jiangxi China 97 H2
Jinxian Liaoning China see Linghai
Jinxiang China 95 I5
Jinyun China 97 I2
Jinz, Qā' al salt flat Jordan 107 C4
Jinzhai China 97 G2
Jinzhong China 95 H4
Jinzhou Liaoning China 95 J3
Jinzhou Liaoning China 95 J4
Jinzhou Wan b. China 95 J4
Jinzhu China see Daocheng
Jinzū-gawa r. Japan 92 D2
Ji-Paraná Brazil 176 F6
Jipijapa Ecuador 176 B4
Ji Qu r. China 99 G7
Jiquilisco El Salvador 166 [inset] H6
Jiquiriçá Brazil 179 D1
Jiquitaia Brazil 179 D2
Jirā', Wādī watercourse Egypt 107 A5
Jirānīyāt, Shi'bān al watercourse Saudi Arabia 107 D4
Jirgatol Tajik. 111 H2
Jiri r. India 86 A1
Jirin Gol China 95 I2
Jirmeng China 94 D4
Jīroft Iran 110 E4
Jirriiban Somalia 122 E3
Jirwān Saudi Arabia 110 C6
Jirwan well Saudi Arabia 110 C6
Jishan China 95 G5
Jishi China see Xunhua
Jishishan China 94 E5
Jishou China 97 F2
Jisr ash Shughūr Syria 107 C2
Jitian China see Lianshan
Jitotol Mex. 167 G5
Jitra Malaysia 84 C1
Jiu r. Romania 69 J3
Jiuchenggong China see Linyou
Jiudengkou China 94 F4
Jiuding Shan mt. China 96 D2
Jiujiang Jiangxi China 97 G2
Jiujiang Jiangxi China 97 H2
Jiulian China see Mojiang
Jiuling Shan mts China 97 G2
Jiulong H.K. China see Kowloon
Jiulong Sichuan China 96 D2
Jiumiao China 95 J3
Jiuqian China 97 F3
Jiuquan China 94 D4
Jiuxian China 95 G4
Jiuxu China 96 E3
Jiuzhou Jiang r. China 97 F4
Jiwani Pak. 111 F5
Jiwen China 95 J1
Jixi Anhui China 97 H2
Jixi Heilong. China 90 C3
Jixian Hebei China see Jizhou
Jixian Heilong. China 90 C3
Jixian Henan China see Weihui
Jixian Shanxi China 95 G4
Jiyuan China 95 H5
Jīzah, Ahrāmāt al tourist site Egypt see Pyramids of Giza
Jīzān Saudi Arabia 108 F6
Jizhou China 95 H4
Jizō-dake mt. Japan 93 F2
Jizzakh Uzbek. see Jizzax
Jizzax Uzbek. 111 G1
Joaçaba Brazil 179 A4
Joaíma Brazil 179 C2
João Belo Moz. see Xai-Xai
João de Almeida Angola see Chibia
João Pessoa Brazil 177 L5
João Pinheiro Brazil 179 B2
Joaquín V. González Arg. 178 D3
Jōban Japan 93 G2
Jobo Point Mindanao Phil. 82 D4
Job Peak NV U.S.A. 158 D2
Jocketa Germany 63 M4
Jocotán Guat. 167 H6
Joda India 105 F5
Jodhpur India 104 C4
Jodiya India 104 B5
Joensuu Fin. 54 P5
Jōetsu Japan 93 E1
Jofane Moz. 123 D6
Joffre, Mount Canada 150 H5
Jōganji-gawa r. Japan 92 D2
Jōga-shima i. Japan 93 F3
Jogbura Nepal 104 E3
Jõgeva Estonia 55 O7
Jogjakarta Indon. see Yogyakarta
Jōhana Japan 92 C2
Johannesburg S. Africa 125 H4
Johannesburg CA U.S.A. 158 E4
Johan Peninsula Canada 147 K2
Johi Pak. 111 G5
John r. AK U.S.A. 149 J2
John Day OR U.S.A. 156 D3

John Day r. OR U.S.A. 156 C3
John D'Or Prairie Canada 150 H3
John F. Kennedy airport NY U.S.A. 165 I3
John H. Kerr Reservoir VA U.S.A. 165 F5
John Jay, Mount Canada/U.S.A. 149 O4
John o' Groats U.K. 60 F2
Johnson KS U.S.A. 160 C4
Johnsonburg PA U.S.A. 165 F3
Johnson City NY U.S.A. 165 H2
Johnson City TN U.S.A. 162 D4
Johnson City TX U.S.A. 161 D6
Johnsondale CA U.S.A. 158 D4
Johnson Draw watercourse TX U.S.A. 161 C6
Johnson's Crossing Canada 149 N3
Johnston, Lake salt flat Australia 135 C8
Johnston and Sand Islands terr. N. Pacific Ocean see Johnston Atoll

▶Johnston Atoll terr. N. Pacific Ocean 186 I4
United States Unincorporated Territory.

Johnstone U.K. 60 E5
Johnstone Lake Canada see Old Wives Lake
Johnston Range hills Australia 135 B7
Johnstown Ireland 61 E5
Johnstown NY U.S.A. 165 H2
Johnstown PA U.S.A. 165 F3
Jōhoku Japan 93 G2
Johor state Malaysia 84 C2
Johor, Selat strait Malaysia/Sing. 87 [inset]
Johor, Sungai r. Malaysia 87 [inset]
Johor Bahru Malaysia 84 C2
Jõhvi Estonia 55 O7
Joinville Brazil 179 A4
Joinville France 66 G2
Joinville Island Antarctica 188 A2
Jojutla Mex. 167 F5
Jokkmokk Sweden 54 K3
Jökulsá r. Iceland 54 [inset 1]
Jökulsá á Fjöllum r. Iceland 54 [inset 1]
Jökulsá í Fljótsdal r. Iceland 54 [inset 1]
Jolfa Iran 110 B2
Joliet IL U.S.A. 164 A3
Joliet, Lac l. Canada 152 F4
Joliette Canada 153 G5
Jolly Lake Canada 151 H1
Jolo Phil. 82 C5
Jolo i. Phil. 82 C5
Jomalig i. Phil. 82 C3
Jombang Jawa Indon. 85 F4
Jomda China 96 C2
Jōmine-san mt. Japan 93 F2
Jonancy KY U.S.A. 164 D5
Jonathan Point Belize 167 H5
Jonava Lith. 55 N9
Jonê China 94 E5
Jōnen-dake mt. Japan 92 D2
Jonesboro AR U.S.A. 161 F5
Jonesboro LA U.S.A. 161 E5
Jones Islands AK U.S.A. 149 J1
Jones Sound sea chan. Canada 147 J2
Jonesville MI U.S.A. 164 C3
Jonesville VA U.S.A. 164 D5
Jonglei Canal South Sudan 108 D8
Jönköping Sweden 55 I8
Jonquière Canada 153 H4
Jonuta Mex. 167 G5
Joplin MO U.S.A. 161 E4
Joppa Israel see Tel Aviv-Yafo
Jora India 104 D4
Jordan country Asia 107 C4
Jordan r. Asia 107 B4
Jordan MT U.S.A. 156 G3
Jordan r. OR U.S.A. 156 D4
Jordânia Brazil 179 C1
Jordet Norway 55 H6
Jorhat India 105 H4
Jor Hu l. China 98 B5
Jork Germany 63 J1
Jörn Sweden 54 L4
Joroinen Fin. 54 O5
Jorong Kalimantan Indon. 85 F3
Jørpeland Norway 55 E7
Jos Nigeria 120 D4
Jose Abad Santos Mindanao Phil. 82 D5
José Cardel Mex. 167 F5
José de San Martín Arg. 178 B6
Jose Panganiban Luzon Phil. 82 C3
Joseph, Lac l. Canada 153 I3
Joseph Bonaparte Gulf Australia 134 E3
Joseph City AZ U.S.A. 159 H4
Joshimath India 104 D3
Jōshinetsu-kōgen Kokuritsu-kōen nat. park Japan 93 E2
Joshipur India 106 E1
Joshua Tree National Park CA U.S.A. 159 F5
Jos Plateau Nigeria 120 D4
Jostedalsbreen Nasjonalpark nat. park Norway 55 E6
Jotunheimen Nasjonalpark nat. park Norway 55 F6
Jouaiya Lebanon 107 B3
Joubertina S. Africa 124 F7
Jouberton S. Africa 125 H4
Jõuga Estonia 55 O7
Joûnié Lebanon 107 B3
Joure Neth. 62 F2
Joutsa Fin. 55 O6
Joutseno Fin. 55 P6
Jouy-aux-Arches France 62 G5
Jovellanos Cuba 163 D8
Jowai India 105 H4
Jowand Afgh. 111 G3
Jowr Deh Iran 110 C2
Jowzak Iran 111 F4
Joy, Mount Canada 149 N3
Joya de Cerén tourist site El Salvador 167 H6
Joyce's Country reg. Ireland 61 C4
Jōyō Japan 92 B4
Joypurhat Bangl. 105 G4
Juan Aldama Mex. 161 C7
Juancheng China 95 H5
Juan de Fuca Strait Canada/U.S.A. 154 C2
Juan Escutia Mex. 166 D4
Juan Fernández, Archipiélago is S. Pacific Ocean 187 O8
Juan Fernández Islands S. Pacific Ocean see Juan Fernández, Archipiélago
Juanjuí Peru 176 C5
Juankoski Fin. 54 P5
Juan Mata Ortíz Mex. 166 C2
Juárez Mex. 167 E3
Juárez, Sierra de mts Mex. 166 A1
Juazeiro Brazil 177 J5
Juazeiro do Norte Brazil 177 K5
Juba r. Somalia see Jubba

▶Juba South Sudan 121 G4
Capital of South Sudan.

Jubany research station Antarctica 188 A2
Jubba r. Somalia 122 E4
Jubbah Saudi Arabia 113 F5
Jubbulpore India see Jabalpur
Jubilee Lake salt flat Australia 135 D7
Juby, Cap c. Morocco 120 B2
Juchatengo Mex. 167 F5
Juchitán Mex. 168 E5
Jucuruçu Brazil 179 D2
Jucuruçu r. Brazil 179 D2
Judaberg Norway 55 D7
Judaidat al Hamir Iraq 113 F5
Judayyidat 'Ar'ar well Iraq 113 F5
Judenburg Austria 57 O7
Judian China 96 C3
Judith Gap MT U.S.A. 156 F3
Juegang China see Rudong
Juelsminde Denmark 55 G9
Juerana Brazil 179 D2
Jugar China see Sêrxü
Juh China 95 G4
Juhongtu China 94 D4
Juigalpa Nicaragua 166 [inset] I6
Juillet, Lac l. Canada 153 J3
Juína Brazil 177 G6
Juist i. Germany 62 H1
Juiz de Fora Brazil 179 C3
Jujuhan r. Indon. 84 C3
Ju Ju Klu Turkm. 111 F2
Jukkoku-tōge pass Japan 93 E2
Julaca Bol. 176 E8
Julesburg CO U.S.A. 160 C3
Julia Brazil 176 E4
Juliaca Peru 176 D7
Julia Creek Australia 136 C4
Julian CA U.S.A. 158 E5
Julian, Lac l. Canada 152 F3
Julianadorp Neth. 62 E2
Julian Alps mts Slovenia see Julijske Alpe
Julianatop mt. Indon. see Mandala, Puncak
Juliana Top mt. Suriname 177 G3
Julianehåb Greenland see Qaqortoq
Jülich Germany 62 G4
Julijske Alpe mts Slovenia 68 E1
Julimes Mex. 166 D2
Juliomagus France see Angers
Julius, Lake Australia 136 B4
Jullundur India see Jalandhar
Juma Uzbek. 111 G2
Jumbilla Peru 176 C5
Jumilla Spain 67 F4
Jumla Nepal 105 E3
Jümme r. Germany 63 H1
Jumna r. India see Yamuna
Jump r. WI U.S.A. 160 F2
Junagadh India 104 B5
Junagarh India 106 D2
Junan China 95 I5
Junayfah Egypt 107 A4
Junbuk Iran 110 E3
Jun Bulen China 95 I2
Junction TX U.S.A. 161 D6
Junction UT U.S.A. 159 G2
Junction City KS U.S.A. 160 D4
Junction City KY U.S.A. 164 C5
Junction City OR U.S.A. 156 C3
Jundiaí Brazil 179 B3
Jundian China 97 F1

▶Juneau AK U.S.A. 149 N4
Capital of Alaska.

Juneau WI U.S.A. 160 F3
Juneau Icefield Canada 149 N4
Junee Australia 138 C5
Jûn el Khudr b. Lebanon 107 B3
Jungar Qi China see Xuejiawan
Jungfrau mt. Switz. 66 H3
Junggar Pendi basin China 102 G2
Jungsi China 99 E6
Juniata r. PA U.S.A. 165 G3
Junín Arg. 178 D4
Junín Peru 176 C6
Junior WV U.S.A. 164 F4
Juniper Mountain CO U.S.A. 159 I1
Juniper Mountains AZ U.S.A. 159 G4
Junipero Serro Peak CA U.S.A. 158 C3
Junlian China 96 E2
Junmenling China 97 G3
Juno TX U.S.A. 161 C6
Junsele Sweden 54 J5
Junshan Hu l. China 97 H2
Junxi China see Datian
Junxian China see Danjiangkou
Ju'nyung China 96 C1
Ju'nyunggoin China see Ju'nyung
Jūō Japan 93 G2
Juodupė Lith. 55 N8
Jupiá Brazil 179 A3
Jupía, Represa resr Brazil 179 A3
Jupiter FL U.S.A. 163 D7
Juquiá r. Brazil 179 B4
Jur r. South Sudan 108 C8
Jura mts France/Switz. 66 G4
Jura i. U.K. 60 D4
Jura, Sound of sea chan. U.K. 60 D5
Juraci Brazil 179 C1
Juradó Col. 166 [inset] K8
Jurbarkas Lith. 55 M9
Jurf ad Darāwīsh Jordan 107 B4
Jürgenstorf Germany 63 M1
Jurh Nei Mongol China 95 J2
Jurh Nei Mongol China 95 J2
Jurhen Ul mts China 99 E6
Jūrmala Latvia 55 M8
Jurmu Fin. 54 O4
Jurong Sing. 87 [inset]
Jurong, Sungai r. Sing. 87 [inset]
Jurong Island reg. Sing. 87 [inset]
Juruá r. Brazil 176 E4
Juruena r. Brazil 177 G5
Juruti Brazil 177 G4
Jurva Fin. 54 L5
Jūshiyama Japan 92 C3
Jūshqān Iran 110 E2
Jūsīyah Syria 107 C2
Jussara Brazil 179 A1
Justice WV U.S.A. 164 E5
Jutaí Brazil 176 E5
Jutaí r. Brazil 176 E4
Jüterbog Germany 63 N3
Jutiapa Guat. 167 H6
Jutiapa Hond. 166 [inset] I6
Juticalpa Hond. 166 [inset] I6
Jutis Sweden 54 J3
Jutland pen. Denmark 55 F8
Juuka Fin. 54 P5
Juva Fin. 55 O6
Juwana Jawa Indon. 85 E4
Juxian China 95 I5
Juye China 95 I5
Jūyom Iran 110 D4
Južnoukrajinsk Ukr. see Yuzhnoukrayinsk
Jwaneng Botswana 124 G3
Jylland pen. Denmark see Jutland
Jyrgalang Kyrg. 98 B4
Jyväskylä Fin. 54 N5

K

▶K2 mt. China/Pak. 104 D2
2nd highest mountain in Asia and the world.

Ka r. Nigeria 120 D3
Kaafu Atoll Maldives see Male Atoll
Kaa-Iya del Gran Chaco, Parque Nacional nat. park Bol. 176 F7
Kaakhka Turkm. see Kaka
Ka'ala mt. HI U.S.A. 157 [inset]
Kaapstad S. Africa see Cape Town
Kaarina Fin. 55 M6
Kaarßen Germany 63 L1
Kaarst Germany 62 G3
Kaavi Fin. 54 P5
Kaba China see Habahe
Kaba r. China/Kazakh. 98 D3
Kabaena i. Indon. 83 B4
Kabakly Turkm. see Gabakly
Kabala Sierra Leone 120 B4
Kabale Uganda 122 C4
Kabalega Falls National Park Uganda see Murchison Falls National Park
Kabalo Dem. Rep. Congo 123 C4
Kabambare Dem. Rep. Congo 123 C4
Kabanbay Kazakh. 102 F2
Kabangu Dem. Rep. Congo 123 C5
Kabanjahe Sumatera Indon. 84 B2
Kabara i. Fiji 133 I3
Kabarai Papua Indon. 83 D3
Kabarega National Park Uganda see Murchison Falls National Park
Kabasalan Mindanao Phil. 82 C5
Kaba-san hill Japan 93 G2
Kabaw Valley Myanmar 86 A2
Kabbani r. India 106 C3
Kåbdalis Sweden 54 L3
Kabetan i. Indon. 83 B2
Kabinakagami r. Canada 152 D4
Kabinakagami Lake Canada 152 D4
Kabinda Dem. Rep. Congo 123 C4
Kabir Indon. 83 C5
Kabīr r. Syria 107 B2
Kabīrkūh mts Iran 110 B3
Kabo Cent. Afr. Rep. 122 B3
Kābol Afgh. see Kābul
Kabompo r. Zambia 123 C5
Kabong Sarawak Malaysia 85 E2
Kabongo Dem. Rep. Congo 123 C4
Kaboré Tambi, Parc National de nat. park Burkina Faso 120 C3
Kabūdeh Iran 111 F3
Kabūd Gonbad Iran 111 E2
Kabūd Rāhang Iran 110 C3
Kabugao Luzon Phil. 82 C2

▶Kābul Afgh. 111 H3
Capital of Afghanistan.

Kābul r. Afgh. 111 I3
Kabuli P.N.G. 81 L7
Kabunda Dem. Rep. Congo 123 C5
Kabunduk Sumba Indon. 83 A5
Kabuntalan Mindanao Phil. 82 D5
Kabura-gawa r. Japan 93 F2
Kaburuang i. Indon. 83 C2
Kabūtar Khān Iran 110 E4
Kabwe Zambia 123 C5
Kacepi Maluku Indon. 83 D3
Kāchā Kūh mts Iran/Pak. 111 F4
Kachalinskaya Rus. Fed. 53 J6
Kachchh, Great Rann of marsh India see Kachchh, Rann of
Kachchh, Gulf of India 104 B5
Kachchh, Little Rann of marsh India 104 B5
Kachchh, Rann of marsh India 104 B4
Kachemak Bay AK U.S.A. 149 J4
Kachia Nigeria 120 D4
Kachkanar Rus. Fed. 51 R4
K'ach'reti Georgia 113 G2
Kachug Rus. Fed. 88 J2
Kaçkar Dağı mt. Turkey 113 F2
Kada Japan 92 B4
Kadaingti Myanmar 86 B3
Kadaiyanallur India 106 C4
Kadanai r. Afgh./Pak. 111 G4
Kadan Kyun i. Myanmar 87 B4
Kadapa India see Cuddapah
Kadapongan i. Indon. 85 F4
Kadatuang i. Indon. 83 B4
Kadavu i. Fiji 133 H3
Kadavu Passage Fiji 133 H3
Kadaya Rus. Fed. 95 I1
Kaddam l. India 106 C2
Kade Ghana 120 C4
Kādhimain Iraq 113 G4
Kadi India 104 C5
Kadıköy Turkey 69 M4
Kadınhanı Turkey 112 D3
Kadiolo Mali 120 C3
Kadiri India 106 C3
Kadirli Turkey 112 E3
Kadiyevka Ukr. see Stakhanov
Kadmat atoll India 106 B4
Ka-do i. N. Korea 91 B5
Kadok Malaysia 84 C1
Kadoka SD U.S.A. 160 C3
Kadoma Zimbabwe 123 C5
Kadonkani Myanmar 86 A4
Kadu Myanmar 86 B1
Kadugli Sudan 108 C7
Kaduna Nigeria 120 D3
Kaduna r. Nigeria 120 D4
Kadusam mt. China/India 105 I3
Kaduy Rus. Fed. 52 H4
Kadyy Rus. Fed. 52 I4
Kadzherom Rus. Fed. 52 L2
Kaédi Mauritania 120 B3
Kaélé Cameroon 121 E3
Kaeng Krachan National Park Thai. 87 B4
Kaesŏng N. Korea 91 B5
Kāf Saudi Arabia 107 C4
Kafa Ukr. see Feodosiya
Kafakumba Dem. Rep. Congo 123 C4
Kafan Armenia see Kapan
Kafanchan Nigeria 120 D4

▶Kaffeklubben Ø i. Greenland 189 I1
Most northerly point of North America.

Kaffrine Senegal 120 B3
Kafiau i. Papua Indon. 83 D3
Kafireas, Akra pt Greece see Ntoro, Kavo
Kafiristan reg. Pak. 111 H3
Kafr ash Shaykh Egypt 112 C5
Kafr el Sheikh Egypt see Kafr ash Shaykh
Kafue Zambia 123 C5
Kafue r. Zambia 123 C5
Kafue National Park Zambia 123 C5
Kaga Japan 92 C2
Kaga Bandoro Cent. Afr. Rep. 122 B3
Kagan Pak. 111 I3
Kagan Uzbek. see Kogon
Kagang China 94 E5
Kaganovichabad Tajik. see Kolkhozobod
Kaganovichi Pervyye Ukr. see Polis'ke
Kagarlyk Ukr. see Kaharlyk
Kåge Sweden 54 L4
Kağızman Turkey 113 F2
Kaglik Lake Canada 149 O1
Kagmar Sudan 108 D7
Kagologolo Indon. 84 B3
Kagosaka-tōge pass Japan 93 E3
Kagoshima Japan 91 C7
Kagoshima pref. Japan 91 C7
Kagul Moldova see Cahul
Kaguyak AK U.S.A. 148 I4
Kahama Tanz. 122 D4
Kaharlyk Ukr. 53 F6
Kahatola i. Maluku Indon. 83 C2
Kahayan r. Indon. 85 F3
Kaherekoau Mountains N.Z. 139 A7
Kahīrī Iran 111 F5
Kahla Germany 63 L4
Kahnūj Iran 110 E4
Kahoka MO U.S.A. 160 F3
Kahoku-gata l. Japan 92 C2
Kaho'olawe i. HI U.S.A. 157 [inset]
Kahperusvaarat mts Fin. 54 L2
Kahramanmaraş Turkey 112 E3
Kahror Pakka Pak. 111 H4
Kâhta Turkey 112 E3
Kahuku HI U.S.A. 157 [inset]
Kahuku Point HI U.S.A. 157 [inset]
Kahulaui i. HI U.S.A. see Kaho'olawe
Kahurangi National Park N.Z. 139 D5
Kahurangi Point N.Z. 139 D5
Kahuta Pak. 111 I3
Kahuzi-Biega, Parc National du nat. park Dem. Rep. Congo 122 C4
Kai, Kepulauan is Indon. 81 I8
Kaiapoi N.Z. 139 D6
Kaibab AZ U.S.A. 159 G3
Kaibab Plateau AZ U.S.A. 159 G3
Kaibamardang China 94 D4
Kaibara Japan 92 B3
Kai Besar i. Indon. 81 I8
Kaibito Plateau AZ U.S.A. 159 H3
Kaida Japan 92 D3
Kaidu He r. China 98 D4
Kaifeng Henan China 95 H5
Kaifeng Henan China see Huanglongsi
Kaihua Yunnan China see Wenshan
Kaihua Zhejiang China 97 H2
Kaiingveld reg. S. Africa 124 E5
Kaijiang China 96 E2
Kai Kecil i. Indon. 81 I8
Kai Keung Leng H.K. China 97 [inset]
Kaikoura N.Z. 139 D6
Kailas mt. China see Kangrinboqê Feng
Kailasahar India see Kailashahar
Kailashahar India 105 H4
Kailas Range mts China see Gangdisê Shan
Kaili China 96 E3
Kailu China 95 J3
Kailua HI U.S.A. 157 [inset]
Kailua-Kona HI U.S.A. 157 [inset]
Kaimana Indon. 81 I7
Kaimanawa Mountains N.Z. 139 E4
Kaimar China 96 B1
Kaimganj India 99 B8
Kaimur Range hills India 104 E4
Käina Estonia 55 M7
Kainan Japan 92 B4
Kainda Kyrg. see Kayyngdy
Kainji Lake National Park Nigeria 120 D4
Kaipara Harbour N.Z. 139 E3
Kaiparowits Plateau UT U.S.A. 159 H3
Kaiping China 97 G4
Kaipokok Bay Canada 153 K3
Kairana India 104 D3
Kairatu Seram Indon. 83 D3
Kairiru Island P.N.G. 81 K7
Kaironi Indon. 81 I7
Kairouan Tunisia 68 D7
Kaiserslautern Germany 63 H5
Kaiser Wilhelm II Land reg. Antarctica 188 E2
Kait, Tanjung pt Indon. 84 D3
Kaitaia N.Z. 139 D2
Kaitangata N.Z. 139 B8
Kaitawa N.Z. 139 F4
Kaithal India 104 D3
Kaitong China see Tongyu
Kaitum Sweden 54 L3
Kaiwatu Maluku Indon. 83 C5
Kaiwi Channel HI U.S.A. 157 [inset]
Kaixian China 97 F2
Kaiyang China 96 E3
Kaiyuan Liaoning China 95 K3
Kaiyuan Yunnan China 96 D4
Kaiyuh Mountains AK U.S.A. 148 H3
Kaizu Japan 92 C3
Kaizuka Japan 92 B4
Kajaani Fin. 54 O4
Kajabbi Australia 136 C4
Kajaki Suflá Afgh. 111 G3
Kajang Malaysia 84 C2
Kajarabie, Lake Australia 138 D1
Kajikazawa Japan 93 E3
Kajrān Afgh. 111 G3
Kajy-Say Kyrg. 98 B4
Kaka Turkm. 111 E2
Kakaban i. Indon. 85 G2
Kakabeka Falls Canada 152 C4
Kakabia i. Indon. 83 B4
Kakadu National Park Australia 134 F3
Kakagi Lake Canada 151 M5
Kakal r. Mindanao Phil. 82 D5
Kakali Sulawesi Barat Indon. 83 A3
Kakamas S. Africa 124 E5
Kakamega Kenya 122 D3
Kakamigahara Japan 92 C3
Kakana India 87 A5
Kakar Pak. 111 G5
Kakata Liberia 120 B4
Kake AK U.S.A. 149 N4
Kakegawa Japan 93 E4
Kakenge Dem. Rep. Congo 123 C4
Kakerbeck Germany 63 L2
Kakhi Azer. see Qax
Kakhonak AK U.S.A. 148 I4
Kakhovka Ukr. 69 O1
Kakhovs'ke Vodoskhovyshche resr Ukr. 53 G7
Kakhul Moldova see Cahul
Kākī Iran 110 C4
Kakinada India 106 D2
Kakisa Canada 150 G2
Kakisa r. Canada 150 G2
Kakisa Lake Canada 150 G2
Kakogawa Japan 92 A4
Kakori India 104 E4
Kakpak Kuduk well China 94 B2
Kakshaal-Too mts China/Kyrg. 102 E3
Kaktovik AK U.S.A. 149 L1
Kakul Pak. 111 I3
Kakus r. Malaysia 85 F2
Kakwa r. Canada 150 G4
Kala Pak. 111 H4
Kala Tanz. 123 D4
Kalaâ Kebira Tunisia 68 D7
Kalaallit Nunaat terr. N. America see Greenland
Kalabahi Indon. 83 C5
Kalabáka Greece see Kalampaka
Kalabakan Sabah Malaysia 85 G1
Kalabgur India 106 C2
Kalabo Zambia 123 C5
Kalābust Afgh. 111 G4
Kalach Rus. Fed. 53 I6
Kalacha Dida Kenya 122 D3
Kalach-na-Donu Rus. Fed. 53 I6
Kaladan r. India/Myanmar 86 A2
Kaladar Canada 165 G1
Ka Lae pt HI U.S.A. 157 [inset]
Kalaena r. Indon. 83 B3
Kalagwe Myanmar 86 B2
Kalahari Desert Africa 124 F2
Kalahari Gemsbok National Park S. Africa 124 E3
Kalaikhum Tajik. see Qal'aikhum
Kalai-Khumb Tajik. see Qal'aikhum
Kalajoki Fin. 54 M4
Kalaliok Sulawesi Indon. 83 B3
Kalalusu i. Indon. 83 C1
Kalam India 106 C1
Kalam Pak. 111 I3
Kalámai Greece see Kalamata
Kalamare Botswana 125 H2
Kalamaria Greece 69 J4
Kalamata Greece 69 J6
Kalamazoo MI U.S.A. 164 C2
Kalambau i. Indon. 85 F4
Kalampaka Greece 69 I5
Kalanchak Ukr. 69 O1
Kalandi Pak. 111 F4
Kalandula Angola see Calandula
Kalanguy Rus. Fed. 95 I1
Kalannie Australia 135 B7
Kalanshiyū ar Ramlī al Kabīr, Sarīr des. Libya 108 B3
Kālān Zīād Iran 111 E5
Kalao i. Indon. 83 B4
Kalaong Mindanao Phil. 82 D5
Kalaotoa i. Indon. 83 B4
Kalapa Indon. 84 D3
Kalapana (abandoned) HI U.S.A. 157 [inset]
Kalār Iraq 113 G4
Kalār, Kūh-e mt. Iran 110 C4
Kalasin Thai. 86 C3
Kalāt Afgh. 111 G3
Kalāt Khorāsān-e Razavī Iran see Kabūd Gonbad
Kalāt Sīstān va Balūchestān Iran 111 E5
Kalat Balochistan Pak. 111 G4
Kalat Balochistan Pak. 111 G5
Kalāt, Kūh-e mt. Iran 110 E3
Kalaupapa HI U.S.A. 157 [inset]
Kalaus r. Rus. Fed. 53 J7
Kalaw Myanmar 86 B2
Kalba, Khrebet mts Kazakh. 98 C2
Kälbäcär Azer. 113 G2
Kalbarri Australia 135 A6
Kalbarri National Park Australia 135 A6
Kalbe (Milde) Germany 63 L2
Kalburgi India see Gulbarga
Kale Turkey 69 M6
Kalecik Turkey 112 D2
Kaledupa i. Indon. 83 B4
Kalefeld Germany 63 K3
Kaleindaung inlet Myanmar 86 A3
Kalélé Benin 120 D3
Kalemie Dem. Rep. Congo 123 C4
Kalemyo Myanmar 86 A2
Käl-e Namak Iran 110 D3
Kalevala Rus. Fed. 54 Q4
Kalewa Myanmar 86 A2
Kaleybar Iran 110 B2
Kalga Rus. Fed. 95 I1
Kalgan China see Zhangjiakou
Kalghatgi India 106 B3
Kalgoorlie Australia 135 C7
Kāl Gūsheh Iran 110 E4
Kali Croatia 68 F2
Kali r. India/Nepal 104 E3
Kaliakra, Nos pt Bulg. 69 M3
Kalianda Sumatera Indon. 84 D4
Kalibo Panay Phil. 82 C4
Kaliet Indon. 84 B3
Kali Gandaki r. Nepal 105 F4
Kaligiri India 106 C3
Kalikata India see Kolkata
Kalima Dem. Rep. Congo 122 C4
Kalimantan reg. Indon. 85 E3
Kalimantan Barat prov. Indon. 85 E2
Kalimantan Selatan prov. Indon. 85 F3
Kalimantan Tengah prov. Indon. 85 F3
Kalimantan Timur prov. Indon. 85 G2
Kalimantan Utara prov. Indon. 85 G2
Kálimnos i. Greece see Kalymnos
Kali Nadi r. India 99 C8
Kalinin Rus. Fed. see Tver'
Kalinin Adyndaky Tajik. see Cheshtebe
Kaliningrad Rus. Fed. 55 L9
Kalinino Armenia see Tashir
Kalinino Rus. Fed. 52 I4
Kalininsk Rus. Fed. 53 J6
Kalininskaya Rus. Fed. 53 H7
Kalinjara India 104 C5
Kalinkavichy Belarus 53 F5
Kalinkovichi Belarus see Kalinkavichy
Kalisat Jawa Indon. 85 F5
Kalisch Poland see Kalisz
Kalispell MT U.S.A. 156 E2
Kalisz Poland 57 Q5
Kalitva r. Rus. Fed. 53 I6
Kaliua Tanz. 123 D4
Kaliujar India 104 E4
Kalix Sweden 54 M4
Kalkalighat India 105 H4
Kalkalpen, Nationalpark nat. park Austria 57 O7
Kalkan Turkey 69 M6
Kalkaska MI U.S.A. 164 C1
Kalkfeld Namibia 123 B6
Kalkfonteindam dam S. Africa 125 G5
Kalkudah Sri Lanka 106 D5
Kall Germany 62 G4
Kallang r. Sing. 87 [inset]
Kallaste Estonia 55 O7
Kallavesi l. Fin. 54 O5
Kallsedet Sweden 54 H5
Kallsjön l. Sweden 54 H5
Kallur India 106 C2
Kalmar Sweden 55 J8
Kalmarsund sea chan. Sweden 55 J8
Kalmit hill Germany 63 I5
Kalmūkh Qal'eh Iran 110 E2
Kalmunai Sri Lanka 106 D5
Kalmykia aut. rep. Rus. Fed. see Kalmykiya-Khalm'g-Tangch, Respublika
Kalmykiya-Khalm'g-Tangch, Respublika aut. rep. Rus. Fed. 113 G1
Kalmykovo Kazakh. see Taypak
Kalmytskaya Avtonomnaya Oblast' aut. rep. Rus. Fed. see Kalmykiya-Khalm'g-Tangch, Respublika
Kalnai India 105 E5
Kalodnaye Belarus 55 O11
Kalol India 104 C5
Kaloma i. Indon. 83 C2
Kalomo Zambia 123 C5
Kalone Peak Canada 150 E4
Kalongan Sulawesi Indon. 83 C1
Kalpa India 104 D3
Kalpeni atoll India 106 B4
Kalpetta India 106 C4
Kalpi India 104 D4
Kalpin China 98 B4
Kalsi India 99 B7
Kaltag AK U.S.A. 148 H2
Kaltensundheim Germany 63 K4
Kaltukatjara Australia 135 E6
Kalu India 111 I4
Kaluga Rus. Fed. 53 H5
Kalukalukuang i. Indon. 85 G4
Kaluku Sulawesi Barat Indon. 83 A3
Kalulong, Bukit mt. Malaysia 85 F2
Kalundborg Denmark 55 G9
Kalupis Falls Malaysia 85 G1
Kalush Ukr. 53 E6
Kalvakol India 106 C2
Kälviä Fin. 54 M5
Kal'ya Rus. Fed. 51 R3
Kalyan India 106 B2
Kalyandurg India 109 M7
Kalyansingapuram India 106 D2
Kalyazin Rus. Fed. 52 H4
Kalymnos i. Greece 69 L6
Kalzhat Kazakh. 98 C4
Kama Dem. Rep. Congo 122 C4
Kama Myanmar 86 A3

▶Kama r. Rus. Fed. 52 L4
4th longest river in Europe.

Kamagaya Japan 93 F3
Kamaishi Japan 91 F5
Kamakura Japan 93 F3
Kamalia Pak. 111 I4
Kaman India 99 B8
Kaman Turkey 112 D3
Kamanashi-gawa r. Japan 93 E3
Kamanashi-yama mt. Japan 93 E3
Kamaniskeg Lake Canada 165 G1
Kamanjab Namibia 123 B5
Kamarān i. Yemen 108 F6
Kamaran Island Yemen see Kamarān
Kamard reg. Afgh. 111 G3
Kamarod Pak. 111 F5
Kamaron Sierra Leone 120 B4
Kamashi Uzbek. see Qamashi
Kamasin India 104 E4
Kambaiti Myanmar 86 B1
Kambalda Australia 135 C7
Kambam India 106 C4
Kambang Sumatera Indon. 84 C3
Kambangan i. Indon. 85 E5
Kambara i. Fiji see Kabara
Kambara Japan see Kanbara
Kambardi China 98 C4
Kambia Sierra Leone 120 B4
Kambing, Pulau i. East Timor see Ataúro, Ilha de
Kambo-san mt. N. Korea see Kwanmo-bong
Kambove Dem. Rep. Congo 123 C5
Kambuno, Bukit mt. Indon. 83 B3
Kambūt Libya 112 B5
Kamchatka, Poluostrov pen. Rus. Fed. see Kamchatka Peninsula
Kamchatka Basin sea feature Bering Sea 186 H2
Kamchatka Peninsula Rus. Fed. 77 Q4
Kamchiya r. Bulg. 69 L3

Kasumiga-ura l. Japan 93 G2
Kasumkent Rus. Fed. 113 H2
Kasungu Malawi 123 D5
Kasungu National Park Malawi 123 D5
Kasur Pak. 111 I4
Katâdtlit Nunât terr. N. America see Greenland
Katahdin, Mount ME U.S.A. 162 G2
Katah Sang Srah Afgh. 111 G3
Kataklik India 104 D2
Katako-Kombe Dem. Rep. Congo 122 C4
Katakwi Uganda 122 D3
Katalla AK U.S.A. 149 K3
Katana India 104 C5
Katangi India 104 D5
Katanning Australia 135 B8
Katano Japan 92 B4
Katashina Japan 93 F2
Katashina-gawa r. Japan 93 F2
Katata Japan 92 B3
Katavi National Park Tanz. 123 D4
Katāwāz reg. Afgh. 111 G3
Katchall i. India 87 A6
Katea Dem. Rep. Congo 123 C4
Kateel r. AK U.S.A. 148 H2
Katerini Greece 69 J4
Katesh Tanz. 123 D4
Kate's Needle mt. Canada/U.S.A. 149 N4
Katete Zambia 123 D5
Katherîna, Gebel mt. Egypt see Kātrīnā, Jabal
Katherine Australia 134 F3
Katherine Gorge National Park Australia see Nitmiluk National Park
Kathi India 111 I6
Kathiawar pen. India 104 B5
Kathihar India see Katihar
Kathiraveli Sri Lanka 106 D4
Kathiwara India 104 C5
Kathleen Falls Australia 134 E3

►Kathmandu Nepal 105 F4
Capital of Nepal.

Kathu S. Africa 124 F4
Kathua India 104 C2
Kati Mali 120 C3
Katibas r. Malaysia 85 F2
Katihar India 105 F4
Katikati S. Africa 125 H7
Katima Mulilo Namibia 123 C5
Katimik Lake Canada 151 L4
Katiola Côte d'Ivoire 120 C4
Kā Tiritiri o te Moana mts N.Z. see Southern Alps
Katkop Hills S. Africa 124 E6
Katlehong S. Africa 125 I4
Katma China 99 D5
Katmai National Park and Preserve AK U.S.A. 146 C4
Katmandu Nepal see Kathmandu
Kato Achaïa Greece 69 I5
Kat O Chau H.K. China see Crooked Island
Kat O Hoi b. H.K. China see Crooked Harbour
Katonkaragay Kazakh. 98 D2
Katoomba Australia 138 E4
Katoposa, Gunung mt. Indon. 83 B3
Katowice Poland 57 Q5
Katoya India 105 G5
Katrancık Dağı mts Turkey 69 M6
Kātrīnā, Jabal mt. Egypt 112 D5
Katrine, Loch l. U.K. 60 E4
Katrineholm Sweden 55 J7
Katse Dam Lesotho 125 I5
Katsina Nigeria 120 D3
Katsina-Ala Nigeria 120 D4
Katsunuma Japan 93 E3
Katsura-gawa r. Japan 93 F3
Katsuragi-san hill Japan 92 B4
Katsuura Japan 93 G3
Katsuyama Japan 92 C2
Kattaktoc, Cap c. Canada 153 I2
Kattamudda Well Australia 134 D5
Kattaqo'rg'on Uzbek. 111 G2
Kattaqŭrghon Uzbek. see Kattaqo'rg'on
Kattegat strait Denmark/Sweden 55 G8
Kattowitz Poland see Katowice
Katumbar India 104 D4
Katun' r. Rus. Fed. 98 D1
Katunino Rus. Fed. 52 J4
Katunskiy Khrebet mts Rus. Fed. 98 D2
Katuri Pak. 111 H4
Katwa India see Katoya
Katwijk aan Zee Neth. 62 E2
Katzenbuckel hill Germany 63 J5
Kaua'i i. HI U.S.A. 157 [inset]
Kaua'i Channel HI U.S.A. 157 [inset]
Kaub Germany 63 H4
Kaufungen Germany 63 J3
Kauhajoki Fin. 54 M5
Kauhava Fin. 54 M5
Kaukauna WI U.S.A. 164 A1
Kaukkwè Hills Myanmar 86 B1
Kaukonen Fin. 54 N3
Ka'ula i. HI U.S.A. 157 [inset]
Kaulakahi Channel HI U.S.A. 157 [inset]
Kaumajet Mountains Canada 153 J2
Kaunakakai HI U.S.A. 157 [inset]
Kaunas Lith. 55 M9
Kaunata Latvia 55 O8
Kaundy, Vpadina depr. Kazakh. 113 I2
Kaunia Bangl. 105 G4
Kaura-Namoda Nigeria 120 D3
Kau Sai Chau i. H.K. China 97 [inset]
Kaustinen Fin. 54 M5
Kautokeino Norway 54 M2
Kau-ye Kyun i. Myanmar 87 B5
Kavadarci Macedonia 69 J4
Kavak Turkey 112 E2
Kavaklıdere Turkey 69 M6
Kavala Greece 69 K4
Kavalas, Kolpos b. Greece 69 K4
Kavalerovo Rus. Fed. 90 D3
Kavali India 106 D3
Kavār Iran 110 D4
Kavaratti India 106 B4
Kavaratti atoll India 106 B4
Kavarna Bulg. 69 M3
Kavendou, Mont mt. Guinea 120 B3
Kaveri r. India 106 C4
Kavīr Iran 110 C3
Kavīr, Dasht-e des. Iran 110 D3
Kavīr Kūshk well Iran 110 E3
Kavkasioni mts Asia/Europe see Caucasus
Kawa Seram Indon. 83 D3
Kawa Myanmar 86 B3
Kawabe Gifu Japan 92 D3
Kawabe Wakayama Japan 92 B5
Kawachi Ibaraki Japan 93 G3
Kawachi Ishikawa Japan 92 C2
Kawachi Tochigi Japan 93 F2
Kawachi-Nagano Japan 92 B4
Kawagama Lake Canada 165 F1
Kawage Japan 92 C4
Kawagoe Japan 93 F3
Kawaguchi Japan 93 F3
Kawaguchiko Japan 93 E3
Kawaguchi-ko l. Japan 93 E3
Kawai Japan 92 D2
Kawaihae HI U.S.A. 157 [inset]
Kawaikini HI U.S.A. 157 [inset]
Kawakami Nagano Japan 93 E3
Kawakami Nara Japan 92 B4
Kawakawa N.Z. 139 E2
Kawakita Japan 92 C2
Kawambwa Zambia 123 C4
Kawamoto Japan 93 F2
Kawana Zambia 123 C5
Kawanakajima Japan 93 E2
Kawana-zaki pt Japan 93 F4
Kawane Japan 93 E4
Kawangkoan Sulawesi Indon. 83 C2
Kawanishi Japan 92 B3
Kawarazawa-gawa r. Japan 93 F2
Kawardha India 104 E5
Kawartha Lakes Canada 165 F1
Kawasaki Japan 93 F3
Kawashima Japan 92 C3
Kawato Sulawesi Indon. 83 B3
Kawaue Japan 92 D3
Kawau Island N.Z. 139 E3
Kawawachikamach Canada 153 I3
Kawazu Japan 93 E4
Kawdut Myanmar 86 B4
Kawe i. Papua Indon. 83 D2
Kawerau N.Z. 139 F4
Kawhia N.Z. 139 E4
Kawhia Harbour N.Z. 139 E4
Kawich Peak NV U.S.A. 158 E3
Kawich Range mts NV U.S.A. 158 E3
Kawinaw Lake Canada 151 L4
Kawinda Sumbawa Indon. 85 G5
Kawio i. Indon. 83 C1
Kaw Lake OK U.S.A. 161 D4
Kawlin Myanmar 86 A2
Kawm Umbū Egypt 108 D5
Kawngmeum Myanmar 86 B2
Kawthaung Myanmar 87 B5
Kaxgar China see Kashi
Kaxgar He r. China 98 B5
Kax He r. China 98 C4
Kaxtax Shan mts China 99 C5
Kaya Burkina Faso 120 C3
Kayadibi Turkey 112 E3
Kayaga-take mt. Japan 93 E3
Kayak Island AK U.S.A. 149 K4
Kayan r. Indon. 85 E3
Kayan r. Indon. 85 G2
Kayangel Atoll Palau 82 [inset]
Kayangel Passage Palau 82 [inset]
Kayankulam India 106 C4
Kayan Mentarang, Taman Nasional nat. park Indon. 85 F2
Kayar India 106 C2
Kayasa Halmahera Indon. 83 C2
Kaycee WY U.S.A. 156 G4
Kaydak, Sor dry lake Kazakh. 113 I1
Kaydanovo Belarus see Dzyarzhynsk
Kayembe-Mukulu Dem. Rep. Congo 123 C4
Kayenta AZ U.S.A. 159 H3
Kayes Mali 120 B3
Kayigyalik Lake AK U.S.A. 148 G3
Kaylahgay (abandoned) Afgh. 111 H3
Kaymaz Turkey 69 N5
Kaynar Vostochnyy Kazakhstan Kazakh. 102 E2
Kaynar Zhambylskaya Oblast' Kazakh. 98 A4
Kaynar Turkey 112 E3
Kayo Japan 92 B3
Kayoa i. Maluku Indon. 83 C2
Kay Point pt Canada 149 M1
Kayseri Turkey 112 D3
Kayuadi i. Indon. 83 B4
Kayuagung Sumatera Indon. 84 D3
Kayuyu Dem. Rep. Congo 122 C4
Kayyngdy Kyrg. 102 D3
Kazach'ye Rus. Fed. 77 O2
Kazakh Azer. see Qazax
Kazakhskaya S.S.R. country Asia see Kazakhstan
Kazakhskiy Zaliv b. Kazakh. 113 I2

►Kazakhstan country Asia 100 F2
4th largest country in Asia and 9th in the world.

Kazakhstan Kazakh. see Aksay
Kazakh Steppe plain Kazakh. see Saryarka
Kazakstan country Asia see Kazakhstan
Kazan r. Canada 151 M2
Kazan' Rus. Fed. 52 K5
Kazandzhik Turkm. see Bereket
Kazanka r. Rus. Fed. 52 K5
Kazanlı Turkey 107 B1
Kazanlŭk Bulg. 69 K3
Kazan-rettō is Japan see Volcano Islands
Kazanshunkyr Kazakh. 98 C2
Kazatin Ukr. see Kozyatyn

►Kazbek mt. Georgia/Rus. Fed. 53 J8
4th highest mountain in Europe.

Kaz Dağı mts Turkey 69 L5
Kāzerūn Iran 110 C4
Kazhym Rus. Fed. 52 K3
Kazidi Tajik. see Qozideh
Kazi Magomed Azer. see Qazımämmäd
Kazincbarcika Hungary 53 D6
Kaziranga National Park India 105 H4
Kazo Japan 93 F2
Kazret'i Georgia 113 G2
Kaztalovka Kazakh. 51 P6
Kazusa Japan 93 G3
Kazy Turkm. 110 E2
Kazym r. Rus. Fed. 51 T3
Kazym-Mys Rus. Fed. 51 T3
Kea i. Greece see Tzia
Keady U.K. 61 F3
Keams Canyon AZ U.S.A. 159 H4
Kéamu i. Vanuatu see Anatom
Kearney NE U.S.A. 160 D3
Kearny AZ U.S.A. 159 H5
Keban Turkey 112 E3
Keban Barajı resr Turkey 112 E3
Kebatu i. Indon. 85 E3
Kébémèr Senegal 120 B3
Kebili Tunisia 64 F5
Kebīr, Nahr al r. Lebanon/Syria 107 B2
Kebkabiya Sudan 121 F3
Kebnekaise mt. Sweden 54 K3
Kebock Head hd U.K. 60 C2
K'ebrī Dehar Eth. 122 E3
Kebumen Jawa Indon. 85 E4
Kebur Sumatera Indon. 84 C3
Kech reg. Pak. 111 F5
Kecheng China 94 D4
Kechika r. Canada 149 P4
Keçiborlu Turkey 69 N6
Kecskemét Hungary 69 H1
Keda Georgia 113 F2
Kedah state Malaysia 84 C1
Kėdainiai Lith. 55 M9
Kedairu Passage Fiji see Kadavu Passage
Kedarnath Peak India 99 B7
Kedgwick Canada 153 I5
Kedian China 97 G2
Kediri Jawa Indon. 85 F4
Kedong China 90 B3
Kédougou Senegal 120 B3
Kedva r. Rus. Fed. 52 L2
Kędzierzyn-Koźle Poland 57 Q5
Keele r. Canada 149 P2
Keele Peak Canada 149 O3
Keeler CA U.S.A. 158 E3
Keeley Lake Canada 151 I4
Keeling Islands terr. Indian Ocean see Cocos Islands
Keen, Mount hill U.K. 60 G4
Keenapusan i. Phil. 82 B5
Keene CA U.S.A. 158 D4
Keene KY U.S.A. 164 C5
Keene NH U.S.A. 165 I2
Keene OH U.S.A. 164 E3
Keeper Hill hill Ireland 61 D5
Keepit, Lake resr Australia 138 E3
Keep River National Park Australia 134 E3
Keerbergen Belgium 62 E3
Keer-weer, Cape Australia 136 C2
Keetmanshoop Namibia 124 D4
Keewatin Canada 151 M5
Kefallinía i. Greece see Cephalonia
Kefallonia i. Greece see Cephalonia
Kefamenanu Timor Indon. 83 C5
Kefe Ukr. see Feodosiya
Keffi Nigeria 120 D4
Keflavík Iceland 54 [inset 1]
Kê Ga, Mui pt Vietnam 87 E5
Kegalla Sri Lanka 106 D5
Kegen Kazakh. 102 E3
Kegeti Kyrg. 98 A4
Keglo, Baie de b. Canada 153 I2
Keg River Canada 150 G3
Kegul'ta Rus. Fed. 53 J7
Kehra Estonia 55 N7
Kehsi Mansam Myanmar 86 B2
Keighley U.K. 58 F5
Keihoku Japan 92 B3
Keila Estonia 55 N7
Keimoes S. Africa 124 E5
Keitele Fin. 54 O5
Keitele l. Fin. 54 O5
Keith Australia 137 C8
Keith U.K. 60 G3
Keith Arm b. Canada 149 Q2
Kejimkujik National Park Canada 153 I5
Kekachi-yama mt. Japan 92 D2
Kekaha HI U.S.A. 157 [inset]
Kékes mt. Hungary 57 R7
Kekik i. Maluku Indon. 83 D3
Keklau Palau 82 [inset]
Kekri India 104 C4
Kelaa i. Maldives 106 B5
K'elafo Eth. 122 E3
Kelan China 95 G4
Kelang i. Maluku Indon. 83 C3
Kelang Malaysia see Klang
Kelantan r. Malaysia 84 C1
Kelantan state Malaysia 84 C1
Kelapa i. Maluku Indon. 83 D5
Kelara r. Indon. 83 A4
Kelawar i. Indon. 85 E3
Kelberg Germany 62 G4
Kel'demurat Kazakh. 98 C3
Kelheim Germany 63 L6
Kelibia Tunisia 68 D6
Kelif Uzboýy marsh Turkm. 111 F2
Kelīrī Iran 110 E5
Kelkheim (Taunus) Germany 63 I4
Kelkit Turkey 113 E2
Kelkit r. Turkey 112 E2
Kéllé Congo 122 B4
Keller Lake Canada 150 F2
Kellett, Cape Canada 146 F2
Kelleys Island OH U.S.A. 164 D3
Kelliher Canada 151 K5
Kellosalkä Fin. 54 P3
Kells Ireland 61 F4
Kells r. U.K. 61 F3
Kelly KY U.S.A. 164 B5
Kelly r. AK U.S.A. 148 G2
Kelly, Mount hill AK U.S.A. 148 G1
Kelly Lake Canada 149 P2
Kelly Range hills Australia 135 C6
Kelmė Lith. 55 M9
Kelmis Belgium 62 G4
Kélo Chad 121 E4
Kelowna Canada 150 G5
Kelp Head hd Canada 150 E5
Kelseyville CA U.S.A. 158 B2
Kelso U.K. 60 G5
Kelso CA U.S.A. 159 F4
Kelso WA U.S.A. 156 C3
Keluang Malaysia 84 C2
Kelvington Canada 151 K4
Kem' Rus. Fed. 52 G2
Kem' r. Rus. Fed. 52 G2
Kemabung Sabah Malaysia 85 F1
Ke Macina Mali see Massina
Kemah Turkey 112 E3
Kemaliye Turkey 112 E3
Kemalpaşa Turkey 69 L5
Kemano (abandoned) Canada 150 E4
Kemasik Malaysia 84 C1
Kembayan Kalimantan Indon. 85 E2
Kembé Cent. Afr. Rep. 122 C3
Kemeneshát hills Hungary 68 G1
Kemer Antalya Turkey 69 N6
Kemer Muğla Turkey 69 M6
Kemer Barajı resr Turkey 69 M6
Kemerovo Rus. Fed. 76 J4
Kemi Fin. 54 N4
Kemijärvi Fin. 54 O3
Kemijärvi l. Fin. 54 O3
Kemijoki r. Fin. 54 N4
Kemin Kyrg. 98 A4
Kemiö Fin. see Kimito
Kemir Turkm. see Keymir
Kemmerer WY U.S.A. 156 F4
Kemnath Germany 63 L5
Kemnay U.K. 60 G3
Kemp Coast reg. Antarctica see Kemp Land
Kempele Fin. 54 N4
Kempen Germany 62 G3
Kempisch Kanaal canal Belgium 62 F3
Kemp Land reg. Antarctica 188 D2
Kemp Peninsula Antarctica 188 A2
Kemp's Bay Bahamas 163 E7
Kempsey Australia 138 F3
Kempt, Lac l. Canada 152 G5
Kempten (Allgäu) Germany 57 M7
Kempton IN U.S.A. 164 B3
Kempton Park S. Africa 125 I4
Kemptville Canada 165 H1
Kemujan i. Indon. 85 E4
Ken r. India 104 E4
Kenai AK U.S.A. 149 J3
Kenai Fiords National Park AK U.S.A. 149 J4
Kenai Lake AK U.S.A. 149 J3
Kenai Mountains AK U.S.A. 149 J4
Kenai National Wildlife Refuge nature res. AK U.S.A. 149 J3
Kenai Peninsula AK U.S.A. 149 J3
Kenam, Tanjung pt Indon. 84 D4
Kenamu r. Canada 153 K3
Kenansville NC U.S.A. 163 E5
Kenâyis, Râs el pt Egypt see Ḥikmah, Ra's al
Kenbridge VA U.S.A. 165 F5
Kencong Jawa Indon. 85 F5
Kendal Jawa Indon. 85 E4
Kendal U.K. 58 E4
Kendall Australia 138 F3
Kendall, Cape Canada 147 J3
Kendall Island Bird Sanctuary nature res. Canada 149 N1
Kendallville IN U.S.A. 164 C3
Kendari Sulawesi Indon. 83 B3
Kendawangan Kalimantan Indon. 85 E3
Kendawangan r. Indon. 85 E3
Kendégué Chad 121 E3
Kendirli-Kiyasan, Plato plat. Kazakh. 113 I2
Kendrapara India 105 F5
Kendraparha India see Kendrapara
Kendrick Peak AZ U.S.A. 159 H4
Kendujhar India see Keonjhar
Kendujhargarh India see Keonjhar
Kendyktas mts Kazakh. 98 A4
Kendyrlisor, Solonchak salt l. Kazakh. 113 I2
Kenebri Australia 138 D3
Kenedy TX U.S.A. 161 D6
Kenema Sierra Leone 120 B4
Kenepai, Gunung mt. Indon. 85 E2
Kenge Dem. Rep. Congo 123 B4
Keng Lap Myanmar 86 C2
Kengtung Myanmar 86 B2
Kenhardt S. Africa 124 E5
Kéniéba Mali 120 B3
Kénitra Morocco 64 C5
Kenli China 95 I4
Kenmare Ireland 61 C6
Kenmare ND U.S.A. 160 C1
Kenmare River inlet Ireland 61 B6
Kenmore NY U.S.A. 165 F2
Kenn Germany 62 G5
Kenna NM U.S.A. 161 C5
Kennebec SD U.S.A. 160 D3
Kennebec r. ME U.S.A. 162 G2
Kennebunkport ME U.S.A. 165 J2
Kennedy, Cape FL U.S.A. see Canaveral, Cape
Kennedy Entrance sea channel AK U.S.A. 148 I4
Kennedy Range National Park Australia 135 A6
Kennedy Town H.K. China 97 [inset]
Kenner LA U.S.A. 161 F6
Kennet r. U.K. 59 G7
Kenneth Range hills Australia 135 B5
Kennett MO U.S.A. 161 F4
Kennewick WA U.S.A. 156 D3
Kennicott AK U.S.A. 149 L3
Kenn Reef Australia 136 F4
Kenny Lake AK U.S.A. 149 K3
Kenogami r. Canada 152 D4
Keno Hill Canada 149 N3
Kenora Canada 151 M5
Kenosha WI U.S.A. 164 B2
Kenozero, Ozero l. Rus. Fed. 52 H3
Kent r. U.K. 58 E4
Kent OH U.S.A. 164 E3
Kent TX U.S.A. 161 B6
Kent VA U.S.A. 164 E5
Kent WA U.S.A. 156 C3
Kentani S. Africa 125 I7
Kent Group is Australia 137 [inset]
Kentland IN U.S.A. 164 B3
Kenton OH U.S.A. 164 D3
Kent Peninsula Canada 146 H3
Kentucky state U.S.A. 164 C5
Kentucky Lake KY U.S.A. 161 F4
Kentwood LA U.S.A. 167 H2
Kenya country Africa 122 D3

►Kenya, Mount Kenya 122 D4
2nd highest mountain in Africa.

Kenyir, Tasik resr Malaysia 84 C1
Ken-zaki pt Japan 93 F3
Keokuk IA U.S.A. 160 F3
Keoladeo National Park India 104 D4
Keonjhar India 105 F5
Keonjhargarh India see Keonjhar
Keosauqua IA U.S.A. 160 F3
Keowee, Lake resr SC U.S.A. 163 D5
Kepahiang Sumatera Indon. 84 C3
Kepina r. Rus. Fed. 52 I2
Keppel Bay Australia 136 E4
Kepsut Turkey 69 M5
Kepulauan Bangka-Belitung prov. Indon. see Bangka-Belitung
Kera India 105 F5
Kerāh Iran 110 E4
Kerala state India 106 B4
Kerang Australia 138 A5
Kerava Fin. 55 N6
Kerba Alg. 67 G5
Kerbau, Tanjung pt Indon. 84 C3
Kerbela Iraq see Karbalā'
Kerben Kyrg. 102 D3
Kerbi r. Rus. Fed. 90 E1
Kerbodot, Lac l. Canada 153 I3
Kerch Ukr. 112 E1
Kerchem"ya Rus. Fed. 52 L3
Kerema P.N.G. 81 L8
Keremeos Canada 150 G5
Kerempe Burun pt Turkey 112 D2
Keren Eritrea 108 E6
Kerepakupai Merú waterfall Venez. see Angel Falls
Kerewan Gambia 120 B3
Kergeli Turkm. 110 E2
Kerguélen, Îles is Indian Ocean 185 M9
Kerguelen Islands Indian Ocean see Kerguélen, Îles
Kerguelen Plateau sea feature Indian Ocean 185 M9
Kericho Kenya 122 D4
Kerihun mt. Indon. 85 F2
Kerikeri N.Z. 139 D2
Kerimäki Fin. 54 P6
Kerinci, Danau l. Indon. 84 C3
Kerinci, Gunung vol. Indon. 84 C3
Kerinci Seblat, Taman Nasional nat. park Indon. 84 C3
Kerintji vol. Indon. see Kerinci, Gunung
Keriya China see Yutian
Keriya He watercourse China 99 C5
Keriya Shankou pass China 99 C6
Kerken Germany 62 G3
Kerkennah, Îles is Tunisia 68 D7
Kerkiçi Turkm. 111 G2
Kerkini, Limni l. Greece 69 J4
Kerkinitis, Limni l. Greece see Kerkini, Limni
Kérkira i. Greece see Corfu
Kerkouane tourist site Tunisia 68 D6
Kerkyra Greece 69 H5
Kerkyra i. Greece see Corfu
Kerma Sudan 108 D6
Kermadec Islands S. Pacific Ocean 133 I5

►Kermadec Trench sea feature S. Pacific Ocean 186 I8
4th deepest trench in the world.

Kermān Iran 110 E4
Kerman CA U.S.A. 158 C3
Kermān, Biābān-e Iran 110 E4
Kermānshāh Kermānshāh Iran 110 B3
Kermānshāh Yazd Iran 110 D4
Kermine Uzbek. see Navoiy
Kermit TX U.S.A. 161 C6
Kern r. CA U.S.A. 158 D4
Kernertut, Cap c. Canada 153 I2
Keroh Malaysia see Pengkalan Hulu
Keros i. Greece 69 K6
Keros Rus. Fed. 52 L3
Kérouané Guinea 120 C4
Kerpen Germany 62 G4
Kerr, Cape Antarctica 188 H1
Kerrobert Canada 151 I5
Kerrville TX U.S.A. 161 D6
Kerry Head hd Ireland 61 C5
Kerteh Malaysia 84 C1
Kerteminde Denmark 55 G9
Kertosono Jawa Indon. 85 F4
Keruak Lombok Indon. 85 G5
Kerulen r. China/Mongolia see Herlen Gol
Kerumutan, Suaka Margasatwa nature res. Indon. 84 C3
Kerur India 106 B2
Keryneia Cyprus see Kyrenia
Kerzaz Alg. 120 C2
Kerzhenets r. Rus. Fed. 52 J4
Kesagami Lake Canada 152 E4
Kesälahti Fin. 54 P6
Keşan Turkey 69 L4
Keşap Turkey 53 H8
Kesariya India 105 F4
Kesennuma Japan 91 F5
Keshan China 90 B2
Keshena WI U.S.A. 164 A1
Keshod India 104 B5
Keshvar Iran 110 C3
Keskin Turkey 112 D3
Keskozero Rus. Fed. 52 G3
Kesova Gora Rus. Fed. 52 H4
Kessel Neth. 62 G3
Kestell S. Africa 125 I5
Kesten'ga Rus. Fed. 54 Q4
Kestilä Fin. 54 O4
Keswick Canada 164 F1
Keswick U.K. 58 D4
Keszthely Hungary 68 G1
Ketahun Sumatera Indon. 84 C3
Ketapang Jawa Indon. 85 F4
Ketapang Kalimantan Indon. 85 E3
Ketchikan AK U.S.A. 149 O5
Ketian China 99 E6
Keti Bandar Pak. 111 G5
Ketik r. AK U.S.A. 148 H1
Ketlkede Mountain hill AK U.S.A. 148 H2
Ketmen', Khrebet mts China/Kazakh. 102 F3
Kettering U.K. 59 G6
Kettering OH U.S.A. 164 C4
Kettle r. Canada 150 G5
Kettle Creek r. PA U.S.A. 165 G3
Kettle Falls WA U.S.A. 156 D2
Kettleman City CA U.S.A. 158 D3
Kettle River Range mts WA U.S.A. 156 D2
Ketungau r. Indon. 85 E2
Keuka NY U.S.A. 165 G2
Keuka Lake NY U.S.A. 165 G2
Keumgang, Mount N. Korea see Kumgang-san
Keuruu Fin. 54 N5
Kew Turks and Caicos Is 163 F8
Kewanee IL U.S.A. 160 F3
Kewapante Flores Indon. 83 B5
Kewaunee WI U.S.A. 164 B1
Keweenaw Bay MI U.S.A. 160 F2
Keweenaw Peninsula MI U.S.A. 160 F2
Keweenaw Point MI U.S.A. 162 C2
Key, Lough l. Ireland 61 D3
Keyala South Sudan 121 G4
Keyano Canada 153 G3
Keya Paha r. NE U.S.A. 160 D3
Key Harbour Canada 152 E5
Keyi China 98 C4
Keyihe China 95 J1
Key Largo FL U.S.A. 163 D7
Keymir Turkm. 110 D2
Keynsham U.K. 59 E7
Keyser WV U.S.A. 165 F4
Keystone Lake OK U.S.A. 161 D4
Keystone Peak AZ U.S.A. 159 H6
Keysville VA U.S.A. 165 F5
Keytesville MO U.S.A. 160 E4
Keyvy, Vozvyshennost' hills Rus. Fed. 52 H2
Key West FL U.S.A. 163 D7
Kez Rus. Fed. 51 Q4
Kezi Zimbabwe 123 C6
Kgalagadi admin. dist. Botswana 124 E3
Kgalagadi Transfrontier National Park Botswana/S. Africa 125 D2
Kgalazadi admin. dist. Botswana see Kgalagadi
Kgatlen admin. dist. Botswana see Kgatleng
Kgatleng admin. dist. Botswana 125 H3
Kgomofatshe Pan salt pan Botswana 124 E2
Kgoro Pan salt pan Botswana 124 G3
Kgotsong S. Africa 125 H4
Kgun Lake AK U.S.A. 148 G3
Khabab Syria 107 C3
Khabar Iran 110 D4
Khabarikha Rus. Fed. 52 L2
Khabarovsk Rus. Fed. 90 D2
Khabarovskiy Kray admin. div. Rus. Fed. 90 D2
Khabarovsk Kray admin. div. Rus. Fed. see Khabarovskiy Kray
Khabary Rus. Fed. 88 D2
Khabis Iran see Shahdād
Khabody Pass Afgh. 111 F3
Khachmas Azer. see Xaçmaz
Khadar, Jabal mt. Oman 110 E6
Khadīr Afgh. 111 G3
Khadro Pak. 111 H5
Khadzhiolen Turkm. 110 E2
Khāf Iran 111 F3
Khafs Banbān well Saudi Arabia 110 B5
Khagaria India 105 F4
Khagrachari Bangl. 105 G5
Khagrachhari Bangl. see Khagrachari
Khairgarh Pak. 111 H4
Khairpur Punjab Pak. 111 I4
Khairpur Sindh Pak. 111 H5
Khāīz, Kūh-e mt. Iran 110 C4
Khajuha India 104 E4
Khāk-e Jabār Afgh. 111 H3
Khakhea Botswana 124 F3
Khāk Rayz Afgh. 111 G4
Khākrīz reg. Afgh. 111 G4
Khalajestan reg. Iran 110 C3
Khalatse India 104 D2
Khalifat mt. Pak. 111 G4
Khalīj Surt g. Libya see Sirte, Gulf of
Khalilabad India 105 E4
Khalīlī Iran 110 D5
Khalkabad Turkm. 111 F1
Khalkhāl Iran 110 C2
Khálki i. Greece see Chalki
Khalkís Greece see Chalkida
Khallikot India 106 E2
Khalturin Rus. Fed. see Orlov
Khamar-Daban, Khrebet mts Rus. Fed. 94 E1
Khamaria India 106 D1
Khambhat India 104 C5
Khambhat, Gulf of India 106 A2
Khamgaon India 106 C1
Khamir Yemen 108 F6
Khamis Mushayṭ Saudi Arabia 108 F6
Khamkeut Laos 86 D3
Khamma well Saudi Arabia 110 B5
Khammam India 106 D2
Khammouan Laos see Thakèk
Khamra Rus. Fed. 77 M3
Khamseh reg. Iran 110 C3
Khan, Nâm r. Laos 86 C3
Khānābād Afgh. 111 H2
Khān al Baghdādī Iraq 113 F4
Khān al Mashāhidah Iraq 113 G4
Khān al Muṣallá Iraq 113 G4
Khanapur India 106 B2
Khān ar Raḥbah Iraq 113 G5
Khanasur Pass Iran/Turkey 113 G3
Khanbalik China see Beijing
Khānch Iran 110 B2
Khandagayty Rus. Fed. 94 C1
Khandu India 111 I6
Khandwa India 104 D5
Khandyga Rus. Fed. 77 O3
Khanewal Pak. 111 H4
Khan Hung Vietnam see Soc Trăng
Khaniá Greece see Chania
Khānī Yek Iran 110 D4
Khanka, Lake China/Rus. Fed. 90 D3
Khanka, Ozero l. China/Rus. Fed. see Khanka, Lake
Khankendi Azer. see Xankändi
Khanna India 104 D3
Khannā, Qā' salt pan Jordan 107 C3
Khanpur Balochistan Pak. 111 H4
Khanpur Punjab Pak. 111 H4
Khān Ruḥābah Iraq see Khān ar Raḥbah
Khansar Pak. 111 H4
Khān Shaykhūn Syria 107 C2
Khantau Kazakh. 98 A3
Khantayskoye, Ozero l. Rus. Fed. 76 K3
Khan-Tengri, Pik mt. Kazakh./Kyrg. 98 C4
Khanthabouli Laos see Savannakhét
Khanty-Mansiysk Rus. Fed. 76 H3
Khān Yūnis Gaza 107 B4
Khanzi admin. dist. Botswana see Ghanzi
Khao Ang Rua Nai Wildlife Reserve nature res. Thai. 87 C4
Khao Banthat Wildlife Reserve nature res. Thai. 87 B6
Khao Chum Thong Thai. 87 B5
Khaoen Si Nakarin National Park Thai. 87 B4
Khao Laem, Ang Kep Nam Thai. 86 B4
Khao Laem National Park Thai. 86 B4
Khao Luang National Park Thai. 87 B5
Khao Pu-Khao Ya National Park Thai. 87 B6
Khao Soi Dao Wildlife Reserve nature res. Thai. 87 C4
Khao Sok National Park Thai. 87 B5
Khao Yai National Park Thai. 87 C4
Khapcheranga Rus. Fed. 95 H1
Khaplu Pak. 102 E4
Khaptad National Park Nepal 104 E3
Kharabali Rus. Fed. 53 J7
Kharagpur Bihar India 105 F4
Kharagpur W. Bengal India 105 F5
Khārān r. Iran 109 I4
Kharānaq, Kūh-e mt. Iran 110 D3
Kharanor Rus. Fed. 95 I1

Kharari India see Abu Road
Kharda India 106 B2
Khardi India 104 C6
Khardong La pass India see Khardung La
Khardung La pass India 104 D2
Kharfiyah Iraq 113 G5
Kharga Egypt see Al Khārijah
Kharga r. Rus. Fed. 90 D1
Khârga, El Wâhât el oasis Egypt see Khārijah, Wāḥāt al
Kharga Oasis Egypt see Khārijah, Wāḥāt al
Kharg Islands Iran 110 C4
Khargon India 104 C5
Khari r. Rajasthan India 104 C4
Khari r. Rajasthan India 104 C4
Kharian Pak. 111 I3
Khariar India 106 D1
Khārijah, Wāḥāt al oasis Egypt 108 D5
Kharīm, Gebel hill Egypt see Kharīm, Jabal
Kharīm, Jabal hill Egypt 107 A4
Kharkhara r. India 104 E5
Kharkhauda India 99 B7
Kharkiv Ukr. 53 H6
Khar'kov Ukr. see Kharkiv
Khār Kūh mt. Iran 110 D4
Kharlovka Rus. Fed. 52 H1
Kharlu Rus. Fed. 54 Q6
Kharmanli Bulg. 69 K4
Kharōtī reg. Afgh. 111 H3
Kharovsk Rus. Fed. 52 I4
Kharsia India 105 E5

▶Khartoum Sudan 108 D6
Capital of Sudan. 4th most populous city in Africa.

Kharwār reg. Afgh. 111 H3
Khasavyurt Rus. Fed. 113 G2
Khāsh Iran 111 F4
Khāsh, Dasht-e Afgh. 111 F4
Khashgort Rus. Fed. 51 T2
Khashm el Girba Sudan 108 E7
Khashm Şana' Saudi Arabia 112 E6
Khāsh Rōd r. Afgh. 111 F4
Khāsh Rūd Afgh. 111 F4
Khashuri Georgia 113 F2
Khasi Hills India 105 G4
Khaskovo Bulg. 69 K4
Khatanga Rus. Fed. 77 L2
Khatanga, Gulf of Rus. Fed. see Khatangskiy Zaliv
Khatangskiy Zaliv b. Rus. Fed. 77 L2
Khatayakha Rus. Fed. 52 M2
Khatinza Pass Pak. 111 H2
Khatmat al Malāha Oman 110 E5
Khatyrka Rus. Fed. 77 S3
Khaur Pak. 111 I3
Khavda India 104 B5
Khāwāk, Kōtal-e Afgh. 111 H3
Khayamnandi S. Africa 125 G6
Khaybar Saudi Arabia 108 E4
Khayelitsha S. Africa 124 D8
Khayrān, Ra's al pt Oman 110 E6
Khedrī Iran 110 E3
Khefa Israel see Haifa
Khehuene, Ponta pt Moz. 125 L2
Khemis Miliana Alg. 67 H5
Khemmarat Thai. 86 D3
Khenchela Alg. 68 B7
Khenifra Morocco 64 C5
Kherāmeh Iran 110 D4
Kherrata Alg. 67 I5
Kherreh Iran 110 D5
Khersan r. Iran 110 C4
Kherson Ukr. 69 O1
Kheta r. Rus. Fed. 77 L2
Kheyrābād Iran 110 D4
Khezerābād Iran 110 D2
Khiching India 105 F5
Khilok Rus. Fed. 95 G1
Khilok r. Rus. Fed. 95 F1
Khinganskiy Zapovednik nature res. Rus. Fed. 90 C2
Khinsar Pak. 111 H5
Khíos i. Greece see Chios
Khipro Pak. 111 H5
Khirbat Isrīyah Syria 107 C2
Khisrow Afgh. 111 G3
Khitai Dawan pass Aksai Chin 99 B6
Khīyāv Iran 110 B2
Khiytola Rus. Fed. 55 P6
Khlevnoye Rus. Fed. 53 H5
Khlong, Mae r. Thai. 87 C4
Khlong Saeng Wildlife Reserve nature res. Thai. 87 B5
Khlong Wang Chao National Park Thai. 86 B3
Khlung Thai. 87 C4
Khmel'nik Ukr. see Khmil'nyk
Khmel'nitskiy Ukr. see Khmel'nyts'kyy
Khmel'nyts'kyy Ukr. 53 E6
Khmer Republic country Asia see Cambodia
Khmil'nyk Ukr. 53 E6
Khoai, Hon i. Vietnam 87 D5
Khobda Kazakh. 102 A1
Khobi Georgia 113 F2
Khodā Āfarīd spring Iran 110 E3
Khodzha-Kala Turkm. see Hojagala
Khodzhambaz Turkm. see Hojambaz
Khodzhent Tajik. see Khŭjand
Khodzheyli Uzbek. see Xo'jayli
Khojand Tajik. see Khŭjand
Khokhowe Pan salt pan Botswana 124 E3
Khokhropar Pak. 111 H5
Khoksar India 104 D2
Kholm Afgh. 111 G2
Kholm Poland see Chełm
Kholm Rus. Fed. 52 F4
Kholmsk Rus. Fed. 90 F3
Kholon Israel see Ḥolon
Kholtoson Rus. Fed. 94 E1
Kholzun, Khrebet mts Kazakh./Rus. Fed. 98 D2
Khomas admin. reg. Namibia 124 C2
Khomas Highland hills Namibia 124 B2
Khomeyn Iran 110 C3
Khomeynīshahr Iran 110 C3
Khong, Mae Nam r. Asia 86 D4 see Mekong
Khonj Iran 110 D5
Khonj, Kūh-e mts Iran 110 D5
Khon Kaen Thai. 86 C3
Khon Kriel Cambodia see Phumĭ Kon Kriel
Khonsa India 105 H4
Khonuu Rus. Fed. 77 P3
Khoper r. Rus. Fed. 53 I6
Khor Rus. Fed. 90 D3
Khor r. Rus. Fed. 90 D3
Khorat Plateau Thai. 86 C3
Khorda India see Khurda
Khordha India see Khurda
Khorey-Ver Rus. Fed. 52 M2
Khorinsk Rus. Fed. 89 J2
Khorixas Namibia 123 B6
Khormūj, Kūh-e mt. Iran 110 C4
Khorog Tajik. see Khorugh
Khorol Rus. Fed. 90 D3
Khorol Ukr. 53 G6
Khoroslū Dāgh hills Iran 110 B2
Khorramābād Iran 110 C3
Khorramshahr Iran 110 C4
Khorugh Tajik. 111 H2
Khosheutovo Rus. Fed. 53 J7
Khōst Afgh. 111 H3
Khōst reg. Afgh./Pak. 111 H3
Khosūyeh Iran 110 D4
Khotan China see Hotan
Khotang Nepal 99 D8
Khotol Mountain hill AK U.S.A. 148 H2
Khouribga Morocco 64 C5
Khovaling Tajik. 111 H2
Khowrjān Iran 110 D4
Khreum Myanmar 86 A2
Khri r. India 99 E8
Khroma r. Rus. Fed. 77 P2
Khromtau Kazakh. 102 A1
Khru r. India 99 F8
Khrushchev Ukr. see Svitlovods'k
Khrysokhou Bay Cyprus see Chrysochou Bay
Khrystynivka Ukr. 53 F6
Khudumelapye Botswana 124 G2
Khudzhand Tajik. see Khŭjand
Khufaysah, Khashm al hill Saudi Arabia 110 B6
Khugiana Afgh. see Pīrzada
Khuis Botswana 124 E4
Khŭjand Tajik. 102 C3
Khŭjayli Uzbek. see Xo'jayli
Khu Khan Thai. 87 D4
Khulays Saudi Arabia 108 E5
Khulkhuta Rus. Fed. 53 J7
Khulm, Daryā-ye r. Afgh. 111 G2
Khulna Bangl. 105 G5
Khulo Georgia 113 F2
Khuma S. Africa 125 H4
Khūm Batheay Cambodia 87 D5
Khunayzīr, Jabal al mts Syria 107 C2
Khūnīk Bālā Iran 110 E3
Khūnīnshahr Iran see Khorramshahr
Khunjerab Pass China/Pak. 104 C1
Khun Yuam Thai. 86 B3
Khūr Iran 110 E3
Khūran sea chan. Iran 110 D5
Khurayş Saudi Arabia 108 G4
Khurda India 106 E1
Khurdha India see Khurda
Khurja India 104 D3
Khurmāliq Afgh. 111 F3
Khurmuli Rus. Fed. 90 E2
Khūrrāb Iran 110 D4
Khushab Pak. 111 I3
Khushalgarh Pak. 111 H3
Khushshah, Wādī al watercourse Jordan/Saudi Arabia 107 C5
Khust Ukr. 53 D6
Khutse Game Reserve nature res. Botswana 124 G2
Khutsong S. Africa 125 H4
Khutu r. Rus. Fed. 90 E2
Khuzdar Pak. 111 G5
Khvāf reg. Iran 111 F3
Khvājeh Iran 110 B2
Khvājeh Do Kūh hill Afgh. 111 G2
Khvājeh Moḥammad, Kūh-e mts Afgh. 111 H2
Khvalynsk Rus. Fed. 53 K5
Khvānsār Iran 110 C3
Khvodrān Iran 110 D4
Khvord Nārvan Iran 110 E3
Khvormūj Iran 110 C4
Khvors Iran 110 D3
Khvoy Iran 110 B2
Khvoynaya Rus. Fed. 52 G4
Khwaja Amran mt. Pak. 111 G4
Khyber Pakhtunkhwa prov. Pak. 111 H3
Khyber Pass Afgh./Pak. 111 H3
Kiama Australia 138 E5
Kiamba Mindanao Phil. 82 D5
Kiamichi r. OK U.S.A. 161 E5
Kiana AK U.S.A. 148 G2
Kiangsi prov. China see Jiangxi
Kiangsu prov. China see Jiangsu
Kiantajärvi l. Fin. 54 P4
Kiari India 99 B6
Kīāsar Iran 110 D2
Kiatassuaq i. Greenland 147 M2
Kibaha Tanz. 123 D4
Kibali r. Dem. Rep. Congo 122 C3
Kibangou Congo 122 B4
Kibawe Mindanao Phil. 82 D5
Kibaya Tanz. 123 D4
Kibi Japan 92 B4
Kiboga Uganda 122 D3
Kibombo Dem. Rep. Congo 122 C4
Kibondo Tanz. 122 D4
Kibre Mengist Eth. 121 G4
Kibris country Asia see Cyprus
Kibungo Rwanda 122 D4
Kičevo Macedonia 69 I4
Kichmengskiy Gorodok Rus. Fed. 52 J4
Kiçik Qafqaz mts Asia see Lesser Caucasus
Kicking Horse Pass Canada 150 G5
Kidal Mali 120 D3
Kidapawan Phil. 82 D5
Kidderminster U.K. 59 E6
Kidepo Valley National Park Uganda 122 D3
Kidira Senegal 120 B3
Kidmang India 104 D2
Kidnappers, Cape N.Z. 139 F4
Kidsgrove U.K. 59 E5
Kidurong, Tanjung pt Malaysia 85 F2
Kiel Germany 57 M3
Kiel WI U.S.A. 164 A2
Kiel Canal Germany 57 L3
Kielce Poland 57 R5
Kielder Water resr U.K. 58 E3
Kieler Bucht b. Germany 57 M3
Kienge Dem. Rep. Congo 123 C5
Kierspe Germany 63 H3

▶Kiev Ukr. 53 F6
Capital of Ukraine.

Kiffa Mauritania 120 B3
Kifisia Greece 69 J5
Kifrī Iraq 113 G4

▶Kigali Rwanda 122 D4
Capital of Rwanda.

Kigalik r. AK U.S.A. 148 I1
Kiğı Turkey 113 F3
Kiglapait Mountains Canada 153 J2
Kigluaik Mountains AK U.S.A. 148 F2
Kigoma Tanz. 123 C4
Kihambatang Kalimantan Indon. 85 F3
Kihlanki Fin. 54 M3
Kihniö Fin. 54 M5
Kiholo HI U.S.A. 157 [inset]
Kii-hantō pen. Japan 92 B5
Kiik Kazakh. 98 A3
Kiiminki Fin. 54 N4
Kii-Nagashima Japan 92 C4
Kii-sanchi mts Japan 92 B5
Kii-suidō sea chan. Japan 91 D6
Kijimadaira Japan 93 E2
Kikerino Rus. Fed. 55 P7
Kikiakrorak r. AK U.S.A. 149 J1
Kikinda Serbia 69 I2
Kikki Pak. 111 F5
Kikládhes is Greece see Cyclades
Kikmiktalikamiut AK U.S.A. 148 F3
Kiknur Rus. Fed. 52 J4
Kikonai Japan 90 F4
Kikori P.N.G. 81 K8
Kikori r. P.N.G. 81 K8
Kikugawa Japan 93 E4
Kikwit Dem. Rep. Congo 123 B4
Kilafors Sweden 55 J6
Kilar India 104 D2
Kilauea HI U.S.A. 157 [inset]
Kīlauea Volcano HI U.S.A. 157 [inset]
Kilbon Seram Indon. 83 D3
Kilbuck Mountains AK U.S.A. 148 H3
Kilchu N. Korea 90 C4
Kilcoole Ireland 61 F4
Kilcormac Ireland 61 E4
Kilcoy Australia 138 F1
Kildare Ireland 61 F4
Kil'dinstroy Rus. Fed. 54 R2
Kilekale Lake Canada 149 Q2
Kilemary Rus. Fed. 52 J4
Kilembe Dem. Rep. Congo 123 B4
Kilfinan U.K. 60 D5
Kilgore TX U.S.A. 161 E5
Kilham U.K. 58 E3
Kilia Ukr. see Kiliya
Kılıç Dağı mt. Syria/Turkey see Aqra', Jabal al
Kilifi Kenya 122 D4
Kilik Pass China 99 A5

▶Kilimanjaro vol. Tanz. 122 D4
Highest mountain in Africa.

Kilimanjaro National Park Tanz. 122 D4
Kilinailau Islands P.N.G. 132 F2
Kilindoni Tanz. 123 D4
Kilingi-Nõmme Estonia 55 N7
Kilis Turkey 107 C1
Kilis prov. Turkey 107 C1
Kiliuda Bay AK U.S.A. 148 I4
Kiliya Ukr. 69 M2
Kilkee Ireland 61 C5
Kilkeel U.K. 61 G3
Kilkenny Ireland 61 E5
Kilkhampton U.K. 59 C8
Kilkis Greece 69 J4
Killala Ireland 61 C3
Killala Bay Ireland 61 C3
Killaloe Ireland 61 D5
Killam Canada 151 I4
Killarney N.T. Australia 134 E4
Killarney Qld Australia 138 F2
Killarney Canada 152 E5
Killarney Ireland 61 C5
Killarney National Park Ireland 61 C6
Killary Harbour b. Ireland 61 C4
Killbuck OH U.S.A. 164 E3
Killeen TX U.S.A. 161 D6
Killenaule Ireland 61 E5
Killik r. AK U.S.A. 148 I1
Killimor Ireland 61 D4
Killin U.K. 60 E4
Killinchy U.K. 61 G3
Killíni mt. Greece see Kyllini
Killinick Ireland 61 F5
Killorglin Ireland 61 C5
Killurin Ireland 61 F5
Killybegs Ireland 61 D3
Kilmacrenan Ireland 61 E2
Kilmaine Ireland 61 C4
Kilmallock Ireland 61 D5
Kilmaluag U.K. 60 C3
Kilmarnock U.K. 60 E5
Kilmelford U.K. 60 D4
Kil'mez' Rus. Fed. 52 K4
Kil'mez' r. Rus. Fed. 52 K4
Kilmona Ireland 61 D6
Kilmore Australia 138 B6
Kilmore Quay Ireland 61 F5
Kilosa Tanz. 123 D4
Kilpisjärvi Fin. 54 L2
Kilrea U.K. 61 F3
Kilrush Ireland 61 C5
Kilsyth U.K. 60 E5
Kiltan atoll India 106 B4
Kiltullagh Ireland 61 D4
Kilwa Masoko Tanz. 123 D4
Kilwinning U.K. 60 E5
Kim CO U.S.A. 161 C4
Kimanis, Teluk b. Malaysia 85 F1
Kimba Australia 135 G8
Kimba Congo 122 B4
Kimball NE U.S.A. 160 C3
Kimball, Mount AK U.S.A. 149 K3
Kimbe P.N.G. 132 F2
Kimberley S. Africa 124 G5
Kimberley Plateau Australia 134 D4
Kimberley Range hills Australia 135 B6
Kimch'aek N. Korea 91 C4
Kimch'ŏn S. Korea 91 C5
Kimhae S. Korea 91 C6
Kimhandu mt. Tanz. 123 D4
Kimhwa S. Korea 91 B5
Kími Greece see Kymi
Kimito Fin. 55 M6
Kimitsu Japan 93 F3
Kimmirut Canada 147 L3
Kimolos i. Greece 69 K6
Kimovsk Rus. Fed. 53 H5
Kimpese Dem. Rep. Congo 123 B4
Kimpoku-san mt. Japan see Kinpoku-san
Kimry Rus. Fed. 52 H4
Kimsquit Canada 150 E4
Kimvula Dem. Rep. Congo 123 B4
Kinabalu, Gunung mt. Sabah Malaysia 85 G1
Kinabalu National Park Malaysia 85 G1
Kinabatangan r. Malaysia 85 G1
Kinabatangan, Kuala r. mouth Malaysia 85 G1
Kinango Kenya 123 D4
Kinasa Japan 93 E2
Kinaskan Lake Canada 149 O4
Kinbasket Lake Canada 150 G4
Kinbrace U.K. 60 F2
Kincaid Canada 151 J5
Kincardine Canada 164 E1
Kincardine U.K. 60 F4
Kinchega National Park Australia 137 C7
Kincolith Canada see Gingolx
Kinda Dem. Rep. Congo 123 C4
Kindat Myanmar 86 A2
Kinde MI U.S.A. 164 D2
Kinder LA U.S.A. 167 G2
Kinder Scout hill U.K. 58 F5
Kindersley Canada 151 I5
Kindia Guinea 120 B3
Kindu Dem. Rep. Congo 122 C4
Kinegnak AK U.S.A. 148 G4
Kinel' Rus. Fed. 53 K5
Kineshma Rus. Fed. 52 I4
Kingaroy Australia 138 E1
King Christian Island Canada 147 H2
King City CA U.S.A. 158 C3
King Cove AK U.S.A. 148 G5
King Edward VII Land pen. Antarctica see Edward VII Peninsula
Kingfield ME U.S.A. 165 J1
Kingfisher OK U.S.A. 161 D5
King George VA U.S.A. 165 G4
King George, Mount Canada 156 E2
King George Island Antarctica 188 A2
King George Islands Canada 152 F2
King George Islands Fr. Polynesia see Roi Georges, Îles du
King Hill hill Australia 134 C5
Kingisepp Rus. Fed. 55 P7
King Island Australia 137 [inset]
King Island Canada 150 E4
King Island Myanmar see Kadan Kyun
King Island AK U.S.A. 148 E2
Kingisseppa Estonia see Kuressaare
Kinglake National Park Australia 138 B6
King Leopold and Queen Astrid Coast Antarctica 188 E2
King Leopold Range National Park Australia 134 D4
King Leopold Ranges hills Australia 134 D4
Kingman AZ U.S.A. 159 F4

▶Kingman Reef terr. N. Pacific Ocean 186 J5
United States Unincorporated Territory.

King Mountain Canada 149 O4
King Mountain hill TX U.S.A. 161 C6
Kingoonya Australia 137 A6
King Peak Antarctica 188 L1
King Peninsula Antarctica 188 K2
Kingri Pak. 111 H4
Kings r. Ireland 61 E5
Kings r. CA U.S.A. 158 C3
Kings r. NV U.S.A. 156 D4
King Salmon AK U.S.A. 148 H4
King Salmon r. AK U.S.A. 148 H4
Kingsbridge U.K. 59 D8
Kingsburg CA U.S.A. 158 D3
Kings Canyon National Park CA U.S.A. 158 D3
Kingscliff Australia 138 F2
Kingscote Australia 137 B7
Kingscourt Ireland 61 F4
King Sejong research station Antarctica 188 A2
King's Lynn U.K. 59 H6
Kingsmill Group is Kiribati 133 H2
Kingsnorth U.K. 59 H7
King Sound b. Australia 134 C4
Kings Peak UT U.S.A. 159 H1
Kingsport TN U.S.A. 162 D4
Kingston Australia 137 [inset]
Kingston Canada 165 G1

▶Kingston Jamaica 169 I5
Capital of Jamaica.

▶Kingston Norfolk I. 133 G4
Capital of Norfolk Island.

Kingston MO U.S.A. 160 E4
Kingston NY U.S.A. 165 H3
Kingston OH U.S.A. 164 D4
Kingston PA U.S.A. 165 H3
Kingston Peak CA U.S.A. 159 F4
Kingston South East Australia 137 B8
Kingston upon Hull U.K. 58 G5

▶Kingstown St Vincent 169 L6
Capital of St Vincent.

Kingstree SC U.S.A. 163 E5
Kingsville TX U.S.A. 161 D7
Kingswood U.K. 59 E7
Kington U.K. 59 D6
Kingungi Dem. Rep. Congo 123 B4
Kingurutik r. Canada 153 J2
Kingussie U.K. 60 E3
King William VA U.S.A. 165 G5
King William Island Canada 147 I3
King William's Town S. Africa 125 H7
Kingwood TX U.S.A. 161 E6
Kingwood WV U.S.A. 164 F4
Kinloch N.Z. 139 B7
Kinloss U.K. 60 F3
Kinmen Taiwan see Chinmen
Kinmen i. Taiwan see Chinmen Tao
Kinmount Canada 165 F1
Kinna Sweden 55 H8
Kinnegad Ireland 61 E4
Kinneret, Yam l. Israel see Galilee, Sea of
Kinniyai Sri Lanka 106 D4
Kinnula Fin. 54 N5
Kinoje r. Canada 152 E3
Kino-kawa r. Japan 92 B4
Kinomoto Japan 92 C3
Kinoosao Canada 151 K3
Kinosaki Japan 92 A3
Kinpoku-san mt. Japan 91 E5
Kinross U.K. 60 F4
Kinsale Ireland 61 D6
Kinsale VA U.S.A. 165 G4

▶Kinshasa Dem. Rep. Congo 123 B4
Capital of the Democratic Republic of the Congo. 3rd most populous city in Africa.

Kinsley KS U.S.A. 160 D4
Kinsman OH U.S.A. 164 E3
Kinston NC U.S.A. 163 E5
Kintom Sulawesi Indon. 83 B3
Kintop Kalimantan Indon. 85 F3
Kintore U.K. 60 G3
Kintyre pen. U.K. 60 D5
Kin-U Myanmar 86 A2
Kinu-gawa r. Japan 93 G3
Kinunuma-yama mt. Japan 93 F2
Kinushseo r. Canada 152 E3
Kinyeti mt. South Sudan 121 G4
Kinzig r. Germany 63 I4
Kiowa CO U.S.A. 156 G5
Kiowa KS U.S.A. 161 D4
Kipahigan Lake Canada 151 K4
Kiparissía Greece see Kyparissia
Kipawa, Lac l. Canada 152 F5
Kipchak Pass China 98 B4
Kipling Canada 151 K5
Kipling Station Canada see Kipling
Kipnuk AK U.S.A. 148 F4
Kiptopeke VA U.S.A. 165 H5
Kipungo Angola see Quipungo
Kipushi Dem. Rep. Congo 123 C5
Kira Japan 92 D4
Kirakira Solomon Is 133 G3
Kirandul India 106 D2
Kirchdorf Germany 63 I2
Kirchheim-Bolanden Germany 63 I5
Kirchheim unter Teck Germany 63 J6
Kircubbin U.K. 61 G3
Kirdimi Chad 121 E3
Kirenga r. Rus. Fed. 89 J1
Kirensk Rus. Fed. 77 L4
Kireyevsk Rus. Fed. 53 H5
Kirghizia country Asia see Kyrgyzstan
Kirghiz Range mts Kazakh./Kyrg. 102 D3
Kirgizskaya S.S.R. country Asia see Kyrgyzstan
Kirgizskiy Khrebet mts Kazakh./Kyrg. see Kirghiz Range
Kirgizstan country Asia see Kyrgyzstan
Kiri Dem. Rep. Congo 122 B4
Kiribati country Pacific Ocean 186 I6
Kiriga-mine mt. Japan 93 E2
Kırıkhan Turkey 107 C1
Kırıkkale Turkey 112 D3
Kirikkuduk China 94 B2
Kirillov Rus. Fed. 52 H4
Kirillovo (abandoned) Rus. Fed. 90 F3
Kirin China see Jilin
Kirin prov. China see Jilin
Kirinda Sri Lanka 106 D5
Kirinyaga mt. Kenya see Kenya, Mount
Kirishi Rus. Fed. 52 G4
Kirishima-Yaku Kokuritsu-kōen Japan 91 C7
Kirishima-yama vol. Japan 91 C7
Kiritimati atoll Kiribati 187 J5
Kiriwina Islands P.N.G. see Trobriand Islands
Kırkağaç Turkey 69 L5
Kirk Bulāg Dāgi mt. Iran 110 B2
Kirkby U.K. 58 E5
Kirkby in Ashfield U.K. 59 F5
Kirkby Lonsdale U.K. 58 E4
Kirkby Stephen U.K. 58 E4
Kirkcaldy U.K. 60 F4
Kirkcolm U.K. 60 D6
Kirkcudbright U.K. 60 E6
Kirkenær Norway 55 H6
Kirkenes Norway 54 Q2
Kirkfield Canada 165 F1
Kirkintilloch U.K. 60 E5
Kirkkonummi Fin. 55 N6
Kirkland AZ U.S.A. 159 G4
Kirkland Lake Canada 152 E4
Kırklareli Turkey 69 L4
Kirklin IN U.S.A. 164 B3
Kirk Michael Isle of Man 58 C4
Kirkoswald U.K. 58 E4
Kirkpatrick, Mount Antarctica 188 H1
Kirksville MO U.S.A. 160 E3
Kirkūk Iraq 113 G4
Kirkwall U.K. 60 G2
Kirkwood S. Africa 125 G7
Kirman Iran see Kermān
Kirn Germany 63 H5
Kirov Kaluzhskaya Oblast' Rus. Fed. 53 G5
Kirov Kirovskaya Oblast' Rus. Fed. 52 K4
Kirova, Zaliv b. Azer. see Qızılağac Körfäzi
Kirovabad Azer. see Gäncä
Kirovabad Tajik. see Panj
Kirovakan Armenia see Vanadzor
Kirovo Ukr. see Kirovohrad
Kirovo-Chepetsk Rus. Fed. 52 K4
Kirovo-Chepetskiy Rus. Fed. see Kirovo-Chepetsk
Kirovograd Ukr. see Kirovohrad
Kirovohrad Ukr. 53 G6
Kirovsk Leningradskaya Oblast' Rus. Fed. 52 F4
Kirovsk Murmanskaya Oblast' Rus. Fed. 54 R3
Kirovsk Turkm. see Badabaýhan
Kirovs'ke Ukr. 112 D1
Kirovskiy Amurskaya Oblast' Rus. Fed. 90 B1
Kirovskiy Primorskiy Kray Rus. Fed. 90 D3
Kirovskoye Ukr. see Kirovs'ke
Kırpaşa pen. Cyprus see Karpasia
Kirpili Turkm. 110 E2
Kirriemuir U.K. 60 F4
Kirs Rus. Fed. 52 L4
Kirsanov Rus. Fed. 53 I5
Kırşehir Turkey 112 D3
Kirthar National Park Pak. 111 G5
Kirthar Range mts Pak. 111 G5
Kirtland NM U.S.A. 159 I3
Kirtorf Germany 63 J4
Kiruna Sweden 54 L3
Kirundu Dem. Rep. Congo 122 C4
Kirwan Escarpment Antarctica 188 B2
Kiryū Japan 93 F2
Kisa Sweden 55 I8
Kisama, Parque Nacional de nat. park Angola see Quiçama, Parque Nacional do
Kisandji Dem. Rep. Congo 123 B4
Kisangani Dem. Rep. Congo 122 C3
Kisantu Dem. Rep. Congo 123 B4
Kisar i. Maluku Indon. 83 C5
Kisaralik r. AK U.S.A. 148 G3
Kisaran Sumatera Indon. 84 B2
Kisarazu Japan 93 F3
Kisei Japan 92 C4
Kiselevka Rus. Fed. 90 E2
Kiselevsk Rus. Fed. 88 F2
Kish i. Iran 110 D5
Kishanganj India 105 F4
Kishangarh Madh. Prad. India 104 D4
Kishangarh Rajasthan India 104 B4
Kishangarh Rajasthan India 104 C4
Kishangarh Rajasthan India 104 D4
Kishi Nigeria 120 D4
Kishigawa Japan 92 B4
Kishi-gawa r. Japan 92 B4
Kishim Afgh. 111 H2
Kishindih-ye Bālā Afgh. 111 G2
Kishinev Moldova see Chişinău
Kishiwada Japan 92 B4
Kishkenekol' Kazakh. 101 G1
Kishoreganj Bangl. 105 G4
Kishorganj Bangl. see Kishoreganj
Kisi Nigeria see Kishi
Kisii Kenya 122 D4
Kiska Island AK U.S.A. 148 [inset] B6
Kiskittogisu Lake Canada 151 L4
Kiskitto Lake Canada 151 L4
Kiskunfélegyháza Hungary 69 H1
Kiskunhalas Hungary 69 H1
Kiskunsági nat. park Hungary 69 H1
Kislovodsk Rus. Fed. 113 F2
Kismaayo Somalia 122 E4
Kismayu Somalia see Kismaayo
Kiso Japan 93 D3
Kisofukushima Japan 92 D3
Kisogawa Japan 92 C3
Kiso-gawa r. Japan 92 C3
Kiso-gawa r. Japan 93 E3
Kisoro Uganda 121 F5
Kisosaki Japan 92 C3
Kiso-sanmyaku mts Japan 93 D3
Kispiox Canada 150 E4
Kispiox r. Canada 150 E4
Kissamos Greece 69 J7
Kisseraing Island Myanmar see Kanmaw Kyun
Kissidougou Guinea 120 B4
Kissimmee FL U.S.A. 163 D6
Kissimmee, Lake FL U.S.A. 163 D7
Kississing Lake Canada 151 K4
Kistendey Rus. Fed. 53 I5
Kistigan Lake Canada 151 M4
Kistna r. India see Krishna
Kisumu Kenya 122 D4
Kisykkamys Kazakh. see Dzhangala
Kita Hyōgo Japan 92 B4
Kita Kyōto Japan 92 B3
Kita Mali 120 C3
Kitab Uzbek. see Kitob
Kita-Daitō-jima i. Japan 89 O7
Kitagata Japan 92 C3
Kitaibaraki Japan 93 G2
Kita-Iō-jima vol. Japan 81 K1
Kitakami Japan 91 F5
Kita-Kyūshū Japan 91 C6
Kitale Kenya 122 D3
Kitami Japan 90 F4
Kitamimaki Japan 93 E2
Kitamoto Japan 93 F2
Kitatachibana Japan 93 F2
Kitaura Japan 93 G2
Kita-ura l. Japan 93 G3
Kitayama Japan 92 B5
Kit Carson CO U.S.A. 160 C4
Kitchener Canada 164 E2
Kitchigama r. Canada 152 F4
Kitee Fin. 54 Q5
Kitgum Uganda 122 D3
Kíthira i. Greece see Kythira
Kíthnos i. Greece see Kythnos
Kiti, Cape Cyprus see Kition, Cape
Kitimat Canada 150 D4
Kitinen r. Fin. 54 O3
Kition, Cape Cyprus 107 A2
Kitiou, Akra c. Cyprus see Kition, Cape
Kitkatla Canada 149 O5
Kitob Uzbek. 111 G2
Kitsault Canada 149 O5
Kitsuregawa Japan 93 G2
Kittanning PA U.S.A. 164 F3
Kittatinny Mountains hills NJ U.S.A. 165 H3
Kittery ME U.S.A. 165 J2
Kittilä Fin. 54 N3
Kittur India 106 B3
Kitty Hawk NC U.S.A. 162 F4
Kitui Kenya 122 D4
Kitwanga Canada 150 D4
Kitwe Zambia 123 C5
Kitzbüheler Alpen mts Austria 57 N7
Kitzingen Germany 63 K5
Kitzscher Germany 63 M3
Kiukpalik Island AK U.S.A. 148 I4
Kiu Lom, Ang Kep Nam Thai. 86 B3
Kiunga P.N.G. 81 K8
Kiuruvesi Fin. 54 O5
Kivak Rus. Fed. 148 D2
Kivalina AK U.S.A. 148 F2
Kividlo AK U.S.A. 148 F2
Kivijärvi Fin. 54 N5
Kiviõli Estonia 55 O7
Kivu, Lac Dem. Rep. Congo/Rwanda 122 C4
Kiwaba N'zogi Angola 123 B4
Kiwai Island P.N.G. 81 K8
Kiwalik AK U.S.A. 148 G2
Kiwalik r. AK U.S.A. 148 G2
Kiyev Ukr. see Kiev
Kiyevskoye Vodokhranilishche resr Ukr. see Kyyivs'ke Vodoskhovyshche
Kıyıköy Turkey 69 M4
Kiyomi Japan 92 D2
Kiyosumi-yama hill Japan 93 G3
Kiyotsu-gawa r. Japan 93 E1
Kizel Rus. Fed. 51 R4
Kizema Rus. Fed. 52 J3
Kizha Rus. Fed. 95 G1
Kizil China 98 C4
Kizilawat China 98 B5
Kızılcadağ Turkey 69 M6
Kızılca Dağ mt. Turkey 112 C3
Kızılcahamam Turkey 112 D2
Kızıldağ mt. Turkey 107 A1

Kızıldağ mt. Turkey 107 B1
Kızıl Dağı mt. Turkey 112 E3
Kızılırmak Turkey 112 D2
Kızılırmak r. Turkey 112 D2
Kızıltepe Turkey 113 F3
Kizilyurt Rus. Fed. 113 G2
Kızkalesi Turkey 107 B1
Kizlyar Rus. Fed. 113 G2
Kizlyarskiy Zaliv b. Rus. Fed. 113 G1
Kizner Rus. Fed. 52 K4
Kizu Japan 92 B4
Kizu-gawa r. Japan 92 B4
Kizyl-Arbat Turkm. see Serdar
Kizyl-Atrek Turkm. see Etrek
Kizyl Jilga Aksai Chin 99 B6
Kjøllefjord Norway 54 O1
Kjøpsvik Norway 54 J2
Kladno Czech Rep. 57 O5
Klagan Sabah Malaysia 85 G1
Klagenfurt Austria 57 O7
Klagetoh AZ U.S.A. 159 I4
Klaipėda Lith. 55 L9
Klaksvík Faroe Is 54 [inset 2]
Klamath CA U.S.A. 156 B4
Klamath r. CA U.S.A. 146 F5
Klamath Falls OR U.S.A. 156 C4
Klamath Mountains CA U.S.A. 156 C4
Klampo Kalimantan Indon. 85 G2
Klang Malaysia 84 C2
Klappan r. Canada 149 O4
Klarälven r. Sweden 55 H7
Klaten Jawa Indon. 85 E4
Klatovy Czech Rep. 57 N6
Klawer S. Africa 124 D6
Klawock AK U.S.A. 149 N5
Klazienaveen Neth. 62 G2
Kleides Islands Cyprus 107 B2
Kleinbegin S. Africa 124 E5
Klein Karas Namibia 124 D4
Klein Nama Land reg. S. Africa see Namaqualand
Klein Roggeveldberge mts S. Africa 124 E7
Kleinsee S. Africa 124 C5
Klemtu Canada 150 D4
Klerksdorp S. Africa 125 H4
Klery Creek AK U.S.A. 148 G2
Kletnya Rus. Fed. 53 G5
Kletsk Belarus see Klyetsk
Kletskaya Rus. Fed. 53 I6
Kletskiy Rus. Fed. see Kletskaya
Kleve Germany 62 G3
Klichka Rus. Fed. 95 I1
Klidhes Islands Cyprus see Kleides Islands
Klimkovka Rus. Fed. 52 K4
Klimovo Rus. Fed. 53 G5
Klin Rus. Fed. 52 H4
Kling Mindanao Phil. 82 D5
Klingenberg am Main Germany 63 J5
Klingenthal Germany 63 M4
Klingkang, Banjaran mts Indon./Malaysia 85 E2
Klink Germany 63 M1
Klínovec mt. Czech Rep. 63 N4
Klintehamn Sweden 55 K8
Klintsy Rus. Fed. 53 G5
Ključ Bos.-Herz. 68 G2
Kłodzko Poland 57 P5
Klondike r. Canada 149 M2
Klondike Gold Rush National Historical Park nat. park AK U.S.A. 149 N4
Kloosterhaar Neth. 62 G2
Klosterneuburg Austria 57 P6
Klotz, Mount Canada 149 L2
Klötze (Altmark) Germany 63 L2
Kluane Game Sanctuary nature res. Canada 149 L3
Kluane Lake Canada 149 M3
Kluane National Park Canada 149 M3
Kluang Malaysia see Keluang
Kluang, Tanjung pt Indon. 85 E3
Kluczbork Poland 57 Q5
Klukhori Rus. Fed. see Karachayevsk
Klukhorskiy, Pereval Georgia/Rus. Fed. 113 F2
Klukwan AK U.S.A. 149 N4
Klumpang, Teluk b. Indon. 85 G3
Klungkung Bali Indon. 85 F5
Klutina Lake AK U.S.A. 149 K3
Klyetsk Belarus 55 O10
Klyosato Japan 93 E1
Klyuchevskaya Sopka, Vulkan vol. Rus. Fed. 77 R4
Klyuchi Rus. Fed. 90 B2
Knåda Sweden 55 I6
Knaresborough U.K. 58 F4
Knee Lake Man. Canada 151 M4
Knee Lake Sask. Canada 151 J4
Knetzgau Germany 63 K5
Knife r. ND U.S.A. 160 C2
Knight Inlet Canada 150 E5
Knighton U.K. 59 D6
Knights Landing CA U.S.A. 158 C2
Knightstown IN U.S.A. 164 C4
Knin Croatia 68 G2
Knittelfeld Austria 57 O7
Knjaževac Serbia 69 J3
Knob Lake Canada see Schefferville
Knob Lick KY U.S.A. 164 C5
Knob Peak hill Australia 134 E3
Knock Ireland 61 D4
Knockalongy hill Ireland 61 D3
Knockalough Ireland 61 C5
Knockanaffrin hill Ireland 61 E5
Knockboy hill Ireland 61 C6
Knock Hill hill U.K. 60 G3
Knockmealdown Mountains hills Ireland 61 D5
Knocknaskagh hill Ireland 61 D5
Knokke-Heist Belgium 62 D3
Knorrendorf Germany 63 N1
Knowle U.K. 59 F6
Knowlton Canada 165 I1
Knox IN U.S.A. 164 B3
Knox PA U.S.A. 164 F3
Knox, Cape Canada 149 N5
Knox Coast Antarctica 188 F2
Knoxville GA U.S.A. 163 D5
Knoxville TN U.S.A. 162 D5
Knud Rasmussen Land reg. Greenland 147 L2
Knysna S. Africa 124 F8
Ko, Gora mt. Rus. Fed. 90 E3
Koartac Canada see Quaqtaq
Koba Indon. 84 D3
Kobbfoss Norway 54 P2
Kobe Halmahera Indon. 83 C2
Kōbe Japan 92 B4
København Denmark see Copenhagen
Kobenni Mauritania 120 C3
Kobi Seram Indon. 83 D3
Koblenz Germany 63 H4
Koboldo Rus. Fed. 90 D1
Kobrin Belarus see Kobryn
Kobroör i. Indon. 81 I8
Kobryn Belarus 55 N10
Kobuchizawa Japan 93 E3
Kobuk AK U.S.A. 148 H2
Kobuk r. AK U.S.A. 148 G2
Kobuk Valley National Park AK U.S.A. 148 H2
Kobuleti Georgia 113 F2
Kobushiga-take mt. Japan 93 E3
Kocaeli Turkey see İzmit
Kocaeli Yarımadası pen. Turkey 69 M4
Kočani Macedonia 69 J4
Kocasu r. Turkey 69 M4
Kocê China 94 E5
Kočevje Slovenia 68 F2
Koch Bihar India 105 G4
Kocher r. Germany 63 J5
Kochevo Rus. Fed. 51 Q4
Kochi India 106 C4
Kōchi Japan 91 D6
Koçhisar Turkey see Kızıltepe
Koch Island Canada 147 K3
Kochkor Kyrg. 102 E3
Kochkorka Kyrg. see Kochkor
Kochkurovo Rus. Fed. 53 J5
Kochubeyevskoye Rus. Fed. 113 F1
Kod India 106 B3
Kodaira Japan 93 F3
Kodala India 106 E2
Kodama Japan 93 F2
Kodarma India 105 F4
Kōdera Japan 92 A4
Koderma India see Kodarma
Kodiak AK U.S.A. 148 I4
Kodiak Island AK U.S.A. 148 I4
Kodiak National Wildlife Refuge nature res. AK U.S.A. 148 I4
Kodibeleng Botswana 125 H2
Kodino Rus. Fed. 52 H3
Kodiyakkarai India 106 C4
Kodok South Sudan 108 D8
Kodyma Ukr. 53 F6
Kodzhaele mt. Bulg./Greece 69 K4
Koedoesberg mts S. Africa 124 E7
Koegrabie S. Africa 124 E5
Koekenaap S. Africa 124 D6
Koersel Belgium 62 F3
Koës Namibia 124 D3
Kofa Mountains AZ U.S.A. 159 G5
Koffiefontein S. Africa 124 G5
Koforidua Ghana 120 C4
Kōfu Japan 93 E3
Koga Japan 93 F2
Kogaluc r. Canada 152 F2
Kogaluc, Baie de b. Canada 152 F2
Kogaluk r. Canada 153 J2
Kogaly Kazakh. 98 B3
Kogan Australia 138 E1
Køge Denmark 55 H9
Kogon r. Guinea 120 B3
Kogon Uzbek. 111 G2
Kohan Pak. 111 G5
Kohat Pak. 111 H3
Kōh-e Şayyād Afgh. 111 G2
Kohila Estonia 55 N7
Kohima India 105 H4
Kōhistān Afgh. 111 F3
Kohistan reg. Pak. 111 I3
Kohler Range mts Antarctica 188 K2
Kohlu Pak. 111 H4
Kohtla-Järve Estonia 55 O7
Kohŭng S. Korea 91 B6
Koidern Canada 149 L3
Koidern Mountain Canada 149 L3
Koidu Sierra Leone see Sefadu
Koihoa India 87 A5
Koikyim Qu r. China 99 F6
Koilkonda India 106 C2
Koin N. Korea 91 B4
Koin r. Rus. Fed. 52 K3
Koi Sanjaq Iraq 113 G3
Koito-gawa r. Japan 93 F3
Kŏje-do i. S. Korea 91 C6
Kojonup Australia 135 B8
Kōka Japan 92 C4
Kokai-gawa r. Japan 93 G3
Kokand Uzbek. see Qo'qon
Kökar Fin. 55 L7
Kök-Art Kyrg. 98 A4
Kokawa Japan 92 B4
Kök-Aygyr Kyrg. 98 A4
Kokchetav Kazakh. see Kokshetau
Kokemäenjoki r. Fin. 55 L6
Kokerboom Namibia 124 D5
Ko Kha Thai. 86 B3
Kokkilai Sri Lanka 106 D4
Kokkola Fin. 54 M5
Kok Kuduk well China 98 D3
Koko Nigeria 120 D3
Kokolik r. AK U.S.A. 148 G1
Kokomo IN U.S.A. 164 B3
Kokong Botswana 124 F3
Kokos i. Indon. 87 A7
Kokosi S. Africa 125 H4
Kokpekty Kazakh. 102 F2
Kokrines AK U.S.A. 148 I2
Kokrines Hills AK U.S.A. 148 I2
Kokruagarok AK U.S.A. 148 I1
Koksan N. Korea 91 B5
Kokshaal-Tau, Khrebet mts China/Kyrg. see Kakshaal-Too
Koksharka Rus. Fed. 52 J4
Kokshetau Kazakh. 101 F1
Koksoak r. Canada 153 H2
Kokstad S. Africa 125 I6
Koksu Almatinskaya Oblast' Kazakh. 98 B3
Koksu Almatinskaya Oblast' Kazakh. 98 B3
Koktal Kazakh. 102 E3
Koktas Kazakh. 98 A2
Kokterek Almatinskaya Oblast' Kazakh. 98 B3
Kokterek Zapadnyy Kazakhstan Kazakh. 53 K6
Koktokay Xinjiang China see Fuyun
Koktokay Xinjiang China 94 B2
Koktuma Kazakh. 98 C3
Koku, Tanjung pt Indon. 83 B4
Kokubunji Japan 93 F2
Kokufu Japan 92 D2
Kokushiga-take mt. Japan 93 E3
Koküy China 94 B2
Kokyar China 99 B5
Kokzhayyk Kazakh. 98 C2
Kola i. Indon. 81 I8
Kola Rus. Fed. 54 R2
Kolachi r. Pak. 111 G5
Kolahoi mt. India 104 C2
Kolaka Sulawesi Indon. 83 B4
Kolambugan Mindanao Phil. 82 C4
Kolana Indon. 83 C5
Ko Lanta Thai. 87 B6
Kola Peninsula Rus. Fed. 52 H2
Kolar Chhattisgarh India 106 D2
Kolar Karnataka India 106 C3
Kolār, Kūh-e hill Iran 110 C4
Kolaras India 104 D4
Kolar Gold Fields India 106 C3
Kolari Fin. 54 M3
Kolarovgrad Bulg. see Shumen
Kolasib India 105 H4
Kolayat India 104 C4
Kolbano Timor Indon. 83 C5
Kolberg Poland see Kołobrzeg
Kol'chugino Rus. Fed. 52 H4
Kolda Senegal 120 B3
Kolding Denmark 55 F9
Kole Kasaï-Oriental Dem. Rep. Congo 122 C4
Kole Orientale Dem. Rep. Congo 122 C3
Koléa Alg. 67 H5
Koler Sweden 54 L4
Kolguyev, Ostrov i. Rus. Fed. 52 K1
Kolhan reg. India 105 F5
Kolhapur India 106 B2
Kolhumadulu Atoll Maldives 103 D11
Koliganek AK U.S.A. 148 H4
Kolikata India see Kolkata
Kõljala Estonia 55 M7
Kolkasrags pt Latvia 55 M8

▶Kolkata India 105 G5
5th most populous city in Asia and 8th in the world.

Kolkhozabad Khatlon Tajik. see Vose
Kolkhozabad Khatlon Tajik. see Kolkhozobod
Kolkhozobod Tajik. 111 H2
Kollam India 106 C4
Kolleru Lake India 106 D2
Kollum Neth. 62 G1
Kolmanskop (abandoned) Namibia 124 B4
Köln Germany see Cologne
Köln-Bonn airport Germany 63 H4
Kołobrzeg Poland 57 O3
Kologriv Rus. Fed. 52 J4
Kolokani Mali 120 C3
Kolombangara i. Solomon Is 133 F2
Kolomea Ukr. see Kolomyya
Kolomna Rus. Fed. 53 H5
Kołomyja Ukr. see Kolomyya
Kolomyya Ukr. 53 E6
Kolondiéba Mali 120 C3
Kolonedale Sulawesi Indon. 83 B3
Koloni Cyprus 107 A2
Kolonkwaneng Botswana 124 E4
Kolono Sulawesi Indon. 83 B4
Kolowana Watobo, Teluk b. Indon. 83 B4
Kolozsvár Romania see Cluj-Napoca
Kolpashevo Rus. Fed. 76 J4
Kolpos Messaras b. Greece 69 K7
Kol'skiy Poluostrov pen. Rus. Fed. see Kola Peninsula
Kölük Turkey see Kâhta
Koluli Eritrea 108 F7
Kolumadulu Atoll Maldives see Kolhumadulu Atoll
Kolva r. Rus. Fed. 52 M2
Kolvan India 106 B2
Kolvereid Norway 54 G4
Kolvik Norway 54 N1
Kolvitskoye, Ozero l. Rus. Fed. 54 R3
Kolwa reg. Pak. 111 G5
Kolwezi Dem. Rep. Congo 123 C5
Kolyma r. Rus. Fed. 77 R3
Kolyma Lowland Rus. Fed. see Kolymskaya Nizmennost'
Kolyma Range mts Rus. Fed. see Kolymskiy, Khrebet
Kolymskaya Nizmennost' lowland Rus. Fed. 77 Q3
Kolymskiy, Khrebet mts Rus. Fed. 77 R3
Kolyshley Rus. Fed. 53 J5
Kolyuchaya, Gora mt. Rus. Fed. 148 A2
Kolyuchin, Ostrov i. Rus. Fed. 148 D2
Kolyuchinskaya Guba b. Rus. Fed. 148 D2
Kom mt. Bulg. 69 J3
Kom China 98 D2
Komadugu-Gana watercourse Nigeria 120 E3
Komae Japan 93 F3
Komaga-dake mt. Japan 93 D3
Komagane Japan 93 D3
Komaga-take mt. Japan 93 F1
Komaggas S. Africa 124 C5
Komaio P.N.G. 81 K8
Komaki Japan 92 C3
Komandnaya, Gora mt. Rus. Fed. 90 E2
Komandorskiye Ostrova is Rus. Fed. 77 R4
Komárno Slovakia 57 Q7
Komati r. Swaziland 125 J3
Komatipoort S. Africa 125 J3
Komatsu Japan 92 C2
Komba i. Indon. 83 B4
Kombakomba Sulawesi Indon. 83 B3
Komebail Lagoon Palau 82 [inset]
Komering r. Indon. 84 D3
Komga S. Africa 125 H7
Komintern Ukr. see Marhanets'
Kominternivs'ke Ukr. 69 N1
Komiža Croatia 68 G3
Komló Hungary 68 H1
Kommunarsk Ukr. see Alchevs'k
Komodo i. Indon. 83 A5
Komodo, Taman Nasional nat. park Indon. 83 A5
Kôm Ombo Egypt see Kawm Umbū
Komono Congo 122 B4
Komono Japan 92 C3
Komoran i. Indon. 81 J8
Komoro Japan 93 E2
Komotini Greece 69 K4
Kompong Cham Cambodia see Kâmpóng Cham
Kompong Chhnang Cambodia see Kâmpóng Chhnăng
Kompong Kleang Cambodia see Kâmpóng Khleăng
Kompong Som Cambodia see Sihanoukville
Kompong Speu Cambodia see Kâmpóng Spœ
Kompong Thom Cambodia see Kâmpóng Thum
Komrat Moldova see Comrat
Komsberg mts S. Africa 124 E7
Komsomol Kazakh. see Karabalyk
Komsomolabad Tajik. see Komsomolobod
Komsomolets Kazakh. see Karabalyk
Komsomolets, Ostrov i. Rus. Fed. 76 K1
Komsomolobod Tajik. 111 H2
Komsomol's'k Ukr. 53 G6
Komsomol'skiy Chukotskiy Avtonomnyy Okrug Rus. Fed. 189 C2
Komsomol'skiy Respublika Kalmykiya-Khalm'g-Tangch Rus. Fed. 53 J7
Komsomol'skiy Tyumenskaya Oblast' Rus. Fed. see Yugorsk
Komsomol'sk-na-Amure Rus. Fed. 90 E2
Komsomol'skoye Kazakh. 102 B1
Komsomol'skoye Rus. Fed. 53 J6
Kömürlü Turkey 113 F2
Kon India 105 E4
Konacık Turkey 107 B1
Konada India 106 D2
Kōnan Aichi Japan 92 C3
Kōnan Shiga Japan 92 C4
Konarak India see Konarka
Konarka India 105 F6
Konch India 104 D4
Konda Japan 92 B3
Kondagaon India 106 D2
Kondinin Australia 135 B8
Kondinskoye Rus. Fed. see Oktyabr'skoye
Kondoa Tanz. 123 D4
Kondol' Rus. Fed. 53 J5
Kondopoga Rus. Fed. 52 G3
Kondoz Afgh. see Kunduz
Kondrovo Rus. Fed. 53 G5
Konergino Rus. Fed. 148 C2
Köneürgenç Turkm. see Köneürgenç
Köneürgenç Turkm. 109 I1
Kong Cameroon 120 E4
Kŏng, Kaôh i. Cambodia 87 C5
Kông, Tônlé r. Cambodia 87 D4
Kong, Xé r. Laos 86 D4
Kongakut r. AK U.S.A. 149 L1
Kongauru i. Palau 82 [inset]
Kong Christian IX Land reg. Greenland 147 O3
Kong Christian X Land reg. Greenland 147 P2
Kongelab atoll Marshall Is see Rongelap
Kong Frederik IX Land reg. Greenland 147 M3
Kong Frederik VI Kyst coastal area Greenland 147 N3
Kongiganak AK U.S.A. 148 G4
Kong Kat hill Indon. 85 G2
Kongkemul mt. Indon. 85 G2
Kongōdo-san mt. Japan 92 D2
Kongō-Ikoma Kokutei-kōen park Japan 92 B4
Kongolo Dem. Rep. Congo 123 C4
Kongor South Sudan 121 G4
Kong Oscars Fjord inlet Greenland 147 P2
Kongoussi Burkina Faso 120 C3
Kongsberg Norway 55 F7
Kongsvinger Norway 55 H6
Kongur Shan mt. China 98 A5
Königsberg Rus. Fed. see Kaliningrad
Königsee Germany 63 L4
Königswinter Germany 63 H4
Königs Wusterhausen Germany 63 N2
Konimekh Uzbek. see Konimex
Konimex Uzbek. 111 G1
Konin Poland 57 Q4
Konjic Bos.-Herz. 68 G3
Konkiep watercourse Namibia 124 C5
Könnern Germany 63 L3
Konnevesi Fin. 54 O5
Kōno Japan 92 C3
Konosha Rus. Fed. 52 I3
Kōnosu Japan 93 F2
Konotop Ukr. 53 G6
Konpara India 105 E5
Kon Plông Vietnam 87 E4
Konqi He r. China 98 E4
Konrei Palau 82 [inset]
Konsei-tōge pass Japan 93 F2
Konso Eth. 122 D3
Konso Cultural Landscape tourist site Eth. 121 G4
Konstantinograd Ukr. see Krasnohrad
Konstantinovka Rus. Fed. 90 B2
Konstantinovka Ukr. see Kostyantynivka
Konstantinovy Lázně Czech Rep. 63 M5
Konstanz Germany 57 L7
Kontha Myanmar 86 B2
Kontiolahti Fin. 54 P5
Konttila Fin. 54 O4
Kon Tum Vietnam 87 D4
Kon Tum, Cao Nguyên Vietnam 87 E4
Könugard Ukr. see Kiev
Konus mt. Rus. Fed. 148 B2
Konushin, Mys pt Rus. Fed. 52 I2
Konya Turkey 112 D3
Konyrat Karagandinskaya Oblast' Kazakh. 98 A3
Konyrat Karagandinskaya Oblast' Kazakh. 98 A3
Konyrolen Kazakh. 98 B3
Konz Germany 62 G5
Konzhakovskiy Kamen', Gora mt. Rus. Fed. 51 R4
Koocanusa, Lake resr Canada/U.S.A. 150 H5
Kooch Bihar India see Koch Bihar
Kookynie Australia 135 C7
Koolyanobbing Australia 135 B7
Koondrook Australia 138 B5
Koorawatha Australia 138 D5
Koordarrie Australia 134 A5
Kootenay r. Canada 150 G5
Kootenay Lake Canada 150 G5
Kootenay National Park Canada 150 G5
Kootjieskolk S. Africa 124 E6
Koozata Lagoon AK U.S.A. 148 E3
Kopa Almatinskaya Oblast' Kazakh. 98 A4
Kopa Vostochnyy Kazakhstan Kazakh. 98 B3
Kópasker Iceland 54 [inset 1]
Kopbirlik Kazakh. 102 E2
Koper Slovenia 68 E2
Kopet Dag mts Iran/Turkm. 110 E2
Kopet-Dag, Khrebet mts Iran/Turkm. see Kopet Dag
Köpetdag Gershi mts Iran/Turkm. see Kopet Dag
Köping Sweden 55 J7
Köpmanholmen Sweden 54 K5
Kopong Botswana 125 G3
Koppal India 106 C3
Koppang Norway 55 G6
Kopparberg Sweden 55 I7
Koppeh Dāgh mts Iran/Turkm. see Kopet Dag
Köppel hill Germany 63 H4
Koppi r. Rus. Fed. 90 F2
Koppies S. Africa 125 H4
Koppieskraal Pan salt pan S. Africa 124 E4
Koprivnica Croatia 68 G1
Köprülü Turkey 107 A1
Köprülü Kanyon Milli Parkı nat. park Turkey 69 N6
Kopyl' Belarus see Kapyl'
Kora India 104 E4
Kōra Japan 92 C3
Korablino Rus. Fed. 53 I5
K'orahē Eth. 122 E3
Korak Pak. 111 G5
Koramlik China 99 D5
Korangal India 106 C2
Korangi Pak. 111 G5
Koraput India 106 D2
Korat Thai. see Nakhon Ratchasima
Koratla India 106 C2
Korba India 105 E5
Korbach Germany 63 I3
Korbu, Gunung mt. Malaysia 84 C1
Korçë Albania 69 I4
Korčula Croatia 68 G3
Korčula i. Croatia 68 G3
Korčulanski Kanal sea chan. Croatia 68 G3
Korday Kazakh. 102 D3
Kord Kūy Iran 110 D2
Kords reg. Iran 111 F5
Korea, North country Asia 91 B5
Korea, South country Asia 91 B5
Korea Bay g. China/N. Korea 91 B5
Korea Strait Japan/S. Korea 91 C6
Koregaon India 106 B2
Korenovsk Rus. Fed. 113 E1
Korenovskaya Rus. Fed. see Korenovsk
Korepino Rus. Fed. 51 R3
Korets' Ukr. 53 E6
Körfez Turkey 69 M4
Korff Ice Rise Antarctica 188 L1
Korfovskiy Rus. Fed. 90 D2
Korgalzhyn Kazakh. 102 D1
Korgas China 98 C3
Korgen Norway 54 H3
Korhogo Côte d'Ivoire 120 C4
Koribundu Sierra Leone 120 B4
Kori Creek inlet India 104 B5
Korinthiakos Kolpos sea chan. Greece see Corinth, Gulf of
Korinthos Greece see Corinth
Kőris-hegy hill Hungary 68 G1
Koritnik mt. Albania 69 I3
Koritsa Albania see Korçë
Kōriyama Japan 91 F5
Korkuteli Turkey 69 N6
Korla China 98 D4
Kormakitis, Cape Cyprus 107 A2
Körmend Hungary 68 G1
Kornati, Nacionalni Park nat. park Croatia 68 F3
Korneyevka Kazakh. 98 A2
Korneyevka Rus. Fed. 53 K6
Koro Côte d'Ivoire 120 C4
Koro i. Fiji 133 H3
Koro r. Indon. 83 B3
Koro Mali 120 C3
Koroc r. Canada 153 I2
Köroğlu Dağları mts Turkey 69 O4
Köroğlu Tepesi mt. Turkey 112 D2
Korogwe Tanz. 123 D4
Koronadal Phil. 82 D5
Koroneia, Limni l. Greece 69 J4
Korong Vale Australia 138 A6
Koronia, Limni l. Greece see Koroneia, Limni

▶Koror Palau 82 [inset]
Former capital of Palau.

Koror i. Palau 82 [inset]
Koro Sea b. Fiji 133 H3
Korosten' Ukr. 53 F6
Korostyshiv Ukr. 53 F6
Koro Toro Chad 121 E3
Korovin Bay AK U.S.A. 148 [inset] D5
Korovin Volcano AK U.S.A. 148 [inset] D5
Korpilahti Fin. 54 N5
Korpo Fin. 55 L6
Korppoo Fin. see Korpo
Korsakov Rus. Fed. 90 F3
Korsnäs Fin. 54 L5
Korsør Denmark 55 G9
Korsun'-Shevchenkivs'kyy Ukr. 53 F6
Korsun'-Shevchenkovskiy Ukr. see Korsun'-Shevchenkivs'kyy
Korsze Poland 57 R3
Kortesjärvi Fin. 54 M5
Korti Sudan 108 D6
Kortkeros Rus. Fed. 52 K3
Kortrijk Belgium 62 D4
Korvala Fin. 54 O3
Koryakskaya, Sopka vol. Rus. Fed. 77 Q4
Koryakskoye Nagor'ye mts Rus. Fed. 77 S3
Koryazhma Rus. Fed. 52 J3
Kōryō Japan 92 B4
Koryŏng S. Korea 91 C6
Kos i. Greece 69 L6
Kosa Rus. Fed. 51 Q4
Kosai Japan 92 D4
Kosam India 104 E4
Kosan N. Korea 91 B5
Kościan Poland 57 P4
Kosciusko, Mount Australia see Kosciuszko, Mount
Kosciuszko, Mount Australia 138 D6
Kosciuszko National Park Australia 138 D6
Köse Turkey 113 E2
Köseçobanlı Turkey 107 A1
Kōsei Japan 92 C3
Kosgi India 106 C2
Kosh-Agach Rus. Fed. 94 B1
Kosh-Döbö Kyrg. 98 A4
Koshigaya Japan 93 F3
Koshikijima-rettō is Japan 91 C7
Koshino Japan 92 C2
Koshk Afgh. 111 F3
Koshkarkol', Ozero l. Kazakh. 98 C3
Koshki Rus. Fed. 53 K5
Kōshoku Japan 93 E2
Kosi r. India 99 B7
Kosi Bay S. Africa 125 K4
Košice Slovakia 53 D6
Kosigi India 106 C3
Kosi Reservoir Nepal 99 D8
Koskudyk Kazakh. 98 B3
Koskullskulle Sweden 54 L3
Köslin Poland see Koszalin
Kosma r. Rus. Fed. 52 K2
Koson Uzbek. 111 G2
Kosŏng N. Korea 91 C5
Kosova prov. Europe see Kosovo

▶Kosovo country Europe 69 I3
Gained independence from Serbia in February 2008.

Kosovo-Metohija prov. Europe see Kosovo
Kosovska Mitrovica Kosovo see Mitrovicë
Kosrae atoll Micronesia 186 G5
Kosrap China 99 B5
Kösseine hill Germany 63 L5
Kossol Passage Palau 82 [inset]
Kossol Reef Palau 82 [inset]
Kosta-Khetagurovo Rus. Fed. see Nazran'
Kostanay Kazakh. 100 F1
Kostenets Bulg. 69 J3
Kosti Sudan 108 D7
Kostinbrod Bulg. 69 J3
Kostino Rus. Fed. 76 J3
Kostomuksha Rus. Fed. 54 Q4
Kostopil' Ukr. 53 E6
Kostopol' Ukr. see Kostopil'
Kostroma Rus. Fed. 52 I4
Kostrzyn Poland 57 O4
Kostyantynivka Ukr. 53 H6
Kostyukovichi Belarus see Kastsyukovichy
Kosuge Japan 93 E3
Kosugi Japan 92 D2
Kos'yu Rus. Fed. 51 R2
Koszalin Poland 57 P3
Kőszeg Hungary 68 G1
Kota Andhra Prad. India 106 D3
Kota Chhattisgarh India 105 E5
Kota Rajasthan India 104 C4
Kōta Japan 92 D4
Kotaagung Sumatera Indon. 84 D4
Kota Baharu Malaysia see Kota Bharu
Kotabaru Kalimantan Indon. 85 E3
Kotabaru Kalimantan Indon. 85 G3
Kotabaru Sumatera Indon. 84 B2
Kota Belud Sabah Malaysia 85 G1
Kotabesi Kalimantan Indon. 85 F3
Kota Bharu Malaysia 84 C1
Kotabumi Sumatera Indon. 84 D4
Kotabunan Sulawesi Indon. 83 C2
Kot Addu Pak. 111 H4
Kota Kinabalu Sabah Malaysia 85 G1
Kotamobagu Sulawesi Indon. 83 C2
Kotaneelee Range mts Canada 150 E2
Kotanemel', Gora mt. Kazakh. 98 B3
Kotaparh India 106 D2
Kotapinang Sumatera Indon. 84 C2
Kota Samarahan Sarawak Malaysia 85 E2
Kotatengah Sumatera Indon. 84 C2
Kota Tinggi Malaysia 84 C2
Kotawaringin Kalimantan Indon. 85 E3
Kotcho r. Canada 150 F3
Kotcho Lake Canada 150 F3
Kot Diji Pak. 111 H5
Kotdwara India 99 B7
Kotel'nich Rus. Fed. 52 K4
Kotel'nikovo Rus. Fed. 53 I7
Kotel'nyy, Ostrov i. Rus. Fed. 77 O2
Kotgar India 106 D2
Kotgarh India 104 D3
Kothagudem India see Kottagudem
Köthen (Anhalt) Germany 63 L3
Kotido Uganda 121 G4
Kotikovo Rus. Fed. 90 D3
Kot Imamgarh Pak. 111 H5
Kotka Fin. 55 O6
Kot Kapura India 104 C3
Kotkino Rus. Fed. 52 K2
Kotlas Rus. Fed. 52 J3
Kotli Pak. 111 I3
Kotlik AK U.S.A. 148 G3
Kötlutangi pt Iceland 54 [inset 1]
Kotly Rus. Fed. 55 P7
Kotō Japan 92 C3
Kotovo Rus. Fed. 53 J6
Kotovsk Rus. Fed. 53 I5
Kotra India 104 C4
Kotra Pak. 111 G4
Kotri r. India 106 D2
Kot Sarae Pak. 111 G6
Kottagudem India 106 D2
Kottarakara India 106 C4
Kottayam India 106 C4
Kotte Sri Lanka see Sri Jayewardenepura Kotte
Kotto r. Cent. Afr. Rep. 122 C3
Kotturu India 106 C3
Kotuy r. Rus. Fed. 77 L2
Kotzebue AK U.S.A. 148 G2
Kotzebue Sound sea channel AK U.S.A. 148 G2
Kötzting Germany 63 M5
Kouango Cent. Afr. Rep. 122 C3
Koubia Guinea 120 B3
Kouchibouguac National Park Canada 153 I5
Koudougou Burkina Faso 120 C3
Kouebokkeveld mts S. Africa 124 D7
Koufey Niger 120 E3
Koufonisi i. Greece 69 L7
Kougaberge mts S. Africa 124 F7
Koukourou r. Cent. Afr. Rep. 122 B3
Koulen Cambodia see Kulen
Koulikoro Mali 120 C3
Koumac New Caledonia 133 G4
Koumenzi China 94 C3
Koumi Japan 93 E2
Koumpentoum Senegal 120 B3
Koundâra Guinea 120 B3
Kountze TX U.S.A. 161 E6
Koupéla Burkina Faso 120 C3
Kourou Fr. Guiana 177 H2
Kouroussa Guinea 120 C3
Kousséri Cameroon 121 E3
Koutiala Mali 120 C3
Kouvola Fin. 55 O6
Kovallberget Sweden 54 J4
Kovdor Rus. Fed. 54 Q3
Kovel' Ukr. 53 E6
Kovernino Rus. Fed. 52 I4
Kovilpatti India 106 C4
Kovno Lith. see Kaunas
Kovrov Rus. Fed. 52 I4
Kovylkino Rus. Fed. 53 I5
Kovzhskoye, Ozero l. Rus. Fed. 52 H3
Kowangge Sumbawa Indon. 85 G5

Lankao China 95 H5
Länkäran Azer. 113 H3
Lannion France 66 C2
La Noria Mex. 166 D4
Lanping China 96 C3
Lansån Sweden 54 M3
L'Anse MI U.S.A. 160 F2
Lanshan China 97 G3

▶Lansing MI U.S.A. 164 C2
Capital of Michigan.

Lanta, Ko i. Thai. 87 B6
Lantau Island H.K. China 97 [inset]
Lantau Peak hill H.K. China 97 [inset]
Lantian China 95 G5
Lanuza Bay Mindanao Phil. 82 D4
Lanxi Heilong. China 90 B3
Lanxi Zhejiang China 97 H2
Lanxian China 95 G4
Lan Yü i. Taiwan 97 I4
Lanzarote i. Canary Is 120 B2
Lanzhou China 94 E4
Lanzijing China 95 J2
Laoag City Luzon Phil. 82 C2
Laoang Phil. 82 D3
Laobie Shan mts China 96 C4
Laobu China 97 F3
Lao Cai Vietnam 86 C2
Laodicea Syria see Latakia
Laodicea Turkey see Denizli
Laodicea ad Lycum Turkey see Denizli
Laodicea ad Mare Syria see Latakia
Laofengkou China 98 C3
Laoha He r. China 95 J3
Laohekou China 97 F1
Laohutun China 95 J4
Laojie China see Yongping
Laojunmiao China 94 D4
La Okapi, Parc National de nat. park Dem. Rep. Congo 122 C3
Lao Ling mts China 90 B4
Lao Mangnai China 99 E5
Laon France 62 D5
Laoqitai China 94 B3
La Oroya Peru 176 C6
Laos country Asia 86 C3
Laoshan China 95 J4
Laoshawan China 98 D3
Laotieshan Shuidao sea chan. China see Bohai Haixia
Laotougou China 90 C4
Laotuding Shan hill China 90 B4
Laowohi pass India see Khardung La
Laoximiao China 94 E3
Laoyacheng China 94 E4
Laoye Ling mts Heilongjiang/Jilin China 90 B3
Laoye Ling mts Heilongjiang/Jilin China 90 C4
Laoyemiao China 94 C2
Lapa Brazil 179 A4
Lapac i. Phil. 82 C5
La Palma i. Canary Is 120 B2
La Palma Guat. 167 H5
La Palma Panama 166 [inset] K7
La Palma AZ U.S.A. 159 H5
La Palma del Condado Spain 67 C5
La Panza Range mts CA U.S.A. 158 C4
La Paragua Venez. 176 F2
Laparan i. Phil. 82 B5
La Parilla Mex. 161 B8
La Paya, Parque Nacional nat. park Col. 176 D3
La Paz Arg. 178 E4

▶La Paz Bol. 176 E7
Joint capital (with Sucre) of Bolivia.

La Paz Hond. 166 [inset] I6
La Paz Mex. 166 C3
La Paz Nicaragua 166 [inset] I6
La Paz, Bahía b. Mex. 166 C3
La Pedrera Col. 176 E4
Lapeer MI U.S.A. 164 D2
La Pendjari, Parc National de nat. park Benin 120 D3
La Perla Mex. 166 D2
La Pérouse Strait Japan/Rus. Fed. 90 F3
La Pesca Mex. 161 D8
La Piedad Mex. 166 E4
Lapinig Samar Phil. 82 D3
Lapinlahti Fin. 54 O5
La Pintada Panama 166 [inset] J7
Lapithos Cyprus 107 A2
Laplace LA U.S.A. 167 H2
Lap Lae Thai. 86 C3
La Plant SD U.S.A. 160 C2
La Plata Arg. 178 E4
La Plata MD U.S.A. 165 G4
La Plata MO U.S.A. 160 E3
La Plata, Isla i. Ecuador 176 B4

▶La Plata, Río de sea chan. Arg./Uruguay 178 E4
Part of the Río de la Plata - Paraná, 2nd longest river in South America and 9th in the world.

La Plonge, Lac l. Canada 151 J4
Lapmežciems Latvia 55 M8
Lapominka Rus. Fed. 52 I2
La Porte IN U.S.A. 164 B3
Laporte PA U.S.A. 165 G3
Laporte, Mount Canada 149 P3
Laposo, Bukit mt. Indon. 83 A4
La Potherie, Lac l. Canada 153 G2
La Poza Grande Mex. 166 B3
Lappajärvi Fin. 54 M5
Lappajärvi l. Fin. 54 M5
Lappeenranta Fin. 55 P6
Lappersdorf Germany 63 M5
Lappi Fin. 55 L6
Lappland reg. Europe 54 K3
La Pryor TX U.S.A. 161 D6
Lâpseki Turkey 69 L4
Laptevo Rus. Fed. see Yasnogorsk
Laptev Sea Rus. Fed. 77 N2
Lapua Fin. 54 M5
Lapuko Sulawesi Indon. 83 B4
Lapu-Lapu Phil. 82 C4
Lapurdum France see Bayonne
La Purísima Mex. 166 B3
Laqiya Arbain well Sudan 108 C5
La Quiaca Arg. 178 C2
L'Aquila Italy 68 E3
La Quinta CA U.S.A. 158 E5
Lār Iran 110 D5
Larache Morocco 67 C6
Lārak i. Iran 110 E5
Laramie WY U.S.A. 156 G4
Laramie r. WY U.S.A. 156 G4
Laramie Mountains WY U.S.A. 156 G4
Laranda Turkey see Karaman
Laranjal Paulista Brazil 179 B3
Laranjeiras do Sul Brazil 178 F3
Laranjinha r. Brazil 179 A3
Larantuka Flores Indon. 83 B5
Larat Indon. 134 E1
Larat i. Indon. 134 E1
Larba Alg. 67 H5
Lärbro Sweden 55 K8
L'Archipélago de Mingan, Réserve du Parc National de nat. park Canada 153 J4
L'Ardenne, Plateau de plat. Belgium see Ardennes
Laredo Spain 67 E2
Laredo TX U.S.A. 161 D7
La Reforma Mex. 167 F4
La Reina Adelaida, Archipiélago de is Chile 178 B8
Largeau Chad see Faya
Largo FL U.S.A. 163 D7
Largs U.K. 60 E5
Lārī Iran 110 B2
L'Ariana Tunisia 68 D6
Lariang Sulawesi Barat Indon. 83 A3
Lariang r. Indon. 83 A3
Larimore ND U.S.A. 160 D2
La Rioja Arg. 178 C3
La Rioja aut. comm. Spain 67 E2
Larisa Greece 69 J5
Larissa Greece see Larisa
Laristan reg. Iran 110 E5
Larkana Pak. 111 H5
Lark Harbour Canada 153 K4
Lark Passage Australia 136 D2
L'Arli, Parc National de nat. park Burkina Faso 120 D3
Larnaca Cyprus 107 A2
Larnaka Cyprus see Larnaca
Larnaka Bay Cyprus 107 A2
Larnakos, Kolpos b. Cyprus see Larnaka Bay
Larne U.K. 61 G3
Larned KS U.S.A. 160 D4
La Robe Noire, Lac de l. Canada 153 J4
La Robla Spain 67 D2
La Roche-en-Ardenne Belgium 62 F4
La Rochelle France 66 D3
La Roche-sur-Yon France 66 D3
La Roda Spain 67 E4
La Romana Dom. Rep. 169 K5
La Ronge Canada 151 J4
La Ronge, Lac l. Canada 151 J4
La Rosa Mex. 167 E3
La Rosita Mex. 167 E2
Larrey Point Australia 134 B4
Larrimah Australia 134 F3
Lars Christensen Coast Antarctica 188 E2
Larsen Bay AK U.S.A. 148 I4
Larsen Ice Shelf Antarctica 188 L2
Larsmo Fin. 54 M5
Larvik Norway 55 G7
Las Adjuntas, Presa de resr Mex. 161 D8
Lasahau Sulawesi Indon. 83 B4
La Sal UT U.S.A. 159 I2
LaSalle Canada 165 I1
La Salle IL U.S.A. 152 C6
La Salonga Nord, Parc National de nat. park Dem. Rep. Congo 122 C4
La Sambre à l'Oise, Canal de France 62 D5
Lasan Kalimantan Indon. 85 F2
Las Animas CO U.S.A. 160 C4
Las Ánimas, Punta pt Mex. 166 B2
Las Anod Somalia see Laascaanood
La Sarre Canada 152 F4
Las Avispas Mex. 166 C2
La Savonnière, Lac l. Canada 153 G3
La Scie Canada 153 L4
Las Cruces Mex. 166 D2
Las Cruces CA U.S.A. 158 C4
Las Cruces NM U.S.A. 157 G6
La Selle, Pic mt. Haiti 169 J5
La Serena Chile 178 B3
Las Esperanças Mex. 167 E3
La Seu d'Urgell Spain 67 G2
Las Flores Arg. 178 E5
Las Guacamatas, Cerro mt. Mex. 157 F7
Lāshār, Rūd-e r. Iran 111 F5
Lashburn Canada 151 I4
Lāsh-e Joway Afgh. 111 F4
Las Heras Arg. 178 C4
Las Herreras Mex. 166 D3
Lashio Myanmar 86 B2
Lashkar India 104 D4
Lashkar Gāh Afgh. 111 G4
Las Juntas Chile 178 C3
Las Lavaderos Mex. 167 F4
Las Lomitas Arg. 178 D2
Las Marismas marsh Spain 67 C5
Las Martinetas Arg. 178 C7
Las Mesteñas Mex. 166 D2
Las Minas, Cerro de mt. Hond. 167 H6
Las Mulatas is Panama see San Blas, Archipiélago de
Las Nieves Mex. 166 D3
Las Nopaleras, Cerro mt. Mex. 166 E3
La Société, Archipel de is Fr. Polynesia see Society Islands
Lasolo, Teluk b. Indon. 83 B3
La Somme, Canal de France 62 C5
Las Palmas watercourse Mex. 158 E5
Las Palmas Panama 166 [inset] J7

▶Las Palmas de Gran Canaria Canary Is 120 B2
Joint capital of the Canary Islands.

Las Petas Bol. 177 G7
La Spezia Italy 68 C2
Las Piedras, Río de r. Peru 176 E6
Las Planchas Hond. 166 [inset] I6
Las Plumas Arg. 178 C6
Laspur Pak. 111 I2
Lassance Brazil 179 B2
Lassen Peak vol. CA U.S.A. 158 C1
Lassen Volcanic National Park CA U.S.A. 158 C1
Las Tablas Mex. 167 F4
Las Tablas Panama 166 [inset] J8
Las Tablas de Daimiel, Parque Nacional de nat. park Spain 67 E4
Last Chance CO U.S.A. 160 C4
Las Termas Arg. 178 D3
Last Mountain Lake Canada 151 J5
Las Tórtolas, Cerro mt. Chile 178 C3
Lastoursville Gabon 122 B4
Lastovo i. Croatia 68 G3
Las Tres Vírgenes, Volcán vol. Mex. 166 B3
Lastrup Germany 63 H2
Las Tunas Cuba 169 I4
Las Varas Chihuahua Mex. 166 D2
Las Varas Nayarit Mex. 168 C4
Las Varillas Arg. 178 D4
Las Vegas NM U.S.A. 157 G6
Las Vegas NV U.S.A. 159 F3
Las Viajas, Isla de i. Peru 176 C6
Las Villuercas mt. Spain 67 D4
La Tabatière Canada 153 K4
Latacunga Ecuador 176 C4
Latady Island Antarctica 188 L2
Latakia Syria 107 B2
Latalata i. Maluku Indon. 83 C3
La Teste-de-Buch France 66 D4
La Tetilla, Cerro mt. Mex. 166 D4
Latham Australia 135 B7
Lathen Germany 63 H2
Latheron U.K. 60 F2
Lathi India 104 B4
Latho India 104 D2
Lathrop CA U.S.A. 158 C3
Latina Italy 68 E4
La Tortuga, Isla i. Venez. 176 E1
Latouche AK U.S.A. 149 K3
Latouche Island AK U.S.A. 149 K3
La Trinidad Nicaragua 166 [inset] I6
La Trinidad Luzon Phil. 82 C2
La Trinitaria Mex. 167 G5
Latrobe PA U.S.A. 164 F3
Latrun West Bank 107 B4
Lattaquié Syria see Latakia
Lattrop Neth. 62 G2
La Tuque Canada 153 G5
Latur India 106 C2
Latvia country Europe 55 N8
Latvija country Europe see Latvia
Latviyskaya S.S.R. country Europe see Latvia
Lauca, Parque Nacional nat. park Chile 176 E7
Lauchhammer Germany 57 N5
Lauder U.K. 60 G5
Laudio Spain 67 E2
Lauenbrück Germany 63 J1
Lauenburg (Elbe) Germany 63 K1
Lauf an der Pegnitz Germany 63 L5
Laufen Switz. 66 H3
Lauge Koch Kyst reg. Greenland 147 L2
Laughlen, Mount Australia 135 F5
Laughlin Peak NM U.S.A. 157 G5
Lauka Estonia 55 M7
Launceston Australia 137 [inset]
Launceston U.K. 59 C8
Laune r. Ireland 61 C5
Launggyaung Myanmar 86 B1
Launglon Myanmar 87 B4
Launglon Bok Islands Myanmar 87 B4
La Unidad Mex. 167 G6
La Unión Bol. 176 F7
La Unión El Salvador 166 [inset] I6
La Unión Hond. 166 [inset] I6
La Unión Mex. 167 E5
Laur Luzon Phil. 82 C3
Laura Australia 136 D2
Laurel DE U.S.A. 165 H4
Laurel MS U.S.A. 161 F6
Laurel MT U.S.A. 156 F3
Laureldale PA U.S.A. 165 H3
Laurel Hill hills PA U.S.A. 164 F4
Laurencekirk U.K. 60 G4
Laurieton Australia 138 F3
Laurinburg NC U.S.A. 163 E5
Lauru i. Solomon Is see Choiseul
Lausanne Switz. 66 H3
Laut i. Indon. 85 E1
Laut i. Indon. 85 E3
Laut i. Indon. 85 G3
Laut, Selat sea chan. Indon. 85 F3
Lautem East Timor 83 C5
Lautersbach (Hessen) Germany 63 J4
Laut Kecil, Kepulauan is Indon. 85 F4
Lautoka Fiji 133 H3
Lauttawar, Danau l. Indon. 84 B1
Lauvuskylä Fin. 54 P5
Lauwersmeer l. Neth. 62 G1
Lava Beds National Monument nat. park CA U.S.A. 156 C4
Laval Canada 152 G5
Laval France 66 D2
La Vall d'Uixó Spain 67 F4
Lāvān i. Iran 110 D5
La Vanoise, Massif de mts France 66 H4
La Vanoise, Parc National de nat. park France 66 H4
Lavapié, Punta pt Chile 178 B5
Lāvar Iran 110 C4
Laveaga Peak CA U.S.A. 158 C3
La Vega Dom. Rep. 169 J5
La Venta Hond. 166 [inset] I6
Laverne OK U.S.A. 161 D4
Laverton Australia 135 C7
La Víbora Mex. 166 E3
La Vila Joíosa Spain see Villajoyosa-La Vila Joíosa
La Viña Peru 176 C5
Lavongai i. P.N.G. see New Hanover
Lavras Brazil 179 B3
Lavrentiya Rus. Fed. 148 E2
Lavumisa Swaziland 125 J4
Lavushi-Manda National Park Zambia 123 D5
Lawa India 104 C4
Lawa Myanmar 86 B1
Lawa Pak. 111 H3
Lawang i. Indon. 85 G5
Lawas Sarawak Malaysia 85 F1
Lawashi r. Canada 152 E3
Law Dome ice feature Antarctica 188 F2
Lawele Sulawesi Indon. 83 B4
Lawin i. Maluku Indon. 83 D3
Lawit, Gunung mt. Indon./Malaysia 85 F2
Lawit, Gunung mt. Malaysia 84 C1
Lawksawk Myanmar 86 B2
Lawn Hill National Park Australia 136 B3
La Woëvre, Plaine de plain France 62 F5
Lawra Ghana 120 C3
Lawrence IN U.S.A. 164 B4
Lawrence KS U.S.A. 160 E4
Lawrence MA U.S.A. 165 J2
Lawrenceburg IN U.S.A. 164 C4
Lawrenceburg KY U.S.A. 164 C4
Lawrenceburg TN U.S.A. 162 C5
Lawrenceville GA U.S.A. 163 D5
Lawrenceville IL U.S.A. 164 B4
Lawrenceville VA U.S.A. 165 G5
Lawrence Wells, Mount hill Australia 135 C6
Lawton OK U.S.A. 161 D5
Lawu, Gunung vol. Indon. 85 E4
Lawz, Jabal al mt. Saudi Arabia 112 D5
Laxå Sweden 55 I7
Laxey Isle of Man 58 C4
Laxgalts'ap Canada 149 O5
Lax Kw'alaams Canada 149 O5
Laxo U.K. 60 [inset]
Laxong Co l. China 99 D6
Laya r. Rus. Fed. 52 M2
Layar, Tanjung pt Indon. 85 G4
Laydennyy, Mys c. Rus. Fed. 52 J1
Layeni Maluku Indon. 83 D4
Laylā Saudi Arabia 108 G5
Laylā salt pan Saudi Arabia 107 D4
Laysan Island HI U.S.A. 186 I4
Laysu China 98 C4
Laytonville CA U.S.A. 158 B2
Layyah Pak. 111 H4
Laza Myanmar 86 B1
La Zacatosa, Picacho mt. Mex. 166 C4
Lazarev Rus. Fed. 90 F1
Lazarevac Serbia 69 I2
Lázaro Cárdenas Baja California Mex. 166 B2
Lázaro Cárdenas Baja California Mex. 166 B2
Lázaro Cárdenas Michoacán Mex. 168 D5
Lazcano Uruguay 178 F4
Lazdijai Lith. 55 M9
Lazhuglung China 99 C6
Lazikou China 96 D1
Lazo Primorskiy Kray Rus. Fed. 90 D4
Lazo Respublika Sakha (Yakutiya) Rus. Fed. 77 O3
Lead SD U.S.A. 160 C2
Leader Water r. U.K. 60 G5
Leadville Australia 138 D4
Leaf r. MS U.S.A. 161 F6
Leaf Bay Canada see Tasiujaq
Leaf Rapids Canada 151 K3
Leakey TX U.S.A. 161 D6
Leaksville NC U.S.A. see Eden
Leamington Canada 164 D2
Leamington Spa, Royal U.K. 59 F6
Leane, Lough l. Ireland 61 C5
Leap Ireland 61 C6
Leatherhead U.K. 59 G7
L'Eau Claire, Lac à l. Canada 152 G2
L'Eau Claire, Rivière à r. Canada 152 G2
L'Eau d'Heure l. Belgium 62 E4
Leavenworth IN U.S.A. 164 B4
Leavenworth KS U.S.A. 160 E4
Leavenworth WA U.S.A. 156 C3
Leavitt Peak CA U.S.A. 158 D2
Lebach Germany 62 G5
Lebak Mindanao Phil. 82 D5
Lebanon country Asia 107 B2
Lebanon IN U.S.A. 164 B3
Lebanon KY U.S.A. 164 C5
Lebanon MO U.S.A. 160 E4
Lebanon NH U.S.A. 165 I2
Lebanon OH U.S.A. 164 C4
Lebanon OR U.S.A. 156 C3
Lebanon PA U.S.A. 165 G3
Lebanon TN U.S.A. 162 C4
Lebanon VA U.S.A. 164 D5
Lebanon Junction KY U.S.A. 164 C5
Lebanon Mountains Lebanon see Liban, Jebel
Lebbeke Belgium 62 E3
Lebec CA U.S.A. 158 D4
Lebedyan' Rus. Fed. 53 H5
Lebel-sur-Quévillon Canada 152 F4
Le Blanc France 66 E3
Lebo Sulawesi Indon. 83 B4
Lębork Poland 57 P3
Lebowakgomo S. Africa 125 I3
Lebrija Spain 67 C5
Łebsko, Jezioro lag. Poland 57 P3
Lebu Chile 178 B5
Lebyazh'ye Kazakh. see Akku
Lebyazh'ye Rus. Fed. 52 K4
Le Caire Egypt see Cairo
Le Cateau-Cambrésis France 62 D4
Le Catelet France 62 D4
Lecce Italy 68 H4
Lecco Italy 68 C2
Lech r. Austria/Germany 57 M7
Lechaina Greece 69 I6
Lechang China 97 G3
Le Chasseron mt. Switz. 66 H3
Le Chesne France 62 E5
Lechtaler Alpen mts Austria 57 M7
Leck Germany 57 L3
Lecompte LA U.S.A. 161 E6
Le Creusot France 66 G3
Le Crotoy France 62 B4
Lectoure France 66 E5
Ledang, Gunung mt. Malaysia 84 C2
Ledbury U.K. 59 E6
Ledesma Spain 67 D3
Ledmore U.K. 60 E2
Ledmozero Rus. Fed. 54 R4
Ledo Kalimantan Indon. 85 E2
Ledong Hainan China 86 E3
Ledong Hainan China 97 F5
Le Dorat France 66 E3
Ledu China 94 E4
Leduc Canada 150 H4
Lee r. Ireland 61 D6
Lee IN U.S.A. 164 B3
Lee MA U.S.A. 165 I2
Leech Lake MN U.S.A. 160 E2
Leeds U.K. 58 F5
Leedstown U.K. 59 B8
Leek Neth. 62 G1
Leek U.K. 59 E5
Leende Neth. 62 F3
Leer (Ostfriesland) Germany 63 H1
Leesburg FL U.S.A. 163 D6
Leesburg GA U.S.A. 163 C6
Leesburg OH U.S.A. 164 D4
Leesburg VA U.S.A. 165 G4
Leese Germany 63 J2
Lee Steere Range hills Australia 135 C6
Leesville LA U.S.A. 161 E6
Leesville Lake OH U.S.A. 164 E3
Leesville Lake VA U.S.A. 164 F5
Leeton Australia 138 C5
Leeu-Gamka S. Africa 124 E7
Leeuwarden Neth. 62 F1
Leeuwin, Cape Australia 135 A8
Leeuwin-Naturaliste National Park Australia 135 A8
Lee Vining CA U.S.A. 158 D3
Leeward Islands Caribbean Sea 169 L5
Lefka Cyprus 107 A2
Lefkada Greece 69 I5
Lefkada i. Greece 69 I5
Lefkás Greece see Lefkada
Lefke Cyprus see Lefka
Lefkimmi Greece 69 I5
Lefkoniko Cyprus see Lefkonikon
Lefkonikon Cyprus 107 A2
Lefkoşa Cyprus see Nicosia
Lefkosia Cyprus see Nicosia
Lefroy r. Canada 153 H2
Lefroy, Lake salt flat Australia 135 C7
Legarde r. Canada 152 D4
Legazpi Luzon Phil. 82 C3
Legden Germany 62 H2
Legges Tor mt. Australia 137 [inset]
Leghorn Italy see Livorno
Legnago Italy 68 D2
Legnica Poland 57 P5
Legohli Canada see Norman Wells
Le Grand CA U.S.A. 158 C3
Legune Australia 134 E3
Leh India 104 D2
Le Havre France 66 E2
Lehi UT U.S.A. 159 H1
Lehighton PA U.S.A. 165 H3
Lehmo Fin. 54 P5
Lehre Germany 63 K2
Lehrte Germany 63 J2
Lehtimäki Fin. 54 M5
Lehututu Botswana 124 E2
Leibnitz Austria 57 O7
Leicester U.K. 59 F6
Leichhardt r. Australia 132 B3
Leichhardt Falls Australia 136 B3
Leichhardt Range mts Australia 136 D4
Leiden Neth. 62 E2
Leie r. Belgium 62 D3
Leigh N.Z. 139 E3
Leigh U.K. 58 E5
Leighton Buzzard U.K. 59 G7
Leiktho Myanmar 86 B3
Leimen Germany 63 I5
Leine r. Germany 63 J2
Leinefelde Germany 63 K3
Leinster Australia 135 C6
Leinster reg. Ireland 61 F4
Leinster, Mount hill Ireland 61 F5
Leipsic OH U.S.A. 164 D3
Leipsoi i. Greece 69 L6
Leipzig Germany 63 M3
Leipzig-Halle airport Germany 63 M3
Leiranger Norway 54 I3
Leiria Port. 67 B4
Leirvik Norway 55 D7
Leishan China 97 F3
Leisler, Mount hill Australia 135 E5
Leisnig Germany 63 M3
Leitchfield KY U.S.A. 164 B5
Leith Hill hill U.K. 59 G7
Leiva, Cerro mt. Col. 176 D3
Leixlip Ireland 61 F4
Leiyang China 97 G3
Leizhou China 97 F4
Leizhou Bandao pen. China 97 F4
Leizhou Wan b. China 97 F4
Lek r. Neth. 62 E3
Leka Norway 54 G4
Lékana Congo 122 B4
Le Kef Tunisia 68 C6
Lekhainá Greece see Lechaina
Lekitobi Maluku Indon. 83 C3
Lekkersing S. Africa 124 C5
Lékoni Gabon 122 B4
Leksand Sweden 55 I6
Leksozero, Ozero l. Rus. Fed. 54 Q5
Leksula Buru Indon. 83 C3
Lelai, Tanjung pt Halmahera Indon. 83 D2
Leland MI U.S.A. 164 C1
Leli China see Tianlin
Leling China 95 I4
Lelinta Papua Indon. 83 D3
Lelogama Timor Indon. 83 B5
Lélouma Guinea 120 B3
Lelystad Neth. 62 F2
Le Maire, Estrecho de sea chan. Arg. 178 C9
Léman, Lac l. France/Switz. see Geneva, Lake
Le Mans France 66 E2
Le Mars IA U.S.A. 160 D3
Lembeh i. Indon. 83 C2
Lemberg France 63 H5
Lemberg Ukr. see L'viv
Lembruch Germany 63 I2
Lembu Kalimantan Indon. 85 G2
Lembu, Gunung mt. Indon. 84 B1
Lembubut Kalimantan Indon. 85 G1
Lemdiyya Alg. see Médéa
Leme Brazil 179 B3
Lemele Neth. 62 G2
Lemesos Cyprus see Limassol
Lemgo Germany 63 I2
Lemhi Range mts ID U.S.A. 156 E3
Lemi Fin. 55 O6
Lemieux Islands Canada 147 L3
Lemmenjoen kansallispuisto nat. park Fin. 54 N2
Lemmer Neth. 62 F2
Lemmon SD U.S.A. 160 C2
Lemmon, Mount AZ U.S.A. 159 H5
Lemnos i. Greece see Limnos
Lemoncove CA U.S.A. 158 D3
Lemoore CA U.S.A. 158 D3
Le Moyne, Lac l. Canada 153 H2
Lemro r. Myanmar 86 A2
Lemtybozh Rus. Fed. 51 R3
Lemukutan i. Indon. 85 E2
Le Murge hills Italy 68 G4
Lemvig Denmark 55 F8
Lem"yu r. Rus. Fed. 52 M3
Lena r. Rus. Fed. 88 J1
Lena WI U.S.A. 164 A1
Lena, Mount UT U.S.A. 159 I1
Lenadoon Point Ireland 61 C3
Lenangguar Sumbawa Indon. 85 G5
Lenchung Tso salt l. China 105 E2
Lencóis Brazil 179 C1
Lençóis Maranhenses, Parque Nacional dos nat. park Brazil 177 J4
Lendery Rus. Fed. 54 Q5
Le Neubourg France 59 H9
Lengerich Germany 63 H2
Lenghu China 98 F5
Lenglong Ling mts China 94 E4
Lengshuijiang China 97 F3
Lengshuitan China 97 F3
Lenham U.K. 59 H7
Lenhovda Sweden 55 I8
Lenin Tajik. 111 H2
Lenin, Qullai mt. Kyrg./Tajik. see Lenin Peak
Lenina, Pik mt. Kyrg./Tajik. see Lenin Peak
Leninabad Tajik. see Khŭjand
Leninakan Armenia see Gyumri
Lenin Atyndagy Choku mt. Kyrg./Tajik. see Lenin Peak
Lenine Ukr. 112 D1
Leningrad Rus. Fed. see St Petersburg
Leningrad Tajik. 111 H2
Leningrad Oblast admin. div. Rus. Fed. see Leningradskaya Oblast'
Leningradskaya Rus. Fed. 53 H7
Leningradskaya Oblast' admin. div. Rus. Fed. 55 R7
Leningradskiy Rus. Fed. 77 S3
Leningradskiy Tajik. see Leningrad
Lenino Ukr. see Lenine
Leninobod Tajik. see Khŭjand
Lenin Peak Kyrg./Tajik. 111 I2
Leninsk Kazakh. see Baykonyr
Leninsk Rus. Fed. 53 J6
Leninskiy Rus. Fed. 53 H5
Leninsk-Kuznetskiy Rus. Fed. 76 J4
Leninskoye Kirovskaya Oblast' Rus. Fed. 52 J4
Leninskoye Yevreyskaya Avtonomnaya Oblast' Rus. Fed. 90 D3
Lenkoran' Azer. see Länkäran
Lenne r. Germany 63 H3
Lennoxville Canada 165 J1
Lenoir NC U.S.A. 162 D5
Lenore WV U.S.A. 164 D5
Lenore Lake Canada 151 J4
Lenox MA U.S.A. 165 I2
Lens France 62 C4
Lensk Rus. Fed. 77 M3
Lenti Hungary 68 G1
Lentini Sicily Italy 68 F6
Lenya Myanmar 87 B5
Lenzen Germany 63 L1
Léo Burkina Faso 120 C3
Leoben Austria 57 O7
Leodhais, Eilean i. U.K. see Lewis, Isle of
Leok Sulawesi Indon. 83 B2
Leominster U.K. 59 E6
Leominster MA U.S.A. 165 J2
León Mex. 168 D4
León Nicaragua 166 [inset] I6
León Spain 67 D2
Leon r. TX U.S.A. 161 D6
Leonardtown MD U.S.A. 165 G4
Leonardville Namibia 124 D2
Leona Vicario Mex. 167 I4
Leongatha Australia 138 B7
Leonidi Greece see Leonidio
Leonidio Greece 69 J6
Leonidovo Rus. Fed. 90 F2
Leonora Australia 135 C7
Leontovich, Cape AK U.S.A. 148 G5
Leopold WV U.S.A. 164 E4
Leopold and Astrid Coast Antarctica see King Leopold and Queen Astrid Coast
Léopold II, Lac l. Dem. Rep. Congo see Mai-Ndombe, Lac
Leopoldina Brazil 179 C3
Leopoldo de Bulhões Brazil 179 A2
Léopoldville Dem. Rep. Congo see Kinshasa
Leoti KS U.S.A. 160 C4
Leoville Canada 151 J4
Lepalale S. Africa see Lephalale
Lepar i. Indon. 84 D3
Lepaya Latvia see Liepāja
Lepel' Belarus see Lyepyel'
Lepellé r. Canada 153 H1
Lephalala r. S. Africa 125 H2
Lephalale S. Africa 125 H2
Lephepe Botswana 125 G2
Lephoi S. Africa 125 G6
Leping China 97 H2
Lepontine, Alpi mts Italy/Switz. 68 C1
Leppävirta Fin. 54 O5
Lepreau, Point Canada 153 I5
Lepsa Kazakh. see Lepsy
Lepsi Kazakh. 98 C3
Lepsi r. Kazakh. 98 B3
Lepsy Kazakh. 102 E2
Le Puy France see Le Puy-en-Velay
Le Puy-en-Velay France 66 F4
Le Quesnoy France 62 D4
Lerala Botswana 125 H2
Leratswana S. Africa 125 H5
Léré Mali 120 C3
Lereh Indon. 81 J7
Lereh, Tanjung pt Indon. 83 A3
Leribe Lesotho see Hlotse
Lérida Col. 176 D4
Lérida Spain see Lleida
Lerik Azer. 113 H3
Lerma Mex. 167 H5
Lerma Spain 67 E2
Lermontov Rus. Fed. 113 F1
Lermontovka Rus. Fed. 90 D3
Lermontovskiy Rus. Fed. see Lermontov
Leros i. Greece 69 L6
Le Roy NY U.S.A. 165 G2
Le Roy, Lac l. Canada 152 G2
Lerum Sweden 55 H8
Lerwick U.K. 60 [inset]
Les Amirantes is Seychelles see Amirante Islands
Lesbos i. Greece 69 K5
Les Cayes Haiti 169 J5
Leshan China 96 D2
Leshou China see Xianxian
Leshukonskoye Rus. Fed. 52 J2
Lesi watercourse South Sudan 121 F4
Leskhimstroy Ukr. see Syeverodonets'k
Leskovac Serbia 69 I3
Leslie MI U.S.A. 164 C2
Lesneven France 66 B2
Lesnoy Kirovskaya Oblast' Rus. Fed. 52 L4
Lesnoy Murmanskaya Oblast' Rus. Fed. see Umba

Lugau Germany 63 M4
Lügde Germany 63 J3
Lugdunum France see Lyon
Lugg r. U.K. 59 E6
Luggudontsen mt. China 99 E7
Lugnaquilla hill Ireland 61 F5
Lugo Italy 68 D2
Lugo Spain 67 C2
Lugoj Romania 69 I2
Lugu China 99 D6
Lugus i. Phil. 82 C5
Luhans'k Ukr. 53 H6
Luhe China 97 H1
Lu He r. China 95 G4
Luhe r. Germany 63 K1
Luḩfī, Wādī watercourse Jordan 107 C3
Luhin Sum China 95 I2
Luhit r. China/India see Zayü Qu
Luhit r. India 105 H4
Luhua China see Heishui
Luhuo China 96 D2
Luhyny Ukr. 53 F6
Luia Angola 123 C4
Luiana Angola 123 C5
Luichow Peninsula China see Leizhou Bandao
Luik Belgium see Liège
Luimneach Ireland see Limerick
Luiro r. Fin. 54 O3
Luis Echeverría Álvarez Mex. 158 E5
Luis L. León, Presa resr Mex. 166 D2
Luis Moya Mex. 166 E4
Luitpold Coast Antarctica 188 A1
Luiza Dem. Rep. Congo 123 C4
Lujiang China 97 H2
Lüjing China 94 F5
Lukachek Rus. Fed. 90 D1
Lukapa Angola see Lucapa
Lukavac Bos.-Herz. 68 H2
Lukenga, Lac l. Dem. Rep. Congo 123 C4
Lukenie r. Dem. Rep. Congo 122 B4
Lukeville AZ U.S.A. 166 B2
Lukh r. Rus. Fed. 52 I4
Lukhī Afgh. 111 F4
Lukhovitsy Rus. Fed. 53 H5
Luk Keng H.K. China 97 [inset]
Lukou China see Zhuzhou
Lukovit Bulg. 69 K3
Łuków Poland 53 D6
Lukoyanov Rus. Fed. 53 J5
Lükqün China 98 E4
Luksagu Sulawesi Indon. 83 B3
Lukusuzi National Park Zambia 123 D5
Luleå Sweden 54 M4
Luleälven r. Sweden 54 M4
Lüleburgaz Turkey 69 L4
Lüliang China 95 G4
Lüliang China 96 D3
Lüliang Shan mts China 95 G4
Lulimba Dem. Rep. Congo 123 C4
Luling TX U.S.A. 161 D6
Lulong China 95 I4
Lulonga r. Dem. Rep. Congo 122 B3
Luluabourg Dem. Rep. Congo see Kananga
Lülung China 99 D7
Lumachomo China 99 D7
Lumajang Jawa Indon. 85 F5
Lumajangdong Co salt l. China 99 C6
Lumbala Moxico Angola see Lumbala Kaquengue
Lumbala Moxico Angola see Lumbala N'guimbo
Lumbala Kaquengue Angola 123 C5
Lumbala N'guimbo Angola 123 C5
Lumberton NC U.S.A. 163 E5
Lumbini Nepal 105 E4
Lumbis Kalimantan Indon. 85 G1
Lumbrales Spain 67 C3
Lumezzane Italy 68 D2
Lumi P.N.G. 81 K7
Lumphăt Cambodia 87 D4
Lumpkin GA U.S.A. 163 C5
Lumsden Canada 151 J5
Lumsden N.Z. 139 B7
Lumut Malaysia 84 C1
Lumut, Gunung mt. Indon. 85 F3
Lumut, Tanjung pt Indon. 84 D3
Lün Mongolia 94 F2
Luna Luzon Phil. 82 C2
Luna NM U.S.A. 159 I5
Lunan China see Shilin
Lunan Bay U.K. 60 G4
Lunan Lake Canada 151 M1
Lunan Shan mts China 96 D3
Luna Pier MI U.S.A. 164 D3
Lund Pak. 111 H5
Lund Sweden 55 H9
Lund NV U.S.A. 159 F2
Lund UT U.S.A. 159 G2
Lundar Canada 151 L5
Lundu Sarawak Malaysia 85 E2
Lundy U.K. 59 C7
Lune r. Germany 63 I1
Lune r. U.K. 58 E4
Lüneburg Germany 63 K1
Lüneburger Heide reg. Germany 63 K1
Lünen Germany 63 H3
Lunenburg VA U.S.A. 165 F5
Lunéville France 66 H2
Lunga r. Zambia 123 C5
Lungdo China 105 E2
Lunggar China 99 C7
Lunggar Shan mts China 99 C7
Lung Kwu Chau i. H.K. China 97 [inset]
Lungleh India see Lunglei
Lunglei India 105 H5
Lungmari mt. China 99 D7
Lungmu Co salt l. China 99 C6
Lung-tzu China see Lhünzê
Lungwebungu r. Zambia 123 C5
Lunh Nepal 105 E3
Luni India 104 C4
Luni r. India 104 B4
Luni r. Pak. 111 H4
Luninets Belarus see Luninyets
Luning NV U.S.A. 158 D2
Luninyets Belarus 55 O10
Lunkaransar India 104 C3
Lunkha India 104 C3
Lünne Germany 63 H2
Lunsar Sierra Leone 120 B4
Lunsklip S. Africa 125 I3
Luntai China 98 D4
Lunyuk Sumbawa Indon. 85 G5
Luobei China 90 C3
Luobuzhuang China 98 E5
Luocheng Fujian China see Hui'an
Luocheng Gansu China 94 D4
Luocheng Guangxi China 97 F3
Luochuan China 95 G5
Luodian China 96 E3
Luoding China 97 F4
Luodou Sha i. China 97 F4
Luohe China 97 G1
Luo He r. Henan China 95 H5
Luo He r. Shaanxi China 95 G5
Luoma Hu l. China 95 I5
Luonan China 95 G5
Luoning China 95 G5
Luoping China 96 E3
Luotian China 97 G2
Luoto Fin. see Larsmo
Luotuoquan China 94 D3
Luoxiao Shan mts China 97 G3
Luoxiong China see Luoping
Luoyang Guangdong China see Boluo
Luoyang Henan China 95 H5
Luoyang Zhejiang China see Taishun
Luoyuan China 97 H3
Luozigou China 90 C4
Lupane Zimbabwe 123 C5
Lupanshui China see Liupanshui
Lupar r. Malaysia 85 E2
L'Upemba, Parc National de nat. park Dem. Rep. Congo 123 C4
Lupeni Romania 69 J2
Lupilichi Moz. 123 D5
Lupon Mindanao Phil. 82 D5
Lupton AZ U.S.A. 159 I4
Luqiao China see Luding
Luqu China 94 E5
Lu Qu r. China see Tao He
Luquan Hebei China 95 H4
Luquan Yunnan China 86 C1
Luray VA U.S.A. 165 F4
Luremo Angola 123 B4
Lurgan U.K. 61 F3
Lúrio Moz. 123 E5
Lurio r. Moz. 123 E5
Lūr Kōh mt. Afgh. 111 F3

▶Lusaka Zambia 123 C5
Capital of Zambia.

Lusambo Dem. Rep. Congo 123 C4
Lusancay Islands and Reefs P.N.G. 132 F2
Lusangi Dem. Rep. Congo 123 C4
Luseland Canada 151 I4
Lush, Mount hill Australia 134 D4
Lushar China see Huangzhong
Lushi China 95 G5
Lushnja Albania see Lushnjë
Lushnjë Albania 69 H4
Lushui China see Luzhang
Lushuihe China 90 B4
Lüshun China 95 J4
Lüsi China 97 I1
Lusi r. Indon. 85 E4
Lusikisiki S. Africa 125 I6
Lusk WY U.S.A. 156 G4
Luso Angola see Luena
Lussvale Australia 138 C1
Lut, Bahrat salt l. Asia see Dead Sea
Lūt, Dasht-e des. Iran see Lūt, Kavīr-e
Lūt, Kavīr-e des. Iran 110 E4
Lutai China see Ninghe
Lü Tao i. Taiwan 97 I4
Lutetia France see Paris
Lūt-e Zangī Aḩmad des. Iran 110 E4
Luther MI U.S.A. 164 C1
Luther Lake Canada 164 E2
Lutherstadt Wittenberg Germany 63 M3
Luton U.K. 59 G7
Lutong Sarawak Malaysia 85 F1
Łutselk'e Canada 151 I2
Luts'k Ukr. 53 E6
Luttelgeest Neth. 62 F2
Luttenberg Neth. 62 G2
Lutto r. Fin./Rus. Fed. see Lotta
Lutz FL U.S.A. 163 D6
Lützelbach Germany 63 J5
Lützow-Holm Bay Antarctica 188 D2
Lutzputs S. Africa 124 E5
Lutzville S. Africa 124 D6
Luuk Phil. 82 C5
Luumäki Fin. 55 O6
Luuq Somalia 122 E3
Luverne AL U.S.A. 163 C6
Luverne MN U.S.A. 160 D3
Luvuei Angola 123 C5
Luvuvhu r. S. Africa 125 J2
Luwero Uganda 122 D3
Luwingu Zambia 123 C5
Luwuhuyu Kalimantan Indon. 85 E3
Luwuk Sulawesi Indon. 83 B3
Luxembourg country Europe 62 G5

▶Luxembourg Lux. 62 G5
Capital of Luxembourg.

Luxemburg country Europe see Luxembourg
Luxeuil-les-Bains France 66 H3
Luxi Hunan China see Wuxi
Luxi Yunnan China 96 C3
Luxi Yunnan China 96 D3
Luxolweni S. Africa 125 G6
Luxor Egypt 108 D4
Luya Shan mts China 95 G4
Luyi China 97 G1
Luyksgestel Neth. 62 F3
Luyuan China see Gaoling
Luza Rus. Fed. 52 J3
Luza r. Rus. Fed. 52 J3
Luza r. Rus. Fed. 52 M2
Luzern Switz. see Lucerne
Luzhai China 97 F3
Luzhang China 96 C3
Luzhou China 96 E2
Luziânia Brazil 179 B2
Luzon i. Phil. 82 C3
Luzon Strait Phil. 82 C1
Luzy France 66 F3
L'viv Ukr. 53 E6
L'vov Ukr. see L'viv
Lwów Ukr. see L'viv
Lyady Rus. Fed. 55 P7
Lyakhavichy Belarus 55 O10
Lyakhovichi Belarus see Lyakhavichy
Lyallpur Pak. see Faisalabad
Lyamtsa Rus. Fed. 52 H2
Lycia reg. Turkey 69 M6
Lyck Poland see Ełk
Lycksele Sweden 54 K4
Lycopolis Egypt see Asyūţ
Lydd U.K. 59 H8
Lydda Israel see Lod
Lyddan Island Antarctica 188 B2
Lydia reg. Turkey 69 L5
Lydney U.K. 59 E7
Lyel'chytsy Belarus 53 F6
Lyell, Mount CA U.S.A. 158 D3
Lyell Brown, Mount hill Australia 135 E5
Lyell Island Canada 149 O5
Lyepyel' Belarus 55 P9
Lykens PA U.S.A. 165 G3
Lyman WY U.S.A. 156 F4
Lyme Bay U.K. 59 E8
Lyme Regis U.K. 59 E8
Lymington U.K. 59 F8
Lynchburg OH U.S.A. 164 D4
Lynchburg TN U.S.A. 162 C5
Lynchburg VA U.S.A. 164 F5
Lynchville ME U.S.A. 165 J1
Lyndhurst N.S.W. Australia 138 D4
Lyndhurst Qld Australia 136 D3
Lyndhurst S.A. Australia 137 B6
Lyndon Australia 135 A5
Lyndon r. Australia 135 A5
Lyndonville VT U.S.A. 165 I1
Lyne r. U.K. 58 D4
Lyness U.K. 60 F2
Lyngdal Norway 55 E7
Lynn U.K. see King's Lynn
Lynn IN U.S.A. 164 C3
Lynn MA U.S.A. 165 J2
Lynndyl UT U.S.A. 159 G2
Lynn Lake Canada 151 K3
Lynton U.K. 59 D7
Lynx Lake Canada 151 J2
Lyon France 66 G4
Lyon r. U.K. 60 F4
Lyon Mountain NY U.S.A. 165 I1
Lyons Australia 135 F7
Lyons France see Lyon
Lyons GA U.S.A. 163 D5
Lyons NY U.S.A. 165 G2
Lyons Falls NY U.S.A. 165 H2
Lyozna Belarus 53 F5
Lyra Reef P.N.G. 132 F2
Lys r. France 62 D4
Lysekil Sweden 55 G7
Lyskovo Rus. Fed. 52 J4
Ly Sơn, Đao i. Vietnam 86 E4
Lys'va Rus. Fed. 51 R4
Lysychans'k Ukr. 53 H6
Lysyye Gory Rus. Fed. 53 J6
Lytham St Anne's U.K. 58 D5
Lytton Canada 150 F5
Lyuban' Belarus 55 P10
Lyubertsy Rus. Fed. 51 N4
Lyubeshiv Ukr. 53 E6
Lyubim Rus. Fed. 52 I4
Lyubytino Rus. Fed. 52 G4
Lyudinovo Rus. Fed. 53 G5
Lyunda r. Rus. Fed. 52 J4
Lyzha r. Rus. Fed. 52 M2

M

Ma r. Myanmar 86 B2
Ma, Nâm r. Laos 86 C2
Ma'agan Israel 107 B3
Maale Maldives see Male
Maale Atholhu atoll Maldives see Male Atoll
Maalhosmadulu Atholhu Uthuruburi atoll Maldives see North Maalhosmadulu Atoll
Maalhosmadulu Atoll Maldives 106 B5
Ma'ān Jordan 107 B4
Maan Turkey see Nusratiye
Maaninka Fin. 54 O5
Maaninkavaara Fin. 54 P3
Maanĭt Bulgan Mongolia see Hishig-Öndör
Maanĭt Töv Mongolia see Bayan
Ma'anshan China 97 H2
Maardu Estonia 55 N7
Maarianhamina Fin. see Mariehamn
Ma'arrat an Nu'mān Syria 107 C2
Maarssen Neth. 62 F2
Maas r. Neth. 62 E3
also known as Meuse (Belgium/France)
Maaseik Belgium 62 F3
Maasin Leyte Phil. 82 D4
Maasmechelen Belgium 62 F4
Maas-Schwalm-Nette, Naturpark nat. park Germany/Neth. 62 F3
Maastricht Neth. 62 F4
Maaza Plateau Egypt 112 C6
Maba Guangdong China see Qujiang
Maba Jiangsu China 97 H1
Maba Halmahera Indon. 83 D2
Mabai China see Maguan
Mabalacat Luzon Phil. 82 C3
Mabalane Moz. 125 K2
Mabana Dem. Rep. Congo 122 C3
Mabaruma Guyana 176 G2
Mabein Myanmar 86 B2
Mabel Creek Australia 135 F7
Mabel Downs Australia 134 D4
Mabella Canada 152 C4
Mabel Lake Canada 150 G5
Maberly Canada 165 G1
Mabian China 96 D2
Mabja China 99 D7
Mablethorpe U.K. 58 H5
Mabopane S. Africa 125 I3
Mabote Moz. 125 L2
Mabou Canada 153 J5
Mabrak, Jabal mt. Jordan 107 B4
Mabuasehube Game Reserve nature res. Botswana 124 F3
Mabudis i. Phil. 82 C1
Mabule Botswana 124 G3
Mabutsane Botswana 124 F3
Macá, Monte mt. Chile 178 B7
Macadam Plains Australia 135 B6
Macaé Brazil 179 C3
Macajalar Bay Mindanao Phil. 82 D4
Macajuba Brazil 179 C1
Macaloge Moz. 123 D5
MacAlpine Lake Canada 147 H3
Macamic Canada 152 F4
Macan, Kepulauan atolls Indon. see Taka'Bonerate, Kepulauan
Macandze Moz. 125 K2
Macao China 97 G4
Macao aut. reg. China 97 G4
Macapá Brazil 177 H3
Macará Ecuador 176 C4
Macaracas Panama 166 [inset] J8
Macarani Brazil 179 C1
Macas Ecuador 176 C4
Macassar Sulawesi Indon. see Makassar
Macassar Strait Indon. see Makassar, Selat
Macau Brazil 177 K5
Macau China see Macao
Macaúba Brazil 177 H6
Macauley Island N.Z. 133 I5
Macau Special Administrative Region aut. reg. China see Macao
Maccaretane Moz. 125 K3
Macclenny FL U.S.A. 163 D6
Macclesfield U.K. 58 E5
Macdiarmid Canada 152 C4
Macdonald, Lake salt flat Australia 135 E5
Macdonald Range hills Australia 134 D3
Macdonnell Ranges mts Australia 135 E5
MacDowell Lake Canada 151 M4
Macduff U.K. 60 G3
Macedo de Cavaleiros Port. 67 C3
Macedon mt. Australia 138 B6
Macedon country Europe see Macedonia
Macedonia country Europe 69 I4
Maceió Brazil 177 K5
Macenta Guinea 120 C4
Macerata Italy 68 E3
Macfarlane, Lake salt flat Australia 137 B7
Macgillycuddy's Reeks mts Ireland 61 C6
Machachi Ecuador 176 C4
Machaila Moz. 125 K2
Machakos Kenya 122 D4
Machala Ecuador 176 C4
Machali China see Madoi
Machan Sarawak Malaysia 85 F2
Machanga Moz. 123 D6
Machar Marshes South Sudan 108 D8
Machattie, Lake salt flat Australia 136 B5
Machatuine Moz. 125 K3
Machault France 62 E5
Machaze Moz. see Chitobe
Macheng China 97 G2
Macherla India 106 C2
Machhagan India 105 F5
Machias ME U.S.A. 162 H2
Machias NY U.S.A. 165 F2
Machida Japan 93 F3
Machilipatnam India 106 D2
Machiques Venez. 176 D1
Māch Kowr Iran 111 F5
Machrihanish U.K. 60 D5
Machu Picchu tourist site Peru 176 D6
Machynlleth U.K. 59 D6
Macia Moz. 125 K3
Macias Nguema i. Equat. Guinea see Bioco
Măcin Romania 69 M2
Macintyre r. Australia 138 E2
Macintyre Brook r. Australia 138 E2
Mack CO U.S.A. 159 I2
Maçka Turkey 113 E2
Mackay Australia 136 E4
MacKay r. Canada 151 I3
Mackay ID U.S.A. 156 E3
Mackay, Lake salt flat Australia 134 E5
MacKay Lake Canada 151 I2
Mackenzie r. Australia 136 E4
Mackenzie Canada 150 F4

▶Mackenzie r. Canada 149 N1
Part of the Mackenzie-Peace-Finlay, the 2nd longest river in North America.

Mackenzie Guyana see Linden
Mackenzie atoll Micronesia see Ulithi
Mackenzie Bay Antarctica 188 E2
Mackenzie Bay Canada 149 M1
Mackenzie Highway Canada 150 G2
Mackenzie King Island Canada 147 G2
Mackenzie Mountains Canada 149 N2

▶Mackenzie-Peace-Finlay r. Canada 146 E3
2nd longest river in North America

Mackillop, Lake salt flat Australia see Yamma Yamma, Lake
Mackintosh Range hills Australia 135 D6
Macklin Canada 151 I4
Macksville Australia 138 F3
Maclean Australia 138 F2
Maclear S. Africa 125 I6
MacLeod Canada see Fort Macleod
MacLeod, Lake imp. l. Australia 135 A6
Macmillan r. Canada 149 N3
Macmillan Pass Canada 149 O3
Macomb IL U.S.A. 160 F3
Macomer Sardinia Italy 68 C4
Mâcon France 66 G3
Macon GA U.S.A. 163 D5
Macon MO U.S.A. 160 E4
Macon MS U.S.A. 161 F5
Macon OH U.S.A. 164 D4
Macondo Angola 123 C5
Macoun Lake Canada 151 K3
Macpherson Robertson Land reg. Antarctica see Mac. Robertson Land
Macpherson's Strait India 87 A5
Macquarie r. Australia 138 C3
Macquarie, Lake b. Australia 138 E4

▶Macquarie Island S. Pacific Ocean 186 G9
Part of Australia. Most southerly point of Oceania.

Macquarie Marshes Australia 138 C3
Macquarie Mountain Australia 138 D4
Macquarie Ridge sea feature S. Pacific Ocean 186 G9
MacRitchie Reservoir Sing. 87 [inset]
Mac. Robertson Land reg. Antarctica 188 E2
Macroom Ireland 61 D6
Mactún Mex. 167 H5
Macumba Australia 137 A5
Macumba watercourse Australia 137 B5
Macuspana Mex. 167 G5
Macuzari, Presa resr Mex. 166 C3
Mādabā Jordan 107 B4
Madadeni S. Africa 125 J4

▶Madagascar country Africa 123 E6
Largest island in Africa and 4th in the world.

Madagascar Basin sea feature Indian Ocean 185 L7
Madagascar Ridge sea feature Indian Ocean 185 K8
Madagasikara country Africa see Madagascar
Madakasira India 106 C3
Madalai Palau 82 [inset]
Madama Niger 121 E2
Madan Bulg. 69 K4
Madanapalle India 106 C3
Madang P.N.G. 81 L8
Madaoua Niger 120 D3
Madaripur Bangl. 105 G5
Madau Turkm. see Madaw
Madaw Turkm. 110 D2
Madawaska Canada 165 G1
Madawaska r. Canada 165 G1
Madaya Myanmar 86 B2
Madded India 106 D2

▶Madeira r. Brazil 176 G4
4th longest river in South America.

▶Madeira terr. N. Atlantic Ocean 120 B1
Autonomous Region of Portugal.

Madeira, Arquipélago da terr. N. Atlantic Ocean see Madeira
Maden Turkey 113 E3
Madeniyet Kazakh. 98 B3
Madera Mex. 166 C2
Madera CA U.S.A. 158 C3
Madgaon India 106 B3
Madha India 106 B2
Madhavpur India 104 B5
Madhepura India 105 F4
Madhipura India see Madhepura
Madhubani India 105 F4
Madhya Pradesh state India 104 D5
Madi, Dataran Tinggi plat. Indon. 85 F2
Madibogo S. Africa 125 G4
Madidi r. Bol. 176 E6
Madikeri India 106 B3
Madikwe Game Reserve nature res. S. Africa 125 H3
Madill OK U.S.A. 161 D5
Madīnat ash Shamāl town Qatar 110 C5
Madīnat ath Thawrah Syria 107 D2
Madingo-Kayes Congo 123 B4
Madingou Congo 123 B4
Madison FL U.S.A. 163 D6
Madison GA U.S.A. 163 D5
Madison IN U.S.A. 164 C4
Madison ME U.S.A. 165 K1
Madison NE U.S.A. 160 D3
Madison SD U.S.A. 160 D2
Madison VA U.S.A. 165 F4

▶Madison WI U.S.A. 160 F3
Capital of Wisconsin.

Madison WV U.S.A. 164 E4
Madison r. MT U.S.A. 156 F3
Madison Heights VA U.S.A. 164 F5
Madisonville KY U.S.A. 164 B5
Madisonville TX U.S.A. 161 E6
Madita Sumba Indon. 83 B5
Madiun Jawa Indon. 85 E4
Madley, Mount hill Australia 135 C6
Madoc Canada 165 G1
Mado Gashi Kenya 122 D3
Madoi China 94 D5
Madona Latvia 55 O8
Madpura India 104 B4
Madra Dağı mts Turkey 69 L5
Madrakah Saudi Arabia 108 E5
Madrakah, Ra's c. Oman 109 I6
Madras India see Chennai
Madras state India see Tamil Nadu
Madras OR U.S.A. 156 C3
Madre, Laguna lag. Mex. 161 D7
Madre, Laguna lag. TX U.S.A. 161 D7
Madre, Sierra mt. Luzon Phil. 82 C2
Madre de Chiapas, Sierra mts Mex. 167 G5
Madre de Dios r. Peru 176 E6
Madre de Dios, Isla i. Chile 178 A8
Madre del Sur, Sierra mts Mex. 168 D5
Madre Mountain NM U.S.A. 159 J4
Madre Occidental, Sierra mts Mex. 157 F7
Madre Oriental, Sierra mts Mex. 161 C7
Madrid Mindanao Phil. 82 D4

▶Madrid Spain 67 E3
Capital of Spain. 5th most populous city in Europe.

Madridejos Phil. 82 C4
Madridejos Spain 67 E4
Madruga Cuba 163 D8
Madu i. Indon. 83 B4
Madugula India 106 D2
Madura i. Indon. 85 F4
Madura, Selat sea chan. Indon. 85 F4
Madurai India 106 C4
Madurantakam India 106 C3
Madvār, Kūh-e mt. Iran 110 D4
Madwas India 105 E4
Maé i. Vanuatu see Émaé
Maebashi Japan 93 F2
Mae Hong Son Thai. 86 B3
Maelang Sulawesi Indon. 83 B2
Mae Ping National Park Thai. 86 B3
Mae Ramat Thai. 86 B3
Mae Sai Thai. 86 B2
Mae Sariang Thai. 86 B3
Mae Sot Thai. 86 B3
Maestre de Campo i. Phil. 82 C3
Mae Suai Thai. 86 B3
Mae Tuen Wildlife Reserve nature res. Thai. 86 B3
Maevatanana Madag. 123 E5
Maéwo i. Vanuatu 133 G3
Mae Wong National Park Thai. 86 B4
Mae Yom National Park Thai. 86 C3
Mafa Halmahera Indon. 83 C2
Mafadi mt. S. Africa 125 I5
Mafeking Canada 151 K4
Mafeking S. Africa see Mafikeng
Mafeteng Lesotho 125 H5
Maffra Australia 138 C6
Mafia Island Tanz. 123 D4
Mafikeng S. Africa 125 G3
Mafinga Tanz. 123 D4
Mafra Brazil 179 A4
Mafraq Jordan see Al Mafraq
Magabeni S. Africa 125 J6
Magadan Rus. Fed. 77 Q4
Magadi Kenya 122 D4
Magaiza Moz. 125 K2
Magallanes Chile see Punta Arenas
Magallanes Luzon Phil. 82 C3
Magallanes, Estrecho de Chile see Magellan, Strait of
Magangué Col. 176 D2
Mağara Dağı mt. Turkey 107 A1
Magaramkent Rus. Fed. 113 H2
Magaria Niger 120 D3
Magarida P.N.G. 136 E1
Magas Rus. Fed. 113 G2
Magat r. Luzon Phil. 82 C2
Magazine Mountain hill AR U.S.A. 161 E5
Magdagachi Rus. Fed. 90 B1
Magdalena Bol. 176 F6
Magdalena r. Col. 176 D1
Magdalena Baja California Sur Mex. 166 B3
Magdalena Sonora Mex. 166 C2
Magdalena r. Mex. 166 C2
Magdalena, Bahía b. Mex. 166 C3
Magdalena, Isla i. Chile 178 B6
Magdalena, Isla i. Mex. 166 B3
Magdaline, Gunung mt. Malaysia 85 G1
Magdeburg Germany 63 L2
Magdelaine Cays atoll Australia 136 E3
Magelang Jawa Indon. 85 E4
Magellan, Strait of Chile 178 B8
Magellan Seamounts sea feature N. Pacific Ocean 186 F4
Magenta, Lake salt flat Australia 135 B8
Magerøya i. Norway 54 N1
Maggiorasca, Monte mt. Italy 68 C2
Maggiore, Lago Italy see Maggiore, Lake
Maggiore, Lake Italy 68 C2
Maghāgha Egypt see Maghāghah
Maghāghah Egypt 112 C5
Maghama Mauritania 120 B3
Maghâra, Gebel hill Egypt see Maghārah, Jabal
Maghārah, Jabal hill Egypt 107 A4
Maghera U.K. 61 F3
Magherafelt U.K. 61 F3
Maghnia Alg. 67 F6
Maghull U.K. 58 E5
Magilligan Point U.K. 61 F2
Magiscatzín Mex. 167 F4
Magitang China see Jainca
Magma AZ U.S.A. 159 H5
Magna Grande mt. Sicily Italy 68 F6
Magnetic Island Australia 136 D3
Magnetic Passage Australia 136 D3
Magnetity Rus. Fed. 54 R2
Magnitogorsk Rus. Fed. 76 G4
Magnolia AR U.S.A. 161 E5
Magnolia MS U.S.A. 161 F6
Magny-en-Vexin France 62 B5
Mago Rus. Fed. 90 F1
Màgoé Moz. 123 D5
Magog Canada 165 I1
Mago National Park Eth. 122 D3
Magosa Cyprus see Famagusta
Magozal Mex. 167 F4
Magpie r. Canada 153 I4
Magpie, Lac l. Canada 153 I4
Magta' Laḩjar Mauritania 120 B3
Magu Tanz. 122 D4
Magu, Khrebet mts Rus. Fed. 90 E1
Maguan China 96 E4
Magude Moz. 125 K3
Magueyal Mex. 166 E3
Magura Bangl. 105 G5
Maguse Lake Canada 151 M2
Magway Myanmar see Magwe
Magwe Myanmar 86 A2
Magyar Köztársaság country Europe see Hungary
Magyichaung Myanmar 86 A2
Mahābād Iran 110 B2
Mahabharat Range mts Nepal 105 F4
Mahaboobnagar India see Mahbubnagar
Mahad India 106 B2
Mahadeo Hills India 104 D5
Mahaffey PA U.S.A. 165 F3
Mahai China 99 F5
Mahajan India 104 C3
Mahajanga Madag. 123 E5
Mahakam r. Indon. 85 G3
Mahalapye Botswana 125 H2
Mahale Mountains National Park Tanz. 123 C4
Mahalevona Madag. 123 E5
Mahallāt-e Bālā Iran 110 C3
Māhān Iran 110 E4
Mahanadi r. India 106 E1
Mahanoro Madag. 123 E5
Maha Oya Sri Lanka 106 D5
Maharajganj Bihar India 99 D8
Maharajganj Uttar Prad. India 99 C8
Maharashtra state India 106 B2
Maha Sarakham Thai. 86 C3
Mahasham, Wādī el watercourse Egypt see Muhashsham, Wādī al
Mahaxai Laos 86 D3
Mahbubabad India 106 D2
Mahbubnagar India 106 C2
Mahd adh Dhahab Saudi Arabia 108 F5
Mahdia Alg. 67 G6
Mahdia Guyana 177 G2
Mahdia Tunisia 68 D7
Mahe China 94 F5
Mahé i. Seychelles 185 L6
Mahendragiri mt. India 106 E2
Mahendranagar Nepal 99 C7
Mahendranagar Nepal 104 E3
Mahenge Tanz. 123 D4
Mahesana India 104 C5
Mahgawan India 99 B8
Mahi r. India 104 C5
Mahia Peninsula N.Z. 139 F4
Mahilyow Belarus 53 F5
Mahim India 106 B2
Mah Jān Iran 110 D4
Mahlabatini S. Africa 125 J5
Mahlsdorf Germany 63 L2
Maḩmūdābād Iran 110 D2

Maḩmūd-e 'Erāqī Afgh. see Maḩmūd-e Rāqī
Maḩmūd-e Rāqī Afgh. 111 H3
Mahnomen MN U.S.A. 160 D2
Maho Sri Lanka 106 D5
Mahoba India 104 D4
Maholi India 104 E4
Mahón Spain 67 I4
Mahony Lake Canada 149 P2
Mahrauni India 104 D4
Mahrès Tunisia 68 D7
Mahrūd Iran 111 F3
Mahsana India see Mahesana
Mahuanggou China 99 F5
Mahudaung mts Myanmar 86 A2
Māhukona HI U.S.A. 157 [inset]
Mahur India 106 C2
Mahuva India 104 B5
Mahwa India 104 D4
Mahya Dağı mt. Turkey 69 L4
Mai i. Maluku Indon. 83 C4
Mai i. Vanuatu see Émaé
Maiaia Moz. see Nacala
Maibang India 86 A1
Maicao Col. 176 D1
Maicasagi r. Canada 152 F4
Maicasagi, Lac l. Canada 152 F4
Maichen China 97 F4
Maidenhead U.K. 59 G7
Maidi Halmahera Indon. 83 C2
Maidstone Canada 151 I4
Maidstone U.K. 59 H7
Maiduguri Nigeria 120 E3
Maiella, Parco Nazionale della nat. park Italy 68 F3
Mai Gudo mt. Eth. 122 D3
Maigue r. Ireland 61 D5
Maihar India 104 E4
Maihara Japan 92 C3
Maiji China 94 F5
Maiji Shan mt. China 96 E1
Maikala Range hills India 104 E5
Maiko r. Dem. Rep. Congo 122 C3
Mailan Hill mt. India 105 E5
Mailani India 99 C7
Maileppe Indon. 84 B3
Mailly-le-Camp France 62 E6
Mailsi Pak. 111 I4
Maïmanah Afgh. 111 G3
Main r. Germany 63 I4
Main r. U.K. 61 F3
Main Brook Canada 153 L4
Mainburg Germany 63 L6
Main Channel lake channel Canada 164 E1
Maindargi India 106 C2
Mai-Ndombe, Lac l. Dem. Rep. Congo 122 B4
Main-Donau-Kanal canal Germany 63 K5
Main Duck Island Canada 165 G2
Maine state U.S.A. 165 K1
Maine, Gulf of Canada/U.S.A. 165 K2
Mainé Hanari, Cerro hill Col. 176 D4
Maïné-Soroa Niger 120 E3
Maingkaing Myanmar 86 A1
Maingkwan Myanmar 86 B1
Maingy Island Myanmar 87 B4
Mainhardt Germany 63 J5
Mainit Mindanao Phil. 82 D4
Mainit, Lake Mindanao Phil. 82 D4
Mainkung China 96 C2
Mainland i. Scotland U.K. 60 F1
Mainland i. Scotland U.K. 60 [inset]
Mainleus Germany 63 L4
Mainling China 99 F7
Mainoru Australia 134 F3
Mainpat reg. India 105 E5
Mainpuri India 104 D4
Main Range National Park Australia 138 F2
Maintenon France 62 B6
Maintirano Madag. 123 E5
Mainz Germany 63 I4
Maio i. Cape Verde 120 [inset]
Maipú Arg. 178 E5
Maisaka Japan 92 D4
Maiskhal Island Bangl. 105 G5
Maisons-Laffitte France 62 C6
Maitengwe Botswana 123 C6
Maitland N.S.W. Australia 138 E4
Maitland S.A. Australia 137 B7
Maitland r. Australia 134 B5
Maitland, Banjaran mts Malaysia 85 G1
Maitland Point pt Canada 149 O1
Maitri research station Antarctica 188 C2
Maiwo i. Vanuatu see Maéwo
Maiyu, Mount hill Australia 134 E4
Maíz, Islas del is Nicaragua 166 [inset] J6
Maizar Pak. 111 H3
Maizhokunggar China 99 E7
Maizuru Japan 92 B3
Maja Jezercë mt. Albania 69 H3
Majdel Aanjar tourist site Lebanon 107 B3
Majene Sulawesi Barat Indon. 83 A3
Majestic KY U.S.A. 164 D5
Majḩūd well Saudi Arabia 110 C6
Majī Eth. 122 D3
Majia He r. China 95 I4
Majiang Guangxi China 97 F4
Majiang Guizhou China 96 E3
Majiawan China see Huinong
Majiazi China 90 B2
Majnābād Iran 111 F3
Majōl country N. Pacific Ocean see Marshall Islands
Major, Puig mt. Spain 67 H4
Majorca i. Spain 67 H4
Mājro atoll Marshall Is see Majuro
Majuli Island India 99 F8
Majunga Madag. see Mahajanga
Majuro atoll Marshall Is 186 H5
Majwemasweu S. Africa 125 H5
Makabana Congo 122 B4
Makabe Japan 93 G2
Makale Sulawesi Indon. 83 A3
Makalehi i. Indon. 83 C2

▶Makalu mt. China/Nepal 105 F4
5th highest mountain in Asia and the world.

Makalu Barun National Park Nepal 105 F4
Makanchi Kazakh. 102 F2
Makanpur India 104 E4
Makari Mountain National Park Tanz. see Mahale Mountains National Park
Makarov Rus. Fed. 90 F2
Makarov Basin sea feature Arctic Ocean 189 B1
Makarska Croatia 68 G3
Makarwal Pak. 111 H3
Makar'ye Rus. Fed. 52 K4
Makar'yev Rus. Fed. 52 I4
Makassar Sulawesi Indon. 83 A4
Makassar, Selat str. Indon. 83 A3
Makat Kazakh. 100 E2
Makatini Flats lowland S. Africa 125 K4
Makedonija country Europe see Macedonia
Makelulu hill Palau 82 [inset]
Makeni Sierra Leone 120 B4
Makete Tanz. 123 D4
Makeyevka Ukr. see Makiyivka
Makgadikgadi depr. Botswana 123 C6
Makgadikgadi Pans National Park Botswana 123 C6
Makhachkala Rus. Fed. 113 G2
Makhad Pak. 111 H3
Makhado S. Africa 125 I2
Makhāzin, Kathīb al des. Egypt 107 A4
Makhâzin, Kathîb el des. Egypt see Makhāzin, Kathīb al
Makhazine, Barrage El dam Morocco 67 D6
Makhmūr Iraq 113 F4
Makhtal India 106 C2
Maki Japan 93 E1
Makian vol. Maluku Indon. 83 C2
Makihata-yama mt. Japan 93 E2
Makin atoll Kiribati see Butaritari
Makindu Kenya 122 D4
Makino Japan 92 C3
Makinsk Kazakh. 101 G1
Makioka Japan 93 E3
Makira i. Solomon Is see San Cristobal
Makiyivka Ukr. 53 H6
Makkah Saudi Arabia see Mecca
Makkovik Canada 153 K3
Makkovik, Cape Canada 153 K3
Makkum Neth. 62 F1
Makó Hungary 69 I1
Makokou Gabon 122 B3
Makopong Botswana 124 F3
Makotipoko Congo 121 E5
Makran reg. Iran/Pak. 111 F5
Makrana India 104 C4
Makran Coast Range mts Pak. 111 F5
Makri India 106 D2
Maksatikha Rus. Fed. 52 G4
Maksi India 104 D5
Maksimovka Rus. Fed. 90 E3
Maksotag Iran 111 F4
Maksudangarh India 104 D5
Mākū Iran 110 B2
Makunguwiro Tanz. 123 D5
Makurdi Nigeria 120 D4
Makushin Bay AK U.S.A. 148 F5
Makwassie S. Africa 125 G4
Mal India 105 G4
Mala Ireland see Mallow
Mala i. Solomon Is see Malaita
Malå Sweden 54 K4
Mala, Punta pt Panama 166 [inset] J8
Malabang Mindanao Phil. 82 D5
Malabar Coast India 106 B3

▶Malabo Equat. Guinea 120 D4
Capital of Equatorial Guinea.

Malabuñgan Palawan Phil. 82 B4
Malaca Spain see Málaga
Malacca Malaysia see Melaka
Malacca state Malaysia see Melaka
Malacca, Strait of Indon./Malaysia 84 B1
Malad City ID U.S.A. 156 E4
Maladzyechna Belarus 55 O9
Malá Fatra nat. park Slovakia 57 Q6
Málaga Spain 67 D5
Malaga NM U.S.A. 161 B5
Malagasy Republic country Africa see Madagascar
Malahar Sumba Indon. 83 B5
Málainn Mhóir Ireland 61 D3
Malaita i. Solomon Is 133 G2
Malaka mt. Sumbawa Indon. 85 G5
Malakal South Sudan 108 D8
Malakal Palau 82 [inset]
Malakal Passage Palau 82 [inset]
Malakanagiri India see Malkangiri
Malakheti Nepal 104 E3
Malakula i. Vanuatu 133 G3
Malamala Sulawesi Indon. 83 B3
Malampaya Sound sea chan. Palawan Phil. 82 B4
Malan, Ras pt Pak. 111 G5
Malang Jawa Indon. 85 F4
Malangana Nepal see Malangwa
Malange Angola see Malanje
Malangwa Nepal 105 F4
Malanje Angola 123 B4
Malappuram India 106 C4
Mälaren l. Sweden 55 J7
Malargüe Arg. 178 C5
Malartic Canada 152 F4
Malasoro, Teluk b. Indon. 83 A4
Malaspina Glacier AK U.S.A. 149 L4
Malatayur, Tanjung pt Indon. 85 F3
Malatya Turkey 112 E3
Malavalli India 106 C3
Malawali i. Malaysia 85 G1
Malawi country Africa 123 D5
Malawi, Lake Africa see Nyasa, Lake
Malawi National Park Zambia see Nyika National Park
Malaya pen. Malaysia see Peninsular Malaysia
Malaya Pera Rus. Fed. 52 L2
Malaya Vishera Rus. Fed. 52 G4
Malaybalay Mindanao Phil. 82 D4
Malāyer Iran 110 C3
Malay Peninsula Asia 87 B4
Malay Reef Australia 136 E3
Malaysary Kazakh. 98 B3
Malaysia country Asia 80 D5
Malaysia, Semenanjung pen. Malaysia see Peninsular Malaysia
Malazgirt Turkey 113 F3
Malbon Australia 136 C4
Malbork Poland 57 Q3
Malborn Germany 62 G5
Malchin Germany 57 N4
Malcolm Australia 135 C7
Malcolm, Point Australia 135 C8
Malcolm Island Myanmar 87 B5
Maldegem Belgium 62 D3
Malden MO U.S.A. 161 F4
Malden Island Kiribati 187 J6
Maldives country Indian Ocean 103 D10
Maldon Australia 138 B6
Maldon U.K. 59 H7
Maldonado Uruguay 178 F4
Maldonado, Punta pt Mex. 167 F5

▶Male Maldives 103 D11
Capital of the Maldives.

Maleas, Akra pt Greece see Maleas, Akrotirio
Maleas, Akrotirio pt Greece 69 J6
Male Atoll Maldives 103 D11
Malebogo S. Africa 125 G5
Malegaon Mahar. India 106 B1
Malegaon Mahar. India 106 C2
Malé Karpaty hills Slovakia 57 P6
Malek Sīāh Kūh mt. Afgh. 111 F4
Malele Dem. Rep. Congo 123 B4
Maler Kotla India 104 C3
Maleševske Planine mts Bulg./Macedonia 69 J4
Maleta Rus. Fed. 95 G1
Malgobek Rus. Fed. 113 G2
Malgomaj l. Sweden 54 J4
Malḩa, Naqb mt. Egypt see Māliḩah, Naqb
Malhada Brazil 179 C1
Malheur r. OR U.S.A. 156 D3
Malheur Lake OR U.S.A. 156 D4
Mali country Africa 120 C3
Mali Dem. Rep. Congo 122 C4
Mali Guinea 120 B3
Maliana East Timor 83 C5
Malianjing Gansu China 94 C3
Malianjing Gansu China 94 E4
Maligay Bay Mindanao Phil. 82 C5
Malihabad India 99 C8
Māliḩah, Naqb mt. Egypt 107 A5
Malik Naro mt. Pak. 111 F4
Maliku Sulawesi Indon. 83 B3
Mali Kyun i. Myanmar 87 B4
Malili Sulawesi Indon. 83 B3
Malin Ukr. see Malyn
Malindi Kenya 122 E4
Malines Belgium see Mechelen
Maling China 95 F4
Malin Head hd Ireland 61 E2
Malino Sulawesi Indon. 83 A4
Malino, Gunung mt. Indon. 83 B2
Malipo China 96 E4
Mali Raginac mt. Croatia 68 F2
Malita Mindanao Phil. 82 D5
Malitbog Leyte Phil. 82 D4
Malka r. Rus. Fed. 113 G2
Malkangiri India 106 D2
Malkapur India 106 B2
Malkara Turkey 69 L4
Mal'kavichy Belarus 55 O10
Malkhanskiy Khrebet mts Rus. Fed. 95 G1
Malko Tŭrnovo Bulg. 69 L4
Mallacoota Australia 138 D6
Mallacoota Inlet b. Australia 138 D6
Mallaig U.K. 60 D4
Mallani reg. India 111 H5
Mallawī Egypt 112 C6
Mallee Cliffs National Park Australia 137 C7
Mallery Lake Canada 151 L1
Mallét Brazil 179 A4
Mallorca i. Spain see Majorca
Mallow Ireland 61 D5
Mallowa Well Australia 134 D5
Mallwyd U.K. 59 D6
Malm Norway 54 G4
Malmberget Sweden 54 L3
Malmédy Belgium 62 G4
Malmesbury S. Africa 124 D7
Malmesbury U.K. 59 E7
Malmö Sweden 55 H9
Malmyzh Rus. Fed. 52 K4
Malo i. Indon. 83 C1
Maloca Brazil 177 G3
Malolos Luzon Phil. 82 C3
Malone NY U.S.A. 165 H1
Malonje mt. Tanz. 123 D4
Maloshuyka Rus. Fed. 52 H3
Malosmadulu Atoll Maldives see Maalhosmadulu Atoll
Malovodnoye Kazakh. 98 B4
Måløy Norway 54 D6
Maloyaroslavets Rus. Fed. 53 H5
Malozemel'skaya Tundra lowland Rus. Fed. 52 K2
Malpaso Mex. 166 E4
Malpelo, Isla de i. N. Pacific Ocean 169 H8
Malprabha r. India 106 C2
Malta country Europe 68 F7
Malta Latvia 55 O8
Malta ID U.S.A. 156 E4
Malta MT U.S.A. 156 G2
Malta Channel Italy/Malta 68 F6
Maltahöhe Namibia 124 C3
Maltby U.K. 58 F5
Maltby le Marsh U.K. 58 H5
Malton U.K. 58 G4
Maluku is Indon. 83 C2
Maluku is Indon. see Moluccas
Maluku prov. Indon. 83 D3
Maluku, Laut sea Indon. 83 C3
Maluku Utara prov. Indon. 83 C3
Ma'lūlā, Jabal mts Syria 107 C3
Malung Sweden 55 H6
Maluti Mountains Lesotho 125 I5
Malu'u Solomon Is 133 G2
Malvan India 106 B2
Malvasia Greece see Monemvasia
Malvern U.K. see Great Malvern
Malvern AR U.S.A. 161 E5
Malvérnia Moz. see Chicualacuala
Malvinas, Islas terr. S. Atlantic Ocean see Falkland Islands
Malyn Ukr. 53 F6
Malyy Anyuy r. Rus. Fed. 77 R3
Malyye Derbety Rus. Fed. 53 J7
Malyy Kavkaz mts Asia see Lesser Caucasus
Malyy Kunaley Rus. Fed. 95 F1
Malyy Lyakhovskiy, Ostrov i. Rus. Fed. 77 P2
Malyy Uzen' r. Kazakh./Rus. Fed. 53 K6
Mamadysh Rus. Fed. 52 K5
Mamafubedu S. Africa 125 I4
Mamasa Sulawesi Barat Indon. 83 A3
Mamatān Nāvar l. Afgh. 111 G4
Mamba China 99 F7
Mamba Japan see Manba
Mambahenauhan i. Phil. 82 B5
Mambai Brazil 179 B1
Mambajao Phil. 82 D4
Mambasa Dem. Rep. Congo 122 C3
Mambi Sulawesi Barat Indon. 83 A3
Mamburao Mindoro Phil. 82 C3
Mamelodi S. Africa 125 I3
Mamfe Cameroon 120 D4
Mamit India 105 H5
Mammoth AZ U.S.A. 159 H5
Mammoth Cave National Park KY U.S.A. 164 B5
Mammoth Reservoir CA U.S.A. 158 D3
Mamonas Brazil 179 C1
Mamoré r. Bol./Brazil 176 E6
Mamou Guinea 120 B3
Mampikony Madag. 123 E5
Mampong Ghana 120 C4
Mamuju Sulawesi Barat Indon. 83 A3
Mamuno Botswana 124 E2
Man Côte d'Ivoire 120 C4
Man India 106 B2
Man r. India 106 B2
Man WV U.S.A. 164 E5

▶Man, Isle of terr. Irish Sea 58 C4
United Kingdom Crown Dependency.

Manacapuru Brazil 176 F4
Manacor Spain 67 H4
Manado Sulawesi Indon. 83 C2
Manadotua i. Indon. 83 C2

▶Managua Nicaragua 166 [inset] I6
Capital of Nicaragua.

Managua, Lago de l. Nicaragua 166 [inset] I6
Manakara Madag. 123 E6
Manakau mt. N.Z. 139 D6
Manākhah Yemen 108 F6

▶Manama Bahrain 110 C5
Capital of Bahrain.

Manamadurai India 106 C4
Mana Maroka National Park S. Africa 125 H5
Manamelkudi India 106 C4
Manam Island P.N.G. 81 L7
Mananara Avaratra Madag. 123 E5
Manangoora Australia 136 B3
Mananjary Madag. 123 E6
Manantali, Lac de l. Mali 120 B3
Manantenina Madag. 123 E6
Mana Pass China/India 99 B7
Mana Pools National Park Zimbabwe 123 C5

▶Manapouri, Lake N.Z. 139 A7
Deepest lake in Oceania.

Manas China 98 D3
Manasa India 104 C4
Manas He r. China 98 D3
Manas Hu l. China 98 D3
Manāşīr reg. U.A.E. 110 D6

▶Manaslu mt. Nepal 105 F3
8th highest mountain in Asia and the world.

Manassas VA U.S.A. 165 G4
Manastir Macedonia see Bitola
Manas Wildlife Sanctuary nature res. Bhutan 105 G4
Manatang Indon. 83 C5
Manatsuru Japan 93 F3
Manatuto East Timor 83 C5
Man-aung Myanmar 86 A3
Man-aung Kyun Myanmar 86 A3
Manaus Brazil 176 F4
Manavgat Turkey 112 C3
Manay Mindanao Phil. 82 D5
Manazuru-misaki pt Japan 93 F3
Manba Japan 93 E2
Manbazar India 105 F5
Manbij Syria 107 C1
Manby U.K. 58 H5
Mancelona MI U.S.A. 164 C1
Manchar India 106 B2
Manchester U.K. 58 E5
Manchester CT U.S.A. 165 I3
Manchester IA U.S.A. 160 F3
Manchester KY U.S.A. 164 D5
Manchester MD U.S.A. 165 G4
Manchester MI U.S.A. 164 C2
Manchester NH U.S.A. 165 J2
Manchester OH U.S.A. 164 D4
Manchester TN U.S.A. 162 C5
Manchester VT U.S.A. 165 I2
Mancılık Turkey 112 E3
Mand Pak. 111 F5
Mand, Rūd-e r. Iran 110 C4
Manda Tanz. 123 D4
Manda, Jebel mt. South Sudan 121 F4
Manda, Parc National de nat. park Chad 121 E4
Mandabe Madag. 123 E6
Mandah Sumatera Indon. 84 C3
Mandah Mongolia 95 G2
Mandai Sing. 87 [inset]
Mandal Bulgan Mongolia see Orhon
Mandal Töv Mongolia see Batsümber
Mandal Norway 55 E7

▶Mandala, Puncak mt. Indon. 81 K7
3rd highest mountain in Oceania.

Mandalay Myanmar 86 B2
Mandale Myanmar see Mandalay
Mandalgovĭ Mongolia 94 F2
Mandalī Iraq 113 G4
Mandal-Ovoo Mongolia 94 F2
Mandalt China 95 H3
Mandalt Sum China 95 H2
Mandan ND U.S.A. 160 C2
Mandaon Masbate Phil. 82 C3
Mandar, Teluk b. Indon. 83 A3
Mandas Sardinia Italy 68 C5
Mandasa India 106 E2
Mandasor India see Mandsaur
Mandav Hills India 104 B5
Mandera Kenya 122 E3
Manderfield UT U.S.A. 159 G2
Manderscheid Germany 62 G4
Mandeville Jamaica 169 I5
Mandeville N.Z. 139 B7
Mandha India 104 B4
Mandhoúdhíon Greece see Mantoudi
Mandi India 104 D3
Mandiana Guinea 120 C3
Mandi Angin, Gunung mt. Malaysia 84 C1
Mandié Moz. 123 D5
Mandini S. Africa 125 J5
Mandioli i. Maluku Indon. 83 C3
Mandira Dam India 105 F5
Mandla India 104 E5
Mandleshwar India 104 C5
Mandor Kalimantan Indon. 85 E2
Mandor, Cagar Alam nature res. Indon. 85 E2
Mandrael India 104 D4
Mandritsara Madag. 123 E5
Mandsaur India 104 C4
Mandul i. Indon. 85 G2
Mandurah Australia 135 A8
Manduria Italy 68 G4
Mandvi India 104 B5
Mandya India 106 C3
Manerbio Italy 68 D2
Manevychi Ukr. 53 E6
Manfalūţ Egypt 112 C6
Manfredonia Italy 68 F4
Manfredonia, Golfo di g. Italy 68 G4
Manga Brazil 179 C1
Manga Burkina Faso 120 C3
Mangabeiras, Serra das hills Brazil 177 I6
Mangai Dem. Rep. Congo 122 B4
Mangaia i. Cook Is 187 J7
Mangakino N.Z. 139 E4
Mangalagiri India 106 D2
Mangaldai India 86 A1
Mangaldoi India see Mangaldai
Mangalia Romania 69 M3
Mangalmé Chad 121 E3
Mangalore India 106 B3
Mangaon India 106 B2
Mangareva Islands Fr. Polynesia see Gambier, Îles
Mangaung Free State S. Africa 125 H5
Mangaung Free State S. Africa see Bloemfontein
Mangawan India 105 E4
Ma'ngê China see Luqu
Mangea i. Cook Is see Mangaia
Manggar Indon. 85 E3
Mangghyshlaq Kazakh. see Mangystau
Mangghystaū Kazakh. see Mangystau
Mangghystaū admin. div. Kazakh. see Mangistauskaya Oblast'
Mangghyt Uzbek. see Mang'it
Manghāl Afgh. 111 F3
Manghit Uzbek. see Mang'it
Mangin Range mts Myanmar see Mingin Range
Mangistau Kazakh. see Mangystau
Mangistauskaya Oblast' admin. div. Kazakh. 113 I2
Mang'it Uzbek. 102 B3
Mangkalihat, Tanjung pt Indon. 85 G2
Mangkutup r. Indon. 85 F3
Mangla Bangl. see Mongla
Mangla Pak. 111 I3
Mangnai China 99 E5
Mangochi Malawi 123 D5
Mangoky r. Madag. 123 E6
Mangole i. Indon. 83 C3
Mangole, Selat sea chan. Indon. 83 C3
Mangoli India 106 B2
Mangotsfield U.K. 59 E7
Mangqystaū Shyghanaghy b. Kazakh. see Mangyshlakskiy Zaliv
Mangra China see Guinan
Mangrol India 104 B5
Mangrul India 106 C1
Mangshi China see Luxi
Mangualde Port. 67 C3
Manguéni, Plateau du Niger 120 E2
Mangui China 90 A2
Mangula Zimbabwe see Mhangura
Mangulile Hond. 166 [inset] I6
Mangum OK U.S.A. 161 D5
Mangupung i. Indon. 83 C1
Mangut Rus. Fed. 95 H1
Mangyshlak Kazakh. see Mangystau
Mangyshlak, Poluostrov pen. Kazakh. 113 H1
Mangyshlak Oblast admin. div. Kazakh. see Mangistauskaya Oblast'
Mangyshlakskaya Oblast' admin. div. Kazakh. see Mangistauskaya Oblast'
Mangyshlakskiy Zaliv b. Kazakh. 113 H1
Mangystau Kazakh. 113 H2
Manhā Brazil 179 B1
Manhan Hovd Mongolia 94 C2
Manhan Hövsgöl Mongolia see Alag-Erdene
Manhattan KS U.S.A. 160 D4
Manhica Moz. 125 K3
Manhoca Moz. 125 K4
Manhuaçu Brazil 179 C3
Manhuaçu r. Brazil 179 C2
Mani China 99 D6
Mania r. Madag. 123 E5
Maniago Italy 68 E1
Manicouagan Canada 153 H4
Manicouagan r. Canada 153 H4
Manicouagan, Réservoir resr Canada 153 H4
Manic Trois, Réservoir resr Canada 153 H4
Manīfah Saudi Arabia 110 C5
Maniganggo China 96 C2
Manigotagan Canada 151 L5
Manihiki atoll Cook Is 186 J6
Maniitsoq Greenland 147 M3
Manikchhari Bangl. 105 H5
Manikgarh India see Rajura

▶Manila Luzon Phil. 82 C3
Capital of the Philippines.

Manila UT U.S.A. 156 F4
Manila Bay Luzon Phil. 82 C3
Manildra Australia 138 D4
Manilla Australia 138 E3
Manimbaya, Tanjung pt Indon. 83 A3
Maningrida Australia 134 F3
Maninjau, Danau l. Indon. 84 C3
Manipa i. Maluku Indon. 83 C3
Manipa, Selat sea chan. Maluku Indon. 83 C3
Manipur India see Imphal
Manipur state India 105 H4
Manisa Turkey 69 L5
Manismata Kalimantan Indon. 85 E3
Manistee MI U.S.A. 164 B1
Manistee r. MI U.S.A. 164 B1
Manistique MI U.S.A. 162 C2
Manitoba prov. Canada 151 L4
Manitoba, Lake Canada 151 L5
Manito Lake Canada 151 I4
Manitou Canada 151 L5
Manitou, Lake IN U.S.A. 164 B3
Manitou Beach NY U.S.A. 165 G2
Manitou Falls Canada 151 M5
Manitou Islands MI U.S.A. 164 B1
Manitoulin Island Canada 152 E5
Manitouwadge Canada 152 D4
Manitowoc WI U.S.A. 164 B1
Maniwaki Canada 152 G5
Manizales Col. 176 C2
Manja Madag. 123 E6
Manjarabad India 106 B3
Manjeri India 106 C4
Manjhand Pak. 111 H5
Manjhi India 105 F4
Manjra r. India 106 C2
Man Kabat Myanmar 86 B1
Mankaiana Swaziland see Mankayane
Mankato KS U.S.A. 160 D4
Mankato MN U.S.A. 160 E2
Mankayane Swaziland 125 J4
Mankera Pak. 111 H4
Mankono Côte d'Ivoire 120 C4
Mankota Canada 151 J5
Manlay Mongolia 94 F2
Manley Hot Springs AK U.S.A. 149 J2
Manmad India 106 B1
Mann r. Australia 134 F3
Mann, Mount Australia 135 E6
Manna Sumatera Indon. 84 C4
Man Na Myanmar 86 B2
Mannahill Australia 137 B7
Mannar Sri Lanka 106 C4
Mannar, Gulf of India/Sri Lanka 106 C4
Manneru r. India 106 D3
Mannessier, Lac l. Canada 153 H3
Mannheim Germany 63 I5
Mannicolo Islands Solomon Is see Vanikoro Islands
Manning r. Australia 138 F3
Manning Canada 150 G3
Manning SC U.S.A. 163 D5
Mannington WV U.S.A. 164 E4
Manningtree U.K. 59 I7
Mann Ranges mts Australia 135 E6
Mannsville KY U.S.A. 164 C5
Mannsville NY U.S.A. 165 G2
Mannu, Capo c. Sardinia Italy 68 C4
Mannville Canada 151 I4
Man-of-War Rocks is HI U.S.A. see Gardner Pinnacles
Manoharpur India 99 B8
Manohar Thana India 104 D4
Manokotak AK U.S.A. 148 H4
Manokwari Indon. 81 I7
Manoron Myanmar 87 B5
Manosque France 66 G5
Manouane r. Canada 153 H4
Manouane, Lac l. Canada 153 H4
Manouba town Tunisia 68 D6
Manovo-Gounda Saint Floris, Parc National du nat. park Cent. Afr. Rep. 122 C3
Man Pan Myanmar 86 B2
Manp'o N. Korea 90 B4
Manra i. Kiribati 133 I2
Manresa Spain 67 G3
Mansa Gujarat India 104 C5
Mansa Punjab India 104 C3
Mansa Zambia 123 C5
Mansalean Sulawesi Indon. 83 B3
Man Sam Myanmar 86 B2
Mansehra Pak. 109 L3
Mansel Island Canada 147 K3
Mansfield Australia 138 C6
Mansfield U.K. 59 F5
Mansfield LA U.S.A. 161 E5
Mansfield OH U.S.A. 164 D3
Mansfield PA U.S.A. 165 G3
Mansfield, Mount VT U.S.A. 165 I1
Man Si Myanmar 86 B1
Mansi Myanmar 86 A1
Manso r. Brazil see Mortes, Rio das
Mansuela Seram Indon. 83 D3
Manta Ecuador 176 B4
Mantalingajan, Mount Palawan Phil. 82 B4
Mantarara Maluku Indon. 83 C3
Mantaro r. Peru 176 D6
Manteca CA U.S.A. 158 C3
Mantehage i. Indon. 83 C2
Mantena Brazil 179 C2
Manteo NC U.S.A. 162 F5
Mantes-la-Jolie France 62 B6
Mantiqueira, Serra da mts Brazil 179 B3
Manto Hond. 166 [inset] I6
Manton MI U.S.A. 164 C1
Mantoudi Greece 69 J5
Mantova Italy see Mantua
Mäntsälä Fin. 55 N6
Mänttä Fin. 54 N5
Mantua Cuba 163 C8
Mantua Italy 68 D2
Mantuan Downs Australia 136 D5
Manturovo Rus. Fed. 52 J4
Mäntyharju Fin. 55 O6
Mäntyjärvi Fin. 54 O3
Manú Peru 176 D6
Manu, Parque Nacional nat. park Peru 176 D6
Manuae atoll Fr. Polynesia 187 J7
Manu'a Islands American Samoa 133 I3
Manuel Ribas Brazil 179 A4
Manuel Vitorino Brazil 179 C1
Manuelzinho Brazil 177 H5
Manui i. Indon. 83 B3
Manuk i. Maluku Indon. 83 D4
Manukan Mindanao Phil. 82 C4
Manukau N.Z. 139 E3
Manukau Harbour N.Z. 139 E3
Manuk Manka i. Phil. 82 B5
Manunda watercourse Australia 137 B7
Manusela, Taman Nasional nat. park Seram Indon. 83 D3
Manus Island P.N.G. 81 L7
Manvi India 106 C3
Many LA U.S.A. 161 E6
Manyana Botswana 125 G3
Manyas Turkey 69 L4
Manyas Gölü l. Turkey see Kuş Gölü
Many Island Lake Canada 151 I5
Manyoni Tanz. 123 D4
Manzai Pak. 111 H3
Manzanares Spain 67 E4
Manzanillo Cuba 169 I4
Manzanillo Mex. 168 D5
Manzanillo, Punta pt Panama 166 [inset] K7

Manzhouli China 95 I1
Manzini Swaziland 125 J4
Mao Chad 121 E3
Maó Spain see Mahón
Maoba Guizhou China 96 E3
Maoba Hubei China 97 F2
Mao'ergai China 96 D1
Maojiachuan China 94 F4
Maojing China 94 F4
Maoke, Pegunungan mts Indon. 81 J7
Maokeng S. Africa 125 H4
Maokui Shan mt. China 90 A4
Maolin China 95 J3
Maomao Shan mt. China 94 E4
Maoming China 97 F4
Maoniupo China 99 D6
Maoniushan China 94 D4
Ma On Shan hill H.K. China 97 [inset]
Maopi T'ou c. Taiwan 97 I4
Maopora i. Maluku Indon. 83 C4
Maotou Shan mt. China 96 D3
Mapai Moz. 125 J2
Mapam Yumco l. China 99 C7
Mapane Sulawesi Indon. 83 B3
Mapanza Zambia 123 C5
Mapastepec Mex. 167 G6
Maphodi S. Africa 125 G6
Mapimí Mex. 166 E3
Mapinhane Moz. 125 L2
Mapiri Bol. 176 E7
Maple r. MI U.S.A. 164 C2
Maple r. ND U.S.A. 160 D2
Maple Creek Canada 151 I5
Maple Heights OH U.S.A. 164 E3
Maple Peak AZ U.S.A. 159 I5
Mapmaker Seamounts sea feature N. Pacific Ocean 186 H4
Mapoon Australia 136 C1
Mapor i. Indon. 84 D2
Mapoteng Lesotho 125 H5
Maprik P.N.G. 81 K7
Mapuera r. Brazil 177 G4
Mapulanguene Moz. 125 K3
Mapungubwe National Park S. Africa 125 I2

▶Maputo Moz. 125 K3
Capital of Mozambique.

Maputo prov. Moz. 125 K3
Maputo r. Moz./S. Africa 125 K4
Maputo, Baía de b. Moz. 125 K4
Maputsoe Lesotho 125 H5
Maqanshy Kazakh. see Makanchi
Maqar an Na'am well Iraq 113 F5
Maqat Kazakh. see Makat
Maqên Qinghai China 94 E5
Maqên Xizang China 99 E7
Maqên Kangri mt. China 94 D5
Maqiao China 98 D3
Maqnā Saudi Arabia 112 D5
Maqṭeïr reg. Mauritania 120 B2
Maqu China 96 D1
Ma Qu r. China see Yellow River
Maquan He r. China 99 D7
Maqueda Channel Phil. 82 C3
Maquela do Zombo Angola 123 B4
Maquinchao Arg. 178 C6
Mar r. Pak. 111 G5
Mar, Serra do mts Rio de Janeiro/São Paulo Brazil 179 B3
Mar, Serra do mts Rio Grande do Sul/Santa Catarina Brazil 179 A5
Mara r. Canada 151 I1
Mara India 105 E5
Mara S. Africa 125 I2
Maraã Brazil 176 E4
Marabá Brazil 177 I5
Marabahan Kalimantan Indon. 85 F3
Marabatua i. Indon. 85 F4
Maraboon, Lake resr Australia 136 E4
Maracá, Ilha de i. Brazil 177 H3
Maracaibo Venez. 176 D1
Maracaibo, Lago de Venez. see Maracaibo, Lake
Maracaibo, Lake Venez. 176 D2
Maracaju Brazil 178 E2
Maracaju, Serra de hills Brazil 178 E2
Maracanda Uzbek. see Samarqand
Maracás Brazil 179 C1
Maracás, Chapada de hills Brazil 179 C1
Maracay Venez. 176 E1
Marādah Libya 121 E2
Maradi Niger 120 D3
Marāgheh Iran 110 B2
Maragondon Luzon Phil. 82 C3
Marahuaca, Cerro mt. Venez. 176 E3
Marajó, Baía de est. Brazil 177 I4
Marajó, Ilha de i. Brazil 177 H4
Marakele National Park S. Africa 125 H3
Maralal Kenya 122 D3
Maralbashi China see Bachu
Maralinga Australia 135 E7
Maralwexi China see Bachu
Maramasike i. Solomon Is 133 G2
Maramba Zambia see Livingstone
Marambio research station Antarctica 188 A2
Marampit i. Indon. 83 C1
Maran Malaysia 84 C2
Marana AZ U.S.A. 159 H5
Marand Iran 110 B2
Marandellas Zimbabwe see Marondera
Marang Malaysia 84 C1
Marang Myanmar 87 B5
Maranhão r. Brazil 179 A1
Maranoa r. Australia 138 D1
Marañón r. Peru 176 D4
Marão Moz. 125 L3
Marão mt. Port. 67 C3
Marapi, Gunung vol. Sumatera Indon. 84 C3
Mara Rosa Brazil 179 A1
Maraş Turkey see Kahramanmaraş
Marasende i. Indon. 85 G4
Marathon Canada 152 D4
Marathon FL U.S.A. 163 D7
Marathon NY U.S.A. 165 G2
Marathon TX U.S.A. 161 C6
Maratua i. Indon. 85 G2
Maraú Brazil 179 D1
Marau Kalimantan Indon. 85 E3
Maravillas Creek watercourse TX U.S.A. 161 C6
Marawi Mindanao Phil. 82 D4
Mārāzā Azer. 113 H2
Marbella Spain 67 D5
Marble Bar Australia 134 B5
Marble Canyon AZ U.S.A. 159 H3
Marble Canyon gorge AZ U.S.A. 159 H3
Marble Hall S. Africa 125 I3
Marble Hill MO U.S.A. 161 F4
Marble Island Canada 151 N2
Marbul Pass India 104 C2
Marburg S. Africa 125 J6
Marburg Slovenia see Maribor
Marburg an der Lahn Germany 63 I4
Marca, Ponta do pt Angola 123 B5
Marcala Hond. 166 [inset] H6
Marcali Hungary 68 G1
Marcelino Ramos Brazil 179 A4
March U.K. 59 H6
Marche reg. France 66 E3
Marche-en-Famenne Belgium 62 F4
Marchena Spain 67 D5
Marchinbar Island Australia 136 B1
Mar Chiquita, Laguna l. Arg. 178 D4
Marchtrenk Austria 57 O6
Marco FL U.S.A. 163 D7
Marcoing France 62 D4
Marcona Peru 176 C7
Marcopeet Islands Canada 152 F2
Marcus Baker, Mount AK U.S.A. 149 K3
Marcy, Mount NY U.S.A. 165 I1
Mardan Pak. 111 I3
Mar del Plata Arg. 178 E5
Mardin Turkey 113 F3
Mardzad Mongolia see Hayrhandulaan
Maré i. New Caledonia 133 G4
Maree, Loch l. U.K. 60 D3
Mareh Iran 111 E5
Marengo IA U.S.A. 160 E3
Marengo IN U.S.A. 164 B4
Marevo Rus. Fed. 52 G4
Marfa TX U.S.A. 161 B6
Margai Caka l. China 99 D6
Margam Ri mts China 99 D6
Marganets Ukr. see Marhanets'
Margao India see Madgaon
Margaret r. Australia 134 D4
Margaret watercourse Australia 137 B6
Margaret, Mount hill Australia 134 B5
Margaret Lake Alta Canada 150 H3
Margaret Lake N.W.T. Canada 150 G1
Margaret River Australia 135 A8
Margaretville NY U.S.A. 165 H2
Margarita, Isla de i. Venez. 176 F1
Margaritovo Rus. Fed. 90 D4
Margate U.K. 59 I7
Margherita, Lake Eth. see Abaya, Lake

▶Margherita Peak Dem. Rep. Congo/Uganda 122 C3
3rd highest mountain in Africa.

Marghilon Uzbek. see Marg'ilon
Marg'ilon Uzbek. 102 D3
Mārgo, Dasht-i des. Afgh. see Māragow, Dasht-e
Margog Caka l. China 99 D6
Margosatubig Mindanao Phil. 82 C5
Mārgow, Dasht-e des. Afgh. 111 F4
Margraten Neth. 62 F4
Marguerite Canada 150 F4
Marguerite, Pic mt. Dem. Rep. Congo/Uganda see Margherita Peak
Marguerite Bay Antarctica 188 L2
Margyang China 99 E7
Marhaj Khalīl Iraq 113 G4
Marhanets' Ukr. 53 G7
Marhoum Alg. 64 D5
Mari Myanmar 86 B1
Maria atoll Fr. Polynesia 187 J7
María Cleofas, Isla i. Mex. 166 D4
María Elena Chile 178 C2
Maria Island Australia 136 A2
Maria Island Myanmar 87 B5
Maria Island National Park Australia 137 [inset]
Mariala National Park Australia 137 D5
María Madre, Isla i. Mex. 166 D4
María Magdelena, Isla i. Mex. 166 D4
Mariana Brazil 179 C3
Marianao Cuba 163 D8
Mariana Ridge sea feature N. Pacific Ocean 186 F4

▶Mariana Trench sea feature N. Pacific Ocean 186 F5
Deepest trench in the world.

Mariani India 105 H4
Mariánica, Cordillera mts Spain see Morena, Sierra
Marian Lake Canada 150 G2
Marianna AR U.S.A. 161 F5
Marianna FL U.S.A. 163 C6
Mariano Machado Angola see Ganda
Mariánské Lázně Czech Rep. 63 M5
Marias r. MT U.S.A. 156 F3
Marías, Islas is Mex. 168 C4

▶Mariato, Punta pt Panama 166 [inset] J8
Most southerly point of North America.

Maria van Diemen, Cape N.Z. 139 D2
Ma'rib Yemen 108 G6
Maribor Slovenia 68 F1
Marica r. Bulg. see Maritsa
Maricopa AZ U.S.A. 159 G5
Maricopa CA U.S.A. 158 D4
Maricopa Mountains AZ U.S.A. 159 G5
Maridi South Sudan 121 F4
Marie Byrd Land reg. Antarctica 188 J1
Marie-Galante i. Guadeloupe 169 L5
Mariehamn Fin. 55 K6
Mariembero r. Brazil 179 A1
Marienbad Czech Rep. see Mariánské Lázně
Marienberg Germany 63 N4
Marienburg Poland see Malbork
Marienhafe Germany 63 H1
Mariental Namibia 124 C3
Marienwerder Poland see Kwidzyn
Mariestad Sweden 55 H7
Mariet r. Canada 152 F2
Marietta GA U.S.A. 163 C5
Marietta OH U.S.A. 164 E4
Marietta OK U.S.A. 161 D5
Marignane France 66 G5
Marii, Mys pt Rus. Fed. 78 G2
Mariinsk Rus. Fed. 76 J4
Mariinskiy Posad Rus. Fed. 52 J4
Marijampolė Lith. 55 M9
Marília Brazil 179 A3
Marillana Australia 134 B5
Marimba Angola 123 B4
Marimun Kalimantan Indon. 85 F3
Marín Mex. 167 E3
Marin mt. Pak. 111 G4
Marín Spain 67 B2
Marina CA U.S.A. 158 C3
Marina di Gioiosa Ionica Italy 68 G5
Mar'ina Gorka Belarus see Mar"ina Horka
Mar"ina Horka Belarus 55 P10
Marinduque i. Phil. 82 C3
Marinette WI U.S.A. 164 B1
Maringá Brazil 179 A3
Maringa r. Dem. Rep. Congo 122 B3
Maringo OH U.S.A. 164 D3
Marinha Grande Port. 67 B4
Marion AL U.S.A. 163 C5
Marion AR U.S.A. 161 F5
Marion IL U.S.A. 160 F4
Marion IN U.S.A. 164 C3
Marion KS U.S.A. 160 D4
Marion MI U.S.A. 164 C1
Marion NY U.S.A. 165 G2
Marion OH U.S.A. 164 D3
Marion SC U.S.A. 163 E5
Marion VA U.S.A. 164 E5
Marion, Lake SC U.S.A. 163 D5
Marion Reef Australia 136 F3
Maripa Venez. 176 E2
Mariposa CA U.S.A. 158 D3
Marisa Sulawesi Indon. 83 B2
Mariscala Mex. 167 F5
Mariscal José Félix Estigarribia Para. 178 D2
Maritime Alps mts France/Italy 66 H4
Maritime Kray admin. div. Rus. Fed. see Primorskiy Kray
Maritimes, Alpes mts France/Italy see Maritime Alps
Maritsa r. Bulg. 69 L4
also known as Evros (Greece), Marica (Bulgaria), Meriç (Turkey)
Marittime, Alpi mts France/Italy see Maritime Alps
Mariupol' Ukr. 53 H7
Mariusa, Parque Nacional nat. park Venez. 176 F2
Marīvān Iran 110 B3
Marjan Afgh. see Wazi Khwa
Marjayoûn Lebanon 107 B3
Marka Somalia 122 E3
Markakol', Ozero l. Kazakh. 98 D2
Markala Mali 120 C3
Markam China 96 C2
Markaryd Sweden 55 H8
Markaz-e Sayyidābād Afgh. 111 H3
Markdale Canada 164 E1
Marken S. Africa 125 I2
Markermeer l. Neth. 62 F2
Market Deeping U.K. 59 G6
Market Drayton U.K. 59 E6
Market Harborough U.K. 59 G6
Markethill U.K. 61 F3
Market Weighton U.K. 58 G5
Markha r. Rus. Fed. 77 M3
Markham Canada 164 F2
Markit China 98 B5
Markkleeberg Germany 63 M3
Markleeville CA U.S.A. 158 D2
Marklohe Germany 63 J2
Markog Qu r. China 96 D1
Markounda Cent. Afr. Rep. 122 B3
Markovo Rus. Fed. 77 S3
Markranstädt Germany 63 M3
Marks Rus. Fed. 53 J6
Marks MS U.S.A. 161 F5
Marksville LA U.S.A. 161 E6
Marktheidenfeld Germany 63 J5
Marktredwitz Germany 63 M4
Marl Germany 62 H3
Marla Australia 135 F6
Marlborough Downs hills U.K. 59 F7
Marle France 62 D5
Marlette MI U.S.A. 164 D2
Marlin TX U.S.A. 161 D6
Marlinton WV U.S.A. 164 E4
Marlo Australia 138 D6
Marmagao India 106 B3
Marmande France 66 E4
Marmara, Sea of g. Turkey 69 M4
Marmara Denizi g. Turkey see Marmara, Sea of
Marmara Gölü l. Turkey 69 M5
Marmarica reg. Libya 112 B5
Marmaris Turkey 69 M6
Marmarth ND U.S.A. 160 C2
Marmê China 99 C6
Marmet WV U.S.A. 164 E4
Marmion, Lake salt l. Australia 135 C7
Marmion Lake Canada 151 N5
Marmolada mt. Italy 68 D1
Marmot Bay AK U.S.A. 148 I4
Marmot Island AK U.S.A. 149 J4
Marne r. France 62 C6
Marne-la-Vallée France 62 C6
Marnitz Germany 63 L1
Maroantsetra Madag. 123 E5
Maroc country Africa see Morocco
Marol Pak. 104 D2
Maroldsweisach Germany 63 K4
Maromokotro mt. Madag. 123 E5
Marondera Zimbabwe 123 D5
Maroochydore Australia 138 F1
Maroonah Australia 135 A5
Maroon Peak CO U.S.A. 156 G5
Maros Sulawesi Indon. 83 A4
Maros r. Indon. 83 A4
Marosvásárhely Romania see Târgu Mureş
Marot Pak. 111 I4
Maroua Cameroon 121 E3
Marovoay Madag. 123 E5
Marowali Sulawesi Indon. 83 B3
Marqādah Syria 113 F4
Mar Qu r. China see Markog Qu
Marquard S. Africa 125 H5
Marquesas Islands Fr. Polynesia 187 K6
Marquesas Keys is FL U.S.A. 163 D7
Marquês de Valença Brazil 179 C3
Marquette MI U.S.A. 162 C2
Marquez TX U.S.A. 161 D6
Marquion France 62 D4
Marquise France 62 B4
Marquises, Îles is Fr. Polynesia see Marquesas Islands
Marra Australia 138 A3
Marra r. Australia 138 C3
Marra, Jebel mt. Sudan 121 F3
Marra, Jebel Sudan 121 F3
Marracuene Moz. 125 K3
Marrakech Morocco 64 C5
Marrakesh Morocco see Marrakech
Marrangua, Lagoa l. Moz. 125 L3
Marrar Australia 138 C5
Marrawah Australia 137 [inset]
Marree Australia 137 B6
Marrowbone KY U.S.A. 164 C5
Marruecos country Africa see Morocco
Marrupa Moz. 123 D5
Marryat Australia 135 F6
Marsá al 'Alam Egypt 108 D4
Marsa 'Alam Egypt see Marsá al 'Alam
Marsa al Burayqah Libya 121 E1
Marsabit Kenya 122 D3
Marsala Sicily Italy 68 E6
Marsá Maṭrūḥ Egypt 112 B5
Marsberg Germany 63 I3
Marsciano Italy 68 E3
Marsden Australia 138 C4
Marsden Canada 151 I4
Marsdiep sea chan. Neth. 62 E2
Marseille France 66 G5
Marseilles France see Marseille
Marsfjället mt. Sweden 54 I4
Marshall watercourse Australia 136 B4
Marshall AK U.S.A. 148 G3
Marshall AR U.S.A. 161 E5
Marshall IL U.S.A. 164 B4
Marshall MI U.S.A. 164 C2
Marshall MN U.S.A. 160 E2
Marshall MO U.S.A. 160 E4
Marshall TX U.S.A. 161 E5
Marshall Islands country N. Pacific Ocean 186 H5
Marshalltown IA U.S.A. 160 E3
Marshfield MO U.S.A. 161 E4
Marshfield WI U.S.A. 160 F2
Marsh Harbour Bahamas 163 E7
Mars Hill ME U.S.A. 162 H2
Marsh Island LA U.S.A. 161 F6
Marsh Lake Canada 149 N3
Marsh Lake l. Canada 149 N3
Marsh Peak UT U.S.A. 159 I1
Marsh Point Canada 151 M3
Marsing ID U.S.A. 156 D4
Märsta Sweden 55 J7
Marsyaty Rus. Fed. 51 S3
Martaban, Gulf of Myanmar see Mottama, Gulf of
Martanai Besar i. Malaysia 85 G1
Martapura Kalimantan Indon. 85 F3
Martapura Sumatera Indon. 84 D4
Marten River Canada 152 F5
Marte R. Gómez, Presa resr Mex. 167 F3
Martha's Vineyard i. MA U.S.A. 165 J3
Martigny Switz. 66 H3
Martim Vaz, Ilhas is S. Atlantic Ocean see Martin Vas, Ilhas
Martin r. Canada 150 F2
Martin Slovakia 57 Q6
Martin MI U.S.A. 164 C2
Martin SD U.S.A. 160 C3
Martínez Mex. 167 F4
Martinez Lake AZ U.S.A. 159 F5
Martinho Campos Brazil 179 B2

▶Martinique terr. West Indies 169 L6
French Overseas Department.

Martinique Passage Dominica/Martinique 169 L5
Martin Peninsula Antarctica 188 K2
Martin Point pt AK U.S.A. 149 L1
Martinsburg WV U.S.A. 165 G4
Martins Ferry OH U.S.A. 164 E3
Martinsville IL U.S.A. 164 B4
Martinsville IN U.S.A. 164 B4
Martinsville VA U.S.A. 164 F5

▶Martin Vas, Ilhas is S. Atlantic Ocean 184 G7
Most easterly point of South America.

Martin Vaz Islands S. Atlantic Ocean see Martin Vas, Ilhas
Martök Kazakh. see Martuk
Marton N.Z. 139 E5
Martorell Spain 67 G3
Martos Spain 67 E5
Martuk Kazakh. 100 E1
Martuni Armenia 113 G2
Maru China 94 E5
Marudi Sarawak Malaysia 85 F1
Marudu, Teluk b. Malaysia 85 G1
Ma'rūf Afgh. 111 G4
Maruim Brazil 177 K6
Marukhis Ugheltekhili pass Georgia/Rus. Fed. 113 F2
Maruko Japan 93 E2
Marulan Australia 138 D5
Maruoka Japan 92 C2
Marusthali reg. India 111 H5
Maruyama Japan 93 F3
Maruyama-gawa r. Japan 92 A3
Marvast Iran 110 D4
Marv Dasht Iran 110 D4
Marvejols France 66 F4
Marvine, Mount UT U.S.A. 159 H2
Marwayne Canada 151 I4
Mary r. Australia 134 E3
Mary Turkm. 111 F2
Maryborough Qld Australia 137 F5
Maryborough Vic. Australia 138 A6
Marydale S. Africa 124 F5
Mary Frances Lake Canada 151 J2
Mary Lake Canada 151 K2
Maryland state U.S.A. 165 G4
Maryport U.K. 58 D4
Mary's Harbour Canada 153 L3
Marys Igloo AK U.S.A. 148 F2
Marysvale UT U.S.A. 159 G2
Marysville CA U.S.A. 158 C2
Marysville KS U.S.A. 160 D4
Marysville OH U.S.A. 164 D3
Maryvale N.T. Australia 135 F6
Maryvale Qld Australia 136 D3
Maryville MO U.S.A. 160 E3
Maryville TN U.S.A. 162 D5
Marzagão Brazil 179 A2
Marzahna Germany 63 M2
Masachapa Nicaragua 166 [inset] I7
Masada tourist site Israel 107 B4
Masagua Guat. 167 H6
Masāhūn, Kūh-e mt. Iran 110 D4
Masai Steppe plain Tanz. 123 D4
Masaka Uganda 122 D4
Masakhane S. Africa 125 H6
Masalembu Besar i. Indon. 85 F4
Masalembu Kecil i. Indon. 85 F4
Masallı Azer. 113 H3
Masamba Sulawesi Indon. 83 B3
Masamba mt. Indon. 83 B3
Masan S. Korea 91 C6
Masapun Maluku Indon. 83 C4
Masasi Tanz. 123 D5
Masavi Bol. 176 F7
Masaya Nicaragua 166 [inset] I7
Masaya, Volcán vol. Nicaragua 166 [inset] I7
Masbate Masbate Phil. 82 C3
Masbate i. Phil. 82 C3
Mascara Alg. 67 G6
Mascarene Basin sea feature Indian Ocean 185 L7
Mascarene Plain sea feature Indian Ocean 185 L7
Mascarene Ridge sea feature Indian Ocean 185 L6
Mascota Mex. 166 D4
Mascote Brazil 179 D1
Masein Myanmar 86 A2
Ma Sekatok b. Indon. 85 G2
Masela Maluku Indon. 83 D5
Masela i. Maluku Indon. 83 D5
Masepe i. Indon. 83 B3

▶Maseru Lesotho 125 H5
Capital of Lesotho.

Mashai Lesotho 125 I5
Mashan China 97 F4
Masherbrum mt. Pak. 104 D2
Mashhad Iran 111 E2
Mashiko Japan 93 G2
Mashishing S. Africa 125 J3
Mashkel, Rudi-i r. Pak. 111 F5
Mashki Chah Pak. 111 F4
Masi Norway 54 M2
Masiáca Mex. 166 C3
Masibambane S. Africa 125 H6
Masīlah, Wādī al watercourse Yemen 108 H6
Masilo S. Africa 125 H5
Masi-Manimba Dem. Rep. Congo 123 B4
Masimbu Sulawesi Barat Indon. 83 A3
Masindi Uganda 122 D3
Masinloc Luzon Phil. 82 B3
Masinyusane S. Africa 124 F6
Masira, Gulf of Oman see Maşīrah, Khalīj
Maşīrah, Jazīrat i. Oman 109 I5
Maşīrah, Khalīj b. Oman 109 I6
Masira Island Oman see Maşīrah, Jazīrat
Masiwang r. Seram Indon. 83 D3
Masjed-e Soleymān Iran 110 C4
Mask, Lough l. Ireland 61 C4
Maskūtān Iran 111 E5
Maslovo Rus. Fed. 51 S3
Masoala, Tanjona c. Madag. 123 F5
Masohi Seram Indon. 83 D3
Mason MI U.S.A. 164 C2
Mason OH U.S.A. 164 C4
Mason TX U.S.A. 161 D6
Mason, Lake salt flat Australia 135 B6
Mason Bay N.Z. 139 A8
Mason City IA U.S.A. 160 E3
Masoni i. Indon. 83 C3
Masontown PA U.S.A. 164 F4
Masqaţ Oman see Muscat
Masqaţ reg. Oman see Muscat
'Masrūg well Oman 110 D6
Massa Italy 68 D2
Massachusetts state U.S.A. 165 I2
Massachusetts Bay MA U.S.A. 165 J2
Massadona CO U.S.A. 159 I1
Massafra Italy 68 G4
Massakory Chad 121 E3
Massa Marittimo Italy 68 D3
Massangena Moz. 123 D6
Massango Angola 123 B4
Massawa Eritrea 108 E6
Massawippi, Lac l. Canada 165 I1
Massena NY U.S.A. 165 H1
Massenya Chad 121 E3
Masset Canada 149 N5
Massieville OH U.S.A. 164 D4
Massif Central mts France 66 F4
Massilia France see Marseille
Massillon OH U.S.A. 164 E3
Massina Mali 120 C3
Massinga Moz. 125 L2
Massingir Moz. 125 K2
Massingir, Barragem de resr Moz. 125 K2
Masson Island Antarctica 188 F2
Mastchoh Tajik. 111 H2
Masteksay Kazakh. 53 K6
Masterton N.Z. 139 E5
Masticho, Akra pt Greece see Oura, Akrotirio
Mastung Pak. 100 F4
Mastūrah Saudi Arabia 108 E5
Masty Belarus 55 N10
Masuda Japan 91 C6
Masuho Japan 93 E3
Masuku Gabon see Franceville
Masulipatam India see Machilipatnam
Masulipatnam India see Machilipatnam
Masuna i. American Samoa see Tutuila
Masurai, Bukit mt. Indon. 84 C3
Masvingo Zimbabwe 123 D6
Masvingo prov. Zimbabwe 125 J1
Maswa Tanz. 122 D4
Maswaar i. Indon. 81 I7
Maşyāf Syria 107 C2
Mat, Nam r. Laos 86 D3
Mata Myanmar 86 B1
Matabeleland South prov. Zimbabwe 125 I1
Matachewan Canada 152 E5
Matachic Mex. 166 D2
Matad Mongolia 95 H2
Matadi Dem. Rep. Congo 123 B4
Matador TX U.S.A. 161 C5
Matagalpa Nicaragua 166 [inset] I6
Matagami Canada 152 F4
Matagami, Lac l. Canada 152 F4
Matagorda TX U.S.A. 167 F2
Matagorda Island TX U.S.A. 161 D6
Mataigou China see Taole
Matak i. Indon. 84 D2
Matak Kazakh. 98 A2
Matakana Island N.Z. 139 F3
Matala Angola 123 B5
Maţāli', Jabal hill Saudi Arabia 113 F6
Matam Senegal 120 B3
Matamey Niger 120 D3
Matamoras PA U.S.A. 165 H3
Matamoros Coahuila Mex. 166 E3
Matamoros Tamaulipas Mex. 167 F3
Matana, Danau l. Indon. 83 B3
Matanal Point Phil. 82 C5
Matandu r. Tanz. 123 D4
Matane Canada 153 I4
Matanuska AK U.S.A. 149 J3
Matanzas Cuba 169 H4
Matapalo, Cabo c. Costa Rica 166 [inset] J7
Matapan, Cape pt Greece see Tainaro, Akrotirio
Matapédia, Lac l. Canada 153 I4
Maţār well Saudi Arabia 110 B5
Matara Sri Lanka 106 D5
Mataram Lombok Indon. 85 G5
Matarani Peru 176 D7
Mataranka Australia 134 F3
Matarape, Teluk b. Indon. 83 B3
Matarinao Bay Samar Phil. 82 D4
Matarípe Brazil 179 D1
Mataró Spain 67 H3
Matarombea r. Indon. 83 B3
Matasiri i. Indon. 85 F4
Matatiele S. Africa 125 I6
Matatila Reservoir India 104 D4
Mataura N.Z. 139 B8
Mata-Utu Wallis and Futuna Is see Matā'utu

▶Matā'utu Wallis and Futuna Is 133 I3
Capital of Wallis and Futuna Islands.

Matawai N.Z. 139 F4
Matay Kazakh. 102 E2
Matcha Tajik. see Mastchoh
Mat Con, Hon i. Vietnam 86 D3
Mategua Bol. 176 F6
Matehuala Mex. 161 C8
Matemanga Tanz. 123 D5
Matera Italy 68 G4
Mateur Tunisia 68 C6
Mathaji India 104 B4
Matheson Canada 152 E4
Mathews VA U.S.A. 165 G5
Mathis TX U.S.A. 161 D6
Mathoura Australia 138 B5
Mathura India 104 D4
Mati Mindanao Phil. 82 D5
Matiali India 105 G4
Matias Cardoso Brazil 179 C1
Matías Romero Mex. 168 E5
Matimekosh Canada 153 I3
Matin India 105 E5
Matina Costa Rica 166 [inset] J7
Matinenda Lake Canada 152 E5
Matizi China 96 D1
Matla r. India 105 G5
Matlabas r. S. Africa 125 H2
Matli Pak. 111 H5
Matlock U.K. 59 F5
Mato, Cerro mt. Venez. 176 E2
Matobo Hills Zimbabwe 123 C6
Mato Grosso Brazil 176 G7
Mato Grosso state Brazil 179 A1
Mato Grosso, Planalto do plat. Brazil 177 H7
Matopo Hills Zimbabwe see Matobo Hills
Matos Costa Brazil 179 A4
Matosinhos Port. 67 B3
Mato Verde Brazil 179 C1
Maţraḩ Oman 110 E6
Matroosberg mt. S. Africa 124 D7
Matsesta Rus. Fed. 113 E2
Matsubara Japan 92 B4
Matsuda Japan 93 F3
Matsudai Japan 93 E1
Matsudo Japan 93 F3
Matsue Japan 91 D6
Matsuida Japan 93 E2
Matsukawa Nagano Japan 93 D2
Matsukawa Nagano Japan 93 D3
Matsumoto Japan 93 D2
Matsunoyama Japan 93 E1
Matsuo Japan 93 G3
Matsuoka Japan 92 C2
Matsusaka Japan 92 C4
Matsushiro Japan 93 E2
Matsu Tao i. Taiwan 97 I3
Matsuyama Japan 91 D6
Matsuzaki Japan 93 E4
Mattagami r. Canada 152 E4
Mattamuskeet, Lake NC U.S.A. 162 E5
Mattawa Canada 152 F5
Matterhorn mt. Italy/Switz. 68 B2
Matterhorn mt. NV U.S.A. 156 E4
Matthew Town Bahamas 169 J4
Maţţī, Sabkhat salt pan Saudi Arabia 110 D6
Mattō Japan 92 C2
Mattoon IL U.S.A. 160 F4
Matturai Sri Lanka see Matara
Matu Sarawak Malaysia 85 E2
Matuku i. Fiji 133 H3
Matumbo Angola 123 B5
Maturín Venez. 176 F2
Matusadona National Park Zimbabwe 123 C5
Matutuang i. Indon. 83 C1
Matutum, Mount vol. Phil. 82 D5
Matwabeng S. Africa 125 H5
Maty Island P.N.G. see Wuvulu Island
Mau India see Maunath Bhanjan
Maúa Moz. 123 D5
Maubeuge France 62 D4
Maubin Myanmar 86 A3
Ma-ubin Myanmar 86 B1
Maubourguet France 66 E5
Mauchline U.K. 60 E5
Maudaha India 104 E4
Maude Australia 137 D7
Maud Seamount sea feature S. Atlantic Ocean 184 I10
Mau-é-ele Moz. see Marão
Maués Brazil 177 G4
Maughold Head hd Isle of Man 58 C4
Maug Islands N. Mariana Is 81 L2
Maui i. HI U.S.A. 157 [inset]
Maukkadaw Myanmar 86 A2
Maulbronn Germany 63 I6
Maule r. Chile 178 B5
Maulvi Bazar Bangl. see Moulvibazar
Maumee OH U.S.A. 164 D3

Maumee Bay MI/OH U.S.A. 164 D3
Maumere Flores Indon. 83 B5
Maumturk Mountains hills Ireland 61 C4
Maun Botswana 123 C5
Mauna Kea vol. HI U.S.A. 157 [inset]
Mauna Loa vol. HI U.S.A. 157 [inset]
Maunath Bhanjan India 105 E4
Maunatlala Botswana 125 H2
Mauneluk r. AK U.S.A. 148 H2
Maungaturoto N.Z. 139 E3
Maungdaw Myanmar 86 A2
Maungmagan Islands Myanmar 87 B4
Maunoir, Lac l. Canada 149 P2
Maurepas, Lake LA U.S.A. 161 F6
Mauriac France 66 F4
Maurice country Indian Ocean see Mauritius
Maurice, Lake salt flat Australia 135 E7
Maurik Neth. 62 F3
Mauritania country Africa 120 B3
Mauritanie country Africa see Mauritania
Mauritius country Indian Ocean 185 L7
Maurs France 66 F4
Mauston WI U.S.A. 160 F3
Mava Dem. Rep. Congo 122 C3
Mavago Moz. 123 D5
Mavan, Kūh-e hill Iran 110 E3
Mavanza Moz. 125 L2
Mavinga Angola 123 C5
Mavrovo nat. park Macedonia 69 I4
Mavume Moz. 125 L2
Mavuya S. Africa 125 H6
Mawa, Bukit mt. Indon. 85 F2
Ma Wan i. H.K. China 97 [inset]
Māwān, Khashm hill Saudi Arabia 110 B6
Mawana India 104 D3
Mawanga Dem. Rep. Congo 123 B4
Ma Wang Dui tourist site China 97 G2
Mawasangka Sulawesi Indon. 83 B4
Mawei China 97 H3
Mawjib, Wādī al r. Jordan 107 B4
Mawkmai Myanmar 86 B2
Mawlaik Myanmar 86 A2
Mawlamyaing Myanmar 86 B3
Mawlamyine Myanmar see Mawlamyaing
Mawqaq Saudi Arabia 113 F6
Mawson research station Antarctica 188 E2
Mawson Coast Antarctica 188 E2
Mawson Escarpment Antarctica 188 E2
Mawson Peninsula Antarctica 188 H2
Maw Taung mt. Myanmar 87 B5
Mawza Yemen 108 F7
Maxán Arg. 178 C3
Maxcanú Mex. 167 H4
Maxhamish Lake Canada 150 F3
Maxia, Punta mt. Sardinia Italy 68 C5
Maxixe Moz. 125 L2
Maxmo Fin. 54 M5
May, Isle of i. U.K. 60 G4
Maya i. Indon. 85 E3
Maya r. Rus. Fed. 77 O3
Mayaguana i. Bahamas 163 F8
Mayaguana Passage Bahamas 163 F8
Mayagüez Puerto Rico 169 K5
Mayahi Niger 120 D3
Mayak Rus. Fed. 90 E2
Mayakovskiy, Qullai mt. Tajik. 111 H2
Mayakovskogo, Pik mt. Tajik. see Mayakovskiy, Qullai
Mayalibit, Teluk b. Papua Indon. 83 D3
Mayama Congo 122 B4
Maya Mountains Belize/Guat. 167 H5
Mayan China see Mayanhe
Mayang China 97 F3
Mayanhe China 94 F5
Mayar hill U.K. 60 F4
Maya-san hill Japan 92 B4
Maybeury WV U.S.A. 164 E5
Maybole U.K. 60 E5
Maych'ew Eth. 122 D2
Maydān Shahr Afgh. see Meydān Shahr
Maydh Somalia 108 G7
Maydos Turkey see Eceabat
Mayen Germany 63 H4
Mayenne France 66 D2
Mayenne r. France 66 D3
Mayer AZ U.S.A. 159 G4
Mayêr Kangri mt. China 99 D6
Mayersville MS U.S.A. 161 F5
Mayerthorpe Canada 150 H4
Mayfield N.Z. 139 C6
Mayhan Mongolia see Sant
Mayhill NM U.S.A. 166 D1
Mayi He r. China 90 C3
Maykamys Kazakh. 98 B3
Maykop Rus. Fed. 113 F1
Mayna Respublika Khakasiya Rus. Fed. 76 K4
Mayna Ul'yanovskaya Oblast' Rus. Fed. 53 J5
Mayni India 106 B2
Maynooth Canada 165 G1
Mayo Canada 149 N3
Mayo r. Mex. 166 C3
Mayo FL U.S.A. 163 D6
Mayo Alim Cameroon 120 E4
Mayoko Congo 122 B4
Mayo Lake Canada 149 N3
Mayon vol. Luzon Phil. 82 C3
Mayor, Puig mt. Spain see Major, Puig
Mayor Island N.Z. 139 F3
Mayor Pablo Lagerenza Para. 178 D1

▶Mayotte terr. Africa 123 E5
French Overseas Department.

Mayraira Point Luzon Phil. 82 C2
Mayskiy Amurskaya Oblast' Rus. Fed. 90 C1
Mayskiy Kabardino-Balkarskaya Respublika Rus. Fed. 113 G2
Mays Landing NJ U.S.A. 165 H4
Mayson Lake Canada 151 J3
Maysville KY U.S.A. 164 D4
Maytag China see Dushanzi
Mayu i. Maluku Indon. 83 C2
Mayumba Gabon 122 B4
Mayum La pass China 99 C7
Mayuram India 106 C4
Mayville MI U.S.A. 164 D2
Mayville ND U.S.A. 160 D2
Mayville NY U.S.A. 164 F2
Mayville WI U.S.A. 164 A2
Mazabuka Zambia 123 C5
Mazaca Turkey see Kayseri
Mazagan Morocco see El Jadida
Mazapil Mex. 167 E3
Mazar China 99 B5
Mazār, Kūh-e mt. Afgh. 111 G3
Mazara, Val di valley Sicily Italy 68 E6
Mazara del Vallo Sicily Italy 68 E6
Mazār-e Sharīf Afgh. 111 G2
Mazāri' reg. U.A.E. 110 D6
Mazartag China 98 C5
Mazartag mt. China 98 B5
Mazatán Mex. 166 C2
Mazatenango Guat. 167 H6
Mazatlán Mex. 168 C4
Mazatzal Peak AZ U.S.A. 159 H4
Mazdaj Iran 113 H4
Mazdāvand Iran 111 F2
Maze Japan 92 D3
Maze-gawa r. Japan 92 D3
Mažeikiai Lith. 55 M8
Maẓhūr, 'Irq al des. Saudi Arabia 110 A5
Mazīm Oman 110 E6
Mazocahui Mex. 166 C2
Mazocruz Peru 176 E7
Mazomora Tanz. 123 D4
Mazongshan China 94 D3
Mazong Shan mt. China 94 D3
Mazong Shan mts China 94 C3
Mazu Dao i. Taiwan see Matsu Tao
Mazunga Zimbabwe 123 C6
Mazyr Belarus 53 F5
Mazzouna Tunisia 68 C7

▶Mbabane Swaziland 125 J4
Capital of Swaziland.

Mbahiakro Côte d'Ivoire 120 C4
Mbaïki Cent. Afr. Rep. 122 B3
Mbakaou, Lac de l. Cameroon 120 E4
Mbala Zambia 123 D4
Mbale Uganda 122 D3
Mbalmayo Cameroon 120 E4
Mbam r. Cameroon 120 E4
Mbandaka Dem. Rep. Congo 122 B4
M'banza Congo Angola 123 B4
Mbarara Uganda 121 G5
Mbari r. Cent. Afr. Rep. 122 C3
Mbaswana S. Africa 125 K4
Mbemkuru r. Tanz. 123 D4
Mbeya Tanz. 123 D4
Mbinga Tanz. 123 D5
Mbini Equat. Guinea 120 D4
Mbizi Zimbabwe 123 D6
Mboki Cent. Afr. Rep. 122 C3
Mbombela S. Africa 125 J3
Mbomo Congo 122 B3
Mbouda Cameroon 120 E4
Mbour Senegal 120 B3
Mbout Mauritania 120 B3
Mbozi Tanz. 123 D4
Mbrès Cent. Afr. Rep. 122 B3
Mbuji-Mayi Dem. Rep. Congo 123 C4
Mbulu Tanz. 122 D4
Mburucuyá Arg. 178 E3
McAdam Canada 153 I5
McAlester OK U.S.A. 161 E5
McAlister mt. Australia 138 D5
McAllen TX U.S.A. 161 D7
McArthur r. Australia 136 B2
McArthur OH U.S.A. 164 D4
McArthur Mills Canada 165 G1
McBain MI U.S.A. 164 C1
McBride Canada 150 F4
McCall ID U.S.A. 156 D3
McCamey TX U.S.A. 161 C6
McCammon ID U.S.A. 156 E4
McCarthy AK U.S.A. 149 L3
McCauley Island Canada 149 O5
McClintock, Mount Antarctica 188 H1
McClintock Channel Canada 147 H2
McClintock Range hills Australia 134 D4
McClure, Lake CA U.S.A. 158 C3
McClure Strait Canada 146 G2
McClusky ND U.S.A. 160 C2
McComb MS U.S.A. 161 F6
McConaughy, Lake NE U.S.A. 160 C3
McConnell Range mts Canada 149 P2
McConnellsburg PA U.S.A. 165 G4
McConnelsville OH U.S.A. 164 E4
McCook NE U.S.A. 160 C3
McCormick SC U.S.A. 163 D5
McCrea r. Canada 150 H2
McCreary Canada 151 L5
McCullum, Mount Canada 149 M2
McDame Canada 150 D3
McDermitt NV U.S.A. 156 D4
McDonald Islands Indian Ocean 185 M9
McDonald Peak MT U.S.A. 156 E3
McDonough GA U.S.A. 163 C5
McDougall AK U.S.A. 149 J3
McDougall's Bay S. Africa 124 C5
McDowell Peak AZ U.S.A. 159 H5
McFarland CA U.S.A. 158 D4
McGill NV U.S.A. 159 F2
McGivney Canada 153 I5
McGrath AK U.S.A. 148 I3
McGrath MN U.S.A. 160 E2
McGraw NY U.S.A. 165 G2
McGregor r. Canada 150 F4
McGregor S. Africa 124 D7
McGregor, Lake Canada 150 H5
McGregor Range hills Australia 137 C5
McGuire, Mount ID U.S.A. 156 E3
Mchinga Tanz. 123 D4
Mchinji Malawi 123 D5
McIlwraith Range hills Australia 136 C2
McInnes Lake Canada 151 M4
McIntosh SD U.S.A. 160 C2
McKay Range hills Australia 134 C5
McKean i. Kiribati 133 I2
McKee KY U.S.A. 164 C5
McKenzie r. OR U.S.A. 156 C3
McKinlay r. Australia 136 C4

▶McKinley, Mount AK U.S.A. 149 J3
Highest mountain in North America.

McKinley Park AK U.S.A. 149 J3
McKinney TX U.S.A. 161 D5
McKittrick CA U.S.A. 158 D4
McLaughlin SD U.S.A. 160 C2
McLeansboro IL U.S.A. 160 F4
McLennan Canada 150 G4
McLeod r. Canada 150 H4
McLeod Bay Canada 151 I2
McLeod Lake Canada 150 F4
McLoughlin, Mount OR U.S.A. 156 C4
McMillan, Lake NM U.S.A. 161 B5
McMinnville OR U.S.A. 156 C3
McMinnville TN U.S.A. 162 C5
McMurdo research station Antarctica 188 H1
McMurdo Sound b. Antarctica 188 H1
McNary AZ U.S.A. 159 I4
McNaughton Lake Canada see Kinbasket Lake
McPherson KS U.S.A. 160 D4
McQuesten r. Canada 149 M3
McRae GA U.S.A. 163 D5
McTavish Arm b. Canada 150 G1
McVeytown PA U.S.A. 165 G3
McVicar Arm b. Canada 150 F1
Mdantsane S. Africa 125 H7
M'Daourouch Alg. 68 B6
M'Đrăk Vietnam 87 E4
Mê, Hon i. Vietnam 86 D3
Mead, Lake resr NV U.S.A. 159 F3
Meade KS U.S.A. 161 C4
Meade r. AK U.S.A. 146 C2
Meade r. AK U.S.A. 148 H1
Meadow Australia 135 A6
Meadow SD U.S.A. 160 C2
Meadow UT U.S.A. 159 G2
Meadow Lake Canada 151 I4
Meadville MS U.S.A. 161 F6
Meadville PA U.S.A. 164 E3
Meaford Canada 164 E1
Meaken-dake vol. Japan 90 G4
Mealhada Port. 67 B3
Mealy Mountains Canada 153 K3
Meandarra Australia 138 D1
Meander River Canada 150 G3
Meares i. Indon. 83 C1
Meaux France 62 C6
Mebulu, Tanjung pt Bali Indon. 85 F5
Mecca Saudi Arabia 108 E5
Mecca CA U.S.A. 158 E5
Mecca OH U.S.A. 164 E3
Mechanic Falls ME U.S.A. 165 J1
Mechanicsville VA U.S.A. 165 G5
Mechelen Belgium 62 E3
Mechelen Neth. 62 F4
Mecherchar i. Palau see Eil Malk
Mecheria Alg. 64 D5
Mechernich Germany 62 G4
Mechigmen Rus. Fed. 148 D2
Mecitözü Turkey 112 D2
Meckenheim Germany 62 H4
Mecklenburger Bucht b. Germany 57 M3
Mecklenburg-Vorpommern land Germany 63 M1
Mecklenburg - West Pomerania land Germany see Mecklenburg-Vorpommern
Meda r. Australia 134 C4
Meda Port. 67 C3
Medak India 106 C2
Medan Sumatera Indon. 84 B2
Medang i. Indon. 85 G5
Medanosa, Punta pt Arg. 178 C7
Médanos de Coro, Parque Nacional nat. park Venez. 176 E1
Medawachchiya Sri Lanka 106 D4
Médéa Alg. 67 H5
Medebach Germany 63 I3
Medellín Col. 176 C2
Meden r. U.K. 58 G5
Medenine Tunisia 64 G5
Mederdra Mauritania 120 B3
Medford NY U.S.A. 165 I3
Medford OK U.S.A. 161 D4
Medford OR U.S.A. 156 C4
Medford WI U.S.A. 160 F2
Medfra AK U.S.A. 148 I3
Medgidia Romania 69 M2
Media PA U.S.A. 165 H4
Mediaş Romania 69 K1
Medicine Bow r. WY U.S.A. 156 G4
Medicine Bow Mountains WY U.S.A. 156 G4
Medicine Bow Peak WY U.S.A. 156 G4
Medicine Hat Canada 151 I5
Medicine Lake MT U.S.A. 156 G2
Medicine Lodge KS U.S.A. 161 D4
Medina Brazil 179 C2
Medina Saudi Arabia 108 E5
Medina ND U.S.A. 160 D2
Medina NY U.S.A. 165 F2
Medina OH U.S.A. 164 E3
Medinaceli Spain 67 E3
Medina del Campo Spain 67 D3
Medina de Rioseco Spain 67 D3
Medina Lake TX U.S.A. 161 D6
Medinipur India 105 F5
Mediolanum Italy see Milan
Mediterranean Sea 64 K5
Mednyy, Ostrov i. Rus. Fed. 186 H2
Médoc reg. France 66 D4
Mêdog China 99 F7
Medora ND U.S.A. 160 C2
Medstead Canada 151 I4
Medu Kongkar China see Maizhokunggar
Meduro atoll Marshall Is see Majuro
Medvedevo Rus. Fed. 52 J4
Medveditsa r. Rus. Fed. 53 I6
Medvednica mts Croatia 68 F2
Medvezh'i, Ostrova is Rus. Fed. 77 R2
Medvezh'ya vol. Rus. Fed. 90 H3
Medvezh'ya, Gora mt. Rus. Fed. 90 E3
Medvezh'yegorsk Rus. Fed. 52 G3
Medway r. U.K. 59 H7
Meekatharra Australia 135 B6
Meeker CO U.S.A. 159 J1
Meeker OH U.S.A. 164 D3
Meelpaeg Reservoir Canada 153 K4
Meemu Atoll Maldives see Mulaku Atoll
Meerane Germany 63 M4
Meerlo Neth. 62 G3
Meerut India 104 D3
Mega i. Indon. 84 C3
Mega Escarpment Eth./Kenya 122 D3
Megalopoli Greece 69 J6
Megamo Indon. 81 I7
Mégantic, Lac l. Canada 153 H5
Megara Greece 69 J5
Megezez mt. Eth. 122 D3

▶Meghalaya state India 105 G4
Highest mean annual rainfall in the world.

Meghasani mt. India 105 F5
Meghri Armenia 113 G3
Megin Turkm. 110 E2
Megisti i. Greece 69 M6
Megri Armenia see Meghri
Mehamn Norway 54 O1
Mehar Pak. 111 G5
Meharry, Mount Australia 135 B5
Mehbubnagar India see Mahbubnagar
Mehdia Tunisia see Mahdia
Meherpur Bangl. 105 G5
Meherrin VA U.S.A. 165 F5
Meherrin r. VA U.S.A. 165 G5
Mehlville MO U.S.A. 160 F4
Mehrakān salt marsh Iran 110 D5
Mehrān Hormozgān Iran 110 D5
Mehrān Īlām Iran 110 B3
Mehren Germany 62 G4
Mehrīz Iran 110 D4
Mehsana India see Mahesana
Mehtar Lām Afgh. 111 H3
Meia Ponte r. Brazil 179 A2
Meicheng China see Minqing
Meichuan China 94 F5
Meiganga Cameroon 121 E4
Meighen Island Canada 147 I2
Meigu China 96 D2
Meihekou China 90 B4
Meihō Japan 92 D3
Meikeng China 97 G3
Meikle r. Canada 150 G3
Meikle Says Law hill U.K. 60 G5
Meiktila Myanmar 86 A2
Meilin China see Ganxian
Meilleur r. Canada 150 E2
Meilü China see Wuchuan
Meine Germany 63 K2
Meinersen Germany 63 K2
Meiningen Germany 63 K4
Meishan Anhui China see Jinzhai
Meishan Sichuan China 96 D2
Meishan Shuiku resr China 97 G2
Meißen Germany 57 N5
Meister r. Canada 149 O3
Meitan China 96 E3
Meiwa Gunma Japan 93 F2
Meiwa Mie Japan 92 C4
Meixi China 90 C3
Meixian Guangdong China see Meizhou
Meixian Shaanxi China 95 F5
Meixing China see Xiaojin
Meizhou China 97 H3
Mej r. India 104 D4
Mejicana mt. Arg. 178 C3
Mejillones Chile 178 B2
Mékambo Gabon 122 B3
Mek'elē Eth. 122 D2
Mekele Eth. see Mek'elē
Mékhé Senegal 120 B3
Mekhtar Pak. 111 H4
Meknassy Tunisia 68 C7
Meknès Morocco 64 C5
Mekong r. Asia 86 D4
also known as Lancang Jiang (China), Mae Nam Khong (Laos/Thailand)
Mekong, Mouths of the Vietnam 87 D5
Mekoryuk AK U.S.A. 148 F3
Melaka Malaysia 84 C2
Melaka state Malaysia 84 C2
Melalap Sabah Malaysia 85 F1
Melalo, Tanjung pt Indon. 84 D3
Melanau, Gunung hill Indon. 87 E7
Melanesia is Pacific Ocean 186 G6
Melanesian Basin sea feature Pacific Ocean 186 G5
Melawi r. Indon. 85 E2

▶Melbourne Australia 138 B6
Capital of Victoria. 2nd most populous city in Oceania.

Melbourne FL U.S.A. 163 D6
Melby U.K. 60 [inset]
Melchor de Mencos Guat. 167 H5
Melchor Ocampo Mex. 167 E3
Meldorf Germany 57 L3

▶Melekeok Palau 82 [inset]
Capital of Palau.

Melekess Rus. Fed. see Dimitrovgrad
Melenki Rus. Fed. 53 I5
Melet Turkey see Mesudiye
Mélèzes, Rivière aux r. Canada 153 H2
Melfa VA U.S.A. 165 H5
Melfi Chad 121 E3
Melfi Italy 68 F4
Melfort Canada 151 J4
Melhus Norway 54 G5
Meliadine Lake Canada 151 M2
Meliau Kalimantan Indon. 85 E3
Melide Spain 67 C2
Melilis i. Indon. 83 B3

▶Melilla N. Africa 67 E6
Autonomous Community of Spain.

Melimoyu, Monte mt. Chile 178 B6
Melintang, Danau l. Indon. 85 G3
Meliskerke Neth. 62 D3
Melita Canada 151 K5
Melitene Turkey see Malatya
Melitopol' Ukr. 53 G7
Melk Austria 57 O6
Melka Guba Eth. 122 D3
Melksham U.K. 59 E7
Mellakoski Fin. 54 N3
Mellansel Sweden 54 K5
Melle Germany 63 I2
Mellerud Sweden 55 H7
Mellette SD U.S.A. 160 D2
Mellid Spain see Melide
Mellilia N. Africa see Melilla
Mellor Glacier Antarctica 188 E2
Mellrichstadt Germany 63 K4
Mellum i. Germany 63 I1
Melmoth S. Africa 125 J5
Mel'nichoye Rus. Fed. 90 D3
Melo Uruguay 178 F4
Meloco Moz. 123 D5
Melolo Sumba Indon. 83 B5
Melozitna r. AK U.S.A. 148 I2
Melrhir, Chott salt l. Alg. 64 F5
Melrose Australia 135 C6
Melrose U.K. 60 G5
Melrose MN U.S.A. 160 E2
Melsungen Germany 63 J3
Melta, Mount Malaysia see Tawai, Bukit
Melton Australia 138 B6
Melton Mowbray U.K. 59 G6
Meluan Sarawak Malaysia 85 E2
Melun France 66 F2
Melville Canada 151 K5
Melville, Cape Australia 136 D2
Melville, Cape Phil. 82 B5
Melville, Lake Canada 153 K3
Melville Bugt b. Greenland see Qimusseriarsuaq
Melville Hills Canada 149 Q1
Melville Island Australia 134 E2
Melville Island Canada 147 H2
Melville Peninsula Canada 147 J3
Melvin IL U.S.A. 164 A3
Melvin, Lough l. Ireland/U.K. 61 D3
Mêmar Co salt l. China 99 C6
Memba Moz. 123 E5
Memberamo r. Indon. 81 J7
Memboro Sumba Indon. 83 A5
Memel Lith. see Klaipėda
Memel S. Africa 125 I4
Memmelsdorf Germany 63 K5
Memmingen Germany 57 M7
Mempawah Kalimantan Indon. 85 E2
Memphis tourist site Egypt 112 C5
Memphis MI U.S.A. 164 D2
Memphis TN U.S.A. 161 F5
Memphis TX U.S.A. 161 C5
Memphrémagog, Lac l. Canada 165 I1
Mena Timor Indon. 83 C5
Mena Ukr. 53 G6
Mena AR U.S.A. 161 E5
Ménaka Mali 120 D3
Menanga Maluku Indon. 83 C3
Menard TX U.S.A. 161 D6
Menasha WI U.S.A. 164 A1
Mendanau i. Indon. 84 D3
Mendanha Brazil 179 C2
Mendarik i. Indon. 84 D2
Mendawai Kalimantan Indon. 85 F3
Mendawai r. Indon. 85 F3
Mende France 66 F4
Mendefera Eritrea 108 E7
Mendeleyev Ridge sea feature Arctic Ocean 189 B1
Mendeleyevsk Rus. Fed. 52 L5
Mendenhall MS U.S.A. 161 F6
Mendenhall, Cape AK U.S.A. 148 F4
Mendenhall Glacier AK U.S.A. 149 N4
Méndez Mex. 167 F3
Mendī Eth. 122 D3
Mendi P.N.G. 81 K8
Mendip Hills U.K. 59 E7
Mendocino CA U.S.A. 158 B2
Mendocino, Cape CA U.S.A. 158 A1
Mendocino, Lake CA U.S.A. 158 B2
Mendooran Australia 138 D3
Mendota CA U.S.A. 158 C3
Mendota IL U.S.A. 160 F3
Mendoza Arg. 178 C4
Menemen Turkey 69 L5
Ménerville Alg. see Thenia
Mengalum i. Malaysia 85 F1
Mengba China 95 F5
Mengban China 96 D4
Mengcheng China 97 H1
Menggala Sumatera Indon. 84 D4
Menghai China 96 D4
Mengjin China 97 G1
Mengkatip Kalimantan Indon. 85 F3
Mengkiang r. Indon. 85 E2
Mengkoka, Gunung mt. Indon. 83 B3
Mengla China 96 D4
Menglang China see Lancang
Menglie China see Jiangcheng
Mengxian China see Mengzhou
Mengyang China see Mingshan
Mengyin China 95 I5
Mengzhou China 95 H5
Mengzi China 96 D4
Menihek Canada 153 I3
Menihek Lakes Canada 153 I3
Menindee Australia 137 C7
Menindee, Lake Australia 137 C7
Ménistouc, Lac l. Canada 153 I3
Menkere Rus. Fed. 77 N3
Mennecy France 62 C6
Menominee MI U.S.A. 164 B1
Menomonee Falls WI U.S.A. 164 A2
Menomonie WI U.S.A. 160 F2
Menongue Angola 123 B5
Menorca i. Spain see Minorca
Mensalong Kalimantan Indon. 85 G2
Mentakab Malaysia 84 C2
Mentarang r. Indon. 85 G2
Mentasta Lake AK U.S.A. 149 L3
Mentasta Mountains AK U.S.A. 149 K3
Mentawai, Kepulauan is Indon. 84 B3
Mentawai, Selat sea chan. Indon. 84 C3
Mentaya r. Indon. 85 F3
Menteroda Germany 63 K3
Mentmore NM U.S.A. 159 I4
Mentok Indon. 84 D3
Menton France 66 H5
Mentone TX U.S.A. 161 C6
Mentuba r. Indon. 85 F3
Menuf Egypt see Minūf
Menukung Kalimantan Indon. 85 F3
Menuma Japan 93 F2
Menunu Sulawesi Indon. 83 B2
Menyapa, Gunung mt. Indon. 85 G2
Menyuan China 94 E4
Menza Rus. Fed. 95 G1
Menza r. Rus. Fed. 95 G1
Menzel Bourguiba Tunisia 68 C6
Menzelet Barajı resr Turkey 112 E3
Menzelinsk Rus. Fed. 51 Q4
Menzel Temime Tunisia 68 D6
Menzies Australia 135 C7
Menzies, Mount Antarctica 188 E2
Meobbaai b. Namibia 124 B3
Meoqui Mex. 166 D2
Meppel Neth. 62 G2
Meppen Germany 63 H2
Mepuze Moz. 125 K2
Meqheleng S. Africa 125 H5
Mequon WI U.S.A. 164 B2
Merah Kalimantan Indon. 85 G2
Merak Jawa Indon. 84 D4
Meråker Norway 54 G5
Merano Italy 68 D1
Merapi, Gunung vol. Jawa Indon. 85 E4
Meratswe r. Botswana 124 G2
Meratus, Pegunungan mts Indon. 85 F3
Merauke Indon. 81 K8
Merbau Sumatera Indon. 84 C2
Merca Somalia see Marka
Mercantour, Parc National du nat. park France 66 H4
Merced CA U.S.A. 158 C3
Merced r. CA U.S.A. 158 C3
Mercedes Arg. 178 E3
Mercedes Uruguay 178 E4
Mercer ME U.S.A. 165 K1
Mercer PA U.S.A. 164 E3
Mercer WI U.S.A. 160 F2
Mercês Brazil 179 C3
Mercury Islands N.Z. 139 E3
Mercy, Cape Canada 147 L3
Merdenik Turkey see Göle
Mere Belgium 62 D4
Mere U.K. 59 E7
Meredith NH U.S.A. 165 J2
Meredith, Lake TX U.S.A. 161 C5
Merefa Ukr. 53 H6
Merga Oasis Sudan 108 C6
Mergui Myanmar see Myeik
Mergui Archipelago is Myanmar 87 B5
Meriç r. Turkey 69 L4
also known as Evros (Greece), Marica, Maritsa (Bulgaria)
Mérida Mex. 167 H4
Mérida Spain 67 C4
Mérida Venez. 176 D2
Mérida, Cordillera de mts Venez. 176 D2
Meriden CT U.S.A. 165 I3
Meridian MS U.S.A. 161 F5
Meridian TX U.S.A. 161 D6
Mérignac France 66 D4
Merijärvi Fin. 54 N4
Merikarvia Fin. 55 L6
Merimbula Australia 138 D6
Merín, Laguna l. Brazil/Uruguay see Mirim, Lagoa
Meringur Australia 137 C7
Merir i. Palau 81 I6
Merit Sarawak Malaysia 85 F2
Merjayoun Lebanon see Marjayoûn
Merkel TX U.S.A. 161 C5
Merluna Australia 136 C2
Mermaid Reef Australia 134 B4
Meron, Har mt. Israel 107 B3
Merowe Sudan 108 D6
Mêrqung Co l. China 105 F3
Merredin Australia 135 B7
Merrick hill U.K. 60 E5
Merrickville Canada 165 H1
Merrill MI U.S.A. 164 C2
Merrill WI U.S.A. 160 F2
Merrill, Mount Canada 150 E2
Merrillville IN U.S.A. 164 B3
Merriman NE U.S.A. 160 C3
Merritt Canada 150 F5
Merritt Island FL U.S.A. 163 D6
Merriwa Australia 138 E4
Merrygoen Australia 138 D3
Mersa Fatma Eritrea 108 F7
Mersa Maṭrūḥ Egypt see Marsá Maṭrūḥ
Mersch Lux. 62 G5
Merseburg (Saale) Germany 63 L3
Mersey est. U.K. 58 E5
Mersin Turkey 107 B1
Mersin prov. Turkey 107 A1
Mersing Malaysia 84 C2
Mersing, Bukit mt. Malaysia 85 F2
Mērsrags Latvia 55 M8
Merta India 104 C4
Merthyr Tydfil U.K. 59 D7
Mértola Port. 67 C5
Mertz Glacier Antarctica 188 G2
Mertz Glacier Tongue Antarctica 188 G2
Mertzon TX U.S.A. 161 C6
Méru France 62 C5

▶Meru vol. Tanz. 122 D4
4th highest mountain, and highest active volcano, in Africa.

Meru Betiri, Taman Nasional nat. park Indon. 85 F5
Merui Pak. 111 F4
Merutai Sabah Malaysia 85 G1
Merv Turkm. see Mary
Merweville S. Africa 124 E7
Merzifon Turkey 112 D2
Merzig Germany 62 G5
Merz Peninsula Antarctica 188 L2
Mesa Halmahera Indon. 83 D2
Mesa AZ U.S.A. 159 H5
Mesa NM U.S.A. 157 G6
Mesabi Range hills MN U.S.A. 160 E2
Mesagne Italy 68 G4
Mesa Mountain hill AK U.S.A. 148 I3
Mesanak i. Indon. 84 D2
Mesa Negra mt. NM U.S.A. 159 J4
Mesara, Ormos b. Greece see Kolpos Messaras
Mesa Verde National Park CO U.S.A. 159 I3
Mescalero Apache Indian Reservation res. NM U.S.A. 166 D1
Meschede Germany 63 I3
Mese Myanmar 86 B3
Meselefors Sweden 54 J4
Mesgouez, Lac Canada 152 G4
Meshed Iran see Mashhad
Meshkān Iran 110 E2
Meshra'er Req South Sudan 108 C8
Mesick MI U.S.A. 164 C1
Mesimeri Greece 69 J4
Mesolongi Greece 69 I5
Mesolóngion Greece see Mesolongi
Mesopotamia reg. Iraq 113 F4
Mesquita Brazil 179 C2
Mesquite NV U.S.A. 159 F3
Mesquite TX U.S.A. 161 D5
Mesquite Lake CA U.S.A. 159 F4
Messaad Alg. 64 E5
Messana Sicily Italy see Messina
Messina Sicily Italy 68 F5
Messina, Strait of Italy 68 F5
Messina, Stretta di Italy see Messina, Strait of
Messini Greece 69 J6
Messiniakos Kolpos b. Greece 69 J6
Mesta r. Bulg. 69 K4
Mesta r. Greece see Nestos
Mesta, Akrotirio pt Greece 69 K5
Mestghanem Alg. see Mostaganem
Mestlin Germany 63 L1
Meston, Akra pt Greece see Mesta, Akrotirio
Mestre Italy 68 E2

Morrin Canada 151 H5
Morrinhos Brazil 179 A2
Morris Canada 151 L5
Morris IL U.S.A. 160 F3
Morris MN U.S.A. 160 E2
Morris PA U.S.A. 165 G3
Morrison IL U.S.A. 160 F3
Morristown AZ U.S.A. 159 G5
Morristown NJ U.S.A. 165 H3
Morristown NY U.S.A. 165 H1
Morristown TN U.S.A. 162 D4
Morrisville NY U.S.A. 165 H2
Morro Brazil 179 B2
Morro Bay CA U.S.A. 158 C4
Morro d'Anta Brazil 179 D2
Morro de Papanoa hd Mex. 167 E5
Morro de Petatlán hd Mex. 167 E5
Morro do Chapéu Brazil 177 J6
Morro Grande hill Brazil 177 H4
Morrosquillo, Golfo de b. Col. 176 C2
Morrumbene Moz. 125 L2
Morschen Germany 63 J3
Morse Canada 151 J5
Morse TX U.S.A. 161 C4
Morse, Cape Antarctica 188 G2
Morse Reservoir IN U.S.A. 164 B3
Morshanka Rus. Fed. 53 I5
Morshansk Rus. Fed. see Morshanka
Morsott Alg. 68 C7
Mort watercourse Australia 136 C4
Mortagne-au-Perche France 66 E2
Mortagne-sur-Sèvre France 66 D3
Mortara Italy 68 C2
Mortehoe U.K. 59 C7
Morteros Arg. 178 D4
Mortes, Rio das r. Brazil 179 A1
Mortimer's Bahamas 163 F8
Mortlake Australia 138 A7
Mortlock Islands Micronesia 186 G5
Mortlock Islands P.N.G. see Takuu Islands
Morton U.K. 59 G6
Morton TX U.S.A. 161 C5
Morton WA U.S.A. 156 C3
Morton National Park Australia 138 E5
Morundah Australia 138 C5
Morupule Botswana 125 H2
Moruroa atoll Fr. Polynesia see Mururoa
Moruya Australia 138 E5
Morven Australia 137 D5
Morven hill U.K. 60 F2
Morvern reg. U.K. 60 D4
Morvi India see Morbi
Morwell Australia 138 C7
Morzhovets, Ostrov i. Rus. Fed. 52 I2
Morzhovoi Bay AK U.S.A. 148 G5
Mosbach Germany 63 J5
Mosborough U.K. 58 F5
Mosby MT U.S.A. 156 G3

►Moscow Rus. Fed. 52 H5
Capital of the Russian Federation. 3rd most populous city in Europe.

Moscow ID U.S.A. 156 D3
Moscow PA U.S.A. 165 H3
Moscow University Ice Shelf Antarctica 188 G2
Mosel r. Germany 63 H4
Moselebe watercourse Botswana 124 F3
Moselle r. France 62 G5
Möser Germany 63 L2
Moses, Mount NV U.S.A. 158 E1
Moses Lake WA U.S.A. 156 D3
Moses Point AK U.S.A. 148 G2
Mosgiel N.Z. 139 C7
Moshaweng watercourse S. Africa 124 F4
Moshchnyy, Ostrov i. Rus. Fed. 55 O7
Moshi Tanz. 122 D4
Mosh'yuga Rus. Fed. 52 L2
Mosi-oa-Tunya waterfall Zambia/Zimbabwe see Victoria Falls
Mosjøen Norway 54 H4
Moskal'vo Rus. Fed. 90 F1
Moskenesøy i. Norway 54 H3
Moskva Rus. Fed. see Moscow
Moskva Tajik. 111 H2
Mosonmagyaróvár Hungary 57 P7
Mosquera Col. 176 C3
Mosquero NM U.S.A. 157 G6
Mosquitia reg. Hond. 166 [inset] J6
Mosquito r. Brazil 179 C1
Mosquito Creek Lake OH U.S.A. 164 E3
Mosquito Lake Canada 151 K2
Mosquito Mountain hill AK U.S.A. 148 H3
Mosquitos, Golfo de los b. Panama 166 [inset] J7
Moss Norway 55 G7
Mossâmedes Angola see Namibe
Mossat U.K. 60 G3
Mossburn N.Z. 139 B7
Mosselbaai S. Africa see Mossel Bay
Mossel Bay S. Africa 124 F8
Mossel Bay b. S. Africa 124 F8
Mossgiel Australia 138 B4
Mossman Australia 136 D3
Mossoró Brazil 177 K5
Moss Vale Australia 138 E5
Mossy r. Canada 151 K4
Most Czech Rep. 57 N5
Mostaganem Alg. 67 G6
Mostar Bos.-Herz. 68 G3
Mostoos Hills Canada 151 I4
Mostovskoy Rus. Fed. 113 F1
Mosty Belarus see Masty
Mostyn Sabah Malaysia 85 G1
Mosul Iraq 113 F3
Mosuowan China 98 D3
Møsvatnet l. Norway 55 F7
Motagua r. Guat. 167 H6
Motala Sweden 55 I7
Motaze Moz. 125 K3
Motegi Japan 93 G2
Motetema S. Africa 125 I3
Moth India 104 D4
Motherwell U.K. 60 F5
Moti i. Maluku Indon. 83 C2
Motian Ling hill China 90 A4
Motihari India 105 F4
Motilla del Palancar Spain 67 F4
Motiti Island N.Z. 139 F3
Motokwe Botswana 124 F3
Motono Japan 93 G3
Motosu Japan 92 C3
Motosu-ko l. Japan 93 E3
Motozintla Mex. 167 G6
Motril Spain 67 E5
Motru Romania 69 J2
Mott ND U.S.A. 160 C2
Mottama Myanmar 86 B3
Mottama, Gulf of Myanmar 86 B3
Motu Ihupuku i. N.Z. see Campbell Island
Motul Mex. 167 H4
Mouaskar Alg. see Mascara
Mouding China 96 D3
Moudjéria Mauritania 120 B3
Moudros Greece 69 K5
Mouhijärvi Fin. 55 M6
Mouila Gabon 122 B4
Moulamein Australia 138 B5
Moulamein Creek r. Australia 138 A5
Moulavibazar Bangl. see Moulvibazar
Mould Bay Canada 146 G2
Moulèngui Binza Gabon 122 B4
Moulins France 66 F3
Moulmein Myanmar see Mawlamyaing
Moulouya r. Morocco 64 D4
Moultrie GA U.S.A. 163 D6
Moultrie, Lake SC U.S.A. 163 E5
Moulvibazar Bangl. 105 G4
Mound City KS U.S.A. 160 E4
Mound City SD U.S.A. 160 C2
Moundou Chad 121 E4
Moundsville WV U.S.A. 164 E4
Moŭng Rœssei Cambodia 87 C4
Mount Abu India 104 C4
Mountain r. Canada 149 O2
Mountainair NM U.S.A. 157 G6
Mountain Brook AL U.S.A. 163 C5
Mountain City TN U.S.A. 164 E5
Mountain Home AR U.S.A. 161 E4
Mountain Home ID U.S.A. 156 E4
Mountain Home UT U.S.A. 159 H1
Mountain Lake Park MD U.S.A. 164 F4
Mountain View AR U.S.A. 161 E5
Mountain Village AK U.S.A. 148 G3
Mountain Zebra National Park S. Africa 125 G7
Mount Airy NC U.S.A. 162 D4
Mount Aspiring National Park N.Z. 139 B7
Mount Assiniboine Provincial Park Canada 150 H5
Mount Ayliff S. Africa 125 I6
Mount Ayr IA U.S.A. 160 E3
Mountbellew Ireland 61 D4
Mount Buffalo National Park Australia 138 C6
Mount Carmel IL U.S.A. 164 B4
Mount Carmel Junction UT U.S.A. 159 G3
Mount Coolon Australia 136 D4
Mount Darwin Zimbabwe 123 D5
Mount Denison Australia 134 F5
Mount Desert Island ME U.S.A. 162 G2
Mount Dutton Australia 137 A5
Mount Eba Australia 137 A6
Mount Elgon National Park Uganda 122 D3
Mount Fletcher S. Africa 125 I6
Mount Forest Canada 164 E2
Mount Frankland National Park Australia 135 B8
Mount Frere S. Africa 125 I6
Mount Gambier Australia 137 C8
Mount Gilead OH U.S.A. 164 D3
Mount Hagen P.N.G. 81 K8
Mount Holly NJ U.S.A. 165 H4
Mount Hope Australia 138 B4
Mount Hope WV U.S.A. 164 E5
Mount Howitt Australia 137 C5
Mount Isa Australia 136 B4
Mount Jackson VA U.S.A. 165 F4
Mount Jewett PA U.S.A. 165 F3
Mount Joy PA U.S.A. 165 G3
Mount Kaputar National Park Australia 138 E3
Mount Keith Australia 135 C6
Mount Lofty Range mts Australia 137 B7
Mount Magnet Australia 135 B7
Mount Manara Australia 138 A4
Mount McKinley National Park AK U.S.A. see Denali National Park and Preserve
Mount Meadows Reservoir CA U.S.A. 158 C1
Mountmellick Ireland 61 E4
Mount Moorosi Lesotho 125 H6
Mount Morgan Australia 136 E4
Mount Morris MI U.S.A. 164 D2
Mount Morris NY U.S.A. 165 G2
Mount Murchison Australia 138 A3
Mount Nebo WV U.S.A. 164 E4
Mount Olivet KY U.S.A. 164 C4
Mount Pearl Canada 153 L5
Mount Pleasant Canada 153 I5
Mount Pleasant IA U.S.A. 160 F3
Mount Pleasant MI U.S.A. 164 C2
Mount Pleasant TX U.S.A. 161 E5
Mount Pleasant UT U.S.A. 159 H2
Mount Rainier National Park WA U.S.A. 156 C3
Mount Remarkable National Park Australia 137 B7
Mount Revelstoke National Park Canada 150 G5
Mount Robson Provincial Park Canada 150 G4
Mount Rogers National Recreation Area park VA U.S.A. 164 E5
Mount St Helens National Volcanic Monument nat. park WA U.S.A. 156 C3
Mount Sanford Australia 134 E4
Mount's Bay U.K. 59 B8
Mount Shasta CA U.S.A. 156 C4
Mountsorrel U.K. 59 F6
Mount Sterling KY U.S.A. 164 D4
Mount Swan Australia 136 A4
Mount Union PA U.S.A. 165 G3
Mount Vernon Australia 135 B6
Mount Vernon AL U.S.A. 167 H2
Mount Vernon IL U.S.A. 160 F4
Mount Vernon IN U.S.A. 162 C4
Mount Vernon KY U.S.A. 164 C5
Mount Vernon MO U.S.A. 161 E4
Mount Vernon OH U.S.A. 164 D3
Mount Vernon TX U.S.A. 161 E5
Mount Vernon WA U.S.A. 156 C2
Mount William National Park Australia 137 [inset]
Mount Willoughby Australia 135 F6
Moura Australia 136 E5
Moura Brazil 176 F4
Moura Port. 67 C4
Mourdi, Dépression du depr. Chad 121 F3
Mourdiah Mali 120 C3
Mourne r. U.K. 61 E3
Mourne Mountains hills U.K. 61 F3
Mousa i. U.K. 60 [inset]
Mouscron Belgium 62 D4
Mousgougou Chad 122 B2
Moussafoyo Chad 121 E4
Moussoro Chad 121 E3
Moutamba Congo 122 B4
Mouth of the Yangtze China 97 I2
Moutong Sulawesi Indon. 83 B2
Mouy France 62 C5
Mouydir, Monts du plat. Alg. 120 D2
Mouzon France 62 F5
Movas Mex. 166 C2
Mowbullan, Mount Australia 138 E1
Moxey Town Bahamas 163 E7
Moy r. Ireland 61 C3
Moyahua Mex. 166 E4
Moyale Eth. 122 D3
Moyen Atlas mts Morocco 64 C5
Moyen Congo country Africa see Congo
Moyeni Lesotho 125 H6
Moynalyk Rus. Fed. 102 I1
Moynaq Uzbek. see Mo'ynoq
Mo'ynoq Uzbek. 102 A3
Moyo i. Indon. 85 G5
Moyobamba Peru 176 C5
Moyock NC U.S.A. 165 G5
Moyola r. U.K. 61 F3
Moyu China 99 B5
Moyynkum Kazakh. 102 D3
Moyynkum, Peski des. Kazakh. 102 C3
Moyynty Kazakh. 102 D2
Mozambique country Africa 123 D6
Mozambique Channel Africa 123 E6
Mozambique Ridge sea feature Indian Ocean 185 K7
Mozdok Rus. Fed. 113 G2
Mozhaysk Rus. Fed. 53 H5
Mozhga Rus. Fed. 52 L4
Mozo Myanmar 96 B4
Mozyr' Belarus see Mazyr
Mpaathutlwa Pan salt pan Botswana 124 E3
Mpanda Tanz. 123 D4
Mpen India 105 I4
Mpika Zambia 123 D5
Mpolweni S. Africa 125 J5
Mporokoso Zambia 123 D4
Mpulungu Zambia 123 D4
Mpumalanga prov. S. Africa 125 I4
Mpunde mt. Tanz. 123 D4
Mpwapwa Tanz. 123 D4
Mqanduli S. Africa 125 I6
Mqinvartsveri mt. Georgia/Rus. Fed. see Kazbek
Mrauk-U Myanmar 86 A2
Mrewa Zimbabwe see Murehwa
Mrkonjić-Grad Bos.-Herz. 68 G2
M'Saken Tunisia 68 D7
Mshinskaya Rus. Fed. 55 P7
M'Sila Alg. 67 I6
Msta r. Rus. Fed. 52 F4
Mstislavl' Belarus see Mstsislaw
Mstsislaw Belarus 53 F5
Mtelo Kenya 122 D3
Mthatha S. Africa 125 I6
Mtoko Zimbabwe see Mutoko
Mtorwi Tanz. 123 D4
Mtsensk Rus. Fed. 53 H5
Mts'ire Kavkasioni Asia see Lesser Caucasus
Mtubatuba S. Africa 125 K5
Mtunzini S. Africa 125 J5
Mtwara Tanz. 123 E5
Mu r. Myanmar 86 A2
Mu'āb, Jibāl reg. Jordan see Moab
Muanda Dem. Rep. Congo 123 B4
Muang Ham Laos 86 D2
Muang Hiam Laos 86 C2
Muang Hinboun Laos 86 D3
Muang Hôngsa Laos 86 C3
Muang Khi Laos 86 C3
Muang Không Laos 87 D4
Muang Khoua Laos 86 C2
Muang Lamam Laos see Lamam
Muang Mok Laos 86 D3
Muang Ngoy Laos 86 C2
Muang Ou Nua Laos 86 C2
Muang Pakbeng Laos 86 C3
Muang Paktha Laos 86 C2
Muang Pakxan Laos see Pakxan
Muang Phalan Laos 80 D3
Muang Phin Laos 86 D3
Muang Sam Sip Thai. 86 D4
Muang Sing Laos 86 C2
Muang Soum Laos 86 C3
Muang Souy Laos 86 C3
Muang Thadua Laos 86 C3
Muang Thai country Asia see Thailand
Muang Va Laos 86 C2
Muang Vangviang Laos 86 C3
Muang Xon Laos 86 C2
Muar Malaysia 84 C2
Muar r. Malaysia 84 C2
Muara Brunei 85 F1
Muaraancalong Kalimantan Indon. 85 G2
Muaraatap Kalimantan Indon. 85 G2
Muarabeliti Sumatera Indon. 84 C3
Muarabulian Sumatera Indon. 84 C3
Muarabungo Sumatera Indon. 84 C3
Muaradua Sumatera Indon. 84 D4
Muaraenim Sumatera Indon. 84 C3
Muarainu Kalimantan Indon. 85 F3
Muarajawa Kalimantan Indon. 85 G3
Muarakaman Kalimantan Indon. 85 G3
Muara Kaman Sedulang, Cagar Alam nature res. Kalimantan Indon. 85 G2
Muaralabuh Sumatera Indon. 84 C3
Muaralakitan Sumatera Indon. 84 C3
Muaralaung Kalimantan Indon. 85 F3
Muaralesan Kalimantan Indon. 85 G2
Muaramayang Kalimantan Indon. 85 G2
Muaranawai Kalimantan Indon. 85 G2
Muararupit Sumatera Indon. 84 C3
Muarasabak Sumatera Indon. 84 C3
Muarasiberut Indon. 84 B3
Muarasipongi Sumatera Indon. 84 B2
Muarasoma Sumatera Indon. 84 B2
Muaras Reef Indon. 85 G2
Muaratebo Sumatera Indon. 84 C3
Muaratembesi Sumatera Indon. 84 C3
Muarateweh Kalimantan Indon. 85 F3
Muara Tuang Sarawak Malaysia see Kota Samarahan
Muarawahau Kalimantan Indon. 85 G2
Muari i. Maluku Indon. 83 C3
Muari, Ras pt Pak. 111 G5
Mu'ayqil, Khashm al hill Saudi Arabia 110 C5
Mubarek Uzbek. see Muborak
Mubarraz well Saudi Arabia 113 F5
Mubende Uganda 122 D3
Mubi Nigeria 120 E3
Muborak Uzbek. 111 G2
Mubur i. Indon. 84 D2
Mucajaí, Serra do mts Brazil 176 F3
Mucalic r. Canada 153 I2
Muccan Australia 134 C5
Much Germany 63 H4
Mucheng China see Wuzhi
Muchinga Escarpment Zambia 123 D5
Muchuan China 96 D2
Muck i. U.K. 60 C4
Mucojo Moz. 123 E5
Muconda Angola 123 C5
Mucubela Moz. 123 D5
Mucugê Brazil 179 C1
Mucur Turkey 112 D3
Mucuri Brazil 179 D2
Mucuri r. Brazil 179 D2
Muda r. Malaysia 84 C1
Mudabidri India 106 B3
Mudan China see Heze
Mudanjiang China 90 C3
Mudan Jiang r. China 90 C3
Mudan Ling mts China 90 B4
Mudanya Turkey 69 M4
Muḍaybī Oman 110 E6
Mudaysīsāt, Jabal al hill Jordan 107 C4
Muddus nationalpark nat. park Sweden 54 K3
Muddy r. NV U.S.A. 159 F3
Muddy Gap WY U.S.A. 156 G4
Muddy Peak NV U.S.A. 159 F3
Mūd-e Dahanāb Iran 110 E3
Mudersbach Germany 63 H4
Mudgal India 106 C3
Mudgee Australia 138 D4
Mudhol India 106 B2
Mudigere India 106 B3
Mudjatik r. Canada 151 J3
Mud Lake NV U.S.A. 158 E3
Mudraya country Africa see Egypt
Mudurnu Turkey 69 N4
Mud'yuga Rus. Fed. 52 H3
Mueda Moz. 123 D5
Mueller Range hills Australia 134 D4
Muerto, Mar lag. Mex. 167 G5
Muertos Cays is Bahamas 163 D7
Muftyuga Rus. Fed. 52 J2
Mufulira Zambia 123 C5
Mufumbwe Zambia 123 C5
Mufu Shan mts China 97 G2
Muğan Düzü lowland Azer. 113 H3
Mugarripug China 105 F2
Mugegawa Japan 92 C3
Mughalbhin Pak. see Jati
Mughal Kot Pak. 111 H4
Mughal Sarai India 105 E4
Mūghār Iran 110 D3
Mughayrā' Saudi Arabia 107 C5
Mughayrā' well Saudi Arabia 110 B5
Mugi Japan 92 D3
Muğla Turkey 69 M6
Mugodzhary, Gory mts Kazakh. 102 A2
Mug Qu r. China 94 C5
Mugu Karnali r. Nepal 99 C7
Mugur-Aksy Rus. Fed. 94 B1
Mugxung China 99 F6
Muḩ, Sabkhat imp. l. Syria 107 D2
Muhala China see Yutian
Muhammad Ashraf Pak. 111 H5
Muhammad Qol Sudan 108 E5
Muhammarah Iran see Khorramshahr
Muhar China 94 D4
Muhashsham, Wādī al watercourse Egypt 107 B4
Muḩaysh, Wādī al watercourse Jordan 107 C5
Muhaysin Syria 107 D1
Mühlanger Germany 63 M3
Mühlberg Germany 63 N3
Mühlhausen (Thüringen) Germany 63 K3
Mühlig-Hofmann Mountains Antarctica 188 C2
Muhos Fin. 54 N4
Muḩradah Syria 107 C2
Mui Bai Bung c. Vietnam see Mui Ca Mau
Mui Ba Lang An pt Vietnam 86 E4
Mui Ca Mau c. Vietnam 87 D5
Mui Độc pt Vietnam 86 D3
Muié Angola 123 C5
Muika Japan 93 E1
Muiliyk i. Maluku Indon. 83 D3
Muineachán Ireland see Monaghan
Muir MI U.S.A. 164 C2
Muirkirk U.K. 60 E5
Muir of Ord U.K. 60 E3
Mui Ron hd Vietnam 86 D3
Muite Moz. 123 D5
Mujeres, Isla i. Mex. 167 I4
Muji China 99 B5
Mujong r. Malaysia 85 F2
Muju S. Korea 91 B5
Mukacheve Ukr. 53 D6
Mukachevo Ukr. see Mukacheve
Mukah Sarawak Malaysia 85 F2
Mukah r. Malaysia 85 F2
Mukalla Yemen 108 G7
Mukandwara India 104 D4
Mukawa Japan 93 E3
Mukdahan Thai. 86 D3
Mukden China see Shenyang
Mukeru Palau 82 [inset]
Muketei r. Canada 152 D3
Mukhen Rus. Fed. 90 E2
Mukhino Rus. Fed. 90 B1
Mukhorshibir' Rus. Fed. 95 G1
Mukhtuya Rus. Fed. see Lensk
Mukinbudin Australia 135 B7
Mukō Japan 92 B4
Mu Ko Chang Marine National Park Thai. 87 C5
Mukojima-rettō is Japan 91 F8
Mukomuko Sumatera Indon. 84 C3
Mukry Turkm. 111 G2
Muktsar India 104 C3
Mukutawa r. Canada 151 L4
Mukwonago WI U.S.A. 164 A2
Mukyr Kazakh. 98 C2
Mula r. India 106 B2
Mulakatholhu atoll Maldives see Mulaku Atoll
Mulaku Atoll Maldives 103 D11
Mulan China 90 C3
Mulanay Luzon Phil. 82 C3
Mulanje, Mount Malawi 123 D5
Mulapula, Lake salt flat Australia 137 B6
Mulatos Mex. 166 C2
Mula-tupo Panama 166 [inset] K7
Mulayḩ Saudi Arabia 110 B5
Mulayḩah, Jabal hill U.A.E. 110 D5
Mulayz, Wādī al watercourse Egypt 107 A4
Mulchatna r. AK U.S.A. 148 H3
Mulde r. Germany 63 M3
Mule Creek NM U.S.A. 159 I5
Mule Creek WY U.S.A. 156 G4
Mulegé Mex. 166 B3
Mules i. Indon. 83 B5
Muleshoe TX U.S.A. 161 C5
Mulga Park Australia 135 E6
Mulgathing Australia 135 F7
Mulgrave Hills AK U.S.A. 148 G2
Mulhacén mt. Spain 67 E5
Mülhausen France see Mulhouse
Mülheim an der Ruhr Germany 62 G3
Mulhouse France 66 H3
Muli China 96 D3
Muli Rus. Fed. see Vysokogorniy
Mulia Indon. 81 J7
Muling Heilong. China 90 C3
Muling Heilong. China 90 C3
Muling He r. China 90 D3
Mull i. U.K. 60 D4
Mull, Sound of sea chan. U.K. 60 C4
Mullaghcleevaun hill Ireland 61 F4
Mullaittivu Sri Lanka 106 D4
Mullaley Australia 138 D3
Mullengudgery Australia 138 C3
Mullens WV U.S.A. 164 E5
Muller watercourse Australia 134 F5
Muller, Pegunungan mts Indon. 85 F2
Mullett Lake MI U.S.A. 164 C1
Mullewa Australia 135 A7
Mullica r. NJ U.S.A. 165 H4
Mullingar Ireland 61 E4
Mullion Creek Australia 138 D4
Mull of Galloway c. U.K. 60 E6
Mull of Kintyre hd U.K. 60 D5
Mull of Oa hd U.K. 60 C5
Mullumbimby Australia 138 F2
Mulobezi Zambia 123 C5
Mulshi Lake India 106 B2
Multai India 104 D5
Multan Pak. 111 H4
Multia Fin. 54 N5
Multien reg. France 62 C6
Mulu, Gunung mt. Malaysia 85 F1
Mulug India 106 C2

►Mumbai India 106 B2
3rd most populous city in Asia and the world.

Mumbil Australia 138 D4
Mumbwa Zambia 123 C5
Muminabad Tajik. see Leningrad
Mŭ'minobod Tajik. see Leningrad
Mun, Mae Nam r. Thai. 86 D4
Muna i. Indon. 83 B4
Muna Mex. 167 H4
Muna r. Rus. Fed. 77 N3
Munabao Pak. 111 H5
Munaðarnes Iceland 54 [inset 1]
Münchberg Germany 63 L4
München Germany see Munich
München-Gladbach Germany see Mönchengladbach
Münchhausen Germany 63 I4
Muncho Lake Canada 150 E3
Muncie IN U.S.A. 164 C3
Muncoonie West, Lake salt flat Australia 136 B5
Muncy PA U.S.A. 165 G3
Munda Pak. 111 H4
Mundel Lake Sri Lanka 106 C5
Mundesley U.K. 59 I6
Mundford U.K. 59 H6
Mundiwindi Australia 135 C5
Mundra India 104 B5
Mundrabilla Australia 132 C5
Munds Park AZ U.S.A. 159 H4
Mundubbera Australia 137 E5
Mundwa India 104 C4
Munfordville KY U.S.A. 164 C5
Mungallala Australia 137 D5
Mungana Australia 136 D3
Mungári Moz. 123 D5
Mungbere Dem. Rep. Congo 122 C3
Mungeli India 105 E5
Munger India 105 F4
Mu Nggava i. Solomon Is see Rennell
Mungguresak, Tanjung pt Indon. 85 E2
Mungindi Australia 138 D2
Mungla Bangl. see Mongla
Mungo Angola 123 B5
Mungo, Lake Australia 138 A4
Mungo National Park Australia 138 A4
Munich Germany 57 M6
Munising MI U.S.A. 162 C2
Munjpur India 104 B5
Munkács Ukr. see Mukacheve
Munkebakken Norway 54 P2
Munkedal Sweden 55 G7
Munkfors Sweden 55 H7
Munkhafaḑ al Qaţţārah depr. Egypt see Qattara Depression
Munku-Sardyk, Gora mt. Mongolia/Rus. Fed. 94 E1
Münnerstadt Germany 63 K4
Munnik S. Africa 125 I2
Munroe Lake Canada 151 L3
Munsan S. Korea 91 B5
Munse Sulawesi Indon. 83 B4
Münster Hessen Germany 63 I5
Münster Niedersachsen Germany 63 K2
Münster Nordrhein-Westfalen Germany 63 H3
Munster reg. Ireland 61 D5
Münsterland reg. Germany 63 H3
Muntadgin Australia 135 B7
Munte Sulawesi Indon. 83 A2
Muntervary hd Ireland 61 C6
Munyal-Par sea feature India see Bassas de Pedro Padua Bank
Munzur Vadisi Milli Parkı nat. park Turkey 65 L4
Muojärvi l. Fin. 54 P4
Mương Nhe Vietnam 86 C2
Muong Sai Laos see Oudômxai
Muonio Fin. 54 M3
Muonioälven r. Fin./Sweden 54 M3
Muonionjoki r. Fin./Sweden see Muonioälven
Muor i. Maluku Indon. 83 D2
Mupa, Parque Nacional da nat. park Angola 123 B5
Muping Shandong China 95 J4
Muping Sichuan China see Baoxing
Muqaynimah well Saudi Arabia 110 C6
Muqdisho Somalia see Mogadishu
Muquem Brazil 179 A1
Muqui Brazil 179 C3
Muqur Bādghīs Afgh. 111 F3
Muqur Ghaznī Afgh. 111 G3
Mur r. Austria 57 P7
also known as Mura (Croatia/Slovenia)
Mura r. Austria see Mur
Murai, Tanjong pt Sing. 87 [inset]
Murai Reservoir Sing. 87 [inset]
Murakami Japan 91 E5
Murallón, Cerro mt. Chile 178 B7
Muramvya Burundi 122 C4
Murashi Rus. Fed. 52 K4
Murat r. Turkey 113 E3
Muratlı Turkey 69 L4
Muraysah, Ra's al pt Libya 112 B5
Murchison watercourse Australia 135 A6
Murchison, Mount Antarctica 188 H2
Murchison, Mount hill Australia 135 B6
Murchison Falls National Park Uganda 122 D3
Murcia Spain 67 F5
Murcia aut. comm. Spain 67 F5
Murcielagos Bay Mindanao Phil. 82 C4
Murdāin Afgh. 111 G2
Murdo SD U.S.A. 160 C3
Mure Japan 93 E2
Murehwa Zimbabwe 123 D5
Mureşul r. Romania 69 I1
Muret France 66 E5
Murewa Zimbabwe see Murehwa
Murfreesboro AR U.S.A. 161 E5
Murfreesboro TN U.S.A. 162 C5
Murg r. Germany 63 I6
Murgab Tajik. see Murghob
Murgab Turkm. see Murgap
Murgab r. Turkm. see Murgap
Murgap Turkm. 111 F2
Murgap r. Turkm. 109 J2
Murgh, Kōtal-e Afgh. 111 H3
Murgha Kibzai Pak. 111 H4
Murghob Tajik. 111 I2
Murgon Australia 137 E5
Murgoo Australia 135 B6
Muri Qinghai China 94 D4
Muri Qinghai China 94 E4
Muri India 105 F5
Muria, Gunung mt. Indon. 85 E4
Muriaé Brazil 179 C3
Murid Pak. 111 G4
Muriege Angola 123 C4
Murih, Pulau i. Indon. 85 E2
Müritz l. Germany 63 M1
Müritz, Nationalpark nat. park Germany 63 N1
Murmansk Rus. Fed. 54 R2
Murmanskaya Oblast' admin. div. Rus. Fed. 54 S2
Murmanskiy Bereg coastal area Rus. Fed. 52 G1
Murmansk Oblast admin. div. Rus. Fed. see Murmanskaya Oblast'
Muro Japan 92 C4
Muro, Capo di c. Corsica France 66 I6
Murō-Akame-Aoyama Kokutei-kōen park Japan 92 C4
Murom Rus. Fed. 52 I5
Muromagi-gawa r. Japan 92 D2
Muroran Japan 90 F4
Muros Spain 67 B2
Muroto Japan 91 D6
Muroto-zaki pt Japan 91 D6
Murphy ID U.S.A. 156 D4
Murphy NC U.S.A. 163 D5
Murphysboro IL U.S.A. 160 F4
Murrah reg. Saudi Arabia 110 C6
Murrah al Kubrá, Al Buḩayrah al l. Egypt see Great Bitter Lake
Murrah aş Şughrá, Al Buḩayrah al l. Egypt see Little Bitter Lake
Murramarang National Park nat. park Australia 138 I5
Murra Murra Australia 138 C2
Murrat el Kubra, Buheirat l. Egypt see Great Bitter Lake
Murrat el Sughra, Buheirat l. Egypt see Little Bitter Lake

►Murray r. S.A. Australia 137 B7
3rd longest river in Oceania, and a major part of the longest (Murray-Darling).

Murray r. W.A. Australia 135 A8
Murray KY U.S.A. 161 F4
Murray UT U.S.A. 159 H1
Murray, Lake P.N.G. 81 K8
Murray, Lake SC U.S.A. 163 D5
Murray, Mount Canada 149 O3
Murray Bridge Australia 137 B7

►Murray-Darling r. Australia 132 E5
Longest river in Oceania.

Murray Downs Australia 134 F5
Murray Range hills Australia 135 E6
Murraysburg S. Africa 124 F6
Murray Sunset National Park Australia 137 C7
Murrhardt Germany 63 J6
Murrieta CA U.S.A. 158 E5
Murringo Australia 138 D5
Murrisk reg. Ireland 61 C4
Murroogh Ireland 61 C4

►Murrumbidgee r. Australia 138 A5
4th longest river in Oceania.

Murrumburrah Australia 138 D5
Murrurundi Australia 138 E3
Mursan India 104 D4
Murshidabad India 105 G4
Murska Sobota Slovenia 68 G1
Mūrt Iran 111 F5
Murtoa Australia 137 C8
Murua i. P.N.G. see Woodlark Island
Murud India 106 B2
Murud, Gunung mt. Indon. 85 F2
Murui r. Indon. 85 F3

Muruin Sum Shuiku *resr* China **95** J3
Murung *r.* Indon. **85** F3
Murung *r.* Indon. **85** F3
Murunkan Sri Lanka **106** D4
Murupara N.Z. **139** F4
Mururoa *atoll* Fr. Polynesia **187** K7
Murviedro Spain *see* **Sagunto**
Murwara India **104** E5
Murwillumbah Australia **138** F2
Murzechirla Turkm. **111** F2
Murzūq Libya **121** E2
Mürzzuschlag Austria **57** O7
Muş Turkey **113** F3
Mūsā, Khowr-e *b.* Iran **110** C4
Musakhel Pak. **111** H4
Musala *mt.* Bulg. **69** J3
Musala *i.* Indon. **84** B2
Musan N. Korea **90** C4
Musandam Peninsula Oman/U.A.E. **110** E5
Musashino Japan **93** F3
Musay'īd Qatar *see* **Umm Sa'id**

▶**Muscat** Oman **110** E6
Capital of Oman.

Muscat *reg.* Oman **110** E5
Muscat and Oman *country* Asia *see* **Oman**
Muscatine *IA* U.S.A. **160** F3
Musgrave Australia **136** C2
Musgrave Harbour Canada **153** L4
Musgrave Ranges *mts* Australia **135** E6
Mushāsh al Kabid *well* Jordan **107** C5
Mushayyish, Wādī al *watercourse* Jordan **107** C4
Mushie Dem. Rep. Congo **122** B4
Mushkaf Pak. **111** G4
Musi *r.* Indon. **84** D3
Music Mountain *AZ* U.S.A. **159** G4
Musina S. Africa **125** J2
Musinia Peak *UT* U.S.A. **159** H2
Muskeg *r.* Canada **150** F2
Muskeget Channel *MA* U.S.A. **165** J3
Muskegon *MI* U.S.A. **164** B2
Muskegon *r. MI* U.S.A. **164** B2
Muskegon Heights *MI* U.S.A. **164** B2
Muskeg River Canada **150** G4
Muskogee *OK* U.S.A. **161** E5
Muskoka, Lake Canada **164** F1
Muskrat Dam Lake Canada **151** N4
Musmar Sudan **108** E6
Musoma Tanz. **122** D4
Musquanousse, Lac *l.* Canada **153** J4
Musquaro, Lac *l.* Canada **153** J4
Mussau Island P.N.G. **81** L7
Musselburgh U.K. **60** F5
Musselkanaal Neth. **62** H2
Musselshell *r. MT* U.S.A. **156** G3
Mussende Angola **123** B5
Mustafabad India **99** C8
Mustafakemalpaşa Turkey **69** M4
Mustau, Gora *mt.* China **98** D3
Mustjala Estonia **55** M7
Mustvee Estonia **55** O7
Musu-dan *pt* N. Korea **90** C4
Muswellbrook Australia **138** E4
Mūţ Egypt **108** C4
Mut Turkey **107** A1
Mutá, Ponta do *pt* Brazil **179** D1
Mutare Zimbabwe **123** D5
Mutayr *reg.* Saudi Arabia **110** B5
Mutina Italy *see* **Modena**
Muting Indon. **81** K8
Mutis Col. **176** C2
Mutis, Gunung *mt. Timor* Indon. **83** C5
Mutnyy Materik Rus. Fed. **52** L2
Mutoko Zimbabwe **123** D5
Mutsamudu Comoros **123** E5
Mutsu Japan **90** F4
Mutsuzawa Japan **93** G3
Muttaburra Australia **136** D4
Mutton Island Ireland **61** C5
Muttukuru India **106** D3
Muttupet India **106** C4
Mutum Brazil **179** C2
Mutunópolis Brazil **179** A1
Mutur Sri Lanka **106** D4
Mutusjärvi *r.* Fin. **54** O2
Muurola Fin. **54** N3
Mu Us Shamo *des.* China **95** G4
Muxaluando Angola **123** B4
Muxi China *see* **Muchuan**
Muxima Angola **123** B4
Muyezerskiy Rus. Fed. **54** R5
Muyinga Burundi **122** D4
Mŭynoq Uzbek. *see* **Mo'ynoq**
Muyu China **97** F2
Muyumba Dem. Rep. Congo **123** C4
Muyunkum, Peski *des.* Kazakh. *see* **Moyynkum, Peski**
Muzaffarabad Pak. **111** I3
Muzaffargarh Pak. **111** H4
Muzaffarnagar India **104** D3
Muzaffarpur India **105** F4
Muzamane Moz. **125** K2
Muzat He *r.* China **98** C4
Muzhi Rus. Fed. **51** S2
Mūzīn Iran **111** F5
Muzon, Cape *AK* U.S.A. **149** N5
Múzquiz Mex. **167** E3
Muztag *mt.* China **99** C6
Muz Tag *mt.* China **99** D5
Muztagata *mt.* China **98** A5
Muztor Kyrg. *see* **Toktogul**
Mvadi Gabon **122** B3
Mvolo South Sudan **121** F4
Mvuma Zimbabwe **123** D5
Mwanza Malawi **123** D5
Mwanza Tanz. **122** D4
Mweelrea *hill* Ireland **61** C4
Mweka Dem. Rep. Congo **123** C4
Mwene-Ditu Dem. Rep. Congo **123** C4
Mwenezi Zimbabwe **123** D6
Mwenga Dem. Rep. Congo **122** C4
Mweru, Lake Dem. Rep. Congo/Zambia **123** C4
Mweru Wantipa National Park Zambia **123** C4
Mwimba Dem. Rep. Congo **123** C4
Mwinilunga Zambia **123** C5
Myadaung Myanmar **86** B2
Myadzyel Belarus **55** O9
Myajlar India **104** B4
Myall Lakes National Park Australia **138** F4
Myanaung Myanmar **86** A3
Myanmar *country* Asia **86** A2
Myauk-U Myanmar *see* **Mrauk-U**
Myaungmya Myanmar **86** A3
Myawadi Thai. **86** B3
Mybster U.K. **60** F2
Myebon Myanmar **86** A2
Myede Myanmar *see* **Aunglan**
Myeik Myanmar **87** B4
Myingyan Myanmar **86** A2
Myinkyado Myanmar **86** B2
Myinmoletkat *mt.* Myanmar **87** B4
Myitkyina Myanmar **86** B1
Myitson Myanmar **86** B2
Myitta Myanmar **87** B4
Myittha Myanmar **86** B2
Mykolayiv Ukr. **69** O1
Mykonos *i.* Greece **69** K6
Myla Rus. Fed. **52** K2
Myla *r.* Rus. Fed. **52** K2
Mylae *Sicily* Italy *see* **Milazzo**
Mylasa Turkey *see* **Milas**
Mymensing Bangl. *see* **Mymensingh**
Mymensingh Bangl. **105** G4
Mynämäki Fin. **55** M6
Mynaral Kazakh. **98** A3
Myōgi Japan **93** E2
Myōgi-Arafune-Saku-kōgen Kokutei-kōen *park* Japan **93** E2
Myōgi-san *mt.* Japan **93** E2
Myōken-yama *hill* Japan **92** A4
Myōkō Japan **93** E2
Myōkō-kōgen Japan **93** E2
Myŏnggan N. Korea **90** C4
Myory Belarus **55** O9
My Phước Vietnam **87** D5
Mýrdalsjökull *ice cap* Iceland **54** [inset 1]
Myre Norway **54** I2
Myrheden Sweden **54** L4
Myrhorod Ukr. **53** G6
Myrnam Canada **151** I4
Myronivka Ukr. **53** F6
Myrtle Beach *SC* U.S.A. **163** E5
Myrtleford Australia **138** C6
Myrtle Point *OR* U.S.A. **156** B4
Myrtoo Pelagos *sea* Greece **69** J6
Mys Chelyuskin Rus. Fed. **189** E1
Mysia *reg.* Turkey **69** L5
Mys Lazareva Rus. Fed. *see* **Lazarev**
Myślibórz Poland **57** O4
My Son Sanctuary *tourist site* Vietnam **86** E4
Mysore India **106** C3
Mysore *state* India *see* **Karnataka**
Mys Shmidta Rus. Fed. **77** T3
Mysuru India *see* **Mysore**
Mysy Rus. Fed. **52** L3
My Tho Vietnam **87** D5
Mytikas *mt.* Greece *see* **Olympus, Mount**
Mytilene *i.* Greece *see* **Lesbos**
Mytilini Greece **69** L5
Mytilini Strait Greece/Turkey **69** L5
Mytishchi Rus. Fed. **52** H5
Myton *UT* U.S.A. **159** H1
Myyeldino Rus. Fed. **52** L3
Mzamomhle S. Africa **125** H6
Mže *r.* Czech Rep. **63** M5
Mzimba Malawi **123** D5
Mzuzu Malawi **123** D5

N

Naab *r.* Germany **63** M5
Nā'ālehu *HI* U.S.A. **157** [inset]
Naantali Fin. **55** M6
Naas Ireland **61** F4
Naba Myanmar **86** B1
Nababeep S. Africa **124** C5
Nababganj Bangl. *see* **Nawabganj**
Nabadwip India *see* **Navadwip**
Nabarangapur India **106** D2
Nabarangpur India *see* **Nabarangapur**
Nabari Japan **92** C4
Nabari-gawa *r.* Japan **92** C4
Nabas *Panay* Phil. **82** C4
Nabatîyé et Tahta Lebanon **107** B3
Nabatiyet et Tahta Lebanon *see* **Nabatîyé et Tahta**
Nabberu, Lake *salt flat* Australia **135** C6
Nabburg Germany **63** M5
Naberera Tanz. **123** D4
Naberezhnyye Chelny Rus. Fed. **51** Q4
Nabesna *AK* U.S.A. **149** L3
Nabesna *r. AK* U.S.A. **149** L3
Nabesna Glacier *AK* U.S.A. **148** I3
Nabesna Village *AK* U.S.A. **149** L3
Nabeul Tunisia **68** D6
Nabha India **104** D3
Nabil'skiy Zaliv *lag.* Rus. Fed. **90** F2
Nabire Indon. **81** J7
Nabi Younés, Ras en *pt* Lebanon **107** B3
Nāblus West Bank **107** B3
Naboomspruit S. Africa **125** I3
Nabq Reserve *nature res.* Egypt **112** D5
Nābulus West Bank *see* **Nāblus**
Nabunturan Phil. **82** D5
Nacajuca Mex. **167** G5
Nacala Moz. **123** E5
Nacaome Hond. **166** [inset] I6
Nachalovo Rus. Fed. **53** K7
Nachicapau, Lac *l.* Canada **153** I2
Nachingwea Tanz. **123** D5
Nachna India **104** B4
Nachuge India **87** A5
Nacimiento Reservoir *CA* U.S.A. **158** C4
Naco *AZ* U.S.A. **157** F7
Nacogdoches *TX* U.S.A. **161** E6
Nacozari de García Mex. **166** C2
Nada China *see* **Danzhou**
Nadachi Japan **93** E1
Nadaleen *r.* Canada **150** C2
Nadbai India **99** B8
Nådendal Fin. *see* **Naantali**
Nadezhdinskoye Rus. Fed. **90** D2
Nadiad India **104** C5
Nadol India **104** C4
Nador Morocco **67** E6
Nadqān, Qalamat *well* Saudi Arabia **110** C6
Nadūshan Iran **110** D3
Nadvirna Ukr. **53** E6
Nadvoitsy Rus. Fed. **52** G3
Nadvornaya Ukr. *see* **Nadvirna**
Nadym Rus. Fed. **76** I3
Næstved Denmark **55** G9
Nafarroa *aut. comm.* Spain *see* **Navarra**
Nafas, Ra's an *mt.* Egypt **107** B5
Nafha, Har *hill* Israel **107** B4
Nafpaktos Greece **69** I5
Nafplio Greece **69** J6
Naftalan Azer. **113** G2
Naft-e Sefīd Iran **110** C4
Naft-e Shāh Iran *see* **Naft Shahr**
Naft Shahr Iran **110** B3
Nafūd ad Daḩl *des.* Saudi Arabia **110** B6
Nafūd al Ghuwayṭah *des.* Saudi Arabia **107** D5
Nafūd al Jur'ā *des.* Saudi Arabia **110** B5
Nafūd as Sirr *des.* Saudi Arabia **110** B5
Nafūd as Surrah *des.* Saudi Arabia **110** A6
Nafūd Qunayfidhah *des.* Saudi Arabia **110** B5
Nafūsah, Jabal *hills* Libya **120** E1
Nafy Saudi Arabia **108** F4
Nag, Co *l.* China **99** E6
Naga Japan **92** B4
Naga *Luzon* Phil. **82** C3
Nagagami *r.* Canada **152** D4
Nagagami Lake Canada **152** D4
Nagahama *Ehime* Japan **91** D6
Nagahama *Shiga* Japan **92** C3
Naga Hills India **105** H4
Naga Hills *state* India *see* **Nagaland**
Nagai Island *AK* U.S.A. **148** G5
Nagaizumi Japan **93** E3
Nagakute Japan **92** D3
Nagaland *state* India **105** H4
Nagamangala India **106** C3
Nagambie Australia **138** B6
Nagano Japan **93** E2
Nagano *pref.* Japan **93** D2
Naganohara Japan **93** E2
Nagaoka Japan **91** E5
Nagaokakyō Japan **92** B4
Nagaon India **105** H4
Nagapatam India *see* **Nagapattinam**
Nagapattinam India **106** C4
Nagar *r.* Bangl./India **99** E8
Nagar *Hima. Prad.* India **109** M3
Nagar *Karnataka* India **106** B3
Nagara Japan **93** G3
Nagara-gawa *r.* Japan **92** C3
Nagaram India **106** D2
Nagareyama Japan **93** F3
Nagari Hills India **106** C3
Nagarjuna Sagar Reservoir India **106** C2
Nagar Parkar Pak. **111** H5
Nagar Untari India **105** E4
Nagarzê China **99** E7
Nagasaka Japan **93** E3
Nagasaki Japan **91** C6
Nagashima Japan **92** C3
Nagato *Nagano* Japan **93** E2
Nagato *Yamaguchi* Japan **91** C6
Nagatoro Japan **93** F2
Nagaur India **104** C4
Nagawa Japan **92** D2
Nagbhir India **106** C1
Nagda India **104** C5
Nageezi *NM* U.S.A. **159** J3
Nagercoil India **106** C4
Nagha Kalat Pak. **111** G5
Nag' Ḩammādī Egypt *see* **Naj' Ḩammādī**
Nagina India **104** D3
Nagiso Japan **92** D3
Nagjog China **99** G7
Nagold *r.* Germany **63** I6
Nagong Chu *r.* China *see* **Parlung Zangbo**

▶**Nagorno-Karabakh** *terr.* Azer. **113** G3
Disputed Territory.

Nagornyy Rus. Fed. **148** B3
Nagornyy Karabakh *terr.* Azer. *see* **Nagorno-Karabakh**
Nagorsk Rus. Fed. **52** K4
Nagoya Japan **92** C3
Nagpur India **104** D5
Nagqu China **99** F7
Nag Qu *r.* China **99** F7
Nagurskoye Rus. Fed. **76** F1
Nagyatád Hungary **68** G1
Nagybecskerek Serbia *see* **Zrenjanin**
Nagyenyed Romania *see* **Aiud**
Nagykanizsa Hungary **68** G1
Nagyvárad Romania *see* **Oradea**
Naha Japan **89** N7
Nahan India **104** D3
Nahanni Butte Canada **150** F2
Nahanni National Park Reserve Canada **149** P3
Nahanni Range *mts* Canada **150** F2
Naharāyim Jordan **107** B3
Nahariyya Israel **107** B3
Nahāvand Iran **110** C3
Nahr Dijlah *r.* Asia **113** G5 *see* **Tigris**
Nahrīn Afgh. **111** H2
Nahrīn *reg.* Afgh. **111** H2
Nahuel Huapi, Parque Nacional *nat. park* Arg. **178** B6
Nahunta *GA* U.S.A. **163** D6
Naic *Luzon* Phil. **82** C3
Naica Mex. **166** D3
Nai Ga Myanmar **96** C3
Naij Tal China **94** C5
Naikliu *Timor* Indon. **83** B5
Nailung China **99** F7
Naiman Qi China *see* **Daqin Tal**
Naimin Shuiquan *well* China **94** B2
Nain Canada **153** J2
Nā'īn Iran **110** D3
Naini Tal India *see* **Nainital**
Nainital India **104** D3
Nairn U.K. **60** F3
Nairn *r.* U.K. **60** F3

▶**Nairobi** Kenya **122** D4
Capital of Kenya.

Naissus Serbia *see* **Niš**
Naivasha Kenya **122** D4
Najaf Iraq **113** G5
Najafābād Iran **110** C3
Na'jān Saudi Arabia **110** B5
Najd *reg.* Saudi Arabia **108** F4
Nájera Spain **67** E2
Naj' Ḩammādī Egypt **108** D4
Naji China **95** J1
Najibabad India **104** D3
Najin N. Korea **90** C4
Najitun China *see* **Naji**
Najrān Saudi Arabia **108** F6
Naka *Hyōgo* Japan **92** A3
Naka *Ibaraki* Japan **93** G2
Nakadōri-shima *i.* Japan **91** C6
Na Kae Thai. **86** D3
Nakagawa Japan **93** D3
Naka-gawa *r.* Japan **93** G2
Nakagō Japan **93** E2
Nakai Japan **93** F3
Nakaizu Japan **93** F4
Nakajima *Fukushima* Japan **93** G1
Nakajima *Ishikawa* Japan **92** C1
Nakajō Japan **93** E2
Nakakawane Japan **93** E3
Nakambé *r.* Burkina Faso/Ghana *see* **White Volta**
Nakamichi Japan **93** E3
Nakaminato Japan **93** G2
Nakanbe *r.* Burkina Faso/Ghana *see* **White Volta**
Nakanno Rus. Fed. **77** L3
Nakano Japan **93** E2
Nakanojō Japan **93** E2
Nakano-shima *i.* Japan **91** D5
Nakano-take *mt.* Japan **93** F1
Nakasato *Gunma* Japan **93** E2
Nakasato *Niigata* Japan **93** E1
Nakasongola Uganda **121** G4
Nakatomi Japan **93** E3
Nakatsu *Ōita* Japan **91** C6
Nakatsu *Wakayama* Japan **92** B5
Nakatsugawa Japan **92** D3
Nakatsu-gawa *r.* Japan **93** E2
Nakfa Eritrea **108** E6
Nakhichevan' Azer. *see* **Naxçıvan**
Nakhl Egypt **107** A5
Nakhodka Rus. Fed. **90** D4
Nakhola India **105** H4
Nakhon Nayok Thai. **87** C4
Nakhon Pathom Thai. **87** C4
Nakhon Phanom Thai. **86** D3
Nakhon Ratchasima Thai. **86** C4
Nakhon Sawan Thai. **86** C4
Nakhon Si Thammarat Thai. **87** B5
Nakhtarana India **104** B5
Nakina Canada **152** D4
Nakina *r.* Canada **149** N4
Naknek *AK* U.S.A. **148** H4
Naknek Lake *AK* U.S.A. **148** H4
Nakodar India **99** A7
Nakonde Zambia **123** D4
Nakoso Japan **93** G2
Nakskov Denmark **55** G9
Naktong-gang *r.* S. Korea **91** C6
Nakuru Kenya **122** D4
Nakusp Canada **150** G5
Nal Pak. **111** G5
Nal *r.* Pak. **111** G5
Na-lang Myanmar **86** B2
Nalayh Mongolia **95** F2
Naláži Moz. **125** K3
Nalbari India **105** G4
Nal'chik Rus. Fed. **113** F2
Naldurg India **106** C2
Nalgonda India **106** C2
Naliya India **104** B5
Nallamala Hills India **106** C3
Nallıhan Turkey **69** N4
Nālūt Libya **120** E1
Namaa, Tanjung *pt Seram* Indon. **83** D3
Namaacha Moz. **125** K3
Namacurra Moz. **123** D5
Namadgi National Park Australia **138** D5
Namahadi S. Africa **125** I4
Namai Bay Palau **82** [inset]
Namak, Daryācheh-ye *salt flat* Iran **110** C3
Namak, Kavīr-e *salt flat* Iran **110** E3
Namakkal India **106** C4
Namakwaland *reg.* Namibia *see* **Great Namaqualand**
Namakzar-e Shadad *salt flat* Iran **110** E4
Namaland *reg.* Namibia *see* **Great Namaqualand**
Namang Indon. **84** D3
Namangan Uzbek. **102** D3
Namaqualand *reg.* Namibia *see* **Great Namaqualand**
Namaqualand *reg.* S. Africa **124** C5
Namaqua National Park S. Africa **124** C6
Namas Indon. **81** K8
Namatanai P.N.G. **132** F2
Nambour Australia **138** F1
Nambu Japan *see* **Nanbu**
Nambucca Heads Australia **138** F3
Nambung National Park Australia **135** A7
Năm Căn Vietnam **87** D5
Namcha Barwa *mt.* China *see* **Namjagbarwa Feng**
Namche Bazar Nepal **105** F4
Namco China **99** E7
Nam Co *salt l.* China **99** E7
Namdalen *valley* Norway **54** H4
Namdalseid Norway **54** G4
Nam Đinh Vietnam **86** D2
Namegawa Japan **93** F2
Namelaki Passage Palau **82** [inset]
Namen Belgium *see* **Namur**
Namerikawa Japan **92** D2
Nam-gang *r.* N. Korea **91** B5
Namhae-do *i.* S. Korea **91** B6
Namhsan Myanmar **86** B2
Namiai Japan **92** D3
Namib Desert Namibia **124** B3
Namibe Angola **123** B5
Namibia *country* Africa **123** B6
Namibia Abyssal Plain *sea feature* N. Atlantic Ocean **184** I8
Namib-Naukluft Game Park *nature res.* Namibia **124** B3
Namie Japan **91** F5
Namīn Iran **113** H3
Namjagbarwa Feng *mt.* China **99** F7
Namka China **99** E7
Namlan Myanmar **86** B2
Namlang *r.* Myanmar **86** B2
Namlea *Buru* Indon. **83** C3
Namling China **99** E7
Nam Loi *r.* China *see* **Nanlei He**
Nam Nao National Park Thai. **86** C3
Nam Ngum Reservoir Laos **86** C3
Namoding China **99** D7
Namoi *r.* Australia **138** D3
Namoku Japan **93** E2
Namonuito *atoll* Micronesia **81** L5
Nampa *mt.* Nepal **104** E3
Nampa *ID* U.S.A. **156** D4
Nampala Mali **120** C3
Nam Phong Thai. **86** C3
Namp'o N. Korea **91** B5
Nampula Moz. **123** D5
Namrole *Buru* Indon. **83** C3
Namsai Myanmar **86** B1
Namsang Myanmar **86** B2
Namsen *r.* Norway **54** G4
Nam She Tsim *hill H.K.* China *see* **Sharp Peak**
Namsos Norway **54** G4
Namti Myanmar **86** B1
Namtok Myanmar **86** B3
Nam Tok Chattakan National Park Thai. **86** C3
Namton Myanmar **86** B2
Namtsy Rus. Fed. **77** N3
Namtu Myanmar **86** B2
Namu Canada **150** E5
Namuli, Monte *mt.* Moz. **123** D5
Namuno Moz. **123** D5
Namur Belgium **62** E4
Namutoni Namibia **123** B5
Namwŏn S. Korea **91** B6
Namya Ra Myanmar **86** B1
Namyit Island S. China Sea **80** E4
Nan Thai. **86** C3
Nana Bakassa Cent. Afr. Rep. **122** B3
Nanaimo Canada **150** F5
Nanakai Japan **93** G2
Nanam N. Korea **90** C4
Nan'an China **97** H3
Nanango Australia **138** F1
Nananib Plateau Namibia **124** C3
Nanao Japan **92** C1
Nanatsuka Japan **92** C2
Nanatsu-shima *i.* Japan **91** E5
Nanbai China *see* **Zunyi**
Nanbaxian China **99** F5
Nanbin China *see* **Shizhu**
Nanbu China **96** E2
Nanbu Japan **93** E3
Nancha China **90** C3
Nanchang *Jiangxi* China **97** G2
Nanchang *Jiangxi* China **97** G2
Nanchangshan China *see* **Changdao**
Nanchong China **96** E2
Nanchuan China **96** E2
Nancowry *i.* India **87** A6
Nancun *Henan* China **95** H5
Nancun *Shanxi* China *see* **Zezhou**
Nancy France **62** G6
Nancy (Essey) *airport* France **62** G6
Nanda Devi *mt.* India **104** E3
Nanda Kot *mt.* India **104** E3
Nandan China **96** E3
Nandapur India **106** D2
Nanded India **106** C2
Nander India *see* **Nanded**
Nandewar Range *mts* Australia **138** E3
Nandod India **106** B1
Nandurbar India **104** C5
Nandyal India **106** C3
Nanfeng *Guangdong* China **97** F4
Nanfeng *Jiangxi* China **97** H3
Nang China **99** F7
Nanga Eboko Cameroon **120** E4
Nangah Dedai *Kalimantan* Indon. **85** E3
Nangahembaloh *Kalimantan* Indon. **85** F2
Nangahkemangai *Kalimantan* Indon. **85** F3
Nangahketungau *Kalimantan* Indon. **85** E2
Nangahmau *Kalimantan* Indon. **85** E3
Nangah Merakai *Kalimantan* Indon. **85** E2
Nangahpinoh *Kalimantan* Indon. **85** E3
Nangahsuruk *Kalimantan* Indon. **85** F2
Nangahtempuai *Kalimantan* Indon. **85** F2
Nangalao *i.* Phil. **82** C4

▶**Nanga Parbat** *mt.* Pak. **104** C2
9th highest mountain in Asia and the world.

Nangar National Park Australia **138** D4
Nangataman *Kalimantan* Indon. **85** E3
Nangatayap *Kalimantan* Indon. **85** E3
Nangdoi China **94** E4
Nangin Myanmar **87** B5
Nangnim-sanmaek *mts* N. Korea **91** B4
Nangong China **95** H4
Nangqên China **96** C1
Nangsin Sum China **95** G4
Nangulangwa Tanz. **123** D4
Nanguneri India **106** C4
Nanhu *Gansu* China **94** C4
Nanhu *Xinjiang* China **94** C3
Nanhua *Gansu* China **94** D4
Nanhua *Yunnan* China **96** D3
Nanhui China **97** I2
Nanjian China **96** D3
Nanjiang China **96** E1
Nanjing China **97** H1
Nanji Shan *i.* China **97** I3
Nanjō Japan **92** C3
Nanka Jiang *r.* China **96** C4
Nankang China **97** G3
Nanking China *see* **Nanjing**
Nankova Angola **123** B5
Nanle China **95** H4
Nanlei He *r.* China **96** C4
also known as Nam Loi (Myanmar)
Nanling China **97** H2
Nan Ling *mts* China **97** F3
Nanliu Jiang *r.* China **97** F4
Nanlong China *see* **Nanbu**
Nanma China *see* **Yiyuan**
Nanmulingzue China *see* **Namling**
Nannilam India **106** C4
Nannine Australia **135** B6
Nanning China **97** F4
Nanniwan China **95** G4
Nannō Japan **92** C3
Nannup Australia **135** A8
Na Noi Thai. **86** C3
Nanortalik Greenland **147** N3
Nanouki *atoll* Kiribati *see* **Nonouti**
Nanouti *atoll* Kiribati *see* **Nonouti**
Nanpan Jiang *r.* China **96** E3
Nanpi China **95** I4
Nanpiao China **95** J3
Nanping China **97** H3
Nanpu China *see* **Pucheng**
Nanri Dao *i.* China **97** H3
Nansei Japan **92** C4
Nansei-shotō *is* Japan *see* **Ryukyu Islands**
Nansei-shotō Trench *sea feature* N. Pacific Ocean *see* **Ryukyu Trench**
Nansen Basin *sea feature* Arctic Ocean **189** H1
Nansen Sound *sea chan.* Canada **147** I1
Nan-sha Ch'ün-tao *is* S. China Sea *see* **Spratly Islands**
Nanshan China **97** [inset]
Nanshan Island S. China Sea **80** F4
Nanshankou *Qinghai* China **94** C4
Nanshankou *Xinjiang* China **94** C3
Nansha Qundao *is* S. China Sea *see* **Spratly Islands**
Nansio Tanz. **122** D4
Nantai-san *hill* Japan **93** G2
Nantai-san *mt.* Japan **93** F2
Nantes France **66** D3
Nantes à Brest, Canal de France **66** C3
Nanteuil-le-Haudouin France **62** C5
Nanthi Kadal Lagoon *lag.* Sri Lanka **106** D4
Nanticoke Canada **164** E2
Nanticoke *MD* U.S.A. **165** H4
Nantō Japan **92** C4
Nantong China **97** I2
Nant'ou Taiwan **97** I4
Nantucket *MA* U.S.A. **165** J3
Nantucket Island *MA* U.S.A. **165** K3
Nantucket Sound *g. MA* U.S.A. **165** J3
Nantwich U.K. **59** E5
Nanumaga *i.* Tuvalu *see* **Nanumanga**
Nanumanga *i.* Tuvalu **133** H2
Nanumea *atoll* Tuvalu **133** H2
Nanuque Brazil **179** C2
Nanusa, Kepulauan *is* Indon. **83** C1
Nanushuk *r. AK* U.S.A. **149** J1
Nanxi China **96** E2
Nanxian China **97** G2
Nanxiong China **97** G3
Nanyang China **97** G1
Nanyuki Kenya **122** D4
Nanzamu China **95** K3
Nanzhang China **97** F2
Nanzhao China *see* **Zhao'an**
Nanzhou China *see* **Nanxian**
Naococane, Lac *l.* Canada **153** H3
Naoero *country* S. Pacific Ocean *see* **Nauru**
Naogaon Bangl. **105** G4
Naoli He *r.* China **90** D3
Nāomīd, Dasht-e *des.* Afgh./Iran **111** F3
Naong, Bukit *mt.* Malaysia **85** F2
Naoshera India **104** C2
Napa *CA* U.S.A. **158** B2
Napaimiut *AK* U.S.A. **148** H3
Napakiak *AK* U.S.A. **148** G3
Napaktulik Lake Canada **151** H1
Napanee Canada **165** G1
Napaskiak *AK* U.S.A. **148** G3
Napasoq Greenland **147** M3
Naperville *IL* U.S.A. **164** A3
Napier N.Z. **139** F4
Napier Range *hills* Australia **134** D4
Napierville Canada **165** I1
Naples Italy **68** F4
Naples *FL* U.S.A. **163** D7
Naples *ME* U.S.A. **165** J2
Naples *TX* U.S.A. **161** E5
Naples *UT* U.S.A. **159** I1
Napo China **96** E4
Napoleon *IN* U.S.A. **164** C4
Napoleon *ND* U.S.A. **160** D2
Napoleon *OH* U.S.A. **164** C3
Napoli Italy *see* **Naples**
Naqadeh Iran **110** B2
Nara India **104** B5
Nara Japan **92** B4
Nara *pref.* Japan **92** B4
Nara Mali **120** C3
Narach Belarus **55** O9
Naracoorte Australia **137** C8
Naradhan Australia **138** C4
Narai-gawa *r.* Japan **93** D2
Narainpur India **106** D2
Narakawa Japan **93** D2
Naralua India **105** F4
Naran Mongolia **95** H2
Naranbulag *Dornod* Mongolia *see* **Bayandun**
Naranbulag *Uvs* Mongolia **94** C1
Naranjal Ecuador **176** C4
Naranjo Mex. **157** F8
Naranjos Mex. **167** F4
Naran Sebstein Bulag *spring* China **94** D3
Narasapur India **106** D2
Narasaraopet India **106** D2
Narashino Japan **93** G3
Narasinghapur India **106** E1
Narasun Rus. Fed. **95** H1
Narat China **98** D4
Narathiwat Thai. **87** C6
Narat Shan *mts* China **98** C4
Nara Visa *NM* U.S.A. **161** C5
Narayanganj Bangl. **105** G5
Narayanganj India **104** E5
Narayangarh India **104** C4
Narbada *r.* India *see* **Narmada**
Narberth U.K. **59** C7
Narbo France *see* **Narbonne**
Narbonne France **66** F5
Narborough Island *Galápagos* Ecuador *see* **Fernandina, Isla**
Narcea *r.* Spain **67** C2
Narcondam Island India **87** A4
Nardò Italy **68** H4
Narechi *r.* Pak. **111** H4
Narembeen Australia **135** B8
Nares Abyssal Plain *sea feature* S. Atlantic Ocean **184** D4
Nares Deep *sea feature* N. Atlantic Ocean **184** D4
Nares Strait Canada/Greenland **147** K2
Naretha Australia **135** D7
Narew *r.* Poland **57** R4
Narib Namibia **124** C3
Narikel Jinjira *i.* Bangl. *see* **St Martin's Island**
Narimanov Rus. Fed. **53** J7
Narimskiy Khrebet *mts* Kazakh. *see* **Narymskiy Khrebet**
Narin China **95** G4
Narince Turkey **112** E3
Narin Gol *watercourse* China **99** F5
Narita Japan **93** G3
Narita *airport* Japan **93** G3
Nariu-misaki *pt* Japan **92** B4
Nariynteel Mongolia **94** E2
Narizon, Punta *pt* Mex. **166** C3
Narkher India **104** D5
Narmada *r.* India **104** C5
Narman Turkey **113** F2
Narnaul India **104** D3
Narni Italy **68** E3

Narnia Italy see Narni
Narodnaya, Gora mt. Rus. Fed. 51 S3
Naro-Fominsk Rus. Fed. 53 H5
Narok Kenya 122 D4
Narooma Australia 138 E6
Narovchat Rus. Fed. 53 I5
Narowlya Belarus 53 F6
Närpes Fin. 54 L5
Narrabri Australia 138 D3
Narragansett Bay RI U.S.A. 165 J3
Narran r. Australia 138 C2
Narrandera Australia 138 C5
Narran Lake Australia 138 C2
Narrogin Australia 135 B8
Narromine Australia 138 D4
Narrows VA U.S.A. 164 E5
Narrowsburg NY U.S.A. 165 H3
Narsapur India 106 C2
Narsaq Greenland 147 N3
Narshingdi Bangl. see Narsingdi
Narsimhapur India see Narsinghpur
Narsingdi Bangl. 105 G5
Narsinghpur India 104 D5
Narsipatnam India 106 D2
Nart China 95 H3
Nart Mongolia see Orhon
Nartkala Rus. Fed. 113 F2
Narusawa Japan 93 E3
Narutō Japan 93 G3
Naruto Japan 91 D6
Narva Estonia 55 P7
Narva Bay Estonia/Rus. Fed. 55 O7
Narvacan Luzon Phil. 82 C2
Narva laht b. Estonia/Rus. Fed. see Narva Bay
Narva Reservoir resr Estonia/Rus. Fed. see Narvskoye Vodokhranilishche
Narva veehoidla resr Estonia/Rus. Fed. see Narvskoye Vodokhranilishche
Narvik Norway 54 J2
Narvskiy Zaliv b. Estonia/Rus. Fed. see Narva Bay
Narvskoye Vodokhranilishche resr Estonia/Rus. Fed. 55 P7
Narwana India 104 D3
Nar'yan-Mar Rus. Fed. 52 L2
Narymskiy Khrebet mts Kazakh. 102 F2
Naryn Kyrg. 102 E3
Naryn admin. div. Kyrg. 98 A4
Naryn r. Kyrg./Uzbek. 98 A4
Naryn Rus. Fed. 94 C1
Narynkol Kazakh. 98 C4
Näsåker Sweden 54 J5
Nash Harbor AK U.S.A. 148 F3
Nashik India 106 B1
Nashua NH U.S.A. 165 J2
Nashville AR U.S.A. 161 E5
Nashville GA U.S.A. 163 D6
Nashville IN U.S.A. 164 B4
Nashville NC U.S.A. 162 E5
Nashville OH U.S.A. 164 D3

▶Nashville TN U.S.A. 162 C4
Capital of Tennessee.

Naṣīb Syria 107 C3
Näsijärvi l. Fin. 55 M6
Nasik India see Nashik
Nasilat Kalimantan Indon. 85 E2
Nasinu Fiji 133 H3
Nasir Pak. 111 H4
Nasir South Sudan 108 D8
Nasirabad Bangl. see Mymensingh
Nasirabad India 104 C4
Nāṣirīyah Iraq 113 G5
Naskaupi r. Canada 153 J3
Naṣr Egypt 112 C5
Nasratabad Iran see Zābol
Naṣrīān-e Pā'īn Iran 110 B3
Nass r. Canada 149 O5
Nassau r. Australia 136 C2

▶Nassau Bahamas 163 E7
Capital of The Bahamas.

Nassau i. Cook Is 133 J3
Nassau NY U.S.A. 165 I2
Nassawadox VA U.S.A. 165 H5
Nasser, Lake resr Egypt 108 D5
Nässjö Sweden 55 I8
Nassuttooq inlet Greenland 147 M3
Nastapoca r. Canada 152 F2
Nastapoka Islands Canada 152 F2
Nasu Japan 93 G1
Nasu-dake vol. Japan 93 F1
Nasugbu Luzon Phil. 82 C3
Nasva Rus. Fed. 52 F4
Nata Botswana 123 C6
Nataboti Buru Indon. 83 C3
Natal Brazil 177 K5
Natal Sumatera Indon. 84 B2
Natal prov. S. Africa see KwaZulu-Natal
Natal Basin sea feature Indian Ocean 185 K8
Naṭanz Iran 110 C3
Natashō Japan 92 B3
Natashquan Canada 153 J4
Natashquan r. Canada 153 J4
Natazhat, Mount AK U.S.A. 149 L3
Natchez MS U.S.A. 161 F6
Natchitoches LA U.S.A. 161 E6
Nathalia Australia 138 B6
Nathia Gali Pak. 111 I3
Nati, Punta pt Spain 67 H3
Natillas Mex. 167 E3
Nation AK U.S.A. 149 L2
National City CA U.S.A. 158 E5
National West Coast Tourist Recreation Area park Namibia 124 B2
Natitingou Benin 120 D3
Natividad, Isla i. Mex. 166 B3
Natividade Brazil 177 I6
Natkyizin Myanmar 86 B4
Natla r. Canada 149 O3
Natmauk Myanmar 86 A2
Nator Bangl. see Natore
Nátora Mex. 157 F7
Natore Bangl. 105 G4
Natori Japan 91 F5
Natron, Lake salt l. Tanz. 122 D4
Nattai National Park Australia 138 E5
Nattalin Myanmar 86 A3
Nattaung mt. Myanmar 86 B3
Na'tū Iran 111 F3
Natuashish Canada 153 J3
Natuna, Kepulauan is Indon. 85 D1
Natuna Besar i. Indon. 85 E1
Natural Bridges National Monument nat. park UT U.S.A. 159 H3
Naturaliste, Cape Australia 135 A8
Naturaliste Plateau sea feature Indian Ocean 185 P8
Naturita CO U.S.A. 159 I2
Nauchas Namibia 124 C2
Nau Co l. China 99 C6
Nauen Germany 63 M2
Naufragados, Ponta dos pt Brazil 179 A4
Naujan Mindoro Phil. 82 C3
Naujoji Akmenė Lith. 55 M8
Naukh India 104 C4
Naukot Pak. 111 H5
Naumburg (Hessen) Germany 63 J3
Naumburg (Saale) Germany 63 L3
Naunglon Myanmar 86 B3
Naungpale Myanmar 86 B3
Naupada India 106 E2
Na'ūr Jordan 107 B4
Nauroz Kalat Pak. 111 G4
Naurskaya Rus. Fed. 113 G2
Nauru i. Nauru 133 G2
Nauru country S. Pacific Ocean 133 G2
Naushki Rus. Fed. 94 F1
Naustdal Norway 55 D6
Nauta Peru 176 D4
Nautaca Uzbek. see Qarshi
Nautanwa India 99 C8
Naute Dam Namibia 124 C4
Nautla Mex. 167 F4
Nava Mex. 167 E2
Navadwip India 105 G5
Navahrudak Belarus 55 N10
Navajo Lake NM U.S.A. 159 J3
Navajo Mountain UT U.S.A. 159 H3
Naval Phil. 82 D4
Navalmoral de la Mata Spain 67 D4
Navalvillar de Pela Spain 67 D4
Navan Ireland 61 F4
Navangar India see Jamnagar
Navapolatsk Belarus 55 P9
Nāvar, Dasht-e depr. Afgh. 111 G3
Navarin, Mys c. Rus. Fed. 77 S3
Navarra aut. comm. Spain 67 F2
Navarra, Comunidad Foral de aut. comm. Spain see Navarra
Navarre Australia 138 A6
Navarre aut. comm. Spain see Navarra
Navarro r. CA U.S.A. 158 B2
Navashino Rus. Fed. 52 I5
Navasota TX U.S.A. 161 D6
Navasota r. TX U.S.A. 167 F2

▶Navassa Island terr. West Indies 169 I5
United States Unincorporated Territory.

Naver r. U.K. 60 E2
Näverede Sweden 54 I5
Navi Mumbai India 109 L6
Navlakhi India 104 B5
Navlya Rus. Fed. 53 G5
Năvodari Romania 69 M2
Navoi Uzbek. see Navoiy
Navoiy Uzbek. 111 G1
Navojoa Mex. 166 C3
Navolato Mex. 166 D3
Návpaktos Greece see Nafpaktos
Návplion Greece see Nafplio
Navşar Turkey see Şemdinli
Navsari India 106 B1
Navy Town AK U.S.A. 148 [inset] A5
Nawá Syria 107 C3
Nawabganj Bangl. 105 G4
Nawabshah Pak. 111 H5
Nawada India 105 F4
Nāwah Afgh. 111 G3
Nāwah-ye Gurz Afgh. 111 G3
Nawalgarh India 104 C4
Nawanshahr India 104 D3
Nawan Shehar India see Nawanshahr
Nawar, Dasht-i depr. Afgh. see Nāvar, Dasht-e
Nawarangpur India see Nabarangapur
Nawngcho Myanmar see Nawnghkio
Nawnghkio Myanmar 86 B2
Nawng Hpa Myanmar 86 B2
Nawngleng Myanmar 86 B2
Nawoiy Uzbek. see Navoiy
Naxçıvan Azer. 113 G3
Naxos i. Greece 69 K6
Nayag China 99 F6
Nayagarh India 106 E1
Nayak Afgh. 111 G3
Nayar Mex. 168 D4
Nayarit state Mex. 166 D4
Nāy Band, Kūh-e mt. Iran 110 E3
Nayong China 96 E3
Nayoro Japan 90 F3

▶Nay Pyi Taw Myanmar 86 B3
Joint capital (with Rangoon) of Myanmar.

Nazaré Brazil 179 D1
Nazareno Mex. 166 E3
Nazareth Israel see Naẕerat
Nazário Brazil 179 A2
Nazas Mex. 166 D3
Nazas r. Mex. 166 D3
Nazca Peru 176 D6
Nazca Ridge sea feature S. Pacific Ocean 187 O7
Naẕerat Israel 107 B3
Nāzīl Iran 111 F4
Nazilli Turkey 69 M6
Nazimabad Pak. 111 G5
Nazımiye Turkey 113 E3
Nazir Hat Bangl. 105 G5
Nazko Canada 150 F4
Nazran' Rus. Fed. 113 G2
Nazrēt Eth. 122 D3
Nazwá Oman 110 E6
Ncojane Botswana 124 E2
N'dalatando Angola 123 B4
Ndao i. Indon. 83 B5
Ndélé Cent. Afr. Rep. 122 C3
Ndendé Gabon 122 B4
Ndende i. Solomon Is see Ndeni
Ndeni i. Solomon Is 133 G3

▶Ndjamena Chad 121 E3
Capital of Chad.

N'Djamena Chad see Ndjamena
Ndjouani i. Comoros see Nzwani
Ndoi i. Fiji see Doi
Ndola Zambia 123 C5
Nduke i. Solomon Is see Kolombangara
Ndwedwe S. Africa 125 J5
Ne, Hon i. Vietnam 86 D3
Neabul Creek r. Australia 138 C1
Neagari Japan 92 C2
Neagh, Lough l. U.K. 61 F3
Neah Bay WA U.S.A. 156 B2
Neale, Lake salt flat Australia 135 E6
Nea Liosia Greece 69 J5
Neapoli Greece 69 J6
Neapolis Italy see Naples
Near Islands AK U.S.A. 148 [inset] 5
Nea Roda Greece 69 J4
Neath U.K. 59 D7
Neath r. U.K. 59 D7
Neba Japan 92 D3
Nebbi Uganda 122 D3
Nebesnaya, Gora mt. China 98 C4
Nebine Creek r. Australia 138 C2
Neblina, Pico da mt. Brazil 176 E3
Nebo Australia 136 E4
Nebo, Mount UT U.S.A. 159 H2
Nebolchi Rus. Fed. 52 G4
Nebraska state U.S.A. 160 C3
Nebraska City NE U.S.A. 160 E3
Nebrodi, Monti mts Sicily Italy 68 F6
Neches r. TX U.S.A. 161 E6
Nechisar National Park Eth. 122 D3
Nechranice, Vodní nádrž resr Czech Rep. 63 N4
Neckar r. Germany 63 I5
Neckarsulm Germany 63 J5
Necker Island HI U.S.A. 186 J4
Necochea Arg. 178 E5
Nederland country Europe see Netherlands
Neder Rijn r. Neth. 62 F3
Nedlouc, Lac l. Canada 153 G2
Nedluk Lake Canada see Nedlouc, Lac
Nedre Soppero Sweden 54 L2
Nédroma Alg. 67 F6
Neeba-san mt. Japan 93 E2
Needle Mountain WY U.S.A. 156 F3
Needles CA U.S.A. 159 F4
Neemach India see Neemuch
Neemuch India 104 C4
Neenah WI U.S.A. 164 A1
Neepawa Canada 151 L5
Neergaard Lake Canada 147 J2
Neerijnen Neth. 62 F3
Neerpelt Belgium 62 F3
Neftçala Azer. 113 H3
Neftechala Azer. see Uzboy
Neftechala Azer. see Neftçala
Neftegorsk Sakhalinskaya Oblast' Rus. Fed. 90 F1
Neftegorsk Samarskaya Oblast' Rus. Fed. 53 K5
Neftekamsk Rus. Fed. 51 Q4
Neftekumsk Rus. Fed. 113 G1
Nefteyugansk Rus. Fed. 76 I3
Neftezavodsk Turkm. see Seýdi
Neftezawodsk Turkm. see Seýdi
Nefyn U.K. 59 C6
Nefza Tunisia 68 C6
Negage Angola 123 B4
Negār Iran 110 E4
Negara Bali Indon. 85 F5
Negara Kalimantan Indon. 85 F3
Negara r. Indon. 85 F3
Negēlē Eth. 122 D3
Negeri Sembilan state Malaysia 84 C2
Negev des. Israel 107 B4
Negomane Moz. 123 D5
Negombo Sri Lanka 106 C5
Negotino Macedonia 69 J4
Negra, Cordillera mts Peru 176 C5
Negra, Punta pt Peru 176 B5
Negra, Serra mts Brazil 179 C2
Negrais, Cape Myanmar 86 A4
Négrine Alg. 68 B7
Negri Sembilan state Malaysia see Negeri Sembilan
Negro r. Arg. 178 D6
Negro r. Mato Grosso do Sul Brazil 177 G7
Negro r. Paraná/Santa Catarina Brazil 179 A4
Negro r. S. America 176 G4
Negro, Cabo c. Morocco 67 D6
Negroponte i. Greece see Evvoia
Negros i. Phil. 82 C4
Negru Vodă, Podișul plat. Romania 69 M3
Nehbandān Iran 111 F4
Nehe China 95 K1
Neiguanying China 94 F5
Neijiang China 96 E2
Neilburg Canada 151 I4
Neimenggu aut. reg. China see Nei Mongol Zizhiqu
Nei Mongol Zizhiqu aut. reg. China 95 E3
Neinstedt Germany 63 L3
Neiqiu China 95 H4
Neiva Col. 176 C3
Neixiang China 97 F1
Nejanilini Lake Canada 151 L3
Nejapa Mex. 167 G5
Nejd reg. Saudi Arabia see Najd
Nekā Iran 110 D2
Nek'emtē Eth. 122 D3
Neko-zaki pt Japan 92 A3
Nekrasovskoye Rus. Fed. 52 I4
Neksø Denmark 55 I9
Nelang India 104 D3
Nelia Australia 136 C4
Nelidovo Rus. Fed. 52 G4
Neligh NE U.S.A. 160 D3
Nel'kan Rus. Fed. 77 P3
Nelligere India 106 C3
Nellore India 106 C3
Nelluz watercourse Turkey 107 D1
Nel'ma Rus. Fed. 90 E3
Nelson Canada 150 G5
Nelson r. Canada 151 M3
Nelson N.Z. 139 D5
Nelson U.K. 58 E5
Nelson AZ U.S.A. 159 G4
Nelson, Cape Australia 137 C8
Nelson, Cape P.N.G. 81 L8
Nelson, Estrecho strait Chile 178 A8
Nelson Bay Australia 138 F4
Nelson Forks Canada 150 F3
Nelsonia VA U.S.A. 165 H5
Nelson Island AK U.S.A. 148 F3
Nelson Lagoon AK U.S.A. 148 G5
Nelson Lakes National Park N.Z. 139 D6
Nelson Reservoir MT U.S.A. 156 G2
Nelspruit S. Africa see Mbombela
Néma Mauritania 120 C3
Nema Rus. Fed. 52 K4
Neman r. Belarus/Lith. see Nyoman
Neman Rus. Fed. 55 M9
Nemausus France see Nîmes
Nemawar India 104 D5
Nemed Rus. Fed. 52 L3
Nementcha, Monts des mts Alg. 68 B7
Nemetocenna France see Arras
Nemetskiy, Mys c. Rus. Fed. 54 Q2
Nemirov Ukr. see Nemyriv
Nemiscau r. Canada 152 F4
Nemiscau, Lac l. Canada 152 F4
Nemor He r. China 95 K1
Nemours Alg. see Ghazaouet
Nemours France 66 F2
Nemrut Dağı mt. Turkey 113 F3
Nemunas r. Belarus/Lith. see Nyoman
Nemuro Japan 90 G4
Nemuro-kaikyō sea chan. Japan/Rus. Fed. 90 G4
Nemyriv Ukr. 53 F6
Nenagh Ireland 61 D5
Nenan China 95 K1
Nenana AK U.S.A. 149 J2
Nenana r. AK U.S.A. 149 J2
Nene r. U.K. 59 H6
Nenjiang China 95 K1
Nen Jiang r. China 95 K2
Neo Japan 92 C3
Neo-gawa r. Japan 92 C3
Neosho MO U.S.A. 161 E4
Nepal country Asia 105 E3
Nepalganj Nepal 105 E3
Nepean Canada 165 H1
Nepean, Point Australia 138 B7
Nephi UT U.S.A. 159 H2
Nephin hill Ireland 61 C3
Nephin Beg Range hills Ireland 61 C3
Nepisiguit r. Canada 153 I5
Nepoko r. Dem. Rep. Congo 122 C3
Nérac France 66 E4
Neragon Island AK U.S.A. 148 F3
Nerang Australia 138 F1
Nera Tso l. China 105 H3
Nerchinsk Rus. Fed. 89 L2
Nerekhta Rus. Fed. 52 I4
Néret, Lac l. Canada 153 H3
Neretva r. Bos.-Herz./Croatia 68 G3
Nêri Pünco l. China 99 E7
Neriquinha Angola 123 C5
Neris r. Lith. 55 M9
also known as Viliya (Belarus/Lithuania)
Nerl' r. Rus. Fed. 52 H4
Nerópolis Brazil 179 A2
Neryungri Rus. Fed. 77 N4
Nes Neth. 62 F1
Nes Norway 55 F6
Nes' Rus. Fed. 52 J2
Nesbyen Norway 55 F6
Neshkan Rus. Fed. 148 D2
Neshkenpil'khyn, Laguna lag. Rus. Fed. 148 D2
Neskaupstaður Iceland 54 [inset 1]
Nesle France 62 C5
Nesna Norway 54 H3
Nesri India 106 B2
Ness r. U.K. 60 E3
Ness, Loch l. U.K. 60 E3
Ness City KS U.S.A. 160 D4
Nesse r. Germany 63 K4
Nesselrode, Mount Canada/U.S.A. 149 N4
Nestor Falls Canada 151 M5
Nestos r. Greece 69 K4
also known as Mesta
Nesvizh Belarus see Nyasvizh
Netanya Israel 107 B3
Netherlands country Europe 62 F2

▶Netherlands Antilles West Indies 169 K6
The Netherlands Antilles was dissolved into 5 constituent dependencies of the Netherlands in Oct. 2010.

Netphen Germany 63 I4
Netrakona Bangl. 105 G4
Netrokona Bangl. see Netrakona
Nettilling Lake Canada 147 K3
Neubrandenburg Germany 63 N1
Neuburg an der Donau Germany 63 L6
Neuchâtel Switz. 66 H3
Neuchâtel, Lac de l. Switz. 66 H3
Neuendettelsau Germany 63 K5
Neuenhaus Germany 62 G2
Neuenkirchen Germany 63 J1
Neuenkirchen (Oldenburg) Germany 63 I2
Neufchâteau Belgium 62 F5
Neufchâteau France 66 G2
Neufchâtel-en-Bray France 62 B5
Neufchâtel-Hardelot France 62 B4
Neuharlingersiel Germany 63 H1
Neuhausen Rus. Fed. see Gur'yevsk
Neuhof Germany 63 J4
Neu Kaliß Germany 63 L1
Neukirchen Hessen Germany 63 J4
Neukirchen Sachsen Germany 63 M4
Neukuhren Rus. Fed. see Pionerskiy
Neumarkt in der Oberpfalz Germany 63 L5
Neumayer III research station Antarctica 188 B2
Neumünster Germany 57 L3
Neunburg vorm Wald Germany 63 M5
Neunkirchen Austria 57 P7
Neunkirchen Germany 63 H5
Neuquén Arg. 178 C5
Neuruppin Germany 63 M2
Neu Sandez Poland see Nowy Sącz
Neuse r. NC U.S.A. 163 E5
Neusiedler See l. Austria/Hungary 57 P7
Neusiedler See Seewinkel, Nationalpark nat. park Austria 57 P7
Neuss Germany 62 G3
Neustadt am Rübenberge Germany 63 J2
Neustadt an der Aisch Germany 63 K5
Neustadt an der Hardt Germany see Neustadt an der Weinstraße
Neustadt an der Waldnaab Germany 63 M5
Neustadt an der Weinstraße Germany 63 I5
Neustadt bei Coburg Germany 63 L4
Neustadt-Glewe Germany 63 L1
Neustadt (Wied) Germany 63 H4
Neustrelitz Germany 63 N1
Neutraubling Germany 63 M6
Neuville-lès-Dieppe France 62 B5
Neuwied Germany 63 H4
Neu Wulmstorf Germany 63 J1
Nevada IA U.S.A. 160 E3
Nevada MO U.S.A. 160 E4
Nevada state U.S.A. 156 D5
Nevada, Sierra mts Spain 67 E5
Nevada, Sierra mts CA U.S.A. 158 C1
Nevada City CA U.S.A. 158 C2
Nevado, Cerro mt. Arg. 178 C5
Nevado, Sierra del mts Arg. 178 C5
Nevado de Colima, Parque Nacional nat. park Mex. 166 E5
Nevasa India 106 B2
Nevatim Israel 107 B4
Nevdubstroy Rus. Fed. see Kirovsk
Nevel' Rus. Fed. 52 F4
Nevel'sk Rus. Fed. 90 F3
Never Rus. Fed. 90 B1
Nevers France 66 F3
Nevertire Australia 138 C3
Nevesinje Bos.-Herz. 68 H3
Nevinnomyssk Rus. Fed. 113 F1
Nevşehir Turkey 112 D3
Nevskoye Rus. Fed. 90 D3
New r. CA U.S.A. 159 F5
New r. WV U.S.A. 164 E5
Newala Tanz. 123 D5
New Albany IN U.S.A. 164 C4
New Albany MS U.S.A. 161 F5
New Amsterdam Guyana 177 G2
New Amsterdam NY U.S.A. see New York
New Angledool Australia 138 C2
Newark DE U.S.A. 165 H4
Newark NJ U.S.A. 165 H3
Newark NY U.S.A. 165 G2
Newark OH U.S.A. 164 D3
Newark Lake NV U.S.A. 159 F2
Newark Liberty airport NJ U.S.A. 162 F3
Newark-on-Trent U.K. 59 G5
Newberg OR U.S.A. 156 C3
New Berlin NY U.S.A. 165 H2
New Bern NC U.S.A. 163 E5
Newberry IN U.S.A. 164 B4
Newberry MI U.S.A. 162 C2
Newberry SC U.S.A. 163 D5
Newberry National Volcanic Monument nat. park OR U.S.A. 156 C4
Newberry Springs CA U.S.A. 158 E4
New Bethlehem PA U.S.A. 164 F3
Newbiggin-by-the-Sea U.K. 58 F3
New Bight Bahamas 163 F7
New Bloomfield PA U.S.A. 165 G3
Newboro Canada 165 G1
New Boston OH U.S.A. 164 D4
New Boston TX U.S.A. 161 E5
New Braunfels TX U.S.A. 161 D6
Newbridge Ireland 61 F4
New Britain i. P.N.G. 81 L8
New Britain CT U.S.A. 165 I3
New Britain Trench sea feature S. Pacific Ocean 186 G6
New Brunswick prov. Canada 153 I5
New Brunswick NJ U.S.A. 165 H3
New Buffalo MI U.S.A. 164 B3
Newburgh Canada 165 G1
Newburgh U.K. 60 G3
Newburgh NY U.S.A. 165 H3
Newbury U.K. 59 F7
Newburyport MA U.S.A. 165 J2
New Busuanga Phil. 82 B3
Newby Bridge U.K. 58 E4

▶New Caledonia terr. S. Pacific Ocean 133 G4
French Overseas Collectivity.

New Caledonia Trough sea feature Tasman Sea 186 G7
New Carlisle Canada 153 I4
Newcastle Australia 138 E4
Newcastle Canada 165 F2
Newcastle Ireland 61 F4
Newcastle S. Africa 125 I4
Newcastle U.K. 61 G3
New Castle CO U.S.A. 159 J2
New Castle IN U.S.A. 164 C4
New Castle KY U.S.A. 164 C4
New Castle PA U.S.A. 164 E3
Newcastle UT U.S.A. 159 G3
New Castle VA U.S.A. 164 E5
Newcastle WY U.S.A. 156 G3
Newcastle Emlyn U.K. 59 C6
Newcastle-under-Lyme U.K. 59 E5
Newcastle upon Tyne U.K. 58 F4
Newcastle Waters Australia 134 F4
Newcastle West Ireland 61 C5
Newchwang China see Yingkou
New City NY U.S.A. 165 I3
Newcomb NM U.S.A. 159 I3
New Concord OH U.S.A. 164 E4
New Cumberland WV U.S.A. 164 E3
New Cumnock U.K. 60 E5
New Deer U.K. 60 G3

▶New Delhi India 104 D3
Capital of India.

New Don Pedro Reservoir CA U.S.A. 158 C3
Newell SD U.S.A. 160 C2
Newell, Lake salt flat Australia 135 D6
Newell, Lake Canada 151 I5
New England National Park Australia 138 F3
New England Range mts Australia 138 E3
New England Seamounts sea feature N. Atlantic Ocean 184 E3
Newenham, Cape AK U.S.A. 148 G4
Newent U.K. 59 E7
New Era MI U.S.A. 164 B2
Newfane NY U.S.A. 165 F2
Newfane VT U.S.A. 165 I2
New Forest National Park nat. park U.K. 59 F8
Newfoundland i. Canada 153 K4
Newfoundland prov. Canada see Newfoundland and Labrador
Newfoundland and Labrador prov. Canada 153 K3
Newfoundland Evaporation Basin salt l. UT U.S.A. 159 G1
New Galloway U.K. 60 E5
New Georgia i. Solomon Is 133 F2
New Georgia Islands Solomon Is 133 F2
New Georgia Sound sea chan. Solomon Is 133 F2
New Glasgow Canada 153 J5

▶New Guinea i. Indon./P.N.G. 81 K8
Largest island in Oceania and 2nd in the world.

Newhalen AK U.S.A. 148 I4
New Halfa Sudan 108 E6
New Hamilton AK U.S.A. 148 G3
New Hampshire state U.S.A. 165 J1
New Hampton IA U.S.A. 160 E3
New Hanover i. P.N.G. 132 F2
Newhaven town U.K. 59 H8
New Haven CT U.S.A. 165 I3
New Haven IN U.S.A. 164 C3
New Haven WV U.S.A. 164 E4
New Hebrides country S. Pacific Ocean see Vanuatu
New Hebrides Trench sea feature S. Pacific Ocean 186 H7
New Holstein WI U.S.A. 164 A2
New Iberia LA U.S.A. 161 F6
Newington S. Africa 125 J3
Newinn Ireland 61 E5
New Ireland i. P.N.G. 132 F2
New Jersey state U.S.A. 165 H4
New Kensington PA U.S.A. 164 F3
New Kent VA U.S.A. 165 G5
Newkirk OK U.S.A. 161 D4
New Lanark U.K. 60 F5
Newland Range hills Australia 135 C7
New Lexington OH U.S.A. 164 D4
New Liskeard Canada 152 F5
New London CT U.S.A. 165 I3
New London MO U.S.A. 160 F4
New Madrid MO U.S.A. 161 F4
Newman Australia 135 B5
Newman CA U.S.A. 158 C3
Newmarket Canada 164 F1
Newmarket Ireland 61 C5
Newmarket U.K. 59 H6
New Market VA U.S.A. 165 F4
Newmarket-on-Fergus Ireland 61 D5
New Martinsville WV U.S.A. 164 E4
New Meadows ID U.S.A. 156 D3
New Mexico state U.S.A. 157 G6
New Miami OH U.S.A. 164 C4
New Milford PA U.S.A. 165 H3
Newnan GA U.S.A. 163 C5
New Orleans LA U.S.A. 161 F6
New Paris IN U.S.A. 164 C3
New Paris OH U.S.A. 164 C4
New Philadelphia OH U.S.A. 164 E3
New Pitsligo U.K. 60 G3
New Plymouth N.Z. 139 E4
Newport Mayo Ireland 61 C4
Newport North Tipperary Ireland 61 D5
Newport England U.K. 59 E6
Newport England U.K. 59 F8
Newport Wales U.K. 59 D7
Newport AR U.S.A. 161 F5
Newport IN U.S.A. 164 B4
Newport KY U.S.A. 164 C4
Newport MI U.S.A. 164 D3
Newport NH U.S.A. 165 I2
Newport NJ U.S.A. 165 H4
Newport OR U.S.A. 156 B3
Newport RI U.S.A. 165 J3
Newport VT U.S.A. 165 I1
Newport WA U.S.A. 156 D2
Newport Beach CA U.S.A. 158 E5
Newport News VA U.S.A. 165 G5
Newport Pagnell U.K. 59 G6
New Port Richey FL U.S.A. 163 D6
New Providence i. Bahamas 163 E7
Newquay U.K. 59 B8
New Roads LA U.S.A. 161 F6
New Rochelle NY U.S.A. 165 I3
New Rockford ND U.S.A. 160 D2
New Romney U.K. 59 H8
New Ross Ireland 61 F5
Newry Australia 134 E4
Newry U.K. 61 F3
New Siberia Islands Rus. Fed. 77 P2
New Smyrna Beach FL U.S.A. 163 D6
New South Wales state Australia 138 C4
New Stanton PA U.S.A. 164 F3
New Stuyahok AK U.S.A. 148 H4
Newtok AK U.S.A. 148 F3
Newton U.K. 58 E5
Newton GA U.S.A. 163 C6
Newton IA U.S.A. 160 E3
Newton IL U.S.A. 160 F4
Newton KS U.S.A. 160 D4
Newton MA U.S.A. 165 J2
Newton MS U.S.A. 161 F5
Newton NC U.S.A. 162 D5
Newton NJ U.S.A. 165 H3
Newton TX U.S.A. 161 E6
Newton Abbot U.K. 59 D8
Newton Mearns U.K. 60 E5
Newton Stewart U.K. 60 E6
Newtown Ireland 61 D5
Newtown England U.K. 59 E6
Newtown Wales U.K. 59 D6
Newtown KY U.S.A. 164 C4
New Town ND U.S.A. 160 C1
Newtownabbey U.K. 61 G3
Newtownards U.K. 61 G3
Newtownbarry Ireland see Bunclody
Newtownbutler U.K. 61 E3
Newtown Mount Kennedy Ireland 61 F4
Newtown St Boswells U.K. 60 G5
Newtownstewart U.K. 61 E3
New Ulm MN U.S.A. 160 E2
Newville PA U.S.A. 165 G3
New World Island Canada 153 L4

▶New York NY U.S.A. 165 I3
2nd most populous city in North America and 6th in the world.

New York state U.S.A. 165 H2

▶New Zealand country Oceania 139 D5
3rd largest and 3rd most populated country in Oceania.

Neya Rus. Fed. 52 I4
Neyagawa Japan 92 B4
Ney Bīd Iran 110 E4
Neyrīz Iran 110 D4

Neyshābūr Iran 110 E2
Nezahualcóyotl, Presa resr Mex. 167 G5
Nezhin Ukr. see Nizhyn
Nezperce ID U.S.A. 156 D3
Ngabang Kalimantan Indon. 85 E2
Ngabé Congo 122 B4
Nga Chong, Khao mt. Myanmar/Thai. 86 B4
Ngadubolu Sumba Indon. 83 A5
Ngagahtawng Myanmar 96 C3
Ngagau mt. Tanz. 123 D4
Ngajangel i. Palau 82 [inset]
Ngalipaëng Sulawesi Indon. 83 C2
Ngalu Sumba Indon. 83 B5
Ngamegei Passage Palau 82 [inset]
Ngamring China 99 D7
Ngangla Ringco salt l. China 99 C7
Nganglong Kangri mt. China 99 C6
Nganglong Kangri mts China 99 C6
Ngangzê Co salt l. China 99 D7
Ngangzê Shan mts China 99 D7
Nganjuk Jawa Indon. 85 E4
Ngân Sơn Vietnam 86 D2
Ngaoundal Cameroon 120 E4
Ngaoundéré Cameroon 121 E4
Ngape Myanmar 86 A2
Ngaputaw Myanmar 86 A3
Ngaras Sumatera Indon. 84 D4
Ngardmau Palau 82 [inset]
Ngardmau Bay Palau 82 [inset]
Ngaregur i. Palau 82 [inset]
Ngariungs i. Palau 82 [inset]
Ngateguil, Point Palau 82 [inset]
Ngathainggyaung Myanmar 86 A3
Ngau i. Fiji see Gau
Ngawa China see Aba
Ngawi Jawa Indon. 85 E4
Ngazidja i. Comoros 123 E5
Ngcheangel atoll Palau see Kayangel Atoll
Ngeaur i. Palau see Angaur
Ngemelachel Palau see Malakal
Ngemelis Islands Palau 82 [inset]
Ngergoi i. Palau 82 [inset]
Ngeruangel i. Palau 81 I5
Ngerulmud Palau 82 [inset]
Ngesebus i. Palau 82 [inset]
Ngga Pulu mt. Indon. see Jaya, Puncak
Ngiap r. Laos 86 C3
Ngilmina Timor Indon. 83 C5
Ngimbang Jawa Indon. 85 F4
Ngiva Angola see Ondjiva
Ngo Congo 122 B4
Ngoako Ramalepe S. Africa see Duiwelskloof
Ngobasangel i. Palau 82 [inset]
Ngofakiaha Maluku Indon. 83 C2
Ngoichogê China 99 F7
Ngoin, Co salt l. China 99 E7
Ngok Linh mt. Vietnam 86 D4
Ngoko r. Cameroon/Congo 121 E4
Ngola Shan mts China 94 D4
Ngola Shankou pass China 94 D5
Ngom Qu r. China 99 G7
Ngong Shuen Chau pen. H.K. China see Stonecutters' Island
Ngoqumaima China 99 D6
Ngoring China 94 D5
Ngoring Hu l. China 94 D5
Ngourti Niger 120 E3
Nguigmi Niger 120 E3
Nguiu Australia 134 E2
Ngükang China 99 F7
Ngukurr Australia 134 F3
Ngulu atoll Micronesia 81 J5
Ngunju, Tanjung pt Sumba Indon. 83 B5
Ngunza Angola see Sumbe
Ngunza-Kabolu Angola see Sumbe
Ngura China 94 E5
Nguru Nigeria 120 E3
Ngwaketse admin. dist. Botswana see Southern
Ngwane country Africa see Swaziland
Ngwathe S. Africa 125 H4
Ngwavuma r. S. Africa/Swaziland 125 K4
Ngwelezana S. Africa 125 J5
Nhachengue Moz. 125 L2
Nhamalabué Moz. 123 D5
Nha Trang Vietnam 87 E4
Nhecolândia Brazil 177 G7
Nhill Australia 137 C8
Nhlangano Swaziland 125 J4
Nho Quan Vietnam 86 D2
Nhow i. Fiji see Gau
Nhulunbuy Australia 136 B2
Niacam Canada 151 J4
Niafounké Mali 120 C3
Niagara WI U.S.A. 162 C2
Niagara Falls Canada 164 F2
Niagara Falls NY U.S.A. 164 F2
Niagara-on-the-Lake Canada 164 F2
Niagzu Aksai Chin 99 B6
Niah Sarawak Malaysia 85 F2
Niakaramandougou Côte d'Ivoire 120 C4

▶Niamey Niger 120 D3
Capital of Niger.

Nīām Kand Iran 110 E5
Niampak Indon. 81 H6
Nianbai China see Ledu
Niangara Dem. Rep. Congo 122 C3
Niangay, Lac l. Mali 120 C3
Nianyuwan China see Xingangzhen
Nianzishan China 95 J2
Nias i. Indon. 84 B2
Niassa, Lago l. Africa see Nyasa, Lake
Niaur i. Palau see Angaur
Nīāzābād Iran 111 F3
Nibil Well Australia 134 D5
Nīca Latvia 55 L8

▶Nicaragua country Central America 169 G6
4th largest country in North America.

Nicaragua, Lago de l. Nicaragua 166 [inset] I7
Nicaragua, Lake Nicaragua see Nicaragua, Lago de
Nicastro Italy 68 G5
Nice France 66 H5
Nice CA U.S.A. 158 B2
Nicephorium Syria see Ar Raqqah
Niceville FL U.S.A. 163 C6
Nichicun, Lac l. Canada 153 H3
Nicholas Channel Bahamas/Cuba 163 D8
Nicholasville KY U.S.A. 164 C5
Nichols WI U.S.A. 164 A1
Nicholson r. Australia 136 B3
Nicholson Lake Canada 151 K2
Nicholson Range hills Australia 135 B6
Nicholville NY U.S.A. 165 H1
Nicobar Islands India 87 A5
Nicolás Bravo Mex. 167 H5
Nicolaus CA U.S.A. 158 C2
Nicomedia Turkey see İzmit

▶Nicosia Cyprus 107 A2
Capital of Cyprus.

Nicoya Costa Rica 166 [inset] I7
Nicoya, Golfo de b. Costa Rica 166 [inset] I7
Nicoya, Península de pen. Costa Rica 166 [inset] I7
Nida Lith. 55 L9
Nidagunda India 106 C2
Nidd r. U.K. 58 F4
Nidda Germany 63 J4
Nidder r. Germany 63 I4
Nidzica Poland 57 R4
Niebüll Germany 57 L3
Nied r. France 62 G5
Niederanven Lux. 62 G5
Niederaula Germany 63 J4
Niedere Tauern mts Austria 57 N7
Niedersachsen land Germany 63 I2
Niedersächsisches Wattenmeer, Nationalpark nat. park Germany 62 G1
Niefang Equat. Guinea 120 E4
Niellé Côte d'Ivoire 120 C3
Nienburg (Weser) Germany 63 J2
Niers r. Germany 62 F3
Nierstein Germany 63 I5
Nieuwe-Niedorp Neth. 62 E2
Nieuwerkerk aan de IJssel Neth. 62 E3
Nieuw Nickerie Suriname 177 G2
Nieuwolda Neth. 62 G1
Nieuwoudtville S. Africa 124 D6
Nieuwpoort Belgium 62 C3
Nieuw-Vossemeer Neth. 62 E3
Nif Seram Indon. 83 D3
Niğde Turkey 112 D3
Niger country Africa 120 D3

▶Niger r. Africa 120 D4
3rd longest river in Africa.

Niger, Mouths of the Nigeria 120 D4
Niger Cone sea feature S. Atlantic Ocean 184 I5

▶Nigeria country Africa 120 D4
Most populous country in Africa and 7th in the world.

Nighthawk Lake Canada 152 E4
Nightmute AK U.S.A. 148 F3
Nigrita Greece 69 J4
Nihing Pak. 111 G4
Nihon country Asia see Japan
Niigata Japan 91 E5
Niigata pref. Japan 93 E1
Niigata-yake-yama vol. Japan 93 E2
Niihama Japan 91 D6
Niihari Japan 93 E2
Ni'ihau i. HI U.S.A. 157 [inset]
Nii-jima i. Japan 93 F4
Niimi Japan 91 D6
Niitsu Japan 91 E5
Niiza Japan 93 F3
Nijil, Wādī watercourse Jordan 107 B4
Nijkerk Neth. 62 F2
Nijmegen Neth. 62 F3
Nijverdal Neth. 62 G2
Nikel' Rus. Fed. 54 Q2
Nikiniki Timor Indon. 83 C5
Nikiski AK U.S.A. 149 J3
Nikki Benin 120 D4
Nikkō Japan 93 F2
Nikkō Kokuritsu-kōen nat. park Japan 93 F2
Nikolaevsk AK U.S.A. 149 J4
Nikolai AK U.S.A. 148 I3
Nikolayev Ukr. see Mykolayiv
Nikolayevka Rus. Fed. 53 J5
Nikolayevsk Rus. Fed. 53 J6
Nikolayevskiy Rus. Fed. see Nikolayevsk
Nikolayevsk-na-Amure Rus. Fed. 90 F1
Nikol'sk Rus. Fed. 52 J4
Nikolski AK U.S.A. 148 E5
Nikol'skiy Kazakh. see Satpayev
Nikol'skoye Kamchatskiy Kray Rus. Fed. 77 R4
Nikol'skoye Vologod. Obl. Rus. Fed. see Sheksna
Nikopol' Ukr. 53 G7
Niksar Turkey 112 E2
Nīkshahr Iran 111 F5
Nikšić Montenegro 68 H3
Nīkū Jahān Iran 111 F5
Nikumaroro atoll Kiribati 133 I2
Nikunau i. Kiribati 133 H2
Nīl, Bahr el r. Africa see Nile
Nila vol. Maluku Indon. 83 D4
Nilagiri India 105 F5
Niland CA U.S.A. 159 F5
Nilande Atoll Maldives see Nilandhoo Atoll
Nilandhe Atoll Maldives see Nilandhoo Atoll
Nilandhoo Atoll Maldives 103 D11
Nilang India see Nelang
Nilanga India 106 C2
Nilaveli Sri Lanka 106 D4

▶Nile r. Africa 112 C5
Longest river in Africa and the world.

Niles MI U.S.A. 164 B3
Niles OH U.S.A. 164 E3
Nilgiri Hills India 106 C4
Nīlī Afgh. 111 G3
Nilka China 98 C4
Nīl Kōtal Afgh. 111 G3
Nilphamari Bangl. 105 G4
Nilsiä Fin. 54 P5
Nimach India see Neemuch
Niman r. Rus. Fed. 90 D2
Nimba, Monts mts Africa see Nimba, Mount
Nimba, Mount Africa 120 C4
Nimbal India 106 B2
Nimberra Well Australia 135 C5
Nimelen r. Rus. Fed. 90 E1
Nîmes France 66 G5
Nimmitabel Australia 137 E8
Nimrod Glacier Antarctica 188 H1
Nimu India 104 D2
Nimule South Sudan 121 G4
Nimwegen Neth. see Nijmegen
Nindigully Australia 138 D2
Nine Degree Channel India 106 B4
Nine Islands P.N.G. see Kilinailau Islands
Ninepin Group is H.K. China 97 [inset]
Ninetyeast Ridge sea feature Indian Ocean 185 N8
Ninety Mile Beach Australia 138 C7
Ninety Mile Beach N.Z. 139 D2
Nineveh NY U.S.A. 165 H2
Ningaloo Coast tourist site Australia 134 A5
Ning'an China 90 C3
Ningbo China 97 I2
Ningcheng China 95 I3
Ningde China 97 H3
Ning'er China see Pu'er
Ningguo China 97 H2
Ninghai China 97 I2
Ninghe China 95 I4
Ninghsia Hui Autonomous Region aut. reg. China see Ningxia Huizu Zizhiqu
Ninghua China 97 H3
Ningjiang China see Songyuan
Ningjing Shan mts China 96 C2
Ninglang China 96 D3
Ningling China 95 H5
Ningming China 96 E4
Ningnan China 96 D3
Ningqiang China 96 E1
Ningwu China 95 H4
Ningxia aut. reg. China see Ningxia Huizu Zizhiqu
Ningxia Huizu Zizhiqu aut. reg. China 94 F4
Ningxian China 95 F5
Ningxiang China 97 G2
Ningyang China 95 I5
Ningzhou China see Huaning
Ninh Bình Vietnam 86 D2
Ninh Hoa Vietnam 87 E4
Ninigo Group atolls P.N.G. 81 K7
Ninilchik AK U.S.A. 149 J3
Ninnis Glacier Antarctica 188 G2
Ninnis Glacier Tongue Antarctica 188 H2
Ninohe Japan 91 F4
Ninomiya Kanagawa Japan 93 F3
Ninomiya Tochigi Japan 93 F2
Niobrara r. NE U.S.A. 160 D3
Nioko India 99 F8
Niokolo Koba, Parc National du nat. park Senegal 120 B3
Nioro Mali 120 C3
Nioro Mali 120 C3
Niort France 66 D3
Nipani India 106 B2
Nipanipa, Tanjung pt Indon. 83 B3
Nipawin Canada 151 J4
Niphad India 106 B1
Nipigon Canada 147 J5
Nipigon, Lake Canada 147 J5
Nipishish Lake Canada 153 J3
Nipissing, Lake Canada 152 F5
Nippon country Asia see Japan
Nippon Hai sea N. Pacific Ocean see Japan, Sea of
Nipton CA U.S.A. 159 F4
Niquelândia Brazil 179 A1
Nir Ardabīl Iran 110 B2
Nir Yazd Iran 110 D4
Nira r. India 106 B2
Nirasaki Japan 93 E3
Nirayama Japan 93 E3
Nirji China 95 K1
Nirmal India 106 C2
Nirmali India 105 F4
Nirmal Range hills India 106 C2
Niš Serbia 69 I3
Nisa Port. 67 C4
Nisarpur India 106 B1
Niscemi Sicily Italy 68 F6
Nishan China 99 D6
Nīshāpūr Iran see Neyshābūr
Nishiazai Japan 92 C3
Nishiizu Japan 93 E4
Nishikata Japan 93 F2
Nishikatsura Japan 93 E3
Nishi-maizuru Japan 92 B3
Nishinasuno Japan 93 F2
Nishinomiya Japan 92 B4
Nishino-shima vol. Japan 91 F8
Nishio Japan 92 D4
Nishi-Sonogi-hantō pen. Japan 91 C6
Nishiwaki Japan 92 A4
Nishiyoshino Japan 92 B4
Nisibis Turkey see Nusaybin
Nisiharu Japan 92 C3
Nisiros i. Greece see Nisyros
Niskibi r. Canada 151 N3
Nisling r. Canada 149 M3
Nispen Neth. 62 E3
Nissan r. Sweden 55 H8
Nisshin Japan 92 D3
Nistru r. Ukr. 69 N1 see Dniester
Nisutlin r. Canada 149 N3
Nisyros i. Greece 69 L6
Niṭā Saudi Arabia 110 C5
Nitchequon Canada 153 H3
Nitendi i. Solomon Is see Ndeni
Niterói Brazil 179 C3
Nith r. U.K. 60 F5
Nitibe East Timor 83 C5
Niti Pass China/India 104 D3
Niti Shankou pass China/India see Niti Pass
Nitmiluk National Park Australia 134 F3
Nitra Slovakia 57 Q6
Nitro WV U.S.A. 164 E4
Nitta Japan 93 F2
Niuafo'ou i. Tonga 133 I3
Niuatoputopu i. Tonga 133 I3
Niubiziliang China 98 F5

▶Niue terr. S. Pacific Ocean 133 J3
Self-governing New Zealand Overseas Territory.

Niujing China see Binchuan
Niulakita i. Tuvalu 133 H3
Niur, Pulau i. Indon. 84 C3
Niushan China see Donghai
Niutao i. Tuvalu 133 H2
Niutoushan China 97 H2
Niuzhuang China 95 J3
Nivala Fin. 54 N5
Nive watercourse Australia 136 D5
Nivelles Belgium 62 E4
Niwai India 104 C4
Niwas India 104 E5
Nixia China see Sêrxü
Nixon NV U.S.A. 158 D2
Niya China see Minfeng
Niya He r. China 99 C5
Niyut, Gunung mt. Indon. 85 E2
Nizamabad India 106 C2
Nizam Sagar l. India 106 C2
Nizhnedevitsk Rus. Fed. 53 H6
Nizhnekamsk Rus. Fed. 52 K5
Nizhnekamskoye Vodokhranilishche resr Rus. Fed. 51 Q4
Nizhnekolymsk Rus. Fed. 77 R3
Nizhnetambovskoye Rus. Fed. 90 E2
Nizhneudinsk Rus. Fed. 88 H2
Nizhnevartovsk Rus. Fed. 76 I3
Nizhnevolzhsk Rus. Fed. see Narimanov
Nizhneyansk Rus. Fed. 77 O2
Nizhneye Giryunino Rus. Fed. 95 I1
Nizhniy Baskunchak Rus. Fed. 53 J6
Nizhniye Kresty Rus. Fed. see Cherskiy
Nizhniy Lomov Rus. Fed. 53 I5
Nizhniy Novgorod Rus. Fed. 52 I4
Nizhniy Odes Rus. Fed. 52 L3
Nizhniy Pyandzh Tajik. see Panji Poyon
Nizhniy Tagil Rus. Fed. 51 R4
Nizhniy Torey Rus. Fed. 94 F1
Nizhniy Tsasuchey Rus. Fed. 95 H1
Nizhnyaya Mola Rus. Fed. 52 J2
Nizhnyaya Omra Rus. Fed. 52 L3
Nizhnyaya Pirenga, Ozero l. Rus. Fed. 54 R3
Nizhnyaya Tunguska r. Rus. Fed. 76 J3
Nizhnyaya Tura Rus. Fed. 51 R4
Nizhyn Ukr. 53 F6
Nizina r. AK U.S.A. 150 A2
Nizina Mazowiecka reg. Poland 57 R4
Nizip Turkey 107 C1
Nízke Tatry nat. park Slovakia 57 Q6
Nizkiy, Mys hd Rus. Fed. 148 B2
Nizwā Oman see Nazwá
Nizza France see Nice
Njallavarri mt. Norway 54 L2
Njavve Sweden 54 K3
Njombe Tanz. 123 D4
Njurundabommen Sweden 54 J5
Nkambe Cameroon 120 E4
Nkandla S. Africa 125 J5
Nkawkaw Ghana 120 C4
Nkhata Bay Malawi 123 D5
Nkhotakota Malawi 123 D5
Nkondwe Tanz. 123 D4
Nkongsamba Cameroon 120 D4
Nkululeko S. Africa 125 H6
Nkwenkwezi S. Africa 125 H7
Noakhali Bangl. 105 G5
Noatak AK U.S.A. 148 G2
Noatak r. AK U.S.A. 148 G2
Noatak National Preserve nature res. AK U.S.A. 148 H1
Nobber Ireland 61 F4
Nobeoka Japan 91 C6
Noblesville IN U.S.A. 164 B3
Noboribetsu Japan 90 F4
Noccundra Australia 137 C5
Nochistlán Mex. 166 E4
Nochixtlán Mex. 167 F5
Nockatunga Australia 137 C5
Nocona TX U.S.A. 161 D5
Noda Japan 93 F3
Nodagawa Japan 92 B3
Noel Kempff Mercado, Parque Nacional nat. park Bol. 176 F6
Noelville Canada 152 E5
Nogales Mex. 166 C2
Nogales AZ U.S.A. 157 F7
Nōgata Japan 91 C6
Nogent-le-Rotrou France 66 E2
Nogent-sur-Oise France 62 C5
Nogi Japan 93 F2
Noginsk Rus. Fed. 52 H5
Nogliki Rus. Fed. 90 F2
Nogoa r. Australia 136 E4
Nōgōhaku-san mt. Japan 92 C3
Nogon Toli China 94 F4
Noguchigorō-dake mt. Japan 92 D2
Nohalal Mex. 167 H5
Nohar India 104 C3
Noheji Japan 90 F4
Nohfelden Germany 62 H5
Nohoit China 94 C4
Noida India 104 D3
Noirmoutier, Île de i. France 66 C3
Noirmoutier-en-l'Île France 66 C3
Noisseville France 62 G5
Nojima-zaki c. Japan 93 F4
Nojiri-ko l. Japan 93 E2
Nokami Japan 92 B4
Nokhowch, Kūh-e mt. Iran 111 F5
Nōkis Uzbek. see Nukus
Nok Kundi Pak. 111 F4
Nokomis Canada 151 J5
Nokomis Lake Canada 151 K3
Nokou Chad 121 E3
Nokrek Peak India 105 G4
Nola Cent. Afr. Rep. 122 B3
Nolin River Lake KY U.S.A. 164 B5
Nolinsk Rus. Fed. 52 K4
No Mans Land i. MA U.S.A. 165 J3
Nome AK U.S.A. 148 F2
Nome, Cape AK U.S.A. 148 F2
Nomgon Mongolia 94 F3
Nomhon China 94 D4
Nomhon He r. China 94 C4
Nomin Gol r. China 95 K1
Nomoi Islands Micronesia see Mortlock Islands
Nomonde S. Africa 125 H6
Nömrög Mongolia 94 D1
Nomto Rus. Fed. 94 F1
Nomugi-tōge pass Japan 92 D2
Nomzha Rus. Fed. 52 I4
Nonacho Lake Canada 151 I2
Nondalton AK U.S.A. 148 I4
Nondweni S. Africa 125 J5
Nong'an China 90 B3
Nonghui China see Guang'an
Nong Khai Thai. 86 C3
Nongoma S. Africa 125 J4
Nongstoin India 105 G4
Nonidas Namibia 124 B2
Nonni r. China see Nen Jiang
Nonning Australia 137 B7
Nonnweiler Germany 62 G5
Nonoava Mex. 166 D3
Nonoichi Japan 92 C2
Nonouti atoll Kiribati 133 H2
Nonthaburi Thai. 87 C4
Nonvianuk Lake AK U.S.A. 148 I4
Nonzwakazi S. Africa 124 G6
Noolyeanna Lake salt flat Australia 137 B5
Noondie, Lake salt flat Australia 135 B7
Noonkanbah Australia 134 D4
Noonthorangee Range hills Australia 137 C6
Noorama Creek watercourse Australia 138 B1
Noordbeveland i. Neth. 62 D3
Noorderhaaks i. Neth. 62 E2
Noordoost Polder Neth. 62 F2
Noordwijk-Binnen Neth. 62 E2
Noorvik AK U.S.A. 148 G2
Nootka Island Canada 150 E5
Nora r. Rus. Fed. 90 C2
Norak Tajik. 111 H2
Norak, Obanbori resr Tajik. 111 H2
Norala Mindanao Phil. 82 D5
Noranda Canada 152 F4
Nor-Bayazet Armenia see Gavarr
Norberg Sweden 55 I6
Norcang China 99 D7
Nord Greenland see Station Nord
Nord, Canal du France 62 D4
Nordaustlandet i. Svalbard 76 D2
Nordegg Canada 150 G4
Norden Germany 63 H1
Nordenshel'da, Arkhipelag is Rus. Fed. 76 K2
Nordenskjold Archipelago is Rus. Fed. see Nordenshel'da, Arkhipelag
Norderney Germany 63 H1
Norderstedt Germany 63 K1
Nordfjordeid Norway 54 D6
Nordfold Norway 54 I3
Nordfriesische Inseln Germany see North Frisian Islands
Nordhausen Germany 63 K3
Nordholz Germany 63 I1
Nordhorn Germany 62 H2
Nordkapp c. Norway see North Cape
Nordkinnhalvøya i. Norway 54 O1
Nordkjosbotn Norway 54 K2
Nordli Norway 54 H4
Nördlingen Germany 63 K6
Nordmaling Sweden 54 K5
Nord- og Østgrønland, Nationalparken i nat. park Greenland 147 O2

▶Nordøstrundingen c. Greenland 189 I1
Most easterly point of North America.

Nord-Ostsee-Kanal Germany see Kiel Canal
Norðoyar i. Faroe Is 50 E3
Nord-Pas-de-Calais admin. reg. France 62 C4
Nordpfälzer Bergland reg. Germany 63 H5
Nordre Strømfjord inlet Greenland see Nassuttooq
Nordrhein-Westfalen land Germany 63 H3
Nordvik Rus. Fed. 77 M2
Nore r. Ireland 61 F5
Nore, Pic de mt. France 66 F5
Noreg country Europe see Norway
Norfolk NE U.S.A. 160 D3
Norfolk NY U.S.A. 165 H1
Norfolk VA U.S.A. 165 G5

▶Norfolk Island terr. S. Pacific Ocean 133 G4
Territory of Australia.

Norfolk Island Ridge sea feature Tasman Sea 186 H7
Norfork Lake AR U.S.A. 161 E4
Norg Neth. 62 G1
Norge country Europe see Norway
Norheimsund Norway 55 E6
Norikura-dake vol. Japan 92 D2
Noril'sk Rus. Fed. 76 J3
Norkyung China 99 E7
Norland Canada 165 F1
Norma Co l. China 99 E6
Norman OK U.S.A. 161 D5
Norman, Lake resr NC U.S.A. 162 D5
Normanby Island P.N.G. 136 E1
Normandes, Îles is English Chan. see Channel Islands
Normandia Brazil 177 G3
Normandie reg. France see Normandy
Normandie, Collines de hills France 66 D2
Normandy reg. France 66 D2
Normanton Australia 136 C3
Norman Wells Canada 149 P2
Norogachic Mex. 166 D3
Norovlin Mongolia 95 G1
Norquay Canada 151 K5
Ñorquinco Arg. 178 B6
Norra Kvarken strait Fin./Sweden 54 L5
Norra Storfjället mts Sweden 54 I4
Norrent-Fontes France 62 C4
Norris Lake TN U.S.A. 164 D5
Norristown PA U.S.A. 165 H3
Norrköping Sweden 55 J7
Norrtälje Sweden 55 K7
Norseman Australia 135 C8
Norsjö Sweden 54 K4
Norsk Rus. Fed. 90 C1
Norsup Vanuatu 133 G3
Norte, Punta pt Arg. 178 E5
Norte, Serra do hills Brazil 177 G6
Nortelândia Brazil 177 G6
Nörten-Hardenberg Germany 63 J3
North, Cape Antarctica 188 H2
North, Cape Canada 153 J5
Northallerton U.K. 58 F4
Northam Australia 135 B7
Northampton Australia 132 B4
Northampton U.K. 59 G6
Northampton MA U.S.A. 165 I2
Northampton PA U.S.A. 165 H3
North Andaman i. India 87 A4
North Anna r. VA U.S.A. 165 G5
North Arm b. Canada 150 H2
North Atlantic Ocean Atlantic Ocean 155 O4
North Augusta SC U.S.A. 163 D5
North Aulatsivik Island Canada 153 J2
North Australian Basin sea feature Indian Ocean 185 P6
North Balabac Strait Phil. 82 B4
North Baltimore OH U.S.A. 164 D3
North Battleford Canada 151 I4
North Bay Canada 152 F5
North Belcher Islands Canada 152 F2
North Berwick U.K. 60 G4
North Berwick ME U.S.A. 165 J2
North Borneo state Malaysia see Sabah
North Bourke Australia 138 B3
North Branch MN U.S.A. 160 E2
North Caicos i. Turks and Caicos Is 163 G8
North Canton OH U.S.A. 164 E3
North Cape Canada 153 I5
North Cape Norway 54 N1
North Cape N.Z. 139 D2
North Cape AK U.S.A. 148 [inset] D5
North Caribou Lake Canada 151 N4
North Carolina state U.S.A. 162 E4
North Cascades National Park WA U.S.A. 156 C2
North Channel lake channel Canada 152 E5
North Channel U.K. 61 G2
North Charleston SC U.S.A. 163 E5
North Chicago IL U.S.A. 164 B2
North China Plain plain China see Huabei Pingyuan
Northcliffe Glacier Antarctica 188 F2
North Collins NY U.S.A. 165 F2
North Concho r. TX U.S.A. 161 C6
North Conway NH U.S.A. 165 J1
North Dakota state U.S.A. 160 C2
North Downs hills U.K. 59 G7
North East PA U.S.A. 164 F2
Northeast Cape AK U.S.A. 148 E3
Northeast Foreland c. Greenland see Nordøstrundingen
North-East Frontier Agency state India see Arunachal Pradesh
Northeast Pacific Basin sea feature N. Pacific Ocean 187 J4
Northeast Point Bahamas 163 F8
Northeast Providence Channel Bahamas 163 E7
North Edwards CA U.S.A. 158 E4
Northeim Germany 63 J3
North Entrance sea chan. Palau 82 [inset]
Northern prov. S. Africa see Limpopo
Northern Areas admin. div. Pak. see Gilgit-Baltistan
Northern Cape prov. S. Africa 124 D5
Northern Donets r. Rus. Fed./Ukr. see Severskiy Donets
Northern Dvina r. Rus. Fed. see Severnaya Dvina
Northern Indian Lake Canada 151 L3
Northern Ireland prov. U.K. 61 F3
Northern Lau Group is Fiji 133 I3
Northern Light Lake Canada 152 C4

▶Northern Mariana Islands terr. N. Pacific Ocean 81 K3
United States Commonwealth.

Northern Rhodesia country Africa see Zambia
Northern Sporades is Greece see Voreies Sporades
Northern Territory admin. div. Australia 132 D3
Northern Transvaal prov. S. Africa see Limpopo
North Esk r. U.K. 60 G4
Northfield MN U.S.A. 160 E2
Northfield VT U.S.A. 165 I1
North Foreland c. U.K. 59 I7
North Fork CA U.S.A. 158 D3
North Fork Pass Canada 149 M2
North French r. Canada 152 E4
North Frisian Islands Germany 57 L3
North Geomagnetic Pole Arctic Ocean 147 K2
North Grimston U.K. 58 G4
North Haven CT U.S.A. 165 I3
North Head hd N.Z. 139 E3
North Henik Lake Canada 151 L2
North Hero VT U.S.A. 165 I1
North Horr Kenya 122 D3
North Island India 106 B4

▶North Island N.Z. 139 D4
3rd largest island in Oceania.

North Island Phil. 82 C1
North Islet rf Phil. 82 C4
North Jadito Canyon gorge AZ U.S.A. 159 H4
North Judson IN U.S.A. 164 B3
North Kingsville OH U.S.A. 164 E3
North Knife r. Canada 151 M3
North Knife Lake Canada 151 L3
North Korea country Asia 91 B5
North Lakhimpur India 105 H4
North Las Vegas NV U.S.A. 159 F3
North Little Rock AR U.S.A. 161 E5
North Loup r. NE U.S.A. 160 D3
North Luangwa National Park Zambia 123 D5
North Maalhosmadulu Atoll Maldives 106 B5
North Magnetic Pole Canada 189 A1
North Malosmadulu Atoll Maldives see North Maalhosmadulu Atoll
North Mam Peak CO U.S.A. 159 J2
North Muskegon MI U.S.A. 164 B2
North Palisade mt. CA U.S.A. 158 D3
North Perry OH U.S.A. 164 E3
North Platte NE U.S.A. 160 C3
North Platte r. NE U.S.A. 160 C3
North Pole Arctic Ocean 189 I1
North Pole AK U.S.A. 149 K2
North Port FL U.S.A. 163 D7
North Reef Island India 87 A4
North Rhine - Westphalia land Germany see Nordrhein-Westfalen
North Rim AZ U.S.A. 159 G3
North Rona i. U.K. see Rona
North Ronaldsay i. U.K. 60 G1
North Ronaldsay Firth sea chan. U.K. 60 G1
North Saskatchewan r. Canada 151 J4
North Schell Peak NV U.S.A. 159 F2
North Sea Europe 56 H2
North Seal r. Canada 151 L3
North Sentinel Island India 87 A5
North Shields U.K. 58 F3
North Shoal Lake Canada 151 L5
North Shoshone Peak NV U.S.A. 158 E2
North Siberian Lowland Rus. Fed. 76 L2
North Sinai governorate Egypt see Shamāl Sīnā'
North Slope plain AK U.S.A. 149 J1
North Somercotes U.K. 58 H5
North Spirit Lake Canada 151 M4
North Stradbroke Island Australia 138 F1
North Sunderland U.K. 58 F3
North Syracuse NY U.S.A. 165 G2
North Taranaki Bight b. N.Z. 139 E4
North Terre Haute IN U.S.A. 164 B4
Northton U.K. 60 B3
North Tonawanda NY U.S.A. 165 F2

North Trap reef N.Z. 139 A8
North Troy VT U.S.A. 165 I1
North Tyne r. U.K. 58 E4
North Ubian i. Phil. 82 C5
North Uist i. U.K. 60 B3
Northumberland National Park U.K. 58 E3
Northumberland Strait Canada 153 I5
North Vancouver Canada 150 F5
North Verde i. Phil. 82 B4
North Vernon IN U.S.A. 164 C4
Northville NY U.S.A. 165 H2
North Wabasca Lake Canada 150 H3
North Walsham U.K. 59 I6
Northway Junction AK U.S.A. 149 L3
North West prov. S. Africa 124 G4
Northwest Atlantic Mid-Ocean Channel N. Atlantic Ocean 184 E1
North West Cape Australia 134 A5
Northwest Cape AK U.S.A. 148 E3
North West Frontier prov. Pak. see Khyber Pakhtunkhwa
North West Nelson Forest Park nat. park N.Z. see Kahurangi National Park
Northwest Pacific Basin sea feature N. Pacific Ocean 186 G3
Northwest Providence Channel Bahamas 163 E7
North West River Canada 153 K3
Northwest Territories admin. div. Canada 150 J2
Northwich U.K. 58 E5
North Wildwood NJ U.S.A. 165 H4
North Windham ME U.S.A. 165 J2
Northwind Ridge sea feature Arctic Ocean 189 B1
Northwood NH U.S.A. 165 J2
North York Canada 164 F2
North York Moors moorland U.K. 58 G4
North York Moors National Park U.K. 58 G4
Norton U.K. 58 G4
Norton KS U.S.A. 160 D4
Norton VA U.S.A. 164 D5
Norton VT U.S.A. 165 J1
Norton Bay AK U.S.A. 148 G2
Norton de Matos Angola see Balombo
Norton Shores MI U.S.A. 164 B2
Norton Sound sea channel AK U.S.A. 148 G3
Nortonville KY U.S.A. 164 B5
Norutak Lake AK U.S.A. 148 I2
Norvegia, Cape Antarctica 188 B2
Norwalk CT U.S.A. 165 I3
Norwalk OH U.S.A. 164 D3
Norway country Europe 54 E6
Norway ME U.S.A. 165 J1
Norway House Canada 151 L4
Norwegian Basin sea feature N. Atlantic Ocean 184 H1
Norwegian Bay Canada 147 I2
Norwegian Sea N. Atlantic Ocean 189 H2
Norwich Canada 164 E2
Norwich U.K. 59 I6
Norwich CT U.S.A. 165 I3
Norwich NY U.S.A. 165 H2
Norwood CO U.S.A. 159 I2
Norwood NY U.S.A. 165 H1
Norwood OH U.S.A. 164 C4
Norzagaray Luzon Phil. 82 C3
Nosaka Japan 93 G3
Nose Japan 92 B4
Nosegawa Japan 92 B4
Nose Lake Canada 151 I1
Noshiro Japan 91 F4
Nosovaya Rus. Fed. 52 L1
Nosratābād Iran 111 E4
Noss, Isle of i. U.K. 60 [inset]
Nossebro Sweden 55 H7
Nossen Germany 63 N3
Nossob watercourse Africa 124 D2 also known as Nosop
Notakwanon r. Canada 153 J2
Notch Peak UT U.S.A. 159 G2
Noteć r. Poland 57 O4
Notikewin r. Canada 150 G3
Noto, Golfo di g. Sicily Italy 68 F6
Notodden Norway 55 F7
Notogawa Japan 92 C3
Noto-hantō pen. Japan 91 E5
Notojima Japan 92 D1
Noto-jima i. Japan 92 D1
Notre-Dame, Monts mts Canada 153 H5
Notre Dame Bay Canada 153 L4
Notre-Dame-de-Koartac Canada see Quaqtaq
Nottawasaga Bay Canada 164 E1
Nottaway r. Canada 152 F4
Nottingham U.K. 59 F6
Nottingham Island Canada 147 K3
Nottoway r. VA U.S.A. 165 G5
Nottuln Germany 63 H3
Notukeu Creek r. Canada 151 J5
Nou Japan 93 D1
Nouabalé-Ndoki, Parc National de nat. park Congo 122 B3
Nouâdhibou Mauritania 120 B2
Nouâdhibou, Râs c. Mauritania 120 B2
▶Nouakchott Mauritania 120 B3 Capital of Mauritania.
Nouâmghâr Mauritania 120 B3
Nouei Vietnam 86 D4
▶Nouméa New Caledonia 133 G4 Capital of New Caledonia.
Nouna Burkina Faso 120 C3
Noupoort S. Africa 124 G6
Nousu Fin. 54 P3
Nouveau-Brunswick prov. Canada see New Brunswick
Nouveau-Comptoir Canada see Wemindji
Nouvelle Calédonie i. S. Pacific Ocean 133 G4
Nouvelle Calédonie terr. S. Pacific Ocean see New Caledonia
Nouvelle-France, Cap de c. Canada 147 K3
Nouvelles Hébrides country S. Pacific Ocean see Vanuatu
Nova América Brazil 179 A1
Nova Chaves Angola see Muconda
Nova Freixa Moz. see Cuamba
Nova Friburgo Brazil 179 C3
Nova Gaia Angola see Cambundi-Catembo
Nova Goa India see Panaji
Nova Gradiška Croatia 68 G2
Nova Iguaçu Brazil 179 C3
Nova Kakhovka Ukr. 69 O1
Nova Lima Brazil 179 C2
Nova Lisboa Angola see Huambo
Novalukoml' Belarus 53 F5
Nova Mambone Moz. 123 D6
Nova Nabúri Moz. 123 D5
Nova Odesa Ukr. 53 F7
Nova Pilão Arcado Brazil 177 J5
Nova Ponte Brazil 179 B2
Nova Ponte, Represa resr Brazil 179 B2
Novara Italy 68 C2
Nova Roma Brazil 179 B1
Nova Scotia prov. Canada 153 I6
Nova Sento Sé Brazil 177 J5
Novato CA U.S.A. 158 B2
Nova Trento Brazil 179 A4
Nova Venécia Brazil 179 C2
Nova Xavantino Brazil 177 H6
Novaya Kakhovka Ukr. see Nova Kakhovka
Novaya Kazanka Kazakh. 51 P6
Novaya Ladoga Rus. Fed. 52 G3
Novaya Lyalya Rus. Fed. 51 S4
Novaya Odessa Ukr. see Nova Odesa
Novaya Sibir', Ostrov i. Rus. Fed. 77 P2
Novaya Zemlya is Rus. Fed. 76 G2
Nova Zagora Bulg. 69 L3
Novelda Spain 67 F4
Nové Zámky Slovakia 57 Q7
Novgorod Rus. Fed. see Velikiy Novgorod
Novgorod-Severskiy Ukr. see Novhorod-Sivers'kyy
Novgorod-Volynskiy Ukr. see Novohrad-Volyns'kyy
Novhorod-Sivers'kyy Ukr. 53 G6
Novi Grad Bos.-Herz. see Bosanski Novi
Novi Iskŭr Bulg. 69 J3
Novikovo Rus. Fed. 90 F3
Novi Kritsim Bulg. see Stamboliyski
Novi Ligure Italy 68 C2
Novillero Mex. 166 D4
Novi Pazar Bulg. 69 L3
Novi Pazar Serbia 69 I3
Novi Sad Serbia 69 H2
Novo Acre Brazil 179 C1
Novoalekseyevka Kazakh. see Khobda
Novoaltaysk Rus. Fed. 88 E2
Novoanninskiy Rus. Fed. 53 I6
Novo Aripuanã Brazil 176 F5
Novoazovs'k Ukr. 53 H7
Novocheboksarsk Rus. Fed. 52 J4
Novocherkassk Rus. Fed. 53 I7
Novo Cruzeiro Brazil 179 C2
Novodugino Rus. Fed. 52 G5
Novodvinsk Rus. Fed. 52 I2
Novoekonomicheskoye Ukr. see Dymytrov
Novogeorgiyevka Rus. Fed. 90 B2
Novogrudok Belarus see Navahrudak
Novo Hamburgo Brazil 179 A5
Novohradské hory mts Czech Rep. 57 O6
Novohrad-Volyns'kyy Ukr. 53 E6
Novokhopersk Rus. Fed. 53 I6
Novokiyevskiy Uval Rus. Fed. 90 C2
Novokubansk Rus. Fed. 113 F1
Novokubanskiy Rus. Fed. see Novokubansk
Novokuybyshevsk Rus. Fed. 53 K5
Novokuznetsk Rus. Fed. 88 F2
Novolazarevskaya research station Antarctica 188 C2
Novolukoml' Belarus see Novalukoml'
Novo Mesto Slovenia 68 F2
Novomikhaylovskiy Rus. Fed. 112 E1
Novomoskovsk Rus. Fed. 53 H5
Novomoskovs'k Ukr. 53 G6
Novonikolayevsk Rus. Fed. see Novosibirsk
Novonikolayevskiy Rus. Fed. 53 I6
Novooleksiyivka Ukr. 53 G7
Novo Paraíso Brazil 176 F3
Novopashiyskiy Rus. Fed. see Gornozavodsk
Novopavlovka Rus. Fed. 95 G1
Novopokrovka Kazakh. 98 C2
Novopokrovka Rus. Fed. 90 D3
Novopokrovskaya Rus. Fed. 53 I7
Novopolotsk Belarus see Navapolatsk
Novopskov Ukr. 53 H6
Novo Redondo Angola see Sumbe
Novorossiysk Rus. Fed. 112 E1
Novorybnaya Rus. Fed. 77 L2
Novorzhev Rus. Fed. 52 F4
Novoselenginsk Rus. Fed. 94 F1
Novoselovo Rus. Fed. 88 G1
Novosel'skoye Rus. Fed. see Achkhoy-Martan
Novosel'ye Rus. Fed. 55 P7
Novosergiyevka Rus. Fed. 51 Q5
Novoshakhtinsk Rus. Fed. 53 H7
Novosheshminsk Rus. Fed. 52 K5
Novosibirsk Rus. Fed. 76 J4
Novosibirskiye Ostrova is Rus. Fed. see New Siberia Islands
Novosil' Rus. Fed. 53 H5
Novosokol'niki Rus. Fed. 52 F4
Novospasskoye Rus. Fed. 53 J5
Novotroyits'ke Ukr. 53 G7
Novoukrainka Ukr. see Novoukrayinka
Novoukrayinka Ukr. 53 F6
Novoussuri (abandoned) Rus. Fed. 90 E2
Novouzensk Rus. Fed. 53 K6
Novovolyns'k Ukr. 53 E6
Novovoronezh Rus. Fed. 53 H6
Novovoronezhskiy Rus. Fed. see Novovoronezh
Novovoskresenovka Rus. Fed. 90 B1
Novovoznesenovka Kyrg. 98 B4
Novoye Chaplino Rus. Fed. 148 D2
Novozybkov Rus. Fed. 53 F5
Nový Jičín Czech Rep. 57 P6
Novyy Afon Georgia see Akhali Ap'oni
Novyy Bor Rus. Fed. 52 L2
Novyy Donbass Ukr. see Dymytrov
Novyye Petushki Rus. Fed. see Petushki
Novyy Kholmogory Rus. Fed. see Archangel
Novyy Margelan Uzbek. see Farg'ona
Novyy Nekouz Rus. Fed. 52 H4
Novyy Oskol Rus. Fed. 53 H6
Novyy Port Rus. Fed. 76 I3
Novyy Urengoy Rus. Fed. 76 I3
Novyy Urgal Rus. Fed. 90 D2
Novyy Uzen' Kazakh. see Zhanaozen
Novyy Zay Rus. Fed. 52 L5
Now Iran 110 D4
Nowabganj Bangl. see Nawabganj
Nowata OK U.S.A. 161 E4
Nowdī Iran 110 C2
Nowgong India see Nagaon
Nowitna r. AK U.S.A. 148 I2
Nowitna National Wildlife Refuge nature res. AK U.S.A. 148 I2
Now Kharegan Iran 110 D2
Nowleye Lake Canada 151 K2
Nowogard Poland 57 O4
Noworadomsk Poland see Radomsko
Nowra Australia 138 E5
Nowrangapur India see Nabarangapur
Nowshera Pak. 111 I3
Nowyak Lake Canada 151 L2
Nowy Sącz Poland 57 R6
Nowy Targ Poland 57 R6
Now Zād Afgh. 111 G3
Noxen PA U.S.A. 165 G3
Noy, Xé r. Laos 86 D3
Noyabr'sk Rus. Fed. 76 I3
Noyes Island AK U.S.A. 149 N5
Noyon France 62 C5
Noyon Mongolia 94 E3
Nozawaonsen-mura Japan 93 E2
Nozizwe S. Africa 125 G6
Nqamakwe S. Africa 125 H7
Nqutu S. Africa 125 J5
Nsanje Malawi 123 D5
Nsombo Zambia 123 C5
Nsukka Nigeria 120 D4
Nsumbu National Park Zambia see Sumbu National Park
Ntambu Zambia 123 C5
Ntha S. Africa 125 H4
Ntoro, Kavo pt Greece 69 K5
Ntoum Gabon 122 A3
Ntungamo Uganda 122 D4
Nuanetsi Zimbabwe see Mwenezi
Nuangan Sulawesi Indon. 83 C2
Nu'aym reg. Oman 110 D6
Nuba Mountains Sudan 108 D7
Nubian Desert Sudan 108 D5
Nubra r. India 99 B6
Nüden Mongolia see Ulaanbadrah
Nudo Coropuna mt. Peru 176 D7
Nueces r. TX U.S.A. 161 D7
Nueltin Lake Canada 151 L2
Nueva Arcadia Hond. 166 [inset] H6
Nueva Ciudad Guerrero Mex. 161 D7
Nueva Gerona Cuba 169 H4
Nueva Harberton Arg. 178 C8
Nueva Imperial Chile 178 B5
Nueva Loja Ecuador see Lago Agrio
Nueva Ocotepeque Hond. 166 [inset] H6
Nueva Rosita Mex. 167 E3
Nueva San Salvador El Salvador 167 H6
Nueva Villa de Padilla Mex. 161 D7
Nueve de Julio Arg. see 9 de Julio
Nuevitas Cuba 169 I4
Nuevo, Cayo i. Mex. 167 H4
Nuevo, Golfo g. Arg. 178 D6
Nuevo Casas Grandes Mex. 166 D2
Nuevo Ideal Mex. 166 D3
Nuevo Laredo Mex. 167 F3
Nuevo León Mex. 159 F5
Nuevo León state Mex. 161 D7
Nuevo Rocafuerte Ecuador 176 C4
Nuga Mongolia see Dzavhanmandal
Nugaal watercourse Somalia 122 E3
Nugget Point N.Z. 139 B8
Nugur India 106 D2
Nuguria Islands P.N.G. 132 F2
Nuh, Ras pt Pak. 111 F5
Nuhaka N.Z. 139 F4
Nui atoll Tuvalu 133 H2
Nui Con Voi r. Vietnam see Red
Nuiqsut AK U.S.A. 149 J1
Nui Thanh Vietnam 86 E4
Nui Ti On mt. Vietnam 86 D4
Nujiang China 96 C2
Nu Jiang r. China/Myanmar see Salween
Nukata Japan 92 D4
Nukey Bluff hill Australia 137 A7
Nukha Azer. see Şäki
▶Nuku'alofa Tonga 133 I4 Capital of Tonga.
Nukufetau atoll Tuvalu 133 H2
Nukuhiva i. Fr. Polynesia see Nuku Hiva
Nuku Hiva i. Fr. Polynesia 187 K6
Nukuhu P.N.G. 81 L8
Nukulaelae atoll Tuvalu 133 H2
Nukulailai atoll Tuvalu see Nukulaelae
Nukumanu Islands P.N.G. 133 F2
Nukunau i. Kiribati see Nikunau
Nukunono atoll Tokelau see Nukunonu
Nukunonu atoll Tokelau 133 I2
Nukus Uzbek. 102 A3
Nulato AK U.S.A. 148 H2
Nullagine Australia 134 C5
Nullarbor Australia 135 E7
Nullarbor National Park Australia 135 E7
Nullarbor Plain Australia 135 E7
Nullarbor Regional Reserve park Australia 135 E7
Nuluarniavik, Lac l. Canada 152 F2
Nulu'erhu Shan mts China 95 I3
Num i. Indon. 81 J7
Num Nepal 99 D8
Numalla, Lake salt flat Australia 138 B2
Numan Nigeria 122 B3
Numanuma P.N.G. 136 E1
Numata Japan 93 F2
Numazu Japan 93 E3
Numbulwar Australia 136 A2
Numedal valley Norway 55 F6
Numfoor i. Indon. 81 I7
Numin He r. China 90 B3
Numurkah Australia 138 B6
Nunachuak AK U.S.A. 148 H4
Nunaksaluk Island Canada 153 J3
Nunakuluut i. Greenland 147 N3
Nunap Isua c. Greenland see Farewell, Cape
Nunapitchuk AK U.S.A. 148 G3
Nunarsuit i. Greenland see Nunakuluut
Nunavakpak Lake AK U.S.A. 148 G3
Nunavaugaluk, Lake AK U.S.A. 148 H4
Nunavik reg. Canada 152 G1
Nunavut admin. div. Canada 151 L2
Nunda NY U.S.A. 165 G2
Nundle Australia 138 E3
Nuneaton U.K. 59 F6
Nungba India 105 H4
Nungesser Lake Canada 151 M5
Nungnain Sum China 95 I2
Nunivak Island AK U.S.A. 148 F4
Nunkapasi India 106 E1
Nunkun mt. India 104 D2
Nunligran Rus. Fed. 148 D2
Nuñomoral Spain 67 C3
Nunspeet Neth. 62 F2
Nunukan i. Indon. 85 G2
Nunyamo Rus. Fed. 148 E2
Nuojiang China see Tongjiang
Nuoro Sardinia Italy 68 C4
Nupani i. Solomon Is 133 G3
Nuqrah Saudi Arabia 108 F4
Nur China 99 C5
Nura Almatinskaya Oblast' Kazakh. 98 B4
Nura Karagandinskaya Oblast' Kazakh. 98 A2
Nura r. Kazakh. 98 A2
Nūrābād Iran 110 C4
Nurakita i. Tuvalu see Niulakita
Nurata Uzbek. see Nurota
Nur Dağları mts Turkey 107 B1
Nurek Tajik. see Norak
Nurek Reservoir Tajik. see Norak, Obanbori
Nurekskoye Vodokhranilishche resr Tajik. see Norak, Obanbori
Nuremberg Germany 63 L5
Nūrestān reg. Afgh. 111 H3
Nuri Mex. 166 C2
Nuri, Teluk b. Indon. 85 E3
Nurla India 104 D2
Nurlat Rus. Fed. 53 K5
Nurmes Fin. 54 P5
Nurmo Fin. 54 M5
Nürnberg Germany see Nuremberg
Nurota Uzbek. 102 C3
Nurri, Mount hill Australia 138 C3
Nür Rūd r. Iran 110 D2
Nur Turu China 99 F5
Nusa Kambangan, Cagar Alam nature res. Jawa Indon. 85 E4
Nusa Laut i. Maluku Indon. 83 D3
Nusa Tenggara Barat prov. Indon. 85 G5
Nusawulan Indon. 81 I7
Nusaybin Turkey 113 F3
Nusela, Kepulauan is Papua Indon. 83 D3
Nushagak r. AK U.S.A. 148 H4
Nushagak Bay AK U.S.A. 148 H4
Nushagak Peninsula AK U.S.A. 148 H4
Nu Shan mts China 96 C3
Nu-shima i. Japan 92 A4
Nushki Pak. 111 G4
Nusratiye Turkey 107 D1
Nutak Canada 153 J2
Nutarawit Lake Canada 151 L2
Nutauge, Laguna lag. Rus. Fed. 148 C2
Nutepel'men Rus. Fed. 148 D2
Nutrioso AZ U.S.A. 159 I5
Nuttal Pak. 111 H4
Nutwood Downs Australia 134 F3
Nutzotin Mountains AK U.S.A. 149 K2
▶Nuuk Greenland 147 M3 Capital of Greenland.
Nuupas Fin. 54 O3
Nuussuaq Greenland 147 M2
Nuussuaq pen. Greenland 147 M2
Nuwaybi' al Muzayyinah Egypt 112 D5
Nuweiba el Muzeina Egypt see Nuwaybi' al Muzayyinah
Nuwerus S. Africa 124 D6
Nuweveldberge mts S. Africa 124 E7
Nuwuk AK U.S.A. 148 H1
Nuyakuk r. AK U.S.A. 148 H4
Nuyakuk Lake AK U.S.A. 148 H4
Nuyts, Point Australia 135 B8
Nuyts Archipelago is Australia 135 F8
Nuzvid India 106 D2
Nwanedi Nature Reserve S. Africa 125 J2
Nxai Pan National Park Botswana 123 C5
Nyaän, Bukit hill Indon. 85 F2
Nyac AK U.S.A. 148 H3
Nyagan' Rus. Fed. 51 T3
Nyagquka China see Yajiang
Nyagrong China see Xinlong
Nyahururu Kenya 122 D3
Nyah West Australia 138 A5
Nyaimai China 99 F7
Nyainqêntanglha Feng mt. China 99 E7
Nyainqêntanglha Shan mts China 99 E7
Nyainrong China 99 F6
Nyåker Sweden 54 K5
Nyakh Rus. Fed. see Nyagan'
Nyaksimvol' Rus. Fed. 51 S3
Nyala Sudan 121 F3
Nyalam China see Congdü
Nyalikungu Tanz. see Maswa
Nyamandhlovu Zimbabwe 123 C5
Nyamtumbo Tanz. 123 D5
Nyande Zimbabwe see Masvingo
Nyandoma Rus. Fed. 52 I3
Nyandomskaya Vozvyshennost' hills Rus. Fed. 52 H3
Nyanga Congo 122 B4
Nyanga Zimbabwe 123 D5
Nyangani mt. Zimbabwe 123 D5
Nyangbo China 99 F7
Nyang Qu r. China 99 F7
Nyapa, Gunung mt. Indon. 85 G2
Nyar r. India 99 B7
Nyarling r. Canada 150 H2
▶Nyasa, Lake Africa 123 D4 3rd largest lake in Africa and 9th in the world.
Nyasaland country Africa see Malawi
Nyashabozh Rus. Fed. 52 L2
Nyasvizh Belarus 55 O10
Nyaungdon Myanmar see Yandoon
Nyaunglebin Myanmar 86 B3
Nyborg Denmark 55 G9
Nyborg Norway 54 P1
Nybro Sweden 55 I8
Nyeboe Land reg. Greenland 147 M1
Nyêmo China 99 E7
Nyenchen Tanglha Range mts China see Nyainqêntanglha Shan
Nyeri Kenya 122 D4
Nygchigen, Mys c. Rus. Fed. 148 D2
Nyi, Co l. China 99 D6
Nyika National Park Zambia 123 D5
Nyima Xizang China 99 D7
Nyima Xizang China 99 F7
Nyimba Zambia 123 D5
Nyingchi Xizang China 99 F7
Nyingchi Xizang China 99 F7
Nyingzhong China 99 E7
Nyinma China see Maqu
Nyíregyháza Hungary 53 D7
Nyiru, Mount Kenya 122 D3
Nykarleby Fin. 54 M5
Nykøbing Denmark 55 G9
Nykøbing Sjælland Denmark 55 G9
Nyköping Sweden 55 J7
Nyland Sweden 54 J5
Nylsvley nature res. S. Africa 125 I3
Nymagee Australia 138 C4
Nymboida National Park Australia 138 F2
Nynäshamn Sweden 55 J7
Nyngan Australia 138 C3
Nyogzê China 99 C7
Nyohō-san mt. Japan 93 F2
Nyoman r. Belarus/Lith. 55 M10 also known as Neman or Nemunas
Nyon Switz. 66 H3
Nyons France 66 G4
Nýřany Czech Rep. 63 N5
Nyrob Rus. Fed. 51 R3
Nysa Poland 57 P5
Nysh Rus. Fed. 90 F2
Nyssa OR U.S.A. 156 D4
Nystad Fin. see Uusikaupunki
Nytva Rus. Fed. 51 R4
Nyūgasa-yama mt. Japan 93 E3
Nyūkawa Japan 92 D2
Nyuksenitsa Rus. Fed. 52 J3
Nyunzu Dem. Rep. Congo 123 C4
Nyurba Rus. Fed. 77 M3
Nyūzen Japan 92 D2
Nyyskiy Zaliv lag. Rus. Fed. 90 F1
Nzambi Congo 122 B4
Nzega Tanz. 123 D4
Nzérékoré Guinea 120 C4
N'zeto Angola 123 B4
Nzwani i. Comoros 123 E5

O

Oahe, Lake SD U.S.A. 160 C2
O'ahu i. HI U.S.A. 157 [inset]
Oaitupu i. Tuvalu see Vaitupu
Oak Bluffs MA U.S.A. 165 J3
Oak City UT U.S.A. 159 G2
Oak Creek CO U.S.A. 159 J1
Oakdale LA U.S.A. 161 E6
Oakes ND U.S.A. 160 D2
Oakey Australia 138 E1
Oak Grove KY U.S.A. 164 B5
Oak Grove LA U.S.A. 161 F5
Oak Grove MI U.S.A. 164 C1
Oakham U.K. 59 G6
Oak Harbor OH U.S.A. 164 D3
Oak Hill OH U.S.A. 164 D4
Oak Hill WV U.S.A. 164 E5
Oakhurst CA U.S.A. 158 D3
Oak Lake Canada 151 K5
Oakland CA U.S.A. 158 B3
Oakland MD U.S.A. 164 F4
Oakland ME U.S.A. 165 K1
Oakland NE U.S.A. 160 D3
Oakland OR U.S.A. 156 C4
Oakland airport CA U.S.A. 158 B3
Oakland City IN U.S.A. 164 B4
Oaklands Australia 138 C5
Oak Lawn IL U.S.A. 164 B3
Oakley KS U.S.A. 160 C4
Oakover r. Australia 134 C5
Oak Park IL U.S.A. 164 B3
Oak Park MI U.S.A. 164 C2
Oak Park Reservoir UT U.S.A. 159 I1
Oakridge OR U.S.A. 156 C4
Oak Ridge TN U.S.A. 162 C4
Oakvale Australia 137 C7
Oak View CA U.S.A. 158 D4
Oakville Canada 164 F2
Oakwood OH U.S.A. 164 C3
Oakwood TN U.S.A. 164 B5
Oamaru N.Z. 139 C7
Ōamishirasato Japan 93 G3
Ōarai Japan 93 G2
Oaro N.Z. 139 D6
Ōashi-gawa r. Japan 93 F2
Oasis CA U.S.A. 158 E3
Oasis NV U.S.A. 156 E4
Oates Coast reg. Antarctica see Oates Land
Oates Land reg. Antarctica 188 H2
Oaxaca Mex. 168 E5
Oaxaca state Mex. 167 F5
Oaxaca de Juárez Mex. see Oaxaca
▶Ob' r. Rus. Fed. 88 E2 Part of the Ob'-Irtysh, the 2nd longest river in Asia.
Ob, Gulf of sea chan. Rus. Fed. see Obskaya Guba
Oba Canada 152 D4
Oba r. Kazakh. 98 C2
Oba i. Vanuatu see Aoba
Obako-dake mt. Japan 92 B4
Obala Cameroon 120 E4
Obama Japan 92 B3
Obama-wan b. Japan 92 B3
Oban U.K. 60 D4
Obara Japan 92 D3
O Barco Spain 67 C2
Obata Japan 92 C4
Obbia Somalia see Hobyo
Obdorsk Rus. Fed. see Salekhard
Óbecse Serbia see Bečej
Obed Canada 150 G4
Oberaula Germany 63 J4
Oberdorla Germany 63 K3
Oberhausen Germany 62 G3
Oberlin KS U.S.A. 160 C4
Oberlin LA U.S.A. 161 E6
Oberlin OH U.S.A. 164 D3
Obermoschel Germany 63 H5
Oberon Australia 138 D4
Oberpfälzer Wald mts Germany 63 M5
Obersinn Germany 63 J4
Oberthulba Germany 63 J4
Obertshausen Germany 63 I4
Oberwälder Land reg. Germany 63 J3
Obi i. Maluku Indon. 83 C3
Obi, Kepulauan is Maluku Indon. 83 C3
Obi, Selat sea chan. Maluku Indon. 83 C3
Óbidos Brazil 177 G4
Obihiro Japan 90 F4
Obilatu i. Maluku Indon. 83 C3
Obil'noye Rus. Fed. 53 J7
▶Ob'-Irtysh r. Rus. Fed. 76 H3 2nd longest river in Asia and 5th in the world.
Obitsu-gawa r. Japan 93 F3
Obluch'ye Rus. Fed. 90 C2
Obninsk Rus. Fed. 53 H5
Obo Cent. Afr. Rep. 122 C3
Obo China 94 E4
Obock Djibouti 108 F7
Ŏbŏk N. Korea 90 C4
Obokote Dem. Rep. Congo 122 C4
Obo Liang China 98 F5
Obong, Gunung mt. Malaysia 85 F1
Obouya Congo 122 B4
Oboyan' Rus. Fed. 53 H6
Obozerskiy Rus. Fed. 52 I3
Obregón, Presa resr Mex. 166 C3
Obrenovac Serbia 69 I2
Obruk Turkey 112 D3
Observatory Hill hill Australia 135 F7
Obshchiy Syrt hills Rus. Fed. 51 Q5
Obskaya Guba sea chan. Rus. Fed. 76 I3
Ōbu Japan 92 C3
Obuasi Ghana 120 C4
Obuse Japan 93 E2
Ob''yachevo Rus. Fed. 52 K3
Ocala FL U.S.A. 163 D6
Ocampo Chihuahua Mex. 166 C2
Ocampo Coahuila Mex. 166 E3
Ocaña Col. 176 D2
Ocaña Spain 67 E4
Occidental, Cordillera mts Chile 176 E7
Occidental, Cordillera mts Col. 176 C3
Occidental, Cordillera mts Peru 176 D7
Oceana WV U.S.A. 164 E5
Ocean Cape AK U.S.A. 149 M4
Ocean Cay i. Bahamas 163 E7
Ocean City MD U.S.A. 165 H4
Ocean City NJ U.S.A. 165 H4
Ocean Falls Canada 150 E4
Ocean Island Kiribati see Banaba
Ocean Island atoll HI U.S.A. see Kure Atoll
Oceanside CA U.S.A. 158 E5
Ocean Springs MS U.S.A. 161 F6
Ochakiv Ukr. 69 N1
Och'amchire Georgia 113 F2
Ocher Rus. Fed. 51 Q4
Ochiishi-misaki pt Japan 90 G4
Ochil Hills U.K. 60 F4
Ochito r. Pak. 111 G5
Ochrida, Lake Albania/Macedonia see Ohrid, Lake
Ochsenfurt Germany 63 K5
Ochtrup Germany 63 H2
Ocilla GA U.S.A. 163 D6
Ockelbo Sweden 55 J6
Ocolaşul Mare, Vârful mt. Romania 69 K1
Oconomowoc WI U.S.A. 164 A2
Oconto WI U.S.A. 164 B1
Ocoroni Mex. 166 C3
Ocos Guat. 167 G6
Ocosingo Mex. 167 G5
Ocotal Nicaragua 166 [inset] I6
Ocotlán Mex. 167 F5
Ocozocoautla Mex. 167 G5
Octeville-sur-Mer France 59 H9
October Revolution Island Rus. Fed. see Oktyabr'skoy Revolyutsii, Ostrov
Ocú Panama 166 [inset] J8
Ocussi enclave East Timor 134 D2
Ocussi-Ambeno enclave East Timor see Ocussi
Oda, Jebel mt. Sudan 108 E5
Ódáðahraun lava field Iceland 54 [inset 1]
Ŏdaejin N. Korea 90 C4
Odae-san National Park S. Korea 91 C5
Ōdai Japan 92 C4
Ōdaigahara-zan mt. Japan 92 C4
Odaira-tōge pass Japan 92 D3
Ōdate Japan 91 F4
Odawara Japan 93 F3
Odda Norway 55 E6
Odei r. Canada 151 L3
Odell IN U.S.A. 164 B3
Odem TX U.S.A. 161 D7
Odemira Port. 67 B5
Ödemiş Turkey 69 L5
Ödenburg Hungary see Sopron
Odense Denmark 55 G9
Odenwald reg. Germany 63 I5
Oder r. Germany 63 J3 also known as Odra (Poland)
Oderbucht b. Germany 57 O3
Oder-Havel-Kanal canal Germany 63 N2
Ödeshog Sweden 55 I7
Odessa Ukr. 69 N1
Odessa TX U.S.A. 161 C6
Odessa WA U.S.A. 156 D3
Odessus Bulg. see Varna
Odiel r. Spain 67 C5
Odienné Côte d'Ivoire 120 C4
Odintsovo Rus. Fed. 52 H5
Odisha state India 106 E1
Ŏdŏngk Cambodia 87 D5
Odra r. Germany/Poland 57 Q6 also known as Oder (Germany)
Odzala, Parc National d' nat. park Congo 122 B3
Ōe Japan 92 B3
Oea Libya see Tripoli
Oé-Cusse enclave East Timor see Ocussi
Oecussi enclave East Timor see Ocussi
Oeiras Brazil 177 J5
Oekussi enclave East Timor see Ocussi
Oelsnitz Germany 63 M4
Oenkerk Neth. 62 F1
Oenpelli Australia 134 F3
Oesel i. Estonia see Hiiumaa
Oeufs, Lac des l. Canada 153 G3
Ōe-yama hill Japan 92 B3
Of Turkey 113 F2
O'Fallon r. MT U.S.A. 156 G3
Ofanto r. Italy 68 G4
Ofaqim Israel 107 B4
Offa Nigeria 120 D4
Offenbach am Main Germany 63 I4
Offenburg Germany 57 K6
Oga r. Indon. 85 F2
Oga Japan 91 E5
Oga-dake mt. Japan 93 F1
Ogadēn reg. Eth. 122 E3
Oga-hantō pen. Japan 91 E5

Ōgaki Japan 92 C3
Ogallala NE U.S.A. 160 C3
Ogan r. Indon. 84 D3
Ogano Japan 93 F2
Ogasa Japan 93 E4
Ogasawara-shotō is Japan see Bonin Islands
Ōga-tō mt. Japan 93 E2
Ogawa Ibaraki Japan 93 G2
Ogawa Ibaraki Japan 93 G2
Ogawa Nagano Japan 93 D2
Ogawa Saitama Japan 93 F2
Ōgawa Japan 93 G2
Ogbomosho Nigeria 120 D4
Ogbomoso Nigeria see Ogbomosho
Ogden IA U.S.A. 160 E3
Ogden UT U.S.A. 156 F4
Ogden, Mount Canada 149 N4
Ogdensburg NY U.S.A. 165 H1
Ogidaki Canada 152 D5
Ogilvie r. Canada 149 M2
Ogilvie Mountains Canada 149 L2
Ögiynuur Mongolia 94 E2
Oglala Pass sea channel AK U.S.A. 148 [inset] B6
Oglethorpe, Mount GA U.S.A. 163 C5
Oglio r. Italy 68 D2
Oglongi Rus. Fed. 90 E1
Ogmore Australia 136 E4
Ōgo Japan 93 F2
Ogoamas, Gunung mt. Indon. 83 B2
Ogōchi-damu dam Japan 93 F3
Ogodzha Rus. Fed. 90 D1
Ogoja Nigeria 120 D4
Ogoki r. Canada 152 D4
Ogoki Lake Canada 160 G1
Ogoki Reservoir Canada 152 C4
Ogoron Rus. Fed. 90 C1
Ogose Japan 93 F3
Ogosta r. Bulg. 69 J3
Ogre Latvia 55 N8
Ōguchi Japan 92 C3
Ogulin Croatia 68 F2
Ogurchinskiy, Ostrov i. Turkm. see Ogurjaly Adasy
Ogurjaly Adasy i. Turkm. 110 D2
Oğuzeli Turkey 107 C1
Ohai N.Z. 139 A7
Ohakune N.Z. 139 E4
Ohanet Alg. 120 D2
Ōhara Japan 93 G3
Ōhata Japan 90 F4
Ohcejohka Fin. see Utsjoki
O'Higgins, Lago l. Chile 178 B7
O'Higgins (Chile) research station Antarctica 188 A2
Ohio r. OH/WV U.S.A. 164 A5
Ohio state U.S.A. 164 D3
Ōhira Japan 93 F2
Ōhito Japan 93 E3
Ohm r. Germany 63 I4
Ohogamiut AK U.S.A. 148 G3
Ohrdruf Germany 63 K4
Ohře r. Czech Rep. 63 N4
Ohre r. Germany 63 L2
Ohrid Macedonia 69 I4
Ohrid, Lake Albania/Macedonia 69 I4
Ohridsko Ezero l. Albania/Macedonia see Ohrid, Lake
Ohrigstad S. Africa 125 J3
Öhringen Germany 63 J5
Ohrit, Liqeni i l. Albania/Macedonia see Ohrid, Lake
Ohura N.Z. 139 E4
Ōi Japan 92 B3
Oich r. U.K. 60 E3
Oiga China 99 F7
Ōigawa Japan 93 E4
Ōi-gawa r. Japan 92 B3
Ōi-gawa r. Japan 93 E4
Oignies France 62 C4
Oil City PA U.S.A. 164 F3
Oise r. France 62 C6
Ōiso Japan 93 F3
Ōita Japan 91 C6
Oiti mt. Greece 69 J5
Ōizumi Japan 93 E3
Oizuruga-dake mt. Japan 92 C2
Ojai CA U.S.A. 158 D4
Ojalava i. Samoa see 'Upolu
Ōji Japan 92 B4
Ojinaga Mex. 166 D2
Ojitlán Mex. 167 F5
Ojiya Japan 91 E5
Ojo Caliente NM U.S.A. 157 G5
Ojo de Laguna Mex. 166 D2
Ojo de Liebre, Lago b. Mex. 166 B3

▶Ojos del Salado, Nevado mt. Arg./Chile 178 C3
2nd highest mountain in South America.

Ojuelos de Jalisco Mex. 167 E4
Oka r. Rus. Fed. 53 I4
Oka r. Rus. Fed. 88 I1
Okabe Saitama Japan 93 F2
Okabe Shizuoka Japan 93 E4
Okahandja Namibia 124 C1
Okahukura N.Z. 139 E4
Okakarara Namibia 123 B6
Okak Islands Canada 153 J2
Okanagan Lake Canada 150 G5
Okanda Sri Lanka 106 D5
Okano r. Gabon 122 B4
Okanogan WA U.S.A. 156 D2
Okanogan r. WA U.S.A. 156 D2
Okara Pak. 111 I4
Okarem Turkm. see Ekerem
Okataina vol. N.Z. see Tarawera, Mount
Okaukuejo Namibia 123 B5
Okavango r. Africa 123 C5

▶Okavango Delta swamp Botswana 123 C5
Largest oasis in the world.

Okavango Swamps Botswana see Okavango Delta
Ōkawachi Japan 92 A3
Okaya Japan 93 E2
Okayama Japan 91 D6
Okazaki Japan 92 D4
Okeechobee FL U.S.A. 163 D7
Okeechobee, Lake FL U.S.A. 163 D7
Okeene OK U.S.A. 161 D4
Okefenokee Swamp GA U.S.A. 163 D6
Okegawa Japan 93 F2
Okehampton U.K. 59 C8
Okemah OK U.S.A. 161 D5
Oker r. Germany 63 K2
Okha India 104 B5
Okha Rus. Fed. 90 F1
Okha Rann marsh India 104 B5
Okhotsk Rus. Fed. 77 P4
Okhotsk, Sea of Japan/Rus. Fed. 90 G3
Okhotskoye More sea Japan/Rus. Fed. see Okhotsk, Sea of
Okhtyrka Ukr. 53 G6
Okinawa i. Japan 91 B8
Okinawa-guntō is Japan see Okinawa-shotō
Okinawa-shotō is Japan 91 B8
Okino-Daitō-jima i. Japan 89 O8
Okino-shima i. Japan 92 B4
Okino-Tori-shima i. Japan 89 P8
Oki-shotō is Japan 91 D5
Okkan Myanmar 86 A3
Oklahoma state U.S.A. 161 D5

▶Oklahoma City OK U.S.A. 161 D5
Capital of Oklahoma.

Okmok sea feature N. Pacific Ocean 148 E5
Okmulgee OK U.S.A. 161 D5
Okolona KY U.S.A. 164 C4
Okolona MS U.S.A. 161 F5
Okondja Gabon 122 B4
Okovskiy Les for. Rus. Fed. 52 G5
Okoyo Congo 122 B4
Okpan, Gora hill Kazakh. 113 H1
Okpekty, Gora mt. Kazakh. 98 C3
Øksfjord Norway 54 M1
Oktemberyan Armenia see Armavir
Oktwin Myanmar 86 B3
Oktyabr' Kazakh. see Kandyagash
Oktyabr'sk Kazakh. see Kandyagash
Oktyabr'skiy Belarus see Aktsyabrski
Oktyabr'skiy Amurskaya Oblast' Rus. Fed. 90 C1
Oktyabr'skiy Arkhangel'skaya Oblast' Rus. Fed. 52 I3
Oktyabr'skiy Kamchatskiy Kray Rus. Fed. 77 Q4
Oktyabr'skiy Respublika Bashkortostan Rus. Fed. 51 Q5
Oktyabr'skiy Volgogradskaya Oblast' Rus. Fed. 53 I7
Oktyabr'skoye Rus. Fed. 51 T3
Oktyabr'skoy Revolyutsii, Ostrov i. Rus. Fed. 77 K2
Okuchi Japan 92 C2
Okulovka Rus. Fed. 52 G4
Oku-sangai-dake mt. Japan 92 D3
Okushiri-tō i. Japan 90 E4
Okusi enclave East Timor see Ocussi
Okuta Nigeria 120 D4
Okutadami-ko resr Japan 93 F1
Okutama Japan 93 F3
Okutama-ko l. Japan 93 F3
Okutango-hantō pen. Japan 92 B3
Okutone-ko resr Japan 93 F2
Ōkuwa Japan 92 D3
Okwa watercourse Botswana 124 G1
Ólafsvík Iceland 54 [inset 1]
Olakkur India 106 C3
Olancha CA U.S.A. 158 D3
Olancha Peak CA U.S.A. 158 D3
Olanchito Hond. 166 [inset] I6
Öland i. Sweden 55 J8
Olary Australia 137 C7
Olathe CO U.S.A. 159 J2
Olathe KS U.S.A. 160 E4
Olavarría Arg. 178 D5
Oława Poland 57 P5
Olbernhau Germany 63 N4
Olbia Sardinia Italy 68 C4
Old Bahama Channel Bahamas/Cuba 163 E8
Old Bastar India 106 D2
Oldcastle Ireland 61 E4
Old Cork Australia 136 C4
Old Crow Canada 149 M2
Old Crow r. Canada 149 M2
Oldeboorn Neth. see Aldeboarn
Oldenburg Germany 63 I1
Oldenburg in Holstein Germany 57 M3
Oldenzaal Neth. 62 G2
Olderdalen Norway 54 L2
Old Forge NY U.S.A. 165 H2
Old Gidgee Australia 135 B6
Oldham U.K. 58 E5
Old Harbor AK U.S.A. 148 I4
Old Head of Kinsale hd Ireland 61 D6
Old John Lake AK U.S.A. 149 K1
Oldman r. Canada 150 I5
Oldmeldrum U.K. 60 G3
Old Perlican Canada 153 L5
Old Rampart AK U.S.A. 149 L2
Old River CA U.S.A. 158 D4
Olds Canada 150 H5
Old Speck Mountain ME U.S.A. 165 J1
Old Station CA U.S.A. 158 C1
Old Wives Lake Canada 151 J5
Öldziyt Arhangay Mongolia 94 E1
Öldziyt Arhangay Mongolia see Erdenemandal
Öldziyt Bayanhongor Mongolia 94 E2
Öldziyt Dornogovĭ Mongolia see Sayhandulaan
Öldziyt Dundgovĭ Mongolia 94 F2
Olean NY U.S.A. 165 F2
Olecko Poland 57 S3
Olekma r. Rus. Fed. 77 N3
Olekminsk Rus. Fed. 77 N3
Olekminskiy Stanovik mts Rus. Fed. 89 M2
Oleksandrivs'k Ukr. see Zaporizhzhya
Oleksandriya Ukr. 53 G6
Ølen Norway 55 D7
Olenegorsk Rus. Fed. 54 R2
Olenek Rus. Fed. 77 M3
Olenek r. Rus. Fed. 77 M2
Olenek Bay Rus. Fed. see Olenekskiy Zaliv
Olenekskiy Zaliv b. Rus. Fed. 77 N2
Olenino Rus. Fed. 52 G4
Olenitsa Rus. Fed. 52 G2
Olenivs'ki Kar"yery Ukr. see Dokuchayevs'k
Olentuy Rus. Fed. 95 H1
Olenya Rus. Fed. see Olenegorsk
Oleshky Ukr. see Tsyurupyns'k
Olet Tongo mt. Sumbawa Indon. 85 G5
Olevs'k Ukr. 53 E6
Ol'ga Rus. Fed. 90 D4
Olga, Lac l. Canada 152 F4
Olga, Mount Australia 135 E6
Ol'ginsk Rus. Fed. 90 D1
Olginskoye Rus. Fed. see Kochubeyevskoye
Ölgiy Mongolia 94 B1
Olhão Port. 67 C5
Olia Chain mts Australia 135 E6
Olifants r. Moz./S. Africa 125 J3
also known as Elefantes
Olifants watercourse Namibia 124 D3
Olifants S. Africa 125 J2
Olifants r. W. Cape S. Africa 124 D6
Olifants r. W. Cape S. Africa 124 E7
Olifantshoek S. Africa 124 F4
Olifantsrivierberge mts S. Africa 124 D7
Olimarao atoll Micronesia 81 L5
Olimbos hill Cyprus see Olympos
Olimbos mt. Greece see Olympus, Mount
Olimpos Beydağları Milli Parkı nat. park Turkey 69 N6
Olinalá Mex. 167 F5
Olinda Brazil 177 L5
Olinga Moz. 123 D5
Olio Australia 136 C4
Oliphants Drift S. Africa 125 H3
Olisipo Port. see Lisbon
Oliva Spain 67 F4
Oliva, Cordillera de mts Arg./Chile 178 C3
Olivares, Cerro de mt. Arg./Chile 178 C4
Olive Hill KY U.S.A. 164 D4
Olivehurst CA U.S.A. 158 C2
Oliveira dos Brejinhos Brazil 179 C1
Olivença Moz. see Lupilichi
Olivenza Spain 67 C4
Oliver Lake Canada 151 K3
Olivet MI U.S.A. 164 C2
Olivet SD U.S.A. 160 D3
Olivia MN U.S.A. 160 E2
Oljoq China 98 C4
Ol'khovka Rus. Fed. 53 J6
Ollagüe Chile 178 C2
Ollombo Congo 122 B4
Olmaliq Uzbek. 102 C3
Olmos Peru 176 C5
Olmütz Czech Rep. see Olomouc
Olney U.K. 59 G6
Olney IL U.S.A. 160 F4
Olney MD U.S.A. 165 G4
Olney TX U.S.A. 161 D5
Olofström Sweden 55 I8
Olomane r. Canada 153 J4
Olomouc Czech Rep. 57 P6
Olonets Rus. Fed. 52 G3
Olongapo Luzon Phil. 82 C3
Olongliko Kalimantan Indon. 85 F3
Oloron-Ste-Marie France 66 D5
Olosenga atoll American Samoa see Swains Island
Olot Spain 67 H2
Olot Uzbek. 111 F2
Olovyannaya Chukotskiy Avtonomnyy Okrug Rus. Fed. 148 C2
Olovyannaya Zabaykal'skiy Kray Rus. Fed. 95 H1
Oloy r. Rus. Fed. 77 Q3
Oloy, Qatorkŭhi mts Asia see Alai Range
Olpe Germany 63 H3
Olsztyn Poland 57 R4
Olt r. Romania 69 K3
Olten Switz. 66 H3
Olteniţa Romania 69 L2
Oltu Turkey 113 F2
Oluan Pi c. Taiwan 97 I4
Olutanga i. Phil. 82 C5
Ol'viopol' Ukr. see Pervomays'k
Olymbos hill Cyprus see Olympos

▶Olympia WA U.S.A. 156 C3
Capital of Washington state.

Olympic National Park WA U.S.A. 156 C3
Olympos hill Cyprus 107 A2
Olympos Greece see Olympus, Mount
Olympos nat. park Greece see Olympou, Ethnikos Drymos
Olympou, Ethnikos Drymos nat. park Greece 69 J4
Olympus, Mount Greece 69 J4
Olympus, Mount WA U.S.A. 156 C3
Olyutorskiy, Mys c. Rus. Fed. 77 S4
Olyutorskiy Zaliv b. Rus. Fed. 77 R4
Olzheras Rus. Fed. see Mezhdurechensk
Oma China 99 C6
Oma r. Rus. Fed. 52 J2
Ōmachi Japan 93 D2
Omaezaki Japan 93 E4
Omae-zaki pt Japan 93 E4
Omagh U.K. 61 E3
Omaha NE U.S.A. 160 E3
Omaheke admin. reg. Namibia 124 D2
Omal'skiy Khrebet mts Rus. Fed. 90 E1
Ōmama Japan 93 F2
Oman country Asia 109 I6
Oman, Gulf of Asia 110 E5
Omaruru Namibia 123 B6
Omate Peru 176 D7
Omaweneno Botswana 124 F3
Omba i. Vanuatu see Aoba
Ombai, Selat sea chan. Indon. 83 C5
Ombalantu Namibia see Uutapi
Ombolata Indon. 84 B2
Omboué Gabon 122 A4
Ombu China 99 D7
Omdraaisvlei S. Africa 124 F6
Omdurman Sudan 108 D6
Ōme Japan 93 F3
Omeo Australia 138 C6
Omer MI U.S.A. 164 D1
Ometepe, Isla de i. Nicaragua 166 [inset] I7
Ometepec Mex. 168 E5
Omgoy Wildlife Reserve nature res. Thai. 86 B3
Om Hajēr Eritrea 108 E7
Ōmi Japan 93 E2
Ōmi Niigata Japan 93 D1
Ōmi Shiga Japan 92 C3
Omīdīyeh Iran 110 C4
Omigawa Japan 93 G3
Ōmihachiman Japan 92 C3
Omineca Mountains Canada 150 E3
Omirzak Kazakh. 113 H2
Omitara Namibia 124 C2
Ōmiya Ibaraki Japan 93 G2
Ōmiya Kyōto Japan 92 B3
Ōmiya Mie Japan 92 C4
Ōmiya Saitama Japan 93 F3
Ommaney, Cape AK U.S.A. 149 N4
Ommen Neth. 62 G2
Ömnödelger Mongolia 95 G2
Ömnögovĭ prov. Mongolia 94 F3
Omoi-gawa r. Japan 93 F2
Omolon Rus. Fed. 77 R3
Omo National Park Eth. 122 D3
Omon Gol watercourse China 94 E3
Omotegō Japan 93 G1
Omsk Rus. Fed. 76 I4
Omsukchan Rus. Fed. 77 Q3
Ōmū Japan 90 F3
O-mu Myanmar 86 B2
Omu, Vârful mt. Romania 69 K2
Ōmura Japan 91 C6
Ōmuro-yama hill Japan 93 F4
Ōmuro-yama mt. Japan 93 E3
Ōmuro-yama mt. Japan 93 F3
Omutninsk Rus. Fed. 52 L4
Onaman Lake Canada 152 D4
Onamia MN U.S.A. 160 E2
Onancock VA U.S.A. 165 H5
Onang Sulawesi Barat Indon. 83 A3
Onangué, Lac l. Gabon 122 B4
Onaping Lake Canada 152 E5
Onatchiway, Lac l. Canada 153 H4
Onavas Mex. 166 C2
Onawa IA U.S.A. 160 D3
Onaway MI U.S.A. 164 C1
Ōnay, Kōtal-e Afgh. 111 H3
Onbingwin Myanmar 87 B4
Oncativo Arg. 178 D4
Onchan Isle of Man 58 C4
Oncócua Angola 123 B5
Öncül Turkey 107 D1
Ondal India see Andal
Ondangwa Namibia 123 B5
Onderstedorings S. Africa 124 E6
Ondjiva Angola 123 B5
Ondo Nigeria 120 D4
Öndörhaan Mongolia 95 G2
Ondor Had China 95 J2
Öndörhushuu Mongolia see Bulgan
Ondorkara China 94 B2
Ondor Mod China 94 F3
Öndörshil Mongolia 95 G2
Ondor Sum China 95 H3
Öndör-Ulaan Mongolia 94 E1
Ondozero Rus. Fed. 52 G3
One Botswana 124 E2
One and a Half Degree Channel Maldives 103 D11
Onega Rus. Fed. 52 H3
Onega r. Rus. Fed. 52 H3

▶Onega, Lake Rus. Fed. 52 G3
3rd largest lake in Europe.

Onega Bay g. Rus. Fed. see Onezhskaya Guba
One Hundred and Fifty Mile House Canada see 150 Mile House
One Hundred Mile House Canada see 100 Mile House
Oneida NY U.S.A. 165 H2
Oneida TN U.S.A. 164 C5
Oneida Lake NY U.S.A. 165 H2
O'Neill NE U.S.A. 160 D3
Onekama MI U.S.A. 164 B1
Onekotan, Ostrov i. Rus. Fed. 77 Q5
Oneonta AL U.S.A. 163 C5
Oneonta NY U.S.A. 165 H2
Oneşti Romania 69 L1
Onezhskaya Guba g. Rus. Fed. 52 G2
Onezhskoye Ozero l. Rus. Fed. see Onega, Lake
Ong r. India 106 D1
Onga Gabon 122 B4
Ongers watercourse S. Africa 124 F5
Onggot China 95 J1
Ongi Dundgovĭ Mongolia see Sayhan-Ovoo
Ongi Övörhangay Mongolia see Uyanga
Ongiyn Gol r. Mongolia 94 E2
Ongjin N. Korea 91 B5
Ongniud Qi China see Wudan
Ongole India 106 D3
Ongon Mongolia see Bürd
Ongt Gol China 94 E3
Onguday Rus. Fed. 98 D2
Onida SD U.S.A. 160 C2
Oniishi Japan 93 F2
Onilahy r. Madag. 123 E6
Onistagane, Lac l. Canada 153 H4
Onitsha Nigeria 120 D4
Onjati Mountain Namibia 124 C2
Onjiva Angola see Ondjiva
Onjuku Japan 93 G3
Ōno Fukui Japan 92 C3
Ōno Gifu Japan 92 C3
Ono Japan 92 A4
Ōnohara-jima i. Japan 93 F4
Ono-i-Lau i. Fiji 133 I4
Onomichi Japan 91 D6
Onon atoll Micronesia see Namonuito
Onon Mongolia see Binder
Onon r. Rus. Fed. 95 H1
Onon Gol r. Mongolia 95 H1
Onor, Gora mt. Rus. Fed. 90 F2
Onotoa atoll Kiribati 133 H2
Onseepkans S. Africa 124 D5
Onslow Australia 134 A5
Onslow Bay NC U.S.A. 163 E5
Onstwedde Neth. 62 H1
Ontake-san vol. Japan 92 D3
Ontaratue r. Canada 149 O2
Ontario prov. Canada 164 E1
Ontario CA U.S.A. 158 E4
Ontario, Lake Canada/U.S.A. 165 G2
Ontong Java Atoll Solomon Is 133 F2
Onutu atoll Kiribati see Onotoa
Onverwacht Suriname 177 G2
Onyx CA U.S.A. 158 D4
Oodnadatta Australia 137 A5
Oodweyne Somalia 122 E3
Ōoka Japan 93 D2
Oolambeyan National Park Australia 137 D7
Ooldea Australia 135 E7
Ooldea Range hills Australia 135 E7
Oologah Lake resr OK U.S.A. 161 E4
Ooratippra r. Australia 136 B4
Oos-Londen S. Africa see East London
Oostburg Neth. 62 D3
Oostende Belgium see Ostend
Oostendorp Neth. 62 F2
Oosterhout Neth. 62 E3
Oosterschelde est. Neth. 62 D3
Oosterwolde Neth. 62 G2
Oostvleteren Belgium 62 C4
Oost-Vlieland Neth. 62 F1
Ootacamund India see Udagamandalam
Ootsa Lake Canada 150 E4
Ootsa Lake l. Canada 150 E4
Opal Mex. 161 C7
Opala Dem. Rep. Congo 122 C4
Oparino Rus. Fed. 52 K4
Oparo i. Fr. Polynesia see Rapa
Opasatika r. Canada 152 E4
Opasatika Lake Canada 152 E4
Opasquia Canada 151 M4
Opataca, Lac l. Canada 152 G4
Opava Czech Rep. 57 P6
Opel hill Germany 63 H5
Opelika AL U.S.A. 163 C5
Opelousas LA U.S.A. 161 E6
Opeongo Lake Canada 152 F5
Opheim MT U.S.A. 156 G2
Ophir, Gunung vol. Indon. 84 C2
Opienge Dem. Rep. Congo 122 C3
Opin Seram Indon. 83 D3
Opinaca r. Canada 152 F3
Opinaca, Réservoir resr Canada 152 F3
Opinnagau r. Canada 152 E3
Opiscotéo, Lac l. Canada 153 H3
Op Luang National Park Thai. 86 B3
Opmeer Neth. 62 E2
Opochka Rus. Fed. 55 P8
Opocopa, Lac l. Canada 153 I3
Opodepe Mex. 166 C2
Opole Poland 57 P5
Oporto Port. 67 B3
Opotiki N.Z. 139 F4
Opp AL U.S.A. 163 C6
Oppdal Norway 54 F5
Oppeln Poland see Opole
Opportunity WA U.S.A. 156 D3
Opunake N.Z. 139 D4
Opuwo Namibia 123 B5
Oqsu r. Tajik. 111 I2
Oquitoa Mex. 166 C2
Ōra Japan 93 F2
Oracle AZ U.S.A. 159 H5
Oradea Romania 69 I1
Orahovac Kosovo see Rahovec
Orai India 104 D4
Oraibi AZ U.S.A. 159 H4
Oraibi Wash watercourse AZ U.S.A. 159 H4
Oral Kazakh. see Ural'sk
Oran Alg. 67 F6
Orán Arg. 178 D2
O Rang Cambodia 87 D4
Orang India 105 H4
Ōrang N. Korea 90 C4
Orange Australia 138 D4
Orange France 66 G4
Orange r. Namibia/S. Africa 124 C5
Orange CA U.S.A. 158 E5
Orange MA U.S.A. 165 I2
Orange TX U.S.A. 161 E6
Orange VA U.S.A. 165 F4
Orange, Cabo c. Brazil 177 H3
Orangeburg SC U.S.A. 163 D5
Orange City IA U.S.A. 160 D3
Orange Cone sea feature S. Atlantic Ocean 184 I8
Orange Free State prov. S. Africa see Free State
Orangeville Canada 164 E2
Orange Walk Belize 167 H5
Orani Luzon Phil. 82 C3
Oranienburg Germany 63 N2
Oranje r. Namibia/S. Africa see Orange
Oranje Gebergte hills Suriname 177 G3
Oranjemund Namibia 124 C5

▶Oranjestad Aruba 169 J6
Capital of Aruba.

Oranmore Ireland 61 D4
Orapa Botswana 123 C6
Oras Samar Phil. 82 D3
Oras Bay Samar Phil. 82 D3
Orăştie Romania 69 J2
Oraşul Stalin Romania see Braşov
Oratia, Mount AK U.S.A. 148 G4
Oravais Fin. 54 M5
Orba Co l. China 99 C6
Orbetello Italy 68 D3
Orbost Australia 138 D6
Orca Bay AK U.S.A. 149 K3
Orcadas research station S. Atlantic Ocean 188 A2
Orchard City CO U.S.A. 159 J2
Orchha India 104 D4
Orchila, Isla i. Venez. 176 E1
Orchy r. U.K. 60 D4
Orcutt CA U.S.A. 158 C4
Ord r. Australia 134 E3
Ord NE U.S.A. 160 D3
Ord, Mount hill Australia 134 D4
Órdenes Spain see Ordes
Orderville UT U.S.A. 159 G3
Ordes Spain 67 B2
Ordesa y Monte Perdido, Parque Nacional de nat. park Spain 67 G2
Ord Mountain CA U.S.A. 158 E4
Ordos China 95 G4
Ord River Dam Australia 134 E4
Ordu Hatay Turkey see Yayladağı
Ordu Ordu Turkey 112 E2
Ordubad Azer. 113 G3
Ordway CO U.S.A. 160 C4
Ordzhonikidze Rus. Fed. see Vladikavkaz
Ore Nigeria 120 D4
Oreana NV U.S.A. 158 D1
Örebro Sweden 55 I7
Oregon IL U.S.A. 160 F3
Oregon OH U.S.A. 164 D3
Oregon state U.S.A. 156 C4
Oregon City OR U.S.A. 156 C3
Orekhov Ukr. see Orikhiv
Orekhovo-Zuyevo Rus. Fed. 52 H5
Orel' Kazakh. 102 G2
Orel Rus. Fed. 53 H5
Orel, Gora mt. Rus. Fed. 90 E1
Orel', Ozero l. Rus. Fed. 90 E1
Orem UT U.S.A. 159 H1
Ore Mountains Czech Rep./Germany see Erzgebirge
Orenburg Rus. Fed. 76 G4
Orense Spain see Ourense
Oreor Palau see Koror
Oreor i. Palau see Koror
Orepuki N.Z. 139 A8
Öresund strait Denmark/Sweden 55 H9
Oretana, Cordillera mts Spain see Toledo, Montes de
Orewa N.Z. 139 E3
Oreye Belgium 62 F4
Orfanou, Kolpos b. Greece 69 J4
Orford Australia 137 [inset]
Orford U.K. 59 I6
Orford Ness hd U.K. 59 I6
Organabo Fr. Guiana 177 H2
Organ Pipe Cactus National Monument nat. park AZ U.S.A. 159 G5
Orge r. France 62 C6
Orgil Mongolia see Jargalant
Orgon Tal China 95 H3
Orhaneli Turkey 69 M5
Orhangazi Turkey 69 M4
Orhon Bulgan Mongolia 94 E1
Orhon Selenge Mongolia 94 F1
Orhon Gol r. Mongolia 94 F1
Orhontuul Mongolia 94 F1
Orichi Rus. Fed. 52 K4
Oriental, Cordillera mts Bol. 176 E7
Oriental, Cordillera mts Col. 176 D2
Oriental, Cordillera mts Peru 176 E6
Orihuela Spain 67 F4
Orikhiv Ukr. 53 G7
Orillia Canada 164 F1
Orimattila Fin. 55 N6
Orin WY U.S.A. 156 G4
Orinoco r. Col./Venez. 176 F2
Orinoco, Delta del Venez. 176 F2
Orissa state India see Odisha
Orissaare Estonia 55 M7
Oristano Sardinia Italy 68 C5
Orivesi Fin. 55 N6
Orivesi l. Fin. 54 P5
Oriximiná Brazil 177 G4
Orizaba Mex. 168 E5

▶Orizaba, Pico de vol. Mex. 168 E5
Highest active volcano and 3rd highest mountain in North America.

Orizona Brazil 179 A2
Orkanger Norway 54 F5
Örkelljunga Sweden 55 H8
Orkhon Valley tourist site Mongolia 94 E2
Orkla r. Norway 54 F5
Orkney S. Africa 125 H4
Orkney Islands is U.K. 60 F1
Orla TX U.S.A. 161 C6
Orland CA U.S.A. 158 B2
Orlândia Brazil 179 B3
Orlando FL U.S.A. 163 D6
Orland Park IL U.S.A. 164 B3
Orleaes Brazil 179 A5
Orléans France 66 E3
Orleans IN U.S.A. 164 B4
Orleans VT U.S.A. 165 I1
Orléans, Île d' i. Canada 153 H5
Orléansville Alg. see Chlef
Orlik Rus. Fed. 88 H2
Orlov Rus. Fed. 52 K4
Orlov Gay Rus. Fed. 53 K6
Orlovskiy Rus. Fed. 53 I7
Ormara Pak. 111 G5
Ormara, Ras hd Pak. 111 G5
Ormiston Canada 151 J5
Ormoc Leyte Phil. 82 D4
Ormskirk U.K. 58 E5
Ormstown Canada 165 I1
Ornach Pak. 111 G5
Ornain r. France 62 E6
Orne r. France 66 D2
Ørnes Norway 54 H3
Örnsköldsvik Sweden 54 K5
Orobie, Alpi mts Italy 68 C1
Orobo, Serra do hills Brazil 179 C1
Orodara Burkina Faso 120 C3
Orofino ID U.S.A. 156 D3
Orog Nuur salt l. Mongolia 94 E2
Oro Grande CA U.S.A. 158 E4
Orogrande NM U.S.A. 157 G6
Orol Dengizi salt l. Kazakh./Uzbek. see Aral Sea
Oromocto Canada 153 I5
Oromocto Lake Canada 153 I5
Oron Israel 107 B4
Orona atoll Kiribati 133 I2
Orono ME U.S.A. 162 G2
Orontes r. Asia 112 E3 see 'Āṣī, Nahr al
Orontes r. Lebanon/Syria 107 C2
Oroqen Zizhiqi China see Alihe
Oroquieta Mindanao Phil. 82 C4
Orós, Açude resr Brazil 177 K5
Orosei, Golfo di b. Sardinia Italy 68 C4
Orosháza Hungary 69 I1
Oroville CA U.S.A. 158 C2
Oroville, Lake CA U.S.A. 158 C2
Orqohan China 95 J1
Orr MN U.S.A. 160 E1
Orsa Sweden 55 I6
Orsha Belarus 53 F5
Orshanka Rus. Fed. 52 J4
Orsk Rus. Fed. 76 G4
Ørsta Norway 54 E5
Orta Toroslar plat. Turkey 107 A1
Ortegal, Cabo c. Spain 67 C2
Orthez France 66 D5
Ortigueira Spain 67 C2
Ortíz Mex. 166 C2
Ortles mt. Italy 68 D1
Orton U.K. 58 E4
Ortona Italy 68 F3
Ortonville MN U.S.A. 160 D2
Ortospana Afgh. see Kābul
Orto-Tokoy Kyrg. 98 A4
Orukuizu i. Palau 82 [inset]
Orulgan, Khrebet mts Rus. Fed. 77 N3
Orumbo Namibia 124 C2
Orūmīyeh Iran see Urmia
Oruro Bol. 176 E7
Orvieto Italy 68 E3
Orville Coast Antarctica 188 L1
Orwell OH U.S.A. 164 E3
Orwell VT U.S.A. 165 I2
Orxon Gol r. China 95 I1
Oryol Rus. Fed. see Orel
Os Norway 54 G5
Osa Rus. Fed. 51 R4
Osa, Península de pen. Costa Rica 166 [inset] J7
Osage IA U.S.A. 160 E3
Osage WV U.S.A. 164 E4
Osage WY U.S.A. 156 G3
Osaka Japan 92 D3

▶**Pamana** *i.* Indon. **83** B5
Most southerly point of Asia.

Pamana Besar *i.* Indon. **83** B5
Pamanukan *Jawa* Indon. **85** D4
Pambarra Moz. **125** L1
Pambero *Sulawesi* Indon. **83** A2
Pambula Australia **138** D6
Pamekasan *Jawa* Indon. **85** F4
Pameungpeuk *Jawa* Indon. **85** D4
Pamidi India **106** C3
Pamiers France **66** E5
Pamir *mts* Asia **111** I2
Pamlico Sound *sea chan. NC* U.S.A. **163** E5
Pamouscachiou, Lac *l.* Canada **153** H4
Pampa *TX* U.S.A. **161** C5
Pampa de Infierno Arg. **178** D3
Pampanua *Sulawesi* Indon. **83** B4
Pampas *reg.* Arg. **178** D5
Pampeluna Spain *see* **Pamplona**
Pamphylia *reg.* Turkey **69** N6
Pamplin *VA* U.S.A. **165** F5
Pamplona Col. **176** D2
Pamplona *Negros* Phil. **82** C4
Pamplona Spain **67** F2
Pampow Germany **63** L1
Pamukan, Teluk *b.* Indon. **85** G3
Pamukova Turkey **69** N4
Pamzal India **104** D2
Pana *IL* U.S.A. **160** F4
Panabá Mex. **167** H4
Panabo *Mindanao* Phil. **82** D5
Panabutan Bay *Mindanao* Phil. **82** C5
Panaca *NV* U.S.A. **159** F3
Panache, Lake Canada **152** E5
Panagtaran Point *Palawan* Phil. **82** B4
Panagyurishte Bulg. **69** K3
Panaitan *i.* Indon. **84** D4
Panaji India **106** B3
Panama *country* Central America **169** H7
Panamá Panama *see* **Panama City**
Panamá, Bahía de *b.* Panama **166** [inset] K7
Panamá, Golfo de *g.* Panama **166** [inset] K8
Panama, Gulf of Panama *see* **Panamá, Golfo de**
Panama, Isthmus of Panama **169** I7
Panamá, Istmo de Panama *see* **Panama, Isthmus of**
Panama Canal Panama **166** [inset] K7

▶**Panama City** Panama **166** K7
Capital of Panama.

Panama City *FL* U.S.A. **163** C6
Panamint Range *mts CA* U.S.A. **158** E3
Panamint Valley *CA* U.S.A. **158** E3
Pananjung Pangandaran, Taman Wisata *nat. park* Indon. **85** E4
Panao Peru **176** C5
Panar *r.* India **99** E8
Panarea, Isola *i.* Italy **68** F5
Panarik Indon. **85** E2
Panarukan *Jawa* Indon. **85** F4
Panay *i.* Phil. **82** C4
Panay Gulf Phil. **82** C4
Pancake Range *mts NV* U.S.A. **159** F2
Pančevo Serbia **69** I2
Panchagarh Bangl. **105** G4
Pancingapan, Bukit *mt.* Indon. **85** F2
Pancsova Serbia *see* **Pančevo**
Pancurbatu *Sumatera* Indon. **84** B2
Panda Moz. **125** L3
Pandan Phil. **82** D3
Pandan, Selat *strait* Sing. **87** [inset]
Pandan Bay *Panay* Phil. **82** C4
Pandang *Kalimantan* Indon. **85** F3
Pandan Reservoir Sing. **87** [inset]
Pandeglang *Jawa* Indon. **84** D4
Pandeiros *r.* Brazil **179** B1
Pandharpur India **106** B2
Pandora Costa Rica **166** [inset] J7
Pandy U.K. **59** E7
Paneas Syria *see* **Bāniyās**
Panevėžys Lith. **55** N9
Panfilov Kazakh. *see* **Zharkent**
Pang, Nam *r.* Myanmar **86** B2
Pangandaran *Jawa* Indon. **85** E4
Panganiban Phil. **82** D3
Pangean *Sulawesi Barat* Indon. **83** A3
Panghsang Myanmar **86** B2
Pangi Range *mts* Pak. **111** I3
Pangjiabu China **95** H3
Pangkah, Tanjung *pt* Indon. **85** F4
Pangkajene *Sulawesi* Indon. **83** A4
Pangkalanbuun *Kalimantan* Indon. **85** E3
Pangkalanlunang *Sumatera* Indon. **84** B2
Pangkalansusu *Sumatera* Indon. **84** B1
Pangkal Kalong Malaysia **84** C1
Pangkalpinang Indon. **84** D3
Pangkalsiang, Tanjung *pt* Indon. **83** B3
Panglang Myanmar **86** B1
Panglao *i.* Phil. **82** C4
Panglima Sugala Phil. **82** B5
Pangman Canada **151** J5
Pangnirtung Canada **147** L3
Pangody Rus. Fed. **76** I3
Pangong Tso *salt l.* China/India *see* **Bangong Co**
Pangrango *vol.* Indon. **84** D4
Pang Sida National Park Thai. **87** C4
Pang Sua, Sungai *r.* Sing. **87** [inset]
Pangtara Myanmar **96** C4
Pangu He *r.* China **90** B1
Panguitch *UT* U.S.A. **159** G3
Pangujon, Tanjung *pt* Indon. **85** E3
Pangururan *Sumatera* Indon. **84** B2
Pangutaran *i.* Phil. **82** C5
Pangutaran Group *is* Phil. **82** C5
Panhandle *TX* U.S.A. **161** C5
Panipat India **104** D3
Panir Pak. **111** G4
Panitian *Palawan* Phil. **82** B4
Panj Tajik. **111** H2
Panjāb Afgh. **111** G3
Panjakent Tajik. **111** G2
Panjang *Sumatera* Indon. **84** D4
Panjang *i.* Indon. **85** E2
Panjang *i.* Indon. **85** G2
Panjang, Bukit Sing. **87** [inset]
Panjang, Selat *sea chan.* Indon. **84** C2
Panjgur Pak. **111** G5
Panjim India *see* **Panaji**
Panjin China *see* **Panshan**
Panji Poyon Tajik. **111** H2
Panjnad *r.* Pak. **111** H4
Panjshayr *reg.* Afgh. **111** H3
Pankakoski Fin. **54** Q5
Pankof, Cape *AK* U.S.A. **148** G5
Panlian China *see* **Miyi**
Panna India **104** E4
Panna *reg.* India **104** D4
Pannawonica Australia **134** B5
Pano Lefkara Cyprus **107** A2
Panopah *Kalimantan* Indon. **85** E3
Panorama Brazil **179** A3
Panormus *Sicily* Italy *see* **Palermo**
Panshan China **95** J3
Panshi China **90** B4
Panshui China *see* **Pu'an**
Pantai *Kalimantan* Indon. **85** G3
Pantaicermin, Gunung *mt.* Indon. **84** C3

▶**Pantanal** *marsh* Brazil **177** G7
Largest area of wetlands in the world.

Pantanal Matogrossense, Parque Nacional do *nat. park* Brazil **177** G7
Pantano *AZ* U.S.A. **159** H6
Pantar *i.* Indon. **83** C5
Pantelaria *Sicily* Italy *see* **Pantelleria**
Pantelleria *Sicily* Italy **68** D6
Pantelleria, Isola di *i. Sicily* Italy **68** E6
Pante Macassar East Timor **83** C5
Pantemakassar East Timor *see* **Pante Macassar**
Pantha Myanmar **86** A2
Panther *r. KY* U.S.A. **164** B5
Panth Piploda India **104** C5
Panticapaeum Ukr. *see* **Kerch**
Pantonlabu *Sumatera* Indon. **84** B1
Pantukan *Mindanao* Phil. **82** D5
Panua, Cagar Alam *nature res.* Indon. **83** B2
Pánuco *Sinaloa* Mex. **161** B8
Pánuco *Veracruz* Mex. **168** E4
Pánuco *r.* Mex. **167** F4
Panwari India **104** D4
Panxian China **96** E3
Panyu China **97** G4
Panzhihua China **96** D3
Panzi Dem. Rep. Congo **123** B4
Panzos Guat. **167** H6
Paola Italy **68** G5
Paola *KS* U.S.A. **160** E4
Paoli *IN* U.S.A. **164** B4
Paoni *Seram* Indon. **83** D3
Paoua Cent. Afr. Rep. **122** B3
Paôy Pêt Cambodia **87** C4
Pápa Hungary **68** G1
Papa, Monte del *mt.* Italy **68** F4
Papagni *r.* India **106** C3
Papahānaumokuākea *tourist site* U.S.A. **186** I4
Pāpā'ikou *HI* U.S.A. **157** [inset]
Papakura N.Z. **139** E3
Papanasam India **106** C4
Papanoa Mex. **167** E5
Papantla Mex. **168** E4
Papar *Sabah* Malaysia **85** F1
Paparoa National Park N.Z. **139** C6
Papa Stour *i.* U.K. **60** [inset]
Papa Westray *i.* U.K. **60** G1
Papay *i.* U.K. *see* **Papa Westray**

▶**Papeete** Fr. Polynesia **187** K7
Capital of French Polynesia.

Papenburg Germany **63** H1
Paphos Cyprus **107** A2
Paphus Cyprus *see* **Paphos**
Papillion *NE* U.S.A. **160** D3
Papoose Lake *NV* U.S.A. **159** F3
Pappenheim Germany **63** K6
Papua, Gulf of P.N.G. **81** K8
Papua Barat *prov.* Indon. **83** D3

▶**Papua New Guinea** *country* Oceania **132** E2
2nd largest and 2nd most populous country in Oceania.

Pa Qal'eh Iran **110** D4
Par U.K. **59** C8
Pará *r.* Brazil **179** B2
Para *i.* Indon. **83** C2
Pará, Rio do *r.* Brazil **177** I4
Paraburdoo Australia **135** B5
Paracale *Luzon* Phil. **82** C3
Paracatu Brazil **179** B2
Paracatu *r.* Brazil **179** B2
Paracel Islands S. China Sea **80** E3
Parachilna Australia **137** B6
Parachute *CO* U.S.A. **159** I2
Paraćin Serbia **69** I3
Paracuru Brazil **177** K4
Pará de Minas Brazil **179** B2
Paradis Canada **152** F4
Paradise *r.* Canada **153** K3
Paradise *AK* U.S.A. **148** G3
Paradise *CA* U.S.A. **158** C2
Paradise Hill Canada **151** I4
Paradise Peak *NV* U.S.A. **158** E2
Paradise River Canada **153** K3
Parado *Sumbawa* Indon. **85** G5
Paradwip India **105** F5
Paraetonium Egypt *see* **Marsá Maṭrūḥ**
Paragominas Brazil **177** I4
Paragould *AR* U.S.A. **161** F4
Paragua *i.* Phil. *see* **Palawan**
Paraguaçu Paulista Brazil **179** A3
Paraguay *r.* Arg./Para. **178** E3
Paraguay *country* S. America **178** E2
Paraíba do Sul *r.* Brazil **179** C3
Parainen Fin. *see* **Pargas**
Paraíso *Tabasco* Mex. **167** G5
Paraíso *Tabasco* Mex. **167** G5
Paraíso do Norte Brazil **177** I6
Paraisópolis Brazil **179** B3
Parak Iran **110** D5
Parakou Benin **120** D4
Paralakhemundi India **106** E2
Paralkot India **106** D2
Paramagudi India *see* **Paramakkudi**
Paramakkudi India **106** C4

▶**Paramaribo** Suriname **177** G2
Capital of Suriname.

Paramillo, Parque Nacional *nat. park* Col. **176** C2
Paramirim Brazil **179** C1
Paramo Frontino *mt.* Col. **176** C2
Paramus *NJ* U.S.A. **165** H3
Paramushir, Ostrov *i.* Rus. Fed. **77** Q4
Paran *watercourse* Israel **107** B4
Paraná Arg. **178** D4
Paranã Brazil **179** B1
Paraná *r.* Brazil **179** A1
Paraná *state* Brazil **179** A4

▶**Paraná** *r.* S. America **178** E4
Part of the Río de la Plata - Paraná, 2nd longest river in South America.

Paraná, Serra do *hills* Brazil **179** B1
Paranaguá Brazil **179** A4
Paranaíba Brazil **179** A2
Paranaíba *r.* Brazil **179** A3
Paranapiacaba, Serra *mts* Brazil **179** A4
Paranas *Samar* Phil. **82** D4
Paranavaí Brazil **178** F2
Parang *i.* Indon. **85** E4
Parang Phil. **82** C5
Parangi Aru *r.* Sri Lanka **106** D4
Parang Pass India **104** D2
Parângul Mare, Vârful *mt.* Romania **69** J2
Parantan Sri Lanka **106** D4
Paraopeba Brazil **179** B2
Parapara *Halmahera* Indon. **83** C2
Pārapāra Iraq **113** G4
Paraparaumu N.Z. **139** E5
Paras Mex. **161** D7
Paras Pak. **111** I3
Paraspori, Akra *pt* Greece *see* **Paraspori, Akrotirio**
Paraspori, Akrotirio *pt* Greece **69** L7
Parateca Brazil **179** C1
Paratinga Brazil **179** C1
Parāū, Kūh-e *mt.* Iraq **113** G4
Paraúna Brazil **179** A2
Parbhani India **106** C2
Parchim Germany **63** L1
Parc National André Félix *nat. park* Cent. Afr. Rep. **122** C3
Parding China **105** G2
Pardo *r. Bahia* Brazil **179** D1
Pardo *r. Mato Grosso do Sul* Brazil **178** F2
Pardo *r. São Paulo* Brazil **179** A3
Pardoo Australia **134** B5
Pardubice Czech Rep. **57** O5
Parece Vela *i.* Japan *see* **Okino-Tori-shima**
Pare Chu *r.* China **99** B6
Parecis, Serra dos *hills* Brazil **176** F6
Paredón Mex. **167** E3
Pareh Iran **110** B2
Parenda India **106** B2
Parenggean *Kalimantan* Indon. **85** F3
Parent Canada **152** G5
Parent, Lac *l.* Canada **152** F4
Pareora N.Z. **139** C7
Parepare *Sulawesi* Indon. **83** A4
Parga Greece **69** I5
Pargas Fin. **55** M6
Parghelia Italy **68** F5
Pargi India **106** C2
Paria, Gulf of Trin. and Tob./Venez. **169** L6
Paria, Península de *pen.* Venez. **176** F1
Pariaman *Sumatera* Indon. **84** C3
Paria Plateau *AZ* U.S.A. **159** G3
Parida, Isla *i.* Panama **166** [inset] J7
Parigi *Sulawesi* Indon. **83** B3
Parikkala Fin. **55** P6
Parikud Islands India **106** E2
Parima, Serra *mts* Brazil **176** F3
Parima-Tapirapecó, Parque Nacional *nat. park* Venez. **176** F3
Parintins Brazil **177** G4
Paris Canada **164** E2

▶**Paris** France **62** C6
Capital of France. 2nd most populous city in Europe.

Paris *IL* U.S.A. **164** B4
Paris *KY* U.S.A. **164** C4
Paris *MO* U.S.A. **160** E4
Paris *TN* U.S.A. **161** F4
Paris *TX* U.S.A. **161** E5
Paris (Charles de Gaulle) *airport* France **62** C5
Paris Crossing *IN* U.S.A. **164** C4
Paris (Orly) *airport* France **62** C6
Parit Buntar Malaysia **84** C1
Pārīz Iran **110** D4
Pārk Iran **111** F5
Park U.K. **61** E3
Parkano Fin. **55** M5
Park City *KY* U.S.A. **164** B5
Parke Lake Canada **153** K3
Parker *AZ* U.S.A. **159** F4
Parker *CO* U.S.A. **156** G5
Parker Dam *CA* U.S.A. **159** F4
Parker Lake Canada **151** M2
Parker Range *hills* Australia **135** B8
Parkersburg *WV* U.S.A. **164** E4
Parkers Lake *KY* U.S.A. **164** C5
Parkes Australia **138** D4
Park Falls *WI* U.S.A. **160** F2
Park Forest *IL* U.S.A. **164** B3
Parkhar Tajik. *see* **Farkhor**
Parkhill Canada **164** E2
Park Rapids *MN* U.S.A. **160** E2
Parkutta Pak. **104** D2
Park Valley *UT* U.S.A. **156** E4
Parla Kimedi India *see* **Paralakhemundi**
Parlakimidi India *see* **Paralakhemundi**
Parli Vaijnath India **106** C2
Parlung Zangbo *r.* China **96** B2
Parma Italy **68** D2
Parma *ID* U.S.A. **156** D4
Parma *OH* U.S.A. **164** E3
Parnaíba Brazil **177** J4
Parnaíba *r.* Brazil **177** J4
Parnassos *mt.* Greece *see* **Liakoura**
Parnassus N.Z. **139** D6
Parner India **106** B2
Parnon *mts* Greece *see* **Parnonas**
Parnonas *mts* Greece **69** J6
Pärnu Estonia **55** N7
Pärnu-Jaagupi Estonia **55** N7
Paro Bhutan **105** G4
Paroikia Greece **69** K6
Parona Turkey *see* **Fındık**
Paroo *watercourse* Australia **138** A3
Paroo Channel *watercourse* Australia **138** A3
Paroo-Darling National Park Australia **137** C6
Paroreang, Bukit *mt.* Indon. **83** A3
Paros Greece *see* **Paroikia**
Paros *i.* Greece **69** K6
Parowan *UT* U.S.A. **159** G3
Parral Chile **178** B5
Parramatta Australia **138** E4
Parramore Island *VA* U.S.A. **165** H5
Parras Mex. **166** E3
Parrett *r.* U.K. **59** D7
Parrita Costa Rica **166** [inset] I7
Parry, Cape Canada **149** P1
Parry, Kap *c.* Greenland *see* **Kangaarsussuaq**
Parry, Lac *l.* Canada **152** G2
Parry Bay Canada **147** J3
Parry Channel Canada **147** G2
Parry Islands Canada **147** G2
Parry Peninsula Canada **149** P1
Parry Range *hills* Australia **134** A5
Parry Sound Canada **164** E1
Parsnip Peak *NV* U.S.A. **159** F2
Parsons *KS* U.S.A. **161** E4
Parsons *WV* U.S.A. **164** F4
Parsons Lake Canada **149** N1
Parsons Range *hills* Australia **134** F3
Parta China **99** E7
Partabgarh India **106** B2
Partabpur India **105** E5
Partenstein Germany **63** J4
Parthenay France **66** D3
Partida, Isla *i.* Mex. **166** C3
Partizansk Rus. Fed. **90** D4
Partney U.K. **58** H5
Partridge *r.* Canada **152** E4
Partry Ireland **61** C4
Partry Mountains *hills* Ireland **61** C4
Paru *r.* Brazil **177** H4
Pārūd Iran **111** F5
Paryang China **99** C7
Parygino Kazakh. **98** D2
Parys S. Africa **125** H4
Pasa Dağı *mt.* Turkey **112** D3
Pasadena *CA* U.S.A. **158** D4
Pasadena *TX* U.S.A. **161** E6
Pasado, Cabo *c.* Ecuador **176** B4
Pa Sang Thai. **86** B3
Pasangkayu *Sulawesi Barat* Indon. **83** A3
Pasarbantal *Sumatera* Indon. **84** C3
Pasarseblat *Sumatera* Indon. **84** C3
Pasarseluma *Sumatera* Indon. **84** C4
Pasarwajo *Sulawesi* Indon. **83** B4
Pasawng Myanmar **86** B3
Pascagama *r.* Canada **152** G4
Pascagoula *MS* U.S.A. **161** F6
Pascagoula *r. MS* U.S.A. **161** F6
Paşcani Romania **69** L1
Pasco *WA* U.S.A. **156** D3
Pascoal, Monte *hill* Brazil **179** D2
Pascua, Isla de *i.* S. Pacific Ocean *see* **Easter Island**
Pas de Calais *strait* France/U.K. *see* **Dover, Strait of**
Pasewalk Germany **57** O4
Pasfield Lake Canada **151** J3
Pāsgāh-e Gol Vardeh Iran **111** F3
Pasha Rus. Fed. **52** G3
Pashih Haihsia *sea chan.* Phil./Taiwan *see* **Bashi Channel**
Pashkovo Rus. Fed. **90** C2
Pashkovskiy Rus. Fed. **53** H7
Pashū'īyeh Iran **110** E4
Pasig *Luzon* Phil. **82** C3
Pasi Ga Myanmar **86** B1
Pasige *i.* Indon. **83** C2
Pasighat India **105** H3
Pasinler Turkey **113** F3
Pasir Gudang Malaysia **87** [inset]
Pasirian *Jawa* Indon. **85** F5
Pasir Mas Malaysia **84** C1
Pasirpangarayan *Sumatera* Indon. **84** C2
Pasir Putih Malaysia **84** C1
Pasitelu, Pulau-pulau *is* Indon. **83** B4
Paskūh Iran **111** F5
Pasni Pak. **185** M4
Paso Caballos Guat. **167** H5
Paso de los Toros Uruguay **178** E4
Paso de San Antonio Mex. **161** C6
Pasok Myanmar **86** A2
Paso Real Hond. **166** [inset] I6
Paso Robles *CA* U.S.A. **158** C4
Pasquia Hills Canada **151** K4
Passaic *NJ* U.S.A. **165** H3
Passa Tempo Brazil **179** B3
Passau Germany **57** N6
Passi *Panay* Phil. **82** C4
Passo del San Gottardo Switz. *see* **St Gotthard Pass**
Passo Fundo Brazil **178** F3
Passos Brazil **179** B3
Passur *r.* Bangl. *see* **Pusur**
Passuri Nadi *r.* Bangl. *see* **Pusur**
Pastavy Belarus **55** O9
Pastaza *r.* Peru **176** C4
Pasto Col. **176** C3
Pastol Bay *AK* U.S.A. **148** G3
Pastora Peak *AZ* U.S.A. **159** I3
Pastos Bons Brazil **177** J5
Pasu Pak. **104** C1
Pasuquin *Luzon* Phil. **82** C2
Pasur Turkey *see* **Kulp**
Pasuruan *Jawa* Indon. **85** F4
Pasvalys Lith. **55** N8
Pasvikelva *r.* Europe *see* **Patsoyoki**
Pata *i.* Phil. **82** C5
Patache, Punta *pt* Chile **178** B2
Patagonia *reg.* Arg. **178** B8
Pataliputra India *see* **Patna**
Patan *Gujarat* India *see* **Somnath**
Patan *Gujarat* India **104** C5
Patan *Mahar.* India **106** B2
Patan Nepal **105** F4
Patan Pak. **111** I3
Patandar, Koh-i- *mt.* Pak. **111** G5
Patani *Halmahera* Indon. **83** D2
Patavium Italy *see* **Padua**
Patea N.Z. **139** E4
Patea *inlet* N.Z. *see* **Doubtful Sound**
Pate Island Kenya **122** E4
Pateley Bridge U.K. **58** F4
Patensie S. Africa **124** G7
Patera India **104** D4
Paterson Australia **138** E4
Paterson *r.* Australia **138** C2
Paterson *NJ* U.S.A. **165** H3
Paterson Range *hills* Australia **134** C5
Pathanamthitta India **106** C4
Pathankot India **104** C2
Pathari India **104** D5
Pathein Myanmar *see* **Bassein**
Pathfinder Reservoir *WY* U.S.A. **156** G4
Pathiu Thai. **87** B5
Pathum Thani Thai. **87** C4
Pati *Jawa* Indon. **85** E4
Patía *r.* Col. **176** C3
Patiala India **104** D3
Patinti, Selat *sea chan. Maluku* Indon. **83** C3
Patiro, Tanjung *pt* Indon. **83** B4
Patkai Bum *mts* India/Myanmar **105** H4
Patkaklik China **99** D5
Patmos *i.* Greece **69** L6
Patna *Bihar* India **105** F4
Patna *Odisha* India **105** F5
Patnagarh India **105** E5
Patnanongan *i.* Phil. **82** C3
Patnos Turkey **113** F3
Pato Branco Brazil **178** F3
Patoda India **106** B2
Patoka *r. IN* U.S.A. **164** B4
Patoka Lake *IN* U.S.A. **164** B4
Patos Albania **69** H4
Patos Brazil **177** K5
Patos, Lagoa dos *l.* Brazil **178** F4
Patos de Minas Brazil **179** B2
Patquía Arg. **178** C4
Patra Greece *see* **Patras**
Patrae Greece *see* **Patras**
Pátrai Greece *see* **Patras**
Patras Greece **69** I5
Patreksfjörður Iceland **54** [inset 1]
Patricio Lynch, Isla *i.* Chile **178** A7
Patrick Creek *watercourse* Australia **136** D4
Patrimônio Brazil **179** A2
Patrocínio Brazil **179** B2
Paṭrū Iran **111** E3
Patsoyoki *r.* Europe **54** Q2
Pattadakal *tourist site* India **106** B2
Pattani Thai. **87** C6
Pattani, Mae Nam *r.* Thai. **84** C1
Pattaya Thai. **87** C4
Pattensen Germany **63** J2
Patterson *CA* U.S.A. **158** C3
Patterson *LA* U.S.A. **161** F6
Patterson, Mount Canada **149** N2
Patti India **105** E4
Patti *Maluku* Indon. **83** C5
Pattijoki Fin. **54** N4
Pättikkä Fin. **54** L2
Patton *PA* U.S.A. **165** F3
Pattullo, Mount Canada **149** O4
Patu Brazil **177** K5
Patuakhali Bangl. **105** G5
Patuanak Canada **151** J4
Patuca *r.* Hond. **166** [inset] I6
Patuca, Punta *pt* Hond. **166** [inset] I6
Patucas, Parque Nacional *nat. park* Hond. **166** [inset] I6
Patur India **106** C1
Patuxent *r. MD* U.S.A. **165** G4
Patuxent Range *mts* Antarctica **188** L1
Patvinsuon kansallispuisto *nat. park* Fin. **54** Q5
Pátzcuaro Mex. **167** E5
Pau France **66** D5
Pauhunri *mt.* China/India **105** G4
Pauillac France **66** D4
Pauini Brazil **176** E5
Pauini *r.* Brazil **176** E5
Pauk Myanmar **86** A2
Paukkaung Myanmar **86** A3
Paulatuk Canada **149** Q1
Paulatuuq Canada *see* **Paulatuk**
Paulden *AZ* U.S.A. **159** G4
Paulding *OH* U.S.A. **164** C3
Paulicéia Brazil **179** A3
Paulis Dem. Rep. Congo *see* **Isiro**
Paul Island Canada **153** J2
Paulo Afonso Brazil **177** K5
Paulo de Faria Brazil **179** A3
Paluoff Harbor *AK* U.S.A. **148** G5
Paulpietersburg S. Africa **125** J4
Paul Roux S. Africa **125** H5
Pauls Valley *OK* U.S.A. **161** D5
Paumotu, Îles *is* Fr. Polynesia *see* **Tuamotu Islands**
Paung Myanmar **86** B3
Paungbyin Myanmar **86** A1
Paungde Myanmar **86** A3
Pauni India **106** C1
Pauri India **104** D3
Pavagada India **106** C3
Pavão Brazil **179** C2
Pāveh Iran **110** B3
Pavia Italy **68** C2
Pāvilosta Latvia **55** L8
Pavino Rus. Fed. **52** J4
Pavlikeni Bulg. **69** K3
Pavlodar Kazakh. **102** E1
Pavlodarskaya Oblast' *admin. div.* Kazakh. **98** B1
Pavlof Bay *AK* U.S.A. **148** G5
Pavlof Islands *AK* U.S.A. **148** G5
Pavlof Volcano *AK* U.S.A. **148** [inset] 5
Pavlograd Ukr. *see* **Pavlohrad**
Pavlohrad Ukr. **53** G6
Pavlovka Rus. Fed. **53** J5
Pavlovo Rus. Fed. **52** I5
Pavlovsk *Altayskiy Kray* Rus. Fed. **88** E2
Pavlovsk *Voronezhskaya Oblast'* Rus. Fed. **53** I6
Pavlovskaya Rus. Fed. **53** H7
Pawahku Myanmar **86** B1
Pawai India **104** E4
Pawan *r.* Indon. **85** E3
Pawayan India **99** C7
Pawnee *OK* U.S.A. **161** D4
Pawnee *r. KS* U.S.A. **160** D4
Pawnee City *NE* U.S.A. **160** D3
Paw Paw *MI* U.S.A. **164** C2
Paw Paw *WV* U.S.A. **165** F4
Pawtucket *RI* U.S.A. **165** J3
Pawut Myanmar **87** B4
Paxson *AK* U.S.A. **149** K3
Paxton *IL* U.S.A. **164** A3
Payahe *Halmahera* Indon. **83** C2
Payakumbuh *Sumatera* Indon. **84** C3
Paya Lebar Sing. **87** [inset]
Pāy Bōldak Ghar *mt.* Afgh. **111** G4
Payette *ID* U.S.A. **156** D3
Pay-Khoy, Khrebet *hills* Rus. Fed. **76** H3
Payne Canada *see* **Kangirsuk**
Payne, Lac *l.* Canada **152** G2
Paynes Creek *CA* U.S.A. **158** C1
Payne's Find Australia **135** B7
Paynesville *MN* U.S.A. **160** E2
Paysandú Uruguay **178** E4
Pays de Bray *reg.* France **62** B5
Payshanba Uzbek. **111** G1
Payson *AZ* U.S.A. **159** H4
Payung, Tanjung *pt* Malaysia **85** F2
Payzawat China *see* **Jiashi**
Pazar Turkey **113** F2
Pazarcık Turkey **112** E3
Pazardzhik Bulg. **69** K3
Pazin Croatia **68** E2
Pe Myanmar **87** B4
Peabody *KS* U.S.A. **160** D4
Peabody *MA* U.S.A. **165** J2

▶**Peace** *r.* Canada **150** I3
Part of the Mackenzie-Peace-Finlay, the 2nd longest river in North America.

Peace Point Canada **151** H3
Peace River Canada **150** G3
Peach Creek *WV* U.S.A. **164** E5
Peach Springs *AZ* U.S.A. **159** G4
Peacock Hills Canada **151** I1
Peak Charles *hill* Australia **135** C8
Peak Charles National Park Australia **135** C8
Peak District National Park U.K. **58** F5
Peake *watercourse* Australia **137** B6
Peaked Mountain *hill ME* U.S.A. **162** G2
Peak Hill *N.S.W.* Australia **138** D4
Peak Hill *W.A.* Australia **135** B6
Peale, Mount *UT* U.S.A. **159** I2
Peanut *CA* U.S.A. **158** B1
Pearce *AZ* U.S.A. **159** I6
Pearce Point Australia **134** E3
Peard Bay *AK* U.S.A. **148** H1
Pearisburg *VA* U.S.A. **164** E5
Pearl *r. MS* U.S.A. **161** F6
Pearl Harbor *inlet HI* U.S.A. **157** [inset]
Pearsall *TX* U.S.A. **161** D6
Pearson *GA* U.S.A. **163** D6
Pearston S. Africa **125** G7
Peary Channel Canada **147** I2
Peary Land *reg.* Greenland **189** J1
Pease *r. TX* U.S.A. **161** D5
Peawanuck Canada **152** D3
Pebane Moz. **123** D5
Pebas Peru **176** D4
Pebengko *Sulawesi* Indon. **83** B3
Peć Kosovo *see* **Pejë**
Peçanha Brazil **179** C2
Pecan Island *LA* U.S.A. **167** G2
Peças, Ilha das *i.* Brazil **179** A4
Pechenga Rus. Fed. **54** Q2
Pechora Rus. Fed. **52** M2
Pechora *r.* Rus. Fed. **52** L1
Pechora Sea Rus. Fed. *see* **Pechorskoye More**
Pechorskaya Guba *b.* Rus. Fed. **52** L1
Pechorskoye More *sea* Rus. Fed. **189** G2
Pechory Rus. Fed. **55** O8
Peck *MI* U.S.A. **164** D2
Pecos *TX* U.S.A. **161** C6
Pecos *r. NM/TX* U.S.A. **161** C6
Pécs Hungary **68** H1
Pedasí Panama **166** [inset] J8
Pedda Vagu *r.* India **106** C2
Pedder, Lake Australia **137** [inset]
Peddie S. Africa **125** H7
Pedernales Dom. Rep. **169** J5
Pedersöre Fin. **54** M5
Pediaios *r.* Cyprus **107** A2
Pediva Angola **123** B5
Pediwang *Halmahera* Indon. **83** C2
Pedra Azul Brazil **179** C1
Pedra Preta, Serra da *mts* Brazil **179** A1
Pedras de Maria da Cruz Brazil **179** B1
Pedregal Panama **166** [inset] J7
Pedregulho Brazil **179** B3
Pedreiras Brazil **177** J4
Pedriceña Mex. **166** E3
Pedro, Point Sri Lanka **106** D4
Pedro Bay *AK* U.S.A. **148** I4
Pedro Betancourt Cuba **163** D8
Pedro II, Ilha *reg.* Brazil/Venez. **176** E3
Pedro Juan Caballero Para. **178** E2
Peebles U.K. **60** F5
Peebles *OH* U.S.A. **164** D4
Pee Dee *r. SC* U.S.A. **163** E5
Peekskill *NY* U.S.A. **165** I3
Peel *r.* Australia **138** E3
Peel *r.* Canada **149** N1
Peel Isle of Man **58** C4
Peel River Game Preserve *nature res.* Canada **149** N2
Peer Belgium **62** F3
Peera Peera Poolanna Lake *salt flat* Australia **137** B5
Peerless Lake Canada **150** H3
Peerless Lake *l.* Canada **150** H3
Peers Canada **150** G4
Peery Lake *salt flat* Australia **138** A3
Pegasus Bay N.Z. **139** D6
Pegnitz Germany **63** L5
Pegu Myanmar **86** B3
Pegunungan Latimojong *nature res.* Indon. **83** B3
Pegunungan Peruhumpenai *nature res.* Indon. **83** B3
Pegu Yoma *mts* Myanmar **86** A3
Pegysh Rus. Fed. **52** K3
Pehuajó Arg. **178** D5
Peikang Taiwan **97** I4
Peine Chile **178** C2
Peine Germany **63** K2
Peint India **106** B1
Peipsi järv *l.* Estonia/Rus. Fed. *see* **Peipus, Lake**
Peipus, Lake Estonia/Rus. Fed. **55** O7
Peiraias Greece *see* **Piraeus**
Pei Shan *mts* China *see* **Bei Shan**
Peißen Germany **63** L3
Peixe Brazil **177** I6
Peixe *r.* Brazil **179** A1
Peixian *Jiangsu* China *see* **Pizhou**
Peixian *Jiangsu* China **95** I5
Peixoto de Azevedo Brazil **177** H6
Pejantan *i.* Indon. **84** D2
Pejë Kosovo **69** I3
Pèk Laos *see* **Phônsavan**
Peka Lesotho **125** H5
Pekabata *Sulawesi* Indon. **83** A3
Pekalongan *Jawa* Indon. **85** E4
Pekan Malaysia **84** C2

Pekanbaru *Sumatera* Indon. 84 C2
Pekin *IL* U.S.A. 160 F3
Peking China *see* **Beijing**
Pekinga Benin 120 D3
Pelabuhan Klang Malaysia 84 C2
Pelagie, Isole *is Sicily* Italy 68 E7
Pelaihari *Kalimantan* Indon. 85 F3
Pelalawan *Sumatera* Indon. 84 C2
Pelapis *i.* Indon. 85 E3
Pelawanbesar *Kalimantan* Indon. 85 G2
Peleaga, Vârful *mt.* Romania 69 J2
Pelee Island Canada 164 D3
Pelee Point Canada 164 D3
Peleliu *i.* Palau 82 [inset]
Peleng *i.* Indon. 83 B3
Peleng, Selat *sea chan.* Indon. 83 B3
Peleng, Teluk *b.* Indon. 83 B3
Peles Rus. Fed. 52 K3
Pélican, Lac du *l.* Canada 153 G2
Pelican Lake Canada 151 K4
Pelican Lake *MN* U.S.A. 160 E1
Pelican Narrows Canada 151 K4
Pelkosenniemi Fin. 54 O3
Pella S. Africa 124 D5
Pellatt Lake Canada 151 I1
Pelleluhu Islands P.N.G. 81 K7
Pello Fin. 54 M3
Pelly *r.* Canada 150 C2
Pelly Crossing Canada 149 M3
Pelly Island Canada 149 N1
Pelly Lake Canada 151 K1
Pelly Mountains Canada 149 N3
Pelokang *is* Indon. 85 G4
Peloponnese *admin. reg.* Greece 69 J6
Pelopónnesos *admin. reg.* Greece *see* **Peloponnese**
Peloponnisos *admin. reg.* Greece *see* **Peloponnese**
Pelotas Brazil 178 F4
Pelotas, Rio das *r.* Brazil 179 A4
Pelusium *tourist site* Egypt 107 A4
Pelusium, Bay of Egypt *see* **Ţīnah, Khalīj aţ**
Pemalang *Jawa* Indon. 85 E4
Pemangkat *Kalimantan* Indon. 85 E2
Pemarung, Pulau *i.* Indon. 85 G3
Pematangsiantar *Sumatera* Indon. 84 B2
Pemba Moz. 123 E5
Pemba Island Tanz. 123 D4
Pemberton Canada 150 F5
Pembina *r.* Canada 150 H4
Pembina *r. ND* U.S.A. 160 D1
Pembine *WI* U.S.A. 162 C2
Pembre Indon. 81 J8
Pembroke Canada 152 F5
Pembroke U.K. 59 C7
Pembroke *GA* U.S.A. 163 D5
Pembrokeshire Coast National Park U.K. 59 B7
Pembuanghulu *Kalimantan* Indon. 85 F3
Pemuar *Kalimantan* Indon. 85 E3
Pen India 106 B2
Peña Cerredo *mt.* Spain *see* **Torrecerredo**
Peñalara *mt.* Spain 67 E3
Penamar Brazil 179 C1
Penambo Range *mts* Malaysia *see* **Tama Abu, Banjaran**
Penampang *Sabah* Malaysia 85 G1
Peña Nevada, Cerro *mt.* Mex. 168 E4
Penang *state* Malaysia *see* **Pinang**
Penápolis Brazil 179 A3
Peñaranda de Bracamonte Spain 67 D3
Penarie Australia 138 A5
Penarlâg U.K. *see* **Hawarden**
Peñarroya *mt.* Spain 67 F3
Peñarroya-Pueblonuevo Spain 67 D4
Penarth U.K. 59 D7
Peñas, Cabo de *c.* Spain 67 D2
Penas, Golfo de *g.* Chile 178 A7
Peñas Blancas Nicaragua 166 [inset] I7
Penasi, Pulau *i.* Indon. 87 A6
Peña Ubiña *mt.* Spain 67 D2
Pender *NE* U.S.A. 160 D3
Pendle Hill *hill* U.K. 58 E5
Pendleton *OR* U.S.A. 156 D3
Pendleton Bay Canada 150 E4
Pendopo *Sumatera* Indon. 84 C3
Pend Oreille *r. WA* U.S.A. 156 D2
Pend Oreille Lake *ID* U.S.A. 156 D2
Pendra India 105 E5
Penduv India 106 B2
Pendzhikent Tajik. *see* **Panjakent**
Penebangan *i.* Indon. 85 E3
Peneda Gerês, Parque Nacional da *nat. park* Port. 67 B3
Penetanguishene Canada 164 F1
Penfro U.K. *see* **Pembroke**
Peng'an China 96 E2
Penganga *r.* India 106 C2
Peng Chau *i. H.K.* China 97 [inset]
P'engchia Yü *i.* Taiwan 97 I3
Penge Dem. Rep. Congo 123 C4
Penge S. Africa 125 J3
P'enghu Ch'üntao *is* Taiwan 97 H4
P'enghu Liehtao *is* Taiwan *see* **P'enghu Ch'üntao**
P'enghu Tao *i.* Taiwan 97 H4
Pengiki *i.* Indon. 85 E2
Pengkalan Hulu Malaysia 84 C1
Peng Kang *hill* Sing. 87 [inset]
Penglai China 95 J4
Penglaizhen China *see* **Daying**
Pengshan China 96 D2
Pengshui China 97 F2
Pengwa Myanmar 86 A2
Pengxi China 96 E2
Penha Brazil 179 A4
Penhoek Pass S. Africa 125 H6
Penhook *VA* U.S.A. 164 F5
Peniche Port. 67 B4
Penicuik U.K. 60 F5
Penida *i.* Indon. 85 F5
Penig Germany 63 M4
Peninga Rus. Fed. 54 R5
Peninsular Malaysia Malaysia 84 C2
Penitente, Serra do *hills* Brazil 177 I5
Penn *PA* U.S.A. *see* **Penn Hills**
Pennell Coast Antarctica 188 H2
Penn Hills *PA* U.S.A. 164 F3
Pennine, Alpi *mts* Italy/Switz. 68 B2
Pennine Alps *mts* Italy/Switz. *see* **Pennine, Alpi**
Pennines *hills* U.K. 58 E4
Pennington Gap *VA* U.S.A. 164 D5
Pennsburg *PA* U.S.A. 165 H3
Penns Grove *NJ* U.S.A. 165 H4
Pennsville *NJ* U.S.A. 165 H4
Pennsylvania *state* U.S.A. 164 F3
Pennville *IN* U.S.A. 164 C3
Penn Yan *NY* U.S.A. 165 G2
Penny Icecap Canada 147 L3
Penny Point Antarctica 188 H1
Penola Australia 137 C8
Peñón Blanco Mex. 166 D3
Penong Australia 135 F7
Penonomé Panama 166 [inset] J7
Penrhyn *atoll* Cook Is 187 J6
Penrhyn Basin *sea feature* S. Pacific Ocean 187 J6
Penrith Australia 138 E4
Penrith U.K. 58 E4
Pensacola *FL* U.S.A. 163 C6
Pensacola Mountains Antarctica 188 L1
Pensiangan *Sabah* Malaysia 85 G1
Pensi La *pass* India 104 D2
Pentadaktylos Range *mts* Cyprus 107 A2
Pentakota India 106 D2
Pentecost Island Vanuatu 133 G3
Pentecôte, Île *i.* Vanuatu *see* **Pentecost Island**
Penticton Canada 150 G5
Pentire Point U.K. 59 B8
Pentland Australia 136 D4
Pentland Firth *sea chan.* U.K. 60 F2
Pentland Hills U.K. 60 F5
Pentwater *MI* U.S.A. 164 B2
Penuba Indon. 84 D3
Penuguan *Sumatera* Indon. 84 D3
Penunjuk, Tanjung *pt* Malaysia 84 C1
Penwegon Myanmar 86 B3
Pen-y-Bont ar Ogwr U.K. *see* **Bridgend**
Penygadair *hill* U.K. 59 D6
Penylan Lake Canada 151 J2
Penyu, Kepulauan *is Maluku* Indon. 83 C4
Penza Rus. Fed. 53 J5
Penzance U.K. 59 B8
Penzhinskaya Guba *b.* Rus. Fed. 77 R3
Peoria *AZ* U.S.A. 159 G5
Peoria *IL* U.S.A. 160 F3
Peotone *IL* U.S.A. 164 B3
Peper, Teluk *b.* Indon. *see* **Lada, Teluk**
Pequeña, Punta *pt* Mex. 166 B3
Pequop Mountains *NV* U.S.A. 159 F1
Peradeniya Sri Lanka 106 D5
Pera Head *hd* Australia 136 C2
Perak *i.* Malaysia 84 B1
Perak *r.* Malaysia 84 C1
Perak *state* Malaysia 84 C1
Perales del Alfambra Spain 67 F3
Perambalur India 106 C4
Perämeren kansallispuisto *nat. park* Fin. 54 N4
Peranap *Sumatera* Indon. 84 C3
Peräseinäjoki Fin. 54 M5
Percé Canada 153 I4
Percival Lakes *salt flat* Australia 134 D5
Percy *NH* U.S.A. 165 J1
Percy Isles Australia 136 E4
Percy Reach *l.* Canada 165 G1
Perdizes Brazil 179 B2
Perdu, Lac *l.* Canada 153 H4
Peregrebnoye Rus. Fed. 51 T3
Pereira Col. 176 C3
Pereira Barreto Brazil 179 A3
Pereira de Eça Angola *see* **Ondjiva**
Pere Marquette *r. MI* U.S.A. 164 B2
Peremul Par *reef* India 106 B4
Peremyshlyany Ukr. 53 E6
Perenjori Australia 135 B7
Pereslavl'-Zalesskiy Rus. Fed. 52 H4
Pereslavskiy Natsional'nyy Park *nat. park* Rus. Fed. 52 H4
Pereyaslavka Rus. Fed. 90 D3
Pereyaslav-Khmel'nitskiy Ukr. *see* **Pereyaslav-Khmel'nyts'kyy**
Pereyaslav-Khmel'nyts'kyy Ukr. 53 F6
Perforated Island Thai. *see* **Bon, Ko**
Pergamino Arg. 178 D4
Perhentian Besar, Pulau *i.* Malaysia 84 C1
Perho Fin. 54 N5
Péribonka, Lac *l.* Canada 153 H4
Perico Arg. 178 C2
Pericos Mex. 166 D3
Peridot *AZ* U.S.A. 159 H5
Périgueux France 66 E4
Perijá, Parque Nacional *nat. park* Venez. 176 D2
Perijá, Sierra de *mts* Venez. 176 D2
Peringat Malaysia 84 C1
Periyar India *see* **Erode**
Perkasie *PA* U.S.A. 165 H3
Perkat, Tanjung *pt* Indon. 84 D3
Perlas, Archipiélago de las *is* Panama 166 [inset] K7
Perlas, Laguna de *lag.* Nicaragua 166 [inset] J6
Perlas, Punta de *pt* Nicaragua 166 [inset] J6
Perleberg Germany 63 L1
Perlis *state* Malaysia 84 C1
Perm' Rus. Fed. 51 R4
Permas Rus. Fed. 52 J4
Pernambuco Brazil *see* **Recife**
Pernambuco Plain *sea feature* S. Atlantic Ocean 184 G6
Pernatty Lagoon *salt flat* Australia 137 B6
Pernem India 106 B3
Pernik Bulg. 69 J3
Pernov Estonia *see* **Pärnu**
Perojpur Bangl. *see* **Pirojpur**
Peron Islands Australia 134 E3
Péronne France 62 C5
Perote Mex. 167 F5
Perpignan France 66 F5
Perranporth U.K. 59 B8
Perrégaux Alg. *see* **Mohammadia**
Perris *CA* U.S.A. 158 E5
Perros-Guirec France 66 C2
Perrot, Île *i.* Canada 165 I1
Perry *FL* U.S.A. 163 D6
Perry *GA* U.S.A. 163 D5
Perry *MI* U.S.A. 164 C2
Perry *OK* U.S.A. 161 D4
Perry Lake *KS* U.S.A. 160 E4
Perryton *TX* U.S.A. 161 C4
Perryville *AK* U.S.A. 148 H5
Perryville *MO* U.S.A. 160 F4
Perseverancia Bol. 176 F6
Pershore U.K. 59 E6
Persia *country* Asia *see* **Iran**
Persian Gulf Asia *see* **The Gulf**
Pertek Turkey 113 E3

▶**Perth** Australia 135 A7
Capital of Western Australia. 4th most populous city in Oceania.

Perth Canada 165 G1
Perth U.K. 60 F4
Perth Amboy *NJ* U.S.A. 165 H3
Perth-Andover Canada 153 I5
Perth Basin *sea feature* Indian Ocean 185 P7
Pertominsk Rus. Fed. 52 H2
Pertunmaa Fin. 55 O6
Pertusato, Capo *c. Corsica* France 66 I6
Peru *atoll* Kiribati *see* **Beru**

▶**Peru** *country* S. America 176 D6
3rd largest and 5th most populous country in South America.

Peru *IL* U.S.A. 160 F3
Peru *IN* U.S.A. 164 B3
Peru *NY* U.S.A. 165 I1
Peru-Chile Trench *sea feature* S. Pacific Ocean 187 O6
Perugia Italy 68 E3
Peruru India 106 C3
Perusia Italy *see* **Perugia**
Péruwelz Belgium 62 D4
Pervomay Kyrg. 98 A4
Pervomaysk Rus. Fed. 53 I5
Pervomays'k Ukr. 53 F6
Pervomayskiy Kazakh. 102 F1
Pervomayskiy *Arkhangel'skaya Oblast'* Rus. Fed. *see* **Novodvinsk**
Pervomayskiy *Tambovskaya Oblast'* Rus. Fed. 53 I5
Pervomays'kyy Ukr. 53 H6
Pervorechenskiy Rus. Fed. 77 R3
Pervyy Brat, Gora *hill* Rus. Fed. 90 F1
Pesaguan *Kalimantan* Indon. 85 E3
Pesaguan *r.* Indon. 85 E3
Pesaro Italy 68 E3
Pescadores *is* Taiwan *see* **P'enghu Ch'üntao**
Pescara Italy 68 F3
Pescara *r.* Italy 68 F3
Peschanokopskoye Rus. Fed. 53 I7
Peschanoye Rus. Fed. *see* **Yashkul'**
Peschanyy, Mys *pt* Kazakh. 113 H2
Pesé Panama 166 [inset] J8
Pesha *r.* Rus. Fed. 52 J2
Peshawar Pak. 111 H3
Peshkopi Albania 69 I4
Peshtera Bulg. 69 K3
Peski Turkm. 111 F2
Peskovka Rus. Fed. 52 L4
Pesnica Slovenia 68 F1
Pespire Hond. 166 [inset] I6
Pesqueira Mex. 166 C2
Pessac France 66 D4
Pessin Germany 63 M2
Pestovo Rus. Fed. 52 G4
Pestravka Rus. Fed. 53 K5
Petah Tiqwa Israel 107 B3
Petäjävesi Fin. 54 N5
Petak, Tanjung *pt Halmahera* Indon. 83 D2
Petaling Jaya Malaysia 87 C7
Petalion, Kolpos *sea chan.* Greece 69 K5
Petaluma *CA* U.S.A. 158 B2
Pétange Lux. 62 F5
Petangis *Kalimantan* Indon. 85 F3
Petatlán Mex. 168 D5
Petauke Zambia 123 D5
Petén Itzá, Lago *l.* Guat. 167 H5
Petenwell Lake *WI* U.S.A. 160 F2
Peterbell Canada 152 E4
Peterborough Australia 137 B7
Peterborough Canada 165 F1
Peterborough U.K. 59 G6
Peterborough *NH* U.S.A. 165 J2
Peterculter U.K. 60 G3
Peterhead U.K. 60 H3
Peter I Island Antarctica 188 K2
Peter I Øy *i.* Antarctica *see* **Peter I Island**
Peter Lake Canada 151 M2
Peterlee U.K. 58 F4
Petermann Bjerg *nunatak* Greenland 147 P2
Petermann Ranges *mts* Australia 135 E6
Peter Pond Lake Canada 151 I4
Peters, Lac *l.* Canada 153 H2
Petersberg Germany 63 J4
Petersburg *AK* U.S.A. 149 N4
Petersburg *IL* U.S.A. 160 F4
Petersburg *IN* U.S.A. 164 B4
Petersburg *NY* U.S.A. 165 I2
Petersburg *VA* U.S.A. 165 G5
Petersburg *WV* U.S.A. 164 F4
Petersfield U.K. 59 G7
Petershagen Germany 63 I2
Petersville *AK* U.S.A. 149 J3
Peter the Great Bay Rus. Fed. *see* **Petra Velikogo, Zaliv**
Peth India 106 B2
Petilia Policastro Italy 68 G5
Petit Atlas *mts* Morocco *see* **Anti Atlas**
Petitcodiac Canada 153 I5
Petitjean Morocco *see* **Sidi Kacem**
Petit Lac Manicouagan *l.* Canada 153 I3
Petit Mécatina *r.* Canada 153 K4
Petit Mécatina, Île du *i.* Canada 153 K4
Petit Morin *r.* France 62 D6
Petitot *r.* Canada 150 F2
Petit St-Bernard, Col du *pass* France 66 H4
Petit Saut, Barrage du *resr* Fr. Guiana 177 H3
Peto Mex. 167 H4
Petoskey *MI* U.S.A. 162 C2
Petra *tourist site* Jordan 107 B4
Petra Velikogo, Zaliv *b.* Rus. Fed. 90 C4
Petre, Point Canada 165 G2
Petrich Bulg. 69 J4
Petrified Forest National Park *AZ* U.S.A. 159 I4
Petrikau Poland *see* **Piotrków Trybunalski**
Petrikov Belarus *see* **Pyetrykaw**
Petrinja Croatia 68 G2
Petroaleksandrovsk Uzbek. *see* **To'rtko'l**
Petroglyphic Complexes *tourist site* Mongolia 102 G2
Petrograd Rus. Fed. *see* **St Petersburg**
Petrokhanski Prokhod *pass* Bulg. 69 J3
Petrokov Poland *see* **Piotrków Trybunalski**
Petrolia Canada 164 D2
Petrolia *CA* U.S.A. 158 A1
Petrolina Brazil 177 J5
Petrolina de Goiás Brazil 179 A2
Petropavl Kazakh. *see* **Petropavlovsk**
Petropavlovka Kazakh. 98 C3
Petropavlovka Rus. Fed. 94 F1
Petropavlovsk Kazakh. 101 F1
Petropavlovsk Rus. Fed. *see* **Petropavlovsk-Kamchatskiy**
Petropavlovsk-Kamchatskiy Rus. Fed. 77 Q4
Petrópolis Brazil 179 C3
Petroşani Romania 69 J2
Petrovsk Rus. Fed. 53 J5
Petrovskoye Rus. Fed. *see* **Svetlograd**
Petrovsk-Zabaykal'skiy Rus. Fed. 95 G1
Petrozavodsk Rus. Fed. 52 G3
Petrus Steyn S. Africa 125 I4
Petrusville S. Africa 124 G6
Petsamo Rus. Fed. *see* **Pechenga**
Pettau Slovenia *see* **Ptuj**
Petten Neth. 62 E2
Pettigo U.K. 61 E3
Petukhovo Rus. Fed. 76 H4
Petushki Rus. Fed. 52 H5
Petzeck *mt.* Austria 57 N7
Peuetsagu, Gunung *vol.* Indon. 84 B1
Peureula *Sumatera* Indon. 84 B1
Pevek Rus. Fed. 77 S3
Pêxung China 99 F6
Pey Ostān Iran 110 E3
Peza *r.* Rus. Fed. 52 J2
Pezinok Slovakia 57 P6
Pezu Pak. 111 H3
Pfälzer Wald *hills* Germany 63 H5
Pforzheim Germany 63 I6
Pfungstadt Germany 63 I5
Phagameng S. Africa 125 I3
Phagwara India 104 C3
Phahameng S. Africa 125 H5
Phalaborwa S. Africa 125 J2
Phalodi India 104 C4
Phalsund India 104 B4
Phalta India 105 G5
Phaluai, Ko *i.* Thai. 87 B5
Phalut Peak India/Nepal 105 G4
Phan Thai. 86 B3
Phanat Nikhom Thai. 87 C4
Phangan, Ko *i.* Thai. 87 C5
Phang Hoei, San Khao *mts* Thai. 86 C3
Phangnga Thai. 87 B5
Phăng Xi Păng *mt.* Vietnam 86 C2
Phanom Dong Rak, Thiu Khao *mts* Cambodia/Thai. 87 D4
Phan Rang-Thap Cham Vietnam 87 E5
Phan Thiêt Vietnam 87 E5
Phapon Myanmar *see* **Pyapon**
Phat Diêm Vietnam 86 D2
Phatthalung Thai. 87 C6
Phayam, Ko *i.* Thai. 87 B5
Phayao Thai. 86 B3
Phayuhakhiri Thai. 86 C4
Phek India 105 H4
Phelps Lake Canada 151 K3
Phen Thai. 86 C3
Phenix *VA* U.S.A. 165 F5
Phenix City *AL* U.S.A. 163 C5
Phet Buri Thai. 87 B4
Phetchabun Thai. 86 C3
Phiafai Laos 86 D4
Phichai Thai. 86 C3
Phichit Thai. 86 C3
Philadelphia Jordan *see* **'Ammān**
Philadelphia Turkey *see* **Alaşehir**
Philadelphia *MS* U.S.A. 161 F5
Philadelphia *NY* U.S.A. 165 H1
Philadelphia *PA* U.S.A. 165 H4
Philip *SD* U.S.A. 160 C2
Philip Atoll Micronesia *see* **Sorol**
Philippeville Alg. *see* **Skikda**
Philippeville Belgium 62 E4
Philippi *WV* U.S.A. 164 E4
Philippi, Lake *salt flat* Australia 136 B5
Philippine Neth. 62 D3
Philippine Basin *sea feature* N. Pacific Ocean 186 E4
Philippines *country* Asia 82 C3
Philippine Sea N. Pacific Ocean 81 G3

▶**Philippine Trench** *sea feature* N. Pacific Ocean 186 E4
3rd deepest trench in the world.

Philippolis S. Africa 125 G6
Philippopolis Bulg. *see* **Plovdiv**
Philippsburg Germany 63 I5
Philipsburg *MT* U.S.A. 156 E3
Philipsburg *PA* U.S.A. 165 F3
Philip Smith Mountains *AK* U.S.A. 149 J2
Philipstown S. Africa 124 G6
Phillip Island Australia 138 B7
Phillips *ME* U.S.A. 165 J1
Phillips *WI* U.S.A. 160 F2
Phillipsburg *KS* U.S.A. 160 D4
Phillips Range *hills* Australia 134 D4
Philmont *NY* U.S.A. 165 I2
Philomelium Turkey *see* **Akşehir**
Phiritona S. Africa 125 H4
Phitsanulok Thai. 86 C3

▶**Phnom Penh** Cambodia 87 D5
Capital of Cambodia.

Phnum Pénh Cambodia *see* **Phnom Penh**
Pho, Laem *pt* Thai. 87 C6
Phoenicia *NY* U.S.A. 165 H2

▶**Phoenix** *AZ* U.S.A. 157 E6
Capital of Arizona.

Phoenix Island Kiribati *see* **Rawaki**
Phoenix Islands Kiribati 133 I2
Phô Lu Vietnam 86 D2
Phon Thai. 86 C4
Phong Nha Vietnam 86 D3
Phôngsali Laos 86 C2
Phong Saly Laos *see* **Phôngsali**
Phong Thô Vietnam 86 C2
Phon Phisai Thai. 86 C3
Phônsavan Laos 86 C3
Phon Thong Thai. 86 C3
Phosphate Hill Australia 136 C4
Phrae Thai. 86 C3
Phra Nakhon Si Ayutthaya Thai. *see* **Ayutthaya**
Phrao Thai. 86 B3
Phra Saeng Thai. 87 B5
Phrom Phiram Thai. 86 C3
Phsar Réam Cambodia 87 C5
Phu Bai Vietnam 86 D3
Phuchong-Nayoi National Park Thai. 87 D4
Phu Cuong Vietnam *see* **Thu Dâu Môt**
Phuket Thai. 87 B6
Phuket, Ko *i.* Thai. 87 B6
Phu Khieo Wildlife Reserve *nature res.* Thai. 86 C3
Phulabani India *see* **Phulbani**
Phulbani India 106 E1
Phulchhari Ghat Bangl. *see* **Fulchhari**
Phulji Pak. 111 G5
Phu Lôc *Soc Trăng* Vietnam 87 D5
Phu Lôc *Thn-Huê* Vietnam 86 D3
Phu Luang National Park Thai. 86 C3
Phu Ly Vietnam 86 D2
Phumĭ Bŏeng Méaléa Cambodia 87 D4
Phumĭ Chhlong Cambodia 87 D4
Phumĭ Kaôh Kŏng Cambodia 87 C5
Phumĭ Kon Kriel Cambodia 87 C4
Phumĭ Mlu Prey Cambodia 87 D4
Phumĭ Moŭng Cambodia 87 C4
Phumiphon, Khuan Thai. 86 B3
Phumĭ Prêk Kak Cambodia 87 D4
Phumĭ Sâmraông Cambodia 87 C4
Phumĭ Trâm Kak Cambodia 87 D5
Phumĭ Veal Renh Cambodia 87 C5
Phu My Vietnam 87 E4
Phung Hiêp Vietnam 87 D5
Phươc Bưu Vietnam 87 D5
Phươc Hai Vietnam 87 D5
Phu Phac Mo *mt.* Vietnam 86 C2
Phu Phan National Park Thai. 86 C3
Phu Quôc, Đao *i.* Vietnam 87 C5
Phu Quy, Đao *i.* Vietnam 87 E5
Phu Tho Vietnam 86 D2
Phu Vinh Vietnam *see* **Tra Vinh**
Phyu Myanmar 86 B3
Piabung, Gunung *mt.* Indon. 85 F2
Piaca Brazil 177 I5
Piacenza Italy 68 C2
Piacouadie, Lac *l.* Canada 153 H4
Piagochioui *r.* Canada 152 F3
Piai, Tanjung *pt* Malaysia 84 C2
Pian *r.* Australia 138 D3
Pianguan China 95 G4
Pianosa, Isola *i.* Italy 68 D3
Piatra Neamţ Romania 69 L1
Piave *r.* Italy 68 E2
Pibor Post South Sudan 121 G4
Pic *r.* Canada 152 D4
Picacho *AZ* U.S.A. 159 H5
Picachos, Cerro dos *mt.* Mex. 166 B2
Picardie *admin. reg.* France 62 C5
Picardie *reg.* France *see* **Picardy**
Picardy *admin. reg.* France *see* **Picardie**
Picardy *reg.* France 62 B5
Picauville France 59 F9
Picayune *MS* U.S.A. 161 F6
Piceance Creek *r. CO* U.S.A. 159 I1
Pich Mex. 167 H5
Picháchic Mex. 166 D2
Pichanal Arg. 178 D2
Pichhor India 104 D4
Pichilemu Chile 178 B4
Pichilingue Mex. 166 C3
Pichucalco Mex. 167 G5
Pickens *WV* U.S.A. 164 E4
Pickering Canada 164 F2
Pickering U.K. 58 G4
Pickering, Vale of *valley* U.K. 58 G4
Pickle Lake Canada 147 I4
Pico Bonito, Parque Nacional *nat. park* Hond. 166 [inset] I6
Pico da Neblina, Parque Nacional do *nat. park* Brazil 176 E3
Pico de Orizaba, Parque Nacional *nat. park* Mex. 167 F5
Pico de Tancítaro, Parque Nacional *nat. park* Mex. 166 E5
Picos Brazil 177 J5
Pico Truncado Arg. 178 C7
Picton Australia 138 E5
Picton Canada 165 G2
Picton N.Z. 139 E5
Pictou Canada 153 J5
Picture Butte Canada 151 H5
Pidarak Pak. 111 F5
Pidurutalagala *mt.* Sri Lanka 106 D5
Piedade Brazil 179 B3
Piedra de Águila Arg. 178 B6
Piedras, Punta *pt* Arg. 178 E5
Piedras Blancas Point *CA* U.S.A. 158 C4
Piedras Negras Guat. 167 H5
Piedras Negras *Coahuila* Mex. 167 E2
Piedras Negras *Veracruz* Mex. 167 F5
Pie Island Canada 152 C4
Pieksämäki Fin. 54 O5
Pielavesi Fin. 54 O5
Pielinen *l.* Fin. 54 P5
Pieljekaise nationalpark *nat. park* Sweden 54 J3
Pienaarsrivier S. Africa 125 I3
Pieniński Park Narodowy *nat. park* Poland 57 R6
Pieninský *nat. park* Slovakia 57 R6
Pierce *NE* U.S.A. 160 D3
Pierce Lake Canada 151 M4
Pierceland Canada 151 I4
Pierceton *IN* U.S.A. 164 C3
Pieria *mts* Greece 69 J4
Pierowall U.K. 60 G1
Pierpont *OH* U.S.A. 164 E3

▶**Pierre** *SD* U.S.A. 160 C2
Capital of South Dakota.

Pierrelatte France 66 G4
Pietermaritzburg S. Africa 125 J5
Pietersaari Fin. *see* **Jakobstad**
Pietersburg S. Africa *see* **Polokwane**
Pie Town *NM* U.S.A. 159 I4
Pietra Spada, Passo di *pass* Italy 68 G5
Piet Retief S. Africa *see* **eMkhondo**
Pietrosa *mt.* Romania 69 K1
Pigeon *MI* U.S.A. 164 D2
Pigeon Bay Canada 164 D3
Pigeon Lake Canada 150 H4
Piggott *AR* U.S.A. 161 F4
Pigg's Peak Swaziland 125 J3
Pigs, Bay of Cuba 163 D8
Piguicas *mt.* Mex. 167 F4
Pihij India 104 C5
Pihkva järv *l.* Estonia/Rus. Fed. *see* **Pskov, Lake**
Pihlajavesi *l.* Fin. 54 P6
Pihlava Fin. 55 L6
Pihtipudas Fin. 54 N5
Piippola Fin. 54 N4
Piispajärvi Fin. 54 P4
Pijijiapan Mex. 167 G6
Pikalevo Rus. Fed. 52 G4
Pike *WV* U.S.A. 164 E4
Pike Bay Canada 164 E1
Pikelot *i.* Micronesia 81 L5
Pikes Peak *CO* U.S.A. 156 G5
Piketon *OH* U.S.A. 164 D4
Pikeville *KY* U.S.A. 164 D5
Pikeville *TN* U.S.A. 162 C5
Pikinni *atoll* Marshall Is *see* **Bikini**
Pikmiktalik *AK* U.S.A. 148 G3
Pikou China 95 J4
Piła Poland 57 P4
Pilanesberg National Park S. Africa 125 H3
Pilar Arg. 178 E4
Pilar Para. 178 E3
Pilar Phil. 82 D4
Pilar de Goiás Brazil 179 A1
Pilas *i.* Phil. 82 C5
Pilas Channel Phil. 82 C5
Pilaya *r.* Bol. 176 F8
Pilcomayo *r.* Bol./Para. 176 F8
Pile Bay Village *AK* U.S.A. 148 I4
Piler India 106 C3
Pilgrim Springs *AK* U.S.A. 148 F2
Pili *Luzon* Phil. 82 C3
Pili, Cerro *mt.* Chile 178 C2
Pilibangan India 104 C3
Pilibhit India 104 D3
Pilipinas *country* Asia *see* **Philippines**
Pillau Rus. Fed. *see* **Baltiysk**
Pillcopata Peru 176 D6
Pilliga Australia 138 D3
Pillsbury, Lake *CA* U.S.A. 158 B2
Pil'na Rus. Fed. 52 J5
Pil'nya, Ozero *l.* Rus. Fed. 52 M1
Pilões, Serra dos *mts* Brazil 179 B2
Pílos Greece *see* **Pylos**
Pilot Knob *mt. ID* U.S.A. 156 E3
Pilot Peak *NV* U.S.A. 158 E2
Pilot Point *AK* U.S.A. 148 H4
Pilot Station *AK* U.S.A. 148 G3
Pilottown *LA* U.S.A. 167 H2
Pilsen Czech Rep. *see* **Plzeň**
Piltene Latvia 55 L8
Pil'tun, Zaliv *lag.* Rus. Fed. 90 F1
Pilu Pak. 111 H5
Pima *AZ* U.S.A. 159 I5
Pimenta Bueno Brazil 176 F6
Pimento *IN* U.S.A. 164 B4
Pimpalner India 106 B1
Pin *r.* India 104 D2
Pin *r.* Myanmar 86 A2
Pinahat India 104 D4
Pinaleno Mountains *AZ* U.S.A. 159 H5
Pinamalayan *Mindoro* Phil. 82 C3
Pinamar Arg. 178 E5
Pinang Malaysia *see* **George Town**
Pinang *i.* Malaysia 84 C1
Pinang *state* Malaysia 84 C1
Pinangah *Sabah* Malaysia 85 G1
Pınarbaşı Turkey 112 E3
Pinar del Río Cuba 169 H4
Pinarhisar Turkey 69 L4
Piñas Ecuador 176 C4
Pincher Creek Canada 150 H5
Pinckneyville *IL* U.S.A. 160 F4
Pinconning *MI* U.S.A. 164 D2
Pińczów Poland 57 R5
Pindaí Brazil 179 C1
Pindamonhangaba Brazil 179 B3
Pindar Australia 135 A7
Pindar *r.* India 99 B7
Pindaré *r.* Brazil 177 J4
Píndhos Óros *mts* Greece *see* **Pindus Mountains**
Pindos *mts* Greece *see* **Pindus Mountains**
Pindrei India 104 E5
Pindus Mountains Greece 69 I5
Pine *watercourse* Australia 137 C7
Pine *r. MI* U.S.A. 164 C1
Pine *r. MI* U.S.A. 164 C2
Pine Bluff *AR* U.S.A. 161 E5
Pine Bluffs *WY* U.S.A. 156 G4
Pine Creek Australia 134 E3
Pine Creek *r. PA* U.S.A. 165 G3
Pinecrest *CA* U.S.A. 158 C2
Pinedale *NM* U.S.A. 159 I4
Pinedale *WY* U.S.A. 156 F4
Pine Dock Canada 151 L5
Pine Falls Canada 151 L5
Pine Flat Lake *CA* U.S.A. 158 D3
Pinega Rus. Fed. 52 I2
Pinega *r.* Rus. Fed. 52 I2
Pinegrove Australia 135 A6
Pine Grove *PA* U.S.A. 165 G3
Pine Hills *FL* U.S.A. 163 D6
Pinehouse Lake Canada 151 J4
Pinehouse Lake *l.* Canada 151 J4
Pineimuta *r.* Canada 151 N4
Pineios *r.* Greece 69 J5
Pine Island Bay Antarctica 187 N10
Pine Island Glacier Antarctica 188 K1
Pine Islands *FL* U.S.A. 163 D7
Pine Islands *FL* U.S.A. 163 D7
Pine Knot *KY* U.S.A. 164 C5
Pineland *TX* U.S.A. 161 E6
Pine Mountain *CA* U.S.A. 158 C4
Pine Peak *AZ* U.S.A. 159 G4
Pine Point *pt* Canada 150 H2
Pine Point (abandoned) Canada 150 H2
Pineridge *CA* U.S.A. 158 D3
Pine Ridge *SD* U.S.A. 160 C3
Pinerolo Italy 68 B2
Pines, Akrotirio *pt* Greece 69 K4
Pines, Isle of *i.* Cuba *see* **La Juventud, Isla de**
Pines, Isle of *i.* New Caledonia *see* **Pins, Île des**
Pines, Lake o' the *TX* U.S.A. 167 G1
Pinetop *AZ* U.S.A. 159 I4
Pinetown S. Africa 125 J5
Pine Valley *NY* U.S.A. 165 G2
Pineville *KY* U.S.A. 164 D5
Pineville *LA* U.S.A. 167 G2
Pineville *MO* U.S.A. 161 E4
Pineville *WV* U.S.A. 164 E5
Ping, Mae Nam *r.* Thai. 86 C4
Ping'an China 94 E4
Ping'anyi China *see* **Ping'an**
Pingba China 96 E3
Pingbian China 96 D4
Ping Dao *i.* China 95 I5
Pingding China 95 H4

Pingdingbu China see Guyuan
Pingdingshan China 97 G1
Pingdong Taiwan see P'ingtung
Pingdu Jiangxi China see Anfu
Pingdu Shandong China 95 I4
Pinggang China 90 B4
Pinggu China 95 I3
Pinghe China 97 H3
Pinghu China see Pingtang
Pingjiang China 97 G2
Pingjin China 96 E2
Pingle China 97 F3
Pingli China 97 F1
Pingliang China 94 F5
Pinglu China 95 G5
Pingluo China 94 F4
Pingma China see Tiandong
Pingnan China 97 H3
Pingqiao China 97 G1
Pingquan China 95 I3
Pingshan Hebei China 95 H4
Pingshan Sichuan China 96 E2
Pingshan Yunnan China see Luquan
Pingshi China 97 G3
Pingshu China see Daicheng
Pingtan China 97 H3
Pingtan Dao i. China see Haitan Dao
Pingtang China 96 E3
P'ingtung Taiwan 97 I4
Pingxi China see Yuping
Pingxiang Gansu China see Tongwei
Pingxiang Guangxi China 96 E4
Pingxiang Jiangxi China 97 G3
Pingyang Heilong. China 95 K1
Pingyang Zhejiang China 97 I3
Pingyao China 95 H4
Pingyi China 95 I5
Pingyin China 95 I4
Pingyu China 97 G1
Pingyuan Shandong China 95 I4
Pingyuan Yunnan China 96 D4
Pingzhai China see Liuzhi
Pinhal Brazil 179 B3
Pinheiro Brazil 177 I4
Pinhoe U.K. 59 D8
Pini i. Indon. 84 B2
Piniós r. Greece see Pineios
Pinjin Australia 135 C7
Pink Mountain Canada 150 F3
Pinlaung Myanmar 86 B2
Pinlebu Myanmar 86 A1
Pinnacle hill VA/WV U.S.A. 165 F4
Pinnacle Island AK U.S.A. 148 D3
Pinnacles National Monument nat. park CA U.S.A. 158 C3
Pinnau r. Germany 63 J1
Pinneberg Germany 63 J1
Pinnes, Akra pt Greece see Pines, Akrotirio
Pinoh r. Indon. 85 E3
Pinon Hills CA U.S.A. 158 E4
Pinos, Isla de i. Cuba see La Juventud, Isla de
Pinos, Mount CA U.S.A. 158 D4
Pinotepa Nacional Mex. 168 E5
Pinrang Sulawesi Indon. 83 A3
Pinrang Sulawesi Indon. 83 B3
Pins, Île des i. New Caledonia 133 G4
Pins, Pointe aux pt Canada 164 E2
Pinsk Belarus 55 O10
Pinta, Sierra hill AZ U.S.A. 159 G5
Pintada Creek watercourse NM U.S.A. 157 G6
Pintados Chile 178 C2
Pintasan Sabah Malaysia 85 G1
Pintura UT U.S.A. 159 G3
Pioche NV U.S.A. 159 F3
Piodi Dem. Rep. Congo 123 C4
Pioneer Mountains MT U.S.A. 156 E3
Pioner, Ostrov i. Rus. Fed. 76 K2
Pionerskiy Kaliningradskaya Oblast' Rus. Fed. 55 L9
Pionerskiy Tyumenskaya Oblast' Rus. Fed. 51 S3
Pionki Poland 57 R5
Piopio N.Z. 139 E4
Piopiotahi inlet N.Z. see Milford Sound
Piorini, Lago l. Brazil 176 F4
Piotrków Trybunalski Poland 57 Q5
Pipa Dingzi mt. China 90 C4
Pipar India 104 C4
Pipar Road India 104 C4
Piperi i. Greece 69 K5
Piper Peak NV U.S.A. 158 E3
Pipestone Canada 151 K5
Pipestone r. Canada 151 N4
Pipestone MN U.S.A. 160 D3
Pipli India 104 C3
Pipmuacan, Réservoir resr Canada 153 H4
Piqan China see Shanshan
Piqanlik China 98 C4
Piqua OH U.S.A. 164 C3
Piquiri r. Brazil 179 A4
Pira Benin 120 D4
Piracanjuba Brazil 179 A2
Piracicaba Brazil 179 B3
Piracicaba r. Brazil 179 C2
Piraçununga Brazil 179 B3
Piracuruca Brazil 177 J4
Piraeus Greece 69 J6
Piraí do Sul Brazil 179 A4
Piráievs Greece see Piraeus
Piraju Brazil 179 A3
Pirajuí Brazil 179 A3
Pirallahı Adası Azer. 113 H2
Piranhas Bahia Brazil 179 C1
Piranhas Goiás Brazil 177 H7
Piranhas r. Goiás Brazil 179 A2
Piranhas r. Rio Grande do Norte Brazil 177 K5
Pirapora Brazil 179 B2
Pirari Nepal 99 D8
Piraube, Lac l. Canada 153 H4
Pirawa India 104 D4
Pirenópolis Brazil 179 A1
Pires do Rio Brazil 179 A2
Pírgos Greece see Pyrgos
Pirin, Natsionalen Park nat. park Bulg. 69 J4
Pirineos mts Europe see Pyrenees
Piripiri Brazil 177 J4
Pirlerkondu Turkey see Taşkent
Pirmasens Germany 63 H5
Pirojpur Bangl. 105 G5
Pir Panjal Pass India 104 C2
Pir Panjal Range mts India/Pak. 111 I3
Piru Seram Indon. 83 D3
Piru, Teluk b. Seram Indon. 83 D3
Piryatin Ukr. see Pyryatyn
Pirzada Afgh. 111 G4
Pisa Italy 68 D3
Pisae Italy see Pisa
Pisagua Chile 176 D7
Pisang i. Maluku Indon. 83 D3
Pisang, Kepulauan is Indon. 81 I7
Pisau, Tanjung pt Malaysia 85 G1
Pisaurum Italy see Pesaro
Pisco Peru 176 C6
Písek Czech Rep. 57 O6
Pisha China see Ningnan
Pishan China 99 B5
Pīshīn Iran 102 B6
Pishin Pak. 111 G4
Pīshīn Jān Afgh. 111 F3
Pishin Lora r. Pak. 111 G4
Pishpek Kyrg. see Bishkek
Pisidia reg. Turkey 112 C3
Pising Sulawesi Indon. 83 B4

▶Pissis, Cerro Arg. 178 C3
4th highest mountain in South America.

Pisté Mex. 167 H4
Pisticci Italy 68 G4
Pistoia Italy 68 D3
Pistoriae Italy see Pistoia
Pisuerga r. Spain 67 D3
Pita Guinea 120 B3
Pitaga Canada 153 I3
Pital Mex. 167 H5
Pitanga Brazil 179 A4
Pitangui Brazil 179 B2
Pitar India 104 B5
Pitarpunga Lake imp. l. Australia 138 A5
Pitcairn, Henderson, Ducie and Oeno Islands terr. S. Pacific Ocean see Pitcairn Islands
Pitcairn Island Pitcairn Is 187 L7

▶Pitcairn Islands terr. S. Pacific Ocean 187 L7
United Kingdom Overseas Territory.

Piteå Sweden 54 L4
Piteälven r. Sweden 54 L4
Pitelino Rus. Fed. 53 I5
Piterka Rus. Fed. 53 J6
Piteşti Romania 69 K2
Pithoragarh India 104 E3
Pitihra India 104 D5
Pitiquito Mex. 166 B2
Pitkas Point AK U.S.A. 148 G3
Pitkyaranta Rus. Fed. 52 F3
Pitlochry U.K. 60 F4
Pitong China see Pixian
Pitsane Siding Botswana 125 G3
Pitti i. India 106 B4
Pitt Island Canada 149 O5
Pitt Island N.Z. 133 I6
Pitt Islands Solomon Is see Vanikoro Islands
Pittsboro MS U.S.A. 161 F5
Pittsburg KS U.S.A. 161 E4
Pittsburg TX U.S.A. 161 E5
Pittsburgh PA U.S.A. 164 F3
Pittsfield MA U.S.A. 165 I2
Pittsfield ME U.S.A. 165 K1
Pittsfield VT U.S.A. 165 I2
Pittston PA U.S.A. 165 H3
Pittsworth Australia 138 E1
Pitz Lake Canada 151 L2
Piumhí Brazil 179 B3
Piura Peru 176 B5
Piute Mountains CA U.S.A. 159 F4
Piute Peak CA U.S.A. 158 D4
Piute Reservoir UT U.S.A. 159 G2
Piuthan Nepal 105 E3
Pivabiska r. Canada 152 E4
Pivka Slovenia 68 F2
Pixa China 99 B5
Pixariá mt. Greece see Pyxaria
Pixian China 96 D2
Pixley CA U.S.A. 158 D4
Pixoyal Mex. 167 H5
Piz Bernina mt. Italy/Switz. 68 C1
Piz Buin mt. Austria/Switz. 57 M7
Pizhanka Rus. Fed. 52 K4
Pizhi Nigeria 120 D4
Pizhma Rus. Fed. 52 J4
Pizhma r. Rus. Fed. 52 K4
Pizhma r. Rus. Fed. 52 L2
Pizhou China 95 I5
Pkulagalid Point Palau 82 [inset]
Pkulagasemieg pt Palau 82 [inset]
Pkulngril pt Palau 82 [inset]
Pkurengei pt Palau 82 [inset]
Placentia Canada 153 L5
Placentia Italy see Piacenza
Placentia Bay Canada 153 L5
Placer Masbate Phil. 82 C4
Placer Mindanao Phil. 82 D4
Placerville CA U.S.A. 158 C2
Placerville CO U.S.A. 159 I2
Placetas Cuba 163 E8
Plácido de Castro Brazil 176 E6
Plain Dealing LA U.S.A. 161 E5
Plainfield CT U.S.A. 165 J3
Plainfield IN U.S.A. 164 B4
Plainfield VT U.S.A. 165 I1
Plains KS U.S.A. 161 C4
Plains TX U.S.A. 161 C5
Plainview TX U.S.A. 161 C5
Plainville IN U.S.A. 164 B4
Plainville KS U.S.A. 160 D4
Plainwell MI U.S.A. 164 C2
Plaju Sumatera Indon. 84 D3
Plaka, Akra pt Greece see Plaka, Akrotirio
Plaka, Akrotirio pt Greece 69 L7
Plakoti, Cape Cyprus 107 B2
Plamondon Canada 151 H4
Plampang Sumbawa Indon. 85 G5
Planá Czech Rep. 63 M5
Plana Cays is Bahamas 163 F8
Planada CA U.S.A. 158 C3
Planaltina Brazil 179 B1
Plane r. Germany 63 M2
Plankinton SD U.S.A. 160 D3
Plano TX U.S.A. 161 D5
Planura Brazil 179 A3
Plaquemine LA U.S.A. 161 F6
Plasencia Spain 67 C3
Plaster City CA U.S.A. 159 F5
Plaster Rock Canada 153 I5
Plastun Rus. Fed. 90 E3
Platani r. Sicily Italy 68 E6
Platberg mt. S. Africa 125 I5

▶Plateau Research Station Antarctica
Lowest recorded annual mean temperature in the world.

Plateros Mex. 166 E4
Platina CA U.S.A. 158 B1
Platinum AK U.S.A. 148 G4
Plato Col. 176 D2
Platón Sánchez Mex. 167 F4
Platte r. NE U.S.A. 160 E3
Platte City MO U.S.A. 160 E4
Plattling Germany 63 M6
Plattsburgh NY U.S.A. 165 I1
Plattsmouth NE U.S.A. 160 E3
Plau Germany 63 M1
Plauen Germany 63 M4
Plauer See l. Germany 63 M1
Plavsk Rus. Fed. 53 H5
Playa Azul Mex. 166 E5
Playa Noriega, Lago l. Mex. 157 F7
Playas Ecuador 176 B4
Playas Lake NM U.S.A. 159 I6
Plây Ku Vietnam 87 E4
Playón Mex. 166 C3
Pleasant, Lake AZ U.S.A. 159 G5
Pleasant Bay MA U.S.A. 165 K3
Pleasant Grove UT U.S.A. 159 H1
Pleasant Hill Lake OH U.S.A. 164 D3
Pleasanton TX U.S.A. 161 D6
Pleasant Point N.Z. 139 C7
Pleasantville NJ U.S.A. 165 H4
Pleasure Ridge Park KY U.S.A. 164 C4
Pleaux France 66 F4
Pledger Lake Canada 152 E4
Plei Doch Vietnam 87 D4
Pleihari Martapura, Suaka Margasatwa nature res. Indon. 85 F3
Pleihari Tanah, Suaka Margasatwa nature res. Kalimantan Indon. 85 F4
Plei Kân Vietnam 86 D4
Pleinfeld Germany 63 K5
Pleiße r. Germany 63 M3
Plenty watercourse Australia 136 B5
Plenty, Bay of g. N.Z. 139 F3
Plentywood MT U.S.A. 156 G2
Plesetsk Rus. Fed. 52 I3
Pleshchentsy Belarus see Plyeshchanitsy
Plétipi, Lac l. Canada 153 H4
Plettenberg Germany 63 H3
Plettenberg Bay S. Africa 124 F8
Pleven Bulg. 69 K3
Plevna Bulg. see Pleven
Plieran r. Malaysia 85 F2
Pljevlja Montenegro 69 H3
Płock Poland 57 Q4
Pločno mt. Bos.-Herz. 68 G3
Plodovoye Rus. Fed. 52 F3
Ploemeur France 66 C3
Ploeşti Romania see Ploieşti
Ploieşti Romania 69 L2
Plomb du Cantal mt. France 66 F4
Ploskoye Rus. Fed. see Stanovoye
Płoty Poland 57 O4
Ploudalmézeau France 66 B2
Plouzané France 66 B2
Plovdiv Bulg. 69 K3
Plover Cove Reservoir H.K. China 97 [inset]
Plover Islands AK U.S.A. 148 I1
Plozk Poland see Płock
Plum PA U.S.A. 164 F3
Plumridge Lakes salt flat Australia 135 D7
Plungė Lith. 55 L9
Plutarco Elías Calles, Presa resr Mex. 157 F7
Plutarco Elís Calles, Presa resr Mex. 166 C2
Pluto, Lac l. Canada 153 H3
Plyeshchanitsy Belarus 55 O9
Ply Huey Wati, Khao mt. Myanmar/Thai. 86 B3
Plymouth U.K. 59 C8
Plymouth CA U.S.A. 158 C2
Plymouth IN U.S.A. 164 B3
Plymouth MA U.S.A. 165 J3
Plymouth NC U.S.A. 162 E5
Plymouth NH U.S.A. 165 J2
Plymouth WI U.S.A. 164 B2

▶Plymouth (abandoned) Montserrat 169 L5
Capital of Montserrat, abandoned in 1997 owing to volcanic activity. Temporary capital established at Brades.

Plymouth Bay MA U.S.A. 165 J3
Plynlimon hill U.K. 59 D6
Plyussa Rus. Fed. 55 P7
Plzeň Czech Rep. 57 N6
Pô Burkina Faso 120 C3
Po r. Italy 68 E2
Po, Tanjung pt Malaysia 85 E2
Poás, Volcán vol. Costa Rica 166 [inset] I7
Poat i. Indon. 83 B3
Pobeda Peak China/Kyrg. 98 C4
Pobedy, Pik mt. China/Kyrg. see Pobeda Peak
Pocahontas AR U.S.A. 161 F4
Pocatello ID U.S.A. 156 E4
Pochala South Sudan 121 G4
Pochayiv Ukr. 53 E6
Pochep Rus. Fed. 53 G5
Pochinki Rus. Fed. 53 J5
Pochinok Rus. Fed. 53 G5
Pochutla Mex. 168 E5
Pock, Gunung hill Malaysia 85 G1
Pocking Germany 57 N6
Pocklington U.K. 58 G5
Poções Brazil 179 C1
Pocomoke City MD U.S.A. 165 H4
Pocomoke Sound b. MD/VA U.S.A. 165 H5
Poconé Brazil 177 G7
Pocono Mountains hills PA U.S.A. 165 H3
Pocono Summit PA U.S.A. 165 H3
Poco Ranakah vol. Flores Indon. 83 B5
Poços de Caldas Brazil 179 B3
Podanur India 106 C4
Poddor'ye Rus. Fed. 52 F4
Podgorenskiy Rus. Fed. 53 H6

▶Podgorica Montenegro 69 H3
Capital of Montenegro

Podgornoye Rus. Fed. 76 J4
Podile India 106 C3
Podişul Transilvaniei plat. Romania see Transylvanian Basin
Podkamennaya Tunguska r. Rus. Fed. 77 K3
Podocarpus, Parque Nacional nat. park Ecuador 176 C4
Podol'sk Rus. Fed. 53 H5
Podporozh'ye Rus. Fed. 52 G3
Podujevë Kosovo 69 I3
Podujevo Kosovo see Podujevë
Podz' Rus. Fed. 52 K3
Poelela, Lagoa l. Moz. 125 L3
Poeppel Corner salt flat Australia 137 B5
Poetovio Slovenia see Ptuj
Pofadder S. Africa 124 D5
Pogar Rus. Fed. 53 G5
Poggibonsi Italy 68 D3
Poggio di Montieri mt. Italy 68 D3
Pogradec Albania 69 I4
Pogranichnyy Rus. Fed. 90 C3
Poh Sulawesi Indon. 83 B3
Po Hai g. China see Bo Hai
P'ohang S. Korea 91 C5
Pohnpei atoll Micronesia 186 G5
Pohri India 104 D4
Poi India 105 H4
Poiana Mare Romania 69 J3
Poigar Sulawesi Indon. 83 C2
Poinsett, Cape Antarctica 188 F2
Point Arena CA U.S.A. 158 B2
Point au Fer Island LA U.S.A. 161 F6
Pointe a la Hache LA U.S.A. 161 F6
Pointe-à-Pitre Guadeloupe 169 L5
Pointe-Noire Congo 123 B4
Point Hope AK U.S.A. 148 F1
Point Lake Canada 150 H1
Point Lay AK U.S.A. 148 G1
Point of Rocks WY U.S.A. 156 F4
Point Pelee National Park Canada 164 D3
Point Pleasant NJ U.S.A. 165 H3
Point Pleasant WV U.S.A. 164 D4
Poitiers France 66 E3
Poitou reg. France 66 E3
Poix-de-Picardie France 62 B5
Pojuca r. Brazil 179 D1
Pokaran India 104 B4
Pokataroo Australia 138 D2
Pokcha Rus. Fed. 51 R3
Pokhara Nepal 105 E3
Pokhran Landi Pak. 111 G5
Pokhvistnevo Rus. Fed. 51 Q5
Pok Liu Chau i. H.K. China see Lamma Island
Poko Dem. Rep. Congo 122 C3
Poko Mountain hill AK U.S.A. 148 G1
Pokosnoye Rus. Fed. 88 I1
P'ok'r Kovkas mts Asia see Lesser Caucasus
Pokrovka Primorskiy Kray Rus. Fed. 90 C4
Pokrovka Zabaykal'skiy Kray Rus. Fed. 90 A1
Pokrovsk Respublika Sakha (Yakutiya) Rus. Fed. 77 N3
Pokrovsk Saratovskaya Oblast' Rus. Fed. see Engel's
Pokrovskoye Rus. Fed. 53 H7
Pokshen'ga r. Rus. Fed. 52 J3
Pol India 104 C5
Pola Croatia see Pula
Pola Mindoro Phil. 82 C3
Polacca Wash watercourse AZ U.S.A. 159 H4
Pola de Lena Spain 67 D2
Pola de Siero Spain 67 D2
Poland country Europe 50 J5
Poland NY U.S.A. 165 H2
Poland OH U.S.A. 164 E3
Polar Plateau Antarctica 188 A1
Polatlı Turkey 112 D3
Polatsk Belarus 55 P9
Polavaram India 106 D2
Polcirkeln Sweden 54 L3
Pol-e 'Alam Afgh. 111 H3
Polee i. Papua Indon. 83 D3
Pol-e Fāsā Iran 110 D4
Pol-e Khātūn Iran 111 F2
Pol-e Safīd Iran 110 D2
Polessk Rus. Fed. 55 L9
Poles'ye marsh Belarus/Ukr. see Pripet Marshes
Polewali Sulawesi Barat Indon. 83 A3
Polgahawela Sri Lanka 106 D5
Poli China 95 I5
Poli Cyprus see Polis
Políaigos i. Greece see Polyaigos
Police Poland 57 O4
Policoro Italy 68 G4
Poligny France 66 G3
Políkastron Greece see Polykastro
Polillo i. Phil. 82 C3
Polillo Islands Phil. 82 C3
Polillo Strait Phil. 82 C3
Polis Cyprus 107 A2
Polis'ke Ukr. 53 F6
Polis'kyy Zapovidnyk nature res. Ukr. 53 F6
Politovo Rus. Fed. 52 K2
Políyiros Greece see Polygyros
Polkowice Poland 57 P5
Pollachi India 106 C4
Pollard Islands HI U.S.A. see Gardner Pinnacles
Polle Germany 63 J3
Pollino, Monte mt. Italy 68 G5
Pollino, Parco Nazionale del nat. park Italy 68 G5
Polloc Harbour b. Mindanao Phil. 82 C5
Pollock Pines CA U.S.A. 158 C2
Pollock Reef Australia 135 C8
Polmak Norway 54 O1
Polnovat Rus. Fed. 51 T3
Polo Fin. 54 P4
Poloat atoll Micronesia see Puluwat
Pologi Ukr. see Polohy
Polohy Ukr. 53 H7
Polokwane S. Africa 125 I2
Polomolok Mindanao Phil. 82 D5
Polonne Ukr. 53 E6
Polonnoye Ukr. see Polonne
Polotsk Belarus see Polatsk
Polperro U.K. 59 C8
Polska country Europe see Poland
Polson MT U.S.A. 156 E3
Polta r. Rus. Fed. 52 I2
Poltava Ukr. 53 G6
Poltoratsk Turkm. see Aşgabat
Põltsamaa Estonia 55 N7
Polunochnoye Rus. Fed. 51 S3
Põlva Estonia 55 O7
Polvadera NM U.S.A. 157 G6
Polvijärvi Fin. 54 P5
Polvoxal Mex. 167 H5
Polyaigos i. Greece 69 K6
Polyanovgrad Bulg. see Karnobat
Polyarnyy Chukotskiy Avtonomnyy Okrug Rus. Fed. 77 S3
Polyarnyy Murmanskaya Oblast' Rus. Fed. 54 R2
Polyarnyye Zori Rus. Fed. 54 R3
Polyarnyy Ural mts Rus. Fed. 51 S2
Polygyros Greece 69 J4
Polykastro Greece 69 J4
Polynesia is Pacific Ocean 186 I6
Polynésie Française terr. S. Pacific Ocean see French Polynesia
Pom Indon. 81 J7
Pomarkku Fin. 55 M6
Pombal Pará Brazil 177 H4
Pombal Paraíba Brazil 177 K5
Pombal Port. 67 B4
Pomene Moz. 125 L2
Pomeranian Bay Poland 57 O3
Pomeroy S. Africa 125 J5
Pomeroy U.K. 61 F3
Pomeroy OH U.S.A. 164 D4
Pomeroy WA U.S.A. 156 D3
Pomezia Italy 68 E4
Pomfret S. Africa 124 F3
Pomona Belize 167 H5
Pomona Namibia 124 B4
Pomona CA U.S.A. 158 E4
Pomorie Bulg. 69 L3
Pomorskie, Pojezierze reg. Poland 57 O4
Pomorskiy Bereg coastal area Rus. Fed. 52 G2
Pomorskiy Proliv sea chan. Rus. Fed. 52 K1
Pomos Point Cyprus 107 A2
Pomo Tso l. China see Puma Yumco
Pomou, Akra pt Cyprus see Pomos Point
Pomozdino Rus. Fed. 52 L3
Pompain China 99 F7
Pompano Beach FL U.S.A. 163 D7
Pompei Italy 68 F4
Pompéia Brazil 179 A3
Pompey France 62 G6
Pompeyevka Rus. Fed. 90 C2
Ponape atoll Micronesia see Pohnpei
Ponask Lake Canada 151 M4
Ponazyrevo Rus. Fed. 52 J4
Ponca City OK U.S.A. 161 D4
Ponce Puerto Rico 169 K5
Ponce de Leon Bay FL U.S.A. 163 D7
Poncheville, Lac l. Canada 152 F4
Pondichéry India see Puducherry
Pond Inlet Canada 189 K2
Ponds Bay Canada see Pond Inlet
Poneloya Nicaragua 166 [inset] I6
Ponente, Riviera di coastal area Italy 68 B3
Poneto IN U.S.A. 164 C3
Ponferrada Spain 67 C2
Pongara, Pointe pt Gabon 122 A3
Pongaroa N.Z. 139 F5
Pongda China 99 F7
Pongo watercourse South Sudan 121 F4
Pongola r. S. Africa 125 K4
Pongolapoort Dam l. S. Africa 125 J4
Poniki, Gunung mt. Indon. 83 B2
Ponindilisa, Tanjung pt Indon. 83 B3
Ponnagyun Myanmar 86 A2
Ponnaivar r. India 106 C4
Ponnampet India 106 B3
Ponnani India 106 B4
Ponnyadaung Range mts Myanmar 86 A2
Pono Indon. 81 I8
Ponoka Canada 150 H4
Ponorogo Jawa Indon. 85 E4
Ponoy r. Rus. Fed. 52 I2
Pons r. Canada 153 H2

▶Ponta Delgada Arquipélago dos Açores 184 G3
Capital of the Azores.

Ponta Grossa Brazil 179 A4
Pontal Brazil 179 A3
Pontalina Brazil 179 A2
Pont-à-Mousson France 62 G6
Ponta Porã Brazil 178 E2
Pontarfynach U.K. see Devil's Bridge
Pont-Audemer France 59 H9
Pontault-Combault France 62 C6
Pontax r. Canada 152 F4
Pontchartrain, Lake LA U.S.A. 161 F6
Pontcysyllte Aqueduct tourist site U.K. 59 D6
Pont-de-Loup Belgium 62 E4
Ponte Alta do Norte Brazil 177 I6
Ponte de Sor Port. 67 B4
Ponte Firme Brazil 179 B2
Pontefract U.K. 58 F5
Ponteix Canada 151 J5
Ponteland U.K. 58 F3
Ponte Nova Brazil 179 C3
Pontes-e-Lacerda Brazil 177 G7
Pontevedra Spain 67 B2
Ponthierville Dem. Rep. Congo see Ubundu
Pontiac IL U.S.A. 160 F3
Pontiac MI U.S.A. 164 D2
Pontiae is Italy see Ponziane, Isole
Pontianak Kalimantan Indon. 85 E3
Pontine Islands is Italy see Ponziane, Isole
Pont-l'Abbé France 66 B3
Pontoise France 62 C5
Ponton watercourse Australia 135 C7
Ponton Canada 151 L4
Pontotoc MS U.S.A. 161 F5
Pont-Ste-Maxence France 62 C5
Pontypool U.K. 59 D7
Pontypridd U.K. 59 D7
Ponza, Isola di i. Italy 68 E4
Ponziane, Isole is Italy 68 E4
Poochera Australia 135 F8
Poole U.K. 59 F8
Poole KY U.S.A. 164 B5
Poolowanna Lake salt flat Australia 137 B5
Poona India see Pune
Pooncarie Australia 137 C7
Poonch India see Punch
Poopelloe Lake salt l. Australia 138 B3
Poopó, Lago de l. Bol. 176 E7
Poor Knights Islands N.Z. 139 E2
Poorman AK U.S.A. 148 I2
Popayán Col. 176 C3
Poperinge Belgium 62 C4
Popigay r. Rus. Fed. 77 L2
Popiltah Australia 137 C7
Popilta Lake imp. l. Australia 137 C7
Poplar r. Canada 151 L4
Poplar MT U.S.A. 156 G2
Poplar Bluff MO U.S.A. 161 F4
Poplar Camp VA U.S.A. 164 E5
Poplarville MS U.S.A. 161 F6

▶Popocatépetl, Volcán vol. Mex. 168 E5
5th highest mountain in North America.

Popoh Jawa Indon. 85 E5
Popokabaka Dem. Rep. Congo 123 B4
Popondetta P.N.G. 81 L8
Popovichskaya Rus. Fed. see Kalininskaya
Popovo Bulg. 69 L3
Popovo Polje plain Bos.-Herz. 68 G3
Poppberg hill Germany 63 L5
Poppenberg hill Germany 63 K3
Poprad Slovakia 57 R6
Poptún Guat. 167 H5
Poquoson VA U.S.A. 165 G5
Porali r. Pak. 111 G5
Porangahau N.Z. 139 F5
Porangatu Brazil 179 A1
Porbandar India 104 B5
Porcher Island Canada 149 O5
Porcos r. Brazil 179 B1
Porcupine r. Canada/U.S.A. 149 K2
Porcupine, Cape Canada 153 K3
Porcupine Abyssal Plain sea feature N. Atlantic Ocean 184 G2
Porcupine Gorge National Park Australia 136 D4
Porcupine Hills Canada 151 K4
Porcupine Mountains MI U.S.A. 160 F2
Poreč Croatia 68 E2
Porecatu Brazil 179 A3
Poretskoye Rus. Fed. 53 J5
Porgyang China 99 C6
Pori Fin. 55 L6
Porirua N.Z. 139 E5
Porkhov Rus. Fed. 55 P8
Porlamar Venez. 176 F1
Pormpuraaw Australia 136 C2
Pornic France 66 C3
Poro i. Phil. 82 D4
Poronaysk Rus. Fed. 90 F2
Porong China 99 E7
Poros Greece 69 J6
Porosozero Rus. Fed. 52 G3
Porpoise Bay Antarctica 188 G2
Porsangerfjorden sea chan. Norway 54 N1
Porsangerhalvøya pen. Norway 54 N1
Porsgrunn Norway 55 F7
Porsuk r. Turkey 69 N5
Portadown U.K. 61 F3
Portaferry U.K. 61 G3
Portage MI U.S.A. 164 C2
Portage PA U.S.A. 165 F3
Portage WI U.S.A. 160 F3
Portage Creek AK U.S.A. 148 H4
Portage Lakes OH U.S.A. 164 E3
Portage la Prairie Canada 151 L5
Portal ND U.S.A. 160 C1
Port Alberni Canada 150 E5
Port Albert Australia 138 C7
Portalegre Port. 67 C4
Portales NM U.S.A. 161 C5
Port-Alfred Canada see La Baie
Port Alfred S. Africa 125 H7
Port Alice Canada 150 E5
Port Allegany PA U.S.A. 165 F3
Port Allen LA U.S.A. 161 F6
Port Alma Australia 136 E4
Port Alsworth AK U.S.A. 148 I3
Port Angeles WA U.S.A. 156 C2
Port Antonio Jamaica 169 I5
Portarlington Ireland 61 E4
Port Arthur Australia 137 [inset]
Port Arthur China see Lüshun
Port Arthur TX U.S.A. 161 E6
Port Askaig U.K. 60 C5
Port Augusta Australia 137 B7

▶Port-au-Prince Haiti 169 J5
Capital of Haiti.

Port Austin MI U.S.A. 164 D1
Port aux Choix Canada 153 K4
Portavogie U.K. 61 G3
Port Barton b. Palawan Phil. 82 B4
Port Beaufort S. Africa 124 E8
Port Blair India 87 A5
Port Bolster Canada 164 F1
Portbou Spain 67 H2
Port Brabant Canada see Tuktoyaktuk
Port Burwell Canada 164 E2
Port Campbell Australia 138 A7
Port Campbell National Park Australia 138 A7
Port Carling Canada 164 F1
Port-Cartier Canada 153 I4
Port Chalmers N.Z. 139 C7
Port Charlotte FL U.S.A. 163 D7
Port Clarence b. AK U.S.A. 148 F2
Port Clements Canada 149 N5
Port Clinton OH U.S.A. 164 D3
Port Credit Canada 164 F2
Port-de-Paix Haiti 169 J5
Port Dickson Malaysia 84 C2
Port Douglas Australia 136 D3
Port Edward Canada 149 O5
Port Edward S. Africa 125 J6
Porteira Brazil 177 G4
Porteirinha Brazil 179 C1
Portel Brazil 177 H4
Port Elgin Canada 164 E1
Port Elizabeth S. Africa 125 G7
Port Ellen U.K. 60 C5
Port Erin Isle of Man 58 C4
Porter Lake N.W.T. Canada 151 J2
Porter Lake Sask. Canada 151 J3
Porter Landing Canada 149 O4
Porterville S. Africa 124 D7
Porterville CA U.S.A. 158 D3
Port Étienne Mauritania see Nouâdhibou
Port Everglades FL U.S.A. see Fort Lauderdale
Port Fitzroy N.Z. 139 E3
Port Francqui Dem. Rep. Congo see Ilebo
Port-Gentil Gabon 122 A4
Port Gibson MS U.S.A. 167 H2
Port Glasgow U.K. 60 E5
Port Graham AK U.S.A. 149 J4
Port Harcourt Nigeria 120 D4
Port Harrison Canada see Inukjuak
Porthcawl U.K. 59 D7
Port Hedland Australia 134 B5
Port Heiden AK U.S.A. 148 H4
Port Heiden b. AK U.S.A. 148 H4

Port Henry NY U.S.A. 165 I1
Port Herald Malawi see Nsanje
Porthleven U.K. 59 B8
Porthmadog U.K. 59 C6
Port Hope Canada 165 F2
Port Hope Simpson Canada 153 L3
Port Hueneme CA U.S.A. 158 D4
Port Huron MI U.S.A. 164 D2
Portimão Port. 67 B5
Port Jackson Australia see Sydney
Port Jackson inlet Australia 138 E4
Port Keats Australia see Wadeye
Port Klang Malaysia see Pelabuhan Klang
Port Láirge Ireland see Waterford
Portland N.S.W. Australia 138 D4
Portland Vic. Australia 137 C8
Portland IN U.S.A. 164 C3
Portland ME U.S.A. 165 J2
Portland MI U.S.A. 164 C2
Portland OR U.S.A. 156 C3
Portland TN U.S.A. 164 B5
Portland, Isle of pen. U.K. 59 E8
Portland Bill hd U.K. see Bill of Portland
Portland Creek Pond l. Canada 153 K4
Portland Roads Australia 136 C2
Port-la-Nouvelle France 66 F5
Portlaoise Ireland 61 E4
Port Lavaca TX U.S.A. 161 D6
Portlaw Ireland 61 E5
Portlethen U.K. 60 G3
Port Lincoln Australia 137 A7
Port Lions AK U.S.A. 148 I4
Portlock AK U.S.A. 149 J4
Port Loko Sierra Leone 120 B4

▶Port Louis Mauritius 185 L7
Capital of Mauritius.

Port-Lyautrey Morocco see Kénitra
Port Macquarie Australia 138 F3
Portmadoc U.K. see Porthmadog
Port McNeill Canada 150 E5
Port-Menier Canada 153 I4
Port Moller AK U.S.A. 148 G5
Port Moller b. AK U.S.A. 148 G5

▶Port Moresby P.N.G. 81 L8
Capital of Papua New Guinea.

Portnaguran U.K. 60 C2
Portnahaven U.K. 60 C5
Port nan Giúran U.K. see Portnaguran
Port Neill Australia 137 B7
Portneuf r. Canada 153 H4
Port Nis U.K. see Port of Ness
Port Noarlunga Australia 137 B7
Port Nolloth S. Africa 124 C5
Port Norris NJ U.S.A. 165 H4
Port-Nouveau-Québec Canada see Kangiqsualujjuaq
Porto Port. see Oporto
Porto Acre Brazil 176 E5
Porto Alegre Brazil 179 A5
Porto Alexandre Angola see Tombua
Porto Amboim Angola 123 B5
Porto Amélia Moz. see Pemba
Porto Artur Brazil 177 G6
Porto Belo Brazil 179 A4
Portobelo Panama 166 [inset] K7
Portobelo, Parque Nacional nat. park Panama 166 [inset] K7
Port O'Brien AK U.S.A. 148 I4
Porto de Moz Brazil 177 H4
Porto de Santa Cruz Brazil 179 C1
Porto dos Gaúchos Óbidos Brazil 177 G6
Porto Esperança Brazil 177 G7
Porto Esperidião Brazil 177 G7
Portoferraio Italy 68 D3
Port of Ness U.K. 60 C2
Porto Franco Brazil 177 I5

▶Port of Spain Trin. and Tob. 169 L6
Capital of Trinidad and Tobago.

Porto Grande Brazil 177 H3
Portogruaro Italy 68 E2
Porto Jofre Brazil 177 G7
Portola CA U.S.A. 158 C2
Portomaggiore Italy 68 D2
Porto Mendes Brazil 178 F2
Porto Murtinho Brazil 178 E2
Porto Nacional Brazil 177 I6

▶Porto-Novo Benin 120 D4
Capital of Benin.

Porto Novo Cape Verde 120 [inset]
Porto Primavera, Represa resr Brazil 178 F2
Port Orchard WA U.S.A. 156 C3
Port Orford OR U.S.A. 156 B4
Porto Rico Angola 123 B4
Porto Santo, Ilha de i. Madeira 120 B1
Porto Seguro Brazil 179 D2
Porto Tolle Italy 68 E2
Porto Torres Sardinia Italy 68 C4
Porto União Brazil 179 A4
Porto-Vecchio Corsica France 66 I6
Porto Velho Brazil 176 F5
Portoviejo Ecuador 176 B4
Porto Walter Brazil 176 D5
Portpatrick U.K. 60 D6
Port Perry Canada 165 F1
Port Phillip Bay Australia 138 B7
Port Pirie Australia 137 B7
Port Radium Canada see Echo Bay
Portreath U.K. 59 B8
Portree U.K. 60 C3
Port Rexton Canada 153 L4
Port Royal VA U.S.A. 165 G4
Port Royal Sound inlet SC U.S.A. 163 D5
Portrush U.K. 61 F2
Port Safaga Egypt see Būr Safājah
Port Safety AK U.S.A. 148 F2
Port Said Egypt 107 A4
Port St Joe FL U.S.A. 163 C6
Port St Lucie City FL U.S.A. 163 D7
Port St Mary Isle of Man 58 C4
Portsalon Ireland 61 E2
Port Sanilac MI U.S.A. 164 D2
Port Severn Canada 164 F1
Port Shepstone S. Africa 125 J6
Port Simpson Canada see Lax Kw'alaams
Portsmouth U.K. 59 F8
Portsmouth NH U.S.A. 165 J2
Portsmouth OH U.S.A. 164 D4
Portsmouth VA U.S.A. 165 G5
Portsoy U.K. 60 G3
Port Stanley Falkland Is see Stanley
Port Stephens b. Australia 138 F4
Portstewart U.K. 61 F2
Port Sudan Sudan 108 E6
Port Sulphur LA U.S.A. 167 H2
Port Swettenham Malaysia see Pelabuhan Klang
Port Talbot U.K. 59 D7
Port Tambang b. Luzon Phil. 82 C3
Porttipahdan tekojärvi l. Fin. 54 O2
Port Townsend WA U.S.A. 156 C2
Portugal country Europe 67 C4
Portugália Angola see Chitato
Portuguese East Africa country Africa see Mozambique
Portuguese Guinea country Africa see Guinea-Bissau
Portuguese Timor country Asia see East Timor
Portuguese West Africa country Africa see Angola
Portumna Ireland 61 D4
Portus Herculis Monoeci country Europe see Monaco
Port-Vendres France 66 F5

▶Port Vila Vanuatu 133 G3
Capital of Vanuatu.

Portville NY U.S.A. 165 F2
Port-Vladimir Rus. Fed. 54 R2
Port Waikato N.Z. 139 E3
Port Washington WI U.S.A. 164 B2
Port William U.K. 60 E6
Porvenir Bol. 176 E6
Porvenir Chile 178 B8
Porvoo Fin. 55 N6
Posada Spain 67 D2
Posada de Llanera Spain see Posada
Posadas Arg. 178 E3
Posen Poland see Poznań
Posen MI U.S.A. 164 D1
Poseyville IN U.S.A. 164 B4
Poshekhon'ye Rus. Fed. 52 H4
Poshekon'ye-Volodarsk Rus. Fed. see Poshekhon'ye
Poshteh-ye Chaqvīr hill Iran 110 E4
Posht-e Kūh mts Iran 110 B3
Posht-e Rūd-e Zamindavar reg. Afgh. see Zamīndāvar
Posht Kūh hill Iran 110 C2
Posio Fin. 54 P3
Poskam China see Zepu
Poso Sulawesi Indon. 83 B3
Poso r. Indon. 83 B3
Poso, Danau l. Indon. 83 B3
Poso, Teluk b. Indon. 83 B3
Posof Turkey 113 F2
Posŏng S. Korea 91 B6
Possession Island Namibia 124 B4
Pößneck Germany 63 L4
Possum Kingdom Lake TX U.S.A. 167 F1
Post TX U.S.A. 161 C5
Postavy Belarus see Pastavy
Poste-de-la-Baleine Canada see Kuujjuarapik
Poste Weygand Alg. 120 D2
Postmasburg S. Africa 124 F5
Poston AZ U.S.A. 159 F4
Postville Canada 153 K3
Postville IA U.S.A. 152 C6
Postysheve Ukr. see Krasnoarmiys'k
Pota Flores Indon. 83 B5
Pótam Mex. 166 C3
Poté Brazil 179 C2
Poteau OK U.S.A. 161 E5
Potegaon India 106 D2
Potentia Italy see Potenza
Potenza Italy 68 F4
Poth TX U.S.A. 161 D6
Poti Georgia 113 F2
Potikal India 106 D2
Potiraguá Brazil 179 D1
Potiskum Nigeria 120 E3
Potlatch ID U.S.A. 156 D3
Pot Mountain ID U.S.A. 156 E3
Po Toi i. H.K. China 97 [inset]
Potomac r. MD/VA U.S.A. 165 G4
Potomana, Gunung mt. Indon. 83 C5
Potosí Bol. 176 E7
Potosi MO U.S.A. 160 F4
Potosi Mountain NV U.S.A. 159 F4
Pototan Panay Phil. 82 C4
Potrerillos Chile 178 C3
Potrerillos Hond. 166 [inset] I6
Potrero del Llano Mex. 166 D2
Potsdam Germany 63 N2
Potsdam NY U.S.A. 165 H1
Potter NE U.S.A. 160 C3
Potterne U.K. 59 E7
Potters Bar U.K. 59 G7
Potter Valley CA U.S.A. 158 B2
Pottstown PA U.S.A. 165 H3
Pottsville PA U.S.A. 165 G3
Pottuvil Sri Lanka 106 D5
Potwar reg. Pak. 111 I3
Pouch Cove Canada 153 L5
Poughkeepsie NY U.S.A. 165 I3
Poulin de Courval, Lac l. Canada 153 H4
Poulton-le-Fylde U.K. 58 E5
Pouso Alegre Brazil 179 B3
Poŭthĭsăt Cambodia 87 C4
Poŭthĭsăt, Stœ̆ng r. Cambodia 87 D4
Považská Bystrica Slovakia 57 Q6
Povenets Rus. Fed. 52 G3
Poverty Bay N.Z. 139 F4
Povlen mt. Serbia 69 H2
Póvoa de Varzim Port. 67 B3
Povorino Rus. Fed. 53 I6
Povorotnyy, Mys hd Rus. Fed. 90 D4
Poway CA U.S.A. 158 E5
Powder r. MT U.S.A. 156 G3
Powder, South Fork r. WY U.S.A. 156 G4
Powder River WY U.S.A. 156 G4
Powell r. TN/VA U.S.A. 164 D5
Powell, Lake resr UT U.S.A. 159 H3
Powell Lake Canada 150 E5
Powell Mountain NV U.S.A. 158 D2
Powell Point Bahamas 163 E7
Powell River Canada 150 E5
Powhatan AR U.S.A. 161 F4
Powhatan VA U.S.A. 165 G5
Powo China 96 C1
Pōwrize Turkm. 110 E2
Poxoréu Brazil 177 H7
Poyang China 97 H2
Poyang Hu l. China 97 H2
Poyan Reservoir Sing. 87 [inset]
Poyarkovo Rus. Fed. 90 C2
Pozantı Turkey 112 D3
Požarevac Serbia 69 I2
Poza Rica Mex. 168 E4
Pozdeyevka Rus. Fed. 90 C2
Požega Croatia 68 G2
Požega Serbia 69 I3
Pozharskoye Rus. Fed. 90 D3
Poznań Poland 57 P4
Pozoblanco Spain 67 D4
Pozo Colorado Para. 178 E2
Pozo Nuevo Mex. 166 C2
Pozsony Slovakia see Bratislava
Pozzuoli Italy 68 F4
Prabumulih Sumatera Indon. 84 D3
Prachatice Czech Rep. 57 O6
Prachi r. India 105 F6
Prachin Buri Thai. 87 C4
Prachuap Khiri Khan Thai. 87 B5
Prades France 66 F5
Prado Brazil 179 D2

▶Prague Czech Rep. 57 O5
Capital of the Czech Republic.

Praha Czech Rep. see Prague

▶Praia Cape Verde 120 [inset]
Capital of Cape Verde.

Praia do Bilene Moz. 125 K3
Prainha Brazil 177 H4
Prairie Australia 136 D4
Prairie r. MN U.S.A. 160 E2
Prairie Dog Town Fork r. TX U.S.A. 161 C5
Prairie du Chien WI U.S.A. 160 F3
Prairie River Canada 151 K4
Pram, Khao mt. Thai. 87 B5
Pran r. Thai. 87 C4
Pran Buri Thai. 87 B4
Prapat Sumatera Indon. 84 B2
Prasonisi, Akra pt Greece see Prasonisi, Akrotirio
Prasonisi, Akrotirio pt Greece 69 L7
Prata Brazil 179 A2
Prata r. Brazil 179 A2
Prat de Llobregat Spain see El Prat de Llobregat
Prathes Thai country Asia see Thailand
Prato Italy 68 D3
Pratt KS U.S.A. 160 D4
Prattville AL U.S.A. 163 C5
Pravdinsk Rus. Fed. 55 L9
Praya Lombok Indon. 85 G5
Preah, Prêk r. Cambodia 87 D4
Preăh Vihéar Cambodia 87 D4
Preble NY U.S.A. 165 G2
Prechistoye Smolenskaya Oblast' Rus. Fed. 53 G5
Prechistoye Yaroslavskaya Oblast' Rus. Fed. 52 I4
Precipice National Park Australia 136 E5
Preeceville Canada 151 K5
Pregolya r. Rus. Fed. 55 L9
Preiļi Latvia 55 O8
Prelate Canada 151 I5
Premer Australia 138 D3
Prémery France 66 F3
Premnitz Germany 63 M2
Prentiss MS U.S.A. 161 F6
Prenzlau Germany 57 N4
Preparis Island Cocos Is 80 A4
Preparis North Channel Cocos Is 80 A4
Preparis South Channel Cocos Is 80 A4
Přerov Czech Rep. 57 P6
Presa de la Amistad, Parque Natural nature res. Mex. 167 E2
Presa San Antonio Mex. 167 E3
Prescelly Mts hills U.K. see Preseli, Mynydd
Prescott Canada 165 H1
Prescott AR U.S.A. 161 E5
Prescott AZ U.S.A. 159 G4
Prescott Valley AZ U.S.A. 159 G4
Preseli, Mynydd hills U.K. 59 C7
Preševo Serbia 69 I3
Presidencia Roque Sáenz Peña Arg. 178 D3
Presidente Dutra Brazil 177 J5
Presidente Hermes Brazil 176 F6
Presidente Manuel A Roxas Mindanao Phil. 82 C4
Presidente Olegário Brazil 179 B2
Presidente Prudente Brazil 179 A3
Presidente Venceslau Brazil 179 A3
Presidio TX U.S.A. 161 B6
Preslav Bulg. see Veliki Preslav
Prešov Slovakia 53 D6
Prespa, Lake Europe 69 I4
Prespansko Ezero l. Europe see Prespa, Lake
Prespës, Liqeni i l. Europe see Prespa, Lake
Prespon, Ethnikos Drymos nat. park Greece 69 I4
Presque Isle ME U.S.A. 162 G2
Presque Isle MI U.S.A. 164 D1
Pressburg Slovakia see Bratislava
Presteigne U.K. 59 D6
Preston U.K. 58 E5
Preston ID U.S.A. 156 F4
Preston MN U.S.A. 160 E3
Preston MO U.S.A. 160 E4
Preston, Cape Australia 134 B5
Prestonpans U.K. 60 G5
Prestonsburg KY U.S.A. 164 D5
Prestwick U.K. 60 E5
Preto r. Bahia Brazil 177 J6
Preto r. Bahia Brazil 179 D1
Preto r. Minas Gerais Brazil 179 B2

▶Pretoria S. Africa 125 I3
Official capital of South Africa.

Pretoria-Witwatersrand-Vereeniging prov. S. Africa see Gauteng
Pretzsch Germany 63 M3
Preussisch-Eylau Rus. Fed. see Bagrationovsk
Preußisch Stargard Poland see Starogard Gdański
Preveza Greece 69 I5
Prewitt NM U.S.A. 159 I4
Prey Vêng Cambodia 87 D5
Priaral'skiy Karakum des. Kazakh. 102 B2
Priargunsk Rus. Fed. 95 I1
Pribilof Islands AK U.S.A. 148 E4
Priboj Serbia 69 H3
Price r. Australia 134 E3
Price NC U.S.A. 164 F5
Price UT U.S.A. 159 H2
Price r. UT U.S.A. 159 H2
Price Island Canada 150 D4
Prichard AL U.S.A. 161 F6
Prichard WV U.S.A. 164 D4
Pridorozhnoye Rus. Fed. see Khulkhuta
Priekule Latvia 55 L8
Priekuļi Latvia 55 N8
Priel'brus'ye, Natsional'nyy Park nat. park Rus. Fed. 53 I8
Prienai Lith. 55 M9
Prieska S. Africa 124 F5
Prievidza Slovakia 57 Q6
Prignitz reg. Germany 63 M1
Prijedor Bos.-Herz. 68 G2
Prijepolje Serbia 69 H3
Prikaspiyskaya Nizmennost' lowland Kazakh./Rus. Fed. see Caspian Lowland
Prilep Macedonia 69 I4
Priluki Ukr. see Pryluky
Přimda Czech Rep. 63 M5
Primero de Enero Cuba 163 E8
Primorsk Rus. Fed. 55 P6
Primorsk Ukr. see Prymors'k
Primorskiy Kray admin. div. Rus. Fed. 90 D3
Primorsko-Akhtarsk Rus. Fed. 53 H7
Primo Tapia Mex. 166 A1
Primrose Lake Canada 151 I4
Prims r. Germany 62 G5
Prince Albert Canada 151 J4
Prince Albert S. Africa 124 F7
Prince Albert Mountains Antarctica 188 H1
Prince Albert National Park Canada 151 J4
Prince Albert Peninsula Canada 146 G2
Prince Albert Road S. Africa 124 E7
Prince Alfred, Cape Canada 146 F2
Prince Alfred Hamlet S. Africa 124 D7
Prince Charles Island Canada 147 K3
Prince Charles Mountains Antarctica 188 E2
Prince Edward Island prov. Canada 153 J5

▶Prince Edward Islands Indian Ocean 185 K9
Part of South Africa.

Prince Edward Point Canada 165 G2
Prince Frederick MD U.S.A. 165 G4
Prince George Canada 150 F4
Prince Harald Coast Antarctica 188 D2
Prince of Wales, Cape AK U.S.A. 148 E2
Prince of Wales Island Australia 136 C1
Prince of Wales Island Canada 147 I2
Prince of Wales Island AK U.S.A. 149 N5
Prince of Wales Strait Canada 146 G2
Prince Patrick Island Canada 146 G2
Prince Regent Inlet sea chan. Canada 147 I2
Prince Rupert Canada 149 O5
Princess Anne MD U.S.A. 165 H4
Princess Astrid Coast Antarctica 188 C2
Princess Charlotte Bay Australia 136 C2
Princess Elisabeth research station Antarctica 188 C2
Princess Elizabeth Land reg. Antarctica 188 E2
Princess Mary Lake Canada 151 L1
Princess Ragnhild Coast Antarctica 188 C2
Princess Royal Island Canada 150 D4
Princeton Canada 150 F5
Princeton CA U.S.A. 158 B2
Princeton IL U.S.A. 160 F3
Princeton IN U.S.A. 164 B4
Princeton MO U.S.A. 160 E3
Princeton NJ U.S.A. 165 H3
Princeton WV U.S.A. 164 E5
Prince William Sound b. AK U.S.A. 149 K3
Príncipe i. São Tomé and Príncipe 120 D4
Prindle, Mount AK U.S.A. 149 K2
Prineville OR U.S.A. 156 C3
Prins Harald Kyst coastal area Antarctica see Prince Harald Coast
Prinzapolca Nicaragua 166 [inset] J6
Priozersk Rus. Fed. 55 Q6
Priozyorsk Rus. Fed. see Priozersk
Pripet r. Belarus/Ukr. 53 F6
also spelt Pryp"yat' (Ukraine) or Prypyats' (Belarus)
Pripet Marshes Belarus/Ukr. 53 E6
Prirechnyy Rus. Fed. 54 Q2

▶Prishtinë Kosovo 69 I3
Capital of Kosovo

Priština Kosovo see Prishtinë
Pritzier Germany 63 L1
Pritzwalk Germany 63 M1
Privas France 66 G4
Privlaka Croatia 68 F2
Privolzhsk Rus. Fed. 52 I4
Privolzhskaya Vozvyshennost' hills Rus. Fed. 53 J6
Privolzhskiy Rus. Fed. 53 J6
Privolzh'ye Rus. Fed. 53 K5
Priyutnoye Rus. Fed. 53 I7
Prizren Kosovo 69 I3
Probolinggo Jawa Indon. 85 F4
Probstzella Germany 63 L4
Probus U.K. 59 C8
Proddatur India 106 C3
Professor van Blommestein Meer resr Suriname 177 G3
Progreso Coahuila Mex. 167 E3
Progreso Hidalgo Mex. 167 F4
Progreso Yucatán Mex. 167 H4
Progress Rus. Fed. 90 C2
Project City CA U.S.A. 156 C4
Prokhladnyy Rus. Fed. 113 G2
Prokop'yevsk Rus. Fed. 88 F2
Prokuplje Serbia 69 I3
Proletarsk Rus. Fed. 53 I7
Proletarskaya Rus. Fed. see Proletarsk
Proletarskoye Vodokhranilishche l. Rus. Fed. 53 I7
Prome Myanmar see Pyè
Promissão Brazil 179 A3
Promissão, Represa resr Brazil 179 A3
Prophet r. Canada 150 F3
Prophet River Canada 150 F3
Propriá Brazil 177 K6
Proskurov Ukr. see Khmel'nyts'kyy
Prosperidad Mindanao Phil. 82 D4
Prosser WA U.S.A. 156 D3
Protem S. Africa 124 E8
Provadiya Bulg. 69 L3
Prøven Greenland see Kangersuatsiaq
Provence reg. France 66 G5
Providence KY U.S.A. 164 B5
Providence MD U.S.A. see Annapolis

▶Providence RI U.S.A. 165 J3
Capital of Rhode Island.

Providence, Cape N.Z. 139 A8
Providence, Cape AK U.S.A. 148 H4
Providencia, Isla de i. Caribbean Sea 169 H6
Provideniya Rus. Fed. 148 D2
Provincetown MA U.S.A. 165 J2
Provo UT U.S.A. 159 H1
Provost Canada 151 I4
Prudentópolis Brazil 179 A4
Prudhoe Bay AK U.S.A. 149 J1
Prudhoe Bay AK U.S.A. 149 J1
Prüm Germany 62 G4
Prüm r. Germany 62 G5
Prunelli-di-Fiumorbo Corsica France 66 I5
Pruntytown WV U.S.A. 164 E4
Prusa Turkey see Bursa
Prushkov Poland see Pruszków
Pruszków Poland 57 R4
Prut r. Europe 53 F7
Prydz Bay Antarctica 188 E2
Pryluky Ukr. 53 G6
Prymors'k Ukr. 53 H7
Prymors'ke Ukr. see Sartana
Pryp"yat' r. Belarus/Ukr. 53 F6 see Pripet
Prypyats' r. Belarus/Ukr. 51 L5 see Pripet
Przemyśl Poland 53 D6
Przheval'sk Kyrg. see Karakol
Przheval'sk Pristany Kyrg. 98 B4
Psara i. Greece 69 K5
Pskov Rus. Fed. 55 P8
Pskov, Lake Estonia/Rus. Fed. 55 O7
Pskov Oblast admin. div. Rus. Fed. see Pskovskaya Oblast'
Pskovskaya Oblast' admin. div. Rus. Fed. 55 P8
Pskovskoye Ozero l. Estonia/Rus. Fed. see Pskov, Lake
Ptolemaïda Greece 69 I4
Ptolemais Israel see 'Akko
Ptuj Slovenia 68 F1
Pu r. Indon. 84 C3
Pua Thai. 86 C3
Puaka hill Sing. 87 [inset]
Pu'an Guizhou China 96 E3
Pu'an Sichuan China 96 E2
Puan S. Korea 91 B6
Pucallpa Peru 176 D5
Pucheng Fujian China 97 H3
Pucheng Shaanxi China 95 G5
Puchezh Rus. Fed. 52 I4
Puch'ŏn S. Korea 91 B5
Pucio Point Panay Phil. 82 C4
Puck Poland 57 Q3
Pudai watercourse Afgh. see Dor
Pūdanū Iran 110 D3
Pudasjärvi Fin. 54 O4
Pudi Kalimantan Indon. 85 G3
Pudimoe S. Africa 124 G4
Pudong China 78 E4
Pudozh Rus. Fed. 52 H3
Pudsey U.K. 58 F5
Pudu China see Suizhou
Puduchcheri India see Puducherry
Puducherry India 106 C4
Puducherry union terr. India 106 C4
Pudukkottai India 106 C4
Puebla Baja California Mex. 159 F5
Puebla Puebla Mex. 168 E5
Puebla state Mex. 167 F5
Puebla de Sanabria Spain 67 C2
Puebla de Zaragoza Mex. see Puebla
Pueblo CO U.S.A. 157 G5
Pueblo Nuevo Mex. 166 D4
Pueblo Nuevo Nicaragua 166 [inset] I6
Pueblo Viejo, Laguna de lag. Mex. 167 F4
Pueblo Yaqui Mex. 166 C3
Puelches Arg. 178 C5
Puelén Arg. 178 C5
Puente de Ixtla Mex. 167 F5
Puente Genil Spain 67 D5
Pu'er China 96 D4
Puerco watercourse AZ U.S.A. 159 H4
Puerto Acosta Bol. 176 E7
Puerto Alegre Bol. 176 F6
Puerto Ángel Mex. 167 F6
Puerto Arista Mex. 167 G6
Puerto Armuelles Panama 166 [inset] J7
Puerto Ayacucho Venez. 176 E2
Puerto Bahía Negra Para. see Bahía Negra
Puerto Baquerizo Moreno Galápagos Ecuador 176 [inset]
Puerto Barrios Guat. 166 [inset] H6
Puerto Cabello Venez. 176 E1
Puerto Cabezas Nicaragua 166 [inset] J6
Puerto Cabo Gracias á Dios Nicaragua 166 [inset] J6
Puerto Carreño Col. 176 E2
Puerto Casado Para. 178 E2
Puerto Cavinas Bol. 176 E6
Puerto Coig Arg. 178 C8
Puerto Cortés Costa Rica 166 [inset] J7
Puerto Cortés Hond. 166 [inset] I6
Puerto Cortés Mex. 166 C3
Puerto de Lobos Mex. 166 B2
Puerto de Los Ángeles, Parque Natural nature res. Mex. 166 D4
Puerto de Morelos Mex. 167 I4
Puerto Escondido Mex. 168 E5
Puerto Francisco de Orellana Ecuador see Coca
Puerto Frey Bol. 176 F6
Puerto Génova Bol. 176 E6
Puerto Guarani Para. 178 E2
Puerto Heath Bol. 176 E6
Puerto Huitoto Col. 176 D3
Puerto Inírida Col. 176 E3
Puerto Isabel Bol. 177 G7
Puerto Juáres Mex. 167 I4
Puerto Leguízamo Col. 176 D4
Puerto Lempira Hond. 166 [inset] J6
Puerto Libertad Mex. 166 B2
Puerto Limón Costa Rica 166 [inset] J7
Puertollano Spain 67 D4
Puerto Lobos Arg. 178 C6
Puerto Madero Mex. 167 G6
Puerto Madryn Arg. 178 C6
Puerto Magdalena Mex. 166 B3
Puerto Maldonado Peru 176 E6
Puerto Máncora Peru 176 B4
Puerto México Mex. see Coatzacoalcos
Puerto Montt Chile 178 B6
Puerto Morazán Nicaragua 166 [inset] I6
Puerto Natales Chile 178 B8
Puerto Nuevo Col. 176 E2
Puerto Peñasco Mex. 166 B2
Puerto Pirámides Arg. 178 D6
Puerto Plata Dom. Rep. 169 J5
Puerto Portillo Peru 176 D5
Puerto Prado Peru 176 D6
Puerto Princesa Palawan Phil. 82 B4
Puerto Princesa Subterranean River National Park Phil. 82 B4
Puerto Quepos Costa Rica 166 [inset] I7
Puerto Quetzal Guat. 166 H6
Puerto Real Mex. 167 H5
Puerto Rico Arg. 178 E3
Puerto Rico Bol. 176 E6

▶Puerto Rico terr. West Indies 169 K5
United States Commonwealth.

▶Puerto Rico Trench sea feature Caribbean Sea 184 D4
Deepest trench in the Atlantic Ocean.

Puerto Sandino Nicaragua 166 [inset] I6
Puerto San José Guat. 167 H6
Puerto Santa Cruz Arg. 178 C8
Puerto Sastre Para. 178 E2
Puerto Saucedo Bol. 176 F6
Puerto Somoza Nicaragua see Puerto Sandino
Puerto Suárez Bol. 177 G7
Puerto Supe Peru 176 C6
Puerto Vallarta Mex. 168 C4
Puerto Victoria Peru 176 D5
Puerto Visser Arg. 178 C7
Puerto Yartou Chile 178 B8
Puerto Ybapobó Para. 178 E2
Pugachev Rus. Fed. 53 K5
Pugal India 104 C3
Puge China 96 D3
Puger Jawa Indon. 85 F5
Pūhāl-e Khamīr, Kūh-e mts Iran 110 D5
Puhiwaero c. N.Z. see South West Cape
Puigmal mt. France/Spain 66 F5
Pui O Wan b. H.K. China 97 [inset]
Pujada Bay Mindanao Phil. 82 D5
Puji Shaanxi China see Wugong
Puji Sichuan China see Puge
Pukaki, Lake N.Z. 139 C7
Pukapuka atoll Cook Is 133 J3
Pukaskwa National Park Canada 152 D4
Pukatawagan Canada 151 K4
Pukchin N. Korea 91 B4
Pukch'ŏng N. Korea 91 C4
Pukekohe N.Z. 139 E3
Puketeraki Range mts N.Z. 139 D6
Pukeuri Junction N.Z. 139 C7
Puksubaek-san mt. N. Korea 90 B4
Pula Croatia 68 E2
Pula Sardinia Italy 68 C5
Pulandian China 95 J4
Pulandian Wan b. China 95 J4
Pulangi r. Mindanao Phil. 82 D5
Pulangpisau Kalimantan Indon. 85 F3
Pulap atoll Micronesia 81 L5
Pulasi i. Indon. 83 B4
Pulaski NY U.S.A. 165 G2
Pulaski VA U.S.A. 164 E5
Pulaski WI U.S.A. 164 A1
Pulaukijang Sumatera Indon. 84 C3
Pulau Pinang state Malaysia see Pinang
Pulau Simeulue, Suaka Margasatwa nature res. Indon. 87 A7
Pul-e Khumrī Afgh. 111 H3
Pulheim Germany 62 G3
Pulicat Lake inlet India 106 D3
Pulivendla India 106 C3
Pulkkila Fin. 54 N4
Pullman WA U.S.A. 156 D3
Pulo Anna i. Palau 81 I6
Pulog, Mount Luzon Phil. 82 C2
Pulozero Rus. Fed. 54 R2
Púlpito, Punta pt Mex. 166 C3
Pulu China 99 C5
Pülümür Turkey 113 E3
Pulusuk atoll Micronesia 81 L5
Pulutan Sulawesi Indon. 83 C1
Puluwat atoll Micronesia 81 L5
Pulwama India 111 I3
Pumasillo, Cerro mt. Peru 176 D6
Puma Yumco l. China 99 E7
Pumiao China see Yongning
Puná, Isla i. Ecuador 176 B4
Punakha Bhutan 105 G4
Punch India 104 C2
Punchaw Canada 150 F4
Punda Maria S. Africa 125 J2
Pundri India 104 D3
Pune India 106 B2
P'ungsan N. Korea 90 C4
Puning China 97 H4
Punjab state India 104 C3
Punjab prov. Pak. 111 H4
Punmah Glacier China/Pak. 104 D2
Puno Peru 176 D7
Punta, Cerro de mt. Puerto Rico 169 K5
Punta Abreojos Mex. 157 E8
Punta Alta Arg. 178 D5
Punta Arenas Chile 178 B8
Punta Balestrieri mt. Italy 68 C4
Punta del Este Uruguay 178 F5
Punta Delgada Arg. 178 D6
Punta Gorda Belize 166 [inset] H5
Punta Gorda Nicaragua 166 [inset] J7
Punta Gorda FL U.S.A. 163 D7
Punta Norte Arg. 178 D6
Punta Prieta Mex. 166 B2
Puntarenas Costa Rica 166 [inset] I7
Puntland area Somalia 122 E3
Punuk Islands AK U.S.A. 148 E3
Punxsutawney PA U.S.A. 165 F3
Puokio Fin. 54 O4
Puolanka Fin. 54 O4
Puqi China see Chibi
Pur r. Rus. Fed. 76 I3
Puracé, Volcán de vol. Col. 176 C3
Purbalingga Jawa Indon. 85 E4
Purcell OK U.S.A. 161 D5
Purcell Mountain AK U.S.A. 148 H2

Rabnabad Islands Bangl. 105 G5
Râbniţa Moldova see Rîbniţa
Rabocheostrovsk Rus. Fed. 52 G2
Racaka China 96 B2
Raccoon Cay i. Bahamas 163 F8
Race, Cape Canada 153 L5
Raceland LA U.S.A. 167 H2
Race Point MA U.S.A. 165 J2
Rachaïya Lebanon 107 B3
Racha Noi, Ko i. Thai. 84 B1
Racha Yai, Ko i. Thai. 84 B1
Rachaya Lebanon see Rachaïya
Rachel NV U.S.A. 159 F3
Rach Gia Vietnam 87 D5
Rach Gia, Vinh b. Vietnam 87 D5
Racibórz Poland 57 Q5
Racine WI U.S.A. 164 B2
Racine WV U.S.A. 164 E4
Rădăuţi Romania 53 E7
Radcliff KY U.S.A. 164 C5
Radde Rus. Fed. 90 C2
Rádeyilíkóé Canada see Fort Good Hope
Radford VA U.S.A. 164 E5
Radili Ko Canada see Fort Good Hope
Radisson Que. Canada 152 F3
Radisson Sask. Canada 151 J4
Radlinski, Mount Antarctica 188 K1
Radnevo Bulg. 69 K3
Radom Poland 57 R5
Radom Sudan 121 F4
Radomir Bulg. 69 J3
Radomsko Poland 57 Q5
Radom National Park Sudan 121 F4
Radomysl Wielki Poland —
Radoviš Macedonia 112 A2
Radstock U.K. 59 E7
Radstock, Cape Australia 135 F8
Raduň' Belarus 55 N9
Radviliškis Lith. 55 M9
Radyvyliv Ukr. 53 E6
Rae Bareli India 104 E4
Raecreek r. Canada 149 M2
Rae-Edzo Canada see Behchokò
Rae Lakes Canada see Gamêtì
Raeside, Lake salt flat Australia 135 C7
Raetihi N.Z. 139 E4
Rāf hill Saudi Arabia 113 E5
Rafaela Arg. 178 D4
Rafaḥ Gaza see Rafiah
Rafaï Cent. Afr. Rep. 122 C3
Rafḥā' Saudi Arabia 113 F5
Rafiah Gaza 107 B4
Rafsanjān Iran 110 D4
Raft r. ID/NV U.S.A. 156 E4
Raga South Sudan 121 F4
Ragang, Mount vol. Mindanao Phil. 82 D5
Ragay Gulf Luzon Phil. 82 C3
Rägelin Germany 63 M1
Ragged, Mount hill Australia 135 C8
Ragged Island Bahamas 163 F8
Rägh Afgh. 111 H2
Rago Nasjonalpark nat. park Norway 54 J3
Ragösen Germany 63 M2
Ragueneau Canada 153 H4
Raguhn Germany 63 M3
Ragusa Croatia see Dubrovnik
Ragusa Sicily Italy 68 F6
Ragxi China 99 F7
Ra'gya China 94 E1
Raha Sulawesi Indon. 83 B4
Rahachow Belarus 53 F5
Rahad r. Sudan 108 D7
Rahaeng Thai. see Tak
Rahden Germany 63 I2
Rahimyar Khan Pak. 111 H4
Rahovec Kosovo 69 I3
Rahuri India 106 B2
Rai, Hon i. Vietnam 87 D5
Raiatea i. Fr. Polynesia 187 J7
Raibu i. Indon. see Air
Raichur India 106 C2
Raiganj India 105 G4
Raigarh Chhattisgarh India 105 E5
Raigarh Chhattisgarh India 106 D2
Raijua i. Indon. 83 B5
Railroad City AK U.S.A. 148 H3
Railroad Pass NV U.S.A. 158 E2
Railroad Valley NV U.S.A. 159 F2
Raimangal r. Bangl. 105 G5
Raimbault, Lac l. Canada 153 H3
Rainbow Lake Canada 150 G3
Raine Island Australia 136 D1
Rainelle WV U.S.A. 164 E4
Raini r. Pak. 111 H4
Rainier, Mount vol. WA U.S.A. 156 C3
Rainis Sulawesi Indon. 83 C1
Rainy r. Canada/U.S.A. 155 I2
Rainy Lake Canada/U.S.A. 155 I2
Rainy River Canada 155 I2
Raipur Chhattisgarh India 105 E5
Raipur W. Bengal India 105 F5
Raisen India 104 D5
Raisio Fin. 55 M6
Raismes France 62 D4
Raitalai India 104 C5
Raivavae i. Fr. Polynesia 187 K7
Raiwind Pak. 111 I4
Raja i. Indon. 85 E4
Raja, Ujung pt Indon. 84 B2
Rajaampat, Kepulauan is Papua Indon. 83 D3
Rajabasa, Gunung vol. Indon. 84 D4
Rajahmundry India 106 D2
Raja-Jooseppi Fin. 54 P2
Rajang Sarawak Malaysia 85 E2
Rajang r. Malaysia 85 E2
Rajanpur Pak. 111 H4
Rajapalayam India 106 C4
Rajapur India 106 B2
Rajasthan state India 104 C4
Rajasthan Canal India see Indira Gandhi Canal
Rajauri India see Rajouri
Rajbiraj Nepal 105 F4
Rajevadi India 106 B2
Rajgarh India 104 D4
Rājijovsset Fin. see Raja-Jooseppi
Rajik Indon. 84 D3
Rajkot India 104 B5
Raj Mahal India 104 C4
Rajmahal Hills India 105 F4
Raj Nandgaon India 104 E5
Rajouri India 104 C2
Rajpipla India 104 C5
Rajpur India 104 C5
Rajpura India 104 D3

Rajputana Agency state India see Rajasthan
Rajsamand India 104 C4
Rajshahi Bangl. 105 G4
Rājū Syria 107 C1
Rajula India 106 A1
Rajura India 106 C1
Raka China 99 D7
Raka Zangbo r. China see Dogxung Zangbo
Rakhiv Ukr. 53 E6
Rakhni Pak. 111 H4
Rakhni r. Pak. 111 H4
Rakhshan r. Pak. 111 F5
Rakit i. Indon. 85 E4
Rakit i. Indon. 85 E4
Rakitnoye Belgorodskaya Oblast' Rus. Fed. 53 G6
Rakitnoye Primorskiy Kray Rus. Fed. 90 D3
Rakiura i. N.Z. see Stewart Island
Rakiura National Park N.Z. 139 A8
Rakke Estonia 55 O7
Rakkestad Norway 55 G7
Rakmanovskie Klyuchi Kazakh. 98 D2
Rakovski Bulg. 69 K3
Rakushechnyy, Mys pt Kazakh. 113 H2
Rakvere Estonia 55 O7
▶Raleigh NC U.S.A. 162 E5
Capital of North Carolina.
Ralla Sulawesi Indon. 83 A4
Ralston PA U.S.A. 165 G3
Ram r. Canada 150 F2
Rama Nicaragua 166 [inset] I6
Ramādī Iraq 113 F4
Ramagiri India 106 E2
Ramah NM U.S.A. 159 I4
Ramalho, Serra do hills Brazil 179 B1
Rāmallāh West Bank 107 B4
Ramanagaram India 106 C3
Ramanathapuram India 106 C4
Ramapo Deep sea feature N. Pacific Ocean 186 F3
Ramapur India 106 D1
Ramas, Cape India 106 B3
Ramatlabama S. Africa 125 G3
Rambhapur India 104 C5
Rambouillet France 62 B6
Rambutyo Island P.N.G. 81 L7
Ramciel South Sudan 121 G4
Rame Head hd Australia 138 D6
Rame Head hd U.K. 59 C8
Rameshki Rus. Fed. 52 H4
Ramezān Kalak Iran 111 F5
Ramganga r. India 99 B8
Ramgarh Jharkhand India 105 F5
Ramgarh Rajasthan India 104 B4
Ramgarh Rajasthan India 104 C3
Rāmhormoz Iran 110 C4
Ramingining Australia 134 F3
Ramitan Uzbek. see Romiton
Ramla Israel 107 B4
Ramlat Rabyānah des. Libya see Rebiana Sand Sea
Ramm, Jabal mts Jordan 107 B5
Ramnad India see Ramanathapuram
Râmnicu Sărat Romania 69 L2
Râmnicu Vâlcea Romania 69 K2
Ramon' Rus. Fed. 53 H6
Ramona CA U.S.A. 158 E5
Ramos r. Mex. 161 B7
Ramos Arizpe Mex. 167 E3
Ramotswa Botswana 125 G3
Rampart AK U.S.A. 149 J2
Rampart of Genghis Khan tourist site Asia 95 H1
Ramparts r. Canada 149 O2
Rampur Hima. Prad. India 99 B7
Rampur Uttar Prad. India 99 B7
Rampur Uttar Prad. India 104 D3
Rampur Boalia Bangl. see Rajshahi
Ramree Myanmar 86 A3
Ramree Island Myanmar 86 A3
Rāmsar Iran 110 C2
Ramsele Sweden 54 J5
Ramsey Isle of Man 58 C4
Ramsey U.K. 59 G6
Ramsey NJ U.S.A. 165 H3
Ramsey Bay Isle of Man 58 C4
Ramsey Island U.K. 59 B7
Ramsey Lake Canada 152 E5
Ramsgate U.K. 59 I7
Rāmshīr Iran 110 C4
Ramu Bangl. 105 H5
Ramusio, Lac l. Canada 153 J3
Ramygala Lith. 55 N9
Ranaghat India 105 G5
Ranai i. HI U.S.A. see Lāna'i
Rana Pratap Sagar resr India 104 C4
Ranapur India 104 C5
Ranasar India 104 B4
Ranau Sabah Malaysia 85 G1
Ranau, Danau l. Indon. 84 C4
Rancagua Chile 178 B4
Rancheria Brazil 179 A3
Rancheria Canada 149 O3
Rancheria r. Canada 149 O3
Ranchi India 105 F5
Rancho Grande Mex. 166 D4
Ranco, Lago l. Chile 178 B6
Rand Australia 138 C5
Randalstown U.K. 61 F3
Randazzo Sicily Italy 68 F6
Randers Denmark 55 G8
Randijaure l. Sweden 54 K3
Randolph ME U.S.A. 165 K1
Randolph UT U.S.A. 156 F4
Randolph VT U.S.A. 165 I2
Randsjö Sweden 54 H5
Râned Sweden 54 M4
Ranérou Senegal 120 B3
Ranfurly N.Z. 139 C7
Ranga r. India 99 F8
Rangae Thai. 87 C6
Rangamati Bangl. 105 H5
Rangapara India 105 H4
Rangas, Tanjung pt Indon. 83 A3
Rangasa, Tanjung pt Indon. 83 A3
Rangeley Lake ME U.S.A. 165 J1
Rangely CO U.S.A. 159 I1
Ranger Lake Canada 152 E5

Rangiora N.Z. 139 D6
Rangitata r. N.Z. 139 C7
Rangitikei r. N.Z. 139 E5
Rangkasbitung Jawa Indon. 84 D4
Rangke China see Zamtang
Rangkūl Tajik. 111 I2
Rangôn Myanmar see Rangoon
▶Rangoon Myanmar 86 B3
Joint capital (with Nay Pyi Taw) of Myanmar.
Rangoon r. Myanmar 86 B3
Rangpur Bangl. 105 G4
Rangsang i. Indon. 84 C2
Rangse Myanmar 86 A1
Ranibennur India 106 B3
Raniganj India 105 F5
Ranipur Pak. 111 H5
Rānsa Iran 110 C3
Ransby Sweden 55 H6
Rantasalmi Fin. 54 P5
Rantau Kalimantan Indon. 85 F3
Rantau i. Indon. 84 C2
Rantaukampar Sumatera Indon. 84 C2
Rantaupanjang Kalimantan Indon. 85 F3
Rantaupanjang Kalimantan Indon. 85 F3
Rantauprapat Sumatera Indon. 84 B2
Rantaupulut Kalimantan Indon. 85 F3
Rantemario, Gunung mt. Indon. 83 B3
Rantepao Sulawesi Indon. 83 A3
Rantoul IL U.S.A. 164 A3
Rantsila Fin. 54 N4
Ranua Fin. 54 O4
Ŗāņya Iraq 113 G3
Ranyah, Wādī watercourse Saudi Arabia 108 F5
Rao Go mt. Laos/Vietnam 86 D3
Raohe China 90 D3
Raoui, Erg er des. Alg. 64 D6
Raoul Island Kermadec Is 133 I4
Rapa i. Fr. Polynesia 187 K7
Rapa-iti i. Fr. Polynesia see Rapa
Rapallo Italy 68 C2
Rapar India 104 B5
Raphoe Ireland 61 E3
Rapidan r. VA U.S.A. 165 G4
Rapid City SD U.S.A. 160 C2
Rapid River MI U.S.A. 162 C2
Rapla Estonia 55 N7
Rappang Sulawesi Indon. 83 A3
Rapti r. India 99 C8
Rapur Andhra Prad. India 106 C3
Rapur Gujarat India 104 B5
Rapurapu i. Phil. 82 D3
Raqqa Syria see Ar Raqqah
Raquette Lake NY U.S.A. 165 H2
Rara National Park Nepal 105 E3
Raritan Bay NJ U.S.A. 165 H3
Rarkan Pak. 111 H4
Raroia atoll Fr. Polynesia 187 K7
Rarotonga i. Cook Is 187 J7
Ras India 104 C4
Rasa i. Phil. 82 B4
Rasa, Punta pt Arg. 178 D6
Ra's ad Daqm Oman 109 I6
Ra's al Ḥikmah Egypt 112 B5
Ras al Khaimah U.A.E. see Ra's al Khaymah
Ra's al Khaymah U.A.E. 110 D5
Ra's an Naqb Jordan 107 B4
Ras Dashen mt. Eth. see Ras Dejen
▶Ras Dejen mt. Eth. 122 D2
5th highest mountain in Africa.
Raseiniai Lith. 55 M9
Rās el Hikma Egypt see Ra's al Ḥikmah
Ra's Ghārib Egypt 112 D5
Rashaant Bayan-Ölgiy Mongolia see Delüün
Rashaant Dundgovĭ Mongolia see Öldziyt
Rashad Sudan 108 D7
Rashid Egypt see Rashid
Rashid Egypt 112 C5
Rasht Iran 110 C2
Raskam mts China 99 A5
Ras Koh mt. Pak. 111 G4
Raskoh mts Pak. 111 G4
Raso, Cabo c. Arg. 178 C6
Rason Lake salt flat Australia 135 D7
Rasony Belarus 55 P9
Rasra India 105 E4
Rasshua, Ostrov i. Rus. Fed. 89 S3
Rass Jebel Tunisia 68 D6
Rasskazovo Rus. Fed. 53 I5
Rastatt Germany 63 I6
Rastede Germany 63 I1
Rastow Germany 63 L1
Rasūl watercourse Iran 110 D5
Rasul Pak. 111 I3
Ratae U.K. see Leicester
Ratai, Gunung mt. Indon. 84 D4
Ratangarh India 104 C3
Ratanda S. Africa 125 I4
Rātānsbyn Sweden 54 I5
Rat Buri Thai. 87 B4
Rathangan Ireland 61 F4
Rathbun Lake IA U.S.A. 160 E3
Rathdowney Ireland 61 E5
Rathdrum Ireland 61 F5
Rathedaung Myanmar 86 A2
Rathenow Germany 63 M2
Rathfriland U.K. 61 F3
Rathkeale Ireland 61 D5
Rathlin Island U.K. 61 F2
Ratibor Poland see Racibórz
Ratingen Germany 62 G3
Ratisbon Germany see Regensburg
Rat Islands AK U.S.A. 148 [inset] B6
Ratiya India 104 C3
Rat Lake Canada 151 L3
Ratlam India 104 C5
Ratmanova, Ostrov i. Rus. Fed. 148 E2

Ratnagiri India 106 B2
Ratnapura Sri Lanka 106 D5
Ratne Ukr. 53 E6
Ratno Ukr. see Ratne
Raton NM U.S.A. 157 G5
Rattray Head hd U.K. 60 H3
Rättvik Sweden 55 I6
Ratz, Mount Canada 149 N4
Ratzeburg Germany 63 K1
Rau i. Maluku Indon. 83 D2
Raub Malaysia 84 C2
Rauch Arg. 178 E5
Rauðamýri Iceland 54 [inset 1]
Raudhatain Kuwait 110 B4
Rauenstein Germany 63 L4
Raufarhöfn Iceland 54 [inset 1]
Raukumara Range mts N.Z. 139 F4
Rauma Fin. 55 L6
Raupelyan Rus. Fed. 148 E2
Raurkela India 105 F5
Rauschen Rus. Fed. see Svetlogorsk
Rausu Japan 90 G3
Rautavaara Fin. 54 P5
Rautjärvi Fin. 55 P6
Rāvar Iran 110 E4
Ravat Kyrg. 111 H2
Ravels Belgium 62 E3
Ravena NY U.S.A. 165 I2
Ravenna Italy see Ravenna
Ravenna Italy 68 E2
Ravenna NE U.S.A. 160 D3
Ravenna OH U.S.A. 164 E3
Ravensburg Germany 57 L7
Ravenshoe Australia 136 D3
Ravensthorpe Australia 135 C8
Ravenswood Australia 136 D4
Ravi r. Pak. 111 H4
Ravnina Turkm. see Rawnina
Rawa Aopa Watumohai, Taman Nasional nat. park Indon. 83 B4
Rāwah Iraq 113 F4
Rawaki i. Kiribati 133 I2
Rawalpindi Pak. 111 I3
Rawalpindi Lake Canada 150 H1
Rāwāndiz Iraq 113 G3
Rawas r. Indon. 84 C3
Rawi, Ko i. Thai. 87 B6
Rawicz Poland 57 P5
Rawlinna Australia 135 D7
Rawlins WY U.S.A. 156 G4
Rawlinson Range hills Australia 135 E6
Rawnina Mary Turkm. 111 F2
Rawnina Mary Turkm. 111 F2
Rawson Arg. 178 C6
Rawu China 99 D7
Raxón, Cerro mt. Guat. 168 G5
Ray, Cape Canada 153 K5
Raya, Bukit mt. Kalimantan Barat Indon. 85 F3
Rayachoti India 106 C3
Rayadurg India 106 C3
Rayagada India 106 D2
Rayagarha India see Rayagada
Rayak Lebanon 107 C3
Raychikhinsk Rus. Fed. 90 C2
Raydah Yemen 108 F6
Rayes Peak CA U.S.A. 158 D4
Rayevskiy Rus. Fed. 51 Q5
Raygay Afgh. 111 H4
Rayleigh U.K. 59 H7
Raymond NH U.S.A. 165 J2
Raymond Terrace Australia 138 E4
Raymondville TX U.S.A. 161 D7
Raymore Canada 151 J5
Ray Mountains AK U.S.A. 148 I2
Rayner Glacier Antarctica 188 D2
Rayones Mex. 167 E3
Rayong Thai. 87 C4
Raystown Lake PA U.S.A. 165 F3
Rayū China 99 F7
Raz, Pointe du pt France 66 B2
Razan Iran 110 C3
Rāzān Iran 110 C3
Razani Pak. 111 H3
Razāzah, Buḩayrat ar l. Iraq 113 F4
Razdan Armenia see Hrazdan
Razdel'naya Ukr. see Rozdil'na
Razdol'noye Rus. Fed. 90 C4
Razeh Iran 110 C3
Razgrad Bulg. 69 L3
Razhēng Zangbo r. China 99 D7
Razim, Lacul lag. Romania 69 M2
Razisi China 96 D1
Razlog Bulg. 69 J4
Razmak Pak. 111 H3
Raz"yezd 3km Rus. Fed. see Novyy Urgal
Ré, Île de i. France 66 D3
Reading U.K. 59 G7
Reading MI U.S.A. 164 C3
Reading OH U.S.A. 164 C4
Reading PA U.S.A. 165 H3
Reagile S. Africa 125 H3
Realicó Arg. 178 D5
Réalmont France 66 F5
Reäng Kesei Cambodia 87 C4
Reata Mex. 167 E3
Reate Italy see Rieti
Rebais France 62 D6
Rebecca, Lake salt flat Australia 135 C7
Rebiana Sand Sea des. Libya 121 F2
Reboly Rus. Fed. 54 Q5
Rebrikha Rus. Fed. 88 E2
Rebun-tō i. Japan 90 F3
Recherche, Archipelago of the is Australia 135 C8
Rechitsa Belarus see Rechytsa
Rechna Doab lowland Pak. 111 I4
Rechytsa Belarus 53 F5
Recife Brazil 177 L5
Recife, Cape S. Africa 125 G8
Recklinghausen Germany 63 H3
Reconquista Arg. 178 E3
Recreo Arg. 178 C3
Rectorville KY U.S.A. 164 D4
Red r. Australia 136 C3
Red r. Canada 150 C3
Red r. Canada/U.S.A. 160 D1
Red r. LA U.S.A. 161 F6
Red r. TN U.S.A. 164 B5
Red r. Vietnam 86 D2
Redang i. Malaysia 84 C1
Red Bank NJ U.S.A. 165 H3
Red Bank TN U.S.A. 163 C5
Red Basin China see Sichuan Pendi
Red Bay Canada 153 K4

Redberry Lake Canada 151 J4
Red Bluff CA U.S.A. 158 B1
Red Bluff Lake TX U.S.A. 161 C6
Red Butte mt. AZ U.S.A. 159 G4
Redcar U.K. 58 F4
Redcliff Canada 156 F2
Redcliffe, Mount hill Australia 135 C7
Red Cliffs Australia 137 C7
Red Cloud NE U.S.A. 160 D3
Red Deer Canada 150 H4
Red Deer r. Alba/Sask. Canada 151 I5
Red Deer r. Man./Sask. Canada 151 K4
Red Deer Lake Canada 151 K4
Reddersburg S. Africa 125 H5
Red Devil AK U.S.A. 148 I3
Redding CA U.S.A. 158 B1
Redditch U.K. 59 F6
Rede r. U.K. 58 E3
Redenção Brazil 177 H5
Redeyef Tunisia 68 C7
Redfield SD U.S.A. 160 D2
Red Granite Mountain Canada 149 M3
Red Hills KS U.S.A. 161 D4
Red Hook NY U.S.A. 165 I3
Red Idol Gorge China 99 E7
Red Indian Lake Canada 153 K4
Redkey IN U.S.A. 164 C3
Redkino Rus. Fed. 52 H4
Red Lake AZ U.S.A. 159 G4
Red Lake Canada 151 M5
Red Lake r. MN U.S.A. 160 D2
Red Lake Falls MN U.S.A. 151 L6
Red Lakes MN U.S.A. 160 E1
Redlands CA U.S.A. 158 E4
Red Lion PA U.S.A. 165 G4
Red Lodge MT U.S.A. 156 F3
Redmesa CO U.S.A. 159 I3
Redmond OR U.S.A. 156 C3
Redmond UT U.S.A. 159 H2
Red Oak IA U.S.A. 160 E3
Redonda Island Canada 150 E5
Redondo Port. 67 C4
Redondo Beach CA U.S.A. 158 D5
Redoubt Volcano AK U.S.A. 148 I3
Red Peak MT U.S.A. 156 F3
Red River, Mouths of the Vietnam 86 D2
Red Rock Canada 152 C4
Red Rock AZ U.S.A. 159 H5
Red Rock PA U.S.A. 165 G3
Redrock NM U.S.A. 159 I5
Red Rock r. MT U.S.A. 156 E3
Redrock Lake Canada 150 H1
Red Sea Africa/Asia 108 D3
Redstone r. Canada 149 P2
Red Sucker Lake Canada 151 M4
Reduzum Neth. 62 F1
Redwater Canada 150 H4
Redway CA U.S.A. 158 B1
Red Wing MN U.S.A. 160 E2
Redwood City CA U.S.A. 158 B3
Redwood Falls MN U.S.A. 160 E2
Redwood National Park CA U.S.A. 156 B4
Redwood Valley CA U.S.A. 158 B2
Ree, Lough l. Ireland 61 E4
Reed KY U.S.A. 164 B5
Reed City MI U.S.A. 164 C2
Reedley CA U.S.A. 158 D3
Reedsport OR U.S.A. 156 B4
Reedsville OH U.S.A. 164 E4
Reedville VA U.S.A. 165 G5
Reedy WV U.S.A. 164 E4
Reedy Glacier Antarctica 188 J1
Reefton N.Z. 139 C6
Rees Germany 62 G3
Reese MI U.S.A. 164 D2
Reese r. NV U.S.A. 158 E1
Refahiye Turkey 112 E3
Refugio TX U.S.A. 161 D6
Regen Germany 63 N6
Regen r. Germany 63 M5
Regência Brazil 179 D2
Regensburg Germany 63 M5
Regenstauf Germany 63 M5
Reggane Alg. 120 D2
Reggio Calabria Italy see Reggio di Calabria
Reggio Emilia-Romagna Italy see Reggio nell'Emilia
Reggio di Calabria Italy 68 F5
Reggio nell'Emilia Italy 68 D2
Reghin Romania 69 K1
▶Regina Canada 151 J5
Capital of Saskatchewan.
Régina Fr. Guiana 177 H3
Registān reg. Afgh. 111 G4
Registro Brazil 178 C3
Registro do Araguaia Brazil 179 A1
Regium Lepidum Italy see Reggio nell'Emilia
Regozero Rus. Fed. 54 Q4
Rehau Germany 63 M4
Rehburg (Rehburg-Loccum) Germany 63 J2
Rehli India 104 D5
Rehoboth Namibia 124 C2
Rehoboth Bay DE U.S.A. 165 H4
Rehovot Israel 107 B4
Reibell Alg. see Ksar Chellala
Reibitz Germany 63 M3
Reichenbach Germany 63 M4
Reichshoffen France 63 H6
Reid Australia 135 E7
Reidh, Rubha a' pt U.K. 60 D3
Reidsville NC U.S.A. 162 E4
Reigate U.K. 59 G7
Reiley Peak AZ U.S.A. 159 H5
Reims France 62 E5
Reinbek Germany 63 K1
Reindeer r. Canada 151 K4
Reindeer Grazing Reserve nature res. Canada 149 O1
Reindeer Island Canada 151 L4
Reindeer Lake Canada 151 K3
Reine Norway 54 H3
Reinosa Spain 67 D2
Reinsfeld Germany 62 G5
Reinøya i. Norway 54 L2
Reisa Nasjonalpark nat. park Norway 54 M2
Reisjärvi Fin. 54 N5
Reitz S. Africa 125 I4
Reivilo S. Africa 124 G5
Rekapalle India 106 D2
Reken Germany 62 H3
Reliance Canada 151 I2

Relizane Alg. 67 G6
Rellano Mex. 166 D3
Rellingen Germany 63 J1
Remagen Germany 63 H4
Remarkable, Mount hill Australia 137 B7
Rembang Jawa Indon. 85 E4
Remedios Cuba 163 E8
Remedios, Punta pt El Salvador 167 H6
Remeshk Iran 110 E5
Remhoogte Pass Namibia 124 C2
Remi France see Reims
Remmel Mountain WA U.S.A. 156 C2
Rempang i. Indon. 84 D2
Remscheid Germany 63 H3
Rena Norway 55 G6
Renaix Belgium see Ronse
Renam Myanmar 96 C3
Renapur India 106 C2
Renchinlhümbe Mongolia 94 D1
Rendsburg Germany 57 L3
René-Levasseur, Île l. Canada 153 H4
Renews Canada 153 L5
Renfrew Canada 165 G1
Renfrew U.K. 60 E5
Rengali Reservoir India 105 F5
Rengat Sumatera Indon. 84 C3
Rengo Chile 178 B4
Ren He r. China 97 F1
Renheji China 97 G2
Renhou China see Tangxian
Renhua China 97 G3
Reni Ukr. 69 M2
Renick WV U.S.A. 164 E5
Renland reg. Greenland see Tuttut Nunaat
Rennell i. Solomon Is 133 G3
Rennerod Germany 63 I4
Rennes France 66 D2
Rennick Glacier Antarctica 188 H2
Rennie Canada 151 M5
Reno r. Italy 68 E2
Reno NV U.S.A. 158 D2
Renovo PA U.S.A. 165 G3
Renqiu China 95 I4
Rensselaer IN U.S.A. 164 B3
Renswoude Neth. 62 F2
Renton WA U.S.A. 156 C3
Réo Burkina Faso 120 C3
Reo Flores Indon. 83 B5
Repalle India 106 D2
Repetek Turkm. 111 F2
Repetek Döwlet Gorugy nature res. Turkm. 111 F2
Repolka Rus. Fed. 55 P7
Republic WA U.S.A. 156 D2
Republican r. NE U.S.A. 160 D4
▶Republic of South Africa country Africa 124 F5
5th most populous country in Africa.
Repulse Bay b. Australia 136 E4
Repulse Bay Canada 147 J3
Requena Peru 176 D5
Requena Spain 67 F4
Reşadiye Turkey 112 E2
Resag, Gunung mt. Indon. 84 D4
Reserva Brazil 179 A4
Reserve NM U.S.A. 159 I5
Reshi China 97 F2
Reshm Iran 110 D3
Reshteh-ye Alborz mts Iran see Elburz Mountains
Reshui China 94 E4
Resistencia Arg. 178 E3
Reşiţa Romania 69 I2
Resolute Canada 147 I2
Resolute Bay Canada see Resolute
Resolution Island Canada 147 L3
Resolution Island N.Z. 139 A7
Resplendor Brazil 179 C2
Restigouche r. Canada 153 I5
Resülayn Turkey see Ceylanpınar
Retalhuleu Guat. 167 H6
Retezat, Parcul Naţional nat. park Romania 69 J2
Retford U.K. 58 G5
Rethel France 62 E5
Rethem (Aller) Germany 63 J2
Réthimnon Greece see Rethymno
Rethymno Greece 69 K7
Retreat Australia 136 C5
Reuden Germany 63 M2
▶Réunion terr. Indian Ocean 185 L7
French Overseas Department.
Reus Spain 67 G3
Reusam, Pulau i. Indon. 84 B2
Reutlingen Germany 57 L6
Reval Estonia see Tallinn
Revda Rus. Fed. 54 S3
Revel Estonia see Tallinn
Revel France 66 E5
Revelstoke Canada 150 G5
Revigny-sur-Ornain France 62 E6
Revillagigedo, Islas is Mex. 166 B5
Revillagigedo Island AK U.S.A. 149 O5
Revin France 62 E5
Revivim Israel 107 B4
Revolyutsii, Pik mt. Tajik. see Revolyutsiya, Qullai
Revolyutsiya, Qullai mt. Tajik. 111 I2
Rewa India 104 E4
Rewari India 104 D3
Rex AK U.S.A. 149 J2
Rexburg ID U.S.A. 156 F4
Rexton Canada 153 I5
Rey, Isla del i. Panama 166 [inset] K7
Reyes, Point CA U.S.A. 158 B2
Reyhanlı Turkey 107 C1
Reykir Iceland 54 [inset 1]
Reykjanes Ridge sea feature N. Atlantic Ocean 184 F2
Reykjanestá pt Iceland 54 [inset 1]
▶Reykjavík Iceland 54 [inset 1]
Capital of Iceland.
Reyneke, Ostrov i. Rus. Fed. 90 E1
Reynoldsburg OH U.S.A. 164 D4
Reynolds Range mts Australia 134 F5
Reynosa Mex. 167 E3
Rezā Iran 110 D3
Rezā'īyeh Iran see Urmia

S

St John, Cape Canada 153 L4
St John Bay Canada 153 K4
St John Island Canada 153 K4

▶St John's Antigua and Barbuda 169 L5
Capital of Antigua and Barbuda.

▶St John's Canada 153 L5
Capital of Newfoundland and Labrador.

St Johns AZ U.S.A. 159 I4
St Johns MI U.S.A. 164 C2
St Johns OH U.S.A. 164 C3
St Johns r. FL U.S.A. 163 D6
St Johnsbury VT U.S.A. 165 I1
St John's Chapel U.K. 58 E4
St Joseph IL U.S.A. 164 A3
St Joseph LA U.S.A. 161 F6
St Joseph MI U.S.A. 164 B2
St Joseph MO U.S.A. 160 E4
St Joseph r. MI U.S.A. 164 C3
St Joseph, Lake Canada 151 N5
St-Joseph-d'Alma Canada see Alma
St Joseph Island Canada 152 E5
St Joseph Island TX U.S.A. 167 F3
St-Junien France 66 E4
St Just U.K. 59 B8
St-Just-en-Chaussée France 62 C5
St Keverne U.K. 59 B8
St Kilda i. U.K. 50 E4
St Kilda is U.K. 56 C2
St Kitts and Nevis country West Indies 169 L5
St-Laurent inlet Canada see St Lawrence
St-Laurent, Golfe du g. Canada see St Lawrence, Gulf of
St-Laurent-du-Maroni Fr. Guiana 177 H2
St Lawrence Canada 153 L5
St Lawrence inlet Canada 153 H4
St Lawrence, Cape Canada 153 J5
St Lawrence, Gulf of Canada 153 J4
St Lawrence Island AK U.S.A. 148 E3
St Lawrence Islands National Park Canada 165 H1
St Lawrence Seaway sea chan. Canada/U.S.A. 165 H1
St-Léonard Canada 153 G5
St Leonard MD U.S.A. 165 G4
St Lewis r. Canada 153 K3
St-Lô France 66 D2
St-Louis Senegal 120 B3
St Louis MI U.S.A. 164 C2
St Louis MO U.S.A. 160 F4
St Louis r. MN U.S.A. 152 B5
St Lucia country West Indies 169 L6
St Lucia, Lake S. Africa 125 K5
St Lucia Estuary S. Africa 125 K5
St Luke's Island Myanmar see Zadetkale Kyun
St Magnus Bay U.K. 60 [inset]
St-Maixent-l'École France 66 D3
St-Malo France 66 C2
St-Malo, Golfe de g. France 66 C2
St-Marc Haiti 169 J5
St Maries ID U.S.A. 156 D3
St Marks S. Africa 125 H7
St Mark's S. Africa see Cofimvaba

▶St-Martin i. West Indies 169 L5
French Overseas Collectivity. The southern part of the island is the Dutch territory of Sint Maarten.

St-Martin terr. West Indies see Sint Maarten
St Martin, Cape S. Africa 124 C7
St Martin, Lake Canada 151 L5
St Martin's i. U.K. 59 A9
St Martin's Island Bangl. 86 A2
St Mary Peak Australia 137 B6
St Mary Reservoir Canada 150 H5
St Mary's Canada 164 E2
St Mary's U.K. 60 G2
St Mary's i. U.K. 59 A9
St Marys AK U.S.A. 148 G3
St Marys PA U.S.A. 165 F3
St Marys WV U.S.A. 164 E4
St Marys r. OH U.S.A. 164 C3
St Mary's, Cape Canada 153 L5
St Mary's Bay Canada 153 L5
St Marys City MD U.S.A. 165 G4
St Matthew Island AK U.S.A. 148 D3
St Matthews KY U.S.A. 164 C4
St Matthew's Island Myanmar see Zadetkyi Kyun
St Matthias Group is P.N.G. 81 L7
St-Maurice r. Canada 153 G5
St Mawes U.K. 59 B8
St-Médard-en-Jalles France 66 D4
St Meinrad IN U.S.A. 164 B4
St Michael AK U.S.A. 148 G3
St Michaels MD U.S.A. 165 G4
St Michael's Bay Canada 153 L3
St-Mihiel France 62 F6
St-Nazaire France 66 C3
St Neots U.K. 59 G6
St-Nicolas Belgium see Sint-Niklaas
St-Nicolas, Mont hill Lux. 62 G5
St-Nicolas-de-Port France 66 H2
St-Omer France 62 C4
Saintonge reg. France 66 D4
St-Pacôme Canada 153 H5
St-Palais France 66 D5
St Paris OH U.S.A. 164 D3
St-Pascal Canada 153 H5
St Paul r. Canada 153 K4
St-Paul atoll Fr. Polynesia see Héréhérétué
St Paul AK U.S.A. 148 E4

▶St Paul MN U.S.A. 160 E2
Capital of Minnesota.

St Paul NE U.S.A. 160 D3
St-Paul, Île i. Indian Ocean 185 N8
St Paul Island AK U.S.A. 148 E4
St Peter and St Paul Rocks is N. Atlantic Ocean see São Pedro e São Paulo

▶St Peter Port Channel Is 59 E9
Capital of Guernsey.

St Peter's N.S. Canada 153 J5
St Peters P.E.I. Canada 153 J5
St Petersburg Rus. Fed. 55 Q7
St Petersburg FL U.S.A. 163 D7
St-Pierre mt. France 66 G5

▶St-Pierre St Pierre and Miquelon 153 L5
Capital of St Pierre and Miquelon.

▶St Pierre and Miquelon terr. N. America 153 K5
French Territorial Collectivity.

St-Pierre-d'Oléron France 66 D4
St-Pierre-le-Moûtier France 66 F3
St-Pol-sur-Ternoise France 62 C4
St-Pourçain-sur-Sioule France 66 F3
St-Quentin France 62 D5
St Regis MT U.S.A. 156 E3
St Regis Falls NY U.S.A. 165 H1
St-Rémi Canada 165 I1
St-Saëns France 62 B5
St Sebastian Bay S. Africa 124 E8
St-Siméon Canada 153 H5
St Simons Island GA U.S.A. 163 D6
St Theresa Point Canada 151 M4
St Thomas Canada 164 E2
St-Trond Belgium see Sint-Truiden
St-Tropez France 66 H5
St-Tropez, Cap de c. France 66 H5
St-Vaast-la-Hougue France 59 F9
St-Valery-en-Caux France 59 H9
St-Véran France 66 H4
St Vincent MN U.S.A. 160 D1
St Vincent country West Indies see St Vincent and the Grenadines
St Vincent, Cape Australia 137 [inset]
St Vincent, Cape Port. see São Vicente, Cabo de
St Vincent, Gulf Australia 137 B7
St Vincent and the Grenadines country West Indies 169 L6
St Vincent Passage St Lucia/St Vincent 169 L6
St-Vith Belgium 62 G4
St Walburg Canada 151 I4
St Williams Canada 164 E2
St-Yrieix-la-Perche France 66 E4
Sain Us China 95 F3
Saioa mt. Spain 67 F2
Saipal mt. Nepal 104 E3
Saipan i. N. Mariana Is 81 L3
Saipan Palau 82 [inset]
Sai Pok Liu Hoi Hap H.K. China see West Lamma Channel
Saitama pref. Japan 93 E3
Saiteli Turkey see Kadınhanı
Saitlai Myanmar 86 A2
Saittanulkki hill Fin. 54 N3
Sai Yok National Park Thai. 87 B4
Sajam Indon. 81 I7
Sajama, Nevado mt. Bol. 176 E7
Sājir Saudi Arabia 110 B5
Sājūr, Nahr r. Syria/Turkey 107 D1
Sak watercourse S. Africa 124 E5
Sakado Japan 93 F3
Sakae Chiba Japan 93 G3
Sakae Nagano Japan 93 E2
Sakai Fukui Japan 92 C2
Sakai Gunma Japan 93 F2
Sakai Ibaraki Japan 93 F2
Sakai Nagano Japan 93 E2
Sakai Ōsaka Japan 92 B4
Sakaide Japan 91 D6
Sakaigawa Japan 93 E3
Sakākah Saudi Arabia 113 F5
Sakakawea, Lake ND U.S.A. 160 C2
Sakaki Japan 93 E2
Sakakita Japan 93 E2
Sakala i. Indon. 85 G4
Sakami Canada 152 G3
Sakami r. Canada 152 F3
Sakami-gawa r. Japan 93 F3
Sakami Lake Canada 152 F3
Sakar mts Bulg. 69 L4
Sakaraha Madag. 123 E6
Sak'art'velo country Asia see Georgia
Sakarya Turkey see Adapazarı
Sakarya r. Turkey 69 N4
Sakashita Japan 92 D3
Sakassou Côte d'Ivoire 120 C4
Sakata Japan 91 E5
Sakauchi Japan 92 C3
Sakchu N. Korea 91 B4
Saken Seyfullin Kazakh. 98 A2
Sakesar Pak. 111 I3
Sakhalin i. Rus. Fed. 90 F2
Sakhalin Oblast admin. div. Rus. Fed. see Sakhalinskaya Oblast'
Sakhalinskaya Oblast' admin. div. Rus. Fed. 90 F2
Sakhalinskiy Zaliv b. Rus. Fed. 90 F1
Sakhi India 104 C3
Sakhile S. Africa 125 I4
Şäki Azer. 113 G2
Saki Nigeria see Shaki
Saki Ukr. see Saky
Šakiai Lith. 55 M9
Sakir mt. Pak. 111 G4
Sakishima-shotō is Japan 89 M8
Sakoli India 104 D5
Sakon Nakhon Thai. 86 D3
Sakrivier S. Africa 124 E6
Saku Nagano Japan 93 E2
Saku Nagano Japan 93 E2
Sakuma Japan 93 D3
Sakura Japan 93 G3
Sakuragawa Japan 93 G3
Sakura-gawa r. Japan 93 G2
Sakurai Japan 92 B4
Saku-shima i. Japan 92 D4
Saky Ukr. 112 D1
Säkylä Fin. 55 M6
Säkzā'ī Afgh. 111 F3
Sal i. Cape Verde 120 [inset]
Sal r. Rus. Fed. 53 I7
Sal, Punta pt Hond. 166 [inset] I6
Sala Sweden 55 J7
Salabangka, Kepulauan is Indon. 83 B3
Salaberry-de-Valleyfield Canada 165 H1
Salacgrīva Latvia 55 N8
Sala Consilina Italy 68 F4
Salada, Laguna salt l. Mex. 166 B1
Saladas Arg. 178 E3
Salado r. Buenos Aires Arg. 178 E5
Salado r. Santa Fe Arg. 178 D4
Salado r. Arg. 178 C5
Salado r. Mex. 167 F3
Salaga Ghana 120 C4
Salairskiy Kryazh ridge Rus. Fed. 88 E2
Salajwe Botswana 124 G2
Şalālah Oman 109 H6
Salamá Guat. 167 H6
Salamá Hond. 166 [inset] I6
Salamanca Mex. 168 D4
Salamanca Spain 67 D3
Salamanca NY U.S.A. 165 F2
Salamanga Moz. 125 K4
Salamantica Spain see Salamanca
Salamat, Bahr r. Chad 121 E4
Salamban Kalimantan Indon. 85 F3
Salamī Iran 111 E3
Salamina i. Greece 69 J6
Salamis tourist site Cyprus 107 A2
Salamís i. Greece see Salamina
Salamīyah Syria 107 C2
Salamonie r. IN U.S.A. 164 C3
Salamonie Lake IN U.S.A. 164 C3
Salang, Tūnel-e Afgh. 111 H3
Salantai Lith. 55 L8
Salaqi China 95 G3
Salar de Pocitos Arg. 178 C2
Salari Pak. 111 G5
Salas Spain 67 C2
Salaspils Latvia 55 N8
Salatiga Jawa Indon. 85 E4
Salavan Laos 86 D4
Salawati i. Papua Indon. 83 D3
Salawin, Mae Nam r. China/Myanmar see Salween
Salay Mindanao Phil. 82 D4
Salaya India 104 B5
Salayar i. Indon. 83 B4
Salayar, Selat sea chan. Indon. 83 B4
Sala y Gómez, Isla i. S. Pacific Ocean 187 M7
Salazar Angola see N'dalatando
Salbris France 66 F3
Salcha r. AK U.S.A. 149 K2
Šalčininkai Lith. 55 N9
Salcombe U.K. 59 D8
Saldae Alg. see Bejaïa
Saldaña Spain 67 D2
Saldanha S. Africa 124 C7
Saldanha Bay S. Africa 124 C7
Saldus Latvia 55 M8
Sale Australia 138 C7
Salea Sulawesi Indon. 83 B3
Saleh, Teluk b. Sumbawa Indon. 85 G5
Şāleḩābād Iran 110 C3
Salekhard Rus. Fed. 76 H3
Salem India 106 C4
Salem AR U.S.A. 161 F4
Salem IL U.S.A. 160 F4
Salem IN U.S.A. 164 B4
Salem MA U.S.A. 165 J2
Salem MO U.S.A. 160 F4
Salem NJ U.S.A. 165 H4
Salem NY U.S.A. 165 I2
Salem OH U.S.A. 164 E3

▶Salem OR U.S.A. 156 C3
Capital of Oregon.

Salem SD U.S.A. 160 D3
Salem VA U.S.A. 164 E5
Salen Scotland U.K. 60 D4
Salen Scotland U.K. 60 D4
Salerno Italy 68 F4
Salerno, Golfo di g. Italy 68 F4
Salernum Italy see Salerno
Salford U.K. 58 E5
Salgótarján Hungary 57 Q6
Salgueiro Brazil 177 K5
Salibabu i. Indon. 83 C2
Salida CO U.S.A. 157 G5
Salies-de-Béarn France 66 D5
Şāliḩān Afgh. 111 F4
Salihli Turkey 69 M5
Salihorsk Belarus 55 O10
Salima Malawi 123 D5
Salimbatu Kalimantan Indon. 85 G2
Salina KS U.S.A. 160 D4
Salina UT U.S.A. 159 H2
Salina, Isola i. Italy 68 F5
Salina Cruz Mex. 168 E5
Salinas Brazil 179 C2
Salinas Ecuador 176 B4
Salinas Mex. 168 D4
Salinas r. Mex. 161 D7
Salinas CA U.S.A. 158 C3
Salinas r. CA U.S.A. 158 C3
Salinas, Cabo de c. Spain see Ses Salines, Cap de
Salinas, Ponta das pt Angola 123 B5
Salinas Peak NM U.S.A. 157 G6
Saline MI U.S.A. 164 D2
Saline r. KS U.S.A. 160 D4
Saline Valley depr. CA U.S.A. 158 E3
Salinópolis Brazil 177 I4
Salinosó Lachay, Punta pt Peru 176 C6
Salisbury U.K. 59 F7
Salisbury MD U.S.A. 165 H4
Salisbury NC U.S.A. 162 D5
Salisbury Zimbabwe see Harare
Salisbury, Mount AK U.S.A. 149 K1
Salisbury Plain U.K. 59 E7
Şalkhad Syria 107 C3
Salla Fin. 54 P3
Sallisaw OK U.S.A. 161 E5
Salluit Canada 189 K2
Sallum, Khalīj as b. Egypt 112 B5
Sallyana Nepal 105 E3
Salmās Iran 110 B2
Salmi Rus. Fed. 52 F3
Salmo Canada 150 G5
Salmon ID U.S.A. 156 E3
Salmon r. ID U.S.A. 156 D3
Salmon Arm Canada 150 G5
Salmon Falls Creek r. ID/NV U.S.A. 156 E4
Salmon Fork r. Canada/U.S.A. 149 L2
Salmon Gums Australia 135 C8
Salmon Reservoir NY U.S.A. 165 H2
Salmon River Mountains ID U.S.A. 156 E3
Salmon Village AK U.S.A. 149 L2
Salmtal Germany 62 G5
Salo Fin. 55 M6
Salome AZ U.S.A. 159 G5
Salon India 104 E4
Salon-de-Provence France 66 G5
Salonica Greece see Thessaloniki
Salonika Greece see Thessaloniki
Saloum Delta tourist site Senegal 120 B3
Salpausselkä reg. Fin. 55 N6
Salqīn Syria 107 C1
Salses, Étang de l. France see Leucate, Étang de
Sal'sk Rus. Fed. 53 I7
Salsomaggiore Terme Italy 68 C2
Salt Jordan see As Salț
Salt watercourse S. Africa 124 F7
Salt r. AZ U.S.A. 159 G5
Salta Arg. 178 C2
Saltaire U.K. 58 F5
Saltash U.K. 59 C8
Saltcoats U.K. 60 E5
Saltee Islands Ireland 61 F5
Saltfjellet Svartisen Nasjonalpark nat. park Norway 54 I3
Saltfjorden sea chan. Norway 54 H3
Salt Flat TX U.S.A. 166 D2
Salt Fork Arkansas r. KS U.S.A. 161 D4
Salt Fork Lake OH U.S.A. 164 E3
Saltillo Mex. 167 E3
Salt Lake India 111 I5

▶Salt Lake City UT U.S.A. 159 H1
Capital of Utah.

Salt Lick KY U.S.A. 164 D4
Salto Brazil 179 B3
Salto Uruguay 178 E4
Salto da Divisa Brazil 179 D2
Salto de Agua Mex. 167 G5
Salto Grande Brazil 179 A3
Salton Sea salt l. CA U.S.A. 159 F5
Salto Santiago, Represa de resr Brazil 178 F3
Salt Range hills Pak. 111 I3
Salt River Canada 151 H2
Saluda VA U.S.A. 165 G5
Saluebesar i. Indon. 83 B3
Saluekecil i. Indon. 83 B3
Salue Timpaus, Selat sea chan. Indon. 83 B3
Sālūk, Kūh-e mt. Iran 110 E2
Salūm Egypt see As Sallūm
Salûm, Khalîg el b. Egypt see Sallum, Khalīj as
Salur India 106 D2
Saluzzo Italy 68 B2
Salvador Brazil 179 D1
Salvador country Central America see El Salvador
Salvador, Lake LA U.S.A. 161 F6
Salvaleón de Higüey Dom. Rep. see Higüey
Salvatierra Mex. 167 E4
Salvation Creek r. UT U.S.A. 159 H2
Salwah Saudi Arabia 122 F1
Salwah, Dawḩat b. Qatar/Saudi Arabia 110 C5
Salween r. China/Myanmar 96 C5
also known as Mae Nam Khong or Mae Nam Salawin or Nu Jiang (China) or Thanlwin (Myanmar)
Salyan Azer. 113 H3
Salyan Nepal see Sallyana
Sal'yany Azer. see Salyan
Salyersville KY U.S.A. 164 D5
Salzbrunn Namibia 124 C3
Salzburg Austria 57 N7
Salzgitter Germany 63 K2
Salzhausen Germany 63 K1
Salzkotten Germany 63 I3
Salzmünde Germany 63 L3
Salzwedel Germany 63 L2
Sam India 104 B4
Samae San, Ko i. Thai. 87 C4
Samagaltay Rus. Fed. 94 C1
Samāh well Saudi Arabia 110 B4
Samaida Iran see Someydeh
Samaixung China 99 C6
Samak, Tanjung pt Indon. 84 D3
Samakhixai Laos see Attapu
Samal i. Phil. 82 D5
Samalanga Sumatera Indon. 84 B1
Samalantan Kalimantan Indon. 85 E2
Samalayuca Mex. 166 D2
Samales Group is Phil. 82 C5
Samalga Pass sea channel AK U.S.A. 148 E5
Samalkot India 106 D2
Samālūț Egypt 112 C5
Samâlût Egypt see Samālūț
Samana Cay i. Bahamas 163 F8
Samanala mt. Sri Lanka see Adam's Peak
Samandağı Turkey 107 B1
Samangān Afgh. see Āybak
Samani Japan 90 F4
Samanlı Dağları mts Turkey 69 M4
Samar Kazakh. see Samarskoye
Samar i. Phil. 82 D4
Samara Rus. Fed. 53 K5
Samara r. Rus. Fed. 51 Q5
Samarahan Sarawak Malaysia see Sri Aman
Samarga Rus. Fed. 90 E3
Samarinda Kalimantan Indon. 85 G3
Samarka Rus. Fed. 90 D3
Samarkand Uzbek. see Samarqand
Samarkand, Pik mt. Tajik. see Samarqand, Qullai
Samarobriva France see Amiens
Samarqand Uzbek. 111 G2
Samarqand, Qullai mt. Tajik. 111 H2
Sāmarrā' Iraq 113 F4
Samar Sea g. Phil. 82 D4
Samarskoye Kazakh. 102 F2
Samarz China 95 H2
Samasata Pak. 111 H4
Samastipur India 105 F4
Samate Papua Indon. 83 D3
Şamaxı Azer. 113 H2
Samba India 104 C2
Samba r. Indon. 85 F3
Sambaliung mts Indon. 85 G2
Sambalpur India 105 E5
Sambar, Tanjung pt Indon. 85 E3
Sambas Kalimantan Indon. 85 E2
Sambat Ukr. see Kiev
Sambava Madag. 123 F5
Sambha India 105 G4
Sambhajinagar India see Aurangabad
Sambhal India 104 D3
Sambhar Lake India 104 C4
Sambiat Sulawesi Indon. 83 B3
Sambir Ukr. 53 D6
Sambit i. Indon. 85 G2
Sambito r. Brazil 177 J5
Sambo Sulawesi Barat Indon. 83 A3
Samboja Kalimantan Indon. 85 G3
Sâmbor Cambodia 87 D4
Sambor Ukr. see Sambir
Samborombón, Bahía b. Arg. 178 E5
Sambre r. Belgium/France 62 E4
Sambu Japan see Sanbu
Samch'ŏk S. Korea 91 C5
Samch'ŏnp'o S. Korea see Sach'on
Same Tanz. 122 D4
Samegawa Japan 93 G1
Samer France 62 B4
Sami India 104 B5
Samia, Tanjung pt Indon. 83 B2
Samīrah Saudi Arabia 108 F4
Samirum Iran see Yazd-e Khvāst
Samizu Japan 93 E2
Samjiyŏn N. Korea 90 C4
Şämkir Azer. 113 G2
Sam Neua Laos see Xam Nua
Samoa country S. Pacific Ocean 133 I3
Samoa Basin sea feature S. Pacific Ocean 186 I7
Samoa i Sisifo country S. Pacific Ocean see Samoa
Samobor Croatia 68 F2
Samoded Rus. Fed. 52 I3
Samokov Bulg. 69 J3
Šamorín Slovakia 57 P6
Samos i. Greece 69 L6
Samosir i. Indon. 84 B2
Samothrace i. Greece see Samothraki
Samothraki i. Greece 69 K4
Samoylovka Rus. Fed. 53 I6
Sampaga Sulawesi Barat Indon. 83 A3
Sampang Jawa Indon. 85 F4
Sampê China see Xiangcheng
Sampit Kalimantan Indon. 85 F3
Sampit r. Indon. 85 F3
Sampit, Teluk b. Indon. 85 F3
Sampolawa Sulawesi Indon. 83 B4
Sam Rayburn Reservoir TX U.S.A. 161 E6
Samrong Cambodia see Phumĭ Sâmraông
Samsang China 99 C7
Sam Sao, Phou mts Laos/Vietnam 86 C2
Samson AL U.S.A. 163 C6
Sâm Sơn Vietnam 86 D3
Samsun Turkey 112 E2
Samsy Kazakh. 98 B4
Samtī Afgh. 111 H2
Samui, Ko i. Thai. 87 C5
Samukawa Japan 93 F3
Samut Prakan Thai. 87 C4
Samut Sakhon Thai. 87 C4
Samut Songkhram Thai. 87 C4
Samyai China 99 E7
San Mali 120 C3
San, Phou mt. Laos 86 C3
San, Tônlé r. Cambodia 87 D4

▶Şan'ā' Yemen 108 F6
Capital of Yemen.

Sanaa Yemen see Şan'ā'
Sanada Japan 93 E2
SANAE IV research station Antarctica 188 B2
Sanage Japan 92 D3
San Agostín FL U.S.A. see St Augustine
San Agustin, Cape Mindanao Phil. 82 D5
San Agustin, Plains of NM U.S.A. 159 I5
Sanak AK U.S.A. 148 G5
Sanak Island AK U.S.A. 148 G5
Sanana Maluku Indon. 83 C3
Sanandaj Iran 110 B3
San Andreas CA U.S.A. 158 C2
San Andrés Guat. 167 H5
San Andres Phil. 82 D3
San Andrés, Isla de i. Caribbean Sea 169 H6
San Andres Mountains NM U.S.A. 157 G6
San Andrés Tuxtla Mex. 167 G5
San Angelo TX U.S.A. 161 C6
San Antonio Belize 167 H5
San Antonio Chile 178 B4
San Antonio Hond. 166 [inset] I6
San Antonio Luzon Phil. 82 C3
San Antonio NM U.S.A. 157 G6
San Antonio TX U.S.A. 161 D6
San Antonio r. TX U.S.A. 161 D6
San Antonio, Cabo c. Cuba 169 H4
San Antonio Bay Palawan Phil. 82 B4
San Antonio del Mar Mex. 166 A2
San Antonio de Oriente Hond. 166 [inset] I6
San Antonio Oeste Arg. 178 D6
San Antonio Reservoir CA U.S.A. 158 C4
San Augustín de Valle Fértil Arg. 178 C4
San Augustine TX U.S.A. 161 E6
San Bartolo Mex. 167 E4
San Benedetto del Tronto Italy 68 E3
San Benedicto, Isla i. Mex. 168 B5
San Benito Guat. 167 H5
San Benito TX U.S.A. 161 D7
San Benito r. CA U.S.A. 158 C3
San Benito Mountain CA U.S.A. 158 C3
San Bernardino CA U.S.A. 158 E4
San Bernardino Mountains CA U.S.A. 158 E4
San Bernardino Strait Phil. 82 D3
San Bernardo Chile 178 B4
San Bernardo Mex. 166 D3
San Blas Nayarit Mex. 166 D4
San Blas Sinaloa Mex. 166 C3
San Blas, Archipiélago de is Panama 166 [inset] K7
San Blas, Cape FL U.S.A. 163 C6
San Blas, Cordillera de mts Panama 166 [inset] K7
San Borja Bol. 176 E6
Sanbornville NH U.S.A. 165 J2
Sanbu China see Kaiping
Sanbu Japan 93 G3
San Buenaventura Mex. 167 E3
San Carlos Chile 178 B5
San Carlos Equat. Guinea see Luba
San Carlos Coahuila Mex. 167 E2
San Carlos Tamaulipas Mex. 161 D7
San Carlos Nicaragua 166 [inset] I7
San Carlos Luzon Phil. 82 C3
San Carlos Negros Phil. 82 C4
San Carlos AZ U.S.A. 159 H5
San Carlos Venez. 176 E2
San Carlos de Bariloche Arg. 178 B6
San Carlos de Bolívar Arg. 178 D5
San Carlos Indian Reservation res. AZ U.S.A. 166 C1
San Carlos Lake AZ U.S.A. 159 H5
Sancha Gansu China 94 F5
Sancha Shanxi China 95 G4
Sanchahe China see Fuyu
Sancha He r. China 96 E3
Sanchakou China 98 B5
Sanchi India 104 D5
San Chien Pau mt. Laos 86 C2
Sanchor India 104 B4
San Ciro de Acosta Mex. 167 F4
San Clemente CA U.S.A. 158 E5
San Clemente Island CA U.S.A. 158 D5
Sanclêr U.K. see St Clears
Sanco Point Mindanao Phil. 82 D4
San Cristóbal Arg. 178 D4
San Cristobal i. Solomon Is 133 G3
San Cristóbal Venez. 176 D2
San Cristóbal, Isla i. Galápagos Ecuador 176 [inset]
San Cristóbal, Volcán vol. Nicaragua 166 [inset] I6
San Cristóbal de las Casas Mex. 167 G5
Sancti Spíritus Cuba 169 I4
Sand r. S. Africa 125 J2
Sanda Japan 92 B4
Sandagou Rus. Fed. 90 D4
Sandai Kalimantan Indon. 85 E3
Sanda Island U.K. 60 D5
Sandakan Sabah Malaysia 85 G1
Sandakan, Pelabuhan inlet Malaysia 85 G1
Sandakphu Peak India 99 E8
Sândăn Cambodia 87 D4
Sandane Norway 54 E6
Sandanski Bulg. 69 J4
Sandaohezi China see Shawan
Sandaré Mali 120 B3
Sandau Germany 63 M2
Sanday i. U.K. 60 G1
Sandbach U.K. 59 E5
Sandborn IN U.S.A. 164 B4
Sand Cay reef India 106 B4
Sandefjord Norway 55 G7
Sandercock Nunataks Antarctica 188 D2
Sanders AZ U.S.A. 159 I4
Sandersleben Germany 63 L3
Sanderson TX U.S.A. 161 C6
Sandfire Roadhouse Australia 134 C4
Sand Fork WV U.S.A. 164 E4
Sandgate Australia 138 F1
Sandhead U.K. 60 E6
Sand Hill r. MN U.S.A. 160 D2
Sand Hills NE U.S.A. 160 C3
Sandia Peru 176 E6
San Diego Mex. 166 D2
San Diego CA U.S.A. 158 E5
San Diego TX U.S.A. 161 D7
San Diego, Sierra mts Mex. 166 C2
Sandıklı Turkey 69 N5
Sandila India 104 E4
Sanding i. Indon. 84 C3
Sand Islands AK U.S.A. 148 F3
Sand Lake Canada 152 D5
Sand Lake l. Canada 151 M5
Sandnes Norway 55 D7
Sandnessjøen Norway 54 H3
Sandoa Dem. Rep. Congo 123 C4
Sandomierz Poland 53 D6
San Donà di Piave Italy 68 E2
Sandover watercourse Australia 136 B4
Sandovo Rus. Fed. 52 H4
Sandoway Myanmar see Thandwè
Sandown U.K. 59 F8
Sandoy i. Faroe Is 54 [inset 2]
Sand Point AK U.S.A. 148 G5
Sandpoint ID U.S.A. 156 D2
Sandray i. U.K. 60 B4
Sandringham Australia 136 B5
Şandrul Mare, Vârful mt. Romania 69 L1
Sandsjö Sweden 55 I6
Sandspit Canada 149 O5
Sand Springs OK U.S.A. 161 D4
Sand Springs Salt Flat NV U.S.A. 158 D2
Sandstone Australia 135 B6
Sandstone MN U.S.A. 160 E2
Sandu Guizhou China 96 E3
Sandu Hunan China 97 G3
Sandur Faroe Is 54 [inset 2]
Sandusky MI U.S.A. 164 D2
Sandusky OH U.S.A. 164 D3
Sandveld mts S. Africa 124 D6
Sandverhaar Namibia 124 C4
Sandvika Akershus Norway 55 G7
Sandvika Nord-Trøndelag Norway 54 H5
Sandviken Sweden 55 J6
Sandwich Bay Canada 153 K3
Sandwich Island Vanuatu see Éfaté
Sandwich Islands is N. Pacific Ocean see Hawai'ian Islands
Sandwick U.K. 60 [inset]
Sandwip Bangl. 105 G5
Sandy UT U.S.A. 159 H1
Sandy r. ME U.S.A. 165 K1
Sandy Bay Canada 151 K4
Sandy Cape Qld Australia 136 F5
Sandy Cape Tas. Australia 137 [inset]
Sandy Hook KY U.S.A. 164 D4
Sandy Hook pt NJ U.S.A. 165 H3
Sandy Island Australia 134 C3
Sandykgachy Turkm. see Sandykgaçy
Sandykgaçy Turkm. 111 F2
Sandykly Gumy des. Turkm. 111 F2
Sandy Lake Alta Canada 150 H4
Sandy Lake Ont. Canada 151 M4
Sandy Lake l. Canada 151 M4
Sandy Springs GA U.S.A. 163 C5
San Estanislao Para. 178 E2
San Esteban, Isla i. Mex. 166 B2
San Felipe Chile 178 B4
San Felipe Baja California Mex. 166 B2
San Felipe Chihuahua Mex. 166 D3
San Felipe Guanajuato Mex. 167 E4
San Felipe Venez. 176 E1
San Felipe, Cayos de is Cuba 163 D8
San Felipe de Puerto Plata Dom. Rep. see Puerto Plata
San Fernando Chile 178 B4
San Fernando Baja California Mex. 166 B2
San Fernando Tamaulipas Mex. 167 F3
San Fernando watercourse Mex. 157 E7
San Fernando Luzon Phil. 82 C2
San Fernando Luzon Phil. 82 C3
San Fernando Spain 67 C5
San Fernando Trin. and Tob. 169 L6
San Fernando CA U.S.A. 158 D4
San Fernando de Apure Venez. 176 E2
San Fernando de Atabapo Venez. 176 E3
San Fernando de Monte Cristi Dom. Rep. see Monte Cristi
Sanford FL U.S.A. 163 D6
Sanford ME U.S.A. 165 J2
Sanford MI U.S.A. 164 C2
Sanford NC U.S.A. 162 E5

Sarempaka, Gunung mt. Indon. 85 F3
Sar-e Pol-e Żahāb Iran 110 B3
Sar-e Pul Afgh. 111 G2
Sar Eskandar Iran see Hashtrud
Sargasso Sea N. Atlantic Ocean 187 P4
Sargodha Pak. 111 I3
Sarh Chad 121 E4
Sarhad reg. Iran 111 F4
Sārī Iran 110 D2
Saria i. Greece 69 L7
Sar-i-Bum Afgh. see Sar-e Būm
Sáric Mex. 166 C2
Sarigan i. N. Mariana Is 81 L3
Sarigh Jilganang Kol salt l. Aksai Chin 104 D2
Sarıgöl Turkey 69 M5
Sarıkamış Turkey 113 F2
Sarikei Sarawak Malaysia 85 E2
Sarikūl, Qatorkūhi mts China/Tajik. see Sarykol Range
Sarila India 104 D4
Sarina Australia 136 E4
Sarıoğlan Kayseri Turkey 112 D3
Sarıoğlan Konya Turkey see Belören
Sariqamish Kuli salt l. Turkm./Uzbek. see Sarykamyshskoye Ozero
Sarīr Tibesti des. Libya 121 E2
Sarita TX U.S.A. 161 D7
Sarıveliler Turkey 107 A1
Sariwŏn N. Korea 91 B5
Sarıyar Barajı resr Turkey 69 N5
Sarıyer Turkey 69 M4
Sarız Turkey 112 E3
Sark i. Channel Is 59 E9
Sarkand Kazakh. 102 E2
Şarkikaraağaç Turkey 69 N5
Şarkışla Turkey 112 E3
Şarköy Turkey 69 L4
Sarlath Range mts Afgh./Pak. 111 G4
Sarmi Indon. 81 J7
Särna Sweden 55 H6
Sarneh Iran 110 B3
Sarnen Switz. 66 I3
Sarni India see Amla
Sarnia Canada 164 D2
Sarny Ukr. 53 E6
Saroako Sulawesi Indon. 83 B3
Sarolangun Sumatera Indon. 84 C3
Saroma-ko l. Japan 90 F3
Saronikos Kolpos g. Greece 69 J6
Saros Körfezi b. Turkey 69 L4
Sarov Rus. Fed. 53 I5
Sarpa, Ozero l. Rus. Fed. 53 J6
Sarpan i. N. Mariana Is see Rota
Sar Passage Palau 82 [inset]
Sarpsborg Norway 55 G7
Sarqant Kazakh. see Sarkand
Sarre r. France 62 H5
Sarrebourg France 62 H6
Sarreguemines France 62 H5
Sarria Spain 67 C2
Sarry France 62 E6
Sartana Ukr. 53 H7
Sartanahu Pak. 111 H5
Sartène Corsica France 66 I6
Sarthe r. France 66 D3
Sartokay China 94 B2
Sartu China see Daqing
Saruna Pak. 111 G5
Sarupsar India 104 C3
Şärur Azer. 113 G3
Saru Tara tourist site Afgh. 111 F4
Sarväbād Iran 110 B3
Sárvár Hungary 68 G1
Sarv-e Bālā Iran 110 D3
Sarwar India 104 C4
Saryarka plain Kazakh. 102 D1
Sar Yazd Iran 110 D4
Sary-Bulak Kyrg. 98 A4
Sarygamysh Köli salt l. Turkm./Uzbek. see Sarykamyshskoye Ozero
Sary-Ishikotrau, Peski des. Kazakh. see Saryyesik-Atyrau, Peski
Sary-Jaz r. Kyrg. 98 B4
Sarykamyshskoye Ozero salt l. Turkm./Uzbek. 113 J2
Sarykol Range mts China/Tajik. 111 I2
Sarykomey Kazakh. 98 A3
Saryozek Kazakh. 102 E3
Saryshagan Kazakh. 102 D2
Sarysu watercourse Kazakh. 102 C2
Sarytash Kazakh. 113 H1
Sary-Tash Kyrg. 111 I2
Sary-Ter, Gora mt. Kyrg. 98 B4
Saryyazy Suw Howdany resr Turkm. 111 F2
Saryyesik-Atyrau, Peski des. Kazakh. 102 E2
Saryzhal Kazakh. 98 B2
Saryzhaz Kazakh. 98 B4
Sarzha Kazakh. 113 H2
Sasak Sumatera Indon. 84 B2
Sasar, Tanjung pt Sumba Indon. 83 A5
Sasaram India 105 F4
Sasayama Japan 92 B3
Sasebo Japan 91 C6
Sashima Japan 93 F2
Saskatchewan prov. Canada 151 J4
Saskatchewan r. Canada 151 K4
Saskatoon Canada 151 J4
Saskylakh Rus. Fed. 77 M2
Saslaya mt. Nicaragua 166 [inset] I6
Saslaya, Parque Nacional nat. park Nicaragua 166 [inset] I6
Sasoi r. India 104 B5
Sasolburg S. Africa 125 H4
Sasovo Rus. Fed. 53 I5
Sass r. Canada 150 H2
Sassandra Côte d'Ivoire 120 C4
Sassari Sardinia Italy 68 C4
Sassenberg Germany 63 I3
Sassnitz Germany 57 N3
Sass Town Liberia 120 C4
Sasykkol', Ozero l. Kazakh. 102 F2
Sasykoli Rus. Fed. 53 J7
Sasyqköl l. Kazakh. see Sasykkol', Ozero
Satahual i. Micronesia see Satawal
Sata-misaki c. Japan 91 C7
Satana India 106 B1
Satan Pass NM U.S.A. 159 I4
Satara India 106 B2
Satara S. Africa 125 J3
Satawal i. Micronesia 81 L5
Sätbaev Kazakh. see Satpayev
Satengar i. Indon. 85 G4
Satevó Mex. 166 D3
Satevó r. Mex. 157 G8
Satırlar Turkey see Yeşilova
Satkania Bangl. 105 H5
Satkhira Bangl. 105 G5
Satluj r. India/Pak. see Sutlej
Satmala Range hills India 106 C2
Satna India 104 E4
Satomi Japan 93 G2
Satonda i. Indon. 85 G5
Satpayev Kazakh. 102 C2
Satpura Range mts India 104 C5
Satsuma-hantō pen. Japan 91 C7
Sattahip Thai. 87 C4
Satte Japan 93 F2
Satteldorf Germany 63 K5
Satthwa Myanmar 86 A3
Satu Mare Romania 53 D7
Satun Thai. 87 C6
Satwas India 104 D5
Saubi i. Indon. 85 F4
Sauceda Mountains AZ U.S.A. 159 G5
Saucillo Mex. 166 D2
Sauda Norway 55 E7
Sauðárkrókur Iceland 54 [inset 1]

▶Saudi Arabia country Asia 108 F4
5th largest country in Asia.

Sauer r. France 63 I6
Saug r. Mindanao Phil. 82 D5
Saugatuck MI U.S.A. 164 B2
Saugeen r. Canada 164 E1
Sāūjbolāgh Iran see Mahābād
Sauk Center MN U.S.A. 160 E2
Saulieu France 66 G3
Saulnois reg. France 62 G6
Sault Sainte Marie Canada 152 D5
Sault Sainte Marie MI U.S.A. 162 C2
Saumalkol' Kazakh. 100 F1
Saumarez Reef Australia 136 F4
Saumlakki Indon. 134 E2
Saumur France 66 D3
Saundatti India 106 B3
Saunders, Mount hill Australia 134 E3
Saunders Coast Antarctica 188 J1
Saurimo Angola 123 C4
Sausu Sulawesi Indon. 83 B3
Sautar Angola 123 B5
Sauvolles, Lac l. Canada 153 G3
Sauyr, Khrebet mts China/Kazakh. 98 D3
Sava r. Europe 68 I2
Savá Hond. 166 [inset] I6
Savage River Australia 137 [inset]
Savai'i i. Samoa 133 I3
Savala r. Rus. Fed. 53 I6
Savalou Benin 120 D4
Savanat Iran see Eşţahbān
Savane r. Canada 153 H4
Savanna IL U.S.A. 160 F3
Savannah GA U.S.A. 163 D5
Savannah OH U.S.A. 164 D3
Savannah TN U.S.A. 161 F5
Savannah r. GA/SC U.S.A. 163 D5
Savannah Sound Bahamas 163 E7
Savannakhét Laos 86 D3
Savanna-la-Mar Jamaica 169 I5
Savant Lake Canada 152 C4
Savant Lake l. Canada 152 C4
Savanur India 106 B3
Sävar Sweden 54 L5
Savaştepe Turkey 69 L5
Savè Benin 120 D4
Save r. Moz./Zimbabwe 123 D6
Säveh Iran 110 C3
Saverne France 63 H6
Saverne, Col de pass France 63 H6
Saviaho Fin. 54 P5
Savinskiy Rus. Fed. 52 I3
Savitri r. India 106 B2
Savli India 104 C5
Savoie reg. France see Savoy
Savona Italy 68 C2
Savonlinna Fin. 54 P6
Savonranta Fin. 54 P5
Savoonga AK U.S.A. 148 E3
Savoy reg. France 66 H3
Şavşat Turkey 113 F2
Sävsjö Sweden 55 I8
Savu i. Indon. 83 B5
Savukoski Fin. 54 P3
Savur Turkey 113 F3
Savu Sea Indon. see Sawu, Laut
Savvo-Borzya Rus. Fed. 95 I1
Saw Myanmar 86 A2
Sawahlunto Sumatera Indon. 84 C3
Sawai, Teluk b. Seram Indon. 83 D3
Sawai Madhopur India 104 D4
Sawan Kalimantan Indon. 85 F3
Sawan Myanmar 86 B1
Sawar India 104 C4
Sawara Japan 93 G3
Sawatch Range mts CO U.S.A. 156 G5
Sawel Mountain hill U.K. 61 E3
Sawi, Ao b. Thai. 87 B5
Sawn Myanmar 86 B2
Sawtell Australia 138 F3
Sawtooth Mountain AK U.S.A. 149 J2
Sawtooth Range mts WA U.S.A. 156 C2
Sawu Indon. 83 B5
Sawu i. Indon. see Savu
Sawu, Laut sea Indon. 83 B5
Sawye Myanmar 86 B2
Sawyer MI U.S.A. 164 B3
Saxilby U.K. 58 G5
Saxman AK U.S.A. 149 O5
Saxmundham U.K. 59 I6
Saxnäs Sweden 54 I4
Saxony land Germany see Sachsen
Saxony-Anhalt land Germany see Sachsen-Anhalt
Saxton PA U.S.A. 165 F3
Say Niger 120 D3
Saya Japan 92 C3
Sayabouri Laos see Xaignabouli
Sayafi i. Maluku Indon. 83 D2
Sayak Kazakh. 102 E2
Sayama Japan 93 F3
Sayang i. Papua Indon. 83 D2
Sayanogorsk Rus. Fed. 88 G2
Sayano-Shushenskoye Vodokhranilishche resr Rus. Fed. 88 G2
Sayansk Rus. Fed. 88 I2
Sayaq Kazakh. see Sayak
Şayat Turkm. 111 F2
Sayat Turkm. see Şaýat
Sayaxché Guat. 167 H5
Şaydā Lebanon see Sidon
Säyen Iran 110 D4
Sayer Island Thai. see Similan, Ko
Sayghān Afgh. 111 G3
Sayhan Mongolia 94 E1
Sayhandulaan Mongolia 95 G2
Sayhan-Ovoo Mongolia 94 E2
Sayḥūt Yemen 108 H6
Sayingpan China 96 D3
Saykhin Kazakh. 51 P6
Saylac Somalia 121 H3
Saylan country Asia see Sri Lanka
Saylyugem, Khrebet mts Rus. Fed. 98 E2
Saynshand Mongolia 95 G2
Sayn-Ust Mongolia see Höhmorīt
Sayoa mt. Spain see Saioa
Sayot Turkm. see Şaýat
Şayqal, Baḩr imp. l. Syria 107 C3
Sayqyn Kazakh. see Saykhin
Sayram Hu salt l. China 98 C3
Sayre OK U.S.A. 161 D5
Sayre PA U.S.A. 165 G3
Sayreville NJ U.S.A. 165 H3
Saysu China 94 C3
Sayula Jalisco Mex. 166 E5
Sayula Veracruz Mex. 168 F5
Sayyod Turkm. see Şaýat
Sazdy Kazakh. 53 K7
Sazin Pak. 111 I3
Sbaa Alg. 64 D6
Sbeitla Tunisia 68 C7
Scaddan Australia 135 C8
Scafell Pike hill U.K. 58 D4
Scalasaig U.K. 60 C4
Scalea Italy 68 F5
Scalloway U.K. 60 [inset]
Scalpaigh, Eilean i. U.K. see Scalpay
Scalpay i. U.K. 60 C3
Scammon Bay AK U.S.A. 148 F3
Scapa Flow inlet U.K. 60 F2
Scarba i. U.K. 60 D4
Scarborough Canada 164 F2
Scarborough Trin. and Tob. 169 L6
Scarborough U.K. 58 G4
Scarborough Shoal sea feature S. China Sea 80 F3
Scariff Island Ireland 61 B6
Scarp i. U.K. 60 B2
Scarpanto i. Greece see Karpathos
Scawfell Shoal sea feature S. China Sea 84 D1
Schaale r. Germany 63 K1
Schaalsee l. Germany 63 K1
Schaerbeek Belgium 62 E4
Schaffhausen Switz. 66 I3
Schafstädt Germany 63 L3
Schagen Neth. 62 E2
Schagerbrug Neth. 62 E2
Schakalskuppe Namibia 124 C4
Schärding Austria 57 N6
Scharendijke Neth. 62 D3
Scharteberg hill Germany 62 G4
Schaumburg IL U.S.A. 164 A2
Schebheim Germany 63 K5
Scheeßel Germany 63 J1
Schefferville Canada 153 I3
Scheibbs Austria 57 O6
Schelde r. Belgium see Scheldt
Scheldt r. Belgium 62 E3
Schell Creek Range mts NV U.S.A. 159 F2
Schellerten Germany 63 K2
Schellville CA U.S.A. 158 B2
Schenectady NY U.S.A. 165 I2
Schenefeld Germany 63 J1
Schermerhorn Neth. 62 E2
Schertz TX U.S.A. 161 D6
Schierling Germany 63 M6
Schiermonnikoog Neth. 62 G1
Schiermonnikoog i. Neth. 62 G1
Schiermonnikoog Nationaal Park nat. park Neth. 62 G1
Schiffdorf Germany 63 I1
Schinnen Neth. 62 F4
Schio Italy 68 D2
Schkeuditz Germany 63 M3
Schleiden Germany 62 G4
Schleiz Germany 63 L4
Schleswig Germany 57 L3
Schleswig-Holstein land Germany 63 K1
Schleswig-Holsteinisches Wattenmeer, Nationalpark nat. park Germany 57 L3
Schleusingen Germany 63 K4
Schlitz Germany 63 J4
Schloss Holte-Stukenbrock Germany 63 I3
Schloss Wartburg tourist site Germany 63 K3
Schlüchtern Germany 63 J4
Schlüsselfeld Germany 63 K5
Schmallenberg Germany 63 I3
Schmidt Island Rus. Fed. see Shmidta, Ostrov
Schmidt Peninsula Rus. Fed. see Shmidta, Poluostrov
Schneeberg Germany 63 M4
Schneidemühl Poland see Piła
Schneidlingen Germany 63 L3
Schneverdingen Germany 63 J1
Schoharie NY U.S.A. 165 H2
Schönebeck Germany 63 M1
Schönebeck (Elbe) Germany 63 L2
Schönefeld airport Germany 63 N2
Schöningen Germany 63 K2
Schöntal Germany 63 J5
Schoolcraft MI U.S.A. 164 C2
Schoonhoven Neth. 62 E3
Schopfloch Germany 63 K5
Schöppenstedt Germany 63 K2
Schortens Germany 63 H1
Schouten Island Australia 137 [inset]
Schouten Islands P.N.G. 81 K7
Schrankogel mt. Austria 57 M7
Schreiber Canada 152 D4
Schroon Lake NY U.S.A. 165 I2
Schröttersburg Poland see Płock
Schulenburg TX U.S.A. 161 D6
Schuler Canada 151 I5
Schull Ireland 61 C6
Schultz Lake Canada 151 L1
Schüttorf Germany 63 H2
Schuyler NE U.S.A. 160 D3
Schuyler Lake NY U.S.A. 165 H2
Schuylkill Haven PA U.S.A. 165 G3
Schwabach Germany 63 L5
Schwäbische Alb mts Germany 57 L7
Schwäbisch Gmünd Germany 63 J6
Schwäbisch Hall Germany 63 J5
Schwaförden Germany 63 I2
Schwalm r. Germany 63 J3
Schwalmstadt-Ziegenhain Germany 63 J4
Schwandorf Germany 63 M5
Schwaner, Pegunungan mts Indon. 85 F3
Schwanewede Germany 63 I1
Schwarmstedt Germany 63 J2
Schwarze Elster r. Germany 63 M3
Schwarzenbek Germany 63 K1
Schwarzenberg Germany 63 M4
Schwarzer Mann hill Germany 62 G4
Schwarzrand mts Namibia 124 C3
Schwarzwald mts Germany see Black Forest
Schwatka, Mount AK U.S.A. 149 K2
Schwatka Mountains AK U.S.A. 148 H2
Schwaz Austria 57 M7
Schwedt an der Oder Germany 57 O4
Schwegenheim Germany 63 I5
Schweich Germany 62 G5
Schweinfurt Germany 63 K4
Schweinitz Germany 63 N3
Schweinrich Germany 63 M1
Schweiz country Europe see Switzerland
Schweizer-Reneke S. Africa 125 G4
Schwelm Germany 63 H3
Schwerin Germany 63 L1
Schweriner See l. Germany 63 L1
Schwetzingen Germany 63 I5
Schwyz Switz. 66 I3
Sciacca Sicily Italy 68 E6
Scicli Sicily Italy 68 F6
Science Hill KY U.S.A. 164 C5
Scilly, Île atoll Fr. Polynesia see Manuae
Scilly, Isles of U.K. 59 A9
Scioto r. OH U.S.A. 164 D4
Scipio UT U.S.A. 159 G2
Scobey MT U.S.A. 156 G2
Scodra Albania see Shkodër
Scofield Reservoir UT U.S.A. 159 H2
Scole U.K. 59 I6
Scone Australia 138 E4
Scone U.K. 60 F4
Scoresby Land reg. Greenland 147 P2
Scoresbysund Greenland see Ittoqqortoormiit
Scoresby Sund sea chan. Greenland see Kangertittivaq
Scorno, Punta dello pt Sardinia Italy see Caprara, Punta
Scorpion Bight b. Australia 135 D8
Scotia Ridge sea feature S. Atlantic Ocean 184 E9
Scotia Sea S. Atlantic Ocean 184 F9
Scotland Canada 164 E2
Scotland admin. div. U.K. 60 F3
Scotland MD U.S.A. 165 G4
Scotstown Canada 153 H5
Scott OH U.S.A. 164 C3
Scott, Cape Australia 134 E3
Scott, Cape Canada 150 D5
Scott, Mount hill OK U.S.A. 161 D5
Scott Base research station Antarctica 188 H1
Scottburgh S. Africa 125 J6
Scott City KS U.S.A. 160 C4
Scott Coast Antarctica 188 H1
Scott Glacier Antarctica 188 I1
Scott Island Antarctica 188 H2
Scott Islands Canada 150 D5
Scott Lake Canada 151 J3
Scott Mountains Antarctica 188 D2
Scott Reef Australia 134 C3
Scottsbluff NE U.S.A. 160 C3
Scottsboro AL U.S.A. 163 C5
Scottsburg IN U.S.A. 164 C4
Scottsville KY U.S.A. 164 B5
Scottsville VA U.S.A. 165 F5
Scourie U.K. 60 D2
Scousburgh U.K. 60 [inset]
Scrabster U.K. 60 F2
Scranton PA U.S.A. 165 H3
Scunthorpe U.K. 58 G5
Scuol Switz. 66 J3
Scupi Macedonia see Skopje
Scutari Albania see Shkodër
Scutari, Lake Albania/Montenegro 69 H3
Seaboard NC U.S.A. 165 G5
Seabrook, Lake salt flat Australia 135 B7
Seaford U.K. 59 H8
Seaforth Canada 164 E2
Seahorse Shoal sea feature Phil. 82 B4
Seal r. Canada 151 M3
Seal, Cape S. Africa 124 F8
Sea Lake Australia 137 C7
Seal Lake Canada 153 J3
Sealy TX U.S.A. 161 D6
Seaman OH U.S.A. 164 D4
Seaman Range mts NV U.S.A. 159 F3
Seamer U.K. 58 G4
Searchlight NV U.S.A. 159 F4
Searcy AR U.S.A. 161 F5
Searles Lake CA U.S.A. 158 E4
Seaside CA U.S.A. 157 C5
Seaside OR U.S.A. 156 C3
Seaside Park NJ U.S.A. 165 H4
Seattle WA U.S.A. 156 C3
Seattle, Mount Canada/U.S.A. 149 M3
Seaview Range mts Australia 136 D3
Seba Indon. 83 B5
Sebaco Nicaragua 166 [inset] I6
Sebago Lake ME U.S.A. 165 J2
Sebakung Kalimantan Indon. 85 G3
Sebangan, Teluk b. Indon. 85 F3
Sebangka i. Indon. 84 D2
Sebastea Turkey see Sivas
Sebastian FL U.S.A. 163 D7
Sebastián Vizcaíno, Bahía b. Mex. 166 B2
Sebasticook r. ME U.S.A. 165 K1
Sebasticook Lake ME U.S.A. 165 K1
Sebastopol Ukr. see Sevastopol'
Sebastopol CA U.S.A. 158 B2
Sebatik i. Indon. 85 G1
Sebauh Sarawak Malaysia 85 F2
Sebayan, Bukit mt. Indon. 85 E3
Sebba Burkina Faso 120 D3
Seben Turkey 69 N4
Sebenico Croatia see Šibenik
Sebeş Romania 69 J2
Sebesi i. Indon. 84 D4
Sebewaing MI U.S.A. 164 D2
Sebezh Rus. Fed. 55 P8
Şebinkarahisar Turkey 112 E2
Seblat, Gunung mt. Indon. 84 C3
Sebree KY U.S.A. 164 B5
Sebring FL U.S.A. 163 D7
Sebrovo Rus. Fed. 53 I6
Sebta N. Africa see Ceuta
Sebuku i. Indon. 85 G3
Sebuku r. Indon. 85 G1
Sebuku, Teluk b. Indon. 85 G2
Sebuku-Sembakung, Taman Nasional nat. park Kalimantan Indon. 85 G1
Sebuyau Sarawak Malaysia 85 E2
Sechelt Canada 150 F5
Sechenovo Rus. Fed. 53 J5
Sechura Peru 176 B5
Sechura, Bahía de b. Peru 176 B5
Seckach Germany 63 J5
Second Mesa AZ U.S.A. 159 H4
Secretary Island N.Z. 139 A7
Secunda S. Africa 125 I4
Secunderabad India 106 C2
Sedalia MO U.S.A. 160 E4
Sedam India 106 C2
Sedan France 62 E5
Sedan KS U.S.A. 161 D4
Sedan Dip Australia 136 C3
Sedanka Island AK U.S.A. 148 F5
Seddon N.Z. 139 E5
Seddonville N.Z. 139 C5
Sedeh Iran 110 E3
Sederot Israel 107 B4
Sédhiou Gambia 120 B3
Sedlčany Czech Rep. 57 O6
Sedlets Poland see Siedlce
Sedom Israel 107 B4
Sedona AZ U.S.A. 159 H4
Sédrata Alg. 68 B6
Sedulang Kalimantan Indon. 85 G2
Šeduva Lith. 55 M9
Seedorf Germany 63 K1
Seehausen Germany 63 L2
Seehausen (Altmark) Germany 63 L2
Seeheim Namibia 124 C4
Seeheim-Jugenheim Germany 63 I5
Seela Pass Canada 149 M2
Seelig, Mount Antarctica 188 K1
Seelze Germany 63 J2
Seenu Atoll Maldives see Addu Atoll
Sées France 66 E2
Seesen Germany 63 K3
Seevetal Germany 63 K1
Sefadu Sierra Leone 120 B4
Sefare Botswana 125 H2
Seferihisar Turkey 69 L5
Sefīd, Kūh-e mt. Iran 110 C3
Sefīd Kūh mts Afgh. 111 G3
Sefid Sang Iran 111 F3
Sefophe Botswana 125 H2
Segalstad Norway 55 G6
Segama r. Malaysia 85 G1
Segamat Malaysia 84 C2
Ségbana Benin 120 D3
Segeletz Germany 63 M2
Segeri Sulawesi Indon. 83 A4
Segezha Rus. Fed. 52 G3
Segontia U.K. see Caernarfon
Segontium U.K. see Caernarfon
Segorbe Spain 67 F4
Ségou Mali 120 C3
Segovia r. Hond./Nicaragua see Coco
Segovia Spain 67 D3
Segozerskoye, Ozero resr Rus. Fed. 52 G3
Seguam Island AK U.S.A. 148 D5
Seguam Pass sea channel AK U.S.A. 148 [inset] D5
Séguédine Niger 120 E2
Séguéla Côte d'Ivoire 120 C4
Seguin TX U.S.A. 161 D6
Segula Island AK U.S.A. 148 [inset] B5
Segura r. Spain 67 F4
Segura, Sierra de mts Spain 67 E5
Segzī Iran 110 D3
Sehithwa Botswana 123 C6
Sehlabathebe National Park Lesotho 125 I5
Seho i. Indon. 83 C3
Sehore India 104 D5
Sehwan Pak. 111 G5
Seibert CO U.S.A. 160 C4
Seignelay r. Canada 153 H4
Seika Japan 92 B4
Seikphyu Myanmar 86 A2
Seiland i. Norway 54 M1
Seille r. France 62 G5
Seinaiji Japan 92 D3
Seinäjoki Fin. 54 M5
Seine r. Canada 151 N5
Seine r. France 62 A5
Seine, Baie de b. France 66 D2
Seine, Val de valley France 66 F2
Seipinang Kalimantan Indon. 85 F3
Seistan reg. Iran see Sīstān
Seiwa Japan 92 C4
Sejaka Kalimantan Indon. 85 G3
Sejangkung Kalimantan Indon. 85 E2
Sejny Poland 55 M9
Sekadau Kalimantan Indon. 85 E2
Sekanak, Teluk b. Indon. 84 D3
Sekatak Bengara Kalimantan Indon. 85 G2
Sekayu Sumatera Indon. 84 C3
Seke China see Sêrtar
Seki Gifu Japan 92 C3
Seki Mie Japan 92 C4
Sekicau, Gunung vol. Indon. 84 D4
Sekidō-san hill Japan 92 C2
Sekigahara Japan 92 C3
Sekijō Japan 93 F2
Sekiyado Japan 93 F2
Sekoma Botswana 124 F3
Sekondi Ghana 120 C4
Sek'ot'a Eth. 122 D2
Sekura Kalimantan Indon. 85 E2
Şela Rus. Fed. see Shali
Selagan r. Indon. 84 C3
Selakau Kalimantan Indon. 85 E2
Selama Malaysia 87 C6
Selangor state Malaysia 84 C2
Selaru i. Maluku Indon. 83 D5
Selassi Indon. 81 I7
Selatan, Tanjung pt Indon. 85 F4
Selatpanjang Sumatera Indon. 84 C2
Selawik AK U.S.A. 148 G2
Selawik r. AK U.S.A. 148 G2
Selawik Lake AK U.S.A. 148 G2
Selawik National Wildlife Refuge nature res. AK U.S.A. 148 H2
Selb Germany 63 M4
Selbekken Norway 54 F5
Selbu Norway 54 G5
Selby U.K. 58 F5
Selby SD U.S.A. 160 C2
Selby, Lake AK U.S.A. 148 I2
Selbyville DE U.S.A. 165 H4
Selden KS U.S.A. 160 C4
Seldovia AK U.S.A. 149 J4
Sele Papua Indon. 83 D3
Sele, Selat sea chan. Papua Indon. 83 D3
Selebi-Phikwe Botswana 123 C6
Selebi-Pikwe Botswana see Selebi-Phikwe
Selemdzha r. Rus. Fed. 90 C1
Selemdzhinsk Rus. Fed. 90 C1
Selemdzhinskiy Khrebet mts Rus. Fed. 90 D1
Selendi Turkey 69 M5
Selenduma Rus. Fed. 94 F1

▶Selenga r. Mongolia/Rus. Fed. 88 J2
Part of the Yenisey-Angara-Selenga, 3rd longest river in Asia.
Also known as Selenga Mörön.

Selenga r. Rus. Fed. 94 G1
Selenga Mörön r. Mongolia/Rus. Fed. see Selenga
Selenge Bulgan Mongolia 94 E1
Selenge Hövsgöl Mongolia see Ih-Uul
Selenge prov. Mongolia 94 F1
Selenge Mörön r. Mongolia 94 F1
Sêlêpug China 99 C7
Seletar Sing. 87 [inset]
Seletar Reservoir Sing. 87 [inset]
Selety r. Kazakh. see Sileti
Seletyteniz, Ozero salt l. Kazakh. see Siletiteniz, Ozero
Seleucia Turkey see Silifke
Seleucia Pieria Turkey see Samandağı
Selfridge ND U.S.A. 160 C2
Sel'gon Rus. Fed. 90 D2
Sélibabi Mauritania 120 B3
Selibe-Phikwe Botswana see Selebi-Phikwe
Seligenstadt Germany 63 I4
Seliger, Ozero l. Rus. Fed. 52 G4
Seligman AZ U.S.A. 159 G4
Selikhino Rus. Fed. 90 E2
Selîma Oasis Sudan 108 C5
Selimbau Kalimantan Indon. 85 F2
Selimiye Turkey 69 L6
Selinsgrove PA U.S.A. 165 G3
Seliu i. Indon. 85 D3
Selizharovo Rus. Fed. 52 G4
Seljord Norway 55 F7
Selkirk Canada 151 L5
Selkirk U.K. 60 G5
Selkirk Mountains Canada 150 G4
Sellafield U.K. 58 D4
Sellersburg IN U.S.A. 164 C4
Sellore Island Myanmar see Saganthit Kyun
Sells AZ U.S.A. 159 H6
Selm Germany 63 H3
Selma AL U.S.A. 163 C5
Selma CA U.S.A. 158 D3
Selmer TN U.S.A. 161 F5
Selong Lombok Indon. 85 G5
Selous, Mount Canada 149 N3
Selseleh-ye Pīr Shūrān mts Iran 111 F4
Selsey Bill hd U.K. 59 G8
Sel'tso Rus. Fed. 53 G5
Selty Rus. Fed. 52 L4
Selu i. Indon. 134 E1
Seluan i. Indon. 85 D1
Selvas reg. Brazil 176 D5
Selvin IN U.S.A. 164 B4
Selway r. ID U.S.A. 156 E3
Selwyn Lake Canada 151 J2
Selwyn Mountains Canada 149 O2
Selwyn Range hills Australia 136 B4
Sel'yb Rus. Fed. 52 K3
Selz r. Germany 63 I5
Semangka, Teluk b. Indon. 84 D4
Semarang Jawa Indon. 85 E4
Sematan Sarawak Malaysia 85 E2
Semau i. Indon. 83 B5
Semayang, Danau l. Indon. 85 G3
Sembakung r. Indon. 85 G2
Sembawang Sing. 87 [inset]
Sembé Congo 122 B3
Şemdinli Turkey 113 G3
Semendire Serbia see Smederevo
Semenivka Ukr. 53 G5
Semenov Rus. Fed. 52 J4
Semenovka Ukr. see Semenivka
Semeru, Gunung vol. Indon. 84 F5
Semey Kazakh. 102 F1
Semidi Islands AK U.S.A. 148 H4
Semikarakorsk Rus. Fed. 53 I7
Semiluki Rus. Fed. 53 H6
Seminoe Reservoir WY U.S.A. 156 G4
Seminole TX U.S.A. 161 C5
Semipalatinsk Kazakh. see Semey
Semirara i. Phil. 82 C3
Semirara Islands Phil. 82 C4
Semīrom Iran 110 C4
Semitau Kalimantan Indon. 85 E2
Semiyarka Kazakh. 98 B2
Semizbuga Kazakh. 98 A2
Sem Kolodezey Ukr. see Lenine
Semnān Iran 110 D3
Semnān va Dāmghān reg. Iran 110 D3
Sêmnyi China 94 E4
Semois r. Belgium/France 62 E5
Semois, Vallée de la valley Belgium/France 62 E5
Semporna Sabah Malaysia 85 G1
Sempu i. Indon. 85 F5
Semyonovskoye Arkhangel'skaya Oblast' Rus. Fed. see Bereznik
Semyonovskoye Kostromskaya Oblast' Rus. Fed. see Ostrovskoye
Sena Bol. 176 E6
Senaja Sabah Malaysia 85 G1
Sena Madureira Brazil 176 E5
Senanga Zambia 123 C5
Senaning Kalimantan Indon. 85 E2
Sendai Kagoshima Japan 91 C7
Sendai Miyagi Japan 91 F5
Sêndo China 99 F7
Senduruhan Kalimantan Indon. 85 E3
Senebui, Tanjung pt Indon. 84 C2
Seneca KS U.S.A. 160 D4
Seneca OR U.S.A. 156 D3
Seneca Lake NY U.S.A. 165 G2
Seneca Rocks WV U.S.A. 164 F4
Senecaville Lake OH U.S.A. 164 E4
Senegal country Africa 120 B3

Sénégal *r.* Mauritania/Senegal **120** B3
Seney *MI* U.S.A. **160** G2
Senftenberg Germany **57** O5
Senga Hill Zambia **123** D4
Sengar *r.* India **99** B8
Sengata *Kalimantan* Indon. **85** G2
Sêngdoi China **99** C7
Sengerema Tanz. **122** D4
Sengeyskiy, Ostrov *i.* Rus. Fed. **52** K1
Sengilen, Khrebet *mts* Rus. Fed. **94** C1
Sengiley Rus. Fed. **53** K5
Sengirli, Mys *pt* Kazakh. *see* **Syngyrli, Mys**
Sêngli Co *l.* China **99** D7
Senhor do Bonfim Brazil **177** J6
Senigallia Italy **68** E3
Senj Croatia **68** F2
Senja *i.* Norway **54** J2
Senjōga-dake *mt.* Japan **92** B4
Senjōga-dake *mt.* Japan **93** E3
Sen'kina Rus. Fed. **52** K2
Şenköy Turkey **107** C1
Senlac S. Africa **124** F3
Senlin Shan *mt.* China **90** C4
Senlis France **62** C5
Senmonorom Cambodia **87** D4
Sennan Japan **92** B4
Sennar Sudan **108** D7
Sennen U.K. **59** B8
Senneterre Canada **152** F4
Sennokura-yama *mt.* Japan **93** E2
Senqu *r.* Lesotho **125** H6
Sens France **66** F2
Sensuntepeque El Salvador **166** [inset] H6
Senta Serbia **69** I2
Senthal India **104** D3
Sentinel *AZ* U.S.A. **159** G5
Sentinel Peak Canada **150** F4
Sentispac Mex. **166** D4
Sentosa *i.* Sing. **87** [inset]
Senwabarwana S. Africa **125** I2
Senyiur *Kalimantan* Indon. **85** G2
Şenyurt Turkey **113** F3
Seo de Urgell Spain *see* **La Seu d'Urgell**
Seonath *r.* India **106** D1
Seoni India **104** D5
Seorinarayan India **105** E5

▶**Seoul** S. Korea **91** B5
Capital of South Korea.

Sepanjang *i.* Indon. **85** F4
Separation Well Australia **134** C5
Sepasu *Kalimantan* Indon. **85** G2
Sepauk *Kalimantan* Indon. **85** E2
Sepik *r.* P.N.G. **81** K7
Sepinang *Kalimantan* Indon. **85** G2
Seping *r.* Malaysia **85** F2
Sep'o N. Korea **91** B5
Sepon India **105** H4
Seppa India **105** H4
Sept-Îles Canada **153** I4
Seputih *r.* Indon. **84** D4
Sequoia National Park *CA* U.S.A. **158** D3
Serafimovich Rus. Fed. **53** I6
Sêraitang China *see* **Baima**
Seram *i. Maluku* Indon. **83** D3
Seram, Laut *sea* Indon. **83** D3
Serang *Jawa* Indon. **84** D4
Serangoon Harbour *b.* Sing. **87** [inset]
Serapi, Gunung *hill* Indon. **87** E7
Serapong, Mount *hill* Sing. **87** [inset]
Serasan *i.* Indon. **85** E2
Serasan, Selat *sea chan.* Indon. **85** E2
Seraya *i.* Indon. **83** A5
Seraya *i.* Indon. **85** E2
Serbâl, Gebel *mt.* Egypt *see* **Sirbāl, Jabal**

▶**Serbia** *country* Europe **69** I3
Formerly known as Yugoslavia and as Serbia and Montenegro. Up to 1993 included Bosnia-Herzegovina, Croatia, Macedonia, Montenegro and Slovenia. Became independent from Montenegro in June 2006. Kosovo declared independence in February 2008.

Sêrbug Co *l.* China **99** E6
Sêrca China **99** F7
Serchhip India **105** H5
Serdar Turkm. **110** E2
Serdica Bulg. *see* **Sofia**
Serdo Eth. **122** E2
Serdoba *r.* Rus. Fed. **53** J5
Serdobsk Rus. Fed. **53** J5
Serdtse-Kamen', Mys *c.* Rus. Fed. **148** E2
Serebryansk Kazakh. **102** F2
Seredka Rus. Fed. **55** P7
Şereflikoçhisar Turkey **112** D3
Seremban Malaysia **84** C2
Serengeti National Park Tanz. **122** D4
Serenje Zambia **123** D5
Serezha *r.* Rus. Fed. **52** I5
Sergach Rus. Fed. **52** J5
Sergelen *Dornod* Mongolia **95** H1
Sergelen *Sühbaatar* Mongolia *see* **Tüvshinshiree**
Sergeyevka Rus. Fed. **90** B2
Sergiyev Posad Rus. Fed. **52** H4
Sergo Ukr. *see* **Stakhanov**
Serh China **94** D4
Serhetabat Turkm. **111** F3
Seria Brunei **85** F1
Serian *Sarawak* Malaysia **85** E2
Seribu, Kepulauan *is* Indon. **84** D4
Serifos *i.* Greece **69** K6
Sérigny *r.* Canada **153** H3
Sérigny, Lac *l.* Canada **153** H3
Serik Turkey **112** C3
Serikbuya China **98** B5
Serikkembelo *Seram* Indon. **83** C3
Seringapatam Reef Australia **134** C3
Sêrkang China *see* **Nyainrong**
Sermata *i. Maluku* Indon. **83** D5
Sermata, Kepulauan *is Maluku* Indon. **83** D5
Sermersuaq *glacier* Greenland **147** M2
Sermilik *inlet* Greenland **147** O3
Sernovodsk Rus. Fed. **53** K5
Sernur Rus. Fed. **52** K4
Sernyy Zavod Turkm. *see* **Kükürtli**
Seronga Botswana **123** C5
Serov Rus. Fed. **51** S4
Serowe Botswana **125** H2
Serpa Port. **67** C5
Serpa Pinto Angola *see* **Menongue**
Serpentine Hot Springs *AK* U.S.A. **148** F2
Serpentine Lakes *salt flat* Australia **135** E7
Serpukhov Rus. Fed. **53** H5
Serra Brazil **179** C3
Serra Alta Brazil **179** A4
Serrachis *r.* Cyprus **107** A2
Serra da Bocaina, Parque Nacional da *nat. park* Brazil **179** B3
Serra da Canastra, Parque Nacional da *nat. park* Brazil **179** B3
Serra da Mesa, Represa *resr* Brazil **179** A1
Serra das Araras Brazil **179** B1
Serra do Divisor, Parque Nacional da *nat. park* Brazil **176** D5
Sérrai Greece *see* **Serres**
Serranía de la Neblina, Parque Nacional *nat. park* Venez. **176** E3
Serraria, Ilha *i.* Brazil *see* **Queimada, Ilha**
Serra Talhada Brazil **177** K5
Serre *r.* France **62** D5
Serres Greece **69** J4
Serrinha Brazil **177** K6
Sêrro Brazil **179** C2
Sers Tunisia **68** C6
Sertanópolis Brazil **179** A3
Sertãozinho Brazil **179** B3
Sêrtar China **96** D1
Sertavul Geçidi *pass* Turkey **107** A1
Sertolovo Rus. Fed. **55** Q6
Serua *vol. Maluku* Indon. **83** D4
Seruai *Sumatera* Indon. **84** B1
Serui Indon. **81** J7
Serule Botswana **123** C6
Seruna India **104** C3
Serutu *i.* Indon. **85** E3
Seruyan *r.* Indon. **85** F3
Serwaru *Maluku* Indon. **83** C5
Sêrwolungwa China **94** C5
Sêrxü China **96** C1
Serykh Gusey, Ostrova *is* Rus. Fed. **148** D2
Seryshevo Rus. Fed. **90** C2
Sesayap *Kalimantan* Indon. **85** G2
Sesayap *r.* Indon. **85** G2
Seseganaga Lake Canada **152** C4
Sese Islands Uganda **122** D4
Sesel *country* Indian Ocean *see* **Seychelles**
Sesepe *Maluku* Indon. **83** C3
Sesfontein Namibia **123** B5
Seshachalam Hills India **106** C3
Seshan Rus. Fed. **148** E2
Sesheke Zambia **123** C5
Sesostris Bank *sea feature* India **106** A3
Ses Salines, Cap de *c.* Spain **67** H4
Sestri Levante Italy **68** C2
Sestroretsk Rus. Fed. **55** P6
Set, Phou *mt.* Laos **86** D4
Sète France **66** F5
Sete Lagoas Brazil **179** B2
Setermoen Norway **54** K2
Setesdal *valley* Norway **55** E7
Seti *r.* Nepal **104** E3
Sétif Alg. **64** F4
Seto Japan **92** D3
Seto-naikai *sea* Japan **89** O6
Seto-naikai Kokuritsu-kōen Japan **91** D6
Setsan Myanmar **86** A3
Settat Morocco **64** C5
Settepani, Monte *mt.* Italy **68** C2
Settle U.K. **58** E4
Setúbal Port. **67** B4
Setúbal, Baía de *b.* Port. **67** B4
Seul, Lac *l.* Canada **151** M5
Seulimeum *Sumatera* Indon. **84** A1
Sevan Armenia **113** G2
Sevan, Lake Armenia **113** G2
Sevan, Ozero *l.* Armenia *see* **Sevan, Lake**
Sevana Lich *l.* Armenia *see* **Sevan, Lake**
Sevastopol' Ukr. **112** D1
Seven Islands Canada *see* **Sept-Îles**
Seven Islands Bay Canada **153** J2
Sevenoaks U.K. **59** H7
Seventy Mile House Canada *see* **70 Mile House**
Sévérac-le-Château France **66** F4
Severn *r.* Australia **138** E2
Severn *r.* Canada **152** D3
Severn S. Africa **124** F4
Severn *r.* U.K. **59** E7
also known as Hafren
Severnaya Dvina *r.* Rus. Fed. **52** I2
Severnaya Sos'va *r.* Rus. Fed. **51** T3
Severnaya Zemlya *is* Rus. Fed. **77** L1
Severn Lake Canada **151** N4
Severnoye Rus. Fed. **51** Q5
Severnyy *Arkhangel'skaya Oblast'* Rus. Fed. **52** K1
Severnyy *Respublika Komi* Rus. Fed. **76** H3

▶**Severnyy, Ostrov** *island* Rus. Fed. **76** G2
4th largest island in Europe.

Severobaykal'sk Rus. Fed. **89** J1
Severo-Baykal'skoye Nagor'ye *mts* Rus. Fed. **77** M4
Severo-Chuyskiy Khrebet *mts* Rus. Fed. **98** D2
Severodonetsk Ukr. *see* **Syeverodonets'k**
Severodvinsk Rus. Fed. **52** H2
Severo-Kuril'sk Rus. Fed. **77** Q4
Severomorsk Rus. Fed. **54** R2
Severoonezhsk Rus. Fed. **52** H3
Severo-Sibirskaya Nizmennost' *lowland* Rus. Fed. *see* **North Siberian Lowland**
Severoural'sk Rus. Fed. **51** R3
Severo-Yeniseyskiy Rus. Fed. **76** K3
Severskaya Rus. Fed. **112** E1
Severskiy Donets *r.* Rus. Fed./Ukr. **53** I7
also known as Northern Donets, Sivers'kyy Donets'
Sevier *UT* U.S.A. **159** G2
Sevier *r. UT* U.S.A. **159** G2
Sevier Desert *UT* U.S.A. **159** G2
Sevier Lake *UT* U.S.A. **159** G2
Sevierville *TN* U.S.A. **162** D5
Sevilla Col. **176** C3
Sevilla Spain *see* **Seville**
Seville Spain **67** D5
Sevlyush Ukr. *see* **Vynohradiv**
Sêwa China **99** E6
Sewani India **104** C3
Seward *AK* U.S.A. **149** J3
Seward *NE* U.S.A. **160** D3
Seward Mountains Antarctica **188** L2
Seward Peninsula *AK* U.S.A. **148** F2
Sexi Spain *see* **Almuñécar**
Sexsmith Canada **150** G4
Sextín Mex. **166** D3
Sextín *r.* Mex. **166** D3
Seya Japan **93** F3
Seyakha Rus. Fed. **189** F2
Seybaplaya Mex. **167** H5
Seychelles *country* Indian Ocean **185** L6
Seydi Turkm. **111** F2
Seydişehir Turkey **112** C3
Seyðisfjörður Iceland **54** [inset 1]
Seyhan Turkey *see* **Adana**
Seyhan *r.* Turkey **107** B1
Seyitgazi Turkey **69** N5
Seym *r.* Rus. Fed./Ukr. **53** G6
Seymchan Rus. Fed. **77** Q3
Seymour Australia **138** B6
Seymour S. Africa **125** H7
Seymour *IN* U.S.A. **164** C4
Seymour *TX* U.S.A. **161** D5
Seymour Inlet Canada **150** E5
Seymour Range *mts* Australia **135** F6
Seypan *i.* N. Mariana Is *see* **Saipan**
Sézanne France **62** D6
Sfakia Greece *see* **Chora Sfakion**
Sfântu Gheorghe Romania **69** K2
Sfax Tunisia **68** D7
Sfikia, Limni *resr* Greece *see* **Sfikias, Limni**
Sfikias, Limni *resr* Greece **69** J4
Sfîntu Gheorghe Romania *see* **Sfântu Gheorghe**
Sgiersch Poland *see* **Zgierz**
's-Graveland Neth. **62** F2
's-Gravenhage Neth. *see* **The Hague**
Sgurr Alasdair *hill* U.K. **60** C3
Sgurr Dhomhnuill *hill* U.K. **60** D4
Sgurr Mòr *mt.* U.K. **60** D3
Sgurr na Ciche *mt.* U.K. **60** D3
Shaanxi *prov.* China **95** G5
Shaartuz Tajik. *see* **Shahrtuz**
Shaban Pak. **111** G4
Shabani Zimbabwe *see* **Zvishavane**
Shabestar Iran **110** B2
Shabībī, Jabal ash *mt.* Jordan **107** B5
Shabla, Nos *pt* Bulg. **69** M3
Shabogamo Lake Canada **153** I3
Shabunda Dem. Rep. Congo **122** C4
Shache China **98** B5
Shacheng China *see* **Huailai**
Shackleton Coast Antarctica **188** H1
Shackleton Glacier Antarctica **188** I1
Shackleton Ice Shelf Antarctica **188** F2
Shackleton Range *mts* Antarctica **188** A1
Shadaogou China **97** F2
Shadaw Myanmar **86** B3
Shādegān Iran **110** C4
Shadihar Pak. **111** G4
Shady Grove *OR* U.S.A. **156** C4
Shady Spring *WV* U.S.A. **164** E5
Shafer, Lake *IN* U.S.A. **164** B3
Shafer Peak Antarctica **188** H2
Shafter *CA* U.S.A. **158** D4
Shaftesbury U.K. **59** E7
Shagamu *r.* Canada **152** D3
Shagan Kazakh. **98** B2
Shagan *watercourse* Kazakh. **98** B2
Shagedu China **95** G4
Shageluk *AK* U.S.A. **148** H3
Shaghyray Üstirti *plat.* Kazakh. *see* **Shagyray, Plato**
Shagonar Rus. Fed. **102** H1
Shag Point N.Z. **139** C7
Shag Rocks *is* S. Georgia **178** H8
Shagyray, Plato *plat.* Kazakh. **102** A2
Shahabad *Karnataka* India **106** C2
Shahabad *Rajasthan* India **104** D4
Shahabad *Uttar Prad.* India **104** E4
Shāhābād Iran *see* **Eslāmābād-e Gharb**
Shah Alam Malaysia **84** C2
Shah Bandar Pak. **111** G5
Shahdād Iran **110** E4
Shahdol India **104** E5
Shahe *Chongqing* China **97** F2
Shahe *Shandong* China **95** I4
Shahejie China *see* **Jiujiang**
Shahepu China *see* **Linze**
Shahezhen *Gansu* China *see* **Linze**
Shahezhen *Jiangxi* China *see* **Jiujiang**
Shāh Fūlādī *mt.* Afgh. **111** G3
Shahid, Ras *pt* Pak. **111** F5
Shāhīn Dezh Iran *see* **Sa'īndezh**
Shāh Jahān, Kūh-e *mts* Iran **110** E2
Shahjahanpur India **104** D4
Shāh Kūh *mt.* Iran **110** E4
Shahousuo China **95** J3
Shāhpūr Iran *see* **Salmās**
Shahrak Afgh. **111** G3
Shāh Rakht Iran **111** F3
Shahr-e Bābak Iran **110** D4
Shahr-e Kord Iran **110** C3
Shahr-e Ṣafā Afgh. **111** G4
Shahrezā Iran **110** C3
Shahrig Pak. **111** G4
Shahrisabz Uzbek. **111** G2
Shahriston Tajik. **111** H2
Shahr Rey Iran **110** C3
Shahr Sultan Pak. **111** H4
Shahrtuz Tajik. **111** H2
Shāhrūd Iran *see* **Emāmrūd**
Shāhrūd, Rūdkhāneh-ye *r.* Iran **110** C2
Shahrud Bustam *reg.* Iran **110** D3
Shāh Savārān, Kūh-e *mts* Iran **110** E4
Shāh Taqī Iran *see* **Emām Taqī**
Shaighalu Pak. **111** H4
Shaikh Husain *mt.* Pak. **111** G4
Shaikhpura India *see* **Sheikhpura**
Shā'īr, Jabal *mts* Syria **107** C2
Sha'īra, Gebel *mt.* Egypt *see* **Sha'īrah, Jabal**
Sha'īrah, Jabal *mt.* Egypt **107** B5
Shaj'ah, Jabal *hill* Saudi Arabia **110** C5
Shajapur India **104** D5
Shajianzi China **90** B4
Shakaga-dake *mt.* Japan **92** B4
Shakaville S. Africa **125** J5
Shakh Tajik. *see* **Shoh**
Shakhbuz Azer. *see* **Şahbuz**
Shākhen Iran **111** E3
Shakhovskaya Rus. Fed. **52** G4
Shakhrisabz Uzbek. *see* **Shahrisabz**
Shakhristan Tajik. *see* **Shahriston**
Shakhtinsk Kazakh. **102** D2
Shakhty *Respublika Buryatiya* Rus. Fed. *see* **Gusinoozersk**
Shakhty *Rostovskaya Oblast'* Rus. Fed. **53** I7
Shakhun'ya Rus. Fed. **52** J4
Shaki Nigeria **120** D4
Shakotan-hantō *pen.* Japan **90** F4
Shaktoolik *AK* U.S.A. **148** G2
Shalakusha Rus. Fed. **52** I3
Shalang China **97** F4
Shali Rus. Fed. **113** G2
Shaliangzi China **94** C4
Shaliuhe China *see* **Gangca**
Shalkar India **104** D3
Shalkar Kazakh. **102** A2
Shalkarteniz, Solonchak *salt marsh* Kazakh. **102** B2
Shalkodesu Kazakh. **98** B4
Shallow Bay Canada **149** M1
Shalqar Kazakh. *see* **Shalkar**
Shaluli Shan *mts* China **96** C2
Shaluni *mt.* India **105** I3
Shama *r.* Tanz. **123** D4
Shamâl Sînâ' *governorate* Egypt *see* **Shamāl Sīnā'**
Shamāl Sīnā' *governorate* Egypt **107** A4
Shāmat al Akbād *des.* Saudi Arabia **113** F5
Shamattawa Canada **151** N4
Shamattawa *r.* Canada **152** D3
Shambār Iran **110** C3
Shamgong Bhutan *see* **Shemgang**
Shamīl Iran **110** E5
Shāmīyah *des.* Iraq/Syria **107** D2
Shamkhor Azer. *see* **Şämkir**
Shamrock *TX* U.S.A. **161** C5
Shancheng *Fujian* China *see* **Taining**
Shancheng *Shandong* China *see* **Shanxian**
Shand Afgh. **111** F4
Shandan China **94** E4
Shandian He *r.* China **95** I3
Shandong *prov.* China **95** I4
Shandong Bandao *pen.* China **95** J4
Shandur Pass Pak. **111** I2
Shangchao China **97** F3
Shangcheng China **97** G2
Shang Chu *r.* China **99** E7
Shangchuan Dao *i.* China **97** G4
Shangdu China **95** H3
Shangganling China **90** C3

▶**Shanghai** China **97** I2
4th most populous city in Asia and 7th in the world.

Shanghai *municipality* China **97** I2
Shanghe China **95** I4
Shangji China *see* **Xichuan**
Shangjie China *see* **Yangbi**
Shangjin China **97** F1
Shangkuli China **95** J1
Shangluo China **97** F1
Shangmei China *see* **Xinhua**
Shangnan China **97** F1
Shangpa China *see* **Fugong**
Shangpai China *see* **Feixi**
Shangpaihe China *see* **Feixi**
Shangqiu China **95** H5
Shangrao China **97** H2
Shangsanshilipu China **98** C3
Shangshui China **97** G1
Shangyou China **97** G3
Shangyou Shuiku *resr* China **98** C4
Shangyu China **97** I2
Shangzhi China **90** B3
Shangzhou China *see* **Shangluo**
Shanhaiguan China **95** I3
Shanhe *Gansu* China *see* **Zhengning**
Shanhe *Heilong.* China **90** B3
Shankou *Guangxi* China **97** F4
Shankou *Xinjiang* China **94** C3
Shanlaragh Ireland **61** C6
Shannon *airport* Ireland **61** D5
Shannon *est.* Ireland **61** D5
Shannon *r.* Ireland **61** D5
Shannon, Mouth of the Ireland **61** C5
Shannon National Park Australia **135** B8
Shannon Ø *i.* Greenland **189** I1
Shan Plateau Myanmar **86** B2
Shanshan China **94** B3
Shanshanzhan China **94** B3
Shansi *prov.* China *see* **Shanxi**
Shan Teng *hill H.K.* China *see* **Victoria Peak**
Shantipur India **105** G5
Shantou China **97** H4
Shantung *prov.* China *see* **Shandong**
Shanwei China **97** G4
Shanxi *prov.* China **95** G4
Shanxian China **95** I5
Shanyang China **97** F1
Shanyin China **95** H4
Shaodong China **97** F3
Shaoguan China **97** G3
Shaowu China **97** H3
Shaoxing China **97** I2
Shaoyang China **97** F3
Shap U.K. **58** E4
Shapa China **97** F4
Shaping China *see* **Ebian**
Shapinsay *i.* U.K. **60** G1
Shapkina *r.* Rus. Fed. **52** L2
Shapshal'skiy Khrebet *mts* Rus. Fed. **98** E2
Shaqiuhe China **98** E3
Shaqrā' Saudi Arabia **108** G4
Shaquanzi China **98** C3
Shar Kazakh. **98** C2
Shār, Jabal *mt.* Saudi Arabia **112** D6
Sharaf *well* Iraq **113** F5
Sharalday Rus. Fed. **95** F1
Sharan Afgh. **111** H3
Sharan Jogizai Pak. **111** H4
Shārb Māh Iran **110** E4
Sharbulag Mongolia *see* **Dzavhan**
Shardara Kazakh. **102** C3
Shardara, Step' *plain* Kazakh. *see* **Chardara, Step'**
Sharga *Govĭ-Altay* Mongolia **94** C2
Sharga *Hövsgöl* Mongolia *see* **Tsagaan-Uul**
Sharhulsan Mongolia *see* **Mandal-Ovoo**
Shari *r.* Cameroon/Chad *see* **Chari**
Shārī, Buḩayrat *imp. l.* Iraq **113** G4
Shari-dake *vol.* Japan **90** G4
Sharīfah Syria **107** C2
Shariff Aguak Phil. **82** D5
Sharjah U.A.E. **110** D5
Sharka-leb La *pass* China **99** E7
Sharkawshchyna Belarus **55** O9
Shark Bay Australia **135** A6
Shark Reef Australia **136** D2
Sharlyk Rus. Fed. **51** Q5
Sharm ash Shaykh Egypt **112** D6
Sharm el Sheikh Egypt *see* **Sharm ash Shaykh**
Sharon *PA* U.S.A. **164** E3
Sharon Springs *KS* U.S.A. **160** C4
Sharpe Lake Canada **151** M4
Sharp Mountain Canada **149** M2
Sharp Peak *hill H.K.* China **97** [inset]
Sharqat Iraq *see* **Ash Sharqāţ**
Sharqī, Jabal ash *mts* Lebanon/Syria **107** B3
Sharqiy Ustyurt Chink *esc.* Uzbek. **102** A3
Sharur Azer. *see* **Şărur**
Shar Us Gol *r.* Mongolia **94** D2
Shar'ya Rus. Fed. **52** J4
Sharyn Kazakh. **98** B4
Sharyn *r.* Kazakh. **98** B4
Shashe *r.* Botswana/Zimbabwe **123** C6
Shashemenē Eth. **122** D3
Shashi China *see* **Jingzhou**
Shashubay Kazakh. **98** A3
Shasta *CA* U.S.A. **158** B1
Shasta, Mount *vol. CA* U.S.A. **156** C4
Shasta Lake *CA* U.S.A. **158** B1
Shatilki Belarus *see* **Svyetlahorsk**
Sha Tin *H.K.* China **97** [inset]
Shatki Rus. Fed. **53** J5
Shaṭnat as Salmās, Wādī *watercourse* Syria **107** D2
Sha Tong Hau Shan *H.K.* China *see* **Bluff Island**
Shatoy Rus. Fed. **113** G2
Shatsk Rus. Fed. **53** I5
Shaṭṭ al 'Arab *r.* Iran/Iraq **113** H5
Shatura Rus. Fed. **53** H5
Shaubak Jordan *see* **Ash Shawbak**
Shaunavon Canada **151** I5
Shaver Lake *CA* U.S.A. **158** D3
Shaviovik *r. AK* U.S.A. **149** K1
Shaw *r.* Australia **134** B5
Shawan China **98** D3
Shawangunk Mountains *hills NY* U.S.A. **165** H3
Shawano *WI* U.S.A. **164** A1
Shawano Lake *WI* U.S.A. **164** A1
Shawinigan Canada **153** G5
Shawnee *OK* U.S.A. **161** D5
Shawnee *WY* U.S.A. **156** G4
Shawneetown *IL* U.S.A. **160** F4
Shaxian China **97** H3
Shaybar, Kōtal-e Afgh. **111** H3
Shay Gap (abandoned) Australia **134** C5
Shaykh, Jabal ash *mt.* Lebanon/Syria *see* **Hermon, Mount**
Shaykh Miskīn Syria **107** C3
Shāzand Iran **110** C3
Shazaoyuan China **98** F5
Shaẓāẓ, Jabal *mt.* Saudi Arabia **113** F6
Shazud Tajik. **111** I2
Shchekino Rus. Fed. **53** H5
Shchel'yayur Rus. Fed. **52** L2
Shcherbakov Rus. Fed. *see* **Rybinsk**
Shchigry Rus. Fed. **53** H6
Shchors Ukr. **53** F6
Shchuchin Belarus *see* **Shchuchyn**
Shchuchyn Belarus **55** N10
Shebalino Rus. Fed. **102** G1
Shebekino Rus. Fed. **53** H6

▶**Shebelē Wenz, Wabē** *r.* Somalia **122** E3
5th longest river in Africa.

Sheboygan *WI* U.S.A. **164** B2
Shebshi Mountains Nigeria **120** E4
Shebunino Rus. Fed. **90** F3
Shecheng China *see* **Shexian**
Shediac Canada **153** I5
Shedin Peak Canada **150** E4
Shedok Rus. Fed. **113** F1
Sheelin, Lough *l.* Ireland **61** E4
Sheenjek *r. AK* U.S.A. **149** K2
Sheep Haven *b.* Ireland **61** E2
Sheepmoor S. Africa **125** J4
Sheep Mountain *CO* U.S.A. **159** J2
Sheep Peak *NV* U.S.A. **159** F3
Sheep's Head *hd* Ireland *see* **Muntervary**
Sheerness U.K. **59** H7
Sheet Harbour Canada **153** J5
Shefar'am Israel **107** B3
Sheffield N.Z. **139** D6
Sheffield U.K. **58** F5
Sheffield *AL* U.S.A. **163** C5
Sheffield *PA* U.S.A. **164** F3
Sheffield *TX* U.S.A. **161** C6
Sheffield Lake Canada **153** K4
Shēgh 'Alāqahdārī Afgh. **111** G4
Sheghnān Afgh. **111** H2
Shegmas Rus. Fed. **52** K2
Shehong China **96** E2
Sheikh, Jebel esh *mt.* Lebanon/Syria *see* **Hermon, Mount**
Sheikhpura India **105** F4
Sheikhupura Pak. **111** I4
Shējā' ul Mulk Kēlay Afgh. **111** H4
Shekak *r.* Canada **152** D4
Shekār Āb Iran **110** D3
Shekhawati *reg.* India **111** I5
Shekhem West Bank *see* **Nāblus**
Shekhpura India *see* **Sheikhpura**
Sheki Azer. *see* **Şäki**
Shekka Ch'ün-Tao *H.K.* China *see* **Soko Islands**
Shek Kwu Chau *i. H.K.* China **97** [inset]
Shekou China **97** [inset]
Sheksna Rus. Fed. **52** H4
Sheksninskoye Vodokhranilishche *resr* Rus. Fed. **52** H4
Shek Uk Shan *mt. H.K.* China **97** [inset]
Shela China **99** F7
Shelagskiy, Mys *pt* Rus. Fed. **77** S2
Shelbina *MO* U.S.A. **160** E4
Shelburn *IN* U.S.A. **164** B4
Shelburne *N.S.* Canada **153** I6
Shelburne *Ont.* Canada **164** E1
Shelburne Bay Australia **136** C1
Shelby *MI* U.S.A. **164** B2
Shelby *MS* U.S.A. **161** F5
Shelby *MT* U.S.A. **156** F2
Shelby *NC* U.S.A. **163** D5
Shelbyville *IL* U.S.A. **160** F4
Shelbyville *IN* U.S.A. **164** C4
Shelbyville *KY* U.S.A. **164** C4
Shelbyville *TN* U.S.A. **162** C5
Sheldon *IA* U.S.A. **160** E3
Sheldon *IL* U.S.A. **164** B3
Sheldon Point *AK* U.S.A. **148** F3
Sheldrake Canada **153** I4
Shelek Kazakh. *see* **Chilik**
Shelikhova, Zaliv *g.* Rus. Fed. **77** Q3
Shelikof Strait *AK* U.S.A. **148** I4
Shell *WY* U.S.A. **160** B2
Shellbrook Canada **151** J4
Shelley *ID* U.S.A. **156** E4
Shellharbour Australia **138** E5
Shell Lake Canada **151** J4
Shell Lake *WI* U.S.A. **160** F2
Shell Mountain *CA* U.S.A. **158** B1
Shelter Bay Canada *see* **Port-Cartier**
Shelter Island *NY* U.S.A. **165** I3
Shelter Point N.Z. **139** B8
Shelton *WA* U.S.A. **156** C3
Shemakha Azer. *see* **Şamaxı**
Shemgang Bhutan **105** G4
Shemonaikha Kazakh. **98** C2
Shemordan Rus. Fed. **52** K4
Shenandoah *IA* U.S.A. **160** E3
Shenandoah *PA* U.S.A. **165** G3
Shenandoah Mountains *VA/WV* U.S.A. **164** F4
Shenandoah National Park *VA* U.S.A. **165** F4
Shenchi China **95** H4
Shendam Nigeria **120** D4
Shending Shan *hill* China **90** D3
Shengel'dy Kazakh. **98** B3
Shengena *mt.* Tanz. **123** D4
Shengli China **97** G2
Shengli Daban *pass* China **98** D4
Shengli Feng *mt.* China/Kyrg. *see* **Pobeda Peak**
Shengli Qichang China **98** B4
Shengli Shibachang China **98** C4
Shengping China **90** B3
Shengrenjian China *see* **Pinglu**
Shengsi China **97** I2
Shengsi Liedao *is* China **97** I2
Shenjiamen China **97** I2
Shenkursk Rus. Fed. **52** I3
Shenmu China **95** G4
Shennong Ding *mt.* China **97** F2
Shennongjia China **97** F2
Shenqiu China **97** G1
Shenshu China **90** C3
Shensi *prov.* China *see* **Shaanxi**
Shentala Rus. Fed. **53** K5
Shenton, Mount *hill* Australia **135** C7
Shenxian *Hebei* China *see* **Shenzhou**
Shenxian *Shandong* China **95** H4
Shenyang China **95** J3
Shenzhen China **97** G4
Shenzhen Wan *b. H.K.* China *see* **Deep Bay**
Shenzhou China **95** H4
Sheopur India **104** D4
Shepetivka Ukr. **53** E6
Shepetovka Ukr. *see* **Shepetivka**
Shepherd Islands Vanuatu **133** G3
Shepherdsville *KY* U.S.A. **164** C5
Shepparton Australia **138** B6
Sheppey, Isle of *i.* U.K. **59** H7
Sheqi China **97** G1
Sherabad Uzbek. *see* **Sherobod**
Sherborne U.K. **59** E8
Sherbro Island Sierra Leone **120** B4
Sherbrooke Canada **153** H5
Sherburne *NY* U.S.A. **165** H2
Shercock Ireland **61** F4
Sherdyayak Kazakh. **98** C2
Shereiq Sudan **108** D6
Shergaon India **105** H4
Shergarh India **104** C4
Sheridan *AR* U.S.A. **161** E5
Sheridan *WY* U.S.A. **156** G3
Sheringham U.K. **59** I6
Sherlovaya Gora Rus. Fed. **95** I1
Sherman *TX* U.S.A. **161** D5
Sherman Mountain *NV* U.S.A. **159** F1
Sherobod Uzbek. **111** G2
Sherpur *Dhaka* Bangl. **105** G4
Sherpur *Rajshahi* Bangl. **105** G4
Sherridon Canada **151** K4
's-Hertogenbosch Neth. **62** F3
Sherwood Forest *reg.* U.K. **59** F5
Sherwood Lake Canada **151** K2
Sheslay Canada **149** O4
Sheslay *r.* Canada **149** N4
Shethanei Lake Canada **151** L3
Shetland Islands *is* U.K. **60** [inset]
Shetpe Kazakh. **100** E2
Sheung Shui *H.K.* China **97** [inset]
Sheung Sze Mun *sea chan. H.K.* China **97** [inset]
Shevchenko Kazakh. *see* **Aktau**
Shevli *r.* Rus. Fed. **90** D1
Shexian *Anhui* China **97** H2
Shexian *Hebei* China **95** H4
Sheyang China **97** I1
Sheyenne *r. ND* U.S.A. **160** D2
Shey Phoksundo National Park Nepal **105** E3
Sheytūr Iran **110** D4
Shezhin II Kazakh. **53** K6
Shiant Islands U.K. **60** C3
Shiashkotan, Ostrov *i.* Rus. Fed. **77** Q5
Shibakawa Japan **93** E3
Shibām Yemen **108** G6
Shibandong Jing *well* China **94** C3
Shiban Jing *well* China **94** D3
Shibaocheng China **94** D4
Shibata Japan **91** E5
Shibayama Japan **93** G3
Shibayama-gata *l.* Japan **92** C2
Shibazhan China **90** B1
Shibh Jazīrat Sīnā' *pen.* Egypt *see* **Sinai**
Shibīn al Kawm Egypt **112** C5
Shibîn el Kôm Egypt *see* **Shibīn al Kawm**
Shibirghān Afgh. **111** G2
Shibogama Lake Canada **152** C3
Shibotsu-jima *i.* Rus. Fed. *see* **Zelenyy, Ostrov**
Shibukawa Japan **93** F2
Shibu-tōge *pass* Japan **93** E2
Shibutsu-san *mt.* Japan **93** F2
Shicheng *Fujian* China *see* **Zhouning**
Shicheng *Jiangxi* China **97** H3
Shicheng Dao *i.* China **95** J4
Shichimen-zan *mt.* Japan **93** E3
Shicun China *see* **Xiangfen**
Shidād al Mismā' *hill* Saudi Arabia **107** D4
Shidao China **95** J4
Shidao Wan *b.* China **95** J4
Shidian China **96** C3
Shidongsi China *see* **Gaolan**
Shiel, Loch *l.* U.K. **60** D4
Shield, Cape Australia **136** B2
Shīeli Kazakh. *see* **Chiili**
Shifa, Jabal ash *mts* Saudi Arabia **112** D5
Shifang China **96** E2
Shiga *Nagano* Japan **93** D2
Shiga *Shiga* Japan **92** B3
Shiga *pref.* Japan **92** B3
Shigaraki Japan **92** C4
Shigatse China *see* **Xigazê**
Shigong China **98** F4

Shiguai China **95** G3
Shiguaigou China *see* **Shiguai**
Shiḩān *mt.* Jordan **107** B4
Shihezi China **98** D3
Shihkiachwang China *see* **Shijiazhuang**
Shijiao China *see* **Fogang**
Shijiazhuang China **95** H4
Shijiu Hu *l.* China **97** H2
Shijiusuo China *see* **Rizhao**
Shika Japan **92** C1
Shikag Lake Canada **152** C4
Shikar *r.* Pak. **111** F4
Shikarpur Pak. **111** H5
Shikengkong *mt.* China **97** G3
Shikhany Rus. Fed. **53** J5
Shiki Japan **93** F3
Shikine-jima *i.* Japan **93** F4
Shikishima Japan **93** E3
Shikohabad India **104** D4
Shikoku *i.* Japan **91** D6
Shikoku-sanchi *mts* Japan **91** D6
Shikotan, Ostrov *i.* Rus. Fed. **90** G4
Shikotan-tō *i.* Rus. Fed. *see* **Shikotan, Ostrov**
Shikotsu-Tōya Kokuritsu-kōen Japan **90** F4
Shildon U.K. **58** F4
Shilega Rus. Fed. **52** J2
Shilianghe Shuiku *resr* China **95** I5
Shiliguri India **105** G4
Shilik *r.* Kazakh. **98** B4
Shilin China **96** D3
Shilipu China **97** G2
Shiliu China *see* **Changjiang**
Shilla *mt.* India **104** D2
Shillelagh Ireland **61** F5
Shillo *r.* Israel **107** B3
Shillong India **105** G4
Shilou China **95** G4
Shilovo Rus. Fed. **53** I5
Shilüüstey Mongolia **94** D2
Shima Japan **92** C4
Shima *spring* Japan **93** E2
Shimada Japan **93** E4
Shimagahara Japan **92** C4
Shima-hantō *pen.* Japan **92** C4
Shimamoto Japan **92** B4
Shimanovsk Rus. Fed. **90** B1
Shimbiris *mt.* Somalia **122** E2
Shimen *Gansu* China **96** D1
Shimen *Hunan* China **97** F2
Shimen *Yunnan* China *see* **Yunlong**
Shimizu *Fukui* Japan **92** C2
Shimizu *Shizuoka* Japan **93** E3
Shimizu *Shizuoka* Japan **93** E3
Shimizu *Wakayama* Japan **92** B4
Shimla India **104** D3
Shimminato Japan *see* **Shinminato**
Shimo Japan **92** D2
Shimobe Japan **93** E3
Shimoda Japan **93** E4
Shimodate Japan **93** F2
Shimofusa Japan **93** G3
Shimoga India **106** B3
Shimoichi Japan **92** B4
Shimojō Japan **93** D3
Shimokita-hantō *pen.* Japan **90** F4
Shimokitayama Japan **92** B4
Shimoni Kenya **123** D4
Shimonita Japan **93** E2
Shimonoseki Japan **91** C6
Shimosuwa Japan **93** E2
Shimotsu Japan **92** B4
Shimotsuma Japan **93** F2
Shimoyama Japan **92** D3
Shimsk Rus. Fed. **52** F4
Shin Japan **93** F2
Shin, Loch *l.* U.K. **60** E2
Shināfīyah Iraq *see* **Ash Shanāfīyah**
Shinan China *see* **Xingye**
Shinano Japan **93** E2
Shin-asahi Japan **92** C3
Shīndand Afgh. **111** F3
Shine-Ider Mongolia **94** D1
Shinejinst Mongolia **94** D2
Shingbwiyang Myanmar **86** B1
Shing-gai Myanmar **86** B1
Shinghshal Pass Pak. **111** I2
Shingletown *CA* U.S.A. **158** C1
Shingū Japan **91** E6
Shingwedzi S. Africa **125** J2
Shingwedzi *r.* S. Africa **125** J2
Shīnkay Afgh. **111** G4
Shīnkay Ghar Afgh. **111** H3
Shinminato Japan **92** D2
Shinnston *WV* U.S.A. **164** E4
Shino-jima *i.* Japan **92** C4
Shinonoi Japan **93** E2
Shinsei Japan **92** C3
Shinshār Syria **107** C2
Shinshiro Japan **92** D4
Shinshūshin Japan **93** E2
Shintō Japan **93** E2
Shintone Japan **93** G3
Shinyanga Tanz. **122** D4
Shio Japan **92** C2
Shiobara Japan **93** F2
Shiocton *WI* U.S.A. **164** A1
Shiogama Japan **91** F5
Shiojiri Japan **93** D2
Shiomi-dake *mt.* Japan **93** E3
Shiono-misaki *c.* Japan **91** D6
Shioya Japan **93** F2
Shioya-zaki *pt* Japan **93** G1
Shiozawa Japan **93** E1
Shipai China **97** H2
Shiping China **96** D4
Shipki Pass China/India **99** B7
Shipman *VA* U.S.A. **165** F5
Shippegan Island Canada **153** I5
Shippensburg *PA* U.S.A. **165** G3
Shippō Japan **92** C3
Shiprock *NM* U.S.A. **159** I3
Shiprock Peak *NM* U.S.A. **159** I3
Shipu *Shaanxi* China *see* **Huanglong**
Shipu *Zhejiang* China **97** I2
Shipunovo Rus. Fed. **88** E2
Shiqian China **97** F3
Shiqiao China *see* **Panyu**
Shiqizhen China *see* **Zhongshan**
Shiquan China **97** F1
Shiquanhe *Xizang* China *see* **Ali**
Shiquanhe *Xizang* China *see* **Gar**
Shiquan Shuiku *resr* China **97** F1
Shira Rus. Fed. **88** F2
Shīrābād Iran **110** C2
Shirahama Japan **93** F4
Shirai-san *hill* Japan **92** C4
Shirakawa *Fukushima* Japan **93** G1
Shirakawa *Gifu* Japan **92** C2
Shirakawa *Gifu* Japan **92** D3
Shirakawa-go and Gokayama *tourist site* Japan **91** E5
Shirake-mine *mt.* Japan **92** D2
Shirako Japan **93** G3
Shirakura-yama *mt.* Japan **92** D3
Shirama-yama *hill* Japan **92** B4
Shiramine Japan **92** C2
Shirane Japan **93** E3
Shirane-san *mt.* Japan **93** E2
Shirane-san *mt.* Japan **93** E3
Shirane-san *vol.* Japan **93** F2
Shirasawa Japan **93** F2
Shirase Coast Antarctica **188** J1
Shirase Glacier Antarctica **188** D2
Shīrāz Iran **110** D4
Shire *r.* Malawi **123** D5
Shireet Mongolia *see* **Bayandelger**
Shireza Pak. **111** G5
Shiriya-zaki *c.* Japan **90** F4
Shirkala *reg.* Kazakh. **102** A2
Shīr Kūh *mt.* Iran **110** D4
Shiroi Japan **93** G3
Shirokura-yama *mt.* Japan **93** D3
Shiroro Reservoir Nigeria **120** D3
Shirotori Japan **92** C3
Shirouma-dake *mt.* Japan **92** D2
Shiroyama Japan **93** F3
Shirpur India **104** C5
Shirten Holoy Gobi *des.* China **94** D3
Shīrvān Iran **110** E2
Shisanjianfang China **94** B3
Shisanzhan China **90** B2
Shishaldin Volcano *AK* U.S.A. **146** B4
Shisha Pangma *mt.* China *see* **Xixabangma Feng**
Shishmaref *AK* U.S.A. **148** F2
Shishmaref Inlet *AK* U.S.A. **148** F2
Shishou China **97** G2
Shisui Japan **93** G3
Shitan China **97** G3
Shitang China **97** I2
Shitanjing China **94** F4
Shitara Japan **92** D3
Shithāthah Iraq **113** F4
Shiv India **104** B4
Shivamogga India *see* **Shimoga**
Shiveluch, Vulkan *vol.* Rus. Fed. **77** R4
Shivpuri India **104** D4
Shivwits *UT* U.S.A. **159** G3
Shivwits Plateau *AZ* U.S.A. **159** G3
Shiwan China **95** G4
Shiwan Dashan *mts* China **96** E4
Shiwan'gandu Zambia **123** D5
Shixing China **97** G3
Shiyan China **97** F1
Shizhu China **97** F2
Shizi *Anhui* China **97** H2
Shizi *Gansu* China **95** F5
Shizilu China *see* **Junan**
Shizong China **96** D3
Shizuishan China **94** F4
Shizuishanzhan China **94** F4
Shizuoka Japan **93** E4
Shizuoka *pref.* Japan **93** E4

▶**Shkhara** *mt.* Georgia/Rus. Fed. **113** F2
3rd highest mountain in Europe.

Shklov Belarus *see* **Shklow**
Shklow Belarus **53** F5
Shkodër Albania **69** H3
Shkodra Albania *see* **Shkodër**
Shkodrës, Liqeni i *l.* Albania/Montenegro *see* **Scutari, Lake**
Shmidta, Ostrov *i.* Rus. Fed. **76** K1
Shmidta, Poluostrov *pen.* Rus. Fed. **90** F1
Shoal Lake Canada **151** K5
Shoals *IN* U.S.A. **164** B4
Shōbara Japan **91** D6
Shōgawa Japan **92** D2
Shō-gawa *r.* Japan **92** D2
Shoh Tajik. **111** H2
Shohi Pass Pak. *see* **Tal Pass**
Shokanbetsu-dake *mt.* Japan **90** F4
Shōkawa Japan **92** C2
Shokpar Kazakh. **98** A4
Sholakkorgan Kazakh. **102** C3
Sholapur India *see* **Solapur**
Sholaqorghan Kazakh. *see* **Sholakkorgan**
Shomba *r.* Rus. Fed. **54** R4
Shomvukovo Rus. Fed. **52** K3
Shōmyō-gawa *r.* Japan **92** D2
Shona Ridge *sea feature* S. Atlantic Ocean **184** I9
Shonzha Kazakh. *see* **Chundzha**
Shor India **104** D2
Shorap Pak. **111** G5
Shorapur India **106** C2
Sho'rchi Uzbek. **111** G2
Shorewood *IL* U.S.A. **164** A3
Shorewood *WI* U.S.A. **164** B2
Shorkot Pak. **111** I4
Shorkozakhly, Solonchak *salt flat* Turkm. **113** J2
Shoshone *CA* U.S.A. **158** E4
Shoshone *ID* U.S.A. **156** E4
Shoshone *r.* *WY* U.S.A. **156** F3
Shoshone Mountains *NV* U.S.A. **158** E2
Shoshone Peak *NV* U.S.A. **158** E3
Shoshong Botswana **125** H2
Shoshoni *WY* U.S.A. **156** F4
Shostka Ukr. **53** G6
Shotor Khūn Afgh. **111** G3
Shouguang China **95** I4
Shouyang China **95** H4
Shouyang Shan *mt.* China **97** F1
Shōwa Japan **93** F2
Showak Sudan **108** E7
Show Low *AZ* U.S.A. **159** H4
Shoyna Rus. Fed. **52** J2
Shpakovskoye Rus. Fed. **113** F1
Shpola Ukr. **53** F6
Shqipëria *country* Europe *see* **Albania**
Shreve *OH* U.S.A. **164** D3
Shreveport *LA* U.S.A. **161** E5
Shrewsbury U.K. **59** E6
Shri Lanka *country* Asia *see* **Sri Lanka**
Shri Mohangarh India **104** B4
Shrirampur India **105** G5
Shu Kazakh. **102** D3
Shü *r.* Kazakh./Kyrg. *see* **Chu**
Shu'ab, Ra's *pt* Yemen **109** H7
Shuajingsi China **96** D1
Shuangbai China **96** D3
Shuangcheng *Fujian* China *see* **Zherong**
Shuangcheng *Heilong.* China **90** B3
Shuanghe *Hubei* China **97** G2
Shuanghe *Sichuan* China **96** E2
Shuanghedagang China **90** C2
Shuanghu China **99** D6
Shuanghuyu China *see* **Zizhou**
Shuangjiang *Guizhou* China *see* **Jiangkou**
Shuangjiang *Hunan* China *see* **Tongdao**
Shuangjiang *Yunnan* China *see* **Eshan**
Shuangliao China **95** J3
Shuangliu China **96** D2
Shuangpai China **97** F3
Shuangshanzi China **95** I3
Shuangshipu China *see* **Fengxian**
Shuangxi China *see* **Shunchang**
Shuangyang China **90** B4
Shuangyashan China **90** C3
Shubarkudyk Kazakh. **102** A2
Shubayḩ *well* Saudi Arabia **107** D4
Shublik Mountains *AK* U.S.A. **149** K1
Shufu China **98** A5
Shugozero Rus. Fed. **52** G4
Shu He *r.* China **95** I5
Shuiding China *see* **Huocheng**
Shuidong China *see* **Dianbai**
Shuiji China *see* **Laixi**
Shuijing China **96** E1
Shuijingkuang China **99** E6
Shuikou *Guangxi* China **96** E4
Shuikou *Hunan* China **97** F3
Shu-Ile, Gory *mts* Kazakh. **102** D3
Shuiluocheng China *see* **Zhuanglang**
Shuiquan China **94** F4
Shuiquanzi China **94** E4
Shuizhai China *see* **Wuhua**
Shuizhan China **99** E5
Shulakpachak Peak *AK* U.S.A. **148** I2
Shulan China **90** B3
Shule China **98** B5
Shulehe China **98** G4
Shule He *r.* China **94** C3
Shule Nanshan *mts* China **94** D4
Shulinzhao China **95** G3
Shulu China *see* **Xinji**
Shumagin Islands *AK* U.S.A. **148** G5
Shumba Zimbabwe **123** C5
Shumen Bulg. **69** L3
Shumerlya Rus. Fed. **52** J5
Shumilina Belarus **53** F5
Shumyachi Rus. Fed. **53** G5
Shunchang China **97** H3
Shuncheng China **90** A4
Shunde China **97** G4
Shungnak *AK* U.S.A. **148** H2
Shunyi China **95** I3
Shuoxian China *see* **Shuozhou**
Shuozhou China **95** H4
Shuqrah Yemen **108** G7
Shūr *r.* Iran **110** D4
Shūr *r.* Iran **111** F3
Shūr *watercourse* Iran **110** D5
Shur *watercourse* Iran **110** E3
Shūr, Rūd-e *watercourse* Iran **110** E4
Shūr Āb *watercourse* Iran **110** D4
Shūrawak *reg.* Afgh. **111** G4
Shūrjestān Iran **110** D4
Shūrū Iran **111** F4
Shuryshkarskiy Sor, Ozero *l.* Rus. Fed. **51** T2
Shūsh Iran **110** C3
Shusha Azer. *see* **Şuşa**
Shushtar Iran **110** C3
Shutfah, Qalamat *well* Saudi Arabia **110** D6
Shuwaysh, Tall ash *hill* Jordan **107** C4
Shuya *Ivanovskaya Oblast'* Rus. Fed. **52** I4
Shuya *Respublika Kareliya* Rus. Fed. **52** G3
Shuyak Island *AK* U.S.A. **148** I4
Shuyang China **95** I5
Shuyskoye Rus. Fed. **52** I4
Shuzenji Japan **93** E4
Shwebo Myanmar **86** A2
Shwedwin Myanmar **86** A1
Shwegun Myanmar **86** B3
Shwegyin Myanmar **86** B3
Shweudaung *mt.* Myanmar **86** B2
Shyghanaq Kazakh. *see* **Chiganak**
Shygys Konyrat Kazakh. **98** A3
Shymkent Kazakh. **102** C3
Shyngystau, Khrebet *mts* Kazakh. **102** E2
Shynkozha Kazakh. **98** C3
Shyok India **104** D2
Shyok *r.* India **99** A6
Shypuvate Ukr. **53** H6
Shyroke Ukr. **53** G7
Sia Indon. **81** I8
Siabu *Sumatera* Indon. **84** B2
Siachen Glacier India/Pak. **99** B6
Siahan Range *mts* Pak. **111** F5
Sīāh Band, Kūh-e *mts* Afgh. **111** F3
Sīāh Chashmeh Iran **110** B2
Sīāh Gird Afgh. **111** G2
Sīāh Kūh *mts* Afgh. **111** G3
Siak *r.* Indon. **84** C2
Siak Sri Inderapura *Sumatera* Indon. **84** C2
Sialkot Pak. **111** I3
Siam *country* Asia *see* **Thailand**
Sian China *see* **Xi'an**
Sian Rus. Fed. **90** B1
Siang *r.* India *see* **Brahmaputra**
Siantan *i.* Indon. **84** D2
Siargao *i.* Phil. **82** D4
Siasi Phil. **82** C5
Siasi *i.* Phil. **82** C5
Siaton *Negros* Phil. **82** C4
Siau *i.* Indon. **83** C2
Šiauliai Lith. **55** M9
Siazan' Azer. *see* **Siyäzän**
Si Bai, Lam *r.* Thai. **86** D4
Sibasa S. Africa **125** J2
Sibati China *see* **Xibet**
Sibay *i.* Phil. **82** C4
Sibayi, Lake S. Africa **125** K4
Sibda China **96** C2
Šibenik Croatia **68** F3
Siberia *reg.* Rus. Fed. **77** M3
Siberut *i.* Indon. **84** B3
Siberut, Selat *sea chan.* Indon. **84** B3
Siberut, Taman Nasional *nat. park* Indon. **84** B3
Sibi Pak. **111** G4
Sibidiri P.N.G. **81** K8
Sibigo Indon. **84** A2
Sibiloi National Park Kenya **122** D3
Sibir' *reg.* Rus. Fed. *see* **Siberia**
Sibiti Congo **122** B4
Sibiu Romania **69** K2
Sibley *IA* U.S.A. **160** E3
Siboa *Sulawesi* Indon. **83** B2
Sibolga *Sumatera* Indon. **84** B2
Siborongborong *Sumatera* Indon. **84** B2
Sibsagar India **105** H4
Sibu *Sarawak* Malaysia **85** E2
Sibuco *Mindanao* Phil. **82** C5
Sibuco Bay *Mindanao* Phil. **82** C5
Sibuguey *r.* *Mindanao* Phil. **82** C5
Sibuguey Bay *Mindanao* Phil. **82** C5
Sibut Cent. Afr. Rep. **122** B3
Sibuti *Sarawak* Malaysia **85** F1
Sibutu *i.* Phil. **82** B5
Sibutu Passage Phil. **82** B5
Sibuyan *i.* Phil. **82** C3
Sibuyan Sea Phil. **82** C3
Sicamous Canada **150** G5
Sicapoo *mt.* *Luzon* Phil. **82** C2
Sicca Veneria Tunisia *see* **Le Kef**
Siccus *watercourse* Australia **137** B6
Sicheng *Anhui* China *see* **Sixian**
Sicheng *Guangxi* China *see* **Lingyun**
Sichon Thai. **87** B5
Sichuan *prov.* China **96** D2
Sichuan Pendi *basin* China **96** E2
Sicié, Cap *c.* France **66** G5
Sicilia *i.* Italy *see* **Sicily**
Sicilian Channel Italy/Tunisia **68** E6
Sicily *i.* Italy **68** F5
Sicuani Peru **176** D6
Sidangoli *Halmahera* Indon. **83** C2
Siddhapur India **104** C5
Siddipet India **106** C2
Sidenreng, Danau *l.* Indon. **83** A3
Sideros, Akra *pt* Greece *see* **Sideros, Akrotirio**
Sideros, Akrotirio *pt* Greece **69** L7
Sidesaviwa S. Africa **124** F7
Sidhauli India **104** E4
Sidhi India **105** E4
Sidhpur India *see* **Siddhapur**
Sidi Aïssa Alg. **67** H6
Sidi Ali Alg. **67** G5
Sīdī Barrānī Egypt **112** B5
Sidi Bel Abbès Alg. **67** F6
Sidi Bennour Morocco **64** C5
Sidi Bou Sa'id Tunisia *see* **Sidi Bouzid**
Sidi Bouzid Tunisia **68** C7
Sidi el Barrâni Egypt *see* **Sīdī Barrānī**
Sidi El Hani, Sebkhet de *salt pan* Tunisia **68** D7
Sidi Ifni Morocco **120** B2
Sidi Kacem Morocco **64** C5
Sidikalang *Sumatera* Indon. **84** B2
Sidi Khaled Alg. **64** E5
Sid Lake Canada **151** J2
Sidlaw Hills U.K. **60** F4
Sidley, Mount Antarctica **188** J1
Sidli India **105** G4
Sidmouth U.K. **59** D8
Sidney *IA* U.S.A. **160** E3
Sidney *MT* U.S.A. **156** G3
Sidney *NE* U.S.A. **160** C3
Sidney *OH* U.S.A. **164** C3
Sidney Lanier, Lake *GA* U.S.A. **163** D5
Sidoan *Sulawesi* Indon. **83** B2
Sidoan *Sulawesi* Indon. **83** B2
Sidoarjo *Jawa* Indon. **85** F4
Sidoktaya Myanmar **86** A2
Sidon Lebanon **107** B3
Sidr Egypt *see* **Sudr**
Siedlce Poland **53** D5
Sieg *r.* Germany **63** H4
Siegen Germany **63** I4
Siĕmréab Cambodia **87** C4
Siem Reap Cambodia *see* **Siĕmréab**
Si'en China *see* **Huanjiang**
Siena Italy **68** D3
Sieradz Poland **57** Q5
Si'erdingka China **99** F7
Sierra Blanca *TX* U.S.A. **157** G7
Sierra Colorada Arg. **178** C6
Sierra de Agalta, Parque Nacional *nat. park* Hond. **166** [inset] I6
Sierra Grande Arg. **178** C6
Sierra Leone *country* Africa **120** B4
Sierra Leone Basin *sea feature* N. Atlantic Ocean **184** G5
Sierra Leone Rise *sea feature* N. Atlantic Ocean **184** G5
Sierra Madre Mountains *CA* U.S.A. **158** C4
Sierra Mojada Mex. **166** E3
Sierra Nevada, Parque Nacional *nat. park* Venez. **176** D2
Sierra Nevada de Santa Marta, Parque Nacional *nat. park* Col. **176** D1
Sierraville *CA* U.S.A. **158** C2
Sierra Vista *AZ* U.S.A. **157** F7
Sierre Switz. **66** H3
Sievi Fin. **54** N5
Sifang Ling *mts* China **96** E4
Sifangtai China **90** B3
Sīfenī Eth. **122** E2
Sifnos *i.* Greece **69** K6
Sig Alg. **67** F6
Sigep, Tanjung *pt* Indon. **84** B3
Sigguup Nunaa *pen.* Greenland **147** M2
Sighetu Marmaţiei Romania **53** D7
Sighişoara Romania **69** K1
Siglap Sing. **87** [inset]
Sigli *Sumatera* Indon. **84** A1
Siglufjörður Iceland **54** [inset 1]
Sigma *Panay* Phil. **82** C4
Signal de Botrange *hill* Belgium **62** G4
Signal de la Ste-Baume *mt.* France **66** G5
Signal Peak *AZ* U.S.A. **159** F5
Signy-l'Abbaye France **62** E5
Sigoisooinan Indon. **84** B3
Sigourney *IA* U.S.A. **160** E3
Sigri, Akra *pt* Greece *see* **Saratsina, Akrotirio**
Sigsbee Deep *sea feature* G. of Mexico **187** N4
Siguatepeque Hond. **167** I6
Sigüenza Spain **67** E3
Siguiri Guinea **120** C3
Sigulda Latvia **55** N8
Sigurd *UT* U.S.A. **159** H2
Sihanoukville Cambodia **87** C5
Sihaung Myauk Myanmar **86** A2
Sihawa India **106** D1
Sihong China **97** H1
Sihora India **104** E5
Sihou China *see* **Changdao**
Sihui China **97** G4
Siikajoki Fin. **54** N4
Siilinjärvi Fin. **54** O5
Siirt Turkey **113** F3
Sijawal Pak. **104** B4
Sijunjung *Sumatera* Indon. **84** C3
Sikaka Saudi Arabia *see* **Sakākah**
Sikakap Indon. **84** C3
Sikandra Rao India **104** D4
Sikanni Chief Canada **150** F3
Sikanni Chief *r.* Canada **150** F3
Sikar India **104** C4
Sīkaram *mt.* Afgh. **111** H3
Sikasso Mali **120** C3
Sikaw Myanmar **86** B2
Sikeli *Sulawesi* Indon. **83** B4
Sikeston *MO* U.S.A. **161** F4
Sikhote-Alin' *mts* Rus. Fed. **90** D4
Sikhote-Alinskiy Zapovednik *nature res.* Rus. Fed. **90** E3
Sikinos *i.* Greece **69** K6
Sikka India **104** B5
Sikkim *state* India **105** G4
Siknik Cape *AK* U.S.A. **148** E3
Siko *i.* *Maluku* Indon. **83** C2
Siksjö Sweden **54** J4
Sikuaishi China **95** J4
Sikuati *Sabah* Malaysia **85** G1
Sil *r.* Spain **67** C2
Şila' *i.* Saudi Arabia **112** D6
Silago *Leyte* Phil. **82** D4
Šilalė Lith. **55** M9
Si Lanna National Park Thai. **86** B3
Sila Point *Samar* Phil. **82** D3
Silas *AL* U.S.A. **161** F6
Silavatturai Sri Lanka **106** C4
Silawaih Agam *vol.* Indon. **84** A1
Silay *Negros* Phil. **82** C4
Silberberg *hill* Germany **63** J1
Silchar India **105** H4
Şile Turkey **69** M4
Sileru *r.* India **106** D2
Silesia *reg.* Czech Rep./Poland **57** P5
Sileti *r.* Kazakh. **88** C2
Siletiteniz, Ozero *salt l.* Kazakh. **101** G1
Silghat India **105** H4
Siliana Tunisia **68** C6
Silifke Turkey **107** A1
Siliguri India *see* **Shiliguri**
Siling Co *salt l.* China **99** E7
Silipur India **104** D4
Silistra Bulg. **69** L2
Silistria Bulg. *see* **Silistra**
Silivri Turkey **69** M4
Siljan *l.* Sweden **55** I6
Silkeborg Denmark **55** F8
Sillajhuay *mt.* Chile **176** E7
Sillamäe Estonia **55** O7
Sille Turkey **112** D3
Silli India **105** F5
Sillod India **106** B1
Silobela S. Africa **125** J4
Silsbee *TX* U.S.A. **167** G2
Silsby Lake Canada **151** M4
Silt *CO* U.S.A. **159** J2
Siltaharju Fin. **54** O3
Siluas *Kalimantan* Indon. **85** E2
Sīlūp *r.* Iran **111** F5
Šilutė Lith. **55** L9
Silvan Turkey **113** F3
Silvânia Brazil **179** A2
Silvassa India **106** B1
Silver Bank Passage Turks and Caicos Is **169** J4
Silver Bay *MN* U.S.A. **160** F2
Silver City *NM* U.S.A. **159** I5
Silver City *NV* U.S.A. **158** D2
Silver City (abandoned) Canada **149** M3
Silver Creek *r.* *AZ* U.S.A. **159** H4
Silver Lake *OR* U.S.A. **156** C4
Silver Lake *l.* *CA* U.S.A. **158** E4
Silvermine Mountains *hills* Ireland **61** D5
Silver Peak Range *mts* *NV* U.S.A. **158** E3
Silver Spring *MD* U.S.A. **165** G4
Silver Springs *NV* U.S.A. **158** D2
Silverthrone Mountain Canada **150** E5
Silvertip Mountain Canada **150** F5
Silverton U.K. **59** D8
Silverton *CO* U.S.A. **159** J3
Silverton *TX* U.S.A. **161** C5
Silvituc Mex. **167** H5
Sima China **99** E7
Simao China **96** D4
Simara *i.* Phil. **82** C3
Simard, Lac *l.* Canada **152** F5
Simaria India **105** F4
Simatang *i.* Indon. **83** B2
Simav Turkey **69** M5
Simav Dağları *mts* Turkey **69** M5
Simawat China **99** C5
Simba Dem. Rep. Congo **122** C3
Simbirsk Rus. Fed. *see* **Ul'yanovsk**
Simcoe Canada **164** E2
Simcoe, Lake Canada **164** F1
Simdega India **106** E1
Simēn *mts* Eth. **122** D2
Simēn Mountains Eth. *see* **Simēn**
Simeonof Island *AK* U.S.A. **148** H5
Simeulue *i.* Indon. **84** B2
Simferopol' Ukr. **112** D1
Sími *i.* Greece *see* **Symi**
Simikot Nepal **105** E3
Similan, Ko *i.* Thai. **87** B5
Simi Valley *CA* U.S.A. **158** D4
Simla India *see* **Shimla**
Simla *CO* U.S.A. **156** G5
Şimleu Silvaniei Romania **69** J1
Simlipal National Park India **105** F5
Simmerath Germany **62** G4
Simmern (Hunsrück) Germany **63** H5
Simmesport *LA* U.S.A. **161** F6
Simms *MT* U.S.A. **156** F3
Simojärvi *l.* Fin. **54** O3
Simon Mex. **161** C7
Simonette *r.* Canada **150** G4
Simon Wash *watercourse* *AZ* U.S.A. **159** I5
Simoom Sound Canada **150** E5
Simoon Sound Canada *see* **Simoom Sound**
Simpang *Sumatera* Indon. **84** D3
Simpang Mangayau, Tanjung *pt* Malaysia **80** F5
Simplício Mendes Brazil **177** J5
Simplon Pass Switz. **66** I3
Simpson Canada **151** J5
Simpson *MT* U.S.A. **156** F2
Simpson Desert Australia **136** B5
Simpson Desert National Park Australia **136** B5
Simpson Desert Regional Reserve *nature res.* Australia **137** B5
Simpson Islands Canada **151** H2
Simpson Lake Canada **149** P1
Simpson Park Mountains *NV* U.S.A. **158** E2
Simpson Peninsula Canada **147** J3
Simrishamn Sweden **55** I9
Simuk *i.* Indon. **84** B3
Simulubek Indon. **84** B3
Simunjan *Sarawak* Malaysia **85** E2
Simunul *i.* Phil. **82** B5
Simushir, Ostrov *i.* Rus. Fed. **89** S3
Sina *r.* India **106** B2
Sinabang Indon. **84** B2
Sinabung *vol.* Indon. **84** B2
Sinai *pen.* Egypt **107** A5
Sinai, Mont *hill* France **62** E5
Sinai al Janûbîya *governorate* Egypt *see* **Janūb Sīnā'**
Sinai ash Shamâlîya *governorate* Egypt *see* **Shamāl Sīnā'**
Si Nakarin, Ang Kep Nam Thai. **86** B4
Sinaloa *state* Mex. **157** F8
Sinalunga Italy **68** D3
Sinan China **97** F3
Sinancha Rus. Fed. *see* **Cheremshany**
Sinbo Myanmar **86** B1
Sinbyubyin Myanmar **87** B4
Sinbyugyun Myanmar **86** A2
Sincan Turkey **112** E3
Sincelejo Col. **176** C2
Sinchu Taiwan *see* **T'aoyüan**
Sinclair Mills Canada **150** F4
Sincora, Serra do *hills* Brazil **179** C1
Sind *r.* India **104** D4
Sind Pak. *see* **Thul**
Sind *prov.* Pak. *see* **Sindh**
Sinda Rus. Fed. **90** E2
Sindañgan *Mindanao* Phil. **82** C4
Sindangan Bay *Mindanao* Phil. **82** C4
Sindangbarang *Jawa* Indon. **84** D4
Sindari India **104** B4
Sindeh, Teluk *b.* *Flores* Indon. **83** B5
Sindelfingen Germany **63** I6
Sindh *prov.* Pak. **111** H5
Sindhuli Garhi Nepal **105** F4
Sindhulimadi Nepal *see* **Sindhuli Garhi**
Sındırgı Turkey **69** M5
Sindor Rus. Fed. **52** K3
Sindou Burkina Faso **120** C3
Sindri India **105** F5
Sind Sagar Doab *lowland* Pak. **111** H4
Sinel'nikovo Ukr. *see* **Synel'nykove**
Sines Port. **67** B5
Sines, Cabo de *c.* Port. **67** B5
Sinettä Fin. **54** N3
Sinfra Côte d'Ivoire **120** C4
Sing Myanmar **86** B2
Singa Sudan **108** D7
Singanallur India **106** C4
Singapore *country* Asia **84** C2

▶**Singapore** Sing. **87** [inset]
Capital of Singapore.

Singapore *r.* Sing. **87** [inset]
Singapore, Strait of Indon./Sing. **87** [inset]
Singapura *country* Asia *see* **Singapore**
Singapura Sing. *see* **Singapore**
Singapuru India **106** D2
Singaraja *Bali* Indon. **85** F5
Sing Buri Thai. **86** C4
Singgimtay China **98** E4
Singhampton Canada **164** E1
Singhana India **104** C3
Singida Tanz. **123** D4
Singidunum Serbia *see* **Belgrade**
Singim China *see* **Singgimtay**
Singkaling Hkamti Myanmar **86** A1
Singkang *Sulawesi* Indon. **83** B4
Singkarak *Sumatera* Indon. **84** C3
Singkawang *Kalimantan* Indon. **85** E2
Singkep *i.* Indon. **84** D3
Singkil *Sumatera* Indon. **84** B2
Singkuang *Sumatera* Indon. **84** B2
Singleton Australia **138** E4
Singleton, Mount *hill* *N.T.* Australia **134** E5
Singleton, Mount *hill* *W.A.* Australia **135** B7
Singora Thai. *see* **Songkhla**
Sin'gosan N. Korea *see* **Kosan**
Singra India **105** G4
Singri India **105** H4
Singu Myanmar **96** B4
Singwara India **106** D1
Sin'gye N. Korea **91** B5
Sinhala *country* Asia *see* **Sri Lanka**
Sinhkung Myanmar **86** B1
Siniloan *Luzon* Phil. **82** C3
Sining China *see* **Xining**
Sinio, Gunung *mt.* Indon. **83** A3
Siniscola *Sardinia* Italy **68** C4
Sinj Croatia **68** G3
Sinjai *Sulawesi* Indon. **83** B4
Sinjār, Jabal *mt.* Iraq **113** F3
Sinkat Sudan **108** E6
Sinkiang *aut. reg.* China *see* **Xinjiang Uygur Zizhiqu**
Sinkiang Uighur Autonomous Region *aut. reg.* China *see* **Xinjiang Uygur Zizhiqu**
Sinmi-do *i.* N. Korea **91** B5
Sinn Germany **63** I4
Sinnamary Fr. Guiana **177** H2
Sinn Bishr, Gebel *hill* Egypt *see* **Sinn Bishr, Jabal**
Sinn Bishr, Jabal *hill* Egypt **107** A5
Sinneh Iran *see* **Sanandaj**
Sinoia Zimbabwe *see* **Chinhoyi**
Sinop Brazil **177** G6
Sinop Turkey **112** D2
Sinope Turkey *see* **Sinop**
Sinoquipe Mex. **166** C2
Sinp'a N. Korea **90** B4
Sinp'o N. Korea **91** C4
Sinsang N. Korea **91** B5
Sinsheim Germany **63** I5
Sintang *Kalimantan* Indon. **85** E2
Sint Eustatius *municipality* West Indies **169** L5
Sint-Laureins Belgium **62** D3

Sørli Norway **54** H4
Soro India **105** F5
Soroca Moldova **53** F6
Sorocaba Brazil **179** B3
Soroki Moldova *see* **Soroca**
Sorol *atoll* Micronesia **81** K5
Sorong *Papua* Indon. **83** D3
Soroti Uganda **122** D3
Sørøya *i.* Norway **54** M1
Sorraia *r.* Port. **67** B4
Sørreisa Norway **54** K2
Sorrento Italy **68** F4
Sorsele Sweden **54** J4
Sorsogon *Luzon* Phil. **82** D3
Sortavala Rus. Fed. **54** Q6
Sortland Norway **54** I2
Sortopolovskaya Rus. Fed. **52** K3
Sorvizhi Rus. Fed. **52** K4
Sŏsan S. Korea **91** B5
Sosenskiy Rus. Fed. **53** G5
Soshanguve S. Africa **125** I3
Sosna *r.* Rus. Fed. **53** H5
Sosneado *mt.* Arg. **178** C4
Sosnogorsk Rus. Fed. **52** L3
Sosnovka Kyrg. **98** A4
Sosnovka *Arkhangel'skaya Oblast'* Rus. Fed. **52** J3
Sosnovka *Kaliningradskaya Oblast'* Rus. Fed. **51** K5
Sosnovka *Murmanskaya Oblast'* Rus. Fed. **52** I2
Sosnovka *Tambovskaya Oblast'* Rus. Fed. **53** I5
Sosnovo Rus. Fed. **55** Q6
Sosnovo-Ozerskoye Rus. Fed. **89** K2
Sosnovyy Rus. Fed. **54** R4
Sosnovyy Bor Rus. Fed. **55** P7
Sosnowiec Poland **57** Q5
Sosnowitz Poland *see* **Sosnowiec**
Sos'va *Sverdlovskaya Oblast'* Rus. Fed. **51** S4
Sos'va *Tyumenskaya Oblast'* Rus. Fed. **51** S3
Sotang China **99** F7
Sotara, Volcán *vol.* Col. **176** C3
Sotkamo Fin. **54** P4
Soto la Marina Mex. **167** F4
Sotteville-lès-Rouen France **62** B5
Sotuta Mex. **167** H4
Souanké Congo **122** B3
Soubré Côte d'Ivoire **120** C4
Souderton *PA* U.S.A. **165** H3
Soufflenheim France **63** H6
Soufli Greece **69** L4
Soufrière St Lucia **169** L6
Soufrière *vol.* St Vincent **169** L6
Sougueur Alg. **67** G6
Souillac France **66** E4
Souilly France **62** F5
Souk Ahras Alg. **68** B6
Souk el Arbaâ du Rharb Morocco **64** C5
Sŏul S. Korea *see* **Seoul**
Soulac-sur-Mer France **66** D4
Soulom France **66** D5
Sounding Creek *r.* Canada **151** I4
Souni Cyprus **107** A2
Soûr Lebanon *see* **Tyre**
Sourdough *AK* U.S.A. **149** K3
Soure Brazil **177** I4
Sour el Ghozlane Alg. **67** H5
Souris Canada **151** K5
Souris *r.* Canada **151** L5
Souriya *country* Asia *see* **Syria**
Sousa Brazil **177** K5
Sousa Lara Angola *see* **Bocoio**
Sousse Tunisia **68** D7
Soustons France **66** D5

▶**South Africa, Republic of** *country* Africa **124** F5
5th most populous country in Africa.

Southampton Canada **164** E1
Southampton U.K. **59** F8
Southampton *NY* U.S.A. **165** I3
Southampton, Cape Canada **147** J3
Southampton Island Canada **147** J3
South Andaman *i.* India **87** A5
South Anna *r. VA* U.S.A. **165** G5
South Anston U.K. **58** F5
South Aulatsivik Island Canada **153** J2
South Australia *state* Australia **132** D5
South Australian Basin *sea feature* Indian Ocean **185** P8
Southaven *MS* U.S.A. **161** F5
South Baldy *mt. NM* U.S.A. **157** G6
South Bank U.K. **58** F4
South Bass Island *OH* U.S.A. **164** D3
South Bend *IN* U.S.A. **164** B3
South Bend *WA* U.S.A. **156** C3
South Bluff *pt* Bahamas **163** F8
South Boston *VA* U.S.A. **165** F5
South Brook Canada **153** K4
South Cape *pt HI* U.S.A. *see* **Ka Lae**
South Carolina *state* U.S.A. **163** D5
South Charleston *OH* U.S.A. **164** D4
South Charleston *WV* U.S.A. **164** E4
South China Sea N. Pacific Ocean **80** F4
South Coast Town Australia *see* **Gold Coast**
South Dakota *state* U.S.A. **160** C2
South Downs *hills* U.K. **59** G8
South Downs National Park *nat. park* U.K. **59** G8
South-East *admin. dist.* Botswana **125** G3
South East Cape Australia **137** [inset]
Southeast Cape *AK* U.S.A. **148** E3
Southeast Indian Ridge *sea feature* Indian Ocean **185** N8
South East Isles Australia **135** C8
Southeast Pacific Basin *sea feature* S. Pacific Ocean **187** M10
South East Point Australia **138** C7
Southend Canada **151** K3
Southend U.K. **60** D5
Southend-on-Sea U.K. **59** H7
Southern *admin. dist.* Botswana **124** G3
Southern Alps *mts* N.Z. **139** C6
Southern Cross Australia **135** B7
Southern Indian Lake Canada **151** L3
Southern Lau Group *is* Fiji **133** I3
Southern National Park South Sudan **121** F4
Southern Ocean **188** C2
Southern Pines *NC* U.S.A. **163** E5
Southern Rhodesia *country* Africa *see* **Zimbabwe**
Southern Uplands *hills* U.K. **60** E5
South Esk *r.* U.K. **60** F4
South Esk Tableland *reg.* Australia **134** D4
Southey Canada **151** J5
Southfield *MI* U.S.A. **164** D2
South Fiji Basin *sea feature* S. Pacific Ocean **186** H7
South Fork *CA* U.S.A. **158** B1
South Geomagnetic Pole Antarctica **188** F1
South Georgia *i.* S. Atlantic Ocean **178** I8

▶**South Georgia and the South Sandwich Islands** *terr.* S. Atlantic Ocean **178** I8
United Kingdom Overseas Territory

South Harris *pen.* U.K. **60** B3
South Haven *MI* U.S.A. **164** B2
South Henik Lake Canada **151** L2
South Hill *VA* U.S.A. **165** F5
South Honshu Ridge *sea feature* N. Pacific Ocean **186** F3
South Indian Lake Canada **151** L3
South Island India **106** B4

▶**South Island** N.Z. **139** D7
2nd largest island in Oceania.

South Islet *rf* Phil. **82** B4
South Junction Canada **151** M5
South Korea *country* Asia **91** B5
South Lake Tahoe *CA* U.S.A. **158** C2
South Luangwa National Park Zambia **123** D5
South Magnetic Pole Antarctica **188** G2
South Mills *NC* U.S.A. **165** G5
Southminster U.K. **59** H7
South Mountains *hills PA* U.S.A. **165** G4
South Naknek *AK* U.S.A. **148** H4
South New Berlin *NY* U.S.A. **165** H2
South Orkney Islands S. Atlantic Ocean **184** F10

▶**South Ossetia** *terr.* Georgia **113** G2
Disputed Territory.

South Paris *ME* U.S.A. **165** J1
South Platte *r. CO* U.S.A. **160** C3
South Point Bahamas **163** F8
South Pole Antarctica **188** C1
Southport *Qld* Australia **138** F1
Southport *Tas.* Australia **137** [inset]
Southport U.K. **58** D5
Southport *NY* U.S.A. **165** G2
South Portland *ME* U.S.A. **165** J2
South Ronaldsay *i.* U.K. **60** G2
South Royalton *VT* U.S.A. **165** I2
South Salt Lake *UT* U.S.A. **159** H1
South Sand Bluff *pt* S. Africa **125** J6

▶**South Sandwich Islands** S. Atlantic Ocean **184** G9
United Kingdom Overseas Territory.

South Sandwich Trench *sea feature* S. Atlantic Ocean **184** G9
South San Francisco *CA* U.S.A. **158** B3
South Saskatchewan *r.* Canada **151** J4
South Seal *r.* Canada **151** L3
South Shetland Islands Antarctica **188** A2
South Shetland Trough *sea feature* S. Atlantic Ocean **188** L2
South Shields U.K. **58** F3
South Sinai *governorate* Egypt *see* **Janūb Sīnā'**
South Solomon Trench *sea feature* S. Pacific Ocean **186** G6

▶**South Sudan** *country* Africa **121** G4
Gained independence from Sudan on 9 July 2011.

South Taranaki Bight *b.* N.Z. **139** E4
South Tasman Rise *sea feature* Southern Ocean **186** F9
South Tent *mt. UT* U.S.A. **159** H2
South Tons *r.* India **105** E4
South Twin Island Canada **152** F3
South Tyne *r.* U.K. **58** E4
South Uist *i.* U.K. **60** B3
South Wellesley Islands Australia **136** B3
South-West Africa *country* Africa *see* **Namibia**
South West Cape N.Z. **139** A8
Southwest Cape *AK* U.S.A. **148** E3
South West Entrance *sea chan.* P.N.G. **136** E1
Southwest Indian Ridge *sea feature* Indian Ocean **185** K8
South West National Park Australia **137** [inset]
Southwest Pacific Basin *sea feature* S. Pacific Ocean **186** I8
Southwest Peru Ridge *sea feature* S. Pacific Ocean *see* **Nazca Ridge**
South West Rocks Australia **138** F3
South Whitley *IN* U.S.A. **164** C3
South Wichita *r. TX* U.S.A. **161** D5
South Windham *ME* U.S.A. **165** J2
Southwold U.K. **59** I6
Southwood National Park Australia **138** E1
Soutpansberg *mts* S. Africa **125** I2
Souttouf, Adrar *mts* W. Sahara **120** B2
Soverato Italy **68** G5
Sovereign Mountain *AK* U.S.A. **149** J3
Sovetsk *Kaliningradskaya Oblast'* Rus. Fed. **55** L9
Sovetsk *Kirovskaya Oblast'* Rus. Fed. **52** K4
Sovetskaya Gavan' Rus. Fed. **90** F2
Sovetskiy *Leningradskaya Oblast'* Rus. Fed. **55** P6
Sovetskiy *Respublika Mariy El* Rus. Fed. **52** K4
Sovetskiy *Tyumenskaya Oblast'* Rus. Fed. **51** S3
Sovetskoye *Chechenskaya Respublika* Rus. Fed. *see* **Shatoy**
Sovetskoye *Stavropol'skiy Kray* Rus. Fed. *see* **Zelenokumsk**
Sovyets'kyy Ukr. **112** D1
Sowa China **96** C2
Sōwa Japan **93** F2
Soweto S. Africa **125** H4
So'x Tajik. **111** H2
Sōya-kaikyō *strait* Japan/Rus. Fed. *see* **La Pérouse Strait**
Sōya-misaki *c.* Japan **90** F3
Soyana *r.* Rus. Fed. **52** I2
Soyma *r.* Rus. Fed. **52** K2
Soyopa Mex. **157** F7
Sozh *r.* Europe **53** F6
Sozopol Bulg. **69** L3
Spa Belgium **62** F4

▶**Spain** *country* Europe **67** E3
4th largest country in Europe.

Spalato Croatia *see* **Split**
Spalatum Croatia *see* **Split**
Spalding U.K. **59** G6
Spanish Canada **152** E5
Spanish Fork *UT* U.S.A. **159** H1
Spanish Guinea *country* Africa *see* **Equatorial Guinea**
Spanish Netherlands *country* Europe *see* **Belgium**
Spanish Sahara *terr.* Africa *see* **Western Sahara**
Spanish Town Jamaica **169** I5
Sparks *NV* U.S.A. **158** D2
Sparta Greece *see* **Sparti**
Sparta *GA* U.S.A. **163** D5
Sparta *KY* U.S.A. **164** C4
Sparta *MI* U.S.A. **164** C2
Sparta *NC* U.S.A. **164** E5
Sparta *TN* U.S.A. **162** C5
Spartanburg *SC* U.S.A. **163** D5
Sparti Greece **69** J6
Spartivento, Capo *c.* Italy **68** G6
Spas-Demensk Rus. Fed. **53** G5
Spas-Klepiki Rus. Fed. **53** I5
Spassk-Dal'niy Rus. Fed. **90** D3
Spassk-Ryazanskiy Rus. Fed. **53** I5
Spata (Eleftherios Venezielos) *airport* Greece **69** J6
Spatha, Akra *pt* Greece *see* **Spatha, Akrotirio**
Spatha, Akrotirio *pt* Greece **69** J7
Spearman *TX* U.S.A. **161** C4
Speedway *IN* U.S.A. **164** B4
Spence Bay Canada *see* **Taloyoak**
Spencer *IA* U.S.A. **160** E3
Spencer *ID* U.S.A. **156** E3
Spencer *IN* U.S.A. **164** B4
Spencer *NE* U.S.A. **160** D3
Spencer *WV* U.S.A. **164** E4
Spencer, Cape *AK* U.S.A. **149** M4
Spencer, Point *pt AK* U.S.A. **148** F2
Spencer Bay Namibia **124** B3
Spencer Gulf *est.* Australia **137** B7
Spencer Range *hills* Australia **134** E3
Spennymoor U.K. **58** F4
Sperrgebiet National Park *nat. park* Namibia **124** B4
Sperrin Mountains *hills* U.K. **61** E3
Sperryville *VA* U.S.A. **165** F4
Spessart *reg.* Germany **63** J5
Spétsai *i.* Greece *see* **Spetses**
Spetses *i.* Greece **69** J6
Spey *r.* U.K. **60** F3
Speyer Germany **63** I5
Spezand Pak. **111** G4
Spice Islands Indon. *see* **Moluccas**
Spijk Neth. **62** G1
Spijkenisse Neth. **62** E3
Spike Mountain *AK* U.S.A. **149** L2
Spilimbergo Italy **68** E1
Spilsby U.K. **58** H5
Spīn Būldak Afgh. **111** G4
Spintangi Pak. **111** H4
Spirit Lake *IA* U.S.A. **160** E3
Spirit River Canada **150** G4
Spirovo Rus. Fed. **52** G4
Spišská Nová Ves Slovakia **53** D6
Spiti *r.* India **104** D3

▶**Spitsbergen** *i.* Svalbard **76** C2
5th largest island in Europe.

Spittal an der Drau Austria **57** N7
Spitzbergen *i.* Svalbard *see* **Spitsbergen**
Split Croatia **68** G3
Split Lake Canada **151** L3
Split Lake *l.* Canada **151** L3
Spokane *WA* U.S.A. **156** D3
Spoletium Italy *see* **Spoleto**
Spoleto Italy **68** E3
Spóng Cambodia **87** D4
Spoon *r. IL* U.S.A. **160** F3
Spooner *WI* U.S.A. **160** F2
Spornitz Germany **63** L1
Spotsylvania *VA* U.S.A. **165** G4
Spotted Horse *WY* U.S.A. **156** G3
Spranger, Mount Canada **150** F4
Spratly Islands S. China Sea **80** E4
Spray *OR* U.S.A. **156** D3
Spree *r.* Germany **57** N4
Sprimont Belgium **62** F4
Springbok S. Africa **124** C5
Springdale Canada **153** L4
Springdale *OH* U.S.A. **164** C4
Springe Germany **63** J2
Springer *NM* U.S.A. **157** G5
Springerville *AZ* U.S.A. **159** I4
Springfield *CO* U.S.A. **160** C4

▶**Springfield** *IL* U.S.A. **160** F4
Capital of Illinois.

Springfield *KY* U.S.A. **164** C5
Springfield *MA* U.S.A. **165** I2
Springfield *MO* U.S.A. **161** E4
Springfield *OH* U.S.A. **164** D4
Springfield *OR* U.S.A. **156** C3
Springfield *TN* U.S.A. **164** B5
Springfield *VT* U.S.A. **165** I2
Springfield *WV* U.S.A. **165** F4
Springfontein S. Africa **125** G6
Spring Glen *UT* U.S.A. **159** H2
Spring Grove *IL* U.S.A. **164** A2
Springhill Canada **153** I5
Spring Hill *FL* U.S.A. **163** D6
Springhouse Canada **150** F5
Spring Mountains *NV* U.S.A. **159** F3
Springs Junction N.Z. **139** D6
Springsure Australia **136** E5
Spring Valley *MN* U.S.A. **160** E3
Spring Valley *NY* U.S.A. **165** H3
Springview *NE* U.S.A. **160** D3
Springville *CA* U.S.A. **158** D3
Springville *NY* U.S.A. **165** F2
Springville *PA* U.S.A. **165** H3
Springville *UT* U.S.A. **159** H1
Sprowston U.K. **59** I6
Spruce Grove Canada **150** H4
Spruce Knob *mt. WV* U.S.A. **162** E4
Spruce Mountain *CO* U.S.A. **159** I2
Spruce Mountain *NV* U.S.A. **159** F1
Spurn Head *hd* U.K. **58** H5
Spurr, Mount *vol. AK* U.S.A. **148** I3
Spuzzum Canada **150** F5
Squam Lake *NH* U.S.A. **165** J2
Square Lake *ME* U.S.A. **153** H5
Squaw Harbor *AK* U.S.A. **148** G5
Squillace, Golfo di *g.* Italy **68** G5
Squires, Mount *hill* Australia **135** D6
Sragen *Jawa* Indon. **85** E4
Srbija *country* Europe *see* **Serbia**
Srbinje Bos.-Herz. *see* **Foča**
Srê Âmběl Cambodia **87** C5
Srebrenica Bos.-Herz. **69** H2
Sredets *Burgas* Bulg. **69** L3
Sredets *Sofiya-Grad* Bulg. *see* **Sofia**
Sredinnyy Khrebet *mts* Rus. Fed. **77** Q4
Sredna Gora *mts* Bulg. **69** J3
Srednekolymsk Rus. Fed. **77** Q3
Sredne-Russkaya Vozvyshennost' *hills* Rus. Fed. *see* **Central Russian Upland**
Sredne-Sibirskoye Ploskogor'ye *plat.* Rus. Fed. *see* **Central Siberian Plateau**
Sredneye Kuyto, Ozero *l.* Rus. Fed. **54** Q4
Sredniy Ural *mts* Rus. Fed. **51** R4
Srednogorie Bulg. **69** K3
Srednyaya Akhtuba Rus. Fed. **53** J6
Sreepur Bangl. *see* **Sripur**
Srê Khtum Cambodia **87** D4
Srê Noy Cambodia **87** D4
Sretensk Rus. Fed. **89** L2
Sri Aman *Sarawak* Malaysia **85** E2
Sriharikota Island India **106** D3

▶**Sri Jayewardenepura Kotte** Sri Lanka **106** C5
Capital of Sri Lanka.

Srikakulam India **106** E2
Sri Kalahasti India **106** C3
Sri Lanka *country* Asia **106** D5
Srinagar India **104** C2
Sri Pada *mt.* Sri Lanka *see* **Adam's Peak**
Sripur Bangl. **105** G4
Srirangam India **106** C4
Sri Thep *tourist site* Thai. **86** C3
Srivardhan India **106** B2
Staaten *r.* Australia **136** C3
Staaten River National Park Australia **136** C3
Stabroek Guyana *see* **Georgetown**
Stade Germany **63** J1
Staden Belgium **62** D4
Stadskanaal Neth. **62** G2
Stadtallendorf Germany **63** J4
Stadthagen Germany **63** J2
Stadtilm Germany **63** L4
Stadtlohn Germany **62** G3
Stadtoldendorf Germany **63** J3
Stadtroda Germany **63** L4
Staffa *i.* U.K. **60** C4
Staffelberg *hill* Germany **63** L4
Staffelstein Germany **63** K4
Stafford U.K. **59** E6
Stafford *VA* U.S.A. **165** G4
Stafford Creek Bahamas **163** E7
Stafford Springs *CT* U.S.A. **165** I3
Stagen *Kalimantan* Indon. **85** G3
Stagg Lake Canada **150** H2
Staicele Latvia **55** N8
Staines U.K. **59** G7
Stakhanov Ukr. **53** H6
Stakhanovo Rus. Fed. *see* **Zhukovskiy**
Stalbridge U.K. **59** E8
Stalham U.K. **59** I6
Stalin Bulg. *see* **Varna**
Stalinabad Tajik. *see* **Dushanbe**
Stalingrad Rus. Fed. *see* **Volgograd**
Staliniri Georgia *see* **Ts'khinvali**
Stalino Ukr. *see* **Donets'k**
Stalinogorsk Rus. Fed. *see* **Novomoskovsk**
Stalinogród Poland *see* **Katowice**
Stalinsk Rus. Fed. *see* **Novokuznetsk**
Stalowa Wola Poland **53** D6
Stamboliyski Bulg. **69** K3
Stamford Australia **136** C4
Stamford U.K. **59** G6
Stamford *CT* U.S.A. **165** I3
Stamford *NY* U.S.A. **165** H2
Stamford *TX* U.S.A. **167** F1
Stampalia *i.* Greece *see* **Astypalaia**
Stampriet Namibia **124** D3
Stamsund Norway **54** H2
Stanardsville *VA* U.S.A. **165** F4
Stanberry *MO* U.S.A. **160** E3
Stancomb-Wills Glacier Antarctica **188** B1
Standard Canada **150** H5
Standdaarbuiten Neth. **62** E3
Standerton S. Africa **125** I4
Standish *MI* U.S.A. **164** D2
Stanfield *AZ* U.S.A. **159** H5
Stanford *KY* U.S.A. **164** C5
Stanford *MT* U.S.A. **156** F3
Stanger S. Africa **125** J5
Stanislaus *r. CA* U.S.A. **158** C3
Stanislav Ukr. *see* **Ivano-Frankivs'k**
Stanke Dimitrov Bulg. *see* **Dupnitsa**
Staňkov Czech Rep. **63** N5
Stanley Australia **137** [inset]
Stanley *H.K.* China **97** [inset]

▶**Stanley** Falkland Is **178** E8
Capital of the Falkland Islands.

Stanley U.K. **58** F4
Stanley *ID* U.S.A. **156** E3
Stanley *KY* U.S.A. **164** B5
Stanley *ND* U.S.A. **160** C1
Stanley *VA* U.S.A. **165** F4
Stanley, Mount *hill N.T.* Australia **134** E5
Stanley, Mount *hill Tas.* Australia **137** [inset]
Stanley, Mount Dem. Rep. Congo/Uganda *see* **Margherita Peak**
Stanleyville Dem. Rep. Congo *see* **Kisangani**
Stann Creek Belize *see* **Dangriga**
Stannington U.K. **58** F3
Stanovoye Rus. Fed. **53** H5
Stanovoye Nagor'ye *mts* Rus. Fed. **89** L1
Stanovoy Khrebet *mts* Rus. Fed. **77** N4
Stansmore Range *hills* Australia **134** E5
Stanthorpe Australia **138** E2
Stanton U.K. **59** H6
Stanton *KY* U.S.A. **164** D5
Stanton *MI* U.S.A. **164** C2
Stanton *ND* U.S.A. **160** C2
Stanton *TX* U.S.A. **161** C5
Stapleton *NE* U.S.A. **160** C3
Starachowice Poland **57** R5
Stara Planina *mts* Bulg./Serbia *see* **Balkan Mountains**
Staraya Russa Rus. Fed. **52** F4
Stara Zagora Bulg. **69** K3
Starbuck Island Kiribati **187** J6
Star City *IN* U.S.A. **164** B3
Starcke National Park Australia **136** D2
Stargard in Pommern Poland *see* **Stargard Szczeciński**
Stargard Szczeciński Poland **57** O4
Staritsa Rus. Fed. **52** G4
Starke *FL* U.S.A. **163** D6
Starkville *MS* U.S.A. **161** F5
Star Lake *NY* U.S.A. **165** H1
Starnberger See *l.* Germany **57** M7
Staroaleyskoye Rus. Fed. **98** C2
Starobel'sk Ukr. *see* **Starobil's'k**
Starobil's'k Ukr. **53** H6
Starogard Gdański Poland **57** Q4
Starokonstantinov Ukr. *see* **Starokostyantyniv**
Starokostyantyniv Ukr. **53** E6
Starominskaya Rus. Fed. **53** H7
Staroshcherbinovskaya Rus. Fed. **53** H7
Star Peak *NV* U.S.A. **158** D1
Start Point U.K. **59** D8
Starve Island Kiribati *see* **Starbuck Island**
Staryya Darohi Belarus **53** F5
Staryye Dorogi Belarus *see* **Staryya Darohi**
Staryy Kayak Rus. Fed. **77** L2
Staryy Oskol Rus. Fed. **53** H6
Staßfurt Germany **63** L3
State College *PA* U.S.A. **165** G3
State Line *MS* U.S.A. **161** F6
Staten Island Arg. *see* **Los Estados, Isla de**
Statenville *GA* U.S.A. **163** D6
Statesboro *GA* U.S.A. **163** D5
Statesville *NC* U.S.A. **162** D5
Statia *municipality* West Indies *see* **Sint Eustatius**
Station *KY* U.S.A. **164** C4
Station Nord Greenland **189** I1
Stauchitz Germany **63** N3
Staufenberg Germany **63** I4
Staunton *VA* U.S.A. **164** F4
Stavanger Norway **55** D7
Staveley U.K. **58** F5
Stavropol' Rus. Fed. **113** F1
Stavropol Kray *admin. div.* Rus. Fed. *see* **Stavropol'skiy Kray**
Stavropol'-na-Volge Rus. Fed. *see* **Tol'yatti**
Stavropol'skaya Vozvyshennost' *hills* Rus. Fed. **113** F1
Stavropol'skiy Kray *admin. div.* Rus. Fed. **113** F1
Stayner Canada **164** E1
Stayton *OR* U.S.A. **156** C3
Steadville S. Africa **125** I5
Steamboat Springs *CO* U.S.A. **156** G4
Stearns *KY* U.S.A. **164** C5
Stebbins *AK* U.S.A. **148** G3
Steele Creek *AK* U.S.A. **149** L2
Steele Island Antarctica **188** L2
Steelville *MO* U.S.A. **160** F4
Steen *r.* Canada **150** G3
Steenderen Neth. **62** G2
Steenkampsberge *mts* S. Africa **125** J3
Steen River Canada **150** G3
Steens Mountain *OR* U.S.A. **156** D4
Steenstrup Gletscher *glacier* Greenland *see* **Sermersuaq**
Steenvoorde France **62** C4
Steenwijk Neth. **62** G2
Steese Highway *AK* U.S.A. **149** K2
Stefansson Island Canada **147** H2
Stegi Swaziland *see* **Siteki**
Steigerwald *mts* Germany **63** K5
Stein Germany **63** L5
Steinach Germany **63** L4
Steinaker Reservoir *UT* U.S.A. **159** I1
Steinbach Canada **151** L5
Steinfeld (Oldenburg) Germany **63** I2
Steinfurt Germany **63** H2
Steinhausen Namibia **123** B6
Steinheim Germany **63** J3
Steinkjer Norway **54** G4
Steinkopf S. Africa **124** C5
Steinsdalen Norway **54** G4
Stella S. Africa **124** G4
Stella Maris Bahamas **163** F8
Stellenbosch S. Africa **124** D7
Steller, Mount *AK* U.S.A. **149** L3
Stello, Monte *mt. Corsica* France **66** I5
Stelvio, Parco Nazionale dello *nat. park* Italy **68** D1
Stenay France **62** F5
Stendal Germany **63** L2
Stenhousemuir U.K. **60** F4
Stenungsund Sweden **55** G7
Steornabhagh U.K. *see* **Stornoway**
Stepanakert Azer. *see* **Xankändi**
Stephens, Cape N.Z. **139** D5
Stephens City *VA* U.S.A. **165** F4
Stephens Lake Canada **151** M3
Stephenville *TX* U.S.A. **161** D5
Stepnoy Kyrg. **98** A4
Stepnoy Rus. Fed. *see* **Elista**
Stepnoye Rus. Fed. **53** J6
Stepovak Bay *AK* U.S.A. **148** G5
Sterkfontein Dam *resr* S. Africa **125** I5
Sterkstroom S. Africa **125** H6
Sterlet Lake Canada **151** I1
Sterlibashevo Rus. Fed. **51** R5
Sterling S. Africa **124** E6
Sterling *CO* U.S.A. **160** C3
Sterling *IL* U.S.A. **160** F3
Sterling *MI* U.S.A. **164** C1
Sterling *UT* U.S.A. **159** H2
Sterling City *TX* U.S.A. **161** C6
Sterling Heights *MI* U.S.A. **164** D2
Sterlitamak Rus. Fed. **76** G4
Stettin Poland *see* **Szczecin**
Stettler Canada **151** H4
Steubenville *KY* U.S.A. **164** C5
Steubenville *OH* U.S.A. **164** E3
Stevenage U.K. **59** G7
Stevenson *WA* U.S.A. **156** C3
Stevenson Entrance *sea channel AK* U.S.A. **148** I4
Stevenson Lake Canada **151** L4
Stevens Point *WI* U.S.A. **160** F2
Stevens Village *AK* U.S.A. **149** J2
Stevensville *MI* U.S.A. **164** B2
Stevensville *PA* U.S.A. **165** G3
Stewart Canada **149** O5
Stewart *r.* Canada **149** M3
Stewart, Isla *i.* Chile **178** B8
Stewart Crossing Canada **149** M3
Stewart Island N.Z. **139** A8
Stewart Islands Solomon Is **133** G2
Stewart Lake Canada **147** J3
Stewarton U.K. **60** E5
Stewarts Point *CA* U.S.A. **158** B2
Stewiacke Canada **153** J5
Steynsburg S. Africa **125** G6
Steyr Austria **57** O6
Steytlerville S. Africa **124** G7
Stiens Neth. **62** F1
Stif Alg. *see* **Sétif**
Stigler *OK* U.S.A. **161** E5
Stikine *r.* Canada **149** N4
Stikine Plateau Canada **149** O4
Stikine Ranges *mts* Canada **149** O4
Stikine Strait *AK* U.S.A. **150** C3
Stilbaai S. Africa **124** E8
Stiles *WI* U.S.A. **164** A1
Stillwater *MN* U.S.A. **160** E2
Stillwater *OK* U.S.A. **161** D4
Stillwater Range *mts NV* U.S.A. **158** D2
Stillwell *IN* U.S.A. **164** B3
Stilton U.K. **59** G6
Stilwell *OK* U.S.A. **161** E5
Stinnett *TX* U.S.A. **161** C5
Štip Macedonia **69** J4
Stirling Australia **134** F5
Stirling Canada **165** G1
Stirling U.K. **60** F4
Stirling Creek *r.* Australia **134** E4
Stirling Range National Park Australia **135** B8
Stittsville Canada **165** H1
Stjørdalshalsen Norway **54** G5
Stockbridge *MI* U.S.A. **164** C2
Stockerau Austria **57** P6
Stockheim Germany **63** L4

▶**Stockholm** Sweden **55** K7
Capital of Sweden.

Stockinbingal Australia **138** C5
Stockport U.K. **58** E5
Stockton *CA* U.S.A. **158** C3
Stockton *KS* U.S.A. **160** D4
Stockton *MO* U.S.A. **160** E4
Stockton *UT* U.S.A. **159** G1
Stockton Islands *AK* U.S.A. **149** K1
Stockton Lake *MO* U.S.A. **160** E4
Stockton-on-Tees U.K. **58** F4
Stockton Plateau *TX* U.S.A. **166** E2
Stockville *NE* U.S.A. **160** C3
Stod Czech Rep. **63** N5
Stœng Trêng Cambodia **87** D4
Stoer, Point of U.K. **60** D2
Stoke-on-Trent U.K. **59** E5
Stokesley U.K. **58** F4
Stokes Point Australia **137** [inset]
Stokes Range *hills* Australia **134** E4
Stokkseyri Iceland **54** [inset 1]
Stokkvågen Norway **54** H3
Stokmarknes Norway **54** I2
Stolac Bos.-Herz. **68** G3
Stolberg (Rheinland) Germany **62** G4
Stolboukha (abandoned) Kazakh. **98** D2
Stolbovoy Rus. Fed. **189** G2
Stolbtsy Belarus *see* **Stowbtsy**
Stolin Belarus **55** O11
Stollberg Germany **63** M4
Stolp Poland *see* **Słupsk**
Stolzenau Germany **63** J2
Stone U.K. **59** E6
Stoneboro *PA* U.S.A. **164** E3
Stonecliffe Canada **152** F5
Stonecutters' Island *pen. H.K.* China **97** [inset]
Stonehaven U.K. **60** G4
Stonehenge Australia **136** C5
Stonehenge *tourist site* U.K. **59** F7
Stoner *CO* U.S.A. **159** I3
Stonewall Canada **151** L5
Stonewall Jackson Lake *WV* U.S.A. **164** E4
Stony *r. AK* U.S.A. **148** H3
Stony Creek *VA* U.S.A. **165** G5
Stony Lake Canada **151** L3
Stony Point *NY* U.S.A. **165** G2
Stony Rapids Canada **151** J3
Stony River *AK* U.S.A. **146** C3
Stooping *r.* Canada **152** E3
Stora Lulevatten *l.* Sweden **54** K3
Stora Sjöfallets nationalpark *nat. park* Sweden **54** J3
Storavan *l.* Sweden **54** K4
Store Bælt *sea chan.* Denmark *see* **Great Belt**
Støren Norway **54** G5
Storfjordbotn Norway **54** O1
Storforshei Norway **54** I3
Storjord Norway **54** I3
Storkerson Peninsula Canada **147** H2
Storm Bay Australia **137** [inset]
Stormberg S. Africa **125** H6
Storm Lake *IA* U.S.A. **160** E3
Stornosa *mt.* Norway **54** E6
Stornoway U.K. **60** C2
Storozhevsk Rus. Fed. **52** L3
Storozhynets' Ukr. **53** E6
Storrs *CT* U.S.A. **165** I3
Storseleby Sweden **54** J4
Storsjön *l.* Sweden **54** I5
Storskrymten *mt.* Norway **54** F5
Storslett Norway **54** L2
Stortemelk *sea chan.* Neth. **62** F1
Storuman Sweden **54** J4
Storuman *l.* Sweden **54** J4
Storvik Sweden **55** J6
Storvorde Denmark **55** G8
Storvreta Sweden **55** J7
Story *WY* U.S.A. **156** G3
Stotfold U.K. **59** G6
Stoughton Canada **151** K5
Stour *r. England* U.K. **59** F6
Stour *r. England* U.K. **59** F8
Stour *r. England* U.K. **59** I7
Stour *r. England* U.K. **59** I7
Stourbridge U.K. **59** E6
Stourport-on-Severn U.K. **59** E6
Stout Lake Canada **151** M4
Stowbtsy Belarus **55** O10
Stowe *VT* U.S.A. **165** I1
Stowmarket U.K. **59** H6
Stoyba Rus. Fed. **90** C1
Strabane U.K. **61** E3
Stradbally Ireland **61** E4

Syowa research station Antarctica 188 D2
Syracusae Sicily Italy see Syracuse
Syracuse Sicily Italy 68 F6
Syracuse KS U.S.A. 160 C4
Syracuse NY U.S.A. 165 G2
Syrdar'ya r. Asia 102 C3
Syrdar'ya Uzbek. see Sirdaryo
Syrdaryinskiy Uzbek. see Sirdaryo
Syria country Asia 112 E4
Syriam Myanmar see Thanlyin
Syrian Desert Asia 112 E4
Syrna i. Greece 69 L6
Syros i. Greece 69 K6
Syrskiy Rus. Fed. 53 H5
Sysmä Fin. 55 N6
Sysola r. Rus. Fed. 52 K3
Syumsi Rus. Fed. 52 K4
Syurkum Rus. Fed. 90 F2
Syurkum, Mys pt Rus. Fed. 90 F2
Syzran' Rus. Fed. 53 K5
Szabadka Serbia see Subotica
Szczecin Poland 57 O4
Szczecinek Poland 57 P4
Szczytno Poland 57 R4
Szechwan prov. China see Sichuan
Szeged Hungary 69 I1
Székesfehérvár Hungary 68 H1
Szekszárd Hungary 68 H1
Szentes Hungary 69 I1
Szentgotthárd Hungary 68 G1
Szigetvár Hungary 68 G1
Szolnok Hungary 69 I1
Szombathely Hungary 68 G1
Sztálinváros Hungary see Dunaújváros

T

Taagga Duudka reg. Somalia 122 E3
Taal, Lake Luzon Phil. 82 C3
Tabaco Luzon Phil. 82 C3
Tābah Saudi Arabia 108 F4
Tabajara Brazil 176 F5
Tabakhmela Georgia see Kazret'i
Tabalo P.N.G. 81 L7
Tabanan Bali Indon. 85 F5
Tabang Kalimantan Indon. 85 G2
Tabang r. Indon. 85 F2
Tabankulu S. Africa 125 I6
Ṭabaqah Ar Raqqah Syria 107 D2
Ṭabaqah Ar Raqqah Syria see Madīnat ath Thawrah
Tabar Islands P.N.G. 132 F2
Tabarka Tunisia 68 C6
Tabasco Mex. 166 E4
Tabasco state Mex. 167 G5
Ṭabas-e Masīnā Iran 111 F3
Tabāsīn Iran 110 E4
Tābask, Kūh-e mt. Iran 110 C4
Tabatinga Amazonas Brazil 176 E4
Tabatinga São Paulo Brazil 179 A3
Tabatinga, Serra da hills Brazil 177 J6
T'abats'q'uri, T'ba l. Georgia 113 F2
Tabayama Japan 93 E3
Tabayin Myanmar 86 A2
Tabayoc, Mount Luzon Phil. 82 C2
Tabbita Australia 138 B5
Tabelbala Alg. 64 D6
Taber Canada 151 H5
Tabet, Nam r. Myanmar 86 B1
Tabia Tsaka salt l. China 99 D7
Tabin Wildlife Reserve nature res. Malaysia 85 G1
Tabir r. Indon. 84 C3
Tabiteuea atoll Kiribati 133 H2
Tabivere Estonia 55 O7
Tablas i. Phil. 82 C3
Tablas Strait Phil. 82 C3
Table Cape N.Z. 139 F4
Table Mountain AK U.S.A. 149 L1
Table Mountain Nature Reserve S. Africa 124 D8
Table Point Palawan Phil. 82 B4
Tabligbo Togo 120 D4
Tábor Czech Rep. 57 O6
Tabora Tanz. 123 D4
Tabou Côte d'Ivoire 120 C4
Tabrīz Iran 110 B2
Tabuaeran atoll Kiribati 187 J5
Tabūk Saudi Arabia 112 E5
Tabulam Australia 138 F2
Tabulan Sulawesi Indon. 83 B3
Tabuyung Sumatera Indon. 84 B2
Tabwémasana, Mount Vanuatu 133 G3
Täby Sweden 55 K7
Tacalé Brazil 177 H3
Tacámbaro Mex. 167 E5
Tacaná, Volcán de vol. Mex. 167 G6
Tachakou China 98 D3
Tacheng China 98 C3
Tachie Canada 150 E4
Tachikawa Japan 93 F3
Tachov Czech Rep. 63 M5
Tacipi Sulawesi Indon. 83 B4
Tacloban Leyte Phil. 82 D4
Tacna Peru 176 D7
Tacna AZ U.S.A. 166 B1
Tacoma WA U.S.A. 156 C3
Taco Pozo Arg. 178 D3
Tacuarembó Uruguay 178 E4
Tacupeto Mex. 166 C2
Tadcaster U.K. 58 F5
Tademaït, Plateau du Alg. 64 E6
Tadenet Lake Canada 149 P1
Tadin New Caledonia 133 G4
Tadjikistan country Asia see Tajikistan
Tadjourah Djibouti 108 F7
Tadmur Syria 107 D2
Tado Japan 92 C3
Tadohae Haesang National Park S. Korea 91 B6
Tadoule Lake Canada 151 L3
Tadoussac Canada 153 H4
Tadpatri India 106 C3
Tadwale India 106 C2
Tadzhikskaya S.S.R. country Asia see Tajikistan
T'aean Haean National Park S. Korea 91 B5
Taech'ŏng-do i. S. Korea 91 B5
Taedasa-do N. Korea 91 B5
Taedong-man b. N. Korea 91 B5
Taegu S. Korea 91 C6
Taehan-min'guk country Asia see South Korea
Taehŭksan-kundo is S. Korea 91 B6
Taejŏn S. Korea 91 B5
Taejŏng S. Korea 91 B6
T'aepaek S. Korea 91 C5
Ta'erqi China 95 J2
Taf r. U.K. 59 C7
Tafahi i. Tonga 133 I3
Tafalla Spain 67 F2
Tafeng China see Lanshan
Tafila Jordan see Aṭ Ṭafīlah
Tafí Viejo Arg. 178 C3
Tafresh Iran 110 C3
Taft Iran 110 D4
Taft CA U.S.A. 158 D4
Taftān, Kūh-e mt. Iran 111 F4
Taftanāz Syria 107 C2
Tafwap India 87 A6
Taga Japan 92 C3
Tagagawik r. AK U.S.A. 148 H2
Taganrog Rus. Fed. 53 H7
Taganrog, Gulf of Rus. Fed./Ukr. 53 H7
Taganrogskiy Zaliv b. Rus. Fed./Ukr. see Taganrog, Gulf of
Tagarev, Gora mt. Iran/Turkm. 110 E2
Tagarkaty, Pereval pass Tajik. 111 I2
Tagaung Myanmar 86 B2
Tagbilaran Bohol Phil. 82 C4
Tagchagpu Ri mt. China 99 C6
Tagdempt Alg. see Tiaret
Taghmon Ireland 61 F5
Tagish Canada 149 N3
Tagish Lake Canada 149 N4
Tagoloan r. Mindanao Phil. 82 D4
Tagtabazar Turkm. 111 F3
Taguchi-zaki pt Japan 92 B4
Tagudin Luzon Phil. 82 C2
Tagula P.N.G. 136 F1
Tagula Island P.N.G. 136 F1
Tagum Mindanao Phil. 82 D5
Tagus r. Port. 67 B4
also known as Tajo (Portugal) or Tejo (Spain)
Taha China 95 K2
Tahaetkun Mountain Canada 150 G5
Tahan, Gunung mt. Malaysia 84 C1
Tahanroz'ka Zatoka b. Rus. Fed./Ukr. see Taganrog, Gulf of
Tahara Japan 92 D4
Tahat, Mont mt. Alg. 120 D2
Tahaurawe i. HI U.S.A. see Kaho'olawe
Tahe China 90 B1
Taheke N.Z. 139 D2
Tahilt Mongolia see Tsogt
Tahiti i. Fr. Polynesia 187 K7
Tahlab, Dasht-i- plain Pak. 111 F4
Tahlequah OK U.S.A. 161 E5
Tahltan Canada 149 O4
Tahoe, Lake CA U.S.A. 158 C2
Tahoe Lake Canada 147 H3
Tahoe Vista CA U.S.A. 158 C2
Tahoka TX U.S.A. 161 C5
Tahoua Niger 120 D3
Tahrūd Iran 110 E4
Tahrūd r. Iran 110 E4
Tahtsa Peak Canada 150 E4
Tahulandang i. Indon. 83 C2
Tahuna Sulawesi Indon. 83 C2
Taï, Parc National de nat. park Côte d'Ivoire 120 C4
Tai'an Liaoning China 95 J3
Tai'an Shandong China 95 I4
Taibai Gansu China 95 G4
Taibai Shaanxi China 95 F5
Taibai Shan mt. China 96 E1
Taibei Taiwan see T'aipei
Taibus Qi China see Baochang
T'aichung Taiwan 97 I3
Taidong Taiwan see T'aitung
Taiei Japan 93 G3
Taigong China see Taijiang
Taigu China 95 H4
Taihang Shan mts China 95 H4
Taihang Shan mts China 95 H4
Taihape N.Z. 139 E4
Taihe Jiangxi China 97 G3
Taihe Sichuan China see Shehong
Taihezhen China see Shehong
Tai Ho Wan H.K. China 97 [inset]
Taihu China 97 H2
Tai Hu l. China 97 I2
Taihuai China 95 H4
Taijiang China 97 F3
Taikang Heilong. China 95 K2
Taikang Henan China 95 H5
Taiko-yama hill Japan 92 B3
Tailaco East Timor 83 C5
Tailai China 95 J2
Tai Lam Chung Shui Tong resr H.K. China 97 [inset]
Taileleo Indon. 84 B3
Tailem Bend Australia 137 B7
Tai Long Wan b. H.K. China 97 [inset]
Taimani reg. Afgh. 111 F3
Tai Mo Shan hill H.K. China 97 [inset]
Tain U.K. 60 F2
T'ainan Taiwan see Hsinying
T'ainan Taiwan 97 I4
Tainaro, Akra pt Greece see Tainaro, Akrotirio
Tainaro, Akrotirio pt Greece 69 J6
Taining China 97 H3
Tai O H.K. China 97 [inset]
Taiobeiras Brazil 179 C1
Taipa Sulawesi Indon. 83 B3
Tai Pang Wan b. H.K. China see Mirs Bay

▶T'aipei Taiwan 97 I3
Capital of Taiwan.

Taiping Guangdong China see Shixing
Taiping Guangxi China see Chongzuo
Taiping Guangxi China 97 F4
Taiping Malaysia 84 C1
Taipingchuan China 95 J2
Taiping Ling mt. China 95 J2
Tai Po H.K. China 97 [inset]
Tai Po Hoi b. H.K. China see Tolo Harbour
Tai Poutini National Park N.Z. see Westland National Park
Taiqian China 95 H5
Taira Japan 92 C2
Tairbeart U.K. see Tarbert
Tai Rom Yen National Park Thai. 87 B5
Tairuq Iran 110 B3
Tais Sumatera Indon. 84 C4
Tais P.N.G. 81 K8
Taishaku-san mt. Japan 93 F2
Taishan China 97 G4
Taishun China 97 H3
Tai Siu Mo To is H.K. China see The Brothers
Taissy France 62 E5
Taitaitanopo i. Indon. 84 C3
Taitao, Península de pen. Chile 178 B7
Tai Tapu N.Z. 139 D6
Tai To Yan mt. H.K. China 97 [inset]
Taitō-zaki pt Japan 93 G3
T'aitung Taiwan 97 I4
Tai Tung Shan hill H.K. China see Sunset Peak
Taivalkoski Fin. 54 P4
Taivaskero hill Fin. 54 N2
Taiwan country Asia 97 I4
T'aiwan Haihsia strait China/Taiwan see Taiwan Strait
Taiwan Haixia strait China/Taiwan see Taiwan Strait
Taiwan Shan mts Taiwan see Chungyang Shanmo
Taiwan Strait China/Taiwan 97 H4
Taixian China see Jiangyan
Taixing China 97 I1
Taiyuan China 95 H4
Tai Yue Shan i. H.K. China see Lantau Island
Taiyue Shan mts China 95 G4
Taizhao China 99 F7
Taizhong Taiwan see Fengyüan
Taizhong Taiwan see T'aichung
Taizhou Jiangsu China 97 H1
Taizhou Zhejiang China 97 I2
Taizhou Liedao i. China 97 I2
Taizhou Wan b. China 97 I2
Taizi He r. China 90 B4
Ta'izz Yemen 108 F7
Tājābād Iran 110 E4
Tajamulco, Volcán de vol. Guat. 167 H6
Tajem, Gunung hill Indon. 85 D3
Tajerouine Tunisia 68 C7
Tajikistan country Asia 111 H2
Tajimi Japan 92 D3
Tajiri Japan 92 B4
Tajitos Mex. 166 B2
Tajjal Pak. 111 H5
Tajo r. Port. 67 C4 see Tagus
Tajrīsh Iran 110 C3
Tak Thai. 86 B3
Takāb Iran 110 B2
Takabba Kenya 122 E3
Taka'Bonerate, Kepulauan atolls Indon. 83 B4
Taka Bonerate, Taman Nasional nat. park Indon. 83 B4
Takagi Japan 93 D3
Takahagi Japan 93 G2
Takahama Aichi Japan 92 C4
Takahama Fukui Japan 92 B3
Takahara-gawa r. Japan 92 D2
Takahashi Japan 91 D6
Takaishi Japan 92 B4
Takaiwa-misaki pt Japan 92 C1
Takamatsu Ishikawa Japan 92 C2
Takamatsu Kagawa Japan 91 D6
Takami-yama mt. Japan 92 C4
Takamori Japan 93 D3
Takane Gifu Japan 92 D2
Takane Yamanashi Japan 93 E3
Takanezawa Japan 93 F2
Takaoka Japan 92 D2
Takapuna N.Z. 139 E3
Takarazuka Japan 92 B4
Ta karpo China 105 G4
Takasago Japan 92 A4
Takasaki Japan 93 F2
Takashima Japan 92 C3
Takashōzu-yama mt. Japan 92 C2
Takasu Japan 92 C3
Takasuma-yama mt. Japan 93 E2
Takasuzu-san hill Japan 93 G2
Takatō Japan 93 E3
Takatokwane Botswana 124 G3
Takatomi Japan 92 C3
Takatori Japan 92 B4
Takatshwaane Botswana 124 E2
Takatsuki Ōsaka Japan 92 B4
Takatsuki Shiga Japan 92 C3
Takatsuki-yama mt. Japan 91 D6
Takayama Gifu Japan 92 D2
Takayama Gunma Japan 93 E2
Tak Bai Thai. 87 C6
Takefu Japan 92 C3
Takengon Sumatera Indon. 84 B1
Takeno Japan 92 A3
Takeo Cambodia see Takêv
Takeshi Japan 93 E2
Take-shima i. N. Pacific Ocean see Liancourt Rocks
Takestān Iran 110 C2
Taketoyo Japan 92 C4
Takêv Cambodia 87 D5
Takhemaret Alg. 67 G6
Takhini Hotspring Canada 149 N3
Ta Khli Thai. 86 C4
Ta Khmau Cambodia 87 D5
Takhta-Bazar Turkm. see Tagtabazar
Takhtah Pul Afgh. 111 G4
Takht Apān, Kūh-e mt. Iran 110 C3
Takhteh Iran 110 D4
Takht-e Soleymān mt. Iran 110 C2
Takht-e Soleymān tourist site Iran 110 B2
Takht-i-Bahi tourist site Pak. 111 H3
Takht-i-Sulaiman mt. Pak. 111 H4
Taki Japan 92 C4
Takijuq Lake Canada see Napaktulik Lake
Takino Japan 92 A4
Takinoue Japan 90 F3
Takisung Kalimantan Indon. 85 F3
Takla Lake Canada 150 E4
Takla Landing Canada 150 E4
Takla Makan des. China see Taklimakan Desert
Taklimakan Desert China 98 C5
Taklimakan Shamo des. China see Taklimakan Desert
Tako Japan 93 G3
Takotna AK U.S.A. 148 H3
Takpa Shiri mt. China 99 F7
Takslesluk Lake AK U.S.A. 148 G3
Taku Canada 150 C3
Taku r. Canada/U.S.A. 149 N4
Takum Nigeria 120 D4
Takuu Islands P.N.G. 133 F2
Talab r. Iran/Pak. 111 F4
Talachyn Belarus 53 F5
Talaja India 104 C5
Talakan Amurskaya Oblast' Rus. Fed. 90 C2
Talakan Khabarovskiy Kray Rus. Fed. 90 D2
Talamanca, Cordillera de mts Costa Rica 166 [inset] J7
Talandzha Rus. Fed. 90 C2
Talang, Gunung vol. Indon. 84 C3
Talangbatu Sumatera Indon. 84 D3
Talangbetutu Sumatera Indon. 84 D3
Talara Peru 176 B4
Talar-i-Band mts Pak. see Makran Coast Range
Talas Kyrg. 102 D3
Talas Ala-Too mts Kyrg. 102 D3
Talas Range mts Kyrg. see Talas Ala-Too
Talasskiy Alatau, Khrebet mts Kyrg. see Talas Ala-Too
Talatakoh i. Indon. 83 B3
Ṭal'at Mūsá mt. Lebanon/Syria 107 C2
Talaud, Kepulauan is Indon. 83 C1
Talavera de la Reina Spain 67 D4
Talawgyi Myanmar 86 B1
Talaya Rus. Fed. 77 Q3
Talayan Mindanao Phil. 82 D5
Talbehat India 104 D4
Talbīsah Syria 107 C2
Talbot, Mount hill Australia 135 D6
Talbotton GA U.S.A. 163 C5
Talbragar r. Australia 138 D4
Talca Chile 178 B5
Talcahuano Chile 178 B5
Taldan Rus. Fed. 90 B1
Taldom Rus. Fed. 52 H4
Taldykorgan Kazakh. 102 E3
Taldy-Kurgan Kazakh. see Taldykorgan
Taldyqorghan Kazakh. see Taldykorgan
Taldy-Suu Kyrg. 98 B4
Tālesh Iran see Hashtpar
Talgar Kazakh. 98 B4
Talgar, Pik mt. Kazakh. 98 B4
Talgarth U.K. 59 D7
Talguppa India 106 B3
Talia Australia 137 A7
Taliabu i. Indon. 83 C3
Talibon Bohol Phil. 82 D4
Talikota India 106 C2
Talikud i. Phil. 82 D5
Talimardzhan Uzbek. see Tollimarjon
Talin Hiag China 95 K2
Taliparamba India 106 B3
Talisay Cebu Phil. 82 C4
Talisayan Kalimantan Indon. 85 G2
Talisayan Mindanao Phil. 82 D4
Taliş Dağları mts Azer./Iran 110 C2
Taliseі i. Indon. 83 C2
Talitsa Rus. Fed. 52 J4
Taliwang Sumbawa Indon. 85 G5
Talkeetna AK U.S.A. 149 J3
Talkeetna r. AK U.S.A. 149 J3
Talkeetna Mountains AK U.S.A. 149 J3
Talkh Āb Iran 110 E3
Tallacootra, Lake salt flat Australia 135 F7
Talladega AL U.S.A. 163 C5

▶Tallahassee FL U.S.A. 163 C6
Capital of Florida.

Tall al Aḥmar Syria 107 D1
Tallassee AL U.S.A. 167 I1
Tall Baydar Syria 113 F3
Tall-e Ḥalāl Iran 110 D4

▶Tallinn Estonia 55 N7
Capital of Estonia.

Tall Kalakh Syria 107 C2
Tall Kayf Iraq 113 F3
Tall Kūjik Syria 113 F3
Tallow Ireland 61 D5
Tallulah LA U.S.A. 161 F5
Tall 'Uwaynāt Iraq 113 F3
Tallymerjen Uzbek. see Tollimarjon
Talmont-St-Hilaire France 66 D3
Tal'ne Ukr. 53 F6
Tal'noye Ukr. see Tal'ne
Taloda India 104 C5
Talodi Sudan 108 D7
Taloga OK U.S.A. 161 D4
Talon, Lac l. Canada 153 I3
Ta-long Myanmar 86 B2
Tāloqān Afgh. 111 H2
Talos Dome ice feature Antarctica 188 H2
Ta Loung San mt. Laos 86 C2
Talovaya Rus. Fed. 53 I6
Taloyoak Canada 147 I3
Talpa Mex. 166 D4
Tal Pass Pak. 111 I3
Talshand Mongolia see Chandmanī
Talsi Latvia 55 M8
Tal Sīyāh Iran 111 F4
Taltal Chile 178 B3
Taltson r. Canada 151 H2
Talu China 99 F7
Talu Sumatera Indon. 84 B2
Taludaa Sulawesi Indon. 83 B2
Taluti, Teluk b. Seram Indon. 83 D3
Talvik Norway 54 M1
Talwood Australia 138 D2
Talyshskiye Gory mts Azer./Iran see Taliş Dağları
Talyy Rus. Fed. 52 L2
Tama Japan 93 F3
Tama Abu, Banjaran mts Malaysia 85 F2
Tamabo Range mts Malaysia see Tama Abu, Banjaran
Tama-gawa r. Japan 93 F3
Tamaki Japan 92 C4
Tamala Australia 135 A6
Tamala Rus. Fed. 53 I5
Tamale Ghana 120 C4
Tamalung Kalimantan Indon. 85 F3
Tamamura Japan 93 F2
Tamana i. Kiribati 133 H2
Taman Nasional Sebangu nat. park Indon. 85 F3
Taman Nasional Tesso Nilo tourist site Indon. 84 C5
Taman Negara National Park Malaysia 84 C1
Tamano Japan 91 D6
Tamanrasset Alg. 120 D2
Tamanthi Myanmar 86 A1
Tamaqua PA U.S.A. 165 H3
Tamar India 105 F5
Tamar Syria see Tadmur
Tamar r. U.K. 59 C8
Tamari Japan 93 G2
Tamarugal, Pampa de plain Chile 176 E7
Tamasane Botswana 125 H2
Tamatave Madag. see Toamasina
Tamatsukuri Japan 93 G2
Tamaulipas state Mex. 161 D7
Tamaulipas, Sierra de mts Mex. 167 F4
Tamazula Durango Mex. 166 D3
Tamazula Jalisco Mex. 166 E5
Tamazulápam Mex. 167 F5
Tamazunchale Mex. 167 F4
Tamba Japan see Tanba
Tambacounda Senegal 120 B3
Tamba-kōchi plat. Japan see Tanba-kōchi
Tambalongang i. Indon. 83 B4
Tambangmunjul Kalimantan Indon. 85 E3
Tambangsawah Sumatera Indon. 84 C3
Tambaqui Brazil 176 F5
Tambar Springs Australia 138 D3
Tambea Sulawesi Indon. 83 B4
Tambelan, Kepulauan is Indon. 84 D2
Tambelan Besar i. Indon. 85 D2
Tamberu Jawa Indon. 85 F4
Tambisan Sabah Malaysia 85 G1
Tambo r. Australia 138 C6
Tambohorano Madag. 123 E5
Tamboli Sulawesi Indon. 83 B3
Tambor Mex. 166 D3

▶Tambora, Gunung vol. Sumbawa Indon. 85 G5
Deadliest recorded volcanic eruption (1815).

Tamboritha mt. Australia 138 C6
Tambov Rus. Fed. 53 I5
Tambovka Rus. Fed. 90 C2
Tambu, Teluk b. Indon. 83 A2
Tambulanan, Bukit hill Malaysia 85 G1
Tambunan Sabah Malaysia 85 G1
Tambura South Sudan 121 F4
Tamburi Brazil 179 C1
Tambuyukon, Gunung mt. Malaysia 85 G1
Tâmchekkeṭ Mauritania 120 B3
Tamdybulak Uzbek. see Tomdibuloq
Tâmega r. Port. 67 B3
Tamenghest Alg. see Tamanrasset
Tamenglong India 105 H4
Tamerza Tunisia 68 B7
Tamgak, Adrar mt. Niger 120 D3
Tamgué, Massif du mt. Guinea 120 B3
Tamiahua Mex. 167 F4
Tamiahua, Laguna de lag. Mex. 168 E4
Tamiang r. Indon. 84 B1
Tamiang, Ujung pt Indon. 84 B1
Tamil Nadu state India 106 C4
Tamirin Gol r. Mongolia 94 E2
Tamitsa Rus. Fed. 52 H2
Ṭāmīya Egypt see Ṭāmīyah
Ṭāmīyah Egypt 112 C5
Tamkuhi India 105 F4
Tam Ky Vietnam 86 E4
Tammarvi r. Canada 151 K1
Tammerfors Fin. see Tampere
Tammisaari Fin. see Ekenäs
Tampa FL U.S.A. 163 D7
Tampa Bay FL U.S.A. 163 D7
Tampang Sumatera Indon. 84 D4
Tampere Fin. 55 M6
Tampico Mex. 168 E4
Tampin Malaysia 84 C2
Tampines Sing. 87 [inset]
Tampo Sulawesi Indon. 83 B4
Tamsagbulag Mongolia 95 I2
Tamsag Muchang China 94 E3
Tamsweg Austria 57 N7
Tamu Myanmar 86 A1
Tamuín Mex. 167 F4
Tamworth Australia 138 E3
Tamworth U.K. 59 F6
Tan Kazakh. 98 B2
Tana r. Fin./Norway see Tenojoki
Tana r. Kenya 122 E4
Tana Madag. see Antananarivo
Tana r. AK U.S.A. 149 L3
Tana i. Vanuatu see Tanna
Tana, Lake Eth. 122 D2
Tanabe Japan 91 D6
Tanabi Brazil 179 A3
Tana Bru Norway 54 P1
Tanacross AK U.S.A. 149 L3
Tanadak Island AK U.S.A. 148 D5
Tanada Lake AK U.S.A. 150 A2
Tanafjorden inlet Norway 54 P1
Tanaga vol. AK U.S.A. 148 [inset] C6
Tanaga Island AK U.S.A. 148 [inset] C6
Tanaga Pass sea channel AK U.S.A. 148 [inset] C6
Tanagura Japan 93 G1
Tanah, Tanjung pt Indon. 85 E4
T'ana Häyk' l. Eth. see Tana, Lake
Tanahbala i. Indon. 84 B3
Tanahgrogot Kalimantan Indon. 85 G3
Tanahjampea i. Indon. 83 B4
Tanahmasa i. Indon. 84 B3
Tanahmerah Kalimantan Indon. 85 G2
Tanah Merah Malaysia 84 C1
Tanahputih Sumatera Indon. 84 C2
Tanah Rata Malaysia 84 C1
Tanakeke i. Indon. 83 A4
Tanambung Sulawesi Barat Indon. 83 A3
Tanami Australia 134 E4
Tanami Desert Australia 134 E4
Tân An Vietnam 87 D5
Tanana AK U.S.A. 148 I2
Tanana r. AK U.S.A. 148 I2
Tananarive Madag. see Antananarivo
Tanandava Madag. 123 E6
Tanauan Leyte Phil. 82 D4
Tanba Japan 92 B3
Tanba-kōchi plat. Japan 92 B3
Tanbu China 97 G4
Tancheng Fujian China see Pingtan
Tancheng Shandong China 95 I5
Tanch'ŏn N. Korea 91 C4
Tanda Côte d'Ivoire 120 C4
Tanda Uttar Prad. India 104 D3
Tanda Uttar Prad. India 105 E4
Tandag Mindanao Phil. 82 D4
Ţăndărei Romania 69 L2
Tandaué Angola 123 B5
Tandek Sabah Malaysia 85 G1
Tandi India 104 D2
Tandil Arg. 178 E5
Tando Adam Pak. 111 H5
Tando Allahyar Pak. 111 H5
Tando Bago Pak. 111 H5
Tandou Lake imp. l. Australia 137 C7
Tandragee U.K. 61 F3
Tandubatu i. Phil. 82 C5
Tandur India 106 C2
Tanduri Pak. 111 G4
Tanega-shima i. Japan 91 C7
Tanen Taunggyi mts Thai. 86 B3
Tanezrouft reg. Alg./Mali 120 C2
Ṭanf, Jabal aṭ hill Syria 107 D3
Tang, Ra's-e pt Iran 111 E5
Tanga Rus. Fed. 95 G1
Tanga Tanz. 123 D4
Tangail Bangl. 105 G4
Tanga Islands P.N.G. 132 F2
Tanganyika country Africa see Tanzania

▶Tanganyika, Lake Africa 123 C4
Deepest and 2nd largest lake in Africa, and 6th largest in the world.

Tangará Brazil 179 A4
Tangasseri India 106 C4
Tangdan China 96 D3
Tangdê China 99 F7
Tangeli Iran 110 D2
Tanger Morocco see Tangier
Tangerang Jawa Indon. 84 D4
Tangerhütte Germany 63 L2
Tangermünde Germany 63 L2
Tang-e Sarkheh Iran 111 E5
Tanggarma China 94 D4
Tanggo China 99 E7
Tanggor China 96 D1
Tanggu China 95 I4
Tanggulashan China 94 C5
Tanggula Shan mt. China 99 E6
Tanggula Shan mts China 99 E6
Tanggula Shankou pass China 99 E6
Tangguo China 99 D7
Tanghai China 95 I4
Tanghe China 97 G1
Tangier Morocco 67 D6
Tangiers Morocco see Tangier
Tangkelemboko, Gunung mt. Indon. 83 B3
Tangkittebak, Gunung mt. Indon. 84 D4
Tang La pass China 99 E8
Tangla India 105 G4
Tanglag China 96 C1
Tanglin Sing. 87 [inset]
Tangmai China 99 F7
Tangnag China 94 E5
Tango Japan 92 B3
Tangorin Australia 136 D4
Tangra Yumco salt l. China 99 D7
Tangse Sumatera Indon. 84 A1
Tangshan Guizhou China see Shiqian
Tangshan Hebei China 95 I4
Tangte mt. Myanmar 86 B2
Tangtse India see Tanktse
Tangub Mindanao Phil. 82 C4
Tangwan China 97 F3
Tangwanghe China 90 C2
Tangxian China 95 H4
Tangyin China 95 H5
Tangyuan China 90 C3
Tangyung Tso salt l. China 105 F3
Tanhaçu Brazil 179 C1
Tanhua Fin. 54 O3
Tani Cambodia 87 D5
Taniantaweng Shan mts China 96 B2
Tanigawa-dake mt. Japan 93 E2
Tanigumi Japan 92 C3
Tanimbar, Kepulauan is Indon. 134 E1
Tanintharī Myanmar see Tenasserim
Tanintharyi Myanmar see Tenasserim
Taninthayi Myanmar see Tenasserim
Taniwel Seram Indon. 83 D3
Tanjah Morocco see Tangier
Tanjay Negros Phil. 82 C4
Tanjiajing China 94 E4
Tanjore India see Thanjavur
Tanjung Kalimantan Indon. 85 F3
Tanjung Sumatera Indon. 84 D3
Tanjungbalai Sumatera Indon. 84 B2
Tanjungbalai Sumatera Indon. 84 C2
Tanjungbaliha Maluku Indon. 83 C3
Tanjungbatu Kalimantan Indon. 85 G2
Tanjungbatu Sumatera Indon. 84 C2
Tanjungbuayabuaya, Pulau i. Indon. 85 G2
Tanjungenim Sumatera Indon. 84 C3
Tanjunggaru Kalimantan Indon. 85 G3
Tanjungkarang-Telukbetung Sumatera Indon. see Bandar Lampung
Tanjungpandan Indon. 85 D3
Tanjungpinang Indon. 84 D2
Tanjungpura Sumatera Indon. 84 B2
Tanjung Puting, Taman Nasional nat. park Indon. 85 F3
Tanjungraja Sumatera Indon. 84 D3
Tanjungredeb Kalimantan Indon. 85 G2
Tanjungsaleh i. Indon. 85 E3
Tanjungsatai Kalimantan Indon. 85 E3
Tanjungselor Kalimantan Indon. 85 G2
Tankhoy Rus. Fed. 94 F1
Tankse India see Tanktse
Tanktse India 104 D2
Tankwa-Karoo National Park S. Africa 124 D7
Tanna i. Vanuatu 133 G3
Tannadice U.K. 60 G4
Tannan Japan 92 B3
Tännäs Sweden 54 H5
Tanner, Mount Canada 150 G5
Tannu-Ola, Khrebet mts Rus. Fed. 94 B1
Tannu Tuva aut. rep. Rus. Fed. see Tyva, Respublika
Tañon Strait Phil. 82 C4
Tanot India 104 B4
Tanout Niger 120 D3
Tanquian Mex. 167 F4
Tansen Nepal 105 E4
Tanshui Taiwan 97 I3
Tansyk Kazakh. 98 B3
Ṭanṭā Egypt 112 C5
Ṭanta Egypt see Ṭanṭā
Tan-Tan Morocco 120 B2
Tantō Japan 92 A3
Tantoyuca Mex. 167 F4
Tantu China 95 J2
Tanuku India 106 D2
Tanuma Japan 93 F2
Tanumbirini Australia 134 F4
Tanumshede Sweden 55 G7
Tanyurer r. Rus. Fed. 148 A2
Tanzania country Africa 123 D4

Tanzawa-Ōyama Kokutei-kōen park Japan 93 F3
Tanzilla r. Canada 149 O4
Tao, Ko i. Thai. 87 B5
Tao'an China see Taonan
Taobh Tuath U.K. see Northton
Taocheng China see Daxin
Taocun China 95 J4
Tao'er He r. China 95 J2
Tao He r. China 94 E5
Taohong China see Longhui
Taohuajiang China see Taojiang
Taohuaping China see Longhui
Taojiang China 97 G2
Taolanaro Madag. see Tôlañaro
Taole China 94 F4
Taonan China 95 J2
Taongi atoll Marshall Is 186 H5
Taos NM U.S.A. 157 G5
Taounate Morocco 64 D5
Taourirt Morocco 64 D5
Taoxi China 97 H3
Taoyang China see Lintao
Taoyuan China 97 F2
T'aoyüan Taiwan 97 I3
Tapa Estonia 55 N7
Tapaan Passage Phil. 82 C5
Tapachula Mex. 167 G6
Tapah Malaysia 87 C6
Tapajós r. Brazil 177 H4
Tapaktuan Sumatera Indon. 84 B2
Tapan Sumatera Indon. 84 C3
Tapanatepec Mex. 167 G5
Tapanuli, Teluk b. Indon. 84 B2
Tapat i. Maluku Indon. 83 C3
Tapauá Brazil 176 F5
Tapauá r. Brazil 176 F5
Taperoá Brazil 179 D1
Tapiau Rus. Fed. see Gvardeysk
Tapijulapa Mex. 167 G5
Tapinbini Kalimantan Indon. 85 E3
Tapis, Gunung mt. Malaysia 84 C1
Tapisuelas Mex. 166 C3
Taplejung Nepal 105 F4
Tap Mun Chau i. H.K. China 97 [inset]
Ta-pom Myanmar 86 B2
Tappahannock VA U.S.A. 165 G5
Tappal India 99 B7
Tappalang Sulawesi Indon. 85 G3
Tappeh, Kūh-e hill Iran 110 C3
Taprobane country Asia see Sri Lanka
Tapti r. India 104 C5
Tapuaenuku mt. N.Z. 139 D5
Tapul Phil. 82 C5
Tapul Group is Phil. 82 C5
Tapulonanjing mt. Indon. 84 B2
Tapung r. Indon. 84 C2
Tapurucuara Brazil 176 E4
Taputeouea atoll Kiribati see Tabiteuea
Ţaqţaq Iraq 113 G4
Taquara Brazil 179 A5
Taquarí Brazil 179 A5
Taquarí r. Brazil 177 G7
Taquaritinga Brazil 179 A3
Tar r. Ireland 61 E5
Tara Australia 138 E1
Ţarābulus Lebanon see Tripoli
Ţarābulus Libya see Tripoli
Taragt Mongolia 94 E2
Tarahuwan India 104 E4
Tarai reg. India 105 G4
Tarakan Kalimantan Indon. 85 G2
Tarakan i. Indon. 85 G2
Tarakki reg. Afgh. 111 G3
Taraklı Turkey 69 N4
Taran, Mys pt Rus. Fed. 55 K9
Tarana Australia 138 D4
Taranagar India 104 C3
Taranaki, Mount vol. N.Z. 139 E4
Tarancón Spain 67 E3
Tarangambadi India 106 C4
Tarangire National Park Tanz. 122 D4
Taranto Italy 68 G4
Taranto, Golfo di g. Italy 68 G4
Taranto, Gulf of Italy see Taranto, Golfo di
Tarapoto Peru 176 C5
Tarapur India 106 B2
Tararua Range mts N.Z. 139 E5
Tarascon-sur-Ariège France 66 E5
Tarasovskiy Rus. Fed. 53 I6
Tarauacá Brazil 176 D5
Tarauacá r. Brazil 176 E5
Tarawera N.Z. 139 F4
Tarawera, Mount vol. N.Z. 139 F4
Taraz Kazakh. 102 D3
Tarazona Spain 67 F3
Tarazona de la Mancha Spain 67 F4
Tarbagatay Kazakh. 98 C3
Tarbagatay Rus. Fed. 95 F1
Tarbagatay, Khrebet mts Kazakh. 102 F2
Tarbat Ness pt U.K. 60 F3
Tarbert Ireland 61 C5
Tarbert Scotland U.K. 60 C3
Tarbert Scotland U.K. 60 D5
Tarbes France 66 E5
Tarboro NC U.S.A. 162 E5
Tarcoola Australia 135 F7
Tarcoon Australia 138 C3
Tarcoonyinna watercourse Australia 135 F6
Tarcutta Australia 138 C5
Tardoki-Yangi, Gora mt. Rus. Fed. 90 E2
Taree Australia 138 F3
Tarella Australia 137 C6
Tarentum Italy see Taranto
Ţarfā', Baţn aţ depr. Saudi Arabia 110 C6
Tarfaya Morocco 120 B2
Targa well Niger 120 D3
Targan China see Talin Hiag
Targhee Pass ID U.S.A. 156 F3
Târgovişte Romania 69 K2
Targuist Morocco 67 D6
Târgu Jiu Romania 69 J2
Târgu Mureş Romania 69 K1
Târgu Neamţ Romania 69 L1
Târgu Secuiesc Romania 69 L1
Targyailing China 99 D7
Targyn Kazakh. 98 C2
Tari P.N.G. 81 K8
Tarian Gol China 95 G4
Tariat Mongolia 94 D1
Tarif U.A.E. 110 D5
Tarifa Spain 67 D5
Tarifa, Punta de pt Spain 67 D5
Tarigtig Point Luzon Phil. 82 C2
Tarija Bol. 176 F8
Tarikere India 106 B3
Tariku r. Indon. 81 J7
Tarim China 98 C4
Tarīm Yemen 108 G6
Tarim Basin China 98 C5
Tarime Tanz. 122 D4
Tarim He r. China 98 D4
Tarim Liuchang China 98 D4
Tarim Pendi basin China see Tarim Basin
Tarim Qichang China 98 D4
Tarīn Kōţ Afgh. 111 G3
Taritatu r. Indon. 81 J7
Taritipan Sabah Malaysia see Tandek
Tarka r. S. Africa 125 G7
Tarkastad S. Africa 125 H7
Tarkio MO U.S.A. 160 E3
Tarko-Sale Rus. Fed. 76 I3
Tarkwa Ghana 120 C4
Tarlac Luzon Phil. 82 C3
Tarlac r. Luzon Phil. 82 C2
Tarlauly Kazakh. 98 B3
Tarlo River National Park Australia 138 D5
Tarma Peru 176 C6
Tarmar China 99 E7
Tarmstedt Germany 63 J1
Tarn r. France 66 E4
Tärnaby Sweden 54 I4
Tarnak Rūd r. Afgh. 111 G4
Târnăveni Romania 69 K1
Tarnobrzeg Poland 53 D6
Tarnogskiy Gorodok Rus. Fed. 52 I3
Tarnopol Ukr. see Ternopil'
Tarnów Poland 53 D6
Tarnowitz Poland see Tarnowskie Góry
Tarnowskie Góry Poland 57 Q5
Taro Co salt l. China 99 C7
Ţārom Iran 110 D4
Taroom Australia 137 E5
Tarō-san mt. Japan 93 F2
Taroudannt Morocco 64 C5
Tarpaulin Swamp Australia 136 B3
Ţarq Iran 110 C3
Tarquinia Italy 68 D3
Tarquinii Italy see Tarquinia
Tarrabool Lake salt flat Australia 136 A3
Tarraco Spain see Tarragona
Tarrafal Cape Verde 120 [inset]
Tarragona Spain 67 G3
Tårrajaur Sweden 54 K3
Tarran Hills hill Australia 138 C4
Tarrant Point Australia 136 B3
Tàrrega Spain 67 G3
Tarso Emissi mt. Chad 121 E2
Tarsus Turkey 107 B1
Tart China 99 F5
Tärtär Azer. 113 G2
Tartu Estonia 55 O7
Ţarţūs Syria 107 B2
Tarui Japan 92 C3
Tarumovka Rus. Fed. 113 G1
Tarung Hka r. Myanmar 86 B1
Tarutao, Ko i. Thai. 87 B6
Tarutao National Park Thai. 87 B6
Tarutung Sumatera Indon. 84 B2
Tarvisium Italy see Treviso
Tarys-Arzhan Rus. Fed. 94 D1
Ţarz Iran 110 E4
Tasai, Ko i. Thai. 87 B5
Tasaral Kazakh. 98 A3
Taschereau Canada 152 F4
Taseko Mountain Canada 150 F5
Tashauz Turkm. see Daşoguz
Tash-Bashat Kyrg. 98 B4
Tashi China 94 C3
Tashi Chho Bhutan see Thimphu
Tashigang Bhutan 105 G4
Tashino Rus. Fed. see Pervomaysk
Tashir Armenia 113 G2
Tashk, Daryācheh-ye l. Iran 110 D4
Tashkent Uzbek. see Toshkent
Tāshqurghān Afgh. see Kholm
Tashtagol Rus. Fed. 88 F2
Tashtyp Rus. Fed. 88 F2
Tasialujjuaq, Lac l. Canada 153 G2
Tasiat, Lac l. Canada 152 G2
Tasiilap Karra c. Greenland 147 O3
Tasiilaq Greenland see Ammassalik
Tasikmalaya Jawa Indon. 85 E4
Tasīl Syria 107 B3
Tasiujaq Canada 153 H2
Tasiusaq Greenland 147 M2
Taskala Kazakh. 51 Q5
Taşkent Turkey 107 A1
Tasker Niger 120 E3
Taskesken Kazakh. 102 F2
Taşköprü Turkey 112 D2
Tasman Abyssal Plain sea feature Tasman Sea 186 G8
Tasman Basin sea feature Tasman Sea 186 G8
Tasman Bay N.Z. 139 D5
▶Tasmania state Australia 137 [inset]
4th largest island in Oceania.
Tasman Islands P.N.G. see Nukumanu Islands
Tasman Mountains N.Z. 139 D5
Tasman Peninsula Australia 137 [inset]
Tasman Sea S. Pacific Ocean 132 H6
Taşova Turkey 112 E2
Tassara Niger 120 D3
Tassialouc, Lac l. Canada 152 G2
Tassili n'Ajjer plat. Alg. 120 D2
Tassili n'Ajjer, Parc National de nat. park Alg. 120 D2
Tasty Kazakh. 102 C3
Taşucu Turkey 107 A1
Tas-Yuryakh Rus. Fed. 77 M3
Tata Morocco 64 C6
Tataba Sulawesi Indon. 83 B3
Tatabánya Hungary 68 H1
Tatalin He r. China 94 C4
Tatamailau, Foho mt. East Timor 83 C5
Tataouine Tunisia 64 G5
Tatarbunary Ukr. 69 M2
Tatarsk Rus. Fed. 76 I4
Tatarskiy Proliv strait Rus. Fed. 90 F2
Tatar Strait Rus. Fed. see Tatarskiy Proliv
Tatau Sarawak Malaysia 85 F2
Tate r. Australia 136 C3
Tatebayashi Japan 93 F2
Tateishi-misaki pt Japan 92 C3
Tateiwa Japan 93 E1
Tateshina Japan 93 E2
Tateshina-yama mt. Japan 93 E2
Tateyama Chiba Japan 93 F4
Tateyama Toyama Japan 92 D2
Tate-yama vol. Japan 92 D2
Tathlina Lake Canada 150 G2
Tathlīth Saudi Arabia 108 F6
Tathlīth, Wādī watercourse Saudi Arabia 108 F5
Tathra Australia 138 D6
Tatinnai Lake Canada 151 L2
Tatishchevo Rus. Fed. 53 J6
Tatitlek AK U.S.A. 149 K3
Tatkon Myanmar 86 B2
Tatla Lake Canada 150 E5
Tatla Lake l. Canada 150 E5
Tatlayoko Lake Canada 150 E5
Tatnam, Cape Canada 151 N3
Tatomi Japan 93 E3
Tatra Mountains Poland/Slovakia 57 Q6
Tatrang China 99 D5
Tatry mts Poland/Slovakia see Tatra Mountains
Tatrzański Park Narodowy nat. park Poland 57 Q6
Tatshenshini r. Canada 149 M4
Tatshenshini-Alsek Provincial Wilderness Park Canada 150 B3
Tatsinskaya Rus. Fed. 53 I6
Tatsuno Japan 93 D3
Tatsunokuchi Japan 92 C2
Tatsuruhama Japan 92 C1
Tatsuyama Japan 93 D4
Tatuí Brazil 179 B3
Tatuk Mountain Canada 150 E4
Tatum NM U.S.A. 161 C5
Tatvan Turkey 113 F3
Tau Norway 55 D7
Taua Brazil 177 J5
Tauapeçaçu Brazil 176 F4
Taubaté Brazil 179 B3
Tauber r. Germany 63 J5
Tauberbischofsheim Germany 63 J5
Taucha Germany 63 M3
Taufstein hill Germany 63 J4
Taukum, Peski des. Kazakh. 102 D3
Taumarunui N.Z. 139 E4
Taumaturgo Brazil 176 D5
Taung S. Africa 124 G4
Taungdwingyi Myanmar 86 A2
Taunggyi Myanmar 86 B2
Taungmaw Myanmar 86 B2
Taung-ngu Myanmar 86 B3
Taungnyo Range mts Myanmar 86 B3
Taungtha Myanmar 86 A2
Taungup Myanmar 96 B5
Taunton U.K. 59 D7
Taunton MA U.S.A. 165 J3
Taunus hills Germany 63 H4
Taupo N.Z. 139 F4
Taupo, Lake N.Z. 139 E4
Tauragė Lith. 55 M9
Tauranga N.Z. 139 F3
Taurasia Italy see Turin
Taureau, Réservoir resr Canada 152 G5
Taurianova Italy 68 G5
Tauroa Point N.Z. 139 D2
Taurus Mountains Turkey 107 A1
Taute r. France 59 F9
Tauz Azer. see Tovuz
Tavas Turkey 69 M6
Tavastehus Fin. see Hämeenlinna
Tavayvaam r. Rus. Fed. 148 B2
Taverham U.K. 59 I6
Taveuni i. Fiji 133 I3
Tavildara Tajik. 111 H2
Tavira Port. 67 C5
Tavistock Canada 164 E2
Tavistock U.K. 59 C8
Tavoy Myanmar 87 B4
Tavoy r. mouth Myanmar 87 B4
Tavoy Island Myanmar see Mali Kyun
Tavoy Point Myanmar 87 B4
Tavricheskoye Kazakh. 98 C2
Tavşanlı Turkey 69 M5
Taw r. U.K. 59 C7
Tawai, Bukit mt. Malaysia 85 G1
Tawakoni, Lake TX U.S.A. 167 G1
Tawang India 105 G4
Tawaramoto Japan 92 B4
Tawas City MI U.S.A. 164 D1
Tawau Sabah Malaysia 85 G1
Tawau, Teluk b. Malaysia 85 G1
Tawè Myanmar see Tavoy
Tawe r. U.K. 59 D7
Tawi r. India 99 A6
Ţawī Ḩafīr well U.A.E. 110 D5
Ţawī Murra well U.A.E. 110 D5
Tawi-Tawi i. Phil. 82 B5
Tawmaw Myanmar 86 B1
Tawu Taiwan 97 I4
Taxco Mex. 167 F5
Taxkorgan China 99 A5
Tay r. Canada 149 N3
Tay r. U.K. 60 F4
Tay, Firth of est. U.K. 60 F4
Tay, Lake salt flat Australia 135 C8
Tay, Loch l. U.K. 60 E4
Tayabas Bay Luzon Phil. 82 C3
Tayan Kalimantan Indon. 85 E2
Tayandu, Kepulauan is Indon. 81 I8
Tāybād Iran 111 F3
Taybola Rus. Fed. 54 R2
Taycheedah WI U.S.A. 164 A2
Taygan Mongolia see Delger
Tayinloan U.K. 60 D5
Taylor Canada 150 F3
Taylor AK U.S.A. 148 F2
Taylor MI U.S.A. 164 D2
Taylor NE U.S.A. 160 D3
Taylor TX U.S.A. 161 D6
Taylor, Mount NM U.S.A. 159 J4
Taylor Mountains AK U.S.A. 148 H3
Taylorsville KY U.S.A. 164 C4
Taylorville IL U.S.A. 160 F4
Taymā' Saudi Arabia 112 E6
Taymura r. Rus. Fed. 77 K3
Taymyr, Ozero l. Rus. Fed. 77 L2
Taymyr, Poluostrov pen. Rus. Fed. see Taymyr Peninsula
Taymyr Peninsula Rus. Fed. 76 J2
Tây Ninh Vietnam 87 D5
Tayoltita Mex. 166 D3
Taypak Kazakh. 51 Q6
Taypaq Kazakh. see Taypak
Tayshet Rus. Fed. 88 H1
Tayshir Mongolia 94 D2
Taytay Luzon Phil. 82 C3
Taytay Palawan Phil. 82 B4
Taytay Bay Palawan Phil. 82 B4
Taytay Point Leyte Phil. 82 D4
Tayu Jawa Indon. 85 E4
Tayuan China 90 B2
Taz r. Rus. Fed. 76 I3
Taza Morocco 64 D5
Tāza Khurmātū Iraq 113 G4
Tazawa Japan 93 D2
Taze Myanmar 86 A2
Tazewell TN U.S.A. 164 D5
Tazewell VA U.S.A. 164 E5
Tazimina Lakes AK U.S.A. 148 I3
Tazin r. Canada 151 I2
Tazin Lake Canada 151 I3
Tāzirbū Libya 121 F2
Tazlina AK U.S.A. 149 K3
Tazlina Lake AK U.S.A. 149 K3
Tazmalt Alg. 67 I5
Tazovskaya Guba sea chan. Rus. Fed. 76 I3
Tbessa Alg. see Tébessa
▶T'bilisi Georgia 113 G2
Capital of Georgia.
Tbilisskaya Rus. Fed. 53 I7
Tchabal Mbabo mt. Cameroon 120 E4
Tchad country Africa see Chad
Tchamba Togo 120 D4
Tchibanga Gabon 122 B4
Tchigaï, Plateau du Niger 121 E2
Tchin-Tabaradene Niger 120 D3
Tcholliré Cameroon 121 E4
Tchula MS U.S.A. 161 F5
Tczew Poland 57 Q3
Te, Prêk r. Cambodia 87 D4
Teacapán Mex. 166 D4
Teague, Lake salt flat Australia 135 C6
Te Anau N.Z. 139 A7
Te Anau, Lake N.Z. 139 A7
Teapa Mex. 167 G5
Te Araroa N.Z. 139 G3
Teate Italy see Chieti
Te Awamutu N.Z. 139 E4
Teba Indon. 81 J7
Tébarat Niger 120 D3
Tebas Kalimantan Indon. 85 E2
Tebay U.K. 58 E4
Tebedu Sarawak Malaysia 85 E2
Tebesjuak Lake Canada 151 L2
Tébessa Alg. 68 C7
Tébessa, Monts de mts Alg. 68 C7
Tebingtinggi Sumatera Indon. 84 B2
Tebingtinggi Sumatera Indon. 84 C3
Tebo r. Indon. 84 C3
Téboursouk Tunisia 68 C6
Tebourba Tunisia 68 C6
Tebulos Mt'a Georgia/Rus. Fed. 113 G2
Tecalitlán Mex. 166 E5
Tecate Mex. 166 A1
Tece Turkey 107 B1
Techiman Ghana 120 C4
Tecka Arg. 178 B6
Tecklenburger Land reg. Germany 63 H2
Tecolutla Mex. 167 F4
Tecomán Mex. 166 E5
Tecoripa Mex. 166 C2
Técpan Mex. 168 D5
Tecuala Mex. 168 C4
Tecuci Romania 69 L2
Tecumseh MI U.S.A. 164 D3
Tecumseh NE U.S.A. 160 D3
Tedori-gawa r. Japan 92 C2
Tedzhen Turkm. see Tejen
Teec Nos Pos AZ U.S.A. 159 I3
Teel Mongolia see Öndör-Ulaan
Teeli Rus. Fed. 98 E2
Tees r. U.K. 58 F4
Teeswater Canada 164 E1
Teet'lit Zhen Canada see Fort McPherson
Tefé r. Brazil 176 F4
Tefenni Turkey 69 M6
Tegal Jawa Indon. 85 E4
Tegel airport Germany 63 N2
Tegid, Llyn l. U.K. see Bala Lake
Tegineneng Sumatera Indon. 84 D4
▶Tegucigalpa Hond. 166 [inset] I6
Capital of Honduras.
Teguidda-n-Tessoumt Niger 120 D3
Tehachapi CA U.S.A. 158 D4
Tehachapi Mountains CA U.S.A. 158 D4
Tehachapi Pass CA U.S.A. 158 D4
Tehek Lake Canada 151 M1
Teheran Iran see Tehrān
Tehery Lake Canada 151 M1
Téhini Côte d'Ivoire 120 C4
Tehoru Seram Indon. 83 D3
▶Tehrān Iran 110 C3
Capital of Iran.
Tehri India see Tikamgarh
Tehuacán Mex. 168 E5
Tehuantepec, Golfo de g. Mex. 167 G6
Tehuantepec, Gulf of Mex. see Tehuantepec, Golfo de
Tehuantepec, Istmo de isthmus Mex. 168 F5
Tehuitzingo Mex. 167 F5
Teide, Pico del vol. Canary Is 120 B2
Teifi r. U.K. 59 C6
Teignmouth U.K. 59 D8
Teixeira de Sousa Angola see Luau
Teixeiras Brazil 179 C3
Teixeira Soares Brazil 179 A4
Tejakula Bali Indon. 85 F5
Tejen Turkm. 111 F2
Tejo r. Port. 67 B4 see Tagus
Tejon Pass CA U.S.A. 158 D4
Tejupan, Punta pt Mex. 166 E5
Tekapo, Lake N.Z. 139 C6
Tekari-dake mt. Japan 93 E3
Tekax Mex. 167 H4
Tekeli Kazakh. 102 E3
Tekes China 98 C4
Tekes Kazakh. 98 C4
Tekes He r. China 98 C4
Tekiliktag mt. China 99 C5
Tekin Rus. Fed. 90 D2
Tekirdağ Turkey 69 L4
Tekka India 106 D2
Tekkali India 106 E2
Teknaf Bangl. 105 H5
Tekong Kechil, Pulau i. Sing. 87 [inset]
Teku Sulawesi Indon. 83 B3
Te Kuiti N.Z. 139 E4
Tel r. India 106 D1
Tela Hond. 166 [inset] I6
Télagh Alg. 67 F6
Telan i. Indon. 84 D2
Telanaipura Sumatera Indon. see Jambi
Telaquana Lake AK U.S.A. 148 I3
Telashi Hu salt l. China 99 F6
Tel Ashqelon tourist site Israel 107 B4
Télataï Mali 120 D3
Tel Aviv-Yafo Israel 107 B3
Telč Czech Rep. 57 O6
Telchac Puerto Mex. 167 H4
Telegapulang Kalimantan Indon. 85 F3
Telekhany Belarus see Tsyelyakhany
Telêmaco Borba Brazil 179 A4
Telen r. Indon. 85 G2
Teleorman r. Romania 69 K3
Telertheba, Djebel mt. Alg. 120 D2
Telescope Peak CA U.S.A. 158 E3
Teles Pires r. Brazil 177 G5
Telford U.K. 59 E6
Telgte Germany 63 H3
Telica, Volcán vol. Nicaragua 166 [inset] I6
Telida AK U.S.A. 148 I3
Télimélé Guinea 120 B3
Teljo, Jebel mt. Sudan 108 C7
Telkwa Canada 150 E4
Tell Atlas mts Alg. see Atlas Tellien
Tell City IN U.S.A. 164 B5
Teller AK U.S.A. 148 F2
Tell es Sultan West Bank see Jericho
Tellicherry India see Thalassery
Tellin Belgium 62 F4
Telloh Iraq 113 G5
Telluride CO U.S.A. 159 J3
Telmen Mongolia 94 D1
Telmen Nuur salt l. Mongolia 94 D1
Tel'novskiy Rus. Fed. 90 F2
Telo Indon. 84 B3
Teloloapán Mex. 167 F5
Telo Martius France see Toulon
Telpoziz, Gora mt. Rus. Fed. 51 R3
Telsen Arg. 178 C6
Telšiai Lith. 55 M9
Teltow Germany 63 N2
Teluk Anson Malaysia see Teluk Intan
Telukbajur Sumatera Indon. see Telukbayur
Telukbatang Kalimantan Indon. 85 E3
Telukbayur Sumatera Indon. 84 C3
Telukbetung Sumatera Indon. see Bandar Lampung
Teluk Cenderawasih, Taman Nasional Indon. 81 I7
Telukdalam Indon. 84 B2
Teluk Intan Malaysia 84 C1
Telukkuantan Sumatera Indon. 84 C3
Telukmelano Kalimantan Indon. 85 E3
Teluknaga Jawa Indon. 84 D4
Telukpakedai Kalimantan Indon. 85 E3
Temagami Lake Canada 152 F5
Temaju i. Indon. 85 E2
Temanggung Jawa Indon. 85 E4
Temapache Mex. 167 F4
Tēmarxung China 99 E6
Temax Mex. 167 H4
Temba S. Africa 125 I3
Tembagapura Indon. 81 J7
Tembenchi r. Rus. Fed. 77 K3
Tembesi r. Indon. 84 C3
Tembilahan Sumatera Indon. 84 C3
Tembisa S. Africa 125 I4
Tembo Aluma Angola 123 B4
Teme r. U.K. 59 E6
Temecula CA U.S.A. 158 E5
Temenchula, Gora mt. Rus. Fed. 94 D1
Temengor, Tasik resr Malaysia 84 C1
Temerluh Malaysia 84 C2
Temiang, Bukit mt. Malaysia 84 C1
Teminabuan Indon. 81 I7
Temirtau Kazakh. 102 D1
Témiscamie r. Canada 153 G4
Témiscamie, Lac l. Canada 153 G4
Témiscaming Canada 152 F5
Témiscamingue, Lac l. Canada 152 F5
Témiscouata, Lac l. Canada 153 H5
Temiyang i. Indon. 84 D2
Temmes Fin. 54 N4
Temnikov Rus. Fed. 53 I5
Temora Australia 138 C5
Temósachic Mex. 166 D2
Tempe AZ U.S.A. 159 H5
Tempe, Danau l. Indon. 83 A4
Tempe Downs Australia 135 F6
Tempino Sumatera Indon. 84 C3
Temple MI U.S.A. 164 C1
Temple TX U.S.A. 161 D6
Temple Bar U.K. 59 C6
Temple Dera Pak. 111 H4
Templemore Ireland 61 E5
Templer Bank sea feature Phil. 82 B4
Temple Sowerby U.K. 58 E4
Templeton watercourse Australia 136 B4
Templin Germany 63 N1
Tempoal Mex. 167 F4
Tempué Angola 123 B5
Tēmpung China 94 D4
Temryuk Rus. Fed. 112 E1
Temryukskiy Zaliv b. Rus. Fed. 53 H7
Temuco Chile 178 B5
Temuka N.Z. 139 C7
Temuli China see Butuo
Tena Ecuador 176 C4
Tenabo Mex. 167 H4
Tenabo, Mount NV U.S.A. 158 E1
Tenakee Springs AK U.S.A. 149 N4
Tenali India 106 D2
Tenango Mex. 167 F5
Tenasserim Myanmar 87 B4
Tenasserim r. Myanmar 87 B4
Tenbury Wells U.K. 59 E6
Tenby U.K. 59 C7
Tendaho Eth. 122 E2
Tende, Col de pass France/Italy 66 H4
Ten Degree Channel India 87 A5
Tendō Japan 91 F5
Tenedos i. Turkey see Bozcaada
Ténenkou Mali 120 C3
Ténéré reg. Niger 120 D2
Ténéré du Tafassâsset des. Niger 120 E2
Tenerife i. Canary Is 120 B2
Ténès Alg. 67 G5
Teng, Nam r. Myanmar 86 B3
Tengah, Kepulauan is Indon. 85 G4
Tengah, Sungai r. Sing. 87 [inset]
Tengahdai Flores Indon. 83 B5
Tengcheng China see Tengxian
Tengchong China 96 C3
Tengeh Reservoir Sing. 87 [inset]
Tenggarong Kalimantan Indon. 85 G3
Tengger Els China 94 F4
Tengger Shamo des. China 94 F4
Tenggul i. Malaysia 84 C1
Tengiz, Ozero salt l. Kazakh. 102 C1
Tengréla Côte d'Ivoire 120 C3
Ten'gushevo Rus. Fed. 53 I5
Tengxian Guangxi China 97 F4
Tengxian Shandong China see Tengzhou
Tengzhou China 95 I5
Teni India see Theni
Teniente Jubany research station Antarctica see Jubany
Tenille FL U.S.A. 163 D6
Tenkawa Japan 92 B4
Tenke Dem. Rep. Congo 123 C5
Tenkeli Rus. Fed. 77 P2
Tenkergynpil'gyn, Laguna lag. Rus. Fed. 148 C1
Tenkodogo Burkina Faso 120 C3
Ten Mile Lake salt flat Australia 135 C6
Ten Mile Lake Canada 153 K4
Tennant Creek Australia 134 F4
Tennessee r. U.S.A. 161 F4
Tennessee state U.S.A. 164 C5
Tennessee Pass CO U.S.A. 156 G5
Tennevoll Norway 54 J2
Tenojoki r. Fin./Norway 54 P1
Tenom Sabah Malaysia 85 F1
Tenosique Mex. 167 H5
Tenpaku Japan 92 C3
Tenri Japan 92 B4
Tenryū Nagano Japan 93 D3
Tenryū Shizuoka Japan 93 D4
Tenryū-gawa r. Japan 93 D3
Tenryū-Okumikawa Kokutei-kōen park Japan 93 D3
Tenteno Sulawesi Indon. 83 B3
Tenterden U.K. 59 H7
Tenterfield Australia 138 F2
Ten Thousand Islands FL U.S.A. 163 D7
Tentolomatinan, Gunung mt. Indon. 83 B2
Tentudia mt. Spain 67 C4
Tentulia Bangl. see Tetulia
Teocelo Mex. 167 F5
Teodoro Sampaio Brazil 178 F2
Teófilo Otoni Brazil 179 C2
Teomabal i. Phil. 82 C5
Teopisca Mex. 167 G5
Teotihuacán tourist site Mex. 167 F5
Tepa Maluku Indon. 83 D4
Tepache Mex. 166 C2
Te Paki N.Z. 139 D2
Tepatitlán Mex. 168 D4
Tepehuanes Mex. 166 D3
Tepeji Mex. 167 F5
Tepeköy Turkey see Karakoçan
Tepelenë Albania 69 I4
Tepelmeme de Morelos Mex. 167 F5
Tepelská vrchovina hills Czech Rep. 63 M5
Tepequem, Serra mts Brazil 169 L8
Tepianlangsat Kalimantan Indon. 85 G2
Tepic Mex. 168 D4
Te Pirita N.Z. 139 C6
Teplá r. Czech Rep. 63 M4
Teplice Czech Rep. 57 N5
Teplogorka Rus. Fed. 52 L3
Teploozersk Rus. Fed. 90 C2
Teploye Rus. Fed. 53 H5
Teploye Ozero Rus. Fed. see Teploozersk
Tepoca, Cabo c. Mex. 157 E7
Tepopa, Punta pt Mex. 166 B2
Tequila Mex. 168 D4
Tequisistlán Mex. 167 G5
Tequisquiapán Mex. 167 F4
Ter r. Spain 67 H2
Téra Niger 120 D3
Terai Japan 92 C2
Teram Kangri mt. China 99 B6
Teramo Italy 68 E3
Terang Australia 138 A7
Ter Apel Neth. 62 H2
Terbang Selatan i. Maluku Indon. 83 D4
Terbang Utara i. Maluku Indon. 83 D4
Tercan Turkey 113 F3
Terebovlya Ukr. 53 E6
Tere-Khol' Rus. Fed. 94 C1
Tere-Khol', Ozero l. Rus. Fed. 94 D1
Terektinskiy Khrebet mts Rus. Fed. 98 D2
Terekty Kazakh. 102 G2
Terengganu r. Malaysia 84 C1
Terengganu state Malaysia 84 C1
Terentang Kalimantan Indon. 85 E3
Terentang, Pulau i. Indon. 85 G3
Teresa Cristina Brazil 179 A4
Tereshka r. Rus. Fed. 53 J6
Teresina Brazil 177 J5
Teresina de Goias Brazil 179 B1
Teresita Col. 176 E3
Teresópolis Brazil 179 C3
Teressa Island India 87 A5
Terezinha Brazil 177 H3
Tergeste Italy see Trieste
Tergnier France 62 D5
Tergun Daba Shan mts China 94 C4
Terhiyn Tsagaan Nuur l. Mongolia 94 D1
Teriberka Rus. Fed. 54 S2
Tering China 99 E7
Termez Uzbek. see Termiz
Termini Imerese Sicily Italy 68 E6
Términos, Laguna de lag. Mex. 167 H5
Termit-Kaoboul Niger 120 E3
Termiz Uzbek. 111 G2
Termo CA U.S.A. 158 C1
Termoli Italy 68 F4
Termonde Belgium see Dendermonde
Tern r. U.K. 59 E6
Ternate Maluku Indon. 83 C2
Ternate i. Maluku Indon. 83 C2
Terneuzen Neth. 62 D3
Terney Rus. Fed. 90 E3
Terni Italy 68 E3
Ternopil' Ukr. 53 E6
Ternopol' Ukr. see Ternopil'
Terpeniya, Mys c. Rus. Fed. 90 G2
Terpeniya, Zaliv g. Rus. Fed. 90 F2

Terra Alta WV U.S.A. 164 F4
Terra Bella CA U.S.A. 158 D4
Terrace Canada 150 D4
Terrace Bay Canada 152 D4
Terra Firma S. Africa 124 F3
Terråk Norway 54 H4
Terralba Sardinia Italy 68 C5
Terra Nova Bay Antarctica 188 H1
Terra Nova National Park Canada 153 L4
Terrazas Mex. 166 D2
Terre Adélie reg. Antarctica see Adélie Land
Terrebonne Bay LA U.S.A. 161 F6
Terre Haute IN U.S.A. 164 B4
Terrell TX U.S.A. 167 F1
Terre-Neuve prov. Canada see Newfoundland and Labrador
Terre-Neuve-et-Labrador prov. Canada see Newfoundland and Labrador
Terrero Mex. 166 D2
Terres Australes et Antarctiques Françaises terr. Indian Ocean see French Southern and Antarctic Lands
Terry MT U.S.A. 156 G3
Terschelling i. Neth. 62 F1
Terskey Ala-Too mts Kyrg. 98 B4
Terskiy Bereg coastal area Rus. Fed. 52 H2
Tertenia Sardinia Italy 68 C5
Terter Azer. see Tärtär
Teruel Spain 67 F3
Tervola Fin. 54 N3
Tes Mongolia 94 C1
Tešanj Bos.-Herz. 68 G2
Teseney Eritrea 108 E6
Tesha r. Rus. Fed. 53 I5
Teshekpuk Lake AK U.S.A. 148 I1
Teshio Japan 90 F3
Teshio-gawa r. Japan 90 F3
Tesiyn Gol r. Mongolia 94 C1
Teslin Canada 149 N3
Teslin r. Canada 149 N3
Teslin Lake Canada 149 N3
Tesouras r. Brazil 179 A1
Tessalit Mali 120 D2
Tessaoua Niger 120 D3
Tessolo Moz. 125 L1
Test r. U.K. 59 F8
Testour Tunisia 68 C6
Tetachuck Lake Canada 150 E4
Tetas, Punta pt Chile 178 B2
Tete Moz. 123 D5
Tetehosi Indon. 84 B2
Te Teko N.Z. 139 F4
Teteriv r. Ukr. 53 F6
Teterow Germany 57 N4
Tetiyev Ukr. see Tetiyiv
Tetiyiv Ukr. 53 F6
Tetlin AK U.S.A. 149 L3
Tetlin Junction AK U.S.A. 149 L3
Tetlin Lake AK U.S.A. 149 L3
Tetlin National Wildlife Refuge nature res. AK U.S.A. 149 L3
Tetney U.K. 58 G5
Teton r. MT U.S.A. 156 F3
Tétouan Morocco 67 D6
Tetovo Macedonia 69 I3
Tetsyeh Mountain AK U.S.A. 149 K1
Tetuán Morocco see Tétouan
Tetulia Bangl. 105 G4
Tetulia sea chan. Bangl. 105 G5
Tetyukhe Rus. Fed. see Dal'negorsk
Tetyukhe-Pristan' Rus. Fed. see Rudnaya Pristan'
Tetyushi Rus. Fed. 53 K5
Teuco r. Arg. 178 D2
Teufelsbach Namibia 124 C2
Teul de González Ortega Mex. 166 E4
Teun vol. Maluku Indon. 83 D4
Teunom Sumatera Indon. 84 A1
Teunom r. Indon. 84 A1
Te Urewera National Park N.Z. 139 F4
Teutoburger Wald hills Germany 63 I2
Teuva Fin. 54 L5
Tevere r. Italy see Tiber
Teverya Israel see Tiberias
Teviot r. U.K. 60 G5
Te Waewae Bay N.Z. 139 A8
Tewah Kalimantan Indon. 85 F3
Te Waipounamu i. N.Z. see South Island
Tewane Botswana 125 H2
Tewantin Australia 137 F5
Teweh r. Indon. 85 F3
Tewkesbury U.K. 59 E7
Têwo Gansu China 94 E5
Têwo Sichuan China 94 E5
Texarkana AR U.S.A. 161 E5
Texarkana TX U.S.A. 161 E5
Texas Australia 138 E2
Texas state U.S.A. 161 D6
Texas City TX U.S.A. 167 G2
Texcoco Mex. 167 F5
Texel i. Neth. 62 E1
Texhoma OK U.S.A. 161 C4
Texoma, Lake OK/TX U.S.A. 161 D5
Teyateyaneng Lesotho 125 H5
Teykovo Rus. Fed. 52 I4
Teza r. Rus. Fed. 52 I4
Teziutlán Mex. 167 F5
Tezpur India 105 H4
Tezu India 105 I4
Tha, Nâm r. Laos 86 C2
Thaa Atoll Maldives see Kolhumadulu Atoll
Tha-anne r. Canada 151 M2
Thabana-Ntlenyana mt. Lesotho 125 I5
Thaba Nchu S. Africa 125 H5
Thaba Putsoa mt. Lesotho 125 H5
Thaba-Tseka Lesotho 125 I5
Thabazimbi S. Africa 125 H3
Thab Lan National Park Thai. 87 C4
Tha Bo Laos 86 C3
Thabong S. Africa 125 H4
Thabyedaung Myanmar 96 C4
Thade r. Myanmar 86 A3
Thagyettaw Myanmar 87 B4
Tha Hin Thai. see Lop Buri
Thai Binh Vietnam 86 D2
Thailand country Asia 86 C4
Thailand, Gulf of Asia 87 C5
Thai Muang Thai. 87 B5
Thai Nguyên Vietnam 86 D2
Thaj Saudi Arabia 110 C5
Thakèk Laos 86 D3
Thakurgaon Bangl. 105 G4
Thakurtola India 104 E5
Thal Germany 63 K4
Thala Tunisia 68 C7
Thalang Thai. 87 B5
Thalassery India 106 B4
Thal Desert Pak. 111 H4
Thale (Harz) Germany 63 L3
Thaliparamba India see Taliparamba
Thallon Australia 138 D2
Thalo Pak. 111 G4
Thamaga Botswana 125 G3
Thamar, Jabal mt. Yemen 108 G7
Thamarīt Oman 109 H6
Thame r. U.K. 59 F7
Thames r. Ont. Canada 155 K3
Thames r. Ont. Canada 164 D2
Thames N.Z. 139 E3
Thames est. U.K. 59 H7
Thames r. U.K. 59 H7
Thamesford Canada 164 E2
Thana India see Thane
Thanatpin Myanmar 86 B3
Thandwè Myanmar 86 A3
Thane India 106 B2
Thanet, Isle of pen. U.K. 59 I7
Thangoo Australia 134 C4
Thangra India 104 D2
Thanh Hoa Vietnam 86 D3
Thanjavur India 106 C4
Than Kyun i. Myanmar 87 B5
Thanlwin r. China/Myanmar see Salween
Thanlyin Myanmar 86 B3
Thaolintoa Lake Canada 151 L2
Tha Pla Thai. 86 C3
Thap Put Thai. 87 B5
Thapsacus Syria see Dibsī
Thap Sakae Thai. 87 B5
Tharabwin Myanmar 87 B4
Tharad Gujarat India 104 B4
Tharad Gujarat India 104 B4
Thar Desert India/Pak. 111 H5
Thargomindah Australia 138 A1
Tharrawaw Myanmar 86 A3
Tharthār, Buḩayrat ath l. Iraq 113 F4
Tharwānīyyah U.A.E. 110 D6
Thasos i. Greece 69 K4
Thatcher AZ U.S.A. 159 I5
Thât Khê Vietnam 86 D2
Thaton Myanmar 86 B3
Thatta Pak. 111 G5
Thaungdut Myanmar 86 A1
Tha Uthen Thai. 86 D3
Thayawthadangyi Kyun i. Myanmar 87 B4
Thayetmyo Myanmar 86 A3
Thazi Magwe Myanmar 86 A3
Thazi Mandalay Myanmar 105 I5
Thazzik Mountain AK U.S.A. 149 K2
The Aldermen Islands N.Z. 139 F3
Theba AZ U.S.A. 159 G5
The Bahamas country West Indies 163 E7
Thebes Greece see Thiva
The Bluff Bahamas 163 E7
The Broads nat. park U.K. 59 I6
The Brothers is H.K. China 97 [inset]
The Calvados Chain is P.N.G. 136 F1
The Cheviot hill U.K. 58 E3
The Dalles OR U.S.A. 156 C3
Thedford NE U.S.A. 160 C3
The Entrance Australia 138 E4
The Faither stack U.K. 60 [inset]
The Fens reg. U.K. 59 G6
The Gambia country Africa 120 B3
Thegon Myanmar 86 A3
The Grampians mts Australia 137 C8
The Great Oasis oasis Egypt see Khārijah, Wāḩāt al
The Grenadines is St Vincent 169 L6
The Gulf Asia 110 C4

▶The Hague Neth. 62 E2
Seat of government of the Netherlands.

The Hunters Hills N.Z. 139 C7
Thekulthili Lake Canada 151 I2
The Lakes National Park Australia 138 C6
Thelon r. Canada 151 L1
The Lynd Junction Australia 136 D3
Themar Germany 63 K4
Thembalihle S. Africa 125 I4
The Minch sea chan. U.K. 60 C2
The Naze c. Norway see Lindesnes
The Needles stack U.K. 59 F8
Theni India 106 C4
Thenia Alg. 67 H5
Theniet El Had Alg. 67 H6
The North Sound sea chan. U.K. 60 G1
Theodore Australia 136 E5
Theodore Canada 151 K5
Theodore Roosevelt Lake AZ U.S.A. 159 H5
Theodore Roosevelt National Park ND U.S.A. 160 C2
Theodosia Ukr. see Feodosiya
The Old Man of Coniston hill U.K. 58 D4
The Paps hill Ireland 61 C5
The Pas Canada 151 K4
The Pilot mt. Australia 138 D6
Thera i. Greece see Santorini
Thérain r. France 62 C5
Theresa NY U.S.A. 165 H1
Thermaïkos Kolpos g. Greece 69 J4
Thermopolis WY U.S.A. 156 F4
The Rock Australia 138 C5
Thérouanne France 62 C4
The Salt Lake salt flat Australia 137 C6

▶The Settlement Christmas I. 80 D9
Capital of Christmas Island.

The Sisters hill AK U.S.A. 148 G3
The Skaw spit Denmark see Grenen
The Skelligs is Ireland 61 B6
The Slot sea chan. Solomon Is see New Georgia Sound
The Solent strait U.K. 59 F8
Thessalon Canada 152 E5
Thessalonica Greece see Thessaloniki
Thessaloniki Greece 69 J4
The Storr hill U.K. 60 C3
Thet r. U.K. 59 H6
The Teeth mt. Palawan Phil. 82 B4
The Terraces hills Australia 135 C7
Thetford U.K. 59 H6
Thetford Mines Canada 153 H5
Thetkethaung r. Myanmar 86 A4
The Triangle mts Myanmar 86 B1
The Trossachs hills U.K. 60 E4
The Twins Australia 137 A6
Theva-i-Ra reef Fiji see Ceva-i-Ra

▶The Valley Anguilla 169 L5
Capital of Anguilla.

Thevenard Island Australia 134 A5
Thévenet, Lac l. Canada 153 H2
Theveste Alg. see Tébessa
The Wash b. U.K. 59 H6
The Weald reg. U.K. 59 H7
The Woodlands TX U.S.A. 161 E6
Thibodaux LA U.S.A. 161 F6
Thicket Portage Canada 151 L4
Thief River Falls MN U.S.A. 160 D1
Thiel Neth. see Tiel
Thiel Mountains Antarctica 188 K1
Thielsen, Mount OR U.S.A. 156 C4
Thielt Belgium see Tielt
Thiérache reg. France 62 D5
Thiers France 66 F4
Thiès Senegal 120 B3
Thika Kenya 122 D4
Thiladhunmathi Atoll Maldives 106 B5
Thiladunmathi Atoll Maldives see Thiladhunmathi Atoll
Thimbu Bhutan see Thimphu

▶Thimphu Bhutan 105 G4
Capital of Bhutan.

Thionville France 62 G5
Thira i. Greece see Santorini
Thirsk U.K. 58 F4
Thirty Mile Lake Canada 151 L2
Thiruvananthapuram India 106 C4
Thiruvannamalai India see Tiruvannamalai
Thiruvarur India 106 C4
Thiruvattiyur India see Tiruvottiyur
Thisted Denmark 55 F8
Thistle Creek Canada 149 M3
Thistle Lake Canada 151 I1
Thityabin Myanmar 86 A2
Thiu Khao Luang Phrabang mts Laos/Thai. see Luang Phrabang, Thiu Khao
Thiva Greece 69 J5
Thívai Greece see Thiva
Thlewiaza r. Canada 151 M2
Thoa r. Canada 151 I2
Thô Chu, Đao i. Vietnam 87 C5
Thoen Thai. 96 C5
Thoeng Thai. 86 C3
Thohoyandou S. Africa 125 J2
Tholen Neth. 62 E3
Tholen i. Neth. 62 E3
Tholey Germany 62 H5
Thomas Hill Reservoir MO U.S.A. 160 E4
Thomas Hubbard, Cape Canada 147 I1
Thomaston CT U.S.A. 165 I3
Thomaston GA U.S.A. 163 C5
Thomastown Ireland 61 E5
Thomasville AL U.S.A. 163 C6
Thomasville GA U.S.A. 163 D6
Thommen Belgium 62 G4
Thompson Canada 151 L4
Thompson r. Canada 150 F5
Thompson UT U.S.A. 159 I2
Thompson r. MO U.S.A. 154 I4
Thompson Falls MT U.S.A. 156 E3
Thompson Peak NM U.S.A. 157 G6
Thompson's Falls Kenya see Nyahururu
Thompson Sound Canada 150 E5
Thomson GA U.S.A. 163 D5
Thon Buri Thai. 87 C4
Thonokied Lake Canada 151 I1
Thoothukudi India see Tuticorin
Thoreau NM U.S.A. 159 I4
Thorn Neth. 62 F3
Thorn Poland see Toruń
Thornaby-on-Tees U.K. 58 F4
Thornapple r. MI U.S.A. 164 C2
Thornbury U.K. 59 E7
Thorne U.K. 58 G5
Thorne NV U.S.A. 158 D2
Thornton r. Australia 136 B3
Thorold Canada 164 F2
Thorshavnfjella reg. Antarctica see Thorshavnheiane
Thorshavnheiane reg. Antarctica 188 C2
Thota-ea-Moli Lesotho 125 H5
Thôt Nôt Vietnam 87 D5
Thouars France 66 D3
Thoubal India 105 H4
Thourout Belgium see Torhout
Thousand Islands Canada/U.S.A. 165 G1
Thousand Lake Mountain UT U.S.A. 159 H2
Thousand Oaks CA U.S.A. 158 D4
Thousandsticks KY U.S.A. 164 D5
Thrace reg. Europe 69 L4
Thraki reg. Europe see Thrace
Thrakiko Pelagos sea Greece 69 K4
Three Gorges Reservoir resr China 97 F2
Three Hills Canada 150 H5
Three Hummock Island Australia 137 [inset]
Three Kings Islands N.Z. 139 D2
Three Oaks MI U.S.A. 164 B3
Three Pagodas Pass Myanmar/Thai. 86 B4
Three Points, Cape Ghana 120 C4
Three Rivers MI U.S.A. 164 C3
Three Rivers TX U.S.A. 167 F2
Three Sisters mt. OR U.S.A. 156 C3
Three Springs Australia 135 A7
Thrissur India 106 C4
Throckmorton TX U.S.A. 161 D5
Throssell, Lake salt flat Australia 135 D6
Throssel Range hills Australia 134 C5
Thrushton National Park Australia 138 C1
Thu Ba Vietnam 87 D5
Thubun Lakes Canada 151 I2
Thu Dâu Môt Vietnam 87 D5
Thuddungra Australia 138 D5
Thu Đuc Vietnam 87 D5
Thuin Belgium 62 E4
Thul Pak. 111 H4
Thulaythawāt Gharbī, Jabal hill Syria 107 D2
Thule Greenland 147 L2
Thun Switz. 66 H3
Thunder Bay Canada 147 J5
Thunder Bay b. MI U.S.A. 164 D1
Thunder Creek r. Canada 151 J5
Thüngen Germany 63 J5
Thung Salaeng Luang National Park Thai. 86 C3
Thung Song Thai. 87 B5
Thung Wa Thai. 84 B1
Thung Yai Naresuan Wildlife Reserve nature res. Thai. 86 B4
Thüringen land Germany 63 K3
Thüringer Becken reg. Germany 63 L3
Thüringer Wald mts Germany 63 K4
Thuringia land Germany see Thüringen
Thuringian Forest mts Germany see Thüringer Wald
Thurles Ireland 61 E5
Thurn, Pass Austria 57 N7
Thursday Island Australia 136 C1
Thurso U.K. 60 F2
Thurso r. U.K. 60 F2
Thurston Island Antarctica 188 K2
Thurston Peninsula i. Antarctica see Thurston Island
Thüster Berg hill Germany 63 J2
Thuthukudi India see Tuticorin
Thwaite U.K. 58 E4
Thwaites Glacier Tongue Antarctica 188 K1
Thyatira Turkey see Akhisar
Thyborøn Denmark 55 F8
Thymerais reg. France 62 B6
Tiancang China 94 D3
Tianchang China 97 H1
Tiancheng Gansu China 94 D4
Tiancheng Hubei China see Chongyang
Tianchi Gansu China 95 F4
Tianchi Sichuan China see Lezhi
Tiandeng China 96 E4
Tiandong China 96 E4
Tianeti Georgia 113 G2
Tianfanjie China 97 H2
Tianguistengo Mex. 167 F4
Tianjin China 95 I4
Tianjin mun. China 95 I4
Tianjun China 94 D4
Tianlin China 96 E3
Tianma China see Changshan
Tianmen China 97 G2
Tianqiaoling China 90 C4
Tianquan China 96 D2
Tianshan China 95 J3
Tian Shan mts China/Kyrg. see Tien Shan
Tianshui China 94 F5
Tianshuibu China 94 F4
Tianshuihai Aksai Chin 99 B6
Tianshuijing China 98 F4
Tiantai China 97 I2
Tiantaiyong China 95 I3
Tiantang China see Yuexi
Tianyang China 96 E4
Tianyi China see Ningcheng
Tianzhen Shandong China see Gaoqing
Tianzhen Shanxi China 95 H3
Tianzhou China see Tianyang
Tianzhu Gansu China 94 E4
Tianzhu Guizhou China 97 F3
Tiaret Alg. 67 G6
Tiassalé Côte d'Ivoire 120 C4
Tibabar Sabah Malaysia see Tambunan
Tibagi Brazil 179 A4
Tibal, Wādī watercourse Iraq 113 F4
Tibati Cameroon 120 E4
Tibba Pak. 111 H4
Tibé, Pic de mt. Guinea 120 C4
Tiber r. Italy 68 E4
Tiberias Israel 107 B3
Tiberias, Lake Israel see Galilee, Sea of
Tiber Reservoir MT U.S.A. 156 F2
Tibesti mts Chad 121 E2
Tibet aut. reg. China see Xizang Zizhiqu
Tibet, Plateau of China 99 D6
Tibi India 111 I4
Tibooburra Australia 137 C6
Tibrikot Nepal 105 E3
Tibro Sweden 55 I7
Tibur Italy see Tivoli
Tiburón, Isla i. Mex. 166 B2
Ticao i. Phil. 82 C3
Ticehurst U.K. 59 H7
Tichborne Canada 165 G1
Tichégami r. Canada 153 G4
Tîchît Mauritania 120 C3
Tichla W. Sahara 120 B2
Ticinum Italy see Pavia
Ticonderoga NY U.S.A. 165 I2
Ticul Mex. 167 H4
Tidaholm Sweden 55 H7
Tiddim Myanmar 86 A2
Tiden India 87 A6
Tidjikja Mauritania 120 B3
Tidore i. Maluku Indon. 83 C2
Tiechanggou China 98 D3
Tiefa China see Diaobingshan
Tiel Neth. 62 F3
Tieli China 90 B3
Tieling China 95 J3
Tielongtan Aksai Chin 99 B6
Tielt Belgium 62 D4
Tienen Belgium 62 E4
Tien Shan mts China/Kyrg. 88 D4
Tientsin China see Tianjin
Tientsin mun. China see Tianjin
Tiên Yên Vietnam 86 D2
Tierp Sweden 55 J6
Tierra Amarilla NM U.S.A. 157 G5
Tierra Blanca Mex. 167 F5
Tierra Colorada Mex. 167 F5

▶Tierra del Fuego, Isla Grande de i. Arg./Chile 178 C8
Largest island in South America.

Tierra del Fuego, Parque Nacional nat. park Arg. 178 C8
Tiétar r. Spain 67 D4
Tiétar, Valle del valley Spain 67 D3
Tietê r. Brazil 179 A3
Tieyon Australia 135 F6
Tiffin OH U.S.A. 164 D3
Tiflis Georgia see T'bilisi
Tifore i. Maluku Indon. 83 C2
Tifton GA U.S.A. 163 D6
Tifu Buru Indon. 83 C3
Tiga i. Malaysia 85 F1
Tigalda Island AK U.S.A. 148 F5
Tigapuluh, Pegunungan mts Indon. 84 C3
Tiga Reservoir Nigeria 120 D3
Tigen Kazakh. 113 H1
Tīgh Āb Iran 111 F5
Tigheciului, Dealurile hills Moldova 69 M2
Tighina Moldova 69 M1
Tigiretskiy Khrebet mts Kazakh./Rus. Fed. 98 C2
Tigiria India 106 E1
Tignère Cameroon 120 E4
Tignish Canada 153 I5
Tigranocerta Turkey see Siirt
Tigre r. Venez. 176 F2
Tigre, Cerro del mt. Mex. 167 F4
Tigris r. Asia 113 G5
also known as Dicle (Turkey) or Nahr Dijlah (Iraq/Syria)
Tigrovaya Balka Zapovednik nature res. Tajik. 111 H2
Tiguidit, Falaise de esc. Niger 120 D3
Tīh, Gebel el plat. Egypt see Tīh, Jabal at
Tīh, Jabal at plat. Egypt 107 A5
Tihuatlán Mex. 167 F4
Tijuana Mex. 166 A1
Tikal tourist site Guat. 167 H5
Tikal, Parque Nacional nat. park Guat. 167 H5
Tikamgarh India 104 D4
Tikanlik China 98 D4
Tikchik Lakes AK U.S.A. 148 H4
Tikhoretsk Rus. Fed. 53 I7
Tikhvin Rus. Fed. 52 G4
Tikhvinskaya Gryada ridge Rus. Fed. 52 G4
Tiki Basin sea feature S. Pacific Ocean 187 L7
Tikokino N.Z. 139 F4
Tikopia i. Solomon Is 133 G3
Tikrīt Iraq 113 F4
Tikse India 104 D2
Tikshozero, Ozero l. Rus. Fed. 54 R3
Tiksi Rus. Fed. 77 N2
Tila r. Nepal 99 C7
Tiladummati Atoll Maldives see Thiladhunmathi Atoll
Tilaiya Reservoir India 105 F4
Tilamuta Sulawesi Indon. 83 B2
Tilbeşar Ovasi plain Turkey 107 C1
Tilbooroo Australia 138 B1
Tilburg Neth. 62 F3
Tilbury Canada 164 D2
Tilbury U.K. 59 H7
Tilcara Arg. 178 C2
Tilcha Creek watercourse Australia 137 C6
Tilden TX U.S.A. 161 D6
Tilemsès Niger 120 D3
Tilemsi, Vallée du watercourse Mali 120 D3
Tilhar India 104 D4
Tilimsen Alg. see Tlemcen
Tilin Myanmar 86 A2
Tillabéri Niger 120 D3
Tillamook OR U.S.A. 156 C3
Tillanchong Island India 87 A5
Tillia Niger 120 D3
Tillicoultry U.K. 60 F4
Tillsonburg Canada 164 E2
Tillyfourie U.K. 60 G3
Tilonia India 111 I5
Tilos i. Greece 69 L6
Tilothu India 105 F4
Tilpa Australia 138 B3
Tilsit Rus. Fed. see Sovetsk
Tilt r. U.K. 60 F4
Tilton IL U.S.A. 164 B3
Tilton NH U.S.A. 165 J2
Tilu, Bukit mt. Indon. 83 B3
Tim Rus. Fed. 53 H6
Ṭimā Egypt 108 D4
Timah, Bukit hill Sing. 87 [inset]
Timakara i. India 106 B4
Timanskiy Kryazh ridge Rus. Fed. 52 K2
Timar Turkey 113 F3
Timaru N.Z. 139 C7
Timashevsk Rus. Fed. 53 H7
Timashevskaya Rus. Fed. see Timashevsk
Timbalier Bay LA U.S.A. 167 H2
Timbedgha Mauritania 120 C3
Timber Creek Australia 132 D3
Timber Mountain NV U.S.A. 158 E3
Timberville VA U.S.A. 165 F4
Timbuktu Mali 120 C3
Timbun Mata i. Malaysia 85 G1
Timétrine reg. Mali 120 C3
Timiaouine Alg. 120 D2
Timimoun Alg. 64 E6
Timirist, Râs pt Mauritania 120 B3
Timiskaming, Lake Canada see Témiscamingue, Lac
Timișoara Romania 69 I2
Timmins Canada 152 E4
Timms Hill hill WI U.S.A. 160 F2
Timon Brazil 177 J5
Timor i. Indon. 83 C5
Timor-Leste country Asia see East Timor
Timor Loro Sae country Asia see East Timor
Timor Sea Australia/Indon. 132 C3
Timor Timur country Asia see East Timor
Timpaus i. Indon. 83 C3
Timperley Range hills Australia 135 C6
Timrå Sweden 54 J5
Tin, Ra's at pt Libya 112 A4
Ṭina, Khalīg el b. Egypt see Ṭīnah, Khalīj aṭ
Tīnah Syria 107 D1
Ṭīnah, Khalīj aṭ b. Egypt 107 A4
Tin Can Bay Australia 137 F5
Tindivanam India 106 C3
Tindouf Alg. 64 C6
Ti-n-Essako Mali 120 D3
Tinggi i. Malaysia 84 D2
Tingha Australia 138 E2
Tingis Morocco see Tangier
Tingo María Peru 176 C5
Tingréla Côte d'Ivoire see Tengréla
Tingri China 99 D7
Tingsryd Sweden 55 I8
Tingvoll Norway 54 F5
Tingwall U.K. 60 F1
Tingzhou China see Changting
Tinharé, Ilha de i. Brazil 179 D1
Tinh Gia Vietnam 86 D3
Tinian i. N. Mariana Is 81 L4
Tini Heke is N.Z. see Snares Islands
Tinjar r. Malaysia 85 F1
Tinjil i. Indon. 84 D4
Tinnelvelly India see Tirunelveli
Tinogasta Arg. 178 C3
Tinompo Sulawesi Indon. 83 B2
Tinos Greece 69 K6
Tinos i. Greece 69 K6
Tinqueux France 62 D5
Tinrhert, Hamada de Alg. 120 D2
Tinsukia India 105 H4
Tintagel U.K. 59 C8
Ţînţâne Mauritania 120 B3
Tintina Arg. 178 D3
Tintinara Australia 137 C7
Tioga ND U.S.A. 160 C1
Tioman i. Malaysia 84 D2
Tionesta PA U.S.A. 164 F3
Tionesta Lake PA U.S.A. 164 F3
Tipasa Alg. 67 H5
Tiphsah Syria see Dibsī
Tipitapa Nicaragua 166 [inset] I6
Tipperary Ireland 61 D5
Tiptala Bhanjyang pass Nepal 99 D8
Tipton CA U.S.A. 158 D3
Tipton IA U.S.A. 160 F3
Tipton IN U.S.A. 164 B3
Tipton MO U.S.A. 160 E4
Tipton, Mount AZ U.S.A. 159 F4
Tiptop VA U.S.A. 164 E5
Tip Top Hill hill Canada 152 D4
Tiptree U.K. 59 H7
Tiptur India 106 C3
Tipturi India see Tiptur
Tiquisate Guat. 167 H6
Tiracambu, Serra do hills Brazil 177 I4
Tirah reg. Pak. 111 H3

▶Tirana Albania 69 H4
Capital of Albania.

Tiranë Albania see Tirana
Tirano Italy 68 D1
Tirari Desert Australia 137 B5
Tiraspol Moldova 69 M1
Tiraz Mountains Namibia 124 C4
Tire Turkey 69 L5
Tirebolu Turkey 113 E2
Tiree i. U.K. 60 C4
Tîrgovişte Romania see Târgovişte
Tîrgu Jiu Romania see Târgu Jiu
Tîrgu Mureş Romania see Târgu Mureş
Tîrgu Neamţ Romania see Târgu Neamţ
Tîrgu Secuiesc Romania see Târgu Secuiesc
Tiri Pak. 111 G4
Tirich Mir mt. Pak. 111 H2
Tirlemont Belgium see Tienen
Tirna r. India 106 C2
Tîrnăveni Romania see Târnăveni
Tírnavos Greece see Tyrnavos
Tiros Brazil 179 B2
Tirourda, Col de pass Alg. 67 I5
Tīr Pul Afgh. 111 F3
Tirreno, Mare sea France/Italy see Tyrrhenian Sea
Tirso r. Sardinia Italy 68 C5
Tirthahalli India 106 B3
Tiruchchendur India 106 C4
Tiruchchirappalli India 106 C4
Tiruchengodu India 106 C4
Tirunelveli India 106 C4
Tirupati India 106 C3
Tiruppattur Tamil Nadu India 106 C3
Tiruppattur Tamil Nadu India 106 C4
Tiruppur India 106 C4
Tiruttani India 106 C3
Tirutturaippundi India 106 C4
Tiruvallur India 106 C3
Tiruvannamalai India 106 C3
Tiruvottiyur India 106 D3
Tiru Well Australia 134 D5
Tisa r. Serbia 69 I2
also known as Tisza (Hungary), Tysa (Ukraine)
Tisdale Canada 151 J4
Tishomingo OK U.S.A. 161 D5
Ţīsīyah Syria 107 C3
Tissemsilt Alg. 67 G6
Tista r. India 99 E8
Tisza r. Serbia see Tisa
Titabar India 99 F8
Titaluk r. AK U.S.A. 148 I1
Titalya Bangl. see Tetulia
Titan Dome ice feature Antarctica 188 H1
Titao Burkina Faso 120 C3
Tit-Ary Rus. Fed. 77 N2
Titawin Morocco see Tétouan
Titicaca, Lago Bol./Peru see Titicaca, Lake

▶Titicaca, Lake Bol./Peru 176 E7
Largest lake in South America.

Titi Islands N.Z. 139 A8
Titiea mt. N.Z. see Aspiring, Mount
Titlagarh India 106 D1
Titograd Montenegro see Podgorica
Titova Mitrovica Kosovo see Mitrovicë
Titovo Užice Serbia see Užice
Titovo Velenje Slovenia see Velenje
Titov Veles Macedonia see Veles
Titov Vrbas Serbia see Vrbas
Ti Tree Australia 134 F5
Titu Romania 69 K2
Titusville FL U.S.A. 163 D6
Titusville PA U.S.A. 164 F3
Tiu Chung Chau i. H.K. China 97 [inset]
Tiumpain, Rubha an hd U.K. see Tiumpan Head
Tiumpan Head hd U.K. 60 C2
Tiva watercourse Kenya 122 D4
Tivari India 104 C4
Tiverton Canada 164 E1
Tiverton U.K. 59 D8
Tivoli Italy 68 E4
Ţīwī Oman 110 E6
Tiwi Aboriginal Land res. Australia 83 D5
Tiworo, Selat sea chan. Indon. 83 B4
Tixtla Mex. 167 F5
Ti-ywa Myanmar 87 B4
Tizi El Arba hill Alg. 67 H5
Tizimín Mex. 167 H4
Tizi N'Kouilal pass Alg. 67 I5
Tizi Ouzou Alg. 67 I5
Tiznap He r. China 99 B5
Tiznit Morocco 120 C2
Tizoc Mex. 166 E3
Tiztoutine Morocco 67 E6
Tjaneni Swaziland 125 J3
Tjappsåive Sweden 54 K4
Tjeukemeer l. Neth. 62 F2
Tjirebon Jawa Indon. see Cirebon
Tjolotjo Zimbabwe see Tsholotsho
Tjorhom Norway 55 E7
Tkibuli Georgia see Tqibuli
Tlacotalpán Mex. 167 G5
Tlacotepec, Cerro mt. Mex. 167 E5

Tlahualilo Mex. 166 E3
Tlalnepantla Mex. 167 F5
Tlancualpican Mex. 167 F5
Tlapa Mex. 167 F5
Tlapacoyan Mex. 167 F5
Tlaxcala Mex. 168 E5
Tlaxcala *state* Mex. 167 F5
Tlaxco Mex. 167 F5
Tlaxiaco Mex. 167 F5
Tl'ell Canada 149 O5
Tlemcen Alg. 67 F6
Tlhakalatlou S. Africa 124 F5
Tlholong S. Africa 125 I5
Tlokweng Botswana 125 G3
Tlyarata Rus. Fed. 113 G2
To *r.* Myanmar 86 B3
Toad *r.* Canada 150 E3
Toad River Canada 150 E3
Toagel Mlungui Palau 82 [inset]
Toamasina Madag. 123 E5
Toana *mts NV* U.S.A. 159 F1
Toano *VA* U.S.A. 165 G5
Toa Payoh Sing. 87 [inset]
Toba China 96 C2
Toba Japan 92 C4
Toba, Danau *l.* Indon. 84 B2
Toba, Lake Indon. *see* Toba, Danau
Toba and Kakar Ranges *mts* Pak. 111 G4
Toba Gargaji Pak. 111 I4
Tobago *i.* Trin. and Tob. 169 L6
Tobelo *Halmahera* Indon. 83 C2
Tobercurry Ireland 61 D3
Tobermorey Australia 136 B4
Tobermory Australia 138 A1
Tobermory Canada 164 E1
Tobermory U.K. 60 C4
Tobi *i.* Palau 81 I6
Tobias Fornier *Panay* Phil. 82 C4
Tobin, Lake *salt flat* Australia 134 D5
Tobin, Mount *NV* U.S.A. 158 E1
Tobin Lake Canada 151 K4
Tobin Lake *l.* Canada 151 K4
Tobishima Japan 92 C3
Tobi-shima *i.* Japan 91 E5
Toboali Indon. 84 D3
Tobol *r.* Kazakh./Rus. Fed. 100 F1
Tobol'sk Rus. Fed. 76 H4
Toboso *Negros* Phil. 82 C4
Tobruk Libya *see* Tubruq
Tobseda Rus. Fed. 52 L1
Tōbu Japan 93 E2
Tobyl *r.* Kazakh./Rus. Fed. *see* Tobol
Tobysh *r.* Rus. Fed. 52 K2
Tocache Nuevo Peru 176 C5
Tocantinópolis Brazil 177 I5
Tocantins *r.* Brazil 179 A1
Tocantins *state* Brazil 179 A1
Tocantinzinha *r.* Brazil 179 A1
Toccoa *GA* U.S.A. 163 D5
Tochi *r.* Pak. 111 H3
Tochigi Japan 93 F2
Tochigi *pref.* Japan 93 F2
Töcksfors Sweden 55 G7
Tocoa Hond. 166 [inset] I6
Tocopilla Chile 178 B2
Tocumwal Australia 138 B5
Tod, Mount Canada 150 G5
Toda Japan 93 F3
Todd *watercourse* Australia 136 A5
Todi Italy 68 E3
Todog China 98 C3
Todoga-saki *pt* Japan 91 F5
Todok China *see* Todog
Todos Santos Mex. 166 C4
Toe Head *hd* U.K. 60 B3
Tōei Japan 92 D3
Tofino Canada 150 E5
Toft U.K. 60 [inset]
Tofua *i.* Tonga 133 I3
Toga Japan 92 D2
Tōgane Japan 93 G3
Togatax China 99 C6
Togi Japan 92 C1
Togiak *AK* U.S.A. 148 G4
Togiak *r. AK* U.S.A. 148 G4
Togiak Bay *AK* U.S.A. 148 G4
Togiak Lake *AK* U.S.A. 148 H4
Togiak National Wildlife Refuge *nature res.* *AK* U.S.A. 148 G4
Togian *i.* Indon. 83 B3
Togian, Kepulauan *is* Indon. 83 B3
Togliatti Rus. Fed. *see* Tol'yatti
Togo *country* Africa 120 D4
Tōgō Japan 92 D3
Tograsay He *r.* China 99 E5
Tögrög *Hovd* Mongolia *see* Manhan
Tögrög *Övörhangay* Mongolia 94 E2
Togrog Ul China 95 H3
Togtoh China 95 G3
Togton He *r.* China 99 F6
Togura Japan 93 E2
Tohatchi *NM* U.S.A. 159 I4
Tohenbatu *mt.* Malaysia 85 F2
Tohoku Japan 92 C3
Toholampi Fin. 54 N5
Tohom China 94 F3
Tōhōm Mongolia *see* Mandah
Tohono O'Odham (Papago) Indian Reservation *res. AZ* U.S.A. 166 B1
Toi Japan 93 E4
Toiba China 99 E7
Toibalewe India 87 A5
Toide Japan 92 C2
Toijala Fin. 55 M6
Toili *Sulawesi* Indon. 83 B3
Toi-misaki *pt* Japan 91 C7
Toin Japan 92 C3
Toineke *Timor* Indon. 83 C5
Toivakka Fin. 54 O5
Toiyabe Range *mts NV* U.S.A. 158 E2
Toja *Sulawesi* Indon. 83 B3
Tojikiston *country* Asia *see* Tajikistan
Tōjō Japan 92 B4
Tok *AK* U.S.A. 149 L3
Tōkai *Aichi* Japan 92 C3
Tōkai *Ibaraki* Japan 93 G2
Tokala, Gunung *mt.* Indon. 83 B3
Tōkamachi Japan 93 E1
Tokar Sudan 108 E6
Tokara-rettō *is* Japan 91 C7
Tokarevka Rus. Fed. 53 I6
Tokat Turkey 112 E2
Tŏkchŏk-to *i.* S. Korea 91 B5
Tokdo *i.* N. Pacific Ocean *see* Liancourt Rocks

▶Tokelau *terr.* S. Pacific Ocean 133 I2
New Zealand Overseas Territory.

Toki Japan 92 D3
Tokigawa Japan 93 F2
Toki-gawa *r.* Japan 92 C3
Tokkuztara China *see* Gongliu
Toklat *AK* U.S.A. 149 J2
Toklat *r. AK* U.S.A. 149 J2
Tokmak Kyrg. *see* Tokmok
Tokmak Ukr. 53 G7
Tokmok Kyrg. 102 E3
Tokomaru Bay N.Z. 139 G4
Tokoname Japan 92 C4
Tokoroa N.Z. 139 E4
Tokorozawa Japan 93 F3
Tokoza S. Africa 125 I4
Toksook Bay *AK* U.S.A. 148 F3
Toksu China *see* Xinhe
Toksun China 98 E4
Tok-tō *i.* N. Pacific Ocean *see* Liancourt Rocks
Toktogul Kyrg. 102 D3
Tokto-ri *i.* N. Pacific Ocean *see* Liancourt Rocks
Tokty Kazakh. 98 C3
Tokur Rus. Fed. 90 D1
Tokushima Japan 91 D6
Tokuyama Japan 91 C6

▶Tōkyō Japan 93 F3
Capital of Japan. Most populous city in Asia and the world.

Tōkyō *mun.* Japan 93 F3
Tōkyō-wan *b.* Japan 93 F3
Tokyrau *watercourse* Kazakh. 98 A3
Tolaga Bay N.Z. 139 G4
Tôlañaro Madag. 123 E6
Tolbo Mongolia 94 B1
Tolbukhin Bulg. *see* Dobrich
Tolbuzino Rus. Fed. 90 B1
Tolé Panama 166 [inset] J7
Tole Bi Kazakh. 98 A4
Toledo Brazil 178 F2
Toledo Spain 67 D4
Toledo *IA* U.S.A. 160 E3
Toledo *OH* U.S.A. 164 D3
Toledo *OR* U.S.A. 156 C3
Toledo, Montes de *mts* Spain 67 D4
Toledo Bend Reservoir *LA/TX* U.S.A. 161 E6
Toletum Spain *see* Toledo
Toli China 98 C3
Toliara Madag. 123 E6
Tolitoli *Sulawesi* Indon. 83 B2
Tol'ka Rus. Fed. 76 J3
Tolleson *AZ* U.S.A. 159 G5
Tollimarjon Uzbek. 111 G2
Tolmachevo Rus. Fed. 55 P7
Tolo Dem. Rep. Congo 122 B4
Toloa Creek Hond. 166 [inset] I6
Tolo Channel *H.K.* China 97 [inset]
Tolochin Belarus *see* Talachyn
Tolo Harbour *b. H.K.* China 97 [inset]
Tolonuu *i. Maluku* Indon. 83 D2
Tolosa France *see* Toulouse
Tolosa Spain 67 E2
Tolovana *r. AK* U.S.A. 149 J2
Toluca Mex. 168 E5
Toluca de Lerdo Mex. *see* Toluca
Tol'yatti Rus. Fed. 53 K5
Tom' *r.* Rus. Fed. 90 B2
Tomaga-shima *i.* Japan 92 B4
Tomagashima-suidō *sea chan.* Japan 92 A4
Tomah *WI* U.S.A. 160 F3
Tomakomai Japan 90 F4
Tomales *CA* U.S.A. 158 B2
Tomali Indon. 81 G7
Tomamae Japan 90 F3
Tomani *Sabah* Malaysia 85 F1
Tomanivi *mt.* Fiji 133 H3
Tomar Brazil 176 F4
Tomar Port. 67 B4
Tomari Rus. Fed. 90 F3
Tomarza Turkey 112 D3
Tomaszów Lubelski Poland 53 D6
Tomaszów Mazowiecki Poland 57 R5
Tomatin U.K. 60 F3
Tomatlán Mex. 168 C5
Tomazina Brazil 179 A3
Tombador, Serra do *hills* Brazil 177 G6
Tombigbee *r. AL* U.S.A. 163 C6
Tomboco Angola 123 B4
Tombouctou Mali *see* Timbuktu
Tombstone *AZ* U.S.A. 157 F7
Tombua Angola 123 B5
Tom Burke S. Africa 125 H2
Tomdibuloq Uzbek. 102 B3
Tome Moz. 125 L2
Tomea *i.* Indon. 83 B4
Tomelilla Sweden 55 H9
Tomelloso Spain 67 E4
Tomengi Kayrakty Kazakh. 98 A2
Tomi Romania *see* Constanța
Tomika Japan 92 C3
Tomingley Australia 138 D4
Tomini, Teluk *g.* Indon. 83 B3
Tominian Mali 120 C3
Tomintoul U.K. 60 F3
Tomioka Japan 93 E2
Tomisato Japan 93 G3
Tomislavgrad Bos.-Herz. 68 G3
Tomiura Japan 93 F3
Tomiyama *Aichi* Japan 93 D3
Tomiyama *Chiba* Japan 93 F3
Tomizawa Japan 93 E3
Tomkinson Ranges *mts* Australia 135 E6
Tømmerneset Norway 54 I3
Tommot Rus. Fed. 77 N4
Tomo *r.* Col. 176 E2
Tomobe Japan 93 G2
Tomóchic Mex. 166 D2
Tomorlog China 99 E5
Tomort *mt.* China 94 C3
Tomortei China 95 H3
Tompira *Sulawesi* Indon. 83 B3
Tompkinsville *KY* U.S.A. 164 C5
Tompo *Sulawesi* Indon. 83 A3
Tom Price Australia 134 B5
Tomra China 99 D7
Tomsk Rus. Fed. 76 J4
Toms River *NJ* U.S.A. 165 H4
Tomtabacken *hill* Sweden 55 I8
Tomtor Rus. Fed. 77 P3
Tomur Feng *mt.* China/Kyrg. *see* Pobeda Peak
Tomuzlovka *r.* Rus. Fed. 53 J7
Tom White, Mount *AK* U.S.A. 149 L3
Tonalá *Chiapas* Mex. 168 F5
Tonalá *Veracruz* Mex. 167 G5
Tonami Japan 92 C2
Tonantins Brazil 176 E4
Tonb-e Bozorg, Jazīreh-ye *i.* The Gulf 110 D5
Tonb-e Kūchek, Jazīreh-ye *i.* The Gulf 110 D5
Tonbridge U.K. 59 H7
Tondabayashi Japan 92 B4
Tondano *Sulawesi* Indon. 83 C2
Tønder Denmark 55 F9
Tondi India 106 C4
Tone *Gunma* Japan 93 F2
Tone *Ibaraki* Japan 93 G3
Tone *r.* U.K. 59 E7
Tone-gawa *r.* Japan 93 G3
Toney Mountain Antarctica 188 K1
Tonga *country* S. Pacific Ocean 133 I4
Tongaat S. Africa 125 J5
Tongariro National Park N.Z. 139 E4
Tongatapu Group *is* Tonga 133 I4

▶Tonga Trench *sea feature* S. Pacific Ocean 186 I7
2nd deepest trench in the world.

Tongbai Shan *mts* China 97 G1
Tongcheng *Anhui* China 97 H2
Tongcheng *Shandong* China *see* Dong'e
T'ongch'ŏn N. Korea 91 B5
Tongchuan *Shaanxi* China 95 G5
Tongchuan *Sichuan* China *see* Santai
Tongdao China 97 F3
Tongde China 94 E5
Tongduch'ŏn S. Korea 91 B5
Tongeren Belgium 62 F4
Tonggu China 97 G2
Tongguan China 95 G5
Tongguzbasti China 98 C5
Tonggu Zui *pt* China 97 F5
Tonghae S. Korea 91 C5
Tonghai China 96 D3
Tonghe China 90 C3
Tonghua *Jilin* China 90 B4
Tonghua *Jilin* China 90 B4
Tongi Bangl. *see* Tungi
Tongjiang *Heilong.* China 90 D3
Tongjiang *Sichuan* China 96 E2
Tongking, Gulf of China/Vietnam 86 E2
Tongko *Sulawesi* Indon. 83 B3
Tongle China *see* Leye
Tongliang China 96 E2
Tongliao China 95 J3
Tongling China 97 H2
Tonglu China 97 H2
Tongo Australia 138 A3
Tongo Lake *salt flat* Australia 138 A3
Tongquil *i.* Phil. 82 C5
Tongren *Guizhou* China 97 F3
Tongren *Qinghai* China 94 E5
Tongres Belgium *see* Tongeren
Tongsa Bhutan 105 G4
Tongshan China *see* Xuzhou
Tongshi China *see* Wuzhishan
Tongta Myanmar 86 B2
Tongtian He *r. Qinghai* China 96 B1 *see* Yangtze
Tongtian He *r. Qinghai* China 96 B1
Tongtian He *r. Qinghai* China 99 G6
Tongue U.K. 60 E2
Tongue *r. MT* U.S.A. 156 G3
Tongue of the Ocean *sea chan.* Bahamas 163 E7
Tongwei China 94 F5
Tongxin China 94 F4
T'ongyŏng S. Korea 91 C6
Tongyu China 95 J2
Tongzhou China 95 I4
Tongzi China 96 E2
Tonhil Mongolia 94 C2
Tónichi Mex. 166 C2
Tonila Mex. 166 E5
Tonk India 104 C4
Tonkābon Iran 110 C2
Tonki Cape *AK* U.S.A. 149 J4
Tonkin *reg.* Vietnam 86 D2
Tônle Repou *r.* Laos 87 D4
Tônlé Sab *l.* Cambodia *see* Tonle Sap

▶Tonle Sap *l.* Cambodia 87 C4
Largest lake in southeast Asia.

Tōno Japan 93 G1
Tonopah *AZ* U.S.A. 159 G5
Tonopah *NV* U.S.A. 158 E2
Tonoshō Japan 93 G3
Tonosí Panama 166 [inset] J8
Tons *r.* India 99 B7
Tønsberg Norway 55 G7
Tonsina *AK* U.S.A. 149 K3
Tonstad Norway 55 E7
Tonto Creek *watercourse AZ* U.S.A. 159 H5
Tonvarjeh Iran 110 E3
Tonzang Myanmar 86 A2
Tonzi Myanmar 86 A1
Toobeah Australia 138 D2
Toobli Liberia 120 C4
Tooele *UT* U.S.A. 159 G1
Toogoolawah Australia 138 F1
Toolik *r. AK* U.S.A. 149 J1
Tooma *r.* Australia 138 D6
Toompine Australia 138 B1
Toora Australia 138 C7
Tooraweenah Australia 138 D3
Toorberg *mt.* S. Africa 124 G7
Toowoomba Australia 138 E1
Tooxin Somalia 122 F2
Tōp Afgh. 111 H3
Topagoruk *r. AK* U.S.A. 148 I1
Top Boğazı Geçidi *pass* Turkey 107 C1

▶Topeka *KS* U.S.A. 160 E4
Capital of Kansas.

Topia Mex. 166 D3
Toplana, Gunung *mt. Seram* Indon. 83 D3
Töplitz Germany 63 M2
Topoľčany Slovakia 57 Q6
Topolobampo Mex. 166 C3
Topolovgrad Bulg. 69 L3
Topozero, Ozero *l.* Rus. Fed. 54 R4
Topsfield *ME* U.S.A. 162 H2
Tor Eth. 121 G4
Torahime Japan 92 C3
Toranggekuduk China 94 B2
Torbalı Turkey 69 L5
Torbat-e Ḩeydarīyeh Iran 110 E3
Torbat-e Jām Iran 111 F3
Torbay Bay Australia 135 B8
Torbert, Mount *AK* U.S.A. 148 I3
Torbeyevo Rus. Fed. 53 I5
Torch *r.* Canada 151 K4
Tordesillas Spain 67 D3
Tordesilos Spain 67 F3
Töre Sweden 54 M4
Torelló Spain 67 H2
Torenberg *hill* Neth. 62 F2
Toreo *Sulawesi* Indon. 83 B3
Toretam Kazakh. *see* Baykonyr
Torgau Germany 63 M3
Torghay Kazakh. *see* Turgay
Torgun *r.* Rus. Fed. 53 J6
Torhout Belgium 62 D3
Toride Japan 93 G3
Torigakubi-misaki *pt* Japan 93 E1
Torigoe Japan 92 C2
Torii-tōge *pass* Japan 93 D3
Torii-tōge *pass* Japan 93 E2
Torikabuto-yama *mt.* Japan 93 E2
Torino Italy *see* Turin
Tori-shima *i.* Japan 91 F7
Torit South Sudan 121 G4
Toriya Japan 92 C2
Torkamān Iran 110 B2
Tör Kham Afgh. 111 H3
Torkovichi Rus. Fed. 52 F4
Tornado Mountain Canada 150 H5
Torneå Fin. *see* Tornio
Torneälven *r.* Sweden 54 N4
Torneträsk *l.* Sweden 54 K2
Torngat, Monts *mts* Canada *see* Torngat Mountains
Torngat Mountains Canada 153 I2
Tornio Fin. 54 N4
Toro Spain 67 D3
Toro, Pico del *mt.* Mex. 161 C7
Torobuku *Sulawesi* Indon. 83 B4
Torom Rus. Fed. 90 D1

▶Toronto Canada 164 F2
Capital of Ontario.

Toro Peak *CA* U.S.A. 158 E5
Toropets Rus. Fed. 52 F4
Tororo Uganda 122 D3
Toros Dağları *mts* Turkey *see* Taurus Mountains
Torphins U.K. 60 G3
Torquay Australia 138 B7
Torquay U.K. 59 D8
Torrance *CA* U.S.A. 158 D5
Torrão Port. 67 B4
Torre *mt.* Port. 67 C3
Torreblanca Spain 67 G3
Torre Blanco, Cerro *mt.* Mex. 166 B1
Torrecerredo *mt.* Spain 67 D2
Torre del Greco Italy 68 F4
Torre de Moncorvo Port. 67 C3
Torrelavega Spain 67 D2
Torremolinos Spain 67 D5

▶Torrens, Lake *imp. l.* Australia 137 B6
2nd largest lake in Oceania.

Torrens Creek Australia 136 D4
Torrent Spain 67 F4
Torrente Spain *see* Torrent
Torreón Mex. 166 E3
Torres Brazil 179 A5
Torres Mex. 166 C2
Torres del Paine, Parque Nacional *nat. park* Chile 178 B8
Torres Islands Vanuatu 133 G3
Torres Novas Port. 67 B4
Torres Strait Australia 132 E2
Torres Vedras Port. 67 B4
Torrevieja Spain 67 F5
Torrey *UT* U.S.A. 159 H2
Torridge *r.* U.K. 59 C8
Torridon, Loch *b.* U.K. 60 D3
Torrijos Spain 67 D4
Torrington Australia 138 E2
Torrington *CT* U.S.A. 162 F3
Torrington *WY* U.S.A. 156 G4
Torsa Chhu *r.* Bhutan 99 E8
Torsby Sweden 55 H6

▶Tórshavn Faroe Is 54 [inset 2]
Capital of the Faroe Islands.

Tortilla Flat *AZ* U.S.A. 159 H5
Törtköl Uzbek. *see* To'rtko'l
To'rtko'l Uzbek. 102 B3
Tortoli *Sardinia* Italy 68 C5
Tortona Italy 68 C2
Tortosa Spain 67 G3
Tortuga, Laguna *l.* Mex. 167 F4
Tortuguero, Parque Nacional *nat. park* Costa Rica 166 [inset] J7
Tortum Turkey 113 F2
Toru-Aygyr Kyrg. 98 B4
Ţorūd Iran 110 D3
Torue *Sulawesi* Indon. 83 B3
Torugart, Pereval *pass* China/Kyrg. *see* Turugart Pass
Torul Turkey 113 E2
Toruń Poland 57 Q4
Tory Island Ireland 61 D2
Tory Sound *sea chan.* Ireland 61 D2
Torzhok Rus. Fed. 52 G4
Torzī Afgh. 111 G4
Tosa Japan 91 D6
Tosbotn Norway 54 H4
Tosca S. Africa 124 F3
Tosca, Punta *pt* Mex. 166 C3
Toscano, Arcipelago *is* Italy 68 C3
Tosham India 104 C3
Tōshi-jima *i.* Japan 92 C4
To-shima *i.* Japan 93 F4
Tōshima-yama *mt.* Japan 91 F4

▶Toshkent Uzbek. 102 C3
Capital of Uzbekistan.

Tosno Rus. Fed. 52 F4
Toson Hu *l.* China 94 D4
Tosontsengel *Dzavhan* Mongolia 94 D1
Tosontsengel *Hövsgöl* Mongolia 94 E1
Tostado Arg. 178 D3
Tostedt Germany 63 J1
Tosya Turkey 112 D2
Totapola *mt.* Sri Lanka 106 D5
Tôtes France 62 B5
Tot'ma Rus. Fed. 52 I4
Totness Suriname 177 G2
Totolapan Mex. 167 F5
Totonicapán Guat. 167 H6
Totsuka Japan 93 F3
Totsukawa Japan 92 B4
Totsu-kawa *r.* Japan 92 B5
Tottenham Australia 138 C4
Totton U.K. 59 F8
Tottori Japan 91 D6
Touba Côte d'Ivoire 120 C4
Touba Senegal 120 B3
Toubkal, Jbel *mt.* Morocco 64 C5
Toubkal, Parc National du *nat. park* Morocco 64 C5
Touboro Cameroon 121 E4
Toudaohu China 94 F4
Tougan Burkina Faso 120 C3
Touggourt Alg. 64 F5
Tougué Guinea 120 B3
Touil Mauritania 120 B3
Toul France 62 F6
Touliu Taiwan 97 I4
Toulon France 66 G5
Toulon *IL* U.S.A. 160 F3
Toulouse France 66 E5
Toumodi Côte d'Ivoire 120 C4
Toupai China 97 F3
Tourane Vietnam *see* Đa Nẵng
Tourcoing France 62 D4
Tourgis Lake Canada 151 J1
Tourlaville France 59 F9
Tournai Belgium 62 D4
Tournon-sur-Rhône France 66 G4
Tournus France 66 A1
Touros Brazil 177 K5
Tours France 66 E3
Tousside, Pic *mt.* Chad 121 E2
Toussoro, Mont *mt.* Cent. Afr. Rep. 122 C3
Toutai China 90 B3
Touwsrivier S. Africa 124 E7
Toužim Czech Rep. 63 M4
Töv *prov.* Mongolia 94 F2
Tovarkovo Rus. Fed. 53 G5
Tovil'-Dora Tajik. *see* Tavildara
Tovuz Azer. 113 G2
Towada Japan 90 F4
Towak Mountain *hill AK* U.S.A. 148 F3
Towanda *PA* U.S.A. 165 G3
Towaoc *CO* U.S.A. 159 I3
Towari *Sulawesi* Indon. 83 B4
Towcester U.K. 59 G6
Tower Ireland 61 D6
Towner *ND* U.S.A. 160 C1
Townes Pass *CA* U.S.A. 158 E3
Townsend *MT* U.S.A. 156 F3
Townsend, Mount Australia 138 D6
Townshend Island Australia 136 E4
Townsville Australia 136 D3
Towori, Teluk *b.* Indon. 83 B3
Towot South Sudan 121 G4
Towson *MD* U.S.A. 165 G4
Towuti, Danau *l.* Indon. 83 B3
Towyn U.K. *see* Tywyn
Toxkan He *r.* China 98 C4
Toy *NV* U.S.A. 158 D1
Toyah *TX* U.S.A. 161 C6
Toyama Japan 92 D2
Toyama *pref.* Japan 92 D2
Toyama-wan *b.* Japan 92 D1
Toyêma China 94 E5
Toygunen Rus. Fed. 148 D2
Toyoake Japan 92 D3
Toyoda Japan 93 D4
Toyohashi Japan 92 D4
Toyokawa Japan 92 D4
Toyo-kawa *r.* Japan 92 D4
Toyonaka Japan 92 B4
Toyone Japan 92 D3
Toyono *Nagano* Japan 93 E2
Toyono *Ōsaka* Japan 92 B4
Toyooka *Hyōgo* Japan 92 A3
Toyooka *Nagano* Japan 93 D3
Toyooka *Shizuoka* Japan 93 D4
Toyoshina Japan 93 D2
Toyota Japan 92 D3
Toyoyama Japan 92 C3
Tozanlı Turkey *see* Almus
Tozê Kangri *mt.* China 99 C6
Tozeur Tunisia 64 F5
Tozi, Mount *AK* U.S.A. 149 J2
Tozitna *r. AK* U.S.A. 148 I2
Tqibuli Georgia 113 F2
Traben Germany 62 H5
Trâblous Lebanon *see* Tripoli
Trabotivište Macedonia 69 J4
Trabzon Turkey 113 E2
Tracy *CA* U.S.A. 158 C3
Tracy *MN* U.S.A. 160 E2
Trading *r.* Canada 152 C4
Traer *IA* U.S.A. 160 E3
Trafalgar *IN* U.S.A. 164 B4
Trafalgar, Cabo de *c.* Spain 67 C5
Traffic Mountain Canada 149 O3
Trail Canada 150 G5
Tràille, Rubha na *pt* U.K. 60 D5
Traill Island Greenland *see* Traill Ø
Traill Ø *i.* Greenland 147 P2
Trainor Lake Canada 150 F2
Trajectum Neth. *see* Utrecht
Trakai Lith. 55 N9
Tra Khuc, Sông *r.* Vietnam 86 E4
Trakiya *reg.* Europe *see* Thrace
Trakt Rus. Fed. 52 K3
Trakya *reg.* Europe *see* Thrace
Tralee Ireland 61 C5
Tralee Bay Ireland 61 C5
Trá Li Ireland *see* Tralee
Tramandaí Brazil 179 A5
Tramán Tepuí *mt.* Venez. 176 F2
Trá Mhór Ireland *see* Tramore
Tramore Ireland 61 E5
Tranås Sweden 55 I7
Trancas Arg. 178 C3
Trancoso Brazil 179 D2
Tranemo Sweden 55 H8
Tranent U.K. 60 G5
Trang Thai. 87 B6
Trangan *i.* Indon. 134 F1
Trangie Australia 138 C4
Trân Ninh, Cao Nguyên Laos 86 C3
Transantarctic Mountains Antarctica 188 H2
Trans Canada Highway Canada 151 H5
Transvase, Canal de Spain 67 E4
Transylvanian Alps *mts* Romania 69 J2
Transylvanian Basin *plat.* Romania 69 K1
Trapani *Sicily* Italy 68 E5
Trapezus Turkey *see* Trabzon
Trapper Creek *AK* U.S.A. 149 J3
Trapper Peak *MT* U.S.A. 156 E3
Trappes France 62 C6
Traralgon Australia 138 C7
Trashigang Bhutan *see* Tashigang
Trasimeno, Lago *l.* Italy 68 E3
Trat Thai. 87 C4
Tratani *r.* Pak. 111 H4
Traunsee *l.* Austria 57 N7
Traunstein Germany 57 N7
Travaillant Lake Canada 149 O2
Travellers Lake *imp. l.* Australia 137 C7
Travers, Mount N.Z. 139 D6
Traverse City *MI* U.S.A. 164 C1
Traverse Peak *hill AK* U.S.A. 148 H2
Tra Vinh Vietnam 87 D5
Travis, Lake *TX* U.S.A. 167 F2
Travnik Bos.-Herz. 68 G2
Trbovlje Slovenia 68 F1
Tre, Hon *i.* Vietnam 87 E4
Treasury Islands Solomon Is 132 F2
Treat Island *AK* U.S.A. 148 H2
Trebbin Germany 63 N2
Trebević, Nacionalni Park *nat. park* Bos.-Herz. 68 H3
Třebíč Czech Rep. 57 O6
Trebinje Bos.-Herz. 68 H3
Trebišov Slovakia 53 D6
Trebizond Turkey *see* Trabzon
Trebnje Slovenia 68 F2
Trebur Germany 63 I5
Trece Martires Phil. 82 C3
Tree Island India 106 B4
Trefaldwyn U.K. *see* Montgomery
Treffurt Germany 63 K3
Treffynnon U.K. *see* Holywell
Trefyclawdd U.K. *see* Knighton
Trefynwy U.K. *see* Monmouth
Tregosse Islets and Reefs Australia 136 E3
Treinta y Tres Uruguay 178 F4
Trelew Arg. 178 C6
Trelleborg Sweden 55 H9
Trélon France 62 E4
Tremblant, Mont *hill* Canada 152 G5
Trembleur Lake Canada 150 E4
Tremiti, Isole *is* Italy 68 F3
Tremont *PA* U.S.A. 165 G3
Tremonton *UT* U.S.A. 156 E4
Tremp Spain 67 G2
Trenance U.K. 59 B8
Trenary *MI* U.S.A. 162 C2
Trenche *r.* Canada 153 G5
Trenčín Slovakia 57 Q6
Trendelburg Germany 63 J3
Trêng Cambodia 87 C4
Trenggalek *Jawa* Indon. 85 E5
Trengganu *state* Malaysia *see* Terengganu
Trenque Lauquén Arg. 178 D5
Trent Italy *see* Trento
Trent *r.* U.K. 59 G5
Trento Italy 68 D1
Trenton Canada 165 G1
Trenton *FL* U.S.A. 163 D6
Trenton *GA* U.S.A. 163 C5
Trenton *KY* U.S.A. 164 B5
Trenton *MO* U.S.A. 160 E3
Trenton *NC* U.S.A. 163 E5
Trenton *NE* U.S.A. 160 C3

▶Trenton *NJ* U.S.A. 165 H3
Capital of New Jersey.

Treorchy U.K. 59 D7
Trepassey Canada 153 L5
Tres Arroyos Arg. 178 D5
Tresco *i.* U.K. 59 A9
Três Corações Brazil 179 B3
Tres Esquinas Col. 176 C3
Tres Forcas, Cabo *c.* Morocco *see* Trois Fourches, Cap des
Três Lagoas Brazil 179 A3
Três Marias, Represa *resr* Brazil 179 B2
Tres Picachos, Sierra *mts* Mex. 157 G7
Tres Picos, Cerro *mt.* Arg. 178 D5
Tres Picos, Cerro *mt.* Mex. 167 G5
Três Pontas Brazil 179 B3
Tres Puntas, Cabo *c.* Arg. 178 C7
Três Rios Brazil 179 C3
Tres Zapotes *tourist site* Mex. 167 G5
Tretten Norway 55 G6
Tretyy Severnyy Rus. Fed. *see* 3-y Severnyy
Treuchtlingen Germany 63 K6
Treuenbrietzen Germany 63 M2
Treungen Norway 55 F7
Treves Germany *see* Trier
Treviglio Italy 68 C2
Treviso Italy 68 E2
Trevose Head *hd* U.K. 59 B8
Tri An, Hồ *resr* Vietnam 87 D5
Triánda Greece *see* Trianta
Triangle *VA* U.S.A. 165 G4
Trianta Greece 69 M6
Tribal Areas *admin. div.* Pak. 111 H3
Tribune *KS* U.S.A. 160 C4
Tricase Italy 68 H5
Trichinopoly India *see* Tiruchchirappalli
Trichur India *see* Thrissur
Tricot France 62 C5
Trida Australia 138 B4
Tridentum Italy *see* Trento
Trier Germany 62 G5
Trieste Italy 68 E2
Trieste, Golfo di *g.* Europe *see* Trieste, Gulf of
Trieste, Gulf of Europe 68 E2
Triglav *mt.* Slovenia 68 E1
Triglavski narodni park *nat. park* Slovenia 68 E1
Trikala Greece 69 I5
Tríkkala Greece *see* Trikala

▶Trikora, Puncak *mt.* Indon. 81 J7
2nd highest mountain in Oceania.

Trim Ireland 61 F4
Trincheras Mex. 166 C2

Ubaitaba Brazil 179 D1
Ubangi r. Cent. Afr. Rep./Dem. Rep. Congo 122 B4
Ubangi-Shari country Africa see Central African Republic
Ubauro Pak. 111 H4
Ubayyiḍ, Wādī al watercourse Iraq/Saudi Arabia 113 F4
Ube Japan 91 C6
Úbeda Spain 67 E4
Uberaba Brazil 179 B2
Uberlândia Brazil 179 A2
Ubin, Pulau i. Sing. 87 [inset]
Ubly MI U.S.A. 164 D2
Ubolratna, Ang Kep Nam Thai. 86 C3
Ubombo S. Africa 125 K4
Ubon Ratchathani Thai. 86 D4
Ubstadt-Weiher Germany 63 I5
Ubundu Dem. Rep. Congo 121 F5
Üçajy Turkm. 111 F2
Ucar Azer. 113 G2
Uçarı Turkey 107 A1
Ucayali r. Peru 176 D4
Uch Pak. 111 H4
Üchajy Turkm. see Üçajy
Ūchān Iran 110 C2
Ucharal Kazakh. 102 F2
Uchigō Japan 93 G1
Uchihara Japan 93 G2
Uchimura-gawa r. Japan 93 E2
Uchinada Japan 92 C2
Uchita Japan 92 B4
Uchiura-wan b. Japan 90 F4
Uchiyama-tōge pass Japan 93 E2
Uchkeken Rus. Fed. 113 F2
Uchkuduk Uzbek. see Uchquduq
Uchquduq Uzbek. 102 B3
Uchte Germany 63 I2
Uchte r. Germany 63 L2
Uchur r. Rus. Fed. 77 O4
Uckermark reg. Germany 63 N1
Uckfield U.K. 59 H8
Ucluelet Canada 150 E5
Ucross WY U.S.A. 156 G3
Ud China 94 F4
Uda r. Rus. Fed. 89 J2
Uda r. Rus. Fed. 90 D1
Udachnoye Rus. Fed. 53 J7
Udachnyy Rus. Fed. 189 E2
Udagamandalam India 106 C4
Udaipur Rajasthan India 104 C4
Udaipur Tripura India 105 G5
Udanti r. India/Myanmar 105 E5
Uday r. Ukr. 53 G6
'Udaynān well Saudi Arabia 110 C6
Uddevalla Sweden 55 G7
Uddingston U.K. 60 E5
Uddjaure l. Sweden 54 J4
'Udeid, Khōr al inlet Qatar 110 C5
Uden Neth. 62 F3
Udgir India 106 C2
Udhagamandalam India see Udagamandalam
Udhampur India 104 C2
Udia-Milai atoll Marshall Is see Bikini
Udimskiy Rus. Fed. 52 J3
Udine Italy 68 E1
Udit India 111 I5
Udjuktok Bay Canada 153 J3
Udmalaippettai India see Udumalaippettai
Udomlya Rus. Fed. 52 G4
Udone-jima i. Japan 93 F4
Udon Thani Thai. 86 C3
Udskaya Guba b. Rus. Fed. 77 O4
Udskoye Rus. Fed. 90 D1
Udumalaippettai India 106 C4
Udupi India 106 B3
Udyl', Ozero l. Rus. Fed. 90 E1
Udzhary Azer. see Ucar
Udzungwa Mountains National Park Tanz. 123 D4
Uéa atoll New Caledonia see Ouvéa
Uebonti Sulawesi Indon. 83 B3
Ueckermünde Germany 57 O4
Ueda Japan 93 E2
Uekuli Sulawesi Indon. 83 B3
Uele r. Dem. Rep. Congo 122 C3
Uelen Rus. Fed. 148 E2
Uel'kal' Rus. Fed. 148 C2
Uelzen Germany 63 K2
Ueno Gunma Japan 93 E2
Ueno Mie Japan 92 C4
Uenohara Japan 93 F3
Uetersen Germany 63 J1
Uettingen Germany 63 J5
Uetze Germany 63 K2
Ufa Rus. Fed. 51 R5
Ufa r. Rus. Fed. 51 R5
Uffenheim Germany 63 K5
Uftyuga r. Rus. Fed. 52 J3
Ugab watercourse Namibia 123 B6
Ugak Bay AK U.S.A. 148 I4
Ugalla r. Tanz. 123 D4
Uganda country Africa 122 D3
Uganik AK U.S.A. 148 I4
Ugashik AK U.S.A. 148 H4
Ugashik Bay AK U.S.A. 148 H4
Ugie S. Africa 125 I6
Ūgīnak Iran 111 F5
Uglegorsk Rus. Fed. 90 F2
Uglich Rus. Fed. 52 H4
Ugljan i. Croatia 68 F2
Uglovoye Rus. Fed. 90 C2
Ugol'noye Rus. Fed. 77 P3
Ugolnyy Rus. Fed. see Beringovskiy
Ugol'nyye Kopi Rus. Fed. 148 B2
Ugra Rus. Fed. 53 G5
Ugtaaltsaydam Mongolia 94 F1
Uher Hudag China 95 G3
Uherské Hradiště Czech Rep. 57 P6
Úhlava r. Czech Rep. 63 N5
Uhrichsville OH U.S.A. 164 E3
Uibhist a' Deas i. U.K. see South Uist
Uibhist a' Tuath i. U.K. see North Uist
Uig U.K. 60 C3
Uíge Angola 123 B4
Ŭijŏngbu S. Korea 91 B5
Ŭiju N. Korea 91 B4
Uimaharju Fin. 54 Q5
Uinta Mountains UT U.S.A. 159 H1
Uis Mine Namibia 123 B6
Uitenhage S. Africa 125 G7
Uithoorn Neth. 62 E2
Uithuizen Neth. 62 G1
Uivak, Cape Canada 153 J2
Ujhani India 104 D4
Uji Japan 92 B4
Uji-gawa r. Japan 92 B4
Uji-guntō is Japan 91 C7
Ujiie Japan 93 F2
Ujitawara Japan 92 B4
Ujiyamada Japan see Ise
Ujjain India 104 C5
Ujohbilang Kalimantan Indon. 85 F2
Ujung Kulon, Taman Nasional nat. park Indon. 84 D4
Ujung Pandang Sulawesi Indon. see Makassar
Újvidék Serbia see Novi Sad
Ukal Sagar l. India 104 C5
Ukata Nigeria 120 D3
'Ukayrishah well Saudi Arabia 110 B5
uKhahlamba-Drakensberg Park nat. park S. Africa 125 I5
Ukholovo Rus. Fed. 53 I5
Ukhrul India 105 H4
Ukhta Respublika Kareliya Rus. Fed. see Kalevala
Ukhta Respublika Komi Rus. Fed. 52 L3
Ukiah CA U.S.A. 158 B2
Ukiah OR U.S.A. 156 D3
Ukkusiksalik National Park Canada 147 J3
Ukkusissat Greenland 147 M2
Ukmergė Lith. 55 N9

▶Ukraine country Europe 53 F6
2nd largest country in Europe.

Ukrainskaya S.S.R. country Europe see Ukraine
Ukrayina country Europe see Ukraine
Uku-jima i. Japan 91 C6
Ukwi Botswana 124 E2
Ukwi Pan salt pan Botswana 124 E2
Ul r. India 99 B7
Ulaanbaatar Mongolia see Ulan Bator
Ulaanbaatar mun. Mongolia 94 F2
Ulaanbadrah Mongolia 95 G3
Ulaan-Ereg Mongolia see Bayanmönh
Ulaangom Mongolia 94 C1
Ulaanhudag Mongolia see Erdenesant
Ulaan Nuur salt l. Mongolia 94 E2
Ulaan-Uul Bayanhongor Mongolia see Öldziyt
Ulaan-Uul Dornogovĭ Mongolia see Erdene
Ulak Island AK U.S.A. 148 [inset] C6
Ulan Australia 138 D4
Ulan Nei Mongol China 95 G4
Ulan Qinghai China 94 D4

▶Ulan Bator Mongolia 94 F2
Capital of Mongolia.

Ulanbel' Kazakh. 102 D3
Ulan Buh Shamo des. China 94 F3
Ulan Erge Rus. Fed. 53 J7
Ulanhad China see Chifeng
Ulanhot China 95 J2
Ulan Hua China 95 G3
Ulan-Khol Rus. Fed. 53 J7
Ulanlinggi China 98 D4
Ulan Mod China 94 F4
Ulan Suhai China 94 F3
Ulansuhai Nur l. China 95 G3
Ulan Tohoi China 94 E3
Ulan-Ude Rus. Fed. 89 J2
Ulan Ul Hu l. China 99 E6
Ulaş Turkey 112 E3
Ulastai China 98 D4
Ulawa Island Solomon Is 133 G2
Ulayyah reg. Saudi Arabia 110 B6
Ul'banskiy Zaliv b. Rus. Fed. 90 E1
Ul'bi Kazakh. 98 C2
Ulchin S. Korea 91 C5
Uldz Mongolia see Norovlin
Uldz r. Mongolia 95 H1
Uleåborg Fin. see Oulu
Ulebsechel i. Palau see Auluptagel
Ulefoss Norway 55 F7
Ulekchin Rus. Fed. 94 F1
Ülenurme Estonia 55 O7
Ulety Rus. Fed. 95 H1
Ulgain Gol r. China 95 I2
Ulhasnagar India 106 B2
Uliastai China 95 I2
Uliastay Mongolia 94 D2
Uliatea i. Fr. Polynesia see Raiatea
Ulicoten Neth. 62 E3
Ulie atoll Micronesia see Woleai
Ulita r. Rus. Fed. 54 R2
Ulithi atoll Micronesia 81 J4
Ul'ken Aksu Kazakh. 98 B4
Ul'ken Boken Kazakh. 98 C2
Ul'ken Naryn Kazakh. 102 F2
Ul'ken Sulutor Kazakh. 98 A4
Ulladulla Australia 138 E5
Ullapool U.K. 60 D3
Ulla Ulla, Parque Nacional nat. park Bol. 176 E6
Ullava Fin. 54 M5
Ullersuaq c. Greenland 147 K2
Ullswater l. U.K. 58 E4
Ullŭng-do i. S. Korea 91 C5
Ulm Germany 57 L6
Ulmarra Australia 138 F2
Ulmen Germany 62 G4
Uloowaranie, Lake salt flat Australia 137 B5
Ulricehamn Sweden 55 H8
Ulrum Neth. 62 G1
Ulsan S. Korea 91 C6
Ulsberg Norway 54 F5
Ulster reg. Ireland/U.K. 61 E3
Ulster PA U.S.A. 165 G3
Ulster Canal Ireland/U.K. 61 E3
Ultima Australia 138 A5
Ulu Sulawesi Indon. 83 C2
Ulúa r. Hond. 166 [inset] I6
Ulubat Gölü l. Turkey 69 M4
Ulubey Turkey 69 M5
Uluborlu Turkey 69 N5
Uludağ mt. Turkey 69 M4
Uludağ Milli Parkı nat. park Turkey 69 M4
Ulugqat China see Wuqia
Ulu Kali, Gunung mt. Malaysia 84 C2
Ulukhaktok Canada 146 G2
Ulukışla Turkey 112 D3
Ulundi S. Africa 125 J5
Ulungur He r. China 98 D3
Ulungur Hu l. China 98 D3
Uluqsaqtuuq Canada see Ulukhaktok
Uluṟu hill Australia 135 E6
Uluṟu-Kata Tjuṯa National Park Australia 135 E6
Uluru National Park Australia see Uluṟu-Kata Tjuṯa National Park
Ulutau Kazakh. see Ulytau
Ulutau, Gory mts Kazakh. see Ulytau, Gory
Ulu Temburong National Park Brunei 85 F1
Uluyatır Turkey 107 C1
Ulva i. U.K. 60 C4
Ulvenhout Neth. 62 E3
Ulverston U.K. 58 D4
Ulvsjön Sweden 55 I6
Ül'yanov Kazakh. see Ul'yanovskiy
Ul'yanovsk Rus. Fed. 53 K5
Ul'yanovskiy Kazakh. 102 D1
Ul'yanovskoye Kazakh. see Ul'yanovskiy
Ulyatuy Rus. Fed. 95 I1
Ulysses KS U.S.A. 160 C4
Ulysses KY U.S.A. 164 D5
Ulytau Kazakh. 102 C2
Ulytau, Gory mts Kazakh. 102 C2
Ulyunkhan Rus. Fed. 89 K2
Uma Rus. Fed. 90 A1
Umal'ta (abandoned) Rus. Fed. 90 D2
'Umān country Asia see Oman
Umán Mex. 167 H4
Uman' Ukr. 53 F6
Umarao Pak. 111 G4
'Umarī, Qā' al salt pan Jordan 107 C4
Umaria India 104 E5
Umarkhed India 106 C2
Umarkot India 106 D2
Umarkot Punjab Pak. 111 H4
Umarkot Sindh Pak. 111 H5
Umaroona, Lake salt flat Australia 137 B5
Umarpada India 104 C5
Umatilla OR U.S.A. 156 D3
Umayan r. Mindanao Phil. 82 D4
Umba Rus. Fed. 52 G2
Umbagog Lake NH U.S.A. 165 J1
Umbeara Australia 135 F6
Umbele i. Indon. 83 B3
Umboi i. P.N.G. 81 L8
Umeå Sweden 54 L5
Umeälven r. Sweden 54 L5
Umera Maluku Indon. 83 D3
Umfolozi r. S. Africa 125 K5
Umfreville Lake Canada 151 M5
Umhlanga Rocks S. Africa 125 J5
Umiat AK U.S.A. 148 I1
Umi-gawa r. Japan 93 D1
Umiiviip Kangertiva inlet Greenland 147 N3
Umingmaktok (abandoned) Canada 189 L2
Umiujaq Canada 152 F2
Umkomaas S. Africa 125 J6
Umkumiut AK U.S.A. 148 F3
Umlaiteng India 105 H4
Umlazi S. Africa 125 J5
Umm ad Daraj, Jabal mt. Jordan 107 B3
Umm al 'Amad Syria 107 C2
Umm al Jamājim well Saudi Arabia 110 B5
Umm al Qaiwain U.A.E. see Umm al Qaywayn
Umm al Qaywayn U.A.E. 110 D5
Umm al Qulbān Saudi Arabia 113 F6
Umm ar Raqabah, Khabrat imp. l. Saudi Arabia 107 C5
Umm az Zumūl well Oman 110 D6
Umm Bāb Qatar 110 C5
Umm Bel Sudan 108 C7
Umm Keddada Sudan 108 C7
Umm Lajj Saudi Arabia 108 E4
Umm Nukhaylah hill Saudi Arabia 107 D5
Umm Qaṣr Iraq 113 G5
Umm Quṣūr i. Saudi Arabia 112 D6
Umm Ruwaba Sudan 108 D7
Umm Sa'ad Libya 112 B5
Umm Sa'id Qatar 110 C5
Umm Ṣalāl Muḥammad town Qatar 110 C5
Umm Shugeira Sudan 108 C7
Umm Wa'āl hill Saudi Arabia 107 D4
Umm Wazīr well Saudi Arabia 110 B6
Umnak Island AK U.S.A. 148 E5
Umnak Pass sea channel AK U.S.A. 148 E5
Um Phang Wildlife Reserve nature res. Thai. 86 B4
Umpqua r. OR U.S.A. 156 B4
Umpulo Angola 123 B5
Umraniye Turkey 69 N5
Umred India 106 C1
Umri India 104 D4
Umtali Zimbabwe see Mutare
Umtata S. Africa see Mthatha
Umtentweni S. Africa 125 J6
Umuahia Nigeria 120 D4
Umuarama Brazil 178 F2
Umvuma Zimbabwe see Mvuma
Umzimkulu S. Africa 125 I6
Una r. Bos.-Herz./Croatia 68 G2
Una Brazil 179 D1
Una India 104 D3
'Unāb, Jabal al hill Jordan 107 C5
'Unāb, Wādī al watercourse Jordan 107 C4
Unaí Brazil 179 B2
Unakami Japan 93 G3
Unalakleet AK U.S.A. 148 G3
Unalakleet r. AK U.S.A. 148 G3
Unalaska AK U.S.A. 148 F5
Unalaska Island AK U.S.A. 148 F5
Unalga Island AK U.S.A. 148 F5
Unapool U.K. 60 D2
Unauna i. Indon. 83 B3
'Unayzah Saudi Arabia 108 F4
'Unayzah, Jabal hill Iraq 113 E4
Unazuki Japan 92 D2
Uncia Bol. 176 E7
Uncompahgre Peak CO U.S.A. 159 J2
Uncompahgre Plateau CO U.S.A. 159 I2
Undara National Park Australia 136 D3
Underberg S. Africa 125 I5
Underbool Australia 137 C7
Underwood IN U.S.A. 164 C4
Undu, Tanjung pt Sumba Indon. 83 B5
Undur Seram Indon. 83 D3
Unecha Rus. Fed. 53 G5
Unga AK U.S.A. 148 G5
Unga Island AK U.S.A. 148 G5
Ungalik AK U.S.A. 148 G2
Ungalik r. AK U.S.A. 148 G2
Ungama Bay Kenya see Ungwana Bay
Ungarie Australia 138 C4
Ungava, Baie d' b. Canada see Ungava Bay
Ungava, Péninsule d' pen. Canada 152 G1
Ungava Bay Canada 153 I2
Ungava Peninsula Canada see Ungava, Péninsule d'
Ungeny Moldova see Ungheni
Ungheni Moldova 69 L1
Unguana Moz. 125 L2
Unguja i. Tanz. see Zanzibar Island
Unguz, Solonchakovyye Vpadiny salt flat Turkm. 110 E2
Üngüz Angyrsyndaky Garagum des. Turkm. 110 E1
Ungvár Ukr. see Uzhhorod
Ungwana Bay Kenya 122 E4
Uni Rus. Fed. 52 K4
União Brazil 177 J4
União da Vitória Brazil 179 A4
União dos Palmares Brazil 177 K5
Uniara India 99 B8
Unimak Bight b. AK U.S.A. 148 F5
Unimak Island AK U.S.A. 148 F5
Unimak Pass sea channel AK U.S.A. 148 F5
Unini r. Brazil 176 F4
Union MO U.S.A. 160 F4
Union WV U.S.A. 164 E5
Union, Mount AZ U.S.A. 159 G4
Union City OH U.S.A. 164 C3
Union City PA U.S.A. 164 F3
Union City TN U.S.A. 161 F4
Uniondale S. Africa 124 F7
Unión de Reyes Cuba 163 D8

▶Union of Soviet Socialist Republics
Divided in 1991 into 15 independent nations: Armenia, Azerbaijan, Belarus, Estonia, Georgia, Latvia, Kazakhstan, Kyrgyzstan, Lithuania, Moldova, the Russian Federation, Tajikistan, Turkmenistan, Ukraine and Uzbekistan.

Union Springs AL U.S.A. 163 C5
Uniontown PA U.S.A. 164 F4
Unionville PA U.S.A. 165 G3
United Arab Emirates country Asia 110 D6
United Arab Republic country Africa see Egypt

▶United Kingdom country Europe 56 G3
4th most populous country in Europe.

United Provinces state India see Uttar Pradesh

▶United States of America country N. America 154 F3
Most populous country in North America and 3rd most populous in the world. Also 2nd largest country in North America and 3rd in the world.

United States Range mts Canada 147 L1
Unity Canada 151 I4
Unjha India 104 C5
Unna Germany 63 H3
Unnao India 104 E4
Unoke Japan 92 C2
Ŭnp'a N. Korea 91 B5
Unsan N. Korea 91 B4
Ŭnsan N. Korea 91 B5
Unst i. U.K. 60 [inset]
Unstrut r. Germany 63 L3
Untor, Ozero l. Rus. Fed. 51 T3
Unuk r. Canada/U.S.A. 149 O4
Unuli Horog China 94 B5
Unzen-dake vol. Japan 91 C6
Unzha Rus. Fed. 52 J4
Uozu Japan 92 D2
Upalco UT U.S.A. 159 H1
Upar Ghat reg. India 105 F5
Upemba, Lac l. Dem. Rep. Congo 123 C4
Uperbada India 105 F5
Upernavik Greenland 147 M2
Upington S. Africa 124 E5
Upland CA U.S.A. 158 E4
Upleta India 104 B5
Upoloksha Rus. Fed. 54 Q3
'Upolu i. Samoa 133 I3
Upper Arlington OH U.S.A. 164 D3
Upper Arrow Lake Canada 150 G5
Upper Chindwin Myanmar see Mawlaik
Upper Fraser Canada 150 F4
Upper Garry Lake Canada 151 K1
Upper Hutt N.Z. 139 E5
Upper Kalskag AK U.S.A. 148 G3
Upper Klamath Lake OR U.S.A. 156 C4
Upper Liard Canada 149 O3
Upper Lough Erne l. U.K. 61 E3
Upper Marlboro MD U.S.A. 165 G4
Upper Mazinaw Lake Canada 165 G1
Upper Missouri Breaks National Monument nat. park MT U.S.A. 160 A2
Upper Peirce Reservoir Sing. 87 [inset]
Upper Red Lake MN U.S.A. 160 E1
Upper Sandusky OH U.S.A. 164 D3
Upper Saranac Lake NY U.S.A. 165 H1
Upper Seal Lake Canada see Iberville, Lac d'
Upper Tunguska r. Rus. Fed. see Angara
Upper Volta country Africa see Burkina Faso
Upper Yarra Reservoir Australia 138 B6
Uppinangadi India 106 B3
Uppsala Sweden 55 J7
Upright, Cape AK U.S.A. 148 D3
Upsala Canada 152 C4
Upshi India 104 D2
Upton MA U.S.A. 165 J2
'Uqayqah, Wādī watercourse Jordan 107 B4
'Uqaybāt Syria 107 C2
'Uqlat al 'Udhaybah well Iraq 113 G5
Uqturpan China see Wushi
Uracas vol. N. Mariana Is see Farallon de Pajaros
Urad Qianqi China see Xishanzui
Urad Zhongqi China see Haliut
Ūrāf Iran 110 E4
Uraga-suidō sea chan. Japan 93 F3
Uragawara Japan 93 E1
Urakawa Japan 90 F4
Ural hill Australia 138 C4
Ural r. Kazakh./Rus. Fed. 100 E2
Uralla Australia 138 E3
Ural Mountains Rus. Fed. 51 S2
Ural'sk Kazakh. 100 E1
Ural'skaya Oblast' admin. div. Kazakh. see Zapadnyy Kazakhstan
Ural'skiye Gory mts Rus. Fed. see Ural Mountains
Ural'skiy Khrebet mts Rus. Fed. see Ural Mountains
Urambo Tanz. 123 D4
Uran India 106 B2
Urana Australia 138 C5
Urana, Lake Australia 138 C5
Urandangi Australia 136 B4
Urandi Brazil 179 C1
Uranium City Canada 151 I3
Uranquinty Australia 138 C5
Uraricoera r. Brazil 176 F3
Urartu country Asia see Armenia
Ura-Tyube Tajik. see Üroteppa
Uravakonda India 106 C3
Uravan CO U.S.A. 159 I2
Urawa Japan 93 F3
Urayasu Japan 93 F3
'Urayf an Nāqah, Jabal hill Egypt 107 B4
Uray'irah Saudi Arabia 110 C5
'Urayq ad Duḥūl des. Saudi Arabia 110 B5
'Urayq Sāqān des. Saudi Arabia 110 B5
Urbana IL U.S.A. 160 F3
Urbana OH U.S.A. 164 D3
Urbino Italy 68 E3
Urbinum Italy see Urbino
Urbs Vetus Italy see Orvieto
Urdoma Rus. Fed. 52 K3
Urd Tamir Gol r. Mongolia 94 E2
Urdyuzhskoye, Ozero l. Rus. Fed. 52 K2
Urdzhar Kazakh. 102 F2
Ure r. U.K. 58 F4
Urek'i Georgia 113 F2
Ureliki Rus. Fed. 148 D2
Uren' Rus. Fed. 52 J4
Urengoy Rus. Fed. 76 I3
Uréparapara i. Vanuatu 133 G3
Ures Mex. 166 C2
Ureshino Japan 92 C4
Urfa Turkey see Şanlıurfa
Urfa prov. Turkey see Şanlıurfa
Urga Mongolia see Ulan Bator
Urgal r. Rus. Fed. 90 D2
Urganch Uzbek. 102 B3
Urgench Uzbek. see Urganch
Urgūn-e Kalān Afgh. 111 H3
Ürgüp Turkey 112 D3
Urgut Uzbek. 111 G2
Urho China 98 D3
Urho Kekkosen kansallispuisto nat. park Fin. 54 O2
Urie r. U.K. 60 G3
Uril Rus. Fed. 90 C2
Uripitijuata, Cerro mt. Mex. 166 E5
Urique Mex. 166 D3
Urisino Australia 138 A2
Urizura Japan 93 G2
Urjala Fin. 55 M6
Urk Neth. 62 F2
Urkan Rus. Fed. 90 B1
Urkan r. Rus. Fed. 90 B1
Urla Turkey 69 L5
Urlingford Ireland 61 E5
Urluk Rus. Fed. 95 F1
Urmā aş Şughrá Syria 107 C1
Urmai China 99 D7
Urmia Iran 110 B2
Urmia, Lake salt l. Iran 110 B2
Urmston Road sea chan. H.K. China 97 [inset]
Uromi Nigeria 120 D4
Uroševac Kosovo see Ferizaj
Urosozero Rus. Fed. 52 G3
Üroteppa Tajik. 111 H2
Urru Co salt l. China 99 D7
Urt Mongolia see Gurvantes
Urt Moron China 99 F5
Urt Moron r. China 94 C4
Uruáchic Mex. 166 C3
Uruaçu Brazil 179 A1
Uruana Brazil 179 A1
Uruapan Baja California Mex. 157 D7
Uruapan Michoacán Mex. 168 D5
Urubamba r. Peru 176 D6
Urucara Brazil 177 G4
Urucu r. Brazil 176 F4
Uruçuca Brazil 179 D1
Uruçuí Brazil 177 J5
Uruçuí, Serra do hills Brazil 177 I5
Urucuia Brazil 179 B2
Urucurituba Brazil 177 G4
Urugi Japan 92 D3
Uruguai r. Arg./Uruguay see Uruguay
Uruguaiana Brazil 178 E3
Uruguay r. Arg./Uruguay 178 E4
also known as Uruguai
Uruguay country S. America 178 E4
Uruhe China 90 B2
Urukthapel i. Palau 82 [inset]
Urumchi China see Ürümqi
Ürümqi China 98 D4
Urundi country Africa see Burundi
Urup, Ostrov i. Rus. Fed. 89 S3
Uru Pass China/Kyrg. 98 B4
Urusha Rus. Fed. 90 A1
Urutaí Brazil 179 A2
Uruzgān Afgh. 111 G3
Uryupino Rus. Fed. 89 M2
Uryupinsk Rus. Fed. 53 I6
Ürzhar Kazakh. see Urdzhar
Urzhum Rus. Fed. 52 K4
Urziceni Romania 69 L2
Usa Japan 91 C6
Usa r. Rus. Fed. 52 M2
Uşak Turkey 69 M5
Usakos Namibia 124 B1
Usarp Mountains Antarctica 188 H2
Usborne, Mount hill Falkland Is 178 E8
Ushakova, Ostrov i. Rus. Fed. 76 I1
Ushanovo Kazakh. 98 C2
Ushant i. France see Ouessant, Île d'
Üsharal Kazakh. see Ucharal
Ush-Bel'dir Rus. Fed. 88 H2
Ushibori Japan 93 G3
Ushiku Japan 93 G2
Ushimawashi-yama mt. Japan 92 B5
Ushkaniy Kryazh mts Rus. Fed. 148 B2
Ushtobe Kazakh. 102 E2
Ush-Tyube Kazakh. see Ushtobe
Ushuaia Arg. 178 C8
Ushumun Rus. Fed. 90 B1
Usingen Germany 63 I4
Usinsk Rus. Fed. 51 R2
Usk U.K. 59 E7
Usk r. U.K. 59 E7
Uskhodni Belarus 55 O10
Uskoplje Bos.-Herz. see Gornji Vakuf
Üsküdar Turkey 69 M4
Uslar Germany 63 J3
Usman' Rus. Fed. 53 H5
Usmanabad India see Osmanabad
Usmas ezers l. Latvia 55 M8
Usogorsk Rus. Fed. 52 K3
Usol'ye-Sibirskoye Rus. Fed. 88 I2
Uspenskoye Kazakh. 98 A2
Ussel France 66 F4
Ussuri r. China/Rus. Fed. 90 D2
Ussuriysk Rus. Fed. 90 C4
Ust'-Abakanskoye Rus. Fed. see Abakan
Usta Muhammad Pak. 111 H4
Ust'-Balyk Rus. Fed. see Nefteyugansk
Ust'-Donetskiy Rus. Fed. 53 I7
Ust'-Dzheguta Rus. Fed. 113 F1
Ust'-Dzhegutinskaya Rus. Fed. see Ust'-Dzheguta
Ustica, Isola di i. Sicily Italy 68 E5
Ust'-Ilimsk Rus. Fed. 77 L4
Ust'-Ilimskoye Vodokhranilishche resr Rus. Fed. 77 L4
Ust'-Ilya Rus. Fed. 95 H1
Ust'-Ilych Rus. Fed. 51 R3
Ústí nad Labem Czech Rep. 57 O5
Ustinov Rus. Fed. see Izhevsk
Üstirt plat. Kazakh./Uzbek. see Ustyurt Plateau
Ustka Poland 57 P3
Ust'-Kamchatsk Rus. Fed. 77 R4
Ust'-Kamenogorsk Kazakh. 102 F2
Ust'-Kan Rus. Fed. 98 D2
Ust'-Koksa Rus. Fed. 98 D2
Ust'-Kulom Rus. Fed. 52 L3
Ust'-Kut Rus. Fed. 77 L4
Ust'-Kuyga Rus. Fed. 77 O2
Ust'-Labinsk Rus. Fed. 113 E1
Ust'-Labinskaya Rus. Fed. see Ust'-Labinsk
Ust'-Lyzha Rus. Fed. 52 M2
Ust'-Maya Rus. Fed. 77 O3
Ust'-Nera Rus. Fed. 77 P3
Ust'-Ocheya Rus. Fed. 52 K3
Ust'-Olenek Rus. Fed. 77 M2
Ust'-Omchug Rus. Fed. 77 P3
Ust'-Ordynskiy Rus. Fed. 88 I2
Ust'-Penzhino Rus. Fed. see Kamenskoye
Ust'-Port Rus. Fed. 76 J3
Ustrem Rus. Fed. 51 T3
Ust'-Tsil'ma Rus. Fed. 52 L2
Ust'-Uda Rus. Fed. 88 I2
Ust'-Ulagan Rus. Fed. 98 D2
Ust'-Umalta (abandoned) Rus. Fed. 90 D2
Ust'-Undurga Rus. Fed. 89 L2
Ust'-Ura Rus. Fed. 52 J3
Ust'-Urgal Rus. Fed. 90 D2
Ust'-Usa Rus. Fed. 52 M2
Ust'-Vayen'ga Rus. Fed. 52 I3
Ust'-Voya Rus. Fed. 51 R3
Ust'-Vyyskaya Rus. Fed. 52 J3
Ust'ya r. Rus. Fed. 52 I3
Ust'ye Rus. Fed. 52 H4
Ustyurt, Plato plat. Kazakh./Uzbek. see Ustyurt Plateau
Ustyurt Plateau Kazakh./Uzbek. 100 E2
Ustyurt Platosi plat. Kazakh./Uzbek. see Ustyurt Plateau
Ustyuzhna Rus. Fed. 52 H4
Usu China 98 D3
Usu i. Indon. 83 B5
Usuda Japan 93 E2
Usulután El Salvador 166 [inset] H6
Usumacinta r. Guat./Mex. 167 G5
Usumbura Burundi see Bujumbura
Usun Apau, Dataran Tinggi plat. Malaysia 85 F2
Usvyaty Rus. Fed. 52 F5
Utah state U.S.A. 156 F5
Utah Lake UT U.S.A. 159 H1
Utajärvi Fin. 54 O4
Utano Japan 92 B4
Utashinai Rus. Fed. see Yuzhno-Kuril'sk
Utata Rus. Fed. 94 E1
'Utaybah, Buḥayrat al imp. l. Syria 107 C3
Utena Lith. 55 N9
Uterlai India 104 B4
Uthai Thani Thai. 86 C4
Uthal Pak. 111 G5
'Uthmānīyah Syria 107 C2
Utiariti Brazil 177 G6
Utica NY U.S.A. 165 H2
Utica OH U.S.A. 164 D3
Utiel Spain 67 F4
Utikuma Lake Canada 150 H4
Utila Hond. 166 [inset] I5
Utlwanang S. Africa 125 G4
Utopia AK U.S.A. 148 I2
Utrecht Neth. 62 F2
Utrecht S. Africa 125 J4
Utrera Spain 67 D5
Utsjoki Fin. 54 O2
Utsugi-dake mt. Japan 93 D3
Utsunomiya Japan 93 F2
Utta Rus. Fed. 53 J7
Uttaradit Thai. 86 C3
Uttarakhand state India see Uttaranchal
Uttaranchal state India 104 D3
Uttarkashi India 104 D3
Uttar Kashi India see Uttarkashi
Uttar Pradesh state India 104 D4
Uttoxeter U.K. 59 F6
Uttranchal state India see Uttaranchal
Utu China see Miao'ergou
Utubulak China 98 D3
Utukok r. AK U.S.A. 148 G1
Utupua i. Solomon Is 133 G3
Uummannaq Greenland see Dundas
Uummannaq Fjord inlet Greenland 189 J2
Uummannarsuaq c. Greenland see Farewell, Cape
Uurainen Fin. 54 N5
Üüreg Nuur salt l. Mongolia 94 B1
Üür Gol r. Mongolia 94 E1
Uusikaarlepyy Fin. see Nykarleby
Uusikaupunki Fin. 55 L6
Uutapi Namibia 123 B5
Uva Rus. Fed. 52 L4
Uvalde TX U.S.A. 161 D6
Uval Karabaur hills Kazakh./Uzbek. 113 I2
Uval Muzbel' hills Kazakh. 113 I2
Uvarovo Rus. Fed. 53 I6
Uvéa atoll New Caledonia see Ouvéa
Uvinza Tanz. 123 D4
Uvs prov. Mongolia 94 C1
Uvs Nuur salt l. Mongolia 94 C1
Uwajima Japan 91 D6
'Uwayrid, Ḥarrat al lava field Saudi Arabia 108 E4
Uwaysiṭ well Saudi Arabia 107 D4
Uweinat, Jebel mt. Sudan 108 C5
Uwi i. Indon. 84 D2
Uxbridge Canada 164 F1

Uxbridge U.K. **59** G7
Uxin Ju China **95** G4
Uxin Qi China *see* **Dabqig**
Uxmal *tourist site* Mex. **167** H4
Uxxaktal China **98** D4
Uyak *AK* U.S.A. **148** I4
Uyaly Kazakh. **102** B3
Uyanga Mongolia **94** E2
Uyar Rus. Fed. **88** G1
Üydzin Mongolia *see* **Manlay**
Uyo Nigeria **120** D4
Üyönch Mongolia **94** C2
Üyönch Gol *r.* China **94** B2
Uyu Chaung *r.* Myanmar **86** A1
Uyuni Bol. **176** E8
Uyuni, Salar de *salt flat* Bol. **176** E8
Uza *r.* Rus. Fed. **53** J5
Uzbekistan *country* Asia **102** B3
Ŭzbekiston *country* Asia *see* **Uzbekistan**
Uzbekskaya S.S.R. *country* Asia *see* **Uzbekistan**
Uzbek S.S.R. *country* Asia *see* **Uzbekistan**
Uzboy Azer. **113** H3
Uzboý Turkm. **110** D2
Uzen' Kazakh. *see* **Kyzylsay**
Uzhgorod Ukr. *see* **Uzhhorod**
Uzhhorod Ukr. **53** D6
Užhorod Ukr. *see* **Uzhhorod**
Užice Serbia **69** H3
Uzlovaya Rus. Fed. **53** H5
Üzöngü Toosu *mt.* China/Kyrg. **98** B4
Üzümlü Turkey **69** M6
Uzun Uzbek. **111** H2
Uzunbulak China **98** D3
Uzun Bulak *spring* China **98** E4
Uzunköprü Turkey **69** L4
Uzynagash *Almatinskaya Oblast'* Kazakh. **98** B4
Uzynagash *Almatinskaya Oblast'* Kazakh. **98** B4
Uzynkair Kazakh. **102** B3

V

Vaaf Atoll Maldives *see* **Felidhu Atoll**
Vaajakoski Fin. **54** N5
Vaal *r.* S. Africa **125** F5
Vaala Fin. **54** O4
Vaalbos National Park S. Africa **124** G5
Vaal Dam S. Africa **125** I4
Vaalwater S. Africa **125** I3
Vaasa Fin. **54** L5
Vaavu Atoll Maldives *see* **Felidhu Atoll**
Vác Hungary **57** Q7
Vacaria Brazil **179** A5
Vacaria, Campo da *plain* Brazil **179** A5
Vacaville *CA* U.S.A. **158** C2
Vachon *r.* Canada **153** H1
Vad Rus. Fed. **52** J5
Vad *r.* Rus. Fed. **53** I5
Vada India **106** B2
Vadakara India **106** B4
Vadla Norway **55** E7
Vadodara India **104** C5
Vadsø Norway **54** P1

▶**Vaduz** Liechtenstein **66** I3
Capital of Liechtenstein.

Værøy *i.* Norway **54** H3
Vaga *r.* Rus. Fed. **52** I3
Vågåmo Norway **55** F6
Vaganski Vrh *mt.* Croatia **68** F2
Vágar *i.* Faroe Is **54** [inset 2]
Vägsele Sweden **54** K4
Vágur Faroe Is **54** [inset 2]
Váh *r.* Slovakia **57** Q7
Vähäkyrö Fin. **54** M5

▶**Vaiaku** Tuvalu **133** H2
Capital of Tuvalu, on Funafuti atoll.

Vaida Estonia **55** N7
Vaiden *MS* U.S.A. **161** F5
Vail *CO* U.S.A. **154** F4
Vailly-sur-Aisne France **62** D5
Vaitupu *i.* Tuvalu **133** H2
Vajrakarur India *see* **Kanur**
Vakhsh Tajik. **111** H2
Vakhsh *r.* Tajik. **111** H2
Vakhstroy Tajik. *see* **Vakhsh**
Vakīlābād Iran **110** E4
Valbo Sweden **55** J6
Valcheta Arg. **178** C6
Valdai Hills Rus. Fed. *see* **Valdayskaya Vozvyshennost'**
Valday Rus. Fed. **52** G4
Valdayskaya Vozvyshennost' *hills* Rus. Fed. **52** G4
Valdecañas, Embalse de *resr* Spain **67** D4
Valdemārpils Latvia **55** M8
Valdemarsvik Sweden **55** J7
Valdepeñas Spain **67** E4
Val-de-Reuil France **62** B5
Valdés, Península *pen.* Arg. **178** D6
Valdez *AK* U.S.A. **149** K3
Valdivia Chile **178** B5
Val-d'Or Canada **152** F4
Valdosta *GA* U.S.A. **163** D6
Valdres *valley* Norway **55** F6
Vale Georgia **113** F2
Vale *OR* U.S.A. **156** D3
Valemount Canada **150** G4
Valença Brazil **179** D1
Valence France **66** G4
Valencia Spain **67** F4
València Spain *see* **Valencia**
Valencia *reg.* Spain **67** F4
Valencia Venez. **176** E1
Valencia, Golfo de *g.* Spain **67** G4
Valencia de Don Juan Spain **67** D2
Valencia Island Ireland **61** B6
Valenciennes France **62** D4
Valensole, Plateau de France **66** H5
Valentia Spain *see* **Valencia**
Valentin Rus. Fed. **90** D4
Valentine *NE* U.S.A. **160** C3
Valentine *TX* U.S.A. **166** D2
Valenzuela *Luzon* Phil. **82** C3
Våler Norway **55** G6
Valera Venez. **176** D2
Vale Verde Brazil **179** D2
Val Grande, Parco Nazionale della *nat. park* Italy **68** C1
Valjevo Serbia **69** H2
Valka Latvia **55** O8
Valkeakoski Fin. **55** N6
Valkenswaard Neth. **62** F3
Valky Ukr. **53** G6
Valkyrie Dome *ice feature* Antarctica **188** D1
Valladolid Mex. **167** H4
Valladolid Spain **67** D3
Vallard, Lac *l.* Canada **153** H3
Valle Norway **55** E7
Vallecillos Mex. **167** F3
Vallecito Reservoir *CO* U.S.A. **159** J3
Valle de Banderas Mex. **166** D4
Valle de la Pascua Venez. **176** E2
Valle de Olivos Mex. **166** D3
Valle de Santiago Mex. **167** E4
Valle de Zaragoza Mex. **166** D3
Valledupar Col. **176** D1
Vallée-Jonction Canada **153** H5
Valle Fértil, Sierra de *mts* Arg. **178** C4
Valle Grande Bol. **176** F7
Valle Hermoso Mex. **167** F3
Vallejo *CA* U.S.A. **158** B2
Valle Nacional Mex. **167** F5
Vallenar Chile **178** B3

▶**Valletta** Malta **68** F7
Capital of Malta.

Valley *r.* Canada **151** L5
Valley U.K. **58** C5
Valley City *ND* U.S.A. **160** D2
Valley Head *hd Luzon* Phil. **82** C2
Valleyview Canada **150** G4
Valls Spain **67** G3
Val Marie Canada **151** J5
Valmiera Latvia **55** N8
Valmy *NV* U.S.A. **158** E1
Valnera *mt.* Spain **67** E2
Valognes France **59** F9
Valona Albania *see* **Vlorë**
Valozhyn Belarus **55** O9
Val-Paradis Canada **152** F4
Valparai India **106** C4
Valparaíso Chile **178** B4
Valparaíso Mex. **166** E4
Valparaiso *FL* U.S.A. **167** I2
Valparaiso *IN* U.S.A. **164** B3
Valpoi India **106** B3
Valréas France **66** G4
Vals, Tanjung *c.* Indon. **81** J8
Valsad India **106** B1
Valspan S. Africa **124** G4
Valtimo Fin. **54** P5
Valuyevka Rus. Fed. **53** I7
Valuyki Rus. Fed. **53** H6
Vammala Fin. **55** M6
Van Turkey **113** F3
Van, Lake *salt l.* Turkey **113** F3
Vanadzor Armenia **113** G2
Van Buren *AR* U.S.A. **161** E5
Van Buren *MO* U.S.A. **161** F4
Van Buren *OH* U.S.A. *see* **Kettering**
Vanceburg *KY* U.S.A. **164** D4
Vanch Tajik. *see* **Vanj**
Vancleve *KY* U.S.A. **164** D5
Vancouver Canada **150** F5
Vancouver *WA* U.S.A. **156** C3
Vancouver, Cape *AK* U.S.A. **148** F3
Vancouver, Mount Canada/U.S.A. **149** M3
Vancouver Island Canada **150** E5
Vanda Fin. *see* **Vantaa**
Vandalia *IL* U.S.A. **160** F4
Vandalia *OH* U.S.A. **164** C4
Vandekerckhove Lake Canada **151** K3
Vanderbijlpark S. Africa **125** H4
Vanderbilt *MI* U.S.A. **164** C1
Vandergrift *PA* U.S.A. **164** F3
Vanderhoof Canada **150** E4
Vanderkloof Dam *resr* S. Africa **124** G6
Vanderlin Island Australia **136** B2
Vanderwagen *NM* U.S.A. **159** I4
Van Diemen, Cape *N.T.* Australia **134** E2
Van Diemen, Cape *Qld* Australia **136** B3
Van Diemen Gulf Australia **134** F2
Van Diemen's Land *state* Australia *see* **Tasmania**
Vändra Estonia **55** N7
Väner, Lake Sweden *see* **Vänern**

▶**Vänern** *l.* Sweden **55** H7
4th largest lake in Europe.

Vänersborg Sweden **55** H7
Vangaindrano Madag. **123** E6
Van Gia Vietnam **87** E4
Van Gölü *salt l.* Turkey *see* **Van, Lake**
Van Horn *TX* U.S.A. **157** G7
Vanikoro Islands Solomon Is **133** G3
Vanimo P.N.G. **81** K7
Vanino Rus. Fed. **90** F2
Vanivilasa Sagara *resr* India **106** C3
Vaniyambadi India **106** C3
Vanj Tajik. **111** H2
Vankarem Rus. Fed. **148** D2
Vankarem *r.* Rus. Fed. **148** C2
Vankarem, Laguna *lag.* Rus. Fed. **148** D2
Vännäs Sweden **54** K5
Vannes France **66** C3
Vannes, Lac *l.* Canada **153** I3
Vannovka Kazakh. *see* **Turar Ryskulov**
Vannøya *i.* Norway **54** K1
Van Rees, Pegunungan *mts* Indon. **81** J7
Vanrhynsdorp S. Africa **124** D6
Vansant *VA* U.S.A. **164** D5
Vansbro Sweden **55** I6
Vansittart Island Canada **147** J3
Van Starkenborgh Kanaal *canal* Neth. **62** G1
Vantaa Fin. **55** N6
Van Truer Tableland *reg.* Australia **135** C6
Vanua Lava *i.* Vanuatu **133** G3
Vanua Levu *i.* Fiji **133** H3
Vanuatu *country* S. Pacific Ocean **133** G3
Van Wert *OH* U.S.A. **164** C3
Vanwyksvlei S. Africa **124** E6
Vanwyksvlei *l.* S. Africa **124** E6
Văn Yên Vietnam **86** D2
Van Zylsrus S. Africa **124** F4
Varadero Cuba **163** D8
Varahi India **104** B5
Varakļāni Latvia **55** O8
Varalé Côte d'Ivoire **120** C4
Varāmīn Iran **110** C3
Varanasi India **105** E4
Varandey Rus. Fed. **52** M1
Varangerfjorden *sea chan.* Norway **54** P1
Varangerhalvøya *pen.* Norway **54** P1
Varaždin Croatia **68** G1
Varberg Sweden **55** H8
Vardar *r.* Macedonia **69** J4
Varde Denmark **55** F9
Vardenis Armenia **113** G2
Vardø Norway **54** Q1
Varel Germany **63** I1
Varėna Lith. **55** N9
Varese Italy **68** C2
Varfolomeyevka Rus. Fed. **90** D3
Vårgårda Sweden **55** H7
Varginha Brazil **179** B3
Varik Neth. **62** F3
Varillas Chile **178** B2
Varkana Iran *see* **Gorgān**
Varkaus Fin. **54** O5
Varna Bulg. **69** L3
Värnamo Sweden **55** I8
Värnäs Sweden **55** H6
Varnavino Rus. Fed. **52** J4
Várnjárg *pen.* Norway *see* **Varangerhalvøya**
Varpaisjärvi Fin. **54** O5
Várpalota Hungary **68** H1
Varsh, Ozero *l.* Rus. Fed. **52** J2
Varto Turkey **113** F3
Várzea da Palma Brazil **179** B2
Vasa Fin. *see* **Vaasa**
Vasai India **106** B2
Vashka *r.* Rus. Fed. **52** J2
Vasht Iran *see* **Khāsh**
Vasilkov Ukr. *see* **Vasyl'kiv**
Vasknarva Estonia **55** O7
Vaslui Romania **69** L1
Vassar *MI* U.S.A. **164** D2
Vas-Soproni-síkság *hills* Hungary **68** G1
Vastan Turkey *see* **Gevaş**
Västerås Sweden **55** J7
Västerdalälven *r.* Sweden **55** I6
Västerfjäll Sweden **54** J3
Västerhaninge Sweden **55** K7
Västervik Sweden **55** J8
Vasto Italy **68** F3
Vasyl'kiv Ukr. **53** F6
Vatan France **66** E3
Vaté *i.* Vanuatu *see* **Éfaté**
Vatersay *i.* U.K. **60** B4
Vathar India **106** B2
Vathí Greece *see* **Vathy**
Vathy Greece **69** L6

▶**Vatican City** Europe **68** E4
Independent papal state, the smallest country in the world.

Vaticano, Città del Europe *see* **Vatican City**
Vatnajökull *ice cap* Iceland **54** [inset 1]
Vatoa *i.* Fiji **133** I3
Vatra Dornei Romania **69** K1
Vätter, Lake Sweden *see* **Vättern**
Vättern *l.* Sweden **55** I7
Vaughn *NM* U.S.A. **157** G6
Vaupés *r.* Col. **176** E3
Vauquelin *r.* Canada **152** F3
Vauvert France **66** G5
Vauxhall Canada **151** H5
Vavatenina Madag. **123** E5
Vava'u Group *is* Tonga **133** I3
Vavitao *i.* Fr. Polynesia *see* **Raivavae**
Vavoua Côte d'Ivoire **120** C4
Vavozh Rus. Fed. **52** K4
Vavuniya Sri Lanka **106** D4
Vawkavysk Belarus **55** N10
Växjö Sweden **55** I8
Vay, Đao *i.* Vietnam **87** C5
Vayenga Rus. Fed. *see* **Severomorsk**
Vazante Brazil **179** B2
Vazáš Sweden *see* **Vittangi**
Veaikevárri Sweden *see* **Svappavaara**
Veal Vêng Cambodia **87** C4
Vecht *r.* Neth. **62** G2
also known as Vechte (Germany)
Vechta Germany **63** I2
Vechte *r.* Germany **63** G2
also known as Vecht (Netherlands)
Veckerhagen (Reinhardshagen) Germany **63** J3
Vedaranniyam India **106** C4
Vedasandur India **106** C4
Veddige Sweden **55** H8
Vedea *r.* Romania **69** K3
Veedersburg *IN* U.S.A. **164** B3
Veendam Neth. **62** G1
Veenendaal Neth. **62** F2
Vega *i.* Norway **54** G4
Vega *TX* U.S.A. **161** C5
Vega de Alatorre Mex. **167** F4
Vega Point *pt AK* U.S.A. **148** [inset] B6
Vegreville Canada **151** H4
Vehari Pak. **111** I4
Vehkalahti Fin. **55** O6
Vehowa Pak. **111** H4
Veinticinco de Mayo *Buenos Aires* Arg. *see* **25 de Mayo**
Veinticinco de Mayo *La Pampa* Arg. *see* **25 de Mayo**
Veirwaro Pak. **111** H5
Veitshöchheim Germany **63** J5
Vejle Denmark **55** F9
Vekil'bazar Turkm. *see* **Wekilbazar**
Velardena Mex. **166** E3
Velas, Cabo *c.* Costa Rica **166** [inset] I7
Velbert Germany **62** H3
Velbŭzhdki Prokhod *pass* Bulg./Macedonia **69** J3
Velddrif S. Africa **124** D7
Velebit *mts* Croatia **68** F2
Velen Germany **62** G3
Velenje Slovenia **68** F1
Veles Macedonia **69** I4
Vélez-Málaga Spain **67** D5
Vélez-Rubio Spain **67** E5
Velhas *r.* Brazil **179** B2
Velibaba Turkey *see* **Aras**
Velika Gorica Croatia **68** G2
Velika Plana Serbia **69** I2
Velikaya *r.* Rus. Fed. **52** K4
Velikaya *r.* Rus. Fed. **55** P8
Velikaya *r.* Rus. Fed. **77** S3
Velikaya Kema Rus. Fed. **90** E3
Veliki Preslav Bulg. **69** L3
Velikiye Luki Rus. Fed. **52** F4
Velikiy Novgorod Rus. Fed. **52** F4
Velikiy Ustyug Rus. Fed. **52** J3
Velikonda Range *hills* India **106** C3
Veliko Tŭrnovo Bulg. **69** K3
Velikoye Rus. Fed. **52** H4
Velikoye, Ozero *l.* Rus. Fed. **53** I5
Veli Lošinj Croatia **68** F2
Velizh Rus. Fed. **52** F5
Vella Lavella *i.* Solomon Is **133** F2
Vellar *r.* India **106** C4
Vellberg Germany **63** J5
Vellmar Germany **63** J3
Vellore India **106** C3
Velpke Germany **63** K2
Vel'sk Rus. Fed. **52** I3
Velsuna Italy *see* **Orvieto**
Velten Germany **63** N2
Veluwezoom, Nationaal Park *nat. park* Neth. **62** F2
Velykyy Tokmak Ukr. *see* **Tokmak**
Vel'yu *r.* Rus. Fed. **52** L3
Vemalwada India **106** C2
Vema Seamount *sea feature* S. Atlantic Ocean **184** I8
Vema Trench *sea feature* Indian Ocean **185** M6
Vempalle India **106** C3
Venado, Isla del *i.* Nicaragua **166** [inset] J7
Venado Tuerto Arg. **178** D4
Venafro Italy **68** F4
Venceslau Bráz Brazil **179** A3
Vendinga Rus. Fed. **52** J3
Vendôme France **66** E3
Venegas Mex. **161** C8
Venetia Italy *see* **Venice**
Venetie *AK* U.S.A. **149** K2
Venetie Landing *AK* U.S.A. **149** K2
Venev Rus. Fed. **53** H5
Venezia Italy *see* **Venice**
Venezia, Golfo di *g.* Europe *see* **Venice, Gulf of**

▶**Venezuela** *country* S. America **176** E2
4th most populous country in South America.

Venezuela, Golfo de *g.* Venez. **176** D1
Venezuelan Basin *sea feature* S. Atlantic Ocean **184** D4
Vengurla India **106** B3
Veniaminof Volcano *AK* U.S.A. **146** C4
Venice Italy **68** E2
Venice *FL* U.S.A. **163** D7
Venice *LA* U.S.A. **167** H2
Venice, Gulf of Europe **68** E2
Vénissieux France **66** G4
Venkatapalem India **106** D2
Venkatapuram India **106** D2
Venlo Neth. **62** G3
Vennesla Norway **55** E7
Venray Neth. **62** F3
Venta *r.* Latvia/Lith. **55** M8
Venta Lith. **55** M8
Ventersburg S. Africa **125** H5
Ventersdorp S. Africa **125** H4
Venterstad S. Africa **125** G6
Ventnor U.K. **59** F8
Ventotene, Isola *i.* Italy **68** E4
Ventoux, Mont *mt.* France **66** G4
Ventspils Latvia **55** L8
Ventura *CA* U.S.A. **158** D4
Venus Bay Australia **138** B7
Venustiano Carranza Mex. **161** C7
Venustiano Carranza, Presa *resr* Mex. **167** E3
Vera Arg. **178** D3
Vera Spain **67** F5
Vera Cruz Brazil **179** A3
Vera Cruz Mex. *see* **Veracruz**
Veracruz Mex. **168** E5
Veracruz *state* Mex. **167** F4
Veraval India **104** B5
Verbania Italy **68** C2
Vercelli Italy **68** C2
Vercors *reg.* France **66** G4
Verdalsøra Norway **54** G5
Verde *r. Goiás* Brazil **179** A2
Verde *r. Goiás/Minas Gerais* Brazil **179** B2
Verde *r. Minas Gerais* Brazil **179** A2
Verde *r. Minas Gerais* Brazil **179** A2
Verde *r.* Mex. **166** D3
Verde *r. AZ* U.S.A. **159** H5
Verde Island Passage Phil. **82** C3
Verden (Aller) Germany **63** J2
Verde Pequeno *r.* Brazil **179** C1
Verdi *NV* U.S.A. **158** D2
Verdon *r.* France **66** G5
Verdun France **62** F5
Vereeniging S. Africa **125** H4
Vereshchagino Rus. Fed. **51** Q4
Vergennes *VT* U.S.A. **165** I1
Véria Greece *see* **Veroia**
Verín Spain **67** C3
Veríssimo Brazil **179** A2
Verkhneberezovskiy Kazakh. **98** C2
Verkhneimbatsk Rus. Fed. **76** J3
Verkhnekolvinsk Rus. Fed. **52** M2
Verkhnespasskoye Rus. Fed. **52** J4
Verkhnetulomskiy Rus. Fed. **54** Q2
Verkhnetulomskoye Vodokhranilishche *resr.* Rus. Fed. **54** Q2
Verkhnevilyuysk Rus. Fed. **77** N3
Verkhneye Kuyto, Ozero *l.* Rus. Fed. **54** Q4
Verkhnezeysk Rus. Fed. **89** N2
Verkhniy Shergol'dzhin Rus. Fed. **95** G1
Verkhniy Ul'khun Rus. Fed. **95** H1
Verkhniy Vyalozerskiy Rus. Fed. **52** G2
Verkhnyaya Khava Rus. Fed. **53** H6
Verkhnyaya Salda Rus. Fed. **51** S4
Verkhnyaya Tunguska *r.* Rus. Fed. *see* **Angara**
Verkhnyaya Tura Rus. Fed. **51** R4
Verkhoshizhem'ye Rus. Fed. **52** K4
Verkhovazh'ye Rus. Fed. **52** I3
Verkhov'ye Rus. Fed. **53** H5
Verkhoyansk Rus. Fed. **77** O3
Verkhoyanskiy Khrebet *mts* Rus. Fed. **77** N2
Verkhuba Kazakh. **98** C2
Vermand France **62** D5
Vermelho *r.* Brazil **179** A1
Vermilion Canada **151** I4
Vermilion Bay *LA* U.S.A. **161** F6
Vermilion Cliffs *AZ* U.S.A. **159** G3
Vermilion Cliffs *UT* U.S.A. **159** G3
Vermilion Cliffs National Monument *nat. park AZ* U.S.A. **159** H3
Vermilion Lake *MN* U.S.A. **160** E2
Vermillion *SD* U.S.A. **160** D3
Vermillion Bay Canada **151** M5
Vermont *state* U.S.A. **165** I1
Vernadsky *research station* Antarctica **188** L2
Vernal *UT* U.S.A. **159** I1
Verner Canada **152** E5
Verneuk Pan *salt pan* S. Africa **124** E5
Vernon Canada **150** G5
Vernon France **62** B5
Vernon *AL* U.S.A. **161** F5
Vernon *IN* U.S.A. **164** C4
Vernon *TX* U.S.A. **161** D5
Vernon *UT* U.S.A. **159** G1
Vernon Islands Australia **134** E3
Vernoye Rus. Fed. **90** C2
Vernyy Kazakh. *see* **Almaty**
Vero Beach *FL* U.S.A. **163** D7
Veroia Greece **69** J4
Verona Italy **68** D2
Verona *VA* U.S.A. **164** F4
Versailles France **62** C6
Versailles *IN* U.S.A. **164** C4
Versailles *KY* U.S.A. **164** C4
Versailles *OH* U.S.A. **164** C3
Versec Serbia *see* **Vršac**
Versmold Germany **63** I2
Vert, Île *i.* Canada **153** H4
Vertou France **66** D3
Verulam S. Africa **125** J5
Verulamium U.K. *see* **St Albans**
Verviers Belgium **62** F4
Vervins France **62** D5
Verwood Canada **151** J5
Verzy France **62** E5
Vescovato *Corsica* France **66** I5
Vesele Ukr. **53** G7
Veselyy Rus. Fed. **53** I7
Veselyy Yar Rus. Fed. **90** D4
Veshenskaya Rus. Fed. **53** I6
Vesle *r.* France **62** D5
Veslyana *r.* Rus. Fed. **52** L3
Vesontio France *see* **Besançon**
Vesoul France **66** H3
Vessem Neth. **62** F3
Vesterålen *is* Norway **54** H2
Vesterålsfjorden *sea chan.* Norway **54** H2
Vestertana Norway **54** O1
Vestfjorddalen *valley* Norway **55** F7
Vestfjorden *sea chan.* Norway **54** H3
Véstia Brazil **179** A3
Vestmanna Faroe Is **54** [inset 2]
Vestmannaeyjar Iceland **54** [inset 1]
Vestmannaeyjar *is* Iceland **54** [inset 1]
Vestnes Norway **54** E5
Vesturhorn *hd* Iceland **54** [inset 1]
Vesuvio *vol.* Italy *see* **Vesuvius**
Vesuvius *vol.* Italy **68** F4
Ves'yegonsk Rus. Fed. **52** H4
Veszprém Hungary **68** G1
Veteli Fin. **54** M5
Veteran Canada **151** I4
Vetlanda Sweden **55** I8
Vetluga Rus. Fed. **52** J4
Vetluga *r.* Rus. Fed. **52** J4
Vetluzhskiy *Kostromskaya Oblast'* Rus. Fed. **52** J4
Vetluzhskiy *Nizhegorodskaya Oblast'* Rus. Fed. **52** J4
Vettore, Monte *mt.* Italy **68** E3
Veurne Belgium **62** C3
Vevay *IN* U.S.A. **164** C4
Vevey Switz. **66** H3
Vexin Normand *reg.* France **62** B5
Veyo *UT* U.S.A. **159** G3
Vézère *r.* France **66** E4
Vezirköprü Turkey **112** D2
Vialar Alg. *see* **Tissemsilt**
Viamao Brazil **179** A5
Viana *Espírito Santo* Brazil **179** C3
Viana *Maranhão* Brazil **177** J4
Viana do Castelo Port. **67** B3
Vianen Neth. **62** F3
Viangchan Laos *see* **Vientiane**
Viangphoukha Laos **86** C2
Viannos Greece **69** K7
Vianópolis Brazil **179** A2
Viareggio Italy **68** D3
Viborg Denmark **55** F8
Viborg Rus. Fed. *see* **Vyborg**
Vibo Valentia Italy **68** G5
Vic Spain **67** H3
Vicam Mex. **166** C3
Vicecomodoro Marambio *research station* Antarctica *see* **Marambio**
Vicente, Point *CA* U.S.A. **158** D5
Vicente Guerrero Mex. **166** A2
Vicenza Italy **68** D2
Vich Spain *see* **Vic**
Vichada *r.* Col. **176** E3
Vichadero Uruguay **178** F4
Vichy France **66** F3
Vicksburg *AZ* U.S.A. **159** G5
Vicksburg *MS* U.S.A. **161** F5
Viçosa Brazil **179** C3
Victor, Mount Antarctica **188** D2
Victor Harbor Australia **137** B7
Victoria Arg. **178** D4
Victoria *r.* Australia **134** E3
Victoria *state* Australia **138** B6

▶**Victoria** Canada **150** F5
Capital of British Columbia.

Victoria Chile **178** B5
Victoria Malaysia *see* **Labuan**
Victoria Malta **68** F6
Victoria *Luzon* Phil. **82** C3

▶**Victoria** Seychelles **185** L6
Capital of the Seychelles.

Victoria *TX* U.S.A. **161** D6
Victoria *VA* U.S.A. **165** F5
Victoria *prov.* Zimbabwe *see* **Masvingo**

▶**Victoria, Lake** Africa **122** D4
Largest lake in Africa and 3rd in the world.

Victoria, Lake Australia **137** C7
Victoria, Mount Fiji *see* **Tomanivi**
Victoria, Mount Myanmar **86** A2
Victoria, Mount P.N.G. **81** L8
Victoria and Albert Mountains Canada **147** K2
Victoria Falls Zambia/Zimbabwe **123** C5
Victoria Harbour *sea chan.* H.K. China *see* **Hong Kong Harbour**

▶**Victoria Island** Canada **146** H2
3rd largest island in North America and 9th in the world.

Victoria Land *coastal area* Antarctica **188** H2
Victoria Peak Belize **168** G5
Victoria Peak *hill* H.K. China **97** [inset]
Victoria Range *mts* N.Z. **139** D6
Victoria River Downs Australia **134** E4
Victoriaville Canada **153** H5
Victoria West S. Africa **124** F6
Victorica Arg. **178** C5
Víctor Rosales Mex. **166** E4
Victorville *CA* U.S.A. **158** E4
Victory Downs Australia **135** F6
Vidalia *LA* U.S.A. **161** F6
Vidal Junction *CA* U.S.A. **159** F4
Videle Romania **69** K2
Vidisha India **104** D5
Vidlin U.K. **60** [inset]
Vidlitsa Rus. Fed. **52** G3
Viechtach Germany **63** M5
Viedma Arg. **178** D6
Viedma, Lago *l.* Arg. **178** B7
Viejo, Cerro *mt.* Mex. **166** B2
Vielank Germany **63** L1
Vielsalm Belgium **62** F4
Vienenburg Germany **63** K3

▶**Vienna** Austria **57** P6
Capital of Austria.

Vienna *MO* U.S.A. **160** F4
Vienna *WV* U.S.A. **164** E4
Vienne France **66** G4
Vienne *r.* France **66** E3

▶**Vientiane** Laos **86** C3
Capital of Laos.

Vieques *i.* Puerto Rico **169** K5
Vieremä Fin. **54** O5
Viersen Germany **62** G3
Vierzon France **66** F3
Viesca Mex. **166** E3
Viesīte Latvia **55** N8
Vieste Italy **68** G4
Vietas Sweden **54** K3
Viêt Nam *country* Asia *see* **Vietnam**
Vietnam *country* Asia **86** D3
Viêt Quang Vietnam **86** D2
Viêt Tri Vietnam **86** D2
Vieux Comptoir, Lac du *l.* Canada **152** F3
Vieux-Fort Canada **153** K4
Vieux Poste, Pointe du *pt* Canada **153** J4
Vigan *Luzon* Phil. **82** C2
Vigevano Italy **68** C2
Vigia Brazil **177** I4
Vigía Chico Mex. **167** I5
Vignacourt France **62** C4
Vignemale *mt.* France **64** D3
Vignola Italy **68** D2
Vigo Spain **67** B2
Vihanti Fin. **54** N4
Vihti Fin. **55** N6
Viipuri Rus. Fed. *see* **Vyborg**
Viitasaari Fin. **54** N5
Vijayadurg India **106** B2
Vijayanagaram India *see* **Vizianagaram**
Vijayapati India **106** C4
Vijayawada India **106** D2
Vík Iceland **54** [inset 1]
Vikajärvi Fin. **54** O3
Vikeke East Timor *see* **Viqueque**
Viking Canada **151** I4
Vikna *i.* Norway **54** G4
Vikøyri Norway **55** E6
Vila Vanuatu *see* **Port Vila**
Vila Alferes Chamusca Moz. *see* **Guija**
Vila Bittencourt Brazil **176** E4
Vila Bugaço Angola *see* **Camanongue**
Vila Cabral Moz. *see* **Lichinga**
Vila da Ponte Angola *see* **Kuvango**
Vila de Aljustrel Angola *see* **Cangamba**
Vila de Almoster Angola *see* **Chiange**
Vila de João Belo Moz. *see* **Xai-Xai**
Vila de María Arg. **178** D3
Vila de Trego Morais Moz. *see* **Chókwé**
Vila Fontes Moz. *see* **Caia**
Vila Franca de Xira Port. **67** B4
Vilagarcía de Arousa Spain **67** B2
Vila Gomes da Costa Moz. **125** K3
Vilalba Spain **67** C2
Vila Luísa Moz. *see* **Marracuene**
Vila Marechal Carmona Angola *see* **Uíge**
Vila Miranda Moz. *see* **Macaloge**
Vilanandro, Tanjona *pt* Madag. **123** E5
Vilanculos Moz. **125** L1
Vila Nova de Gaia Port. **67** B3
Vilanova i la Geltrú Spain **67** G3
Vila Pery Moz. *see* **Chimoio**
Vila Real Port. **67** C3
Vilar Formoso Port. **67** C3
Vila Salazar Angola *see* **N'dalatando**
Vila Salazar Zimbabwe *see* **Sango**
Vila Teixeira de Sousa Angola *see* **Luau**
Vila Velha Brazil **179** C3
Vilcabamba, Cordillera *mts* Peru **176** D6
Vil'cheka, Zemlya *i.* Rus. Fed. **76** H1
Viled' *r.* Rus. Fed. **52** J3
Vileyka Belarus *see* **Vilyeyka**
Vil'gort Rus. Fed. **52** K3
Vilhelmina Sweden **54** J4
Vilhena Brazil **176** F6
Viliya *r.* Lith. *see* **Neris**
Viljandi Estonia **55** N7
Viljoenskroon S. Africa **125** H4
Vilkaviškis Lith. **55** M9
Vilkija Lith. **55** M9
Vil'kitskogo, Proliv *strait* Rus. Fed. **77** K2
Vilkovo Ukr. *see* **Vylkove**
Villa Abecia Bol. **176** E8
Villa Ahumada Mex. **166** D2
Villa Ángela Arg. **178** D3
Villa Bella Bol. **176** E6
Villa Bens Morocco *see* **Tarfaya**
Villablino Spain **67** C2
Villacañas Spain **67** E4
Villach Austria **57** N7
Villacidro *Sardinia* Italy **68** C5
Villa Cisneros W. Sahara *see* **Ad Dakhla**
Villa Comaltitlán Mex. **167** G6
Villa Coronado Mex. **166** D3

Wanshengchang China see Wansheng
Wantage U.K. 59 F7
Wanxian Chongqing China see Wanzhou
Wanxian Chongqing China see Shahe
Wanyuan China 97 F1
Wanzai China 97 G2
Wanze Belgium 62 F4
Wanzhou China 97 F2
Wapakoneta OH U.S.A. 164 C3
Wapawekka Lake Canada 151 J4
Wapello IA U.S.A. 160 F3
Wapikaimaski Lake Canada 152 C4
Wapikopa Lake Canada 152 C3
Wapiti r. Canada 150 G4
Wapotih Buru Indon. 83 C3
Wapusk National Park Canada 151 M3
Waqên China 96 D1
Waqf aş Şawwān, Jibāl hills Jordan 107 C4
War WV U.S.A. 164 E5
Wara Japan 92 D3
Warab South Sudan 108 C8
Warangal India 106 C2
Waranga Reservoir Australia 138 B6
Waratah Bay Australia 138 B7
Warbreccan Australia 136 C5
Warburg Germany 63 J3
Warburton Australia 135 D6
Warburton watercourse Australia 137 B5
Warburton Bay Canada 151 I2
Warche r. Belgium 62 F4
Ward, Mount N.Z. 139 B6
Warden S. Africa 125 I4
Wardenburg Germany 63 I1
Wardha India 106 C1
Wardha r. India 106 C2
Ward Hill hill U.K. 60 F2
Ward Hunt, Cape P.N.G. 81 L8
Ware Canada 150 E3
Ware MA U.S.A. 165 I2
Wareham U.K. 59 E8
Waremme Belgium 62 F4
Waren Germany 63 M1
Warendorf Germany 63 H3
Warginburra Peninsula Australia 136 E4
Wargla Alg. see Ouargla
Warialda Australia 138 E2
Warin Chamrap Thai. 86 D4
Waring Mountains AK U.S.A. 148 G2
Warkum Neth. see Workum
Warkworth U.K. 58 F3
Warli China see Walêg
Warloy-Baillon France 62 C4
Warman Canada 151 J4
Warmbad Namibia 124 D5
Warmbad S. Africa 125 I3
Warmbaths S. Africa see Warmbad
Warminster U.K. 59 E7
Warminster PA U.S.A. 165 H3
Warmond Neth. 62 E2
Warm Springs NV U.S.A. 158 E2
Warm Springs VA U.S.A. 164 F4
Warmwaterberg mts S. Africa 124 E7
Warner Canada 151 H5
Warner Lakes OR U.S.A. 156 D4
Warner Mountains CA U.S.A. 156 C4
Warnes Bol. 176 F7
Warning, Mount Australia 138 F2
Waronda India 106 C2
Warora India 106 C1
Warra Australia 138 E1
Warragamba Reservoir Australia 138 E5
Warragul Australia 138 B7
Warrambool r. Australia 138 C3
Warrandirinna, Lake salt flat Australia 137 B5
Warrandyte Australia 138 B6
Warrawagine Australia 134 C5
Warrego r. Australia 138 B3
Warrego Range hills Australia 136 D5
Warren Australia 138 C3
Warren AR U.S.A. 161 E5
Warren MI U.S.A. 164 D2
Warren MN U.S.A. 160 D1
Warren OH U.S.A. 164 E3
Warren PA U.S.A. 164 F3
Warren Hastings Island Palau see Merir
Warren Island AK U.S.A. 150 C4
Warren Point pt Canada 149 N1
Warrenpoint U.K. 61 F3
Warrensburg MO U.S.A. 160 E4
Warrensburg NY U.S.A. 165 I2
Warrenton S. Africa 124 G5
Warrenton GA U.S.A. 163 D5
Warrenton MO U.S.A. 160 F4
Warrenton VA U.S.A. 165 G4
Warri Nigeria 120 D4
Warriners Creek watercourse Australia 137 B6
Warrington N.Z. 139 C7
Warrington U.K. 58 E5
Warrington FL U.S.A. 163 C6
Warrnambool Australia 137 C8
Warroad MN U.S.A. 160 E1
Warrumbungle National Park Australia 138 D3
Warsaj 'Alāqahdārī Afgh. 111 H2

▶Warsaw Poland 57 R4
Capital of Poland.

Warsaw IN U.S.A. 164 C3
Warsaw KY U.S.A. 164 C4
Warsaw MO U.S.A. 160 E4
Warsaw NY U.S.A. 165 F2
Warsaw VA U.S.A. 165 G5
Warshiikh Somalia 122 E3
Warstein Germany 63 I3
Warszawa Poland see Warsaw
Warta r. Poland 57 O4
Waru Kalimantan Indon. 85 G3
Warwick Australia 138 F2
Warwick U.K. 59 F6
Warwick RI U.S.A. 165 J3
Warzhong China 96 D2
Wasaga Beach Canada 164 E1
Wasatch Range mts UT U.S.A. 156 F5
Wasbank S. Africa 125 J5
Wasco CA U.S.A. 158 D4
Wāshayr Afgh. 111 F3
Washburn ND U.S.A. 160 C2
Washburn WI U.S.A. 160 F2
Washiga-take mt. Japan 92 C3
Washim India 106 C1

▶Washington DC U.S.A. 165 G4
Capital of the United States of America.

Washington GA U.S.A. 163 D5
Washington IA U.S.A. 160 F3
Washington IN U.S.A. 164 B4
Washington MO U.S.A. 160 F4
Washington NC U.S.A. 162 E5
Washington NJ U.S.A. 165 H3
Washington PA U.S.A. 164 E3
Washington UT U.S.A. 159 G3
Washington state U.S.A. 156 C3
Washington, Cape Antarctica 188 H2
Washington, Mount NH U.S.A. 165 J1
Washington Court House OH U.S.A. 164 D4
Washington Island WI U.S.A. 162 C2
Washington Land reg. Greenland 147 L2
Washita r. OK U.S.A. 161 D5
Washpool National Park Australia 138 F2
Washtucna WA U.S.A. 156 D3
Washuk Pak. 111 G5
Wasi India 106 B2
Wasi' Saudi Arabia 110 B5
Wasī' well Saudi Arabia 110 C6
Wasiri Maluku Indon. 83 C4
Wasisi Buru Indon. 83 C3
Waskaganish Canada 152 F4
Waskagheganish Canada see Waskaganish
Waskaiowaka Lake Canada 151 L3
Waskey, Mount AK U.S.A. 148 H4
Waspán Nicaragua 166 [inset] I6
Wassenaar Neth. 62 E2
Wasser Namibia 124 D4
Wasserkuppe hill Germany 63 J4
Wassertrüdingen Germany 63 K5
Wassuk Range mts NV U.S.A. 158 D2
Wasua P.N.G. 81 K8
Wasum P.N.G. 81 L8
Waswanipi r. Canada 152 F4
Waswanipi, Lac l. Canada 152 F4
Watam P.N.G. 81 K7
Watambayoli Sulawesi Indon. 83 B3
Watampone Sulawesi Indon. 83 B4
Watana, Mount AK U.S.A. 149 J3
Watansoppeng Sulawesi Indon. 83 A4
Watapi Lake Canada 151 I4
Watarai Japan 92 C4
Watarase-gawa r. Japan 93 F2
Watarrka National Park Australia 135 E6
Watauchi Japan 93 E2
Watenstadt-Salzgitter Germany see Salzgitter
Waterbury CT U.S.A. 165 I3
Waterbury VT U.S.A. 165 I1
Waterbury Lake Canada 151 J3
Water Cays i. Bahamas 163 E8
Waterdown Canada 164 F2
Wateree r. SC U.S.A. 163 D5
Waterfall AK U.S.A. 149 N5
Waterford Ireland 61 E5
Waterford PA U.S.A. 164 F3
Waterford WI U.S.A. 164 A2
Waterford Harbour Ireland 61 F5
Watergrasshill Ireland 61 D5
Waterhen Lake Canada 151 L4
Waterloo Australia 134 E4
Waterloo Belgium 62 E4
Waterloo Ont. Canada 164 E2
Waterloo Que. Canada 165 I1
Waterloo IA U.S.A. 160 E3
Waterloo IL U.S.A. 160 F4
Waterloo NY U.S.A. 165 G2
Waterlooville U.K. 59 F8
Waterton Lakes National Park Canada 150 H5
Watertown NY U.S.A. 165 H2
Watertown SD U.S.A. 160 D2
Watertown WI U.S.A. 160 F3
Water Valley MS U.S.A. 161 F5
Waterville ME U.S.A. 165 K1
Waterville WA U.S.A. 156 C3
Watford Canada 164 E2
Watford U.K. 59 G7
Watford City ND U.S.A. 160 C2
Wathaman r. Canada 151 K3
Wathaman Lake Canada 151 K3
Watheroo National Park Australia 135 A7
Wathlingen Germany 63 K2
Watino Canada 150 G4
Watīr, Wādī watercourse Egypt 107 B5
Watkins Glen NY U.S.A. 165 G2
Watling Island Bahamas see San Salvador
Watmuri Indon. 134 E1
Watonga OK U.S.A. 161 D5
Watowato, Bukit mt. Halmahera Indon. 83 D2
Watrous Canada 151 J5
Watrous NM U.S.A. 157 G6
Watseka IL U.S.A. 164 B3
Watsi Kengo Dem. Rep. Congo 121 F5
Watson r. Australia 136 C2
Watson Canada 151 J4
Watson Lake Canada 149 O3
Watsontown PA U.S.A. 165 G3
Watsonville CA U.S.A. 158 C3
Watten U.K. 60 F2
Watterson Lake Canada 151 L2
Watton U.K. 59 H6
Watts Bar Lake resr TN U.S.A. 162 C5
Wattsburg PA U.S.A. 164 F2
Watubela, Kepulauan is Indon. 81 I7
Watuwila, Bukit mt. Indon. 83 B3
Wau P.N.G. 81 L8
Wau South Sudan 108 C8
Waubay Lake SD U.S.A. 160 D2
Wauchope N.S.W. Australia 138 F3
Wauchope N.T. Australia 134 F5
Waukara, Gunung mt. Indon. 83 A3
Waukaringa (abandoned) Australia 137 B7
Waukarlycarly, Lake salt flat Australia 134 C5
Waukegan IL U.S.A. 164 B2
Waukesha WI U.S.A. 164 A2
Waupaca WI U.S.A. 160 F2
Waupun WI U.S.A. 160 F3
Waurika OK U.S.A. 161 D5
Wausau WI U.S.A. 160 F2
Wausaukee WI U.S.A. 162 C2
Wauseon OH U.S.A. 164 C3
Wautoma WI U.S.A. 160 F2
Wave Hill Australia 134 E4
Waveney r. U.K. 59 I6
Waverly IA U.S.A. 160 E3
Waverly NY U.S.A. 165 G2
Waverly OH U.S.A. 164 D4
Waverly TN U.S.A. 162 C4
Waverly VA U.S.A. 165 G5
Wavre Belgium 62 E4
Waw Myanmar 86 B3
Wawa Canada 152 D5
Wawalalindu Sulawesi Indon. 83 B3
Wāw al Kabīr Libya 121 E2
Wawasee, Lake IN U.S.A. 164 C3
Wawo Sulawesi Indon. 83 B3
Wawotebi Sulawesi Indon. 83 B3
Waxahachie TX U.S.A. 161 D5
Waxü China 94 E5
Waxxari China 98 D5
Way, Lake salt flat Australia 135 C6
Wayabula Maluku Indon. 83 D2
Wayag i. Papua Indon. 83 D2
Wayamli Halmahera Indon. 83 D2
Wayaobu China see Zichang
Waycross GA U.S.A. 163 D6
Wayhaya Maluku Indon. 83 C3
Way Kambas, Taman Nasional nat. park Indon. 84 D4
Waykilo Maluku Indon. 83 C3
Wayland KY U.S.A. 164 D5
Wayland MI U.S.A. 164 C2
Wayne NE U.S.A. 160 D3
Wayne WV U.S.A. 164 D4
Waynesboro GA U.S.A. 163 D5
Waynesboro MS U.S.A. 161 F6
Waynesboro TN U.S.A. 162 C5
Waynesboro VA U.S.A. 165 F4
Waynesburg PA U.S.A. 164 E4
Waynesville MO U.S.A. 160 E4
Waynesville NC U.S.A. 162 D5
Waynoka OK U.S.A. 161 D4
Waza, Parc National de nat. park Cameroon 121 E3
Wāzah Khwāh Afgh. see Wazi Khwa
Wazi Khwa Afgh. 111 H3
Wazirabad Pak. 111 I3
Wazuka Japan 92 B4
W du Niger, Parc National du nat. park Niger 120 D3
We, Pulau i. Indon. 84 A1
Weagamow Lake Canada 151 N4
Weam P.N.G. 81 K8
Wear r. U.K. 58 F4
Weare NH U.S.A. 165 J2
Weatherford TX U.S.A. 161 D5
Weaver Lake Canada 151 L4
Weaverville CA U.S.A. 156 C4
Webb, Mount hill Australia 134 E5
Webequie Canada 152 D3
Weber, Mount Canada 149 O5
Weber Basin sea feature Laut Banda 186 E6
Webster IN U.S.A. 164 C4
Webster MA U.S.A. 165 J2
Webster SD U.S.A. 160 D2
Webster City IA U.S.A. 160 E3
Webster Springs WV U.S.A. 164 E4
Wecho Lake Canada 150 H2
Weda Halmahera Indon. 83 C2
Weda, Teluk b. Halmahera Indon. 83 D2
Wedau P.N.G. 136 E1
Weddell Abyssal Plain sea feature Southern Ocean 188 A2
Weddell Island Falkland Is 178 D8
Weddell Sea Antarctica 188 A2
Wedderburn Australia 138 A6
Weddin Mountains National Park Australia 138 D4
Wedel (Holstein) Germany 63 J1
Wedge Mountain Canada 150 F5
Wedowee AL U.S.A. 163 C5
Weedville PA U.S.A. 165 F3
Weeim i. Papua Indon. 83 D3
Weenen S. Africa 125 J5
Weener Germany 63 H1
Weert Neth. 62 F3
Weethalle Australia 138 C4
Wee Waa Australia 138 D3
Wegberg Germany 62 G3
Węgorzewo Poland 57 R3
Weichang China 95 I3
Weida Germany 63 M4
Weidenberg Germany 63 L5
Weiden in der Oberpfalz Germany 63 M5
Weidongmen China see Qianjin
Weifang China 95 I4
Weihai China 95 J4
Wei He r. Henan China 95 H4
Wei He r. Shaanxi China 95 G5
Weihui China 95 H5
Weilburg Germany 63 I4
Weilmoringle Australia 138 C2
Weimar Germany 63 L4
Weinan China 95 G5
Weinheim Germany 63 I5
Weining China 96 E3
Weinsberg Germany 63 J5
Weipa Australia 136 C2
Weiqu China see Chang'an
Weir r. Australia 138 D2
Weirong China 94 F5
Weir River Canada 151 M3
Weirton WV U.S.A. 164 E3
Weiser ID U.S.A. 156 D3
Weishan Shandong China 95 I5
Weishan Yunnan China 96 D3
Weishan Hu l. China 95 I5
Weishi China 95 H5
Weiße Elster r. Germany 63 L3
Weißenburg in Bayern Germany 63 K5
Weißenfels Germany 63 L3
Weißkugel mt. Austria/Italy 57 M7
Weissrand Mountains Namibia 124 D3
Weiterstadt Germany 63 I5
Weitzel Lake Canada 151 J3
Weixi China 96 C3
Weixian China 95 H4
Weixin China 96 E3
Weiya China 94 C3
Weiyuan Gansu China 94 F5
Weiyuan Qinghai China see Huzhu
Weiyuan Sichuan China 96 E2
Weiyuan Yunnan China see Jinggu
Weiyuan Jiang r. China 96 D4
Weiz Austria 57 O7
Weizhou Ningxia China 94 F4
Weizhou Sichuan China see Wenchuan
Weizhou Dao i. China 97 F4
Weizi China 95 J3
Wejherowo Poland 57 Q3
Wekilbazar Turkm. 111 F2
Wekusko Canada 151 L4
Wekusko Lake Canada 151 L4
Wekweètì Canada 150 H1
Welatam Myanmar 86 B1
Welbourn Hill Australia 135 F6
Welch WV U.S.A. 164 E5
Weld ME U.S.A. 165 J1
Weldiya Eth. 122 D2
Welford National Park Australia 136 C5
Welk'īt'ē Eth. 122 D3
Welkom S. Africa 125 H4
Welland Canada 164 F2
Welland r. U.K. 59 G6
Welland Canal Canada 164 F2
Wellesley Canada 164 E2
Wellesley Islands Australia 136 B3
Wellesley Lake Canada 149 M3
Wellfleet MA U.S.A. 165 J3
Wellin Belgium 62 F4
Wellingborough U.K. 59 G6
Wellington Australia 138 D4
Wellington Canada 165 G2

▶Wellington N.Z. 139 E5
Capital of New Zealand.

Wellington S. Africa 124 D7
Wellington England U.K. 59 D8
Wellington England U.K. 59 E6
Wellington CO U.S.A. 156 G4
Wellington IL U.S.A. 164 B3
Wellington KS U.S.A. 161 D4
Wellington NV U.S.A. 158 D2
Wellington OH U.S.A. 164 D3
Wellington TX U.S.A. 161 C5
Wellington UT U.S.A. 159 H2
Wellington, Isla i. Chile 178 B7
Wellington Range hills N.T. Australia 134 F3
Wellington Range hills W.A. Australia 135 C6
Wells Canada 150 F4
Wells U.K. 59 E7
Wells NV U.S.A. 156 E4
Wells, Lake salt flat Australia 135 C6
Wellsboro PA U.S.A. 165 G3
Wellsburg WV U.S.A. 164 E3
Wellsford N.Z. 139 E3
Wells-next-the-Sea U.K. 59 H6
Wellston MI U.S.A. 164 C1
Wellsville NY U.S.A. 165 G2
Wellton AZ U.S.A. 159 F5
Wels Austria 57 O6
Welshpool U.K. 59 D6
Welsickendorf Germany 63 N3
Welwitschia Namibia see Khorixas
Welwyn Garden City U.K. 59 G7
Welzheim Germany 63 J6
Wem U.K. 59 E6
Wembesi S. Africa 125 I5
Wembley Canada 150 G4
Wemindji Canada 152 F3
Wenatchee WA U.S.A. 156 C3
Wenatchee Mountains WA U.S.A. 156 C3
Wenchang Hainan China 97 F5
Wenchang Sichuan China see Zitong
Wenchow China see Wenzhou
Wenchuan China 96 D2
Wendelstein Germany 63 L5
Wenden Germany 63 H4
Wenden Latvia see Cēsis
Wenden AZ U.S.A. 159 G5
Wendeng China 95 J4
Wendover UT U.S.A. 159 F1
Wenfengzhen China 94 F5
Weng'an China 96 E3
Wengda China 96 D2
Wengshui China 96 C2
Wengyuan China 97 G3
Wenhua China see Weishan
Wenlan China see Mengzi
Wenling China 97 I2
Wenlock r. Australia 136 C2
Wenping China see Ludian
Wenquan Guizhou China 96 E2
Wenquan Henan China see Wenxian
Wenquan Hubei China see Yingshan
Wenquan Qinghai China 94 D5

▶Wenquan Qinghai China 99 E6
Highest settlement in the world.

Wenquan Xinjiang China 98 C3
Wenshan China 96 E4
Wenshui China 96 E2
Wensu China 98 C4
Wensum r. U.K. 59 I6
Wentorf bei Hamburg Germany 63 K1
Wentworth Australia 137 C7
Wenxi China 97 F1
Wenxian Gansu China 96 E1
Wenxian Henan China 97 G1
Wenxing China see Xiangyin
Wenzhou China 97 I3
Wenzlow Germany 63 M2
Wepener S. Africa 125 H5
Wer India 104 D4
Werben (Elbe) Germany 63 L2
Werda Botswana 124 F3
Werdau Germany 63 M4
Werdër Eth. 122 E3
Werder Germany 63 M2
Werdohl Germany 63 H3
Werinama Seram Indon. 83 D3
Werl Germany 63 H3
Wernberg-Köblitz Germany 63 M5
Werne Germany 63 H3
Wernecke Mountains Canada 149 M2
Wernigerode Germany 63 K3
Werra r. Germany 63 J3
Werris Creek Australia 138 E3
Wertheim Germany 63 J5
Wervik Belgium 62 D4
Werwaru Maluku Indon. 83 D5
Wesel Germany 62 G3
Wesel-Datteln-Kanal canal Germany 62 G3
Wesenberg Germany 63 M1
Wesendorf Germany 63 K2
Weser r. Germany 63 I1
Weser sea chan. Germany 63 I1
Wesergebirge hills Germany 63 I2
Weslaco TX U.S.A. 161 D7
Weslemkoon Lake Canada 165 G1
Wesleyville Canada 153 L4
Wessel, Cape Australia 136 B1
Wessel Islands Australia 136 B1
Wesselsbron S. Africa 125 H4
Wesselton S. Africa 125 I4
Wessington Springs SD U.S.A. 160 D2
West r. Canada 149 P1
Westall, Point Australia 135 F8
West Allis WI U.S.A. 164 A2
West Antarctica reg. Antarctica 188 J1
West Australian Basin sea feature Indian Ocean 185 O7

▶West Bank terr. Asia 107 B3
Disputed Territory.

West Bay Canada 153 K3
West Bay b. LA U.S.A. 167 H2
West Bay inlet FL U.S.A. 163 C6
West Bend WI U.S.A. 164 A2
West Bengal state India 105 F5
West Branch MI U.S.A. 164 C1
West Bromwich U.K. 59 F6
Westbrook ME U.S.A. 165 J2
West Burke VT U.S.A. 165 J1
West Burra i. U.K. see Burra
Westbury U.K. 59 E7
West Caicos i. Turks and Caicos Is 163 F8
West Cape Howe Australia 135 B8
West Caroline Basin sea feature N. Pacific Ocean 186 F5
West Chester PA U.S.A. 165 H4
Westcliffe CO U.S.A. 157 G5
West Coast National Park S. Africa 124 D7
West End Bahamas 163 E7
Westerburg Germany 63 H4
Westerholt Germany 63 H1
Westerland Germany 57 L3
Westerlo Belgium 62 E3
Westerly RI U.S.A. 165 J3
Western r. Canada 151 J1
Western Australia state Australia 135 C6
Western Cape prov. S. Africa 124 E7
Western Desert Egypt 112 C6
Western Dvina r. Europe see Zapadnaya Dvina
Western Ghats mts India 106 B3
Western Lesser Sunda Islands prov. Indon. see Nusa Tenggara Barat
Western Port b. Australia 138 B7

▶Western Sahara terr. Africa 120 B2
Disputed Territory.

Western Samoa country S. Pacific Ocean see Samoa
Western Sayan Mountains reg. Rus. Fed. see Zapadnyy Sayan
Westerschelde est. Neth. 62 D3
Westerstede Germany 63 H1
Westerville OH U.S.A. 164 D3
Westerwald hills Germany 63 H4
West Falkland i. Falkland Is 178 D8
West Fargo ND U.S.A. 160 D2
West Fayu atoll Micronesia 81 L5
Westfield IN U.S.A. 164 B3
Westfield MA U.S.A. 165 I2
Westfield NY U.S.A. 164 F2
Westfield PA U.S.A. 165 G3
West Frisian Islands Neth. see Waddeneilanden
Westgat sea chan. Neth. 62 G1
Westgate Australia 138 C1
West Glacier MT U.S.A. 156 E2
West Grand Lake ME U.S.A. 162 H2
West Hartford CT U.S.A. 165 I3
Westhausen Germany 63 K6
West Haven CT U.S.A. 165 I3
Westhill U.K. 60 G3
Westhope ND U.S.A. 160 C1
West Ice Shelf Antarctica 188 E2
West Indies is Caribbean Sea 169 J4
West Island India 87 A4
Westkapelle Neth. 62 D3
West Kazakhstan Oblast admin. div. Kazakh. see Zapadnyy Kazakhstan
West Kingston RI U.S.A. 165 J3
West Lafayette IN U.S.A. 164 B3
West Lamma Channel H.K. China 97 [inset]
Westland Australia 136 C4
Westland National Park N.Z. 139 C6
Westleigh S. Africa 125 H4
Westleton U.K. 59 I6
West Liberty KY U.S.A. 164 D5
West Linton U.K. 60 F5
West Loch Roag b. U.K. 60 C2
Westlock Canada 150 H4
West Lorne Canada 164 E2
West Lunga National Park Zambia 123 C5
West MacDonnell National Park Australia 135 F5
West Malaysia pen. Malaysia see Peninsular Malaysia
Westmalle Belgium 62 E3
Westmar Australia 138 D1
West Mariana Basin sea feature N. Pacific Ocean 186 F4
West Memphis AR U.S.A. 161 F5
Westminster MD U.S.A. 165 G4
Westmoreland Australia 136 B3
Westmoreland TN U.S.A. 164 B5
Westmorland CA U.S.A. 159 F5
Weston Sabah Malaysia 85 F1
Weston OH U.S.A. 164 D3
Weston WV U.S.A. 164 E4
Weston-super-Mare U.K. 59 E7
West Palm Beach FL U.S.A. 163 D7
West Passage Palau see Toagel Mlungui
West Plains MO U.S.A. 161 F4
West Point pt Australia 137 [inset]
West Point CA U.S.A. 158 C2
West Point KY U.S.A. 164 C5
West Point MS U.S.A. 161 F5
West Point NE U.S.A. 160 D3
West Point VA U.S.A. 165 G5
West Point mt. AK U.S.A. 149 K2
West Point Lake resr AL/GA U.S.A. 163 C5
Westport Canada 165 G1
Westport Ireland 61 C4
Westport N.Z. 139 C5
Westport CA U.S.A. 158 B2
Westport KY U.S.A. 164 C4
Westport NY U.S.A. 165 I1
Westray Canada 151 K4
Westray i. U.K. 60 F1
Westray Firth sea chan. U.K. 60 F1
Westree Canada 152 E5
West Rutland VT U.S.A. 165 I2
West Salem OH U.S.A. 164 D3
West Siberian Plain Rus. Fed. 76 J3
West-Skylge Neth. see West-Terschelling
West Stewartstown NH U.S.A. 165 J1
West-Terschelling Neth. 62 F1
West Topsham VT U.S.A. 165 I1
West Union IA U.S.A. 160 F3
West Union IL U.S.A. 164 B4
West Union OH U.S.A. 164 D4
West Union WV U.S.A. 164 E4
West Valley City UT U.S.A. 159 H1
Westville IN U.S.A. 164 B3
West Virginia state U.S.A. 164 E4
Westwood CA U.S.A. 158 C1
West Wyalong Australia 138 C4
West York PA U.S.A. 165 G4
Westzaan Neth. 62 E2
Wetan i. Maluku Indon. 83 D4
Wetar i. Maluku Indon. 83 C4
Wetar, Selat sea chan. Indon. 83 C5
Wetaskiwin Canada 150 H4
Wete Tanz. 123 D4
Wetter r. Germany 63 I4
Wettin Germany 63 L3
Wetumpka AL U.S.A. 163 C5
Wetwun Myanmar 86 B2
Wetzlar Germany 63 I4
Wevok AK U.S.A. 148 F1
Wewahitchka FL U.S.A. 163 C6
Wewak P.N.G. 81 K7
Wewoka OK U.S.A. 161 D5
Wexford Ireland 61 F5
Wexford Harbour b. Ireland 61 F5
Weyakwin Canada 151 J4
Weybridge U.K. 59 G7
Weyburn Canada 151 K5
Weyhe Germany 63 I2
Weymouth U.K. 59 E8
Weymouth MA U.S.A. 165 J2
Wezep Neth. 62 G2
Whakaari i. N.Z. 139 F3
Whakatane N.Z. 139 F3
Whalan Creek r. Australia 138 D2
Whale r. Canada see La Baleine, Rivière à
Whalsay i. U.K. 60 [inset]
Whampoa China see Huangpu
Whangamata N.Z. 139 E3
Whanganui National Park N.Z. 139 E4
Whangarei N.Z. 139 E2
Whapmagoostui Canada 152 F3
Wharfe r. U.K. 58 F5
Wharfedale valley U.K. 58 F4
Wharton TX U.S.A. 161 D6
Wharton Lake Canada 151 L1
Whatì Canada 149 R3
Wheatland IN U.S.A. 164 B4
Wheatland WY U.S.A. 156 G4
Wheaton IL U.S.A. 164 A3
Wheaton MN U.S.A. 160 D2
Wheaton-Glenmont MD U.S.A. 165 G4
Wheeler TX U.S.A. 161 C5
Wheeler Lake Canada 150 H2
Wheeler Lake resr AL U.S.A. 163 C5
Wheeler Peak NM U.S.A. 157 G5
Wheeler Peak NV U.S.A. 159 F2
Wheelersburg OH U.S.A. 164 D4
Wheeling WV U.S.A. 164 E3
Whernside hill U.K. 58 E4
Whinham, Mount Australia 135 E6
Whiskey Jack Lake Canada 151 K3
Whitburn U.K. 60 F5
Whitby Canada 165 F2
Whitby U.K. 58 G4
Whitchurch U.K. 59 E6
Whitchurch-Stouffville Canada 164 F2
White r. Canada 152 D4
White r. Canada/U.S.A. 149 M3
White r. AR U.S.A. 155 I5
White r. AR U.S.A. 161 F5
White r. CO U.S.A. 159 I1
White r. IN U.S.A. 164 B4
White r. MI U.S.A. 164 B2
White r. NV U.S.A. 159 F3
White r. SD U.S.A. 160 D3
White r. VT U.S.A. 165 I2
White watercourse AZ U.S.A. 159 H5
White, Lake salt flat Australia 134 E5
White Bay Canada 153 K4
White Butte mt. ND U.S.A. 160 C2
White Canyon UT U.S.A. 159 H3
White Cloud MI U.S.A. 164 C2
Whitecourt Canada 150 H4
Whiteface Mountain NY U.S.A. 165 I1
Whitefield NH U.S.A. 165 J1
Whitefish r. Canada 149 P2
Whitefish MT U.S.A. 156 E2
Whitefish Bay WI U.S.A. 164 B1
Whitefish Lake Canada 151 J2
Whitefish Lake AK U.S.A. 148 I3
Whitefish Point MI U.S.A. 162 C2
Whitehall Ireland 61 E5
Whitehall U.K. 60 G1
Whitehall NY U.S.A. 165 I2
Whitehall WI U.S.A. 160 F2
Whitehaven U.K. 58 D4
Whitehead U.K. 61 G3
White Hill hill Canada 153 J5
Whitehill U.K. 59 G7
White Hills AK U.S.A. 149 J1

▶Whitehorse Canada 149 N3
Capital of Yukon.

White Horse NM U.S.A. 159 J4
White Horse, Vale of valley U.K. 59 F7
White Horse Pass NV U.S.A. 159 F1
White House TN U.S.A. 164 B5
White Island Antarctica 188 D2
White Island N.Z. see Whakaari
White Lake Ont. Canada 152 D4
White Lake Ont. Canada 165 G1
White Lake LA U.S.A. 161 E6
White Lake MI U.S.A. 164 B2
Whitemark Australia 137 [inset]
White Mountain AK U.S.A. 148 G2
White Mountain Peak CA U.S.A. 158 D3
White Mountains AK U.S.A. 149 K2
White Mountains NH U.S.A. 165 J1
White Mountains National Park Australia 136 D4
Whitemouth Lake Canada 151 M5
Whitemud r. Canada 150 G3
White Nile r. Africa 108 D6
also known as Bahr el Abiad or Bahr el Jebel
White Nossob watercourse Namibia 124 D2
White Oak KY U.S.A. 164 D5
White Otter Lake Canada 151 N5
White Pass Canada/U.S.A. 149 N4

White Pine Range mts NV U.S.A. 159 F2
White Plains NY U.S.A. 165 I3
White River Canada 152 D4
Whiteriver AZ U.S.A. 159 I5
White River SD U.S.A. 160 C3
White River Valley NV U.S.A. 159 F2
White Rock Peak NV U.S.A. 159 F2
White Russia country Europe see Belarus
Whitesail Lake Canada 150 E4
White Salmon WA U.S.A. 156 C3
Whitesand r. Canada 150 H2
White Sands National Monument nat. park NM U.S.A. 157 G6
Whitesburg KY U.S.A. 164 D5
White Sea Rus. Fed. 52 H2
Whitestone r. Canada 149 M2
White Stone VA U.S.A. 165 G5
White Sulphur Springs MT U.S.A. 156 F3
White Sulphur Springs WV U.S.A. 164 E5
Whitesville WV U.S.A. 164 E5
Whiteville NC U.S.A. 163 E5
White Volta r. Burkina Faso/Ghana 120 C4
also known as Nakambé or Nakanbe or Volta Blanche
Whitewater CO U.S.A. 159 I2
Whitewater Baldy mt. NM U.S.A. 159 I5
Whitewater Lake Canada 152 C4
Whitewood Australia 136 C4
Whitewood Canada 151 K5
Whitfield U.K. 59 I7
Whithorn U.K. 60 E6
Whitianga N.Z. 139 E3
Whitland U.K. 59 C7
Whitley Bay U.K. 58 F3
Whitmore Mountains Antarctica 188 K1
Whitney Canada 165 F1
Whitney, Lake TX U.S.A. 167 F2
Whitney, Mount CA U.S.A. 158 D3
Whitney Point NY U.S.A. 165 H2
Whitstable U.K. 59 I7
Whitsunday Group is Australia 136 E4
Whitsunday Island National Park Australia 136 E4
Whitsun Island Vanuatu see Pentecost Island
Whittemore MI U.S.A. 164 D1
Whittier AK U.S.A. 149 J3
Whittlesea Australia 138 B6
Whittlesey U.K. 59 G6
Whitton Australia 138 C5
Wholdaia Lake Canada 151 J2
Why AZ U.S.A. 159 G5
Whyalla Australia 137 B7
Wiang Sa Thai. 86 C3
Wiarton Canada 164 E1
Wibaux MT U.S.A. 156 G3
Wichelen Belgium 62 D3
Wichita KS U.S.A. 160 D4
Wichita r. TX U.S.A. 161 D5
Wichita Falls TX U.S.A. 161 D5
Wichita Mountains OK U.S.A. 161 D5
Wick U.K. 60 F2
Wick r. U.K. 60 F2
Wickenburg AZ U.S.A. 159 G5
Wickes AR U.S.A. 161 E5
Wickford U.K. 59 H7
Wickham r. Australia 134 E4
Wickham, Cape Australia 137 [inset]
Wickham, Mount hill Australia 134 E4
Wickliffe KY U.S.A. 161 F4
Wicklow Ireland 61 F5
Wicklow Head hd Ireland 61 G5
Wicklow Mountains Ireland 61 F5
Wicklow Mountains National Park Ireland 61 F4
Wide Bay AK U.S.A. 148 H4
Widerøe, Mount Antarctica 188 C2
Widerøefjellet mt. Antarctica see Widerøe, Mount
Widgeegoara watercourse Australia 138 B1
Widgiemooltha Australia 135 C7
Widi, Kepulauan is Maluku Indon. 83 D3
Widnes U.K. 58 E5
Wi-do i. S. Korea 91 B6
Wied r. Germany 63 H4
Wiehengebirge hills Germany 63 I2
Wiehl Germany 63 H4
Wielkopolskie, Pojezierze reg. Poland 57 O4
Wielkopolski Park Narodowy nat. park Poland 57 P4
Wieluń Poland 57 Q5
Wien Austria see Vienna
Wiener Neustadt Austria 57 P7
Wien Lake AK U.S.A. 149 J2
Wierden Neth. 62 G2
Wieren Germany 63 K2
Wieringerwerf Neth. 62 F2
Wiesbaden Germany 63 I4
Wiesenfelden Germany 63 M5
Wiesentheid Germany 63 K5
Wiesloch Germany 63 I5
Wiesmoor Germany 63 H1
Wietze Germany 63 J2
Wietzendorf Germany 63 J2
Wieżyca hill Poland 57 Q3
Wigan U.K. 58 E5
Wiggins MS U.S.A. 161 F6
Wight, Isle of i. U.K. 59 F8
Wigierski Park Narodowy nat. park Poland 55 M9
Wignes Lake Canada 151 J2
Wigston U.K. 59 F6
Wigton U.K. 58 D4
Wigtown U.K. 60 E6
Wigtown Bay U.K. 60 E6
Wijchen Neth. 62 F3
Wijhe Neth. 62 G2
Wilberforce, Cape Australia 136 B1
Wilbur WA U.S.A. 156 D3
Wilburton OK U.S.A. 161 E5
Wilcannia Australia 138 A3
Wilcox PA U.S.A. 165 F3
Wilczek Land i. Rus. Fed. see Vil'cheka, Zemlya
Wildberg Germany 63 M2
Wildcat Peak NV U.S.A. 158 E2
Wild Coast S. Africa 125 I6
Wildeshausen Germany 63 I2
Wild Horse Hill mt. NE U.S.A. 160 C3
Wildspitze mt. Austria 57 M7
Wildwood FL U.S.A. 163 D6
Wildwood NJ U.S.A. 165 H4
Wilge r. Free State S. Africa 125 I4
Wilge r. Gauteng/Mpumalanga S. Africa 125 I3
Wilgena Australia 135 F7

▶Wilhelm, Mount P.N.G. 81 L8
5th highest mountain in Oceania.

Wilhelm II Land reg. Antarctica see Kaiser Wilhelm II Land
Wilhelmina Gebergte mts Suriname 177 G3
Wilhelmina Kanaal canal Neth. 62 F3
Wilhelmshaven Germany 63 I1
Wilhelmstal Namibia 124 C1
Wilkes-Barre PA U.S.A. 165 H3
Wilkesboro NC U.S.A. 162 D4
Wilkes Coast Antarctica 188 G2
Wilkes Land reg. Antarctica 188 G2
Wilkie Canada 151 I4
Wilkins Coast Antarctica 188 L2
Wilkins Ice Shelf Antarctica 188 L2
Wilkinson Lakes salt flat Australia 135 F7
Will, Mount Canada 149 O4
Willand U.K. 59 D8
Willandra Billabong watercourse Australia 138 B4
Willandra National Park Australia 138 B4
Willapa Bay WA U.S.A. 156 B3
Willard Mex. 166 C2
Willard NM U.S.A. 157 G6
Willard OH U.S.A. 164 D3
Willcox AZ U.S.A. 159 I5
Willcox Playa salt flat AZ U.S.A. 159 I5
Willebadessen Germany 63 J3
Willebroek Belgium 62 E3
Willemstad Curaçao 169 K6
Willeroo Australia 134 E3
Willette TN U.S.A. 164 C5
William, Mount Australia 137 C8
William Creek Australia 137 B6
William Lake Canada 151 L4
Williams AZ U.S.A. 159 G4
Williams CA U.S.A. 158 B2
Williamsburg KY U.S.A. 164 C5
Williamsburg OH U.S.A. 164 C4
Williamsburg VA U.S.A. 165 G5
Williams Lake Canada 150 F4
William Smith, Cap c. Canada 153 I1
Williamson NY U.S.A. 165 G2
Williamson WV U.S.A. 164 D5
Williamsport IN U.S.A. 164 B3
Williamsport PA U.S.A. 165 G3
Williamston NC U.S.A. 162 E5
Williamstown KY U.S.A. 164 C4
Williamstown NJ U.S.A. 165 H4
Willimantic CT U.S.A. 165 I3
Willis Group atolls Australia 136 E3
Williston S. Africa 124 E6
Williston ND U.S.A. 160 C1
Williston SC U.S.A. 163 D5
Williston Lake Canada 150 F4
Williton U.K. 59 D7
Willits CA U.S.A. 158 B2
Willmar MN U.S.A. 160 E2
Willoughby, Lake VT U.S.A. 165 I1
Willow AK U.S.A. 149 J3
Willow Beach AZ U.S.A. 159 F4
Willow Bunch Canada 151 J5
Willow Creek AK U.S.A. 149 K3
Willow Hill PA U.S.A. 165 G3
Willow Lake Canada 150 G2
Willowlake r. Canada 150 F2
Willowmore S. Africa 124 F7
Willowra Australia 134 F5
Willows CA U.S.A. 158 B2
Willow Springs MO U.S.A. 161 F4
Willowvale S. Africa 125 I7
Wills, Lake salt flat Australia 134 E5
Wilma FL U.S.A. 163 C6
Wilmington DE U.S.A. 165 H4
Wilmington NC U.S.A. 163 E5
Wilmington OH U.S.A. 164 D4
Wilmore KY U.S.A. 164 C5
Wilmslow U.K. 58 E5
Wilno Lith. see Vilnius
Wilnsdorf Germany 63 I4
Wilpattu National Park Sri Lanka 106 D4
Wilseder Berg hill Germany 63 J1
Wilson watercourse Australia 137 C5
Wilson atoll Micronesia see Ifalik
Wilson KS U.S.A. 160 D4
Wilson NC U.S.A. 162 E5
Wilson NY U.S.A. 165 F2
Wilson, Mount CO U.S.A. 159 J3
Wilson, Mount NV U.S.A. 159 F2
Wilson, Mount OR U.S.A. 156 C3
Wilsonia CA U.S.A. 158 D3
Wilson's Promontory pen. Australia 138 C7
Wilson's Promontory National Park Australia 138 C7
Wilsum Germany 62 G2
Wilton r. Australia 134 F3
Wilton ME U.S.A. 165 J1
Wiltz Lux. 62 F5
Wiluna Australia 135 C6
Wimereux France 62 B4
Wina r. Cameroon see Vina
Winamac IN U.S.A. 164 B3
Winbin watercourse Australia 137 D5
Winburg S. Africa 125 H5
Wincanton U.K. 59 E7
Winchester Canada 165 H1
Winchester U.K. 59 F7
Winchester IN U.S.A. 164 C3
Winchester KY U.S.A. 164 C5
Winchester NH U.S.A. 165 I2
Winchester TN U.S.A. 163 C5
Winchester VA U.S.A. 165 F4
Wind r. Canada 149 N2
Wind r. WY U.S.A. 156 F4
Windau Latvia see Ventspils
Windber PA U.S.A. 165 F3
Wind Cave National Park SD U.S.A. 160 C3
Windermere U.K. 58 E4
Windermere l. U.K. 58 E4
Windham AK U.S.A. 149 N4

▶Windhoek Namibia 124 C2
Capital of Namibia.

Windigo Lake Canada 151 N4
Windlestraw Law hill U.K. 60 G5
Wind Mountain NM U.S.A. 157 G6
Windom MN U.S.A. 160 E3
Windom Peak CO U.S.A. 159 J3
Windorah Australia 136 C5
Window Rock AZ U.S.A. 159 I4
Wind Point WI U.S.A. 164 B2
Wind River Range mts WY U.S.A. 156 F4
Windrush r. U.K. 59 F7
Windsbach Germany 63 K5
Windsor Australia 138 E4
Windsor N.S. Canada 153 I5
Windsor Ont. Canada 164 D2
Windsor U.K. 59 G7
Windsor NC U.S.A. 162 E4
Windsor NY U.S.A. 165 H2
Windsor VA U.S.A. 165 G5
Windsor VT U.S.A. 165 I2
Windsor Locks CT U.S.A. 165 I3
Windward Islands Caribbean Sea 169 L5
Windward Passage Cuba/Haiti 169 J5
Windy AK U.S.A. 146 D3
Windy Fork r. AK U.S.A. 148 I3
Winefred Lake Canada 151 I4
Winfield KS U.S.A. 161 D4
Winfield WV U.S.A. 164 E4
Wingate U.K. 58 F4
Wingen Australia 138 E3
Wingene Belgium 62 D3
Wingen-sur-Moder France 63 H6
Wingham Australia 138 F3
Wingham Canada 164 E2
Wini East Timor 83 C5
Winisk r. Canada 152 D3
Winisk (abandoned) Canada 152 D3
Winisk Lake Canada 152 D3
Winkana Myanmar 86 B4
Winkelman AZ U.S.A. 159 H5
Winkler Canada 151 L5
Winlock WA U.S.A. 156 C3
Winneba Ghana 120 C4
Winnebago, Lake WI U.S.A. 164 A1
Winnecke Creek watercourse Australia 134 E4
Winnemucca NV U.S.A. 158 E1
Winnemucca Lake NV U.S.A. 158 D1
Winner SD U.S.A. 160 C3
Winnett MT U.S.A. 156 F3
Winnfield LA U.S.A. 161 E6
Winnibigoshish, Lake MN U.S.A. 160 E2
Winnie TX U.S.A. 161 E6
Winning Australia 135 A5

▶Winnipeg Canada 151 L5
Capital of Manitoba.

Winnipeg r. Canada 151 L5
Winnipeg, Lake Canada 151 L5
Winnipegosis Canada 151 L5
Winnipegosis, Lake Canada 151 K4
Winnipesaukee, Lake NH U.S.A. 165 J2
Winnsboro LA U.S.A. 167 H1
Winona AZ U.S.A. 159 H4
Winona MN U.S.A. 160 F2
Winona MO U.S.A. 161 F4
Winona MS U.S.A. 161 F5
Winschoten Neth. 62 H1
Winsen (Aller) Germany 63 J2
Winsen (Luhe) Germany 63 K1
Winsford U.K. 58 E5
Winslow AZ U.S.A. 159 H4
Winslow ME U.S.A. 165 K1
Winsop, Tanjung pt Indon. 81 I7
Winsted CT U.S.A. 165 I3
Winston-Salem NC U.S.A. 162 D4
Winterberg Germany 63 I3
Winter Haven FL U.S.A. 163 D6
Winters CA U.S.A. 158 C2
Winters TX U.S.A. 161 D6
Wintersville OH U.S.A. 164 E3
Winterswijk Neth. 62 G3
Winterthur Switz. 66 I3
Winterton S. Africa 125 I5
Winthrop ME U.S.A. 165 K1
Winton Australia 136 C4
Winton N.Z. 139 B8
Winton NC U.S.A. 162 E4
Winwick U.K. 59 G6
Wiralaga Sumatera Indon. 84 D3
Wirral pen. U.K. 58 D5
Wirrulla Australia 137 A7
Wisbech U.K. 59 H6
Wiscasset ME U.S.A. 165 K1
Wisconsin r. WI U.S.A. 160 F3
Wisconsin state U.S.A. 164 A1
Wisconsin Rapids WI U.S.A. 160 F2
Wise VA U.S.A. 164 D5
Wiseman AK U.S.A. 149 J2
Wishaw U.K. 60 F5
Wisher ND U.S.A. 160 D2
Wisil Dabarow Somalia 122 E3
Wisła r. Poland see Vistula
Wismar Germany 57 M4
Wistaria Canada 150 E4
Witbank S. Africa 125 I3
Witbooisvlei Namibia 124 D3
Witham U.K. 59 H7
Witham r. U.K. 59 H6
Witherbee NY U.S.A. 165 I1
Withernsea U.K. 58 H5
Witherspoon, Mount AK U.S.A. 149 K3
Witjira National Park Australia 137 A5
Witmarsum Neth. 62 F1
Witney U.K. 59 F7
Witrivier S. Africa 125 J3
Witry-lès-Reims France 62 E5
Witteberg mts S. Africa 125 H6
Wittenberg Germany see Lutherstadt Wittenberg
Wittenberge Germany 63 L2
Wittenburg Germany 63 L1
Witti, Banjaran mts Malaysia 85 G1
Wittingen Germany 63 K2
Wittlich Germany 62 G5
Wittmund Germany 63 H1
Wittstock Germany 63 M1
Witu Islands P.N.G. 81 L7
Witvlei Namibia 124 D2
Witzenhausen Germany 63 J3
Wivenhoe, Lake Australia 138 F1
Władysławowo Poland 57 Q3
Włocławek Poland 57 Q4
Wobkent Uzbek. see Vobkent
Wodonga Australia 138 C6
Wœrth France 63 H6
Wohlthat Mountains Antarctica 188 C2
Woippy France 62 G5
Wōjjā atoll Marshall Is see Wotje
Wokam i. Indon. 81 I8
Woken He r. China 90 C3
Wokha India 105 H4
Woking U.K. 59 G7
Wokingham watercourse Australia 136 C4
Wokingham U.K. 59 G7
Woko National Park Australia 138 E3
Wolcott IN U.S.A. 164 B3
Wolcott NY U.S.A. 165 G2
Woldegk Germany 63 N1
Wolea atoll Micronesia see Woleai
Woleai atoll Micronesia 81 K5
Wolf r. Canada 149 N3
Wolf r. TN U.S.A. 161 F5
Wolf r. WI U.S.A. 160 F2
Wolf Creek MT U.S.A. 156 E3
Wolf Creek OR U.S.A. 156 C4
Wolf Creek Mountain hill AK U.S.A. 148 G3
Wolf Creek Pass CO U.S.A. 157 G5
Wolfen Germany 63 M3
Wolfenbüttel Germany 63 K2
Wolfhagen Germany 63 J3
Wolf Lake Canada 149 O3
Wolf Mountain AK U.S.A. 148 I2
Wolf Point MT U.S.A. 156 G2
Wolfsberg Austria 57 O7
Wolfsburg Germany 63 K2
Wolfstein Germany 63 H5
Wolfville Canada 153 I5
Wolgast Germany 57 N3
Wolin Poland 57 O4
Wollaston Lake Canada 151 K3
Wollaston Lake l. Canada 151 K3
Wollaston Peninsula Canada 146 G3
Wollemi National Park Australia 138 E4
Wollongong Australia 138 E5
Wolmaransstad S. Africa 125 G4
Wolmirstedt Germany 63 L2
Wolong Reserve nature res. China 96 D2
Wolowaru Flores Indon. 83 B5
Wolseley Australia 137 C8
Wolseley S. Africa 124 D7
Wolsey SD U.S.A. 160 D2
Wolsingham U.K. 58 F4
Woluswālī Behsūd Afgh. 111 G3
Wolvega Neth. 62 G2
Wolvegea Neth. see Wolvega
Wolverhampton U.K. 59 E6
Wolverine r. Canada 149 O1
Wolverine MI U.S.A. 164 C1
Wolya r. Indon. 84 A1
Womens Bay AK U.S.A. 148 I4
Wommelgem Belgium 62 E3
Womrather Höhe hill Germany 63 H5
Wonarah Australia 136 B3
Wondai Australia 137 E5
Wongalarroo Lake salt l. Australia 138 B3
Wongarbon Australia 138 D4
Wong Chuk Hang H.K. China 97 [inset]
Wong Leng hill H.K. China 97 [inset]
Wong Wan Chau H.K. China see Double Island
Wŏnju S. Korea 91 B5
Wonogiri Jawa Indon. 85 E4
Wonosari Indon. 85 E4
Wonosobo Jawa Indon. 85 E4
Wonowon Canada 150 F3
Wonreli Maluku Indon. 83 C5
Wŏnsan N. Korea 91 B5
Wonthaggi Australia 138 B7
Wonyulgunna, Mount hill Australia 135 B6
Woocalla Australia 137 B6
Wood r. AK U.S.A. 149 J2
Wood, Mount Canada 149 L3
Woodbine GA U.S.A. 163 D6
Woodbine NJ U.S.A. 165 H4
Woodbridge U.K. 59 I6
Woodbridge VA U.S.A. 165 G4
Wood Buffalo National Park Canada 150 H3
Woodburn OR U.S.A. 156 C3
Woodbury NJ U.S.A. 165 H4
Woodbury TN U.S.A. 161 G5
Woodchopper Creek AK U.S.A. 149 L2
Wooded Bluff hd Australia 138 F2
Wood Lake Canada 151 K4
Woodlake CA U.S.A. 158 D3
Woodland CA U.S.A. 158 C2
Woodland PA U.S.A. 165 F3
Woodland WA U.S.A. 156 C3
Woodlands Sing. 87 [inset]
Woodlark Island P.N.G. 132 F2
Woodridge Canada 151 L5
Woodroffe watercourse Australia 136 B4
Woodroffe, Mount Australia 135 E6
Woodruff UT U.S.A. 156 F4
Woodruff WI U.S.A. 160 F2
Woods, Lake salt flat Australia 134 F4
Woods, Lake of the Canada/U.S.A. 155 I2
Woodsfield OH U.S.A. 164 E4
Woodside Australia 138 C7
Woodstock N.B. Canada 153 I5
Woodstock Ont. Canada 164 E2
Woodstock IL U.S.A. 160 F3
Woodstock VA U.S.A. 165 F4
Woodstock VT U.S.A. 165 I2
Woodsville NH U.S.A. 165 I1
Woodville Canada 165 F1
Woodville MS U.S.A. 161 F6
Woodville OH U.S.A. 164 D3
Woodville TX U.S.A. 161 E6
Woodward OK U.S.A. 161 D4
Woody CA U.S.A. 158 D4
Woody Island AK U.S.A. 148 I4
Wooler U.K. 58 E3
Woolgoolga Australia 138 F3
Wooli Australia 138 F2
Woollard, Mount Antarctica 188 K1
Woollett, Lac l. Canada 152 G4
Woolyeenyer Hill hill Australia 135 C8
Woomera Australia 137 B6
Woomera Prohibited Area Australia 135 F7
Woonsocket RI U.S.A. 165 J2
Woonsocket SD U.S.A. 160 D2
Woorabinda Australia 136 E5
Wooramel r. Australia 135 A6
Wooster OH U.S.A. 164 E3
Wootton Bassett, Royal town U.K. 59 F7
Worbis Germany 63 K3
Worbody Point Australia 136 C2
Worcester S. Africa 124 D7
Worcester U.K. 59 E6
Worcester MA U.S.A. 165 J2
Worcester NY U.S.A. 165 H2
Wörgl Austria 57 N7
Workai i. Indon. 81 I8
Workington U.K. 58 D4
Worksop U.K. 58 F5
Workum Neth. 62 F2
Worland WY U.S.A. 156 G3
Wörlitz Germany 63 M3
Wormerveer Neth. 62 E2
Worms Germany 63 I5
Worms Head hd U.K. 59 C7
Wortel Namibia 124 C2
Wörth am Rhein Germany 63 I5
Worthing U.K. 59 G8
Worthington IN U.S.A. 164 B4
Worthington MN U.S.A. 160 E3
Wosi Halmahera Indon. 83 C3
Wosu Sulawesi Indon. 83 B3
Wotje atoll Marshall Is 186 H5
Wotu Sulawesi Indon. 83 B3
Woudrichem Neth. 62 E3
Woustviller France 62 H5
Wowoni i. Indon. 83 B4
Wowoni, Selat sea chan. Indon. 83 B3
Wozrojdeniye Oroli i. Uzbek. see Vozrozhdenya Island
Wrangel Island Rus. Fed. 77 T2
Wrangell AK U.S.A. 149 N4
Wrangell, Cape AK U.S.A. 148 [inset] A5
Wrangell, Mount AK U.S.A. 149 K3
Wrangell Island AK U.S.A. 150 C3
Wrangell Mountains AK U.S.A. 148 H4
Wrangell-St Elias National Park and Preserve AK U.S.A. 149 L3
Wrath, Cape U.K. 60 D2
Wray CO U.S.A. 160 C3
Wreake r. U.K. 59 F6
Wreck Point S. Africa 124 C5
Wreck Reef Australia 136 F4
Wrecsam U.K. see Wrexham
Wrestedt Germany 63 K2
Wrexham U.K. 59 E5
Wrightmyo India 87 A5
Wrightson, Mount AZ U.S.A. 157 F7
Wrightwood CA U.S.A. 158 E4
Wrigley Canada 149 Q3
Wrigley KY U.S.A. 164 D4
Wrigley Gulf Antarctica 188 J2
Wrocław Poland 57 P5
Września Poland 57 P4
Wu'an Fujian China see Changtai
Wu'an Hebei China 95 H4
Wubin Australia 135 B7
Wubu China 95 G4
Wuchagou China 95 J2
Wuchang Heilong. China 90 B3
Wuchang Hubei China see Jiangxia
Wuchow China see Wuzhou
Wuchuan Guangdong China 97 F4
Wuchuan Guizhou China 96 E2
Wuchuan Nei Mongol China 95 G3
Wuda China see Ud
Wudalianchi China 90 B2
Wuḍām 'Alwā Oman 110 E6
Wudan China 95 I3
Wudang Shan mt. China 97 F1
Wudao China 95 J4
Wudaoliang China 94 C5
Wudi China 95 I4
Wuding China 96 D3
Wuding He r. China 95 G4
Wudinna Australia 135 F8
Wufeng Hubei China 97 F2
Wufeng Yunnan China see Zhenxiong
Wufo China 94 F4
Wugang China 97 F3
Wugong China 95 G5
Wuhai China 94 F4
Wuhan China 97 G2
Wuhu China 97 H1
Wuhu China 97 H2
Wuhua China 97 G4
Wuhubei China 97 H2
Wūjang China 99 B6
Wu Jiang r. China 96 E2
Wujin Jiangsu China see Changzhou
Wujin Sichuan China see Xinjin
Wukari Nigeria 120 D4
Wulang China 96 B2
Wuleidao Wan b. China 95 J4
Wuli China 94 C5
Wulian Feng mts China 96 D2
Wuliang Shan mts China 96 D3
Wuliaru i. Indon. 134 E1
Wuli Jiang r. China 97 F4
Wulik r. AK U.S.A. 148 F2
Wuling Shan mts China 97 F2
Wulong China 96 E2
Wulongji China see Huaibin
Wulur Maluku Indon. 83 D4
Wumatang China 99 E7
Wumeng Shan mts China 96 D3
Wuming China 97 F4
Wümme r. Germany 63 I1
Wundwin Myanmar 86 B2
Wuning China 97 G2
Wünnenberg Germany 63 I3
Wunnummin Lake Canada 147 J4
Wunsiedel Germany 63 M4
Wunstorf Germany 63 J2
Wupatki National Monument nat. park AZ U.S.A. 159 H4
Wuping China 97 H3
Wuppertal Germany 63 H3
Wuppertal S. Africa 124 D7
Wuqi China 95 G4
Wuqia Xinjiang China 98 A5
Wuqia Xinjiang China 98 A5
Wuqiang China 95 H4
Wuqiao China 95 I4
Wuqing China 95 I4
Wuquan China see Wuyang
Wuranga Australia 135 B7
Wurno Nigeria 120 D3
Würzburg Germany 63 J5
Wurzen Germany 63 M3
Wushan Chongqing China 97 F2
Wushan Gansu China 94 F5
Wu Shan mts China 97 F2
Wushi Guangdong China 97 F4
Wushi Xinjiang China 98 B4
Wüstegarten hill Germany 63 J3
Wusuli Jiang r. China/Rus. Fed. see Ussuri
Wutai Shanxi China 95 H4
Wutai Xinjiang China 98 C3
Wutaishan China 95 H4
Wutai Shan mts China 95 H4
Wutonggou Gansu China 94 D3
Wutonggou Xinjiang China 98 E4
Wutongwozi Quan well China 94 C3
Wuvulu Island P.N.G. 81 K7
Wuwei China 94 E4
Wuxi Chongqing China 97 F2
Wuxi Hunan China 97 F2
Wuxi Hunan China see Qiyang
Wuxi Jiangsu China 97 I2
Wuxia China see Wushan
Wuxian China see Suzhou
Wuxiang China 95 H4
Wuxing China see Huzhou
Wuxu China 97 F4
Wuxuan China 97 F4
Wuxue China 97 G2
Wuyang Guizhou China see Zhenyuan
Wuyang Henan China 97 G1
Wuyang Shanxi China 95 H4
Wuyang Zhejiang China see Wuyi
Wuyi China 97 H2
Wuyiling China 90 C2
Wuyi Shan mts China 97 H3
Wuyuan Jiangxi China 97 H2
Wuyuan Nei Mongol China 95 G3
Wuyuan Zhejiang China see Haiyan
Wuyun China see Jinyun
Wuzhai China 95 G4
Wuzhi China 95 H5
Wuzhishan China 97 F5
Wuzhi Shan mts China 97 F5
Wuzhong China 94 F4
Wuzhou China 97 F4
Wyalkatchem Australia 135 B7
Wyalong Australia 138 C4
Wyandra Australia 138 B1
Wyangala Reservoir Australia 138 D4
Wyara, Lake salt flat Australia 138 B2
Wycheproof Australia 138 A6
Wylliesburg VA U.S.A. 165 F5
Wyloo Australia 134 B5
Wylye r. U.K. 59 F7
Wymondham U.K. 59 I6
Wymore NE U.S.A. 160 D3
Wynbring Australia 135 F7
Wyndham Australia 134 E3
Wyndham-Werribee Australia 138 B6
Wynne AR U.S.A. 161 F5
Wynyard Canada 151 J5
Wyola Lake salt flat Australia 135 E7
Wyoming MI U.S.A. 164 C2
Wyoming state U.S.A. 156 G4
Wyoming Peak WY U.S.A. 156 F4
Wyoming Range mts WY U.S.A. 156 F4
Wyong Australia 138 E4
Wyperfeld National Park Australia 137 C7
Wysox PA U.S.A. 165 G3
Wyszków Poland 57 R4
Wythall U.K. 59 F6
Wytheville VA U.S.A. 164 E5
Wytmarsum Neth. see Witmarsum

X

Xaafuun Somalia 122 F2

▶Xaafuun, Raas pt Somalia 108 H7
Most easterly point of Africa.

Xabyai China 99 G7
Xabyaisamba China 96 C2
Xaçmaz Azer. 113 H2
Xagjang China 99 F7
Xagnag China 99 C6
Xago China 99 E7
Xagquka China 99 F7
Xaidulla China 99 B5
Xaignabouli Laos 86 C3
Xaignabouri Laos see Xaignabouli
Xainza China 99 E7
Xaitongmoin China 99 E7
Xai-Xai Moz. 125 K3
Xakur China 98 B5
Xal, Cerro de hill Mex. 167 H4
Xalapa Mex. 168 E5
Xaltianguis Mex. 167 F5
Xamba China 95 F3
Xambioa Brazil 177 I5
Xam Nua Laos 86 D2
Xá-Muteba Angola 123 B4
Xan r. Laos 86 C3
Xanagas Botswana 124 E2
Xangd China 94 E3
Xangda China see Nangqên
Xangdin Hural China 95 G3
Xangdoring China 99 C6
Xangongo Angola 123 B5
Xangzha China 99 F7
Xanica Mex. 167 F5

▶Xankändi Azer. 113 G3
Capital of Nagorno-Karabakh.

Xanthi Greece 69 K4
Xarag China 94 D4
Xarardheere Somalia 122 E3
Xarba La pass China 99 D7
Xar Burd China see Bayan Nuru
Xardong China 99 D7
Xar Hudag China 95 H2
Xar Moron r. China 95 G3
Xar Moron r. China 95 J3
Xarru China 99 D7
Xarsingma China see Yadong
Xàtiva Spain 67 F4
Xavantes, Serra dos hills Brazil 177 I6
Xaxa China 99 C6
Xayar China 98 C4
Xazgat China 98 D3
Xcalak Mex. 167 I5
X-Can Mex. 167 I4
Xegil China 98 B4
Xekar China 98 B5
Xelva Spain see Chelva
Xenia OH U.S.A. 164 D4
Xênkyêr China 99 E7
Xero Potamos r. Cyprus see Xeros
Xeros r. Cyprus 107 A2
Xhora S. Africa see Elliotdale
Xia Awat China 98 B5
Xiabancheng China see Chengde
Xia Bazar China 98 B5
Xiabole Shan mt. China 90 B2
Xiachuan Dao i. China 97 G4
Xiacun China see Rushan

Yeghegnadzor Armenia 113 G3
Yegindybulak Kazakh. 98 B2
Yegindykol' Kazakh. 102 C1
Yegorlykskaya Rus. Fed. 53 I7
Yegorova, Mys pt Rus. Fed. 90 E3
Yegor'yevsk Rus. Fed. 53 H5
Yei South Sudan 121 G4
Yei r. South Sudan 121 G4
Yeji China 97 G2
Yejiaji China see Yeji
Yekaterinburg Rus. Fed. 76 H4
Yekaterinodar Rus. Fed. see Krasnodar
Yekaterinoslav Ukr. see Dnipropetrovs'k
Yekaterinoslavka Rus. Fed. 90 C2
Yekhegnadzor Armenia see Yeghegnadzor
Yekibastuz Kazakh. 102 E1
Ye Kyun i. Myanmar 86 A3
Yelabuga Khabarovskiy Kray Rus. Fed. 90 D2
Yelabuga Respublika Tatarstan Rus. Fed. 52 K5
Yelan' Rus. Fed. 53 I6
Yelan' r. Rus. Fed. 53 I6
Yelandur India 106 C3
Yelantsy Rus. Fed. 88 J2
Yelarbon Australia 138 E2
Yelbarsli Turkm. 111 F2
Yelenovskiye Kar'yery Ukr. see Dokuchayevs'k
Yelets Rus. Fed. 53 H5
Yeliguan China 94 E5
Yélimané Mali 120 B3
Yelizavetgrad Ukr. see Kirovohrad
Yelkhovka Rus. Fed. 53 K5
Yell i. U.K. 60 [inset]
Yellabina Regional Reserve nature res. Australia 135 F7
Yellandu India 106 D2
Yellapur India 106 B3
Yellowhead Pass Canada 150 G4

▶Yellowknife Canada 150 H2
Capital of the Northwest Territories.

Yellowknife r. Canada 150 H2
Yellow Mountain hill Australia 138 C4

▶Yellow River r. China 95 I4
4th longest river in Asia and 7th in the world.

Yellow Sea N. Pacific Ocean 89 N5
Yellowstone r. MT U.S.A. 160 C2
Yellowstone Lake WY U.S.A. 156 F3
Yellowstone National Park U.S.A. 156 F3
Yell Sound strait U.K. 60 [inset]
Yeloten Turkm. see Ýolöten
Yelovo Rus. Fed. 51 Q4
Yel'sk Belarus 53 F6
Yel'tay Kazakh. 98 C3
Yelucá mt. Nicaragua 166 [inset] I6
Yelva r. Rus. Fed. 52 K3
Yema Nanshan mts China 94 C4
Yema Shan mts China 98 F5
Yematan Qinghai China 94 D4
Yematan Qinghai China 94 D5
Yemel' r. Kazakh. 98 C3
Yemen country Asia 108 G6
Yemetsk Rus. Fed. 52 I3
Yemişenbükü Turkey see Taşova
Yemmiganur India see Emmiganuru
Yemtsa Rus. Fed. 52 I3
Yemva Rus. Fed. 52 K3
Yena Rus. Fed. 54 Q3
Yenagoa Nigeria 120 D4
Yenakiyeve Ukr. 53 H6
Yenakiyevo Ukr. see Yenakiyeve
Yenangyat Myanmar 86 A2
Yenangyaung Myanmar 86 A2
Yenanma Myanmar 86 A3
Yenbek Kazakh. 98 B2
Yenda Australia 138 C5
Yêndum China see Zhag'yab
Yengisar Xinjiang China 98 B5
Yengisar Xinjiang China 98 D4
Yengisu China 98 D4
Yengo National Park Australia 138 E4
Yenice Turkey 69 L5
Yenidamlar Turkey see Demirtaş
Yenihan Turkey see Yıldızeli
Yenije-i-Vardar Greece see Giannitsa
Yenişehir Greece see Larisa
Yenişehir Turkey 69 M4

▶Yenisey r. Rus. Fed. 76 J2
Part of the Yenisey-Angara-Selenga, 3rd longest river in Asia.

▶Yenisey-Angara-Selenga r. Rus. Fed. 76 J2
3rd longest river in Asia and 6th in the world.

Yeniseysk Rus. Fed. 76 K4
Yeniseyskaya Ravnina ridge Rus. Fed. 76 K4
Yeniseyskiy Zaliv inlet Rus. Fed. 189 F2
Yeniugou China 94 D4
Yeniugou Shisuzhan China 94 D5
Yeniyol Turkey see Borçka
Yên Minh Vietnam 86 D2
Yenotayevka Rus. Fed. 53 J7
Yentna r. AK U.S.A. 149 J3
Yeola India 106 B1
Yeo Lake salt flat Australia 135 D6
Yeotmal India see Yavatmal
Yeoval Australia 138 D4
Yeovil U.K. 59 E8
Yeo Yeo r. Australia see Bland
Yepachi Mex. 166 C2
Yeppoon Australia 136 E4
Yeraliyev Kazakh. see Kuryk
Yerbabuena Mex. 167 E4
Yerbent Turkm. 110 E2
Yerbogachen Rus. Fed. 77 L3
Yercaud India 106 C4

▶Yerevan Armenia 113 G2
Capital of Armenia.

Yereymentau Kazakh. 102 D1
Yergara India 106 C2
Yergeni hills Rus. Fed. 53 J7
Yergoğu Romania see Giurgiu
Yeriho West Bank see Jericho
Yerilla Australia 135 C7
Yerington NV U.S.A. 158 D2
Yerköy Turkey 112 D3
Yerla r. India 106 B2
Yermak Kazakh. see Aksu
Yermakovo Rus. Fed. 90 B1
Yermak Plateau sea feature Arctic Ocean 189 H1
Yermentau Kazakh. see Yereymentau
Yermo Mex. 166 D3
Yermo CA U.S.A. 158 E4
Yerofey Pavlovich Rus. Fed. 90 A1
Yerres r. France 62 C6
Yërsha r. Rus. Fed. 52 L2
Yershov Rus. Fed. 53 K6
Yertsevo Rus. Fed. 52 I3
Yeruham Israel 107 B4
Yerupaja mt. Peru 176 C6
Yerushalayim Israel/West Bank see Jerusalem
Yeruslan r. Rus. Fed. 53 J6
Yesagyo Myanmar 86 A2
Yesan S. Korea 91 B5
Yesik Kazakh. 98 B4
Yesil' Kazakh. 100 F1
Yeşilhisar Turkey 112 D3
Yeşilırmak r. Turkey 112 E2
Yeşilova Turkey 69 M6
Yeşilova Turkey see Sorgun
Yespe Kazakh. 98 A4
Yessentuki Rus. Fed. 113 F1
Yessey Rus. Fed. 77 L3
Yes Tor hill U.K. 59 C8
Yêtatang China see Baqên
Yetman Australia 138 E2
Ye-U Myanmar 86 A2
Yeu, Île d' i. France 66 C3
Yevdokimovskoye Rus. Fed. see Krasnogvardeyskoye
Yevlakh Azer. see Yevlax
Yevlax Azer. 113 G2
Yevpatoriya Ukr. 112 D1
Yevreyskaya Avtonomnaya Oblast' admin. div. Rus. Fed. 90 D2
Yexian China see Laizhou
Yeyik China 99 C5
Yeysk Rus. Fed. 53 H7
Yeyungou China 98 D4
Yezhou China see Jianshi
Yezhuga r. Rus. Fed. 52 J2
Yezo i. Japan see Hokkaidō
Yezyaryshcha Belarus 52 F5
Y Fenni U.K. see Abergavenny
Y Fflint U.K. see Flint
Y Gelli Gandryll U.K. see Hay-on-Wye
Yialí i. Greece see Gyali
Yi'allaq, Gebel mt. Egypt see Yu'alliq, Jabal
Yialousa Cyprus see Aigialousa
Yi'an China 90 B3
Yianisádha i. Greece see Gianisada
Yiannitsá Greece see Giannitsa
Yibin Sichuan China 96 E2
Yibin Sichuan China 96 E2
Yibug Caka salt l. China 99 D6
Yichang China 97 F2
Yicheng Henan China see Zhumadian
Yicheng Hubei China 97 G2
Yicheng Shanxi China 95 G5
Yichuan Henan China 95 H5
Yichuan Shaanxi China 95 G5
Yichun Heilong. China 90 C3
Yichun Jiangxi China 97 G3
Yidu Hubei China see Zhicheng
Yidu Shandong China see Qingzhou
Yidun China 96 C2
Yifeng China 97 G2
Yiggêtang Qinghai China see Sêrwolungwa
Yiggêtang Qinghai China 94 D5
Yihatuoli China 94 D3
Yi He r. Henan China 95 H5
Yi He r. Shandong China 95 I5
Yihuang China 97 H3
Yijun China 95 G5
Yilaha China 95 K1
Yilan China 90 C3
Yilan Taiwan see Ilan
Yıldız Dağları mts Turkey 69 L4
Yıldızeli Turkey 112 E3
Yilehuli Shan mts China 90 A2
Yiliang China 96 E3
Yiling China 97 F2
Yiliping China 99 F5
Yilong Heilong. China 90 B3
Yilong Sichuan China 96 E2
Yilong Yunnan China see Shiping
Yilong Hu l. China 96 D4
Yimatu He r. China 95 I3
Yimianpo China 90 C3
Yimin He r. China 95 I1
Yinan China 95 I5
Yinbaing Myanmar 86 B3
Yincheng China see Dexing
Yinchuan China 94 F4
Yindarlgooda, Lake salt flat Australia 135 C7
Yingcheng China 97 G2
Yingde China 97 G3
Yinggehai China 97 F5
Yinggen China see Qiongzhong
Ying He r. China 97 H1
Yingjing China 96 D2
Yingkiong India 105 H3
Yingkou Liaoning China 95 J3
Yingkou Liaoning China see Dashiqiao
Yingpanshui China 94 F4
Yingshan China 97 G2
Yingtan China 97 H2
Yingtaoyuan China 95 H5
Yingxian China 95 H4
Yining Jiangxi China see Xiushui
Yining Xinjiang China 98 C4
Yining Xinjiang China 98 C4
Yinjiang China 97 F3
Yinkeng China see Yinkengxu
Yinkengxu China 97 G3
Yinmabin Myanmar 86 A2
Yinnyein Myanmar 86 B3
Yin Shan mts China 95 G3
Yinxian China see Ningbo
Yi'ong Nongchang China 99 F7
Yi'ong Zangbo r. China 99 F7
Yipinglang China 96 D3
Yiquan China see Meitan
Yiran Co l. China 99 F6
Yirga Alem Eth. 122 D3
Yirol South Sudan 121 G4
Yirshi China 95 I2
Yirtkuq Bulak spring China 98 E4
Yirxie China see Yirshi
Yisa China see Honghe
Yishan Guangxi China see Yizhou
Yishan Jiangsu China see Guanyun
Yi Shan mt. China 95 I4
Yishui China 95 I5
Yishun Sing. 87 [inset]
Yíthion Greece see Gytheio
Yitiaoshan China see Jingtai
Yitong He r. China 90 B3
Yi Tu, Nam r. Myanmar 86 B2
Yiwanquan China 94 C3
Yiwu Xinjiang China 94 C3
Yiwu Yunnan China 96 D4
Yiwulü Shan mts China 95 J3
Yixian China 95 J3
Yixing China 97 H2
Yiyang China 97 G2
Yiyuan China 95 I4
Yizheng China 97 H1
Yizhou Guangxi China 97 F3
Yizhou Liaoning China see Yixian
Yizra'el country Asia see Israel
Yläne Fin. 55 M6
Ylihärmä Fin. 54 M5
Yli-Ii Fin. 54 N4
Yli-Kärppä Fin. 54 N4
Ylikiiminki Fin. 54 O4
Yli-Kitka l. Fin. 54 P3
Ylistaro Fin. 54 M5
Ylitornio Fin. 54 M3
Ylivieska Fin. 54 N4
Ylöjärvi Fin. 55 M6
Ymer Ø i. Greenland 147 P2
Ynys Enlli i. U.K. see Bardsey Island
Ynys Môn i. U.K. see Anglesey
Yoakum TX U.S.A. 161 D6
Yoder IN U.S.A. 164 C3
Yodo-gawa r. Japan 92 B4
Yogan, Cerro mt. Chile 178 B8
Yogo Japan 92 C3
Yogyakarta Indon. 85 E4
Yogyakarta admin. dist. Indon. 85 E5
Yoho National Park Canada 150 G5
Yoigilanglêb Hu r. China 99 G6
Yojoa, Lago de l. Hond. 166 [inset] I6
Yōka Japan 92 A3
Yokadouma Cameroon 121 E4
Yōkaichi Japan 92 C3
Yōkaichiba Japan 93 G3
Yokawa Japan 92 B4
Yokkaichi Japan 92 C4
Yoko Cameroon 120 E4
Yokohama Japan 93 F3
Yokokawa Japan 93 E2
Yokoshiba Japan 93 G3
Yokosuka Japan 93 F3
Yokote Japan 91 F5
Yokoze Japan 93 F3
Yola Nigeria 120 E4
Yolaina, Cordillera de mts Nicaragua 166 [inset] I7
Yolo CA U.S.A. 158 C2
Yolombo Dem. Rep. Congo 122 C4
Ýolöten Turkm. 111 F2
Yoloxóchitl Mex. 167 F5
Yoluk Mex. 167 I4
Yom, Mae Nam r. Thai. 86 C4
Yomou Guinea 120 C4
Yomuka Indon. 81 J8
Yonaguni-jima i. Japan 97 I3
Yŏnan N. Korea 91 B5
Yonezawa Japan 91 F5
Yong'an Chongqing China see Fengjie
Yong'an Fujian China 97 H3
Yongbei China see Yongsheng
Yongchang China 94 E4
Yongcheng China 95 I5
Yongcong China 97 F3
Yongdeng China 94 E4
Yongding Fujian China 97 H3
Yongding Yunnan China see Fumin
Yongding Yunnan China see Yongren
Yongding He r. China 95 I4
Yongfeng Jiangxi China 97 G3
Yongfeng Xinjiang China 98 D4
Yongfu China 97 F3
Yonghe China 95 G4
Yŏnghŭng N. Korea 91 B5
Yŏnghŭng-man b. N. Korea 91 B5
Yŏngil-man b. S. Korea 91 C6
Yongjing Gansu China 94 E5
Yongjing Guizhou China see Xifeng
Yongjing Liaoning China see Xifeng
Yŏngju S. Korea 91 C5
Yongkang Yunnan China 96 C3
Yongkang Zhejiang China 97 I2
Yongle China see Zhen'an
Yongnian China 95 H4
Yongning Guangxi China 97 F4
Yongning Jiangxi China see Tonggu
Yongning Ningxia China 94 F4
Yongning Sichuan China see Xuyong
Yongping China 96 C3
Yongqing China see Qingshui
Yongren China 96 D3
Yongsheng China 96 D3
Yongshou China 95 G5
Yongshun China 97 F2
Yongtai China 97 H3
Yongxi China see Nayong
Yongxin China 97 G3
Yongxing Hunan China 97 G3
Yongxing Shaanxi China 95 G4
Yongxiu China 97 G2
Yongyang China see Weng'an
Yongzhou China 97 F3
Yonkers NY U.S.A. 165 I3
Yopal Col. 176 D2
Yopurga China 98 B5
Yoquivo Mex. 166 D3
Yordu India 104 C2
Yorii Japan 93 F2
York Australia 135 B7
York Canada 164 F2
York U.K. 58 F5
York AL U.S.A. 161 F5
York NE U.S.A. 160 D3
York PA U.S.A. 165 G4
York, Cape Australia 136 C1
York, Kap c. Greenland see Innaanganeq
York, Vale of valley U.K. 58 F4
Yorke Peninsula Australia 137 B7
York Mountains AK U.S.A. 148 F2
Yorkshire Dales National Park U.K. 58 E4
Yorkshire Wolds hills U.K. 58 G5
Yorkton Canada 151 K5
Yorktown VA U.S.A. 165 G5
Yorkville IL U.S.A. 160 F3
Yoro Hond. 166 [inset] I6
Yōrō Japan 92 C3
Yoroi-zaki pt Japan 92 C4
Yoronga i. Maluku Indon. 83 D3
Yöröö Gol r. Mongolia 94 F1
Yorosso Mali 120 C3
Yosemite KY U.S.A. 164 C5
Yosemite National Park CA U.S.A. 158 D3
Yoshida Saitama Japan 93 F2
Yoshida Shizuoka Japan 93 E4
Yoshii Japan 93 E2
Yoshima Japan 93 G1
Yoshino Japan 92 B4
Yoshinodani Japan 92 C2
Yoshino-gawa r. Japan 92 B4
Yoshino-Kumano Kokuritsu-kōen nat. park Japan 92 C5
Yoshkar-Ola Rus. Fed. 52 J4
Yösöndzüyl Mongolia 94 E2
Yos Sudarso i. Indon. see Dolok, Pulau
Yŏsu S. Korea 91 B6
Yotsukaidō Japan 93 G3
Yotsukura Japan 93 G1
Yotvata Israel 107 B5
Youbou Canada 150 E5
Youdunzi China 99 E5
Youghal Ireland 61 E6
Young Australia 138 D5
Young AZ U.S.A. 159 H4
Younghusband, Lake salt flat Australia 137 B6
Younghusband Peninsula Australia 137 B7
Young Island Antarctica 188 H2
Youngstown Canada 151 I5
Youngstown OH U.S.A. 164 E3
Youshashan China 99 E5
You Shui r. China 97 F2
Youssoufia Morocco 64 C5
Youvarou Mali 120 C3
Youxi China 97 H3
Youxian China 97 G3
Youyang China 97 F2
Youyi China 90 C3
Youyi Feng mt. China/Rus. Fed. 98 D2
Yovon Tajik. 111 H2
Yowah watercourse Australia 138 B2
Yozgat Turkey 112 D3
Ypres Belgium see Ieper
Yreka CA U.S.A. 156 C4
Yrghyz Kazakh. see Irgiz
Yrgyz r. Kazakh. 102 B2
Yr Wyddfa mt. U.K. see Snowdon
Yser r. France 62 C4
also known as IJzer (Belgium)
Ysselsteyn Neth. 62 F3
Ystad Sweden 55 H9
Ystwyth r. U.K. 59 C6
Ysyk-Ata Kyrg. 98 A4
Ysyk-Köl Kyrg. see Balykchy
Ysyk-Köl admin. div. Kyrg. 98 B4

▶Ysyk-Köl salt l. Kyrg. 102 E3
5th largest lake in Asia.

Ythan r. U.K. 60 G3
Y Trallwng U.K. see Welshpool
Ytyk-Kyuyel' Rus. Fed. 77 O3
Yu i. Maluku Indon. 83 D3
Yu'alliq, Jabal mt. Egypt 107 A4
Yuan'an China 97 F2
Yuanbaoshan China 95 I3
Yuanbao Shan mt. China 97 F3
Yuanjiang Hunan China 97 G2
Yuanjiang Yunnan China 96 D4
Yuan Jiang r. Hunan China 97 F2
Yuan Jiang r. Yunnan China 96 D4
Yuanjiazhuang China see Foping
Yuanlin China 95 J1
Yuanling China 97 F2
Yuanma China see Yuanmou
Yuanmou China 96 D3
Yuanping China 95 H4
Yuanqu China 95 G5
Yuanquan China see Anxi
Yuanshan China see Lianping
Yuanshanzi China 94 D4
Yuanyang China see Xinjie
Yuasa Japan 92 B4
Yub'ā i. Saudi Arabia 112 D6
Yuba City CA U.S.A. 158 C2
Yubei China 96 E2
Yuben' Tajik. 111 I2
Yucatán pen. Mex. 167 H5
Yucatán state Mex. 167 H4
Yucatan Channel Cuba/Mex. 167 I4
Yucca AZ U.S.A. 159 F4
Yucca Lake NV U.S.A. 158 E3
Yucca Valley CA U.S.A. 158 E4
Yucheng Henan China 95 H5
Yucheng Shandong China 95 I4
Yucheng Sichuan China see Ya'an
Yuci China see Jinzhong
Yudi Shan mt. China 90 A1
Yudu China 97 G3
Yuelai China see Huachuan
Yueliang Pao l. China 95 J2
Yuendumu Australia 134 E5
Yuen Long H.K. China 97 [inset]
Yueqing China 97 I2
Yuexi China 97 H2
Yueyang Hunan China 97 G2
Yueyang Hunan China 97 G2
Yueyang Sichuan China see Anyue
Yug r. Rus. Fed. 52 J3
Yugan China 97 H2
Yugawara Japan 93 F3
Yugê China 99 F6
Yugorsk Rus. Fed. 51 S3

▶Yugoslavia country Europe 69 I2
Former European country. Up to 1993 included Bosnia-Herzegovina, Croatia, Macedonia and Slovenia. Renamed as Serbia and Montenegro in 2003. Serbia and Montenegro became separate independent countries in June 2006, Kosovo declared independence from Serbia in February 2008.

Yuhang China 97 I2
Yuhu China see Eryuan
Yuhuan China 97 I2
Yuhuang Ding mt. China 95 I4
Yui Japan 93 E3
Yuin Australia 135 B6
Yu Jiang r. China 97 F4
Yukagirskoye Ploskogor'ye plat. Rus. Fed. 77 Q3
Yukamenskoye Rus. Fed. 52 L4
Yukarı Sakarya Ovaları plain Turkey 69 N5
Yukarısarıkaya Turkey 112 D3
Yūki Japan 93 F2
Yuki r. AK U.S.A. 148 H2
Yukon admin. div. Canada 149 N3

▶Yukon r. Canada/U.S.A. 148 F3
5th longest river in North America.

Yukon-Charley Rivers National Preserve nature res. AK U.S.A. 149 L2
Yukon Crossing (abandoned) Canada 149 M3
Yukon Delta AK U.S.A. 148 F3
Yukon Flats National Wildlife Refuge nature res. AK U.S.A. 149 K2
Yüksekova Turkey 113 G3
Yulara Australia 135 E6
Yule r. Australia 134 B5
Yuleba Australia 138 D1
Yulee FL U.S.A. 163 D6
Yuli China 98 D4
Yulin Guangxi China 97 F4
Yulin Shaanxi China 95 G4
Yulong Xueshan mt. China 96 D3
Yuma AZ U.S.A. 159 F5
Yuma CO U.S.A. 160 C3
Yuma Desert AZ U.S.A. 159 F5
Yumco China 99 D7
Yumen Gansu China 94 D3
Yumen Gansu China see Laojunmiao
Yumendongzhan China 94 D4
Yumenguan China 98 F4
Yumenzhen China see Yumen
Yumin China 98 C3
Yumt Uul mt. Mongolia 94 D2
Yumurtalık Turkey 107 B1
Yuna Australia 135 A7
Yunak Turkey 112 C3
Yunan China 97 F4
Yunaska Island AK U.S.A. 148 E5
Yuncheng Shandong China 95 H5
Yuncheng Shanxi China 95 G5
Yundamindera Australia 135 C7
Yunfu China 97 G4
Yungas reg. Bol. 176 E7
Yungui Gaoyuan plat. China 96 D3
Yunhe Jiangsu China see Pizhou
Yunhe Yunnan China see Heqing
Yunhe Zhejiang China 97 H2
Yunjinghong China see Jinghong
Yunkai Dashan mts China 97 F4
Yünlin Taiwan see Touliu
Yunling China see Yunxiao
Yun Ling mts China 96 C3
Yunlong China 96 C3
Yunmeng China 97 G2
Yunmenling China see Junmenling
Yunnan prov. China 96 D3
Yunta Australia 137 B7
Yunt Dağı mt. Turkey 107 A1
Yunxi Hubei China 97 F1
Yunxi Sichuan China see Yanting
Yunxian Hubei China 97 F1
Yunxian Yunnan China 96 D3
Yunxiao China 97 H4
Yunyang Chongqing China 97 F2
Yunyang Henan China 97 G1
Yuping Guizhou China see Libo
Yuping Guizhou China 97 F3
Yuping Yunnan China see Pingbian
Yuqing China 96 E3
Yura Japan 92 B5
Yura-gawa r. Japan 92 B3
Yuraygir National Park Australia 138 F2
Yurba Co l. China 99 D6
Yürekli Turkey 107 B1
Yurga Rus. Fed. 76 J4
Yuriria Mex. 168 D4
Yurungkax He r. China 99 C5
Yur'ya Rus. Fed. 52 K4
Yur'yakha r. Rus. Fed. 52 L2
Yuryev Estonia see Tartu
Yur'yevets Rus. Fed. 52 I4
Yur'yev-Pol'skiy Rus. Fed. 52 H4
Yuscarán Hond. 166 [inset] I6
Yushan China 97 H2
Yü Shan mt. Taiwan 97 I4
Yushe China 95 H4
Yushino (abandoned) Rus. Fed. 52 L1
Yushkozero Rus. Fed. 54 R4
Yushu Jilin China 90 B3
Yushu Qinghai China 96 C1
Yushugou China 98 D4
Yushuwan China see Huaihua
Yusufeli Turkey 113 F2
Yus'va Rus. Fed. 51 Q4
Yuta West Bank see Yatta
Yutai China 95 I5
Yutan China see Ningxiang
Yutian Hebei China 95 I4
Yutian Xinjiang China 99 C5
Yutiangao China 95 I3
Yūtō Japan 92 D4
Yuwang China 94 F4
Yuxi Guizhou China see Daozhen
Yuxi Hubei China 97 F2
Yuxi Yunnan China 96 D3
Yuxian Hebei China 95 H4
Yuxian Shanxi China 95 H4
Yuyangguan China 97 F2
Yuyao China 97 I2
Yuzawa Japan 91 F5
Yuzha Rus. Fed. 52 I4
Yuzhno-Kamyshovyy Khrebet ridge Rus. Fed. 90 F3
Yuzhno-Kuril'sk Rus. Fed. 90 G3
Yuzhno-Muyskiy Khrebet mts Rus. Fed. 89 K1
Yuzhno-Sakhalinsk Rus. Fed. 90 F3
Yuzhno-Sukhokumsk Rus. Fed. 113 G1
Yuzhnoukrayinsk Ukr. 53 F7
Yuzhnyy Rus. Fed. see Adyk
Yuzhnyy, Ostrov island Rus. Fed. 76 G2
Yuzhnyy Altay, Khrebet mts Kazakh. 98 D2
Yuzhong China 94 F5
Yuzhou Chongqing China see Chongqing
Yuzhou Hebei China see Yuxian
Yuzhou Henan China 95 H5
Yuzovka Ukr. see Donets'k
Yuzuruha-yama hill Japan 92 A4
Yverdon Switz. 66 H3
Yvetot France 66 E2
Ywamun Myanmar 86 A2

Z

Zaamin Uzbek. see Zomin
Zaandam Neth. 62 E2
Zab, Monts du mts Alg. 67 I6
Zabānābād Iran 110 E3
Zabaykal'sk Rus. Fed. 95 I1
Zabaykal'skiy Kray admin. div. Rus. Fed. 95 H1
Zabīd Yemen 108 F7
Zābol Iran 111 F4
Zabqung China 99 D7
Zacapa Guat. 167 H6
Zacapu Mex. 167 E5
Zacatal Mex. 167 H5
Zacatecas Mex. 168 D4
Zacatecas state Mex. 161 C8
Zacatecoluca El Salvador 166 [inset] H6
Zacatepec Mex. 167 F5
Zacatlán Mex. 167 F5
Zacharo Greece 69 I6
Zacoalco Mex. 168 D4
Zacualpán Mex. 167 F5
Zacynthus i. Greece see Zakynthos
Zadar Croatia 68 F2
Zadetkale Kyun i. Myanmar 87 B5
Zadetkyi Kyun i. Myanmar 87 B5
Zadi Myanmar 87 B4
Zadoi China 99 F6
Zadonsk Rus. Fed. 53 H5
Za'farâna Egypt see Za'farānah
Za'farānah Egypt 112 D5
Zafer Adaları is Cyprus see Kleides Islands
Zafer Burnu c. Cyprus see Apostolos Andreas, Cape
Zafora i. Greece see Sofrana
Zafra Spain 67 C4
Zagazig Egypt see Az Zaqāzīq
Zaghdeh well Iran 110 E3
Zaghouan Tunisia 68 D6
Zagorsk Rus. Fed. see Sergiyev Posad

▶Zagreb Croatia 68 F2
Capital of Croatia.

Zagros, Kūhhā-ye mts Iran see Zagros Mountains
Zagros Mountains Iran 110 B3
Zagunao China see Lixian
Za'gya Zangbo r. China 99 E7
Zāhedān Iran 111 F4
Zahir Pir Pak. 111 H4
Zahlah Lebanon see Zahlé
Zahlé Lebanon 107 B3
Zähmet Turkm. 111 F2
Zahrān Saudi Arabia 108 F6
Zahrez Chergui salt pan Alg. 67 H6
Zahrez Rharbi salt pan Alg. 67 H6
Zainlha China see Xiaojin
Zainsk Rus. Fed. see Novyy Zay
Zaire country Africa see Congo, Democratic Republic of the
Zaïre r. Congo/Dem. Rep. Congo see Congo
Zaječar Serbia 69 J3
Zaka Zimbabwe 123 D6
Zakamensk Rus. Fed. 94 E1
Zakataly Azer. see Zaqatala
Zakháro Greece see Zacharo
Zakhmet Turkm. see Zähmet
Zākhō Iraq 113 F3
Zakhodnyaya Dzvina r. Europe see Zapadnaya Dvina
Zákinthos i. Greece see Zakynthos
Zakopane Poland 57 Q6
Zakouma, Parc National de nat. park Chad 121 E3
Zakwaski, Mount Canada 150 F5
Zakynthos Greece 69 I6
Zakynthos i. Greece 69 I6
Zala China 99 F7
Zalaegerszeg Hungary 68 G1
Zalai-domsag hills Hungary 68 G1
Zalamea de la Serena Spain 67 D4
Zalantun China 95 J2
Zalari Rus. Fed. 88 I2
Zalău Romania 69 J1
Zaleski OH U.S.A. 164 D4
Zalim Saudi Arabia 108 F5
Zalingei Sudan 121 F3
Zalmā, Jabal az mt. Saudi Arabia 108 E4
Zama Japan 93 F3
Zama City Canada 150 G3
Zambales Mountains Luzon Phil. 82 C3
Zambeze r. Africa 123 C5 see Zambezi

▶Zambezi r. Africa 123 C5
4th longest river in Africa.
Also known as Zambeze.

Zambezi Zambia 123 C5
Zambia country Africa 123 C5
Zamboanga Mindanao Phil. 82 C5
Zamboanga Peninsula Mindanao Phil. 82 C5
Zamboanguita Negros Phil. 82 C4
Zamfara watercourse Nigeria 120 D3
Zamīndāvar reg. Afgh. 111 F4
Zamkog China see Zamtang
Zamora Ecuador 176 C4
Zamora Spain 67 D3
Zamora de Hidalgo Mex. 168 D5
Zamość Poland 53 D6
Zamost'ye Poland see Zamość
Zamtang China 96 D1
Zamuro, Sierra del mts Venez. 176 F3
Zanaga Congo 122 B4
Zanatepec Mex. 167 G5
Zancle Sicily Italy see Messina
Zanda China 99 B7
Zandamela Moz. 125 L3
Zandvliet Belgium 62 E3
Zane Hills AK U.S.A. 148 H2
Zanesville OH U.S.A. 164 D4
Zangguy China 99 B5
Zangsêr Kangri mt. China 99 D6
Zangskar reg. India see Zanskar

Zangskar Mountains India see Zanskar Mountains
Zanhuang China 95 H4
Zanjān Iran 110 C2
Zanjān Rūd r. Iran 110 B2
Zannah, Jabal az hill U.A.E. 110 D5
Zanskar r. India 99 B6
Zanskar reg. India 104 D2
Zanskar Mountains India 104 D2
Zante i. Greece see Zakynthos
Zanthus Australia 135 C7
Zanūghān Iran 110 E3
Zanzibar Tanz. 123 D4
Zanzibar Island Tanz. 123 D4
Zaosheng China 95 G5
Zaoshi Hubei China 97 G2
Zaoshi Hunan China 97 G3
Zaouatallaz Alg. 120 D2
Zaouet el Kahla Alg. see Bordj Omer Driss
Zaoyang China 97 G1
Zaoyangzhan China 97 G1
Zaoyuan China 98 D3
Zaozernyy Rus. Fed. 77 K4
Zaozhuang China 95 I5
Zapadnaya Dvina r. Europe 52 F5
also known as Dvina or Zakhodnyaya Dzvina. English form Western Dvina
Zapadnaya Dvina Rus. Fed. 52 G4
Zapadni Rodopi mts Bulg. 69 J4
Zapadno-Kazakhstanskaya Oblast' admin. div. Kazakh. see Zapadnyy Kazakhstan
Zapadno-Sakhalinskiy Khrebet mts Rus. Fed. 90 F2
Zapadno-Sibirskaya Nizmennost' plain Rus. Fed. see West Siberian Plain
Zapadno-Sibirskaya Ravnina plain Rus. Fed. see West Siberian Plain
Zapadnyy Alamedin, Pik mt. Kyrg. 98 A4
Zapadnyy Chink Ustyurta esc. Kazakh. 113 I2
Zapadnyy Kazakhstan admin. div. Kazakh. 51 Q6
Zapadnyy Kil'din Rus. Fed. 54 S2
Zapadnyy Sayan reg. Rus. Fed. 88 F2
Zapata TX U.S.A. 161 D7
Zapata, Península de pen. Cuba 163 D8
Zapiga Chile 176 E7
Zapolyarnyy Rus. Fed. 54 Q2
Zapol'ye Rus. Fed. 52 H4
Zaporizhzhya Ukr. 53 G7
Zaporozh'ye Ukr. see Zaporizhzhya
Zapug China 99 C6
Zaqatala Azer. 113 G2
Zaqên China 99 F6
Za Qu r. China 96 C2
Zaqungngomar mt. China 99 E6
Zara China see Moinda
Zara Croatia see Zadar
Zara Turkey 112 E3
Zarafshan Uzbek. see Zarafshon
Zarafshon Uzbek. 102 B3
Zarafshon, Qatorkŭhi mts Tajik. 111 G2
Zaragoza Mex. 167 E2
Zaragoza Spain 67 F3
Zarand Iran 110 E4
Zarang China 99 B7
Zaranikh Reserve nature res. Egypt 107 B4
Zaranj Afgh. 111 F4
Zarasai Lith. 55 O9
Zárate Arg. 178 E4
Zaraysk Rus. Fed. 53 H5
Zaraza Venez. 176 E2
Zarbdor Uzbek. 111 H1
Zārdab Azer. 53 J8
Zarechensk Rus. Fed. 54 Q3
Zāreh Iran 110 C3
Zarembo Island AK U.S.A. 149 N4
Zargun mt. Pak. 111 G4
Zaria Nigeria 120 D3
Zarichne Ukr. 53 E6
Zarifête, Col des pass Alg. 67 F6
Zarinsk Rus. Fed. 88 E2
Zarmardān Afgh. 111 F3
Zarneh Iran 110 B3
Zărneşti Romania 69 K2
Zarqā' Jordan see Az Zarqā'
Zarqā', Nahr az r. Jordan 107 B3
Zarubino Rus. Fed. 90 C4
Zaruga-dake mt. Japan 93 E3
Żary Poland 57 O5
Zarya Rus. Fed. 53 H5
Zarzis Tunisia 64 G5
Zashchita Kazakh. 98 C2
Zasheyek Rus. Fed. 54 Q3
Zaskar reg. India see Zanskar
Zaskar Range mts India see Zanskar Mountains
Zaslawye Belarus 55 O9
Zastron S. Africa 125 H6
Za'tarī, Wādī az watercourse Jordan 107 C3
Zaterechnyy Rus. Fed. 53 J7
Zauche reg. Germany 63 M2
Zaunguzskiye Karakumy des. Turkm. see Üngüz Angyrsyndaky Garagum
Zautla Mex. 167 F5
Zavalla TX U.S.A. 161 E6
Zavetnoye Rus. Fed. 53 I7
Zavety Il'icha Rus. Fed. 90 F2
Zavidovići Bos.-Herz. 68 H2
Zavitaya Rus. Fed. see Zavitinsk
Zavitinsk Rus. Fed. 90 C2
Zavolzhsk Rus. Fed. 52 I4
Zavolzh'ye Rus. Fed. see Zavolzhsk
Závora, Ponta pt Moz. 125 L3
Zawa Qinghai China 94 E4
Zawa Xinjiang China 99 B5
Zawiercie Poland 57 Q5
Zawilah Libya 121 E2
Zāwīyah, Jabal az hills Syria 107 C2
Zaxoi China 99 E7
Zaybāk Afgh. 104 B1
Zaydī, Wādī az watercourse Syria 107 C3
Zaysan Kazakh. 102 F2
Zaysan, Lake Kazakh. 102 F2
Zaysan, Ozero l. Kazakh. see Zaysan, Lake
Zayü China see Gyigang
Zayü Qu r. China/India 105 I3
Žďár nad Sázavou Czech Rep. 57 O6
Zdolbuniv Ukr. 53 E6
Zdolbunov Ukr. see Zdolbuniv
Zealand i. Denmark 55 G9
Zebulon KY U.S.A. 164 D5
Zedelgem Belgium 62 D3
Zeebrugge Belgium 62 D3
Zeeland MI U.S.A. 164 B2
Zeerust S. Africa 125 H3
Ẕefat Israel 107 B3
Zehdenick Germany 63 N2
Zeil, Mount Australia 135 F5
Zeil am Main Germany 63 K4
Zeist Neth. 62 F2
Zeitz Germany 63 M3
Zêkog China 94 E5
Zekti China 98 C4
Zela Turkey see Zile
Zelennik Rus. Fed. 52 J3
Zelenoborsk Rus. Fed. 51 S3
Zelenoborskiy Rus. Fed. 54 R3
Zelenodol'sk Rus. Fed. 52 K5
Zelenogorsk Rus. Fed. 55 P6
Zelenograd Rus. Fed. 52 H4
Zelenogradsk Rus. Fed. 55 L9
Zelenokumsk Rus. Fed. 113 F1
Zelentsovo Rus. Fed. 52 J4
Zelenyy, Ostrov i. Rus. Fed. 90 G4
Zelinggou China 94 D4
Zell am See Austria 57 N7
Zellingen Germany 63 J5
Zelzate Belgium 62 D3
Žemaitijos nacionalinis parkas nat. park Lith. 55 L8
Zêmdasam China 96 D1
Zemetchino Rus. Fed. 53 I5
Zémio Cent. Afr. Rep. 122 C3
Zemmora Alg. 67 G6
Zempoaltépetl, Nudo de mt. Mex. 168 E5
Zengcheng China 97 G4
Zenica Bos.-Herz. 68 G2
Ẕenifim watercourse Israel 107 B4
Zennor U.K. 59 B8
Zenta Serbia see Senta
Zenzach Alg. 67 H6
Zepu China 99 B5
Zeravshanskiy Khrebet mts Tajik. see Zarafshon, Qatorkŭhi
Zerbst Germany 63 M3
Zerenike Reserve nature res. Egypt see Zaranikh Reserve
Zerf Germany 62 G5
Zernien Germany 63 K1
Zernitz Germany 63 M2
Zernograd Rus. Fed. 53 I7
Zernovoy Rus. Fed. see Zernograd
Zêsum China 99 E7
Zêtang China 99 E7
Zetel Germany 63 H1
Zeulenroda Germany 63 L4
Zeven Germany 63 J1
Zevenaar Neth. 62 G3
Zevgari, Cape Cyprus 107 A2
Zeya Rus. Fed. 90 B1
Zeya r. Rus. Fed. 90 B2
Zeydī Iran 111 F5
Zeyskiy Zapovednik nature res. Rus. Fed. 90 B1
Zeysko-Bureinskaya Vpadina depr. Rus. Fed. 90 C2
Zeyskoye Vodokhranilishche resr Rus. Fed. 90 B1
Zeytin Burnu c. Cyprus see Elaia, Cape
Zêzere r. Port. 67 B4
Zezhou China 95 H5
Zgharta Lebanon 107 B2
Zghorta Lebanon see Zgharta
Zgierz Poland 57 Q5
Zhabinka Belarus 55 N10
Zhaggo China see Luhuo
Zhaglag China 96 C1
Zhag'yab China 96 C2
Zhaksy Sarysu watercourse Kazakh. see Sarysu
Zhalanash Almatinskaya Oblast' Kazakh. 98 B4
Zhalanash Kostanayskaya Oblast' Kazakh. see Damdy
Zhalgyztobe Kazakh. 98 C2
Zhalpaktal Kazakh. 51 P6
Zhalpaqtal Kazakh. see Zhalpaktal
Zhaltyr Kazakh. 102 C1
Zhambyl Karagandinskaya Oblast' Kazakh. 102 D2
Zhambyl Zhambylskaya Oblast' Kazakh. see Taraz
Zhambylskaya Oblast' admin. div. Kazakh. 98 A3
Zhameuka Kazakh. 98 C3
Zhamo China see Bomi
Zhana Kanay Kazakh. 98 C2
Zhanakorgan Kazakh. 102 C3
Zhanang China 99 E7
Zhanaortalyk Kazakh. 98 A3
Zhanaozen Kazakh. 100 E2
Zhanatalan Kazakh. 98 B4
Zhanatas Kazakh. 102 C3
Zhanbei China 90 B2
Zhangaözen Kazakh. see Zhanaozen
Zhanga Qazan Kazakh. see Novaya Kazanka
Zhangaqorghan Kazakh. see Zhanakorgan
Zhangatas Kazakh. see Zhanatas
Zhangbang China 97 G2
Zhangbei China 95 H3
Zhangcheng China see Yongtai
Zhangcunpu China 97 H1
Zhangdian China see Zibo
Zhanggu China see Danba
Zhangguangcai Ling mts China 90 C3
Zhanggutai China 95 J3
Zhanghua Taiwan see Changhua
Zhangjiachuan China 94 F5
Zhangjiajie China 97 F2
Zhangjiakou China 95 H3
Zhangjiang China see Taoyuan
Zhangjiapan China see Jingbian
Zhangla China 96 D1
Zhangling China 90 A1
Zhanglou China 97 H1
Zhangping China 97 H3
Zhangqiangzhen China 90 A4
Zhangqiao China 97 H1
Zhangqiu China 95 I4
Zhangshu China 97 G2
Zhangwu China 95 J3
Zhangxian China 94 F5
Zhangye China 94 E4
Zhangzhou China 97 H3
Zhangzi China 95 H4
Zhanhe China see Zhanbei
Zhanhua China 95 I4
Zhanibek Kazakh. 51 P6
Zhanjiang China 97 F4
Zhanjiang Bei China see Chikan
Zhansugirov Kazakh. 98 B3
Zhao'an China 97 H4
Zhaodong China 90 B3
Zhaoge China see Qixian
Zhaojue China 96 D2
Zhaoliqiao China 97 G2
Zhaoping China 97 F3
Zhaoqing China 97 G4
Zhaoren China see Changwu
Zhaosu China 98 C4
Zhaosutai He r. China 95 J3
Zhaotong China 96 D3
Zhaoxian China 95 H4
Zhaoyang Hu l. China 95 I5
Zhaoyuan Heilong. China 90 B3
Zhaoyuan Shandong China 95 J4
Zhaozhou Hebei China see Zhaoxian
Zhaozhou Heilong. China 90 B3
Zharbulak Kazakh. 98 C3
Zhari Namco salt l. China 99 D7
Zharkamys Kazakh. 102 A2
Zharkent Kazakh. 102 F3
Zharkovskiy Rus. Fed. 52 G5
Zharma Kazakh. 102 F2
Zharsuat (abandoned) Kazakh. 98 C3
Zharyk Kazakh. 98 C2
Zhashkiv Ukr. 53 F6
Zhashkov Ukr. see Zhashkiv
Zhaslyk Uzbek. see Jasliq
Zhaxi China see Weixin
Zhaxi Co salt l. China 99 D6
Zhaxigang Xizang China 99 B6
Zhaxigang Xizang China 99 E7
Zhaxizê China 96 C2
Zhaxizong China 99 D7
Zhayü China 96 C2
Zhayyq r. Kazakh./Rus. Fed. see Ural
Zhdanov Ukr. see Mariupol'
Zhdanovsk Azer. see Beyläqan
Zhecheng China 95 H5
Zhedao China see Lianghe
Zhêhor China 96 D2
Zhejiang prov. China 97 I2
Zhekezhal Kazakh. 98 A2
Zhelaniya, Mys c. Rus. Fed. 76 H2
Zheleznodorozhnyy Rus. Fed. see Yemva
Zheleznodorozhnyy Uzbek. see Qo'ng'irot
Zheleznogorsk Rus. Fed. 53 G5
Zhelou China see Ceheng
Zheltorangy Kazakh. 98 A3
Zheltyye Vody Ukr. see Zhovti Vody
Zhem Kazakh. see Emba
Zhem r. Kazakh. 102 A2
Zhen'an China 97 F1
Zhenba China 96 E1
Zhengding China 95 H4
Zhenghe China 97 H3
Zhengjiakou China see Gucheng
Zhengjiatun China see Shuangliao
Zhengkou China see Gucheng
Zhenglan Qi China see Dund Hot
Zhenglubu China 94 E4
Zhengning China 95 G5
Zhengxiangbai Qi China see Qagan Nur
Zhengyang China 97 G1
Zhengyangguan China 97 H1
Zhengzhou China 95 H5
Zhenhai China 97 I2
Zhenjiang China 97 H1
Zhenjiangguan China 96 D1
Zhenlai China 95 J2
Zhenning China 96 E3
Zhenping China 97 F2
Zhenwudong China see Ansai
Zhenxiong China 96 E3
Zhenyang China see Zhengyang
Zhenyuan Gansu China 95 F5
Zhenyuan Guizhou China 97 F3
Zherdevka Rus. Fed. 53 I6
Zherong China 97 H3
Zheshart Rus. Fed. 52 K3
Zhetikara Kazakh. see Zhitikara
Zhetysuskiy Alatau mts China/Kazakh. 102 E3
Zhêxam China 99 D7
Zhexi Shuiku resr China 97 F2
Zhezkazgan Kazakh. 102 C2
Zhezqazghan Kazakh. see Zhezkazgan
Zhicheng Hubei China 97 F2
Zhicheng Shandong China see Qingzhou
Zhicheng Zhejiang China see Changxing
Zhidan China 95 G4
Zhidoi China 99 F6
Zhifang China see Jiangxia
Zhigalovo Rus. Fed. 88 J2
Zhigansk Rus. Fed. 77 N3
Zhigou China 95 I5
Zhigung China 99 E7
Zhijiang Hubei China 97 F2
Zhijiang Hunan China 86 E1
Zhijin China 96 E3
Zhilong China see Yangxi
Zhiluozhen China 95 G5
Zhi Qu r. China see Yangtze
Zhitikara Kazakh. 100 F1
Zhitkovichi Belarus see Zhytkavichy
Zhitkur Rus. Fed. 53 J6
Zhitomir Ukr. see Zhytomyr
Zhīvār Iran 110 B3
Zhiziluo China 96 C3
Zhlobin Belarus 53 F5
Zhmerinka Ukr. see Zhmerynka
Zhmerynka Ukr. 53 F6
Zhob Pak. 111 H4
Zhob r. Pak. 111 H3
Zholnuskau Kazakh. 98 C2
Zhong'an China see Fuyuan
Zhongba Guangdong China 97 G4
Zhongba Sichuan China see Jiangyou
Zhongba Xizang China 99 D7
Zhongduo China see Youyang
Zhongguo country Asia see China
Zhongguo Renmin Gongheguo country Asia see China
Zhonghe China see Xiushan
Zhongmou China 95 H5
Zhongning China 94 F4
Zhongping China see Huize
Zhongpu China 94 E4
Zhongshan research station Antarctica 188 E2
Zhongshan Guangdong China 97 G4
Zhongshan Guangxi China 97 F3
Zhongshan Guizhou China see Liupanshui
Zhongshu Yunnan China see Luliang
Zhongshu Yunnan China see Luxi
Zhongtai China see Lingtai
Zhongtiao Shan mts China 95 G5
Zhongwei China 94 F4
Zhongxin Guangdong China 97 G3
Zhongxin Yunnan China see Xianggelila
Zhongxin Yunnan China see Huaping
Zhongxing Anhui China 97 H2
Zhongxing Jiangsu China see Siyang
Zhongxinzhan China 94 D5
Zhongyang China 95 G4
Zhongyaozhan China 90 B2
Zhongyicun China see Gucheng
Zhongyuan China 97 F5
Zhongzhai China 96 E1
Zhosaly Kazakh. see Dzhusaly
Zhoucheng China 95 I5
Zhoujiajing China 94 E4
Zhoukou Henan China 97 G1
Zhoukou Sichuan China see Peng'an
Zhoukoudian tourist site China 95 H4
Zhouning China 97 H3
Zhoushan China 97 I2
Zhoushan Dao i. China 97 I2
Zhoushan Qundao is China 97 I2
Zhouzhi China 95 G5
Zhovti Vody Ukr. 53 G6
Zhuanghe China 95 J4
Zhuanglang China 94 F5
Zhubgyügoin China 96 C1
Zhucheng China 95 I5
Zhuchengzi China 90 B3
Zhudong Taiwan see Chutung
Zhugkyung China 94 D4
Zhugla China 99 F7
Zhugqu China 96 E1
Zhuhai China 97 G4
Zhuji China 97 I2
Zhujing China 97 I2
Zhukeng China 97 G4
Zhukovka Rus. Fed. 53 G5
Zhukovskiy Rus. Fed. 53 H5
Zhulong He r. China 95 H4
Zhumadian China 97 G1
Zhuokeji China 96 D2
Zhuolu China 95 H3
Zhuozhou China 95 I4
Zhuozi China 95 H3
Zhuozishan China see Zhuozi
Zhusandala, Step' plain Kazakh. 98 A3
Zhushan Hubei China 97 F1
Zhushan Hubei China see Xuan'en
Zhuxi China 97 F1
Zhuxiang China 97 H1
Zhuyang China see Dazhu
Zhuzhou Hunan China 97 G3
Zhuzhou Hunan China 97 G3
Zhydachiv Ukr. 53 E6
Zhympity Kazakh. 51 Q5
Zhytkavichy Belarus 55 O10
Zhytomyr Ukr. 53 F6
Zīā'ābād Iran 110 C3
Zīārat-e Shāh Esmā'īl Afgh. 111 G4
Žiar nad Hronom Slovakia 57 Q6
Zibā salt pan Saudi Arabia 107 D4
Zibo China 95 I4
Zichang China 95 G4
Zicheng China see Zijin
Zicuirán Mex. 167 E5
Zīdar Iran 110 E2
Zidi Pak. 111 G5
Ziel, Mount Australia see Zeil, Mount
Zielona Góra Poland 57 O5
Ziemelkursas augstiene hills Latvia 55 M8
Zierenberg Germany 63 J3
Ziesar Germany 63 M2
Ziftá Egypt 112 C5
Zigê Tangco l. China 99 E6
Zīghan Libya 121 F2
Zigong China 96 E2
Ziguey Chad 121 E3
Ziguinchor Senegal 120 B3
Žīguri Latvia 55 O8
Zihuatanejo Mex. 168 D5
Zijin China 97 G4
Zijpenberg hill Neth. 62 G2
Ziketan China see Xinghai
Zile Turkey 112 D2
Žilina Slovakia 57 Q6
Zillah Libya 121 E2
Zima Rus. Fed. 88 I2
Zimapán Mex. 167 F4
Zimatlán Mex. 167 F5
Zimba Zambia 123 C5
Zimbabwe country Africa 123 C5
Zimi Sierra Leone see Zimmi
Zimmerbude Rus. Fed. see Svetlyy
Zimmi Sierra Leone 120 B4
Zimnicea Romania 69 K3
Zimniy Bereg coastal area Rus. Fed. 52 H2
Zimovniki Rus. Fed. 53 I7
Zimrīn Syria 107 B2
Ẕin watercourse Israel 107 B4
Zin Pak. 111 H4
Zinave, Parque Nacional do nat. park Moz. 123 D6
Zinder Niger 120 D3
Zindo China 96 D2
Ziniaré Burkina Faso 120 C3
Zinihu China 94 F4
Zinjibār Yemen 108 G7
Zinoyevsk Ukr. see Kirovohrad
Zion IL U.S.A. 164 B2
Zion National Park UT U.S.A. 159 G3
Zionz Lake Canada 151 N5
Zippori Israel 107 B3
Zi Qu r. China 99 G6
Ziqudukou China 96 B1
Zirah, Gōd-e plain Afgh. 111 F4
Zirc Hungary 68 G1
Zirkel, Mount CO U.S.A. 156 G4
Zirkūh i. U.A.E. 110 D5
Zirndorf Germany 63 K5
Ziro India 105 H4
Zirreh Afgh. 111 F4
Zīr Rūd Iran 110 C4
Zi Shui r. China 89 K7
Zistersdorf Austria 57 P6
Zitácuaro Mex. 168 D5
Zitong China 96 E2
Zittau Germany 57 O5
Zitziana r. AK U.S.A. 149 J2
Zixi China 97 H3
Zixing China see Xingning
Ziyang Jiangxi China see Wuyuan
Ziyang Shaanxi China 97 F1
Ziyang Sichuan China 96 E2
Ziyaret Dağı hill Turkey 107 B1
Ziyuan China 97 F3
Ziyun China 96 E3
Ziz, Oued watercourse Morocco 64 D5
Zizhong China 96 E2
Zizhou China 95 G4
Zlatoustovsk Rus. Fed. 90 D1
Zlín Czech Rep. 57 P6
Zmeinogorsk Rus. Fed. 102 F1
Zmiyevka Rus. Fed. 53 H5
Znamenka Kazakh. 98 B2
Znamenka Rus. Fed. 53 I5
Znamenka Ukr. see Znam"yanka
Znam"yanka Ukr. 53 G6
Znojmo Czech Rep. 57 P6
Zoar S. Africa 124 E7
Zoco China 99 C6
Zoetermeer Neth. 62 E2
Zogainrawar China see Huashixia
Zogang China 96 C2
Zogqên China 96 C1
Zoidê Lhai China 99 E6
Zoigê China 96 D1
Zoji La pass India 104 C2
Zola S. Africa 125 H7
Zolder Belgium 62 F3
Zolochev Kharkivs'ka Oblast' Ukr. see Zolochiv
Zolochev L'vivs'ka Oblast' Ukr. see Zolochiv
Zolochiv Kharkivs'ka Oblast' Ukr. 53 G6
Zolochiv L'vivs'ka Oblast' Ukr. 53 E6
Zolotonosha Ukr. 53 G6
Zolotoye Rus. Fed. 53 J6
Zolotoy Khrebet mts Rus. Fed. 148 B2
Zolotukhino Rus. Fed. 53 H5

▶Zomba Malawi 123 D5
Former capital of Malawi.

Zombor Serbia see Sombor
Zomin Uzbek. 111 H2
Zongjiafangzi China 94 D4
Zonguldak Turkey 69 N4
Zongxoi China 105 G3
Zongzhai China 94 D4
Zörbig Germany 63 M3
Zorgho Burkina Faso 120 C3
Zorgo Burkina Faso see Zorgho
Zorn r. France 63 I6
Żory Poland 57 Q5
Zossen Germany 63 N2
Zottegem Belgium 62 D4
Zouar Chad 121 E2
Zoucheng China 95 I5
Zouérat Mauritania 120 B2
Zoulang Nanshan mts China 94 D4
Zouping China 95 I4
Zousfana, Oued watercourse Alg. 64 D5
Zoushi China 97 F2
Zouxian China see Zoucheng
Zrenjanin Serbia 69 I2
Zschopau Germany 63 N4
Zschopau r. Germany 63 N3
Zschornewitz Germany 63 M3
Zubālah, Birkat waterhole Saudi Arabia 113 F5
Zubillaga Arg. 178 D5
Zubova Polyana Rus. Fed. 53 I5
Zubtsov Rus. Fed. 52 G4
Zuénoula Côte d'Ivoire 120 C4
Zug Switz. 66 I3
Zugdidi Georgia 113 F2
Zugspitze mt. Austria/Germany 57 M7
Zugu Nigeria 120 D3
Zuider Zee l. Neth. see IJsselmeer
Zuidhorn Neth. 62 G1
Zuid-Kennemerland Nationaal Park nat. park Neth. 62 E2
Zuitai China see Kangxian
Zuitaizi China see Kangxian
Zuitou China see Taibai
Zújar r. Spain 67 D4
Zuli He r. China 94 F4
Zülpich Germany 62 G4
Zumba Ecuador 176 C4
Zumpango Mex. 167 F5
Zumpango del Río Mex. 167 F5
Zunheboto India 105 H4
Zunhua China 95 I3
Zuni NM U.S.A. 159 I4
Zuni watercourse AZ/NM U.S.A. 159 I4
Zuni Mountains NM U.S.A. 159 I4
Zun-Torey, Ozero l. Rus. Fed. 95 H1
Zunyi Guizhou China 96 E3
Zunyi Guizhou China 96 E3
Zuo Jiang r. China/Vietnam 86 E2
Zuoquan China 95 H4
Zuoyun China 95 H4
Županja Croatia 68 H2
Zūrābād Āzarbāyjān-e Gharbī Iran 110 B2
Zūrābād Khorāsān-e Razavī Iran 111 F3
Zürich Switz. 66 I3
Zurmat reg. Afgh. 111 H3
Zuru Nigeria 120 D3
Zurzuna Turkey see Çıldır
Zushi Japan 93 F3
Zutphen Neth. 62 G2
Zuwārah Libya 120 E1
Zuyevka Rus. Fed. 52 K4
Zūzan Iran 111 E3
Zvishavane Zimbabwe 123 D6
Zvolen Slovakia 57 Q6
Zvornik Bos.-Herz. 69 H2
Zwedru Liberia 120 C4
Zweeloo Neth. 62 G2
Zweibrücken Germany 63 H5
Zweletemba S. Africa 124 D7
Zwelitsha S. Africa 125 H7
Zwethau Germany 63 N3
Zwettl Austria 57 O6
Zwickau Germany 63 M4
Zwochau Germany 63 M3
Zwolle Neth. 62 G2
Zwönitz Germany 63 M4
Zyablovo Rus. Fed. 52 L4
Zygi Cyprus 107 A2
Zyryan Kazakh. see Zyryanovsk
Zyryanka Rus. Fed. 77 Q3
Zyryanovsk Kazakh. 102 F2
Zyyi Cyprus see Zygi

Acknowledgements

Maps and data

Maps, design and origination by Collins Bartholomew Ltd, Westerhill Road, Bishopbriggs, Glasgow G64 2QT Illustrations created by HarperCollins Publishers unless otherwise stated.

Cover image: Planetary Visions Ltd

Earthquake data (pp10-11): United States Geological Survey (USGS) National Earthquakes Information Center, Denver, USA.

Population map (pp16-17): 2005. Gridded Population of the World Version 3 (GPWv3). Palisades, NY: Socioeconomic Data and Applications Center (SEDAC), Columbia University. Available at http://sedac.ciesn.columbia.edu/plue/gpw http://www.ciesin.columbia.edu

Terrorism data (pp26-27): National Consortium for the Study of Terrorism (START) (2011) Global Terrorism Database http://www.start.umd.edu/gtd

Coral reefs data (p31): World Resources Institute (WRI), Washington D.C., USA.

Desertification data (p31): U.S. Department of Agriculture Natural Resources Conservation Service.

Antarctica (p188): Antarctic Digital Database (versions1 and 2), ©Scientific Committee on Antarctic research (SCAR), Cambridge, UK (1993, 1998).

Photographs and images

Page	Image	Satellite/Sensor	Credit	Page	Image	Satellite/Sensor	Credit	Page	Image	Satellite/Sensor	Credit
6–7	Greenland	MODIS	MODIS/NASA		Dubai	ASTER	ASTER/NASA		Lake Victoria	MODIS	MODIS/NASA
8–9	Vatican City	IKONOS	Satellite imagery courtesy of GeoEye	34	Venice main	MODIS	MODIS/NASA	118–119	Cape Town	IKONOS	Satellite imagery courtesy of GeoEye
12–13	Hurricane Ophelia	MODIS	MODIS/NASA/		Venice inset		NASA/GSFC	126–127	Oceania		Blue Marble: Next Generation. NASA's Earth Observatory
14–15	Tokyo	ASTER	ASTER/NASA	35	Venice main	ASTER	NASA/ASTER				
	Cropland, Consuegra		© Rick Barrentine/Corbis		Venice insets	IKONOS	Satellite imagery courtesy of GeoEye	128–129	Heron Island	IKONOS	Satellite imagery courtesy of GeoEye
	Mojave Desert		Keith Moore	36	Namib Desert	Landsat	USGS EROS Data Center	128–129	Banks Peninsula	Space shuttle	NASA
	Larsen Ice Shelf	MODIS	MODIS/NASA	37	Kamchatka Peninsula	MODIS	MODIS/NASA	130–131	Nouméa	ISS	NASA/Johnson Space Center
16–17	Singapore		Courtesy of USGS EROS Data Center	38	London	IKONOS	Satellite imagery courtesy of GeoEye	130–131	Wellington		NZ Aerial Mapping Ltd www.nzam.com
	Kuna Indians		© Danny Lehman/Corbis	39	Cape Canaveral	ASTER	NASA/GSFC/METI/ERSDAC/ JAROS, and US/Japan ASTER Science Team	140–141	North America		Blue Marble: Next Generation. NASA's Earth Observatory
18–19	Hong Kong	IKONOS	Satellite imagery courtesy of GeoEye	40	Lake Natron	ASTER	NASA/GSFC/METI/ERSDAC/ JAROS, and US/Japan ASTER Science Team	142–143	Mississippi Delta	ASTER	ASTER/NASA
24–25	London		QQ7/Shutterstock	41	Yukon Delta	Landsat	NASA/USGS	142–143	Panama Canal	Landsat	Clifton-Campbell Imaging Inc.
	Malawi village		Magdalena Bujak/ Shutterstock	44–45	Europe		Blue Marble: Next Generation. NASA's Earth Observatory	144–145	Mexicali	ASTER	NASA
26–27	Refugee camp in Thailand		Liewluck/Shutterstock	46–47	Iceland	MODIS	MODIS/NASA	144–145	The Bahamas	MODIS	MODIS/NASA
28–29	Opium poppy		forbis/Shutterstock	48–49	Bosporus	ISS	NASA/Johnson Space Center	170–171	South America		Blue Marble: Next Generation. NASA's Earth Observatory
	Water		Tian Zhan/Shutterstock	70–71	Asia		Blue Marble: Next Generation. NASA's Earth Observatory	172–173	Amazon/Rio Negro	Terra/MISR	NASA
30–31	Deforestation, Itaipu	Landsat	Images reproduced by kind permission of UNEP	72–73	Yangtze	MODIS	MODIS/NASA	172–173	Tierra del Fuego	MODIS	MODIS/NASA
	Aral Sea 1973–2001	Landsat	Images reproduced by kind permission of UNEP		Caspian Sea	MODIS	MODIS/NASA	174–175	Galapagos Islands	MODIS	MODIS/NASA
	Aral Sea 2011	MODIS	MODIS/NASA	74–75	Timor	MODIS	MODIS/NASA	174–175	Falkland Islands	MODIS	MODIS/NASA
	Great Barrier Reef	MODIS	MODIS/NASA		Beijing	IKONOS	Satellite imagery courtesy of GeoEye	180–181	Antarctica	USGS/NSF/ NASA/BAS	Landsat Image Mosaic of Antarctica (LIMA) PROJECT
32–33	Lake Chad	Landsat	Images reproduced by kind permission of UNEP	114–115	Africa		Blue Marble: Next Generation. NASA's Earth Observatory	182–183	Larsen Ice Shelf	MODIS	MODIS/NASA
	Tubarjal, Arabian Desert	Landsat	Images reproduced by kind permission of UNEP	116–117	Congo River	Space shuttle	NASA				
	Yellowstone National Park	Landsat	NASA/USGS								
	Athabasca Oil Sands	Landsat	NASA/USGS								

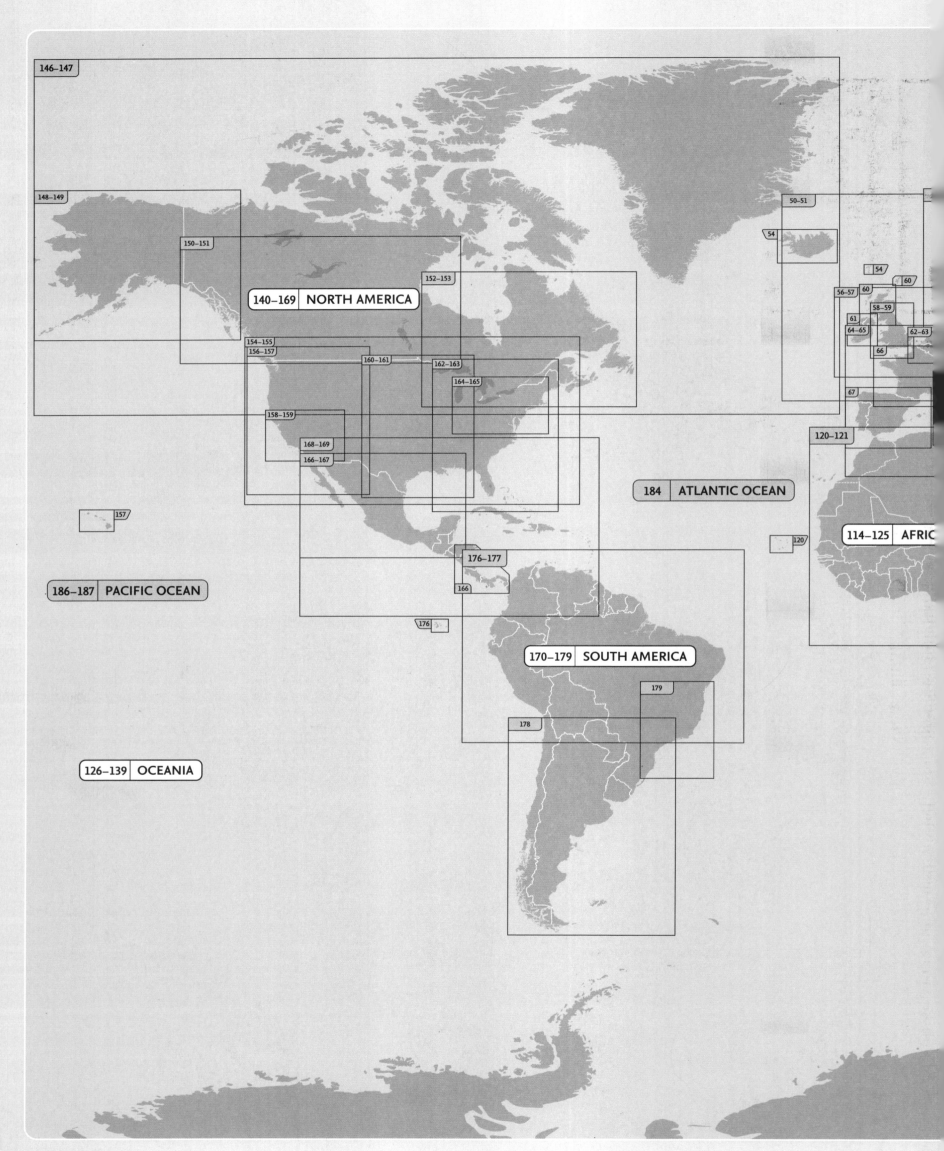

146–147

148–149

150–151

152–153

140–169 NORTH AMERICA

154–155
156–157

160–161

162–163

164–165

158–159

168–169

166–167

157

50–51

54

54

60

60

56–57

58–59

61

64–65

62–63

66

67

120–121

184 ATLANTIC OCEAN

120

114–125 AFRIC

186–187 PACIFIC OCEAN

176–177

166

176

170–179 SOUTH AMERICA

179

178

126–139 OCEANIA

Find your map